T0142191

Handbook of Artificial Intelligence for Music

Eduardo Reck Miranda
Editor

Handbook of Artificial Intelligence for Music

Foundations, Advanced Approaches, and Developments for Creativity

 Springer

Editor
Eduardo Reck Miranda ⓘ
Interdisciplinary Centre for Computer Music
Research (ICCMR)
University of Plymouth
Plymouth, UK

ISBN 978-3-030-72118-3   ISBN 978-3-030-72116-9   (eBook)
https://doi.org/10.1007/978-3-030-72116-9

This Springer imprint is published by the registered company Springer Nature Switzerland AG
The registered company address is: Gewerbestrasse 11, 6330 Cham, Switzerland

Foreword: From Audio Signals to Musical Meaning

In 1957, Lejaren Hiller and Leonard Isaacson stunned the world of music by presenting the first composition constructed by an AI system, called *Illiac Suite* (Hiller and Isaacson 1959).

Illiac was the name of one of the first computers ever built, installed at the University of Illinois in 1952. Hiller and Isaacson were trained as musicians but they were also computer scientists 'avant la lettre' with a solid training in the natural sciences. Their project took place in the wake of the earliest problem-solving programs demonstrated by Allen Newell, Herbert Simon and John Shaw a few years earlier and the enthusiasm generated by John McCarthy and Marvin Minsky at the Dartmouth summer project on AI in 1956 (Nilson, 2010).

Illiac Suite is remarkable from many angles, particularly given the state of computer and software technology at that time. Programs had to be submitted on punched cards, memory was tiny, execution slow, and higher-level programming languages were in their infancy; the first compiler for Fortran became operational only in 1957. One had to be a genius to get anything done at all. The *Illiac Suite* composition was also remarkable because Hiller and Isaacson introduced various paradigms for computer music that are still dominant today.

They were familiar with the canonical techniques of Western composition based on a system of pitches and constraints on how these pitches could best be organized to get a harmonious piece of music, such as use recognizable tonalities, avoid transitions that are boring like parallel fifths or octaves, and so on. Within the heuristic search paradigm initiated by Allen Newell and Herbert Simon (Newell and Simon, 1956), Hiller and Isaacson implemented a generate and test scenario where possible pitches were generated and only those kept that fit with the canonical rules of composition, thus foreshadowing the constraint-based computer composition techniques used today.

To dampen the inevitable combinatorial explosions, they introduced heuristics and higher-level musical representations, such as larger melodic and rhythmic structures. They also experimented with Markovian decision processes that are still at the heart of many efforts in computer music generation and argued that creativity could be modelled by introducing stochasticity, based on a random number generator that could make unexpected choices. To bridge the gap with human-produced music, they introduced higher level structures from the classical music tradition, for example, having different movements like presto, andante, and allegro, and they used human performers and classical instruments to give a recognizable emotional quality to their music.

How did the resulting music sound? You can listen for yourself.[1] The music is certainly intriguing and an adequate performance can add emotional value making it easier (or in some cases harder) for listeners to build some sort of interpretive experience. After all, enjoyable music is not only the task of the composer and the performers but just as much of the listeners who are invited to project structures and meanings on what they are hearing.

At the time, most musicians reacted in an extremely hostile way to this experiment, both because the computer was encroaching on a terrain that was until then the province of human creativity and because of the aesthetics and structure of the music that the computer programs produced. With respect to the latter, we have to remember that the *IlliacSuite* was composed at the time John Cage's experimental music had come in vogue, emphasizing aleatoric elements, processes, and rhythm and tone rather than melody and harmony (Kuhn 2016). From that perspective, *Illiac Suite* is actually more conservative than much of the experimental music, concrete and electronic music that followed. It is more comprehensible to the average listener than the highly complex academic music produced in the 1980s and 90s. Nevertheless, *Illiac Suite* remained an isolated experiment.

Fast forward to today. The field of computer music in general, and the application of AI in music in particular, have blossomed beyond belief. Developments at the level of hardware, software, and the use of AI for composition, tutoring, recording and music distribution have been extraordinary. The papers appearing in the *Computer Music Journal* (started in 1977) and the historical collection of Stephan Schwanauer and David Levitt (1993) are important resources to track these developments. And now we have the collection of chapters in this handbook, brilliantly brought together by Eduardo Reck Miranda. This book gives an excellent survey of more recent achievements and speculates on near-future developments. All the publications, demonstrations and musical works being discussed here establish beyond doubt the very high level of technical and scientific competence and the musicological sophistication of the computer music field and its branch dedicated to the application of AI to music.

The experimental achievements of computer music researchers have been abundant. But equally impressive is the fact that the laboratory experiments have successfully moved into musical practice in the real world. No composer today would work without the help of programs for editing scores and for the tedious process of adapting scores to different instruments. Synthesis from scores has become so good (but certainly not at the level of human performers) to give composers a good idea of what their music will sound when executed by a human orchestra. Performers now practice and play from digital scores and have digital ways to organise and annotate scores. They can even practice on their own with the

[1]https://www.youtube.com/watch?v=n0njBFLQSk8 (Accessed on 02 February 2021).

other instruments synthesized by a computer, in real-time synchrony with what they are playing. The recording and distribution of music are no longer the exclusive work of manual labour only because very sophisticated signal processing intervenes in recording and listening. Moreover, modern-day AI algorithms play a crucial role in how the public gets to know new work. Also in musical education, the results from computer music research are playing increasing roles from simple Apps that help you train your musical competence to MOOCs that allow many more people to learn about music online (Steels, 2015). And moreover, we have many examples of fascinating music composed, and in many cases performed, by computer systems in prestigious venues and launched on a commercial market where until recently only human compositions could be found. This is all very remarkable. The adoption of computer music has even accelerated with the COVID-19 pandemic in 2020, so that you now find choirs that rehearse using Internet streaming technologies, or Jazz musicians that play together over the cloud, with occasionally an AI musician thrown in to play along when a band member is missing.

Research into computer music has not only contributed to music itself. Computer music researchers have also been making steady contributions to software engineering, hardware development, signal processing, embedded systems, and AI methods, particularly in the area of constraint programming, object-oriented programming and, more recently, deep learning. At the moment there are even forays into neuro-technology (integration of electronics and computing with living neural cells) and quantum computing (see Chaps. 8 and 34 this volume). All of these topics are explored in this book with outstanding overviews and reviews.

Given all these incredible advances what could be done next? Pushing the state of the art further in computational creativity is high on the list, and one of the focal topics of the present book, so let me focus on that for the remainder of this essay.

So far most experiments in musical creativity still follow the approach of Hiller and Isaacson, namely to work with templates and add some randomness in instantiating a template to make an audible composition. The difference nowadays is that those templates might be learned using machine learning techniques and the randomness gets heavily constrained both by statistical models and by music theory so that the resulting music often sounds more harmonious and plausible than *Illiac Suite*. But is this the only approach possible?

Although composers certainly use templates that they have either learned explicitly through musical education or implicitly by listening to a lot of music, their creativity obviously goes beyond making random variations to instances of templates or to the templates themselves. And although listeners also have musical memories containing templates, melodies, favourite interpretations of well-known pieces, and so on, they clearly do more than recognize patterns and predict what pattern comes next. I am of the opinion that in order to know what it is that they do more, and hence what creativity requires in the domain of music, we have to address the question of meaning in music. I am probably stating the obvious when I say that *musicians and listeners engage with music because they find music meaningful*.

What are the implications of saying that? Does it make sense actually to talk about meaning in music? What kinds of meanings are we talking about? And how does music accomplish the expression of meaning? How do listeners 'understand' music? Can we build tools to assist composers for the meaning dimension of their work? Can we find computational means to aid listeners in interpreting and experiencing in a richer and deeper way the meanings of a musical work? Most importantly, if we are serious about music creation or co-creation with AI systems, should we address how musicians use music to express meaning? And furthermore, if we are serious about autonomous computational creativity for music, should we investigate how innovative composers or improvisers have found new ways to express meaning through music or opened up new domains of meaning for expression by music?

All these questions are difficult, which might explain why the AI and music community has been avoiding them. In fact, recent work on machine learning and neural networks has moved AI even further away from considerations of meaning because of its behaviourist approach to mind. In the behaviourist tradition, initiated by Watson (1930) and Skinner (1953) and brought into AI in the 1950s by Frank Rosenblatt (1962) and his cybernetic colleagues, intelligence is reduced to pattern recognition and pattern prediction It is acquired through behavioural conditioning, associative learning, reinforcement learning, perceptron-style multi-layered networks and other statistical machine learning techniques. Goals, intentions, beliefs, symbols and perspectives are de-emphasized, and occasionally denied to be relevant for intelligence. The topic of meaning is avoided entirely.

We see this kind of approach not only in applications of AI to music but also for all other applications areas that this kind of data-driven, behaviourist AI has tackled. For example, 'neural' text translation approaches translation by mapping n-grams (sequences of words) from a source to a target language without even trying to do a serious syntactic and semantic analysis, let alone try to understand and reformulate what the author wants to say. Adepts of this approach argue that doing syntactic and semantic analysis is very difficult, which is certainly true, but also that you do not need it. When more data is given to learn from, the glitches and silly translations that we now see will become rare. Another example is 'neural' art generation (Dumoulin et al. 2017). A neural network learning system generates paintings in the style of the impressionist Claude Monet, for example, by regenerating statistical patterns gleaned from Monet's paintings, but without even trying to understand what is depicted on the painting. The system would not have a clue as to why a particular scene was chosen or why Claude Monet made a specific transformation of the original colours and shapes.

We see this same approach in data-driven AI work that explores how deep learning mechanisms can be used for music, for example, in the experiments of MUSENET by OpenAI.[2] Even though it is quite fascinating and a technical tour de force, attempts to create music 'in the same style' as human composers like Chopin,

---

[2]https://openai.com/blog/musenet/ (Accessed on 02 February 2021).

based on a probabilistic transformer model that predicts or generates the next element in a sequence, completely bypasses meaning. What is amazing is that the end result is so close to a Chopin piano piece that commentators often describe it as 'brilliant', but also 'terrifying' and 'having no human element in it'. It suggests that a significant part of the musical experience is imposed by listeners. The composer creates a vehicle for this to happen. And even if the musical piece has been constructed without any consideration of meaning, listeners still manage to impose structure and meaning onto it.

In contrast to the behaviourist tradition, the cognitivist tradition, brought into AI by Allen Newell and Herbert Simon (1956), insisted on topics like goal-directed problem solving, symbolic representations, reasoning, conceptual understanding and Piagetian style constructivist learning. Some research on understanding did indeed take place in the 1960s and 70s, see, for example, Minsky (1968) or Schank (1983), but in general, the cognitivist AI tradition has also tended to shy away from meaning. They have focused instead on syntactic manipulation of formal structures, simply because this is more amenable to computational treatment. The composition and analysis experiments to formalise and codify music using symbolic techniques (see, for example, Chap. 18 in this volume) are technically as impressive as the more recent music generation experiments based on machine learning, particularly when used for real-time support during Jazz improvisation. The results also sound more like real music, even though discerning listeners might still feel a lack of narrative structure, authentic emotions and meaning. Nevertheless, the cognitive AI tradition accepts at least that meaning is important in human intelligence and culture.

Computational music research on meaning has been difficult because there is no clear consensus among musical scholars and practitioners on what musical meaning is. Even the idea that music is about meaning is controversial. For some, there is simply no meaning in music. For instance, consider this quotation from composer Igor Stravinsky: "I consider that music is, by its very nature, essentially powerless to express anything at all, whether a feeling, an attitude of mind, a psychological mood, a phenomenon of nature, etc." (Stravinsky, 1935, p. 53). This quotation is surprising, particularly coming from a composer that has written music for ballet, a few operas, and even music for film. If we take this stance, music becomes similar to mathematics. Musical composition comes to be seen as about designing abstract structures and formal pattern manipulation. Listening in this case amounts to an experience of sound and the recognition of the patterns imposed on sounds. From this perspective, the joy of musical listening consists in recognizing and tracing the development of these structural patterns, similar to looking at mosaic patterns on a floor.

The 'music is like mathematics' metaphor is natural to the many mathematicians and computer scientists, who have been the most active group in computer music research. They feel very much at home in the world of abstract structures and the computer is the ideal tool for exploring this world. This perspective has heavily influenced the development of AI as applied to music. However, equating music with mathematics is nor the view of many practicing musicians nor of most listeners. For them, music is much more than sound sensations and syntactic structures. We are a meaning-seeking species steeped in emotion and intention. We are always trying to figure out why things are the way they are, what motivates somebody to do something, how fragments of an experience fit together into a coherent whole and relate to our earlier experiences.

True, many of the meanings that we impose on reality and on artworks, including music, are not easy to capture in words. They are pre-verbal and non-symbolic, but they still count as meanings. It is also true that even if we would have a clear notion of what musical meaning might be, the set of meanings invoked by one listener would seldom be the same as those invoked by another listener. This is simply because different people have their own personal memory, their own prior experiences of the world and of music, their own social context and psychological state when composing or listening to music. Objectively, there is no 'correct' set of meanings for a given piece of music. Therefore, it does not seem to be a reasonable goal for AI to extract it. It also seems beyond machines to capture the rich embodied and culturally grounded set of meanings that humans effortlessly deal with.

Those who admit that music is meaningful often restrict the meaning of music to be about expressing and invoking emotional states, like sadness or joy (Meyer, 1956). That is certainly one aspect of musical meaning, but there is much more. I suggest that it is helpful to look at other artistic disciplines that have been grappling with meaning in art.

One concept that I have found useful is that of a narrative. It is commonly employed in studies of art and literature. A narrative is a larger scale structure that organizes experiences into multiple levels of description. A painting or a musical composition is not literally a story, like a theatre play or a novel, but it stimulates us to construct narratives. From this perspective, an artist is engaged in a form of cognitive engineering (Dewey, 2018), manipulating the mental processes of viewers by shaping their sensory experiences and memory recalls in order to stimulate narrative construction. This insight is very important because it suggests that a composer or performer is like a designer who has goals at many levels and almost magically manages to transform these goals into a coherent piece of art. It also suggests a rethink of how we might achieve computational creativity in the music domain. It is about finding solutions to compositional problems similar to the way an architect designs a building that has to satisfy many constraints and at the same time has to be done in a creative way. Creativity then is not about introducing some random variations without motivation or insight into the underlying purposes and strategies for achieving them.

Narratives typically segment experiences into a series of events with a temporal, causal, and spatial structure. They describe the different participants in these events their roles, goals, intentions and emotions. They introduce the context and world setting, provide perspectives, an emotional stance, and probe the moral, political and ethical implications of what is happening. When we look intently at a painting or watch a theatre play, we spontaneously construct narratives. We try to fit together the different elements we see or hear until they fall into place. An artistic experience, or even a mundane situation, only 'makes sense' when we can construct a coherent narrative and integrate it with our own personal episodic and semantic memory. Often there are ambiguities, alternative competing interpretations and conflicting perspectives which either get resolved or remain as open-ended multiplicities. As composer Arnold Schoenberg puts it: "A work of art is a labyrinth where, at every point, every knowledgeable person is aware of the entrance and the exit without needing a golden thread to guide him." (Schoenberg, 1995). I think Schoenberg overestimates most listeners who may struggle to hear the structure underlying his 12-tone compositions, but the point is well taken.

Another, complementary, insight which I have found useful, comes from the art historian and semiotician Ervin Panofsky. He has identified five levels of meaning (Panofsky, 1939): the formal, factual, expressional, cultural, and intrinsic level, and applied it principally to painting. Can we apply these Panofskyan distinctions to music as a step towards putting meaning at the heart of AI research into music? Let me try and see what lessons we can learn.

The first Panofskyan level is that of the *form*, the material presence and syntactic structure of an artwork. For a painting, these are the lines and colours which hierarchically aggregate into artistic motifs. The obvious correlation for music are the sounds themselves, which have sensory qualities that may already give aesthetic sensations or a feeling of well-being, and the syntactic structuring of the sounds: their segmentation, categorization and aggregation into tones, melodies, rhythm, meter, harmonic structure, phrases, and the like. They constitute musical motifs, or musical ideas in Schoenberg's terminology (Schoenberg, 1995). They are the building blocks of a composition at the form level.

Composers often already tell a story on this form level, playing around with these musical motifs. They are presented, transformed, repeated and contrasted with other motifs as the music unfolds. Music is unique as an art medium because the musical forms themselves create narratives that are about musical ideas without any reference to emotions or events in the world. Minsky's brilliant essay *Music, mind and meaning* (Minsky, 1981) illustrates this point, using the example of Ludwig van Beethoven's fifth symphony, where the first subject is expressed in its famous first four notes; see also (Guerrieri, 2012). If some musicians, such as Stravinsky, say that music does not have any meaning, I reckon that what they want to convey is that there is no meaning outside of the domain of (musical) form itself in music. I am not entirely convinced about this.

The level of musical form is what most of the AI research into musical composition, interpretation and listening has focused on. Much has been achieved, as the chapters in this book clearly attest, and there are still many ideas floating around on how one can increase the structural depth of compositional work, build better ways to extract from audio signals notes, tempo, measures, rhythms, and harmonic structure or improve the synthesis of music by taking into account its phrasal structure. However, less work has been done on the narrative structure of music at this form level: to recognize the motifs and their transformations, to reconstruct the musical story that the composer is telling us.

The second Panofskyan level is concerned with *factual meanings*. It refers to the capability of images to conjure up memories of objects and events in a real or imaginary world. For example, Michelangelo Merisi da Caravaggio's stunning painting *Presa di Cristo nell'orto* (*The Taking of Christ*, in English) from 1602 directly triggers recognition of a central narrative in the catholic passion story that would have been known by his audience at the time.[3] In the painting we see in the middle Judas giving the fatal kiss and the soldiers ready to take Jesus. To the left, we see one of the apostles crying for help and Jesus retracting to avoid the embrace of Judas. To the far right, we see a person (generally considered to be the painter himself) who shines light on the scene, thus becoming an accomplice to the arrest. The title of a work is usually suggestive of its factual meaning. But it is only the starting point, together with the image itself, for triggering the construction of a narrative that makes sense of what is depicted and why.

Factual meanings are much more common in music than usually thought, although they are less so in twentieth-century music, which commensurate with the rise of abstract art by painters such as Piet Mondriaan and Wassily Kandinsky who wanted to create paintings who were interesting at the level of form only, using music as their guiding example. A figurative component is most evident for vocal music, where the music underscores and augments the verbally expressed narrative, or for opera and film music, where the music underlines the action, the emotional state of the characters and their role.

For example, Johann Sebastian Bach's *St. Matthew Passion* composed in 1727 tells the same story as Carravagio's painting and is equally figurative. The story of the arrest of Christ is first told by the Evangelist without much drama (Recitativo 32). Initially, there is a duet (Duetto 33) with a feeling of sadness and resignation with the choir representing the apostles and interjecting with the cries "Laszt ihn, haltet, bindet nicht!" ("Leave him, don't' keep him, do not tie him!").[4] These cries map straight onto the left-most figure in Caravaggio's painting. But then a storm breaks out: "Sind Blitze und Donner in Wolken verschwunden" ("Lightning and thunder disappear in the clouds"). It is forcefully evoked by the choir in staccato rhythm and totally dramatizes the importance of the arrest.[5] In order to appreciate all this, one has to go beyond the form appearance of this music and take into account what the story is about.

Factual meanings are not only present in vocal works. Music does not necessarily have to imitate literally the sound of an event or situation in the world to be figurative. It is most of the time only suggestive, the same way a painting of the sea by impressionist painter Claude Monnet does not literally reuse the colours of the sea and the sky, or faithfully represents the waves that you actually observe. The

---

[3]https://en.wikipedia.org/wiki/The_Taking_of_Christ_(Caravaggio)#/media/File:The_Taking_of_Christ-Caravaggio_(c.1602).jpg (Accessed on 04 February 2021).

[4]Phlippe Herreweghe, Collegium Vocale: https://www.youtube.com/watch?v=70shLtLxcYA (Accessed on 04 February 2021) Storm starts at 3:33.

[5]Jos van Veldhoven, Nederlandse Bachvereniging: https://www.youtube.com/watch?v=_uLpp6cW7sA (Accessed on 04 February 2021).

relation to reality is iconic: there is a resemblance with what is signified without trying to be realistic. Take Antonio Vivaldi's *Four Seasons* violin concerti composed in 1723. You can of course listen to it purely from a form point of view and discern different musical motifs, and hear how they develop and interact over time. But this ignores that the work is really about the four seasons: Summer, Spring, Winter, and Autumn. Each season is evoked with musical images conjuring up impressions and experiences related to that season. For example, in the Summer movement[6] we hear the laziness that comes with a sizzling hot sun, water flowing, birds, a barking dog, buzzing flies, but also the wind coming up, lightning bolts, thunder and then a violent escalating storm. Is this over-interpretation? Not really. Vivaldi himself wrote sonnets corresponding to each movement. The sonnets describe what experiences he was trying to evoke, helping the listener's imagination. Without considering this figurative aspect, listening to *Four Seasons* becomes an exercise in syntactic recognition that lacks meaning and therefore becomes boring once these sounds and structures have been grasped at their surface level.

Other examples of factual meaning in figurative music are easy to find. Claude Debussy's symphonic sketch *La Mer* (*The Sea*, in English) composed in 1903 is really about the sea. The first movement *De l'aube a midi sur la mer* (*From dawn to midday at the sea*, in English) gives the sensation of the swaying movement of the waves that start timidly but then become bigger with the water splashing as they break.[7] Another example are the so-called tone poems by Richard Strauss. For example, the last one of the *Vier letzte lieder* (*The four last songs*, in English) called *Im Abendrot* (*At Sunset* or more literally *'With the red of the evening'*, in English) was written in 1948 shortly before the composer died.[8] The song for soprano and orchestra evokes the red light of the sun going under but also the end of life depicted as a long walk by a couple. When the soprano sings 'Zwei Lerchen nur noch steigen/nachträumend in den Duft' ('Left are only two larks who climb like in a night dream in the air', in English), we hear singing larks evoked through two flutes. These larks are metaphors for the souls of the couple that are soon to go to heaven. The last phrase is: 'Wie sind wir wandermüde-Ist dies etwa der Tod?' ('We are tired of walking-is this near death?', in English) where Strauss reuses the basic theme of 'Tod und Erklaerung' ('Death and transfiguration', in English), another tone poem he wrote 60 years earlier, which is a musical portrait of a dying man entering into heaven. Clearly, when this broader context is provided the experience of *Im Abendrot* changes completely and goes beyond its remarkable sensual beauty.

The third Panofskyan level is about *expressional meaning*, in other words the psychological states, emotions and affects that are evoked through an artwork. Looking again at Caravaggio's *Presa di Cristo nell'orto* we see that every figure

---

[6]Mari Samuelsen, Trondheim solists: https://www.youtube.com/watch?v=g65oWFMSoK0 (Accesses on 04 February 2021).

[7]Claudio Abbado, Luzern Festival Orchestra: https://www.youtube.com/watch?v=SgSNgzA37To (Accessed on 04 February 2021).

[8]Anja Harteros, Sinfonieorchester des Bayerischen Rundfunks: https://www.youtube.com/watch?v=JwZOXC6_4fE (Accessed on 04 February 2021).

expresses clearly emotional states through the looks of their face, the gestures and body language. The apostle expressing fear while crying for help, Jesus almost saying to Judas: 'What are you doing?', frowning and looking sad, the onlooker to the right being curious and astonished about what is going on. Obviously, expressional meanings are abundant in music as well, and I am not referring now to expressive performance that brings out the music's phrase structure, which is on the form level, but to the expression of affective states, often related to the factual meanings of the musical work. Such expressive meanings are embedded in all the aspects of a piece of music: the tonality, the chords and chord progressions, the choice of instruments, the tempo, dynamics, loudness and articulation. The responsibility for recognizing the affective content in a score and expressing it in performance lies for a large part in the hands of human interpreters. It is the Achilles' heel of synthetic music.

The song by Richard Strauss showed already a magnificent example of a strongly emotional content. But let us listen to George Friedric Haendel's famous aria *Lascia ch'io pianga* from his opera *Rinaldo*[9] as a second example. The aria, composed in 1685 is sung by the character Almerina, who is held captive, away from her lover Rinaldo. The words are as follows: 'Lascia ch'io pianga / Mia cruda sorte, / E che sospiri / La libert'a Il duolo infranga / Queste ritorte, / De' miei martiri / Sol per pietà' (which translates in English as 'Allow that I weep over / my cruel fate, / and that I may sigh / for freedom. Let my sadness shatter / these chains / of my suffering, / if only out of pity'). The aria, in a tonality of F-major, and its orchestration is of utmost simplicity and you do not need to follow or understand the words to share the extreme feeling of sadness of Almerina, the desperation and frustration of being away from her lover, the longing for liberty. Many other magnificent examples of the importance and power of expression in music abound, including in purely instrumental music, and to ignore it is to deprive music of its potent force.

The expressive meaning level has already received considerable attention within AI approaches to musical meaning; see, for example, Widmer and Goebl (2004) and Chap. 19 this volume, because it is so crucial for a good performance. But so far, expression is mostly considered from the viewpoint of making the syntactic structure of the music more legible. This is very important in itself of course, but the expression of affective states and how they embed in a narrative remains almost virgin territory for AI approaches to music.

Next, there is the *cultural meaning* layer. It rests on knowing more about historical events, society, religious systems, myths, other cultural artefacts. For example, the Caravaggio *Presa di Cristo nell'orto* or Bach's *Matthäus Passion* can only be understood when knowing the Bible's narrative of these depicted events. For Christian believers, it has even more significance. They will feel total empathy with the suffering of Christ, the shock of the arrest, the protests of the apostles. Or

---

[9]Joyce Di Donato, Maxim Emelyanychev, *Il Pomo d'Oro*: https://www.youtube.com/watch?v=PrJTmpt43hg (Accessed on 04 February 2021).

consider, for example, the song *To Yelasto Pedi* (*The jovial boy*, in English) composed by Mikis Theodorakis, and performed to a full stadium after the fall of the military dictatorship in Greece in 1974.[10] This song, about the fascist terror exerted on the Greek population, was of enormous significance for the audience, particularly because they were forbidden and Theodorakis was jailed and forced into exile. The unforgettable concert in 1974 was a celebration of the regained freedom.

Similarly, fully experiencing the aria *Va pensiero* from Giuseppe Verdi's opera *Nabucco*, which has become something like an alternative national hymn of Italy, can only be done by understanding that it was written when Lombardy and Veneto were occupied by the Habsburg empire in the nineteenth century and the population felt enslaved like the slaves depicted in the opera. When this aria is performed today, Italian audiences often rise to sing along. The aria resonates because it was at the time a symbol of protest against oppression by the Habsburg armies. More recently it has been appropriated by Italian right-wing parties because of its patriotic symbolism but Ricardo Mutti in 2011 invited the audience to re-appropriate this highly symbolic music to protest against the dismantlement of cultural institutions and to regroup the cultural force of Italy and thus halt the slide in moral decay of Italy during the era of Silvio Berlusconi.[11]

Here is another example: the Jazz standard *Strange Fruit*. You can certainly listen to it—and it is often performed that way—as just another Jazz standard where the different performers give their own interpretations of the melody and harmony. However, this is totally missing the cultural and political significance of this song. It is actually a cry against the injustice of racial oppression that was happening in the south of the US in the 1920s and 30s when this song was conceived and performed. *Strange Fruit* refers to bodies of black people that have been tortured and lynched: 'Southern trees bear a strange fruit / Blood on the leaves and blood at the root / Black bodies swingin' in the Southern breeze / Strange fruit hangin' from the poplar trees'. When watching Billy Holliday's rendition of this song[12] there is raw authentic emotion. At the time, it raised high tensions and there were attempts to silence her, particularly as she sang it before white audiences. Without this historical context, the significance of the song is largely lost.

It is clearly too much to expect from a computer program to take this cultural context into account or to construct an authentic performance with the same cultural background and emotional force that humans bring to bear on such musical experiences. Nevertheless, this is what music in its full extent is all about. As more and more cultural knowledge becomes available through the World Wide Web and as the knowledge graphs and dictionaries (e.g., Wordnet or Propbank) have now

---

[10]Maria Farantouri, Mikis Theodorakis: https://www.youtube.com/watch?v=NLgerQJo7zM (Accessed on 04 February 2021).

[11]Ricardo Mutti, Scala of Milano: https://www.youtube.com/watch?v=5wAXhHrqOzQ&list=RDXg1yRoENqJQ&index=2 (access on 4 February 2021).

[12]Billy Holliday: https://www.youtube.com/watch?v=-_R8xxeMFEU (Accessed 4 February 2021).

become accessible to the AI and music research community for use in meaning-oriented AI, new opportunities will certainly emerge to preserve much more of the cultural context of musical works and to make it more accessible as part of recordings or in educational settings. That is also a task for the future.

Finally, Panofsky talks about the *intrinsic meaning* of an artwork: the motivations of the artist, what does he or she try to accomplish. This can, for example, be a political statement, social commentary, moral advice, community bonding, commemoration of traumatic events, religious and spiritual exaltation, or mere entertainment. The intrinsic meaning of Holliday's *Strange Fruit* or Theodorakis song *To Yelasto Pedi* is political, protesting against injustice. The meaning of Bach's *Matthäus Passion*, and much of his other music, is spiritual. Needless to say, this dimension is entirely lacking in computational musical compositions or synthetic performance, mainly because AI systems, despite claims in the popular press, do not have the kind of autonomous agency and social embedding that humans have. This gap is not a criticism. But it should make us all humble and critical about AI researchers claiming that their computer programs can now make music as good as human composers! They have fallen in the Turing trap: to create music superficially indistinguishable from a real composition by a (usually naïve) human observer. But this is fake music because it lacks the many levels of meaning that are the essence of human music. It is not grounded in identity or human motivation. It does not express affective values. It is not embedded in cultural and societal concerns.

Let me summarize the main point of this essay. Our current computational tools can handle a remarkable number of signal processing and feature recognition aspects for going from sounds to notes, rhythms and phrasal structures. They can represent and enact constraints on harmony, instrumentation or rhythm for musical composition. And they can even approach very difficult issues in performance and audio synthesis. Nevertheless, they rarely address the meanings and musical narratives which underlie music as an art form. Consequently, it makes no sense to call these systems creative in the same way as human composers, performers or listeners are musically creative.

I do not believe that the rich web of meanings that we as humans naturally engage in will ever be captured by an AI system, particularly if it is disembodied and has no social role in a human community. Nevertheless, the fantastic tools we have already today make it conceivable to attempt a significant leap in the direction of meaning. This development would be in line with a current trend in AI research, which considers meaning as the key barrier AI still has to overcome (Mitchell, 2020) and calls for a 'human-centric AI' where only through a proper focus on meaning can we create a more responsible and more robust form of AI than the one underlying many of today's applications (Steels, 2020).

A focus on meaning in AI research into music would allow us to understand better the relation between music and the musical narratives that it can invoke in listeners, and the strategies composers use to design music that can realize this function. I do not think this will happen soon but if it happens it would lead to many new spin-offs for enhancing musical practice, preserving or reconstructing musical heritage, richer musical compositions, and many great musical experiences for all of us. It would also allow us a whole new approach towards musical creativity, now understood as establishing multi-dimensional mappings between a complex web of meanings and musical forms.

Barcelona, Spain   Luc Steels
December 2020

Acknowledgements The writing of this essay was possible by the support of the Catalan Institute for Research and Advanced Studies (ICREA) and partly funded by the European FET Proactive Project MUHAI on Meaning and Understanding in Human-centric AI. I am indebted to Oscar Vilarroya for many discussions about the role of meaning in understanding the human mind and its manifestations in art.

References

Dewey, R. (2018). *Hack the experience. New tools for artists from cognitive science.* Brainstorm books. Goleto, Ca.

Dumoulin, V., Shlens J., Kudlur M. (2017). A learned representation for artistic style. https://arxiv. org/abs/1610.07629 (Accessed on 04 February 2021)

Golio, G. (2017). *Strange Fruit. Billie Holliday and he power of a protest song.* Minneapolis: Milbrook Press.

Guerrieri, M. (2012). *The first four notes. Beethoven's fifth and the musical imagination.* New York: Random House.

Hiller, L., Isaacson L. (1959). *Experimental Music: Composition with an electronic computer.* New York: McGraw-Hill.

Kuhn, L. (Ed.) (2016). *The selected Letters of John Cage.* Middletown, CT: Wesleyan University Press.

Meyer, L. (1956). *Emotion and meaning in music.* University of Chicago Press

Minsky, M. (1968). *Semantic information processing.* Cambridge Ma: The MIT Press.

Minsky, M. (1981). Music, Mind, and Meaning. *Computer Music Journal,* 5(3).

Mitchell, M. (2020). On crashing the barrier of meaning in Artificial Intelligence. *AI magazine,* 41(2).

Newell, A., Simon, H. (1956). The logic theory machine: A complex information processing system. *IRE Transactions of Information Theory* 2:61–79.

Nilson, N. (2010). *The quest for Artificial Intelligence. A history of ideas and achievements.* Cambridge UK: Cambridge University Press.

Panofsky, E. (1939). *Studies in iconology. Humanistic themes in the art of the renaissance.* Oxford: Oxford University Press.

Rosenblatt, F. (1962). *Principles of Neurodynamics: Perceptrons and the Theory of Brain Mechanisms.* Washington DC: Spartan Books.

Schank, R. (1983.) *Dynamic memory a theory of reminding and learning in computers and people.* Cambridge UK: Cambridge University Press.

Schoenberg, A. (1995). *The Musical Idea and the Logic, Technique, and Art of Its Presentation. motive, gestalt, phrase, theme, rhythm, harmony, and form. English translation.* New York: Columbia University Press.

Schwanauer, S. Levitt D. (1984). *Machine models of music.* Cambridge Ma: The MIT Press.

Skinner, B. F. (1953). *Science and human behaviour.* New York: Macmillian.

Steels, L. (2015). *Music learning with Massive Open Online Courses (MOOCS).* Amsterdam: IOS Press.

Steels, L. (2020). Personal Dynamic Memories are Necessary to Deal with Meaning and Understanding in Human-Centric AI. In: Saffiotti, A, L. Serafini and P. Lukowicz (eds). Proceedings of the First International Workshop on New Foundations for Human-Centered AI (NeHuAI) Co-located with 24th European Conference on Artificial Intelligence (ECAI 2020) CEUR Workshop Proceedings (CEUR-WS.org, ISSN 1613-0073) Vol-2659.

Stravinsky, I. (1935). *Igor stravinsky. An autobiography*. New York: Simon and Schuster.

Watson, J. (1930). *Behaviorism*. New York, NU: Norton.

Widmer, G. Goebl W. (2004.) Computational models of expressive music performance: the state of the art. *Journal of New Music Research*. 33(3) 203–216.

Preface

I am delighted to be in a position to write this preface: it is the last task that I need to get done before I submit the manuscript for production. I have just gone through the checklist. All good to go. It was a long, but nevertheless gratifying, journey.

I must confess that I misjudged the magnitude of the job when I signed up to produce this book. It ended up being a much greater project than I had anticipated. And much harder too. The field of Artificial Intelligence (AI) today is overwhelming. It is very difficult to map. And throwing music into the mix makes things even muddier.

It was relatively straightforward to survey the field when I edited the book *Readings in Music and Artificial Intelligence* 20 years ago.[13] There were only a handful of pioneers taking music as a serious domain for AI at the time. Research into applying AI in music was in its infancy. I vividly remember the disdainful looks I used to get at international AI conferences in the 1990s when introducing myself as a musician. And to add insult to injury, musicians used to scoff at the notion of making music with AI. Perceptions have changed. And how!

Back then, neural networks were not much more than a theoretical promise based on toy problems. Practical implementations often failed to impress. Symbolic knowledge representation and logic-based modelling were the norm. Functional programming with LISP and logic programming with PROLOG defined the bastions of AI research at the time; the latter favoured in Europe, notably in France and Scotland, the former in the USA and beyond. From this era, two notable achievements immediately come to mind. David Cope's EMI system emerged as an exemplary LISP-based system, able to learn and compose in the style of classical music composers. And the Continuator system (precursor of the Flow Machines project) led by my former colleague at Sony, François Pachet, took the symbolic approach to an unprecedented level of sophistication.

Since then, neural networks evolved significantly with the emergence of the so-called 'deep learning' methods, which are remarkable. Deep learning has been enjoying considerable publicity. So much so that it has inadvertently become a synonym of AI for some: I often have students coming through the door these days

---

[13]https://www.taylorfrancis.com/books/readings-music-artificial-intelligence-eduardo-reck-miranda/e/10.4324/9780203059746.

thinking that AI and deep learning are the same thing. Yet, deep learning alone is of limited capacity to model and simulate intelligence; depending on what one means by 'intelligence', of course. This book concerns musical intelligence.

In addition to developing technology to building musical systems able to personify aspects of human intelligence, AI is a great tool to study musical intelligence. If anything, AI research has demonstrated that intelligence in general requires more than logical reasoning. It requires creativity, subjectivity, emotions, interaction, embodiment, and all those things that the brain takes care of, consciously and unconsciously, to keep us alive. Music engages a multitude of these human capacities. Hence the reason music has become such an interesting domain for AI research.

This book comprises 34 chapters from leading scholars and practitioners approaching AI in music from a variety of perspectives. There are chapters touching upon sociological, philosophical and musicological issues: Chapters 1–4, 31. Then, we have chapters on understanding our musical brain and body for (and with) AI: Chaps. 5–9. These naturally connect with chapters discussing cognition and modelling thereof: Chapters 10–12 and 15. More technical chapters introduce a variety of applications ranging from improvisation and composition (Chaps. 14, 16 –18), to performance (Chaps. 19, 27), orchestration (Chap. 20), notation (Chaps. 24 , 25), studio production (Chaps. 13, 30) and even lyrics for popular music (Chap. 26). Other important applications of AI represented in this book are sound synthesis and signal processing (Chaps. 21–23), and musical robotics (Chaps. 28, 29).

The field is evolving faster than ever. AI is becoming so ubiquitous in our daily lives that the topic as we know it today is becoming diluted. It is being absorbed by other domains; almost every application of computing involves some form of AI in a way or another. One question that the AI and music community should certainly consider, however, is this: What is next? Has AI research reached the end of the road? Twenty years from now, what would the sequel book be about, if any?

The last three chapters (Chaps. 32–34) consider harnessing biology to develop living processors for 'not-so-Artificial' Intelligence systems and the potential of emerging quantum computing technology for music. The computers that our children will be using in 2050 are likely to be significantly different from the ones we are using today. What will be the impact of these on AI, music and indeed society?

I am grateful to Luc Steels for agreeing to write the foreword. Luc was director of Sony Computer Science Laboratory Paris at the time when I worked there as a member of his Origins of Language team. Luc is well respected internationally for his ground-breaking research on computational modelling of the origins and evolution of language, and robotics. Luc also enjoys composing opera[14] and has made pioneering contributions to the field of computer music in the 1980s. In the foreword, Luc touches upon the problem of making sense of musical meaning, a topic

---

[14]See *Casparo*, a tragi-comic opera in three acts by Luc Steels (music) and Oscar Villaroya Oliver (libretto): https://bit.ly/3obAHuH.

that is seldom discussed in AI and music research. It is an invitation to this research community to take the challenge.

I do not have words to express my gratitude to all contributors to this book. My heartfelt thanks to you all. You taught me a great deal about AI, but even more so about human intelligence, and above all, generosity. Thank you!

Plymouth, UK   Eduardo Reck Miranda
October 2020

Contents

1 Sociocultural and Design Perspectives on AI-Based Music Production: Why Do We Make Music and What Changes if AI Makes It for Us? 1
Oliver Bown

2 Human–Machine Simultaneity in the Compositional Process 21
Hanns Holger Rutz

3 Artificial Intelligence for Music Composition 53
Artemi-Maria Gioti

4 Artificial Intelligence in Music and Performance: A Subjective Art-Research Inquiry 75
Baptiste Caramiaux and Marco Donnarumma

5 Neuroscience of Musical Improvisation 97
Psyche Loui

6 Discovering the Neuroanatomical Correlates of Music with Machine Learning 117
Tatsuya Daikoku

7 Music, Artificial Intelligence and Neuroscience 163
David Cope

8 Creative Music Neurotechnology 195
Eduardo Reck Miranda

9 On Making Music with Heartbeats 237
Elaine Chew

10 Cognitive Musicology and Artificial Intelligence: Harmonic Analysis, Learning, and Generation 263
Emilios Cambouropoulos and Maximos Kaliakatsos-Papakostas

11 On Modelling Harmony with Constraint Programming for Algorithmic Composition Including a Model of Schoenberg's Theory of Harmony 283
Torsten Anders

12   Constraint-Solving Systems in Music Creation   327
     Örjan Sandred

13   AI Music Mixing Systems   345
     David Moffat

14   Machine Improvisation in Music: Information-Theoretical
     Approach   377
     Shlomo Dubnov

15   Structure, Abstraction and Reference in Artificial Musical
     Intelligence   409
     Geraint A. Wiggins

16   Folk the Algorithms: (Mis)Applying Artificial Intelligence
     to Folk Music   423
     Bob L. T. Sturm and Oded Ben-Tal

17   Automatic Music Composition with Evolutionary Algorithms:
     Digging into the Roots of Biological Creativity   455
     Francisco Vico, David Albarracin-Molina, Gustavo Diaz-Jerez
     and Luca Manzoni

18   Assisted Music Creation with Flow Machines: Towards New
     Categories of New   485
     François Pachet, Pierre Roy and Benoit Carré

19   Performance Creativity in Computer Systems for Expressive
     Performance of Music   521
     Alexis Kirke and Eduardo Reck Miranda

20   Imitative Computer-Aided Musical Orchestration
     with Biologically Inspired Algorithms   585
     Marcelo Caetano and Carmine E. Cella

21   Human-Centred Artificial Intelligence in Concatenative Sound
     Synthesis   617
     Noris Mohd Norowi

22   Deep Generative Models for Musical Audio Synthesis   639
     Muhammad Huzaifah and Lonce Wyse

23   Transfer Learning for Generalized Audio Signal Processing   679
     Stavros Ntalampiras

24   From Audio to Music Notation   693
     Lele Liu and Emmanouil Benetos

25   Automatic Transcription of Polyphonic Vocal Music   715
     Rodrigo Schramm

26 Graph-Based Representation, Analysis, and Interpretation of Popular Music Lyrics Using Semantic Embedding Features 737
Mitsunori Ogihara, Brian Manolovitz, Vítor Y. Shinohara, Gang Ren and Tiago F. Tavares

27 Interactive Machine Learning of Musical Gesture 771
Federico Ghelli Visi and Atau Tanaka

28 Human–Robot Musical Interaction 799
Sarah Cosentino and Atsuo Takanishi

29 Shimon Sings-Robotic Musicianship Finds Its Voice 823
Richard Savery, Lisa Zahray and Gil Weinberg

30 AI-Lectronica: Music AI in Clubs and Studio Production 849
Shelly Knotts and Nick Collins

31 Musicking with Algorithms: Thoughts on Artificial Intelligence, Creativity, and Agency 873
Palle Dahlstedt

32 *cellF*: Surrogate Musicianship as a Manifestation of In-Vitro Intelligence 915
Vahri McKenzie, Nathan John Thompson, Darren Moore and Guy Ben-Ary

33 On Growing Computers from Living Biological Cells 933
Eduardo Reck Miranda, Edward Braund and Satvik Venkatesh

34 Quantum Computer: Hello, Music! 963
Eduardo Reck Miranda

Editor and Contributors

About the Editor

Eduardo Reck Miranda is Professor in Computer Music and head the Interdisciplinary Centre for Computer Music Research (ICCMR) at the University of Plymouth, UK. He studied music, philosophy and informatics in Brazil before he graduated with an M.Sc. in Music Technology from the University of York, UK. Subsequently he received a Ph.D. on the topic of sound design with Artificial Intelligence (AI) from the University of Edinburgh, UK. Before joining the University of Plymouth, he worked at Sony Computer Science Laboratory in Paris, France, as a research scientist in the fields of AI, speech and evolution of language. He also is a composer working at the crossroads of music and science. His distinctive music is informed by his unique background as a classically trained composer and AI scientist with an early involvement in electroacoustic and avant-garde pop music. E-mail: eduardo.miranda@plymouth.ac.uk

Contributors

David Albarracin-Molina ETS Ingeniería Informática - Campus de Teatinos, Malaga, Spain

Torsten Anders Aiva Technologies, Luxembourg, Luxembourg

Guy Ben-Ary University of Western Australia, Darlington, WA, Australia

Oded Ben-Tal Department of Performing Arts, Kingston University, London KT1 2EE, UK

Emmanouil Benetos School of Electronic Engineering and Computer Science, Queen Mary University of London, London E1 4NS, UK

Oliver Bown Interactive Media Lab, School of Art & Design, UNSW, Paddington, Australia

Edward Braund Interdisciplinary Centre for Computer Music Research (ICCMR), University of Plymouth, Plymouth PL4 8AA, UK

Marcelo Caetano Schulich School of Music & CIRMMT, McGill University, Montreal, Canada

Emilios Cambouropoulos School of Music Studies, Aristotle University of Thessaloniki, Thermi, Thessaloniki, Greece

Baptiste Caramiaux Sorbonne Université, CNRS, ISIR, Paris, France

Benoit Carré Spotify CTRL, Paris, France

Carmine E. Cella University of California, Berkeley, Berkeley, CA, USA

Elaine Chew CNRS-UMR/STMS (IRCAM), Paris, France

Nick Collins Durham University, Durham DH1 3LE, UK

David Cope Department of Music, University of California, Santa Cruz, La Jolla, CA, USA

Sarah Cosentino Waseda University, Tokyo, Japan

Palle Dahlstedt Department of Computer Science and Engineering, and the Academy of Music and Drama, University of Gothenburg and Chalmers University of Technology, Gothenburg, Sweden

Tatsuya Daikoku International Research Center for Neurointelligence (WPI-IRCN), The University of Tokyo, Tokyo, Japan

Gustavo Diaz-Jerez ETS Ingeniería Informática - Campus de Teatinos, Malaga, Spain

Marco Donnarumma Independent artist based in Berlin, Berlin, Germany

Shlomo Dubnov Department of Music, University of California San Diego, La Jolla, CA, USA

Artemi-Maria Gioti Institute of Electronic Music and Acoustics (IEM), University of Music and Performing Arts Graz, Graz, Austria

Hanns Holger Rutz Reagenz-Association for Artistic Experiments, Morellenfeldgasse 11, 8010 Graz, Austria

Muhammad Huzaifah NUS Graduate School for Integrative Sciences and Engineering, National University of Singapore, Singapore, Singapore

Maximos Kaliakatsos-Papakostas School of Music Studies, Aristotle University of Thessaloniki, Thermi, Thessaloniki, Greece

Alexis Kirke Interdisciplinary Centre for Computer Music Research (ICCMR), University of Plymouth, Plymouth PL4 8AA, UK

Shelly Knotts Durham University, Durham DH1 3LE, UK

Lele Liu School of Electronic Engineering and Computer Science, Queen Mary University of London, London E1 4NS, UK

Psyche Loui Northeastern University, Boston, MA, USA

Brian Manolovitz Department of Computer Science, University of Miami, Coral Gables, FL, USA

Luca Manzoni ETS Ingeniería Informática - Campus de Teatinos, Malaga, Spain

Vahri McKenzie Centre for Creative and Cultural Research, Faculty of Arts and Design, University of Canberra, Canberra, Australia

Eduardo Reck Miranda Interdisciplinary Centre for Computer Music Research (ICCMR), University of Plymouth, Plymouth PL4 8AA, UK

David Moffat Interdisciplinary Centre for Computer Music Research (ICCMR), University of Plymouth, Plymouth PL4 8AA, UK

Darren Moore LaSalle College of the Arts, Singapore, Singapore

Noris Mohd Norowi Faculty of Computer Science and Information Technology, Universiti Putra Malaysia, Serdang, Selangor, Malaysia

Stavros Ntalampiras University of Milan, Milan, Italy

Mitsunori Ogihara Department of Computer Science, University of Miami, Coral Gables, FL, USA

François Pachet Spotify CTRL, Paris, France

Gang Ren Department of Computer Science, University of Miami, Coral Gables, FL, USA

Pierre Roy Spotify CTRL, Paris, France

Örjan Sandred Desautels Faculty of Music, University of Manitoba, Winnipeg, MB, Canada

Richard Savery Georgia Tech Center for Music Technology, Atlanta, GA, USA

Rodrigo Schramm Federal University of Rio Grande do Sul, Porto Alegre, Brazil

Vítor Y. Shinohara School of Electrical and Computer Engineering, University of Campinas, Campinas, Brazil

Bob L. T. Sturm Tal, Musik och Hörsel (Speech, Music and Hearing), School of Electronic Engineering and Computer Science, Royal Institute of Technology KTH, Stockholm, Sweden

Atsuo Takanishi Waseda University, Tokyo, Japan

Atau Tanaka Embodied Audiovisual Interaction, Goldsmiths, University of London, London SE14 6NW, UK

Tiago F. Tavares School of Electrical and Computer Engineering, University of Campinas, Campinas, Brazil

Nathan John Thompson University of Western Australia, Beaconsfield, WA, Australia

Satvik Venkatesh Interdisciplinary Centre for Computer Music Research (ICCMR), University of Plymouth, Plymouth PL4 8AA, UK

Francisco Vico ETS Ingeniería Informática - Campus de Teatinos, Malaga, Spain

Federico Ghelli Visi GEMM))) Gesture Embodiment and Machines in Music, School of Music in Piteå, Luleå University of Technology, Piteå, Sweden

Gil Weinberg Georgia Tech Center for Music Technology, Atlanta, GA, USA

Geraint A. Wiggins Vrije Universiteit Brussel, Brussels, Belgium

Lonce Wyse Communications and New Media Department, National University of Singapore, Singapore, Singapore

Lisa Zahray Georgia Tech Center for Music Technology, Atlanta, GA, USA

Sociocultural and Design Perspectives on AI-Based Music Production: Why Do We Make Music and What Changes if AI Makes It for Us?

1

Oliver Bown

1.1 Introduction

The recent advance α of artificial intelligence (AI) technologies that can generate musical material (e.g. [1–4]) has driven a wave of interest in applications, creative works and commercial enterprises that employ AI in music creation. Most fundamental to these endeavours is research focused on the question of how to create better algorithms that are capable of generating music, but the wider issue of application and use draws on a diverse range of fields including design, psychology, creative practice and sociocultural factors. This chapter takes a closer look at the sociological and design dimensions of AI music generation, and offers researchers in AI and music a number of themes and references that can be used to help frame creative practice and applications, supporting the design and evaluation of creative music systems.

I begin by considering the more practice-based origins of AI-based music generation, which I suggest has traditionally taken a more philosophical orientation towards the question of musical intelligence and creative autonomy in machines. Then I consider how design has given the field a more functional applied focus which has to some extent drawn attention away from the philosophical concerns of earlier creative practitioners. Then I consider how sociological views, which remain relatively marginal to the practice of AI music, are beginning to influence the field and contribute a much-needed vantage point for understanding human musical behaviour.

O. Bown (✉)
Interactive Media Lab, School of Art & Design, UNSW, Paddington, Australia
e-mail: o.bown@unsw.edu.au

© Springer Nature Switzerland AG 2021
E. R. Miranda (ed.), *Handbook of Artificial Intelligence for Music*,
https://doi.org/10.1007/978-3-030-72116-9_1

1.2 The Philosophical Era

In the 1950s, Lejaren Hiller and Leonard Isaacson composed the *Illiac Suite* [5], widely recognised as the first score composed with the creative input of algorithms running on a digital computer, the ILLIAC 1 computer, based at the University of Illinois at Urbana-Champaign. The *Illiac Suite* consists of four movements, each of which explored different methods of algorithmic composition including hand-coded rules and the now widely used stochastic generation method of Markov modelling. It is well over half a century since this first experiment in computer music generation, and the capabilities of computers have advanced unimaginably. Subfields of Computer Science have made great advances, particularly over the last decade in Deep Learning [6] (a summary of Deep Learning applications in music can be found here [1,2]). Programmes far more complex than Hiller and Isaacson's run in real time on $10 credit card-sized computers, and school children are learning to code using programming languages that abstract away the complexities of the machine code they would have had to use. Yet listening to the *Illiac Suite*, you might think that the authors had solved automated music generation on the very first attempt. The music sounds harmonious and richly structured, original and emotional. You might conclude upon listening that automated music generation is not a hard problem.

In fact, on the contrary, this field possesses some of the characteristics of a *wicked problem* [7], that is ill-defined and potentially unsolvable due to its complexity and sociocultural embeddedness. Relevant features of wicked problems include that there is no definitive formulation, no ultimate test and no stopping rule. Researchers are definitely still trying to discover functional music generation algorithms today, that could effectively generate new and original musical works from the ground up. Unsurprisingly, this disconnect between us thinking of the *Illiac Suite* as a success and yet still finding automated music generation a hard problem arises because of the complex context of creative production.

Hiller and Isaacson were composers (amongst other things), and their approach to the *Illiac Suite* took a form that continued for the rest of the century to be, arguably, the predominant approach to computer-generated music experiments; creative practitioners with hacking skills (or with paid programming support) programming computers in tasks of algorithmic composition (there are significant exceptions, of course, like the creation of more traditional end-user tools such as Microsoft's *Songsmith*). Here, the creative interaction between human and software system takes the form of an iterative cycle of programming and reviewing machine output, followed by any further processes the human author wishes to add to complete the work (arranging, orchestrating and performing the work, for example). The process is summarised in a simplified form in Fig. 1.1.

This diagram purposefully highlights the limited scope of the machine and the various ways in which creative authority is maintained by the human composer. For example, if the system produces outputs that don't sound right the first time, the composer can modify the program code or parameters through trial and error—a form of search enacted by the composer. They can cherry-pick outputs, and they can

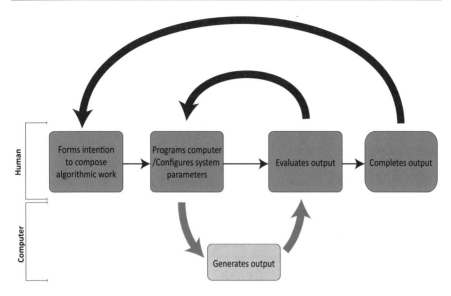

Fig. 1.1 Typical human–computer creative interaction in algorithmic composition where the composer is either the programmer or user of an existing program

perform additional work on the resulting outputs, modifying them or engaging in additional steps such as arranging, orchestrating or rendering the result.

Thus conceived, the challenge of making better algorithmic composition systems could be defined in terms of moving more of these stages and decisions into the computer's scope, to the point where a computer is more autonomous in the creation of music, or alternatively making the computer perform so well in the given role that it minimises the need for the composer to iteratively search for the 'right' output. Historically, this has been the focus of much academic work in computer-generated music, underpinned by a vision of creating machines that fulfil the role of human-equivalent artists. Practitioners of algorithmic composition have endeavoured to create systems that allow them to be as hands-off as possible, intending to hand over autonomy and control to the machine in order to fulfil this vision of the machine performing the artist's job. We can think of this in terms of timescales or levels of a creative agency. At a very low level, we might think of the creative work that goes into the choice of a single note in a sequence. Higher up we might think of the composition of an individual melody. Up and up at the other extreme we might think of the kind of creative development a practitioner engages in over their lifetime involving choices of styles, paradigms and strategies; in theory, these might all be creative processes that could be codified in computer programs.

Such a vision was popularised by writers such as Ray Kurzweil [8] who prophesised that autonomous machine artists were imminent and, as in other areas of AI, would begin to take their place alongside human artists. For many artists, this endeavour to experiment with creative autonomy in machines was primarily grounded in an aesthetic philosophical interest; the creative work acting both as a simulation experiment as well as a kind of cultural probe [9], stimulating reactions. David Cope [10, 11] famously upset musicologists with machine-generated compositions that he disguised as human works. He viewed his works as a proof-of-concept that musical composition could be subjected to mechanical instructions, and that much of the defensiveness found in responses to his work was hubristic and based on an essentialist view that human creativity was profound and inimitable. In the parallel world of generative visual art systems, pioneer Harold Cohen [12] used his work, co-creating with rule-based software of his own making, to explore how we attribute authorial agency to machines:

> If a photographer takes a picture, we do not say that the picture has been made by the camera. If, on the other hand, a man writes a chess-playing program for a computer, and then loses to it, we do not consider it unreasonable to say that he has been beaten by the computer. [12]

But since these composer-centric efforts in algorithmic composition are always ultimately (and heavily—despite various claims made) in the creative control of the practitioner, it becomes tricky to define quite how the system is able to take on creative autonomy, no matter how good the results are and how little, metaphorically speaking, the human artist's hand touched the canvas. For example, Brian Eno's celebrated generative music experiments [13] were purposefully musically simple, constrained to a pleasant melodic space not dissimilar to the output of aeolian harps. The *Illiac Suite*'s fourth movement sounds significantly more abrasive and challenging than the other movements, reflecting the weirder results of their Markov experiments. In both cases, we are hearing the aesthetics that emerge when a composer grapples with algorithmic possibilities; arguably less important is the detail filled in by the algorithm's decisions. It is possible that the trickiness of unpacking and evaluating such efforts—the wickedness of the problem—has, over time, whittled away this once strong interest in making autonomous machine artists.

Moreover, there is a wider context of engagement in the sociocultural environment that frames such cultural production; the human arrives at this interaction having formed an intention to do so, usually with a specific style, agenda and audience in mind, and, importantly, motivated by social objectives such as engagement with a community or social status. They may also exert other forms of influence on the sociocultural environment; for example, if they are successful they may be more empowered to influence what constitutes good music. If all of this culturally grounded activity is part of being an artist, then the full hand-over of being an artist to a machine becomes unimaginably complex and beyond the scope of anyone's capability.

Friction between engineering and sociologically grounded perspectives arises here: from an engineer's perspective, where simplifying first-approximations to problems are used purposefully to scaffold more substantial solutions, it would seem reasonable to separate out such questions of social context from questions of what note goes next or how to arrange a composition for dramatic effect, and the success of music generation tools at mimicking musical style and proposing interesting new content is testament to this approach. However, from a human scientist's perspective, the engineer's simplification may be untenable; the result of their work is a strange beast that does not correspond exactly with anything in the pre-existing world. It is as much a novel hybrid as it is a model of any particular aspect of human behaviour. This is an important difference of perspective that can be hard to fully appreciate.

1.3 Creative Cognition and Lofty Versus Lowly Computational Creativity

In the field of Computational Creativity [14], a common tenet is that the mere generation of creative content, although a critical subcomponent, is far from a complete model of human creative production [15]. An act of creative production, it is held, requires evaluation and iteration of outputs; when humans make music, art and other forms of cultural production, a key component of their process is reflection and iteration. Algorithms that do not do this are deficient and, it could be said, have no sense of the aesthetic and cultural world they act in.

In practical terms, the majority of current generative art practices are situated in the domain of 'mere generation'. This includes most of the work of creative coding artists from Harold Cohen and David Cope onwards, who shepherd their generative systems, but it also includes the bulk of advanced machine learning (ML) systems applied to music that perform predictive modelling of what should come next in a sequence, not involving any creative iteration or evaluation. These 'lowly' forms of generative practice may generate creative works of stunning originality and sophistication, but they have no meta-awareness they are doing so. They are not culturally aware agents and they have no sense of judgement or inherent taste themselves. The 'lofty' goal of Computational Creativity is to create systems that perform genuine human-like creative cognition, which involves a host of cognitive processes and is largely understood as a search process.

1.4 The Design Turn

In recent years, design thinking and design practices have become increasingly fore-grounded in the study of the application of AI to music (e.g. [16–18]). This is in step with design's more general rise to prominence, especially in technology innovation where design methods now enable a richer and more productive cycle of feedback between the work of the engineer and the experience and needs of the human user. It has also arisen naturally within the music AI field in recognition of the importance of interfaces and user interactions even when the ultimate goal is to build an 'autonomous' intelligent system. Everything has an interface, even a sophisticated robot that can converse in natural language, or a real-time improvisational musical agent that interacts via musical sound. As AI-powered systems emerge in multiple different fields, it has become increasingly evident that the design of interactions occurs all the way up the scale of AI sophistication. Even if you are conversing with a machine in plain English, its behaviour is packed with design decisions, from the overall interface and interaction context to the specific responses and behavioural traits. Thus, design considerations clearly extend beyond the graphical and tangible aspects of an interface; non-graphical voice-audio or music-audio interfaces present their own unique challenges for interaction design. For example, the makers of real-time improvisational interfaces must still grapple with designed interactions such as turn-taking strategies or ways for the system to signal to the user that it is responding, whether it is hearing properly, and so on (e.g. as discussed in [19]).

Although they rarely framed their discussion in terms of interaction design, those early innovators such as Hiller and Isaacson, Cope and, in the visual domain, Harold Cohen, could all be seen to be interacting with their systems in a variety of ways, even if through the code interface itself, engaging in heuristic creative strategies, evaluating and iterating. In doing so, their work inevitably highlights many interesting interaction design concepts. Today design thinking horizontally penetrates other fields from business to computer science, with music AI systems as natural an area of application as any other; current creators of AI music systems are more likely to apply design terminology and methods, following the leading work by researchers such as Rebecca Fiebrink [17], Thor Magnusson [20], Nick Collins [21], Andrew Brown [19] and Fraçois Pachet [22] (also see Anna Kantosalo's work in non-music domains [23]). Areas of practice such as 'live coding' have focused more explicitly on the design of usable and creatively productive programming languages and environments, work that has extended into the design of usable generative and AI-based systems. This work draws on research into the design of creatively empowering and productive software systems, such as Blackwell and Green work on the cognitive dimensions of notations [24], Shneiderman, Resnick, Candy, Edmonds and colleagues' work on creativity support tools [25–27] and more general usability principles such as Nielsen's heuristics for user interface design [28] and key interaction design work such as that of Donald Norman [29].

Thus increasingly, the question of how good interaction design can support the creation of successful AI music tools has become more commonly posed (for example, [17,18,20,21,30]), and a general shift can be seen away from the more philosophical concerns of autonomous music composition agents, towards AI tools that support creative production. This is in part due to the maturation of the technology and the potential for business opportunities that invite a user-centered design perspective to solve the problem of making usable technology.

The design of usable AI music systems can be divided very roughly into two categories: tools targeting creators, those people already involved in the production of music; and tools targeting non-musician end-users who need music services, including professionals such as film producers, their equivalent amateur or prosumer creators (such as amateur YouTube contributors) and other types of music consumers. In both cases, as with other areas of technology innovation, the use-cases to which new AI music technologies are applied can be broadly divided into those use-cases that effectively model an existing scenario and those use-cases that are novel.

Regarding tools for creators, there are a number of common creative practice contexts and activities that point to some of the main uses for AI in music. Some major areas that cover a great deal of the scope of creator-based AI music production are as follows:

- Supporting a composition task in an offline context (i.e. not performed live), for example, when working in a Digital Audio Workstation, on a paper score or composing with an instrument.
- Creating, configuring and performing with intelligent performance systems such as improvising musical agents and intelligent augmented instruments, where the system is perceived as having creative agency in some capacity. This has been a popular topic of discussion in communities such as the Live Algorithms for Music and Musical Metacreation research groups.
- Meta-designing musical interfaces to be used in creation or performance. This area is exemplified by the work of Rebecca Fiebrink with her Wekinator software, which can be used for rapid on-the-fly mapping by non-programmer users in a range of contexts [17].
- Developing bespoke systems with niche applications. A recent popular example is Holly Herndon's AI choir, which does not aim for a dominant creative role by AI in the musical composition, but a more specific creative function within her compositional work.

The first area is vast and I will consider it in a bit more detail. AI-supported composition may be a collaborative or solo activity in any number of musical cultural niches from commercial studio production to highly experimental art music to educational contexts. Common tasks include melodic-, chord- or drum-pattern creation, arrangement, orchestration, harmonisation, timbre selection, expressive performance rendering (as in 'groove quantise') and related production tasks such as mixing and mastering (as performed by the successful commercial software service *Landr* (https://www.landr.com/)). Contextual factors for the task may include adaption to existing musical content (e.g. selecting a chord progression to fit a melodic line), and selecting styles and other parameters (e.g. achieved through selecting a training corpus). Two important use-case paradigms here are rapid ideation, as performed by *Aiva* (https://www.aiva.ai/), where the system's main purpose is to support the rapid ideation of potentials; and a producer–session–musician relationship, where the system's main purpose is to provide modular adaptive units for insertion into a composition, as popularised in amateur production by Apple's *Garage Band* software (https://www.apple.com/au/mac/garageband/). Slightly distinct from these two paradigms is the situation in which there is more of a conceptual commitment to the idea of the system being an autonomous independent creator, or more loosely sometimes acting as a 'collaborator' (examples include the Sony CSL-produced *Daddy's Car* track [31]). One other related category is the creation of adaptive compositions such as music for games or VR/AR experiences, where the preparation of a composition is performed offline, but its ultimate structuring occurs at listening time. However, this category of activity is more correctly placed in the 'Tools for Consumers' category.

Tools for consumers might include systems for democratising music production and generative music for games and other interactive experiences. We can imagine that as such tools emerge the specific use-cases in which consumer-based generative music might occur will evolve. For example, with the rise of predictive tools in text messaging and richer text media such as emojis and gifs we can imagine the automation of creative content such as images or music becoming applied to rapid-fire social interactions.

1.4.1 Design Evaluation

The design process is strongly focused on the evaluation of tools in the hands of users, feeding back into improved designs in an iterative cycle. For example, tools to support music ideation can be evaluated in terms of the speed of development of new musical ideas, how well they enable a creator to break a creative block or discover new directions (as reported by the creator, for example), or how well they augment someone's musical skill (for example, could a system that enables style transfer support an expert jazz musician to transfer their skills to Latin music styles?).

Compared to the earlier philosophical perspective, the system's creative autonomy becomes a broader but somewhat more measurable issue from a design perspective:

- Does the system create music well (canonically) under given stylistic or task constraints? In many contexts, such as generating a piece of music for a YouTube video, we aren't necessarily concerned with whether a system is innovative, but whether it can produce functional music that conforms to stylistic requirements. Thus, a need for typicality may be key [32].
- Does the system creatively innovate? Does it evoke a sense of being talented, maverick, surprising or inspiring? This may be more useful in the context of breaking the creative block.
- Does the system give the *impression* of either performative agency (demonstrating autonomy in a performance context) or memetic agency (demonstrating agency over a cultural timescale) [33]? Giving the impression of agency, regardless of what is actually produced, may be an important factor in certain contexts such as interactive performance contexts where liveness is at stake.

Here, the context of the creativity activity has a nuanced impact on how we might judge the importance of any system's intelligence and autonomy. In a performance context, for example, the sense of autonomy may be an important aspect of the experience of the work. In a creative production context, the system's creative autonomy could potentially problematise the author's sense of ownership of the work, if there is a strong relationship between authorship and identity. In a commercial context, this may be less the case if the identity of the work is more anonymous, but creators may nevertheless be concerned about the technicalities of ownership, i.e. issues of copyright.

Such concerns regarding contextual factors in the evaluation of music AI systems, from a design perspective, naturally invite a number of sociological questions, which form the next stage in this discussion.

1.5 The Sociological View

A more recent development that builds in turn on design practices is the introduction of sociological perspectives on how we think about and study creative practices in the AI music space. Sociological perspectives naturally complement design contributing practical extensions to design research with ethnographic methods for the observation of producers or consumers of music. Since designers focus on understanding use in practice, social and cultural factors are naturally important; how we use cars or kitchens, for example, and therefore how they should be designed, is deeply entangled with our social patterns of behaviour, which vary greatly across cultural contexts. Ethnography emphasises situated qualitative research that holistically takes into account the cultural context in which people operate, where 'culture' might refer equally to what differs between bedroom techno producers and commercial pop producers, as to what differs between religious rites in Cuban Catholic and Thai Buddhist groups. Music can safely be considered an exemplary cultural activity; we inhabit niches of musical style specific to our cultural backgrounds, and we find music playing a role in a wide number of critical social activities from funerals and weddings to the formation of friendships and the playing out of everyday shared experiences. Yet a sociological perspective has revealed how even seemingly non-cultural activities such as scientific research are shaped in very important ways by cultural factors (e.g. [34,35]. In this case, whilst the principle of scientific objectivity may be closely adhered to, science is still carried out by individuals with personal ambitions, biases and social relations, and within systems of social organisation that strongly influence behaviour.

A sociological perspective also provides a frame, building on relevant social theory, with which to conceptualise AI music activity. It is not a neutral method but a creative one, where conceptual frameworks can guide how research is done. One of the pioneers of Sociology and Anthropology, Emile Durkheim [36], believed that a social perspective is to psychology what chemistry is to physics: the phenomena of the social are irreducible to explanation at the level of individual human psychology. Durkheim developed the concept of the collective consciousness to capture the notion that societies operate in systems of share beliefs, ideas, habits, styles and attitudes.

In modern work on music, Born [37], for example, considers how social relations—such as those amongst musical collaborators, between themselves and their audiences, or in the wider social environment as reflected upon by musical artists—influence and are influenced by musical practices, styles and cultures in complex but traceable ways that are subject to useful analysis. A band's social organisation may reflect its politics, for example.

1.5.1 Cluster Concepts and Emic Versus Etic Definitions

The sociological perspective is valuable for a number of reasons but one of the most fundamental is how it enables us to distinguish the analysis of the practice, as seen from 'outside', from the perspective that emerges from the practice itself—this is something that distinguishes it from art theory or musicology, for example. In Anthropology, an emic perspective is a perspective from within the system being observed and an etic perspective is that of the (in theory) independent observer. This distinction is immediately enlightening when we consider how we might define two important but ambiguous terms: creativity and art. From an emic perspective, the use of both terms may be observed in practice. For example, we might notice that creativity is closely associated by people with an expression of individuality in some contexts and more closely associated with occasional genius and a high degree of training in others (Anna Jordanous [38] was the first to bring this topic to the fore in the field of Computational Creativity). Likewise, the familiar provocations of conceptual artists to push the boundaries of what is considered art, and the predictable cries of 'this is not art' from some sectors of the population, highlight how there is ongoing movement around that concept. We might therefore note that even when more formal definitions are in play, they are always contestable and blurry at the edges.

This tallies with how psychologists have come to understand how concepts are formed and used by people [39]. Rather than adhere to definitions, in practice, we understand concepts in relation to *prototypes*. Things that are very similar to those prototypes are more likely to fit the concept, and their salient properties more likely to be treated as important to the concept: thus we recognise fluffy dogs as more dog-like than bald dogs. Pablo Picasso and Albert Einstein might serve as prototypical 'creative' people.

Meanwhile, we have to be able to understand what *we* (as researchers) mean by these terms even when their meaning might change from context to context. Although one solution is to seek an operationalisable definition of such terms, as has been attempted in various fields, it is arguably more useful to seek useful technical concepts that inspire an underlying social or psychological phenomenon. Examples include work by researchers such as Dissanayake (art as 'making special' [40]), Blacking (music as 'human organised sound' [41]), Bloom ('essentialism' as a structuring concept [42]) and Blackmore (meme theory [43]), who attempt to seek the essence of the behaviour in question.

1.5.2   Social Perspectives on the Psychology of Creativity

A key concept in the study of the psychology of creativity is that creative tasks are those that inherently involve a process of search for an outcome that has not been considered before. Thus, a strong focus of creative psychology research is the question of what strategies and heuristics support effective search. Wallas' early formulation of creative cognition [44], for example, identified the four stages of preparation, incubation, illumination and verification. During incubation, an unsolved problem goes on the cognitive backburner so to speak, away from conscious attention, but is still being processed and might respond to salient input; as in the tale of Archimedes shouting 'eureka' in the bath. This process outline suggests at least two cycles of trial and error: one internal and subconscious and the other external and overtly evaluated. A substantial body of more recent work may deviate significantly from Wallas' early formulation but shares a common framework of looking at the cognitive heuristics and methods of search.

Meanwhile, a longstanding body of theory has considered equivalent questions formulated through a social frame. In a social system, many individuals performing search are contributing to a higher level collective, parallel search system. Mathematicians trying to prove Fermat's Last Theorem, for example, are in competition with each other, but in doing so are collectively collaborating on the problem being solved faster at that collective level. Thus, the same heuristics of creative search found in Psychology can also be seen operating at the social level, sometimes more overtly constructed in systems like market mechanisms, grand challenges in research, patent law, peer review and open data policies.

When viewed at the social level, it is worth noting that our ability to imitate becomes one of the most important cognitive abilities in the support of creative innovation: if we couldn't learn from each other then creative outcomes would never accumulate and there would be little benefit in individuals being creative (discussed for example in different ways by [43,45,46]). Richerson and Boyd [45] in particular emphasise the importance of social learning to strategic behaviours and to the evolutionary process itself. It is common sense that those most successful in creative spheres must be trained so that they can 'stand on the shoulders of giants'. Furthermore, creative activities operate in cultures of practice which create their own environments of objectives and evaluation (a phenomenon known in evolutionary theory as niche construction [47]). This is especially evident in the arts and there is evidence, discussed below, that the practice of artistic behaviours is tied up with the construction and maintenance of these cultural groups.

Most well known to researchers in Computational Creativity, Mihaly Csikszentmihalyi's systems model of creativity [48] defines such a community as a collective realm in which creativity occurs, the creative individual being one 'owner' of a creative output, but the community of others who evaluate it and hold it up as worthy is just as important. Indeed, analysis by Schaffer in the domain of science suggests that often the attribution of a breakthrough to an individual can be exaggerated, diminishing the collective action of the community, a process of myth-making that may perform some functional role.

Whilst Csikszentmihalyi's work is more well known to Computational Creativity researchers, one of the most extensive bodies of work studying communities of creative practice in Sociology is by Howard Becker [49]. Becker's work is less about predictive theories and more about a rich description of the minutiae of concerns of such communities, prising apart the myriad different individuals and the relationship they each hold to the systems they interact with. For example, he discusses the esoteric musical interests of undergraduate music students inhabiting small closed cliques of extreme experimentalism, a consequence of the intellectual learning environment they inhabit and compete within. Always, importantly, in Becker's studies, the relevant community is never a community of artists but may include business people, lawyers, technicians, marketing people, philanthropists and so on, all contributing to the structures within which any other individual operates. The resulting portrait is one in which any particular individual is pursuing a complex multi-factored goal that might involve money, social status, political intentions, ethnicity, fame, tradition, authorial integrity, friendships, loyalties, relationships, courtship, lifestyle, quality of life and rebellion against one's parents.

Becker's work highlights the very emergent nature of artistic creativity at this social level: artist A's intentions may be very specific to a context that is far beyond their design, and their work might have an effect that goes far beyond those intentions. Whilst creativity in artistic and scientific domains has much in common, it seems fair to say that artistic domains have many more possible and divergent paths of future development.

1.5.3   Social Theories of Taste and Identity

One of the most influential bodies of work in the sociological study of artistic behaviours comes from Pierre Bourdieu [50], who sought to understand amongst other things, artistic taste and its apparent role in social interaction. Bourdieu suggested that the way that taste and embodied knowledge of a cultural milieu is acquired is deeply related to social groups and their identities and boundaries. In essence, we absorb tacit cultural understanding very deeply and at such an early age that it becomes integral to our identity. It is hard to fake one's accent, which indicates one's social background, and the same is true of intimate knowledge, or lack thereof, of a cultural domain. Indeed, Bourdieu notes how some aspects of one's cultural identity can be acquired in education, learning about the arts at school, say, but some are so deeply embedded that they are really only acquired by those whose family life provides the right environment for early in-depth acquisition. These deep cultural acquisitions Bourdieu terms 'habitus'.

For Bourdieu, this acquisition and deep embodiment of taste, in turn, influence social relations in profound ways:

> Taste classifies, and it classifies the classifier. Social subjects, classified by their classifications, distinguish themselves by the distinctions they make, between the beautiful and the ugly, the distinguished and the vulgar, in which their position in the objective classifications is expressed or betrayed. [50]

This fits everyday experience: we gravitate towards people with similar taste or at least we find ourselves situated in filter bubbles of cultures and tastes; we spend time in the same places or listening to the same radio stations as those whose tastes we share. This is a more general instance of the way that shared experience can forge social bonds. Related research has shown that information about a person's taste can influence others' judgements about them, including about their personalities [51].

Bourdieu also introduces the idea of 'cultural capital'. Like financial capital (wealth), this is capital accumulated by a person as embodied in tacit or explicit knowledge, style or status. Cultural capital includes one's knowledge, acquired through education, but also one's taste. By constructing this correspondence with financial capital, Bourdieu is able to show how the cultural qualities of people serve goals and tangible outcomes, and also how the properties of a cultural group define the context in which each individual must compete. The implication that being a consumer of art or music is a competitive activity was radical at the time and still sounds counter-intuitive or at least confrontational to a view of art and music as bringing people together or being of unquestioned benefit to humanity. Bourdieu portrays a more combative and politically charged world of music production and consumption. He says specifically of music; "nothing more clearly affirms one's 'class', nothing more infallibly classifies, than tastes in music" [50].

Such strands of research feed a broader potential that music and other artistic behaviours are functional, in some way, in the formation and maintenance of groups, or more generally, in the construction of individual identities and relations. Briefly, then, I consider the related field of research into music's origins, as viewed from the perspective of Evolutionary Psychology.

1.5.4 Why Do We Make and Listen to Music?

For some, the discussion of social functions for music must go further and seek a theoretical footing regarding why we make and listen to music. One approach is a cultural blank-slate perspective where we understand human behaviour as being so flexible as to adapt to very different cultural potentials. Imagine a child born into a richly musical culture, whether New York jazz or Javanese gamelan music or Irish folk. Through their immersion in this culture, they gain a love of their local music, expertise in it and above all a deep appreciation of its cultural value and therefore potential personal value. Within this context, they may pursue musical activities for a range of reasons. We may say that given the cultural context, the individual's behaviour can be explained in terms of the cultural motivators that have driven them to like the music and perhaps aspire to be a creator or collector of it. But a further goal of a social perspective is to understand how and why this particular cultural context emerged, not just how individuals act given the culture.

As an alternative to a blank-slate approach, we may consider a deep evolutionary perspective, in which we seek to understand how Darwinian evolutionary theory [52–54] may be used to explain how human artistic behaviours and their related social structures emerged. Darwinian evolutionary theory should be understood in the broadest sense—i.e. not simple adaptationism or genetic determinism—instead taking into account the more contemporary concepts of emergence, gene-culture coevolution and niche constructionism, amongst others. It should be noted that such a perspective is not widely popular amongst sociologists. Darwinian explanations of social phenomena were popular in the wake of Darwin's theory but became severely tainted by applications to eugenics and other morally problematic or flawed scientific initiatives.

There are, broadly speaking, four categories of theory of the evolution of human musical behaviour. In all cases, these needn't refer to genetically evolved behaviours, but be understood in terms of a more complex gene-culture coevolutionary framework.

1. **Cognitivist**: theories which posit that music supports cognitive development, helping us think.
2. **Consequentialist**: theories which do not posit a function for music itself, but explain musical behaviour as the consequence of a set of other evolved traits. The most well known of these is Stephen Pinker's [55] position that music is like cheesecake; it combines elements that we evolved to enjoy (like salt and sugar) with novelty and complexity, that we also evolved to enjoy, but neither cheesecake nor music were themselves directly involved in our evolution.
3. **Cohesionist**: theories which posit that music is functional in binding groups, for example, by creating shared rhythmic experiences that reinforce a shared identity [56,57]. One example is Hagen and Bryant's [58] theory of music as a signalling system for a group's coalition strength, representing their ability to fight. This draws on the important handicap principle, or honest signalling theory, which states that a system of communication can evolve as long as it can't be cheated. Hagen and Bryant's theory is that because learning to perform together takes practice, it is an honest indicator of the cohesion of the group.
4. **Competitivist**: theories which posit that music evolved through competition between individuals. The most familiar example of this is the sexual selection theory of music [59], which states that males attract females with their music performance ability, music being here an honest indicator of cognitive ability. But in fact, the same logic that underlies sexual selection theory, based on honest signalling theory, can be applied in many other ways. Of particular interest is the potential to derive a competitivist model based on the work of Bourdieu.

In all cases, it is necessary to consider emergent factors and interactions between these different forms of explanation. Certainly, at some level, a consequentialist view must be foundational to music's evolution, since we wouldn't have music if we didn't first have a hearing apparatus, and some of the auditory perceptual abilities that clearly preceded human evolution [60]. The cohesionist and competitivist perspectives can also be seen to interact: it follows that if music plays a role in supporting cohesion within groups, then it also sets up the conditions for there to be competition within the group on the same grounds.

I only briefly touch on this subject here to highlight some of the ways in which the social nature of music generally exceeds the kinds of factors taken into account in current AI music models. Although sociologists and evolutionary psychologists generally work in different realms, both of these strands provide a footing for thinking about what underlying factors might fundamentally motivate musical enthusiasm and pleasure. This matters a great deal because it influences how we understand individual social motivations and pleasure responses related to our creation and experience of music. These factors draw attention to the great difference between what situated contexts AI systems inhabit when they create music and those that we inhabit.

1.6 Discussion

Just as the design perspective has been thoroughly embraced in AI music practice, the sociological perspective seems to be taking hold and promises to contribute to a far richer multidisciplinary field. What can AI currently do, and what can sociological and design perspectives do to both support and critique the development of AI music systems?

The above discussion points broadly to two related ways in which current state-of-the-art ML systems do not employ 'human-like algorithms' of music creation. Firstly, most do not perform an iteration of search and evaluation. And secondly, they do not perform generative actions grounded in matters of taste, identity and human motivations.

This is not to say that we couldn't very soon derive systems that would satisfy these requirements, especially given the big data resources related to musical culture that are available. This can be achieved by training systems that are not just aware of musical content but also of the context, the cultural associations and meanings of the musical corpus being ingested by an algorithm. This requires a paradigm shift: the currently cutting-edge ML algorithms are still only predictive models (whereas in the Computational Creativity community there are in fact many examples of evaluative and iterative search-based models, such as [61,62]). They take a corpus of music to infer expectations about what the next note will be in a sequence. Anecdotally, I have heard an ML model trained on the music of David Bowie being described as a 'David Bowie simulator', yet this is far from an accurate description: the artist's awareness of the culture and his position in it is completely missing from the model – it is actually absurd to suggest you can model David Bowie, as a system, by looking at the output of that system. Models of taste, identity and motivation will become important as the next step in powering a more human-like AI generation, if this is what we want.

In fact, we might position the current most popular algorithms at the second stage of a possible four-stage hierarchy of more culturally-oriented models of taste acquisition:

1. Universal rules of aesthetics, such as those of [63], which assume that despite differences in taste, there are common rules to what makes something aesthetically pleasing;
2. Experience-specific models, sophisticated versions of which posit a universal cognitive mechanism combined with adaptation. For example, Berlyne [64] proposed models of cultural evolution in which individuals learnt and then became saturated in their preference for certain stylistic traits. Similarly, Ramachandran [65] proposes a number of existing cognitive strategies related to learning about the world stimulate aesthetic pleasure and are, equally, subject to adaptation through learning (this is another consequentialist theory). One example is the peak shift principle, which states that once we've learnt a structural property we tend to seek it in its extreme (explaining how some genres evolve towards more baroque forms);

3. More overtly curiousity-based models, in which we are stimulated by our ability to build effective models of the world, those forms we find most learnable being those we enjoy most. Versions of this concept can be found in Csikszentmihalyi's 'flow' theory [66] and in the work of Schmidthuber [67] and Wiggins (e.g. [68]);
4. Approaches in which all of the above are situated in the context of life strategies that shape an individual's interaction with a musical corpus. Arguably, we don't really have any good models of this. There are some experimental models that have tentatively explored this stage in the hierarchy, such as Saunders' curious design agents [69].

An additional level of complexity comes from the fact that musical styles and genres might embody extremely different sets of rules regarding innovation, authorship, copying, referencing, collaboration and what is considered the fixed and important parts of a composition versus those immaterial and changeable parts. Musical scores in Common Music Notation are treated in some cultures as instances of pieces of music, but many electronic music composers would not consider a score to be a suitable representation of a work, sonic timbre and microtiming being critically defined only in a machine rendering of the work. Regarding authorship, the importance of the author's identity may be far less present in commercial jingle composition than it is in hip hop. Where authorship matters, highly regarded authors are able to create value around their work. Regarding copying and innovation, in Jamaican dancehall, it is common to produce many different variations using the same riddim (backing track), whereas reuse of previous material might be considered lazy in other music scenes. These types of variation impact the kinds of behaviours a human creative practitioner might engage in, cutting to the heart of how they make decisions as simple as, say, what note comes next in a melody. All of these nuances are arguably essential to marking out a music scene's identity; if current ML algorithms are to embody human-like musical behaviours, we have to ask which of these behaviours they are targeting. What type of musical role or musical activity, whether existing in the human realm or not, is the system aiming for?

We should also be conscious of how AI 'disrupts' these various cultural spheres, and recognise cultural applications as just as potentially dangerous as other areas of activity, in terms of the possible damage AI could wreak. Both the sociological and evolutionary perspectives on the potential social function of music suggest that disruption in the means of cultural production or the experience or dissemination of cultural products could, in perhaps very subtle ways, upset core processes underlying the formation and maintenance of communities. Perhaps not in the near future, but in the long term, such technologies could have devastating potential, in line with recent developments in the manipulation of electorates via social media disinformation.

Pointing out the ways in which current ML technologies are not simply comparable to human creators certainly does not mean that such systems are not useful or effective tools. From the design stance—unencumbered by the need to argue for or aspire towards AI human-likeness, and simply focused on how such systems might enhance creativity—such tools may clearly perform a novel and potentially useful function. But I would argue that with the exception of more practical user-interface focused work such as Fiebrink's, or very domain-specific functionality such as the Landr service (my own very much included), many existing music AI projects have been more conceptual than they have been practical and have yet to prove their use value in tangible examples. Whilst it remains easy to generate hype around the use of AI in music, it remains hard to spot more sustained uses of the technology.

A sociological view can also be used to understand AI music systems as creative contributors in social processes of creativity, returning to the discussion surrounding how creators' creative authority interacts with and may give over to the contribution of an AI system (with reference to Fig. 1.1). A system that generates completely novel musical content, even in the hands of an operator who is manipulating settings, datasets and so on, should be understood as technology that extends the basic creative mechanism of search in potentially powerful ways, as has been explored extensively by Computational Creativity researchers [70–72]. It is cognitive machinery of a sort, as seen from the perspective of Clark's extended-mind hypothesis [73]; it can be seen to possess material agency, in the language of Lambros Malafouris [74]; or secondary agency, in the language of Alfred Gell [75].

Richer analysis of such systems might fruitfully attempt to classify and categorise them in terms of what role they play in this bigger system, with a key distinction being between generators and evaluators: systems that generate output under the supervised control of an operator, and systems that analyse output in order to feed directly into a search process or to provide information back to the human operator in a conversational interactive paradigm. Such analysis, in necessary detail, is beginning to emerge and will have a part to play in shaping the algorithmic design and the interaction design of future tools. As such systems start to be used in practice, it would seem likely that the emerging design requirements and applied objectives of such systems will move to outweigh the philosophical questions, but that new philosophical questions will come to the fore.

Acknowledgements I thank Chloe McFadden for her research assistance in the production of this chapter.

References

1. Briot, J. P., Hadjeres, G., & Pachet, F. (2017). *Deep learning techniques for music generation.* Technical report, Sorbonne Universites, UPMC Univ Paris 06, CNRS, LIP6, Paris, France.
2. Briot, J. P., & Pachet, F. (2017). Music generation by deep learning-challenges and directions. *arXiv preprint* arXiv:1712.04371.
3. Engel, J., Resnick, C., Roberts, A., Dieleman, S., Eck, D., Simonyan, K., & Norouzi, M. (2017). Neural audio synthesis of musical notes with wavenet autoencoders. *arXiv preprint* arXiv:1704.01279.
4. Sturm, B. L., Ben-Tal, O., Monaghan, U., Collins, N., Herremans, D., Chew, E., Hadjeres, G., Deruty, E., & Pachet, F. (2019). Machine learning research that matters for music creation: A case study. *Journal of New Music Research, 48*(1), 36–55.

5. Hiller, L. A., jr., & Isaacson, L. M. (1957). Musical composition with a high speed digital computer. In *Audio engineering society convention, 9*. Audio Engineering Society.
6. Schmidhuber, J. (2015). Deep learning in neural networks: An overview. *Neural Networks, 61*, 85–117.
7. Buchanan, R. (1992). Wicked problems in design thinking. *Design Issues, 8*(2), 5–21.
8. Kurzweil, R. (1999). *The age of spiritual machines: How we will live, work and think in the new age of intelligent machines*. Orion.
9. Gaver, B., Dunne, T., & Pacenti, E. (1999). Design: Cultural probes. *interactions, 6*(1), 21–29.
10. Cope, D. (1992). Computer modelling of musical intelligence in EMI. *Computer Music Journal, 16*(2), 69–83.
11. Cope, D. (1996). *Experiments in musical intelligence*. Madison, WI: A-R Editions.
12. Cohen, H. (1973). Parallel to perception: Some notes on the problem of machine-generated art. *Computer Studies, 4*(3/4).
13. Eno, B. (1996). Generative music 1. Software art sleeve notes.
14. Cardoso, A., Veale, T., & Wiggins, G. A. (2009). Converging on the divergent: The history (and future) of the international joint workshops in computational creativity. *AI Magazine, 30*(3), 15.
15. Ventura, D. (20116). Mere generation: Essential barometer or dated concept. In *Proceedings of the Seventh International Conference on Computational Creativity* (pp. 17–24). Sony CSL, Paris.
16. Bown, O. (2014). Empirically grounding the evaluation of creative systems: Incorporating interaction design. In *Proceedings of the 5th International Conference on Computational Creativity*, Ljubljana.
17. Fiebrink, R. (2017). Machine learning as meta-instrument: Human-machine partnerships shaping expressive instrumental creation. In *Musical instruments in the 21st century*, (pp. 137–151).
18. Stowell, D., Plumbley, M. D., & Bryan-Kinns, N. (2008). Discourse analysis evaluation method for expressive musical interfaces. In *NIME* (pp. 81–86).
19. Brown, A., Gifford, T., & Voltz, B. (2013). *Controlling interactive music performance (cim)* (Vol. 221).
20. Magnusson, T. (2010). Designing constraints: Composing and performing with digital musical systems. *Computer Music Journal, 34*(4), 62–73.
21. Collins, N. (2006). *Towards autonomous agents for live computer music: Realtime machine listening and interactive music systems*. Ph.D. thesis, Centre for Science and Music, Faculty of Music, University of Cambridge.
22. Addessi, A. R., & Pachet, F. (2006). Young children confronting the continuator, an interactive reflective musical system. *Musicae Scientiae, 10*(1 suppl), 13–39.
23. Kantosalo, A. A., Toivanen, J. M., Toivonen, H. T. T., et al. (2015). Interaction evaluation for human-computer co-creativity. In *Proceedings of the Sixth International Conference on Computational Creativity*.
24. Blackwell, A., & Green, T. (2003). Notational systems—The cognitive dimensions of notations framework. *HCI models, theories, and frameworks: Toward an interdisciplinary science. Morgan Kaufmann*.
25. Bilda, Z., Edmonds, E., & Candy, L. (2008). Designing for creative engagement. *Design Studies, 29*(6), 525–540.
26. Resnick, M., Myers, B., Nakakoji, K., Shneiderman, B., Pausch, R., Selker, T., & Eisenberg, M. (2005). *Design principles for tools to support creative thinking*.
27. Shneiderman, B., Fischer, G., Czerwinski, M., Resnick, M., Myers, B., Candy, L., et al. (2006). Creativity support tools: Report from a US national science foundation sponsored workshop. *International Journal of Human-Computer Interaction, 20*(2), 61–77.
28. Nielsen, J. (1995). 10 usability heuristics for user interface design. *Nielsen Norman Group, 1*(1).
29. Norman, D. (1988). *The psychology of everyday things*. Basic Books.

30. Bown, O., & Brown, A. R. (2018). Interaction design for meta creative systems. In *New directions in third wave human-computer interaction: Volume 1—Technologies*. Springer.
31. Sony CSL. (2016). *Daddy's car: A song composed by artificial intelligence—In the style of the beatles. YouTube video.*
32. Ritchie, G. (2007). Some empirical criteria for attributing creativity to a computer program. *Minds and Machines, 17*(1), 67–99.
33. Bown, O., Eldridge, A., & McCormack, J. (2009). Understanding interaction in contemporary digital music: From instruments to behavioural objects. *Organised Sound, 14*(02), 188–196.
34. Kuhn, T. S. (1996). *The structure of scientific revolutions*, 3 edn. University of Chicago Press.
35. Latour, B. (2012). *We have never been modern*. Harvard University Press.
36. Durkheim, E. (1972). *Selected writings*. New York: Cambridge University Press.
37. Born, G., Lewis, E., & Straw, W. (2017). *Improvisation and social aesthetics*. Duke University Press.
38. Jordanous, A. K. (2013). *Evaluating computational creativity: A standardised procedure for evaluating creative systems and its application*. Ph.D. thesis, University of Sussex.
39. Murphy, G. (2004). Typicality and the classical view of categories. *The big book of concepts* (pp. 11–41).
40. Dissanayake, E. (2000). *Art and intimacy: How the arts began*. Seattle, USA: University of Washington Press.
41. Blacking, J. (1995). *Music, culture and experience: Selected papers of John blacking*. Chicago: University of Chicago Press.
42. Bloom, P., et al. (2010). *How pleasure works: The new science of why we like what we like*. Random House.
43. Susan, J. (1999). *Blackmore*. New York: The Meme Machine. OUP.
44. Götz, I. L. (1981). On defining creativity. *The Journal of Aesthetics and Art Criticism, 39*(3), 297–301.
45. Richerson, P. J., & Boyd, R. (2005). *Not by genes alone: How culture transformed human evolution*. Chicago, IL, US: University of Chicago Press.
46. Tomasello, M., Carpenter, M., Call, J., Behne, T., & Moll, H. (2005). Understanding and sharing intentions: The origins of cultural cognition. *Behavioral and Brain Sciences, 28*(5), 675–691.
47. Laland, K. N., Odling-Smee, J., & Feldman, M. W. (2000). Niche construction, biological evolution, and cultural change. *Behavioral and Brain Sciences, 23*(01), 131–146.
48. Csikszentmihalyi, M. (2015). *The systems model of creativity: The collected works of Mihaly Csikszentmihalyi*. Springer.
49. Saul Becker, H. (1982). *Art worlds*. Univ of California Press.
50. Bourdieu, P. (1984). *Distinction: A social critique of the judgement of taste*. Harvard University Press.
51. North, A. C., & Hargreaves, D. J. (1999). Music and adolescent identity. *Music Education Research, 1*(1), 75–92.
52. Darwin, C. (1860). *On the origin of species by means of natural selection, or The preservation of favoured races in the struggle for life*. D. Appleton and company.
53. Dawkins, R. (1976). *The selfish gene*. OUP.
54. Smith, J. M., & Szathmáry, E. (1995). *The major transitions in evolution*. New York: Oxford University Press.
55. Pinker, S. (1995). *The language instinct: The new science of language and mind* (vol. 7529). Penguin UK.
56. Brown, S. (2007). Contagious heterophony: A new theory about the origins of music. *Musicæ Scientiæ, 11*(1), 3–26, Springer.
57. Cross, I. (1999). Is music the most important thing we ever did? Music, development and evolution. In S. W. Yi (Ed.), *Music mind and science*. Seoul National University Press, Seoul.
58. Hagen, E. H., & Bryant, G. A. (2003). Music and dance as a coalition signaling system. *Human Nature, 14*(1), 21–51.

59. Miller, G. (2000). Evolution of human music through sexual selection. In N. L. Wallin, B. Merker, & S. Brown (Eds.), *The origins of music* (pp. 329–360). MIT Press, Cambridge, MA, USA.

60. Bregman, A. S. (1990). *Auditory scene analysis*. Cambridge, MA: MIT Press.

61. Gervás, P. (2015). A personal perspective into the future for computational creativity. In *Computational creativity research: Towards creative machines* (pp. 393–406).

62. Ventura, D. (2015). The computational creativity complex. In *Computational creativity research: Towards creative machines* (pp. 65–92). Springer.

63. David Birkhoff, G. (1933). *Aesthetic measure*, (Vol. 9). Harvard University Press Cambridge.

64. Berlyne, D. E. (1971). *Aesthetics and psychobiology*. Appleton-Century-Crofts.

65. Ramachandran, V. S. (2003). *The artful brain. Talk given at the 2003 BBC Reith Lectures*. http://www.bbc.co.uk/radio4/reith2003/lecture3.shtml.

66. Csikszentmihalyi, M. (1990). *Flow: The psychology of optimal experience*. Harper and Row.

67. Schmidhuber, J. (2010). Formal theory of creativity, fun, and intrinsic motivation (1990–2010). *IEEE Transactions on Autonomous Mental Development, 2*(3), 230–247.

68. Forth, J., Agres, K., Purver, M., & Wiggins, G. A. (2016). Entraining idyot: Timing in the information dynamics of thinking. *Frontiers in Psychology, 7*.

69. Saunders, R. (2001). *Curious design agents and artificial creativity*. Ph.D. thesis, Faculty of Architecture, The University of Sydney.

70. Kantosalo, A. & Toivonen, H. (2016). Modes for creative human-computer collaboration: Alternating and task-divided co-creativity. In *Proceedings of the Seventh International Conference on Computational Creativity*.

71. Pachet, F. (2004). Beyond the cybernetic jam fantasy: The continuator. *IEEE Computer Graphics and Applications, 24*(1), 31–35.

72. Sturm, B. L. (2016). The "horse" inside: Seeking causes behind the behaviors of music content analysis systems. *Computers in Entertainment (CIE), 14*(2), 3.

73. Clark, A. (2003). *Natural-born cyborgs: Minds, technologies, and the future of human intelligence*. Oxford University Press.

74. Malafouris, L. (2007). At the potter's wheel: An argument for material agency.

75. Gell, A. (1998). *Art and agency: An anthropological theory*. Oxford: Clarendon Press.

Oliver Bown is associate professor and co-director of the Interactive Media Lab at the Faculty of Arts, Design and Architecture, University of New South Wales, Australia. As an undergraduate he combined studies in both mathematics and social anthropology at the University of Cambridge, UK, and then completed a masters in Evolutionary and Adaptive Systems at Sussex University. He completed his Ph.D. at Goldsmiths College looking further at evolutionary models of the emergence of musical behaviour. Throughout his academic career he has also worked as a practicing musician, music producer and interactive media artist, including in the electronic music duo Icarus, and the Australian ensemble Tangents, as well as co-founding the improvised music label Not Applicable. E-mail: o.bown@unsw.edu.au.

Human–Machine Simultaneity in the Compositional Process

2

Hanns Holger Rutz

2.1 Introduction

How can the exchange processes between human artists and software algorithms as the medium of their work be understood? It is no longer the case that the research value in art is only validated through other disciplines, and this chapter attempts to interrogate the possibilities of artistic research to shed light on this question. I will put a particular computer music system and various pieces and studies made with it into a dialogue with theoretical explorations, focusing on the question how temporal relationships are established that subvert the instrumental reasoning often foregrounded in technological discourses. What happens to the rudiments and failures, and how can turning away and disconnecting from real-time coupling help to think computation as a domain that includes the relations that were built by us through careful and long-term investment? How can the elements that appear in software systems be seen as carrying a transformative potential, and what does it mean to share these elements with others in a togetherness that avoids a regime of cause-and-effect?

I spent much of my adolescence in front of a computer screen. A more appropriate description would be to say that I was *in* the computer. To become immersed does not require a particular technological finesse. I returned from holidays after two or three weeks away from the computer, and I was astonished when I booted up the computer again: The screen had become a flat surface, the plasticity and three-dimensionality that I was used to had vanished, it would require some time for me to reinhabit that virtual space. Computers and computation are complexes that are not exhaustively described in technological terms, in terms of informatics and mathematics, because the relationships we build with them are as important. These

H. H. Rutz (✉)
Reagenz-Association for Artistic Experiments, Morellenfeldgasse 11, 8010 Graz, Austria
e-mail: rutz@reagenz.at

© Springer Nature Switzerland AG 2021
E. R. Miranda (ed.), *Handbook of Artificial Intelligence for Music*,
https://doi.org/10.1007/978-3-030-72116-9_2

relationships in turn are not exhaustively described in terms of cognitive processes that eliminate the materiality of the exchanges, that conflate both sides of the relation by either implying that the computer should be a transparent and generic vehicle supporting the human creative nature, or that in turn human cognition is just a peculiar form of computation. Instead, humans and machines come together as cognitive assemblages [19] in which the exchange processes and dynamics themselves become the central element, and whatever emerges from this connectedness is difficult to separate and attribute to either agent. The idea of a hybrid human–machine agency is central for many thinkers, for instance, Karen Barad describes the objects or phenomena arising from scientific experimentation as coproduced in the coming-together of researcher and apparatus [3].

With this perspective as background, I want to describe what happens in computer music and computer sound art composition, when the human artist forms a connection with their machinery or programming environment, particularly if that environment has been co-created or shaped by the artists themselves, not unlike the tools and arrangements that scientists develop in order to conduct their work. Originating from my research on the temporal relations in the compositional process [34], I will take as example the computer music environment *Mellite* that I have been developing since several years [32], and look at the temporal and cognitive relations between the artist or composer and the computer system. *Mellite* appears as something that vacillates between a technological infrastructure for the composition and performance of sound works, and an often unstable research device that is used to understand these processes through artistic research.

Some of the cases presented are anchored in the project *Algorithms that Matter* [38] which investigated the agency of algorithms as emerging from human–machine interaction, and how the work with algorithms reshapes the way we think about our role as artists. It is implied that algorithms are—like computation—not delimited by narrow technical definitions, but that they are "ontogenetic in nature (always in a state of becoming), teased into being: edited, revised, deleted and restarted, shared with others, passing through multiple iterations stretched out over time and space" [21, p. 18].

The chapter is structured around terms and concepts that, when put together, form a picture of human–machine coproduction in the compositional process. Instead of one concept following from another, they function as simultaneous perspectives that complement each other. Each section breaks down its concept into two levels, a rather theoretical and abstract one, and a technical–practical one rooted in the practice with the computer music system. What the text will work towards is a counterbalance to the compulsivity of the computational medium to force the image of connectedness on us, always being coupled, always moving along arrows provided by the operability of digital objects. The balancing is performed by acts of suspension (to set aside for a time), relaying (to pass on in a shared effort that maintains a critical concern) and searching for states of simultaneity where heterogeneous things can meet in a common reference frame without arrows of causation or asymmetrical dependency.

2.2 Machine as Projection Space

It is an often shared view that machines and technologies extend or substitute our abilities and thereby can be thought of as prostheses. The computer's "memory" and storage media extend or substitute our memory, for example. But beyond being merely mnemotechnical devices, they produce novel operations and novel spaces, which turn familiar at the same time they are inhabited by their users. We project our doing and thinking into these new spaces, which arise not out of thin air but as a result of the investment of work in the infrastructures that bring them about.

Who makes this investment? In the case of computer-based art, there are, first of all, a number of *professional* companies producing software for a user *base* abstracted to a certain degree. Here the investment is primarily an economic one, even though it is driven by "usability" and the valuation of the user base, thus also becoming part of an artistic investment in an indirect way. This relation is inverted when looking at software made by *amateurs*—artists and researchers who are often not professionally trained in programming, mathematics or computer science, who cannot compete in the economical sense, who cannot conduct studies with larger user bases and adjust their software process accordingly, but they rather build software as a direct artistic investment. No software is isolated, it always builds on existing software, in the ultimate case the compiler for the language in which it is written, but more often by extending or incorporating an existing platform. And therefore, artistic software almost always requires a number of software written with other strategies and goals in mind. A useful model for this relation is Hans–Jörg Rheinberger's distinction along the continuum of technical devices and epistemic things [28]. As a technology, a computer and a software system can never be purely epistemic things on their own, this would be a false idealisation, however in their tentative, unfinished form under constant reconfiguration by the researcher or artist, they rely, on the one hand, on the stable subroutines embodied by the existing software they built on, and on the other hand they become crucial elements in an epistemic endeavour (and epistemic can be read as artistic-researching in this context).

While it is absolutely valid for an artist to work with a set of tools purely created by others, there arises the particular situation of an artist working with software created by themselves, as here a reciprocation happens between the creation of an infrastructure for projection spaces and their inhabitation, the population of a space of material representation as Rheinberger calls it. This highly individual perspective is different to one that looks, for example, at the general "conditions of creativity" and how software could support it. It is to make a case for writing software as an irreducible strategy of artistic research where the computer medium is central.

The writing of artistic software is a formal *re-entry*. This term, going back to mathematician George Spencer-Brown, is used by system theorist Niklas Luhmann to ask what happens within a system when a form is distinguished and the "other" of this form is omitted because form and distinction (making form) become the same: We only ever find ourselves on the inner side of the distinction [23]. It is reminiscent of Rheinberger explaining "pure" representations as interventions that lost their correlational reference. In a paradoxical self-reference, there is a writing underlying the creation of the artistic software that in turn makes this underlying writing possible at all. We can analytically distinguish between the two writings, the creation of a software, and the *application* of a software thus created, but this is just a temporal and fluctuating distinction. When I write *Mellite* the software, when I write a piece *in* Mellite, and when I write this text *about* both, the three principle writing processes are entangled and aligned. It means that none of these three can have been written without the other, and also that there is a formal recurrence in the three regarding the way they are written. Thus, there is a moment of selfsame authorship, voluntary or not. The entanglement implies that I can merely make analytical cuts, they are after the fact as there is always a correspondence, a reciprocal exchange between the layers and instances of writing. In the end, it is a contiguous endeavour in artistic production and research in which these three forms are complementary.

Each layer of the writing is excessive in the sense that it will always produce something unexpected, not planned for, and most importantly, something whose use and function is not known yet or ever. This graft or cruft, what has unintendedly grown during the work of writing, can become a crucial topological element in the space, an element that is much more likely to be removed if we had looked at a software written by an organisation for a general user base, much less likely to have even existed in the absence of the personal, artistic investment.[1] The grafting of foreign elements onto the artistic process, this type of contingency, is often part of the artistic strategy, and one should not be ashamed to admit it, indeed one should study the conditions that make it possible.

Workspaces

I now want to look more closely at the particular projection space enabled by *Mellite*. If we think of the representations of the graphematic space afforded by a machine, we may begin with the "handle" by which we refer to them. According to a known bon mot, naming things is one of the hard tasks in computer science. But it is not only hard, but full of consequence, as it shapes how we think about that which obtained the name. What is it that we compose and work with in a computer music system? A *patch* (Max, PD), a *document* (SuperCollider), a *workspace* (OpenMusic) a *project* (Logic Pro), a *session* (Pro Tools)? For a time I alternatingly used the words *session* and *workspace* in *Mellite*, then settling on the latter. Why not session? A session is a meeting delimited in time and space, with an element of repetition, such as musicians coming together in a studio and making music, or the scheduled meeting with a psychiatrist. We do not return to the *same session*, but when we compose, we return to the same set of objects, sketches, sounds, ideas. A workspace, on the other hand, first sounds like a container of varying content and a set of tools. But it is also more specific than a workshop, it includes the particular organisation of the space with respect to a work carried out. In computer software, the term is often

---

[1]The non-removal I also call non-selection, see Rutz [35].

found to describe the set of objects that form a software project within an integrated development environment (IDE) such as *Eclipse* or *Visual Studio*. I describe *Mellite* as an integrated environment for composing and performing.

The comfort of the digital workspace is that one can have multiple of them, each becoming fitted over time with the elements belonging to a particular project. The metaphor of a space with objects is of course as old as graphical user interfaces are for operating systems. If one instals the full operating system image of a Raspberry Pi miniature computer in 2020, one will still be greeted with a "desktop" and a "wastebasket" after booting finishes. In our digital second nature, it feels intuitive to project spaces into these tiny machines. Like physical spaces, we can have them turned into a mess, we can go and invest time to clean them up, and so forth. This is not changed by the fact that the nominal and visual metaphors drift according to trends in software design, and this space still exists in mobile phones that do away with desktop imagery and file system navigation—we simply learned again to inhabit these differently designed spaces.

Is a workspace a volume or a hypertext? Certainly, there is a nesting of spaces within spaces: In the interface, we can open an object to enter a new (sub)space. The space in the workspace is the twofold space of Spencer-Brown: Unmarked space or virtuality on one side, and marked space or carved out forms on the other side [44]. It is an inhabited space, a personal space filled with relations (hypertext), but also a proposition to elaborate it further (an extending volume). The hybrid nature of *Mellite*'s workspace becomes clear when looking at the underlying data structure and its visual representation which, more or less involuntarily, reveals this ambiguity. The data structure is simply a graph of interconnected objects, some of which have classical spatial representations, such as the *Folder* which contains the list of other objects, or the *Timeline* which associates a list of objects with positions along a time axis. The graphical interface uses dedicated renderers for each type of object, and one always begins with a "root" folder, from which one can then access the views of the contained objects, which again could be other folders, or audio files, or a timeline object (Fig. 2.1). However, objects can be associated with more than one container-like object, thus within any one set of currently visually rendered subspaces, the same object may appear multiple times—like a variable in text programming language—thereby breaking with our experience of physical spaces as well as weakening the analogy with patcher-based programs. Clearly indicating those multiplicities for the user is one of the open tasks for the future development of this interface.

Why is the workspace as such important, why not begin with a description of objects that *Mellite* offers for its population? In a conversation, I was recently confronted with the argument that the computational medium always presented itself as a network of dots and arrows and no notion of emptiness or isolation. What was thus crucially missing for the computer artist was the element of horror vacui. But the void here exists both in the ever extending volume as well as in the blank new object (empty folder, empty timeline, empty code fragment). The blank new object has this quality of vacuum. There exists also the opposite sense: Working in a traditional digital audio workstation (DAW) can feel claustrophobic; there is no space to put things other than on dedicated positions in the timeline. Unless it is a supported

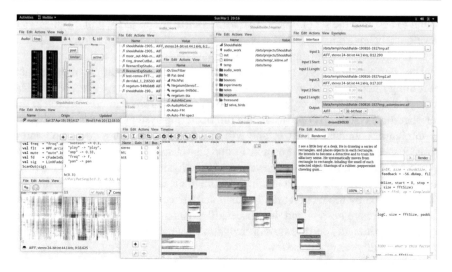

Fig. 2.1 A screenshot of *Mellite*, showing a number of objects in the workspace of the electroacoustic composition *Shouldhalde* (work in progress)

object such as an audio file that can live in a list of audio files. Otherwise one has to organise their space elsewhere. *Mellite*'s workspace is designed to allow for different ways of organisation and heterogeneous objects, more akin to a patcher or the set of source code files in a purely text-based environment.

When marking this intermediate position between a stable technical subroutine and the material embodiment of an always under-determined epistemic endeavour, it implied that I am presenting *Mellite* and its workspace in its current form which may always become subject to slight or more radical change in the future. The aim is, therefore, not to give an explanation of what its workspace is and how to use it, but to understand how and why it came about. From the actual application, there is a gap towards the structure as I imagine it. For example, it *should* be possible to produce any kind of indices into the underlying graph of a workspace, so that a timeline is just a selected index over time spans, but one could as well generate a new index by the duration of contained objects, by their colour attribute or name, by their sonic features, etc. What are all the possible ways in which one may want to organise objects in digital spaces?

2.3 Temporal Interleaving

The sonic arts are largely time-based art forms, and as such capable of producing curious interleaving between the temporal dimension of their performative expressions and the temporal dimension of the production of the artwork. Even in the "most spatial" form, sound installation, in which the work has a relatively weak authority on the temporal ordering of the recipient's perception—equally structured by their exploration of a site or space—most works can still be described in terms of temporally composed elements. In this case, one may place the composer's writing process as an antecedent to the temporal unfolding in the exhibition or performance of the work. If we hypothetically distinguish between a performance time (prescriptive, composed or in its reenactment and actualisation) and a creation time, in which the prescription is written by the artist, these two layers seem neatly separated, so how can we claim their interleaving? The obvious counter case would be improvisation, in which decision-making happens clearly in the temporal vicinity of or simultaneous with what the audience hears. But there are three less obvious and qualitatively different aspects of interleaving.

The first one could be described as a sedimentation of time "in a piece". It begins with the almost trivial assertion that it takes time to make a piece, to select and form its elements, to develop the thoughts and gather the experience that shapes it. It may appear that this time is erased from the piece as it takes its final form, unless there is a manifest way in which temporal context is embedded, for example, through the use of field recordings or references to the events of the day. Or think of Luc Ferrari's piece *Dialogue Ordinaire Avec La Machine* in which one hears him talk in his studio about the composition process [14]. But this time *always* participates, through the way it was invested in the process, in the production of excess that is reflected as ingression into the piece. Because of this participation, it is not possible to see these ingressions as purified and "outside time". Even if one imagines the purity of Iannis Xenakis' outside-time structures that he can manipulate without the constraints of "lexicographic" ordering [47, p. 160 and passim], the conceptualisation of this type of structure, its plain possibility, as well as the manipulations performed, shielded from the audience's ears, are embedded in time. As Sara Ahmed elaborates in her look "behind" phenomenology, in the constitution of the figure of an object, its background is not just what is dimly perceived around a thus isolated or "bracketed" foreground, but it also denotes "the conditions of emergence or an arrival of something as the thing that it appears to be in the present" [1, p. 38], and the arrival takes time that is not hollow but active in forming the direction of the object. This arrival includes us who witness the arrival, thus Ferrari's self-citing does not remain the type of bracketing performed by the reciting "non-serious" actor on stage that Jacques Derrida dismisses as totalisation of intentionality in the speech act theory, and context is not escaped but infinitely produced without originary anchoring, leading to aforementioned excess [9].

The second aspect is the introduction of the computational medium, as yet another writing process that is relocated into the performance. Generation, transformation, selection and rejection are built into the composition as programs to be invoked and actualised in the performance. This does not go as far as the automatic reprogramming of a composition's code, but it must go beyond the pre-established course in which an algorithmic composition unfolds irrespective of a performance context. There must be a sensitivity towards "the unexpected, the singularity of events" [10, 236f].

The third is a rotation of perspective from reception to production. Pieces here become interpunctuation in a long-term process. What is marked as a "piece" is often transverse to the actual writing nexus. We have one body with one set of tentacles. We can only tend to one thing at a time, but we fluctuate across confluent projects, software components, pieces. Pieces are often cut from this fluctuating nexus—just like deciding when to take a developing photo out of the acid bath—and in order to understand the writing process, it may be more useful to establish object-series related to one another, not necessarily in chronological order, through reconfigurations within a set of commonalities (cf. [36]). And finally, the sets of tentacles multiply, as we move towards collaborative works, and a whole new dimension is added to these topological reconfigurations through the simultaneous arrival of multiple agents.

Transactions

When I developed the temporal model that eventually became a fundamental layer of *Mellite*, I was still guided by the techno-optimism of capturing the "entire" compositional process, using as basis the concept of a bi-temporal database, which posits valid time—the temporal information represented by a datum in the database—against user time—the time, when a user modifies the database. It is no coincidence that the former, referring to the "real world", is often represented as durations, time and date intervals, whereas the latter, referring to the digital realm, is often represented as discrete and duration-less instants.[2] From a technical perspective, it is much more difficult and rather useless to think about the process of entering or deleting data as something that takes time. The datum was there; now it is not there; it had value A, now it has value B. There is no space for uncertainty. Of course, every implementation will take time, but logically it must be atomised, especially where concurrency comes into play—multiple actors operating within a common space. It is from this background that the concept of transactions was developed for database systems.

As the name suggests, a transaction is something that spans across actions, "… the actions of a process are grouped into sequences called transactions which are units of consistency." [13] Let us take a simple example: Given a list of elements, move the first element one position down. If the list was realised through single links from cell to cell, where each cell contains a value (element) and a pointer to the next cell (or terminal symbol), the computer might perform three actions: Set the next-pointer of the former first cell to the former third cell. Set the next-pointer of the former second cell to the former first cell. Set the pointer to the list head to the former second cell. To the computer system, and likely to the user as well, only the ensemble of the three actions makes sense, thus forming a transaction. A transaction as a semantic unit, therefore, forms a higher level of atomicity than the actions it is composed of. Concurrent transactions are isolated, so if two users try to move elements in the list, this cannot overlap in time, but parallelism must be coerced into sequential order, possibly aborting and retrying the transaction of one user if it would conflict

---

[2]Compare the opposition of time as passage and time as encounter in Rohrhuber [30].

with the transaction of the other user. These three properties, atomicity, consistency, isolation, along with a guarantee that the effects of transactions are made durable on a secondary storage, define the classic *ACID* acronym of database systems.

Digital systems are transactional through and through. When we type a character in a text editor, we expect the cursor to move in the same instant as the character is inserted. When we save the text buffer, we expect it to *complete* with the entire contents saved (or nothing at all, if there is an error). If saving means the hard disk has to spin up because it had been automatically parked due to inactivity, we accept that during this physically perceivable time span, we cannot do anything useful in the editor. To a certain extent, we become transactional ourselves, in the way we anticipate the machine to work. But perhaps also in the way we consider other elements outside the machine?

Mellite was thought with the orthogonality of performance and creation time in mind, with the goal of being able to observe the latter and the prospect of possibly linking the two in some way. It turns out that both objectives are quite complicated. Automated observation requires a prior definition of a boundary within which provisions for observing (trans)actions are implemented. This happens by extending the transactional object modifications with a history-preserving data model called confluent persistence [15]. In the linked list example, it means that after updating the list, we can determine the point in time preceding this update and view the list at this point in its "old" state. In contrast to delta-based versioning systems such as *git*, an analysis must heuristically reconstruct from this information the changes that happened in between two transactions. This is cumbersome but feasible, as demonstrated in Fig. 2.2 that shows the creation of an electroacoustic music piece, with performance time on the abscissa and creation (transaction) time on the ordinate. For simplicity, what is highlighted are the time spans of objects that were created, deleted, moved, resized or otherwise modified, sufficient to see particular patterns of working with the timeline. While this is an interesting result for the study of the compositional process, two strong limitations arise. The principle idea of the computer music environment rests on the possibility to write code that produces and transforms structures. Arranging audio file snippets on the timeline is a very tight boundary for observation. With code fragments, it is not a priori clear what constitutes a transaction. Versioning systems like *git* avoid this problem by requiring the user to decide when to commit a new transaction. In *Mellite*, the current solution is similar—changes to code fragments have to be explicitly saved. Still, analysing what happens semantically between two versions is difficult. Moreover, since the system is always at the threshold between stable technical component and unstable research device, the development of various sound installations has shown that staying within the confines of prior coded object abstractions is impossible. There is always a moment when implementing a new algorithm or mechanism exceeds what is currently possible with the given objects, and thus one moves from the domain-specific language provided by *Mellite* to the general object language, *Scala*, in which it is implemented and which is not under automated observation itself. Extending the system to accommodate these algorithms in the future also happens outside the provided observation system, confirming the entanglement of the different writing

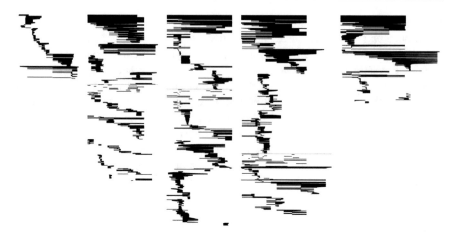

Fig. 2.2 Visualisation of the work on the electroacoustic study *(Inde)terminus* (2013), its five sections are shown as columns. In each column, creation time (transactions) advances from top to bottom, and the horizontal extent covers the section's performance time (duration). Black markings represent the modifications to the piece

processes. Finally, we leave programming languages altogether, whenever our work within the computer is suspended; perhaps we sketch on paper, or we read, write and talk in a natural language, "evil" and messy since it cannot be cast in the stratification of object and meta languages [17].

Secondly, linking the two time domains is difficult, because a relatively complex concept must be represented within a relatively confined embedded language. An attempt was made to explore this option at least as an artistic research experiment rather than a stand-alone composition, creating the étude *(Inde)terminus* in which an explicit mechanism is introduced to manually trigger a recursive replacement of audio files in an electroacoustic composition [33]. It is another example where writing a new abstraction—the representation of the recursive element—is part both of writing the computer music environment and of writing a particular piece. Indeed, it proved to be so specific to this study that the abstraction has since been *removed* again from the software. As a new embedded "glue" language within *Mellite* is shaping up to be able to write more expressive algorithmic couplings within the system, naturally this would be the place to introduce new elements that represent the creation and modification time of objects. To make any sense, this introduction would have to coincide with the composition of a piece that requires the use of this data. So no matter how one looks at this development process, it is clear that apparatus and objects produced from it always coevolve.

Expectedly, building a system based on transactions produced a number of effects accidental to the design goals. For a long time, especially while the system was in a less stable state than it is today, the property that transactions can be rolled back, played an important role in living with error. Transactions are performed in sepa-rate phases in order to guarantee the isolation property. In the first phase, accessing (reading) and updating (writing) objects are recorded in a log. If another transaction tries to access or update the same objects concurrently, the actions recorded in the log are reverted. Only when all actions that make up the transaction have success-fully completed, the changes in the log are made permanent in the second phase or commit phase. Programming errors can now be handled as if they were a conflicting concurrent transaction, reverting the log but not attempting to run the actions again as in a usual conflict. Therefore, if the transactional layer is robust and implemented correctly, the system is relatively immune towards propagating errors in the evolving and more unstable code to places where actual damage is done (such as corrupting the workspace database). It is only this behaviour that permitted the system to be actively used even while parts of it are in precarious state.

Another effect that retroacts on the compositional process is the image we have of ourselves as humans in relation to transactions. We can think transactional and atomic in the small gestures, but in the larger context we are never transactional as humans, we do not "roll back". If there is anything like transactions, we rather abandon them than complete them. A transaction leads from consistent state to consistent state. We are not consistent. But we suspend, we bend. The time the computer actually takes, it is our time of simultaneously doing and thinking other things. There are indications that we perform simultaneous threads in the compositional process, through opera-tions of deferral for which this isolation from the computer transactions is important (see, for example, the process-synthesis model of [7]).

2.4 Work

When we speak of computers as machines, it probably relates back to the tradition of mechanical machines that complemented or replaced physical *work* done by humans (the first computation machines still had mechanical components). Force times dis-placement. As today less and less of our work is physical work, but rather thinking, writing, negotiating, designing and observing machines that do physical work, we employ the term for any form of production and processing, including computational data production and processing. A program is written until "it works". Like the wear of physical machines, a program or configuration of programs may stop to work, something may become broken. Bits rot.

But also: Writing programs is "a lot of work" (and creating systems is even more so) until "they work". There is the work we *invest*, the time we spend setting up, fixing and tuning the system, and the work a running program returns to us is a work that, because of our investment, is not just the functioning of something we took off a shelf or somebody else could have written, but it constitutes a critical work with epistemic value to us. It is *us* who have overcome the frictions and resistances of the computer. This investment and return has been captured by Rheinberger as an opening statement to his theory of experimental systems, which examines the laboratory culture in the natural sciences: The more a scientist "… learns to handle his or her own experimental system, the more it plays out its own intrinsic capacities.

In a certain sense, it becomes independent of the researcher's wishes just because he or she has shaped it with all possible skill." [27, p. 24] The perceived agency *in* the system that we have shaped is, to a significant degree, a result of our engagement with it. Rheinberger employs Lacan's term *extimacy* for this situation, where we are intimately familiar with a machinery even though it is exterior to us. When we say, "it works", it signals that we recognise a form of agency has passed over to the machinery, which is now self-moving or self-governing, even though the overall agency is still extimately shared, because it was us that passed something over.

Ostensibly, work seems indivisible. Either it works or it does not. Using the classical idea of the artwork, it is difficult to imagine half of an artwork. We may say a work is unfinished, thus the thought rests with the completed work. When we think of a *body* of works, we use the word *piece*. The work unites the act of working and the product, in contrast to labour which seems detachable from the product. In industrial production, labour is divided. When we rid ourselves of the masterwork syndrome [12, p. 134], the works of art may be conceived more fragmentary and open-ended. The double meaning of work or composition as both the activity and the result seems to reflect a similar ambiguity in processes, which may either terminate in products or perpetuate as self-sustaining (cf. [31]). This undecidedness is in the artistic process as well; while one works on a piece, one is often not concerned with its termination but with a productive sustainment.

This durational mode, the productive sustainment or suspension of completing the process, allows us to experiment and speculate, and it is here that algorithmic practices appear as particularly appealing, since algorithmic agency shares such experimental and speculative tendencies. That work is durational, that it takes time, is not to say that it is inseparable or indivisible. When we proceed, we make steps, the discreteness of steps is not in contradiction to sustainment. One would think that process happens as bottom-up self-organisation and that divisions have to be top-down, rational, breaking-down. This conceals that the effective motion is vacillation, up and down, forward and backward. The divisibility indeed ensures the sustainment. It allows to put things side-by-side, a spatial projection, a random access to and thus possible rerouting of what has been broken down. For example, Fig. 2.3 shows a sketch of the sections of a catalogue text about the sound installation *Mexican Tumulus* (2018). There is a top-down decision to divide the text into twelve sections, following the number of speakers in the installation, and to produce an overall text length of six thousand characters equally distributed across the sections. Both enable particular movements: First to identify and select twelve subtitles that guide the text production. This is a request for an effort—find twelve items—and at the same time an open-ended step—the liberty to assemble heterogeneous things in no particular order. Also an anticipation: to stop after twelve items and then tend to another part of the production. Note that this part was suspended with a placeholder or hole in the last place—"(it'll come)". Placeholders are available in all types of writing and coding. Furthermore, one can always cancel out an item and replace it with another in the process, or merge two together. It is what happened with the text you are reading, the number of sections shrank over time.

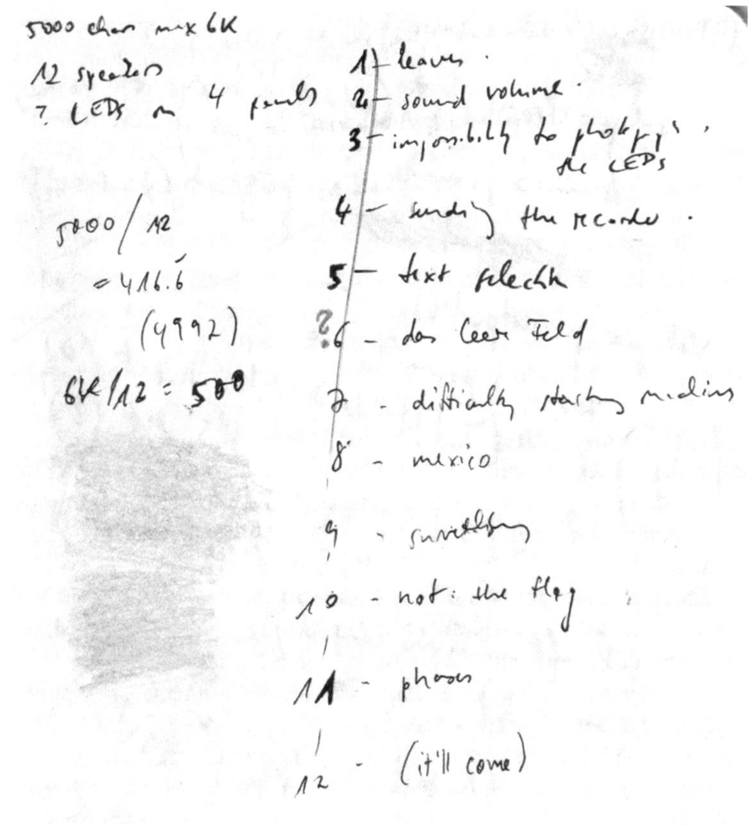

5000 char max 6K

12 speakers
7 LEDs   4 panels

5000 / 12

= 416.6

(4992)

6K / 12 = 500

1 } leaves
2 } sound volume
3 } impossibility to photogr. the LEDs
4 } sending the recorder
5 } text felecht
?6 } das leere Feld
7 } difficulty starting, medium
8 } mexico
9 } surveillance
10 } note: the flag
11 } phases
12 } (it'll come)

Fig. 2.3 A priori partitioning of a catalogue text into sections and number of characters

The division and spatialisation help to handle the simultaneity of things, we fix them in no prescribed order, we tentatively mark the spaces, so we can return to them later. We stay in the hypertext, even if the eventual outcome is a linear text. This suspension of order is not only a quality I can discern in algorithmic practices, but also in the way dreams are memorised. They appear as episodes, and they may have had a sequence, but the sequence's order is often not important or even clear. An effective technique to mark them is to quickly gather them as captions, similar to the section titles of the catalogue text described above. This creates an iterability that allows us to return to each episode and note down its details without complete loss or shadowing of the others.

I have made the connection between writing processes, the algorithmic, and dreams on several occasions—for example, in the installation work *Imperfect Reconstruction* [40] and in the lecture performance *From Data to Process* [39]—which lead me to believe that this connection is quite useful to understand writing processes and algorithmic practices. One aspect in which dreams resemble the algorithmic is in terms of their change. Changes happen both in the discrete (separated) and under discretion (tacit). For example: "the hotel room, now dorm room, now outside field exposed to rain." It is not clear whether this is an essential property of the dream, or it belongs to the mode of their recall, which is challenged with verbalisation, but there are cases that indicate the essential: "I notice the fundamental error – the room; I must have confused it, it unnoticeably changed." Sometimes the discrete has not manifested itself, yet the limbo is not a continuity but an oscillation—"the tram that is not"—or it appears as statement of change without qualification—"the town that changes". The discretion is an ambiguity that is only seemingly resolved through statement, because the statement pretends to resolve something that in fact remains unsaid: "A light source which began moving in space (the performer began moving in the space)." The observation is not innocent. When I correct myself, stating that it is not the light source that moves by itself, but the performer carrying the light source, the observation is responsible for the manifestation of the change. This is one side of the change, in which we are passive or reactive. We make a move, for example, we make the observation and statement "the performer began moving in the space," but this decision is a consequence to an alien agency or will that encircles what is possible.

The other side relates to the forward–backward movement described before as random access. In dreams, this is still constrained and partial. For instance, we jump across a cliff or fall from a cliff. We observe ourselves falling, we then "develop" the landscape beneath us. A river appears, and we may either miss it and hit on a piece of grass next to it, or we reach the water surface without further ado. In the first case, we possess a limited power to repeat—perhaps not from the very beginning, but while already in motion—the jump or fall; a new attempt can be made, to correct the fall's trajectory in order to reach safely the water surface. It is a partial power, because it only extends to "incomplete" things; if I had already hit the ground, the jump or fall could not be repeated. Clocks cannot be fully turned back, instead we can suspend the situation, reconfigure it and resume it in altered state. Substances can be transformed: I am rolling within a wave of water, I need air and thus I can take the required breath of air, thus the water becomes oxygenous or my lungs become amphibious.

In the speculative mode, one tests a proposition and one may revert and redo it slightly differently, one adjusts the rules, thus rules are mutable. For example, in a dream, we travel in space-time, but a problem occurs, a physical impossibility in the contact between the traveller and those who "stay on". Something did not work or would have terminated the dream. We introduce a "solution", perhaps it is better to call it *resolution* to avoid confusion with the concept of problem-solving (a confusion that also applies to the surficial description of algorithmic practice): We were not transparent, thus we speculate and become transparent along with the objects that we take in possession. If I envelop an orb or a box, it belongs to me, passes over into my space-time, becomes transparent with me against those who "stay on". Therefore, the resolution is the boundary that now runs alongside me and the objects in possession.

We are at the middle of the text, and just like in other of my writing processes, the materials develop their own motion of unfolding. The demonstration should suffice, so let us return to understand, how can one relate these kinds of changes and investments to algorithmic practices?

Software Anatomy

To begin with an obvious difference, while in dreams something does not "work" or "figure" only for a short moment before a kind of resolution sets in—as we are in a flux that is similar to music improvisation—when working with algorithms, they are seldom effortless, most of the time they are in the state of "not working" (yet). There seems to be a separation between, on the one hand, my writing or the computer "reading" my code, and, on the other hand, the computer "writing" or producing things which is observed or "read" by me, perhaps captured by the upper half of the phase model of reading–writing relations in Fig. 2.4.

The diaphragm in the figure was originally indicating the separation between composing and performing by the introduction of a manifest element such as a score, but also the separation between observer and observed, through spatio-temporal distance or distinct behaviour. In contrast, the lower half pictures a mode where reading and writing are tightly coupled and interacting to a degree where it is impossible to separate them, symbolised by the needle and the wax disc, in which the needle could either incise the wax or carefully trace its surface. It corresponds with the entangled agency in dreams, where sometimes we are able to suspend and inject our will and direct the fall, whereas at other times we are acceptors of the discrete and tacit changes presented to us (tacit: we are not asked, we are not separated observers).

The important point here is, as indicated by the rotary arrows, a process iterates both types of couplings and distances. Even though most of the time writing software and algorithms is spent in alternating activity—either writing with the system halted, or the system runs tests with us waiting and observing—we also enter a mode in which

Fig. 2.4 Phase model of relations between writing and reading ([34, p. 108])

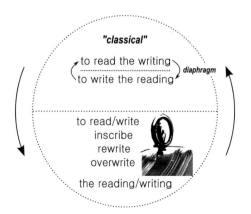

directions are not taken from a distance, but by following hunches in close proximity to the performance of the system, its unexpected responses. As a result, the evolution of a program follows the kind of sprawling and it includes the moments of acceptance and resolution described before.

Before *Mellite* even had its name, one of its starting points was the development of a model of sound processes that were on the one hand "persistent" in the sense of a score, but also reflected in a real-time sound synthesis realisation. The needle/wax model came in as a way to understand the hinge between these two aspects, literally translating into two elements in the software called Scan and Grapheme [34, 280f]. The idea that a "scan" (the action of the needle) had no a priori distinction between reading and writing proved to be very unpractical, and eventually the Scan element itself was removed again, giving way to more traditionally distinguished inputs and outputs, although a trace is still there as one refers to inputs and outputs in the code that defines a sound synthesis program as ScanIn and ScanOut. Another entirely different remnant is an episode of spoken text in the installation piece *Unvorhergesehen–Real–Farblos* (2012) in which the difficulty of understanding the hinge between stored and live sound is addressed. In a way, the difficulty is resolved in this spoken text, whereas it has been scraped off the software framework.

A tacit change happened in my perspective on *Mellite*. In the original research, everything was centred around the sedimentation of traces in creation time; even though it included many thoughts on multiple versions of a piece, branching and merging in the compositional process, the computer only registered human time, its own time was of little consideration. That is kind of surprising, given that the first music software I wrote, beginning in 2001, was *FScape*, a program for "rendering" sounds in non-real-time. Only a few years back did I start to rethink *FScape* as another constituent element within *Mellite* next to its existent real-time sound synthesis, giving more explicit thought to the time it takes to compute a sound, and the human time away from the computer while it is occupied.

The original *FScape* program was developed in the spirit of several other programs that existed at the time—such as *SoundHack* (1991), *Argeïphontes Lyre* (1997/98) or the commercial *sonicWORX* (1994)—which applied lengthy digital signal processing (DSP) to sound files, yielding newly transformed sound files as output. Each transform, called *module*, was either a common DSP algorithm, such as convolution or resampling, or the result of experimenting with a less conventional sonic idea that I had, often arising out of work on a particular piece of music. Since so-called real-time, the alignment of sound processing and audible sound production, was not a requirement, depending on the parameters chosen the modules could often run for a very long time, indicating their internal state through a progress bar and estimation of remaining processing time. Especially in the beginning, when computers were relatively slow compared to today, one had to tend to other activities while expensive processes were running, or even put them to run overnight. At a time when real-time software had become feasible on personal computers, it could be seen as a disadvantage having to wait for results, examining them, possibly adjusting parameters and running the process again, until one arrived at a satisfying output. But on the contrary, it felt liberating to work this way. Clearly, since I had given the computer so

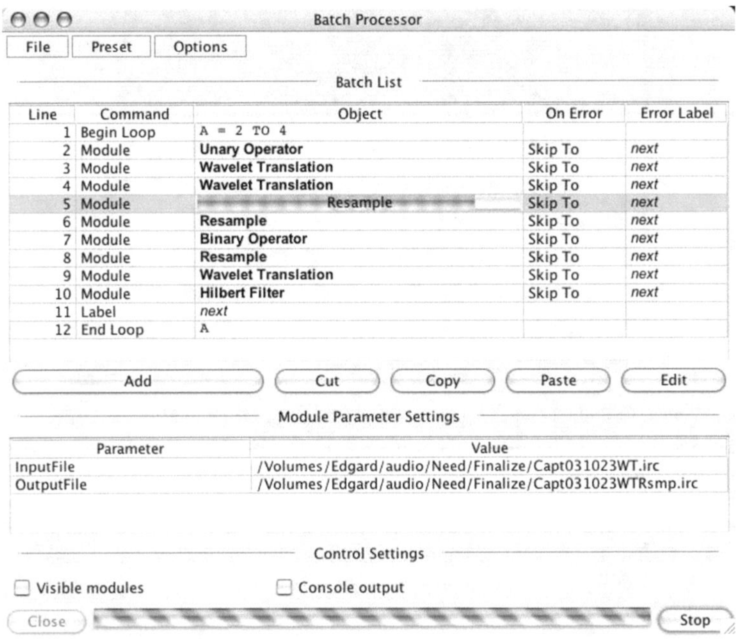
Batch Processor
File
Preset
Options
Batch List
Line
Command
Object
On Error
Error Label
1 Begin Loop A = 2 TO 4
2 Module Unary Operator Skip To next
3 Module Wavelet Translation Skip To next
4 Module Wavelet Translation Skip To next
5 Module Resample Skip To next
6 Module Resample Skip To next
7 Module Binary Operator Skip To next
8 Module Resample Skip To next
9 Module Wavelet Translation Skip To next
10 Module Hilbert Filter Skip To next
11 Label next
12 End Loop A
Add
Cut
Copy
Paste
Edit
Module Parameter Settings
Parameter
Value
InputFile /Volumes/Edgard/audio/Need/Finalize/Capt031023WT.irc
OutputFile /Volumes/Edgard/audio/Need/Finalize/Capt031023WTRsmp.irc
Control Settings
Visible modules
Console output
Close
Stop

Fig. 2.5 Iterating over a number of modules in batch processing mode in *FScape* (2004)

much time to make an effort and waited for so much time to examine it, an entirely different type of valuation is taking place compared to the effortless tweaking of real-time parameters that often leave me with a stronger sense of arbitrariness (if there is no effort, what is the point?). There is a particular way of treating the results as jigsaw pieces, putting them sometimes aside until a position for them is found.

A countermovement was prompted, though, by the fact that while under development, a module might fail or run out of memory, or it would take only a few hours and leave the computer idle for the rest of the night. A simple solution was the introduction of a batch module that could run a list of modules in succession, but also provided a simple variable templating function to iterate a process over a number of uniformly named input files (Fig. 2.5).

Intermediate files would be overwritten in this case and not remain for future examination. This possibility of process division and iteration was not really new, it just automated and systematised a mode of working that I had employed before. Although it was always possible to invoke a remote *FScape* rendering process from *Mellite*, it felt like a shortcoming not to have a genuine integration of the two. A reason this had not happened earlier is that the original modules had been written in a language (*Java*) I was no longer using, and some of the code was so old that I would neither have been able to fully understand all of its details, rendering the task of translating the code too laborious. It was in 2016 during work on a sonification project that the real-time capabilities of *Mellite* alone were too limited to transform the

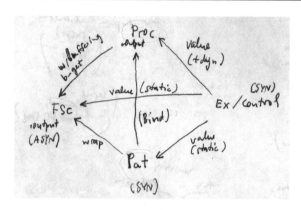

Fig. 2.6 Attempt to understand the passages between the four languages embedded in *Mellite*: Sound Processes or `Proc` for real-time signal processing, FScape or `FSc` for offline signal processing, Patterns or `Pat` for symbolic or numeric sequences, Expressions or `Ex` and `Control` for high-level coordination or "glue" between algorithmic processes. Each lives in their own temporal space, with `FSc` working by rendering asynchronously, `Proc` running on a server in real time, and `Pat` and `Ex` sharing the similarity of returning values or invoking actions synchronously

sonification's input data, and I decided that a worthwhile experiment would be to give *FScape* a new "language form" within *Mellite* in order to formulate these sonification data preparations. This language form was intentionally chosen to resemble the real-time sound synthesis description, using a similar domain-specific language for unit generator descriptions of a signal process, although now I could use the particularities that offline signals would have a finite duration and could be treated in a random access way.

At first, the coupling between the two embedded languages was fixed and designed with the sonification application in mind: *FScape* could be invoked as an auxiliary, preparatory step to the sonification, rendering to temporary sound files which would then be streamed into the real-time process. A year later, *Algorithms that Matter* (ALMAT) was started as an artistic research project with the experimentality of algorithms as its explicit topic, and *Mellite* becoming (again) a research vehicle. One of the experiments was the translation of sketches by guest artist Ron Kuivila, using the *SuperCollider* pattern language, into a language that could be embedded in *Mellite*, in order to understand what happens in this translation process, what it enables, precludes or displaces. The question of how these different sprawling subsystems could be connected became more pressing, and barely another year later, in 2018, a fourth embedded language was introduced, with the explicit goal of acting as a glue between the others. The sketch in Fig. 2.6 shows the quadruple configuration with the glue language appearing on an equal level with the others.

The multiplicity of these, nevertheless interlinked and often structurally similar, languages is not a disadvantage over the monism of other computer music systems. Instead, one could see it as an expression of the becoming-topological of *Mellite*, a surface that produces its own internally organised space [24]. Like the depicted diagram, this space is a mobile as the system evolves, and each new form of notation introduced in either of the sub-languages can have the experimental property of spilling over and "contaminating" the other sub-languages (cf. [5, 36]).

2.5 Artistic Research

Processes of human–machine exchange in sound composition, and algorithmic experimentation can be regarded from a number of disciplines, using their corresponding perspectives and methods. I want to argue here for the sovereignty of artistic research as an appropriate way to understand these processes. We still rely too much on disciplines like musicology, psychology and cognitive science, but also media archaeology, software studies, cultural studies and philosophy, to encircle the topic. All of them produce valid knowledge, but a fundamental difference to artistic research is that the latter is not talking about art and about artists, but now artists articulate research through their practice, challenging the assumption that you have to be distinct from your research subject and that a particular form of written language is the distinguished means of articulation.

The two criteria, attenuation of the prerogative of rational, citational, peer-reviewed text, and of the distance between researcher and researched, are not easy to solve,[3] and the embedding of artistic research in institutional cultures anchored in traditional scholarly practices also contributes to the fact that a lot of artistic research is still articulated in traditional forms. The spatio-temporal persistence of a published text is not easily substituted by a lecture performance, a concert, an exhibited artefact; we cannot really cite them unless we refer to their recordings or catalogues. Text is successful, because it is so connectable. The success of the online platform *Research Catalogue* (RC), which was chosen for the dissemination of the ALMAT project [42], is an indicator that both stable citationality—allowing acceptance within a scholarly culture—and an augmentation to non-linear hypertext with the inclusion of non-textual media—allowing adequate expression of work processes—are strong requirements for the dissemination of artistic research. The RC exposition represents perhaps a current "local optimum", still having an ordering of authors, an abstract, a table-of-contents and the idea of immutability once the exposition is "published" (which has no technological justification and requires but a button click), hence we should strive for much more experimental means of dissemination.

Computer code would seem a good candidate next to natural language text, sharing with it the same properties of persistence, citationality, being even formally specified. Given enough preparation, it may in fact be executable by others, although any non-trivial code would involve difficult to reproduce performance contexts. But there is no literacy we can assume, especially given the vast amount of programming languages available, some even specific to a particular artist/researcher. We want to

---

[3]For a discussion on the problems of language and reflexivity in artistic research, see Crispin [8].

talk not only to our closest peers, but even beyond the boundaries of the discipline, so that a cultural theorist or a musicologist can follow the discourse to a certain extent, and here is perhaps a difference to a computer scientist that can write a paper readable almost exclusively by other computer scientists. Programming languages are likely "inscrutable to the uninitiated" [20], so code has to be contextualised with the products of its performance, with commentary. Gathering multiple formats around each research "item" and interlinking them could be a viable approach, with the implicit assumption that no person can read them exhaustively.

When researcher and researched are intimately linked, the issue of how to write—writing now in an abstract sense that goes beyond logically linguistically structured natural language text—has to be augmented by writing about the writing. As indicated earlier, there is a self-sameness in the writings, this text, the software, the compositions, so why would a re-entry or (simpler) a meta-level be needed? Are not all the crucial elements guaranteed to be present in the text as it is and thus relatable to the other writings? It is obvious that the writings are not reducible to each other, otherwise the plea for new forms of dissemination would not be necessary. A writing is always the coming-together of an assumed author and a material configuration that enables the writing, and it would be a mistake to assume a generality of this configuration, as it happens when researchers talk about general conditions for *creativity*, *creativity support systems*, *artificial creativity* and so on. The suspicion that Rheinberger has about this generality can be extended beyond the artist's workspace that he considers:

> I don't like the notion of creativity. It tends to obscure the materiality of the process, and to locate itself on the spiritual side. An artist's studio is not only an aesthetic space, it is usually also an epistemic work-space with a lot of intellectual as well as material investment, an investment that tends to disappear in the product. But for the artist, it's an integral aspect of his or her work, without which she or he probably would not be motivated to carry out that work. [29, p. 217]

It is this material investment that we are interested in as artists-researchers, it is here that a difference towards "just" artistic work manifests itself. It is important to observe that writing a dream recollection, it makes a difference whether I open the laptop and type characters, or I take my paper notebook and begin to scribble. Two very distinctly structured recollections ensue. "I write on a typewriter … and my machine … is the biggest influence on my work … The type-face is a standard pica; if it were another style I'd write (subtly) different poems. And when a ribbon gets dull my poems I'm sure change" [43, back]. Yes, there is a sameness in the movement, whether I write this text or I write a composition, there is strategic alignment, but at the same time, the word processor feels far more removed to how I imagine to work with text, than *Mellite* feels removed from how I imagine to work with sound. I interrupt, I move from screen to paper and back, I copy and paste materials to future subspaces of the text. A musicologist does not normally write about their desk or how they manage to work on their texts. It may not be needed, because there is no re-entry of the subject, but Ahmed makes clear that there is a problematic disappearance of materiality from the writing when limiting one's focus to what is faced. What is excluded is the background:

> We can think … of the background not simply in terms of what is around what we face, as the 'dimly perceived,' but as produced by acts of relegation: some things are relegated to the background in order *to sustain* a certain direction; in other words, in order to keep attention on what is faced. [1, p. 31]

Beyond the relegation of the familiar, the background can be "understood as that which must take place in order for something to appear" [1, 37f], i.e. the appearance of the research object in the first place. The call for multiple formats is not made for a hermeneutic gain. It does not mean that a recipient gets "nearer" the object, that they uncover more of it. Instead, the object is *constituted* through the complementary forms of arrival (it does not exist prior to each of their performances).

We should strive for rigour, but limit redaction, not in order to create mystification but to preserve what is fragile. In the ALMAT project, we have reviewed its RC exposition, adding meta-data in order to transform it into a database that can be queried. To obtain a partially exterior perspective, we tasked somebody with a reading through the existing material. After this reading, they stated that initially it seemed difficult to get into the text because of its fragmentary, unwieldy character and lack of more common academic style, but that during the course of the reading this impression receded, instead of giving way to an understanding why this fragmentary and dispersed form was chosen, producing a concreteness that resists totalisation [11].

Materiality and Rudiments

How can one not only preserve the materiality of writing, but work with it, share it, if it escapes verbalisation? How would this sharing look like, if it is not simply the display of artefacts *about* which one can then talk? When ALMAT was constructed, one of its foundations were the existing computer music frameworks that the team had developed in the preceding years. In several iterations in which we invited guest artists to work with us, we had envisioned that they could engage with these systems, and thus their epistemic qualities would appear through the difference these systems made when used not by their original authors but by other artists.

The first iteration began in autumn 2017 with composer and sound artist Ron Kuivila joining the project. Kuivila is also a pioneer of computer music, having coauthored *Formula* (Forth Music Language) in the late 1980s, and later the pattern system for *SuperCollider*. I was intrigued by what he would do with *Mellite* whose real-time component is based on a *SuperCollider* dialect, and in return, I tried to translate the pattern system to *Mellite*. What looks much less surprising in retrospect, expecting that after handing a personal system over to someone they can transfer their knowledge and be productive in a short amount of time is unrealistic. Because the system is not a stable technical component—in which case it would be easier to involve an exterior person but one would rather deal with design and engineering questions than with aesthetic-epistemic questions—the extimate relation that I had developed with it concealed that of the large possible design space of this system only those paths were trodden that corresponded to my personal practice, and glitches and problems would appear quickly if one left these paths. Despite some effort to document the paths, the close relationship with my practice also meant that the documentation was insufficient for an exterior person. I recently made a renewed attempt to develop a tutorial that only looks at one aspect of the system, the *FScape* offline rendering component, and even here it was difficult to draw a boundary to the necessary explanations and assumptions about the knowledge somebody would bring to the tutorial. For every statement made, a huge space of unsaid things would open. Sometimes the term *tacit knowledge* is used to describe the implicit aspects of a practice, but the term is wrong in this respect; the problem with sharing knowledge about a technological system rooted in personal investment lies less in an inability to verbalise its aspects, but in their shear amount, interconnectedness and contextualisation. It is literally *impractical*.

The effect was also observable in the reverse case: While I had the literacy to read the code with which Kuivila and the other guest artists were working, often using mainstream languages such as *SuperCollider*, *Java*, *Python* or *C++*, I did not develop a strong interest in being able to run the original pieces of code, but preferred to see how the artists worked with the code, how the code embodied a particular long-term practice, and how I could draw value from it in other ways. In the case of Kuivila's pattern-based piece *The Fifth Root Of Two*,[4] inspired by Gamelan music, a melodic base cell is generated, filtered, permuted, looking for repeated sub-patterns, and from the analyses it produces rhythmical-spatial interleaving. The program that generates the piece is less than 300 lines of code, including the definition of sound synthesis functions and audio routing, with core pattern code taking up around 200 lines. That felt like a reasonable size for a translation experiment, and so I took this as the study case that should be representable in a pattern system written for *Mellite* (for more details on the pattern translations and side-by-side code comparisons, see [41]).

Examining the original code, two things became clear. First, that the boundaries between patterns and ordinary sequence collections were porous. One can quickly translate from a pattern to a stateful stream, from there into a plain collection, and from there back to patterns. A pattern is an immutable description, such as "count the integer numbers, starting with 4"—written `Pseries(start: 4)` in *SuperCollider*. Expanded as a stream this becomes a stateful object that responds to the `next` message. When `next` is called the first time, the stream returns 4, the second time `next` is called, it will return 5, and so on. When collecting the first three results of the invocations of `next`, one obtains the plain collection [4, 5, 6]. A particularity of the *SuperCollider* language is that many operations are defined in the same way for different types, and one can easily and sometimes unknowingly move from one type to another. In his piece, Kuivila moved from patterns to arrays (plain sequences), and back to patterns. As he was explaining in a workshop:

---

[4]Kuivila stressed that it is a project in development, which came into being primarily to give me an example of how he was working with patterns.

I will take every distinct subgrouping of pitches from [the initial] phrase ... And then I will find how to play every one of those notes in combination in that grouping ... It just turns out that doing this in SuperCollider, it took a bunch of code, because although array manipulations are really great, they are not necessarily set up to do exactly this. This kind of idea is atemporal. You do not want to do it in a sequential fashion. You want to take an array and expand all these possibilities. This is a kind of question that probably turns out to be much nicer to do within a functional programming language. [22]

Kuivila talks about shortcomings of the language, although the code certainly looks elegant and concise. He knows how to work around the fact that patterns establish sequential (temporal) relations, implementing his own operations on sets through custom functions. An entirely different aspect of patterns is that they are implemented using coroutines, linking them with *SuperCollider*'s primary way of expressing time-based sequencing. Kuivila is using an abstraction he has written, `Pspawner`, that makes it more easy to formulate temporal structures and interleave parallel patterns. Furthermore, value patterns that generate sequences of scalar parameters and event patterns that configure a sound playing function can be distinguished, and special cases have been introduced to distinguish between notes and rests. Once all these elements are included, the surface area of patterns in *SuperCollider* becomes quite large, evidence of sprawling having taken place in its evolution.

I worked over the course of half a year on the implementation up to the point where *The Fifth Root Of Two* was fully working following the original code. The process was very intriguing as an opportunity to narrow down some solutions, for example, being able to write the piece using only patterns without having to expand them to sequences for manipulations, also having to find solutions where equivalent constructs such as coroutines were not available in the *Scala* language. However, regarding Fig. 2.6, the quadrant had been lying dormant since its creation. I had not understood yet what to *do* with the pattern language. It was an experiment and remained a *rudiment*. A beginning, a first try, a test piece, a vestigial organ in the anatomy of the system. A rudiment does not mean it is nonfunctional matter, that it does not matter. It may be overlooked as too uninteresting or unintelligible, but it has been suggested to adopt "rudimentariness as a mode of thought and practice in approaching an object of investigation", wherein rudimentariness is seen as a way of resisting premature conceptual judgement, as an approach "predisposed to the concept of sensate thinking" [16]. Going beyond sensate thinking, the rudiment could also be approached with new operations, or to stay in the vestige metaphor, one could operate on these software pieces and graft them onto other objects.

The excess produced in the translation of the pattern system manifested itself in at least two instances of novel elements entering into my system, now attaching themselves to the further development of the system. These instances are the abilities to reset and to persist streams. The first came about as a consequence of merging patterns with the breadth of the operations normally available to *Scala* collections, in particular the functional programming concept of functions acting as arguments to operations. For example, one can sort a collection by giving a function argument for the pairwise comparison of elements (a predicate determining whether one element is "less than" another). On a collection `Seq[A]` of element type A, this operation is `def sortWith(lt: (A, A) => Boolean): Seq[A]`, the predicate `lt` comparing two elements, and the result being a new collection of type `Seq[A]`. In the patterns system of *Mellite*, because of the second property—the ability to persist streams (to store them on the hard-drive)—functions passed as arguments have to be destructured into a pattern or a tree of pattern expressions. A trick is to require that the pattern is nested,[5] `Pat[Pat[A]]` or a pattern of patterns of element type A, and thus the predicate has type `(Pat[A], Pat[A]) => Pat[Boolean]`, allowing the evaluation of this *pattern expression* and obtaining a serialisable tree. The predicate has to be "reused" for any pair of elements that need to be compared during the sorting operation. The solution I found is to add a `reset` operation to the stream (expanded pattern), which requires that the stream purges its cached state, internal counters, etc., and recursively calls `reset` on its inputs, thus fetching fresh iteration variables when `next` is called again. Without going into more technical details, the reset mechanism also allows for the nested iteration and mapping over patterns in a way that delimited pattern scopes can be created, blocking the propagation of reset and thereby allowing the kind of array operations Kuivila used in his piece. I was so stunned when finally having made this reset mechanism work that I now plan to implement the same mechanism for *FScape* unit generators. It would mean that the same problem that Kuivila stated in the above quote, escaping the inherent "temporal" coupling of patterns, could be overcome in signal processing, which in the unit generator formalism also suffers from the inability to express larger forms of "stages" of processes and functionally nested processing.

The second instance, making streams persistent, was somewhat premeditated but at the same time a natural choice, because in *Mellite* mutable state is usually represented with software transactional memory, which is only one step away from persistence. In the first implementation, this property remained rudimentary, as one could not do anything yet with the persisted stream. Only recently, persisted streams were integrated as directly accessible objects. Storing their current state in the workspace, they can be resumed at any future point in time. For me, this was a solution to representing very slowly changing and interruptible processes in a sound installation, also having a memory that survives the rebooting of a computer. In this way, persistent streams complement *FScape* which produces such memory or material through its intermediary sound files written to the hard disk. An unexpected, unintended or outright useless sound is not "going away" by rotating some knobs, but lies there on the hard disk. Likewise, data is kept, the human composer can go away and return, examine and consider this data at a later point.

---

[5] You can always transform a pattern into a nested one using the `bubble` operation, and return later using `flatten`.

2.6 Suspension

To understand the nature of human-machine coupling, it is also necessary to look at those situations in which they are *not* coupled, where a causal interaction is suspended: When either the sealed transaction takes longer than required to trick us into perceiving it as instantaneous—a computation is taking place at its intrinsic speed—or we proactively turn away from the computer and towards other things. We are set aside or we set ourselves aside, temporarily. At a research seminar, I was attending in 2019, there was concern that human life and machine operation are often treated, in the discourse, as commensurable. That there is a widespread view that they can be treated equally by some abstract model of computation that runs in both of them. It was instead suggested that computations and algorithms are nothing but applied mathematics, and the world was more than mathematics, and therefore we should be careful not to conflate the human world and the world of computation, since the latter cannot contain the whole of the former.

I believe this assumption to be wrong on two levels. First, is human life commensurable with itself? Do we recognise our kind? I recently heard the story of a mother and her 2 1/2 year-old child riding on the tramway. The child grew up in a small village in rural Austria and was perhaps visiting the city for the first time. It was very shy and clung to its mother as it was anxiously observing another child of African descent sitting across the aisle. Not speaking for a while, it was eventually asking its mother whether "the dog would not bite". It would seem strange to think of this reaction as an expression of racism, but more likely the child had never seen a child of another skin colour and hair type, and just having started to develop its language, it was trying to verbalise its confusion. On the other end of the spectrum, we find the post-human position of Donna Haraway who stresses the potential to communicate beyond the boundaries of otherness and to form a kinship with other species, to think-with as a transformative practice [18].

So yes, if we dismiss both computationalist universality and connectionism, there may be otherness between human life and computational processes, but this is not a distinguished feature of this pair. Computation may be governed by what Luciana Parisi calls "alien mode of thought" [26, p. 240] which cannot nearly be reduced to applied mathematics (not even the application alone would be reducible, but would bring with it performativity and contextuality). If the alienness or otherness is granted a degree of autonomy, the possibility of nevertheless going together with otherness could perhaps be compared to a holobiontic relationship.[6] Biologist Lynn Margulis used the term to denote the formation of a new individual from two, possibly very different bionts, by recognising each other and merging their bodies, eventually dissociating again [25]. The new integrated symbiont is of higher complexity than the constituting former individuals, questioning the concept of individuality itself

---

[6]To be sure, this is an approximation, not to conflate the algorithmic with a living matter, as "life" is beyond the scope of this article. This is why autonomy or self-governance is a less problematic term.

Fig. 2.7 Phase model of coupling between human and machine

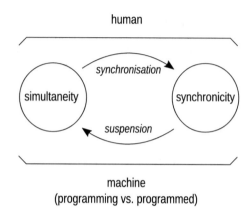

(cf. [6]). Two human arms are put together, next to each other, close to each other. They are squashed, dissected, cut, united on an object slide or a glass. A specimen is created—a confluent investment—the (section of the) double-arm becomes one object. What happens to life? Because formerly life existed separately in each of the arms. To what extent does life unite in the squashed arms, since it can be traced back to two individual lines? Composed systems are made this way: they perform an orientation, they give up something (necessity) to gain something (contingency), they align with each other [2].

An important element in the holobiont is rhythmic; the alignment may be undone, the integrated system may be dissolved, and then later, alignment and composition can be performed again. Today I would develop a phase model different to the one drawn in Fig. 2.4 in 2011–2013, focusing more on this alternation between coupling/alignment and decoupling/suspension instead of the binarism between reading and writing. At the end points, one then finds the two temporal modes of synchronisation and simultaneity (Fig. 2.7).

A movement between both sides is necessary, because on the one hand, there is no knowing from a distance without direct material engagement [3, p. 49], on the other hand memory and reflection require a distance or disengagement. Constantly being close is stressful, as it requires a form of obedience—having to listen. Turning away allows also for an important function of memory, oblivion. When we come back, we have to pick up where we left, remember things, and piece those together anew that we have forgotten. Human–machine agency thus develops in a balance between memory work and synchronised activity. No pure real-time systems and no pure non-real-time systems are likely to exhibit it, but a movement between both.

Simultaneity and Relaying

Why choose simultaneity on the left side instead of asynchronicity or diachronicity? To be sure, diachronicity may also occur, where something happening in the computer forms a relation with what a human is doing at a later point and vice versa. But

I wanted to stress a togetherness-in-independence. The word simultaneity derives from Latin *simul* for "together, at the same time". For example, in the reception of an artwork, the person encountering the work will create meaning from the intersection of the presence of the piece's artefacts or propositions and their past experiences and memories which through mental and bodily acts become co-present. There is no causality involved, it is not one being primary to the other. In physics, simultaneity would be the observation of two events at the "same" time which thus precludes that one event caused the other. In an artistic performance, one might think this ecologically or like Cage's idea of the "unimpeded and interpenetrating" coexistence of sounds [4, p. 46]. When regarding the compositional process, this reference frame may well include human and machine activities that are in spatio-temporal distance when viewed atomically, as long as the reference frame permits to establish a "togetherness, at the same time". One may observe an orientation away from each other, the other becoming latent, as long as one includes an eventual common *arrival* of the two. If I leave the computer rendering, turn away from it for a while tending towards other elements of the compositional process—even sleeping over it, piecing together elements in a dream or recollecting them the next morning—then there is still a togetherness in the compositional process without a clear causal link; finally, I return to the computer and examine the tableau of elements that now coincide.

Simultaneity can become a vehicle for artistic research and collaboration, too. In the fifth and last ALMAT iteration, we were working on a collaborative sound installation between four artists titled *Through Segments* [37]. An early thought was that we could explore the excess of algorithmic agency, manifesting itself as an individuation and differentiation in the process of experimentation and implementation, by departing from the same initial configuration or algorithm. As we would then work in parallel with the common disposition, individuated segments would emerge between which horizontal communicative links could be established, as sketched on the left side of Fig. 2.8. It soon turned out that finding a neutral "uninvested" algorithmic idea as the starting point was very difficult; either someone proposed an idea that others could not connect to or had difficulties to construe with their respective computer music systems (we were all using different systems); or we were left with a feeling of arbitrariness—if nobody had an investment in a particular algorithmic configuration, then why use it at all?

At attempt was thus made to "reset" the planning process. What had also become clear is that even if we did not agree on one specific disposition, we identified common ideas and elements; perhaps these elements could be explicated and serve as a layer of stability on which we could work in a different way. The parallelism seemed the important concept to retain, and so I suggested to discard the common disposition, but to keep the steps from there, inverting the arrows so that we should instead *arrive* at a common site, as sketched in the right side of Fig. 2.8, site meaning the bringing together of our work process—on the RC platform—but also the particular exhibition site. If parallelism was not sufficient to constitute simultaneity, it may be the operation in which we come together, in intervals, or even staying together through the image of the future arrival. The arrival then is not just a cumulative effect of what each individual had done, but it is something that would always already have

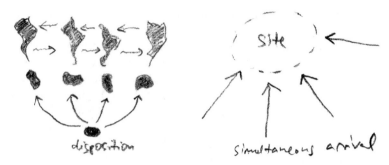

Fig. 2.8 Inversion of the working method on *Through Segments*, from the departure from a common algorithmic disposition (left) to a projected common arrival (right)

configured our prior doing, the "background" as Ahmed would call it. She describes this arrival as follows:

> At least two entities have to arrive to create an encounter, a 'bringing forth' in the sense of an occupation … To 'co-incide' suggests how different things happen at the same moment, a happening that brings things near to other things, whereby the nearness shapes the shape of each thing. Simultaneous arrivals … are determined, at least in a certain way, as a determination that might determine what gets near, even if it does not decide what happens once we are near. If being near to this or that object is not a matter of chance, what happens in the 'now' of this nearness remains open, in the sense that we don't always know things affect each other, or how we will be affected by things …[1, p. 39]

In other words, the arbitrariness is excluded by the intention to get near, while openness and contingency remain in the outcome of the encounter, not unlike Barad's concept of agency arising in the encounters she calls intra-action [3, p. 128], a term also found in the writing of Haraway, both in turn connecting to Margulis' symbiogenesis.

In *Through Segments*, although we wanted the openness of the experiment, we also wanted to prolong the mode of simultaneous working, to have frequent encounters after which each of us would turn away again and work on their layer of sound. The common site should include, as something we were striving for, a sense of differential reproduction of shared ideas, instead of the pure chance of unimpeded interpenetration in Cage's way. A method was put in place for this exchange, by giving each artist dedicated workspaces on the RC to develop their process and layer, while inviting everyone to respond to the others, by either commenting or by answering to open questions put out by each artist; this could be a textual natural language, but also code or rendered sounds. The responses were not merely meant as a reflection on the others, but a move to take what was offered and turn it into a way of continuing one's own trajectory. This attitude is perhaps best described by Isabelle Stengers as *relaying*, in which something is not simply taken from somebody else in indifference, but with a mutual understanding:

… knowing that what you take has been held-out entails a particular thinking 'between'. It does not demand fidelity, still less fealty, rather a particular kind of loyalty, the answer to the trust of the hand held-out. Even if this trust is not in 'you' but in 'creative uncertainty', even if the consequences and meaning of what has been done, thought or written do not belong to you any more than they belonged to the one you take the relay from, one way or another the relay is now in your hands, together with the demand that you do not proceed with 'mechanical confidence'. [45, p. 134]

Staying faithful implies "to feel and think and decide together what a situation is demanding" [46, p. 398], and the action of relaying is transformative, because what is relayed to me know becomes my "concern". In the process, relaying and simultaneity go hand in hand. We are not forming a chain in the sense that one is holding their hands out and keeping them still while the next is taking off the string figure (to use Haraway's metaphor); it is that we have a kind of multiple string figure that is simultaneously produced by each of us.

Relaying in this form is something that can hardly be performed by a computer system, the mutual trust and thinking-with, the shifting of concern, it may be restricted to living forms. However, the situation we created in *Through Segments* could open an important new perspective on human–machine agency which is too often narrowed down to one individual artist interacting with one single computer system. It would allow us to examine the distributed work that happens in this situation, the distributed (work)spaces and temporalities, and above all the simultaneity in the configuration of the different computer music systems, and what happens when they finally come together in the exhibition site.

Acknowledgements This work was supported by the project *Algorithms that Matter* (FWF AR 403-GBL). Thanks to Rusty Demick for making me aware of the texts of Johnston and Saroyan.

References

1. Ahmed, S. (2006). *Queer phenomenology: Orientations, objects, others*. Durham and London: Duke University Press.
2. Baecker, D. (1996). A note on composition. *Systems Research, 13*, 195–203. https://doi.org/10.1002/(SICI)1099-1735(199609)13:3%3c195::AID-SRES97%3e3.0.CO;2-G.
3. Barad, K. (2007). *Meeting the universe halfway: Quantum physics and the entanglement of matter and meaning*. Durham & London: Duke University Press.
4. Cage, J. (1961). Composition as process. In *Silence. Lectures and writings* (pp. 18–55). Middletown, CT: Wesleyan University Press.
5. Châtelet, G. (2006). Interlacing the singularity, the diagram and the metaphor. In S. Duffy (Ed.), *Virtual mathematics: The logic of difference* (pp. 31–45). Manchester: Clinamen Press.
6. Clarke, B. (2017). Planetary immunity. Biopolitics, Gaia theory, the holobiont, and the systems counterculture. In E. Hörl & J. Burton (Eds.), *General ecology: The new ecological paradigm* (pp. 193–216). London: Bloomsbury Publishing.
7. Collins, D. (2005). A synthesis process model of creative thinking in music composition. *Psychology of Music, 33*(2), 193–216.

8. Crispin, D. (2019). Artistic Research as a Process of Unfolding. https://www.researchcatalogue. net/view/503395/503396 (visited on 3 Aug. 2020).

9. Derrida, J. [1972] (1988). Signature event context. In G. Graff (Ed.), *Limited Inc.* (S. Weber, Trans.). (pp. 1–23). Evanston, Illinois: Northwestern University Press.

10. Di Scipio, A. (1998). Compositional models in Xenakis's electroacoustic music. *Perspectives of New Music, 36*(2), 201–243. https://doi.org/10.2307/833529.

11. Döbereiner, L. (2020). *Re-reading the ALMAT documentation.* https://www.researchcatalogue. net/view/381565/960739 (visited on 3 Aug. 2020).

12. Emmerson, S. (1989). Composing strategies and pedagogy. *Contemporary Music Review, 3*(1), 133–144.

13. Eswaran, K. P., Gray, J. N., Lorie, R. A., & Traiger, I. L. (1976). The notions of consistency and predicate locks in a database system. *Communications of the ACM, 19*(11), 624–633. https:// doi.org/10.1145/360363.360369.

14. Ferrari, L. [1984] (2009). Dialogue Ordinaire Avec La Machine Ou Trois Fables Pour Bande Doucement Philosophiques. In *L'OEuvre Électronique. CD 6.* Paris: INA-GRM.

15. Fiat, A., & Kaplan, H. (2003). Making data structures confluently persistent. *Journal of Algorithms, 48*(1), 16–58.

16. Fournier, A. (2017). Rudimentariness: A concept for artistic research. *Journal for Artistic Research, 12.* https://doi.org/10.22501/jar.261526.

17. Goffey, A. (2014). Technology, logistics and logic: Rethinking the problem of fun in software. In O. Goriunova (Ed.), *Fun and software. Exploring pleasure, paradox and pain in computing* (pp. 21–40). New York: Bloomsbury Academic.

18. Haraway, D. J. (2015). A curious practice. *Angelaki, 20*(2), 5–14. https://doi.org/10.1080/ 0969725X.2015.1039817.

19. Hayles, N. K. (2017). *Unthought: The power of the cognitive nonconscious.* Chicago: University of Chicago Press.

20. Johnston, D. (2002). Programming as poetry: A few brief musings on Antiorp, Kurzweil, and Stallman. In *Year01 Forum 10.* http://www.year01.com/archive/issue10/programmer_poet. html (visited on 3 Aug. 2020).

21. Kitchin, R. (2017). Thinking critically about and researching algorithms. In *Information, communication & society* (Vol. 20, No. 1, pp. 14–29). https://doi.org/10.1080/1369118X.2016. 1154087.

22. Kuivila, R. (2018). SuperCollider Meeting @ IEM Graz. https://www.researchcatalogue.net/ view/386118/444476 (visited on 3 Aug. 2020).

23. Luhmann, N. (1999). The paradox of form. In D. Baecker (Ed.), *Problems of form* (pp. 15–26). Stanford: Stanford University Press.

24. Lury, C., Parisi, L., & Terranova, T. (2012). Introduction: The becoming topological of culture. *Theory, Culture & Society, 29*(4/5), 3–35. https://doi.org/10.1177/0263276412454552.

25. Margulis, L. (1990). Words as battle cries: Symbiogenesis and the new field of endocytobiology. *BioScience, 40*(9), 673–677. https://doi.org/10.2307/1311435.

26. Parisi, L. (2013). *Contagious architecture: Computation, aesthetics, and space.* Cambridge, MA: MIT Press.

27. Rheinberger, H.-J. (1997). *Toward a history of epistemic things: Synthesizing proteins in the test tube.* Palo Alto: Stanford University Press.

28. Rheinberger, H.-J. (1998). Experimental systems, graphematic spaces. In T. Lenoir (Ed.), *Inscribing science: Scientific texts and the materiality of communication* (pp. 285–303). Palo Alto: Stanford University Press.

29. Rheinberger, H.-J. (2013). Forming and being informed: Hans-Jörg Rheinberger in conversation with Michael Schwab. In M. Schwab (Ed). *Experimental systems. Future knowledge in artistic research* (pp. 198–219). Leuven: Leuven University Press.

30. Rohrhuber, J. (2018). Algorithmic music and the philosophy of time. In R. T. Dean & A. McLean (Eds.), *The oxford handbook of algorithmic music* (pp. 17–40). Oxford: Oxford University Press. https://doi.org/10.1093/oxfordhb/9780190226992.013.1.

31. Röttgers, K. (1983). Der Ursprung der Prozessidee aus dem Geiste der Chemie. *Archiv für Begriffsgeschichte, 27,* 93–157.
32. Rutz, H. H. (2012). *Mellite.* https://www.sciss.de/mellite (visited on 3 Aug. 2020).
33. Rutz, H. H. (2014a). Sound processes: A new computer music framework. In A. Georgaki & G. Kouroupetroglou (Eds.), *Proceedings of the Joint 11th Sound and Music Computing Conference and the 40th International Computer Music Conference* (pp. 1618–1626). Athens: National and Kapodistrian University of Athens. http://hdl.handle.net/2027/spo.bbp2372.2014.245.
34. Rutz, H. H. (2014b). *Tracing the compositional process. Sound art that rewrites its own past: Formation, praxis and a computer framework.* Ph.D. thesis, Plymouth University, UK. http://hdl.handle.net/10026.1/3116.
35. Rutz, H. H. (2017). Halting operations for algorithmic alignment. *Journal of Science and Technology of the Arts (CITAR), 9*(3), 7–20. https://doi.org/10.7559/citarj.v9i3.416.
36. Rutz, H. H. (2018). Algorithms under reconfiguration. In M. Schwab (Ed.), *Transpositions: Aesthetico-epistemic operators in artistic research* (pp. 149–176). Leuven: Leuven University Press. https://doi.org/10.26530/OAPEN_1000226.
37. Rutz, H. H. (2020). A pattern system for sound processes. In *AM'20: Proceedings of the 15th International Audio Mostly Conference: In Extended Realities.* Graz.
38. Rutz, H. H. & David P. (2017). *Algorithms that matter. On the agency of computational processes in sound composition and performance.* https://almat.iem.at/ (visited on 3 Aug. 2020).
39. Rutz, H. H., Pirrò, D., & Di Scipio, A. (2017). *From data to process.* https://www.researchcatalogue.net/view/381571/860154 (visited on 3 Aug. 2020).
40. Rutz, H. H., Pirrò, D., & Horvath, L. (2016). *Imperfect reconstruction.* https://www.researchcatalogue.net/view/245942/245943 (visited on 3 Aug. 2020).
41. Rutz, H. H., & Pirrò, D., Kang, J. Y., & Pozzi, D. (2020). *Through segments.* https://www.researchcatalogue.net/view/711706/711707 (visited on 3 Aug. 2020).
42. Rutz, H. H., Pirrò, D., & Pozzi, D. (2017). *ALMAT: Continuous exposition.* https://www.researchcatalogue.net/view/381565/381566 (visited on 3 Aug. 2020).
43. Saroyan, A. (1969). *Pages.* New York: Random House.
44. Spencer-Brown, G. [1969] (1979). *Laws of form.* New York: E.P. Dutton.
45. Stengers, I. (2011). Relaying aWar machine? In É. Alliez & A. Goffey (Eds.), *The Guattari effect* (pp. 134–155). London: Continuum.
46. Stengers, I. (2017). Autonomy and the Intrusion of Gaia. *South Atlantic Quarterly, 116*(2), 381–400. https://doi.org/10.1215/00382876-3829467.
47. Xenakis, I. (1992). *Formalized music. Thought and mathematics in composition* (Revised ed.). Stuyvesant, NY: Pendragon Press.

Hanns Holger Rutz is a sound and digital artist, composer, performer and researcher. He worked as senior post-doctoral researcher at the Institute of Electronic Music and Acoustics (IEM) of the University of Music and Performing Arts Graz, Austria. Most recently, he led the artistic research project Algorithms that Matter. He holds a Ph.D. in computer music from the Interdisciplinary Centre for Computer Music Research (ICCMR), University of Plymouth, UK. Prior to Plymouth, he worked as assistant professor at the Studio for electroacoustic Music (SeaM) Weimar, Germany. In his artistic work, the development and research on software and algorithms plays an important role, and he is interested in the materiality of writing processes, and trajectories of aesthetic objects as they travel and transform across different works and different artists. E-mail: rutz@reagenz.at.

Artificial Intelligence for Music Composition

3

Artemi-Maria Gioti

3.1 Introduction

This chapter explores the potential of Artificial Intelligence (AI) for art music composition, focusing on how AI can transform musical tasks and shape compositional ideas. In this context, AI is viewed as an agent contributing to a distributed human–computer co-creativity and extending human capabilities, rather than a replacement for human creativity. The premise behind this approach is that Artificial Intelligence—specifically machine learning algorithms—can shape musical thinking, by opening up the space of compositional possibilities and allowing for the emergence of new artistic concepts and practices. The unique capabilities and compositional "affordances" [19] of machine learning algorithms (i.e., what they afford composers, both technically and conceptually) are illustrated through applications in instrument design, interactive music systems, computational aesthetic evaluation and human–computer co-exploration. Current and future challenges concerning the application of machine learning algorithms in the arts are also considered, particularly the discrepancies between machine learning problems as closed-ended tasks and artistic practices as open-ended, exploratory processes. Re-examining the scope, optimization objectives and interaction capabilities of machine learning algorithms and adopting human-in-the loop design strategies that allow for a closer human–machine collaboration are proposed as first steps in addressing the discrepancies between currently available AI tools and emerging artistic practices and aesthetics.

A.-M. Gioti (✉)
Institute of Electronic Music and Acoustics (IEM), University of Music and Performing Arts Graz, Inffeldgasse 10, 8010 Graz, Austria
e-mail: gioti@iem.at

E. R. Miranda (eds.), *Handbook of Artificial Intelligence for Music*,
https://doi.org/10.1007/978-3-030-72116-9_3

3.2   Artificial Intelligence and Distributed Human–Computer Co-creativity

A common research objective in Music and Artificial Intelligence is the automation of musical tasks and the development of autonomously creative systems, i.e., systems that are able to "compose" music autonomously within specific musical styles (e.g., [8, 9]). Such systems are concerned with the simulation of musical creativity, aiming to produce artifacts that are comparable to those produced by human artists. Recent developments in Deep Learning have brought about a new era for music generation systems, which can now surpass the problem of music representation by learning directly from raw audio data (i.e., waveforms)—albeit at the cost of higher computational power and longer training time (e.g., [42]). While earlier automatic composition systems relied on representations such as MIDI reductions of musical scores or signal-level descriptors, Deep Learning applications like *WaveNet* [42] can learn from unstructured data (raw audio) and by doing so simplify the training process, all the while theoretically broadening the area of application of automatic composition systems to musical idioms that pose challenges for music representation. For instance, spectralist music (e.g., works by Kaija Saariaho or Tristan Murail) cannot be reduced to MIDI representations without significant information loss—indeed, such a reduction would probably defy the very premise of this music.

Despite their differences, both Deep Learning applications operating on unstructured data and systems operating in a symbolic domain share a common principle: that of *style imitation*. Both approaches aim to imitate artifacts produced by humans. While such an objective might be interesting from a music-analytical perspective, it holds limited potential for artistic production per se—let alone for artistic innovation [21]. Additionally, autonomously creative systems are often of limited use to artists, as they lack collaborative and interactive capabilities.

As an alternative to automation, this chapter considers how Artificial Intelligence can be integrated in a more "ecosystemic" [34] approach to musical creativity, including both humans and machines. The purpose of such an approach is to enhance human creativity, by opening up new creative possibilities and challenging traditional notions of authorship and definitions of the musical work. Specifically, the chapter examines how AI can transform creative tasks and, in synergy with human creativity, contribute to artistic innovation. The question being asked here is not whether AI can compose music, but rather, whether it can expand our creative capabilities and have a formative influence on compositional ideas.

This last proposition draws from Latour's ideas on agency as a property of both human and non-human actors. Latour [29] claims that not only humans, but also objects—both material and immaterial—have agency, which he defines as the ability to alter a "state of affairs". Similarly to Latour, Gell [18] regards art as a "system of action" and attributes agency to persons and "things" that can "cause events to happen in their vicinity". For Gell, agency is social in nature and action can only be conceptualized in social terms. He distinguishes between "primary" agents (i.e., intentional beings) and "secondary" agents (objects, works of art, etc.), through which "primary" agents exercise their agency. However, such a distinction does not suggest that material agency is any less important than intentional agency: as human (intentional) agency manifests itself within the material world, "things" are as essential to the exercise of agency as are "states of mind". While Gell is primarily interested in the agency of art objects—or "indices", to use his terminology—his concept of "secondary" agents can be expanded to encompass all types of objects and artifacts, including computational tools.

With new computational tools come new compositional affordances and potentially new artistic concepts and practices. Computational tools then exert a type of agency that has the potential to modify the "state of affairs" [29] in artistic production, by inspiring and contributing to artistic innovation. In that sense, they can be considered as "secondary" agents [18], their agency lying in their potential to expand the space of creative possibilities and influence musical thinking.

The ways in which AI, in particular, can influence creative ideation and practices are multiple and relate to its potential not only to assist creative tasks, but also re-conceptualize them, by providing new compositional affordances. For instance, machine learning algorithms can be used to create custom action-sound mappings, enabling composers to design idiosyncratic digital musical instruments that fit the needs of a specific composition or compositional idea. Admittedly, action-sound mappings do not require the use of machine learning, as they can be explicitly programmed using hand-coded rules. However, working with training examples instead of hand-coded rules can make artistic experimentation with data mappings much more intuitive and efficient, particularly when dealing with high-dimensional input and output data (e.g., when collecting data from a variety of different sensors and mapping them to a large number of interdependent synthesis parameters).

Additionally, machine learning algorithms can be used to explore new interaction paradigms, which are only possible thanks to the affordances of the algorithms themselves. For example, a musical agent can use clustering algorithms to group sounds based on their similarity, or classification algorithms to classify incoming sounds and produce appropriate responses. Such capabilities allow for interaction affordances that go well beyond conventional mapping strategies, such as recognizing and responding to specific timbres or musical gestures, by interpreting high-dimensional streams of signal-level features in real-time. And, while action-sound mappings can be explicitly programmed, hand-coding the rules of a timbre or gesture recognition algorithm would be an extraordinarily challenging task. Such applications illustrate the unique and possibly transformative potential of AI tools for music composition.

The following sections examine this potential more closely, focusing on how Artificial Intelligence can transform musical tasks and shape compositional ideas. In this context, AI is regarded as an agent contributing to a "distributed human–computer co-creativity", rather than a replacement for human creativity [21]. The examples discussed next include applications of AI in instrument design, interactive music systems, computational aesthetic evaluation and human–computer co-exploration. While this list is by no means exhaustive, it is representative of the rich potential of AI capabilities for music composition and their implications for the concept of the musical work, the author construct and creativity itself.

3.3 Machine Learning: Applications in Music and Compositional Potential

As a lot of the applications discussed in this section make use of machine learning algorithms, a quick overview of the different types of algorithms mentioned is provided below (for a more comprehensive review of the different types of machine learning algorithms and their applications in music see [6, 15]). Specifically, the machine learning algorithms discussed in this chapter include *regression, classification, clustering, prediction* and *reinforcement learning*. The first two, regression and classification, are examples of supervised learning algorithms and involve two types of data: *input* and *output* or *target* data. Concretely, each training example consists of an input-output pair: the input is a feature vector describing the training example, while the output or target value is the "correct answer" that the algorithm is expected to "learn". The task of the algorithm is to predict the target value given the inputs. Usually, a separate set of examples than those used to train the algorithm, called the *test set*, is used to assess the algorithm's ability to generalize (i.e., make predictions on previously unseen data).

Regression algorithms produce a continuous-valued output, while classification algorithms produce a discrete-valued output. An example of a music-related classification task is instrument recognition. In such a task, a single training example could consist of a vector of spectral descriptors, such as Mel Frequency Cepstral Coefficients (MFCCs), extracted from a short excerpt of audio and a label (e.g., 1 for flute and 2 for saxophone, in the case of saxophone vs. flute classification). Contrastingly, regression can be used to create continuous input-output mappings by providing the algorithm with just a few examples of input-output pairs (e.g., sensor readings and synthesis parameters). Using these examples, a regression algorithm can approximate a function that maps input to output variables, thereby producing a continuous mapping.

In contrast to supervised learning, unsupervised learning involves input but no output data. The task of the algorithm in this case is to find structure in the data. For example, clustering algorithms can be used to divide a set of sounds into smaller groups (clusters) based on spectral similarity. Another machine learning task with applications in music is prediction, which involves forecasting future events based on historical data [6]. Predictive probabilistic models can be used to learn from and generate new sequence data (e.g., generate melodies using conditional probabilities). Finally, the last type of machine learning discussed in this chapter is reinforcement learning. In reinforcement learning, an agent "acts" in an environment and receives (positive or negative) feedback. The agent selects an action based on its current state and with the purpose to maximize the value of some reward function. Co-exploration tools that navigate parametric spaces (e.g., different parameter settings of a synthesis engine) by generating sounds and receiving feedback from a human user in an iterative fashion are examples of music-related applications of reinforcement learning.

3.3.1 Digital Musical Instruments

One of the most common applications of machine learning in music composition involves data mapping. Machine learning algorithms—particularly regression algorithms—can function as an "interface", allowing artists to build complex mappings between input and output data [15]. Several end-user machine learning toolkits are currently available to artists and instrument designers [1, 5, 7, 16, 39], allowing them to experiment with machine learning algorithms without requiring extensive machine learning knowledge. A widely used machine learning toolkit is *Wekinator* [16]. Fiebrink [14] describes a series of music compositions that use *Wekinator* to map data obtained through sensors such as accelerometers, light sensors and other commercial and custom-made physical interfaces to sound synthesis parameters. The advantage of using a regression algorithm for such an application is that the user can create complex mappings between high-dimensional input and output data without explicitly programming them. Alternative mappings can be created just by recording new examples, rather than changing the code, enabling hands-on experimentation as part of the creative process.

Besides composition-specific action-sound mappings, machine learning is used in the design of Digital Musical Instruments (DMIs) designed for a variety of musical contexts and idioms. These two approaches represent different stances toward instrument design: one that prioritizes idiosyncratic sonic interactions over customizability (e.g., developing a "musical instrument" for the needs of a specific composition or performance) and one that prioritizes broader applicability, by aiming to create instruments that can be used in a variety of compositional and improvisational settings. Machine learning algorithms, particularly end-user machine learning toolkits, allow composers to design idiosyncratic musical instruments, lifting creative limitations that might be posed by customary DMIs and interfaces. At the same time, the integration of machine learning capabilities in non-idiosyncratic—or at least composition-agnostic—DMIs is becoming increasingly common, with applications ranging from purely reactive to partly autonomous instruments with interactive capabilities. Examples of such instruments are *Sansa*, *Phalanger* and *NOISA*.

Sansa [31] is an augmented acoustic instrument, which can be used as a purely acoustic instrument or as a hyper-instrument, extended through various interaction modalities with the use of *Wekinator*. The instrument consists of a Kalimba extended through a series of sensors and machine learning capabilities. *Sansa*'s different operation modes allow the user to choose among "conducting" an ensemble of electronic instruments, navigating a score, shaping electronic sounds through hand gestures, amplifying or processing the signal of the instrument or other sound sources (e.g., the performer's voice) and driving visualizations.

Unlike *Sansa, Phalanger* [27] has no acoustic component. It is an entirely digital interface used to control sound through hand and finger motion. *Phalanger* relies exclusively on video data and uses a Neural Network to detect and separate the user's hand from the background and a Support Vector Machine (SVM) to recognize different hand positions. The Neural Network can be trained using snapshots of the user's hand and the background (without the user) as training examples. This allows the system to be configured for different cameras, lighting conditions and skin tones.

Despite differences regarding sound production and user-customizability, the two instruments mentioned above share a common interaction model based entirely on action-sound mappings: both instruments produce sound exclusively as a response to the performer's control actions; they are reactive but not interactive. In addition to action-sound mappings, machine learning can be used to design musical instruments with interactive capabilities and partly autonomous behavior. *NOISA* (Network of Intelligent Sonic Agents) is an example of such an instrument, which aims to increase the performer's level of engagement by generating autonomous "non-intrusive" sonic responses ("counteractions") [40]. The instrument estimates the performer's level of engagement at any given moment and generates autonomous responses with a probability that is inversely correlated with it. That is, the system is more likely to generate an autonomous response when the musician's level of engagement is estimated as low, a behavior that aims to help the performer maintain high levels of engagement by providing stimuli for interaction. *NOISA* consists of three box-shaped instruments, a computer, an armband sensor and a motion-tracking camera. Each box-shaped instrument features two handles, attached to motorized faders. The instrument monitors the performer's movements, facial expressions and control actions using descriptors such as slider activity, torso inclination, neck and head acceleration. These descriptors are analyzed using movement analysis and the features obtained through this process are fed into a regression algorithm. Additionally, the instrument performs a spectral analysis of sonic gestures and the extracted features are used to inform the selection of autonomous responses, with the purpose to avoid frequency masking between reactions and "counteractions" (autonomously generated responses) and ensure that the latter are spectrally distinct from and quieter than performer-controlled sounds. *NOISA* is a musical instrument meant to be used in idiomatic musical contexts and, as such, its behavior is primarily reactive. However, its interactive capabilities (i.e., deciding when and how to produce autonomous "counteractions" with the purpose of increasing the user's level of engagement) make it a hybrid between musical instrument and interactive music system, a category that is examined more closely in the following section.

3.3.2   Interactive Music Systems

Interactive music systems are computer music systems that can sense their environment by collecting and interpreting sensing data, make decisions and act both in response to human actions and as a result of autonomous internal processes. Their design is based on a decentralized notion of agency in which actions are carried out both by human and non-human actors, while creativity and authorial responsibility are distributed in time and across different actors. Creative decisions are made both "offline", e.g., when the composer creates the software and possibly a score, and in real-time, as part of the interaction between the performer and the software agent.

Agentive behaviors in this setting emerge as a result of a negotiation between compositional intentions and technological directionality. Ihde [23] proposes the term *technological intentionality* to refer to the directionality or scope of technological artifacts. For instance, a tape recorder has a directionality toward sound which differs fundamentally from a human listener's intentionality in that it is unable to focus on some sonic foreground and suppress background noise [44]. Similarly, the output of a pitch detection algorithm differs significantly from pitch perception in humans. Using a pitch detection algorithm as a sensing module in an interactive music system will therefore inevitably introduce artifacts that are a by-product of technological directionality rather than compositional intention. In an interactive music system, compositional intention is rendered through technological directionality. Human intentionality is conveyed through the musical knowledge and aesthetic values embedded in the system, while technological directionality is inherent to the design of customary hardware and software tools (e.g., standard Music Information Retrieval (MIR) tools embedded in the agent's machine listening stage).

This relationship between compositional intentions and technological directionality can potentially be enhanced and refined through the use of AI, enabling more diverse and idiosyncratic sonic interactions. For instance, machine learning can be used to interpret high-dimensional, signal-level data streams and extract context-relevant music information. What qualifies as context-relevant information can be determined by the composer and might depend, among other things, on the musical idiom, the instrumentation and the compositional idea. Doug Van Nort's *Genetically Sonified Organisms* and the author's *Imitation Game* are discussed below as examples of interactive musical works in which software agents utilize machine learning in order to process and interpret auditory information.

Doug Van Nort's *Genetically Sonified Organisms* (GSOs) is a piece of "environmental sound art" consisting of a set of artificial creatures designed to interact with and adapt to their acoustic environment [43]. Each creature is equipped with a lexicon of twenty sounds, produced using physical modeling synthesis techniques based upon wildlife that may be present at the site of the installation (e.g., frogs, flies, bees, etc.). The GSOs are designed to listen to their environment and respond to sounds that are similar to their vocabulary. Specifically, incoming sounds are analyzed and the extracted feature vectors are compared to the GSO's sound lexicon. Using a nearest neighbor approach, incoming sounds are matched to the closest synthesis model, while synthesis parameters are updated incrementally so that with each response the generated sounds come a bit "closer" to the input sounds. The purpose of this process is for the GSOs to eventually converge to a sound output similar to the wildlife that inhibits the site of the installation. Listening and learning are therefore responsible not only for the system's short-term responses, but also for its long-term evolution and adaptation to its acoustic environment.

In the author's *Imitation Game*, a similar classification task is performed by a robotic percussionist as part of its interaction with a human counterpart [20]. The human percussionist's input is analyzed and the extracted features are fed into a feed-forward Neural Network (NN) trained to recognize different instruments (cymbals, bongos and cowbells) and playing techniques (strokes, scraping and bowing). The data collected in the robotic percussionist's auditory processing stage is used to inform its short- and long-term decision-making. Specifically, the robotic percussionist can choose among three different interaction scenarios: "imitate" (play similar material as the human), "initiate" (introduce new sound material) and "repeat" (selectively repeat some of the musician's actions in an improvisatory context). Interaction scenarios are selected based on metrics of rhythmic, timbral and dynamic contrast, which are calculated on a phrase basis. For instance, if the material played by the human percussionist lacks timbral contrast, the robotic percussionist might choose to introduce new timbres (i.e., different instruments or playing techniques). Similarly, if the estimated rhythmic contrast (standard deviation of Inter-Onset Intervals) has remained constant (i.e., around the same value) for a while, the robotic percussionist is less likely to follow the human's lead and more likely to introduce new, contrasting rhythmic material.

These two examples illustrate the flexibility that AI tools afford composers when it comes to designing sonic interactions. Using signal-level features as an input, machine learning algorithms can extract high-level music information, facilitating real-time decision-making in the context of interactive music systems. Most importantly, the composer is free to decide what information is relevant in a certain context and train the algorithm to retrieve that information by providing appropriate examples. This allows for a high degree of creative freedom coupled with a more intuitive approach to sonic interaction design, resulting from the use of training examples as opposed to hand-coded rules.

3.3.3 Computational Aesthetic Evaluation

Computational aesthetic evaluation, i.e., the aesthetic evaluation of (human- or computer-generated) artifacts through computational means, is another field of interest for the application of AI in music composition. Research in the field of computational aesthetics encompasses a wide range of approaches, from formulaic theories to psychological models and empirical studies of aesthetics (for a comprehensive review see [17]). Admittedly, the relevance of such research for the arts has often been questioned—and justifiably so. For instance, empirical studies aiming to identify "universal" aesthetic values (e.g., [33]) have been criticized for lacking relevance for the appreciation of contemporary art and disregarding the role that cultural values and individual taste play in aesthetic judgments [34]. Similarly, research on machine learning based artificial music critics that use popularity as a measure for aesthetic evaluation (e.g., [32]) has been criticized for equating popularity with aesthetic value and disregarding the philosophical discourse around aesthetics, as well as the subjective nature of measures of "beauty" and "pleasantness" [26].

While universal or "context-agnostic" [26] aesthetic values might have limited applicability in the arts, the idea of idiosyncratic musical agents capable of making aesthetically informed decisions can find applications in both human–computer co-exploration tasks and interactive music systems. Machine agents can act based on learned or hand-coded aesthetic values, a capability that brings new dimensions to computational decision-making.

For example, in the author's composition *Bias*, for bass clarinet and interactive music system, a regression algorithm (Neural Network) was trained to predict the composer's aesthetic preferences. Recordings of improvisation sessions, made with the help of the musician, were segmented, analyzed and labeled by the composer based on her subjective aesthetic preferences, using a 5-point Likert-type scale ranging from 1 ("not at all interesting") to 5 ("extremely interesting"). These examples were later used to train the Neural Network. The aim of this process was for the machine learning algorithm to "learn" the composer's aesthetic preferences and be able to extrapolate from them in real-time. During the performance, the interactive music system makes judgments on different time scales and responds to sounds and textures it finds "interesting", but remains silent or proposes new sound material when it loses interest in the musician's input.

The composition is a comment on the disparities between machine learning concepts such as optimization and quantitative performance evaluation, both of which assume that there exist some objectively "right" and "wrong" answers for the algorithm to learn, and aesthetic judgments as inherently subjective and intangible. Furthermore, it explores the extent to which aesthetic preferences can be modeled by machine learning algorithms and aims to blur the boundaries between human and machine agency. The title "Bias" refers to both the inherently subjective nature of aesthetic judgments and the "bias" that results from machine learning algorithms making arbitrary or erroneous assumptions about data. As the composer's preferences are distorted through these arbitrary assumptions, the decision-making taking place during the performance can be attributed neither to the composer nor the machine learning algorithm alone, but rather an emergent, hybrid human–machine agency that is distributed across actors (composer and machine learning algorithm) and time (training and performance).

Computational aesthetic evaluation has been explored in other artistic fields as well, particularly in visual arts. For example, the *DrawBots* project used evolutionary robotics to investigate whether drawing robots can exhibit autonomously creative behavior by developing a creative signature of their own [4]. The project was a continuation of Paul Brown's previously failed attempts to use cellular automata to produce artworks that would transcend his personal signature. After initial experimentation with fitness functions that were meant to minimize the designers' influence on the robots' behavior, such as penalizing robots for crashing into walls and rewarding them for using the whole surface of the drawing area, the *DrawBots* research team opted for a radically different approach, by adopting a fitness function that revolved around fractals. The robots were endowed with a "fractal detector" and a "fractal preference" and were able to evaluate the marks they made based on self-similarity. Brown et al. [4] argue that, while this evaluation might not be aesthetic or artistic in nature, it results in the agents making preference-based choices and that fractals are a broad enough category for the agents to be able to produce diverse and, at times, surprising patterns. While such a fitness function might be far from an autonomously evolved creative signature, the *DrawBots* project is a good example of artificial agents making aesthetically informed decisions—albeit based on predefined rather than autonomously developed rules.

3.3.4 Human–Computer Co-exploration

McCormack [34] conceptualizes the creative process in the context of human–computer co-creativity as a process of search within *creative spaces* and "meta-search" within *spaces of possibility*. Creative spaces are subsets of vast spaces of possibilities and are defined by the scope of the generative mechanisms (i.e., the search methods) used in the creative search. For instance, the different images that can be generated by a piece of code written in Lisp are only a tiny fraction of all the images that can possibly be generated. The process of "meta-search" involves defining and modifying the generative mechanisms and therefore the creative space. In music composition, such a creative space could be defined by the affordances of a sound synthesis algorithm, a rule-based generative system, or other compositional constraints.

The purpose of human–machine co-exploration of creative spaces is to facilitate creative discovery through human–machine interaction. For instance, interactive machine learning can be used to assist the exploration of a sound synthesis algorithm, by allowing for user-customizable search strategies. Most importantly, human–machine co-exploration can help expand human creativity by enhancing the artist's ability to think beyond established creative habits and take new creative paths. For instance, the machine learning algorithm might generate an output that the user/artist would otherwise not have created, guiding the creative process into new territories. Beyond breaking creative habits, sonic human–machine co-exploration can also be a useful tool in reflecting on one's own artistic practice and aesthetic stance [25].

While computer-assisted composition tools have been around for a long time, sonic human–computer co-exploration is a relatively new concept, making use of AI capabilities—specifically, the ability of machine learning algorithms to learn by example. The main difference between traditional computer-assisted composition tools and human–computer co-exploration tools is that the latter have adaptive capabilities; i.e., they are able to adapt their output to the user's preferences through learning. The examples that follow illustrate two different yet related approaches to human–machine co-exploration of synthesis processes, incorporating machine learning and user-provided training examples.

The first example, *Sonic Xplorer*, is a co-exploration tool that uses adjectives for multiparametric control of a sound synthesis engine [41]. Implemented in *Max/MSP* and making use of *Wekinator* [16], *Sonic Xplorer* uses Neural Networks to build correlations between six different adjectives and four perceptual audio features. After providing the system with a series of training examples, the user can use six different sliders to describe the qualities of the sound they want to produce. Each slider corresponds to one of the following adjectives: "warm", "bright", "stable", "thick", "noisy" and "evolving". The user can transition between the *Xplorer* interface and the synthesizer's interface, in order to fine-tune the generated sounds by setting the synthesis parameters directly. Expert evaluation indicated that the tool-assisted creative discovery, but the user's control over the generated sounds lacked precision.

Scurto et al. [38] conducted similar experiments using reinforcement learning. In these experiments, participants were asked to collaborate with artificial agents in the completion of a closed-ended task, by communicating feedback to the agents in an iterative fashion. Concretely, the task entailed human–machine co-exploration of a Virtual Studio Technology (VST) with the aim to discover the parameter settings that produce the brightest sound possible. The VST consisted of an FM synthesis engine with two discrete parameters (modulation index and harmonicity ratio), all possible configurations of which added up to 30 discrete states; i.e., 30 static sounds. At each iteration, the agent would produce a new sound and receive positive feedback if the new sound was brighter than the previously generated one, or negative feedback otherwise. At the end of the task, the participants were asked to evaluate the performance of the artificial agents with respect to different aspects of collaboration. The participants' responses seemed to suggest that, regardless of whether the goal was reached or not, the "path" taken during exploration was decisive to whether the agents were perceived as collaborative. While still far from being applicable to real-world scenarios, these experiments reveal the potential of machine learning for creative exploration. Some of the challenges still to be overcome include the much higher dimensionality of real-world applications in comparison to the two parameters used in the experiments and the open-ended nature of creative tasks. That is to say that creative tasks cannot sufficiently be modeled by closed-ended, goal-directed tasks, as in creative work goals might not necessarily precede the task, but rather evolve as a result of exploration and aesthetic experimentation.

Coincidentally, both of the examples discussed above involve creative experimentation with sound synthesis processes. However, human–computer co-exploration does not need to be limited to the design of static sounds, but can also include experimentation with larger-scale generative processes. The nature of creative tasks as open-ended processes informed by subjective aesthetic values and idiomatic artistic practices suggests that there are still challenges to be overcome in the design of human–computer co-exploration tools. Nevertheless, first experiments in this area show potential for future applications in music composition, promising to assist creative discovery through human–machine collaboration.

3.4 Conceptual Considerations

3.4.1 The Computer as a Compositional Prosthesis

Several of the examples discussed in the previous sections share an understanding of the computer as a "compositional prosthesis" [24]: a tool used to extend the composer's capabilities, by helping them break creative habits [25], or explore conceptual spaces [34]. In cases of co-creativity such as these, the machine functions as an assistant, making "suggestions" that can be adopted or rejected by the composer. Creativity is distributed not only across different actors, but also across different functions, with computational decision-making being mainly explorative and human decision-making being primarily evaluative.

This type of human–computer co-creativity is concerned with assisting the creative process, the product of which might fall within existing paradigms (e.g., a fixed-media composition). The purpose of such applications is to enhance the artist's creativity, by generating surprising sound material and exploring creative paths that the artist might otherwise not have taken. A secondary goal might be to reflect on one's own creative practice and aesthetic values [25]. Defining a conceptual space (e.g., a parametric space within which the algorithm can generate material) and curating (i.e., selecting, rejecting and modifying) computer-generated material are both tasks that can facilitate reflection on, and analysis of, one's aesthetic preferences.

In human–machine co-exploration, or even generative music systems, the ownership of aesthetic components can rarely be questioned, since high-level aesthetic decisions are made by the (human) composer, who assumes a significantly higher degree of authorial responsibility than the computer. Still, traditional notions of authorship have limited applicability here, since the relation between compositional intention and material is mediated through computational decision-making. To that, one must add the agency of the software developer, in case this is someone other than the composer, and possibly a wider community of developers and/or artists; e.g., in case a corpus of musical works was used to train the algorithm.

Impett [24] considers the musical work as an activity that is "distributed in space, technology, society and time". While this is arguably true for all musical practices, it is strongly exemplified in human–computer co-creativity. The concept of distributed human–computer co-creativity invites us to think of musical creativity as a social activity, involving both human and non-human actors. Bown [2] argues that "all human creativity occurs in the context of networks of mutual influence" and that artifacts are produced by networks of interaction involving human and non-human actors. He maintains that creativity lies in collective knowledge and networks of influence rather than isolated individuals, which he refers to as "islands of creativity". Brown [3] holds a similar view, proposing an understanding of creative acts as "networks of agency" that encompass "humans, tools, culture and the physical environment". Creative relationships within these networks are symmetrical ("coupled") with respect to influence, but asymmetrical with respect to contribution, meaning that within co-creative networks degrees of agency can vary. For instance, tools influence creative decisions, even though they might exhibit weaker agency than human actors.

3.4.2 The Computer as a Virtual Player

Human–machine interaction as part of live performance settings is another major area of application of AI tools discussed in this chapter. Whether this interaction falls under Rowe's [37] "instrument" or "player" paradigm has implications not only for the degree of agency assigned to the computer music system, but also for the affordances each paradigm brings to music composition. In the "instrument" paradigm the computer assumes a role similar to a musical instrument, by translating (human) control actions into sound, while in the "player" paradigm it is conceptualized as a virtual performer, interacting with musicians in a reciprocal way. The "instrument" paradigm encompasses DMIs using machine learning to map sensory data to sound synthesis parameters. The "player" paradigm, on the other hand, serves as a frame of reference for interactive music systems, prioritizing system responsiveness and autonomy over controllability.

Arguably, while the "instrument" paradigm falls within familiar conceptual frameworks—"instrument" being a metaphor that pertains to acoustic musical instruments—the "player" paradigm poses a number of conceptual challenges and has implications for both the compositional process and its product. An interactive musical work cannot be understood as a predetermined structure of sounds, but rather a space of sonic possibilities, explored by the performers (both human and virtual) during the performance. In interactive compositions, the practice of musical interpretation is expanded to include decision-making as part of a real-time interaction with a non-human partner, a premise that challenges the composition/improvisation binary, as well as conventional notions of musical form. Composing does not entail creating sequences of sounds, but rather interaction scenarios, designed to be explored in real time during the performance. The object of the compositional process shifts from sound itself to sonic interactions and creative responsibility is shared among the composer, the human and the virtual performer. Both the compositional process and its product are effectively redefined and re-conceptualized.

In interactive musical works, machine intelligence can help enhance the perception and interaction capabilities of computer music systems, enabling new types of sonic human–machine interaction. Machine learning algorithms can be used to equip computer music systems with "music understanding" [10] capabilities, allowing them to recognize and operate based on human musical concepts. Thanks to the ability of machine learning algorithms to learn from examples, these concepts do not need to be limited to features extracted by standard Music Information Retrieval (MIR) tools (e.g., pitch), but can be defined by the composer using appropriate examples and can range from the concrete (e.g., timbral categories) to the abstract (e.g., aesthetic evaluation or perceived levels of engagement during music-making).

3.4.3 Artificial Intelligence as a Secondary Agent

The roles that machines can assume in distributed human–computer co-creativity include but are not limited to those of a compositional prosthesis and a virtual performer. These are only a few of many examples that illustrate the reciprocal relationship between tools and creative ideas. Creative tools are as much tools as they are instruments of thinking—that is, they have a formative potential for creative ideas. This is true not only for AI, but any type of tool involved in creative practices.

The way in which creative tools can form compositional ideas is exemplified strikingly in some of Éliane Radigue's recent works which, though strictly acoustic, are more representative of techniques used in electronic rather than instrumental music composition. For instance, in her composition *OCCAM RIVER XXII* [35] for bass clarinet and alto saxophone, her use of the two woodwind instruments resembles the sound of amplitude-modulated oscillators, recalling some of her slowly unfolding electronic pieces created with the ARP 2500 synthesizer. Indeed, one might argue that her way of musical thinking, deeply rooted in her work with analogue synthesizers, was transferred almost unaltered from electronic to acoustic music composition. The result is a radical approach to instrumental composition, informed by electronic sound production capabilities rather than the traditional repertoire of the respective instruments.

Creative tools can influence not only the musical language of individual composers but also entire artistic movements. For instance, the stark contrast between the aesthetics of *Elektronische Musik* and *musique concrète* is reflected in—and, perhaps, partly attributable to—their use of different sound production means; that is, synthesis and recording technologies, respectively. And while aesthetic choices can never be entirely attributed to the tools themselves, the reciprocal relationship between the two and the influence of the latter on the development of aesthetic movements is undeniable.

Electronic and computational tools therefore have yet another level of agency: through their affordances, they define the space of creative possibilities and inform creative decisions. Such a claim is in line with Latour's [29] and Gell's [18] views of material agency. The agency of machine learning algorithms, as well as AI in general, is not limited to the decision-making that might be delegated to them as part of the compositional process or the performance, but includes opening up the space of compositional possibilities and allowing for the emergence of new artistic concepts and practices. The ability to recognize musical or physical gestures and timbres, perform aesthetic judgments, or adapt to a (human) user's preferences in a co-exploration task are only a few of the unique affordances of machine learning algorithms that have the potential to shape musical thinking. As creative applications of machine learning algorithms become more common, their creative potential will unfold, allowing new interaction paradigms and conceptualization frameworks to emerge.

3.5 Limitations of Machine Learning

Despite their potential, machine learning algorithms have shortcomings and limitations, particularly when it comes to creative applications. A common challenge in machine learning applications is the problem of overfitting. This occurs when the algorithm learns noise specific to the training data and, as a result, is unable to generalize on previously unseen examples. Overfitting leads to models that perform particularly well on the training set (i.e., the examples used for training), but poorly on the test set (a separate data set used to evaluate the algorithm's ability to make predictions on previously unseen examples). Dreyfus ([11]: xxxvi) recalls one of the most well-known, though never confirmed as true, anecdotes around the problem of overfitting:

> For an amusing and dramatic case of creative but unintelligent generalization, consider one of connectionism's first applications. In the early days of this work, the army tried to train an artificial neural network to recognize tanks in a forest. They took a number of pictures of a forest without tanks and then, on a later day, with tanks clearly sticking out from behind trees, and they trained a net to discriminate the two classes of pictures. The results were impressive, and the army was even more impressed when it turned out that the net could generalize its knowledge to pictures that had not been part of the training set. Just to make sure that the net was indeed recognizing partially hidden tanks, however, the researchers took more pictures in the same forest and showed them to the trained net. They were depressed to find out that the net failed to discriminate between the new pictures of trees with tanks behind them and new pictures of just plain trees. After some agonizing, the mystery was finally solved when someone noticed that the original pictures of the forest without tanks were taken on a cloudy day and those with tanks were taken on a sunny day. The net had apparently learned to recognize and generalize the difference between forest with and without shadows!

In music applications, overfitting might result in a machine listening algorithm performing poorly on examples recorded with different microphones than the one used to record the training set, or a video-based gesture recognition algorithm used to control a DMI failing to adapt to different lighting conditions. Overfitting is usually addressed by collecting more training data, preferably from different data distributions (e.g., audio recordings done with different microphones or video recordings of various lighting conditions), in order to help the algorithm learn relevant features and ignore any noise specific to a subset of the data. However, overfitting might also be the result of an imbalanced training set (i.e., a training set in which some classes are overrepresented and others underrepresented), or features that have little or no relevance for the task at hand. Depending on the task, collecting an adequately large, variable and balanced training set and selecting relevant features for learning can be a time-consuming and labor-intensive process and involves a good deal of troubleshooting and expert knowledge of the application domain—albeit not of machine learning per se.

In addition to domain-general problems, such as overfitting, compositional applications of machine learning pose a series of new, domain-specific challenges. For instance, for certain musical tasks overfitting might actually be a desirable feature, while for others existing machine learning algorithms might simply be inapplicable [15]. Most importantly, supervised learning problems are essentially optimization problems, operating on the assumption that there is a "right" answer for the algorithm to learn. This focus on closed-ended tasks and quantitative evaluation metrics stands in stark contrast to artistic practice as an open-ended process of exploration and discovery. This effectively limits the scope of application of supervised learning algorithms to a rather narrow spectrum of music-related tasks. Unsupervised algorithms such as clustering algorithms might not involve labeled data (i.e., "right" and "wrong" answers), but their scope does not differ significantly from that of supervised learning algorithms, as clustering (grouping data points together based on similarity metrics) is essentially a classification task.

Another category of machine learning algorithms that might be of relevance for compositional applications is that of generative models, such as Generative Adversarial Networks (GANs) and *WaveNet* [42]. Such algorithms operate based on probabilistic principles, generating artifacts that "imitate" some sample works. Imitation as an optimization objective, combined with a lack of interactive capabilities, make such models hard to use in the context of human–computer co-creativity. The reason for this is that these algorithms are essentially "black boxes": the user can feed the algorithm with some sample works but is unable to provide any form of feedback on the generated outputs. Additionally, style imitation might not always be a desideratum in human–computer co-exploration tasks. An "ecosystemic" [34] approach to generative music systems would require an interactive, human-in-the-loop design, in which the "fitness" of the generated outputs would be determined by the user's feedback, rather than their proximity to some sample works. In fact, since arguably one of the objectives of human–computer co-creativity is to challenge one's own creative habits and explore new creative paths [25], deviation from, rather than proximity to, some sample works might be an equally valid optimization objective.

3.6   Composition and AI: The Road Ahead

The relationship between computational affordances and compositional ideas is a complex and reciprocal one. Computational affordances can shape compositional ideas by expanding the space of creative possibilities, or by reducing it to what is technically feasible, available or efficient. This negotiation between (technical) means and (aesthetic) ends is an integral part of the creative process and evidence of the aesthetic implications of material agency. Not only are technical means a factor in creative decision-making, but also carriers of aesthetic values. Computational tools are designed with a specific end in mind and are rarely free of aesthetic "bias".

Consider Google Brain's *Magenta* project as an example. The *Magenta* project includes tools such as *MusicVAE*, a model used to blend two different melodies [36], *Onsets and Frames*, a tool for automatic polyphonic piano music transcription [22], and *NSynth*, a deep learning-based algorithm used to create morphings between different timbres [12]. The dataset used by the latter consists of instrumental sounds generated using commercial sample libraries and covering the range of a standard MIDI piano. Users can navigate the timbral space among up to four of these source sounds, using a MIDI input to determine the pitch of the source (and output) sounds.

All three of *Magenta*'s creative tools use musical notes as a basic unit, a design feature that makes them suitable for "note-based" rather than "sound-based" music [28]. While morphing is a very common technique in electroacoustic music composition, the sound material used in the latter can include any recorded sound (e.g., recordings of environmental sounds, or instrumental sounds that include microtones or glissandi) and is not limited to equally tempered, fixed-pitch instrumental sounds. A tool such as *NSynth* in this context would therefore be inadequate. Developing a morphing tool for electroacoustic music composition would require a different design, in which source sounds could be selected directly by the user, while sound generation would not depend on pitch, as that might not always be a relevant parameter; e.g., when morphing between two sounds of indefinite pitch.

Similarly, one might argue that concepts such as melody and harmony are of little relevance to much of contemporary art music. Of course, there is nothing to suggest that *Magenta*'s tools were intended for use within contemporary art music. The latter is just used as a, perhaps extreme, example in order to demonstrate the aesthetic agency of computational tools and point out that, when it comes to creative tools, design decisions are inherently aesthetic.

While the availability and accessibility of AI tools for music has increased significantly over the last few years, the apparent discrepancy between the scope of such tools and contemporary art aesthetics seems to point toward the need for a closer collaboration between machine learning developers and composers and the involvement of the latter in the development process. As part of this collaboration, assumptions underlying the design of AI tools need to be questioned and adapted to reflect the needs of current and emerging artistic practices. Concretely, the relationship between human and computational creativity and the purpose of the latter needs to be re-examined, as the debate on *Intelligence Augmentation* (machines enhancing human intelligence) versus *Artificial Intelligence* (machines replicating human intelligence) [13, 30] seems to be as relevant as ever. Is computational creativity to be understood as a simulation or an extension of human creativity? And how does each of these approaches relate to artistic practices and inform the development of AI-based compositional tools?

If we are to develop tools for artists, then we clearly need to move away from automation and "black box" architectures and toward interactive AI systems that learn from and adapt to human preferences. As far as generative systems are concerned, this would mean adopting human-in-the-loop design strategies that enable users to communicate their preferences and guide AI systems through a process of co-exploration based on their subjective aesthetic judgments. As artistic experimentation is an open-ended rather than a closed-ended process—that is, artistic goals might change, or new ones might evolve as a result of experimentation —optimization objectives should also be examined more closely. Style imitation as an optimization objective is one, but not the only option. As part of human–computer co-exploration, artists might wish to explore new territories that lie beyond established paradigms and challenge their practice and working techniques. Such discrepancies between currently available machine learning models and creative practices point toward the need for further research and development of new tools, designed specifically for artistic applications.

Questions of scope might also be of relevance for future research in music and AI. As "one-fits-all" approaches are rarely possible, the design of AI tools for music should be regarded as artistic in nature. Design decisions, such as choosing to use musical notes, spectral descriptors or audio samples as input units, have aesthetic implications, as each of these units might be relevant for certain musical idioms and applications but not for others. A closer collaboration between developers and artists can ensure that the machine learning models and types of data used by AI tools meet the needs of artistic practice, facilitating their use within idiomatic and idiosyncratic musical contexts.

Acknowledgements The author wishes to thank Eduardo Reck Miranda, Marko Ciciliani and Gerhard Eckel for their critical readings of this manuscript. This research was funded by the Austrian Science Fund (FWF): AR 483-G24.

References

1. Bevilacqua, F., Müller, R., & Schnell, N. (2005). MnM: A Max/MSP mapping toolbox. In *Proceedings of the International Conference on New Interfaces for Musical Expression.*
2. Bown, O. (2015). Attributing creative agency: Are we doing it right? In *Proceedings of the 6th International Conference on Computational Creativity* (pp. 17–22).
3. Brown, A. R. (2016). Understanding musical practices as agency networks. In *Proceedings of the 7th International Conference on Computational Creativity* (pp. 144–151).
4. Brown, P., Bigge, B., Bird, J., Husbands, P., Perris, M., & Stokes, D. (2007). The Drawbots. In *Proceedings of MutaMorphosis: Challenging Arts and Sciences.*
5. Bullock, J., & Momeni, A. (2015). ml.lib : Robust, cross-platform, open-source machine learning for max and pure data. In *Proceedings of the International Conference on New Interfaces for Musical Expression* (pp. 265–270).
6. Caramiaux, B., & Tanaka, A. (2013). Machine learning of musical gestures. In *Proceedings of the International Conference on New Interfaces for Musical Expression* (pp. 513–518).
7. Caramiaux, B., Montecchio, N., Tanaka, A., & Bevilacqua, F. (2015). Adaptive gesture recognition with variation estimation for interactive systems. *ACM Transactions on Interactive Intelligent Systems, 4.* Association for Computing Machinery. https://doi.org/10. 1145/2643204.
8. Collins, N. (2012). Automatic composition of electroacoustic art music utilizing machine listening. *Computer Music Journal, 36,* 8–23.
9. Cope, D. (1992). Computer modeling of musical intelligence in EMI. *Computer Music Journal, 16,* 69. https://doi.org/10.2307/3680717.
10. Dannenberg, R. (2000). Artificial intelligence, machine learning, and music understanding. In *Proceedings of the 2000 Brazilian Symposium on Computer Music: Arquivos do Simpsio Brasileiro de Computao Musical (SBCM).*
11. Dreyfus, H. L. (1992). *What computers still can't do: A critique of artificial reason.* Cambridge, MA: MIT Press.
12. Engel, J., Resnick, C., Roberts, A., Dieleman, S., Eck, D., Simonyan, K., & Norouzi, M. (2017). Neural audio synthesis of musical notes with WaveNet Autoencoders.
13. Engelbart, D. (1962). *Augmenting human intellect: A conceptual framework.* SRI Summary Report AFOSR-3223. (Vol. 1962).
14. Fiebrink, R. A. (2011). *Real-time human interaction with supervised learning algorithms for music composition and performance.*
15. Fiebrink, R., & Caramiaux, B. (2018). The machine learning algorithm as creative musical tool. *The Oxford handbook of algorithmic music* (pp. 181–208). https://doi.org/10.1093/ oxfordhb/9780190226992.013.23.
16. Fiebrink, R., Trueman, D., & Cook, P. R. (2009). A meta-instrument for interactive, on-the-fly machine learning. In *Proceedings of the International Conference on New Interfaces for Musical Expression.*
17. Galanter, P. (2012). Computational aesthetic evaluation: Past and future. In J. McCormack M. D'Inverno (Eds.), *Computers and creativity* (pp. 255–293). Berlin, Heidelberg: Springer. https://doi.org/10.1007/978-3-642-31727-9_10.
18. Gell, A. (1998). *Art and agency: An anthropological theory.* Oxford: Oxford University Press.
19. Gibson, J. (1979). *The ecological approach to visual perception.* Boston: Houghton Mifflin. https://doi.org/10.1002/bs.3830260313.
20. Gioti, A.-M. (2019). Imitation game: An interactive composition for human and robotic percussionist. In *Proceedings of the International Computer Music Conference.*
21. Gioti, A.-M. (2020). From artificial to extended intelligence in music composition. *Organised Sound, 25,* 1–8.

22. Hawthorne, C., Elsen, E., Song, J., Roberts, A., Simon, I., Raffel, C., et al. (2018). Onsets and frames: Dual-objective piano transcription.
23. Ihde, D. (1978). *Technics and praxis* (Vol. 24). Boston Studies in the Philosophy of Science. Dordrecht: Springer Netherlands. https://doi.org/10.1007/978-94-009-9900-8.
24. Impett, J. (2000). Situating the invention in interactive music. *Organised Sound, 5,* 27–34. https://doi.org/10.1017/S1355771800001059.
25. Jones, D., Brown, A. R., & D'Inverno, M. (2012). The extended composer. In J. McCormack & M. D'Inverno (Eds.), *Computers and creativity* (pp. 175–203). Berlin, Heidelberg: Springer. https://doi.org/10.1007/978-3-642-31727-9_7.
26. Kalonaris, S., & Jordanous, A. (2018). Computational music aesthetics: A survey and some thoughts. In *Proceedings of the 3rd Conference on Computer Simulation of Musical Creativity* (pp. 1–15).
27. Kiefer, C., Collins, N., & Fitzpatrick, G. (2009). Phalanger: Controlling music software with hand movement using a computer vision and machine learning approach. In *Proceedings of the International Conference on New Interfaces for Musical Expression* (pp. 246–249).
28. Landy, L. (2019). Re-composing sounds … and other things. *Organised Sound, 24,* 130–138. https://doi.org/10.1017/S1355771819000177.
29. Latour, B. (2005). *Reassembling the social: An introduction to actor-network-theory.* Oxford: Oxford University Press.
30. Licklider, J. C. R. (1960). Man-computer symbiosis. *IRE Transactions on Human Factors in Electronics, HFE-3,* c1–c1. https://doi.org/10.1109/thfe2.1962.4503337.
31. Macionis, M. J., & Kapur, A. (2018). Sansa: A modified Sansula for extended compositional techniques using machine learning. In *Proceedings of the International Conference on New Interfaces for Musical Expression* (pp. 78–81).
32. Manaris, B., Roos, P., Machado, P., Krehbiel, D., Pellicoro, L., & Romero, J. (2007). A corpus-based hybrid approach to music analysis and composition. In *Proceedings of the National Conference on Artificial Intelligence* (pp. 839–845).
33. Martindale, C. (1998). Biological bases of creativity. In R. Sternberg (Ed.), *Handbook of creativity* (pp. 137–152). Cambridge: Cambridge University Press.
34. McCormack, J. (2012). Creative ecosystems. In J. McCormack & M. D'Inverno (Eds.), *Computers and creativity* (pp. 39–60). Berlin, Heidelberg: Springer. https://doi.org/10.1007/978-3-642-31727-9_2.
35. Radigue, E. (2018). *OCCAM RIVER XXII, for bass clarinet and alto saxophone.*
36. Roberts, A., Engel, J., Raffel, C., Hawthorne, C., & Eck, D. (2018). A hierarchical latent vector model for learning long-term structure in music.
37. Rowe, R. (1993). *Interactive music systems. Machine listening and composing.* Cambridge, MA: MIT Press.
38. Scurto, H., Bevilacqua, F., & Caramiaux, B. (2018). Perceiving agent collaborative sonic exploration in interactive reinforcement learning. In *Proceedings of the Sound and Music Computing Conference* (pp. 72–79).
39. Smith, B. D., & Garnett, G. E. (2012). Unsupervised play: Machine learning toolkit for max. In *Proceedings of the International Conference on New Interfaces for Musical Expression* (pp. 66–69).
40. Tahiroglu, K., Vasquez, J. C., & Kildal, J. (2015). Facilitating the musician's engagement with new musical interfaces: Counteractions in music performance. *Computer Music Journal, 41,* 69–82. https://doi.org/10.1162/COM_a_00413.
41. Tsiros, A. (2017). Sonic Xplorer: A machine learning approach for parametric exploration of sound. In *Proceedings of EVA London* (pp. 144–149). https://doi.org/10.14236/ewic/eva2017.34.
42. van den Oord, A., Dieleman, S., Zen, H., Simonyan, K., Vinyals, O., Graves, A., et al. (2016). *WaveNet: A generative model for raw audio.* https://doi.org/10.1109/ICASSP.2009.4960364.

43. Van Nort, D.. (2018). Genetically Sonified organisms: Environmental listening/sounding agents. In *Proceedings of the Musical Metacreation Workshop*.
44. Verbeek, P. P. (2008). Cyborg intentionality: Rethinking the phenomenology of human-technology relations. *Phenomenology and the Cognitive Sciences, 7*, 387–395. https://doi.org/10.1007/s11097-008-9099-x.

Artemi-Maria Gioti is a composer and artistic researcher working in the fields of artificial intelligence, musical robotics and participatory sound art. Her work explores the role of technology as a transformative force in music composition, performance and perception. She holds degrees in Composition (University of Macedonia, Greece) and Computer Music (University of Music and Performing Arts Graz, Austria) and is currently working as a senior scientist at the Institute of Electronic Music and Acoustics of the University of Music and Performing Arts Graz. E-mail: gioti@iem.at.

Artificial Intelligence in Music and Performance: A Subjective Art-Research Inquiry

4

Baptiste Caramiaux and Marco Donnarumma

4.1 Introduction

In many contemporary societies the pervasiveness of technology is constantly expanding. From communication to social networks, digital health and welfare services, every aspect of social life in industrialised societies is being captured by technology with the objective of human enhancement, optimised services, or automated management. Among these technologies, Machine Learning (ML) and the broader field of Artificial Intelligence (AI) received considerable attention in the past decades. In this chapter, we use an autoethnographic approach to present and discuss the hybrid methodology that we developed in five years of collaborative research across computation, science and art. The analysis we offer here combines insight from academic research in Human–Computer Interaction (HCI), in particular body-based interaction, and from aesthetic research in the performing arts to inspect and question the role of ML and AI in our practices.

The past decade has shown that data-driven learning-based algorithms can succeed in many tasks that were unthinkable not too long ago. Since the deep learning breakthrough in 2012 [44], these algorithms have been shown to recognise images as well as humans do, to acquire motor control capacities from few observations, and to understand and respond to several kinds of human languages. These breakthroughs prompted major investments in the field, thus accelerating technological advance at an exponential pace (the number of attendees at major conferences or the number of published papers at online repository like *arxiv* show the radical increase of interest

B. Caramiaux (✉)
Sorbonne Université, CNRS, ISIR, Paris, France
e-mail: baptiste.caramiaux@lri.fr

M. Donnarumma
Independent artist based in Berlin, Berlin, Germany

© Springer Nature Switzerland AG 2021
E. R. Miranda (ed.), *Handbook of Artificial Intelligence for Music*,
https://doi.org/10.1007/978-3-030-72116-9_4

in the topic). A consequence of the impressive advance of the field is a frantic race to embed ML-based algorithms in most digital services, without offering ways for users to acquire a basic literacy of the technology. The general paradigm behind the development of these technologies is based on centralised ownership by tech companies or institutions. By interacting with these technologies, people produce large amount of usage data, which, in turn, is used to train the underlying algorithms. This type of technology is therefore detached from people's control and understanding.

Artists have historically been among the first to question technological innovations (see, for instance, the organisation Experiments in Art and Technology, E.A.T., founded in 1967). They have often been early adopters and disruptors of new technological tools, and ML is not an exception [13]. On one hand, many artists use ML to enrich the way they work with their preferred media. On the other, some artists use ML, and in particular AI, to shed light onto certain facets of these same tools which can be invisible or taken for granted by public opinion, media, or institutions.

Our own path, which we elaborate next, has taken different directions throughout the past five years of collaboration. Initially, our approach was to use ML as a tool to design improvised and markedly physical musical performance, exploring the relation between computation and corporeality. Eventually, our approach shifted to utilise and reflect on AI as an actor in a performance, an entity whose functioning can be used to question the understanding of computational intelligence in Western society. As a team doing research in overlapping fields, we tried to combine our respective methodologies in a zone of encounter, where *practice-based research* meets *artistic intervention in research*. The former involves the use of artistic practice as a means of research. The latter entails that a creative, artistic process acts upon scientific research objectives. Naturally, such a hybrid methodology has been explored by others before us [26, 28].

In this chapter, we intend to extract the subjective aspects of our collaborative works and to discuss the methodological perspective that our particular mode of collaboration offers to the study of ML and AI, as well as to the study of their impact on HCI and the performing arts. The chapter is structured as follows. First, we provide general thoughts on combining scientific and artistic practices; these observations will help us give context to the methodology of our collaborative work. The next two sections discuss the conception and development of our collaborative artworks, two hybrid performances of computational music and choreography, *Corpus Nil* and *Humane Methods*. We present the scientific and artistic drives behind each project, highlighting scientific, artistic and cultural contexts. Finally, we provide a closing discussion where we bring together the core findings emerged from our research.

4.2 Combining Art, Science and Sound Research

A dialogue between scientific research and artistic practice is inclined to generate multiple and often contrasting perspectives, rather than producing an agreement. Important insight can emerge from those contrasts, insight that would have been obscured by a unified and monodisciplinary approach. This is the methodological grounding of the present chapter. We do not strive for objective knowledge. Art, even in its practice-based forms, does not offer any provable truth but creates alternate visions and, sometimes, it is called upon to "contemplate the dark without drawing a resolutely positive lesson", as Fuller and Goriunova put it [33].

4.2.1 Practice-Based Research and Objective Knowledge

The kind of art and science coupling we discuss here is not the use of scientific findings for the creation of an artwork, for that strategy requires an attentive process of translation, as stressed by Stengers [53], and—based on our subjective experience— it can easily feel constraining. As we will elaborate later when discussing our first collaborative project *Corpus Nil*, valid insight or correct measurements achieved in a laboratory setting may not be useful when applied to a musical performance. The motivation lies in the experimental limitations of particular scientific methods found in HCI and other research fields combining natural science, design and engineering. Contrary to the social sciences, for instance, HCI experiments are often conducted in a laboratory context. In controlled studies, every aspect of such studies is thoroughly directed by the experimenters. Whereas the protocols of such HCI experiments aim to ensure scientific rigour and reproducibility, those same protocols create the specific context wherein the collected data and related findings are meaningful. Outside of the specified context, data and findings may not be as meaningful, especially when applying them to an unpredictable and ever-changing situation such as a live artistic performance before a public audience.

For example, during a live performance, sensor measurements that have been validated through a particular experiment may very well vary according to a range of factors, including room temperature, magnetic interferences and the like. Those variables—contrary to a laboratory experiment situation—cannot be controlled. More importantly, the performer experiences her own body, a technological musical instrument and the context in subjective ways; during an artistic performance a per- former is driven by instincts, desires and feelings that arise from the relation with the audience, other performers and a particular musical instrument. Artistic expression in musical performance emerges from the interaction of human actions and desires with the capabilities of a musical instrument.

This emphasises the need for, on one hand, a careful selection and interpretation of the methods of art and science collaboration, and, on the other, a precise definition of the shared knowledge needed by artist and scientist to operate collaboratively; an entanglement that Roger Malina aptly calls "deep art-science coupling" [46]. Practice-based research represents a good framework for the exploration of art and science coupling, for it generates knowledge from action, self-reflection and empir- ical experimentation [6,11], methods that are equally fitting in HCI as in music and the performing arts. Crucially, we believe that the goal of art and science col- laboration is not the production or re-staging of the limits of a normative type of science, but rather is about "working outside current paradigms, taking conceptual risks", following Malina, so as to mindfully merge disciplines towards new practices of experimentation. This can result in contrasts and disimilarities which must be considered and which, in fact, produce the richness of art and science practice.

4.2.2 Artistic Intervention in Scientific Research

As technology has become more ubiquitous, spreading from workplaces to everyday life, the field of HCI has adopted new ways to investigate how we interact with such pervasive technology [23,39]. The so-called third-wave of HCI looks at notions such as experience, emotions, aesthetics and embodiment [9]. The field thus embraces methodological resources from a broader range of fields such as cognitive science, social science, science studies or the Arts. In this context, artistic intervention encourages research practitioners to look at their subject of study under an alternative "hypothesis", through different facets. It is important to underline that, differently from practice-based research, artistic intervention in research emphasises the idea of intervention: the artistic process *acts* upon the research objectives. For example, artistic intervention in scientific research, and more specifically in HCI, can help address a problem (or study a phenomenon) in radically new ways [5]. Such as in the case of Fdili Alaoui [28] who, working between HCI and dance, questions the academic culture of HCI through her expertise in interactive dance performance.

In our research, we use artistic intervention to build and study interactions between people and intelligent systems. This methodological choice is motivated by two factors. On one hand, scientific research practice can feel normative and standardised. As researchers, we employ established methods to structure our investigations on a particular question, as well as to disseminate the outcomes of the research. While this standardisation has its pragmatic rationale (for instance, to help its dissemination), it can be detrimental to scientific research practice in many ways, such as limiting exploration or surprise. A detailed articulation of the pros and cons of it goes beyond the scope of this paper. Here, we stress how artistic intervention in research can complement standard scientific methods in leaving more room for unexpected challenges and nuanced conceptual questioning. As an example, which will be developed in the following section, our study of gestural expressivity in musical performances has shifted the emphasis from characterising gestural variations in kinematic space to characterising variations in muscle coordination space.

On the other hand, the specific field of HCI has its own culture and shortcomings. While the field examines and generates the systems underpinning the technological world with which humans interact daily, its political dimension—that is, the varying balances of power between who produces the technology, who designs it, who uses it, and what socio-cultural impact it may have—is rarely addressed [4,40,42]. By avoiding to explicitly address the politics of technological innovation, one risks to contribute to the creation of forms of technological solutionism. Technological solutionism refers to the idea that technology can solve any problem, including issues which may not exist or which ignore both socio-cultural and political contexts [8]. We found that one method to prevent (at least partially) our research from entering a solutionist discourse is to invoke artistic intervention within the process of scientific research. Critical artistic intervention can explicitly provoke self-reflection about the involvement of a particular technology. Through an analytical and self-reflexive engagement, a critical artistic intervention can question the role of technology and its capacities of meaning-making, forcing artists and researchers to face the inner beliefs that ultimately motivated their choices.

In the following, we discuss how we applied the methods and insight described above to two separate research projects, which led to the creation of two artistic performances and scientific publications. This also serves to illustrate how our collaboration developed iteratively through the intertwining of practice-based research in the art field and artistic intervention in the scientific research.

4.3   Machine Learning as a Tool for Musical Performance

Our first project stemmed from a collaboration started in 2014. The outcomes of this particular project were a performance entitled *Corpus Nil* (premiered in 2016 at ZKM, Center for Art and Media, Germany and still touring internationally) and academic publications [12,22].

4.3.1   Corpus Nil

The piece is a twenty-minute dance and music performance exploring hybrid forms of identity and musicianship. It is an intense and ritualistic interaction between an autonomous musical instrument, a human body, and sound. Figure 4.1 depicts a picture from a live performance. The theatre space is completely dark. The player (Donnarumma in this case), whose body is partly naked and partly painted in black, performs a tense choreography which gradually morphs his body. Two types of wearable biosensors transmit data from his body to our machine learning-based software. Chip microphones capture sounds from muscles and internal organs (mechanomyogram or MMG) and electrodes capture muscle voltages (electromyogram or EMG). The software uses special filters to generate a description of the amplitude and frequencies of all sounds produced within the performer's body (between 1 and 40 Hz), as well as their variations over time. Then, it re-synthesises those sounds by orchestrating a feedback network of twenty digital oscillators. Because the choreography demands slow, subtle and iterative physical movements, the resulting music is equally slow and recursive, mutating across microtonal variations of a minimal set of pitches.

The instrument—here intended as a combination of our chosen hardware and software—analyses the collected data to learn the nuances of the performer's movement (muscular tension, gesture abruptness, rate of relaxation). Upon observing a certain nuance, it chooses whether to mute or activate particular oscillators, how to regulate volumes, phases, glissandos and multi-channel diffusion, and how to adjust

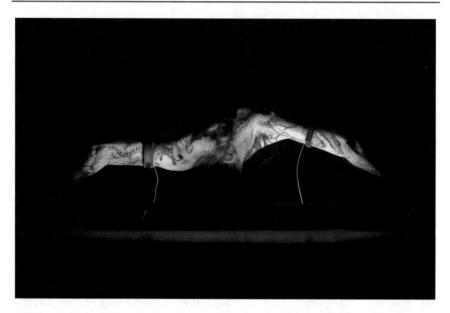

Fig. 4.1 Picture from the performance *Corpus Nil*. Photo courtesy of ONUK Fotografie. The piece evolves through different levels of muscular tension, torsion and articulations of the upper limbs. Aspects of the movements captured by means of two different muscle sensors placed on the arms

feedback amounts within the network. The player cannot control the instrument, but can only learn how to affect it and be affected by it. The piece thus discards conventional performer-instrument relationships—founded on the performer's full control of the instrument—in favour of an unstable corporeal engagement between the two. Through the rhythm of sound, vibration and light, the performer's body and the instrument mutate, physically and conceptually, into something "other"; an unfamiliar creature defying common definition of the human.

The software used in *Corpus Nil*, collaboratively created by the authors, consists of a set of algorithms linked to one another forming a recursive network. The algorithms have different tasks, such as biosignal analysis, learning of movement nuances (through linear regression and statistical methods) and sound resynthesis. A group of algorithms extracts a set of high-level features from the biosignals collected from the player's body (change rate, damping and spectral centroid). This feature set does not represent the movement per se, for it does not account for the shape of movement in space. Rather, it indicates specific traits, such as muscular force, abruptness of a contraction and damping of the muscular tissues, that characterise the articulation of the movement. The combination of analysis, learning and sound synthesis algorithms into a recursive network makes the instrument dynamic enough to provide highly unexpected responses to the player's movements. This, in turn, forces the performer to adapt the choreography "on the fly", establishing thus a continuous and adaptive dialogue with the instrument.

4.3.2   Scientific and Artistic Drives

Here, we present the scientific and artistic contexts, specific to each author, in which our collaboration on *Corpus Nil* took place.

Gesture Expressivity and Interactive Machine Learning When we started the collaboration in 2014, my (first author) research focused on capturing movement expressivity to be creatively used in music performance. A hypothesis was that aspects of the physical expressivity of a performer could be observed by analysing intentional variations in the execution of a movement. A system which would capture such variations could then be used to drive sound synthesis engines. However capturing those variations proved not trivial. Our approach at the time, developed with colleagues at Ircam (Paris) and Goldsmiths College (London), relied on a machine learning-based algorithm—called Gesture Variation Follower (GVF) [14]—which tracks, in real-time, continuous movement variations across space and time. In order to allow artists with radically different movement vocabularies and expressivity to use the system, this was designed to be rapidly calibrated.

This research belongs to a broader line of endeavour where machine learning algorithms are considered as tools to design expressive musical instruments and interactions [15,29,30,32,34,36]. In this type of research, the significant advantage of machine learning is that it leverages advances in computation and data analysis to allow musicians to tackle fairly complex musical scenarios [29]. More precisely, instead of writing rules that govern the criteria of interaction between performed movements and resulting sound, one can provide the algorithmic system with demonstrations of those criteria, which will be automatically learned by the system [31]. This approach involves tight interactions between the performer and the ML algorithm, formalised under the discipline of Interactive Machine Learning (IML) [1,27,55]. Using machine learning as a design tool seemed a natural approach when considering movement inputs to an interactive system. Writing rules that govern the analysis of movement inputs is clearly unfeasible when we consider that the system is expected to handle a wide scope of complex movements, mostly subjective to each performer. In addition, movement literacy is tacit, which means it cannot be easily formalised through words and lines of code of a programming language in a design context [38]. A machine learning-based approach where one can configure a system by demonstration seems a much more efficient approach [35]. In addition, such a system can be more inclusive, meaning that it can be used by novices and people with diverse physical abilities, who may not have previous experience in movement analysis or computer science [41].

Deconstructing a Performer's Body By the time our collaboration began, I (second author) had been working for four years in the field of gestural music as a researcher, composer and performer; in particular, I had been developing a musical performance practice known as *biophysical music* [21]. With this term, I refer to live music pieces based on a combination of physiological technology and markedly physical, gestural performance. The approach of biophysical music differs significantly from previous strands of biosignal-based musical performance [43,49,54] which are largely rooted in the use of physiological signal as a means of control over electronic or digital interfaces. The practice of biophysical music focuses, instead, on designing ways and tools through which the physical and physiological properties of a performer's body are interlaced with the material and computational qualities of the electronic instruments, with varying degrees of mutual influence. Through this method, which I term human–machine *configuration* [20], musical expression arises from an intimate and, often, not fully predictable negotiation of human bodies, instruments, and programmatic musical ideas (an anthology of biophysical music projects can be viewed in [19]).

After several years exploring potentialities and limits of gestural music research, I started questioning—in both my artistic and scientific processes—the kind of human body at the centre of conventional gestural music performances. My concern arouse from both my own work experience in the field and my participation to the HCI community through conferences and research exchanges, as well as from my study of feminist theory, in particular body theory [7] and disability studies [51]. Soon, it became clear to me that the kind of body shown in the performances of gestural music, and new musical instruments in general, was most times a heavily normalised body, that is, a body fitting particular criteria of normality. This triggered me to investigate how elements of gestural music performance and HCI could be exploited—in combination with research on movement and aesthetic—to create a different kind of performance practice; a practice that would account for the human body as an ever-changing, fluid entity with multiple potentials and varying forms of embodiment, instead of a static, controlled and controlling subject as established by our societal regime. Thus, drawing on the artistic work of performers such as Kō Murobushi [47] and Maria Donata D'Urso [25], among others, I developed a particular methodology of movement research that emphasised the combined use of unconventional choreographic methods and intense somatic experimentation towards the physical manipulation and symbolic deconstruction of a performer's body.

The movement experiments I conducted at the time were based on a gesture vocabulary composed of complex torsions, flexions, and contractions of shoulders, upper arms, and neck. No lower arm or hands gesture figured in the movement vocabulary I had designed for the piece (which then became *Corpus Nil*); hands, lower arms and even the head were, in fact, hidden from view and rendered purposely useless. Because the literature and tools in regard to this particular mode of gestural interaction are scarce, we decided to explore muscle activity at a very low level—through choreographic methods and resources from biomedical engineering. This, in turn, led us to investigate complementary sensor modality, with the goal to understand physical expression outside of a frame focused on "control".

4.3.3 Development and Observations

The initial seed of the collaboration was an intuition to investigate applications of interactive machine learning to the analysis of movement in a body-based musical performance. The performance in question, however, relied on the expression of bodily and motion qualities that were uncharted by previous work in the field. This spawned a research of muscle activity, the sensorimotor system and how, through different sensing methods, aspects of expressivity could be observed in human–computer interaction.

Understanding Movement Expressivity Initially, the analysis of movement expressivity as conveyed by the specific kind of muscle torsions, flexions and contractions described in the previous section seemed a good challenge for the Gesture Variation Follower algorithm (GVF) [14]. GVF was originally designed to track variations of movement trajectories in space and time, so we explored fundamental questions about movement expressivity at the level of the muscle activation. What is the trajectory of muscle activity in this context? To what extent information on muscle temporal activity is meaningful to a performer, and how muscle temporal activity can be controlled?

We began by experimenting with Mechanomyogram (MMG) sensors, capturing the mechanical activity of the muscle, built by Donnarumma in previous work [18]. We organised sessions of data capture and post-analysis. It became quickly clear that MMG data captured dynamic transitions between separate muscle contractions and the resulting trajectories calculated by GVF did not make sense. We added a second sensor based on Electromyogram (EMG), which measures the electrical discharges activating the muscle. Here, a new problem emerged, following Donnarumma's feedback about the resulting movement-sound interaction: controlling EMG trajectories was not aesthetically convincing, for it could not allow a highly dynamic mode of interaction, one of our main musical goal. Therefore, we worked on a new way to analyse muscle biosignals. We developed a different tracking system where the tracked parameters were not linked to the movement trajectory but to the parameters of an underlying second-order dynamical system with damping (symbolically representing muscle dynamic as an oscillating string).

How to define gesture expressivity when the gestures in questions operate through a set of symbolic and aesthetic signs? What kind of expressivity emerges from a performer's body that is physically constrained by a given choreography? And how can a ML system actively and subtly support a semi-improvisational physical performance of music where the very notion of "control" is put into question? We felt that these questions were to be tackled through a strategy that combined scientific and artistic methods. Our research forked in two parallel streams of investigation. On one hand, we deepened our understanding of expressivity to take into account involuntary aspects of whole-body gestures. Using real-time analysis of complementary muscle biosignals, EMG and MMG, we began isolating a set of features that could describe relative levels of muscular effort without the need to define in advance the type or the timing of a gesture. This would support the open-ended and semi-improvised nature of the choreography that was being developed. On the other hand, we started exploring the design of a computational music system that would not be tied to conventional mapping techniques, but instead would reflect, through sound, levels of effort intensity, movement abruptness and degree of complexity of particular gestures—i.e. the amount of muscle groups activated by a given gesture.

We finally conducted a controlled experiment to study gestural expressivity from the point of view of motor control (i.e. the ability of users to control gesture variations), using both EMG and MMG interfaces [12]. The main study brought together 12 participants for a session of 45 min each. In these sessions, participants were asked to perform a certain number of gestures (with or without tangible feedback) and then to vary one or more dimensions of expressivity. We showed that the participants consistently characterised dimensions of implicit expressivity (force, tension, etc.) and that the physiological interfaces used made it possible to describe these dimensions. Finally, we showed that participants could control these dimensions under certain conditions linked to constraints from the laws of motion.

Highlighting algorithm's limitation with IML GVF was designed to be quickly trained (or calibrated) by providing one example for each movement that the system has to recognise, and its capacity to track movement variation was meant to give to users a means to explore a movement space. However, its use in a tight interaction loop with the performer's body during experiments and rehearsals felt like a failure. One major factor was that the system felt restrictive rather than extensive. The movement possibilities seemed to shrink rather than extend. In the typical IML workflow, the performer is engaged in a close interaction loop with the movement-based machine learning system. However, if the algorithm has low-capacity (failing to handle a wide range of input movements) with respect to the complexity of the input movement, the performer may ultimately adapt to the system limitations, hence constraining her own movement qualities. Consequently, this adaptation would make the interaction converge towards simplistic movements and interactions.

This phenomenon may have also been emphasised by the absence of clear explanations about the system's prediction behaviour. Incorrect analysis of the GVF was hard to grasp by the performer (second author). Typically, the algorithm could have failed because the beginning of the movement is too different from the pre-recorded ones, but this information was not clearly fed back to the performer. As most temporal gesture recognition systems, GVF recognises a gesture (or movement) from a starting point until an end point. Establishing what defines the beginning of a movement and its ending point during the artistic performance was not trivial and it could definitely not be handled by the algorithm. Moreover, the system was designed to handle continuous and rather slow variations, whereas Donnarumma's muscle activity during the choreography presented types of dynamics that could not be tracked by the system. We needed a more flexible approach and thus we developed a new tracking system. This was designed to estimate in real-time the parameters of a physical model that mimicked the performer's muscular activity, as mentioned above. In doing so, we were not tracking gesture trajectories but movement "regimes". Thus, this method allowed us to explore alternative representations of movement using the input data at hand.

4.4 Artificial Intelligence as Actor in Performance

In 2019, we initiated a second collaboration, which actively involves a group of 13 people, including artists working with new media, biological materials and performance, as well as designers, AI and neurorobotics scientists. The project outcome is a dance-theatre production entitled *Humane Methods*. The first version of the performance premiered at Romaeuropa Festival and, at the time of writing, the project is currently ongoing. As for the previous collaborative project, we begin by describing the piece and then situating it within distinct scientific and artistic contexts.

4.4.1 Humane Methods

Humane Methods is a dance-theatre production exploring the multilayered nature of today's violence. The project departs from the assumption that—through the physical and psychological brutalization of people and non-human beings—the combination of digital technologies and capitalistic urge has driven the natural ecosystem towards impending destruction. The project then aims to dissect the violence of algorithmic societies, where power structures, knowledge creation and normative criteria become means of manipulation. Being an evening-length production, *Humane Methods* is composed of a multitude of elements, including robotic prosthetic limbs driven by their own neural networks, dead plant specimen and fungi growing on costumes, uncompleted or destroyed architectural structures, chimeric creatures, experiments in trauma, actions as rituals. For the sake of clarity, here we focus on the technological aspects of the piece and how they relate to the techniques and implications of AI. Figure 4.2 shows a picture from the performance.

In a landscape of ruined nature and technological relics, a community of nine semi-human figures lives a primal and stern existence. They perform a ritual of prayer in a loop, but with every repetition of the prayer, something in their interpersonal relations or in the world surrounding changes. As variations accumulate, the praying loop is drastically altered and the storyline branches out into a constellation of stories, of hints, of untold events, playing out various degrees of intolerance, isolation and exploitation. Throughout the action, a deep reinforcement learning algorithm tries to learn a meaningless sequence of ten digits.

Our motivation in choosing to work with an AI algorithm performing meaningless calculations lies in a conceptual shift from conventional uses of deep learning techniques in music and performance. What interests us is not the capacity of the algorithm to reach its target, but rather the ways in which the inner (obsessive) logic of this type of computation can be made perceivable at an aesthetic and sensorial level to both performers and audience. To that end, we designed an audiovisual system that links the actions of the AI algorithm to synaesthetic patterns of music and light, so that the algorithm "speaks", as it were, of its actions and choices through sound and light. The result is a dogged, hypnotic stream of sound and light that inundate the venue: the calculations of the AI are turned into perceivable material, auditory and visual pulsating patterns that literally mark the choreographic actions on stage, as well as the spectators' experience of the piece.

Fig. 4.2 Photo courtesy of Giada Spera. Picture from a live performance of Humane Methods at Romaeuropa Festival. Portrayed is one of the iterations of the ritual at the core of the performance. It is possible to observe in detail the lighting generated by the AI

4.4.2 Scientific and Artistic Drives

Human–AI Interaction ML and AI algorithms have known an exponential development in the past decades. Several important works have shown the capacity of learning-based algorithms to outperform humans in specific cognitive tasks such as playing the game Go [52], recognising images [44] or understanding natural language [37].

Simultaneously, the fields of HCI, Humanities, and Social Sciences have started to take seriously the study of the socio-cultural impact of AI and to propose design guidelines or good practices. Several works have recently been published along this line. Among them, some aim to propose a set of guidelines for designers of AI-powered interactive systems [2]. In this context, AI is seen as a tool to improve users' services and generally empower humans [10]. As an extension, AI can be seen as a material that can be appropriated by designers to improve user experience in AI-based applications [24]. However, most of these attempts have highlighted the inherent challenges of this approach due to the difficulty of grasping what AI can and cannot do [56]. In my work (first author), I am exploring how the computational learning mechanisms themselves can become interactive in order to foster exploration and human learning, as we recently explored in the specific domain of sound design [50].

On the other hand, recent works have investigated the complex consequences of the inherent biases in AI-powered applications and their impact when used in health care, education or culture [3,17,45]. This last branch of research is a necessary undertaking that I am currently pushing in my recent research interest, which looks at the socio-cultural impact of technology. Therefore, at a scientific level, the collaboration presented in this section was motivated by an intention to investigate how people understands AI technology and which are the founding beliefs supporting particular forms of such understanding.

Motivations and Artistic Needs The project *Humane Methods* is a collaborative endeavour that involves, aside from the collaboration between myself (second author) and Caramiaux, a shared authorship between Margherita Pevere [48], myself and video artist Andrea Familari. In particular, the artistic concept for the piece was jointly created by Pevere and myself, and then furthered through a close collaboration with Caramiaux. As artists working respectively with biotechnology and AI technology, the first question that Pevere and I asked ourselves was how to situate our artistic practices within the current historical period, one characterised by a generally intolerant and polarised socio-political forces, converging with a serious, technologically-driven disruption of the natural environment. This question led our efforts towards an analysis of the multifaceted nature of human violence, as it is exerted between humans as well as it is enforced by humans on the lives of non-human entities and the natural environment.

Turning to the main topic at hand—AI technology and its use in collaborative art and science projects—we chose to deploy AI algorithms in an unconventional way. Instead of using AI to aid human performers in the creation of sound—as we had done for *Corpus Nil*—or using an AI generative capacity to create a musical automata, we chose to make tangible the "brute force" computing mechanism of AI algorithms. In other words, we chose to highlight how many of the most common learning algorithms being presently developed attempt to reach their targets using a mechanism that is obsessive and raw.

4.4.3 Development and Observations

The collaboration developed through personal exchanges on the general theme of technology and society and particularly on how technology induces violence or empathy on people, to other people and to their environment. We wanted to create an algorithmic behaviour that obsessively learned something and which could autonomously explore different ways to reach its goal. The first trials, in terms of scenography, music, light and algorithms happened in June 2019.

Machine Behaviour The algorithm designed and implemented for *Humane Methods* is based on deep reinforcement learning, which means that the algorithm explores a high-dimensional continuous space and receives positive rewards when approaching the goal. These rewards are used to exploit certain moves within this space that would help the algorithm reach the goal. In *Humane Methods*, the algorithm's target is an arbitrary set of parameter values which—purposely—holds no meaning. The reward is given by its distance to the target. Its actions are moves in the parametric space.

As the algorithm moves in the parametric space, it outputs a list of 10 values—indicating the degree of proximity of its calculations in respect to its target on an integer scale between 1 and 3. Each of the 10 values is then mapped to a musical pattern—which are predefined arpeggios of acoustic piano samples—and a light pulsation pattern. Sonic and light patterns follow relentlessly one after the other, creating the perception of an audiovisual entity morphing continually through a multitude of syncopated variations. This dynamic morphing of sound and light is made more complex by a parallel method linking the algorithm degree of proximity to the target to, on one hand, the loudness of each single musical pattern, and on the other, to the brightness intensity of physical analog lights. The closer a value is to the corresponding target, the quieter is the volume of the related musical pattern and the dimmer is the brightness of the corresponding light pattern.

The algorithm moves within the space are entirely inferred by the learning process. This process consequently makes apparent to the spectators the behaviour of the algorithm. The algorithm becomes thus an actor, a performer on its own. Because neither the human performers nor the technical team behind the piece can control the computation of the algorithm, the latter is the sole entity responsible for the audio-visual dramaturgy of the piece. Interestingly, this role taken by the algorithm made us personify it: we began referring to it by a name, or discussing its contribution to the piece as an actor on its own. Journalists have also asked questions along this line, after seeing the show. This has been all the more striking for us as we were very careful not to anthropomorphize AI, a process that we find counter-creative for it typically impedes a precise understanding of technology by imposing a human worldview onto something which is not human.

Controlling Artificial Intelligence and Being Controlled by It Following our first experiments with the algorithm and, thus, observing the modalities of its interaction with music, light and choreography, it became more interesting to us *how* the algorithm learned rather than what it learned. We tested several strategies to map, more or less directly, the behaviour of the algorithm (the how) to the choreography executed by the human performers—discarding, in the process, any information regarding what the algorithm learned. In doing so, we soon faced a different challenge: how to find a balance between the control of the AI over the piece's narrative and the influence of the performers over the AI's learning process. We explored different strategies. One was to have the algorithm dictate the start and end points of each choreographic action. This, however, felt narratively constraining and aesthetically poor. Another attempt required the AI to describe the movement qualities with which each loop was to be performed by the human actors. This proved cumbersome, for a reliable, real-time communication between the AI and the performers was too complex to design.

At this point we changed our approach. Instead of mapping the AI's behaviour to the actions on stage, we thought of implementing the opposite strategy, that is, to map the actions on stage to the behaviour of the AI. Thus the choreography was re-conceived to mimic the temporal structure of the AI's learning process. One single action (a hybrid form of gestural prayer) is repeated in a loop, but with each repetition comes a more or less drastic variation. This loop structure mirrors the episodic learning of the algorithm: the algorithm learns through episodes—each can take a few minutes—and each episode adds variations to the next iteration of learning. This solution meant to limit the explicit interaction between actors' performance and AI learning process. The interaction between the two elements became thus implicitly intertwined: at conceptual and aesthetic levels the performers' action and the algorithm's learning process were connected, but this connection was not defined by explicit mapping of control signals. While we successfully performed the piece before a public audience in this format, we consider the issue still open. In our view, the piece would have a stronger impact if the performers' actions would be linked *both* implicitly and explicitly to the learning process of the AI.

Audience Perception of Artificial Intelligence In June 2019, we had the opportunity to collect subjective feedback from the audience during an open rehearsal at the Centre des Arts Enghien les Bains (CDA), a co-producer of *Humane Methods* together with Romaeuropa Festival, Italy. Our encounter with the audience in France was important, for it allowed us to open our aesthetics and research to a general public, most of whom had little or no familiarity with the ongoing project or our previous works. Here, we focus on the feedback given by the audience about their perception of the AI, as they observed it during the excerpts of the piece we performed for them. It is important to note that, before the performance, we purposely avoided informing the audience about the presence of an algorithm driving lights and music.

The two most significant comments of the audience were that some spectators did not realise that music and light were driven by an AI algorithm, and that another spectator suggested us to create more explicit interactions between the algorithm and the performers on stage. These comments are perhaps unsurprising if we consider the issue of implicit/explicit interaction discussed above. Nevertheless, they confirmed our early intuition about the challenges of making an AI perceivable to a public audience. Our algorithm manifests itself only indirectly, through lights and music and it lacks a physical embodiment. This was a choice we made in order to reinforce our critical stand on the impact of AI in society; the AIs regulating social media, welfare and warfare are pervasive and ubiquitous, while simultaneously invisible and implicit, integrated seamlessly as they are in institutional structures and interpersonal lives. Our AI was designed with this in mind, and is therefore omnipresent and unobservable.

However, concept aside, on an actual theatre stage it is indeed a challenge to manifest the AI's presence and expressivity while completely avoiding a physical representation of it (and potentially fall into naive anthropomorphism). Thus, while we still believe the concept we explored is meaningful to the overall piece, the audience feedback made us realise that, in order to be perceived as a "real" presence, the AI in *Humane Methods* needs to be embodied and its agency has to be manifested, in a way or another. This is still ongoing research, thus we can only speculate here, but we believe this issue opens a fascinating challenge regarding the fragile balance between "AI in control" versus "humans in control" elaborated in the previous section.

4.5 Discussion

This chapter focused on possible methodological approaches to the use of ML and AI in the context of music and performance creation. We have offered an autoethnographic perspective on a research and creation process spanning five years. Our aim was to open up our process and proffer insight into one possible way of coupling art and science in the application of AI and ML. In closing this chapter, we discuss three main aspects of the research. The first relates to how we approached AI and ML in relation to music and sound creation. The second concerns a shift in terminology that accompanied, and became manifested through, our projects. The third and final one addresses the hybrid methodological approach we developed progressively and contextually to each artwork.

4.5.1 Artificial Intelligence and Music

Many music-related fields are currently facing important changes due to the intervention of machine learning and artificial intelligence technology in music processing. These changes occur at different levels: creation, consumption, production and diffusion [13]. While AI technologies offer increasingly broad options to researchers and artists alike, with the present contribution we stress the importance of acknowledging the historicity of these technologies—where and how they emerged and developed—as well as the increasingly complex implications of their interaction with multiple layers of humans' societies. As we have demonstrated through the review and discussion of our specific collaborative projects, the use of ML and AI in music-related research does not have to be constrained by a paradigm of control—of humans over algorithms, of humans over musical forms, or of humans over other humans. Rather, by nurturing in-depth and long-term art and science collaborations it is possible to define new modalities of interaction across ML, scientific research and artistic creation.

At a musical level, both *Corpus Nil* and *Humane Methods* foster improvisational and unconventional types of interaction between algorithms, human bodies and musical forms. What should be emphasised, however, is that these kinds of musical interactions emerged from the combination of particular scientific and artistic drives which, in turn, evolved out of specific socio-cultural contexts. Artistic intervention into scientific research was coupled with practice-based research in ways that ramified our thoughts and strategies in multiple directions. Our own idea of what computational music can be was heavily affected by the particular paths we chose throughout the past five years of collaborative work. Whereas this allowed the germination of nuanced and technically rigorous interaction systems, it also made the development of satisfying outcomes slower than it could have been, had either of chosen to work alone. Thus, the same combination of practices and approaches which affords us with the capacity to deeply couple art and science is a factor that impedes fast turnarounds and requires mid-large timescales in order to reveal artistically and scientifically valid outcomes.

4.5.2   From Machine Learning to Artificial Intelligence

Our work witnessed a change in terminology that has been occurring since the deep learning breakthrough in 2012, that is, the shift from "machine learning" to "artificial intelligence". Machine learning used to—and, to some extent, still does—refer to the technological underpinnings that allow computational systems to "learn" from data, where learning means extracting structural components from a dataset. The term artificial intelligence is, however, more ambiguous: it was originally coined in the 1950s to designate a symbolic approach for modelling human cognition, but nowadays what is called AI mostly relies on vector-space generated by deep neural networks (which is not a symbolic approach) [16]. The term has its advantage to communicate about the technology and to create research and business incentives. Then, we also believe that the term imposed itself following the recent capacities of machine learning techniques. When AlphaGo [52] won against the world's best Go player, the idiom "machine learning" did not seem comprehensive enough to designate the technology that made it possible, its computational capacities, or the new prospect that such technology had opened up.

While, today, the HCI community often uses the term Artificial Intelligence, in our own research we preferably adopt the term Machine Learning to designate the type of algorithms we develop and use. Nevertheless, in our view, the adoption of the term AI triggers interesting questions into the concepts that are most commonly associated with the term. Speaking of AI triggers a specific and ambiguous imaginary that is worth understanding in detail in order to make better use (or no use at all) of this technology as practitioners and researchers in HCI.

The dialectical shift can be traced in our own work. Our first project, *Corpus Nil*, relied on a low-capacity movement recognition system. In this case, we were certain that Machine Learning was the right designation because the algorithm did not manifest a distinctive behaviour. Rather, its role was to recognise and learn given aspects of a performer's physical expressivity, so as to emphasise elements of human corporeality. On the contrary, the second project, *Humane Methods*, involved a radically different algorithm chosen not for its capacity to achieve a certain goal, but rather for the particular computational behaviour driving its learning mechanism. In this case, the term Machine Learning felt constraining, for it precluded an understanding of the algorithm as a socio-cultural phenomenon, beyond its computational capabilities. The algorithm had almost become a black box, interpretable only by observing its choices and subsequent actions. In this sense, it became observable as an actor.

4.5.3   Hybrid Methodology

By observing the varied methods we deployed in the research presented in this chapter, what comes to the fore is a hybrid methodology, an adaptive range of methods which evolved according to the nature and context of the particular problem at hand. This is illustrated by how, in *Corpus Nil* and *Humane Methods*, learning algorithms were used in two fundamentally different ways, and how, in each case, the coupling of the respective needs of art and science led to unconventional and effective results.

In *Corpus Nil*, we used an algorithmic system to design expressive, body-based musical interactions between a human performer and algorithms. We set out to explore Machine Learning algorithms as a *tool*, therefore our focus was less on the algorithm itself and more on what results the algorithm could achieve during the performance. The particular choreography created for the piece revealed limits of available computational approaches for the design of interactions with sound, and led us to find an ad hoc method based on physiological sensing. This method— triggered by artistic intervention into scientific research—yielded a new approach to the analysis of gesture expressivity, one based on complimentary aspects of muscle physiological data. This allowed us to capture dimensions of expressivity that greatly differ from those obtained through computer vision interfaces, which are the most commonly used in the literature.

In *Humane Methods*, we designed a computational framework which eventually became an actor, an independent entity directing sound and light in a dance-theatre performance according to its own internal functioning. Contrarily to *Corpus Nil*, at the core of this piece was an investigation of AI as a cultural and social *concept*, therefore we were less concerned with the results the algorithm could achieve and more preoccupied with how to manifest the functioning of the algorithm itself and to exhibit its behaviour. On one hand, this shift of focus proved challenging because it forced our research to confront a broad set of (scientific, artistic and popular) expectations surrounding the notion of AI. On the other hand, though, the challenge has opened before us a vast field of investigation, which extends across HCI, performing art and into the socio-political impact of AI. We feel that the prospect for a further entanglement of science, art and politics is, today, perhaps more urgent than ever.

Acknowledgements We would like to thank Frédéric Bevilacqua (IRCAM, Sorbonne Université), Sarah Fdili Alaoui and Margherita Pevere for their helpful comments on the paper. This research was partly supported by the European Research Council under the European Union's Seventh Framework Programme (FP/2007–2013)/ERC Grant Agreement n. 283771; by the CNRS under the programme PEPS/project INTACT; and by La Diagonale Paris-Saclay, under the programme Phares 2019/project Humane Methods.

References

1. Amershi, S., Cakmak, M., Knox, W. B., & Kulesza, T. (2014). Power to the people: The role of humans in interactive machine learning. *AI Mag., 35*(4), 105–120.
2. Amershi, S., Weld, D., Vorvoreanu, M., Fourney, A., Nushi, B., Collisson, P., Suh, J., Iqbal, S., Bennett, P. N., & Inkpen, K. et al. (2019). Guidelines for human-AI interaction. In *Proceedings of the 2019 CHI conference on human factors in computing systems*, pp. 1–13.
3. Angwin, J., Larson, J., Mattu, S., & Kirchner, L. (2016). Machine bias. *ProPublica, 23*.
4. Bardzell, J., Bardzell, S., & Koefoed Hansen, L.: Immodest proposals: Research through design and knowledge. In *Proceedings of the 33rd annual ACM conference on human factors in computing systems*, (pp. 2093–2102).

5. Benford, S., Greenhalgh, C., Giannachi, G., Walker, B., Marshall, J., & Rodden, T. (2012). Uncomfortable interactions. In *Proceedings of the sigchi conference on human factors in computing systems*, (pp. 2005–2014).

6. Biggs, M. (2004). Learning from experience: approaches to the experiential component of practice-based research. *Forskning-Reflektion-Utveckling* (pp. 6–21). Stockholm: Swedish Research Council, Vetenskapsr det.

7. Blackman, L. (2012). *Immaterial bodies: Affect, embodiment, mediation*. London: Sage Publications.

8. Blythe, M., Andersen, K., Clarke, R., & Wright, P. (2016). Anti-solutionist strategies: Seriously silly design fiction. In *Proceedings of the 2016 CHI conference on human factors in computing systems*, (pp. 4968–4978).

9. Bødker, S. (2006). When second wave HCI meets third wave challenges. In *Proceedings of the 4th Nordic conference on Human-computer interaction: changing roles*, (pp. 1–8).

10. Cai, C. J., Winter, S., Steiner, D., Wilcox, L., & Terry, M. (2019). "hello ai": Uncovering the onboarding needs of medical practitioners for human-AI collaborative decision-making. *Proceedings of the ACM on Human-Computer Interaction (CSCW), 3*, 1–24.

11. Candy, L. (2006). Practice based research: A guide. *CCS report, 1*, 1–19.

12. Caramiaux, B., Donnarumma, M., & Tanaka, A. (2015). Understanding gesture expressivity through muscle sensing. *ACM Transactions on Computer-Human Interaction (TOCHI), 21*(6), 1–26.

13. Caramiaux, B., Lotte, F., Geurts, J., Amato, G., Behrmann, M., Bimbot, F., Falchi, F., Garcia, A., Gibert, J., & Gravier, G., et al. (2019). Ai in the media and creative industries. *[Research Report] New European Media (NEM)*, (pp. 1–35).

14. Caramiaux, B., Montecchio, N., Tanaka, A., & Bevilacqua, F. (2015). Adaptive gesture recognition with variation estimation for interactive systems. *ACM Transactions on Interactive Intelligent Systems (TiiS), 4*(4), 1–34.

15. Caramiaux, B., & Tanaka, A. (2013). Machine learning of musical gestures: Principles and review. In *Proceedings of the International Conference on New Interfaces for Musical Expression (NIME)* (pp. 513–518). Graduate School of Culture Technology, KAIST.

16. Cardon, D., Cointet, J.-P., Mazières, A., & Libbrecht, E. (2018). Neurons spike back. *Réseaux, 5*, 173–220.

17. Crawford, K., & Paglen, T. (2019). Excavating AI: The politics of images in machine learning training sets.

18. Donnarumma, M. (2011). XTH sense: A study of muscle sounds for an experimental paradigm of musical performance. In *Proceedings of the International Computer Music Conference*. Huddersfield: Maynooth University.

19. Donnarumma, M. (2015). Biophysical music sound and video anthology. *Computer Music Journal, 39*(4), 132–138.

20. Donnarumma, M. (2017). Beyond the cyborg: Performance, attunement and autonomous computation. *International Journal of Performance Arts and Digital Media, 13*(2), 105–119.

21. Donnarumma, M. (2017). On biophysical music. In E. R. Miranda (Ed.) *Guide to Unconventional Computing for Music*, chapter 3 (pp. 63–83). London: Springer.

22. Donnarumma, M., Caramiaux, B., & Tanaka, A. (2013). *Muscular interactions combining emg and mmg sensing for musical practice*. KAIST: In NIME.

23. Dourish, P. (2004). *Where the action is: The foundations of embodied interaction*. MIT press.

24. Dove, G., Halskov, K., Forlizzi, J., & Zimmerman, J. (2017). Ux design innovation: Challenges for working with machine learning as a design material. In *Proceedings of the 2017 chi conference on human factors in computing systems*, (pp. 278–288).

25. D'Urso, M. D. Artist's website. http://www.disorienta.org/en/.

26. Edmonds, E., & Candy, L. (2010). Relating theory, practice and evaluation in practitioner research. *Leonardo, 43*(5), 470–476.

27. Fails, J. A., & Jr. Olsen, D. R. (2003). Interactive machine learning. In *Proceedings of the 8th international conference on intelligent user interfaces*, (pp. 39–45).
28. Fdili Alaoui, S. (2019). Making an interactive dance piece: Tensions in integrating technology in art. In *Proceedings of the 2019 on designing interactive systems conference*, (pp. 1195–1208).
29. Fiebrink, R., & Caramiaux, B. (2018). The machine learning algorithm as creative musical tool. In: *The Oxford handbook of algorithmic music*. Oxford University Press.
30. Fiebrink, R., Cook, P. R., & Trueman, D. (2011). Human model evaluation in interactive supervised learning. In *Proceedings of the SIGCHI conference on human factors in computing systems*, (pp. 147–156).
31. Françoise, J. (2015). *Motion-sound mapping by demonstration*. PhD thesis, Université Pierre et Marie Curie, Paris.
32. Françoise, J., Schnell, N., Borghesi, R., & Bevilacqua, F. (2014). Probabilistic models for designing motion and sound relationships.
33. Fuller, M., & Goriunova, O. (2019). *Bleak joys*. Minneapolis, MN: University of Minnesota Press.
34. Gillian, N., & Paradiso, J. A. (2014). The gesture recognition toolkit. *The Journal of Machine Learning Research, 15*(1), 3483–3487.
35. Gillies, M. (2019). Understanding the role of interactive machine learning in movement interaction design. *ACM Transactions on Computer-Human Interaction (TOCHI), 26*(1), 1–34.
36. Gillies, M., Fiebrink, R., Tanaka, A., Garcia, J., Bevilacqua, F., Heloir, A., Nunnari, F., Mackay, W., Amershi, S., & Lee, B. et al. (2016). Human-centred machine learning. In *Proceedings of the 2016 CHI conference extended abstracts on human factors in computing systems*, (pp. 3558–3565).
37. Hinton, G., Deng, L., Yu, D., Dahl, G. E., Mohamed, A.-R., Jaitly, N., et al. (2012). Deep neural networks for acoustic modeling in speech recognition: The shared views of four research groups. *IEEE Signal Processing Magazine, 29*(6), 82–97.
38. Höök, K. (2010). Transferring qualities from horseback riding to design. In *Proceedings of the 6th nordic conference on human-computer interaction: Extending boundaries*, (pp. 226–235).
39. Hutchinson, H., Mackay, W., Westerlund, B., Bederson, B. B., Druin, A., Plaisant, C., Beaudouin-Lafon, M., Conversy, S., Evans, H., & Hansen, H. et al. (2003). Technology probes: Inspiring design for and with families. In *Proceedings of the SIGCHI conference on Human factors in computing systems*, (pp. 17–24).
40. Irani, L., Vertesi, J., Dourish, P., Philip, K., & Grinter, R. E. (2010). Postcolonial computing: A lens on design and development. In *Proceedings of the SIGCHI conference on human factors in computing systems*, (pp. 1311–1320).
41. Katan, S., Grierson, M., & Fiebrink, R. (2015). Using interactive machine learning to support interface development through workshops with disabled people. In *Proceedings of the 33rd annual ACM conference on human factors in computing systems*, (pp. 251–254).
42. Keyes, O., Hoy, J., & Drouhard, M. (2019). Human-computer insurrection: Notes on an anarchist HCI. In *Proceedings of the 2019 CHI conference on human factors in computing systems*, (pp. 1–13).
43. Knapp, R. B., & Lusted, H. S. (1990). A bioelectric controller for computer music applications. *Computer Music Journal, 14*(1), 42–47 Apr.
44. Krizhevsky, A., Sutskever, I., & Hinton, G. E. (2012). Imagenet classification with deep convolutional neural networks. In *Advances in neural information processing systems*, (pp. 1097–1105).
45. Kulesz, O. (2018). Culture, platforms and machines: The impact of artificial intelligence on the diversity of cultural expressions. *Intergovernmental committee for the protection and promotion of the diversity of cultural expressions; Paris*.
46. Malina, R. (2006). Welcoming uncertainty: The strong case for coupling the contemporary arts to science and technology. In J. Scott (Ed.), *Artists-in-labs: Process of Inquiry* (p. 15). Wien: Springer.

47. Murobushi, K. Artist's website. https://ko-murobushi.com/eng/.
48. Pevere, M. Artist's website. https://margheritapevere.com.
49. Rosenboom, D., Number, L. M., & Rosenboom, D. (1990). *Extended musical interface with the human nervous system*, vol. 1990–97. Leonardo.
50. Scurto, H., Van Kerrebroeck, B., Caramiaux, B., & Bevilacqua, F. (2019). Designing deep reinforcement learning for human parameter exploration. *arXiv preprint*arXiv:1907.00824.
51. Shildrick, M. (2002). *Embodying the monster: Encounters with the vulnerable self*. London: Sage Publications.
52. Silver, D., Huang, A., Maddison, C. J., Guez, A., Sifre, L., Van Den Driessche, G., Schrittwieser, J., Antonoglou, I., Panneershelvam, V., & Lanctot, M. et al. (2016). Mastering the game of go with deep neural networks and tree search. *nature, 529*(7587), 484.
53. Stengers, I. (2000). *The invention of modern science*. Minneapolis, MN: University of Minnesota Press.
54. Tanaka, A. (1993). Musical technical issues in using interactive instrument technology with application to the BioMuse. In *Proceedings of the International Computer Music Conference*, (pp. 124–126).
55. Ware, M., Frank, E., Holmes, G., Hall, M., & Witten, I. H. (2001). Interactive machine learning: Letting users build classifiers. *The International Journal of Human-Computer, 55*(3), 281–292.
56. Yang, Q., Steinfeld, A., Zimmerman, J. (2020). Re-examining whether, why, and how human-ai interaction is uniquely difficult to design. In *Proceedings of the 2020 CHI conference on human factors in computing systems*.

Baptiste Caramiaux is a Centre National de la Recherche Scientifique (CNRS) researcher at the Institute for Intelligent Systems and Robotics (ISIR), of Sorbonne University in Paris, France. He holds a Ph.D. in Computer Science from University Pierre and Marie Curie also in Paris. His work lies at the intersection of human-computer interaction and machine learning, investigating the use of AI in artistic practice and rehabilitation. Prior to ISIR, he has worked as Research Scientist at Goldsmiths College (London, UK), McGill University (Montreal, Canada) and Mogees Ltd. (London, UK). E-mail: baptiste.caramiaux@lri.fr.

Marco Donnarumma is an artist, performer and scholar weaving together contemporary performance, new media art and computer music since the early 2000s. He has a Ph.D. from Goldsmiths College University of London, UK, and is currently a Research Fellow at the Academy for Theatre and Digitality, Dortmund, Germany. His works embrace performance studies, body theory, aesthetics, human-computer interaction and unconventional computing in music. E-mail: sad@flxer.net.

Neuroscience of Musical Improvisation

5

Psyche Loui

5.1 Introduction

One of the most remarkable abilities of the human brain is to create. Creativity is the cornerstone of human culture, and is the core cognitive capacity that has enabled music throughout history. Much of the act of creating new music, such as in music composition, is an effortful process that requires prolonged persistence, motivation, and dedication. However, other aspects of musical creativity, such as musical improvisation, have an appearance of spontaneity and automaticity, and appear to depend on states of flow that seize the improviser as they encounter musical ideas and produce novel musical output seemingly in real time. How is this real-time creativity possible: how does the brain tackle the problem of musical improvisation, and how does it accomplish this feat? Can improvisation be learned, and if so, how?

In this chapter, I begin with an introduction into the field of the Cognitive Neuroscience of Music. This includes a methodological overview of the tools and techniques commonly used to investigate the key components of music, as well as the relative strengths and limitations of each technique, and their general findings. From this overview, I turn to the core question that is addressed in this chapter: how does the human brain accomplish musical improvisation? This is a question that requires multiple answers, especially considering that musical improvisation is a complex system that necessarily involves many simultaneous excitations and inhibitions across the brain over time. Thus, I take a multi-level approach, discussing different levels of evidence in sequence. I introduce a hierarchical model of musical improvisation as a complex system, which affords multiple levels of description. From there I turn to each level and review the psychological and the neuroscience evidence in some detail. This is followed by a call to action for what

P. Loui (✉)
Northeastern University, 360 Huntington Ave, Boston, MA 02115, USA
e-mail: p.loui@northeastern.edu

© Springer Nature Switzerland AG 2021
E. R. Miranda (eds.), *Handbook of Artificial Intelligence for Music*,
https://doi.org/10.1007/978-3-030-72116-9_5

might be missing, or still to be addressed, in the current state of the psychology and neuroscience of musical improvisation.

5.2   Cognitive Neuroscience of Music

Cognitive Neuroscience is, fundamentally, the biological study of the mind. As its parent fields of Cognitive Neuroscience are Psychology and Biology, it necessarily inherits the overarching questions from these fields, in that the main goal is to link brain structure and function to behavior. The field has made great strides in advancing knowledge, mainly by using emerging technologies to sense and to record brain activity with ever-increasing spatiotemporal precision and accuracy. As part of these advancements, recently there has been much interest in real-time brain processes. As music necessarily unfolds over time, listening to and playing music can be thought of as a quintessential real-time brain process.

Magnetic Resonance Imaging (MRI) is a technique that can provide insight into structure as well as function of the human brain. Structural images include anatomical images and Diffusion Tensor Imaging (DTI). These techniques are powerful when applied together because of their respective foci: anatomical images are best at detecting grey matter whereas DTI at imaging white matter. While grey matter includes cell bodies of neurons and dendrites which provide input to them, they also provide important information such as the thickness of the cortex, the surface area of specific structures, and the volume of cortical and subcortical structures. In contrast, DTI is highly tuned toward white matter, which contains the axonal connections between neurons. Because DTI images the structural connections in the brain, it is an especially useful technique for studies where the hypothesis pertains directly to brain connectivity.

In contrast to the structural imaging techniques, functional techniques are important as they yield time-series data which can then be assessed against EEG, MEG, and other more time-sensitive measures. Functional MRI studies (or fMRI) include task and resting-state studies. Task fMRI studies typically involve the subject engaging in a variety of mental operations in the scanner, and comparisons between brain activations during experimental tasks and control tasks can yield regions and patterns of interest, which may be related to specific mental operations. For example, Limb et al. [34] compared task activations during the spontaneous generation of new musical sequences on an MRI-compatible keyboard, against task activations during a control task of playing a musical scale. The control task does not involve spontaneous music generation but nevertheless does involve interacting with the same keyboard; thus, the motoric component and some aspects of the auditory component are accounted for in the task-fMRI design. By subtracting the brain activity during the control task from the brain activity during the experimental task, researchers can obtain activation patterns that are uniquely driven by the unique aspect of the experimental task; i.e., the cognitive operations that distinguish the experimental task from the control task. For example, by subtracting brain activity during scale-playing from brain activity during the spontaneous generation of new musical sequences, it should be possible to isolate the effect of spontaneity while subtracting away the effect of audiation and motor movements, since the two latter operations are in both experimental and control tasks whereas spontaneity is only a characteristic of the experimental task and not the control task. By assuming this purely linear relationship between different cognitive operations fMRI tasks, this design relies on the assumption that cognitive components are additive in their effects on brain activity, and is known as the cognitive subtraction methodology. Results from this widely used cognitive subtraction methodology have been influential; for instance, in showing isolated activity in the superior temporal lobe areas (the auditory cortex) during auditory tasks. In addition, task-related fMRI has shown attention-related modulations of stimulus-driven processing. For example, when attention that is directed specifically to auditory stimuli is compared to attention to visual stimuli, there is additional involvement from neighboring regions to the auditory cortex [57]. This suggests that the extent of activations due to a predefined perceptual or cognitive operation can be modulated by the conditions of the task. In the study of musical improvisation, activations during the spontaneous generation of musical notes in contrast against motorically performing overlearned sequences (such as musical scales) shows activity in distributed regions throughout the brain, with the largest number of significantly active clusters within the frontal lobe [34]. This pattern of distributed clusters of activity may suggest that the experimental task of musical improvisation, which clearly involves multiple cognitive and perceptual operations, differs from a control task in multiple significant ways. The same results may also imply that different individuals use different strategies or set of cognitive operations to approach the task of musical improvisation.

5.3 Intrinsic Networks of the Brain

Although powerful, the standard model of task-related functional MRI has its own limitations. The predominant model of fMRI work involves cognitive subtraction, but there are caveats to cognitive subtraction as a standard model. In particular, abundant research in the past decade has shown that negative activations may be just as crucial as positive activations for subserving behavior, especially complex behavior such as musical improvisation. Evidence for this comes from the finding that specific regions of the human brain show correlated activity over time. Furthermore, across a variety of tasks in the fMRI, some regions of the brain are positively correlated with each other in activity, whereas other regions are negatively correlated (anticorrelated). The most consistent set of regions that are anticorrelated with task-related activity includes the medial prefrontal cortex and the posterior cingulate cortex, and some regions in the temporal lobe. This network of regions is together known as the Default Mode Network [17]. The Default Mode Network has received intense interest and attention in Cognitive Neuroscience in recent years, partly because it appears to be active when the mind is not actively pursuing a task. In contrast, the Default Mode Network is active during mind-wandering, or during stimulus-independent thought [12, 51]. This set of regions is also deactivated during effortful cognitive tasks, such as attention and memory tasks. The latter set of tasks activate the Executive Control Network and the Dorsal Attention Network, which are centered around the frontal and parietal cortices.

Mind-wandering is also thought to precede creativity [2]. Thus, these anticorrelated networks are useful in thinking about music and improvisation because musical improvisation can be thought of as a real-time creative act. As such, cognitive neuroscientists have found activity in the Default Mode Network during improvisation, that is in flexible exchange with the brain's Executive Control Network [3]. A review of the neuroscience of musical improvisation suggests that multiple large-scale brain networks are involved in improvisation; specifically, a network of prefrontal brain regions is commonly activated, including areas in the motor system (premotor and pre-supplementary motor area), areas in the language network (inferior frontal gyrus), and importantly areas in the classic Default Mode Network (medial prefrontal cortex) and Executive Control Network [4, 15, 47, 58]. Following up on these general findings, Belden et al. [6] asked if findings from task fMRI studies might extend to differences in intrinsic brain networks as assessed by resting-state functional connectivity. Seeding the Default Mode Network and the Executive Control Network in resting-state fMRI, this study compared three groups of different musical training: improvising musicians, classical musicians, and controls with minimal musical training. Improvising musicians showed the highest functional connectivity from the Executive Control Network, whereas both classical and improvising musicians showed higher Default Mode Network connectivity than musically untrained controls. Interestingly, the primary visual network also showed higher functional connectivity to both Default Mode and Executive Control networks in improvising musicians. From this study, the pattern of results that emerges suggests that while classical (non-improvising) musicians had higher connectivity within specific networks, improvising musicians showed higher connectivity between networks, whereas both musically trained groups showed higher resting-state connectivity overall compared to musically untrained controls. This distinction between within-network and between-network connectivity may recur in creativity research more generally, as more research in the network neuroscience of creativity shows that individuals who are more creativity in laboratory tasks tend to simultaneously engage multiple networks (in particular Default Mode, Executive Control, and Salience Networks) that are usually anticorrelated in their activity [5].

While fMRI is a highly effective method at localizing multiple brain networks at once, one shortcoming of fMRI is that the time resolution is quite low, on the order of several seconds. This is because of the inherent properties of fMRI: the technique makes use of the fact that neural activity is coupled with changes in the oxygenation level of the blood flow. Thus, by measuring fluctuations in blood flow (known as the hemodynamic response), we can extract the Blood Oxygenation Level-Dependent (BOLD) response as the signal of interest in fMRI. Although changes in activity of neuronal populations are causally related to the BOLD signal, the BOLD response requires several seconds to reach its peak after its corresponding neural activity. This delay, known as the hemodynamic lag, places limitations on the temporal resolution of fMRI. Since music is an art form that necessarily unfolds over time, temporal resolution is at least as important as spatial resolution for our understanding of neural circuitry that enables musical functions.

5.4 Temporally Precise Indices of Brain Activity in Music

In contrast to fMRI, Electroencephalography (EEG) and Magnetoencephalography (MEG) are methods that enable examining the function of the brain with much higher temporal resolution. EEG relies on the electrical properties of brain activity, and MEG relies on the magnetic fields that are generated as a result of electrical brain activity. When groups of neurons fire they generate electrical changes, known as local field potentials. These local field potentials can be recorded as dipoles, which are separations in electrical charge. These dipoles propagate throughout the head and are recordable on the surface of the scalp using electrodes. The source of the dipole can be identified by taking the second-order derivative of the electrical gradient across different recording sites on the scalp, thus giving a more precise location of the source of electrical activity, which can be interpreted as the neural generators of the activity. Because there are multiple geometric nonlinearities in the mapping between the head shape and the brain, such as due to cerebrospinal fluid as well as the structure of the brain tissue, the mapping between the source of the dipole and the local field potentials is often inconsistent. This places constraints on the spatial acuity of EEG, especially in areas of the brain that are near the inside folds (sulci) of the cortex, and in areas that are deep inside the head beneath the level of the cortex (i.e., subcortical structures). Thus, the spatial resolution of EEG is relatively low. On the other hand, the temporal resolution of EEG is high as it relies on a direct measure of neural firing itself. Established methods in EEG research have capitalized on this temporal resolution to obtain fine-grained time-domain and frequency-domain readouts of brain activity during music processing. One established EEG method is Event-Related Potentials (ERPs). ERPs rely on recordings of EEG during repeated presentations of the same stimulus, or the same category of stimuli, while precisely tagging the time window during which each stimulus is presented. Then, by averaging the EEG time windows of all stimulus presentations, the randomly distributed noise sources in the EEG are averaged out, whereas the neural signal that is associated with the neural processing of the stimulus becomes amplified. This increase in signal-to-noise ratio of the EEG, as a result of time-locked averaging across many trials, results in an electrical potential that is uniquely related to each neural event. The Event-Related Potential (ERP) technique has been influential in Cognitive Neuroscience of Music research, as it is sensitive to cognitive, top-down effects as well as to the bottom-up processing of sensory stimuli. One well-known ERP is the P300, which denotes a positive waveform around 300 ms after the stimulus, and is observed whenever a subject is responding to a stimulus. Another well-known ERP is the Mismatch Negativity (MMN), which is a negative waveform around 200 ms after any stimulus mismatch (i.e., a slightly unexpected stimulus that is different from other stimuli in an ongoing stream of events). Another ERP that is closely related to the MMN is the Early Right Anterior Negativity (ERAN), which is a negative waveform that is largest over the right hemisphere, and occurs around 200 ms after the onset of an unexpected musical chord. Since the ERAN is elicited whenever unexpected chords are presented, it has been known as a neural marker of musical syntax [29]. The ERAN is elicited, albeit smaller in amplitude, even when attention is directed away from music, such as when musical chord progressions are played in the background during a demanding visually presented cognitive task [38]. This finding of attention-dependent modulation of the ERAN suggests that neural processes for syntactic structure in music are partially automatic; in other words, we process musical syntax without needing to allocate attention toward it, but attention certainly enhances the syntax processing. This puts musical syntax in the same category as linguistic syntax, which is also indexed by an early waveform, but one that is left-lateralized: the Early Left Anterior Negativity (ELAN) is usually observed after an unexpected word category, such as when the tense of a verb within a sentence is different from expected [18]. The hemispheric asymmetry— between the ELAN for language and the ERAN for music—may seem to lend support to the popular idea that language is left-lateralized whereas music is right-lateralized; however, in practice the lateralization of these ERP results is much more variable, and is dependent on low-level acoustical properties of the stimuli as well as to higher-level task demands and/or instructions to the subject.

While the ERAN and ELAN are relatively early cortical ERP waveforms, there are other ERPs that occur later in latency during musical and linguistic processing. These mid- and late-latency waveforms include the N400 and the P600. The N400 is a negative waveform largest in central-parietal sites around 400 ms after the onset of a semantic incongruity [32], whereas the P600 is a positive waveform largest in parietal sites around 600 ms. Typically, the N400 is observed in response to semantic incongruity: unexpected semantic sentence stimuli such as "I take my coffee with cream and socks" elicits an N400 after the unexpected word "socks." In contrast, the P600 is elicited during sentences that require syntactic integration, such as when a sentence contains an ambiguous syntactic structure that the brain must resolve [31]. A classic example of this comes from "garden path" sentences, e.g., "The horse raced past the barn fell." In this example, the phrase "raced past the barn" is initially interpreted as a verb phrase (i.e., describing the action of the horse). However, when "fell" is presented, the brain has to re-interpret "raced past the barn" as an adjective phrase that describes a property rather than an action of the horse. This reinterpretation of the garden path sentence is known to elicit the P600 waveform [31]. Because the P600 is similar to the P3 in its waveform shape and topography, it has been suggested that these two effects are from the same neural generators [11]. In music, a similar late positive effect has been observed in response to unexpected melodic changes that require the reinterpretation of chord structure [8, 55]. This suggests some similarity between neural resources for processing language and music, especially in the syntactic structure of music and language.

The P600 or P3 effect is also observed during music cognition experiments when participants are asked to attend and respond specifically to chord structure. In one study, Koelsch et al. [30] presented participants with chord progressions that were either highly expected (tonic endings), or unexpected (Neapolitan chord endings), and asked participants to press a button in response to the unexpected chords [29]. This attentive listening condition was compared against an unattended condition when the same chord progressions were played in the background while participants did another task. ERPs showed a large ERAN during both attended and unattended conditions; however, in the attended condition the ERAN was followed by the P3 which was not observed in the unattended condition [30]. This pattern of results was partially replicated in Loui et al. [38], which also observed that the ERAN was elicited during attended and unattended listening, but with a larger amplitude during attended listening. In Loui et al.'s extension [38], the researchers further added an amplitude change in some of the chords, and participants' task during the attended condition was to respond to the amplitude change. The P3 was observed only during the amplitude change, but not during the syntactically unexpected chord. This finding shows that the P3 is elicited in response to any feature of sounds to which attention is directed, and not to harmony or musical syntax per se. On the other hand, the ERAN is more specifically elicited in response to violations in musical expectancy, especially from violations in chord structure. The effects of musical training can affect neural processing of musical syntax, as indicated by these ERPs. In a study comparing improvising (mostly jazz-trained) musicians and non-improvising (mostly classical) musicians against non-musicians, Przysinda et al. [59] recorded preference ratings for highly expected, slightly unexpected, and very unexpected chord progressions, while EEG was recorded. Behavioral ratings showed that while non-musicians and non-improvising musicians preferred the highly expected chord progressions and disliked the very unexpected chord progressions, improvising musicians preferred the slightly unexpected chord progressions, and did not dislike the very unexpected chord progressions as much as the other two groups. ERPs in response to unexpected chords showed a larger ERAN among improvising musicians. Although all three groups showed the P3, it was the largest among the improvising musicians. However, while the P3 returned to baseline by around 800 ms after the onset of the unexpected chord in both the improvising musicians and the non-musicians, the P3 lingered to a much later latency (800 ms after stimulus onset) in the non-improvising (classical) group only. This late-latency positive effect in classical musicians suggests a rumination, or error-related processing, that lingers in the minds of the classical musicians even after the improvisers have returned to baseline. Taken together, the double dissociation between early processing in improvising musicians and late-latency processing in classical musicians highlights the effects of different genres of musical training: while classical training emphasizes accuracy and precision, training in improvisation emphasizes sensitivity to expectancy and engagement with unexpected events. Methodologically it is useful to have improvising musicians, classical musicians, and non-musicians as multiple control groups, as it enables a direct comparison between different types of musical training. Even though the Cognitive Neuroscience of Music has seen a surge of interest in recent years, with many studies being done on the effects of musical training, the vast majority of these studies have examined western classical musical training as the dominant genre, without much studies done at all on non-classical forms of training. By examining the effects of jazz improvisation training, this study makes a first attempt at quantifying the effects of training on various neural and cognitive outcomes.

In another in-depth study on Western music improvisation, Goldman et al. [20] recorded EEG in musicians with varying levels of improvisation experience while they listened to an oddball task, where standard stimuli are interspersed with occasional deviant stimuli. Standard stimuli were chords, interspersed with occasional deviant chords that either did or did not serve a similar chord function musically. Participants with more improvisation experience showed larger N2 and P3 while processing the functionally deviant chords, suggesting that the ability to engage in creative improvisation is related to differences in knowledge organization.

While ERPs provide accurate time-domain information of brain activity in response to stimuli and cognitive processes, frequency-domain information can also be informative, especially since abundant research in recent years has identified periodic oscillations at multiple frequencies as a fundamental feature of brain activity. Oscillatory activity is especially important in music and speech, as evidence shows that these complex auditory stimuli can engage phase-locked activity in the brain via the process of neural entrainment. When listening to acoustic stimuli with energy at certain frequencies, brain activity also shows activity at the corresponding frequencies. These oscillations at specific frequencies do not only reflect passive processing of stimulus by the auditory system, but in some cases they also reflect the active parsing of stimulus streams. This is demonstrated clearly in a MEG study on the cortical tracking of speech: When meaningful Chinese speech was presented with a syllabic rate of 4 Hz, noun or verb phrases at 2 Hz, and sentences at 1 Hz, only Chinese listeners showed corresponding activity at 1 and 2 Hz. In contrast, English speakers who did not understand Chinese only showed activity at 4 Hz [14]. This finding suggests cortical tracking of linguistic stimuli reflect comprehension, rather than the perceptual processing of acoustic stimuli. Findings such as this one show how informative it can be to take a frequency-based approach instead of a time-domain approach in analyzing and interpreting EEG and MEG data.

The frequency-based approach is especially informative when there are frequency-based hypotheses motivating the collection of the EEG and MEG data. In music, for example, one commonality across musical experiences is that of rhythm, which is a pattern of repeated durations over time. Rhythm is closely related to beat, which is the steady pulse that a listener extracts from the rhythm. The ability to extract a beat from an ongoing pattern of sounds is crucial to musical ability, and thus much of the literature in the Cognitive Neuroscience of Music perception and cognition is dedicated to the perception of rhythm and beat. Since the beat is tied to a specific frequency (e.g., a 1 Hz beat corresponds to 60 beats per minute), a frequency-domain analysis makes the problem of beat perception relatively tractable. Nozaradan et al. [54] recorded EEG from human subjects while they listened to rhythmic patterns that were designed to elicit a sense of beat and meter. They found that the EEG showed peaks of oscillatory activity at the rhythmic frequencies, with peaks observed at beat frequencies even when the acoustic energy was not necessarily strongest [54]. This observation of oscillatory brain activity at the beat frequency without acoustic stimulation is also termed the "missing pulse" phenomenon [69], borrowing from terminology of the "missing fundamental" phenomenon in which pitch can be perceived virtually even without acoustic energy at the corresponding fundamental frequency [70]. Thus, the rhythmic brain activity appears to be an index of how the mind interprets the stimuli, instead of being a faithful mirror of the stimuli themselves. In other words, these findings highlight the importance of oscillatory brain activity in coding not only for bottom-up processing of rhythmic stimuli, but also of top-down brain mechanisms such as attention and memory that are involved in the experience of music.

5.5 Attention Toward Moments in Time

The idea that attention can fluctuate rhythmically over time, especially in sync with music and speech stimuli, is formalized in the Dynamic Attending Theory [33], which is a framework for describing the brain as a series of internal oscillations, known as attending rhythms, that can entrain (i.e., tune in) to external events and focus on expected points in time. This model is especially appropriate as a formal description of the brain during musical experience: As the materials of music (pitch, harmony, melody, rhythm) unfold over time, these same musical materials can reasonably be expected to guide our attention over time as well. Ongoing research is aimed at understanding how the different musical materials guide attention, and the trajectory of the ability and strategies used to attend to these musical features throughout the human lifespan [16].

The ability to sustain attention is also related to the degree of engagement one feels toward a piece of music. For example, if a piece of music urges a person to move, then the act of engaging in movement likely helps to sustain attention over time in a rhythmically oscillatory manner. The pleasurable urge to move to music, also known as "groove," has become an interesting topic that intersects the study of neural oscillations and entrainment, rhythm and beat, and pleasure and reward. In the attempt to understand how rhythmic patterns might activate in the motor system, Stupacher et al. [68] stimulated the motor cortex using Transcranial Magnetic Stimulation (TMS) and measured their resultant Motor Evoked Potentials (MEPs) as a measurability of the motor system [68]. Music that was rated as high-groove showed larger MEPs, suggesting more excitability of the motor system. This finding fits well with fMRI studies showing activity in the motor system during the perception of musical rhythm and beat [22]. Furthermore, people with motor disorders, specifically Parkinson's Disease, are less able than controls to extract the beat from musical rhythms, as shown by a reduced beat-based advantage in discriminating musical rhythms [23]. This provides converging evidence that the motor system is important for beat perception.

While the engagement of the motor system explains the urge to move that one feels when listening to music, the link between pleasure and the urge to move is yet unclear. Insight comes from examining the link between groove and syncopation, which is the shift of acoustic events from metrically strong to metrically weak beats [73], who compared pleasure ratings between drum-beats with varying levels syncopation, and showed that medium degrees of syncopation yielded the highest desire to move and the highest pleasure ratings. Since syncopation is in itself a violation of rhythmic expectations, this preference for a medium level of syncopation is broadly consistent with an inverse u-shaped relationship between expectation and pleasure, which has long been hypothesized in music [52], and also in the psychology and biology of aesthetics more generally [7].

The ability to hone one's expectations toward events at recurrent moments in time is likely a precursor to the ability to the tendency to synchronize with others. Interpersonal synchrony is a fascinating topic of recent investigations, especially since the tendency to synchronize with others seems to be tied to the sense of group identity and group affiliation. The effect of interpersonal synchrony on group affiliation was tested when pairs of participants were asked to rate how well they felt affiliated to each other after tapping either to synchronous or to asynchronous metronomes [26]. As hypothesized, ratings of interpersonal affiliation were higher for participants after tapping to synchronous metronomes. This suggests that the ability to entrain to another individual's rhythmic behaviors is closely tied to social behavior, in particular affiliative behavior.

The link between synchronizing with other people and cooperative behavior appears to be established relatively early in life. This link was tested in 14-month-old infants, who were placed in a standard cooperation task after a rhythmic task. In the rhythmic task, the infants were bounced either in-synchrony or out-of-synchrony with an experimenter. Following this bouncing task, the infants were placed in a room with the experimenter, who "accidentally" drops an object. Cooperation was measured by whether the infant helped by picking up and handing the dropped object to the experimenter. Infants who had bounced with the experimenter were more likely to help the experimenter afterwards. Interestingly, cooperative behavior was observed even when the rhythmic bouncing was done out-of-phase (by still in-synchrony), suggesting that rhythmic synchrony rather than the similarity or symmetry of movement was what drove the cooperative behavior [13]. While this measure of cooperative behavior is important and informative as a measure of prosociality (i.e., behavior that benefits society as a whole), and may thus have optimistic implications for the effects of music on social behavior, it turns out that infants were only more likely to help individuals who had bounced with them; this helping behavior did not extend to other individuals who did not participate in the bouncing [71]. This suggests that rhythmic synchrony in music may help affiliation for the in-group only, rather than promoting altruistic behavior in general. Nevertheless, this cooperative behavior extends to older children (aged 4), who were more likely to cooperate in their behavior after swinging rhythmically with a partner [61], suggesting that the link between rhythmic entrainment and cooperation is likely a stable relationship across the lifespan.

5.6 Prediction and Reward

Given that rhythm directs attention and expectation (as posited by the Dynamic Attending Theory) and relates to enjoyment and group affiliation, it is not surprising that the brain processes expectation in time in the same way that it processes other forms of pleasure and enjoyment. The currency with which the brain processes reward is dopamine, which is a neurotransmitter that is emitted when animals undergo hedonic experiences such as food and sex [60]. The dopaminergic system in the brain includes several way stations: the substantia nigra, ventral tegmental area, nucleus accumbens, caudate, putamen, and orbitofrontal cortex. In particular, the nucleus accumbens, caudate, and putamen are known as the striatum. Together these regions tend to be active when processing extremely pleasurable rewards, such as when winning in gambling tasks [60]. Interestingly, even events that are themselves not rewarding, but that signal rewards (i.e., they provide a cue toward rewards) also activate cells in the dopaminergic system. Furthermore, events that signal rewards, but are then followed by the lack of reward, results in a *decrease* in activity in the dopamine neurons [67]. Thus, the dopaminergic system is known as a code for the difference between the prediction of a reward and the actual experience of the reward; this difference is known as the reward prediction error. Importantly, these same dopaminergic areas are active during the experience of intensely pleasurable moments in music [9, 10]. In a study that specifically related music to activity in the dopaminergic system, Salimpoor et al. [66] injected participants with radioactive raclopride, which is metabolized during dopaminergic activity, and conducted Positron Emission Tomography (PET) scanning combined with functional MRI while people listened to pieces of music that they selected as being intensely pleasurable to them. This combined PET and fMRI was especially useful because it allowed the researchers to simultaneously localize brain activity and establish its link to the dopaminergic system. Results from this study showed a peak of activity in the caudate during the anticipation of intensely pleasurable moments in music, and a peak of activity in the nucleus accumbens during the experience of the intensely pleasurable moment. This finding is exciting for Neuroscience generally and for Music Cognition researchers specifically, because it shows a differentiation between anticipation and experience. Both are important components of the experience of pleasure, but this distinction is especially important for music, which is fundamentally an interplay between expectation and experience. In further work, the same researchers showed that the auditory cortices are coupled in activity with the nucleus accumbens, and that this coupling is stronger during the experience of strongly preferred music [65], thus linking the experience of reward to activity in the auditory system. More evidence for the role of the reward system in music listening comes from musical anhedonia, which is a recently coined abnormal lack of sensitivity to musical reward. People with musical anhedonia feel no desire to listen to music, despite normal hedonic responses to non-auditory senses, such as visual art, food, and monetary reward [50]. Because of this fascinating dissociation between music and monetary reward, musical anhedonia can be considered a model system for examining the link between music and reward, and for examining what it is that makes music special within our culture. In a diffusion tensor imaging study on a striking case of musical anhedonia, Loui et al. [46] showed that compared to a large group of controls, the musical anhedonic had less structural connectivity between auditory areas in the temporal lobe and reward areas in the nucleus accumbens. Looking at individual differences in white matter connectivity across a group of individuals who vary in musical reward responses, Martinez-Molina et al. [49] showed that structural connectivity between auditory and insula, which is an area important for emotional functioning and for interoceptive functions, was correlated with individual differences in self-reported musical reward. Similar differences were seen between people who frequently experience chills, or strong emotional responses, when listening to music, compared with those who rarely experience chills during music listening [63]. Furthermore, when listening to music that a general population rated as rewarding, musical anhedonics showed no functional connectivity between auditory areas and the nucleus accumbens, further providing support for a disconnection between auditory and reward regions in the brain [48]. Reviewing these findings, Belfi and Loui [1] propose an anatomical model for the coupling between the auditory and reward systems, and posit a distinction between multiple types of predictions, only some of which may become rewarding.

The importance of prediction and expectation in the musical experience is the theme of Meyer's seminal work *Emotion and Meaning in* Music [52], and is also the topic of Huron's theory of musical expectation as laid out in his volume *Sweet Anticipation* [27]. Huron articulates the ITPRA model, which conceptualizes five phases of experiencing music (and indeed any experiences that are time-dependent) as Imagination, Tension, Prediction, Reaction, and Appraisal. This five-stage model is useful for thinking about the experience of music, partly because it separates the short-term, or the immediate, predictions and responses surrounding an event, from the longer-term buildup of expectations in the Imagination phase and the follow-up experiences of the Appraisal phase. Computational modeling studies have also begun to quantify the dynamics of information processing in music, and to relate these dynamics to brain activity. In particular, the Information Dynamics of Music (IDyoM) model simulates musical expectation using information-theoretic measures and makes predictions for how much uncertainty there is at each moment in time, and/or surprising each event is on a note-by-note basis [56]. Training this model on corpora of real music, and testing it against human ratings, shows an inverse u-shaped relationship between expectation and preference [19]. Using these computational tools coupled with neuroscientific methods, the field can begin to relate activity in the dopaminergic system to musical expectation in a realistic music-listening context.

Regarding music and reward, one persistent puzzle is that music, unlike food or sex, has no clear evolutionary advantage, yet music consistently ranks among life's greatest pleasures. Why do we find pleasure in experiences that are not necessary for keeping ourselves alive, or for keeping our progeny alive? The answer must come from the interaction between music and inherent properties of the cognitive system. The ability to learn is fundamental to the cognitive system, and is evolutionary advantageous as it enables organisms to adapt flexibly to their environment. As the ability to form correct predictions is likely adaptive, the ability to form predictions must also be learned, and may therefore acquire reward value in and of itself. Thus, the relationship between learning and reward is an active area of research in music and in neuroscience more generally.

5.7 Music and Language Learning

The literature on learning is also heavily influenced by work on language acquisition, which has shown that infants as young as eight months of age are able to learn the transitional probability of events within an acoustic stream (e.g., syllables) [64]. These findings provide evidence for the existence of a statistical learning mechanism as part of our cognitive system that can learn expectations from exposure in much the same way that infants can learn the grammatical structure of linguistic sounds in their environment even without explicit instruction. Music is likely learned in a similar manner. Evidence for the learning of musical structures via passive exposure comes from abundant findings in reaction time, subjective ratings, and neuroimaging and electrophysiological studies showing that even people with no explicit musical training have knowledge of musical structure. For example, the ERAN is observed in response to unexpected musical chords even among non-musicians [29]. When asked to rate their preference for different chord progressions, both musicians and non-musicians rated unexpected chord progressions as less preferred [42], although jazz and classical musicians differed in their preference for unexpected chord progressions [59]. Reaction time is also slower when non-musicians are presented with unexpected musical chords, even when their task is independent of chord structure [42], suggesting that we bring implicitly learned expectation into our experience of music.

While most would agree that these expectations are implicitly learned, much remains unknown in how this musical knowledge is acquired, and to what extent these learned expectations interact with acoustic properties of the musical stimulus (e.g., consonance and dissonance). These questions are challenging to address because the vast majority of participants (at least participants that most music cognition labs can access) have already acquired an internal template or representation of musical structures within their culture. In other words, common-practice Western musical structure is overlearned in most brains. In order to observe the human brain as it is learning musical structure for the first time [72], one can approach younger populations to trace their developmental trajectory of musical knowledge Jacoby and McDermott [28], or one can take a cross-cultural approach in which we can compare the constraints of cognition in the musical systems of different cultures, or one can create a new musical system in order to test how the human brain responds de novo. In an attempt to create a musical system, Loui et al. [39, 44, 2010] turned to the Bohlen-Pierce scale, which differs from existing musical systems of the world in its mathematical ratios. While musical systems of the world commonly recur around the octave, which is a 2:1 ratio in frequency, the Bohlen-Pierce scale recurs around the tritave, which is a 3:1 ratio. The equal-tempered Bohlen-Pierce scale has 13 logarithmically even divisions of the 3:1 frequency ratio (in contrast to the 12 logarithmically even divisions of the equal-tempered Western scale). Using melodies generated from this system, it was shown that participants can rapidly learn melodies after exposure. Furthermore, they can generalize what they had learned after exposure to a sufficiently large set of melodies by choosing new melodies that followed the same grammatical structure. In addition, participants rated melodies that they heard repeatedly during exposure as being more preferable. Because it is a systematic way to test the learning and liking of new music, the finding that humans rapidly identify and prefer grammatical structure in a new musical scale offers optimistic implications for creating new music. EEG recordings made during the course of one hour of listening to the new musical system showed an ERAN in response to infrequent chords in the Bohlen–Pierce scale after around 20 min of listening [44]. These results together show that humans can rapidly learn to form expectations for new music, by being sensitive to the frequencies and probabilities of events in the acoustic environment; in that regard music learning is analogous to language learning [45]. Further follow-up studies showed that the input makes a significant difference in what was learned and preferred: the larger the set of exposure items, the more people learned; on the other hand, the more times each melody was repeated, the more people preferred those specific melodies [43]. Additionally, the ability to learn grammatical structure was found to be correlated with the white matter connections in the arcuate fasciculus, a super highway that connects regions important for auditory perception and sound production, as shown in diffusion tensor imaging studies [40].

This same white matter pathway is implicated in multiple auditory-motor functions. For example, people who are tone-deaf, who have trouble perceiving and producing small differences in pitch (e.g., less than a semitone), have less white matter connectivity in the arcuate fasciculus [37]. These individuals also have difficulty with statistical learning of new musical systems, using the same tasks described above [41]. Furthermore, people with tone-deafness are unaware of their own pitch production: when presented with pairs of pitches, and asked to reproduce them by humming and to tell them apart by pitch height, people who are tone-deaf show a striking mismatch between their production and their perception, frequently singing a pitch interval that is different from what they report hearing [39]. This perception-production mismatch also points to a more general distinction between different pathways, or streams, in the auditory system. These ideas on separable streams in audition are partly inspired by analogous findings in the visual system [21]: for example, people with lesions in their visual cortex, who are blind and have no conscious awareness of what they see, are nevertheless able to scale the size of their grip as they reach toward objects in front of them. These types of findings provide support for dual-stream pathways in the visual system. In the analogous sense, the auditory system is posited to have multiple, separable pathways for processing "where" (location information) and "what" (identity information) [62]. These functional distinctions are also posited specifically for speech processing [25] and for musical functions such as singing [35]. Strong support for the dual-stream pathways comes from a diffusion tensor imaging study which showed that the superior branch of the arcuate fasciculus is less connected in people who are tone-deaf [37]. Furthermore, people with musical training had larger volume in the arcuate fasciculus [24], and a week of performing an auditory-motor task on musical cues (in a motorically controlled form of musical training) resulted in increased integrity of the right arcuate fasciculus [53].

The same statistical learning mechanisms that are involved in language acquisition and music learning may be involved in creativity as well. Although the areas of creativity and statistical learning are commonly thought of as separate lines of research, Zioga et al. [74] tested the relationship between learning and creativity. They trained participants on an artificial musical grammar, using similar methods as presented above regarding the Bohlen-Pierce scale. After each training session, participants created their own musical compositions, which were later evaluated by human experts. Results showed that the individuals who were better learners as defined by the statistical learning task were also better at generating more creative new melodies as judged by experts [74]. These results are first to link statistical learning to creativity. Future studies are needed to examine the extent to which similar neural substrates underlie learning and creativity.

5.8 Conclusions: Creativity at Multiple Levels

Taken together, it is clear that multiple cognitive and neural systems contribute to the brain's ability to improvise creative musical output. Musical improvisation can be thought of as a combination of multiple levels of cognitive and neural computations [36]. At the highest level, musical improvisation serves the computational goal of using musical knowledge to generate auditory-motor patterns that are rewarding. This is accomplished by cognitive algorithms that involve statistical learning mechanisms which help to shape the learned musical structures, including melodies, harmonies, and rhythms. The cognitive algorithms also include idea generation and evaluation, and flexibly switching between the perception of auditory targets and the motor production of those targets. The underlying brain networks that implement these cognitive mechanisms include the auditory-motor, executive control, default mode, and reward networks. Future work may further delineate the relationship between learning and creativity, and between social information (e.g., visual and auditory information that comes from partners in group musical improvisation) and the prediction and reward systems. This social information likely involves neural entrainment of auditory and motor areas, which refine predictions and thus generate rewards. By studying the spatial and temporal dynamics of human brains as they engage in cognitive operations that are linked to musical improvisation, future work may design new biologically informed musical partners that aid improvisation with intellectually and aesthetically satisfying outcomes.

References

1. Belfi, A. M., & Loui, P. (2020). Musical anhedonia and rewards of music listening: current advances and a proposed model. *Annals of the New York Academy of Sciences, 1464*, 99–114.
2. Baird, B., Smallwood, J., Mrazek, M. D., Kam, J. W., Franklin, M. S., & Schooler, J. W. (2012). Inspired by distraction: Mind wandering facilitates creative incubation. *Psychological Science, 23*(10), 1117–1122.
3. Beaty, R. E., Benedek, M., Barry Kaufman, S., & Silvia, P. J. (2015). Default and executive network coupling supports creative idea production. *Scientific Reports, 5*, 10964.
4. Beaty, R. E. (2015). The neuroscience of musical improvisation. *Neuroscience & Biobehavioral Reviews* (in press).
5. Beaty, R. E., Kenett, Y. N., Christensen, A. P., Rosenberg, M. D., Benedek, M., Chen, Q., Silvia, P. J. (2018). Robust prediction of individual creative ability from brain functional connectivity. *Proceedings of the National Academy of Sciences, 115*(5), 1087.
6. Belden, A., Zeng, T., Przysinda, E., Anteraper, S. A., Whitfield-Gabrieli, S., & Loui, P. (2020). Improvising at rest: Differentiatingjazz and classical music training with resting state functional connectivity. *NeuroImage, 207*, 116384.
7. Berlyne, D. E. (1971). *Aesthetics and psychobiology.* . New York: Appleton-Century-Crofts.
8. Besson, M., & Faita, F. (1995). An Event-Related Potential (ERP) study of musical expectancy: Comparison of musicians with nonmusicians. *Journal of Experimental Psychology: Human Perception and Performance, 21*(6), 1278–1296.
9. Blood, A. J., & Zatorre, R. J. (2001). Intensely pleasurable responses to music correlate with activity in brain regions implicated in reward and emotion. *Proceedings of the National Academy of Sciences of the United States of America, 98*(20), 11818–11823.
10. Blood, A. J., Zatorre, R. J., Bermudez, P., & Evans, A. C. (1999). Emotional responses to pleasant and unpleasant music correlate with activity in paralimbic brain regions. *Nature Neuroscience, 2*(4), 382–387.
11. Brouwer, H., Crocker, M. W., Venhuizen, N. J., & Hoeks, J. C. J. (2017). A Neurocomputational model of the N400 and the P600 in language processing. *Cognitive Science, 41* (Suppl 6), 1318–1352.
12. Christoff, K., Gordon, A. M., Smallwood, J., Smith, R., & Schooler, J. W. (2009). Experience sampling during fMRI reveals default network and executive system contributions to mind wandering. *Proceedings of the National Academy of Sciences of the United States of America, 106*(21), 8719–8724.
13. Cirelli, L. K., Einarson, K. M., & Trainor, L. J. (2014). Interpersonal synchrony increases prosocial behavior in infants. *Developmental Science, 17*(6), 1003–1011.
14. Ding, N., Melloni, L., Zhang, H., Tian, X., & Poeppel, D. (2016). Cortical tracking of hierarchical linguistic structures in connected speech. *Nature Neuroscience, 19*(1), 158–164.

15. Donnay, G. F., Rankin, S. K., Lopez-Gonzalez, M., Jiradejvong, P., & Limb, C. J. (2014). Neural substrates of interactive musical improvisation: An fMRI study of 'trading fours' in Jazz. *PLoS ONE, 9*(2), e88665.
16. Fortenbaugh, F. C., DeGutis, J., Germine, L., Wilmer, J. B., Grosso, M., Russo, K., & Esterman, M. (2015). Sustained attention across the life span in a sample of 10,000: Dissociating ability and strategy. *Psychological Science, 26*(9), 1497–1510.
17. Fox, M. D., Snyder, A. Z., Vincent, J. L., Corbetta, M., Van Essen, D. C., & Raichle, M. E. (2005). The human brain is intrinsically organized into dynamic, anticorrelated functional networks. *Proceedings of the National Academy of Sciences of the United States of America, 102*(27), 9673–9678.
18. Friederici, A. D. (2002). Towards a neural basis of auditory sentence processing. *Trends in Cognitive Sciences, 6*(2), 78–84.
19. Gold, B. P., Pearce, M. T., Mas-Herrero, E., Dagher, A., & Zatorre, R. J. (2019). Predictability and uncertainty in the pleasure of music: a reward for learning? *The Journal of Neuroscience*, 0419–0428.
20. Goldman, A., Jackson, T., & Sajda, P. (2018). Improvisation experience predicts how musicians categorize musical structures. *Psychology of Music*, 0305735618779444.
21. Goodale, M. A., & Milner, A. D. (1992). Separate visual pathways for perception and action. *Trends in Neurosciences, 15*(1), 20–25.
22. Grahn, J. A., & Brett, M. (2007). Rhythm and beat perception in motor areas of the brain. *Journal of Cognitive Neuroscience, 19*(5), 893–906.
23. Grahn, J. A., & Brett, M. (2009). Impairment of beat-based rhythm discrimination in Parkinson's disease. *Cortex, 45*(1), 54–61.
24. Halwani, G. F., Loui, P., Rueber, T., & Schlaug, G. (2011). Effects of practice and experience on the arcuate fasciculus: Comparing singers, instrumentalists, and non-musicians. *Frontiers in Psychology, 2.*
25. Hickok, G., & Poeppel, D. (2007). The cortical organization of speech processing. *Nature Reviews Neuroscience, 8*(5), 393–402.
26. Hove, M. J., & Risen, J. L. (2009). It's all in the timing: Interpersonal synchrony increases affiliation. *Social Cognition, 27*(6), 949–960.
27. Huron, D. (2006). *Sweet anticipation: Music and the psychology of expectation* (1 ed., Vol. 1). Cambridge, MA: MIT Press.
28. Jacoby, N., & McDermott, J. H. (2017). Integer ratio priors on musical rhythm revealed cross-culturally by iterated reproduction. *Current Biology.*
29. Koelsch, S., Gunter, T., Friederici, A. D., & Schroger, E. (2000). Brain indices of music processing: "Nonmusicians" are musical. *Journal of Cognitive Neuroscience, 12*(3), 520–541.
30. Koelsch, S., Schroger, E., & Gunter, T. C. (2002). Music matters: Preattentive musicality of the human brain. *Psychophysiology, 39*(1), 38–48.
31. Kuperberg, G. R. (2007). Neural mechanisms of language comprehension: Challenges to syntax. *Brain Research, 1146*, 23–49.
32. Kutas, M., & Hillyard, S. A. (1980). Reading senseless sentences: Brain potentials reflect semantic incongruity. *Science, 207*(4427), 203–205.
33. Large, E. W., & Jones, M. R. (1999). The dynamics of attending: How people track time-varying events. *Psychological Review, 106*(1), 119.
34. Limb, C. J., & Braun, A. R. (2008). Neural substrates of spontaneous musical performance: An FMRI study of jazz improvisation. *PLoS ONE, 3*(2), e1679.
35. Loui, P. (2015). A dual-stream neuroanatomy of singing. *Music Perception, 32*(3), 232–241.
36. Loui, P. (2018). Rapid and flexible creativity in musical improvisation: Review and a model. *Annuals of the New York Academy of Sciences, 1423*(1), 138–145.
37. Loui, P., Alsop, D., & Schlaug, G. (2009). Tone deafness: A new disconnection syndrome? *Journal of Neuroscience, 29*(33), 10215–10220.

38. Loui, P., Grent-'t-Jong, T., Torpey, D., & Woldorff, M. (2005). Effects of attention on the neural processing of harmonic syntax in Western music. *Brain Research Cognitive Brain Research, 25*(3), 678–687.
39. Loui, P., Guenther, F. H., Mathys, C., & Schlaug, G. (2008). Action-perception mismatch in tone-deafness. *Current Biology, 18*(8), R331-332.
40. Loui, P., Li, H. C., & Schlaug, G. (2011). White matter integrity in right hemisphere predicts pitch-related Grammar learning. *NeuroImage, 55*(2), 500–507.
41. Loui, P., & Schlaug, G. (2012). Impaired learning of event frequencies in tone deafness. *Annals of the New York Academy of Sciences, 1252*(1), 354–360.
42. Loui, P., & Wessel, D. (2007). Harmonic expectation and affect in Western music: Effects of attention and training. *Perception & Psychophysics, 69*(7), 1084–1092.
43. Loui, P., & Wessel, D. L. (2008). Learning and liking an artificial musical system: Effects of set size and repeated exposure. *Musicae Scientiae, 12*(2), 207–230.
44. Loui, P., Wu, E. H., Wessel, D. L., & Knight, R. T. (2009). A generalized mechanism for perception of pitch patterns. *Journal of Neuroscience, 29*(2), 454–459.
45. Loui, P. (2012). Statistical learning—What can music tell us? In P. Rebuschat & J. Williams (Eds.), *Statistical learning and language acquisition* (pp. 433–462). Boston/Berlin: Mouton de Gruyter.
46. Loui, P., Wessel, D. L., & Hudson Kam, C. L. (2010). Humans Rapidly Learn Grammatical Structure in a New Musical Scale. *Music Perception, 27*(5), 377–388.
47. de Manzano, Ö., & Ullén, F. (2012). Activation and connectivity patterns of the presupplementary and dorsal premotor areas during free improvisation of melodies and rhythms. *NeuroImage, 63*(1), 272–280.
48. Martinez-Molina, N., Mas-Herrero, E., Rodriguez-Fornells, A., Zatorre, R. J., & Marco-Pallares, J. (2016). Neural correlates of specific musical anhedonia. *Proceedings of the National Academy of Sciences of the United States of America, 113*(46), E7337–E7345.
49. Martinez-Molina, N., Mas-Herrero, E., Rodriguez-Fornells, A., Zatorre, R. J., & Marco-Pallares, J. (2019). White matter microstructure reflects individual differences in music reward sensitivity. *The Journal of Neuroscience.*
50. Mas-Herrero, E., Zatorre, R. J., Rodriguez-Fornells, A., & Marco-Pallares, J. (2014). Dissociation between musical and monetary reward responses in specific musical Anhedonia. *Current Biology, 24*(6), 699–704.
51. Mason, M. F., Norton, M. I., Van Horn, J. D., Wegner, D. M., Grafton, S. T., & Macrae, C. N. (2007). Wandering minds: The default network and stimulus-independent thought. *Science, 315*(5810), 393–395.
52. Meyer, L. (1956). *Emotion and meaning in music.* University of Chicago Press.
53. Moore, E., Schaefer, R. S., Bastin, M. E., Roberts, N., & Overy, K. (2017). Diffusion tensor MRI tractography reveals increased fractional anisotropy (FA) in arcuate fasciculus following music-cued motor training. *Brain and Cognition, 116*, 40–46.
54. Nozaradan, S., Peretz, I., & Mouraux, A. (2012). Selective neuronal entrainment to the beat and meter embedded in a musical rhythm. *Journal of Neuroscience, 32*(49), 17572–17581.
55. Patel, A. D., Gibson, E., Ratner, J., Besson, M., & Holcomb, P. J. (1998). Processing syntactic relations in language and music: An event-related potential study. *Journal of Cognitive Neuroscience, 10*(6), 717–733.
56. Pearce, M. T., & Wiggins, G. A. (2012). Auditory expectation: The information dynamics of music perception and cognition. *Topics in Cognitive Science.*
57. Petkov, C. I., Kang, X., Alho, K., Olivier Bertrand, E., Yund, W., & Woods, D. L. (2004). Attentional modulation of human auditory cortex. *Nature Neuroscience, 7*(1), 658–663.
58. Pinho, A. L., de Manzano, O., Fransson, P., Eriksson, H., & Ullen, F. (2014). Connecting to create: Expertise in musical improvisation is associated with increased functional connectivity between premotor and prefrontal areas. *Journal of Neuroscience, 34*(18), 6156–6163.
59. Przysinda, E., Zeng, T., Maves, K., Arkin, C., & Loui, P. (2017). Jazz musicians reveal role of expectancy in human creativity. *Brain and Cognition, 119*, 45–53.

60. Purves, D., Cabeza, R., Huettel, S. A., LaBar, K. S., Platt, M. L., Woldorff, M. G., & Brannon, E. M. (2008). *Cognitive neuroscience.* Sunderland: Sinauer Associates, Inc.
61. Rabinowitch, T. C., & Meltzoff, A. N. (2017). Synchronized movement experience enhances peer cooperation in preschool children. *Journal of Experimental Child Psychology, 160,* 21–32.
62. Rauschecker, J. P., & Scott, S. K. (2009). Maps and streams in the auditory cortex: Nonhuman primates illuminate human speech processing. *Nature Neuroscience, 12*(6), 718–724.
63. Sachs, M. E., Ellis, R. J., Schlaug, G., & Loui, P. (2016). Brain connectivity reflects human aesthetic responses to music. *Social, Cognitive, and Affective Neuroscience, 11*(6), 884–891.
64. Saffran, J. R., Aslin, R. N., & Newport, E. L. (1996). Statistical learning by 8-month-old infants. *Science, 274*(5294), 1926–1928.
65. Salimpoor, V. N., van den Bosch, I., Kovacevic, N., McIntosh, A. R., Dagher, A., & Zatorre, R. J. (2013). Interactions between the nucleus accumbens and auditory cortices predict music reward value. *Science, 340*(6129), 216–219.
66. Salimpoor, V. N., Benovoy, M., Larcher, K., Dagher, A., & Zatorre, R. J. (2011). Anatomically distinct dopamine release during anticipation and experience of peak emotion to music. *Nature Neuroscience, 14*(2), 257–262.
67. Schultz, W., Dayan, P., & Montague, P. R. (1997). A neural substrate of prediction and reward. *Science, 275*(5306), 1593–1599.
68. Stupacher, J., Hove, M. J., Novembre, G., Schutz-Bosbach, S., & Keller, P. E. (2013). Musical groove modulates motor cortex excitability: A TMS investigation. *Brain and Cognition, 82*(2), 127–136.
69. Tal, I., Large, E. W., Rabinovitch, E., Wei, Y., Schroeder, C. E., Poeppel, D., & Zion Golumbic, E. (2017). Neural entrainment to the beat: The "missing pulse" phenomenon. *The Journal of Neuroscience.*
70. Terhardt, E. (1974). Pitch, consonance, and harmony. *The Journal of the Acoustical Society of America, 55*(5), 1061–1069.
71. Trainor, L. J., & Cirelli, L. (2015). Rhythm and interpersonal synchrony in early social development. *Annals of the New York Academy of Sciences, 1337*(1), 45–52.
72. Winkler, I., Haden, G. P., Ladinig, O., Sziller, I., & Honing, H. (2009). Newborn infants detect the beat in music. *Proceedings of the National Academy of Sciences of the United States of America, 106*(7), 2468–2471.
73. Witek, M. A. G., Clarke, E. F., Wallentin, M., Kringelbach, M. L., & Vuust, P. (2014). Syncopation, body-movement and pleasure in groove music. *PLoS ONE, 9*(4), e94446.
74. Zioga, I., Harrison, P. M. C., Pearce, M. T., Bhattacharya, J., & Luft, C. D. B. (2019). From learning to creativity: Identifying the behavioural and neural correlates of learning to predict human judgements of musical creativity. *NeuroImage*, 116311.

Psyche Loui is interested in the psychology and neuroscience of music perception and cognition. What happens in the brain when we create music? Loui is Director of the Music, Imaging and Neural Dynamics (MIND) Lab at Northeastern University, USA. She holds a Bachelor degrees in Psychology and Music and a certificate in Neuroscience from Duke University (Durham, USA) and a Ph.D. in Psychology the University of California Berkeley (USA). She has since held faculty positions in Psychology, Neuroscience, and Integrative Sciences at Wesleyan University, and in Neurology at the Beth Israel Deaconess Medical Center and Harvard Medical School, USA. Her research has received support from the US National Institutes of Health, National Science Foundation, Imagination Institute, and the Grammy Foundation. E-mail: p.loui@northeastern.edu.

Discovering the Neuroanatomical Correlates of Music with Machine Learning

Tatsuya Daikoku

6.1 Introduction

Music is ubiquitous in our lives yet unique to humans. The interaction between music and the brain is complex, engaging a variety of neural circuits underlying sensory perception, learning and memory, action, social communication, and creative activities. Over the past decades, a growing body of literature has revealed the neural and computational underpinnings of music processing including not only sensory perception (e.g., pitch, rhythm, and timbre) but also local/non-local structural processing (e.g., melody and harmony). These findings have also influenced Artificial Intelligence and Machine Learning systems, enabling computers to possess human-like learning and composing abilities. Despite plenty of evidence, more study is required for a complete account of music knowledge and creative mechanisms in human brain. This chapter reviews the neural correlates of unsupervised learning with regard to the computational and neuroanatomical architectures of music processing. Further, we offer a novel theoretical perspective on the brain's unsupervised learning machinery that considers computational and neurobiological constraints, highlighting the connections between neuroscience and machine learning.

In the past decades, machine learning algorithms have been successfully used in a wide variety of fields including automatic music composition and natural language processing as well as search engine development and social network filtering. Machine Learning implements probabilistic algorithms based on input data to make predictions in the absence of explicit instructions. There are various types of machine learning algorithms (e.g., supervised, unsupervised, and reinforcement learning), each of which gives computers a particular learning ability similar to the

T. Daikoku (✉)

International Research Center for Neurointelligence (WPI-IRCN), The University of Tokyo, 1130033 7-3-1, Hongo, Bunkyo-ku, Tokyo, Japan

e-mail: daikoku.tatsuya@mail.u-tokyo.ac.jp

© Springer Nature Switzerland AG 2021

E. R. Miranda (eds.), *Handbook of Artificial Intelligence for Music*,

https://doi.org/10.1007/978-3-030-72116-9_6

equivalent ability of the human brain. For this reason, these algorithms also enable machines to create interpretable models revealing the brain's learning and prediction mechanisms. This knowledge allows us to design brain-inspired Artificial Intelligence (AI), potentially leading to a harmonized society of humans and computers. For example, statistical learning theory is a framework for machine learning that has given neuroscientists some interpretable ideas contributing toward understanding the implicit learning mechanisms in the human brain [212]. Implicit learning is an "*unsupervised learning*" ability that is innately equipped in the human brain and does not require explicit instructions, intention to learn or awareness of what has been learned [194]. It is believed that the brain's (implicit) statistical learning machinery contributes to the acquisition of a range of auditory knowledge such as that related to music and language. Abundant evidence has suggested that statistical learning functions across different levels of processing phases in perception, memory consolidation, production (i.e., action), and social communication including music sessions and conversations. Recently, a growing body of literature has suggested that auditory knowledge acquired through statistical learning can be stored in different types of memory spaces through data transfer between the cortex and the subcortex and that this knowledge is represented based on semantic/episodic, short/long-term, and implicit/explicit (procedural/declarative) processing. This chapter reviews the neural correlates of these processes with machine learning in the framework of the statistical learning hypothesis, based on a large body of literature across a broad spectrum of research areas including Neuroscience, Psychology, and AI.

6.2 Brain and Statistical Learning Machine

6.2.1 Prediction and Entropy Encoding

The auditory cortex receives external acoustic information through a bottom-up (ascending) pathway via the cochlea, the brainstem, the superior and olivary complex, the inferior colliculus in the midbrain, and the medial geniculate body of the thalamus [154, 216, 259]. For auditory perception, our brain processes space information (originating from the tonotopic organization of the cochlea) and time information (originating from the integer time intervals of neural spiking in the auditory nerve) [189]. Importantly, the auditory pathway consists of top-down (descending) as well as bottom-up (ascending) projections. Indeed, it has been proposed that nuclei such as the dorsal nucleus of the inferior colliculus receive more top-down projections than bottom-up projections from the auditory cortices [119]. Furthermore, even within the neocortical circuits, auditory processing is driven by both top-down and bottom-up systems via dorsal and ventral streams [86]. Here, we focus on the top-down and bottom-up predictive functions of (sub)cortices within the framework of the statistical learning hypothesis.

The brain is inherently equipped with computing machinery that models probability distributions about our environmental conditions. According to the internalized probabilistic model, it can also predict probable future states and optimize both perception and action to resolve any uncertainty over the environmental conditions [215]. Predictive coding, currently one of the dominant theories on sensory perception [89], provides a neurophysiological framework of such predictive processes with regard to auditory functions. According to this theory, neuronal representations in the higher levels of the cortical hierarchies are used to predict plausible representations in the lower levels in a top-down manner and are then compared with the representations in the lower levels to assess prediction error; i.e., a mismatch between sensory information and a prediction [133, 191, 222]. The resulting mismatch signal is passed back up the hierarchy to update higher representations and evince better predictions. Over the long term, this recursive exchange of signals suppresses prediction error and uncertainty to provide a hierarchical explanation for the input information that enters at the lowest (sensory) level. In auditory processing, the lower to higher levels of this hierarchy could comprise the auditory brainstem and thalamus, the primary auditory cortex, the auditory association cortex, the premotor cortex, and the frontal cortex in that order. Thus perceptual processes are driven by active top-down systems (i.e., backward/inverse) as well as passive bottom-up systems (i.e., forward) in a perception–action cycle [90, 226, 275]. Thus, the processing of auditory data such as music and language subsumes a variety of cognitive systems including prediction, learning, planning, and action.

The brain's statistical learning mechanisms appear to agree with this predictive model [110]. Statistical learning is an unsupervised and implicit mechanism by which the brain encodes the probability distributions in sequential information such as music and language [30, 238, 239] and assesses the entropy of the distribution (i.e., the uncertainty of future states, being interpreted as the average surprise of outcomes sampled from a probability distribution) [112]. The brain also predicts probable future states based on an internal statistical model and chooses the optimal action to achieve a given goal [185, 188]. The role of statistical learning was first discovered in the lexical (word) acquisition process [238, 239], but an increasing number of studies has indicated that statistical or probabilistic learning also contributes to various levels of learning such as phonetic, syntactic, and grammatical processing. Statistical learning is a domain-general and species-general principle, occurring for visual as well as auditory information over a wide span of ages [241, 268] and in both primates such as monkeys [240] and non-primates such as songbirds [166, 167] and rats [276]. The statistical learning function is not limited to within the individual but can be expanded to communication between persons [253]. That is, two persons can share a common statistical model, resulting in the interplay between them [188]. Furthermore, the generation of culture [68] and musical creativity and individuality [37] can originate through the interplay of statistical learning. Thus, statistical learning is an indispensable ability in the developing brain that contributes to both music perception and production. Previous studies have shown that pitch prediction of novel melodies is closely linked to probability distribution sampled from a large corpus of music [207–209]. In addition, the brain can process chord sequences accurately and quickly if the predictability of a chord (local event) and the uncertainty of the preceding sequence of six chords (global harmonic phrase) are correlated with each other [272, 273]. Thus, the two levels of statistical learning (i.e., probability and uncertainty encoding) may not function independently but may rather be interdependent. Hansen and Pearce [109] have demonstrated that uncertainty perception in melody is stronger in musicians than in non-musicians. This suggests that long-term musical training allows the brain to optimize/generalize its probabilistic model of music which decreases uncertainty. Thus the development of statistical learning machinery in the brain is indispensable for the generalization of music structure, music proficiency, and predictive processing efficiency.

6.2.2 Learning

6.2.2.1 Timbre, Phoneme, and Pitch: Distributional Learning

Although plenty of statistical learning studies have focused on the lexical acquisition, statistical learning is also used to discover which phonemes, timbres, and pitch contours are important in a given language or in music [105, 148, 198]. It is of note that this type of statistical learning differs from that used in lexical acquisition: the statistics that are learned do not represent transitional probability but rather the distributional regularity of acoustic features (e.g., pitch and formant). This is often referred to as *distributional learning* [290]. Distributional learning has also been proposed as a machine learning algorithm in the framework of computational learning theory [178] although the algorithm differs from that used in psychological and neural studies. Prior to native language acquisition, infants discriminate between phonemes in many different languages regardless of phoneme categories. Through ample exposure to the sounds in their native language, however, they gradually abstract the features of the phonemes and contrasts through statistical learning of the distributional regularities in those sounds. Infants then generalize those features into the same phonetic category even if the phonemes occur at different articulations [173, 174]; thus they become unable to discriminate between phonemes that do not appear in their native language. In contrast, a prototypical phoneme of a native language acts as a magnet for similar phonemes (perceptual magnet effect) [147, 150]. In the end, the brain perceives that those similar phonemes belong to the same category as the prototypical phoneme [148].

6.2.2.2 Chunk and Word: Transitional Probability

Saffran et al. [238, 239] initially reported on human statistical learning ability in lexical acquisition. After four minutes of exposure to speech sequences in which three-syllable pseudo-words were randomly concatenated, infants discriminated the pseudo-words from non-words (non-words consisted of the same syllables but were sequenced in a different order from the pseudo-words). Because there were no cues (such as pauses, intonation, etc.) indicating word boundary information other than transitional probabilities between words, the results indicate that infants can learn words based on statistical learning of adjacent transitional probability. Several studies have demonstrated that statistical learning based on adjacent transitional probability is also indispensable for learning the sequential structures of musical pitches [241, 242], timbre [141], and chord sequences [45, 135]. Actually, this type of statistical learning has frequently been used in machine learning such as natural-language processing and automatic music composition [28, 223]; these models are referred to as *n*-gram or *n*th-order Markov models. The statistical learning that occurs during lexical acquisition has generally been assumed to represent the early stages of native language and music acquisition. Statistical learning based on local dependency (i.e., adjacent transitional probability) alone, however, may not be sufficient to account for all levels of music and language knowledge. In other words, music structures consist of both local and non-local (hierarchically organized and non-adjacent) dependencies. Some reports have indicated that different types of statistical or probabilistic learning can partially explain the acquisition of higher level structures such as syntactic processing [243, 254]. Indeed, in machine learning as well as in natural language processing, the n-gram models of words have been applied to generate artificial sentences (i.e., a word is recognized as one unit and a computer calculates the statistical relationships between words). It is, however, still debatable whether the human brain also performs the same underlying computation used in lexical acquisition to acquire syntactic structure, or whether the two processes tap into different mechanisms. In the next section, we review recent advances in exploring the underpinnings of syntactic learning mechanisms and how nonlocal/nonadjacent (i.e., long-distance) dependency interacts with adjacent dependency.

6.2.2.3 Syntax and Grammar: Local Versus Non-local Dependencies

The important question consists of how statistically chunked words are syntactically ordered and how nonlocal/nonadjacent (i.e., long-distance) dependency interacts with adjacent dependency. In many experimental paradigms, however, the processes of local dependency (e.g., musical expectancy formation between adjacent events) and non-local dependency (hierarchically organized musical structure building) have often been confounded (as is usually the case in real music and language). For example, in the sentence "The books on the desk are old," the plural verb form "are" corresponds to the plural subject "books" occurring several words earlier, creating a nonadjacent hierarchical dependency between "the books" and "are old." Learning such rules can be difficult because the adjacent singular form "desk" must be ignored. Analogous hierarchical structures are found in music. For example, in a wide variety of musical genres (but most commonly by far in Jazz), the subdominant—dominant—tonic progression is referred to as a two–five–one (II–V–I) progression is a common cadential chord progression. Jazz improvisers partially chunk harmony progressions to create the hierarchical structure of a larger phrase. Figure 6.1 shows an example of non-local dependency in a piece of Jazz music entitled *Misty* as played by Errol Garner (a simplified arrangement is shown).

Fig. 6.1 *Misty* by Errol Garner, composed in 1954. This is a simplified arrangement

As can be seen in Fig. 6.1, the chord names and symbols are also simplified (just major/minor, and 7th note) to account for the two-five-one (II–V$^{(7)}$–I) progression. In this phrase, the chord "IV" (E♭maj7) in the fourth measure corresponds to the chord "I" (E♭maj7) in the second measure occurring several chords earlier, creating a nonadjacent hierarchical dependency between the "I" and the "IV" in a recursive fashion. The local dependency between the first and second chords (E♭maj7–B♭m7) is less likely according to traditional music theory, but this second chord lays the groundwork for the non-local dependency between "I" and "IV" by generating a II–V–I progression (i.e., B♭m7–E♭7–A♭maj7). Another type of interaction can be seen in the latter half of the phrase (i.e., adjacent: II–V–VI–IV, non-adjacent: IV–I). Near the end of the piece, the higher hierarchy of the harmony structure "I–IV (–IV)–I" nests the lower hierarchy of the structures "II–V–I" and "II–V–VI–IV." Hofstadter [118] has also indicated that a key change embedded in a superordinate key forms hierarchical nonadjacent structures in a recursive fashion. Thus, composers generally design hierarchical nonadjacent structures in a recursive fashion, potentially using this technique to organize as much as an entire movement of a symphony or sonata [248]. Some researchers have proposed computational and generative models for such hierarchical structures in music; e.g., Generative Theory of Tonal Music (GTTM) by [158] and the Generative Syntax Model (GSM) by [232].

With respect to the question of how nonadjacent dependency interacts with adjacent dependency, categorization [125], non-adjacent (non-local) transitional probabilities [94, 211], and higher order transitional probabilities [38] may be key insights into generating advanced statistical learning models that are as similar as possible to those used for natural music and language processing. For example, humans can learn which words belong to certain categories such as nouns and verbs by tracking the similar contexts in which words of the same category appear and creating templates of possible sentence structures based on the statistical regularities of the ordering of these different categories, regardless of explicit (declarative) knowledge of labels on their categories [125, 153, 168]. For example, when the verb "drink" occurs, the models predict subsequent words referring to things that can be drunk. This hypothesis is partially supported by a behavioral study [105]. In this study, after exposure to novel grammatical and ungrammatical sentences, infants could discriminate between grammatical and ungrammatical sentences even when the individual words were exchanged for others in the same category. This generalization indicates that infants were not learning vocabulary-specific grammatical structures but rather abstracting the general rules of those grammatical structures and applying those rules to novel vocabulary [106]. Furthermore, Gomez demonstrated that both adults and infants can learn non-adjacent transitional probabilities of words [103]. This study also suggested conditions that might lead learners to focus on nonadjacent versus adjacent dependencies. Each learner was exposed to several types of pseudo-word streams (e.g., pel-wadim-rud and pel-kicey-rud). Each type of stream contained the same adjacent dependencies (e.g., P(wadim|pel) = P(kicey|pel) and P(rud|wadim) = P(rud|kicey)), so learners could distinguish among the languages only by acquiring data on dependencies between the first and third elements (the nonadjacent dependencies: P(pel|rud)). The size of the pool from which the middle words were drawn was systematically varied to investigate whether increasing variability (in the form of decreasing predictability between adjacent words) would lead to better detection of nonadjacent dependencies. The participants acquired non-adjacent dependencies only when adjacent dependencies were least predictable. That is, the adjacent elements were recognized as invariant when the adjacent transitional probabilities were high, whereas learners might seek alternative sources of predictability such as non-adjacent transitional probabilities when adjacent dependencies were lower. A similar finding has also been observed from a different viewpoint in a study on the order of transitional probability [42]. In this study, when the variability of transitional probability distribution was increased, participants focused on higher-order transitional probability. For example, in the sentence "the books on the desk are old" mentioned above, an increase in variability could lead to a shift in the statistical learning strategy from a lower order (e.g., first-order: P(are|desk)) to a higher order (e.g., fourth-order: P(are|books-on-the-desk)). In the end, the adjacent singular form "desk" does not have to be ignored when predicting the plural verb form "are" based on a higher-order transitional probability. In other words, "are" accompanied by "desk" (i.e., first-order transitional probability of P(are|desk)) is less likely and the uncertainty of predictability is high, whereas "are" accompanied by "books-on-the-desk" (i.e., first-order transitional probability of P(are|desk)) is likely and the uncertainty of predictability is low. Importantly, Shannon's information theory also offers evidence that a higher order transitional-probability distribution shows lower conditional entropy (i.e., uncertainty). Thus the order of transitional probability may partially represent the relationship between local and non-local dependencies [256]. It is of note, however, that composers sometimes design hierarchical nonadjacent structures, potentially even consisting of "entire" movements of music [248]. It may not be reasonable to create a transitional probability that is long enough and of a high enough order to cover an entire piece of music. In summary, many researchers have suggested a relationship between adjacent and non-adjacent dependency in syntactic structure, but the matter is still open to debate.

6.2.3   Memory

6.2.3.1   Semantic Versus Episodic

It has been suggested that semantic memory is partially acquired through statistical learning of episodic experience [4, 231]. In other words, an individual episodic experience is abstracted on a statistical basis to generate semantic knowledge that captures the statistical common denominator across experienced information [261]. This suggests that statistical learning underlying chunk formation and word acquisition consists in part of statistical accumulation across multiple episodes. On the other hand, an opposing statistical learning process appears to be happening simultaneously: semantic memory can be integrated to generate novel episodic memory through statistical learning [4]. This can be regarded as a syntactic process in contrast to chunking and the lexical process. Altman [4] has suggested that language learning (e.g., semantic tokens) requires a route from episodic experience to semantic representation (via abstraction), while language comprehension (e.g., grammar and sentences) requires a route from semantic to episodic representation. Thus it has been suggested that two interdependent processes should be incorporated to generate a complete account of statistical learning [270]:

(a)   Abstraction (chunking) of statistically coherent events from the input information (i.e., abstraction to generate semantic memory on lexicon
(b)   Comparison and integration between those chunked units (i.e., comparison between semantic memories to generate episodic memory on syntax).

6.2.3.2   Short-Term Versus Long-Term

Recent neurophysiological studies have demonstrated that the statistical learning effect is reflected in neuronal response even after short-duration exposure (5–10 min) [43, 78, 141]. Few studies, however, have investigated how long statistical knowledge can persist [63]. It has been suggested that statistical learning shares properties with artificial grammar learning [227] because of their implicit nature in memory [33, 212]. According to artificial grammar learning studies, implicit memory persists over the long term; as long as two years [3]. Considering its shared properties with artificial grammar learning, implicit memory acquired by statistical learning may also have both short-term and long-term properties. Indeed, some researchers have reported that statistical learning persists for at least 24 h [134]. Recent studies indicate that slow-wave sleep (SWS) contributes to the retention of statistical knowledge [59, 60]. Interestingly, memory consolidation could modulate the structure of short-term memory into different forms of long-term memory in which the information may be minimized, possibly to enhance information efficiency in long-term storage [52, 160]. Furthermore, it has been indicated that memory consolidation transforms implicit memory into explicit memory [73]. In the next section, we review recent studies on consolidation within the statistical learning framework and discuss how memory can be transformed by consolidation.

6.2.3.3 Consolidation

An initially acquired memory is labile and easily forgotten. To retain temporary but important memories over the long term, memory can be stabilized by the memory consolidation system in the brain. This memory consolidation process allows the brain to extract useful knowledge and discard (forget) irrelevant information, contributing to the efficiency of memory capacity in the brain [151]. It is still debatable, however, how the brain discriminates between important and irrelevant knowledge among the massive quantities of information it receives. Recent studies have proposed that the algorithm underlying the brain's memory consolidation will prove to be a key insight for improving the efficiency of information processing in machine learning [291] and understanding the links between neuroscience and machine learning [151].

Active Systems Consolidation (ASC), a leading theory of memory consolidation, proposes a two-stage model of memory consolidation across short- and long-term storage [52]. This model describes a way in which the brain's neuronal networks could overcome the stability–plasticity dilemma; i.e., how it could acquire new information (plasticity) without overriding older knowledge (stability) [81, 171, 176, 224]. The model assumes two types of memory stores: one serves as storage for fast and short-term learning and memory while the other serves as storage for long-term learning and memory. First, novel information is encoded in both stores. Then, the short-term memory is repeatedly re-activated in the fast-learning store. This processing is followed by re-activation in the long-term store to re-organize and strengthen the memory. Through these re-activations of novel information, the short-term learning store acts like an internal trainer for the long-term-learning store, allowing it to gradually adapt the novel information to the pre-existing long-term memories. This process also promotes the extraction of invariant repeating features from the new memories. These processes occur when there is no interference from novel information; i.e., during sleep. Neuronal studies have suggested that these two stores for short-term and long-term learning are reflected in the hippocampus and neocortex activities, respectively [59, 225]. On the other hand, whether memory consolidation merely passively protects memories from decay or actively refreshes memory representations remains an open question [62, 295]. The ASC posits that consolidation during both Slow-Wave Sleep (SWS), which is typically referred to as deep sleep and which consists of stages 3 and 4 of non-rapid Eye Movement (nonREM) sleep, and Rapid Eye Movement (REM) sleep promotes both quantitative and qualitative changes in memory representations [61, 286]. For example, through ASC, memory representation in the short-term space is consolidated and then re-organized in the long-term space. This consolidation also leads to chunking of the memory as a single unit, improvement of performance, and enhancement of novel and creative processing [287, 288]. The consolidated memory can be integrated into the network of pre-existing long-term memories [160], which allows the brain to generate creative information [284]. Furthermore, the consolidation facilitates the inference of relationships between distant (non-local) objects that had not been learned before sleep [61]. Together, the brain's consolidation system may give AI researchers new ideas to use in pursuing an innovative future machine learning algorithm; this will be discussed in more detail in Sect. 6.4.2.

6.2.4   Action and Production

Statistical learning also influences human actions and decision-making [91, 92, 185–187, 214, 252, 299]. Using sequential paradigms based on various-order Markov models, Karlaftis et al. [128] demonstrated that the brain alters its decision strategies and engages dissociable neural circuits in response to changes in statistics pertaining to the environment: the ability to extract exact sequence statistics relates to neural plasticity in the motor corticostriatal circuits, while the ability to select the most probable outcomes relates to plasticity in the motivational and executive corticostriatal circuits. The same study also provided evidence that learning-dependent changes in these circuits predict individual decision strategy. Statistical learning of motor and action sequences is partially supported by the chunking hypothesis [27], i.e., the hypothesis that learning is based on extracting, storing, and combining small chunks of information. Statistical knowledge formed in the cerebral cortex is sent to the cerebellum, which is thought to play important roles in procedural learning such as motor skill learning [120] and habit learning [90] as well as the generalization or abstraction of statistical knowledge [257] and prediction of sequences [159, 182].

6.2.5   Social Communication

Humans are more sensitive to the statistical regularities of action sequences between two persons than to those that occur within one person [186]. This implies that social–communicative interaction facilitates statistical learning [188]. Some evidence also suggests the importance of communication in the distributional learning of phonemes [148]. In these studies, infants who spent time in a laboratory with a native Mandarin speaker could discriminate among Mandarin but not among English phonemes, whereas infants raised under comparable circumstances who were exposed to English rather than Mandarin failed to discriminate among Mandarin phonemes [149]. This shows that, when infants are merely exposed to auditory speech sounds rather than engaged in social interaction, they cannot use the statistical cues included in the sounds. Hence, social and communicative interaction may allow infants to conduct statistical learning more effectively. Within the predictive coding framework, a recent study on human–robot interaction [192] likewise indicated that interacting with other individuals often increases prediction error, which can be minimized by executing one's own action corresponding to others' actions. Using robotic systems, Nagai and colleagues replicated developmental dynamics observed in infants. The abilities of self–other cognition and goal-directed action were acquired through updating an immature predictor through sensorimotor experiences, whereas imitation and prosocial behaviors emerged by executing the action anticipated by the predictor. Thus, social and communicative interaction modulates learning and prediction abilities in the developing brain and may be an important key to developing advanced machine learning algorithms similar to that used by the human brain.

6.3 Computational Model

6.3.1 Mathematical Concepts of the Brain's Statistical Learning

According to the statistical learning hypothesis, the brain automatically computes transitional probability distributions in sequences, grasps uncertainty/entropy in distributions, and predicts probable states based on its internal statistical models to minimize prediction error. Thus statistical learning includes at least two mechanisms:

(a) Probability encoding of each local event
(b) Uncertainty encoding of probability distribution.

The transitional probability is a conditional probability of an event B given that the latest event A has occurred, written as $P(B|A)$. From a psychological perspective, it can be interpreted as positing that the brain predicts a subsequent event B after observing the preceding events A in a sequence. Learners expect an event with a higher transitional probability based on the latest event A, whereas they are likely to be surprised by an event with a lower transitional probability. Entropy can be calculated from the probability distribution and used to evaluate the neurobiology of higher levels of predictive coding and statistical learning [110]. Conditional entropy has been defined as the average surprise (uncertainty) of an outcome [89]. Furthermore, the motivation to resolve uncertainty is sometimes interpreted as curiosity [127]. Curiosity can be regarded as the drive toward novelty-seeking behavior, which has often been evaluated by mutual information $I(X;Y)$ between hidden states (Y) and observations (X) [90, 146, 252, 294]. In general, mutual information is an information-theoretical measure of dependency between two variables. Mutual information corresponds to a reduction in entropy (uncertainty) about hidden states (Y) afforded by observations (X). According to psychological and information-theoretical concepts, mutual information means that the amount of uncertainty remaining about Y after X is known. The brain's prediction ability is correlated with mutual information (uncertainty reduction) [110]. When an observer is curious about sequential information, observation of an event X may lead to stronger (and correct) expectation of Y, resulting in an increase in mutual information (reduction in uncertainty). In contrast, a lack of curiosity about event X can be simply perceived as having no expectation of a subsequent event, resulting in less mutual information (increasing uncertainty). Several researchers have proposed advanced computational models for expressing a variety of brain functions such as reward system and action. The next section discusses these brain-inspired models in the framework of music and language statistical learning.

6.3.2 Statistical Learning and the Neural Network

Computational modeling has been used to understand the brain's statistical learning mechanisms [36, 210, 235, 292]. Although experimental approaches are necessary for understanding the brain's function in the real world, the modeling approaches partially outperform experimental results under conditions that are difficult to replicate in an experimental approach (e.g., long-term statistical variation over the decades within a person and across cultures). Computational modeling can also represent the relevant neural hardware in the sensory cortices [237, 279]. For example, the simple recurrent network (SRN), which is classified as a neural network and was first hypothesized by Elmer [64], learns sequential co-occurrence statistics through error-driven learning in which the gap between the predicted next input and the actual next input drives changes to the weights on its internal connections. The SRN [231] and a modified SRN [5, 53] implement a similarity space in which words referring to similar objects or actions were located more closely to one another than to words referring to dissimilar objects or actions. The neural network and deep learning such as Long-Short Term Memory (LSTM) [117], however, are not intended to serve as a model for the human episodic and semantic memory systems, although they proceed in this direction. Corpus-based approaches such as Hyperspace Analogue to Language (HAL) [168], Bound Encoding of the AGgregate Language Environment (BEAGLE) [125], and Latent Semantic Analysis (LSA) [153] are based on the abstraction of episodic information and encoding in a multidimensional semantic space. These models can also generate semantic similarity spaces in a similar way. For example, when the verb "drink" occurs, the models predict subsequent words referring to things that can be drunk. PARSER [213], Competitive Chunker [255], Information Dynamics of Music (IDyOM) [210], Information Dynamics of Thinking (IDyOT) [292], and other Markovian models including the n-gram and nth-order Markov models [37] incorporate the chunking hypothesis in which learning is based on extracting, storing, and combining small chunks of information. The Markov Decision Process (MDP) [91, 92, 214, 252], which has often been used for reinforcement learning in machine learning and robotics, extends the simple perceptive process by adding an active process (controlling predictability by choice, called 'policy') and rewards (giving motivation). The IDyOM is also an extension of the Markov model (i.e., the variable-order Markov model) for precisely modeling the statistical learning of musical sequences concomitantly combining several types of information such as pitch, duration, onset, scale degree, and so on. The IDyOT takes advantage of information theory to represent statistical learning mechanisms that cover both music and language [292]. This model implements semantic and episodic memory systems and captures the hierarchical learning process from lower to higher levels using boundary entropy: the spectrum of an auditory sequence is chunked into phonemes, then morphemes, then words [292].

Rohrmeier and Cross [233] compared the n-gram Markov, Competitive Chunker, and neural network SRN models to examine how each of these models simulates human implicit learning. They showed a strong learning effect for n-gram models and Competitive Chunker and a weaker effect for SRN. Their results suggest that the SRN and n-gram models represent the abilities of ordinary humans and those of music experts, respectively. These findings are important because they can provide useful information for devising an AI algorithm that simulates the development of learning ability in the human brain. It is of note, however, that such neural networks and deep learning [156] are inscrutable because some integrated components as opposed to independent components may be learned. The statistical (machine) learning model, on the other hand, is time-based and the learning effect is dynamically represented. Importantly, pitch prediction in novel melodies is closely tied with probability distribution sampled from a large corpus of music [207–209]. For example, the transitional probability between two pitches that are a whole-tone apart is higher than other transitional probabilities in Beethoven's piano sonatas [39], Jazz improvisation [37], and Bach's *Well-Tempered Clavier* [40, 41]. These properties are clearer when the order of transitional probabilities is higher (e.g., fifth-order transitional probability: $P(VI|I\text{-}II\text{-}III\text{-}IV\text{-}V)$, corresponding to $P(A|C\text{-}D\text{-}E\text{-}F\text{-}G)$ in C major [39]. The transition probability distribution of chords extracted from a corpus of Bach chorales also captures musical expectancy [234], showing, for example, that a tonic chord follows the dominant seventh chord with the highest transitional probability.

These statistical learning models have also been applied to neurophysiological experiments [38, 208–210, 296, 297], which have consistently indicated that neural activity is higher in response to stimuli with high information content (i.e., low probability) than in response to those with low information content (i.e., high probability), which is in keeping with the predictive coding hypothesis. Furthermore, these statistical learning effects are larger when humans are exposed to stimulus sequences with less information entropy (uncertainty) than when they are exposed to stimulus sequences with more information entropy [42]. This neural phenomenon is in agreement with the *Bayesian* hypothesis in which the brain encodes probabilities (beliefs) about the causes of sensory data and updates these beliefs in response to new sensory evidence based on Bayesian inference [58, 89, 131, 137, 196, 204, 205]. Hence, the statistical (machine) learning model can capture a variety of neurophysiological phenomena pertaining to statistical learning such as prediction and uncertainty. The next section reviews how these statistical learning models are reflected in neurophysiological activity based on the abundant neuroimaging literature.

6.4 Neurobiological Model

6.4.1 Temporal Mechanism

Electroencephalography (EEG) and magnetoencephalography (MEG) directly measure neural activity during statistical learning and represent a more sensitive method as compared to the observation of behavioral effects [141, 202]. When the brain encodes the probability distribution in a stimulus sequence, it expects a probable future stimulus with a high probability and inhibits the neural activity that would occur in response to that predictable stimulus. Finally, the statistical learning effect manifests as a difference in neuronal activity between predicable and unpredictable stimuli (Fig. 6.2). Studies on Event-Related Potentials (ERP) and

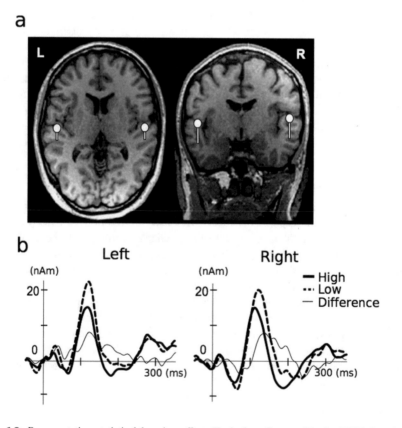

Fig. 6.2 Representative statistical learning effect. Equivalent Current Dipole (ECD) locations (dots) and orientations (bars) for auditory ERP (N1) responses superimposed on the magnetic resonance images (**a**) and the auditory statistical learning effects (**b**). Reprinted from [36–39] with permission

Event-Related Magnetic Fields (ERF) have suggested that statistical learning is reflected in:

(a) Early components, such as

- Auditory Brainstem Response (ABR) [260]

- P5 [45, 46, 202]

- N100 [43, 44, 95, 246]

- MisMatch Negativity (MMN) [78, 141, 183, 278]

(b) Late components such as:

- P200 [13, 35, 79, 95],
- N200–250 [78, 221]
- P300 [155]
- N400 [13, 34, 35, 77, 80, 246]

The suppression of the early components of responses in the lower cortical areas to auditory stimuli with higher transitional probabilities has been interpreted as the transient expression of prediction error that is suppressed by top-down predictions from higher cortical areas [38, 260]. Within the predictive coding framework, neuronal representations in the higher levels of cortical hierarchies predict plausible representations in the lower levels in a top-down manner and are compared with the representations in the lower levels to yield prediction error, usually associated with the activity of superficial pyramidal cells [133, 191, 222]. The resulting mismatch signal is passed back up the hierarchy to update higher representations (associated with the activity of deep pyramidal cells). This recursive exchange of signals suppresses prediction error at each level to provide a hierarchical explanation for inputs that enter at the lowest (sensory) level.

The brain computes the uncertainty/entropy of each probability distribution as well as the probability of each local event. The distinction between the uncertainty and probability encodings may partially be explained by the findings of ERP studies [143]. An early component called MMN (100–200 ms after stimulus onset) is typically elicited by deviant stimuli of oddball sequences and is not affected by explicit and prior knowledge about upcoming deviant stimuli [98, 229, 265, 293]. In contrast, a later component called P300 or P3 is elicited by novel stimuli rather than repeated deviant stimuli [87] and is reduced by prior knowledge of an upcoming syntactic deviant stimulus [230, 265]. This suggests that, if an upcoming stimulus is predictably unpredictable (i.e., the event has a low probability but the sequence has low uncertainty), the later rather than earlier components may be decreased. It has generally been considered that, as compared to earlier components, later components reflect higher levels of auditory processing such as semantic and syntactic learning [99]. Neurophysiological [56, 82] and computational studies [69] suggest that later components reflect a change in context or predictability. For example, N400 reflects a semantic meaning in language and music [142, 152, 274]. Thus, statistical learning's effect on N400 [13, 34, 35, 77, 80, 246] may support the hypothesis that semantic memory can be acquired through statistical learning [4, 231].

N400 and Early Anterior Negativity (EAN) components distinguishing between high and low transitional probability are also influenced by long-term musical experiences [79, 135]. It is widely known that Early Right Anterior Negativity (ERAN) has a larger amplitude in individuals with musical training [139]. ERAN can be elicited not only in harmony processing but also in melody processing [29, 180] and in rhythmic syntactic processing [264]. Importantly, random feedback including false and correct feedback regarding participants' detection of out-of-key tones in melodies may modulate ERAN [285], as could attention-driven changes in the confidence of predictions (i.e., uncertainty). A recent study offered evidence that long-term experience of music also modulates another earlier component called P50. In this study, the effects of statistical learning on P50 were larger in musicians than in non-musicians [202], suggesting that long-term experience may facilitate the prediction of each content type as well as the uncertainty of context. Hence, both the prediction of individual events and the uncertainty of the context can be reflected in many ERP components, but different levels of statistical learning may involve different ERP components.

Statistical learning is reflected in oscillatory activity as well as ERP/ERF. According to neurophysiological studies, low-frequency oscillations in the speech motor cortex track the envelope of the speech signal [203], while high-frequency oscillations dominate in tracking the fine structure of speech [100] and bottom-up processing [76]. Furthermore, in each frequency band, statistical learning and the chunking function control the coupling and synchronization between phase-locked neural oscillations and speech frequencies (e.g., ~ 20 Hz: phoneme, ~ 4 Hz: syllable, ~ 1 Hz: word and phrase) [9, 54]. This has also been suggested by simulations and models based on cochlea function [55, 157]. Furthermore, the N400 and phase-locked coherence (~ 1 Hz: word frequency) as semantic chunking effects can be detected in parallel [15]. Thus a number of electrophysiological experiments have shown that both oscillation and ERP/ERF represent statistical learning processes including probability and uncertainty encodings.

As shown in Fig. 6.2, when the brain encodes the transitional probability in an auditory sequence, it expects a probable future stimulus with a high transitional probability and inhibits the neural response to predictable stimuli. In the end, the statistical learning effects manifest as a difference in amplitudes of neural responses to stimuli with lower and higher transitional probability.

6.4.2 Spatial Mechanism

6.4.2.1 Domain Generality Versus Domain Specificity

It has generally been assumed that the networks that are instrumental in statistical learning involve a variety of brain areas including the neocortex, hippocampus, and corticostriatal systems [102, 176, 228, 247]. In other words, the neuroanatomical mechanisms of statistical learning are associated with both modality-general (e.g., hippocampus and striatum) and modality-specific processing (e.g., auditory: Superior Temporal Gyrus (STG) and Superior Temporal Sulcus (STS); visual: cuneus, fusiform gyrus) [193, 263]. Some studies have suggested that the sensory type of statistical learning modulates the cortical networks. For example, the neuronal system underlying audiovisual statistical learning is partly in common with and partly distinct from the unimodal networks of visual and auditory statistical learning, comprising the right temporal [236] and left inferior frontal sources, respectively [201]. That is, statistical learning essentially reflects contributions from domain-general mechanisms that share brain regions between different modalities yet are constrained to operate in specific modalities [93, 193, 263]. In terms of the two distinct types of statistical learning mechanisms (i.e., encoding probability and uncertainty, presumably corresponding to the prediction of local events and predictability of whole events, respectively), recent studies have consistently shown that the neocortex is likely to play an important role in probability encoding, while the hippocampus is thought to be associated with uncertainty encoding [110, 112, 271]. On the other hand, many other studies have implied that these two levels of statistical learning do not function independently but rather are interdependent [109, 272, 273].

6.4.2.2 Probability Encoding

According to findings obtained through functional magnetic resonance imaging (fMRI) [34], MEG [201], and near-infrared spectroscopy (NIRS) [1], the networks instrumental in statistical learning are associated with a variety of brain areas. For example, recent studies report contributions from motor areas including the Premotor Cortex (PMC) [34] and the primary motor cortex [299] as well as the superior temporal cortex including the STG [277] and the STS [66], areas for speech processing and forward prediction, respectively [116, 200]. The left dorsal stream including the superior temporal areas, auditory-motor areas, PMC, and prefrontal cortex plays an important role in statistical learning [65] in the contexts of infant speech and music processing [197]. The basal ganglia are also thought to be associated with chunk formation, which is underpinned by statistical learning [107, 245]. In particular, the striatum, which is part of the basal ganglia and thought to be associated with motivational circuits, has been proposed as a region implicating prediction [177, 219, 279]. Using sequential paradigms based on various-order Markov models, Karlaftis et al. [128] have demonstrated that individuals alter their decision strategies in response to changes in the statistics of their environments and engage dissociable circuits, extraction of exact sequence statistics is related to neural plasticity in the motor corticostriatal circuits, while the selection of the most probable outcomes is related to plasticity in the motivational and executive corticostriatal circuits. Karlaftis et al. [128] also provided evidence that learning-dependent changes in these circuits predict individual decision strategies.

Previous studies have also reported contributions from functional connectivity between the auditory and motor language networks, that is, from the link between the prefrontal cortex including the IFG and Broca's area, and that between the superior temporal cortex and Wernicke's area [165, 177]. It is important, however, to differentiate between local and non-local processing in prediction [50]. A growing body of literature claims that hierarchically organized (nested) non-local dependencies are processed in the pars opercularis of the posterior IFG corresponding to BA 44v [7], whereas the processing of local dependency violations is mainly associated with the ventral PMC [83, 85, 170, 199]. The ventral parts of Broca's area are involved in left- and right-hemispheric weighting in language- and music-syntactic processing, respectively [85, 170]. Furthermore, the ventral parts of Broca's area are involved not only in language- and music-syntactic processing but also in the hierarchical processing of action sequences [67, 138] and presumably in the processing of hierarchically organized mathematical formulas [88]. Music syntax has both local and non-local regularities. Therefore, there is no doubt that music-syntactic processing involves not only the IFG but also the ventral PMC [121, 206] and the STG [277]. The IFG and ventral PMC, however, are likely to contribute mainly to non-local and local processing, respectively. Dehaene et al. [50] have indicated that tree structures, which are used to explain hierarchical syntactic structures in language and music (e.g., context-free grammar) [113, 158], require a specific recursive neural code. Importantly, the processing of context-free grammar is available to humans but not to non-human primates [74]. Thus this type of processing may be unique to humans, which may explain the singularity of human language and music cognition.

6.4.2.3 Uncertainty Encoding

The mechanisms underlying uncertainty encoding are considered to be partially independent of those underlying prediction [112, 271]. For example, Medial Temporal Lobe (MTL) including the hippocampus [279, 280], and the lateral temporal region [34] including Wernicke's area [24] are considered to play roles in encoding uncertainty [110]. The interactive neuronal networks between prediction and uncertainty may be partially explained by the Complementary Learning System (CLS) [176], which is a model for the memory system in the neocortex and hippocampus. This model suggests that the neocortex contributes slow and long-term encoding of semantic memory based on statistical knowledge through smaller changes in connectivity within the neocortex, whereas the hippocampus contributes rapid, sparse, and long-term encoding of episodic memory through large changes in connectivity between the hippocampus and the neocortex as well as within the hippocampus [93].

6.4.2.4   Consolidation of Statistically Learned Knowledge

Many studies have suggested that neural replay in the MTL contributes to memory consolidation in the cortex [52, 184]. A previous study has demonstrated that, after 24 h of consolidation of statistical knowledge during sleep, the memory system is less dependent on the hippocampus and more dependent on the corticostriatal pathway and the planum temporale [59] in a process known as Active System Consolidation (ASC). That study indicated that, prior to consolidation, the striatum has greater connectivity with both the MTL and the ventromedial prefrontal cortex, whereas after consolidation the striatum is directly connected to the STG. The system of interaction between the hippocampus and the neocortex that is involved in statistical learning has also been discussed from the perspective of a different consolidation system that activates during development, between infancy and adulthood [60, 102, 266]. The ability to predict each type of content improved after 24 h consolidation in adults [60], whereas infants tend to show weak retention of statistical knowledge [102, 266]. Furthermore, infants' statistical knowledge is drastically altered by novel input [20], suggesting that infants, compared with adults, may encode statistical information in a noisier representation, and have more difficulty integrating novel input with pre-existing memory [269]. It has been suggested that the connectivity between hippocampal and other memory systems including the prefrontal cortex [104] develops more fully after two years of age [96]. Prior to two years of age, therefore, the networks that are instrumental in statistical learning involve the cortex, corticostriatal loop, and monosynaptic circuit of the hippocampus. Together, the previous studies suggest that the hippocampus–neocortex loop contributes to the consolidation of statistical knowledge. That hypothesis leads one to wonder how the consolidation networks between the MTL and the neocortex are related to the interactive system between uncertainty and prediction in statistical learning. Again, the CLS and ASC models suggest that the hippocampus plays an important role in the formation of novel episodic memory through rapid, sparse, and short-term encoding, whereas the neocortex contributes to slow and long-term encoding of semantic memory based on statistical knowledge [59, 93]. Thus, to retain a memory, the brain must consolidate a short-term memory in the hippocampus and shift it into long-term memory in the neocortex through the pathway between the hippocampus and the neocortex. Then novel input can be integrated into the consolidated memory without destroying it [160]. According to previous studies, the MTL contributes the abstraction in statistical learning [31, 144, 190] and uncertainty perception [110, 111, 279, 280]. This abstracted information is sparse and represents only a fragment of the whole, but is statistically important and enhances predictability under conditions of limited uncertainty (Fig. 16.1). In contrast, syntactic processing associated with the integration of semantic knowledge depends on neocortical areas including the language network; e.g., IFG, STG, etc. [84] as well as other areas associated with the integration of semantic knowledge, such as the medial prefrontal cortex [282] and the perirhinal cortex [267]. Thus, integration between pre-existing long-term information sent from the MTL through consolidation and novel input information may occur in the neocortex. Statistical knowledge may also be sent to the cerebellum which is thought to play important roles in generalization or abstraction, prediction of sequences [159, 182], motor skill acquisition [120], and transference into novel circumstances [257] to enable more efficient performance in a learned context. A previous study has suggested that the cerebellum, in conjunction with the pre-motor cortex, inferior parietal lobule, and medial occipital cortex, mediates the probabilistic inferences that guide decision-making under conditions of uncertainty [25]. The cerebellum as well as the hippocampus and the cerebellum-hippocampus network [11] may play a role in resolving uncertainty [132] to optimize action and prediction via statistical learning. An fMRI study [129] has suggested that, during statistical learning, participants with strong statistical learning effects of a familiar language on which they had been pretrained (e.g., their native language) exhibited decreased recruitment of the fronto-subcortical and posterior parietal regions, as well as a dissociation between downstream regions and the early auditory cortex. Some studies have indicated that IFG activity may reflect recognition of accumu-lated statistical information [129, 218]. This finding may suggest that, through long-term learning, the brain optimizes probabilistic models with less uncertainty in the long-term space in order to predict input information efficiently. In summary, these previous studies suggest that the dorsal stream (namely, the superior temporal areas, motor areas, PMC, and prefrontal cortex) plays an important role in the online prediction of each event during statistical learning. In addition, these net-works in the neocortex may interact with the functions of the basal ganglia through the corticostriatal pathway. In contrast, the hippocampus may serve as a short-term space associated with perceptive mechanisms of uncertainty. Furthermore, these two distinct systems are not independent but interdependent via the hippocampus-neocortex gateway, which contributes to memory consolidation from short-term to long-term memory.

Within the framework of CLS theory, Kumaran et al. [151] have also asserted the relevance of the hippocampus-neocortex interplay to the design of Artificial Intelligence, highlighting connections between neuroscience and machine learning. The CLS theory proposes two learning systems. The first gradually acquires structured knowledge representations in the neocortex while the second quickly learns the specifics of individual experiences in the hippocampus. Both the brain and AI systems benefit from the second system that stores specific experiences in the hippocampus. That is, once structured knowledge has been acquired in the hippocampus–neocortex networks, new consistent information can be rapidly integrated. The network replays memories stored in the hippocampus, contributing to the integration of new information into the neocortex [195]. It is thought that the replay of recent experiences occurs during offline periods (e.g., during sleep and rest). Furthermore, the hippocampus and the neocortex interact during replay [123]. This recurrent activation of multiple memories can be used to discover links between experiences, supporting generalization and memory-based reasoning. Thus this mechanism could support a variety of cognitive functions, including goal-related manipulation of experience statistics such that the neocortex is not a slave to the statistics of its environment [151]. The fast-learning hippocampal system can circumvent the general statistics of the environment by reweighting experiences that are of unequal significance. This mechanism may link the cognitive and machine learning models in that both operate by computing the similarity of a new input pattern to stored experiences, though the first is an exemplar model and the second is an instance-based model. On the other hand, the hippocampal replay of experiences can be modulated according to each experience's degree of surprise and its novelty, that is, its relative reward value (either positive or negative) and the amount of new informational content that it provides (e.g., its value in terms of reducing uncertainty about the best action to take in a given situation), acting to rebalance the general statistics of the environment [151]. Kumaran et al. [151] have also indicated that the hippocampus plays an important role in marking salient but statistically infrequent experiences, ensuring that such events are not swamped by the wealth of typical experiences but are instead preferentially stabilized and replayed to the neocortex, thereby allowing knowledge structures to incorporate this new information. Importantly, recent machine learning research has been inspired by the role of hippocampal experience replay within the framework of CLS theory. In AI research, experience replay stores experiences including state transitions, rewards, and actions, which are necessary for creating mini-batches to update neural networks and increase learning speed. For example, the implementation of an experience replay mechanism was crucial to developing the neural network called Deep Q-network (DQN). This neural network achieved human-level performance across a wide variety of Atari 2600 games by successfully harnessing the power of deep neural networks and reinforcement learning [181]. In machine-learning research, continual learning, which is the ability to learn successive tasks in a sequential fashion (e.g., tasks A, B, C) without catastrophic forgetting of non-local earlier tasks (e.g., task A), remains a fundamental challenge. This is believed to be a prerequisite to developing artificial agents that we would consider truly intelligent. A principal motivation for incorporating a fast-learning hippocampal system as a complement to the slow neocortical system was to support continual learning in the neocortex: hippocampal replay was proposed to mediate interleaved training of the neocortex (i.e., intermixed examples from tasks A, B, C). In sum, a number of recent studies have identified the neural correlates of music with machine learning. Actually, a number of AI models have been inspired by neural function in the human brain, and compose many genres of music as if human brain does. On the other hand, many computational and neurophysiological studies in music processing had mainly focused into optimal, likelihood, efficient problem-solving. However, the human brain often behaves inefficiently. For example, creative thinking such as music composition is a process by which we resolve an open-ended problem from a different perspective that has not been emerged before. In the next section, we propose future directions for interdisciplinary research in Neuroscience and AI for music processing.

6.5   Future Direction: Creativity

6.5.1   Optimization for Creativity Rather than Efficiency

The brain is generally motivated to optimize prediction and minimize uncertainty for information efficiency [89]. This uncertainty resolution results in rewards. Until the last few decades, many computational and neurophysiological studies in music processing had mainly focused on optimal, likely, and efficient solutions to specific problems. Yet these specific problem-solving approaches are not ideal for revealing how the brain deals with open-ended problems. For example, creative thinking such as music composition is a process by which we resolve a specific or open-ended problem from a different perspective that has not been encountered before. This mechanism has been broadly investigated in a variety of analyses of creative people [97], products [6], creative processes [258], and neuroimaging during creation [19]. For example, *motivation* is a key insight into understanding creativity from both neuronal and computational perspectives. Generally, motivation stems from two different sources: intrinsic and extrinsic motivation [251]. Intrinsic motivation is a drive originating inside an individual toward personal interest, satisfaction, goals, etc., whereas extrinsic motivation is a drive originating outside of a person toward external factors such as specific rewards, approval from others, etc. Although both extrinsic and intrinsic motivation increases creativity in certain cases, extrinsic motivation can sometimes impede creativity [220]. Excessively predictable patterns and very low uncertainty of information essentially give rise to boredom because they do not allow for the pursuit of curiosity rewards. A certain degree of uncertainty may be necessary to maintain curiosity about information and thus the motivation to learn it, given that uncertainty allows the brain to anticipate further rewards through the resolution of the unknown. That is, for sustainable curiosity and motivation, humans may seek a slightly suboptimal solution if it is afforded at a significantly low uncertainty. Recent studies indicate that fluctuations in uncertainty may contribute to esthetic appreciation of art and music [40, 41, 140] and that this phenomenon may encourage humans to create and learn new regularities [250]. This suggests that an algorithm optimizing not for efficiency but for creativity is an important goal in statistical learning (probability and uncertainty encodings) of creative information such as music. Creative information is not just pastiche and replication of previous information but is regarded as an artifact that is difficult to anticipate based on information that is already known.

Over the past decade, however, statistical learning mechanisms have essentially been discussed based on optimization of prediction and information efficiency at the lowest possible informational cost and uncertainty. Creativity, however, does not necessarily generate information-theoretically optimal, efficient, and certain information, but sometimes gives rise to uncertain, unpredictable information. We sometimes derive pleasure from prediction errors under conditions such as music listening due to our curiosity and our drive toward novelty-seeking behavior in connection with our anticipation of the resolution of uncertainties. That is, humans appear to seek certain forms of optimality between uncertain and certain situations through actions from which we expect to receive maximal curiosity rewards, and hence our actions give rise to increasing as well as decreasing uncertainty. Nevertheless, few studies have investigated how creativity interacts with the brain's statistical learning machinery including probability and uncertainty encoding. The next section reviews some computational literature on this challenging question from the viewpoint of the brain's functions including prediction, learning, memory consolidation, and intrinsic/extrinsic rewards systems. Then we discuss the neuroanatomical correlates of creativity and music with machine learning and statistical learning.

6.5.2 Cognitive Architectures

Until a few decades ago, computational modeling was mostly focused on seeking an optimal, likely, and efficient solution to a specific problem by a reductionist means. These problem-solving approaches, however, are not ideal for implementing divergent thinking as humans do. How to deal with open-ended problems is a contemporary challenge in AI studies. Computational creativity and Artificial General Intelligence (AGI) aims at breaking free from the problem-solving approaches [23] and instead of dealing with conditions where there is no solution and no problem. The Dual Process Theory of Intelligence has proposed two types of intelligence models that give rise to creativity [130]. One is a conscious and explicit process in response to a specific goal-directed thought. The other, in contrast, is an unconscious and implicit process of spontaneous cognition associated with implicit learning ability. Hélie and Sun [115] have also proposed the Explicit–Implicit Interaction (EII) theory of creativity as a unified theory of creativity. This theory, which attempts to integrate various fragmentary theories, consists of five basic principles:

(1) The co-existence of and the difference between explicit and implicit knowledge
(2) The simultaneous involvement of implicit and explicit processes in most tasks
(3) The redundant representation of explicit and implicit knowledge
(4) The integration of the results of explicit and implicit processing
(5) The existence of iterative (and possibly bidirectional) processing.

A cognitive architecture called Connectionist Learning with Adaptive Rule Induction On-line (CLARION) [115] computationally implements EII theory and simulates relevant human data. This work represents an initial step in the development of process-based theories of creativity encompassing incubation, insight, and various other related phenomena. For example, explicit knowledge can be encoded as directional associative rules that link chunks (of declarative knowledge), while implicit knowledge is learned by an algorithm related to standard backpropagation using both implicit and explicit networks. In the end, the given explicit knowledge affects the learned implicit knowledge.

Schmidhuber [250, 251] has proposed a theory of learning that affords creativity based on information theory. This theory indicates that creativity and curiosity are by-products of a computational principle for optimizing learning progress. That is, a human's acts afford a *"black box"* optimization through reinforcement learning that maximizes the extrinsic rewards for achieving a given goal. In this model, the intrinsic rewards, i.e., the so-called wow-effect, motivates creative behavior even if there is no specific goal. The agent keeps improving its performance over time because it is invariably predicting and encoding a growing history of actions and sensory information. A sudden improvement in data compression or computational speed, which can be measured as a decrease in computational cost at each time point (e.g., errors, time, number of required synapses, storage size), gives rise to the wow-effect. This effect finally becomes an intrinsic reward signal for the action selector. Thus, unknown (uncertain), novel, and regular information motivates the agent to perform continual, open-ended, active, creative exploration, whereas random data, already known (certain) information, and predictable patterns are essentially boring because they do not give rise to wow-effects and rewards. Recent computational studies on music have found that the conditional entropies (i.e., uncertainties) in Beethoven's music gradually increased [40, 41] with time over the composer's lifetime. These findings were prominent in higher-rather than lower order statistical learning models. Improvisational music also shows a similar phenomenon: lower order statistical learning models represent the general characteristics shared among musicians, whereas higher order statistical learning models detected specific characteristics unique to each musician [37]. These findings may suggest that higher rather than lower order statistical knowledge [36] may be more susceptible to the effects of long-term experience on the brain's probabilistic models and individuality of creativity. In sum, it is thought that new structured information may intrinsically motivate humans to discover the regularities. In response, they perform open-ended and creative exploration due to the absence of pre-established knowledge or instruction on the regularities. This behavior, however, may increase creativity and provide intrinsic rewards when the hidden regularity is finally detected. In terms of statistical learning, "how" and "when" the intrinsic motivation occurs during statistical (machine) learning appears to be a key insight into new frontiers for both neural and computational fields. In the next section, we discuss neuroanatomical mechanisms involved in creativity and music.

6.5.3 Neuroanatomical Correlates

In contrast to a large number of studies on statistical learning and memory, there are few neuronal studies on creativity based on statistical learning theory. On the other hand, behavioral and neuroimaging studies have begun to uncover mechanisms that give rise to novel ideas using various paradigms on divergent thinking, musical improvisation, poetry composition, and art production. Here, we review neural studies on creativity across several paradigms. Then, based on a number of previous findings across neuronal and computational studies, we hypothesize possible mechanisms of creativity within the statistical learning framework including prediction and uncertainty encoding.

6.5.3.1 Frontal Lobe

It is generally considered that frontal lobe function, which is involved in top-down control of executive function and decision-making [47, 57, 101, 114], is one of the most important keys to understanding creativity and statistical learning in the brain [75], although multiple neural networks also interact with each other [175]. For example, EEG [71, 72, 169] and fMRI studies [21, 22, 48, 49, 161] have examined brain activity during exposure to fixed melodies (less creative) or free-improvised melodies (more creative). The results indicate that more creative conditions lead to stronger alpha power [71, 164, 169] in the right frontal and parietal regions [72]. The increased oscillatory activity in the alpha band is considered to reflect inhibition of the top-down process [136] and the dorsal stream [124]. Other studies, in contrast, have suggested that alpha power reflects internally oriented attention in which external bottom-up stimulation is suppressed [70]. One study that investigated both the neural and genetic correlates of creativity has suggested that a system of interaction between strong top-down and weak bottom-up processes underpins creativity, which is modulated by competition between the glutamate and GABA neurotransmitter systems [163]. Furthermore, a computational model [32] inspired the hypothesis that the frontal lobes create an expanding repertoire of flexible behavioral strategies for driving action in uncertain, changing, and open-ended environments and suggested that frontal lobe function including executive control and decision-making supports integration between reasoning, learning, and creativity through uncertainty monitoring. Green et al. [108] have also suggested that neural activity in the frontopolar cortex facilitates creative intelligence. The contradiction between these two opposing findings on inhibition and enhancement of top-down control may be explained by the different tasks set in the different studies [2]. In fMRI studies [217], however, improvisation using a defined pitch set resulted in activation of the dorsolateral Prefrontal Cortex (dlPFC) because participants had to maintain available note choices in the working memory, whereas free improvisation leads to the deactivation of the dlPFC because participants are able to take advantage of their implicit learning systems to create improvisations in which top-down control from the dlPFC would be disadvantageous [51]. Using fMRI, Liu et al. [162] have examined brain mechanisms during poetry composition and the assessment (revision) process. The results indicated that dlPFC activity was attenuated during composition and re-engaged during revision, whereas the Medial Prefrontal Cortex (MPFC), which is associated with multiple cognitive functions such as motivation [145] and unconscious decision-making [262], was active during both phases. Furthermore, expert poets showed significantly stronger deactivation of the dlPFC during composition but no significant difference in activity of the MPFC. Thus expert poets may more effectively suspend top-down control while maintaining their motivation. Together, these findings show that open-ended creative behaviors may suppress top-down controls as expressed through dlPFC activity level while maintaining motivation as expressed through MPFC activity level, whereas fixed behaviors enhance top-down control.

6.5.3.2 Cerebellum

The cerebellum as well as the frontal lobe is known to be an important area in creativity. de Manzano and Ullen [48] found that rhythmic improvisation enhanced connectivity between the Supplementary Motor Area (SMA) and the cerebellum. Furthermore, the cerebellum [244] and the caudate, which is part of the striatum [18, 122], also contribute to creative cognition. Vandervert et al. [283] have explained how the frontal lobes and the cerebellum collaborate to produce creativity. The cerebellum adaptively models all movement and thought [249]. The cerebellum's adaptive models then forward this information to the frontal lobes' working memory which it uses in its control processes [179]. Frontal lobe function then leads to idea generation [283]. Furthermore, the temporal lobe, as a region where idea editing and evaluation occurs [75], triggers creative insight or the "aha" experience [126]. This hypothesis may be partially supported by computational studies [250, 251]. Due to the improvements in performance speed and efficiency and the reduction of uncertainty that occur through repetitive mental prototyping in the cerebro-cerebellar blending process, the human brain receives intrinsic rewards in the form of the so-called wow-effect, which then motivates further creative behavior. Furthermore, statistical learning studies have also suggested that statistical knowledge can be sent to the cerebellum for more efficient performance in a learned context [257]. The cerebellum, in conjunction with the premotor cortex, inferior parietal lobule, and medial occipital cortex, mediates the probabilistic inferences under the control of uncertainty [11, 25, 132].

6.5.3.3 Neural Network

Recently, to explain the dynamics of creativity processes, three types of neuronal networks have been proposed [19]. One is the Default Mode Network (DMN), which consists of the cortical midline and posterior inferior parietal regions and contributes to idea generation via flexible, spontaneous, and self-generated thought involved in mental simulation [298], mind-wandering [172], social cognition, and episodic future thinking. A second proposed network is the Executive Control Network (ECN), which consists of the lateral prefrontal and anterior inferior parietal regions and plays a role in idea evaluation through involvement in cognitive processes that require externally directed attention, working memory, and relational integration [17]. The third is the Salience Network (SN), which consists of the bilateral insula and anterior cingulate cortex and which underpins the dynamic transitions between DMN and ECN [281] and forwards candidate ideas originating from the DMN to the ECN for high-order processing such as idea evaluation, elaboration, or revision [16, 17, 19]. Thus, creative behaviors may involve an interaction between an automatic bottom-up process (DMN) that supplies possible choices and a top-down control process (ECN) that guides those choices according to hierarchical rules [16, 17]. The ECN [10] and the DMN [172] have also been considered to contribute to mind-wandering, which is important for many mental functions such as future planning [14] and creativity [12]. Using a divergent-thinking task, a recent study [16] reported that coupling between the DMN and the SN preceded coupling between the DMN and the ECN, suggesting dynamic shifts in idea generation and evaluation. They also indicated that more creative participants showed higher global efficiency within a network; i.e., a smaller number of paths to traverse between brain regions). This suggests that communication efficiency is higher in more creative people. Interestingly, a recent study has suggested that the hippocampus, which is thought to be related to uncertainty, is linked to the DMN [289]. Thus, it is hypothesized that uncertainty perception and divergent thinking are interdependent with each other. It has generally been considered that the DMN and the ECN usually do not work concurrently [8]. A recent study, however, has demonstrated that creative people have the ability to simultaneously engage these large-scale brain networks [19, 26]. This suggests that individual variation in the ability to simultaneously engage the DMN, ECN, and SN can be a neurophysiological marker of creativity.

In summary, the brain is equipped with unsupervised statistical learning machinery that makes Bayesian predictions without explicit instructions. For this reason, AI algorithms also enable machines to create interpretable models representing the brain's methods of prediction, learning, and memory consolidation in music and language acquisition. These machine learning models, however, are still unable to account for all levels of music and language learning including hierarchically organized and non-local regularities. It also remains an open question how the unsupervised statistical learning machinery in the human brain gives rise to creative information. Hence, an algorithm optimizing not for efficiency but for creativity is a key option to pursue to improve music processing both by the brain and by computers. To understand how and when creativity originates through learning processes, the future interdisciplinary study is needed to verify the present conclusions from both computational and neuronal perspectives.

6.6 Concluding Remarks

A body of studies demonstrated that the brain makes Bayesian predictions without explicit instructions: unsupervised learning. The AI algorithms also enable machines to create interpretable models revealing the brain's predictive and learning function. Nonetheless, it remains unknown how our brains produce creative and innovative ideas, which are an essential capacity unique to natural intelligence and which have recently been an important and challenging topic for advanced machine learning algorithms as they attempt to break free from the specific problem-solving approaches that have been a mainstream of AI. Given that composers do not observe their own brains' activity in writing music, music itself does not necessarily require input from the fields of neuroscience and computing. Yet music offers (computational) neuroscientists a new perspective from which to explore a wide range of the brain's natural intelligence including idea generation and to devise creative machine learning algorithms that can resolve open-ended problems.

In sum, further research is required to generate a complete explanation of music knowledge both in the human brain and in computers. One of the key questions for future research will be how local dependency (e.g., musical expectancy formation between adjacent events) interacts with non-local dependency (hierarchically organized musical structure building) in the computation of music, and whether these interactions can explain both AI models' and the brain's function. A second key question is how music processing benefits from ubiquitous (domain-general) phenomena such as curiosity, creativity, and reward systems. Statistical learning essentially reflects contributions from domain-general mechanisms that share brain regions between different modalities (e.g., auditory, visual, and somatosensory) but are constrained to operate in their respective specific modalities. A third key question is how and when unsupervised statistical learning machinery such as that in the brain computationally and neurophysiologically gives rise to creative information. Creativity is part of human nature and is an important ability for advanced machine learning algorithms that are expected to imitate the human brain. Hence, an algorithm that is optimized not for efficiency but rather for creativity may be a key step toward a complete account of music knowledge both in the brain and in computers, potentially leading to a harmonized society of humans and computers. Here, we offer a novel theoretical perspective on statistical learning, highlighting the connections between Neuroscience and Machine Learning.

Acknowledgements This chapter was supported by Suntory Foundation. The funders had no role in decision to publish and preparation of the manuscript.

References

1. Abla, D., & Okanoya, K. (2008). Statistical segmentation of tone sequences activates the left inferior frontal cortex: A near-infrared spectroscopy study. *Neuropsychologia, 46*(11), 2787–2795. https://doi.org/10.1016/j.neuropsychologia.2008.05.012.
2. Adhikari, B. M., Norgaard, M., Quinn, K. M., Ampudia, J., Squirek, J., & Dhamala, M. (2016). The brain network underpinning novel melody creation. *Brain Connectivity, 6*(10), 772–785. https://doi.org/10.1089/brain.2016.0453.
3. Allen, R., & Reber, A. S. (1980). Very long term memory for tacit knowledge. *Cognition, 8* (2), 175–185. https://doi.org/10.1016/0010-0277(80)90011-6.
4. Altmann, G. (2017). Abstraction and generalization in statistical learning: Implications for the relationship between semantic types and episodic tokens. *Philosophical Transactions of the Royal Society B: Biological Sciences, 372*(1711). https://doi.org/10.1098/rstb.2016.0060.
5. Altmann, G. T. (1999). Rule learning by seven-month-old infants and neural networks. *Science, 284*(5416), 875a–875. https://doi.org/10.1126/science.284.5416.875a.
6. Amabile, T. (1996). *Creativity in context.* CO: Westview Press.
7. Amunts, K., Lenzen, M., Friederici, A. D., Schleicher, A., Morosan, P., Palomero-Gallagher, N., & Zilles, K. (2010). Broca's region: Novel organizational principles and multiple receptor mapping. *PLOS Biology, 8*(9), e1000489. https://doi.org/10.1371/journal.pbio.1000489.

8. Anticevic, A., Cole, M. W., Murray, J. D., Corlett, P. R., Wang, X.-J., & Krystal, J. H. (2012). The role of default network deactivation in cognition and disease. *Trends in Cognitive Sciences, 16*(12), 584–592. https://doi.org/10.1016/j.tics.2012.10.008.

9. Assaneo, M. F., Ripollés, P., Orpella, J., Lin, W. M., de Diego-Balaguer, R., & Poeppel, D. (2019). Spontaneous synchronization to speech reveals neural mechanisms facilitating language learning. *Nature Neuroscience, 22*(4), 627–632. https://doi.org/10.1038/s41593-019-0353-z.

10. Axelrod, V., Rees, G., Lavidor, M., & Bar, M. (2015). Increasing propensity to mind-wander with transcranial direct current stimulation. *Proceedings of the National Academy of Sciences, 112*(11), 3314–3319. https://doi.org/10.1073/pnas.1421435112.

11. Babayan, B. M., Watilliaux, A., Viejo, G., Paradis, A.-L., Girard, B., & Rondi-Reig, L. (2017). A hippocampo-cerebellar centred network for the learning and execution of sequence-based navigation. *Scientific Reports, 7*(1), 17812. https://doi.org/10.1038/s41598-017-18004-7.

12. Baird, B., Smallwood, J., Mrazek, M. D., Kam, J. W. Y., Franklin, M. S., & Schooler, J. W. (2012). Inspired by distraction: Mind wandering facilitates creative incubation. *Psychological Science, 23*(10), 1117–1122. https://doi.org/10.1177/0956797612446024.

13. Balaguer, R. D. D., Toro, J. M., Rodriguez-fornells, A., Psicologia, F. De, Barcelona, U. De, & Hospital, H. M. (2007). *Different neurophysiological mechanisms underlying word and rule extraction from speech.* (11). https://doi.org/10.1371/journal.pone.0001175.

14. Bar, M. (2009). The proactive brain: Memory for predictions. *Philosophical Transactions of the Royal Society of London. Series B, Biological Sciences, 364*(1521), 1235–1243. https://doi.org/10.1098/rstb.2008.0310.

15. Batterink, L. J., & Paller, K. A. (2017). Online neural monitoring of statistical learning. *Cortex.* https://doi.org/10.1016/j.cortex.2017.02.004.

16. Beaty, R. E., Benedek, M., Barry Kaufman, S., & Silvia, P. J. (2015). Default and executive network coupling supports creative idea production. *Scientific Reports, 5*, 10964. https://doi.org/10.1038/srep10964.

17. Beaty, R. E., Benedek, M., Silvia, P. J., & Schacter, D. L. (2016). Creative cognition and brain network dynamics. *Trends in Cognitive Sciences, 20*(2), 87–95. https://doi.org/10.1016/j.tics.2015.10.004.

18. Beaty, R. E., Christensen, A. P., Benedek, M., Silvia, P. J., & Schacter, D. L. (2017). Creative constraints: Brain activity and network dynamics underlying semantic interference during idea production. *NeuroImage, 148*(January), 189–196. https://doi.org/10.1016/j.neuroimage.2017.01.012.

19. Beaty, R. E., Kenett, Y. N., Christensen, A. P., Rosenberg, M. D., Benedek, M., Chen, Q., & Silvia, P. J. (2018). Robust prediction of individual creative ability from brain functional connectivity. *Proceedings of the National Academy of Sciences, 7*, 201713532. https://doi.org/10.1073/pnas.1713532115.

20. Benavides-Varela, S., Gómez, D. M., Macagno, F., Bion, R. A. H., Peretz, I., & Mehler, J. (2011). Memory in the neonate brain. *PLOS ONE, 6*(11), e27497. https://doi.org/10.1371/journal.pone.0027497.

21. Bengtsson, S. L., Csíkszentmihályi, M., & Ullén, F. (2007). Cortical regions involved in the generation of musical structures during improvisation in pianists. *Journal of Cognitive Neuroscience, 19*(5), 830–842. https://doi.org/10.1162/jocn.2007.19.5.830.

22. Berkowitz, A. L., & Ansari, D. (2008). Generation of novel motor sequences: The neural correlates of musical improvisation. *NeuroImage, 41*(2), 535–543. https://doi.org/10.1016/j.neuroimage.2008.02.028.

23. Besold, T., Schorlemmer, M., & Smaill, A. (2015). *Computational creativity research: Towards creative machines* (Atlantis T). Atlantis Press.

24. Bischoff-Grethe, A., Proper, S. M., Mao, H., Daniels, K. A., & Berns, G. S. (2000). Conscious and unconscious processing of nonverbal predictability in Wernicke's area. *The Journal of Neuroscience, 20*(5), 1975–1981. https://doi.org/10.1523/jneurosci.5501-05.2006.

25. Blackwood, N., ffytche, D., Simmons, A., Bentall, R., Murray, R., & Howard, R. (2004). The cerebellum and decision making under uncertainty. *Cognitive Brain Research, 20*(1), 46–53. https://doi.org/10.1016/j.cogbrainres.2003.12.009.

26. Boccia, M., Piccardi, L., Palermo, L., Nori, R., & Palmiero, M. (2015). Where do bright ideas occur in ourbrain? Meta-analytic evidence from neuroimaging studies of domain-specific creativity. *Frontiers in Psychology, 6*(AUG), 1–12. https://doi.org/10.3389/fpsyg.2015.01195.

27. Boyd, L. A., Edwards, J. D., Siengsukon, C. S., Vidoni, E. D., Wessel, B. D., & Linsdell, M. A. (2009). Motor sequence chunking is impaired by basal ganglia stroke. *Neurobiology of Learning and Memory, 92*(1), 35–44. https://doi.org/10.1016/j.nlm.2009.02.009.

28. Brent, M. R. (1999). Speech segmentation and word discovery: A computational perspective. *Trends in Cognitive Sciences, 3*(8), 294–301. https://doi.org/10.1016/S1364-6613(99)01350-9.

29. Carrus, E., Pearce, M. T., & Bhattacharya, J. (2013). Melodic pitch expectation interacts with neural responses to syntactic but not semantic violations. *Cortex, 49*(8), 2186–2200. https://doi.org/10.1016/j.cortex.2012.08.024.

30. Cleeremans, A., Destrebecqz, A., & Boyer, M. (1998). Implicit learning: News from the front. *Trends in Cognitive Sciences, 2*(10), 406–416. https://doi.org/10.1016/S1364-6613(98)01232-7.

31. Cohen, N., & Eichenbaum, H. (1993). *Memory, amnesia, and the hippocampal system.* Cambridge, MA: MIT Press.

32. Collins, A., & Koechlin, E. (2012). Reasoning, learning, and creativity: Frontal lobe function and human decision-making. *PLoS Biology, 10*(3). https://doi.org/10.1371/journal.pbio.1001293.

33. Conway, C. M., & Christiansen, M. H. (2006). *Pages from Revista—Corpo a Corpo—2007-11-8.pdf. 17*(10), 905–912.

34. Cunillera, T., Càmara, E., Toro, J. M., Marco-pallares, J., Sebastián-galles, N., Ortiz, H., et al. (2009). NeuroImage time course and functional neuroanatomy of speech segmentation in adults. *NeuroImage, 48*(3), 541–553. https://doi.org/10.1016/j.neuroimage.2009.06.069.

35. Cunillera, T., Toro, J. M., Sebastián-gallés, N., & Rodríguez-fornells, A. (2006). *The effects of stress and statistical cues on continuous speech segmentation: An event-related brain potential study. 3.* https://doi.org/10.1016/j.brainres.2006.09.046.

36. Daikoku, T. (2018a). Entropy. *Uncertainty, and the depth of implicit knowledge on musical creativity: Computational study of improvisation in melody and rhythm. 12*(December), 1–11. https://doi.org/10.3389/fncom.2018.00097.

37. Daikoku, T. (2018b). Musical creativity and depth of implicit knowledge: Spectral and temporal individualities in improvisation. *Frontiers in Computational Neuroscience, 12* (November), 1–27. https://doi.org/10.3389/fncom.2018.00089.

38. Daikoku, T. (2018c). Neurophysiological markers of statistical learning in music and language: Hierarchy, entropy, and uncertainty. *Brain Sciences, 8*(6). https://doi.org/10.3390/brainsci8060114.

39. Daikoku, T. (2018d). Time-course variation of statistics embedded in music: Corpus study on implicit learning and knowledge. *PLoS ONE, 13*(5). https://doi.org/10.1371/journal.pone.0196493.

40. Daikoku, T. (2019). Depth and the uncertainty of statistical knowledge on musical creativity fluctuate over a composer's lifetime. *Frontiers in computational neuroscience, 13*, 27.

41. Daikoku, T. (2019). Tonality tunes the statistical characteristics in music: Computational approaches on statistical learning. *Frontiers in Computational Neuroscience, 13*, 70. https://www.frontiersin.org/article/10.3389/fncom.2019.00070.

42. Daikoku, T., Okano, T., & Yumoto, M. (2017). Relative difficulty of auditory statistical learning based on tone transition diversity modulates chunk length in the learning strategy. In *Proceedings of the Biomagnetic*, Sendai, Japan, 22–24 May (p.75). https://doi.org/10.1016/j.nlm.2014.11.001.

43. Daikoku, T., Yatomi, Y., & Yumoto, M. (2014). Implicit and explicit statistical learning of tone sequences across spectral shifts. *Neuropsychologia, 63*. https://doi.org/10.1016/j.neuropsychologia.2014.08.028.
44. Daikoku, T., Yatomi, Y., & Yumoto, M. (2015). Statistical learning of music- and language-like sequences and tolerance for spectral shifts. *Neurobiology of Learning and Memory, 118*. https://doi.org/10.1016/j.nlm.2014.11.001.
45. Daikoku, T., Yatomi, Y., & Yumoto, M. (2016). Pitch-class distribution modulates the statistical learning of atonal chord sequences. *Brain and Cognition, 108*. https://doi.org/10.1016/j.bandc.2016.06.008.
46. Daikoku, T., & Yumoto, M. (2017). Single, but not dual, attention facilitates statistical learning of two concurrent auditory sequences. *Scientific Reports, 7*(1). https://doi.org/10.1038/s41598-017-10476-x.
47. Dalley, J. W., Everitt, B. J., & Robbins, T. W. (2011). Impulsivity, compulsivity, and top-down cognitive control. *Neuron, 69*(4), 680–694. https://doi.org/10.1016/j.neuron.2011.01.020.
48. de Manzano, Ö., & Ullén, F. (2012). Activation and connectivity patterns of the presupplementary and dorsal premotor areas during free improvisation of melodies and rhythms. *NeuroImage, 63*(1), 272–280. https://doi.org/10.1016/j.neuroimage.2012.06.024.
49. de Manzano, Ö., & Ullén, F. (2012). Goal-independent mechanisms for free response generation: Creative and pseudo-random performance share neural substrates. *NeuroImage, 59*(1), 772–780. https://doi.org/10.1016/j.neuroimage.2011.07.016.
50. Dehaene, S., Meyniel, F., Wacongne, C., Wang, L., & Pallier, C. (2015). Perspective the neural representation of sequences: From transition probabilities to algebraic patterns and linguistic trees. *Neuron, 88*(1), 2–19. https://doi.org/10.1016/j.neuron.2015.09.019.
51. Dhakal, K., Norgaard, M., Adhikari, B. M., Yun, K. S., & Dhamala, M. (2019). Higher node activity with less functional connectivity during musical improvisation. *Brain Connectivity*. https://doi.org/10.1089/brain.2017.0566.
52. Diekelmann, S., & Born, J. (2010). The memory function of sleep. *Nature Reviews Neuroscience, 11*(2), 114–126. https://doi.org/10.1038/nrn2762.
53. Dienes, Z., Altmann, G., & Gao, S. (1999). Mapping model across domains a neural feedback: Network of implicit of transfer of implicit knowledge. *Cognitive Science, 23*(1), 53–82.
54. Ding, N., Melloni, L., Zhang, H., Tian, X., & Poeppel, D. (2016). Cortical tracking of hierarchical linguistic structures in connected speech. *Nature Neuroscience, 19*(1), 158–164. https://doi.org/10.1038/nn.4186.
55. Ding, N., Patel, A. D., Chen, L., Butler, H., Luo, C., & Poeppel, D. (2017). Temporal modulations in speech and music. *Neuroscience & Biobehavioral Reviews, 81*, 181–187. https://doi.org/10.1016/j.neubiorev.2017.02.011.
56. Donchin, E., & Coles, M. G. H. (1988). Is the P300 component a manifestation of context updating? *Behavioral and Brain Sciences, 11*(3).
57. Dosenbach, N. U. F., Fair, D. A., Cohen, A. L., Schlaggar, B. L., & Petersen, S. E. (2008). A dual-networks architecture of top-down control. *Trends in Cognitive Sciences, 12*(3), 99–105. https://doi.org/10.1016/j.tics.2008.01.001.
58. Doya, K., Ishii, S., Pouget, A., & Rao, R. P. N. (2007). Bayesian brain: Probabilistic approaches to neural coding. *Book, 326*. https://doi.org/10.7551/mitpress/9780262042383.001.0001.
59. Durrant, S. J., Cairney, S. A., & Lewis, P. A. (2013). Overnight consolidation aids the transfer of statistical knowledge from the medial temporal lobe to the striatum. *Cerebral Cortex, 23*(10), 2467–2478. https://doi.org/10.1093/cercor/bhs244.
60. Durrant, S. J., Taylor, C., Cairney, S., & Lewis, P. A. (2011). Sleep-dependent consolidation of statistical learning. *Neuropsychologia, 49*(5), 1322–1331. https://doi.org/10.1016/j.neuropsychologia.2011.02.015.

61. Ellenbogen, J. M., Hu, P. T., Payne, J. D., Titone, D., & Walker, M. P. (2007). Human relational memory requires time and sleep. *Proceedings of the National Academy of Sciences, 104*(18), 7723–7728. https://doi.org/10.1073/pnas.0700094104.

62. Ellenbogen, J. M., Payne, J. D., & Stickgold, R. (2006). The role of sleep in declarative memory consolidation: Passive, permissive, active or none? *Current Opinion in Neurobiology, 16*(6), 716–722. https://doi.org/10.1016/j.conb.2006.10.006.

63. Ellis, R. (2009). Implicitand explicit learning, knowledge and instruction. In R. Ellis, S. Loewen, C. Elder, R. Erlam, J. Philip, & H. Reinders (Eds.), *Implicit and explicit knowledge in second language learning, testing and teaching* (Vol. 27, pp. 3–25). https://doi.org/10. 1002/9780470756492.ch11.

64. Elman, J. L. (1990). Finding structure in time. *Cognitive Science, 14*(2), 179–211. https:// doi.org/10.1016/0364-0213(90)90002-E.

65. Elmer, S., Albrecht, J., Valizadeh, S. A., & François, C. (2018). *Theta coherence asymmetry in the dorsal stream of musicians facilitates word learning.* (March), 1–13. https://doi.org/ 10.1038/s41598-018-22942-1.

66. Farthouat, J., Franco, A., Mary, A., Delpouve, J., Wens, V., Op de Beeck, M., & Peigneux, P. (2017). Auditory magnetoencephalographic frequency-tagged responses mirror the ongoing segmentation processes underlying statistical learning. *Brain Topography, 30*(2), 220–232. https://doi.org/10.1007/s10548-016-0518-y.

67. Fazio, P., Cantagallo, A., Craighero, L., D'Ausilio, A., Roy, A. C., Pozzo, T., & Fadiga, L. (2009). Encoding of human action in Broca's area. *Brain, 132*(7), 1980–1988. https://doi. org/10.1093/brain/awp118.

68. Feher, O., Ljubičić, I., Suzuki, K., Okanoya, K., & Tchernichovski, O. (2016). Statistical learning in songbirds: From self-tutoring to song culture. In K. Suzuki, K. Okanoya, & O. Tchernichovski (Eds.), *Statistical learning in songbirds: from self-tutoring to song culture. Philosophical Transactions of the Royal Society B: Biological Sciences.*

69. Feldman, H., & Friston, K. (2010). Attention, uncertainty, and free-energy. *Frontiers in Human Neuroscience, 4*, 215. https://www.frontiersin.org/article/10.3389/fnhum.2010. 00215.

70. Fink, A., & Benedek, M. (2014). EEG alpha power and creative ideation. *Neuroscience and Biobehavioral Reviews, 44*(100), 111–123. https://doi.org/10.1016/j.neubiorev.2012.12.002.

71. Fink, A., Grabner, R. H., Benedek, M., & Neubauer, A. C. (2006). Divergent thinking training is related to frontal electroencephalogram alpha synchronization. *European Journal of Neuroscience, 23*(8), 2241–2246. https://doi.org/10.1111/j.1460-9568.2006.04751.x.

72. Fink, A., Grabner, R. H., Benedek, M., Reishofer, G., Hauswirth, V., Fally, M., & Neubauer, A. C. (2009). The creative brain: Investigation of brain activity during creative problem solving by means of EEG and FMRI. *Human Brain Mapping, 30*(3), 734–748. https://doi. org/10.1002/hbm.20538.

73. Fischer, S., Drosopoulos, S., Tsen, J., & Born, J. (2006). Implicit learning–explicit knowing: A role for sleep in memory system interaction. *Journal of Cognitive Neuroscience, 18.* https://doi.org/10.1162/089892906775990598.

74. Fitch, W. T., & Hauser, M. D. (2004). Computational constraints on syntactic processing in a nonhuman primate. *Science, 303*(5656), 377–380. https://doi.org/10.1126/science.1089401.

75. Flaherty, A. W. (2005). Frontotemporal and dopaminergic control of idea generation and creative drive. *The Journal of Comparative Neurology, 493*(1), 147–153. https://doi.org/10. 1002/cne.20768.

76. Fontolan, L., Morillon, B., Liegeois-Chauvel, C., & Giraud, A. L. (2014). The contribution of frequency-specific activity to hierarchical information processing in the human auditory cortex. *Nature Communications, 5*(May), 1–10. https://doi.org/10.1038/ncomms5694.

77. François, C., Chobert, J., Besson, M., & Schön, D. (2013). *Music training for the development of speech segmentation.* (September), 2038–2043. https://doi.org/10.1093/ cercor/bhs180.

78. François, C., Cunillera, T., Garcia, E., Laine, M., & Rodriguez-Fornells, A. (2017). Neurophysiological evidence for the interplay of speech segmentation and word-referent mapping during novel word learning. *Neuropsychologia, 98*, 56–67. https://doi.org/10.1016/j.neuropsychologia.2016.10.006.

79. Francois, C., & Schön, D. (2011). Musical expertise boosts implicit learning of both musical and linguistic structures. *Cerebral Cortex, 21*(10), 2357–2365. https://doi.org/10.1093/cercor/bhr022.

80. François, C., & Schön, D. (2014). Neural sensitivity to statistical regularities as a fundamental biological process that underlies auditory learning: The role of musical practice. *Hearing Research, 308*, 122–128. https://doi.org/10.1016/j.heares.2013.08.018.

81. Frankland, P. W., & Bontempi, B. (2005). The organization of recent and remote memories. *Nature Reviews Neuroscience, 6*, 119. https://doi.org/10.1038/nrn1607.

82. Frens, M., & Donchin, O. (2009). Forward models and state estimation in compensatory eye movements. *Frontiers in Cellular Neuroscience, 3*, 13. https://www.frontiersin.org/article/10.3389/neuro.03.013.2009.

83. Friederici, A. D. (2004). Processing local transitions versus long-distance syntactic hierarchies. *Trends in Cognitive Sciences, 8*(6), 245–247. https://doi.org/10.1016/j.tics.2004.04.013.

84. Friederici, A. D. (2011). The brain basis of language processing: From structure to function. *Physiological Reviews, 91*(4), 1357–1392. https://doi.org/10.1152/physrev.00006.2011.

85. Friederici, A. D., Bahlmann, J., Heim, S., Schubotz, R. I., & Anwander, A. (2006). The brain differentiates human and non-human grammars: Functional localization and structural connectivity. *Proceedings of the National Academy of Sciences, 103*(7), 2458–2463. https://doi.org/10.1073/pnas.0509389103.

86. Friederici, A. D., Chomsky, N., Berwick, R. C., Moro, A., & Bolhuis, J. J. (2017). Language, mind and brain. *Nature Human Behaviour, 1*(10), 713–722. https://doi.org/10.1038/s41562-017-0184-4.

87. Friedman, D., Cycowicz, Y. M., & Gaeta, H. (2001). The novelty P3: An event-related brain potential (ERP) sign of the brain's evaluation of novelty. *Neuroscience & Biobehavioral Reviews, 25*(4), 355–373. https://doi.org/10.1016/S0149-7634(01)00019-7.

88. Friedrich, R., & Friederici, A. D. (2009). Mathematical logic in the human brain: Syntax. *PLOS ONE, 4*(5), e5599. https://doi.org/10.1371/journal.pone.0005599.

89. Friston, K. (2010). The free-energy principle: A unified brain theory? *Nature Reviews Neuroscience, 11*(2), 127–138. https://doi.org/10.1038/nrn2787.

90. Friston, K., Fitzgerald, T., Rigoli, F., Schwartenbeck, P., Doherty, J. O., & Pezzulo, G. (2016). Neuroscience and biobehavioral reviews active inference and learning. *Neuroscience and Biobehavioral Reviews, 68*, 862–879. https://doi.org/10.1016/j.neubiorev.2016.06.022.

91. Friston, K., Rigoli, F., Ognibene, D., Mathys, C., Fitzgerald, T., & Pezzulo, G. (2015). Active inference and epistemic value. *Cognitive Neuroscience, 6*(4), 187–224. https://doi.org/10.1080/17588928.2015.1020053.

92. Friston, K., Schwartenbeck, P., FitzGerald, T., Moutoussis, M., Behrens, T., & Dolan, R. J. (2014). *The anatomy of choice: Dopamine and decision-making Subject collections The anatomy of choice: dopamine and decision-making.* Retrieved from http://rstb.royalsociety-publishing.org/content/369/1655/20130481.full.html#related-urls%5Chttp://rstb.royalsoci-etypublishing.org/content/369/1655/20130481.full.html%23ref-list-1%5Chttp://dx.doi.org/10.1098/rstb.2013.0481.

93. Frost, R., Armstrong, B. C., Siegelman, N., & Christiansen, M. H. (2015). Domain generality versus modality specificity: The paradox of statistical learning. *Trends in Cognitive Sciences, 19*(3), 117–125. https://doi.org/10.1016/j.tics.2014.12.010.

94. Frost, R. L. A., & Monaghan, P. (2016). Simultaneous segmentation and generalisation of non-adjacent dependencies from continuous speech. *Cognition.* https://doi.org/10.1016/j.cognition.2015.11.010.

95. Furl, N., Kumar, S., Alter, K., Durrant, S., Shawe-Taylor, J., & Griffiths, T. D. (2011). Neural prediction of higher-order auditory sequence statistics. *NeuroImage, 54*(3), 2267–2277. https://doi.org/10.1016/j.neuroimage.2010.10.038.

96. Gao, W., Zhu, H., Giovanello, K. S., Smith, J. K., Shen, D., Gilmore, J. H., & Lin, W. (2009). Evidence on the emergence of the brain's default network from 2-week-old to 2-year-old healthy pediatric subjects. *Proceedings of the National Academy of Sciences, 106* (16), 6790–6795. https://doi.org/10.1073/pnas.0811221106.

97. Gardner, H. (1993). *Creating minds: An anatomy of creativity seen through the lives of Freud, Einstein, Picasso, Stravinsky, Eliot, Graham, and Gandhi.* Retrieved from https:// books.google.de/books?id=NAyZhZTivckC.

98. Garrido, M. I., Friston, K. J., Kiebel, S. J., Stephan, K. E., Baldeweg, T., & Kilner, J. M. (2008). The functional anatomy of the MMN: A DCM study of the roving paradigm. *NeuroImage, 42*(2), 936–944. https://doi.org/10.1016/j.neuroimage.2008.05.018.

99. Garrido, M. I., Kilner, J. M., Kiebel, S. J., & Friston, K. J. (2007). Evoked brain responses are generated by feedback loops. *Proceedings of the National Academy of Sciences, 104*(52), 20961–20966. https://doi.org/10.1073/pnas.0706274105.

100. Giraud, A. L., & Poeppel, D. (2012). Cortical oscillations and speech processing: Emerging computational principles and operations. *Nature Neuroscience, 15*(4), 511–517. https://doi. org/10.1038/nn.3063.

101. Gold, J. I., & Shadlen, M. N. (2007). The neural basis of decision making. *Annual Review of Neuroscience, 30*(1), 535–574. https://doi.org/10.1146/annurev.neuro.29.051605.113038.

102. Gomez, R. (2017). Do infants retain the statistics of a statistical learning experience? Insights from a developmental cognitive neuroscience perspective. *Philosophical Transactions of the Royal Society B: Biological Sciences, 372*(1711), 20160054. https://doi.org/10.1098/rstb. 2016.0054.

103. Gómez, R. L. (2002). Variability and detection of invariant structure. *Psychological Science, 13*(5), 431–436. https://doi.org/10.1111/1467-9280.00476.

104. Gómez, R. L., & Edgin, J. O. (2016). The extended trajectory of hippocampal development: Implications for early memory development and disorder. *Developmental Cognitive Neuroscience, 18*, 57–69. https://doi.org/10.1016/j.dcn.2015.08.009.

105. Gómez, R. L., & Gerken, L. (2000). Infant artificial language learning and language acquisition. *Trends in Cognitive Sciences, 4*(5), 178–186. https://doi.org/10.1016/S1364-6613(00)01467-4.

106. Gomez, R. L., & Gerken, L. A. (1999). Artificial grammar learning by one-year-olds leads to specific and abstract knowledge. *Cognition, 70*(2), 109–136.

107. Graybiel, A. M. (1998). the basal ganglia and chunking of action repertoires. *Neurobiology of Learning and Memory, 70*(1), 119–136. https://doi.org/10.1006/nlme.1998.3843.

108. Green, A. E., Spiegel, K. A., Giangrande, E. J., Weinberger, A. B., Gallagher, N. M., & Turkeltaub, P. E. (2017). Thinking cap plus thinking zap: Tdcs of frontopolar cortex improves creative analogical reasoning and facilitates conscious augmentation of state creativity in verb generation. *Cerebral Cortex, 27*(4), 2628–2639. https://doi.org/10.1093/ cercor/bhw080.

109. Hansen, N. C., & Pearce, M. T. (2014). Predictive uncertainty in auditory sequence processing. *Frontiers in Psychology, 5*(SEP), 1–17. https://doi.org/10.3389/fpsyg.2014. 01052.

110. Harrison, L. M., Duggins, A., & Friston, K. J. (2006). Encoding uncertainty in the hippocampus. *Neural Networks, 19*(5), 535–546. https://doi.org/10.1016/j.neunet.2005.11. 002.

111. Harrison, L. M., Duggins, A., & Friston, K. J. (2006). *Encoding uncertainty in the hippocampus. 19*, 535–546. https://doi.org/10.1016/j.neunet.2005.11.002.

112. Hasson, U. (2017). The neurobiology of uncertainty: Implications for statistical learning. *Philosophical Transactions of the Royal Society B, 372*, 20160048.
113. Hauser, M. D., Chomsky, N., & Fitch, W. T. (2002). The faculty of language: What is it, who has it, and how did it evolve? *Science, 298*(5598), 1569–1579. https://doi.org/10.1126/science.298.5598.1569.
114. Heekeren, H. R., Marrett, S., & Ungerleider, L. G. (2008). The neural systems that mediate human perceptual decision making. *Nature Reviews Neuroscience, 9*, 467. https://doi.org/10.1038/nrn2374.
115. Hélie, S., & Sun, R. (2010). Incubation, insight, and creative problem solving: A unified theory and a connectionist model. *Psychological Review, 117*. https://doi.org/10.1037/a0019532.
116. Hickok, G. (2012). The cortical organization of speech processing: Feedback control and predictive coding the context of a dual-stream model. *Journal of Communication Disorders, 45*(6), 393–402. https://doi.org/10.1016/j.jcomdis.2012.06.004.
117. Hochreiter, S., & Urgen Schmidhuber, J. (1997). Ltsm. *Neural Computation, 9*(8), 1735–1780. https://doi.org/10.1162/neco.1997.9.8.1735.
118. Hofstadter, D. (1979). Gödel, Escher, Bach: An eternal golden braid. *Critica, 12*(36).
119. Huffman, R. F., & Henson, O. W. (1990). The descending auditory pathway and acousticomotor systems: connections with the inferior colliculus. *Brain Research Reviews, 15*(3), 295–323. https://doi.org/10.1016/0165-0173(90)90005-9.
120. Ito, M. (2008). Control of mental activities by internal models in the cerebellum. *Nature Reviews Neuroscience, 9*, 304. https://doi.org/10.1038/nrn2332.
121. Janata, P., Birk, J. L., Van Horn, J. D., Leman, M., Tillmann, B., & Bharucha, J. J. (2002). The cortical topography of tonal structures underlying western music. *Science, 298*(5601), 2167–2170. https://doi.org/10.1126/science.1076262.
122. Jauk, E., Neubauer, A. C., Dunst, B., Fink, A., & Benedek, M. (2015). Gray matter correlates of creative potential: A latent variable voxel-based morphometry study. *NeuroImage, 111*, 312–320. https://doi.org/10.1016/j.neuroimage.2015.02.002.
123. Ji, D., & Wilson, M. A. (2007). Coordinated memory replay in the visual cortex and hippocampus during sleep. *Nature Neuroscience, 10*(1), 100–107. https://doi.org/10.1038/nn1825.
124. Jokisch, D., & Jensen, O. (2007). Modulation of gamma and alpha activity during a working memory task engaging the dorsal or ventral stream. *The Journal of Neuroscience, 27*(12), 3244–3251. https://doi.org/10.1523/JNEUROSCI.5399-06.2007.
125. Jones, M. N., & Mewhort, D. J. K. (2007). Representing word meaning and order information in a composite holographic lexicon. *Psychological Review, 114*(1), 1–37. https://doi.org/10.1037/0033-295X.114.1.1.
126. Jung-Beeman, M., Bowden, E. M., Haberman, J., Frymiare, J. L., Arambel-Liu, S., Greenblatt, R., Kounios, J. (2004). Neural activity when people solve verbal problems with insight. *PLOS Biology, 2*(4), e97. https://doi.org/10.1371/journal.pbio.0020097.
127. Kagan, J. (1972). Motives and development. *Journal of Personality and Social Psychology, 22*(1), 51–66. Retrieved from https://europepmc.org/abstract/MED/5013358.
128. Karlaftis, V. M., Giorgio, J., Vértes, P. E., Wang, R., Shen, Y., Tino, P., & Kourtzi, Z. (2019). Multimodal imaging of brain connectivity reveals predictors of individual decision strategy in statistical learning. *Nature Human Behaviour, 3*(3), 297–307. https://doi.org/10.1038/s41562-018-0503-4.
129. Karuza, E. A., Li, P., Weiss, D. J., Bulgarelli, F., Zinszer, B. D., & Aslin, R. N. (2016). Sampling over nonuniform distributions: A neural efficiency account of the primacy effect in statistical learning. *Journal of Cognitive Neuroscience, 28*(10), 1484–1500. https://doi.org/10.1162/jocn_a_00990.
130. Kaufman, J. C., Kaufman, S. B., & Plucker, J. A. (2013). *Contemporary theories of intelligence* (D. Reisberg, Ed.). https://doi.org/10.1093/oxfordhb/9780195376746.013.0051.

131. Kersten, D., Mamassian, P., & Yuille, A. (2004). Object perception as Bayesian inference. *Annual Review of Psychology, 55*(1), 271–304. https://doi.org/10.1146/annurev.psych.55. 090902.142005.

132. Khilkevich, A., Canton-Josh, J., DeLord, E., & Mauk, M. D. (2018). A cerebellar adaptation to uncertain inputs. *Science Advances, 4*(5), eaap9660–eaap9660. https://doi.org/10.1126/sciadv.aap9660.

133. Kiebel, S. J., Daunizeau, J., & Friston, K. J. (2008). A hierarchy of time-scales and the brain. *PLoS Computational Biology, 4*(11). https://doi.org/10.1371/journal.pcbi.1000209.

134. Kim, R., Seitz, A., Feenstra, H., & Shams, L. (2009). Testing assumptions of statistical learning: Is it long-term and implicit? *Neuroscience Letters, 461*(2), 145–149. https://doi. org/10.1016/j.neulet.2009.06.030.

135. Kim, S. G., Kim, J. S., & Chung, C. K. (2011). The effect of conditional probability of chord progression on brain response: An MEG study. *PLoS ONE, 6*(2). https://doi.org/10.1371/journal.pone.0017337.

136. Klimesch, W. (2012). α-band oscillations, attention, and controlled access to stored information. *Trends in Cognitive Sciences, 16*(12), 606–617. https://doi.org/10.1016/j.tics. 2012.10.007.

137. Knill, D. C., & Pouget, A. (2004). The Bayesian brain: The role of uncertainty in neural coding and computation. *Trends in Neurosciences, 27*(12), 712–719. https://doi.org/10. 1016/j.tins.2004.10.007.

138. Koechlin, E., & Jubault, T. (2006). Broca's area and the hierarchical organization of human behavior. *Neuron, 50*(6), 963–974. https://doi.org/10.1016/j.neuron.2006.05.017.

139. Koelsch, S. (2012). *Brain and music.* Retrieved from https://books.google.co.uk/books?id= b9OXDpmE9dwC.

140. Koelsch, S. (2014). Brain correlates of music-evoked emotions. *Nature Reviews Neuroscience, 15*(3), 170–180. https://doi.org/10.1038/nrn3666.

141. Koelsch, S., Busch, T., Jentzsche, S., & Rohrmeier, M. (2016). Under the hood of statistical learning: A statistical MMN reflects the magnitude of transitional probabilities in auditory sequences. *Scientific Reports, 6*(February), 1–11. https://doi.org/10.1038/srep19741.

142. Koelsch, S., Kasper, E., Sammler, D., Schulze, K., Gunter, T., & Friederici, A. D. (2004). Music, language and meaning: Brain signatures of semantic processing. *Nature Neuroscience, 7*(3), 302–307. https://doi.org/10.1038/nn1197.

143. Koelsch, S., Vuust, P., & Friston, K. (2018). Predictive processes and the peculiar case of music. *Trends in Cognitive Sciences, 23*(1), 63–77. https://doi.org/10.1016/j.tics.2018.10.006.

144. Konkel, A., Warren, D., Duff, M., Tranel, D., & Cohen, N. (2008). Hippocampal amnesia impairs all manner of relational memory. *Frontiers in Human Neuroscience, 2*, 15. Retrieved from https://www.frontiersin.org/article/10.3389/neuro.09.015.2008.

145. Kouneiher, F., Charron, S., & Koechlin, E. (2009). Motivation and cognitive control in the human prefrontal cortex. *Nature Neuroscience, 12*, 939. https://doi.org/10.1038/nn.2321.

146. Krebs, R. M., Schott, B. H., Schütze, H., & Düzel, E. (2009). The novelty exploration bonus and its attentional modulation. *Neuropsychologia, 47*(11), 2272–2281. https://doi.org/10. 1016/j.neuropsychologia.2009.01.015.

147. Kuhl, P. K. (2000). A new view of language acquisition. *Proceedings of the National Academy of Sciences, 97*(22), 11850–11857. https://doi.org/10.1073/pnas.97.22.11850.

148. Kuhl, P. K. (2004). Early language acquisition: Cracking the speech code. *Nature Reviews Neuroscience.* https://doi.org/10.1038/nrn1533.

149. Kuhl, P. K., Tsao, F.-M., & Liu, H.-M. (2003). Foreign-language experience in infancy: Effects of short-term exposure and social interaction on phonetic learning. *Proceedings of the National Academy of Sciences of the United States of America, 100*(15), 9096–9101. https://doi.org/10.1073/pnas.1532872100.

150. Kuhl, P. K., Williams, K. A., Lacerda, F., Stevens, K. N., & Lindblom, B. (1992). Linguistic experience alters phonetic perception in infants by 6 months of age. *Science, 255*(5044), 606–608. https://doi.org/10.1126/science.1736364.

151. Kumaran, D., Hassabis, D., & McClelland, J. L. (2016). What learning systems do intelligent agents need? Complementary learning systems theory updated. *Trends in Cognitive Sciences, 20*(7), 512–534. https://doi.org/10.1016/j.tics.2016.05.004.

152. Kutas, M., & Federmeier, K. D. (2010). Thirty years and counting: Finding meaning in the N400 component of the event-related brain potential (ERP). *Annual Review of Psychology, 62*(1), 621–647. https://doi.org/10.1146/annurev.psych.093008.131123.

153. Landauer, T. K., & Dumais, S. T. (1997). A solution to Platos problem: The latent semantic analysis theory of acquisition, induction and representation of knowledge. *Psychological Review, 104*(2), 211–240. https://doi.org/10.1037//0033-295X.104.2.211.

154. Langner, G., & Ochse, M. (2006). The neural basis of pitch and harmony in the auditory system. *Musicae Scientiae, 10*(1_suppl), 185–208. https://doi.org/10.1177/102986490601000109.

155. Laura, J. B., Paul, J. R., Helen, J. N., & Ken A. P. (2015). Implicit and explicit contributions to statistical learning. *Journal of Memory and Language, 83*, 62–78. https://doi.org/10.1016/j.jml.2015.04.004.Implicit.

156. LeCun, Y., Bengio, Y., & Hinton, G. (2015). Deep learning. *Nature, 521*, 436. https://doi.org/10.1038/nature14539.

157. Leong, V., & Goswami, U. (2015). Acoustic-emergent phonology in the amplitude envelope of child-directed speech. *PLOS ONE, 10*(12), e0144411. https://doi.org/10.1371/journal.pone.0144411.

158. Lerdahl, F., Jackendoff, R., & Jackendoff, R. S. (1983). *A generative theory of tonal music.* Retrieved from https://books.google.de/books?id=38YcngEACAAJ.

159. Lesage, E., Morgan, B. E., Olson, A. C., Meyer, A. S., & Miall, R. C. (2012). Cerebellar rTMS disrupts predictive language processing. *Current Biology: CB, 22*(18), R794–R795. https://doi.org/10.1016/j.cub.2012.07.006.

160. Lewis, P. A., & Durrant, S. J. (2011). Overlapping memory replay during sleep builds cognitive schemata. *Trends in Cognitive Sciences, 15*(8), 343–351. https://doi.org/10.1016/j.tics.2011.06.004.

161. Limb, C. J., & Braun, A. R. (2008). Neural substrates of spontaneous musical performance: An fMRI study of jazz improvisation. *PLOS ONE, 3*(2), e1679. https://doi.org/10.1371/journal.pone.0001679.

162. Liu, S., Erkkinen, M. G., Healey, M. L., Xu, Y., Swett, K. E., Chow, H. M., & Braun, A. R. (2015). Brain activity and connectivity during poetry composition: Toward a multidimensional model of the creative process. *Human Brain Mapping, 36*(9), 3351–3372. https://doi.org/10.1002/hbm.22849.

163. Liu, Z., Zhang, J., Xie, X., Rolls, E. T., Sun, J., Zhang, K., Feng, J. (2018). Neural and genetic determinants of creativity. *NeuroImage, 174*(November 2017), 164–176. https://doi.org/10.1016/j.neuroimage.2018.02.067.

164. Lopata, J. A., Nowicki, E. A., & Joanisse, M. F. (2017). Creativity as a distinct trainable mental state: An EEG study of musical improvisation. *Neuropsychologia, 99*(March), 246–258. https://doi.org/10.1016/j.neuropsychologia.2017.03.020.

165. Lopez-Barroso, D., Catani, M., Ripolles, P., Dell'Acqua, F., Rodriguez-Fornells, A., & de Diego-Balaguer, R. (2013). Word learning is mediated by the left arcuate fasciculus. *Proceedings of the National Academy of Sciences, 110*(32), 13168–13173. https://doi.org/10.1073/pnas.1301696110.

166. Lu, K., & Vicario, D. S. (2014). *Statistical learning of recurring sound patterns encodes auditory objects in songbird forebrain. 111*(40), 14553–14558. https://doi.org/10.1073/pnas.1412109111.

167. Lu, K., & Vicario, D. S. (2017). *Familiar but unexpected: Effects of sound context statistics on auditory responses in the songbird forebrain. 37*(49), 12006–12017. https://doi.org/10.1523/JNEUROSCI.5722-12.2017.

168. Lund, K., & Burgess, C. (1996). Producing high-dimensional semantic spaces from lexical co-occurrence. *Behavior Research Methods, Instruments, and Computers, 28*(2), 203–208. https://doi.org/10.3758/BF03204766.
169. Lustenberger, C., Boyle, M. R., Foulser, A. A., Mellin, J. M., & Fröhlich, F. (2015). Functional role of frontal alpha oscillations in creativity. *Cortex, 67*, 74–82. https://doi.org/10.1016/j.cortex.2015.03.012.
170. Makuuchi, M., Bahlmann, J., Anwander, A., & Friederici, A. D. (2009). Segregating the core computational faculty of human language from working memory. *Proceedings of the National Academy of Sciences, 106*(20), 8362–8367. https://doi.org/10.1073/pnas.0810928106.
171. Marr, D. (1971). Simple memory: A theory for archicortex. *Philosophical Transactions of the Royal Society of London. B, Biological Sciences, 262*(841), 23–81. https://doi.org/10.1098/rstb.1971.0078.
172. Mason, M. F., Norton, M. I., Van Horn, J. D., Wegner, D. M., Grafton, S. T., & Macrae, C. N. (2007). Wandering minds: The default network and stimulus-independent thought. *Science, 315*(5810), 393–395. https://doi.org/10.1126/science.1131295.
173. Maye, J., Weiss, D., & Aslin, R. (2008). Statistical phonetic learning in infants: Facilitation and feature generalization. *Developmental Science.* https://doi.org/10.1111/j.1467-7687.2007.00653.x.
174. Maye, J., Werkerb, J., & Gerkenc, L. (2002). *Infant sensitivity to distributional information can affect phonetic discrimination. 82,* B101–B111. https://dx.doi.org/10.1016/S0010-0277(01)00157-3.
175. Mayseless, N., Eran, A., & Shamay-Tsoory, S. G. (2015). Generating original ideas: The neural underpinning of originality. *NeuroImage, 116,* 232–239. https://doi.org/10.1016/j.neuroimage.2015.05.030.
176. McClelland, J., McNaughton, B., & O'Reilly, R. (1995). Why there are complementary learning systems in the hippocampus and neocortex: Insights from the successes and failures of connectionist models of learning and memory. *Psychological Review, 102*(3), 419–457.
177. McNealy, K., Mazziotta, J. C., & Dapretto, M. (2006). Cracking the language code: Neural mechanisms underlying speech parsing. *Journal of Neuroscience.* https://doi.org/10.1523/JNEUROSCI.5501-05.2006.
178. Michael, K., Yishay, M., Dana, R., Ronitt, R., Robert, S., & Linda, S. (1994). On the learnability of discrete distributions. In *Proceedings of the Twenty-Sixth Annual ACM Symposium on Theory of Computing (STOC '94)* (pp. 273–282). https://doi.org/10.1145/195058.195155.
179. Miller, E. K., & Cohen, J. D. (2001). An integrative theory of prefrontal cortex function. *Annual Review of Neuroscience, 24*(1), 167–202. https://doi.org/10.1146/annurev.neuro.24.1.167.
180. Miranda, R. A., & Ullman, M. T. (2007). Double dissociation between rules and memory in music: An event-related potential study. *NeuroImage, 38*(2), 331–345. https://doi.org/10.1016/j.neuroimage.2007.07.034.
181. Mnih, V., Kavukcuoglu, K., Silver, D., Rusu, A. A., Veness, J., Bellemare, M. G., Hassabis, D. (2015). Human-level control through deep reinforcement learning. *Nature, 518,* 529. https://doi.org/10.1038/nature14236.
182. Moberget, T., Gullesen, E. H., Andersson, S., Ivry, R. B., & Endestad, T. (2014). Generalized role for the cerebellum in encoding internal models: Evidence from semantic processing. *The Journal of Neuroscience, 34*(8), 2871–2878. https://doi.org/10.1523/JNEUROSCI.2264-13.2014.
183. Moldwin, T., Schwartz, O., & Sussman, E. S. (2017). Statistical learning of melodic patterns influences the brain's response to wrong notes. 2114–2122. https://doi.org/10.1162/jocn.

184. Mölle, M., Marshall, L., Gais, S., & Born, J. (2002). Grouping of spindle activity during slow oscillations in human non-rapid eye movement sleep. *The Journal of Neuroscience, 22* (24), 10941–10947. https://doi.org/10.1523/JNEUROSCI.22-24-10941.2002.
185. Monroy, C. D., Gerson, S. A., Domínguez-Martínez, E., Kaduk, K., Hunnius, S., & Reid, V. (2017). Sensitivity to structure in action sequences: An infant event-related potential study. *Neuropsychologia,* (May), 0–1. https://doi.org/10.1016/j.neuropsychologia.2017.05.007.
186. Monroy, C. D., Gerson, S. A., & Hunnius, S. (2018). Translating visual information into action predictions: Statistical learning in action and nonaction contexts. *Memory and Cognition, 46*(4), 600–613. https://doi.org/10.3758/s13421-018-0788-6.
187. Monroy, C. D., Meyer, M., Schröer, L., Gerson, S. A., & Hunnius, S. (2017). The infant motor system predicts actions based on visual statistical learning. *NeuroImage, 185* (December 2017), 947–954. https://doi.org/10.1016/j.neuroimage.2017.12.016.
188. Monroy, C., Meyer, M., Gerson, S., & Hunnius, S. (2017). Statistical learning in social action contexts. *PLoS ONE, 12*(5), 1–20. https://doi.org/10.1371/journal.pone.0177261.
189. Moore, B. (2003). *An introduction to the psychology of hearing.*
190. Moscovitch, M., Cabeza, R., Winocur, G., & Nadel, L. (2016). Episodic memory and beyond: The hippocampus and neocortex in transformation. *Annual Review of Psychology, 67*(1), 105–134. https://doi.org/10.1146/annurev-psych-113011-143733.
191. Mumford, D. (1992). On the computational architecture of the neocortex—II The role of cortico-cortical loops. *Biological Cybernetics, 66*(3), 241–251. https://doi.org/10.1007/BF00198477.
192. Nagai, Y. (2019). Predictive learning: Its key role in early cognitive development. *Philosophical Transactions of the Royal Society B: Biological Sciences, 374*(1771), 20180030. https://doi.org/10.1098/rstb.2018.0030.
193. Nastase, S., Iacovella, V., & Hasson, U. (2014). Uncertainty in visual and auditory series is coded by modality-general and modality-specific neural systems. *Human Brain Mapping, 35* (4), 1111–1128. https://doi.org/10.1002/hbm.22238.
194. Norris, J. M., & Ortega, L. (2000). Effectiveness of L2 instruction: A research synthesis and quantitative meta-analysis. *Language Learning, 50*(3), 417–528. https://doi.org/10.1111/0023-8333.00136.
195. O'Neill, J., Pleydell-Bouverie, B., Dupret, D., & Csicsvari, J. (2010). Play it again: Reactivation of waking experience and memory. *Trends in Neurosciences, 33*(5), 220–229. https://doi.org/10.1016/j.tins.2010.01.006.
196. O'Reilly, J. X., Jbabdi, S., & Behrens, T. E. J. (2012). How can a Bayesian approach inform neuroscience? *European Journal of Neuroscience, 35*(7), 1169–1179. https://doi.org/10.1111/j.1460-9568.2012.08010.x.
197. Oechslin, M. S., Meyer, M., & Jäncke, L. (2010). Absolute pitch-functional evidence of speech-relevant auditory acuity. *Cerebral Cortex, 20*(2), 447–455. https://doi.org/10.1093/cercor/bhp113.
198. Ong, J. H., Burnham, D., & Stevens, C. (2016). Learning novel musical pitch via distributional learning. *Journal of Experimental Psychology: Learning, Memory, and Cognition, 43*,. https://doi.org/10.1037/xlm0000286.
199. Opitz, B., & Kotz, S. A. (2012). Ventral premotor cortex lesions disrupt learning of sequential grammatical structures. *Cortex, 48*(6), 664–673. https://doi.org/10.1016/j.cortex.2011.02.013.
200. Overath, T., Cusack, R., Kumar, S., Von Kriegstein, K., Warren, J. D., Grube, M., & Griffiths, T. D. (2007). An information theoretic characterisation of auditory encoding. *PLoS Biology, 5*(11), 2723–2732. https://doi.org/10.1371/journal.pbio.0050288.
201. Paraskevopoulos, E., Chalas, N., Kartsidis, P., Wollbrink, A., & Bamidis, P. (2017). Statistical learning of multisensory regularities is enhanced in musicians: An MEG study. *NeuroImage.* https://doi.org/10.1016/j.neuroimage.2018.04.002.

202. Paraskevopoulos, E., Kuchenbuch, A., Herholz, S. C., & Pantev, C. (2012). Statistical learning effects in musicians and non-musicians: An MEG study. *Neuropsychologia, 50*(2), 341–349. https://doi.org/10.1016/j.neuropsychologia.2011.12.007.
203. Park, H., Ince, R. A. A., Schyns, P. G., Thut, G., & Gross, J. (2015). Frontal top-down signals increase coupling of auditory low-frequency oscillations to continuous speech in human listeners. *Current Biology, 25*(12), 1649–1653. https://doi.org/10.1016/j.cub.2015.04.049.
204. Parr, T., & Friston, K. J. (2018). The anatomy of inference: Generative models and brain structure. *Frontiers in Computational Neuroscience, 12*(November). https://doi.org/10.3389/fncom.2018.00090.
205. Parr, T., Rees, G., & Friston, K. J. (2018). Computational neuropsychology and Bayesian inference. *Frontiers in Human Neuroscience, 12*(February), 1–14. https://doi.org/10.3389/fnhum.2018.00061.
206. Parsons, L. M. (2001). Exploring the functional neuroanatomy of music performance, perception, and comprehension. *Annals of the New York Academy of Sciences, 930*(1), 211–231. https://doi.org/10.1111/j.1749-6632.2001.tb05735.x.
207. Pearce, M. (2006). *Expectation in melody.* 377–405.
208. Pearce, M. T., Müllensiefen, D., & Wiggins, G. A. (2010). The role of expectation and probabilistic learning in auditory boundary perception: A model comparison. *Perception, 39* (10), 1367–1391. https://doi.org/10.1068/p6507.
209. Pearce, M. T., Ruiz, M. H., Kapasi, S., Wiggins, G. A., & Bhattacharya, J. (2010). Unsupervised statistical learning underpins computational, behavioural, and neural manifestations of musical expectation. *NeuroImage, 50*(1), 302–313. https://doi.org/10.1016/j.neuroimage.2009.12.019.
210. Pearce, M. T., & Wiggins, G. A. (2012). Auditory expectation: The information dynamics of music perception and cognition. *Topics in Cognitive Science, 4*(4), 625–652. https://doi.org/10.1111/j.1756-8765.2012.01214.x.
211. Pena, M. (2002). Signal-driven computations in speech processing. *Science, 298*(5593), 604–607. https://doi.org/10.1126/science.1072901.
212. Perruchet, P., & Pacton, S. (2006). Implicit learning and statistical learning: One phenomenon, two approaches. *Trends in Cognitive Sciences, 10*(5), 233–238. https://doi.org/10.1016/j.tics.2006.03.006.
213. Perruchet, P., & Vinter, A. (1998). PARSER: A model for word segmentation. *Journal of Memory and Language, 39*(2), 246–263.
214. Pezzulo, G., Rigoli, F., & Friston, K. (2015). Active Inference, homeostatic regulation and adaptive behavioural control. *Progress in Neurobiology, 134*, 17–35. https://doi.org/10.1016/j.pneurobio.2015.09.001.
215. Pickering, M. J., & Clark, A. (2014). Getting ahead: Forward models and their place in cognitive architecture. *Trends in Cognitive Sciences, 18*(9), 451–456. https://doi.org/10.1016/j.tics.2014.05.006.
216. Pickles, J. (2013). *An introduction to the physiology of hearing.*
217. Pinho, A. L., Ullén, F., Castelo-Branco, M., Fransson, P., & de Manzano, Ö. (2015). Addressing a paradox: Dual strategies for creative performance in introspective and extrospective networks. *Cerebral Cortex, 26*(7), 3052–3063. https://doi.org/10.1093/cercor/bhv130.
218. Plante, E., Patterson, D., Dailey, N. S., Kyle, R. A., & Fridriksson, J. (2014). Dynamic changes in network activations characterize early learning of a natural language. *Neuropsychologia, 62*, 77–86. https://doi.org/10.1016/j.neuropsychologia.2014.07.007.
219. Plante, E., Patterson, D., Gómez, R., Almryde, K. R., White, M. G., & Asbjørnsen, A. E. (2015). The nature of the language input affects brain activation during learning from a natural language. *Journal of Neurolinguistics, 36*, 17–34. https://doi.org/10.1016/j.jneuroling.2015.04.005.
220. Prabhu, V., Sutton, C., & Sauser, W. (2008). Creativity and certain personality traits: Understanding the mediating effect of intrinsic motivation. *Creativity Research Journal, 20* (1), 53–66. https://doi.org/10.1080/10400410701841955.

221. Rao, P., Vasuki, M., Sharma, M., Ibrahim, R., & Arciuli, J. (2017). *Clinical neurophysiology statistical learning and auditory processing in children with music training: An ERP study. 128,* 1270–1281. https://doi.org/10.1016/j.clinph.2017.04.010.
222. Rao, R. P. N., & Ballard, D. H. (1999). Predictive coding in the visual cortex: A functional interpretation of some extra-classical receptive-field effects. *Nature Neuroscience, 2,* 79. https://doi.org/10.1038/4580.
223. Raphael, C., & Stoddard, J. (2004). Functional harmonic analysis using probabilistic models. *Computer Music Journal, 28*(3), 45–52. https://doi.org/10.1162/0148926041790676.
224. Rasch, B., & Born, J. (2007). Maintaining memories by reactivation. *Current Opinion in Neurobiology, 17*(6), 698–703. https://doi.org/10.1016/j.conb.2007.11.007.
225. Rasch, B., & Jan, B. (2013). About sleep's role in memory. *Physiological Reviews, 93*(2), 681–766. https://doi.org/10.1152/Physrev.00032.2012.
226. Rauschecker, J. P., & Scott, S. K. (2009). Maps and streams in the auditory cortex: Nonhuman primates illuminate human speech processing. *Nature Neuroscience, 12*(6), 718–724. https://doi.org/10.1038/nn.2331.
227. Reber, A. S. (1967). Implicit learning of artificial grammars. *Journal of Verbal Learning and Verbal Behavior.* https://doi.org/10.1016/S0022-5371(67)80149-X.
228. Reddy, L., Poncet, M., Self, M. W., Peters, J. C., Douw, L., van Dellen, E., & Roelfsema, P. R. (2015). Learning of anticipatory responses in single neurons of the human medial temporal lobe. *Nature Communications, 6,* 8556. https://doi.org/10.1038/ncomms9556.
229. Rinne, T., Antila, S., & Winkler, I. (2001). Mismatch negativity is unaffected by top-down predictive information. *NeuroReport, 12*(10). Retrieved from https://journals.lww.com/neuroreport/Fulltext/2001/07200/Mismatch_negativity_is_unaffected_by_top_down.33.aspx.
230. Ritter, W., Sussman, E., Deacon, D., Cowan, N., Vaughan, J. R., & H. G. . (1999). Two cognitive systems simultaneously prepared for opposite events. *Psychophysiology, 36*(6), 835–838. https://doi.org/10.1111/1469-8986.3660835.
231. Rogers, T. T., & McClelland, J. L. J. (2004). Semantic cognition: A parallel distributed processing approach. *Attention and Performance, 425,* 439. https://doi.org/10.1017/S0140525X0800589X.
232. Rohrmeier, M. (2011). Towards a generative syntax of tonal harmony. *Journal of Mathematics and Music, 5*(1), 35–53. https://doi.org/10.1080/17459737.2011.573676.
233. Rohrmeier, M. A., & Cross, I. (2014). Modelling unsupervised online-learning of artificial grammars: Linking implicit and statistical learning. *Consciousness and Cognition, 27*(1), 155–167. https://doi.org/10.1016/j.concog.2014.03.011.
234. Rohrmeier, M., & Cross, I. (2008). Statistical properties of tonal harmony in Bach's Chorales. In *Proceedings of the 10th International Conference on Music Perception and Cognition* (Vol. 6, no. 4, pp. 123–1319). Retrieved from https://icmpc10.psych.let.hokudai. ac.jp/%5Cnhttps://www.mus.cam.ac.uk/files/2009/09/bachharmony.pdf.
235. Rohrmeier, M., & Rebuschat, P. (2012). Implicit learning and acquisition of music. *Topics in Cognitive Science, 4*(4), 525–553. https://doi.org/10.1111/j.1756-8765.2012.01223.x.
236. Roser, M. E., Fiser, J., Aslin, R. N., & Gazzaniga, M. S. (2011). Right hemisphere dominance in visual statistical learning. *Journal of Cognitive Neuroscience, 23*(5), 1088–1099. https://doi.org/10.1162/jocn.2010.21508.
237. Roux, F., & Uhlhaas, P. J. (2014). Working memory and neural oscillations: Alpha-gamma versus theta-gamma codes for distinct WM information? *Trends in Cognitive Sciences, 18*(1), 16–25. https://doi.org/10.1016/j.tics.2013.10.010.
238. Saffran, J., Aslin, R., & Newport, E. (1996). Statistical learning by 8-month-old infants. *Science, 274*(December), 1926–1928.
239. Saffran, J. R., Aslin, R. N., & Newport, E. L. (1996). Statistical learning by 8-month-old infants. *Science.* https://doi.org/10.1126/science.274.5294.1926.
240. Saffran, J. R., Hauser, M., Seibel, R., Kapfhamer, J., Tsao, F., & Cushman, F. (2008). Grammatical pattern learning by human infants and cotton-top tamarin monkeys. *Cognition, 107*(2), 479–500. https://doi.org/10.1016/j.cognition.2007.10.010.

241. Saffran, J. R., Johnson, E. K., Aslin, R. N., & Newport, E. L. (1999). Statistical learning of tone sequences by human infants and adults. *Cognition, 70*(1), 27–52. https://doi.org/10.1016/S0010-0277(98)00075-4.

242. Saffran, J. R., Reeck, K., Niebuhr, A., & Wilson, D. (2005). Changing the tune: The structure of the input affects infants' use of absolute and relative pitch. *Developmental Science, 8*(1), 1–7. https://doi.org/10.1111/j.1467-7687.2005.00387.x.

243. Saffran, J. R., & Wilson, D. P. (2003). From syllables to syntax: Multilevel statistical learning by 12-month-old infants. *Infancy, 4*(2), 273–284. https://doi.org/10.1207/S15327078IN0402_07.

244. Saggar, M., Quintin, E.-M., Bott, N. T., Kienitz, E., Chien, Y., Hong, D.W.-C., & Reiss, A. L. (2016). Changes in brain activation associated with spontaneous improvization and figural creativity after design-thinking-based training: A longitudinal fMRI study. *Cerebral Cortex, 27*(7), 3542–3552. https://doi.org/10.1093/cercor/bhw171.

245. Sakai, K., Kitaguchi, K., & Hikosaka, O. (2003). Chunking during human visuomotor sequence learning. *Experimental Brain Research, 152*(2), 229–242. https://doi.org/10.1007/s00221-003-1548-8.

246. Sanders, L. D., Newport, E. L., & Neville, H. J. (2002). Segmenting nonsense: An event-related potential index of perceived onsets in continuous speech. *Nature Neuroscience, 5*(7), 700–703. https://doi.org/10.1038/nn873.

247. Schapiro, A. C., Gregory, E., Landau, B., McCloskey, M., & Turk-Browne, N. B. (2014). The Necessity of the medial temporal lobe for statistical learning. *Journal of Cognitive Neuroscience, 26*(8), 1736–1747. https://doi.org/10.1162/jocn_a_00578.

248. Schenker, H., & Jonas, O. (1956). *Neue musikalische Theorien und Phantasien.* Retrieved from https://books.google.de/books?id=rTuKxwEACAAJ.

249. Schmahmann, J. D. (2004). Disorders of the cerebellum: Ataxia, dysmetria of thought, and the cerebellar cognitive affective syndrome. *The Journal of Neuropsychiatry and Clinical Neurosciences, 16*(3), 367–378. https://doi.org/10.1176/jnp.16.3.367.

250. Schmidhuber, J. (2006). Developmental robotics, optimal artificial curiosity, creativity, music, and the fine arts. *Connection Science, 18*(2), 173–187. https://doi.org/10.1080/09540090600768658.

251. Schmidhuber, J. (2010). Formal theory of creativity, fun, and intrinsic motivation (1990–2010). *IEEE Transactions on Autonomous Mental Development, 2*(3), 230–247. https://doi.org/10.1109/TAMD.2010.2056368.

252. Schwartenbeck, P., FitzGerald, T., Dolan, R. J., & Friston, K. (2013). Exploration, novelty, surprise, and free energy minimization. *Frontiers in Psychology, 4*(OCT), 1–5. https://doi.org/10.3389/fpsyg.2013.00710.

253. Scott-Phillips, T., & Blythe, R. (2013). *Why is combinatorial communication rare in the natural world?* Talk first(Abstract): No.

254. Seidenberg, M. S. (1997). Language acquisition and use: Learning and applying probabilistic constraints. *Science.* https://doi.org/10.1126/science.275.5306.1599.

255. Servan-Schreiber, E., & Anderson, J. R. (1990). Learning artificial grammars with competitive chunking. *Journal of Experimental Psychology: Learning, Memory, and Cognition, 16*(4), 592–608. https://doi.org/10.1037/0278-7393.16.4.592.

256. Shannon, C. E. (1948). A mathematical theory of communication. *Bell System Technical Journal, 27*(April 1924), 623–656.

257. Shimizu, R. E., Wu, A. D., Samra, J. K., & Knowlton, B. J. (2017). The impact of cerebellar transcranial direct current stimulation (Tdcs) on learning fine-motor sequences. *Philosophical Transactions of the Royal Society B: Biological Sciences, 372*(1711). https://doi.org/10.1098/rstb.2016.0050.

258. Simonton, D. K. (2010). Creative thought as blind-variation and selective-retention: Combinatorial models of exceptional creativity. *Physics of Life Reviews, 7*(2), 156–179. https://doi.org/10.1016/j.plrev.2010.02.002.

259. Sinex, D. G., Guzik, H., Li, H., & Henderson Sabes, J. (2003). Responses of auditory nerve fibers to harmonic and mistuned complex tones. *Hearing Research, 182*(1), 130–139. https://doi.org/https://doi.org/10.1016/S0378-5955(03)00189-8.

260. Skoe, E., Krizman, J., Spitzer, E., & Kraus, N. (2015). Prior experience biases subcortical sensitivity to sound patterns. *Journal of Cognitive Neuroscience, 27*(1), 124–140. https://doi.org/10.1162/jocn_a_00691.

261. Sloutsky, V. M. (2010). From perceptual categories to concepts: What develops? *Cognitive Science, 34*(7), 1244–1286. https://doi.org/10.1111/j.1551-6709.2010.01129.x.

262. Soon, C. S., Brass, M., Heinze, H.-J., & Haynes, J.-D. (2008). Unconscious determinants of free decisions in the human brain. *Nature Neuroscience, 11*, 543. https://doi.org/10.1038/nn.2112.

263. Strange, B. A., Duggins, A., Penny, W., Dolan, R. J., & Friston, K. J. (2005). Information theory, novelty and hippocampal responses: unpredicted or unpredictable? *Neural Networks, 18*(3), 225–230. https://doi.org/10.1016/j.neunet.2004.12.004.

264. Sun, L., Liu, F., Zhou, L., & Jiang, C. (2018). Musical training modulates the early but not the late stage of rhythmic syntactic processing. *Psychophysiology, 55*(2), e12983. https://doi.org/10.1111/psyp.12983.

265. Sussman, E., Winkler, I., & Schröger, E. (2003). Top-down control over involuntary attention switching in the auditory modality. *Psychonomic Bulletin & Review, 10*(3), 630–637.

266. Swain, I., Zelazo, P., & Clifton, R. (1993). Newborn infants' memory for speech sounds retained over 24 hours. *Developmental Psychology, 29*, 312–323. https://doi.org/10.1037/0012-1649.29.2.312.

267. Taylor, K. I., Moss, H. E., Stamatakis, E. A., & Tyler, L. K. (2006). Binding crossmodal object features in perirhinal cortex. *Proceedings of the National Academy of Sciences, 103*(21), 8239–8244. https://doi.org/10.1073/pnas.0509704103.

268. Teinonen, T., Fellman, V., Näätänen, R., Alku, P., & Huotilainen, M. (2009). *Statistical language learning in neonates revealed by event-related brain potentials. 8.* https://doi.org/10.1186/1471-2202-10-21.

269. Thiessen, E. D. (2017). What's statistical about learning? Insights from modelling statistical learning as a set of memory processes. *Philosophical Transactions of the Royal Society B: Biological Sciences, 372*(1711). https://doi.org/10.1098/rstb.2016.0056.

270. Thiessen, E. D., Kronstein, A. T., & Hufnagle, D. G. (2013). *The extraction and integration framework: A two-process account of statistical learning. 139*(4), 792–814. https://doi.org/10.1037/a0030801.

271. Thiessen, E. D., & Pavlik, P. I. (2013). iMinerva: A mathematical model of distributional statistical learning. *Cognitive Science.* https://doi.org/10.1111/cogs.12011.

272. Tillmann, B., Bharucha, J. J., & Bigand, E. (2000). Implicit learning of tonality: A self-organizing approach. *Psychological Review, 107*(4), 885–913. https://doi.org/10.1037/0033-295X.107.4.885.

273. Tillmann, B., Bigand, E., & Pineau, M. (1998). Effects of global and local contexts on harmonic expectancy. *Music Perception: An Interdisciplinary Journal, 16*(1), 99–117. https://doi.org/10.2307/40285780.

274. Tillmann, B., Koelsch, S., Escoffier, N., Bigand, E., Lalitte, P., Friederici, A. D., & von Cramon, D. Y. (2006). Cognitive priming in sung and instrumental music: Activation of inferior frontal cortex. *NeuroImage, 31*(4), 1771–1782. https://doi.org/10.1016/j.neuroimage.2006.02.028.

275. Tishby, N., & Polani, D. (2011). Information theory of decisions and actions. *Perception-Action Cycle, 601–636.* https://doi.org/10.1007/978-1-4419-1452-1_19.

276. Toro, J. M., Sinnett, S., & Soto-Faraco, S. (2005). Speech segmentation by statistical learning depends on attention. *Cognition, 97*(2), 25–34. https://doi.org/10.1016/j.cognition.2005.01.006.

277. Tremblay, P., Baroni, M., & Hasson, U. (2013). Processing of speech and non-speech sounds in the supratemporal plane: Auditory input preference does not predict sensitivity to statistical structure. *NeuroImage, 66*, 318–332. https://doi.org/10.1016/j.neuroimage.2012. 10.055.

278. Tsogli, V., Jentschke, S., Daikoku, T., & Koelsch, S. (2019). When the statistical MMN meets the physical MMN. *Scientific Reports, 9*(1), 5563. https://doi.org/10.1038/s41598-019-42066-4.

279. Turk-browne, N. B., Scholl, B. J., Chun, M. M., & Johnson, M. K. (2009). Neural evidence of statistical learning: Efficient detection of visual regularities without awareness. *Journal of Cognitive Neuroscience, 21*(10), 1934–1945. https://doi.org/10.1162/jocn.2009.21131.

280. Turk-Browne, N. B., Scholl, B. J., Johnson, M. K., & Chun, M. M. (2010). Implicit perceptual anticipation triggered by statistical learning. *The Journal of Neuroscience, 30*(33), 11177–11187. https://doi.org/10.1523/JNEUROSCI.0858-10.2010.

281. Uddin, L. Q. (2014). Salience processing and insular cortical function and dysfunction. *Nature Reviews Neuroscience, 16*, 55. https://doi.org/10.1038/nrn3857.

282. van Kesteren, M. T. R., Ruiter, D. J., Fernández, G., & Henson, R. N. (2012). How schema and novelty augment memory formation. *Trends in Neurosciences, 35*(4), 211–219. https:// doi.org/10.1016/j.tins.2012.02.001.

283. Vandervert, L. R., Schimpf, P. H., & Liu, H. (2007). How working memory and the cerebellum collaborate to produce creativity and innovation. *Creativity Research Journal, 19* (1), 1–18. https://doi.org/10.1080/10400410709336873.

284. Von Fange, E. K. (1959). *Professional creativity*. Retrieved from https://books.google.de/ books?id=9PMyAAAAMAAJ.

285. Vuvan, D. T., Zendel, B. R., & Peretz, I. (2018). Random feedback makes listeners tone-deaf. *Scientific Reports, 8*(1), 7283. https://doi.org/10.1038/s41598-018-25518-1.

286. Wagner, U., Gais, S., Haider, H., Verleger, R., & Born, J. (2004). Sleep inspires insight. *Nature, 427*, 352. https://doi.org/10.1038/nature02223.

287. Walker, M. P., Liston, C., Hobson, J. A., & Stickgold, R. (2002). Cognitive flexibility across the sleep–wake cycle: REM-sleep enhancement of anagram problem solving. *Cognitive Brain Research, 14*(3), 317–324. https://doi.org/10.1016/S0926-6410(02)00134-9.

288. Walker, M. P., & Stickgold, R. (2006). Sleep, memory, and plasticity. *Annual Review of Psychology, 57*(1), 139–166. https://doi.org/10.1146/annurev.psych.56.091103.070307.

289. Ward, A. M., Schultz, A. P., Huijbers, W., Van Dijk, K. R. A., Hedden, T., & Sperling, R. A. (2014). The parahippocampal gyrus links the default-mode cortical network with the medial temporal lobe memory system. *Human Brain Mapping, 35*(3), 1061–1073. https:// doi.org/10.1002/hbm.22234.

290. Werker, J. F., Yeung, H. H., & Yoshida, K. A. (2012). How do infants become experts at native-speech perception? *Current Directions in Psychological Science*. https://doi.org/10. 1177/0963721412449459.

291. Wiggins, G. A. (2018). Creativity, information, and consciousness: The information dynamics of thinking. *Physics of Life Reviews, 1*, 1–39. https://doi.org/10.1016/j.plrev.2018. 05.001.

292. Wiggins, G. A. (2019). Consolidation as re-representation: Revising the meaning of memory. *Frontiers in Psychology*, 1–22.

293. Winkler, I., & Czigler, I. (2012). Evidence from auditory and visual event-related potential (ERP) studies of deviance detection (MMN and vMMN) linking predictive coding theories and perceptual object representations. *International Journal of Psychophysiology, 83*(2), 132–143. https://doi.org/10.1016/j.ijpsycho.2011.10.001.

294. Wittmann, B. C., Daw, N. D., Seymour, B., & Dolan, R. J. (2008). Striatal activity underlies novelty-based choice in humans. *Neuron, 58*(6), 967–973. https://doi.org/10.1016/j.neuron. 2008.04.027.

295. Wixted, J. T. (2004). The psychology and neuroscience of forgetting. *Annual Review of Psychology, 55*(1), 235–269. https://doi.org/10.1146/annurev.psych.55.090902.141555.

296. Yumoto, M., & Daikoku, T. (2016). Basic function. *Clinical Applications of Magnetoencephalography*. https://doi.org/10.1007/978-4-431-55729-6_5.
297. Yumoto, M., & Daikoku, T. (2018). Neurophysiological studies on auditory statistical learning [in Japanese] 聴覚刺激列の統計学習の神経生理学的研究. *Japanese Journal of Cognitive Neuroscience(認知神経科学)*, *20*(1), 38–43.
298. Zabelina, D. L., & Andrews-Hanna, J. R. (2016). Dynamic network interactions supporting internally-oriented cognition. *Current Opinion in Neurobiology*, *40*, 86–93. https://doi.org/10.1016/j.conb.2016.06.014.
299. Zubicaray, G. De, Arciuli, J., & Mcmahon, K. (2013). *Putting an "End" to the Motor Cortex Representations of Action Words*. 1957–1974. https://doi.org/10.1162/jocn.

Tatsuya Daikoku is an assistant professor at the International Research Center for Neurointelligence, The University of Tokyo, Japan. He is also a composer and is interested in interdisciplinary understanding of human and artificial intelligence, in particular issues pertaining to universality and specificity in music and language. He likes to develop his own music theories to compose original music. E-mail: daikoku.tatsuya@mail.u-tokyo.ac.jp.

Music, Artificial Intelligence and Neuroscience

7

David Cope

7.1 Introduction

Aside from historical references to the Early Greek philosophers and since then a long line of sci-fi authors and stories of mental illnesses running rampant, the fields of Artificial Intelligence (AI) and Neuroscience waited until the mid-twentieth century before gaining their current titles and credence in academia, research, and knowledge of their existence among the populace as a whole [33]. Certainly, people like von Neumann and Turing in AI and Skinner and Chomsky in Psychology had great theories, some of which are still in vogue, but it took John McCarthy to invent the term 'Artificial Intelligence' in his 1955 proposal for the 1956 Dartmouth Conference. Several prominent Neuroscience organizations (study of the human nervous system and brain) were formed during that same period and later: e.g., the International Society for Neurochemistry in 1963, the European Brain and Behaviour Society in 1968, and the Society for Neuroscience in 1969.

Today, both subjects thrive in the arenas of disagreements with AI gaining a growing audience of Deep Learning enthusiasts while the experts begin to doubt the all-encompassing future that many have predicted. Neuroscience, on the other hand, has split into at least fourteen different specialties that often struggle through lean times. Since AI and Neuroscience would seem un-strange bedfellows, logic suggests that the two disciplines would have a great deal to offer one another, and to some extent, that proved true over the sixty-plus years since their official births [47]. However, it has only been recently that collegiate departments have surfaced that pair expert of both studies working together and that a few brave converts have decided to codify their interests in both subjects and frame a single discipline from the two [44]. This should herald a celebration of sorts, for the independence of these

D. Cope (✉)
Department of Music, University of California, Santa Cruz, CA, USA
e-mail: howell@ucsc.edu

© Springer Nature Switzerland AG 2021
E. R. Miranda (ed.), *Handbook of Artificial Intelligence for Music*,
https://doi.org/10.1007/978-3-030-72116-9_7

fields makes no sense at all. In fact, at least in part, the two should have been joined at the hip from the beginning.

Music, interestingly enough, naturally shares overlapping interests for both of these aforementioned disciplines: algorithmic computer music and music psychology and perception being obvious examples of such overlaps. In fact, music, with its more syntactic than semantic base, and strong semiotic ties, provides the former two areas with a strong base for creating a cohesive binding between all three fields [24]. With these thoughts in mind, we will proceed with more information about these areas of study and how important they can be to one another now and in the future.

7.2 Music

> ... experienced listeners show the following expectational tendencies: 1. Pitch proximity Listeners expect an ensuing pitch to be near the current pitch. 2. Post-skip reversal Listeners expect a large interval to be followed by a change in pitch direction. 3. Step inertia Listeners expect a small interval to be followed by a subsequent small interval in the same direction. 4. Late-phrase declination Listeners expect pitches to descend in the latter half of phrases (Huron [25], p. 94).

Music "is the science or art of ordering tones or sounds in succession, in combination, and in temporal relationships to produce a composition having unity and continuity" (Merriam-Webster). Defining music presents many difficulties since it pertains to very different and subtle complications such as pitch, rhythm, dynamics, timbre, transposition, key, texture, form, styles, articulations, meters, tempos, and too many more to continue listing. In brief, however, music relies on *patterns*, a word not unfamiliar to the two other fields proclaimed in the title of this chapter, and the word that will be oft-repeated during the course of describing the manner in which Music, Artificial Intelligence, and Neuroscience intersect regardless of whether we know and/or understand this to be true.

Music, like its brethren Visual Art and Authorship, has, at least since composer Hector Berlioz in the early and mid-nineteenth century, proven itself a medium of experimental works in progress, and, following John Cage, an anything-goes model. Like both AI and Neuroscience, Cage's fixation on chance and combinations of unrelated forms began during the forties and fifties of the twentieth century, mirroring in some respects the formal origins of AI and Neuroscience. Cage's historic composition entitled *4'33"* premiered in 1952 and today represents the first instance of a work of music devoid of deliberate sounds. *Finnigans Wake* by James Joyce, an avant-garde novel, was published in 1939, and Marcel Duchamp's *Fountain*, an actual cement drinking fountain untouched except by those who moved it over the years, was first displayed in 1917, both predating Cage's work but neither having the impact that *4'33"* did.

Human-composed music, even computer-composed and so-called randomly-composed music, depends on the single word: *patterns*. To a degree, patterns exist in everything. Even irrational numbers like π exhibit patterns and, because irrational numbers are infinite in length, these patterns repeat an infinite number of times and infinitely varied in unpredictable ways. Patterns (often called motives) in non-experimental Classical music, however, tend to be the glue that holds works together, even when most of the other elements are changing, sometimes even radically so.

Examples of motives holding music together, even long and large ensemble types, are plentiful in the music of Ludwig van Beethoven as briefly pointed out in an example of the beginning of his famous 5th Symphony (Fig. 7.1).

In music, pattern recognition, when included with techniques of variation such as pitch transposition, proximate rhythmic similarities, interval size variants, and so on, as well as less audible inversions, retrogrades, and metric displacements, require wider search techniques than in most other fields.

In the first example, the beginning of Beethoven's 5th Symphony, the upper strings demonstrate the four-note pattern beginning on the offbeat of beat one of measure one: three repeated notes followed by a major third downward (G to Eb). The motive is then repeated transposed down to already the first variation, a minor third downward preceded by three repeated notes. Beginning in measure 6, then, the music becomes more contrapuntal with repeated statements beginning in the second violins (major third down), the violas a minor second above and moving only a minor second down after the repeated notes, and then a minor third in the first

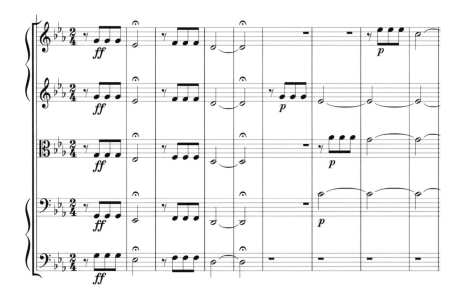

Fig. 7.1 Strings from the beginning of Ludwig van Beethoven's 5th Symphony, Movement 1 (1807). (Dover Publications, Public Domain.)

violins down from the starting notes a minor sixth up from the beginning statement. A single note motive in several intervallic iterations in the first twelve measures of the symphony exhibits an amazing array of variations with no extended melody presented thus far [26].

The short snippet shown in this first example barely begins to indicate how this pattern alters throughout all four movements of the symphony. For example, just a few measures beyond that example, the music displays a two-note beginning of the motive followed by stepwise motion filling in material in the same strings in both the original material and its inversion. The following music presents continuing variation with the original pattern transposed and altered with an expanded interval (perfect fourth) upward.

Fearful that presenting all the manipulations of Beethoven's four-note motive would in themselves create a book-length manuscript, readers should look to the Internet, Bibliography of this book, or your local library for far more extensive portrayals of this and other works by Beethoven, and the many other composers of the eighteenth, nineteenth, and twentieth centuries that made their careers from this kind of pattern recognition in their music, from Antonio Vivaldi and Johann Sebastien Bach to Igor Stravinsky and Arnold Schoenberg).

It would be imprudent here not to include more on music and emotions at this point, especially since emotional states are integral to the activities of the brain. Kate Hevner's 66 words in eight categories have created a kind of model for those theorizing on one-to-one relationships between the elements of music that trigger certain emotional states in at least a majority of those taking part in tests (Hevner in [19]. One version of this model appears in Fig. 7.2. Sometimes called the Adjective Circle, these groups of words tend toward the positive aspects of the human

1.	melancholy	4.	delicate	dramatic
spiritual	frustrated	lyrical	light	passionate
lofty	depressing	leisurely	graceful	sensational
awe-	gloomy	satisfying		agitated
inspiring	heavy	serene	6.	exciting
dignified	dark	tranquil	merry	impetuous
sacred		quiet	joyous	restless
solemn	3.	soothing	gay	
sober	dreamy		happy	8.
serious	yielding	5.	cheerful	vigorous
	tender	humorous	bright	robust
2.	sentimental	playful		emphatic
pathetic	longing	whimsical	7.	martial
doleful	yearning	fanciful	exhilarated	ponderous
sad	pleading	quaint	soaring	majestic
mournful	plaintive	sprightly	triumphant	exalting
tragic				

Fig. 7.2 The hevner adjective list

condition rather than the negative, with only eleven words tending toward the dark side (see the second category).

AI scholars and researchers have tended toward ignoring emotions in their analyses of listener reactions since chemical responses to activations are much more difficult to pin down precisely than judgments on reactions to electrical initializations.

> Emotions are usually considered states of a person. We say that somebody is in a state of fear as they are being chased by a bear, for instance. But we also apply emotions to systems larger than a person. For instance, we can say that 'America was in a state of fear' after the 9/11 terrorist attacks. In this case we might be referring to all or most of the people in America, or to America as a more abstract entity in terms of how the country reacted in news, policy, and so forth. The attribution of a fear state to a single person, or to larger social entity, can both be legitimate, if they adopt the functional perspective... In both examples, there is a situation of threat and various functional consequences of an emotion state that collectively attempt to deal with the threat (Adolphs and Anderson [1], p. 58).

All of these affect the states and cognition of listeners and the human brain's interpretation of almost anything perceived and should never be taken for granted by researchers in areas associated with Music, AI, or Neuroscience.

7.3   Artificial Intelligence

> AI currently encompasses a huge variety of subfields, ranging from the general (learning and perception) to the specific, such as playing chess, proving mathematical theories, writing poetry, driving a car on a crowded street, and diagnosing diseases. AI is relevant to any intellectual task: it is truly a universal field (Norvig and Russell [34], p. 1).

A common definition of Artificial Intelligence is "the capability of a machine to imitate intelligent human behavior" (Merriam- Webster). Since everyone reading this last sentence will have different views on a definition, we will let this stand for the moment since simple and direct views of a complicated matter will help us stay on track.

One of the things we can imply from this definition is that the activity and structure of the human brain plays a significant role, if not the entire role, in what we can surmise from 'intelligent human behavior.' Since the human brain and its corollaries are at least equally important in the field of Neuroscience, we will discuss patterns in AI in terms of programming, and neuroscience in terms of how an actual brain functions.

> Your perceptions and knowledge about the world are built from these patterns. There's no light inside your head. It's dark in there. There's no sound entering your brain either. It's quiet inside. In fact, the brain is the only part of your body that has no senses itself. A surgeon could stick a finger into your brain and you wouldn't feel it. All the information that enters your mind comes in as spatial and temporal patterns on the axons (Hawkins [22], p. 56–57).

Early on in the history of Artificial Intelligence, pattern recognition (the automatic discovery of patterns and their regularity in data through the use of algorithms taking actions such as classifying the data into different groupings) became an important element of computational learning and thus programming. Computational musical pattern recognition can, therefore, reveal otherwise elusive pattern relationships not otherwise obvious or clear. Of the many types of techniques used in machine learning, the following three seem the most often and most successfully used. Note, however, that at the core of each is some manner of a pattern recognition program, regardless of whether it's explicitly stated here or not.

The first is Linear Regression. This is an approach to modeling relationships between a dependent variable and one or more independent variables. In simple terms, this process could be described as someone asking you to rate the first ten people you see walking around a corner in order of their yearly salaries without knowing or being able to ask them what their salaries were. One way to do this would be to judge their clothing: the better and more or less expensive their suits or dresses, the more or less money they make. While not always correct, this approach, a linear 45° line on a graph representing the dependent variable and points where the well-dressed and not so well-dressed people were situated would be one way to statistically answer the question [29].

The second are supervised machine learning algorithms referred to as Decision Trees. Again, in simple terms, one way to view this type of computational learning could be a problem that needs solving. In an example case, you know ten people who have never been to Death Valley before and would like to schedule an event there such that all ten will attend. You would like to do this without causing a problem such as having to cancel it when you discover that only five can come. Based on past experience, you could create a tree structure in which all ten people sit at the top and the layers (branches) below it attempt to indicate under what weather conditions, likability among other members of the group will get along, and who does not like to walk in warm weather (the event would take place in the early spring).

And then, there is the Naive Bayes method which is based on a simple formula

$$P(h|d) = (P(d|h) * P(h)) / P(d)$$

where **P(h|d)** is the probability of hypothesis **h** given the data **d**, called the posterior probability, **P(d|h)** is the probability of data **d** given that the hypothesis **h** is true, **P (h)** is the probability of hypothesis **h** being true called the prior probability of **h**, and **P(d)** is the probability of the data (regardless of the hypothesis). In brief, we are interested in the posterior probability of **P(h|d)** from the prior probability **p(h)** with **P(D)** and **P(d|h)**. The title usually given this approach (Naive Bayes) is also termed 'Idiot Bayes' due to the probabilities for each hypothesis being simplified to make their calculation manageable. Using our example above, with a new instance of the *weather* of *sunny*, we can calculate

$$go - out = \mathbf{P}(weather = sunny|class = go - out) * \mathbf{P}(class = go - out)$$

$$\text{stay} - \text{home} = \mathbf{P}(\text{weather} = \text{sunny}|\text{class} = \text{stay} - \text{home})$$
$$* \, \mathbf{P}(\text{class} = \text{stay} - \text{home})$$

We can also choose the class that has the largest calculated value, and can then turn the values into probabilities by normalizing them as follows:

$$\mathbf{P}(\text{go} - \text{out}|\text{weather} = \text{sunny}) = \text{go} - \text{out} \, / \, (\text{go} - \text{out} + \text{stay} - \text{home})$$

$$\mathbf{P}(\text{stay} - \text{home}|\text{weather} = \text{sunny}) = \text{stay} - \text{home} \, / \, (\text{go} - \text{out} + \text{stay} - \text{home})$$

Other algorithms for machine learning include Logistic Regression, SVM, kNN, K-Means, Random Forests, Dimensionality Reduction Algorithms, Gradient Boosting Algorithms, Markov Techniques, and many more.

There are many other processes aside from these three machine learning algorithms that deserve mentioning here. For example, machine creativity (particularly in the areas of music composition and art) has come a long way from its beginnings in the 1950s. While most of the programs that succeed in these areas remain typically in the 'shadows' of what some might say have more business-oriented or neurological-research points of view, computational visual arts, in particular, have proven amazingly robust both in longevity and in the world of financial sales [35].

Pattern recognition also plays a significant role in today's computational neural networks, particularly Convolutional Neural Networks (CNNs) making it possible to recognize visual patterns directly from raw pixels with little to no preprocessing [21]. It may, therefore, be surprising to some that the history of Artificial Neural Networks (ANNs) and Deep Learning Neural Networks (DNNs) goes back more than sixty years, well before the invention of the seemingly ubiquitous computers that we carry with us in our phones, watches, briefcases, and maybe even still our desktops. ANNs began in 1943 when neurophysiologist Warren McCulloch and mathematician Walter Pitts portrayed a simple electrical circuit as having brain-like potentials. Donald Hebb's book, The *Organization of Behaviour* in 1949 then proposed that neural pathways strengthen over repeated use, especially between neurons that fire at the same time, thus beginning a long journey towards quantifying some of the complex processes of the human brain. The first Hebbian network was successfully implemented at MIT in 1954. Four years later, Frank Rosenblatt, a psychologist at Cornell University, proposed the idea of the Perceptron calling it the Mark 1 version, modeled on a McCulloch-Pitts neuron, proposed in 1943.

To say that from then until today, the road has been rocky for ANNs would be doing its history an injustice. ANNs have gone from hardware to software, guesses to whether they are similar to the human brain or nothing like it have come and gone with prolific rapidity, and yearly AI conferences have occurred with some years boasting *no* papers on the subject, and other years having *only* papers on the subject. As of 2020, however, Deep Learning will have remained the hottest ticket on the market with assumptions that the next breakthroughs in AI will surely originate with these virtual machines.

Amazingly enough, though, these advanced multi-layered hidden-unit programs are still basically simple machines that often produce astonishing results. Add to that, the fact that many designers, programmers, and users are still not precisely sure what makes them work, and the history becomes even more confusing. Questions remain, however: Do they really mimic the manner in which the human brain works? Do their outputs simply recognize and categorize inputs, and in some cases, produce surprisingly strange images, but have nothing much related to the current goal of AI or that of AGI (Artificial General Intelligence). That is, the notion that computers could act more like the human mind in being able to solve problems with which they have not been specifically human trained.

There are three types of layers in an ANN: The Input Layer, Hidden Layer(s), and the Output Layer. To train a neural network, you will need a very large data set. The fundamental internal structure of Deep Learning uses a neural network with two or more hidden layers to mimic human intelligence (to be discussed more fully under Neuroscience in this chapter). Each of these ranks of hidden units tend to specialize in different aspects of the problem confronted. Interconnections between neurons are associated with neuronal weights which dictate the importance of input values. The artificial neurons in Deep Learning each apply an Activation Function to the data to regulate its output. Comparing the outputs produces a Cost Function, indicating how much it is off mark from the desired outputs. Following every iteration through the data set, weights between the neurons in the hidden layers are adjusted to reduce the difference between the desired result and the current result. Eventually, the desired result finally appears when the weights are properly self-adjusted [7].

Put more simply, each of deep learning's hidden units contains summational math sensitive to the success or failure of the current output. Each unit (non-linearly) sums all of its input to achieve its weight (between 0 and 1). As the program begins, if the algorithm's output improves, unit increase or decrease values until the output begins to fail. Then the program weights to discover what happens. This goes on for thousands of iterations until finally one assembly of weights hits pay dirt and the formula (the numerical weights themselves) is memorized and the DNN has successfully achieved its goal with no help from a human whatsoever. DNNs (Deep), RNNs (Recurrent), and CNNs (Convolutional) typically have thousands of units and millions of connections, significantly less than human brains [39].

Figure 7.3 presents an example of one of many different configurations for a Deep Learning program. This facial recognition example disassembles and then reconstructs to compare likely candidates with names attached. Using Deep Learning for these kinds of problems can prove effective, and there is no question that Deep Learning will find a place in future AI regardless of its occasional failures in moving beyond complex but limited tasks. These successes have made it extremely valuable in today's market for technical resources to solve certain problems that no other machine learning program can deal with as effectively.

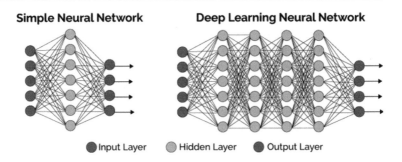

Fig. 7.3 A diagram of an ANN and a simple deep learning program. Public domain

Anyone with small children or grandchildren and paying attention to how they learn will tell you that they mimic those around them. This is particularly noticeable by adults watching youngsters learning language and their resultant reactions when hearing words that they do not yet fully understand. To us, their elders, this process seems slow and cumbersome, repetitious, and at times obnoxious, but once learned correctly in pronunciation and parsed correctly, it can last a lifetime. Deep Learning derives its repetitive processes from these types of examples and represents one of the most important reference points for the success of fundamental principles involved in DNN's success [18].

Many AI professionals, however, have become skeptical about the ability of the various incarnations of software versions of Deep Learning to ever become a good example of AGI as opposed to AI. So far at least, the outputs of such programs can be singularly unique but universally silent. They can certainly recognize a particular face out of thousands of photos and pin names and other details on that face, a useful process to be sure, but they cannot yet create a human face from scratch without simply recombining parts from different faces. As well, patterns or strategies extracted by Deep Learning may be more superficial than they appear. The well-known 'Atari model' (2600) that learned to break walls and win games can be 'over interpreted' to the extent that many believe the model truly understood the concept of a wall or of winning, while the model merely learned to break walls to maximize a highly constrained objective.

Some AI experts believe that Deep Learning has more disadvantages than advantages. For example, inputs when applied to, say, music, language, and the sciences require different tunings of the system itself (i.e., hidden units and I/O). Also, Deep Learning does not, as of yet at least, deal with AI's primary aim of AGI where machines can, using just one implementation, deal with different problems without reworking the fundamentals of the program. At present, each design is typically useful for one or possibly a few types of problems. Human brains can deal with almost any problem, at least in understanding what the central patterns of those problems mean.

Another aspect of Deep Learning encompasses the number of examples necessary for this type of ANN to tolerably capture the nature (typically visual) of an image or images. Humans, even children of younger ages, can perceive a photograph of, say, an animal like a lion and told its name a single time, and then call it by name when seeing it a second time. Deep Learning requires thousands of such images and beyond to replicate the same experience. These processes may require similar amounts of time since computers now function so quickly, but it's clear that the two processes vary significantly, and that the notion of Deep Learning as working similarly to the human brain has become more and more problematic to defend.

Yet no one knows what the future may bring, and the surprises provided by Deep Learning systems have been strikingly remarkable at times. Thus, the few criticisms mentioned above may be too soon in coming and even shortsighted. Regardless of the lack of match between DL and the human brain's operation (especially since they do not resemble one another in terms of mechanical and biological construction), many well-schooled futurists tend toward declaring future dates and goals with amazing rewards in mind.

After having used Deep Learning programs and attempted more than several outputs, I am cautiously hopeful that it may eventually be part of an AGI explanation, but not the major solution. Jeff Hawkins' belief in 'memory and prediction' evolving from pattern matching in the neocortex's cortical columns soon to be discussed, while completely abstracted from its sources (a perfect example of AGI), seems a much better human meme to achieve which, until now, seemed like a bridge-too-far. Interestingly, some other neuroscientists now believe that our five senses (sight, hearing, touch, smell, and taste) can work simultaneously in combinations producing AGI, and with added deep memory what has seemed like an insoluble computational problem can be soluble. Only time will tell.

7.4 Neuroscience

... in visionary volumes called *Description of the Human Body*, *Passions of the Soul*, and *L'homme* (Man), Descartes presented a resolutely mechanical perspective on the inner operation of the body. We are sophisticated automata, wrote this bold philosopher. Our bodies and brains literally act as a collection of "organs": musical instruments comparable to those found in the churches of his time, with massive bellows forcing a special fluid called "animal spirits" into reservoirs, then a broad variety of pipes, whose combinations generate all the rhythms and music of our actions (Dehaene [14], pp. 3–4).

Neuroscience "is a branch of the life sciences that deals with the anatomy, physiology, biochemistry, or molecular biology of nerves and nervous tissue and especially with their relation to behavior and learning" (Merriam-Webster). Even without direct reference to the major set of organs that constitute the human *brain*, this definition of Neuroscience demonstrates the collection of different scientific specialties that contribute to a more or less recent discipline that represents one of the most important branches of science.

There are basically fourteen types of Neuroscience (though counting subtypes will account for many more):

- Cognitive Neuroscience: study of the biological underpinnings of cognition
- Computational Neuroscience: studies information processing in the brain
- Behavioral Neuroscience: study of biological psychology and behavior
- Molecular Neuroscience: study of the biology of the nervous system
- Neurology: study of disorders of the nervous system
- Neurophysiology: study of the nervous system
- Neuroanatomy: study of the nervous tissue and neural structures of the nervous system
- Systems Neuroscience: studies the function of neural circuits and systems
- Neuropsychology: studies the brain related to psychological behavior
- Neuroevolution: studies the evolution of the nervous system
- Neurophilosophy: studies the philosophy of neuroscience
- Developmental Neuroscience: study of the cellular basis of brain development
- Neuropharmacology: study of how drugs affect the cellular function in the nervous system
- Affective Neuroscience: researches emotions and the human brain.

As mentioned previously, and noting that the human brain is complex enough to afford this number of specialties, the overlaps between these various research groups can cause many complications if not difficulties in Neuroscience. Since many relatively new fields of study have suffered from such complicated municipalities and survived, we can expect that these too will gather together to form more useful units of study.

Figure 7.4 shows a representation of the neocortex and the brain's older, less intelligent, but still necessary organs which it surrounds. The neocortex (translation: 'new bark' since it resembles the bark of a tree due to its large size forcing the wrinkles) controls language, cognition, motor commands, reasoning, and sensory perception. Commonly the neocortex is divided into four lobes demarcated by the cranial sutures in the surrounding skull: the frontal lobe, the parietal lobe, the occipital lobe, and the temporal lobe. Each of these lobes performs different functions, the temporal lobe, for example, contains the primary auditory cortex and the occipital lobe acts as the primary visual cortex (in the rear).

The neocortex is usually described as containing a large number of vertical structures called cortical columns, each with diameters of approximately 0.5 mm and a depth of 2 mm. These columns are considered the basic repeating functional units of the neocortex, but their varying definitions in terms of anatomy and function are generally not consistent, leading to many different opinions regarding their purpose or even their definitions in terms of columns.

Fig. 7.4 The four principal
areas of the Neocortex and the
Neocortex in relation to its
two other quite older brains
which it surrounds (Sensory
Cortex and Motor Cortex).
Public domain

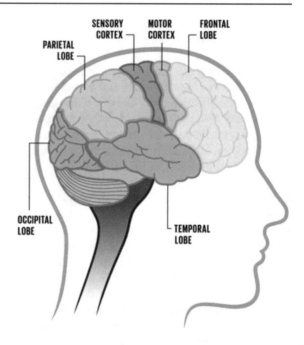

Brains are pattern machines. It's not incorrect to express the brain's functions in terms of
hearing or vision, but at the most fundamental level, patterns are the name of the game. No
matter how different the activities of various cortical areas may seem from each other, the
same basic cortical algorithm is at work. The cortex doesn't care if the patterns originated in
vision, hearing, or another sense. It doesn't care if you happened to perceive the world with
sonar, radar, or magnetic fields, or if you had tentacles rather than hands, or even if you
lived in a world of four dimensions rather than three (Hawkins [22], p. 62).

What is so interesting about these patterns, as they reach their ultimate analytical
destination, is that they have lost their origins and treated as simple abstract entities.
It would seem that those origins would be important, at least as much as they would
keep the neocortex from mistaking visual from oral sources. Since these patterns are
coincident with one another, sight mirroring sound and vice versa, we must assume
that one pattern can stand for many simultaneously, and thus produce much faster
and more accurate responses to what could be dangerous situations.

… the most important thing to understand about the neocortex is that it has an extremely
uniform structure. This was first hypothesized by American neuroscientist Vernon
Mountcastle in 1978. You would think a region responsible for much of the color and
subtlety of human experience would be chaotic, irregular, and unpredictable. Instead, we've
found the **cortical column**, a basic structure that is repeated throughout the neocortex. Each
of the approximately 500,000 cortical columns is about two millimeters high and a half
millimeter wide, and contains about 60,000 neurons (for a total of about 30 billion neurons
in the neocortex) [16].

There are many useful concepts of pattern recognition currently. The five principal theories include analysis of features, template matching, prototype similarities, recognition by components theory, and bottom-up/top-down processing. Each of these approaches pertains to various areas where patterns prove important, even critical. Music, language, and visual image recognition are a few of such subjects. Facial recognition occurs through encrypting visual patterns, while language and music recognition benefit from the encoding of auditory information [4].

Feature analysis suggests that the central nervous system filters incoming stimuli that allows us to understand the evidence. This tactic involves feature detectors which include groups of neurons encoding perceptual structures. The theory proposes an increasing complexity between detectors and other descriptors. Basic detectors respond to simple properties of the stimuli. Further along the perceptual pathways, detectors may respond to even more multifaceted and specific stimuli. When features repeat or occur in sequences, we can identify these patterns because of our feature analysis system.

Template theory defines a basic methodology for human pattern recognition. The model assumes that most perceived entities are kept as a *template* in long-term memory. Incoming patterns are compared with these templates to reveal an exact match. In simpler terms, all sensory input is matched to multiple representations of a pattern to form one model. This defines perception as a fundamental pattern recognition process. It assumes that everything we see, we understand through past experiences, which then informs our future perceptions of the world around us. This perspective is limited, however, in clarifying how completely new experiences are understood without being compared to internal memory templates [42].

Prototype matching associates incoming patterns to one common prototype exposed to a series of related stimuli leading to the formation of a *typical* prototype based on shared features. It reduces the number of stored templates by standardizing them into a single representation. The prototype supports perceptual flexibility since, unlike template matching, it tolerates variability in the recognition of unique stimuli. For instance, if a child had never seen a lawn chair, s/he would likely still recognize it as a chair because of their understanding of chairs having four supports and a seat. This idea, however, limits the concept of objects that cannot necessarily be "averaged" into one. Even though dogs, wolves, and foxes are all typically furry, four-legged, moderate sized animals with ears and a tail, they are not all the same, and thus cannot be strictly perceived with respect to this theory.

Like feature detection theory, the recognition by components (RBC) approach proposed by Irving Biederman (1987) states that humans recognize objects by breaking them down into their basic geometric forms called geons. For example, we deconstruct a cup by recognizing the cylinder that holds the liquid and the curved handle that allows us to hold it. While not every coffee cup is exactly the same, these basic components help us to recognize the regularity across examples (or patterns). RBC implies that there are fewer than 36 unique geons that when combined form a virtually unlimited number of objects. RBC then proposes we focus on two specific features: edges and concavities. Edges enable observers to maintain a consistent representation of the object, regardless of the angle of sight and lighting conditions. Concavities are where two edges meet and enable observers to perceive where one geon ends and another begins [3].

Bottom-up processing originated with the stimulation of the sensory receptors and was proposed by psychologist James Gibson. He opposed the top-down model by arguing that perception is direct and not subject to hypothesis testing. He identified sensation as perception and there was no need for extra interpretation. Further, he maintained that there is more than enough information in our environment to make sense of the world in a direct way. His theory is also known as the 'ecological theory' because he claimed that perception can be described solely in terms of the environment.

The opposite of the bottom-up approach, top-down processing commences by utilizing an individual's previous experience and then makes predictions according to the earlier acquired information. Psychologist Richard Gregory estimated that most of the information is lost during the time it takes to get from the eye to the brain which is why our brains must guess what a person sees based on past experiences. In short, we create a perception of reality, and these observations produce hypotheses or propositions based on past experiences.

> ... superior pattern processing (SPP) as the fundamental basis of most, if not all, unique features of the human brain including intelligence, language, imagination, invention, and the belief in imaginary entities such as ghosts and gods. SPP involves the electrochemical, neuronal network-based, encoding, integration, and transfer to other individuals of perceived or mentally-fabricated patterns. During human evolution, pattern processing capabilities became increasingly sophisticated as the result of expansion of the cerebral cortex, particularly the prefrontal cortex and regions involved in processing of images [30].

Given a paragraph written with difficult handwriting, it is easier to understand what a writer wishes to convey if one reads a whole paragraph rather than just the words as separate terms. Brains may perceive and even understand the substance of the paragraph due to the context supplied by nearby words [43].

> In the neocortex which forms the convoluted outer surface of the (for example) human brain, neurons lie in six vertical layers highly coupled within cylindrical columns. Such columns have been suggested as basic functional units, and stereotypical patterns of connections both within a column and between columns are repeated across cortex (Dayan and Abbott [13], p. 229).

> Every one of the approximately 300 million pattern recognizers in our neocortex is recognizing and defining a pattern and giving it a name, which in the case of the neocortical pattern recognition modules is simply the axon emerging from the pattern recognizer that will fire when that pattern is found. That symbol in turn then becomes part of another pattern. Each one of these patterns is essentially a metaphor. The recognizers can fire up to 100 times a second, so we have the potential of recognizing up to 30 billion metaphors a second. Of course, not every module is firing in every cycle—but it is fair to say that we are indeed recognizing millions of metaphors a second (Kurzweil [28], p. 113).

Pattern recognition, a significant part but not all of the memory process just described, involves an automated computational process that recognizes the similarity between two similar but not equivalent patterns [10]. The process of PR proves highly useful in areas such as computer-aided diagnosis in medicine, speech recognition, matching handwritten postal addresses, and image recognition. Pattern recognition can also be useful in Bayesian networks and Markov analyses [4].

> One can, for example, define a musical event as an input pattern of activation that is then transformed by a network of interconnected processing units into an output pattern of activation representing an interpretation of the event (Gjerdingen [17], p. 138).

In *"A Pattern Recognition Program That Generates, Evaluates, and Adjusts Its Own Operators"* [45], pp. 555), the authors describe one of the first machine learning programs that adaptively acquires and modifies features such that they overcome the limitations of a simple perceptron (a predecessor of neural networks) by Rosenblatt.

> The human brain has evolved to recognize patterns, perhaps more than any other single function. Our brain is weak at processing logic, remembering facts, and making calculations, but pattern recognition is its deep core capability. Deep Blue, the computer that defeated the chess champion Garry Kasparov in 1997, was capable of analyzing 200 million board positions every second. Kasparov was asked how many positions he could analyze each second. His answer was "less than one." So how was this even a remotely close match? Because Kasparov's 30 billion neurons, while relatively slow, are able to work *in parallel*. He is able to look at a chess board and compare what he sees with *all* the (estimated) 100,000 positions he has mastered *at the same time*. Each of these positions is a pattern of pieces on a board, and they are all available as potential matches within seconds. This is how Kasparov's brain can go head to head against a computer that "thinks" 10 million times faster than him (and also is millions of times more precise): his processing is slow, but *massively parallel*. This doesn't just happen in the brains of world chess champions [16].

Before leaving this cursory examination of what our brains are responsible for, we must pay homage to the central nervous system (Fig. 7.7). Our spinal cords, miracles in themselves, carry and receive messages to and from ganglia and nerves, and along with those the various muscles, veins, and critical organs of our bodies. For the most part, these signals emanate from ancient parts of our brains buried deep inside and below the cortex that keep our hearts going, lungs breathing, and to some degree our emotional approaches to life. Therefore, lest we forget, the command-center of the human body is the human brain. We can exchange a dying heart or lung or kidney with the recently dead in the case of a heart, or a part of a lung from a living donor but, to date at least, no one has figured out how to replace a person's brain.

Figure 7.5 presents a drawing of the human body and a severely reduced number of ganglia and nerves (we have several thousand times those shown) that control the movement and reactions of our bodes to counter danger (attacks, weather, and so on) and should remind us that the machines of AI are mostly metal and, as Marvin Minsky allegedly once said: "We are indeed meat. With no disrespect meant toward robots and androids, meat may have shorter lifetimes, but, so far at least, its ability to create those robots and androids puts it a step ahead of the pack."

Not all of the human memory resides in the brain. The memory of the body's immune system, for example, resides outside the brain in certain cells (called the B and T cells) that routinely exist everywhere in the body, but gather around invading

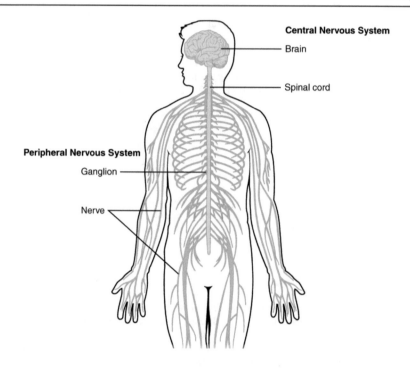

Fig. 7.5 How the brain services the human body as well as its own learning. (OpenStax Anatomy and Physiology:Creative Commons Attribution 4.0 International license)

bacteria to fend them off. These special cells (antibodies) immediately begin dividing and within the bloodstream spread throughout the body. When the battle concludes, most of these added immune cells, no longer required, die off to allow the body's normal blood cells (red and white) to continue maintaining the natural blood flow. Fortunately, not all of these new cells disappear, and the remainder carries with them the memories of what or who won the battles. These few and simple immune cells, therefore, maintain the memories of what keeps us alive.

Interestingly, 'muscle memory' primarily occurs in the brain rather than with muscles themselves. Words can often be deceiving and this group of two is a primary example. Interestingly, though, the slim number of memories our muscles do have are often stored without much conscious awareness, and the skilled actions are performed automatically. The body can play a major role in Artificial Intelligence though it has not made much of an impression thus far. The worlds of dance, acting, and sports tend to be left behind in research, most likely due to robotic complexities that pose so many problems for those intent on including such on their agendas. The lack of professional and academic papers on this subject, as well as books, is testimony to the so far almost nonexistent research taking place [6].

A limbic system is a complex group of nerves and networks in the brain located near the boundary of the neocortex that controls instinct, mood, and especially fear, pleasure, and anger. The amygdala is also critical to emotional reactions. The Hypothalamus helps produce physical responses to emotions, and the Cingulate gyrus is important with respect to subjective emotional awareness. The prefrontal cortex, ventral striatum, insula, and cerebellum also contribute to emotions and emotional regulation. Recent studies have indicated that emotions play a significant role in our higher-level cognitive processes. A popular view of this problem as some researchers have put it, would be like owning a Maserati but not being able to drive it.

Known as Emotional Intelligence (EI), Emotional Quotient (EQ), or Affective Neuroscience, studying and publishing in the field of emotions of the brain has recently become a significant new approach to intelligence within the world of neuroscience, and adding neuroplasticity to the mix has made the brain a flexible and malleable organ that, in good health, has proven by far that the brain is far and away from the most powerful living organism on the face of the Earth. "Neuroplasticity can be seen in various forms at every level of nervous system organization, from the lowest levels of molecular activity to the highest level of brain-wide systems and behavior" (Costandi [9], pp. 11–13).

7.5 Music and Neuroscience

Music (with its music cognition and music perception journals, psychoacoustics, conferences, and academic courses) uses Neuroscience as a significant foundation for understanding aspects of composition, performance, and listening. These latter aspects of music become extremely important when neuroscience links particularly with music performance and composition. Recognition of patterns in the human brain becomes also extraordinarily important during listening when the listener is beset by so many variants that s/he can no longer follow the fundamental shape and direction of the music.

The diagram in Fig. 7.6 shows one possible version of how the ears and brain process the sounds involved in music. The ears take the input through the first ring, that being the outside world of sound through to the second ring. The first ring includes whether the owner of the brain is paying attention to the sound, whether it's loud or soft (dynamics), the sound's timbre (voice, cello, guitar, and so on), what kind of immediate sensation the sound produces in the brain, what the meter (beats per measure) might be, any incidental noise in the environment, any other sensual correlations such as vision competing for notice, and the immediate recognition of musical form involved. The input then penetrates the neocortex with the second ring noting the pitches (intervals), rhythmic, phrase lengths, and cadence types, and feeds those into the third ring where the cortical columns reduce the input to patterns where they can be compared with patterns in memory and send the results back out through the same but retrograde process where the sounds regain

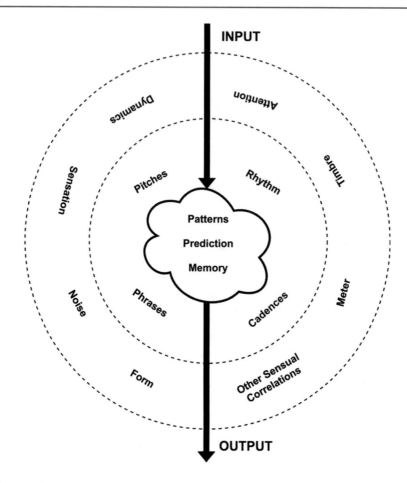

Fig. 7.6 One possible version of how the brain processes musical sounds. Based on [32], Fig. 4, p. 22

their input attributes with the added (learned) correlates so that, for example, the person involved can whistle the tune, speak to the artist's style, or compare one actor's propensities with another.

> The auditory system may be divided into two pathways, or stages: early auditory pathways, which lead from the outer ear through a number of subcortical regions and terminate in the primary auditory cortex, and cortical auditory pathways, which pass out activation from the primary auditory cortex to a number of other cortical areas. Whereas the early pathways are essentially the same for all types of sounds (i.e., in the sense that pretty much everything we hear passes through the same path), the cortical pathways largely depend on the nature of the auditory signal; that is, sounds may go through different cortical pathways depending on their specific characteristics (Miranda [32], p. 14).

The millions and millions of cortical columns in the neocortex can become confused by patterns so altered by mathematical and rigid controls (see music by Anton von Webern, for example) that the resultant music sounds foreign and inimical to the brain. While in part based on lack of experience with such music, some listener reactions are adversely affected based on complexity alone. What's interesting in this case particularly (e.g., Webern's *integral serialism* method), is that music previous to the twentieth century relies primarily on intuitive generation and the many composers after Webern and influenced by him use pure logic [20]. Why music based on the fundamental nature of the human brain (logic) would be so negatively charged by serialism seems beyond rational understanding.

Music also plays an obvious role in Neuroscience through its vast investment of people in music therapy and participating in the ranks of those involved with administering care to those with neurological problems. The education of a music therapist not only allows the study of music, but also encourages examination of one's self as well as others. An undergraduate curriculum includes coursework in music therapy, psychology, music, biological, social, behavioral sciences, disabilities, and general studies. Students learn to assess the needs of patients, develop and implement treatment plans, and evaluate and document clinical changes. At the completion of the American Music Therapy Association AMTA-approved academic training and internship, a student is eligible for admission to the certification exam administered by the Certification Board for Music Therapists (CBMT) Inc. Upon passing the national examination administered by the CBMT, the student acquires the credential Music Therapist-Board Certified (MT-BC).

Figure 7.7 presents a simple scale-illusion (top) and the manner in which a listener might hear a performance (bottom) as Diana Deutsch's famed audio illusions. In the top staff for piano, the first note of each bar when played without the second note of each bar will sound as a whole-tone scale in downward motion (top staff) and upward motion (bottom staff)—as in C-A#-G#-F#-E-D-C (top) and C-D-E–F#-G#-A#-C (bottom). The top two staves and the bottom pair, played

Fig. 7.7 A fast two-hand sound-pattern above and the resultant sounding scales heard by most listeners (Diana Deutsch, Public Domain)

correctly, will sound the same. With the top line of each pair performed, say, by a saxophone and the bottom line of each pair performed by a flute, will sound as written (in other words, due to their different timbres, each instrument will leap back and forth except near the middle in the top staves and stepwise half-octave chromatic scales in the bottom two staves).

Many similar illusions exist in the palette of composers and orchestrators such as a flute diminuendo simultaneous with a clarinet crescendo on the same pitch never heard as such in Claude Debussy's orchestra music, Beethoven's Fifth Symphony motive which should begin on a softer note metrically and work its way to the louder downbeat but is almost always performed as if all four of its notes accented equally, and six-note chords often sounding like two different triads (polytonality) rather than one chord even if not intended that way by the composer.

7.6 Artificial Intelligence and Neuroscience

It is hard to imagine Artificial Intelligence and Neuroscience not interrelated. Experts in either of these fields must rely on experts in the other field or having expertise in both areas of study. How can one research AI without having intimate knowledge of neuroscience and vice versa?

AI depends on neuroscience for its fundamental understanding of the human brain. Neuroscience depends on AI for its ability to build machines and software to carry out its necessary experiments to make both their studies possible. A perfect example of how this would work is the following:

> Technology that translates neural activity into speech would be transformative for people who are unable to communicate as a result of neurological impairments. Decoding speech from neural activity is challenging because speaking requires very precise and rapid multi-dimensional control of vocal tract articulators. Here we designed a neural decoder that explicitly leverages kinematic and sound representations encoded in human cortical activity to synthesize audible speech. Recurrent neural networks first decoded directly recorded cortical activity into representations of articulatory movement, and then transformed these representations into speech acoustics. In closed vocabulary tests, listeners could readily identify and transcribe speech synthesized from cortical activity. Intermediate articulatory dynamics enhanced performance even with limited data. Decoded articulatory representations were highly conserved across speakers, enabling a component of the decoder to be transferrable across participants [2].

Figure 7.8 provides an example where brain and machine can be studied together for positive and negative aspects of both may be measured and otherwise compared. In this particular case, White moves first and wins in two moves. What initially appears as a relatively simple endgame puzzle, proves difficult for many, at least for those relatively unfamiliar with the game. Both AI and human brains will benefit from discovering the algorithm involved (answer deliberately not provided here).

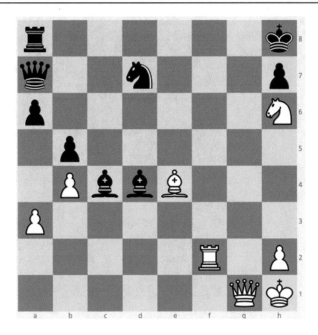

Fig. 7.8 White moves first and wins in two moves. (Public domain)

For those interested in White's apparently weak situation, Black is winning 26 to 23 points and has, was it his/her turn to move, the possibility of either taking White's rook or queen if they attempt to check Black's king and making the score either 31–23 or 35–23, a thoroughly impossible deficit to overcome even though White could counter these moves by taking Black's rook or bishop/knight. Imaginative analysis, however, can provide far too much information for those still seeking an answer, and therefore, good luck on this one.

The mathematical theory of games was invented by John von Neumann and Oskar Morgenstern in 1944. While Fig. 7.9 and the previous chess puzzle may seem strange for a chapter on Music, Artificial Intelligence, and Neuroscience, it can provide significant insights for those experienced enough to infer valuable information on how to make sense of apparently impossible to solve situations. Let's begin by saying that this chess endgame requires more than several moves and that White, who moves first and eventually wins, must know precisely what s/he is doing. As well, the solution to this puzzle is given the name of Saavedra after the priest who discovered it over 100 years ago [41].

It is placed here because of its brilliance in regard to a retrograde solution (i.e., find the perfect checkmate with you the winner, and see if you can work your way back to this position).

Fig. 7.9 The Saavedra
solution (White to move first
and win). (Public domain)

My freedom will be so much the greater and more meaningful the more narrowly I limit my
field of action and the more I surround myself with obstacles. Whatever diminishes constraint, diminishes strength. The more constraints one imposes, the more one frees oneself
of the chains that shackle the spirit [40].

"Artificial Intelligence (AI) is full of questions that cannot be answered and
answers that cannot be assigned to the correct questions" (Nisioti 2018). Game
theory share common goals. It can lend AI the tools to guide learning algorithms in
these settings. While game theory and neurology can both explain what motivates
human decision-making, it is the intersection of the two studies that develop deeper
understandings of how brains make choices.

Here is a list of equations without answers. Your job is to determine what the
question is that prompted these equations and to do that you will have to figure out
the answers to the equations, or at least the answers to two of them.

$$A.\ (2 + \sqrt{3}) + (2 - \sqrt{3})$$
$$B.\ \pi + (1 - \pi))$$
$$C.\ (2 + \sqrt{3}) \times (2 - \sqrt{3})$$
$$D.\ \pi + \pi$$
$$E.\ 22 - (\sqrt{3})^2$$

For those that find mathematics difficult, a good hint would be rational and
irrational numbers; i.e., Can combinations of one turn into the other?

The correct answer, to avoid spending too much time on this, would be something like 'Which of the following equations would produce an irrational number?'
The answer would be *D* based on the assumption that adding two irrational numbers

that wouldn't cancel one another (i.e., $[\pi - \pi] = 0$ which *is* a rational number) would definitely produce an irrational number. The other equations would all, amazingly enough, produce rational numbers.

While game theory brings to mind economics more than any other discipline, it is a subject that can benefit almost everyone's interest. For example, take the sentence "He looked like he'd been to hell and _____." Finding the missing word would not be that difficult with 'back' and 'gone' being the top contenders. On the other hand, the sentence "I looked to see what it was and saw that I'd angled toward the very edge of the cliffs between Cloud Peak and Bomber Mountain and almost stepped blithely into the limitless _____" needs the perfect ending. Is the missing word 'canyon', 'gorge', 'ravine', 'valley', 'abyss', 'crevasse', 'void', 'chasm', or 'depths' [27]? The actual word chosen is 'void' (complete emptiness), one that perfectly describes the nothingness that the author of this passage hopes readers will appreciate more than the other choices.

Some readers declare that writers filling the spaces with unpredictable verbiage (word[s]) represent the best (taking time to study their prose as they write and finishing with a more or less epic poem rather than simple prose) and writers grabbing whatever comes to mind quickly represent the worst. Whatever the case, Game Theory can underscore the understanding of literature as well as many otherwise difficult to analyze styles of authorship [38].

It is actually not widely known among AI scientists that many of today's machine learning algorithms come from research covering animal learning. Recent findings in neuroscience show that the hippocampus—a seahorse-shaped configuration that acts as a center for pre-encoding memory—replays those experiences during sleep. This allows the brain to learn anew from successes or failures that occurred in the past. Depending on the specific tasks involved, machine learning algorithms are established with specific mathematical structures. Through millions of examples, artificial neural networks learn to fine-tune the strength of their connections until they achieve the state that lets them complete a task with high accuracy—may it be identifying faces or translating languages. Because each algorithm is highly tailored to the task at hand, relearning a new task often erases established connections. This leads to *catastrophic forgetting*, and while AI learns a new task, it can overwrite the previous one, thus nullifying memories of past successes that may be required in the future.

While Deep Learning affords significantly more such memory than available in the past, the human mind is capable of enormous numbers of cortical cylinders that can memorize significantly more than the current best versions of Deep Learning programs. As the differential of the volume of memories increases, however, the manifold combinations of parallel procedures occurring simultaneously (part of the AI versus AGI conflict) will replace the memory problem. Some AI experts see this as an infinite regress situation that can only be set straight by fully understanding the human brain's solutions to these problems. Since the ANN concepts at the base of Deep Learning, and Deep Learning not actually mirroring the human brain in design, many AI researchers see a serious obstacle occurring in the not-so-distant future.

7.7 Music and Artificial Intelligence

When desktop computers became popular in the late 1970s, digital synthesis was not far behind. Where previously analog machines like the Moog synthesizer had driven the market, computer software began to take over. John Chowning's revolutionary frequency modulation (FM) software [8] initially led the way, followed by the programming language Csound [5] and many others, and by the late twentieth century synthesis had taken over the market not only because the results were amazing, but the software was a fraction of the cost of the earlier Moogs and other types of hardware computational devices. From 1976 on, computers and music became no longer strange bedfellows. Although it took more time for computer music composition to catch up to synthesis, this too has now become popular, and thus music and AI are now integrated with many college students either majoring in both subjects, or music departments offering courses in their own versions of both fields.

Another valuable aspect of AI and music is analysis. Counting intervals instead of pitches in single lines of a multi-instrument work (say string quartet up to full orchestra) can indicate a great deal about the nature of a work's chromatic versus diatonic nature (intervals void the necessity to account for modulations and transpositions in music). Computational analysis can indicate textural changes, repetitions, and variations as well as dozens of other characteristics of music; e.g., dynamics, rhythm, articulations, tempi, and meter (time signature) shifts.

Pattern matching (recognition), a seminal aspect of AI, can produce fundamental properties of form, structure, and techniques used during composition that no other technique can reveal as well. The short-short-short-long motive in Beethoven's Fifth Symphony we have previously discussed proves invaluable when computationally analyzed, for example, and will be proven thus later in this chapter when writing code that responds to rhythm rather than pitch.

The world of AI and music has grown in status over the past few years with many new startups incorporating a variety of methods to create music in different styles. Google's Magenta initially led the field with OpenAI a recent convert. Controversial since their first appearances due to legal possibilities and stealing jobs from humans in the same fields, they signal the onset of what is bound to be at least a cheaper way to produce music for films, television sitcoms, and dramas, and for those backed-up on iPhone lines, elevators, and medical waiting rooms; in short, for any situation requiring a backdrop of pleasantly, pleasing music.

AIVA (Artificial Intelligence Virtual Artist, https://www.aiva.ai/about) 'has been learning the art of music composition by reading through a large collection of music written by the greatest composers (Mozart, Beethoven, Bach, etc.) to create a mathematical representation of what music is.' This program was developed for creating film scores, with both composition and performance built into the algorithm, and a well-constructed interface that allows users the ability to alter almost every aspect of the output they wish to with ease. The results, at the end of a half-hour of entertaining work, are as professional and as convincing as the music of composers of previous eras taking hundreds of hours to produce.

OpenAI is a not-for-profit artificial intelligence company backed by Elon Musk and Reid Hoffman among others, with a mission to "ensure that Artificial General Intelligence (AGI)—by which we mean highly autonomous systems that outperform humans at most economically valuable work—benefits all of humanity" (https://openai.com/about/). OpenAI made quite a splash when it demonstrated an AI model capable of writing news and fiction so convincingly-human that the company declined to release the research publicly in case the system would be misused. Anyway, OpenAI is now entering AI-generated music. "We've created MuseNet, a deep neural network that can generate four-minute musical compositions with ten different instruments, and can combine styles from country and western to Mozart and the Beatles," announced the company recently. "MuseNet was not explicitly programmed with our understanding of music, but instead discovered patterns of harmony, rhythm, and style by learning to predict the next token in hundreds of thousands of MIDI files" [15].

7.8 Music, AI, and Neuroscience: A Test

Since we began with Beethoven's 5th Symphony earlier in this chapter, it may be a good idea to continue and finish this chapter with the same work. The title of this section more than suggests that you, the reader, will be included in this bit of research. The rules of the test are simple: if you are not familiar with the first movement of Beethoven's 5th Symphony, you must listen to it several times in order that the cortical columns in your neocortex will have stored the simple four-note pattern and some of the variations that take place in this first movement (or maybe the entire symphony where it returns at certain points). The next rule requires that you now listen to as many works in the more than hundred-year period of roughly 1780 to, say, 1920 (more likely the second half of that period) as you can. The last rule requires that once you have done this and written down those composers and works in which your ears, minds, and bodies have recognized clear references to the original, you send them to my email address (Howell@ucsc.edu) so that the world might take notice of what you've accomplished (including your name is optional). I will then collect these once a month and make the results available on my website (https://artsites.ucsc.edu/faculty/cope/) for all to see.

While this may seem like a trick to get those not familiar with classical music to become familiar with it, it's much more than that. You will be testing your own abilities to hear, think, and feel music by realizing how pitch, rhythm, texture, timbre, meter, beat positioning, phrasing, variations on motives, articulations, cadences, orchestration, harmony, counterpoint, and many other features of music of many different types. You'll also realize how you entrust your brain (both in your head and in your body physically) to compare, recognize, process, and memorize materials in ways that will astound you.

This test will further demonstrate how Music, AI, and Neuroscience operate in a significantly hand in glove manner to deepen your appreciation of the world around you and how important your senses are to that appreciation in light of the sounds you hear, whether originating from birds, bears, or human brains and relevant senses.

The questions remaining at this point are: What does this test prove, if anything? The answer requires that all three of this chapter's focal points must be influenced by the results in important ways. Thus, we will take them in order beginning with music.

- Do the slowly-appearing and increasing-in-complexity variations of Beethoven's Fifth Symphony's motive make his music so distinctive that it almost immediately becomes inimitable to all who hear it and no matter the number of times we listen to the unpredictable variants output from the test music you probably hear at least once a week?
- Patterns and their recognition in language, music, and data of any kind represent the single most important constituent in artificial intelligence. Do patterns transcend their originating sources and represent the basis upon which intelligence, creativity, and perception are based?
- Do we continue to recognize Beethoven's 5th Symphony's source no matter how often we play different versions of other music, or do we discover Diana Deutsch's audio illusion techniques playing roles in confusing our neurology's pattern memories [26]? Can corruptions of patterns in memory lead to mental disorders and problems in perception that could be dangerous and should be avoided?

Clearly, questions should not supplant answers as seems to be the case in the above situations. However, these particular questions deserve asking and point to answers both important and relevant to all three of the disciplines discussed herein: music, artificial intelligence, and neuroscience.

Therefore, as previously asked, what does this test prove, if anything? The answer requires that all three of this chapter's focus points must be influenced by the results in important ways. Thus, we will take them in order beginning with music.

- Do the slowly-appearing and increasing-in-complexity variations of Beethoven's 5th Symphony's motive make his music so distinctive that it almost immediately becomes inimitable to all who hear it and no matter the number of times we listen to the unpredictable variants output from the test program it claims as dominance?
- Patterns and their recognition in language, music, and data of any kind represent the single most important constituent in artificial intelligence. Do patterns transcend their originating sources and represent the basis upon which intelligence, creativity, and perception are based?

- Do we continue to recognize Beethoven's Fifth Symphony's source no matter how often we play different outputs of the simple program's tests, or do we discover Diana Deutsch's audio illusion techniques playing roles in confusing our neurology's pattern memories [26]? Can corruptions of patterns in memory lead to mental disorders and problems in perception that could be dangerous and avoided?

Clearly, questions should not supplant answers as seems to be the case in the above cases. However, these particular questions deserve asking and point to answers both important and relevant to all three of the disciplines discussed herein: music, artificial intelligence, and neuroscience.

7.9   Concluding Discussion

When people are free to do as they please, they usually imitate each other. Eric Hoffer (Cox [12], p. 13).

Music, Artificial Intelligence, and Neuroscience, as discussed herein, share many important properties. Music perception and cognition, for example, reveal researchers whose original interests lay exclusively in Neuroscience and Artificial Intelligence. Artificial Intelligence and Neuroscience now rely upon one another since at least one of the two's definition depends on an expertise in the other. Music and Neuroscience contribute to one another in the understanding of shared interests such as Music Therapy, perception, and cognition, and Neuroscience finding language and music so close relatives that at certain points in pattern recognition, it is difficult to know their differences.

What all three disciplines in the title of this chapter, and more importantly their obvious and subtle relationships over the past several years, is that no matter how much we pat ourselves on our backs, not only are these specialties significantly behind their proclaimed target dates, but woefully so. Researchers are not too busy making names for themselves and attempting to get tenure, full professorships, and their photos on the covers of disciplinary journals, but they have often gravely misjudged the complexities of the subjects they study and particularly the ways in which those subjects interact with one another.

This said, and without the prognostications of futurists hell-bent on suggesting the end is near, we have still come a long way. Unfortunately, AI is nowhere near AGI and further yet from understanding consciousness and self-awareness no less how to create them in machines. We have, however, come a long way toward understanding elements of the human brain, though we remain far from the goals set by science-fiction authors a hundred years ago. And Music, no one knows much of anything about where it is headed and how it might affect the human race on its way there.

On the other hand, we have gained a great deal of knowledge about what we do not know. Putting it in a slightly different way, we now know the names of things we do not know much or anything about and wish to share that with you. Here, then, is a numbered list in no particular order that could not possibly be complete or thorough but may present a place to start.

1. Artificial Intelligence is currently mired in projects attracting funding to keep their research going. Deep learning represents a perfect example of that. On one hand, the initial exemplars of recognition and classification have proved useful to solving a number of real-world problems. On the other hand, these solutions, as valuable as they may be, actually do more to prove the failures of their goals than their successes. The AI versus AGI problem previously discussed is but one of these. Its initial successes and provocative results gained world attention, yet at the same time, as the rave reviews play themselves out, it may be that we are facing another AI winter as we begin to understand the limitations of Deep Learning.

   Once you unleash it on large data, deep learning has its own dynamics, it does its own repair and its own optimization, and it gives you the right results most of the time. But when it doesn't, you don't have a clue about what went wrong and what should be fixed (Pearl [37], p. 15).

2. Up until the twentieth century, classical music had a deep historical practice of producing at least one or two so-called masters per century. Cultural stylistic traditions changed slowly and even then, often produced severe audience negative reactions. With Claude Debussy around as the nineteenth century changed into the twentieth century and with Igor Stravinsky soon to follow, matters quickly changed, and by mid-century all manner of sound and non-sounding works appeared, and at such rapid paces that audiences shrunk in size and the future likewise shrunk in terms of what was left with which to experiment. One of the composer's most important draws depended on gaining attention by outrageous acts, yet unfortunately, even by 1970, such acts seemed already aged and certainly no longer outrageous, and thus came the neo-avant-garde. New and outrageous by being old. These bits of tradition, no matter what happened with style, involved musical patterns saving the day. And, as with AI (above), musicians find themselves knowing less about the subject and craft than they should, and with popular music more performed and recorded than ever, yet further behind in what people listen to [11].

3. Neurology, like all the natural sciences, has been lost in the complexity of its discipline. It, like the two others facing off in this presentation, struggling against over-specialization and lack of agreement on even the simplest of theories, routinely creating massive and highly complex tomes of research summaries that often confuse rather than elucidate their readers and colleagues. As Einstein once purportedly said: "Any intelligent fool can make things bigger and more complex... It takes a touch of genius – and a lot of courage to move in the opposite direction."

4. While not knowing all of the previous research done in the combined subjects of Music, AI, and Neuroscience, many quickly discover a number of papers delivered on these three subjects that evidence a lack of familiarity with their overlapping concepts. The following proves the point:

> In the experiment, six volunteers heard 40 pieces of classical music, rock, pop, jazz, and others. The neural fingerprint of each song on participants' brains were captured by the MR machine while a computer was learning to identify the brain patterns elicited by each musical piece. Musical features such as tonality, dynamics, rhythm and timbre were taken into account by the computer. After that, researchers expected that the computer would be able to do the opposite: identify which song participants were hearing based on their brain activity – a technique known as brain decoding. When confronted with two options, the computer showed up to 85% accuracy in identifying the correct song, which is a great performance, comparing to previous studies [23].

Once again, the word 'pattern' occurs just enough times in the above that we are aware of its importance in the study of cross-disciplinary research and how important its recurrence is to understand seemingly isolated subjects by taking a multidisciplinary approach. The significance of patterns, whether their sources (sound, sight, etc.) are known or not, appear to exist in every aspect of the natural world and therefore must, if any understanding of that world is to take place, be the basic foundation of any research that is to lead to any true achievement.

> The central role of music and language in human existence and the fact that both involve complex and meaningful sound sequences naturally invite comparison between the two domains. Yet from the standpoint of modern cognitive science, music-language relations have barely begun to be explored. This situation appears to be poised to change rapidly, as researchers from diverse fields are increasingly drawn to this interdisciplinary enterprise. The appeal of such research is easy to understand. Humans are unparalleled in their ability to make sense out of sound (Patel [36], p. 3).

As a final thought, the simple diagram in Fig. 7.10 will point out both the problems and the solution potentials presented in this chapter.

Woody Allen was once quoted as saying: "Life is divided into the horrible and the miserable" (Allen playing Alvy Singer in Annie Hall, 1977, screenplay by Woody Allen and Marshall Brickman). This is included here because not only is every human brain different from every other human brain, but also that each and every human brain has faults that make it malfunction at least occasionally. Sometimes these faults can cause a human to commit suicide, at other times murder, at still other times produce great acts of courage and love. All of these problems should remind us that nothing we compose, create, or feel (Music, Artificial Intelligence, Neuroscience) will be shy of those mistakes. We pass them on. No matter how we attempt to avoid this from occurring, we cannot escape the inevitable. The best we can do is to act responsibly and sensitively as we study as many different disciplines as make sense and hope that our results will prove fruitful.

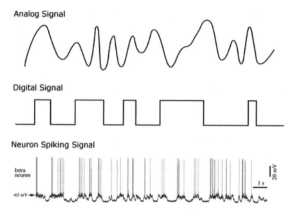

Fig. 7.10 Analog (music), digital (today's computers), and signals (the human brain's method of thinking, communicating, and creating) demonstrating the differences and similarities of the three profound problems and solutions presented in this chapter (Cope)

References

1. Adolphs, R., & Anderson, D. J. (2018). *The neuroscience of emotion: A new synthesis.* . Princeton, NJ: Princeton University Press.
2. Anumanchipalli, G. K., Chartier, J., & Chang, E. F. (2019). Speech synthesis from neural decoding of spoken sentences. *Nature, 568,* 493–498.
3. Banich, M. (2018). *Cognitive neuroscience.* (4th ed.). Cambridge, UK: Cambridge University Press.
4. Bishop, C. (2011). *Pattern recognition and machine learning.* . London: Springer-Verlag.
5. Boulanger, R. (Ed.). (2000). *The csound book: Perspectives in software synthesis, sound design, signal processing, and programming.* . Cambridge, MA: MIT Press.
6. Brooks, R. (2003). *Flesh and machines: How robots will change Us.* . New York: Vintage.
7. Charniak, E. (2019). *Introduction to deep learning.* . Oxford, UK: Oxford University Press.
8. Chowning, J. M. (1973). The synthesis of complex audio spectra by means of frequency modulation. *Journal of the Audio Engineering Society, 7*(21), 526–534.
9. Costandi, M. (2016). *Neuroplasticity.* . Cambridge, MA: MIT Press.
10. Cope, D. (1996). *Experiments in musical intelligence.* . Madison, WI: A-R Editions.
11. Cope, D. (2000). *New directions in music.* (7th ed.). Long Grove, Ill: Waveland Press Inc.
12. Cox, A. (2016). *Music and embodied cognition: Listening, moving, feeling, and thinking (musical meaning and interpretation).* . Bloomington, Indiana: Indiana University Press.
13. Dayan, P., & Abbott, L. F. (2001). *Theoretical neuroscience: Computational and mathematical modeling of neural systems.* Cambridge, MA.
14. Dehaene, S. (2014). *Consciousness and the brain: Deciphering how the brain codes our thoughts.* . NY: Penguin Books.
15. Dredge, S. (2019). https://musically.com/2019/04/26/openai-musenet-music-generating-ai/.
16. Forte, T. (2018). A pattern recognition theory of mind. *Praxis.* https://praxis.fortelabs.co/a-pattern-recognition-theory-of-mind/.
17. Gjerdingen, R. (1991). Using connectionist models to explore complex musical patterns. In P. Todd and G. Loy (Eds.), *Music and Connectionism.* Cambridge, MA: The MIT Press.
18. Goodfellow, I., Bengio, Y., & Courville, A. (2016). *Deep learning.* . Cambridge, MA: MIT Press.

19. Grekow, J. (2018). *From content-based music emotion recognition to emotion maps of musical pieces.* . Cham, Switzerland: Springer International Publishing.
20. Griffiths, P. (1979). *Boulez.* . Oxford, UK: Oxford University Press.
21. Gu, J., et al. (2017). *Recent advances in convolutional neural networks* (Introduction). Arxiv. org/pdf/1512.07108.
22. Hawkins, J. (2004). *On intelligence: How a new understanding of the brain will lead to the creation of truly intelligent machines.* . New York: Henry Holt and Company LLC.
23. Hoefle, S., Engel, A., Basilio, R., Alluri, V., Toiviainen, P., Cagy, M. & Moll, J. (2018). *Identifying musical pieces from fMRI data using encoding and decoding models.* Scientific Reports 8, Article number: 2266.
24. Hofstadter, D. (1979). *Gödel, escher, bach: An eternal golden braid.* . New York: Basic Books Inc.
25. Huron, D. (2006). *Sweet anticipation: Music and the psychology of expectation.* . Cambridge, MA: The MIT Press.
26. Hurwitz, D. (2008). *Beethoven's fifth and seventh symphonies: A closer look.* . New York: The Continuum International Publishing Group.
27. Johnson, C. (2011). *Hell is empty.* . London, UK: Penguin Group.
28. Kurzweil, R. (2013). *How to create a mind.* . New York: Penguin Books.
29. Kutner, M., Nachtsheim, C., & Neter, J. (2004). *Applied linear regression models.* (4th ed.). NY: McGraw-Hill Education.
30. Mattson, M. P. (2014). Superior pattern processing is the essence of the evolved human brain. *Frontiers in Neuroscience.* Vol. 8. PMC4141622.
31. Merriam Webster. https://merriam-webster.com/dictionary/neuroscience.
32. Miranda, E. (2010). Organised sound, mental imageries and the future of music technology: A neuroscience outlook. Interdisciplinary Centre for Computer Music Research (ICCMR), Faculty of Arts, University of Plymouth, Plymouth PL4 8AA, UK. Vol. 15, Issue 1.
33. Nilsson, N. (2010). *The quest for artificial intelligence: A history of ideas and achievements.* . Cambridge, UK: Cambridge University Press.
34. Norvig, P., & Russell, S. (2009). *Artificial intelligence: A modern approach.* (3rd ed.). New York: Pearson.
35. Parker, J. (2019). *Generative art: Algorithms as artistic tool.* . New York: Durville.
36. Patel, A. D. (2008). *Music, language, and the brain.* . Oxford, UK: Oxford University Press.
37. Pearl, J. (2019). In J. Brockman (Ed.), *Possible minds: Twenty-five ways of looking at AI.* NY: Penguin Press.
38. Roughgarden, T. (2016). *Algorithmic game theory.* . Cambridge, UK: Cambridge University Press.
39. Sejnowski, T. (2018). *The deep learning revolution.* . Cambridge, MA: The MIT Press.
40. Stravinsky, I. (1947). *Poetics of music.* . New York: Vintage Books.
41. Talwalkar, P. (2014). *The joy of game theory: An introduction to strategic thinking.* Amazon Createspace.
42. Tsinaslanidis, P., & Zapranis, A. (2016). *Technical analysis for algorithmic pattern recognition.* . New York: Springer International Publishing.
43. Theodoridis, S., & Koutroumbas, K. (2009). *Pattern recognition.* (4th ed.). Boston, MA: Elsevier.
44. Topol, E. (2019). *Deep medicine: How artificial intelligence can make healthcare human again.* . New York: Hachette Book Group.
45. Uhr, L., & Vossler, C. (1961). *A pattern recognition program that generates, evaluates and adjusts its own operators, managing requirements knowledge, international workshop on AFIPS,* p. 555. Los Angeles, CA.

46. Waldrop, M. M. (2019). What are the limits of deep learning? *PNAS, 116*(4), 1074–1077. Retrieved January 22, 2019, fromhttps://doi.org/10.1073/pnas.1821594116.
47. Wickens, A. (2015). *A history of the brain: From stone age surgery to modern neuroscience.* London, UK: Psychology Press.

David Cope David Cope is Professor Emeritus of Music at the University of California at Santa Cruz, California, USA. His books on the intersection of music and computer science include *Computers and Musical Style, Experiments in Musical Intelligence, The Algorithmic Composer, Virtual music, Computer Models of Musical Creativity, Hidden Structure*, and describe the computer program *Experiments in Musical Intelligence* which he created in 1981. Experiments in Musical Intelligence's works include three operas, a symphony and piano concerto in the style of Mozart, a seventh *Brandenburg Concerto* in the style of Bach, and several thousand other shorter works in various styles. Compositions composed in his own style include ten symphonies, six string quartets, several chamber orchestra pieces, and a host of other works, most of which have been performed around the world and all of which are available on recordings. Cope also is a visual artist with many paintings on display in galleries and in homes around the world, an author (seven plays, thirty-three published novels, and ten books of short stories to date). He also writes books on his own created board games, artificial intelligence, computer programming, and music theory. E-mail: howell@ucsc.edu.

Creative Music Neurotechnology

8

Eduardo Reck Miranda

8.1 Introduction

Artificial Intelligence is aimed at endowing machines with some form of intelligence. Not surprisingly, AI scientists take much inspiration from the ways in which the brain and/or the mind works to build intelligent systems [15]. Hence, studies in Philosophy, Psychology, Cognitive Science and more recently, the Neurosciences have been nourishing AI research since the field emerged in the 1950s, including, of course, AI for music. Indeed, whereas chapters by David Cope, Tatsuya Daikoku and Psyche Louis in this volume discuss the relationship of AI with the Neurosciences, Geraint Wiggins and Emilios Cambouropolous offer a Cognitive Science perspective to AI.

The Neurosciences have led to a deeper understanding of the behaviour of individual and large groups of biological neurons and we can now begin to apply biologically informed neuronal functional paradigms to problems of design and control, including applications pertaining to music technology and creativity. Artificial Neuronal Networks (ANN) technology owes much of its development to burgeoning neuroscientific insight.

However, this chapter introduces a different angle to harness the Neurosciences for music technology. Rather than discuss how to build musical ANN informed by the functioning of real biological neuronal networks, I shall introduce my forays into harnessing the latter to create music with.

Is it possible to build programmable processors using living biological neurones? Can we harness information in physiological brain data to make music? How could we couple computers with our brains? What new musical systems might we be able to build with these? These are some of the questions that will be addressed below.

E. R. Miranda (✉)
Interdisciplinary Centre for Computer Music Research (ICCMR), University of Plymouth, Plymouth PL4 8AA, UK
e-mail: eduardo.miranda@plymouth.ac.uk

© Springer Nature Switzerland AG 2021
E. R. Miranda (eds.), *Handbook of Artificial Intelligence for Music*,
https://doi.org/10.1007/978-3-030-72116-9_8

8.2   Sound Synthesis with Real Neuronal Networks

There has been a growing interest in research into the development of neurochips coupling living brain cells and silicon circuits together. The ambition is to harness the intricate dynamics of in vitro neuronal networks to perform computations.

Engineers have been looking into developing ways to culture brain cells in mini Petri-like dishes measuring only a few square millimetres. These devices are referred to as MEA (short for Multi-Electrode Array) devices. They are embedded with electrodes that detect the electrical activity of aggregates of cells and stimulate them with electrical pulses. It has been observed that in vitro cultures of brain cells spontaneously branch out, even if they are left to themselves without external input. They have a strong disposition to form synapses, even more so if subjected to electrical stimulation [16].

DeMarse et al. [3] reported the pioneering development of a neuronally-controlled artificial animal—or Animat—using dissociated cortical neurons from rats cultured on a MEA device. Distributed patterns of neuronal activity, also referred to as spike trains, controlled somewhat the behaviour of the Animat in a computer-simulated virtual environment. The Animat provided electrical feedback about its movement within its virtual environment to the cells on the MEA device. Changes in Animat's behaviour were studied together with the neuronal processes that produced those changes in an attempt to understand how information was encoded and processed by the cultured neurones.

I am curious about the possibility of developing interactive musical computers based on such neurochips. As an entry point to kick-start the research towards this end, I collaborated with scientists at the University of the West of England (UWE), Bristol, to develop methods for rendering the temporal behaviour of in vitro neuronal tissue into sound [9]. The dynamics of in vitro neuronal tissue represent a source of rich temporal behaviour, which inspired me to develop and test a number of rendering methods using different sound synthesis techniques, one of which will be introduced below.

The UWE team developed a method to extract brain cells from hen embryos at day seven in ovo and maintain them for relatively long periods of time, typically several months [19]. Figure 8.1 shows a typical hen embryo aggregate neuronal culture, also referred to as a *spheroid*.

In our experiments, spheroids were grown in culture in an incubator for 21 days. Then, they were placed into a MEA device in such a way that at least two electrodes made connections into the neurones inside the spheroid. One electrode was designated as the input by which we applied electrical stimulation and the other as the output from which we recorded the effects of the stimulation on the spheroid's spiking behaviour.

Electrical stimulation at the input electrode consisted of a train of biphasic pulses of 300 mv each, coming once every 300 ms. This induced change in the stream of spikes at the output electrode, which was recorded and saved into a file.

Fig. 8.1 Images of a typical hen embryo aggregate neuronal culture on a scanning electron microscope magnified 448 times (Courtesy of Prof Larry Bull, University of the West of England)

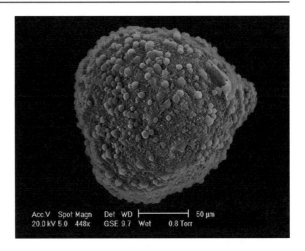

The resulting neuronal activity for each session was saved on separate files. Figure 8.2 plots an excerpt lasting for 1 s of typical neuronal activity from one of the sessions. Note that the neurones are constantly firing spontaneously. The noticeable spikes of higher amplitude indicate concerted increases of firing activity by groups of neurones in response to input stimuli.

We developed a number of methods to render the activity of the living neurones into sound. The method introduced below combines aspects of granular synthesis and additive synthesis [14].

An additive synthesizer was implemented with nine sinusoidal oscillators. The synthesizer requires three input values to generate a tone: frequency (*freq*), amplitude (*amp*) and duration (*dur*). It was established that the data would produce *freq* and *amp* values for the first oscillator only. Then the values for the other

Fig. 8.2 Plotting of the first second of a data file showing the activity of the spheroid in terms of μV against time. Induced spikes of higher amplitudes took place between 400 and 600 ms

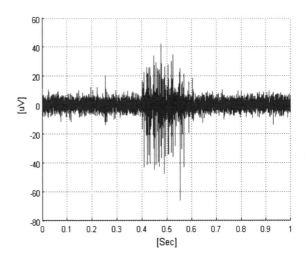

oscillators would be calculated relative to the values of the first oscillator; e.g., $freq_{osc2} = freq_{osc}1 \times 0.7$, $freq_{osc}3 = freq_{osc}1 \times 0.6$ and so on.

Initially, the system synthesized a tone for every datum. However, this produced excessively long sounds. In order to address this problem, a data compression technique was developed, which preserved the behaviour that I was interested to make sounds with, namely patterns of neuronal activity and induced spikes. For clarity, I firstly introduce the method whereby a tone is produced for every datum. Then the method using data compression is described.

Each datum yielded three values for the synthesizer: frequency (*freq*), amplitude (*amp*) and duration (*dur*). The frequency value is calculated in Hz as follows: $freq = (datum \times 20) + \alpha$. We set $\alpha = 440$ as an arbitrary reference to 440 Hz; changes to this value produce sounds at different registers.

The synthesizer's amplitude parameter is a number between 0 and 10. The amplitude is calculated as follows: $amp = 2 \times \log_{10}(abs(datum) + 0.01) + 4.5$. This produces a value between 0.5 and 9.5. In order to avoid negative amplitudes, the system takes the absolute value of the datum. Then, 0.01 is added in order to avoid the case of logarithm of 0, which cannot be computed.

The duration of the sound is calculated in secs; it is proportional to the absolute value of the datum, which is divided by a constant c, as follows:

$$dur = \frac{abs(datum)}{c} + t$$

In the case of the present example, c was set equal to 100. The higher the value of c, the grainy the results. In order to account for excessively short or possibly null durations, t is added to the result; e.g., $t = 0.05$.

The compression algorithm was implemented as follows: it begins by creating a set with the value of a datum. To start with, this will be the first sample of the data. Then it feeds in the second sample, the third and so on. The value of each incoming sample is compared with the value of the first sample in order to check if they are close to each other according to a given distance threshold Δ. If the difference between them is lower than Δ, then the incoming datum is stored in the set. Otherwise, the values of all data stored in the set are averaged and used to generate a tone. Then, a new set is created, whose first value is the value of the datum that prompted the creation of the last tone, and so forth. In this case, the frequency of a tone is calculated as follows, where n is the minimum value found in the data set and x is the maximum value:

$$freq\left(\frac{(set\_average - n) \times 900}{x - n}\right) + 100$$

In the equation above, the values of n and x do not necessarily need to be the minimum and maximum values in the data file; they can be set arbitrarily, with the condition that $n < x$. The result is scaled in order to fall in the range between 100 and 1 kHz. The amplitude is calculated as for the case of one tone per datum, as

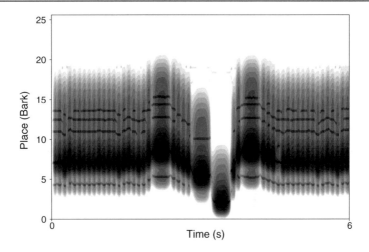

Fig. 8.3 Cochleagram of an excerpt of a sonification where spikes of higher amplitude can be visually seen just after the middle of the diagram

described above, with the only difference that the *datum* is replaced by the *set average*. The duration is also calculated as described above with the difference that a bandwidth defined by minimum and maximum duration thresholds is introduced. If the calculated duration of a tone falls outside the bandwidth, then the system assigns a predetermined duration value; e.g., the tone is assigned a duration of 0.1 s if its calculated duration is below the minimum threshold.

Figure 8.3 shows the cochleagram of an excerpt of a sound produced with the system, where one can clearly observe sonic activity corresponding to induced spiking activity.

It turns out that experiments with in vitro neurones are very difficult to conduct. And they require specialist resources that are not readily available for musicians to fiddle with. While research in this area develops, what musicians can do is to work with computer simulations of spiking neurones.

The next section introduces a composition technique that I had envisaged for using in vitro neuronal tissue to generate a piece of orchestral music. For practical reasons, I use simulation instead.

8.3 *Raster Plot*: Making Music with Spiking Neurones

Raster Plot is a piece for orchestra, choir and a solo mezzo-soprano, which was generated with computer simulations of spiking neurons. The choir and the soloist sing extracts from the diary of British explorer, Robert Falcon Scott, on the final moments of his expedition to the South Pole, before he died in March of 1912.

The piece was generated by a computer simulation of a network of interconnected neurones. The simulation was implemented in collaboration with Etienne Roesch, a cognitive scientist at the University of Reading, UK. It is based on a model that simulates the spiking behaviour of biological neurones, developed by computational neuroscientist Izhikevich [5].

When the network is stimulated, each neurone of the network produces sequences of bursts of activity, referred to as spikes, forming streams of patterns. A *raster plot* is a graph plotting the spikes; hence the title of the composition.

In a nutshell, I orchestrated raster plots by allocating each instrument of the orchestra to a different neurone of the network. Each time a neurone produced a spike, its respective instrument was prompted to play a certain note. The notes were assigned based upon a series of chords, which served as frames to make simultaneous spikes sound in harmony.

A biological neurone aggregates the electrical activity of its surroundings over time, until it reaches a threshold, at which point it generates a sudden burst of electricity, referred to as an *action potential*. Izhikevich's model is interesting because it produces spiking behaviours that are identical to the spiking behaviour of neurones in real brains. Also, its equations are relatively easier to understand and program on a computer, compared to other, more complex models. The equations of this model represent the electrical activity at the level of the membrane of neurones over time and are able to reproduce several properties of biological spiking neurones commonly observed in real neuronal tissue.

The simulation contains two types of neurones, excitatory and inhibitory, that interact and influence the network as a whole. Each action potential produced by a neurone is registered, and transmitted to the whole network, therefore, producing waves of activation as the electrical activity of one neurone yields a cascade of action potentials, which then spread. A raster plot showing an example of such collective firing behaviour taken from a simulation of a network of 1000 neurones, is shown in Fig. 8.4. This is a simulation of the activity of this group of 1000 artificial neurones over a period of one second: the neurones are numbered on the y-axis (with neurone number 1 at the bottom, and neurone number 1000 at the top) and time, which runs from zero to 1000 ms is on the x-axis. Every time one such neurone fires, a dot is placed on the graph at the appropriate time on a line horizontally drawn from that particular neurone.

In Fig. 8.4, one can observe periods of intense collective spiking activity separated by quieter moments. These moments of relative quietness in the network are due to both the action of the inhibitory neurones, and the refractory period during which a neurone that has spiked remains silent whilst its electrical potential decays back to baseline. In addition to this intrinsic activity, the network receives external stimulation in the form of a sinusoidal signal that is input to all neurones of the network. Generally speaking, the amplitude of this signal controls the overall intensity of firing. For instance, the bottom of Fig. 8.5 shows a raster plot generated by a network of 50 spiking neurones stimulated by the sinusoid shown at the top of the figure. As the undulating line rises, the spiking activity is intensified. Conversely, as the undulating line falls, the spiking activity becomes quieter.

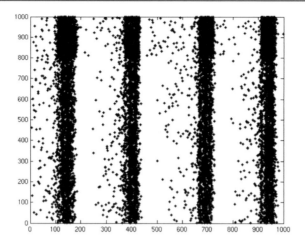

Fig. 8.4 A raster plot illustrating collective firing behaviour of a simulated network of spiking neurones. Neurone numbers are plotted (y-axis) against time (x-axis) for a simulation of 1000 neurones over a period of one second. Each dot represents a firing event

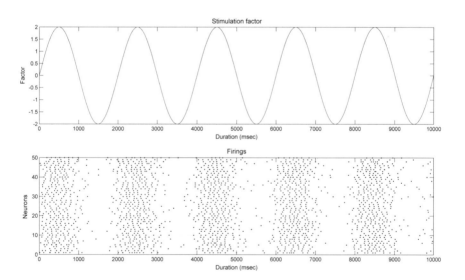

Fig. 8.5 At the top is a sinusoid signal that stimulated the network that produced the spiking activity represented by the raster plot at the bottom

Compositionally, to me, the top of Fig. 8.5 suggests musical form, whereas the bottom suggests musical content.

In order to compose *Raster Plot*, I set up a network with 50 neurones and ran the simulation 12 times, lasting 10 s each. For all runs of the simulation, I set the stimulating sinusoid to a frequency of 0.0005 Hz, which means that each cycle of the wave lasted for 2 s. Therefore, each simulation took five cycles of the wave, which can be seen at the top of Figs. 8.5 and 8.6.

For each run, I varied the amplitude of the sinusoid, that is, the power of the stimulating signal, and the sensitivity of the neurones to fire. The power of the stimulating signal could be varied from 0.0 (no power at all) to 5.0 (maximum power) and the sensitivity of the neurones could be varied from 0.0 (no sensitivity at all; would never fire) to 5.0 (extremely sensitive). For instance, for the first run of the simulation, I set the power of the signal to 1.10 and sensitivity of the neurones to 2.0, whereas in the tenth run I set these to 2.0 and 4.4, respectively. One can see that the higher the power of the stimuli and the higher the sensitivity, the more likely the neurones are to fire, and therefore, more and more spikes the network produces overall. In Fig. 8.6, there are only a few spikes. In Fig. 8.5, one can observe an increase in spiking activity. Table 8.1 shows the values for the 12 runs. I envisaged a composition where the music would become increasingly complex and tense, towards a climax.

I established that each cycle of the stimulating sinusoid would produce spiking data for three measures of music, with the following time signatures: 4/4, 3/4 and 4/4, respectively. Therefore, each run of the simulation would produce spiking data for fifteen measures of music. Twelve runs resulted in a total of 180 measures.

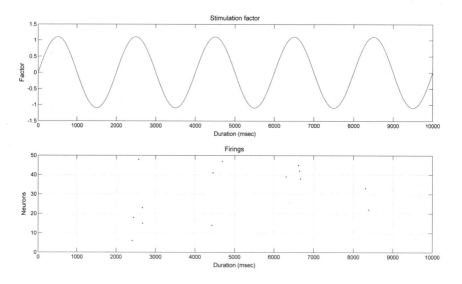

Fig. 8.6 The density of spikes is proportional to the amplitude of the stimulating sinewave

Table 8.1 The parameters for the 12 runs of the spiking neurones network

Run	1	2	3	4	5	6	7	8	9	10	11	12
Stimulating power	1.10	1.11	1.12	1.13	1.14	1.2	1.21	1.22	1.3	2.0	2.2	3.0
Network sensitivity	2.0	2.3	2.6	2.9	3.2	3.5	3.8	4.0	4.2	4.4	4.8	5.0

I noticed that with the settings shown in Table 8.1, none of the neurones produced more than 44 spikes in one cycle of the stimulating sinusoid. This meant that if I turned each spike into a musical note, then each cycle of the sinusoid could produce up to 44 notes.

In order to transcribe the spikes as musical notes, I quantized them to fit a metric of semiquavers, where the first and the last of the three measures could hold up to 16 spikes each, and the second measure could hold up to 12 (Fig. 8.8). Next, I associated each instrument of the orchestra, excepting the voices, to a neurone or group of neurones, as shown in Table 8.2. From the 50 neurones of the network, I ended up using only the first 40, counting from the bottom of the raster plots upwards. Instruments that are associated with a group of neurones (e.g., Organ) can play more than one note simultaneously.

The compositional process continued in three major steps: the establishment of a rhythmic template, the assignment of pitches to the template and the articulation of the musical material.

Table 8.2 Instruments are associated with neurones. Each instrument plays the spikes produced by its respective neurone or group of neurones

Neurones	Instruments	Neurones	Instruments
1	Contrabass 2	17	1st Violin 1
2	Contrabass 2	18, 19, 20, 21	Organ
3	Cello 3	22, 23, 24, 25, 26	Celesta
4	Cello 2	27, 28, 29	Vibraphone, Timpani
5	Cello 1	30	Snare drum, Cymbal, Tam-tam
6	Viola 3	31	Tuba
7	Viola 2	32	Trombone 3
8	Viola 1	33	Trombone 2
9	2nd Violin 4	34	Trombone 1
10	2nd Violin 3	35	Trumpet 2
11	2nd Violin 2	36	Trumpet 1
12	2nd Violin 1	37	Horn 3
13	1st Violin 5	38	Horn 2
14	1st Violin 4	39	Horn 1
15	1st Violin 3	40	Clarinet Bass clarinet
16	1st Violin 2		

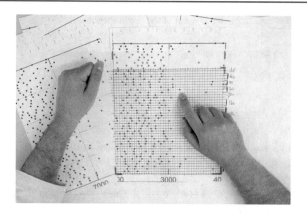

Fig. 8.7 Transcribing the raster plot spikes into musical notes

Fig. 8.8 Transcribing spikes from a raster plot as semiquavers on a score

In order to establish the rhythmic template, firstly I transcribed the spikes as semiquavers on the score (Fig. 8.7). Figure 8.8 shows an excerpt of the result of this transcription for a group of eight instruments. In order to forge more musically plausible rhythmic figures, I altered the duration of the notes and rests, whilst preserving the original spiking pattern as much as I could. Fig. 8.9 shows the new version of Fig. 8.8 after this process. Figure 8.10 shows the final result of the compositional process, with pitches and articulation.

In order to assign pitches to the rhythmic template, I defined a series of 36 chords of 12 notes each, as shown in Fig. 8.11. Each chord provided pitch materials for 3 measures, that is, corresponding to one cycle of the stimulating sinusoid. Those figures to be played by instruments of lower tessitura were assigned the lower pitches of the chords and those to be played by instruments of higher tessitura

Fig. 8.9 Resulting rhythmic figure

Fig. 8.10 The resulting music

were assigned the higher pitches, and so on. An example is shown in Fig. 8.12, illustrating the assignment of pitches from the G clef portion of chord number 22 to certain rhythmic figures for the violins. There were occasions where I decided to transpose pitches one octave upwards or downwards in order to best fit specific

Fig. 8.11 Series of chords

contexts or technical constraints. Other adjustments also occurred during the process of articulating the musical materials.

A detailed explanation of the process of articulating the musical material is beyond the intended scope of this chapter. Essentially, a number of non-standard playing techniques were employed.

The vocal part was composed at the same time as I worked on the articulations. It was not constrained by the rhythmic template or by the chords. The mezzo-soprano sings in sprechgesang mode in measures corresponding to periods of rarefactive spiking activity. A sample of the full score is provided in the Appendix.

As a gross generalization, if one thinks of the spiking neuronal network model above as the brain of some sort of organism, the stimulating sinusoid would represent perceived sensory information. Albeit simplistic, I find this idea rather

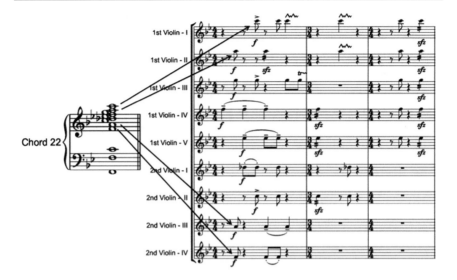

Fig. 8.12 An excerpt from *Raster Plot* illustrating the assignment of pitches to rhythmic figures

inspiring in the sense that it captures the essence of how our brain represents sensorial information; in this case a sinusoidal signal. And this signal could well be a sound. Metaphorically, *Raster Plot* is a representation (a rather convoluted one, I must admit) of how the 'organism's brain' listened to the sinusoid. Would it be possible to develop a similar paradigm to musically represent how our brain listens to music? This question inspired the composition *Symphony of Minds Listening*, introduced below.

8.4 *Symphony of Minds Listening*: Listening to the Listening Mind

Similar to the fact that we have unique fingerprints, which differ from one person to another, our brains are also unique. Even though all human brains share a common basic biological blueprint, the detailed neurological circuitry of the mechanisms whereby we make sense of music differ from person to person. And they are continually changing, making scientific research into unveiling how the brain listens to music to very difficult. Paradoxically, it seems that the more we study the brain, the more difficult it becomes to draw firm conclusions.

Symphony of Minds Listening is an artistic expression of how different brains construct their own unique reality. It is an experimental symphonic piece in three movements based on the fMRI brain scans taken from three different persons whilst they listened to the 2nd movement of Ludwig van Beethoven's *Seventh Symphony*: a ballerina, a philosopher and I.

In simple terms, I deconstructed the Beethoven movement to its essential elements and stored them with information representing their structural features. Then, I reassembled these elements into a new composition, using the same instrumentation as for Beethoven's 7th symphony, but with a twist: the fMRI information of each listener influenced the process of reassembling the music.

The fMRI brain scanning method measures brain activity by detecting changes in blood flow. The measurements can be presented graphically by colour-coding the strength of activation across the brain. Figure 8.13 shows a representation of an fMRI scan of my brain listening to Beethoven's music at a specific window of time, lasting for 2 s.

Figure 8.13 shows planar surfaces, or slices, from the top to the bottom of my brain, my face is facing upwards. Figure 8.14 shows an example of a 3D rendition of such a two-second fMRI snapshot, using a bespoke piece of software developed by Dan Lloyd, at Trinity College in Hartford, USA: it displays different areas of the brain, represented by different colours, responding in a coordinate manner to the music.

Each scanning session generated sets of fMRI data, each of which is associated with a measure of the 2nd movement of Beethoven's piece. This is shown schematically in Fig. 8.15.

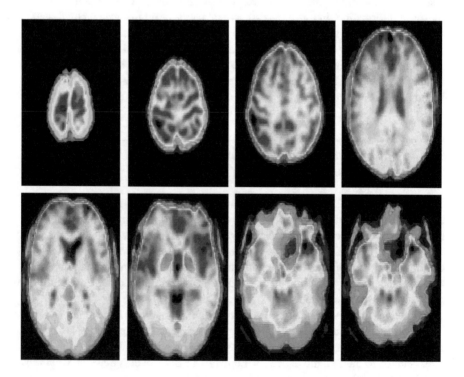

Fig. 8.13 A typical representation of an fMRI snapshot, showing 8 transversal slices of the brain

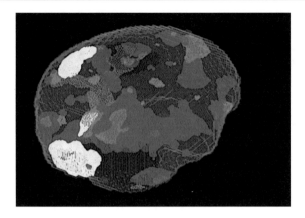

Fig. 8.14 An artistic 3D rendering of an fMRI scan by Dan Lloyd

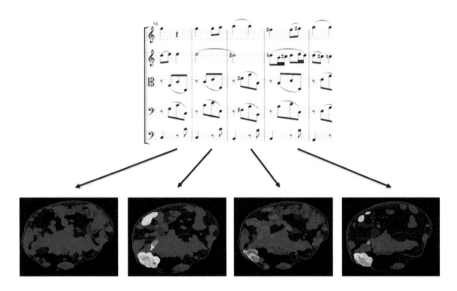

Fig. 8.15 The result of a scanning section is a set of fMRI data for each measure of Beethoven's piece (*Note* this is only a schematic representation; the brain imaging does not correspond to the actual music shown)

The score of Beethoven's movement was deconstructed with a custom-made piece of software, which extracted statistical information about the structure of the music. Then, I used this information to reconstruct the Beethoven movement, also aided by AI, but the process of reconstruction was influenced by the fMRI data. In a nutshell, during the reconstruction process, the fMRI data altered the original music

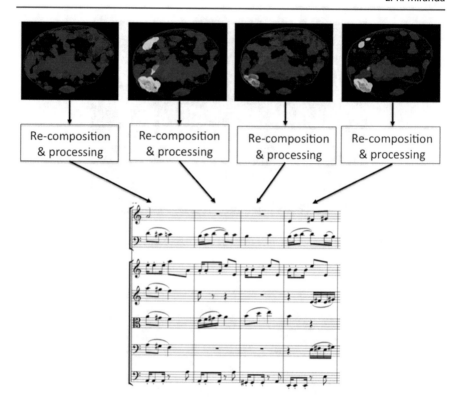

Fig. 8.16 The fMRI data inform the re-assemblage of the piece

(Fig. 8.16). Not surprisingly, the fMRI scans differed amongst the three listeners. Therefore, brain activity from three different minds yielded three different movements for the resulting composition, each of which displaying varying degrees of resemblance to the original symphony. Each movement is named after the profession of the respective persons that were scanned: *Ballerina*, *Philosopher* and *Composer*. The instrumentation is the same as for Beethoven's original instrumentation.

8.4.1 Brain Scanning and Analysis

The brain images were collected using a Siemens Allegra 3T head-only scanner at the University of New York ("T" stands for Tesla, a measure of magnetic field strength.) Each full-brain image took two seconds to collect, to yield 36 image slices of the brain. Each slice comprised 64×64 picture elements, known as voxels or volume pixels. Thus, each image comprised approximately 150,000 continuously varying voxels.

Subjects heard the second movement of Beethoven's *Seventh Symphony* twice. The subjects were instructed to attend to the music with their eyes closed. The fMRI recording began with 30 s without music, then 460 s of Beethoven, then 18 s without music, and finally the same 460 s of Beethoven previously heard. Thus, each run generated 484 images.

The raw fMRI images were first pre-processed following usual procedures for functional neuroimaging. These included correcting for head motion, morphing the individual brains to conform to a standard anatomical atlas and spatial smoothing, which is a procedure that reduces random fluctuations by calculating a moving average of each voxel in the context of its spatial neighbours. These pre-processing steps were implemented using Statistical Parametric Mapping software [1].

Each of the 484 images produced 150,000 voxels, which are very complex for direct analysis. Instead, the image series were further processed with Independent Component Analysis [18]. Informally, ICA separates ensembles of voxels that oscillate in unison. These are unified as supervoxels that represent temporally coherent networks of brain activity. The coloured patches in Fig. 8.14 are examples of independent components. A total of 25 components were calculated for the three subjects in the experiment.

In order to select which of these components might be musically significant, the activity of each component during the first pass through the Beethoven listening was compared to that same component during the second pass. If these two segments of a component time series were correlated, it was hypothesized that the activity was at least partly musically driven, since the stimulus, that is, the music would be identical at the corresponding time points in the two passes through the music. Although 25 independent component time series were identified, only the strongest 15 were selected to influence the compositional process. The order of strength of the selected 15 ICA components is as follows: 25, 15, 14, 8, 5, 10, 11, 18, 6, 2, 4, 1, 17, 16 and 13.

The time series were normalized to range from 1 to 9. As the last step, the varying components were resampled to match the timing of the Beethoven score measure by measure. Thus, each time point was indexed to a measure of the Beethoven score. The movement comprises 278 measures, therefore, each ICA component comprises a time series of 278 values, ranging from 0 (meaning lowest fMRI intensity) to 9 (highest fMRI intensity). As an example, Table 8.3 shows the values of the first 5 strongest ICA components (that is, 25, 15, 14, 8 and 5) for the first 10 measures of Beethoven's music, yielded by the fMRI of my own brain during the first listening pass in the scanner.

8.4.2 The Compositional Process

The compositional process involved manual and computer-automated procedures. The composition of the piece evolved in tandem with the development of a piece of software called MusEng. MusEng was programmed to learn musical information from given examples and use this information to generate new music.

Table 8.3 The values of the strongest 5 ICA components for the first 10 measures of Beethoven's music

Beethoven measure	ICA 25	ICA 15	ICA 14	ICA 8	ICA 5
1	7	5	5	5	2
2	5	5	8	5	8
3	7	3	5	5	6
4	5	8	3	5	2
5	5	7	4	4	4
6	6	6	4	5	3
7	7	8	5	6	3
8	4	6	3	4	3
9	6	6	4	5	4
10	5	7	5	5	3

The first step of the compositional process was to deconstruct the score of Beethoven's music into a set of basic materials for processing. These materials were subsequently given to MusEng as input for a Machine Learning algorithm, which will be explained in more detail below.

First of all, Beethoven's piece was divided into 13 sections, manually:

- Section 1: from measure 1 to measure 26
- Section 2: from measure 26 to measure 50
- Section 3: from measure 51 to measure 74
- Section 4: from measure 75 to measure 100
- Section 5: from measure 101 to measure 116
- Section 6: from measure 117 to measure 138
- Section 7: from measure 139 to measure 148
- Section 8: from measure 149 to measure 183
- Section 9: from measure 184 to measure 212
- Section 10: from measure 213 to measure 224
- Section 11: from measure 225 to measure 247
- Section 12: from measure 248 to measure 253
- Section 13: from measure 254 to measure 278.

The 13 sections informed the overarching form of each movement of my new symphony. This provided a scaffold for the new piece, which preserved the overall form of the original Beethoven movement.

MusEng did not learn the whole Beethoven piece at once. Rather, it was trained on a section by section basis. And the musical sequences for the respective new sections of the new movements were generated independently from each other. For instance, Section 1 of the movement *Ballerina* has 26 measures and was composed based on materials from the first 26 measures of Beethoven's music. Next, Section 2 has 24 measures and was composed based on materials from the next 24 measures (26–50) of Beethoven's music, and so on.

Fig. 8.17 The first 10 measures of Section 1 of Beethoven's music, showing the viola, violoncello and double bass parts

A discussion of manual handling is beyond the scope of this chapter. As an example, the transformation of Section 1 of Beethoven's original music into the opening section of *Ballerina* is shown in Fig. 8.18. Figure 8.17 shows the first 10 measures of Beethoven's music focusing on the parts of the violas, violoncellos and double basses. And Fig. 8.18 shows how those measures were 'recomposed' to form 10 measures for the opening of the first movement of my new symphony. Note the rhythmic transformation of measures 4, 6, 8 and 10.

Fig. 8.18 Ten measures from the opening of *Ballerina*, the first movement of *Symphony of Minds Listening*, showing the viola, violoncello and double bass parts

Once a new segment is generated, it is orchestrated and appended to the respective score of the new movement accordingly. The fMRI also influenced instrumentation, playing techniques and other musical parameters (Fig. 8.17).

8.4.3 The Musical Engine: MusEng

MusEng has three distinct phases of operation: a *learning phase*, a *generative phase* and a *transformative phase*.

The learning phase extracts a number of musical features from a given musical score. A dataset comprising these features and rules representing the likelihood of given features appearing in the music are then stored.

At the generative phase, the system uses the extracted to inform the generation of new sequences. These sequences will bear close resemblance to the sequences that were used to train the system in the first phase.

Finally, at the transformative phase, the outcome from the generative phase is modified by transformation algorithms. It is in this phase that the fMRI information is used to influence the resulting music.

The transformative phase was added to further modify the results from the generative phase. The role of fMRI information is to control the extent of the transformations. Essentially, stronger activity in a given ICA component of the fMRI data results in larger amounts of transformation in the resulting music.

MusEng reads and outputs musical scores coded in the MIDI format. This is useful because outputs can be loaded into any suitable music notation software for inspection and put together the composition.

MusEng only processes monophonic musical sequences, that is, sequences of one note at a time. Obviously, Beethoven's piece is a polyphonic orchestral symphony. In order to circumvent MusEng's monophonic limitation, I developed two approaches to process the music. The first approach is to train the system with the part of one instrumental voice of the orchestra at a time (violins, violoncellos, etc.) and then generate sequences for those respective parts individually. The second approach is to reduce the orchestral music to one monophonic voice and then generate various monophonic sequences, which are subsequently orchestrated. I generated materials for *Symphony of Minds Listening* using both approaches.

8.4.3.1 Learning Phase

MusEng implements an abridged version of a system called iMe, developed at ICCMR by Miranda and Gimenes [10]. MusEng takes a MIDI file as an input and extracts the following 5 features from the encoded music:

- Pitches of the notes
- Melody directions between successive notes in a sequence
- Melody intervals; i.e., the amount of change between the pitches of successive notes in a sequence
- Note durations
- Tonality implied by groups of notes in the sequence.

Table 8.4 Musicodes for the first two measures of the musical sequence in Fig. 8.19. The rows correspond to the event number, or in this case, number of notes in the sequence: the first two measures comprise a total of 9 notes

	1	2	3	4	5	6	7	8	9
Melody direction	0	−1	+1	−1	0	+1	+1	−1	−1
Melody interval	0	8	3	7	0	1	2	2	1
Event duration	120	120	120	120	60	60	120	60	60
Note pitch	E5	G#4	B4	E4	B4	C5	D5	C5	B5
Modality	E Maj, A harm min				A min, C Maj				

Fig. 8.19 An example of a musical sequence

These features are stored as event-based vectors, referred to as *musicodes*. Table 8.4 shows the musicodes for the first two measures (initial nine notes) of the musical excerpt shown in Fig. 8.19.

Melody direction can value −1, 0, or +1, referring to descending, motionless, or ascending movement, respectively. The current note in a sequence is compared with the previous note; in this example, the first note in a measure returns a value equal to 0.

Melody intervals are represented in terms of half steps, which are also calculated with reference to the current note's distance from the previous note. Again, the first note in the measure returns a value equal to 0.

As for note durations, the value 240 is assigned to quarter notes, and other durations are calculated with reference to this value; e.g., half notes are equal to 480 and eighth notes are equal to 120.

In general, the number −2 is used to represent the absence of data in a musicode vector. That is, the note pitch musicode for a musical rest would be equal to −2. With respect to the implied tonality of segments, the system creates a label specifying a tonal pattern and indicates when the estimation is ambiguous. For example, in the first measure of the music shown in Fig. 8.19, the system sees E, G#, and B, as an 'E Major' chord, but the note G# implies it could be an 'A harmonic minor' chord.

As we shall see below, MusEng builds a musical memory in terms of small segments of music. Ideally, the system would segment the music based on perceptual criteria. The original iMe system sported such a method, inspired by Gestalt psychology [4]. However, for this composition, MusEng was programmed to segment the music according to a given number of measures, e.g., every measure, or every two measures, or every three and so on. The rationale for this decision is that I wanted to be able to synchronize the fMRI analysis to the input score by handling the fMRI data on a measure-by-measure basis, as it was shown schematically in Fig. 8.15.

MusEng's memory consists of a series of Feature Tables (FTs), which comprise vectors of musicodes. As the musicodes are extracted from the measures, one after another, the system may or may not create new FTs. This depends on whether the respective musicodes have already been seen by the system or not. If a certain vector of musicodes is identical to one that has been previously seen by the system, then it updates the relevant FT by increasing a weighting factor, represented by the variable ω in the equation

$$\omega(x) = \frac{\Sigma_x FT}{\Sigma_n FT}$$

This variable ω is generated by summing the total number of FTs, and then dividing the number of instances of each individual FT by the total. In essence, this becomes a simple moving average. The variable x represents the number of instances of a given FT in the series, and n the total number of all FT in the series so far. This moving average has the effect of lowering the value of ω for vectors of musicodes that do not appear as often as more frequent ones, in the same way, that it raises the value of ω for more commonly used vectors, to a maximum value of 1.0.

The value of ω informs the probability of a given musical segment being generated later on by the system. Typically, a decrease in the value of ω causes the system to avoid using the corresponding FT entry in the subsequent generative phase.

In order to illustrate how MusEng's memory is built, let us examine a hypothetical run through the sequence previously shown in Fig. 8.19, commencing with an empty memory. The first measure (Fig. 8.20) is analyzed and the respective musicodes are generated. For the sake of clarity, this example will focus on only three of the five features: melody direction (*dir*), melody interval (*int*) and event duration (*dur*).

MusEng creates in its memory the first feature table, FT1, with musicodes derived from the first measure (Fig. 8.20) of the training sequence as follows:

Fig. 8.20 The first measure for the example analysis

Fig. 8.21 The second measure for the example analysis

$$dir = \{0, -1, +1, -1\}$$
$$int = \{0, 8, 3, 7\}$$
$$dur = \{120, 120, 120, 120\}$$
$$\omega = 1/1 \text{ or } 1.0$$

Then, the system creates FT2 with musicodes extracted from the second measure of the training sequence (Fig. 8.21) as follows:

$$dir = \{0, +1, +1, -1, -1\}$$
$$int = \{0, 1, 2, 2, 1\}$$
$$dur = \{60, 60, 120, 60, 60\}$$
$$\omega = 1/2 \text{ or } 0.5$$

Next, MusEng creates FT3, with musicodes from the third measure of the training sequence (Fig. 8.22) as follows:

$$dir = \{0, +1, 0\}$$
$$int = \{0, 1, 0\}$$
$$dur = \{120, 120, 240\}$$
$$\omega = 1/3 \text{ or } 0.33$$

The fourth and fifth measures are processed next. However, MusEng does not create new FTs in these cases because they are repetitions of previous measures; that is, their respective musicodes have already been seen by the system. In this case, only the values of ω for the respective FTs are adjusted accordingly. Thus, at this point of the training phase, the ω values for each FT are as shown in Table 8.5.

MusEng's memory after the training phase, complete with 3 FTs is shown in Table 8.6. It is important to stress that particular FTs gain or lose perceptual

Fig. 8.22 The third measure for the example analysis

Table 8.5 Values of ω after three FTs have been created and stored in memory, calculated by dividing the number of instances of a given FT by the total number of FTs analyzed

	FT1	FT2	FT3
ω	1/5 = 0.2	2/5 = 0.4	2/5 = 0.4

Table 8.6 MusEng's memory after being trained with the musical sequence shown in Fig. 8.19

	dir	int	dur	ω
FT1	0, −1, +1, −1	0, 8, 3, 7	120, 120, 120, 120	0.2
FT2	0, +1, +1, −1, −1	0, 1, 2, 2, 1	60, 60, 120, 60, 60	0.4
FT3	0, +1, 0	0, 1, 0	120, 120, 240	0.4

importance depending on how often the system is exposed to them. Notice, therefore, that FT2 and FT3 have higher ω values than that of FT1 because they appeared twice.

8.4.3.2 Generative Phase

At the generative phase, MusEng generates new FTs by mutating the musicodes: an existing FT (source) is mutated towards another FT (target). Mutations are influenced by the values of ω: FTs with larger ω values are selected more often than FTs with smaller ω values.

The very first measure of a newly generated structure is typically informed by the first FT in memory (FT1). Let us consider this as the source FT for the mutation. A second FT, the target FT, is selected from memory according to the values held in memory for the variable ω. FTs with higher ω values tend to be selected as targets more often than those with lower ω values.

The generative process is illustrated below by means of an example using the learned memory shown in Table 8.6. For clarity, the example considers only one of the musicodes: melodic direction (*dir*). Therefore, assume the memory scenario shown in Table 8.7.

To generate a new measure, the *dir* musicode of the source FT1 will be mutated towards the respective musicode values of a target FT. In this case, both FT2 and FT3 have the same ω. Thus, there is an equal chance of FT2 or FT3 being selected as the target. Let us assume that FT2 is selected. In this case, FT2's *dir* musicode is applied to FT1's *dir* musicode to produce a mutation (the mutated element is written in bold) as follows:

Table 8.7 A memory scenario with three FTs

	FT1	FT2	FT3
dir	0, −1, +1, −1	0, +1, +1, −1, −1	0, +1, 0
ω	0.2	0.4	0.4

Fig. 8.23 The musical rendering of the new FT that was generated by mutating the *dir* musicode from FT1 towards FT2

$$\{0, \ +1, \ +1, \ -1, \ -1\} + \{0, \ -1, \ +1, \ -1\} = \{0, \mathbf{0}, \ +1, \ -1, \ -1\}$$

Note that the *dir* musicode has outlying maximum and minimum values of +1 and −1, hence only the second value is actually mutated $(+1) + (−1) = 0$. Therefore, the newly generated FT contains a *dir* musicode equal to $\{0, 0, +1, −1, −1\}$.

Obviously, mutating other musicodes would yield more variation. Mutations are possible across all musicodes in the FTs in a similar manner, with the only exception being mutations in modality. These are accomplished by a process of transformation whereby the intervals between successive absolute pitches in the given FTs are forced to conform to pre-set intervals for major, minor, or diminished modes.

Finally, the new FT is rendered into a musical measure (Fig. 8.23) and saved into a MIDI file.

8.4.3.3 Transformative Phase

The transformative phase comprises a dozen of transformation algorithms that modify a given musical sequence, two of which will be explained in this section.

Although there are some differences in the specific processing undertaken by each algorithm, the basic signal flow is fairly identical for all of them. The generated input signal is modified towards values given by a transformation algorithm. The amount of modification is scaled according to the fMRI data. The fMRI data, or more specifically the data extrapolated from the fMRI scans by ICA analysis, is referred to as the *fMRI_index*.

The *fMRI_index* is given on a ten-point scale with values between 0 and 9. In order to use the fMRI index as a Control Signal (*CS*) for the transformation algorithms, MusEng first scales the data to a range between 0.1 and 1.0. In order to do this, the system applies the following simple scaling process to the value of the *fMRI_index*:

$$CS = \{(fMRI\_index + 1) * 0.1\}$$

A difference value (*d*) between the input and the transformed musicodes is also calculated. This difference is then multiplied by the *CS* to give a final Scaled Modifier Value: *SMV*.

The *SMV* is summed with the input signal to transform the output. This gives a degree of fMRI-controlled variability in each transformation: a high *fMRI_index* value will result in larger transformations, whereas a low *fMRI_index* value will result in smaller transformations.

Below are examples of two of the transformation algorithms available, showing the effect of varying the *fMRI_index*: pitch inversion and pitch scrambling.

Pitch Inversion Algorithm

Given an input musical sequence, the pitch inversion algorithm creates a new sequence, which is effectively the input sequence turned upside-down. For instance, a sequence rising in pitch would descend in pitch after this transformation. In order to illustrate this, let us consider the measure shown in Fig. 8.23.

The melody interval musicode for this measure is {0, 0, 3, 2, 1} and the note pitch musicode is {B4, B4, D5, C5, B4}. Bear in mind that the pitch values need to be converted into MIDI representations in order to be processed by the system. In this case, the MIDI values are 71, 71, 74, 72 and 71, respectively.

There are a variety of ways to accomplish a pitch inversion, including diatonic and chromatic options, or inversions around a specific sounding pitch. MusEng processes pitch inversion simply by subtracting the current MIDI pitch value from 128 (MIDI uses a range of 128 pitch values). For instance, the transformed pitch values for our example created using this technique would be as follows: (128 − 71 = 57), (128 − 71 = 57), (128 − 74 = 54), (128 − 72 = 56) and (128 − 71 = 57).

The resulting MIDI values are 57, 57, 54, 56 and 57, yielding the following pitch sequence {A4, A4, F#4, G#4, A4}. Note that the inverted sequence maintains the original melody interval musicode of {0, 0, 3, 2, 1}, whilst giving an upside-down melody, as shown in Fig. 8.24.

The example above assumed a maximal fMRI index value of 9, which once scaled to create a *CS* gives 1.0. However, as mentioned earlier, varied degrees of transformations are also possible by scaling the amount of transformation according to the value of the *fMRI_index*. The difference between the input and the transformed pitches is multiplied by *CS*, before being summed with the input to create the final transformed output value.

$$New\_pitch = \{Input\_pitch + ((Input\_pitch - transf\_pitch) * [(fMRI\_index + 1) * 0.1])\}$$

Let us examine what happens if we assume an *fMRI_index* equal to 5, which yields a *CS* equal to 0.6. In this case, we would expect an output approximately halfway between the original pitch and the inversion; in other words, an almost

Fig. 8.24 Newly inverted sequence, after transformation of measure in Fig. 8.23

neutral set of intervals. First, the difference d between the maximal inversion and the input signal for each of the musicode values needs to be calculated as follows:

$$d = \{(57-71), (57-71), (54-74), (56-72), (57-71)\}$$
$$d = \{-14, -14, -20, -16, -14\}$$

Then, the scaled modifier values are calculated by multiplying the difference values by the value of CS

$$SMV = \{(-14 * 0.6), (-14 * 0.6), (-20 * 0.6), (-16 * 0.6), (-14 * 0.6)\}$$
$$SMV = \{-8.4, -8.4, -12, -9.6, -8.4\}$$

Finally, the SMV values are summed with the original input to give a transformed set of output values

$$New\_pitches = \{(71 - 8.4), (71 - 8.4), (74-12), (72 - 9.6), (71 - 8.4)\}$$
$$New\_pitches = \{62.6, 62.6, 62, 62, 62.6\}$$

Pitch values are rounded up to the nearest whole number as per the MIDI standard, giving a transformed set of pitch values equal to $\{63, 63, 62, 62, 63\}$, which is rendered as $\{D\#4, D\#4, D4, D4, D\#4\}$, as shown in Fig. 8.25.

Pitch Scrambling Algorithm

In simple terms, the pitch scrambling algorithm orders the pitch values of the input signal into a numerical list, which is then re-ordered randomly. Using the same input as for the previous example (Fig. 8.23), let us examine the result of applying this transformation. The process is as follows:

- Input pitches: $\{71, 71, 74, 72, 71\}$
- Order pitches in ascending order: $\{71, 71, 71, 72, 74\}$
- Scramble the order of pitches randomly: $\{74, 72, 71, 71, 71\}$
- Output pitches: $\{74, 72, 71, 71, 71\}$.

In this case, the output would be rendered as $\{D5, C5, B4, B4, B4\}$. Re-running the transformation, a further three times would give further variants, for example: $\{72, 74, 71, 71, 71\}$, $\{71, 74, 72, 71, 71\}$ and $\{71, 74, 71, 72, 71\}$, rendered as $\{C5,$

Fig. 8.25 Sequence after inversion with *fMRI_index* = 5, giving a nearly neutral set of pitch intervals

Fig. 8.26 The result from applying the pitch scrambling algorithm four times on the same input

D5, B4, B4, B4}, {B4, D5, C5, B4, B4} and {B4, D5, B4, C5, B4}, respectively, as illustrated in Fig. 8.26.

As with the pitch inversion algorithm, the value of *fMRI_index* can be used to create a control signal with which the amount of transformation can be varied. In order to illustrate this, let us assume an *fMRI_index* equal to 3. This gives a *CS* value of 0.4.

Again, considering the same input as before and the transformed values from the first pitch scramble shown in Fig. 8.26, the value of *d*, between the first scramble transformation (first measure) and the input signal is calculated as follows:

$$d = \{(74-71), (72-71), (71-74), (71-72), (71-71)\}$$
$$d = \{3, 1, -3, -1, 0\}$$

The scaled modifier values are then calculated by multiplying the difference values by *CS* = 0.4

$$SMV = \{(3 * 0.4), (1 * 0.4), (-3 * 0.4), (-1 * 0.4), (0 * 0.4)\}$$
$$SMV = \{1.2, 0.4, -1.2, -0.4, 0\}$$

Finally, the *SMV* values are summed with the values of the original input to give a transformed set of output values

$$New\_pitches = \{(71+1.2), (71+0.4), (74-1.2), (72-0.4), (71-0)\}$$
$$New\_pitches = \{72.2, 71.4, 72.8, 71.6, 71\}$$

As before, pitch values are rounded up to the nearest whole number as per the MIDI standard, giving a transformed set of pitch values of {72, 71, 73, 72, 71}, which is rendered as {C5, B4, C#5, C5, B4}, as shown in Fig. 8.27. Note that the output is significantly closer in the overall structure to the unscrambled input than the first scrambled transformation in Fig. 8.26.

Fig. 8.27 Transformed output created by pitch scrambling algorithm assuming *fMRI_index* = 3

The transformation examples above give a glimpse of how the addition of control by means of fMRI enhances the potential of MusEng. As I mentioned earlier, the composition of *Symphony of Minds Listening* involved automatic and manual processes. Whereas I deployed MusEng heavily to remix Beethoven's Symphony, there was a great deal of manual work to reject and/or amend the outputs from the system. However, I consistently remained faithful to the fMRI of the respective subjects in order to yield the differentiated movements accordingly. I worked on the assumption that a great proportion of my manual interventions, if not all, could in principle be automated in MusEng.

Symphony of Minds Listening insinuates the possibility of coupling musical systems with our brain. A better understanding of the brain combined with the emergence of increasingly sophisticated devices for scanning the brain is enabling the development of musical interfaces with our neuronal systems, which would have been unthinkable until very recently. These interfaces have tremendous potential to enable access to active music making to people with severe motor impairments, such as severe paralysis after a severe stroke or accident damaging the spinal cord, in addition, to open the doors to completely new ways to harness creative practices.

8.5 Brain-Computer Music Interfacing

A Brain-Computer Interface (BCI) is a device that enables users to control systems with signals from their brains. I coined the term Brain-Computer Music Interfacing (BCMI) to refer to BCI systems to control music (Fig. 8.28). BCMI systems have the potential to be used as recreational devices for people with severe motor impairment and music therapy, in addition, to innovative applications in composition and music performance [12].

Fig. 8.28 A BCMI system extracts information from the user's EEG to control musical systems. In this photo, a person is playing a Disklavier MIDI piano through a BCMI

The most commonly used brain signal in BCMI is the EEG, which stands for electroencephalogram. The fMRI scanning method used for *Symphony of Minds Listening* is not practical, and its timing resolution is not suitable for real-time systems.

In a nutshell, brain cells communicate with each other through electrical impulses. The EEG is a recording of this electrical activity with electrodes placed on the scalp. The EEG expresses the overall activity of millions of neurones in the brain in terms of charge movement. However, the electrodes can detect this only in the most superficial regions of the cerebral cortex.

The EEG is a difficult signal to handle because it is filtered by the meninges (the membranes that separate the cortex from the skull), the skull and the scalp before it reaches the electrodes. Furthermore, the signals arriving at the electrodes are sums of signals arising from many possible sources, including artefacts like the heartbeat and eye blinks. This signal needs to be scrutinized with signal processing and analysis techniques in order to be of any use for a BCI system.

In general, power spectrum analysis is the most commonly used method to analyze the EEG. In simple terms, power spectrum analysis breaks the EEG signal into different frequency bands and reveals the distribution of power between them. This is useful because it is believed that specific distributions of power in the spectrum of the EEG can encode different cognitive behaviours.

In BCI research, it is often assumed that:

- There is information in the EEG that corresponds to different cognitive tasks, or at least a function of some sort
- This information can be detected
- Users can be trained to produce such EEG information voluntarily.

Typically, users must learn ways to voluntarily produce specific patterns of EEG signals to be able to control something. This informs the hard approach to BCMI: a system whereby the user actively controls music.

It is arguable that voluntary control may not be always necessary for creating music. For instance, a system may simply react to the mental states of the user, producing music that is not necessarily explicitly controlled. We shall refer to such systems as *soft BCMI*, as opposed to *hard BCMI*. In this chapter, however, I shall focus on hard BCMI because I am interested in active, voluntary control of music with the brain.

There basically are two approaches to control the EEG for a hard BCMI: *conscious effort* and *operant conditioning* [11]. Conscious effort induces changes in the EEG by engaging in specific cognitive tasks designed to produce specific EEG activity [2, 8]. The cognitive task that is most often used in this case is motor imagery because it is relatively straightforward to detect changes in the EEG of a subject imagining the movement of a limb such as, for instance, the left hand. Other forms of imagery, such as auditory, visual and navigation imagery, have also been used.

Operant conditioning involves the presentation of a task in conjunction with some form of feedback, which allows the user to develop unconscious control of the EEG. Once the brain is conditioned, the user is able to accomplish the task without being conscious of the EEG activity that needs to be generated [6].

On both aforementioned approaches, the system often has some form of AI to recognize patterns in the EEG signal and activate the system to perform the required tasks accordingly.

Somewhere in between the conscious effort and operant conditioning, there is a method referred to as evoked potentials.

Evoked Potentials (EPs) are spikes that appear in the EEG in response to external stimuli. EPs can be evoked from auditory, visual or tactile stimuli producing auditory (AEP), visual (VEP) and somatosensory (SSEP) evoked potentials, respectively. It is not trivial to detect the electrophysiological response to a single event in an ongoing EEG stream. However, if the person is subjected to repeated stimulation at short intervals (e.g., nine repetitions per second, or 9 Hz) then the brain's response to each subsequent stimulus is evoked before the response to the prior stimulus has decayed. This prevents the signal to return to a baseline state. Rather, it produces a steady-state response, which can be detected in the EEG with no major difficulties [17].

Steady-State Visual Evoked Potential (SSVEP) is a robust paradigm for a BCI, provided the user is not severely visually impaired. Typically, visual targets are presented to a user on a computer monitor representing tasks to be performed. These could be spelling words from an alphabet, or selecting directions for a wheelchair to move and so on. Each target is encoded by a flashing visual pattern reversing at a unique frequency; usually lower than 30 Hz.

In order to select a target, the user must simply direct their gaze at the flashing pattern corresponding to the action they would like to perform. As the user's spotlight of attention falls over a particular target, the frequency of the unique pattern reversal rate can be accurately detected in their EEG through spectral analysis. It is possible to classify not only a user's choice of target, but also the extent to which they are attending it. Effectively, each target of a SSVEP system can be implemented as a switch with a potentiometer.

8.5.1 ICCMR's First SSVEP-Based BCMI System

In 2011, the ICCMR team completed the implementation of its first SSVEP-based BCMI system, which was trialled with a person with locked-in syndrome at the Royal Hospital for Neuro-disability, in London.

The system comprised four flashing images, or targets, as shown on the computer screen in front of the users in Fig. 8.29. Each target image represents a different musical instrument and a sequence of notes (Fig. 8.30). Each image flashes reversing its colour (in this case the colour is red) at different frequencies: 7 Hz, 9 Hz, 11 Hz and 15 Hz, respectively.

Fig. 8.29 A person with locked-in syndrome testing the BCMI

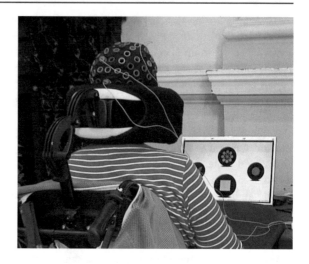

Fig. 8.30 Each target image is associated with a musical instrument and a sequence of notes

Thus, for instance, if the user gazes at the image flashing at 15 Hz, then the system will activate the xylophone instrument and will produce a melody using the sequence of six notes that was associated with this target. These notes are modifiable: they are set beforehand and the number of notes can be other than six. The more the person attends to this icon, the more prominent is the magnitude of their brain's SSVEP response to this stimulus, and vice-versa. This produces a varying control signal, which is used to produce the melody. Also, it provides a visual feedback to the user; the size of the icon increases or decreases as a function of this control signal.

The melody is generated as follows: the sequence of six notes is stored in an array, whose index varies from one to six. The amplitude of the SSVEP signal is normalized so that it can be used as an index that slides up and down through the array. As the signal varies, the corresponding index triggers the respective musical notes stored in the array (Fig. 8.31).

Fig. 8.31 Notes are selected according to the level of the SSVEP signal

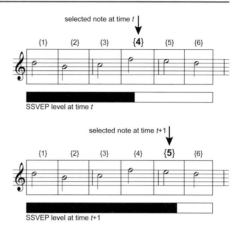

The system requires just three electrodes on the scalp of the user: a pair placed on the region of the visual cortex and a ground electrode placed on the front head. Filters are used to reduce interference of AC mains noise and undesired spurious signals, such as those generated by blinking eyes or moving facial muscles. SSVEP data is then analyzed in order to extract band power across the frequencies correlating to the flashing stimuli.

The person at the hospital trialled the system during a two-hour session. Being familiar with eye gaze technology for her alternative communication system, she grasped the concept quickly and rapidly demonstrated her skills at playing the system with minimal practice. It took approximately 15 min to learn how to use the system and she was able to quickly learn how to make melodies by increasing and decreasing the level of her SSVEP signal.

Suggestions and criticism from the staff of the hospital, carers and the user, with respect to improvements and potential further developments were collected. Two important challenges emerged from this exercise:

- The system produced synthesized sounds, which were not enjoyed. And the music sounded mechanical; it lacked expressivity. It was suggested that it would be much more desirable if the music could be played on real acoustic musical instruments.
- The system enabled a one-to-one interaction with a machine. However, it was immediately apparent that it would be desirable to design a system that would promote interaction amongst people. Similar resident patients of the hospital wished for something that would enable them to do something socially, as a group. Making music is the ideal activity for this. Therefore, a BCMI should enable a group of patients to make music together.

The possibilities for applying the system within group settings were immediately apparent and an exciting prospect for people with limited opportunities for participating as an equal partner in a group.

8.5.2 *Activating Memory* and *The Paramusical Ensemble*

In order to address the abovementioned challenges, I adopted a slightly different research methodology. I started by dreaming a musical composition and a performance scenario first and then I considered how that would work in practice with the BCMI technology.

In order to address the problem of lack of expressivity, I came up with the idea that the patient would generate a score on the fly for a human musician to sight-read, instead of relaying it to a synthesizer. Another idea would be to build a robotic contraption to play a musical instrument. However, this would require developments that were beyond the remits of the research that ICCMR was developing at that time. There is much potential to be explored, however, combining BCMI technology with musical robotics.

In order to promote group interaction, I established that the composition would have to be generated collectively by a group of participants. Moreover, the generative process would have to be simple and clearly understood by the participants. Also, the controlling-brain participants would need to clearly feel that they have control of what is happening with the music. The concept of a musical ensemble emerged, where severely motor-impaired participants and motor-able professional musicians make music together: *The Paramusical Ensemble* (Fig. 8.32).

The end result is a new version of the SSVEP-based BCMI system and a bespoke composition entitled *Activating Memory*: piece for a string quartet and a BCMI quartet. Each member of the BCMI quartet is furnished with the new SSVEP-based BCMI system, which enables them to generate a musical score in real-time. Each member of the BCMI quartet generates a part for the string quartet,

Fig. 8.32 A rehearsal of *The Paramusical Ensemble*, with a quartet of locked-in syndrome patients performing *Activating Memory*

Fig. 8.33 Photo of our new SSVEP stimuli device. In this photograph, the LCD screens are showing numbers, but in *Activating Memory* they display short musical phrases, such as the ones shown in Fig. 8.34

LCD screen   Flashing LEDs

which is displayed on a computer screen for the respective performer to sight-read during a performance (Fig. 8.34).

The new BCMI system works similarly to the one described above, with the fundamental difference that the visual targets are associated with short musical phrases. Moreover, instead of flashing images on a computer monitor, the ICCMR team designed a device with flashing LEDs and LCD screens displaying what the LEDs represent (Figs. 8.33 and 8.34). The LCD provides an efficient way to change the set of options available for selection. Also, this device increases the SSVEP response to the stimuli because it produces flashing rates with greater precision than the rates that were produced using standard computer monitors. Subliminally, it promotes the notion that one is using a bespoke musical device to interact with others, rather than interacting via a computer.

I composed *Activating Memory* as a musical game involving four players, but it is a cooperative game. There are no winners. The composition method is inspired by *Arca Musurgica*, an extraordinary musical device built in 1650, in Rome, by Jesuit Father Athanasius Kircher, and described in his book *Musurgia Universalis* [7]. Kircher's device consisted of a box holding a number of wooden slats. Each of them contained a set of numbers, corresponding to sets of notes and rhythmic patterns. These materials could be combined in a number of ways to form compositions. In the eighteenth century, a number of musical dice games inspired by

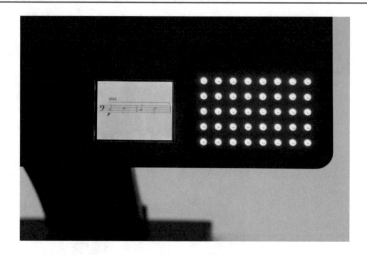

Fig. 8.34 Detail from the SSVEP stimuli device, showing a short musical phrase displayed on the LDC screen

Arca Musurgica, appeared in Europe, the most famous of which is Wolfgang Amadeus Mozart's *Musikalisches Würfelspiel*, or musical dice games.

Activating Memory is generated on the fly by sequencing four voices of pre-determined musical sections simultaneously. For each section, the system provides four choices of musical phrases, or riffs, for each part of the string quartet, which are selected by the BCMI quartet (Fig. 8.35). The selected riffs for each instrument are relayed to the computer monitors facing the string quartet for sight-reading. While the string quartet is playing the riffs for a section, the system provides the BCMI quartet with another set of choices for the next section. Once the current

Fig. 8.35 An example of two sets of four musical riffs on offer for two subsequent sections the violoncello part

section has been played, the chosen new riffs for each instrument are subsequently relayed to the musicians, and so on. In order to give enough time for the BCMI quartet to make choices, the musicians repeat the respective riffs until the next set of options are available for selection. The system follows an internal metronome, which guarantees synchronization.

Activating Memory has been publicly performed on a number of occasions before we performed with *The Paramusical Ensemble*. This allowed us to make final adjustments to the system and music. *The Paramusical Ensemble*'s first public performance of *Activating Memory* took place on 17 July 2015, at the Royal Hospital for Neuro-disability in Putney, London.

A new system is currently being designed to cater for a larger number of participants and an increased number of choices for the 'musical game'. In addition to the increased sophistication of the signal processing and pattern matching methods, AI is being deployed to increase the sophistication of the generative music method. Instead of working with pre-composed musical phrases, I am developing a system that generates those musical phrases from scratch. Machine learning methods are being tested in order to endow the system with the ability to learn generative music rules from examples and build the sequencing options automatically.

8.6 Concluding Discussion and Acknowledgements

In a paper which I co-authored for *Computer Music Journal* [9], I coined the term *Music Neurotechnology* to refer to a new area of research at the crossroads of Neurobiology, Engineering Sciences and Music. This chapter introduced the work I have been developing to champion this field. I deliberately focused on my own work here. However, this is not to say that there is nothing else being developed by others. On the contrary. Research into BCMI is burgeoning [12]. And indeed, the chapter by Vahri McKenzie, Nathan Thompson, Darren Moore and Guy Ben-Ary in this volume presented an awesome approach to harnessing living neurones to build a music system.

I consider the four pieces of work introduced above as different paths converging to two intertwined long-term objectives. One is the development of programmable processors based on cultured neuronal tissue. And the other is the development of increasingly more sophisticated coupling between our natural brain and artificial ones. Of course, I am interested in how these will impact music. However, the impact of such developments traverses a much wider range of applications.

The first development is bound to lead to new kinds of computers, combining silicon-based chips and biological tissue. What advantages these may bring about that current computing technology does not offer are unclear. Nevertheless, attributes commonly found in biological systems, such as energy efficiency, reproduction, self-repairing, holism and massive parallelism, to cite but a few can be desirable for certain AI applications, although they are problematical to endow digital computers with.

The SSVEP method used in the BCMI system introduced above is the best currently available. A number of other methods have been proposed, but they are not as reliable for deployment in the real world as SSVEP is. The great majority of BCI systems developed to date exist in the realm of research laboratories only. Such systems will become useful when they become controllable with signals produced voluntarily and reliably from within the brain, rather than in response to external sensorial stimuli. Research continues.

In the future we may be able to tightly couple hybrid biological computers with our brains, as some sort of *brain prostheses*; e.g., to mitigate the consequences of brain impairment or perhaps for human enhancement. Musical brain prosthesis? That is a far-fetched thought. But it is not an implausible one.

Acknowledgements The work presented in the chapter would not have been possible to be developed without the expertise and active input from a number of collaborators, including Dan Lloyd (Trinity College, Hartford, USA), Zoran Josipovic (New York University, USA), Larry Bull (University of the West of England, UK), Etienne Roesch (University of Reading, UK), Wendy Magee (Royal Hospital for Neuro-disability, London, UK), Julian O'Kelly (Royal Hospital for Neuro-disability, London, UK), John Wilson (University of Sussex, UK), Ramaswamy Palaniappan (University of Sussex, UK), Duncam Wililams (University of Plymouth, UK), François Guegen (University of Plymouth) and Joel Eaton (University of Plymouth, UK).

Appendix: Two Pages of *Raster Plot*

The full score is available in [13].

References

1. Ashburner, J., & The FIL Methods Group at UCL. (2013). *SMP8 manual*. London: Institute of Neurology, University College London. Retrieved November 4, 2013, from https://www.fil.ion.ucl.ac.uk/spm/.
2. Curran, E. A., & Stokes, M. J. (2003). Learning to control brain activity: A review of the production and control of EEG components for driving brain-computer interface (BCI) systems. *Brain and Cognition, 51*(3), 326–336.
3. DeMarse, T., Wagenaar, D. A., Blau, A. W., & Potter, S. M. (2001). The neurally controlled animat: Biological brains acting with simulated bodies. *Autonomous Robots, 11*(3), 305–310.
4. Eysenck, M. W., & Keane, M. T. (2005). *Cognitive psychology: A student's handbook*. Hove and New York: Psychology Press (Taylor and Francis).
5. Izhikevich, E. R. (2007). *Dynamical systems in neuroscience*. Cambridge, MA: The MIT Press. ISBN 978-0262090438.
6. Kaplan, A., Ya Kim, J. J., Jin, K. S., Park, B. W., Byeon, J. G., & Tarasova, S. U. (2005). Unconscious operant conditioning in the paradigm of brain-computer interface based on color perception. *International Journal of Neurosciences, 115*, 781–802.
7. Kircher, A. (1650). *Musurgia Universalis* (2 Vols.). Rome, Italy: Ex typographia Haeredum F. Corbellitti.
8. Miranda, E. R. (2006). Brain-Computer music interface for composition and performance. *International Journal on Disability and Human Development, 5*(2), 119–125.
9. Miranda, E. R., Bull, L., Gueguen, F., & Uroukov, I. S. (2009). Computer music meets unconventional computing: Towards sound synthesis with in vitro neural networks. *Computer Music Journal, 33*(1), 09–18.
10. Miranda, E. R., & Gimenes, M. (2011). An ontomemetic approach to musical intelligence. In E. R. Miranda (Ed.), *A-life for music: Music and computer models of living systems.* (pp. 261–286). Middleton, WI: A-R Editions.
11. Miranda, E. R., Magee, W., Wilson, J. J., Eaton, J., & Palaniappan, R. (2011). Brain-computer music interfacing (BCMI): From basic research to the real world of special needs. *Music and Medicine, 3*(3), 134–140.
12. Miranda, E. R., & Castet, J. (Eds.). (2014). *Guide to brain-computer music interfacing*. London, UK: Springer.
13. Miranda, E. R. (2014). *Thinking music*. Plymouth, UK: University of Plymouth Press.
14. Miranda, E. R. (2002). *Computer sound design: Synthesis techniques and programming*. Oxford, UK: Elsevier/Focal Press.
15. Miranda, E. R. (Ed.). (2000). *Readings in music and artificial intelligence*. Abingdon, UK: Routledge.
16. Potter, A. M., DeMarse, T. B., Bakkum, D. J., Booth, M. C., Brumfield, J. R., Chao, Z., Madhavan, R., Passaro, P. A., Rambani, K., Shkolnik, A. C., Towal R. B., & Wagenaar, D. A. (2004). Hybrots: Hybrids of living neurons and robots for studying neural computation. In *Proceedings of Brain Inspired Cognitive Systems*. Stirling, UK.
17. Regan, D. (1989). *Human brain electrophysiology: Evoked potentials and evoked magnetic fields in science and medicine*. Oxford, UK: Elsevier.
18. Stone, J. V. (2004). *Independent component analysis: A tutorial introduction*. Cambridge, MA: The MIT Press.
19. Uroukov, I., Ma, M., Bull, L., & Purcell, W. (2006). Electrophysiological measurements in 3-dimensional *In Vivo*-mimetic organotypic cell cultures: Preliminary studies with hen embryo brain spheroids. *Neuroscience Letters, 404*, 33–38.

Eduardo Reck Miranda is Professor in Computer Music and head the Interdisciplinary Centre for Computer Music Research (ICCMR) at the University of Plymouth, UK. He studied music, philosophy and informatics in Brazil before he graduated with an M.Sc. in Music Technology from the University of York, UK. Subsequently he received a Ph.D. on the topic of sound design with Artificial Intelligence (AI) from the University of Edinburgh, UK. Before joining the University of Plymouth, he worked at Sony Computer Science Laboratory in Paris, France, as a research scientist in the fields of AI, speech and evolution of language. He also is a composer working at the crossroads of music and science. His distinctive music is informed by his unique background as a classically trained composer and AI scientist with an early involvement in electroacoustic and avant-garde pop music. E-mail: eduardo.miranda@plymouth.ac.uk.

On Making Music with Heartbeats

9

Elaine Chew

9.1 Introduction

Representation and analysis of musical structures in heart signals can benefit understanding of cardiac electrophysiology aberrations such as arrhythmias, which can in turn aid in the diagnosis and treatment of cardiac arrhythmias.

The typical time–frequency analysis of electrocardiographic recordings of cardiac arrhythmias yields descriptive statistics that provide useful features for classification, but fails to capture the actual rhythms of the physiological phenomena. Here, I propose to use music notation to represent beat-to-beat and morphological feature-to-feature durations of abnormal cardiac rhythms, using articulation markings when emphasis is warranted. The rhythms and articulations captured in these representations may provide cues to differentiate between individual experiences of cardiac arrhythmia, with potential impact on personalising diagnostics and treatment decisions.

Music generation is presented as an application of these rhythm transcriptions. The physiological origins ensure that the music based on heart rhythms, even abnormal ones, sound natural. The two-part music creation process draws inspiration from music collage practices and comprises of a retrieval component followed by transformation processes, which can be applied at the melody or block levels, and complex combinations thereof.

The music thus created can not only be used to identify distinct heart signatures and what they mean for different cardiac conditions but can also provide a visceral record of the experience of an arrhythmic episode. The pounding and fluttering of arrhythmia

E. Chew (✉)
CNRS-UMR9912/STMS (IRCAM), 1 place Igor-Stravinsky, 75004 Paris, France
e-mail: elaine.chew@ircam.fr

© Springer Nature Switzerland AG 2021
E. R. Miranda (ed.), *Handbook of Artificial Intelligence for Music*,
https://doi.org/10.1007/978-3-030-72116-9_9

can often be physically uncomfortable. The music created from arrhythmic traces is not easy listening; it is often provocative, but potentially instructive.

Music generated from arrhythmic hearts can have interesting implications for the development of intelligent heart–brain–computer interfaces. Music has been shown to have direct impact on cardiac response [1, 2]. This heart–brain response offers a window into the listener's true state of emotion, with potential for integration into emotive interfaces for music performance. Like respiration, and with the appropriate sensors, heart rhythms can also provide a feedback mechanism during music performance, driven by, and influencing autonomic response [3].

An understanding of how abnormal heart rhythms can be precisely and organically rendered into music thus opens up new opportunities and challenges for music and Artificial Intelligence (AI). The goal here is to propose some ideas and examples of these opportunities and challenges and to offer some possible solution approaches.

9.1.1 Why Cardiac Arrhythmias

The worldwide prevalence of cardiovascular disease (CVD) is high and is expected to increase substantially in the future. In the United States, nearly half (48%, 121.5 million in 2016) of all adults have some form of cardiovascular disease [4]. According to the World Health Organization, of the 56.9 million global deaths in 2016, 40.5 million (71%) were due to NCD, and the leading cause of NCD is CVD (17.9 million, or 44% of NCD deaths) [5]. CVD is the cause of more than half of all deaths in the European Region [6]. Hence, there is great interest in characterizing heart disease so as to benefit CVD diagnostics and therapeutics.

Like other conditions that affect the heart, abnormalities in heart rhythms (arrhythmias) are associated with morbidity and substantial economic costs. A study using over half a million records in the UK Biobank ascertained that abnormalities of cardiac rhythm affect >2% of adults, and the incidence rate of 0.5% per year is similar to that of stroke, myocardial infarction and heart failure [7]. Another study based on the Swedish National Study on Aging and Care (SNAC) data of adults aged 60 and older, shows that the prevalence and incidence of arrhythmias rapidly increase with age [8]. Baseline prevalence of atrial fibrillation (AF) was 4.9%, other arrhythmias including premature ventricular complexes or ventricular ectopics (VEs), supraventricular tachycardia (SVT) and supraventricular extrasystoles or ectopics (SVEs) were 8.4%, first- or second-degree atrioventricular (AV) block was 7.1%. AF is the most common arrhythmia, with a global prevalence of 33.5 million in 2010 [9].

There have been significant advances in the diagnosis and management of cardiac arrhythmias over the past two decades [10], but the classification and description of arrhythmias remain crude and often bear little relation to the symptoms and treatment outcomes. Arrhythmias are classified according to the source (atrial/supraventricular, ventricular, junctional), rate (bradycardia is slow and tachycardia is fast) and regularity (fibrillations are fast and irregular, and tachycardias are fast and regular).

Consider the case of AF. AF is irregular and often rapid, and is subdivided according to duration: paroxysmal AF is sporadic, lasting more than 30 s but less than a week; early persistent AF is continuous for more than a week but less than a year; longstanding persistent AF is continuous for more than a year; and, permanent AF is chronic and ongoing. These coarse descriptions fail to capture the actual rhythms and feature variations in individual occurrences of AF. The classifications also have little bearing on patients' symptoms or the likelihood of success of ablations or other treatments.

With the move towards precision medicine and the customisation of health care, it will become increasingly important to be able to distinguish between individual experiences of different arrhythmias.

9.1.2 Why Music Representation

Arrhythmias and other heart conditions are highly musical, with their innate periodicity and time-varying musical structures. The rhythms of arrhythmia closely resemble those of music rhythms, both the natural ones encountered in performance and more stylised ones found in musical scores. The episodic nature of many arrhythmias, their time evolution and the local patterns, have direct musical equivalents. The musical language we use to describe these structures, therefore, offers tools to describe cardiac anomalies in far greater detail than currently practiced.

Musicians have over the centuries developed a rich vocabulary for describing frequency (pitch) and time (rhythm), and how these attributes change over time, notating them so that they can be reproduced with high fidelity [11]. Over time, music notation has gained in sophistication to represent almost any imaginable rhythmic pattern, pushing the limits of rhythm notation, rendering, and perception. Virtuosic uses of notation include Haydn's incongruous metric and harmonic groupings [12], Brahms' creative use of hemiolas and metrical shifts [13], Stravinsky's playing with metrical changes while the rhythm remained untouched [14](p.61), Elliott Carter's invention of metric modulation [15] and Brian Ferneyhough's breathtakingly complex notations [16], just to name a few.

This rich vocabulary has been used to describe birdsong. In the nineteenth century, Lunn showed brief notated examples of cuckoo and blackbird calls in a short piece about the history of musical notation [17]. Composer Messiaen incorporated many birdsongs into his compositions like [18]. For bird enthusiasts, Saunders systematically transcribed the songs of 201 birds from the Eastern United States [19], representing pitch on the y-axis, duration on the x-axis, intensity with thick and thin lines, pronunciation with loops for consonant sounds and wavy lines to indicate trills and quality, but ignoring rhythm and repetitions of accented syllables [20]. These are features that can be captured using music notation.

Music has also been used to capture linguistic prosody. Joseph Steele was one of the earliest protagonists of this idea. He notated accent (pitch inflection), duration, pause, cadence and force (loudness) using symbols on a five-line staff inspired by that used in music [21]. In the early 1900s, Scripture notated the general melody and length of sounds using the height placement and lengths of symbols and by the number and heaviness of marks [22]. In opera, Arnold Schoenberg and Leoš Janáček used speech melody, not has an accurate representation of natural speech, but as an approximate guide to singers to follow the pitch inflexions of speech. Research developments in representing speech rarely used music notation. Noting that work in speech rhythm is predominantly driven by a desire to classify languages than to elucidate actual rhythms of spoken language, recent work by Brown, Pfordresher, and Chow builds on that of Steele to represent spoken meter using music notation [23]. Independently, Simões and Meireles have been using music notation to transcribe speech prosody in Spanish, Portuguese and English, but with only a 4/4 meter [24].

Given its flexibility and power to render strange and varied rhythms, using music to represent the fine variations in arrhythmia is not a far-fetched idea. Scholars and physicians have long noted the close connections between music and the heart. In the Middle Ages, academic physicians wrote about the music of the human pulse [25]. The first use of music notation to describe cardiovascular anomalies was applied to heart murmurs, first by the inventor of the stethoscope Réne Laennec [26] and more recently by nephrologist Michael Field [27], reflecting the close listening necessary for cardiac auscultation. These first instances of representing cardiac disorders using music notation will be described in greater detail in later sections. As far as we know, music representation of heart rhythm disorders like that in cardiac auscultation has been shown only recently by Chew in [28]. The focus on details of actual rhythms could potentially provide cues to the physiological phenomena of arrhythmias, and make a difference in how arrhythmia is viewed, described and discussed, beyond simple categories.

Music representation of heart rhythm disorders can give a detailed description of the actual rhythms, and can potentially provide tools for characterising individual cases of the arrhythmias and the forms they take within a person. For example, music notation can provide quick, visual information about differences between different kinds of ventricular premature beats or specific kinds of rhythmic irregularities encountered in experiences of atrial fibrillation that could potentially be linked to the severity of symptoms or treatment outcomes.

To make music representation scalable, transcriptions will need to be automated. While many rhythm quantisation techniques exist, the specifics of the methods will need to be tailored and fine-tuned for the new applications. The music representations can also form the basis for further comparisons such as similarity assessment and classification. These problems present new opportunities and challenges for music and AI.

9.1.3   Hearts Driving Music

Taking the parallels between music and heart signals one step further, *the strong similarities between the human pulse and music means that heart data can be readily mapped to music.*

Using heart rate time series data calculated over 300-beat heartbeat windows and mapping the numbers to 18 notes on a diatonic scale, Goldberger (alias Davids) generated a set of melodies that, augmented with improvised accompaniment, were recorded in the Heartsongs CD [29]. More complex mapping techniques have followed in the sonification of cardiac data. An example is Yokohama [30]'s work, which maps cardiac data to melodic pitches: each heartbeat interval corresponds to a Musical Instrument Digital Interface (MIDI) note, with intervallic changes such as premature beats triggering more significant pitch changes. In [31], Orzessek and Falkner passed heartbeat intervals through a bandpass filter and mapped them to MIDI note onsets, pitch, and/or loudness to sonify heart rate variability (HRV). Ballora et al. [32] further maps HRV data to pitch, timbre and pulses over a course of hours for medical diagnosis.

Heart rate variability parameters have been used to guide music generation. In [33], Fukumoto et al. used the high-frequency component of HRV, linked to autonomic nervous activity—as a fitness value in their Interactive Evolutionary Computation system to generate music chord progressions. Heart data has also been used to shape interactive performances in real time. In Votava and Berger [34]'s Heart Chamber Orchestra, interpretations of its 12 musicians' heartbeats, detected through ECG monitors, and relationships between them influence a real-time score that is then read and performed by the musicians from a computer screen. Related to this, physiological measures like respiration, blood pressure and heart rate have been shown to increase with music tempo [1], and decrease with lower tempo [3]. Prior work has mainly focused on non-arrhythmic hearts.

Arrhythmia rhythms arise naturally in music; it is but a small step from rhythm notation of cardiac pathologies to turning them into collage music. Since arrhythmia rhythms arise naturally in music, finding music that matches the rhythms of a segment of recorded arrhythmia then becomes a matter of retrieval. And the task of creating a musical piece then becomes one of re-combining these retrieved segments in elegant and interesting ways to form a collage composition.

Collage is a common compositional technique, one that is commonly used in AI systems for music generation. David Cope's EMI (Experiments in Musical Intelligence) [35] is a classic example using the idea of recombinancy [36]. EMI takes fragments of existing music and recombines them into new logical sequences to produce music in the style of composers ranging from Bach to Scott Joplin. In [35], Cope argues that recombinancy transcends music, citing that great books in English comprise of recombinations of the 26 alphabet letters, and Western art music consists of recombinations of 12 equal-tempered scale pitch classes. The quality of the work then depends on the 'subtlety and elegance of their recombination'.

The OMax family of human-machine co-improvisors by Gérard Assayag et al. [37] provides another example of recombinant music. The OMax systems generate music sequences stylistically similar to that produced by the human co-improvisor. The systems use factor oracles and create new music by recombining subsequences from the original material. Pachet's Continuator similarly generates stylistically consistent music from a human improvisor but using variable Markov models [38]. Mimi [39] is another factor oracle-based system, with the addition of visual feedback. In Mimi4x [40], the user can structurally engineer four recombination processes by simultaneously controlling four Mimi instances. This was inspired, in part, by John Zorn's Cobra, where a composition consists of a set of cue cards with rules instructing players what to do; a prompter decides on the combination sequence for the performance.

In the same vein of musical material re-use, the RhythmCAT system [41] creates new loops that mimic the rhythmic pattern and timbral qualities of a target loop using a corpus of existing sound material. Audio inpainting is a specific instance of collaging. Long audio signal gaps are patched using segments from other parts of a recording that can be smoothly inserted using similarity graphs [42]; deep neural networks are used to restore missing audio content at a smaller scale [43]. At the extreme end, small grains of sonic elements are joined together to form larger acoustic events in granular synthesis [44].

Collage music created based on heart rhythms will adhere to the extracted rhythms. Music generation to fit a rhythm template has been practiced in Herremans and Chew's Morpheus music generation system [45], which randomly assigns notes to the rhythms of an existing piece, then alters them iteratively to more closely fit the tension profile. Dabby's chaos theory-driven music generation technique also systematically transforms an existing composition by degrees [46]. Transcriptions of sight-reading consist of faithfully notating flawed performances of pitches and rhythms [28, 47], not unlike the accurate transcription of abnormal heart rhythms.

Music based on arrhythmias provides a visceral way to communicate the experience of an arrhythmia. The interrupted rhythms, the skipped beats, the sharp transitions, can all be captured and rendered through music. For some listeners, this might be pleasurable. For others, it might be discomforting and disorienting. But it will hopefully provide a lasting impression of what an arrhythmia feels like. The upcoming sections will present historic notations of heart murmurs, followed by an introduction to music notation of cardiac arrhythmias, then music created from the rhythm transcriptions, and a short conclusion.

9.2 Music Notation in Cardiac Auscultation

Heart sounds form important cues for diagnosing valvular disorders. The opening and closing of heart valves and the flow of blood through the valves produce the rhythmic lubdub and periodic swooshing sounds of the beating heart. Here, we review and discuss some of the earliest examples of applying music notation to representing heart murmurs heard in the process of auscultation, before introducing notation for cardiac arrhythmias in the next section.

9.2.1 Venous Hum

The inventor of the stethoscope, Réne Laennec, who was both a physician and a flute player, provided one of the earliest examples for using music notation to describe a cardiac disorder, in this case, a benign heart murmur called the venous hum [26].

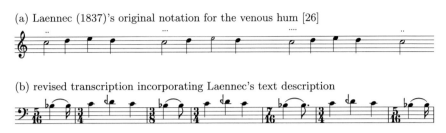

(a) Laennec (1837)'s original notation for the venous hum [26]

(b) revised transcription incorporating Laennec's text description

Fig. 9.1 The first music representation of a heart murmur, the venous hum, **a** as proposed by physician-musician Laennec; and, **b** following Laennec's text description accompanying the initial notation

Laennec integrated music notation into the description of the venous hum. His original notation is shown in Fig. 9.1a, which will be adapted to Fig. 9.1b based on his remarks. In his text, Laennec describes the undulating sequence of tones as passing through three notes over a range of a major third: the highest note was a little too low for a major third, but not quite low enough to warrant a flat. Duration-wise, the notes were of roughly the same length, with the tonic being a little longer, but of variable duration. The relative durations were denoted by dots atop the empty noteheads. The revised transcription in Fig. 9.1b is at a lower register, ascribes a quarter flat to the third and assigns actual note values to the longer tonic. It further approximates the note values from Laennec's notation, taking into account the fact that he mentioned that the notes were of roughly equal but variable durations.

9.2.2 Heart Murmurs

More recently, another physician-musician Michael Field, a nephrologist and flutist, also used music notation to describe heart murmurs, as well as regular heart sounds [27]. Figure 9.2 re-creates Field's transcriptions of four left-sided heart murmurs. In contrast to Laennec's notation, Field's transcriptions are unpitched but include fine details such as grace notes, articulations and dynamic markings to more precisely indicate the shaping and evolution of the sounds. Acciacaturas mark the initial snap in mitral stenosis; trills capture the rumbling quality of aortic and mitral stenosis; decrescendo signs indicate the diminishing sound of aortic regurgitation.

Field observes that the close listening to musical rhythms, articulation and dynamics essential to deep enjoyment of musical performance are the same skills needed to identify the characteristic patterns of heart sounds and valvular murmurs. The music notation designed to represent performance variations such as articulations and dynamics conveys the variations audible in common heart murmurs. Motivated by a desire to teach student doctors how to identify these heart murmurs, Field uses the music transcriptions in his teaching of cardiac auscultation. He further proposes that the exercise be extended to other murmurs and cardiac conditions.

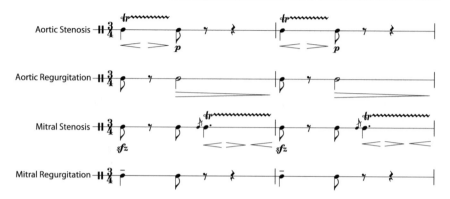

Fig. 9.2 Representation of heart murmurs by Field [27] using music notation

9.3 Music Notation of Cardiac Arrhythmias

Pathologic heart rhythms map to recognisable musical rhythms that serve as defining characteristics of different arrhythmias. This section demonstrates the feasibility of using music notation to represent different cardiac arrhythmias. In [28], I presented a few such examples. Here, these examples are further expanded and the notation of other cardiac rhythm disorders is introduced.

9.3.1 Premature Ventricular and Atrial Contractions

Premature contractions, a.k.a. ectopics, are some of the most basic and common arrhythmias that produce a distinctive abnormal heart rhythm.

Figure 9.3 shows examples of rhythms produced by premature contractions. Figure 9.3a presents a transcription of sinus rhythm, normal beats marked N, with premature ventricular contractions, also called ventricular ectopics marked VE. Ectopics

(a) Ectopics (V) followed by fully compensatory post-extrasystolic pauses

(b) Ectopics (V) followed by non-compensatory post-extrasystolic pauses

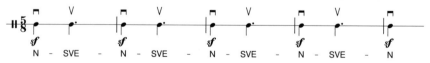

Fig. 9.3 Ectopics, marked VE or SVE and indicated by upbow (V) marks, with **a** compensatory and **b** non-compensatory post-extrasystolic pauses

can be atrial, ventricular or junctional, but the musical rhythm representation, apart from the labels, does not distinguish between the three.

In the figure, each ectopic is followed by a characteristic prolonged post-extrasystolic pause, the time between the VE and the next N. The pause is fully compensatory as the time between the preceding N to the subsequent N after the ectopic is double the length of the preceding NN interval—the crotchet plus minim equals three beats, which is two times the dotted crotchet.

In these examples, the onsets have also been marked as upbow (a V above the notehead) or downbow (a square bracket above a notehead). A premature contraction is shown with an upbow because its onset is often imperceptible, whereas the normal beats are marked downbow to indicate that they are strong onsets. The ones following an ectopic have an even stronger emphasis, marked by the sforzandos because the post-extrasystolic pause allows the heart to fill up with more blood than normal and the next beat is especially strong.

Figure 9.3b shows a transcription of premature atrial contractions. The ectopics are marked SVE (supraventricular ectopic) and the normal contractions are marked N. Because the time between the N onset just before and after each SVE is less than double the length of the preceding NN (normal) interval, the pause is not compensatory. Note that post-extrasystolic pauses following VEs can be non-compensatory and those following SVEs can be compensatory.

Premature contractions can recur in periodic patterns: every other beat (bigeminy), every third beat (trigeminy), every fourth beat (quadrigeminy), etc.; they can also occur in quick succession, in couplets or triplets. Figure 9.3b shows a bigeminy rhythm. Figure 9.4 shows the electrocardiographic trace of a trigeminy with compensatory pauses and two possible ways to transcribe the rhythm: one in simple triple time, and the other in compound triple time.[1]

9.3.2   A Theory of Beethoven and Arrhythmia

The characteristic syncopated rhythms of premature contractions can be found in composed music, such as that of Beethoven. Because of this striking similarity, cardiologists Lüderitz [48, 49], Cheng [50] and more recently Goldberger et al. [51] amongst others, have speculated that Beethoven may have suffered from arrhythmia, and that distinctive rhythms in his compositions represent musical electrograms of his abnormal heart rhythms. The commonly cited example is the dotted rhythm that features prominently in the opening to his piano Sonata in E♭ ("Les Adieux"), Op. 81a, shown in Fig. 9.5. An interpretation of this dotted rhythm as that of premature beats would suggest that the main beats are the ectopic beats, marked 'E' in the figure, followed by (non-compensatory) pauses; normal beats are marked 'N'. If the normal beat is three 16 notes' duration, then the extra-systolic pause, at five 16 notes, is not quite twice the normal beat, and so is not fully compensatory.

---

[1]ECG of trigeminal premature ventricular contractions [Online image]. (2013). Retrieved April 16, 2017, from http://floatnurse-mike.blogspot.com/2013/05/ekg-rhythm-strip-quiz-123.html.

(a) Electrocardiographic trace[1] with trigeminy rhythm

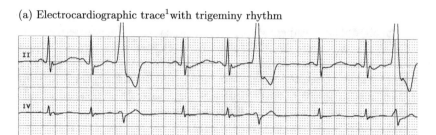

(b) Two possible transcriptions of the trigeminy rhythm

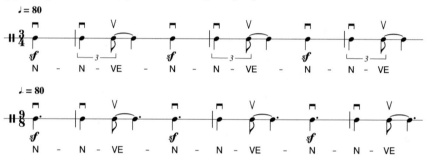

Fig. 9.4 Electrocardiographic trace and transcriptions of a trigeminy rhythm

Fig. 9.5 Dotted rhythm in Beethoven's "Les Adieux" Sonata, Op. 81a

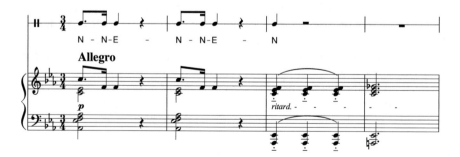

Fig. 9.6 Dotted rhythm in Beethoven's Sonata No. 18 in E♭, Op. 31 No. 3

Another example of such a dotted rhythm can be seen in an earlier sonata, Op. 31 No. 3 shown in Fig. 9.6. Again, the normal and ectopic beats are marked 'N' and 'E' in the score. It is worth noting that many rhythms of arrhythmia can be found in music, so ascribing such rhythms to a composer's possible cardiac condition may lead to false positive conclusions.

9.3.3 Ventricular and Supraventricular Tachycardias

Tachycardia is an abnormal heart rhythm where the heart beats regularly but faster than normal, even when the body is at rest. Tachycardias are labelled according to their source: ventricular or supraventricular.

Tachycardias can be triggered by ectopics or induced with short bursts of fast pacing, as was the case for the recording shown in Fig. 9.7. Figure 9.7b shows only the electrocardiographic (ECG) signal from Lead II; Fig. 9.7a displays the same ECG segment with an added layer showing the short burst of fast pacing (the three vertical lines) that triggered the ventricular tachycardia. The steady crotchet rhythm at about 71 bpm breaks into a fast trot with quavers at about 85 bpm, i.e. a pulse

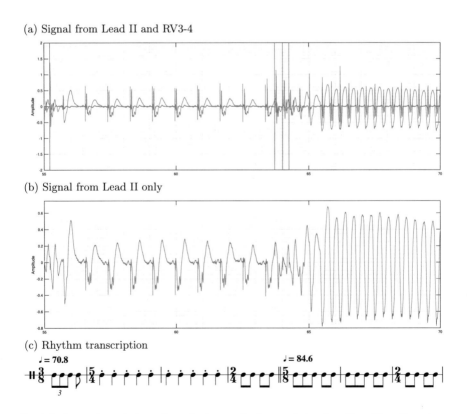

(a) Signal from Lead II and RV3-4

(b) Signal from Lead II only

(c) Rhythm transcription

Fig. 9.7 Onset of ventricular tachycardia (anonymised research data from Barts Heart Centre)

rate of nearly 170 bpm, as shown in Fig. 9.7c. The tachycardia, the fast rhythm, continues for over 30 s before it is terminated with anti-tachycardia pacing (not shown). Supraventricular tachycardia produces a similar kind of rhythm, but the ECG trace has a different morphology.

9.3.4 Atrial Fibrillation

Atrial fibrillation (AF) is a common condition characterised by fast and irregular rhythms. On the ECG, an additional clue is the lack of P waves. Figures 9.8 through 9.10 show excerpts of ECG recordings of AF sequences extracted from a single Holter monitor recording, with timestamps 16:52:59, 17:38:26 and 20:07:45. These examples were first introduced in [28]. Each shows some irregular rhythms typical of AF.

Music transcriptions of AF rhythms require many more metric and tempo changes as a result of this irregularity. Figure 9.8 contains a metric modulation, a proportional change in tempo, between bars one and two, like that used by Elliot Carter. To capture the rhythmic variation, the tempo went from 94 bpm to 126 bpm, a 3:4 tempo ratio; as notated, a dotted quaver in the previous tempo (94 bpm) is equivalent to a crotchet in the new tempo (126 bpm). All three examples contain frequent meter changes, like in the music of Stravinsky. The first transcription, Fig. 9.8, goes from $\frac{3}{4}$ to $\frac{4}{4}$ to $\frac{2}{4}$ to $\frac{3}{8}$. The second transcription, Fig. 9.9, alternates between $\frac{4}{4}$ and $\frac{7}{8}$. And, finally, Fig. 9.10, goes from $\frac{7}{8}$ to $\frac{3}{4}$ back to $\frac{7}{8}$ to $\frac{5}{8}$ to $\frac{6}{8}$ to $\frac{5}{8}$ to $\frac{6}{8}$. There are high degrees of variability in the duration contrast but also in the underlying tempo of the transcriptions. The notated tempi shown range from 94 bpm in Fig. 9.8 to 125 bpm and 188 bpm in Fig. 9.9 to 214 bpm in Fig. 9.10.

Because these are subsequences retrieved from a long recording for human inspection, they also embed anomalous behaviours, such as strings of broad complex beats labeled 'V' (ventricular) in the ECG strip. A series of broad complex beats is usually labelled VT (ventricular tachycardia) but they can also arise in AF.

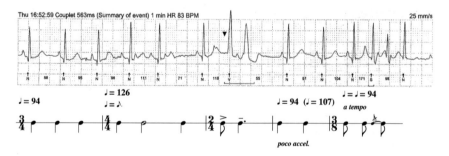

Fig. 9.8 ECG and transcription of AF excerpt Thu 16-52-59 Couplet 563ms (Summary of event) 1 min HR 83 BPM

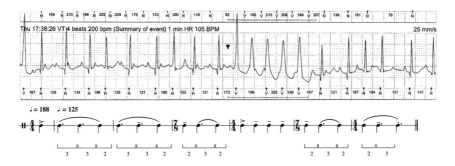

Fig. 9.9 ECG and transcription of AF excerpt Thu 17-38-26 VT 4 beats 200 bpm (summary of event) 1 min HR 105 BPM

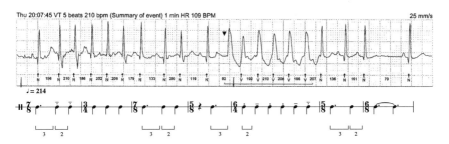

Fig. 9.10 ECG and transcription of AF excerpt Thu 20-07-45 VT 5 beats 210 bpm (summary of event) 1 min HR 109 BPM

Fig. 9.11 Atrial flutter with 3:1 block and 4:1 block

9.3.5 Atrial Flutter

Atrial flutter is an arrhythmia caused by a re-entry circuit in the right atrium that causes the atria to pulse at a rapid rate. The atrial rate is determined by the size of the atrium. As a result, it settles reliably around 300 bpm. Only some of these impulses are conducted to the lower chambers of the heart, the ventricles, due to the heart's own gating mechanism, the atrioventricular (AV) node. The ventricular rate is determined by the AV conduction ratio—whether every other atrial beat is conducted to the ventricles, every third beat or every fourth beat, etc. For example, a 2:1 AV conduction ratio leads to a ventricular rate of 150 bpm, and a 4:1 ratio leads to a rate of 75 bpm.

Figure 9.11 gives an example of atrial flutter; notes depicting the atrial contractions have stems pointing up, and notes marking ventricular contractions have stems pointing down. The first bar demonstrates a 3:1 block; the second bar a 4:1 block and so on. The underlying atrial rate of 300 bpm is indicated in the tempo marking.

This concludes the discussion on notating heart rhythms. The next section describes the collage and transformation processes involved in generating music from abnormal heartbeats.

9.4 Music Generation from Abnormal Heartbeats

Drawing from a growing collection of collage music based on cardiac electrophysiology aberrations, this section will introduce two main ideas underlying the creation of these pieces. The examples are selected from a collection of seven *Little Etudes* for beginner-to-intermediate piano players released for World Heart Rhythm Week 2020, the *Arrhythmia Suite* (2017–2018), and the *Holter Highlights* introduced in [28].

The following sections discuss the retrieval task involved in finding appropriate source material for the arrhythmia pieces, and the matter of musical transformation to make the retrieved segments fit smoothly.

Table 9.1 Collage music based on cardiac electrophysiology aberrations

	Title	Source
	Little etudes (2020) [52]	
1.	Atrial fibrillation [53]	Chopin: Nocturne Op.62, No.1 in B
2.	Atrial flutter [54]	N/A
3.	Bigeminy Sea-snatch [55]	Barber: *Hermit Songs*: Sea-Snatch
4.	The Girl with the Labile T Waves [56]	N/A
5.	Per Torsade [57]	N/A
6.	A La Bru Rondo Turk [58] (Ventricular Ectopics)	Brubeck: Blue Rondo A La Turk
7.	Wenckebach Lullaby [59]	Brahms-Godowsky: Wiegenlied
	Arrhythmia suite (2017–2018)	
I.	161122 VT before during after ECG [60]	Holst: *The Planets*: Mars
II.	161102 VT4 before after UNI [61]	Chopin: Ballade No. 2 in F
	Holter highlights (2017)	
I.	Mixed meters [62, 63]	Larsen: *Penta Metrics*: III
II.	Siciliane [64, 65]	Bach: Flute Son No.2 in E♭: Siciliane
III.	Tango [66, 67]	Piazzolla: Le Grand Tango

9.4.1   A Retrieval Task

Selected pieces created from ECG recordings of cardiac arrhythmias are catalogued in Table 9.1. Alongside the name of each arrhythmia piece is the music source for the piece when one exists. The pieces were collaged by Chew; rhythm for the *Arrhythmia Suite* were transcribed using a combination of automated tools and manual revisions by Krishna, Soberanes and Ybarra, and Orini and Lambiase provided the source sequences. Included in the table are links to audio and video recordings of these pieces. The YouTube videos show performances of the pieces. For the *Little Etudes*, the blogpost and their individual YouTube video descriptions also contain links to the full scores. The Vimeo videos for the *Holter Highlights* show the correspondence between the ECG and the rhythm transcription, and between the modified source and the ECG.

The very first task in the process of creating the pieces is the identification of an appropriate source piece from which to draw music material for recombination and transformation. The choice of pieces not only relied on matching the most salient rhythmic patterns, the pitch patterns in the chosen pieces must also fit the kinds of duration prolongations and reductions found in the particular ECG sequence. Only one piece is used in order to ensure stylistic coherence through consistency of musical language use. Thus, it is important that the source piece can encompass the variations in the rhythms of the arrhythmia ECG.

While transcribing the rhythm sequence for the first piece in the *Arrhythmia Suite*, Ashwin Krishna noted that the short bursts of fast pacing used to induce the ventricular tachycardia in ECG sequence 161122 produced the same rhythm as that in Mars in *The Planets*, Op. 32, by Holst–see Fig. 9.12. Thus, Mars became the source piece for Arrhythmia Suite: I. 161122 VT before during after ECG. The militant regularity and ratcheting intensity of Mars provided good material suitable for adapting to the ventricular tachycardia episode in the piece.

In the *Little Etudes*, beginning with the ectopics, the 2:3 pattern of the ventricular bigeminy in No. 3 is captured by the $\frac{5}{8}$ rhythm of Samuel Barber's Sea-snatch from his *Hermit Songs*, Op. 29, see Fig. 9.13a. Extra emphasis, a sforzando (*sf*), is put on the forceful regular beat following the early ventricular beat and pause. Recall that during the pause, the heart fills up with more blood than usual, causing the next heartbeat to be particularly forceful. The $2 + 2 + 2 + 3$ rhythm of Dave Brubeck's *Blue Rondo A La Turk* renders perfectly the rhythmic sequence of ventricular ectopics with compensatory post-extra-systolic pauses in Little Etude No. 6. This rhythmic ostinato corresponds exactly to the middle portion of Fig. 9.3a.

It is not common that a pre-existing musical rhythm fits the arrhythmia rhythm exactly, as in the above examples. Often, rhythmic adjustments or re-arrangements have to be made. The next section presents some of the transformations required and how this impacts the choice of the source music.

9.4.2 A Matter of Transformation

Here, we explore a few of the techniques that were used to adapt existing musical rhythms to those extracted from the ECGs.

Melodic Transformations The Siciliane in the *Holter Highlights*, Fig. 9.15, is based on Bach's Siciliane from the Flute Sonata BWV 1031. The flute melody is particularly adept at fitting to the rhythm of the ECG sequence of Fig. 9.8. This is because the note at the top of the upward leap of a fourth lends itself to flexible elongation in order to fit the couplet (two wider ventricular beats) in the ECG, which is followed by a pause (Fig. 9.14).

The Wenckebach Lullaby, Little Etude No. 7, presents another example of a warped melody. The Wenckebach block is a second-degree atrioventricular heart block where there is some obstruction of the conduction from the atria to ventricles. It is characterised by progressively elongating PR intervals that reset when a complete beat is dropped. The Brahms Lullaby is chosen because the melody not only fits rhythmically but also lends itself to the intervallic prolongation characteristic of the Wenckebach block, leading to a dramatic dropped beat at the end of the phrase, as shown in Fig. 9.16.

In the unmetered Little Etude No. 1, the irregular rhythms of slow atrial fibrillation fits the elastic rhythms of romantic playing styles, which tend to flexibly bend time through musical rubato. To depict the fibrillatory waves of AF, Chopin's Nocturne Op. 62 No. 1, which has many trills, is used as source material. Figure 9.17 shows (a)

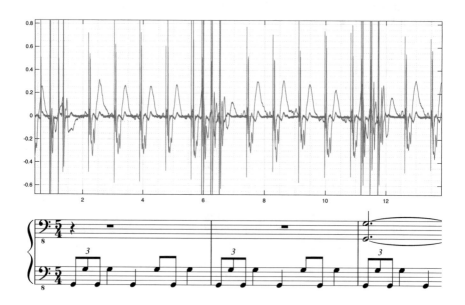

Fig. 9.12 Sources for *Arrhythmia Suite*: I. 161122 VT before during after ECG—ECG showing fast pacing bursts to trigger ventricular tachycardia (signal from Lead II and RV3-4) and beginning of Holst's Mars for two pianos (condensed to two staffs)

(a) adaptation of Samuel Barber's Sea-snatch to highlight ventricular bigeminy rhythm, with emphasis on the more forceful normal beat following a pause

(b) adaptation of Dave Brubeck's Blue Rondo A La Turk to emphasise the ventricular ectopics with compensatory pause embedded in the rhythm

Fig. 9.13 Excerpts from Little Etude No. 3: Bigeminy Sea-snatch and Little Etude No.6: Ventricular Ectopics incorporating different ventricular ectopic rhythms

(a) original melody (and rhythm)

(b) melody adjusted to fit the transcribed rhythm

Fig. 9.14 Excerpt from Bach's "Siciliane" and its modification to fit the AF rhythm

Fig. 9.15 Siciliane: Thu 16-52-59 Couplet 563ms (Summary of event) 1 min HR 83 BPM and J. S. Bach's "Siciliane" from his *Flute Sonata No. 2 in E♭ major*, BWV 1031

the original Chopin nocturne excerpt and (b) its transformed version. Although the two sound very similar, they are visually quite different. To simplify the physical

(a) bars 5-9 of the Wenckebach Lullaby (Little Etude 7)

(b) bars 2-6 of the Brahms-Godowsky Wiegenlied

Fig. 9.16 Excerpts from a Little Etude No.7: Wenckebach Lullaby, showing the lengthening PR intervals leading up to the dropped beat; and, (b) the corresponding Brahms-Godowsky Wiegenlied segment

movements, the right-hand melody with the trills has been split between the right and left hands in the little etude. The original nocturne has regular notated rhythms. The written melodic notes of the little etude are explicitly of irregular lengths. When rendered as written, the little etude actually closely resembles how the original nocturne might be performed.

Block Recombination *Holter Highlights*: I. Mixed Meters, Fig. 9.18, is based on the third of Libby Larsen's *Penta Metrics*. The frequent $\frac{7}{8}$ and $\frac{5}{8}$ meters in the ECG sequence shown in Fig. 9.10 fit naturally into Larsen's pedagogical piece, which is written in $\frac{7}{8}$ time. The *Holter Highlights* piece is based on a re-combination of the elements of Larsen's original music shown in Fig. 9.19: (a) the $\frac{7}{8}$ motif (truncated in the $\frac{5}{8}$ bar); (b) the descending octaves; and, (c) right hand repeated chord pairs with step-wise moving left hand octaves.

Composite Methods The transition to ventricular tachycardia in the Arrhythmia Suite: I (161122 VT before during after ECG) occurs in bars 19–25, shown in Fig. 9.20. These bars employ a combination of melodic transformation and multi-block recombination. This transition corresponds to the ECG shown in Fig. 9.7. The note material in the initial bar with the triplet figure is derived from bar 70 in Holst's Mars, shown in Fig. 9.21a. The chords preceding the onset of tachycardia quote from the Piano I part in bars 118–124 in the original Mars. To join the first bar of the *Arrhythmia Suite* excerpt with the ensuing chord sequence, the pitch class of the first chord is altered from G to G♯ to fit with the preceding harmonic context while acting as A♭ to fit with the subsequent chords. The left-hand quaver G's mark the start of the tachycardia, and the right hand joins in by re-iterating the chord pattern. The repeated quaver octaves are a simplification of the original rhythmic ostinato in the Piano II part.

(a) Excerpt from Chopin's Nocturne Op.62 No.1 in B major

(b) Corresponding transformed version in Little Etude No.1

Fig. 9.17 Excerpts from Little Etude No. 1: Atrial Fibrillation showing flexible, unmetered rhythms embellished with trills representing fibrillatory waves

Fig. 9.18 Mixed meters: based on Thu 20-07-45 VT 5 beats 210 bpm (Summary of event) 1 min HR 109 BPM and Libby Larsen's *Penta Metrics*, movement III

(a) bars 55-56: recurrent motif

(b) bars 42-44: descending octaves

(c) bars 57-60: repeated RH chords with moving LH bass

Fig. 9.19 Excerpts from Libby Larsen's *Penta Metrics*, movement III, source material for Mixed Meters

Fig. 9.20 Excerpt from Arrhythmia Suite: I. 161122 VT before during after ECG (bars 19–25), corresponding to ECG sequence shown in Fig. 9.7

(a) bar 70

(b) bars 118-124

Fig. 9.21 Excerpts from Mars from *The Planets*, Op. 32, by Gustav Holst

9.5 Conclusions and Discussion

The preceding sections have given an introduction to the representation of cardiac rhythms using music notation, beginning by motivating the study of abnormal heart rhythms, and proposing that music representation of actual heart rhythms may offer insights into arrhythmia variations and subtypes. After a short introduction to uses of music notation to represent heart murmurs, examples of musical representations of arrhythmias followed, covering ectopics, tachycardias, atrial fibrillation, and atrial flutter. These transcriptions, deployed at scale, could potentially yield cues for arrhythmia symptoms and treatment.

Music generation from abnormal heartbeats was then described as a two-part process of music retrieval followed by musical transformation, which can be applied at the melodic or block levels, and complex combinations thereof. The generation process draws inspiration from AI techniques for music generation by sampling from and transforming existing compositions. It also presents interesting new problems not yet a staple of music information research.

Together, the challenges of representing arrhythmias with music and those in turning rhythm transcriptions to music include accurate, reproducible, yet flexible and comparable representations of ECG features of abnormal heartbeats using music; stratification of transcriptions into subclasses; elegant solutions to combining and transforming music to fit arrhythmia rhythms; creative matching of arrhythmia sequences to music sources. The success of these tasks relies on understanding the nuances of these new problems in a new domain and finding appropriate and efficient solutions to them.

Being able to render abnormal heart rhythms precisely and accurately into music has far-reaching consequences not only for gaining insights into cardiac conditions but also for expanding the scope of biologically sourced music. The physiology of the heart constrains music generated from heartbeats to natural-sounding rhythms, even in states of arrhythmia, thus ensuring satisfactory and often provocative musical results. Furthermore, the importance of heart–brain interactions in cardiac arrhythmias [68] suggests future possibilities for integrating affective considerations into the making of music with heartbeats.

Acknowledgements These results are part of a project that has received funding from the European Research Council (ERC) under the European Union's Horizon 2020 research and innovation programme (Grant agreement No. 788960).

References

1. Bernardi, L., Porta, C., & Sleight, P. (2006). Cardiovascular, cerebrovascular, and respiratory changes induced by different types of music in musicians and non-musicians: the importance of silence. *Heart, 92*(4), 445–52.
2. Chew, E., Taggart, P., & Lambiase, P. (2020). Cardiac response to live music performance: effect of large-scale musical structure on action potential duration. EHRA Essentials 4 You: EHRA Publication #41218 (2020). https://youtu.be/TJs9TBa7pFM. Accessed 26 June 2020
3. Leslie, G., Ghandeharioun, A., Zhou, D., & Picard, R.W. (2019). Engineering music to slow breathing and invite relaxed physiology. In *Proceedings of the 8th international conference on affective computing and intelligent interaction*
4. American Heart Association: Heart and Stroke Statistics (2020). https://www.heart.org/en/about-us/heart-and-stroke-association-statistics. Accessed 25 May 2020
5. World Health Organization: Global Health Observatory (GHO) data: NCD mortality and morbidity. https://www.who.int/gho/ncd/mortality_morbidity/en/. Accessed 3 Jun 2020
6. World Health Organization (2020). Health topics: Non-communicable diseases: Cardiovascular diseases: Data and statistics. http://www.euro.who.int/en/health-topics/noncommunicable-diseases/cardiovascular-diseases/data-and-statistics. Accessed 25 May 2020

7. Khurshid, S., Choi, S.H., Weng, L.-C., Wang, E.Y., Trinquart, L., Benjamin, E.J., Ellinor P.T., & Lubitz, S.A. (2018). Frequency of cardiac rhythm abnormalities in a half million adults. *Circulation: Arrhythmia and Electrophysiology, 11*(7)
8. Lindberg, T., Wimo, A., Elmstahl, S., Qiu, C., Bohman, D., & Sanmartin Berglund, J. (2019). Prevalence and incidence of atrial fibrillation and other arrhythmias in the general older population: Findings from the Swedish National Study on aging and care. *Gerontology and geriatric medicine, 2333–7214*, 5.
9. Chugh, S. S., Havmoeller, R., Forouzanfar, M. H., Naghavi, M., Mensah, G. A., Ezzati, M., et al. (2014). Worldwide epidemiology of atrial fibrillation: A global burden of disease 2010 study. *Circulation, 129*(8), 837–847.
10. Aro, A.L., & Chugh, S.S. (2018). Epidemiology and global burden of arrhythmias. In A.J. Camm & T.F. Lüscher, G. Maurer, P.W. Serruys (Eds.) *ESC CardioMed* (3 edn). Oxford University Press
11. Kelly, T. F. (2014). *Capturing music: The story of notation.* New York City: W. W. Norton & Company.
12. Grave, F. (1995). Metrical dissonance in Haydn. *The Journal of Musicology, 13*(2), 158–202.
13. Wick, N. L. (1994). Shifted downbeats in classic and romantic music. *Indiana Theory Review, 15*(2), 73–87.
14. Haieff, A., Carter, Piston, E.W., Krenek, E., Milhaud, D., Fromm, P., Sessions, R., Shostakovitch, D., Stravinsky, S., Johnston, B., Fortner, W., Mennin, P., Finney, R.L., Rochberg, G., Tippett, M., Searle, H., Ussachevsky, V., Petrassi, G., Palmer, R., Weber, B., Diamond, D., Evangelisti, F., Shifrin, S., Lieberson, G., Chavez, C., Imbrie, A., Cone, E.T., Babbitt, M., Spies, C., Persichetti, V., Foss, L, Haubenstock-Ramati, R., Martino, D., Weisgall, H., Kohn, K., Fricker, P.R., Gaburo, K., Sollberger, H., Berger, A., des Marais, P., Talma, L., Smit, L., Moevs, R., Harris, D., Spiegelman, J., Wuorinen, C., Berio, L., Xenakis, I., Powell, M., Luening, O., Randall, J.K., Pousseur, H., Brün, H., Hamilton, I., Wood, H., Kraft, L., Kupferman, M., Boretz, B., Heiss J., & Hamilton, D. (1971). Stravinsky (1882–1971): A composers' memorial. *Perspectives of New Music, 9*(2), 1–180
15. Tingley, G. P. (1981). Metric modulation and Elliott carter's "First String Quartet". *Indiana Theory Review, 4*(3), 3–11.
16. Duncan, S. P. (2010). Re-complexifying the function(s) of notation in the music of brian Ferneyhough and the "New Complexity". *Perspectives of New Music, 48*(1), 136–172.
17. Lunn, H. C. (1866). The history of musical notation. *The Musical Times and Singing Class Circular, 12*(278), 261–263.
18. Messiaen, O. (1956). *Oiseaux Exotique for piano and small orchestra* (Universal ed.). Vienna: Austria.
19. Saunders, A. A. (1951). *A guide to bird songs* (rev ed.). Garden City, New York: Doubleday and Company Inc.
20. Smith, K. G. (2015). 100 years ago in the American Ornithologists' union. *The Auk, 132*(4), 953–954.
21. Steele, J. (1779). Prosodia rationalis or, An essay towards establishing the melody and measure of speech, to be expressed and perpetuated by peculiar symbols.
22. Scripture, E. W. (1901). Phonetic notation. *Modern Language Notes, 16*(6), 161–164.
23. Brown, S., Pfordresher, P.Q., & Chow, I. (2017). A musical model of speech rhythm. *Psychomusicology: Music, Mind, and Brain, 27*(2), 95–112
24. Simões, A. R. M., & Meireles, A. R. (2016). *Speech prosody in musical notation: Spanish.* Boston, USA: Portuguese and English Speech Prosody.
25. Siraisi, N. G. (1975). The music of pulse in the writings of Italian Academic Physicians (Fourteenth and Fifteenth Centuries). *Speculum, 50*(4), 689–710.
26. Segall, H. N. (1962). Evolution of graphic symbols for cardiovascular sounds and murmurs. *British Heart Journal, 24*(1), 1–10.
27. Field, M. (2010). Music of the heart. *The Lancet, 376*, 2074.

28. Chew, E. (2018). Notating disfluencies and temporal deviations in music and arrhythmia. *Music and Science.* https://doi.org/10.1177/2059204318795159.
29. Davids, Z. (1995). *Heartsongs: Musical mappings of the heartbeat.* Wellesley, Massachusetts: Ivory Moon Recordings.
30. Yokohama, K. (2002). Heart rate indication using musical data. *IEEE Transactions on Biomedical Engineering., 49*(7), 729–733.
31. Orzessek B., & Falkner M. (2006). Sonification of autonomic rhythms in the frequency spectrum of heart rate variability. In *12th international conference on auditory display.* London, UK
32. Ballora, M., Pennycook, B., Ivanov, P. C., Glass, L., & Goldberger, A. L. (2006). Heart rate sonification: A new approach to medical diagnosis. *Leonardo, 37*(1), 41–46.
33. Fukumoto, M., Nakashima, S., Ogawa, S., & Imai, J. (2011). An extended interactive evolutionary computation using heart rate variability as fitness value for composing music chord progression. *Journal of Advanced Computational Intelligence and Intelligent Informatics, 15*(9), 1329–1336.
34. Votava P., & Berger E. (2011). The heart chamber orchestra: An audio-visual real-time performance for chamber orchestra based on heartbeats. *Journal of the Canadian Electroacoustic Community, 14*(2). http://econtact.ca/14_2/votava-berger_hco.html.
35. Cope, D. (1996). *Experiments in musical intelligence.* A-R Editions: Computer Music & Digital Audio Series.
36. Experiments in Musical Intelligence (2020). http://artsites.ucsc.edu/faculty/cope/experiments.htm. Accessed 1 June 2020
37. Assayag, G., Bloch, G., Chemillier, M., Cont, A., & Dubnov, S. (2006). OMax brothers: A dynamic topology of agents for improvization learning. In *First ACM workshop on audio and music computing multimedia*, pp. 125–132. New York: ACM Press
38. Pachet, F. (2003). The Continuator: Musical Interaction With Style. *Journal of New Music, 32*(3), 333–341.
39. François, A.R.J., Chew, E., & Thurmond, D. (2007). Visual feedback in performer-machine interaction for musical improvisation. In *Proceedings of new interfaces for musical expression.*
40. Schankler, I., Chew, E., & François, A.R.J., (2014). Improvising with digital auto-scaffolding: How mimi changes and enhances the creative process. In Digital Da Vinci (Ed.), *Newton Lee.* Berlin: Springer Verlag.
41. Nuanáin, C.Ó., Herrera, P., & Jordá, S. (2017). Rhythmic concatenative synthesis for electronic music: Techniques, implementation, and evaluation. *Computer Music Journal, 41*(2), 21–37.
42. Perraudin, N., Holighaus, N., Majdak, P., & Balazs, P. (2018). Inpainting of long audio segments with similarity graphs. *IEEE/ACM Transactions on Audio, Speech, and Language Processing, 26*(6), 1083–1094.
43. Marafioti, A., Perraudin, N., Holighaus, N., & Majdak, P. (2019). A context encoder for audio inpainting. *IEEE/ACM Transactions on Audio, Speech, and Language Processing, 27*(12), 2362–2372.
44. Road, C. (1988). Introduction to granular synthesis. *Computer Music Journal, 12*(2), 11–13.
45. Herremans, D., & Chew, E. (2019). MorpheuS: Generating structured music with constrained patterns and tension. *IEEE Transactions on Affective Computing, 10*(4), 510–523.
46. Dabby, D. S. (1996). Musical variations from a chaotic mapping. *Chaos, 6,* 95.
47. Didkovsky, N. (2004). Recent compositions and performance instruments realized in Java Music Specification Language. In *Proceedings of the international computer music conference*
48. Lüderitz, B. (1994). *History of the disorders of cardiac rhythm.* Armonk, NY: Futura.
49. Barnes, D. J., von Herbay, A., Schuhmacher, F., Ditton, H. J., Maiwald, M., Lüderitz, B., Kubba, A. K., Hofbauer, L. C., Heufelder, A. E., & Joy, M. (1996). Beethoven's final illness. *The Lancet, 347*(9003), 766–767. https://doi.org/10.1016/S0140-6736(96)90119-1
50. Cheng, T. O. (1998). Cardiac arrhythmias set to music. *Postgraduate Medicine, 103*(4), 25.

51. Goldberger, Z. D., Whiting, S. M., & Howell, J. D. (2014). The heartfelt music of Ludwig van Beethoven. *Perspectives in Biology and Medicine, 57*(2), 285–294.
52. Chew, E. (2020). *Little Etudes* based on cardiac electrophysiology aberrations. http://cosmos.cnrs.fr/?p=1471. Accessed 26 June 2020
53. Chew, E. (2020). Atrial Fibrillation (based on Chopin's Nocturne Op.62, No.1 in B) (8 May 2020). https://youtu.be/7hwvfoxtuCM. Accessed 26 June 2020
54. Chew, E. (2020). Atrial Flutter (12 April 2020). https://youtu.be/6N0R1nmYimU. Accessed 26 June 2020
55. Chew, E. (2020). Bigeminy Sea-snatch (based on Samuel Barber's Sea-Snatch from *Hermit Songs*) (7 April 2020). https://youtu.be/7xF0dyXz4Xw. Accessed 26 June 2020
56. Chew, E. (2020). The Girl With The Labile T Waves (7 April 2020). https://youtu.be/-6_1AhlgQMc. Accessed 26 June 2020
57. Chew, E. (2020). Per Torsade (16 May 2020). https://youtu.be/s7M9vMq1HEA. Accessed 26 June 2020
58. Chew, E. (2020). A La Bru Rondo Turk (Ventricular Ectopics) (based on Dave Brubeck's Blue Rondo A La Turk) (5 April 2020). https://youtu.be/LXZEFooqaQw. Accessed 26 June 2020
59. Chew, E. (2020). Wenckebach Lullaby (based on Brahms-Godowsky's Wiegenlied) (21 May 2020). https://youtu.be/vy-3UCjyuxk. Accessed 26 June 2020
60. Chew, E. (2020). Arrhythmia Suite I. 161122 VT before during after ECG (based on Mars from Holst's *The Planets*) (2017–2018). https://youtu.be/dgdo-BQJEBY. Accessed 26 June 2020
61. Chew, E. (2020). Arrhythmia Suite II. 161102 VT4 before after UNI (based on Chopin's Ballade No. 2 in F) (2017–2018). https://youtu.be/fBtpO6oJJp4. Accessed 26 June 2020
62. Chew, E. (2017). Holter Highlights I. Mixed Meters (based on Libby Larsen's Penta Metrics: III) (2017) on the Bösendorfer Enspire. https://youtu.be/A0eRWzQ-WnQ. Accessed 26 June 2020
63. Chew, E. (2017). Holter Highlights I. Mixed Meters (based on Libby Larsen's Penta Metrics: III). https://vimeo.com/257248109. Accessed 26 June 2020
64. Chew, E. (2017). Holter Highlights II. Siciliane (based on the Siciliane from Bach's Flute Sonata No.2 in E♭ (2017) on the Bösendorfer Enspire. https://youtu.be/VT7lY2nOveY. Accessed 26 June 2020
65. Chew, E. (2017). Holter Highlights II. Siciliane (based on the Siciliane from Bach's Flute Sonata No.2 in E♭. https://vimeo.com/221351463. Accessed 26 June 2020
66. Chew, E. (2017). Holter Highlights III. Tango (based on Piazzolla's Le Grand Tango) on the Bösendorfer Enspire. https://youtu.be/iQhCWvHkXkA. Accessed 26 June 2020
67. Chew, E. (2017). Holter Highlights III. Tango (based on Piazzolla's Le Grand Tango). https://vimeo.com/257253528. Accessed 26 June 2020
68. Taggart, P., Critchley, H., & Lambiase, P. D. (2011). Heart-brain interactions in cardiac arrhythmia. *Heart, 97*, 698–708.

Elaine Chew is a pianist and mathematician who proposed the spiral array model, a geometric model for tonality, in her MIT doctoral thesis. Having suffered from arrhythmia, she was inspired to turn its rhythms into music, and to draw parallels between music and arrhythmia. She is currently a Centre National de la Recherche Scientifique (CNRS) researcher at the Sciences et Technologies de la Musique et du Son (STMS) Laboratory located at the Institut de Recherche et Coordination Acoustique/Musique (IRCAM) in Paris, France, and Visiting Professor of Engineering in the Faculty of Natural & Mathematical Sciences at King's College London, UK. E-mail: elaine.chew@ircam.fr.

Cognitive Musicology and Artificial Intelligence: Harmonic Analysis, Learning, and Generation

10

Emilios Cambouropoulos and Maximos Kaliakatsos-Papakostas

10.1 Introduction

A listener is able to discern diverse aspects of music when exposed to musical stimuli: from elementary features of the musical surface (e.g., a discrete note or a chord or a certain timbre), to salient musical patterns (e.g., motives, themes, cadences), and even, high-level composer or stylistic features. A listener may find, for instance, a particular harmonic progression intriguing, inducing new exciting responses, even though the listener is not able to identify constituent chords and scale degrees, or a melody might sound emotionally moving to a listener, even if (s) he is not able to name the individual notes or intervals. Harmony, melody, rhythm, texture, and timbre (among others) are aspects of music that a listener is able to appreciate, encode, and remember, despite not having explicit access to underlying components.

Through the centuries, music theorists, analysts, philosophers have attempted to describe (via introspection) and to formalize, core musical concepts and processes, such as scales, chord types, harmonic functions, tonality, rhythmic structures, types of texture, form, and so on. In more recent years, computational methodology, and more specifically Artificial Intelligence (AI) has offered new means of precision and formalization, enabling the development of models that emulate musical intelligent behaviors. This way, musical theories and hypotheses drawing not only on traditional music knowledge, but also on research in music cognition, linguistics, semiotics, logic reasoning, neuroscience, and so on, have given rise to actual

E. Cambouropoulos (✉) · M. Kaliakatsos-Papakostas
School of Music Studies, Aristotle University of Thessaloniki, 57001 Thermi, Thessaloniki, Greece
e-mail: emilios@mus.auth.gr

M. Kaliakatsos-Papakostas
e-mail: maxk@mus.auth.gr

© Springer Nature Switzerland AG 2021
E. R. Miranda (eds.), *Handbook of Artificial Intelligence for Music*,
https://doi.org/10.1007/978-3-030-72116-9_10

musical analytic/compositional/performance computer programs that may be tested in a more systematic manner and may give rise to useful computational applications.

Nowadays, Artificial Neural Network (ANN) architectures, and more specifically Deep Learning methods, appear in the minds of many researchers to have superseded the Good Old-Fashioned Artificial Intelligence (GOFAI) paradigm; for many younger AI researchers, Artificial Intelligence *is* Deep Learning. The hypothesis is that given sufficient amounts of data represented appropriately, and adequate deep learning algorithms, any musical intelligent behavior can be emulated successfully. So, what is the point of developing sophisticated AI programs that employ ad hoc knowledge-engineering approaches (drawing on music theory or music cognition) when a generic ANN approach may be at least equally effective (not to mention that it is more flexible and adaptive)?

In this chapter, we discuss aspects of Cognitive Musicology with a view to presenting reasons why it is relevant in the context of current developments in the field of AI. Laske [31] states that "cognitive musicology has as its goal the modeling of musical intelligence in its many forms." (p. 44). According to Laske, "computer programs serve to substantiate hypotheses regarding musical knowledge, and second, they are the medium for designing structured task environments (such as programs for interactive composition). While it is not a prerequisite for building intelligent systems to have a fully-fledged theory of the activity one wants to support, it is certainly more effective to design such systems on as much theory as one can harness." (p. 45). We assert that the insights drawn from cognitive psychology, and also music theory, play an important role in building musical models (combining symbolic AI with statistical learning) that can serve both as a means to broaden our understanding of music per se, and also to create robust sophisticated systems for music analysis, composition, and performance. Computational modeling, as a means to test musical hypotheses, has enriched musical knowledge in the domain of musical analysis [34] and music cognition [42], enabling, at the same time, the development of useful musical systems and applications.

In the next section, we discuss briefly general issues regarding the advantages and disadvantages of symbolic versus deep learning methodologies. Then, we present two case studies that show the effectiveness of classical symbolic AI in music modeling (coupled with simple statistical learning techniques): firstly, we examine the modeling of melodic harmonization showing strengths and weaknesses of both the standard AI and deep learning methodologies, and secondly, we present a creative melodic harmonization system based on Conceptual Blending Theory [11] that operates on a high reasoning level allowing sophisticated combination of abstract chord features with a view to generating novel harmonic spaces. In both of these cases, we argue that the classical symbolic approach to musical intelligence drawing on music cognition research, coupled with simple statistical learning techniques, provides a reasonable way to address complex phenomena of musical listening, performance, and creativity effectively.

10.2   Classical Artificial Intelligence Versus Deep Learning

Before attempting to give reasons for pursuing cognitive musicology research following the more traditional symbolic AI approach (or at least a hybrid AI and statistical learning approach), a brief discussion on core cognitive processes of acquiring knowledge is due. Such processes involve, among other things, abstraction, categorization, inference, use of prior knowledge, encoding, and transmission of knowledge at a high-level symbolic level.

Information abstraction or compression appears to be a universal innate mechanism of cognition and consciousness. It is essential not only for humans in their everyday interaction with the surrounding environment and with other humans, but for other non-human animals as well. Feinberg and Mallatt [12] maintain that the reduction of information received from the visual sensory system to a more abstract representation of the visible world facilitates the involvement of memory in decision making, this applies to the auditory and other sensory systems as well. For example, a predator with the ability to form abstractions of the perceived world requires significantly less memory capacity to remember the existence of prey at a specific location while having no visual contact with it. This allows the predator to develop stealth hunting techniques that do not require constant visual contact with the prey, giving the predator an advantage in species evolution. While hunting techniques are irrelevant to music cognition, the aforementioned example shows that abstraction in representing elements in the perceived world, and the advantages in memory requirements that this abstraction yields, is part of a fundamental mechanism in the evolution of species.

Information abstraction, or more formally put, information compression, is a cognitive mechanism constantly at play at all levels of music understanding. Not only the extraction of the musical surface per se (i.e., the actual note pitches/durations/beats) from the actual audio signal involves a very sophisticated information abstraction process, but also the extraction of higher-level meaningful structures from the musical surface. This abstraction mechanism allows listeners to move beyond the information layer that the musical surface offers and focus on holistic aspects of the musical stimulus, identifying or appreciating elements that form on higher levels of information organization, such as a harmonic style, or thematic material or a cadential pattern.

Compressed data and information (learned from data or taken as prior knowledge) may be represented by symbols. Symbols point to (signify) something quite complicated in all its fine detail such as a physical object, an event, an idea. Humans use symbols to communicate between them, transferring rich information in a succinct manner (just a few words may convey rich meanings that would otherwise require extremely large and complex data structures to pass on the same meanings).

The so-called "deep neural networks" present the important ability to build knowledge on higher-levels of representation. Deep learning is essentially a statistical technique for classifying patterns, based on sample data. It maps a set of inputs to any set of outputs; for instance, in speech recognition, an Artificial Neural

Network (ANN) learns a mapping between a set of speech sounds and a set of phonemes. Deep learning systems work particularly well for parsing and classifying raw sensory input data in the visual and/or auditory domain.

The success of ANNs learning from data is restricted by the specific training dataset context. The efficiency of such methods deteriorates when insufficient amounts of training data are available, when the domain of application is shifted, and when intelligent reasoning is required for rapid adaptation to new environments [48]. But how can humans, who also learn from stimuli in their environment, so easily perform domain shift and zero-shot learning (i.e., identification of an element based on specifications that do not appear in the training data)? For instance, how is a child able to identify that an animal is a zebra at first sight, having available only the description that "zebra is a horse with black and white stripes"?

In a study presented by Dubey et al. [8], a similar question was asked: Why do humans perform well in games they play for the first time—or at least better than machine learning systems trained to perform well at other games? In this study, human participants were asked to play different versions of a platformer retro-style computer game (with similar goals and level design as Atari's "Montezuma's Revenge"), in each version, alternative visual textures were devised for masking the functionality of different components of the game. The aim of this study was to explore the importance of "human priors", e.g., prior knowledge on the functionality of stage components, in game performance. The alternative textures were used as a means to "camouflage" different visual components, gradually disabling visual identification of the function these components imply; e.g., ladders for climbing, enemies to avoid, keys to open doors, etc. Some versions also included altered physical qualities (e.g., effect of gravity) and interactions between game agents, but with preservation of the underlying structure, goals, and rewards.

Dubey et al. [8] showed that as the visual interface of the game was altered, the performance of the human players degraded. This fact indicates that prior knowledge is a crucial factor that allows humans to achieve good performances in first-time encountered games. Reinforcement learning systems need to build a model for identifying the functionality of all components of the environment from scratch, after numerous "blind" trial and error simulations; and this hard-earned knowledge is strictly domain-dependent, rendered worthless for new games. There are promising signs that task-agnostic priors can be acquired from data in dynamical systems [9]. However, ad hoc modeling remains to this day an effective way of tackling various problems, since it offers the possibility to model elements in an environment through a "hand-crafted" definition of what the priors are.

Human perception of music relies on prior knowledge organized in complex networks of concepts on many levels. The human brain groups together the numerous harmonics of a plucked string into an single integrated tone. Multiple notes occurring simultaneously are grouped into a chord, which is an entity in its own right, carrying functions, meaning, even emotions, that extend beyond the isolated role of each constituent note. The notion of the root of a chord, for instance, is attributed to a note (often missing from the simultaneity that constitutes the chord) depending on complex psychoacoustic phenomena. Such concepts can be modeled as priors in a computational system; for instance, the General Chord Type (GCT) representation enables automatic encoding of note simultaneities in a form that is close to traditional chord types based on consonance/dissonance optimization, root, and scale degree identification [4]. Of course, such priors can be learned implicitly from data, at the cost of having to collect and annotate enough data. Having such priors, however, explicitly available in symbolic models, makes it possible to develop creative systems that can tackle complex tasks with access to relatively small datasets—or even with toy-example models of musical spaces.

Symbolic AI's strengths lie in the fact that symbolic representations are abstract and can, therefore, be generalized and transferred in different tasks, and additionally, due to their affinity to language, they can be easily interpreted and understood by humans. Symbols enable transferring knowledge to other occasions/problems, since knowledge embodied in a symbol is abstract and can be applied to other actual instances; for instance, characterizing a newly heard piece as Jazz transfers our broader knowledge of Jazz to that specific piece.

Reasoning involves combining and manipulating symbols allowing arguments and inferences to be made. Symbolic AI implements symbolic reasoning in rule-based or knowledge engineering systems. In such systems, humans must first study, learn, and model how certain input relates to a specific output, and then hand-craft the rules into a program. Such rules may rely on distilled knowledge acquired through experience and/or on general cognitive principles. Symbolic AI has a number of drawbacks the most important of which is that, as it requires manual coding, it does not allow dynamic change and it cannot capture the complexity of the real world (see [36] on pros and cons of symbol systems). This problem can be partly addressed by introducing statistical learning that allows some amount of adaption of rules to specific contexts.

Deep learning models, on the contrary, are flexible, adaptive, easy to build as they do not require fully fleshed-out models, and they are resilient to noise or incomplete information. They have, however, limitations particularly in high-level cognitive tasks where generalization is required; ANNs tend to fail disastrously when exposed to data outside the pool of data they are trained on. As they are black-boxes, it is not clear how they work, what is learned and how intermediate activation patterns may be interpreted. Additionally, they are data-hungry requiring huge amounts of data to capture even simple concepts and need enormous computing power and storage space (see [33] for a critical appraisal).

Recently, attempts are made to reconcile symbolic systems, that are strong in abstraction and inference, with deep learning that excels in perceptual classification [13]. Combining symbolic AI with deep learning may assist in addressing the fundamental challenges of reasoning, hierarchical representations, transfer learning, robustness in the face of adversarial examples, and interpretability (or explanatory power).

The different approaches of Symbolic AI and ANNs in music research are discussed in [44, 50] and in the volume on Music and Artificial Intelligence [35].

In this chapter, emphasis is given to the advantages of traditional symbolic computational modeling of musical tasks. Building computational systems that rely on cognitive-based and/or music-theoretic-based systematic descriptions of processes involved in mapping certain input to certain output, enables the development of sophisticated models that may have both theoretical and practical merits. In terms of theory, our understanding of music per se is enriched, traditional assumptions are tested, empirically-derived cognitive principles are evaluated, and new musical knowledge is acquired. As knowledge is explicit in such AI models, sophisticated practical systems can be created that allow intelligent interaction with musicians/users through the manipulation of meaningful symbolic representations (e.g., educational systems, compositional assistants, interactive performers, content-based music search engines, and so on). Such systems make use of prior sophisticated knowledge acquired through years (or even centuries) of experience and introspection, and also capitalize on findings resulting from empirical work in music cognition. This way, sophisticated models can be built relatively quickly combining diverse components on different hierarchical levels of organization. Additionally, symbolic systems reinforced with simple statistical learning capacities can adapt to different contexts based on relatively small training datasets allowing this way a certain degree of flexibility. Furthermore, such models can bridge different conceptual spaces enabling the invention of novel concepts not present in the initial input spaces. All these qualities will be discussed in more detail in the following sections, focusing on computation models in the domain of musical harmony (analysis and generation).

10.3 Melodic Harmonization: Symbolic and Subsymbolic Models

Various methods for music analysis and generation—and specifically harmonization—following the classical AI approach have been presented during the past decades. The first score generated by a computer, the *Illiac Suite* string quartet composition in 1957 [19], included a mix of rule-based approaches and Markov transition matrices for composing cantus firmus music, rhythmic sequences, and four voice segments. The first attempts in building cognitively-inspired computational models should probably be attributed to the pioneering work of Christopher Longuet-Higgins, a cognitive scientist that proposed among others, a key-finding [28] and a meter-finding [29] model that processes notes in a left-to-right fashion based on fundamental music theoretic and cognitive concepts (collected essays can be found in [30]).

Among the most complete approaches to modeling four-part chorales in the style of Johann Sebastian Bach was presented by Ebcioglu [10] in the CHORAL expert system, which comprised of 270 rules to represent the knowledge for harmonizing a melody. A review of such purely hand-crafted rule-based approaches can be found in Pachet and Roy [37], while a more recent study of such systems was presented by Phon-Anmuaisuk et al. [39]. Rule-based methods are useful for examining the nuts and bolts of a musical style and for studying how several components or musical concepts are interrelated towards forming what listeners identify as a coherent musical style.

A more generic approach to rule-based modeling of harmony, is to model a wider range of harmonic genres through generative grammars. Rohrmeier [47] and Koops et al. [27] have presented grammars that model tonal harmony and Granroth-Wilding and Steedman [14] develop grammars that describe Jazz style harmony. Grammars offer a clear and powerful interpretation of how high-level harmonic concepts are hierarchically organized and what their relations and functions are. Harmonic grammars so far enable primarily describing musical surfaces in terms of chord symbols, generated symbols, however, cannot be rendered to actual musical surfaces. It is, also, still difficult to adapt such grammars to diverse styles, since their formulation is based on specific alphabets of chord labels and (manually-constructed) hierarchical relations between them.

The methods discussed so far are not adaptive, in the sense that specific rule-sets represent specific musical styles; representing new styles would require to come up with new sets of rules. Probabilistic generative models can capture probabilities of occurrence of specific elements in a dataset, therefore, offering a way of adaptation to specific styles. Among the most popular probabilistic AI approaches are Hidden Markov Models (HMM). Regarding harmonization, and specifically melodic harmonization, HMM model conditional relations between chords, melodic notes or other information of interest (e.g., chord functions). After learning from data, new harmonies that reflect learned characteristics can be generated by sampling from the distribution of such learned conditional probabilities, or traversing paths of optimal probabilities over a given set of conditions (e.g., composing the optimal harmonic path over a given melody).

Among many examples of employing HMMs for melodic harmonization, the approaches of Allan and Williams [2] and Raphael and Stoddard [40] incorporated a dual HMM for four-part harmonization: role of the first HMM was to define a coarse functional layout over a given melody, while the second HMM assigned specific chord symbols given the functional labeling and the melody. The idea of layering additional information in HMM-based models was also discussed by Raczynski et al. [45], where information about local tonality was incorporated as conditions for defining chord symbols over a given melody. In the original "MySong" application [41], users could sing a melody and then select a mixing rate between classical and jazz harmonies, two HMM models trained on classical and jazz music data, respectively, were then be combined into a single model for generating the desired harmonic mix.

Music composed by humans incorporates meaning on many structural levels. For instance, tonal music includes sections, periods, phrases with sub-phrases, conveying the essence of closure on different levels. An important weakness of the Markov-based models is that they cannot capture long-term structure since their conditional context includes information on fixed-size window frames in time. Even though the context can be increased (Markov models of higher order; i.e., conditioning their prediction based on information further back in the past), this increase quickly leads to highly specialized models that actually model specific segments in the training data, rather than stylistic properties in the data.

One way to overcome the "locality" effect in the prediction of Markov-based models is to employ a hierarchical stratification of Markov models, where layers on top capture information about what model parts should be used in lower layers. Thereby, dependencies further away in time are captured in the top layers, while the generalization capabilities of low order Markov are preserved in the bottom. For example, Thornton [43] presented a Hierarchical Markov model for harmonic generation, where the top model would define the succession or repetition of chord-generating hidden states. Hierarchical relations in combination with proba-bilistic modeling are also achieved with Probabilistic grammars, which offer a way to learn and model alternate hierarchical properties of strings of musical sequences [1]. Additionally, more complex, probabilistic models have been proposed that incorporate information about the metric position in the chord [7] or voice [49] decision process—for melodic and four-part harmonization, respectively.

Another approach to overcome the locality problem of Markov-based models is to "tie" the generative process on structure-inducing landmarks that indicate har-monic structural closings or phrase endings, i.e., cadences. To this end, methods have been proposed that focus on generating chord sequences that end with proper cadences. An approach that has been examined by Yi and Goldsmith [51] and Borrel-Jensen and Hjortgaard Danielsen [3] is to incorporate a special cadence evaluation scheme for rating/discarding entire melodic harmonizations generated by a Markov-based system. Other approaches examined learning chord sequences from start to end [2, 17], making sure that the conditional probability for "starting" the chord sequence would allow only valid endings with proper cadences. If positions of intermediate cadences that determine lower-level phrases are known, then Markov models with constraints can be employed [38].

A simple approach for composing melodic harmonizations under this scheme was presented by Kaliakatsos-Papakostas and Cambouropoulos [23], where con-straints are added at phrase boundaries ensuring appropriate cadential schemata at structurally important positions, intermediate chord progressions are filled in according to the learned chord transition matrices. This method is incorporated in the CHAMELEON melodic harmonization assistant [24, 25] that is adaptive (learns from data), general (can cope with any tonal or non-tonal harmonic idiom), and modular (learns and encodes explicitly different components of harmonic structure: chord types, chord transitions, cadences, bass line voice-leading). This system preserves the merits of rule-based systems in its overall hierarchical modular out-look and at the same time, it is enhanced with statistical learning mechanisms that extract context-sensitive harmonic information enabling adaptation to different harmonic idioms. Two examples of melodic harmonization of a traditional Greek diatonic melody in the Bach chorale and jazz idioms is presented in Fig. 10.1. In CHAMELEON, cadence locations are given by the user (or assumed by default only at the end of the harmonization), automatic methods, however, for identifying potential intermediate phrase boundaries and cadence positions can be employed.

Fig. 10.1 Harmonization of the traditional Greek melody *Milo Mou Kokkino* (repetition of phrases omitted) by CHAMELEON in: **a** Bach chorale idiom, and **b** Jazz idiom. Voice-leading is incomplete and erroneous as only the bass line movement is modeled

Symbolic AI modeling requires manual encoding of information in the form of explicit rules about note/chord relations. These rules can be probabilistic, and therefore, adaptive to peculiarities of specific datasets; nonetheless, these rules still capture specific aspects of the richly diverse and hierarchically structured information that is incorporated in musical surfaces. In relation to the harmonization methods discussed above, in most cases, the composition process ends at the point where chord symbols are generated. Converting chord symbols to actual notes, or implementing voice leading [22] with the generated chord symbols, requires further complicated models that take into account auditory stream and voice separation principles, segmentation and phrase structure, metric structure and harmonic rhythm, dissonance and consonance, and so on. Probabilistic approaches have been examined for determining the bass voice in a generated chord sequence [32], but the problem of proper and complete voice leading is still very complicated even in the extensively studied case of the Bach chorales (see problems with voice-leading in Fig. 10.1a). Therefore, symbolic models do not offer a "holistic" description of the music they model, since they are only able to model and generate specific aspects of information that are described by explicit representation. A holistic musical model that is general enough to describe diverse musical styles and sophisticated enough to generate high quality musical surfaces in different idioms is still an elusive goal. Deep learning techniques seem to promise a faster way to accomplish such holistic behavior or at least give the illusion that this goal is easier to achieve with ANNs.

Deep learning and ANNs have also been used for generating harmonizations. DeepBach [16] is an example of combining LSTM (looking both forward and backward in time) and feedforward components for capturing different modes of musical information from the score. This system learns from Bach chorales that are encoded using information about each voice separately, including also information about the metric structure (time signature and beat position), key signature, and locations of the fermata symbol (indicating phrase endings). After DeepBach is trained with multiple Bach chorales that include annotations for all the aforementioned information modes, it can generate new Bach chorales either from scratch or by completing certain parts of a given score (e.g., harmonize a melody or fill specific parts on a given score). To generate from scratch, DeepBach needs an input that contains information about the metric structure, key signature, and locations of fermatas. With this input, the system follows a process similar to Gibbs sampling: it initially generates random notes for each voice and during many iterations (on a magnitude of tens of thousands), single random notes from random voices are selected and readjusted with a sampling process, based on the joint distribution reflected by the system according to each current setup of notes. As iterations evolve, the initially random setup of notes slowly converges to a new setup that follows the style of Bach chorales. Score-filling is performed in a similar manner, but the notes given in the input are not subject to change by the sampling process.

Even though there are errors in the end results, DeepBach is able to learn important elements of high-level information including chords and cadences. An impressive aspect of how ANNs learn is the ability of this system to learn high-level features implicitly, meaning that such information is not encoded explicitly in the data, but it emerges inside the latent variables of the network. Any time DeepBach composes a new piece, either from scratch or by filling a given excerpt, it effectively explores the space of all possible Bach chorales, with a (considerably high) degree of accuracy on many diverse levels (chords, chord progressions, cadences, etc.). This is achieved by starting from different random note setups (in the part it is expected to fill) and then converging with random sampling to a new piece that reflects the overall characteristics of a Bach chorale.

Another approach for exploring harmonizations has been presented by Google in the "Bach doodle" application [21] that appeared on the interface of the popular search engine in 2019 (on J. S. Bach's birthday). This approach is based on two-dimensional convolutional neural networks that have been very effective in image recognition tasks, since they can capture two-dimensional spatial patterns. Bach doodle is based on a musical adaptation of the Coconet [20], that is able to find patterns in the two-dimensional time-pitch space. Even though this approach does not process temporal information in the way that DeepBach does, that is, time is considered only in the context of two-dimensional pattern rather than accumulated dynamics within in a sequence, the principles of music generation are similar: new compositions are explored by sampling on probability spaces that are formed by combining learned convolutional filters. DeepBach and the Bach doodle are two among numerous examples of deep learning systems that exhibit the impressive ability to infer high-level features from musical surfaces and generate new music by effectively exploring new possible materializations of musical surfaces based on the learned latent spaces.

A trained ANN involves symbol manipulation in the sense that the input data are encoded as strings of symbols and labels. Musical knowledge is manually incorporated in the training data; for instance, in DeepBach, notes are encoded explicitly in separate voices, metrical structure and tonality are given, and phrase structure is explicitly annotated. The more information is annotated explicitly in the training data, the better the resulting learning and performance of the system. This, however, comes at the expense of making the initial representation and symbolic preprocessing more complex, compromising thus the simplicity of the Deep Learning approach. Deep learning is not miraculous. It requires meaningful data to learn from. Humans may learn Bach chorale harmony simply by being exposed to Bach chorales. Human listeners, however, have prior knowledge regarding beat, meter, and rhythm, have the ability to separate auditory stimuli into separate streams, knowledge regarding tuning and scale systems, can parse sequences of notes to smaller phrases, have a latent understanding of consonance and dissonance, and a whole system of chord hierarchies; all this knowledge plays a role in learning Bach chorale structure through mere exposure. A computational system (either symbolic AI or deep learning) needs one way or another such information. Bringing closer together symbolic reasoning and connectionist approaches may be a good way to deal more effectively with highly complex data such as musical data (abstract, multi-parametric, hierarchical, multi-layered).

10.4 Inventing New Concepts: Conceptual Blending in Harmony

Conceptual blending is a cognitive theory developed by Fauconnier and Turner [11] whereby elements from diverse, but structurally-related, mental spaces are blended giving rise to new conceptual spaces that often possess new powerful interpretative properties allowing better understanding of known concepts or the emergence of novel concepts altogether. In the context of the COINVENT project [6], a formal model has been developed inspired by category theory, wherein two input spaces (I1 and I2) that share a number of common properties (Generic space) are combined into a new blended concept (Blend) after incompatibilities, inconsistencies, and contradictions have been eliminated [6]. As an illustration of the model's potential, the proof-of-concept computational creative assistant CHAMELEON that performs melodic harmonization and blending has been developed [5, 25].

What concepts are there to be blended in music? Focusing on harmonic structural blending (rather than cross-domain blends between; e.g., text and music, image and music, or physical motion and music), musical concepts are taken to be generalizations of harmonic entities and relations, derived from a corpus of harmonic annotated data via statistical learning. This data-driven approach ensures that learned concepts reflect adequately the characteristics of diverse harmonic idioms.

Fig. 10.2 Bach Chorale melody harmonized in medieval Fauxbourdon style with inserted tonal cadences

From each independent harmonic space (e.g., modal, common-practice tonal, jazz, atonal, organum, etc.), represented by a set of characteristic annotated music pieces, the following structural characteristics are learned and explicitly encoded: chord types, chord transitions (probabilistic distributions), cadences (i.e., chord transitions on designated phrase endings at different hierarchic levels), and voice-leading (i.e., bass line motion in relation to melody, bass-melody distance, chord inversion). This structural information sometimes corresponds to standard musicological linguistic terms (e.g., "cadence", "perfect cadence", "dominant", "leading-note", etc.), bringing the learned musical concepts closer to the standard notion of "concept" in the domain of cognitive linguistics. Such features drawn from diverse idioms may be combined so as to create new harmonic blended styles; for instance, tonal cadences may be assigned to phrase endings and modal chord transitions may be employed for filling in the rest of the phrase chords Fig. 10.2.

Take, for instance, the concept of *perfect cadence* in common-practice harmony and the *phrygian cadence* of renaissance music. The former has some salient features appearing in all instances found in, for instance, the Bach chorale dataset: leading note resolved upwards to tonic, seventh (in dominant chord) resolved downward by step, leap from the root of dominant chord to tonic chord in the bass line. The latter contains always a downward leading tone moving by semitone to the tonic, and an upward movement of the seventh degree by tone to the tonic. If these two cadential concepts are imported in the formal blending model (as I1 and I2), the highest rating blend in terms of preserving salient features from both input cadences and also ensuring that the resulting chord types are acceptable in these idioms (e.g., major triad, minor triad, major seventh chord, etc.), is the *tritone substitution* progression which is commonly found in jazz music (it contains both upward and downward leading notes). In this case, by blending two established harmonic concepts, a new concept is invented that has not been seen in the training data [52].

The above cadence blending process is generalized to any two input chord transitions, allowing the creative blending of entire chord transition matrices from different idioms. Let us assume a "toy" harmonic space, where, within a major tonality, only three chords exist, namely, the tonic, subdominant, and dominant seventh chords. It is clear that such "toy" chord transition spaces of, for instance, C major and F# major tonalities have no common chords and do not communicate, so it is not possible to move from one space to the other. Can the proposed chord transition methodology "invent" new transitions and possibly new chords that may connect the two spaces in a meaningful way? The chord transition blending methodology is applied to all the chord transitions in the C major and F# major tables, i.e., each chord transition in the first matrix is blended with each chord transition in the second matrix producing a list of resulting blends. The resulting blends are ranked according to criteria that take into account the number of salient features from each input space preserved in the blend and the balance of the contribution of each input chord transition in the blend. The highest ranking chord transition blends include a sort of tritone substitution or German sixth chord transition (i.e., G7 → F# or Db7 → C), and the diminished seventh chord (i.e., B°7 C or E#°7 → F# where E#°7 is enharmonically identical to B°7). The first blended transition establishes a connection between existing chords of the two input spaces, whereas the second proposes a new chord, a diminished seventh chord, that constitutes a bridge between the two tonal spaces—see detailed description in [25]. If more transition blends are allowed, the resulting transition table is augmented and populated with more connections between the two spaces.

The special purpose-made melody in Fig. 10.3 contains a remote modulation from C major to F# major and back again to C major. This rather awkward melody cannot be harmonized correctly by the learned Bach Chorale harmonic style as chord transitions in C major cannot cope with the transitions to/in the F# major region (and vice versa). Even if a key-finding algorithm indicates the exact positions of the modulations so that the relevant keys may be employed in the appropriate regions, the transitions between the regions would remain undefined (random chord transitions). Chord transition matrix blending of the sort previously discussed, creates meaningful connections between the two tonal regions and the melody can be harmonized correctly by the blended transition table Fig. 10.3.

Blending different tonal spaces (different keys) in the same harmonic style can be used creatively for introducing chromaticism and more advanced harmonies that go beyond the initial tonal spaces. The traditional Greek melody *Milo Mou Kokkino* in D major can be harmonized in many different ways, with blended variations of the Bach Chorale major harmonic idiom in various shifted tonalities. In Fig. 10.4a, b, D major is blended with G# major (tritone distance between keys) and D major is blended with A major (7 semitone distance). In these examples, harmony deviates from common practice functional progressions towards free chromaticism. The

Fig. 10.3 Melody with distant modulation between C major and F# major is successfully harmonized by CHAMELEON after applying blending between the two tonal spaces (from [25], Fig. 8b)

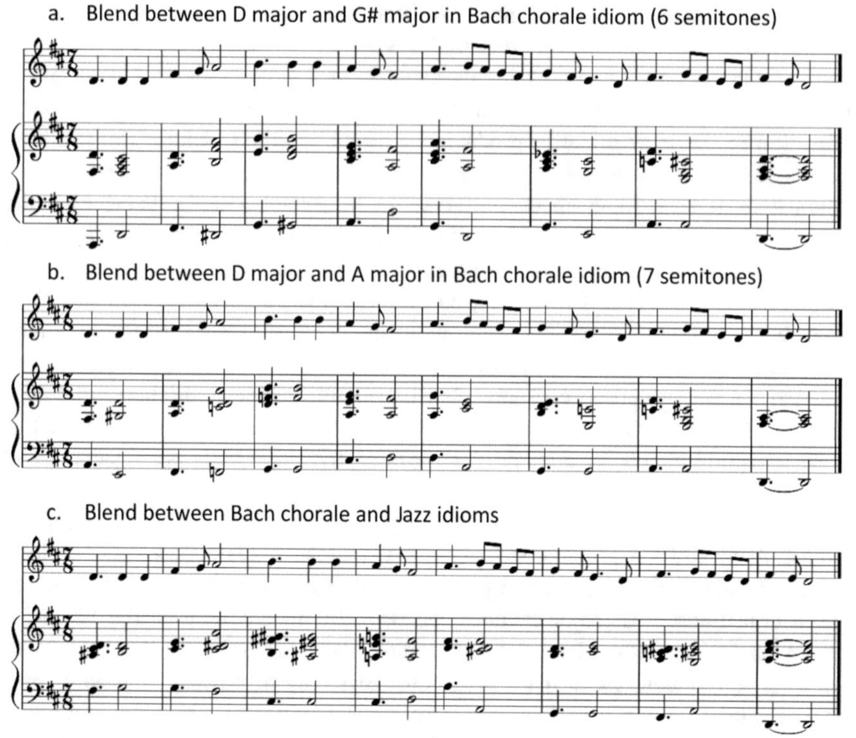

a. Blend between D major and G# major in Bach chorale idiom (6 semitones)

b. Blend between D major and A major in Bach chorale idiom (7 semitones)

c. Blend between Bach chorale and Jazz idioms

Fig. 10.4 Harmonization of the traditional Greek melody *Milo Mou Kokkino* (repetition of phrases omitted) by CHAMELEON in: **a** blend between two major tonalities 6 semitones apart, **b** blend between two major tonalities 7 semitones apart, and **c** blend between Bach chorale and Jazz idioms

produced chords cannot always be explicitly identified as belonging to one of the blended spaces. It is also interesting that the blended tonal spaces can produce such a diverse range of forced harmonic chromaticism, with elements of tonal mixture and chords of ambiguous functionality, even though the melody is purely diatonic (without any chromatic elements). In this case, blending produces novel harmonic spaces that go well beyond the initial diatonic input spaces.

An example of blending different harmonic spaces, namely Bach chorale tonal with Jazz is shown in Fig. 10.4c. This example illustrates a harmonization that is neither plain tonal (as in Fig. 10.1a) nor Jazz (as in Fig. 10.1b), this harmonization has a distinct character with a mixture of simple and extended triads and shows a high degree of originality in relation to the more well established contributing idioms.

Deep learning techniques can be used for generating morphs between different spaces. Why employ symbolic AI techniques if this is possible? "Interpolated" music generation has been explored by leveraging the spatially interpretational capabilities of the latent space in the Variational Autoencoder (VAE) [26]. Examples in image generation [15] have shown that a continuum of new images can be generated that include intermediate-morphed characteristics between two input images. This continuum is constructed by a specialized training process that includes two phases steps, divided by an intermediate sampling step. Similar to the "vanilla" Autoencoder, one goal of the training process is to perform accurate reconstruction of the input, while a parallel goal is to construct latent representations that follow a Gaussian distribution. Given enough data, the latent space obtains continuous characteristics, and thereby, sampling between any two points is made possible. Images generated by points on the line that connects any two points in the latent space, exhibit the effect of morphing between the characteristics of the images that correspond to the two extremes.

In music, both interpolation and extrapolation from two given excerpts has been examined by [46]. For instance, if the melodies corresponding to two extreme points in the latent space were a major and a minor melody, sampling from interpolated points between the latent representations of the inputs would generate new melodies with intermediate levels of major and minor characteristics. Sampling from latent points that are closer to, for instance, the major excerpt would generate a melody that is closer to a major melody than sampling closer to the minor end. Even though this system learns from data that represent musical surfaces, the "morphing continuum" that is being formed between any two points in the latent space includes high-level information as, for example, tonality.

Exploring spaces in-between two learned spaces is possible, as with the Variational Autoencoder; in case the two learned spaces are two musical styles, morphing between the two styles is made possible. There are, however, some shortcomings with this morphing approach. Firstly, extensive amounts of data are required for learning two styles, with a view to creating the continuous latent space. Secondly, high-level features in the latent spaces are not transparent, in the sense that it is not clear which features are represented by which latent space variables. For instance, it is not possible to force such a system to generate a major melody without providing an example of how a major melody looks like. The beta-VAE variation [18] potentially allows disentanglement of prominent features, but again, concrete features are not necessarily clearly divisible.

Except for the above shortcomings, there is also an inherent limitation: musical materialization of latent space points only happens by rehashing material in the musical surface of the (numerous) examples that were encountered during training. Therefore, such systems are able to interpolate (and even, to some extent, extrapolate) between musical styles, but they are able to do so only by reproducing elements of what already exists in the training data. This approach does not enable the creation of new concepts that allow creative connections between two seemingly disjoint spaces. The creation of such concepts is possible using Conceptual Blending, which allows the creation of combinational components that connect disjoint spaces, with very few (if any) training and with transparent access to what concepts are combined (however, at a cost in hand-crafting the relations between low-to-high-level features).

10.5 Conclusions

In this chapter, recent research in the domain of melodic harmonization and computational creativity has been presented with a view to highlighting strengths and weaknesses of the classical cognitively-inspired symbolic AI approach (often in juxtaposition to contemporary deep learning methodologies). A modular melodic harmonization system that learns chord types, chord transitions, cadences, and bass line voice-leading from diverse harmonic datasets is presented. Then, it is shown that the harmonic knowledge acquired by this system, can be used creatively in a cognitively-inspired conceptual blending model that creates novel harmonic spaces combining in meaningful ways the various harmonic components of different styles. This system is essentially a proof-of-concept creative model that demonstrates that new concepts can be invented which transcend the initial harmonic input spaces. It is argued that such original creativity is more naturally accommodated in the world of symbolic reasoning that allows links and inferences between diverse concepts at highly abstract levels. Moreover, symbolic representations and processing facilitate interpretability and explanation that are key components of musical knowledge advancement. Finally, reconciling symbolic AI with deep learning may be the way forward to combine the strengths of both approaches towards building more sophisticated robust musical systems that connect sensory auditory data to abstract musical concepts.

References

1. Abdallah, S., Gold, N., & Marsden, A. (2016). Analysing symbolic music with probabilistic grammars. In *Computational music analysis* (pp. 157–189). Cham: Springer.
2. Allan, M., & Williams, C. K. I. (2004). Harmonising chorales by probabilistic inference. In *Advances in neural information processing systems* (Vol. 17, pp. 25–32). MIT Press.
3. Borrel-Jensen, N., & Hjortgaard Danielsen, A. (2010). Computer-assisted music composition —A database-backed algorithmic composition system. B.S. Thesis, Department of Computer Science, University of Copenhagen, Copenhagen, Denmark. B.S. Thesis.
4. Cambouropoulos, E., Kaliakatsos-Papakostas, M., & Tsougras, C. (2014). An idiom-independent representation of chords for computational music analysis and generation. In *Proceedings of the Joint ICMC-SMC*, Athens, Greece.
5. CHAMELEON. (2020). Retrieved April 22, 2020, from https://ccm.web.auth.gr/chameleonmain.html.
6. Confalonieri, R., Pease, A., Schorlemmer, M., Besold, T. R., Kutz, O., Maclean, E., & Kaliakatsos-Papakostas, M. (Eds.). (2018). *Concept invention: Foundations, implementation, social aspects and applications*. Springer.
7. Dixon, S., Mauch, M., & Anglade, A. (2010). Probabilistic and logic-based modelling of harmony. In *International Symposium on Computer Music Modeling and Retrieval* (pp. 1–19). Berlin, Heidelberg: Springer.
8. Dubey, R., Agrawal, P., Pathak, D., Griffiths, T. L., & Efros, A. A. (2018). Investigating human priors for playing video games. arXiv preprint. arXiv:1802.10217.

9. Du, Y., & Narasimhan, K. (2019). Task-agnostic dynamics priors for deep reinforcement learning. arXiv preprint. arXiv:1905.04819.
10. Ebcioglu, K. (1988). An expert system for harmonizing four-part chorales. *Computer Music Journal, 12*(3), 43–51. ISSN 01489267.
11. Fauconnier, G., & Turner, M. (2003). *The way we think: Conceptual blending and the mind's hidden complexities.* (reprint). New York, NY: Basic Books.
12. Feinberg, T. E., & Mallatt, J. (2013). The evolutionary and genetic origins of consciousness in the Cambrian Period over 500 million years ago. *Frontiers in Psychology, 4*, 667.
13. Garnelo, M., & Shanahan, M. (2019). Reconciling deep learning with symbolic artificial intelligence: Representing objects and relations. *Current Opinion in Behavioral Sciences, 29*, 17–23.
14. Granroth-Wilding, M., & Steedman, M. (2014). A robust parser-interpreter for jazz chord sequences. *Journal of New Music Research, 43*(4), 355–374.
15. Gulrajani, I., Kumar, K., Ahmed, F., Taiga, A. A., Visin, F., Vazquez, D., & Courville, A. (2016). Pixelvae: A latent variable model for natural images. arXiv preprint. arXiv:1611.05013.
16. Hadjeres, G., Pachet, F., & Nielsen, F. (2017). Deepbach: A steerable model for Bach chorales generation. In *Proceedings of the 34th International Conference on Machine Learning* (Vol. 70, pp. 1362–1371).
17. Hanlon, M., & Ledlie, T. (2002). Cpubach: An automatic chorale harmonization system. https://www.timledlie.org/cs/CPUBach.pdf.
18. Higgins, I., Matthey, L., Pal, A., Burgess, C., Glorot, X., Botvinick, M., Mohamed, S., & Lerchner, A. (2017). beta-VAE: Learning basic visual concepts with a constrained variational framework. In *International Conference on Learning Representations* (Vol. 2, No. 5, p. 6).
19. Hiller, L. A., & Isaacson, L. M. (1979). *Experimental music; composition with an electronic computer.* Greenwood Publishing Group Inc.
20. Huang, C. Z. A., Cooijmans, T., Roberts, A., Courville, A., & Eck, D. (2019a). Counterpoint by convolution. arXiv preprint. arXiv:1903.07227.
21. Huang, C.Z.A., Hawthorne, C., Roberts, A., Dinculescu, M., Wexler, J., Hong, L., & Howcroft, J. (2019b). The bach doodle: Approachable music composition with machine learning at scale. arXiv preprint. arXiv:1907.06637.
22. Huron, D. (2016). *Voice leading: The science behind a musical art.* MIT Press.
23. Kaliakatsos-Papakostas, M., & Cambouropoulos, E. (2014). Probabilistic harmonisation with fixed intermediate chord constraints. In *Proceedings of the Joint ICMC–SMC 2014*, Athens, Greece.
24. Kaliakatsos-Papakostas, M., Makris, D., Tsougras, C., & Cambouropoulos, E. (2016). Learning and creating novel harmonies in diverse musical idioms: An adaptive modular melodic harmonisation system. *Journal of Creative Music Systems, 1*(1).
25. Kaliakatsos-Papakostas, M., Queiroz, M., Tsougras, C., & Cambouropoulos, E. (2017). Conceptual blending of harmonic spaces for creative melodic harmonisation. *Journal of New Music Research, 46*(4), 305–328.
26. Kingma, D. P., & Welling, M. (2013). Auto-encoding variational bayes. arXiv preprint. arXiv:1312.6114.
27. Koops, H. V., Magalhaes, J. P., & De Haas, W. B. (2013). A functional approach to automatic melody harmonisation. In *Proceedings of the First ACM SIGPLAN Workshop on Functional Art, Music, Modeling & Design* (pp. 47–58). ACM.
28. Longuet-Higgins, H. C., & Steedman, M. J. (1971). On interpreting Bach. *Machine Intelligence, 6*, 221–241.
29. Longuet-Higgins, H. C., & Lee, C. S. (1984). The rhythmic interpretation of monophonic music. *Music Perception, 1*(4), 424–441.
30. Longuet-Higgins, H. C. (1987). *Mental processes: Studies in cognitive science.* . Cambridge, MA: MIT Press.

31. Laske, O. E. (1988). Introduction to cognitive musicology. *Computer Music Journal, 12*(1), 43–57.
32. Makris, D., Kaliakatsos-Papakostas, M. A., & Cambouropoulos, E. (2015). Probabilistic modular bass voice leading in melodic harmonisation. In *Proceedings of ISMIR 2015* (pp. 323–329).
33. Marcus, G. (2018). Deep learning: A critical appraisal. arXiv preprint. arXiv:1801.00631.
34. Meredith, D. (Ed.). (2016). *Computational music analysis* (Vol. 62). Berlin: Springer.
35. Miranda, E. R. (Ed.). (2013). *Readings in music and artificial intelligence*. Routledge.
36. Nilsson, N. J. (2017). The physical symbol system hypothesis: Status and prospects. *SpringerLink, 2007*, 9–17. https://doi.org/10.1007/978-3-540-77296-5_2.
37. Pachet, F., & Roy, P. (2001). Musical harmonization with constraints: A survey. *Constraints, 6*(1), 7–19.
38. Pachet, F., Roy, P., & Barbieri, G. (2011). Finite-length markov processes with constraints. In *Twenty-Second International Joint Conference on Artificial Intelligence*.
39. Phon-Amnuaisuk, S., Smaill, A., & Wiggins, G. (2006). Chorale harmonization: A view from a search control perspective. *Journal of New Music Research, 35*(4), 279–305.
40. Raphael, C., & Stoddard, J. (2004). Functional harmonic analysis using probabilistic models. *Computer Music Journal, 28*(3), 45–52.
41. Simon, I., Morris, D., & Basu, S. (2008). MySong: Automatic accompaniment generation for vocal melodies. In *Proceedings of the SIGCHI Conference on Human Factors in Computing Systems* (pp. 725–734). ACM.
42. Temperley, D. (2012). Computational models of music cognition. *The psychology of music* (pp. 327–368).
43. Thornton, C. (2009). Hierarchical markov modeling for generative music. In *Proceedings of the International Computer Music Conference* (ICMC2009).
44. Toiviainen, P. (2013). Symbolic AI versus connectionism in music research. In *Readings in music and artificial intelligence* (pp. 57–78). Routledge.
45. Raczynski, S. A., Fukayama, S., & Vincent, E. (2013). Melody harmonization with interpolated probabilistic models. *Journal of New Music Research, 42*(3), 223–235.
46. Roberts, A., Engel, J., Raffel, C., Hawthorne, C., & Eck, D. (2018). A hierarchical latent vector model for learning long-term structure in music. arXiv preprint. arXiv:1803.05428.
47. Rohrmeier, M. (2011). Towards a generative syntax of tonal harmony. *Journal of Mathematics and Music, 5*(1), 35–53.
48. Rosenfeld, A., & Tsotsos, J. K. (2018). Bridging cognitive programs and machine learning. arXiv preprint. arXiv:1802.06091.
49. Whorley, R. P., Wiggins, G. A., Rhodes, C., & Pearce, M. T. (2013). Multiple viewpoint systems: Time complexity and the construction of domains for complex musical viewpoints in the harmonization problem. *Journal of New Music Research, 42*(3), 237–266.
50. Wiggins, G., & Smaill, A. (2013). Musical knowledge: What can artificial intelligence bring to the musician? In *Readings in music and artificial intelligence* (pp. 39–56). Routledge.
51. Yi, L., & Goldsmith, J. (2007). Automatic generation of four-part harmony. In K. B. Laskey, S. M. Mahoney, & J. Goldsmith (Eds.), *CEUR Workshop Proceedings* (p. 268). BMA.
52. Zacharakis, A., Kaliakatsos-Papakostas, M., Tsougras, C., & Cambouropoulos, E. (2017). Creating musical cadences via conceptual blending: Empirical evaluation and enhancement of a formal model. *Music Perception, 35*(2), 211–234.

Emilios Cambouropoulos is Professor of Musical Informatics at the School of Music Studies, Aristotle University of Thessaloniki, Greece. He studied Physics, Music and Music Technology, and obtained his Ph.D. in 1998 on Artificial Intelligence and Music at the University of Edinburgh.

His research interests focus on cognitive musicology, artificial intelligence and music, computational models of musical structure, expression and creativity. He is director of the Cognitive and Computational Musicology Group at the School of Music Studies at Aristotle University of Thessaloniki. E-mail: emilios@mus.auth.gr.

Maximos Kaliakatsos-Papakostas works as a researcher and a lecturer in the field of music informatics at Aristotle University of Thessaloniki, Greece. His research focuses on the combination of mathematical and cognitive models for computational analysis and generation of musical signals. He has a background in mathematics (B.Sc.), Artificial Intelligence (M.Sc. and Ph.D.), music and software development. He has been teaching courses on a wide range of fields, ranging from pure mathematics to interactive music systems. E-mail: maxk@mus.auth.gr.

11 On Modelling Harmony with Constraint Programming for Algorithmic Composition Including a Model of Schoenberg's Theory of Harmony

Torsten Anders

11.1 Introduction

This chapter introduces the use of Constraint Programming for modelling the algorithmic generation of harmonic progressions for composition. Constraint Programming (CP) is a paradigm based on explicitly encoded compositional rules. The paradigm allows to directly implement traditional rules, such as rules found in music theory textbooks, as well as non-standard rules, e.g., rules formulated by composers to model their own composition techniques when using this paradigm. CP has been highly attractive for researchers and composers since decades because of its high degree of abstraction and not least because constraint solvers can efficiently find solutions that fulfil all the stated constraints.

In a comprehensive survey, Fernández and Vico [28] present a hierarchical taxonomy of Artificial Intelligence (AI) methods for algorithmic composition. They categorise these methods into symbolic AI, optimisation techniques based on Evolutionary Algorithms and related methods, and Machine Learning. CP is one of the symbolic AI methods alongside, e.g., Case-Based Reasoning and grammars such as Lindenmayer systems.

The survey by Herremans et al. [33] suggest a functional taxonomy of algorithmic composition systems. The authors organise their discussion of systems according to compositional "dimensions": rhythm, melody, harmony and timbre/orchestration. While their survey subsumes under harmony any combination of multiple simultaneous pitches (e.g., also counterpoint), the preset chapter focuses on modelling what traditional textbooks on harmony usually mean by this term: a progression of chords.

T. Anders (✉)
Aiva Technologies, Luxembourg, Luxembourg
e-mail: torstenanders@gmx.de

© Springer Nature Switzerland AG 2021
E. R. Miranda (ed.), *Handbook of Artificial Intelligence for Music*,
https://doi.org/10.1007/978-3-030-72116-9_11

Besides providing an introduction into its field, this chapter offers two contributions to knowledge. Firstly, it implements large parts of Arnold Schoenberg's textbook on tonal harmony. The chapter presents formal details on how to model harmonic concepts such as diatonic chords, chord inversions, root progressions, cadences, dissonance treatment and modulation with constrain programming. To the knowledge of the author, Schoenberg's theory of harmony has not been computationally modelled before, neither with constraints programming nor in any other way.

Secondly, the Schoenberg model is implemented with a more general and style-neutral harmonic framework that was designed with the capabilities of modern constraint solvers in mind. This research proposes a harmony framework that supports various analytical information to allow for modelling complex theories of harmony at a high level of abstraction, and whose design is at the same time suitable for propagation-based constraint solvers. Using constraint propagation allows for efficiently solving constraint problems with a large search space.

11.2 Application Examples

We will start our introduction into modelling harmony with CP by looking at three concrete examples. These examples are all realised with a harmony framework introduced formally later (Sect. 11.4). The first example automatically finds a fitting harmony for a given melody. The second example introduces a larger-scale constraint model: it implements large parts of Schoenberg's comprehensive tonal theory of harmony [57]. Formal details of this model are discussed towards the end of this chapter in Sect. 11.5. The last example uses CP for realising a composition by the author.

11.2.1 Automatic Melody Harmonisation

The first example creates a harmonisation for a given melody. The example is comparatively simple and is therefore discussed in some detail.

CP controls relations between variables, which are here the parameters of notes and chords (e.g., their pitches). There is no principle distinction between the input and the output in this approach. The variables whose values are known initially are the input and the variables whose values are found by the constraint solver are the output. Therefore, a framework originally developed for music composition, but explicitly modelling the underlying harmony can also be used for analysis by setting the parameters of the actual music before the search starts but leaving the parameters of the underlying harmony unset.

This example actually combines analysis and composition. It performs an automatic harmonic analysis of a given folk tune, but additional compositional rules are applied to the resulting harmonies. Voicing is irrelevant in this example; only the chord symbols are searched for.

The harmonic rhythm is slower than the melody, as common in classical, folk and popular music. By contrast, most automatic harmonisation examples in the literature are choral-like with one chord per note.

For simplicity, this example defines relatively rigid basic conditions. Only major, minor and dominant seventh chords are permitted, and all chords must be diatonic in C major. The harmonic rhythm is fixed, and all chords share the same duration (e.g., a whole bar), but chord repetitions are permitted.

The example distinguishes between harmonic and nonharmonic tones, but for simplicity only a few cases of nonharmonic tones are permitted (passing and neighbour tones). All other melody notes must be chord pitches.

The example further borrows a few harmonic rules from Schoenberg [57] in order to ensure musically reasonable solutions. The example assumes that the given melody starts and ends with the tonic—these chords are constrained to be equal. A seventh chord must be resolved by a "fourth upwards the fundament" (e.g., $V^7 \rightarrow$ I), the simplest resolution form for seventh chords. Also, all chords share at least one common pitch class with their predecessor (harmonic band, a simpler form of Schoenberg's directions for producing favourable chord progressions).

Figure 11.1 shows all solutions for the first phrase of the German folksong "Horch was kommt von draussen rein" that fulfil the given rules. All these solutions work well musically. An x on top of a note denotes a nonharmonic pitch.

Because of the relative simplicity of this example, it works only well for some melodies and less good for others. The harmonic rhythm of the melody must fit the harmonic rhythm specified for the example (at least chords can last longer, as repetitions are permitted). This is easily addressed by turning the currently fixed chord durations into variables, but doing so increases the size of the search space. Further, the nonharmonic pitches of the melody must fit the cases defined (passing and neighbour tones). An extension could define further cases, like suspensions and

Fig. 11.1 For the given melody this simple harmonisation model has four solutions (the chords shown above the melody)

anticipations. Also, the melody currently cannot modulate. This can be solved by additionally modelling scales, and applying modulation constraints between chords and scales (as shown in the next example).

11.2.2 Modelling Schoenberg's Theory of Harmony

The next example implements large parts of Schoenberg's textbook on tonal harmony originally published in 1911 [57]—a particular comprehensive harmony textbook. This example demonstrates that the underlying framework is capable of modelling complex conventional theories. A brief summary of main ideas of Schoenberg's 1911 harmony textbook can be found in the introduction of his later text on harmony [56, pp. 4–14]. The present section introduces this example from a musical point of view, while below Sect. 11.5 presents formal details.

To the knowledge of the author, Schoenberg's theory of harmony has not been computationally modelled before, neither with constraints programming nor in any other way. Also, this example implements modulation, which has rarely been done with CP before. Among constraint-based harmony models, Ebcioğlu's CHORAL [25] is the only system the author is aware of that supports modulation.

The example modulates from C major to G major, but features an extended pitch set that allows for non-diatonic tones. Figure 11.2 shows a solution.

The example applies Schoenberg's directions on chord root progressions designed to help obtaining better progressions. Schoenberg distinguishes between three kinds of root progressions. In *strong* or *ascending* progressions the chord root progresses by a fourth up (harmonically the same as a fifth down) or a third down. For example, in Fig. 11.2 chord 1 progresses to chord 2 by a third down (I → vi), while chord 2 progresses to chord 3 by a fourth up or fifth down (vi → ii). *Descending* root progressions form the second type. They are the inversion of ascending progressions: a fourth down (fifth up) or a third up. These are not allowed in this example. Finally, in *superstrong* progressions the root moves a second up or down, as the chords in the penultimate bar do (IV → V).

The chords are related to underlying scales, which change during the modulation. The first five chords relate to the C major scale, and the rest to G major. However,

Fig. 11.2 A solution of the Schoenberg harmony model modulating from C to G major featuring some non-diatonic tones; Roman numerals added manually here for clarity (altered chords are crossed out)

the example also allows for non-diatonic tones. Schoenberg introduces these as accidentals from church modes, namely the raised 1st, 2nd, 4th, 5th and the flattened 7th degree. These are always resolved stepwise in the direction of their alteration (e.g., raised degrees go up). In order to support the intended direction of the modulation (C to G), only raised degrees are allowed in this example. In the solution above, e.g., chord 4 contains a raised 4th degree of C major (F♯) that is chromatically introduced and resolves upwards by a step. Chord 7 contains a raised 5th degree of G major (D♯).

A modulation constraint requires that chord 5 is a *neutral chord*, i.e., a chord shared by both keys. In the solution above this chord is iii in C and vi in G major. The modulation constraint further requires that the neutral chord is followed by the *modulatory chord*, which is only part of the target key (vii$^{\varnothing 7}$ in the solution). For clarity, the modulatory chord progresses by an ascending root progression a fourth upwards (into iii above).

The example also applies part writing rules. Open and hidden parallel fifths and octaves are not permitted. Also, the upper three voices are restricted to small melodic intervals and small harmonic intervals between voices (larger harmonic intervals are allowed between tenor and bass).

Root positions and first inversions can occur freely. For example, in Fig. 11.2 chord 4 is in first inversion. The number of first inversions has not been constrained and it is rather high in the shown solution (6 out of 11 chords). More generally, statistical properties such as the likelihood of certain chords are difficult to control by CP (e.g., their overall number can be restricted, but they then may be bunched early or late in the search process).

11.2.3   A Compositional Application in Extended Tonality

The last example discusses the 7 min composition *Pfeifenspiel* by the author, which was composed for the two organs of the Kunst-Station St. Peter in Cologne and premiered at the Computing Music VIII series in 2012. Figure 11.3 shows a passage from the piece at the boundary between two sections.

The music is tonal in the extended sense of Tymoczko [62]: melodic intervals tend to be small; the dissonance degree of the harmony is rather consistent; relatively consonant chords are used in moments of musical stability; sections of the piece are limited to certain scales; and for specific sections one tone is particularly important (root).

However, the piece is clearly non-diatonic. Suitable scales where found by first searching with an ad hoc constraint program through about 200 scales and 50 chord types for scales that contain many chords with a similar dissonance degree (measured with an experimental algorithm). Solution scales were further evaluated manually by considering all chords that can be built on each scale degree, and by judging the melodic quality of scales. In the end, three scales that are all somewhat similar to the whole tone scale where selected: Takemitsu's *Tree Line* mode 2,

Fig. 11.3 Passage from the composition *Pfeifenspiel* composed by the author. The upper three staves show the actual composition, and the lower two an analysis of the underlying harmony. Chord and scale tones are shown like an appoggiatura and roots as normal notes. Nonharmonic tones are marked by an x

Messiaen's mode 3, and Messiaen's mode 6. Two of these scales are shown in Fig. 11.3 in the analysis in the lowest stave (e.g., Takemitsu's *Tree Line* mode 2 on D in measures 6–7).

Based on these scales, a global harmonic and formal plan was composed by hand, but concrete harmonic progressions were generated algorithmically with custom harmony models for different sections. Also, contrapuntal sections rendering the harmony were algorithmically generated (and slightly manually revised), while some other sections were composed manually (e.g., in Fig. 11.3 the septuplets in the Great division, and the triplets in the pedal were composed manually).

Some example constraints are outlined. Chords have at least four tones, which all belong to the simultaneous scale. The first and last chord root of a section is often the tonic of its scale. To ensure smooth transitions between chords, the voice-leading distance between consecutive chords is low (at most 3 semitones in the excerpt). The voice-leading distance is the minimal sum of absolute intervals between the tones of two chords. For example, the voice-leading distance between the C and A♭ major triads is 2 (C → C = 0, E → E♭ = 1, G → A♭ = 1). Also, any three consecutive chords must be distinct.

The actual notes (in staves 1–3) must express the underlying harmony (stave 4). Nonharmonic tones (marked with an x in Fig. 11.3) are prepared and resolved by small intervals. Across the section starting in measure 8, the contrapuntal lines in the swell division rise gradually (pitch domain boundaries are rising), and melodic intervals are getting smaller (this section lasts over 10 bars, so this is not obvious from the few bars shown). The contrapuntal voices are never more than an octave apart; they don't cross; they avoid open and hidden parallels; they avoid perfect consonances between simultaneous notes (one is there in Fig. 11.3 after manual revisions); and voice notes sound all tones of the underlying harmony. Also, the lines are composed of motifs; and durational accents are constrained [5].

11.3   Overview: Constraint Programming for Modelling Harmony

After a few application examples in the previous section, this section motivates and introduces Music Constraint Programming (MCP) in general. Several surveys already study this field. Pachet and Roy [45] focus on harmonic constraint problems. Fernández and Vico [28] provide a detailed list of music constraint problems and systems and situate this field in the wider context of AI-based methods. Anders and Miranda [12] present a comprehensive overview of the field in general and in particular carefully compare MCP systems designed to implement custom models of music theory and composition with CP. Finally, Anders [7] complements these more technical reviews by a more artistic point of view and examines how several composers employed CP systems and techniques when realising specific pieces.

11.3.1   Why Constraint Programming for Music Composition?

For centuries, compositional rules have been one of the central devices in music theory and education for explaining compositional knowledge. For example, already in the ninth century the anonymous treatise *Musica enchiriadis* explained the composition of an important polyphonic form of its time—the organum—by compositional rules [37]. Even though the music notation and musical style of that time was very different to later centuries, this early music textbook already presents a fundamental compositional concern that is shared by later developments of tonal music: the distinction between consonance and dissonance which leads to compositional rules controlling their treatment (though consonances are restricted to the fourth, fifth and octave in this early music). Since then and through the centuries until today, compositional rules have been a central method in music theory when describing how to compose in a certain musical style—complemented by musical examples.

Rules are such a central device, because rules allow to describe aspects of composition in both a declarative and modular way. Instead of procedurally specifying how to create a certain result, rules are declarative in the sense that they only describe certain features or aspects of the intended result. Rules are modular in the sense that they allow to focus on only one compositional aspect at the time. The description of a musical style is simplified when it can be broken down into separate rules on aspects of rhythm, melody, harmony and so forth.

CP carries the advantages of compositional rules into the world of algorithmic composition: it helps to realise music theory models that are also declarative and modular. A computer program using a declarative programming paradigm describes *what* the program does—its logic and results (e.g., *what* a composition system does in a musical sense), without the need to state *how* this is done—the procedural details are covered by its search algorithm. Further, CP can model music theories and composition in a modular way. A single musical parameter can be affected by multiple rules defined separately. For example, a single pitch can be affected simultaneously by multiple melodic and harmonic rules. No rule necessarily determines the pitch, but a search algorithm finds a pitch that meets all the rules.

Due to the importance of rules in music theory and education, programming paradigms supporting rules have also been highly attractive for composers and scholars since the earliest days of algorithmic composition. Already the *Illiac Suite* (1956) for string quartet—widely considered the first computer-composed score—used a rule-based approach [36]. Different movements of this piece are considered separate experiments and are composed in different styles: the composition process for the second movement (in strict counterpoint) and the third movement (chromatic music) used a generate-and-test algorithm for filtering randomly generated notes that meet stated rules. The algorithms implementing rules became more refined over time. Most likely, Ebcioglu [23] was the first proposing a composition system (creating florid counterpoint for a given cantus firmus) that employed a systematic search algorithm.

11.3.2   What Is Constraint Programming?

Constraint Programming [14] is a programming paradigm—a particular way to approach programming in general—that has been especially successful for implementing ruled-based composition systems. The attraction of CP is easily explained. It allows users to implement rule-based music theories rather easily by directly formalising sets of modular compositional rules.

CP is a descendant of the Logic Programming paradigm. Virtually all programming paradigms support variables, usually in the sense of an identifier given to a certain storage location. Variables in Logic Programming [19] are more like variables in mathematics. Logic variables can name unknown or partially known quantities; a logic program expresses relations between logic variables. As all the variables can be unknown, they can also all act as either input or output (in contrast to functions in other paradigms, where the function result cannot be used as an input to deduce one of the function arguments). However, Logic Programming is best suited for symbolic computations, it does not work well with numeric relations.

CP is a kinsman of Logic Programming that supports numeric relations in addition to logic relations. It introduces techniques to solve combinatorial problems. A *constraint satisfaction problem* (CSP) is defined by a set of *decision variables* (in the following *variables* for brevity) and mathematical relations between these variables, called *constraints*. The value of variables is initially only partially known: they have a *domain* of their possible values. A constraint *solver* then searches for one or more *solutions* that reduces the domain of each variable to one value that is consistent with all its constraints. A CP system allows user to define and solve constraint problems.

11.3.3 Music Constraint Systems for Algorithmic Composition

Due to the great interest of composers in CP, a number of CP systems have been developed, which are designed for composing music that meets compositional rules expressed as constraints. These systems help composers programming their custom CSPs, which then assist them in their compositional work. The pioneering system of this kind was Carla [20]. Anders and Miranda[12] compare five MCP systems in detail. PWConstraints [39,53] offer two constraint solvers. A more generic one searches for sequences of values (e.g., pitch or chord sequences), and the other one finds pitches for polyphonic scores. Situation [15,53] was originally designed for solving harmonic CSPs in a French compositional tradition. The music representation MusES [43,44] and the constraint solver BackTalk [52] have been combined for solving various compositional tasks including automatic melody harmonisation. OMClouds [60] implements a heuristic solver that finds approximate solutions even for over-constrained CSPs. Strasheela [1] is a library that offers building blocks for a particularly wide range of musical CSPs, though this flexibility makes it a bit harder to use than some other systems, which effectively offer CSP templates. More recent solvers are PWMC [55] and its successor Cluster Engine with the extension Cluster Rules [6]. They support polyphonic CSPs where both the rhythm and the pitches are searched for. Chapter 12 by Örjan Sandred in this volume discusses the solver Cluster Engine further.

Various algorithms exist for CP solvers [21], and various algorithms have been used in music constraint systems [12]. The classical search algorithm for CP is chronological backtracking, which systematically visits one variable after another. It assigns a variable a value from its domain and then checks whether this partial solution complies with all the constraints on this variable. If it does, the search progresses to the next variable, and otherwise it tries a different domain value. If all domain values of a variable fail a constraint then the search backtracks to the previously visited variable and tries different domain values of that previous variable.

Chronological backtracking works well for relatively simple music constrain problems, but music constraint systems usually support refinements of this principal algorithm for solving more complex problems with reasonable efficiency. Anders and Miranda [12] discuss in detail different search algorithms used by music constraint systems; here we only provide a brief summary.

The order in which variables are visited during the search process can have a great impact on the efficiency (as does the order in which we make decisions in daily live), and music constraint systems therefore commonly offer custom or even user-definable variable orderings. Some systems support dynamic variable orderings, where the solver decides which variable to visit next only at the moment when that decision is due—taking the current stage of the partial solution into account [2].

Back jumping is an optimisation of chronological backtracking. In case the solver needs to backtrack, back jumping tries to skip intermediate unrelated variables when going back and instead continues with a variable that actually conflicts with a failed constraint; the solver avoids unnecessary work this way.

Constraint propagation [59] reduces the size of the search tree by shrinking domains without search to exclude domain values that contradict some constraints and cannot be part of any solution. Constraint propagation is triggered during the search process whenever a new variable is visited and may affect all variables that have not been visited so far. To speed up the propagation process itself, it commonly only affects variable domain boundaries (i.e., reduces the domain range of an integer domain without cutting "holes" into the domain). Constraint propagation can greatly speed up the search and is therefore widely used in academia and industry in general. However, it is rarely used for MCP, likely because it somewhat restricts the constraints that can be expressed. The highly specialised propagation algorithms that reduce variable domains without search are designed for specific decision variable "types" (kinds of variable domains, e.g., Booleans, integers and sets of integers), and therefore all variables in a constraint system using propagation must be "typed" accordingly. Nevertheless, the harmony framework proposed later in this chapter is designed in such a way that it can be implemented with a constraint system using propagation, because this framework is designed with such "typed" variables in mind.

11.3.4 Harmony Modelling

In the field of algorithmic composition, harmony is a challenging area to address. Theories of harmony can be rather complex, as the mere size of standard harmony textbooks indicates. Also, different theories vary considerably depending on the musical style they address such as classical music [49,57], Jazz [40], contemporary classical music in extended tonality [46] or microtonal music [22].

Due to this complexity, techniques of Machine Learning are a suitable way for modelling harmony. For example, Hild et al. [35] present a neural net that—given a melody—generates a four-part choral, imitating the style of Johann Sebastian Bach. The system breaks this task down into multiple steps, starting with a harmonic skeleton (the bass plus harmonic functions), progressing to a chord skeleton (four-part voicings) and finally adding ornamenting quavers. Boulanger-Lewandowski et al. [18] propose an often-cited recursive neural network (with different network architectures) that learns to compose polyphonic music from corpora of varying complexity (folk tunes, chorals, piano music and orchestral music). The model composes musical sequences that demonstrate learnt knowledge of harmony and how to shape melodic lines, though long-term structure is missing. Eigenfeldt and Pasquier [27] describe a method for generating harmonic progressions in real time that uses Markov chains. The system learns from Jazz standards from the Real Book.

While Machine Learning works well for generating chord progressions of existing styles, composers are interested in developing their own musical language and commonly prefer avoiding pastiche. A rule-based approach allows composers to define their own harmonic language (e.g., using non-conventional or microtonal scales), even if this language is rather complex. Besides, a rule-based model is comprehensible for humans, which is rarely the case for models resulting from Machine Learning.

11.3.5   Constraint-Based Harmony Systems

As CP is well suited for modelling rule-based compositional knowledge, and as much compositional knowledge is available on harmony in standard textbooks, harmony is a music theory area that has particularly often been addressed when modelling composition with CP. Only counterpoint, which is also codified in detail by rules in the literature, attracted similar attention, while other areas of music theory (rhythm, melody, musical form, orchestration) have been addressed comparatively less often. Some of the above-mentioned surveys on MCP also cover specifically how harmony has been modelled [12,45]. Below, we look at a few particularly relevant examples.

Tsang and Aitken [61] presented an often-cited harmonisation system with only 20 rules for creating four-part harmonisations of a choral melody.

By contrast, the harmonisation system CHORAL [25,26] received great attention due to the musical quality of its results, which were realised by over 300 constraints. CHORAL generates four-part choral harmonisations for given melodies in the style of Johann Sebastian Bach. While Ebcioglu also extracted rules from a number of traditional harmony treatises, he derived much compositional knowledge by a detailed analysis of Bach's music, and then formalised this knowledge by a large number of rules.

The system applies rules to what Ebcioglu calls multiple *viewpoints* of the score, i.e., different variable combinations (elsewhere, this chapter uses the term *score context* for a very similar notion). Rules on the *chord skeleton* view constrain the rhythmless sequence of chord symbols of the underlying harmony. These include, e.g., rules controlling chord progressions. The *fill in* view provides access to the four voices including the duration and metric weight of notes, and it is used for controlling nonharmonic tones like passing tones. Rules on the *Schenkerian analysis* view and *melodic string* view control melodic developments, in particular of the bass. Due to the large amount of modelled compositional knowledge in CHORAL, its results can be harmonically more complex than most other constraint-based harmonisation systems. For example, CHORAL features modulations, as mentioned earlier.

To meet his purpose in an efficient way, Ebcioglu first designed and implemented the CP language BSL, which is short for Backtracking Specification Language [24]. BSL allows for strict constraints but also heuristics. It implements a search algorithm that features backjumping as an optimisation.

Phon-Amnuaisuk also proposed a system for Bach choral harmonisations [47,48]. Phon-Amnuaisuk criticises the design of CHORAL, pointing out that this system is hard to modify. To realise a more adaptable constraint system design, he proposes a design that separates the logic of the compositional knowledge and the search, so that the temporal order in which variables are visited during the search process (variable ordering) can be changed independently of the problem definition. For example, for the four-voice Bach choral example, the search process may first create the harmonic skeleton for the given melody, then outline the bass skeleton, create a draft of the other voices and eventually create the final version of each voice by adding ornamentations such as passing notes.

While most constraint-based harmony systems harmonise a given melody—often creating a new chord for each melody note—[9] present a system for creating a harmonic progression from scratch. The work models Schoenberg's directions for convincing chord progressions, which is a subset of the model presented below in Sect. 11.5. However, this research models Schoenberg's explanation of his recommendations instead of the actual rules, and that way generalises these recommendations beyond diatonic progressions and even for microtonal music.

11.4 Case Study: A Constraint-Based Harmony Framework

The next two sections present a case study in some detail. The present section describes formal details of a proposed framework for defining harmonic constraint applications. The applications in Sect. 11.2 above are all defined with this framework. The following section then returns to one of these application examples. Based on the framework presented in the present section, the following section models core parts of Schoenberg's comprehensive tonal theory of harmony.

There is no agreement on a single theory of harmony; there exist various harmonic styles. Therefore, a flexible algorithmic composition environment should allow users to create their own style by modelling their own theory of harmony. This section proposes a framework with which users can model their own theory of harmony, and then let the system generate harmonic progressions that follow it. If the harmonic rules are complemented by rules controlling the melody, counterpoint and so forth, then they can also be used more generally to generate music that follows given or generated progressions.

The framework provides building blocks common to many theories of harmony and that way simplifies the definition of custom theories from scratch. The proposed framework provides flexible representations of harmonic concepts (e.g., chords, scales, notes, as well as their parameters like a note's pitch or a chord root), which allow users to define their own harmony models declaratively at a high level of abstraction with modular rules implemented by constraints that restrict the relations between these parameters.

Users can freely declare chord and scale types (e.g., major and minor triads and scales) by specifying pitch class intervals among chord or scale tones and their root/tonic. A number of different pitch representations are supported including pitch numbers (e.g., MIDI key numbers), pitch classes, enharmonic note representations, scale degrees of notes and chords, and specific chord tones such as the fifth or the third of a triad. All these representations are freely constrainable. The framework supports the common 12-tone temperament and arbitrary other equal divisions of the octave.

Much of the information represented by the framework is analytical information. Notes are concrete musical objects that produce sound when the score is played, but chord and scale objects represent analytical information—the underlying harmony.

Notes, chords and scales are represented by tuples of decision variables. Variables represent score parameters (like a note's start time, pitch, etc.) or analytical information (e.g., the pitch class set of a chord, or its root). When users define harmony models with this framework, they employ these objects and apply constraints between their variables. However, some well-formedness constraints must always hold between these variables and are automatically applied for convenience. This section discusses the variables of these objects, as well as the well-formedness constraints.

For clarity and portability, this section shows core definitions of the framework in mathematical notation instead of using any programming language. For simplicity, we leave out some auxiliary variables (intermediate results in larger constraint expressions represented by extra variables).

11.4.1 Declaration of Chord and Scale Types

In the proposed framework, the chord and scale types supported globally by a constraint model (e.g., major and minor triads and scales) can be declared independently of the rest of the model. The ordered sequence $\mathcal{CT}$ consists of tuples, where each tuple specifies one chord type with a set of features as shown in the example below (11.1). The first tuple declares the major triad type: it specifies the pitch class integer 0 representing the untransposed chord root (C), and the pitch classes of the untransposed chord—in this case the C major triad, $\{C, E, G\}$—as the set of pitch class integers $\{0, 4, 7\}$. Implicitly, such declarations state the intervals between the chord tones. The given *name* is a useful annotation, but not directly used by the framework.

Most values of the proposed framework are variables, e.g., the temporal or pitch parameters of notes and chords can be initially unknown, constrained and are searched for. By contrast, all values in chord type declarations (i.e., the different chord types involved in a harmonic constraint application) are usually constants that are known from the outset.

$$
\mathcal{CT} = \begin{array}{l} [\langle name \text{ major}, \quad root \ 0, \quad PCs \{0, 4, 7\}\rangle, \\ \langle name \text{ minor}, \quad root \ 0, \quad PCs \{0, 3, 7\}\rangle, \\ \dots]. \end{array} \tag{11.1}
$$

Scale types are declared in the same way in an extra sequence of tuples $\mathcal{ST}$. For example, the pitch class set of the major scale type is $\{0, 2, 4, 5, 7, 9, 11\}$, while its tonic (also represented under variable name *root* for consistency) is 0.

Users can declare the global number of pitches per octave (*psPerOct*), and that way specify the meaning of all integers representing pitches and pitch classes in the constraint model. A useful default value for *psPerOct* is 12, which results in the common 12 equal division of the octave (12-EDO), and which was used for the chord and scale type examples above. Only equal temperaments that evenly subdivide the octave are supported. However, just intonation or irregular temperaments can be closely approximated by setting *psPerOct* to a high value (e.g., *psPerOct* = 1200 results in cent resolution).

Instead of specifying pitch classes by integers as shown, it can be more convenient to specify note names, which are then automatically mapped ($\mapsto$) to the corresponding pitch class integers, depending on *psPerOct*. In 12-EDO, C $\mapsto$ 0, C♯ $\mapsto$ 1 and so on. Alternatively, pitch classes can be specified by frequency ratios as a useful approximation of just intonation intervals for different temperaments. Again in 12-EDO, the prime $\frac{1}{1} \mapsto 0$, the fifth $\frac{3}{2} \mapsto 7$, etc. Remember that for the frequency ratio r, the corresponding pitch class is $round((\log_2 r) \cdot psPerOct)$.

The format of chord and scale declarations is extendable. Users can add further chord or scale type features (e.g., a measure of the dissonance degree of each chord type), which would then result in further variables in the chord and scale representation. Some additional features are already predefined for convenience and are discussed in the Sect. 11.4.3 below.

11.4.2 Temporal Music Representation

The underlying harmony can change over time. Temporal relations are a suitable way to express dependencies: all notes simultaneous to a certain chord or scale depend on that object (i.e., those notes fall into their harmony).

The framework shows its full potential when combined with a music representation where multiple events can happen simultaneously. A chord sequence (or scale sequence or both) can run in parallel to the actual score, as shown in the score example discussed above (Fig. 11.3).

Score objects are organised in time by hierarchic nesting. A sequential container implicitly constrains its contained objects (e.g., notes, chords, or other containers) to follow each other in time. The objects in a simultaneous container start at the same time (by default). All temporal score objects represent temporal parameters like their *start* time, *end* time and *duration* by integer variables. A rest before a score object is represented by its temporal parameter *offset* time (another integer variable), which allows for arbitrary rests between objects in a sequential container, and before objects in a simultaneous container.

Equation (11.2) shows the constraints between the temporal variables of a simultaneous container sim and its contained objects object$_1$ ... object$_n$. Any contained object—object$_i$—starts at the start time of the container sim plus the offset time of the contained object. The end time of sim is the maximum end time of any contained object.

$$start_{object_i} = start_{sim} + offset_{object_i}$$

$$end_{sim} = \max(end_{object_1}, \ldots, end_{object_n}). \tag{11.2}$$

The relations between temporal variables of a sequential container and its contained objects are constrained correspondingly, and every temporal object is constrained by the obvious relation that the sum of its start time and duration is its end time. The interested reader is referred to [1, Chap. 5] for further details.

Temporal relations can be defined with these temporal parameters. For example, we can constrain that (or whether, by further constraining the resulting truth value) two objects o_1 and o_2 are simultaneous by constraining their start and ($\wedge$) end times (11.3). For clarity, this constraint is simplified here by leaving out the offset times of these objects.

$$start_{o_1} < end_{o_2} \ \wedge \ start_{o_2} < end_{o_1}. \tag{11.3}$$

Remember that all these relations are constraints—relations that work either way. The temporal structure of a score can be unknown in the definition of a harmonic CSP. Users can apply constraints, e.g., to control the harmonic rhythm in their model, or the rhythm of the notes in a harmonic counterpoint.

If other constraints depend on which objects are simultaneous to each other (e.g., harmonic relations between notes and chords), then the search should find temporal parameters relatively early during the search process [2].

11.4.3 Chords and Scales

The proposed model represents the underlying harmony of music with chord and scale objects. This section introduces the representation of these objects, their variables, and the implicit constraints on these variables. The representation of chords and scales is identical, except that chords depend on the declaration of chord types CT, and scales on scale types ST (see Sect. 11.4.1). Therefore, the rest of this subsection only discusses the definition of chords.

A chord c is represented by a tuple of four variables (11.4)—in addition to the temporal variables mentioned above (Sect. 11.4.2), which are indicated with the ellipsis "…". Internally, some additional auxiliary variables are used in the implementation: *untransposedRoot* and *untransposedPitchClasses*. The integer variable *type* denotes the chord type. Formally, it is the position of the respective chord in the sequence of chord type declarations CT, see Eq. (11.1) above. The integer variable *transp* specifies by how much the chord is transposed with respect to its declaration in CT. The set of integer variables PCs represents the set of (transposed) pitch classes of the chord, and the integer variable *root* is the (transposed) root pitch class of the chord.

$$c = \langle type, transp, PCs, root, \ldots \rangle. \tag{11.4}$$

For chords where the *root* is 0 (C) in the declaration, *transp* and *root* are equal. In a simplified framework, the variable *transp* could therefore be left out. However, sometimes it is more convenient to declare a chord where the root is not C (e.g., leaving a complex chord from the literature untransposed, or stating the pitch classes of a chord by fractions where the root is not $\frac{1}{1}$). Therefore this flexibility is retained here with the separate variables *transp* and *root*.

Implicitly applied constraints restrict the relation between the variables of any chord object c, and the collection of chord type declarations $\mathcal{CT}$. Note that $\mathcal{CT}$ (and $\mathcal{ST}$) are internally rearranged for these constraints. $root_{\mathcal{CT}}$ is the sequence of all chord roots (in the order of the chord declarations) and $PCs_{\mathcal{CT}}$ is the sequence of the pitch class sets of all chord declarations.

Equations (11.5) and (11.6) show the implicit constraints. The *element constraint* is a key here. It accesses in an ordered sequence of variables a variable at a specific index, but the index is also a variable. The element constraint is notated here like accessing an element in a sequence. $x = xs[i]$ constrains x to the element at position i in xs, where i is an integer variable, x is either an integer or a set variable, and xs is a sequence of integer or set variables. In (11.5), $root_{\mathcal{CT}}[type_{c}]$ is the untransposed root of the chord type $type_{c}$. The (transposed) chord $root_{c}$ is this untransposed root—pitch class transposed with the constraint *transp-pc* by the transposition interval of the chord. A corresponding constraint for pitch class sets is expressed in (11.6).

When chords are extended by further variables (e.g., a chord type specific dissonance degree), the chord declarations and chord object variables are simply linked by further element constraints (e.g., $feat_{c} = feat_{\mathcal{CT}}[type_{c}]$).

$$root_{c} = transp\text{-}pc(root_{\mathcal{CT}}[type_{c}], transp_{c}) \qquad (11.5)$$

$$PCs_{c} = transp\text{-}PCs(PCs_{\mathcal{CT}}[type_{c}], transp_{c}). \qquad (11.6)$$

The pitch class transposition constraint used here is defined in (11.7). Pitch class transposition in 12-EDO with mod 12 is well known in the literature [31]. The definition here slightly deviates to support arbitrary equal temperaments (*psPerOct* was introduced in Sect. 11.4.1 above). The function *transp-pc* expects a pitch class *pc* and a transposition interval t and returns a transposed pitch class. *transpPCs* does the equivalent for a set of pitch classes, transposing them all by the same interval.

$$transp\text{-}pc(pc, t) := (pc + t) \bmod psPerOct. \qquad (11.7)$$

Note that functions in this chapter—like *transp-pc* and *transpPCs*—must be read as relations; they apply constraints between the decision variables involved. For example, their "results" can also be used as inputs. We can effectively ask *transp-pc* by which interval t we need to transpose the pitch class 2 (D in 12-EDO) to reach 9 (A), and the constraint solver deduces that $t = 7$ (a perfect fifth).

Side note: constraint propagation of the framework is improved with the redundant constraint (11.8): the *root* of a chord is always an element ($\in$) of its pitch class set. Remember that the root of a chord is always a chord tone—which is not necessarily true for its fundamental. For example, the root of the diminished triad $\{C, E\flat, G\flat\}$ is C, which is a chord tone, while its fundamental is A$\flat$, which is not a chord tone.

$$root_{c} \in PCs_{c}. \qquad (11.8)$$

11.4.4 Notes with Analytical Information

Note objects represent the actual notes in the score. A note n is represented by a tuple of variables as shown in (11.9). As with chords, temporal variables are left out for simplicity and are only indicated with an ellipsis.

$$n = \langle pitch,\ pc,\ oct,\ inChord?,\ inScale?,\ \dots \rangle. \qquad (11.9)$$

The note's *pitch* (integer variable) is essential for melodic constraints. It is a MIDI note number [50] in case of 12-EDO. The *pc* (integer variable) represents the pitch class (chroma) independent of the *oct* (octave, integer variable) component, which is useful for harmonic constraints. The relation between a note's *pitch*, *pc* and *oct* is described by (11.10). The octave above middle C is 4, as in scientific pitch notation [63].

$$pitch = psPerOct \cdot (oct + 1) + pc. \qquad (11.10)$$

The Boolean variable *inChord?* distinguishes between a harmonic and nonharmonic tone, i.e., expresses whether the *pc* of a note n is an element of the *PCs* of its simultaneous chord c. This relation is implemented with a *reified constraint* (a meta-constraint, which constrains whether or not other constraints hold), namely, a reified set membership constraint (11.11). In the harmonic analysis discussed in Sect. 11.2.1 above and in the composition example of Sect. 11.2.3, the variable *inChord?* is used for constraining that nonharmonic tones are treated adequately (e.g., as passing tones). The Boolean variable *inScale?* denotes equivalently whether the note is inside or outside its simultaneous scale.

$$inChord?_n = pc_n \in PCs_c. \qquad (11.11)$$

11.4.5 Degrees, Accidentals and Enharmonic Spelling

So far, we used two common pitch representations: the single variable *pitch* and the pair $\langle pc, oct \rangle$. Further pitch-related representations can be useful to denote scale degrees (including deviations from the scale), tones in a chord (and their deviations), and to express enharmonic spelling.

Enharmonic spelling is represented with a pair of integer variables $\langle nominal, accidental \rangle$, where *nominal* represents one of the seven-pitch nominals (C, D, E, ..., B) as integers: 1 means C, 2 means D, ... and 7 means B. The choice to start with C and not A (or any other tone) as 1 is arbitrary, and it is very easy to change that when desired. C is represented by 1 and not 0 for consistency with the common use of Roman numerals for scale degrees, where the lowest degree is notated with the Roman numeral I. The variable *accidental* is an integer where 0 means ♮, and 1 means raising by the smallest step of the current equal temperament. In 12-EDO, 1 means ♯, −1 means ♭, −2 is ♭♭ and so on. This representation can also be implemented in a constraint system that only supports positive integer variables by adding a constant offset to all accidental variables.

The representation of the enharmonic spelling depends on the pitch classes of the C major scale: the *nominal* 1 is a reference to the pitch class at the first scale degree of C major, 2 refers to the second degree and so on. The same scheme can be used with any other scale to express scale degrees with a pair of integer variables ⟨*scaleDegree*, *scaleAccidental*⟩. The variable *scaleDegree* denotes the position of a pitch class in the declaration of the pitch classes of a given scale in $\mathcal{ST}$. If the variable *scaleAccidental* is 0 (♮), then the expressed pitch class is part of that scale. Otherwise, *scaleAccidental* denotes how far the expressed pitch class deviates from the pitch class at *scaleDegree*. This representation is used in the Schoenberg example described in Sect. 11.2.2 to constrain the raised scale degrees I, II, IV and V.

This schéme can further be used for chords with a pair of integer variables ⟨*chordDegree*, *chordAccidental*⟩. The integer variable *chordDegree* denotes a specific tone of a chord, e.g., its root, third, fifth, etc.; it is the position of a chord tone in its chord type declaration in $\mathcal{CT}$ (11.1), while *chordAccidental* indicates whether and how much the note deviates from a chord tone. This representation is also used in the model of Schoenberg's theory of harmony discussed above to recognise dissonances that should be resolved (e.g., any seventh in a seventh chord).

These representations are closely related. They all "split" the pitch class component *pc* into a tuple ⟨*degree*, *accidental*⟩. They only differ in the pitch class set they relate to (i.e., the seven-pitch nominals, a certain scale or a chord). The constraint between this pitch class set, the tuple ⟨*degree*, *accidental*⟩ and the pitch class of the *degree* is implemented in a uniform way by the constraint *degreeToPC*.

For example, let us consider the D major scale $PCs_{\text{D-major}}$, which in 12-EDO is the pitch class set {2, 4, 6, 7, 9, 11, 1}. The scale degree V♭ is A♭ in D major, which corresponds to the pitch class 8. This scale degree is represented by the degree-accidental-tuple ⟨5, −1⟩ (scale degree V flattened by a semitone). The relation between the underlying scale, the scale degree (including its accidental) and the corresponding pitch class is expressed by the constraint *degreeToPC*: *degreeToPC*($PCs_{\text{D-major}}$, ⟨5, −1⟩) = 8.

The constraint between the pitch classes of a chord, a "chord degree" (with its "chord accidental") and the corresponding pitch class is formally the same. It is also defined with the constraint *degreeToPC*, only that it depends on another pitch class set, the pitch classes of a given chord.

The definition of *degreeToPC* is shown in (11.12). It simply constrains the resulting pitch class to the pitch class in *PCs* at position *degree*—plus the corresponding *accidental*, but the modulus constraint with *psPerOct* ensures that the pitch class range is not exceeded. For example, in C major and 12-EDO, the degree I♭ results in the pitch class 11 and not −1, thanks to the modulus constraint. In (11.12), the element constraint actually requires a sequence of integers. Instead, the set *PCs* is notated here directly for simplicity. In the implementation of this constraint, the set

PCs is complemented by a matching sequence containing the elements of the set. Note that the order of elements is important.

$$degreeToPC(PCs, \langle degree, accidental \rangle) := \quad\quad (11.12)$$
$$(PCs[degree] + accidental) \bmod psPerOct.$$

Similar to the transposition of pitches and pitch classes, we need to complement our degree representation by a constraint that defines how degrees are transposed. For example, in the Schoenberg harmony model intervals between chord root scale degrees are controlled by constraints (e.g., remember that a descending progression is either a third down or fourth up between chord roots expressed by scale degrees).

It is sufficient that a degree transposition constraint restricts only the relation between pitch classes and their corresponding scale degrees. The accidentals are automatically constrained as well, as the constraint *degreeToPC* must still hold between every combination of degree, accidental and corresponding pitch class.

Consider again the D major scale $PCs_{\text{D-major}}$: transposing the degree V (A, pitch class 9) down by two scale degrees leads to the degree III (F♯, pitch class 6). We can express this relation with the constraint *transposeDegree*, where both tones and the transposition interval are represented by tuples of the form $\langle degree, pc \rangle$. Assuming that the accidentals of both tones are 0 (♮) and the transposition interval is diatonic (i.e., its accidental is also 0), we can state the transposition of degree V by two scale degrees downwards as follows: $transposeDegree(PCs_{\text{D-major}}, \langle 5, pc_1 \rangle,$ $\langle -2, pc_t \rangle) = \langle degree_2, pc_2 \rangle$. The solver can then automatically deduce that $pc_1 = 9$, the transposition interval $pc_t = 3$, the resulting scale degree $degree_2 = 3$ and its pitch class $pc_2 = 6$.

The definition of *transposeDegree* (11.13) binds the number of elements in the pitch class set (its cardinality, $|PCs|$) to l (e.g., 7 for a diatonic scale). It then computes from the untransposed degree $degree_1$, the degree transposition interval $degree_t$ and l with *modl* the transposed degree $degree_2$. The constraint *modl* (11.14) is a variation of the modulus constraint that returns numbers in $[1, l]$. That way, the lowest degree (the prime) is 1 and not 0. The transposed pitch class is computed with the constraint *transp-pc* discussed earlier (11.7).

$$transposeDegree(PCs, \langle degree_1, pc_1 \rangle, \langle degree_t, pc_t \rangle) := \quad\quad (11.13)$$
$$\textbf{let } l = |PCs|$$
$$degree_2 = modl(degree_1 + degree_t - 1, l)$$
$$pc_2 = transp\text{-}pc(pc, pc_t)$$
$$\textbf{in } \langle degree_2, pc_2 \rangle$$

$$modl(x, l) := (x - 1 \bmod l) + 1. \quad\quad (11.14)$$

The degree transposition for enharmonic notation, scale degrees and "chord degrees" are all done this way. As said before, they differ only in their relevant pitch class set, but of course they need separate variables for their degrees, accidentals and pitch classes that are then related to each other with *degreeToPC*.

11.4.6 Efficient Search with Constraint Propagation

The proposed framework has been designed with modern constraint solvers in mind, which employ constraint propagation for efficiency. Some music constraint systems already use as search algorithms a limited form of constraint propagation, which reduce variable domains before visiting these variables. Situation's constraint solver implements a variation of forward-checking [54]. The combination of BackTalk and MusES supports several classic arc-consistency enforcing algorithms (AC-3, AC-4, ..., AC-7), but only at the first stage of the search [52].

However, the author is not aware of a prior system for harmonic CSPs whose design is suitable for propagation-based constraint solvers. The efficient propagation algorithms of these solvers require that decision variables are restricted to a few types like Booleans, integers and sets of integers. By contrast, the music representation MusES has originally not been designed with CP in mind; and the variable domains of CSPs defined with MusES consist of complex SmallTalk objects.

Further, the explicit representation of analytic harmonic information by the proposed framework can speed up the search process by supporting propagation. Constraints on these explicit variables allow to interchange information that can help reducing domains. For example, if a certain harmonic CSP only allows for specific chord types, then this limits the possible pitch and pitch class interval combinations. Similarly, once the search determines a certain pitch class and related octave, then constraint propagation can automatically and without any further search determine the related pitch, scale degree and so forth.

An efficient search with the proposed framework is further helped by a suitable dynamic variable ordering. For example, for efficiency the implementation of the Schoenberg model visits variables in the following order. It completes all parts of the score parallel in score time, i.e., the undetermined variables of the score object with smallest start time are visited first. In case of ties (multiple variables belonging to objects with the same start time), first temporal variables are determined, then variables that belong to the underlying harmony (chords and scales), then note pitch classes and finally octaves (pitches are then automatically deduced by propagation as discussed above). In case there is still a tie (e.g., multiple note pitch classes belonging to objects with the same start time), then the variable with the smallest domain is visited first according to the *first fail* principle, a standard advice for designing variable orderings (for a variable with smaller domain it is more difficult to find a fitting value, and difficult cases are best handled first).

11.4.7 Implementation

The presented framework is implemented in the music constraint system Strasheela [4] on top of the Oz programming language [51]. Unfortunately, the development of the Oz programming language [42] slowed down over the years, which also affects Strasheela (e.g., CP is only supported by the old version 1 of Mozart, the Oz implementation).

Anyway, the presented framework can be implemented with any other constraint system that supports the following features found in various propagation-based constraint systems (e.g., Gecode, Choco, JaCoP, MiniZinc): the variable domains Boolean, integer and set of integers; constraints including reified constraints on integers and sets; and the element constraint. For details on the element constraint see [16] and also Sect. 11.4.3. Of course, the framework could also be implemented with a constraint system that does *not* support propagation, but then the search will be less efficient.

11.5   An Example: Modelling Schoenberg's Theory of Harmony

The proposed framework consists primarily of the constrainable harmony representation presented in the previous section. Developing concrete harmony models with this foundation is relatively straightforward: the variables in the representation are further constrained.

To show the framework in action with a real-live example, this section explains important details of the model of Schoenberg's tonal theory of harmony introduced above (Sect. 11.2.2). While we cannot discuss such an extensive model in full detail in the limited space of this chapter, we will cover the main ideas and how they are expressed formally within the proposed framework. The full source code is available online at [3].

11.5.1   Score Topology

The music representation of this example provides the score contexts necessary for applying all relevant rules. Figure 11.4 shows a schematic overview of this representation.

Four voices, each implemented as a sequential container (see Sect. 11.4.2) of notes, present the melodic contexts (for clarity called soprano, alto, tenor and bass in Fig. 11.4). These voices run simultaneously in time by being wrapped in a simultaneous container (again, see Sect. 11.4.2) called score in the figure alongside two further sequential containers. One sequence contains as many chords (underlying harmonies) as there are notes in each voice. Another sequence contains scales for expressing modulations. There are less scales necessary than notes or chords, as the underlying scale changes less often. The representation of the individual chords, scales and notes was introduced above in the Sects. 11.4.3 and 11.4.4.

The harmonic context of a note is represented by its simultaneous objects: the notes of the other voices, one simultaneous chord and one simultaneous scale. For example, $note_1$ of each voice as well as $chord_1$ and $scale_1$ are simultaneous in Fig. 11.4. The formalisation of the notion of simultaneous objects was define above (Sect. 11.4.2).

Fig. 11.4 Topology of the music representation for modelling Schoenberg's theory of harmony

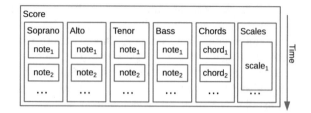

11.5.2 Pitch Resolution

This example is implemented in 31-tone equal temperament (31-EDO) instead of the standard 12-EDO, which Schoenberg so stunningly exhausted in his compositions. 31-EDO [30] is virtually the same as quarter-comma meantone, a common tuning in the sixteenth and seventeenth centuries. It can be notated with standard accidentals (♯, ♭, ♭♭ …). 31-EDO has been chosen, because it distinguishes enharmonic variants, e.g., C♯ and D♭ are different numeric pitch classes. At the same time, this representation allows for convenient pitch class calculations with consistent interval sizes much like 12-EDO, but with 31 different pitch class integers. More generally, the use of this temperament demonstrates that the presented framework supports microtonal music [10], though the intervals of this example are limited to the intervals of common practice music.

Other representations using a single number for pitch classes that distinguish enharmonically equivalent tones and where distances between tones consistently map to notated interval names could have been used as well, e.g., 41-EDO or the base-40 system [34]. Anyway, the meantone temperament of 31-EDO works better for tertian harmony. By contrast, while the enharmonic spelling representation introduced above (Sect. 11.4.5) would represent the same information, it would have been somewhat less economical, because two further variables (the nominal and accidental) would have been added to every note (and certain transposition intervals).

11.5.3 Chord Types

In his harmony book, Schoenberg starts with the purely consonant triads major and minor, and by and by introduces the diminished triad, various seventh chords, the augmented triad (when discussing minor keys), ninth chords and so on up to chords with six or more tones. Arbitrary collections of chord types can be declared with the proposed framework as discussed above (see Sect. 11.4.2), and chord types can be easily added to or removed from a constraint model. For example, for relatively conventional results the four triad types (major, minor, diminished and augmented) and several seventh chords (dominant 7th, major 7th, minor 7th, diminished 7th and halve-diminished 7th) can be declared in this model.

11.5.4   Part Writing Rules

Several score contexts involving only notes and not chords and scales are controlled by part writing rules in this model. Such rules constrain the pitches of consecutive notes in a single voice (e.g., restricting melodic intervals), simultaneous notes across voices (e.g., restricting the intervals between voices), and a combination of these cases (e.g., for prohibiting parallels, and voice crossing). Such rules are typically inherited from counterpoint and are often discussed in the music constraints literature, e.g., by Ebcioglu [23], Schottstaedt [58] and Laurson [39, p. 229ff], while Sandred [55] and Anders and Miranda [11] present how arbitrary rules can be applied to various score contexts.

The proposed framework explicitly represents all relevant note information as variables, i.e., their temporal parameters and pitches, and the music representation provides access to score contexts such as consecutive and simultaneous notes. Arbitrary part writing rules can therefore also be defined with this framework by restricting these note variables.

As such rules are discussed elsewhere in the literature, we only present formal details for one simple example rule here. Voice crossing is prohibited by constraining the notes of an upper voice to be higher than the notes of a lower voice. For clarity, Eq. 11.15 defines this rule only between two specific parts, the *tenor* and the *bass*. The rule simply restricts the pitch of the bass note to never be higher than the simultaneous tenor note (the note with the same index i).

$$getPitch(bass_i) \leq getPitch(tenor_i). \tag{11.15}$$

We are slightly changing the notation here from the former subscript notation (e.g., $pitch_n$) to a function-call notation (e.g., $getPitch(n)$). While the former notation is convenient for shorter formulas, this latter notation is better suited as a pseudo-code notation for a more complex model, e.g., to avoid nesting indices like $pitch_{n_i}$. Nevertheless, we are not switching to a strict functional notation, e.g., still conveniently notate the index with a subscript (e.g., $bass_i$).

11.5.5   Simplified Root Progression Directions: Harmonic Band

A particular instructive aspect of Schoenberg's harmony textbook for composers when compared with most other such textbooks are his directions on composing chord root progressions (Piston [49] provides somewhat similar guidance, though less systematic). In his typical educational approach, Schoenberg introduces his guidance gradually in steps, starting with a more restricted rule set and later refining the rule set to allow for a wider range of solutions.

The initial harmonic progression rule is straightforward. For a smooth connection, consecutive chords should share at least one common tone. Schoenberg talks about their "harmonic band". For example, in D major, the degrees I (D major triad) and V (A major triad) share the common tone A.

Fig. 11.5 Harmonic solution of the Schoenberg model introduced so far: harmonic phrase of diatonic major and minor triads connected by a "harmonic band"; see text for details

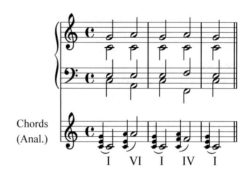

Chords (Anal.)

I   VI   I   IV   I

This rule can be formalised by a constraint between the pitch class sets of chords. The two consecutive chords $c1$ and $c2$ share common pitch classes if the intersection ($\cap$) between their pitch class sets is not empty ($\varnothing$) (11.16).

$$PCs_{c1} \cap PCs_{c2} \neq \varnothing. \tag{11.16}$$

Figure 11.5 shows a possible result of our CSP so far. The score topology is shown with the four homorhythmic voices in the two upper staves, but also the chords of the underlying harmony are notated on a third stave, again with chord tones like an appoggiatura and roots as normal notes. The scale is constant C major, which is not notated for simplicity, but it is explicitly represented in the CSP. The solution of a later version of the CSP showing a modulation and involving two scales also notates the underlying scales (see Fig. 11.11). The internal music representation stores various further analytical information as discussed before, at least the scale degrees are also translated into notation by the model.

In terms of chord types, this first example only uses major (primary) and minor (secondary) triads that are part of the underlying scale. You can also see the effect of the part writing rules. For example, all voices except for the bass only move stepwise, if at all; parallel fifths and octaves are avoided; the voices sound all tones of each triad; and voices don't cross.

To express the underlying key, this result starts and ends with the tonic: the roots of the first and last chords are constrained to the tonic of the underlying scale. Also, all chords are in root position here: all bass notes are set to the root of their underlying harmony. Finally, all consecutive chords are connected by a "harmonic band": the rule of Eq. (11.16) above is applied to all pairs of consecutive chords. For example, the first two chords in Fig. 11.5 both feature the tones C (in the bass, and held in the alto) and E (held in the tenor).

Note that this result could be one of the first harmonic phrases a student of Schoenberg's textbook writes—after having studied diatonic primary and secondary triads in the major scale, how they can be arranged for four sung voices, and how they can be connected pairwise when preserving a harmonic band between them. The result corresponds to Schoenberg's recommendations at the stage of chapter IV section "Connection of the Diatonic Primary and Secondary Triads in Short Phrases" of his textbook [57]. However, the following subsections progress in a different order than Schoenberg's textbook to simplify the pseudo-code by some code reuse and to reduce the length of the discussion overall.

11.5.6 Chord Inversions

Schoenberg initially asks his harmony students to write only chords in root position, which can be simply modelled by constraining the pitch classes of all notes in the bass to equal the root of their simultaneous chord. In later sections of his textbook, Schoenberg allows students to freely use chords in root position and first inversion for more flexibility of an expressive bass voice and more harmonic diversity.

With the means introduced in the discussion of the framework above, this is easily modelled with chords that also represent their *chordDegree* (Sect. 11.4.5). In a choral-like texture, the pitch class of the i-th bass note $bass_i$ is restricted to only certain tones of the chord c_i (the simultaneous chord), see Eq. (11.17). We restrict the pitch class of the bass note to one of the pitch class corresponding to either the first or the second chord degree (the root or the third) by a decision variable *chordDegree* with a domain restricted to the set $\{1, 2\}$. The previously defined constraint *degreeToPC* (11.12) controls the relation between the pitch classes of the chord c_i, its *chordDegree* (with the accidental set to 0, i.e., ♮) and the pitch class of the bass note $bass_i$.

$$
\textbf{let } chordDegree \in \{1, 2\} \tag{11.17}
$$
$$
\textbf{in } getPC(bass_i) = degreeToPC(getPCs(c_i), \langle chordDegree, 0 \rangle).
$$

You can see a possible solution in Fig. 11.6. It is a result of the same CSP discussed in the previous subsection, only that bass notes are no longer simply set to the root of their underlying harmony. Instead, the pitch classes of most bass tones are now constrained as defined in Eq. (11.17); only the first and last bass tones are still restricted to root position. In the shown solution, several chords happen to be in second inversion, namely, the second, third and fourth chord (the corresponding annotations of the Roman numerals in the score were done manually for clarity). Either inversion can occur freely here.

Fig. 11.6 A solution where now first and second inversions are permitted

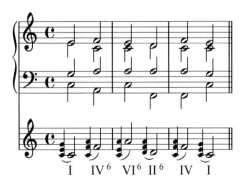

In a more complex texture, only certain bass notes might be constrained this way (e.g., only the lowest note of a phrase above a longer chord), and the condition whether a bass note is constrained this way or not can be implemented with a reified constraint (e.g., implication, where the constrained is only applied when the condition is true).

11.5.7 Refined Root Progression Rules

In his refined directions on chord root progressions, Schoenberg distinguishes between *ascending, descending* and *superstrong* progressions, as outlined in Sect. 11.2.2. In short, Schoenberg advices to primarily use ascending progressions, to save superstrong progressions for situations when strong means are desired (e.g., in cadences including deceptive cadences, see below) and to generally avoid descending progressions (except two consecutive descending progressions form together a strong progression).

The three different root progression cases can be formalised by constraints on the scale degree intervals between chord roots. In an *ascending* root progression, the interval between chord roots is either a fourth upwards or a third downwards. The constraint *fourthUpProgression* (11.18) restricts the interval between the scale degrees of the roots of the chords c_1 and c_2 to a fourth upwards. By restricting the scale degrees and not the pitch classes of the roots this definition covers also the augmented fourth (e.g., between the scale degrees IV and VII in major). The constraint *fourthUpProgression* constrains this interval by simply calling the previously defined constraint *transposeDegree* (11.13) with the pitch classes of the underlying scale PCs_s (again a sequence represented by a pitch class set for brevity), tuples with the scale degrees and roots of the two chords and the scale degree transposition interval 4 (a fourth upwards). The variable name_ stands for an ignored variable whose value is irrelevant (it is deduced automatically depending on the accidentals of the degrees involved, and these are all ♮, i.e., 0, here).

$$fourthUpProgression(c_1, c_2) :=$$
$$\langle scaleDegree(c_2), root(c_2)\rangle = transposeDegree(PCs_s,$$
$$\langle scaleDegree(c_1), root(c_1)\rangle,$$
$$\langle 4, \_\rangle).$$

$$(11.18)$$

The constraint *thirdDownProgression* (11.19) is a copy of *fourthUpProgression* except for a different scale degree transposition interval. The constraint *ascending* can then be defined simply as a disjunction (logical *or*, $\vee$) between *fourthUpProgression* and *thirdDownProgression* (11.20). The other root progression cases can be defined in the same way, only with different intervals: fourth down or third up for *descending* and second up or down for *superstrong*.

Fig. 11.7 A solution with only ascending progressions

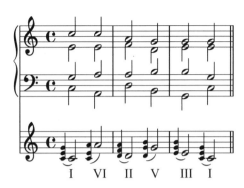

$$thirdDownProgression(c_1, c_2) :=$$
$$\langle scaleDegree(c_2), root(c_2)\rangle = transposeDegree(PCs_s,$$
$$\langle scaleDegree(c_1), root(c_1)\rangle,$$
$$\langle -3, \_\rangle).$$

$$(11.19)$$

$$ascending_1(c_1, c_2) := \quad fourthUpProgression(c_1, c_2) \qquad (11.20)$$
$$\vee \ thirdDownProgression(c_1, c_2).$$

Schoenberg discusses his directions on root progressions in detail (and colourful images) reasoning, e.g., why an ascending V–I progressions feels like a resolution: the first chord yields to the power of the second chord with a root a fifth below as it is absorbed in the second chord. Schoenberg talks of a prince who yields to the stronger power of his king.

Only ascending progressions where allowed in the next solution (Fig. 11.7) to first clearly demonstrate the effect of this progression constraint. This solution first progresses a third down (from degree I to VI), then a fourth up (or fifth down, VI to II), another fourth up (II to V) and so on.

Instead of modelling the directions on root progressions by constraints on scale degree intervals, we can also formally model Schoenberg's reasoning by constrains between chord pitch class sets and their roots. In an ascending progression, the root of the first chord c_1 is an element of the pitch class set of the second chord c_2, but not the other way round (expressed by a logical *and*, $\wedge$)—the root of c_2 is a new tone (11.21). For triads, this second rule formalisation leads to the same results as the rule implemented with scale degree intervals, but for other chords (e.g., seventh chords) this is not necessarily the case. However, this second formalisation is more generic and can also be used for non-diatonic scales and microtonal music. Anders and Miranda [9] presents a formalisation of all of Schoenberg's root progressions directions using this second approach.

$$ascending_2(c_1, c_2) := \quad root(c_2) \notin PCs(c_1) \qquad (11.21)$$
$$\wedge \ root(c_1) \in PCs(c_2).$$

Fig. 11.8 A solution featuring ascending, superstrong and descending progressions, but the treatment of descending progressions follows Schoenberg's directions (see text)

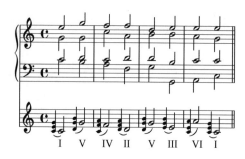

I   V   IV   II   V   III   VI   I

Ascending progressions are rather smoothly connected and Schoenberg recommends using them primarily. An occasional superstrong progression—where consecutive chords do not share common tones—creates some contrast. Schoenberg advises his harmony students to avoid descending progressions except for cases where in a quasi "passing chord" a descending progression and a neighbour progression together form an ascending or superstrong progression.

These directions are implemented in the next CSP; Fig. 11.8 displays a solution. The chord sequence starts with descending progressions a fifth up (I–V) and proceeds with a superstrong progression (V–IV). However, if the second chord is considered a "passing chord", the progression from the first chord I to the third chord IV is ascending (a fourth up).

You might note that some chords occur more than once (the second and fifth chords are both V), but these chords happen to be in different inversions thanks to the randomised search process, which leads to more variety. You might also note that by and by the solutions become longer. With increased harmonic means we are now able to generated somewhat longer chord progressions that retain interest.

11.5.8 Cadences

Schoenberg's textbook explicates that a key is expressed by the exclusive use of all its tones. To clearly express a key (tonality in Schoenberg's words), it must be clearly distinguished from other keys, in particular those that are closest to it. For example, the C major scale is distinguished from F major by the tone B (instead of the B♭ of F major) and from G major by the tone F (instead of the F♯ of G major). Further, to conclude a piece the cadence leads to I, the chord over the scale's tonic,

These two restrictions alone allow for a wide range of chord progressions, including solutions beyond Schoenberg's recommendations for a cadence, but they are a useful foundation for later refinements. Equation (11.22) formalises these restrictions. The constraint *cadenceFoundation* expects a chord sequence cs (besides a scale s), so that this constraint can be applied to an arbitrarily long chord progression to ensure that it ends in a cadence. The root (tonic) of the scale s equals the root of the last chord (bound to the local variable c_{last}). In addition, the union ($\cup$) of all pitch classes of the last n chords (cs_{lastN}) equals the pitch class set of the scale s; n

defaults to three. This last expression enforces that the cadence chords express all tones of the scale s (the tonality) and no other tone.

$$cadenceFoundation(s, cs, n = 3) :=$$ (11.22)

$$\textbf{let } c_{last} = \text{last element in } cs$$
$$cs_{lastN} = \text{last } n\text{element in } cs$$
$$\textbf{in } \quad getRoot(s) = getRoot(c_{last})$$
$$\wedge \ getPCs(s) = \bigcup getPCs(cs_{lastN}).$$

The above definition can be expanded to describe an authentic cadence, the most commonly used cadence. The definition *authenticCadence* (11.23) constrains again the end of an arbitrarily long chord progression cs. The constraint allows for an ending with the chords II–V–I or IV–V–I. For convenience, the last three chords are bound to local variables, c_{ante}, c_{pen} and c_{last}. The progression from the antepenultimate to the penultimate chord must be either ascending or superstrong (see Sect. 11.5.7). Together with the other constraints of this definition, this restricts the antepenultimate chord to either II or IV. We could directly set the chords to these scale degrees, but the constraints applied here better clarify the harmonic relations. Also, changes of the overall definition, e.g., removing the restriction that all scale pitch classes must be expressed, allow for further variants.

The last harmonic progression should be decisive, and the most decisive progression is the interval of a fourth upwards between chord roots, an ascending harmonic progression. Together with the other constraints, the constraint *fourthUpProgression* (11.18) enforces the last two chords to V–I. Finally, the scale and chords are restricted by the above-discussed constraint *cadenceFoundation*. For harmonic clarity, we could additionally restrict the dominant (the penultimate chord) and/or tonic (last chord) to root position by constraining their bass note chord degrees to 1 in a variant of the constraint in Eq. (11.17).

$$authenticCadence(s, cs) :=$$ (11.23)

$$\textbf{let } c_{ante} = \text{antepenultimate chord of } cs$$
$$c_{pen} = \text{penultimate chord of } cs$$
$$c_{last} = \text{last chord of } cs$$
$$\textbf{in } \quad (ascending(c_{ante}, c_{pen})$$
$$\vee \ superstrong(c_{ante}, c_{pen}))$$
$$\wedge \ fourthUpProgression(c_{pen}, c_{last})$$
$$\wedge \ cadenceFoundation(s, cs).$$

A solution with an authentic cadence is depicted in Fig. 11.9: the harmonic progression ends with the chords II–V–I (D minor, G major, C major). It is by chance a perfect authentic cadence (the cadence chords are in root position and the last soprano note is also the tonic, C), but this is not enforced by our CSP.

The constraint *cadenceFoundation* (11.22) restricts the cadence chords to contain together all pitch classes of the scale and no others, which can be confirmed in Fig. 11.9. The union of the pitch classes of the last three chords is C, D, E, F, G, A, B, which are the pitch classes of the C major scale. The present

Fig. 11.9 A solution where an authentic cadence is now enforced

CSP version also somewhat loosened the restriction on melodic intervals and allows for slightly larger intervals.

The deceptive cadence can be defined similarly to *authenticCadence*, but the progression between the last two chords is controlled by the constraint *superstrong* instead—and the root of the last chord is not constrained to the root (tonic) of the scale. To limit the deceptive cadence to the standard cases V–VI and V–IV, the scale degree of the root of the penultimate chord must also be set to 5.

An extension of the definition *authenticCadence* inserts a $^6_4$-chord before the dominant. A $^6_4$-chord is enforced by restricting the bass note to the pitch class that corresponds to the *chordDegree* of this chord set to 3—like we previously restricted the result to either root positions or inversions (see Sect. 11.5.6). The $^6_4$-chord is then also constrained to the scale degree I (the tonic of the scale), as we already did with the last chord in the definition *cadenceFoundation* (11.22).

11.5.9 Dissonance Treatment

Schoenberg's textbook teaches as musically "safest" form of dissonance treatment the preparation and resolution of a dissonance. A dissonance is, e.g., the diminished fifths of a diminished triad or the seventh of a seventh chord. The dissonance is prepared by including it as a consonance in the previous chord. It is resolved commonly by a downward step into the next chord. For a strong feeling of a resolution, the chord root may progress from the dissonant chord by a fourth upwards into the next chord (e.g., from the dominant into the tonic).

To prepare or resolve a dissonant note in an individual voice, we need to detect whether the pitch class of a note is a dissonance in the underlying chord. This information depends on the *chordDegree* of the note's pitch class with respect to the underlying chord, but also on the *type* of the underlying chord. When we represent chord degrees in the order *root, third, fifth, seventh, ...*, then any chord degree that is larger than 3 is a dissonance. However, if we also allow for chords like the diminished triad or diminished seventh chords, then already the chord degree 3 is a dissonance. We therefore need to take both the *chordDegree* and the *type* of the chord into account.

The dissonance resolution of a note n_i is formalised in Eq. (11.24), where i is the position of the note in its voice. This rule is expressed by an implication ($\Rightarrow$, a reified constraint). The left-hand side of the implication expresses the condition; it tests whether n_i is a dissonance. The right-hand side expresses the consequence how n_i has to be resolved if it is indeed a dissonance.

The dissonance test (left-hand side of the implication) takes both the *chordDegree* and the chord *type* into account as just discussed. The chord c_i is the underlying harmony of the potentially dissonant note n_i (they share the same position and are simultaneous). The function call *getMinDissChordDegree*(c_i) returns the lowest chord degree that is dissonant for this chord type: if the type of this chord is a diminished (or augmented) chord it returns 3, and 4 for a seventh chord, etc. (this information is stored in an extended version of $\mathcal{CT}$, and is also accessed by the element constraint). The function *getChordDegree* applied to a note returns the chord degree of the simultaneous chord object that corresponds with the note's pitch class. If the note's chord degree is equal or greater than the lowest chord degree that is dissonant for this chord, then this note is a dissonance.

The implication's consequence (right-hand side) constrains the pitch intervals into and out of the dissonance. For better legibility it first introduces three auxiliary variables for the pitches of the three consecutive notes, where p_{i-1} is the pitch of the predecessor note in the same voice, p_i is the pitch of the potentially dissonant note and p_{i+1} the successor's pitch. If n_i is a dissonance, then it must share the pitch of the previous note. Also, the pitch interval (absolute difference) to the successor note must be a step, i.e., less than or equal *maxStep* (e.g., 2 semitones for 12-EDO, or 6 for 31-EDO), and it must be a downward interval, i.e., p_i is greater than p_{i+1}.

$$
\begin{aligned}
getChordDegree(n_i) &\geq getMinDissChordDegree(c_i) \Rightarrow \\
\textbf{let}\ \ p_{i-1} &= getPitch(n_{i-1}) \\
p_i &= getPitch(n_i) \\
p_{i+1} &= getPitch(n_{i+1}) \\
\textbf{in}\quad\ \ p_{i-1} &= p_i \qquad\qquad\ \text{(same pitch as predecessor note)} \\
\wedge\ |p_{i+1} - p_i| &\leq maxStep \quad \text{(step to successor)} \\
\wedge\ \ p_i &> p_{i+1} \qquad\quad\ \text{(downward interval to successor)}
\end{aligned}
\tag{11.24}
$$

We can enforce a strong harmonic progression by an additional constraint between a dissonant chord and its successor as expressed in Eq. (11.25). The constraint *isConsonant* checks whether the type of a given chord is a consonant triad (again, this information is stored in an extended version of $\mathcal{CT}$ and accessed by the element constraint). If it is not ($\neg$), then *fourthUpProgression* (11.18) is applied between the chords. We could have used here the more general constraint *ascending* defined above (Sect. 11.5.7), but *fourthUpProgression* is a particularly convincing harmonic resolution in this context, which Schoenberg initially recommends when introducing dissonance treatment.

$$
\neg isConsonant(type_{c_i}) \Rightarrow fourthUpProgression(c_i, c_{i+1}).
\tag{11.25}
$$

At a later stage in his textbook, Schoenberg relaxes these constraints to allow for more harmonic flexibility. The dissonance is then not necessarily prepared

Fig. 11.10 A solution with diminished triads and seventh chords with resolved dissonances

I   IV   VII VI   IV   III   II   V   I

anymore and the harmony can progress into other chords more freely, but the reso-lution of the dissonance by a downward step is still recommended, until later also that recommendation is loosened.

The solution in Fig. 11.10 features multiple dissonant chords, three seventh chords (easily recognisable by four instead of three appoggiatura tones in the chords stave: the second chord, IV, and at the end II and V) and a diminished triad (VII). In this CSP version, the dissonance treatment is already relaxed and only a stepwise dissonance resolution is enforced, but the other recommendations (dissonance preparation and progression by a fourth upwards) happen to also still be fulfilled in most cases.

For each dissonant chord, the dissonance is resolved by a downward step. For example, in the second chord (IV, F major) the dissonant seventh is E (in the alto), which is resolved by a step downwards into D in the following chord. This dissonance also happens to be prepared: the E is already present in the previous chord. The root progression from this second chord into the following chord also happens by a fourth up into the chord VII. This root progression interval is actually a tritone, but in his textbook Schoenberg treats such a root progression like a progression a fourth up, which is consistent with the treatment of this progression, e.g., in a descending fifths sequence. In the VII chord now in turn the dissonance is the diminished fifth (F), which again is resolved by a downward step into E in the following chord. This dissonant F is coincidentally also prepared in the previous chord. However, this VII chord is not resolved by a fourth up root progression here (which would lead into III), but instead by a superstrong progression a second down. Further on, the dissonance of the chord II (the C of the D minor chord) is also resolved by a downward step. Yet, this dissonance is not prepared by the strict condition of being already present in the previous chord, but instead in the more relaxed way of a semitone step from the B of the previous chord into the dissonant C.

There are rather many superstrong chord progressions in this particular solution: the chord roots of VII, IV and III all progress by a downward step. As mentioned above, such progressions lack common pitches between consecutive chords, which make them less connected, and Schoenberg recommends to use them sparingly. We could (and actually do in other CSP versions in this chapter) reduce their occurrence by simply limiting their number with a constraint applied across multiple chords. It is worth noting, however, that in general probabilities are difficult to control with CP.

11.5.10 Modulation

For modulations between close keys, Schoenberg presents a scheme that consists of three parts. After establishing the original key, the modulation starts by one or more neutral chords, i.e., chords that are part of both keys. For example, when modulating from C major to G major, all diatonic chords without the tones F or F♯ could serve as neutral chords. Next, the actual modulation follows with the modulation chord, which is part of the new key only. An ascending root progression can help making the movement from the modulatory chord on to its successor more convincing. Finally, the new key is confirmed with a cadence.

Our definition below (11.26) assumes for brevity that the original key has been established before (as Schoenberg does when teaching modulation). It defines a modulation over a sequence of chords cs from the initial scale s_1 to the target scale s_2. The variable $neutralLength$ sets the (minimum) number of neutral chords that belong to both scales and occur before the modulation chord. The last three chords that will form the cadence are $cs_{cadence}$.

Most constraints of this definition have been introduced earlier. After the actual modulation (discussed in a minute), Eq. (11.26) requires that the modulatory chord is left by a strong root progression, specifically, by a fourth upwards (11.18). The modulation chord is the chord just after the neutral chords, i.e., the chord in cs at position $neutralLength + 1$. The last three chords are constrained to form a cadence, e.g., an authentic cadence (11.23).

$$
\begin{aligned}
\textbf{let } cs &= \text{sequence of chords} \qquad\qquad\qquad\qquad (11.26)\\
s_1 &= \text{original scale}\\
s_2 &= \text{target scale}\\
neutralLength &= 1\\
cs_{cadence} &= \text{last 3 elements of } cs\\
\textbf{in } \ & modulation(cs, s_1, s_2, neutralLength)\\
& fourthUpProgression(c_{neutralLength+1}, c_{neutralLength+2})\\
& authenticCadence(s, cs_{cadence}).
\end{aligned}
$$

The actual modulation is defined by the constraint $modulation$ (11.27), which restricts the relation between the sequence of chords cs, the original scale s_1, the target scale s_2 and the number of neutral chords $neutralLength$. The constraint defines several auxiliary variables. The variable $neutralPCs$ is bound to the pitch classes that belong to both scales (s_1 and s_2), namely, the intersection between the pitch classes of these scales, while $neutralChords$ are the chords from cs that will be constrained to form the neutral chords. The constraint restricting neutral chords follows after the keyword **in** in Eq. (11.27): the pitch classes of every ($\forall$) chord c from the $neutralChords$ is a subset ($\subset$) of the set of neutral pitch classes $neutralPCs$.

$$modulation(cs, s_1, s_2, neutralLength) :=$$ (11.27)

  let $neutralPCs = getPCs(s_1) \cap getPCs(s_2)$
      $neutralChords =$ the first $neutralLength$ elements of cs
      $modulationPCs = getPCs(s_2) \setminus getPCs(s_1)$
      $modulationPC$
  in $\forall c \in neutralChords : getPCs(c) \subset neutralPCs.$
      $modulationPC \in modulationPCs$
      $modulationPC \in getPCs(cs_{neutralLength+1})$

The auxiliary variable *modulationPCs* are the pitch classes of the target scale s_2 that are *not* part of the original scale s_1, which is implemented by the set difference ($\setminus$) between the pitch class sets of these scales. The auxiliary variable *modulationPC* is just one arbitrary element of the set *modulationPCs*. This modulation pitch class *modulationPC* must be an element of the modulation chord (the chord just after the neutral chords).

We previously in Fig. 11.2 saw a solution modulating a fifth upwards from C major to G major, but that example used already richer harmonic means with non-diatonic tones originating from church modes, which we do not have the room to formally model here. We also do not have the space to introduce minor and the special treatment Schoenberg recommends for its raised sixth and seventh degrees. The only modulation to a very close key that is outstanding is therefore the modulation a fifth downwards, e.g., from C major to F major.

Figure 11.11 shows a solution to such a modulation. This score example now shows the topology of the music representation more fully: it displays not only the chords of the underlying harmony on a third stave, but also the scales on a fourth stave. Similar to the chords, the scale tones are notated like an appoggiatura and the tonics as normal notes.

Fig. 11.11 A solution for modulating a fifth down from C major to F major

Schoenberg notes that the modulation a fifth down may feel "too easy", as the I of the initial key is already the dominant of the target key (e.g., C major is V of F major). He recommends to use richer means, e.g., at least the dominant seventh chord as modulation chord. The solution in Fig. 11.11 uses that chord in the final cadence in the target key (penultimate chord in Fig. 11.11).

This CSP enforces at least one neutral chord directly before the modulation chord. In the present solution coincidentally there are three neutral chords, as chords before the enforced neutral chord are free to be neutral chords as well: I, II and IV. These chords only use the six tones that are shared by both initial and target key, i.e., avoid both B and B♭. The modulation chord in this example is II^7 of the new key, which is followed by the new V (the former I, C major) and the new I, but this tonic happens to be a seventh chord I^7. These three chords clearly express the new key, but the I^7 is not conclusive and the chord progression continues until a final cadence.

11.6 Discussion

This section compares the presented framework with previous systems and discusses the limitations of the framework. The section then details which concepts of Schoenberg's harmony textbook are omitted by the example presented in the previous section.

11.6.1 Comparison with Previous Systems

Quite a number of constraint-based harmony models have been proposed. However, only some of these systems allow users to define their own harmonic rules so that they are relevant for the algorithmic composer.

In contrast to most previous music constraint systems for algorithmic composition, the framework proposed in Sect. 11.4 explicitly represents analytical information like chord and scale types, their root/tonic and so forth. The representation of such harmonic pieces of information by explicit variables allows to directly constrain such information, which simplifies complex harmony models.

Constraint-based systems that represent polyphonic music such as Score-PMC (part of PWConstraints) and Cluster Engine do in principle allow for defining harmonic CSPs, where the underlying harmony is simply represented by concrete chords consisting of actual notes with pitches. Certain analytical information like the chord type can be deduced in such case (e.g., by extracting the pitch classes of chords with the modulus operator and then deducing the normal form of these pitch class sets). However, other information, like the root of a chord, or scale and chord degrees and their corresponding accidentals are more difficult to deduced from a representation that explicitly only represents pitches. As a consequence, complex harmonic CSPs are more difficult to define in these systems—due to their lack of explicitly represented analytical information.

The combination of MusES and BackTalk is the only music constraint system (besides Stasheela, see Sect. 11.4.7) with an explicit representation of analytic harmonic information of which the author is aware. The framework proposed here is largely comparable in terms of its flexibility with the combination of MusES and BackTalk, although it has a different stylistic focus. MusES was designed for Jazz, while this research focuses on classical tonal music and contemporary music in an extended tonality and also supports microtonal music.

11.6.2 Limitations of the Framework

The proposed design of the framework is best suited for tonal music. For example, any atonal pitch class set can be declared as well, but then information like the chord root is redundant (it can simply be ignored in a model, though).

While the framework supports tonal music in an extended sense (see Sect. 11.2.3) and also microtonal music, it is less suitable for spectral music composition. Spectral music [29] is based on absolute frequencies (and their intervals) translated into pitches. This approach preserves the octave of each pitch and that way the order of pitches in a chord. By contrast, in the proposed model chord and scale types are expressed by pitch classes. Individual chord or scale pitches can thus be freely octave transposed while retaining the chord or scale identity. Such an approach allows to control melodic and harmonic aspects independently with constraints.

The proposed model could be changed to better support spectral music by expressing chords with absolute pitches instead of pitch classes, and by disregarding all information based on pitch classes (chord roots, scale degrees, etc.), but then tonal music theories depending on such analytical information that is independent of an octave component cannot be modelled anymore. The music constraint system PWMC [55] and its successor Cluster Engine implement such an approach.

A compromise could be special rules that constrain specific chord tones—e.g., tones at or above a certain *chordDegree*—into or above certain octaves, or above other chord tones, like some popular music voicing recommendations do (e.g., in a $V^{\sharp 9}$ chord, the augmented ninth is preferred above the major third).

The framework supports microtonal music, but only equal divisions of the octave. Specifically, just intonation intervals are best represented by ratios, and unequal temperaments with floats, but the proposed framework only uses integers, because constraint propagation works very efficiently for those. Nevertheless, just intonation intervals can be approximated by equal temperaments (e.g., with cent precision using 1200-EDO).

11.6.3 Completeness of Schoenberg Model

The presented example models core ideas of Schoenberg's harmony textbook (see Sect. 11.5), but it does not implement it fully. Even though much of Schoenberg's textbook is spend reflecting and reasoning about ideas and directions given (and also on polemic remarks), its 500 pages are far beyond the scope of this chapter. More specifically, the code used for generating results like the one shown in Fig. 11.2 models the main ideas of about the first half of Schoenberg's textbook.

For completeness, here we briefly summarise details that have been left out. We ignored guidelines on the spacing and voicing of chords (e.g., details on the pitch range of voices or which tones can be doubled in certain situations). Also, the treatment of second inversions is slighty simplified (its more liberal treatment as a "passing chord" is left out). We skipped modelling minor keys. The minor keys introduce optionally raised VI♯ and VII♯ degrees, which leads to 9 scale tones and 13 triads in the minor scale. However, Schoenberg recommends that the natural and the raised degrees should not be mixed to preserve the character of the minor scale. This requires careful treatment of the raised and non-raised tones. This treatment can be modelled rather easily in the presented framework with constraints on scale degrees and their corresponding accidentals. Support for minor keys is already included in the implementation source.

The result shown in Sect. 11.2.2 already allowed for secondary dominants and other non-diatonic tones derived from church modes (implemented with constraints on scale degrees and the corresponding accidentals), but we did not discuss the formal details of such non-diatonic tones.

Further, the model presented here ignores the second half of the textbooks, starting with a chapter on rhythm (metre) and harmony. These skipped details include modulation into more remote keys, further alterations (e.g., derived from the minor subdominant with a flat VI♭ degree), ninth chords, etc. For example, for modulations into three or four degrees alongside the circle of fifth (e.g., from C to A or E major) Schoenberg recommends using the relation of parallel keys; modulations two "circles" upwards or downwards (e.g., from C to D major) or five to six "circles" are performed via intermediate keys (somewhat simplified).

11.7 Future Research

This section offers two suggestions for future research directions in the field of modelling harmony with CP.

11.7.1 Supporting Musical Form with Harmony

Existing constraint-based models of harmony tend to treat harmony in a way that is either independent of considerations of musical form, or which is limited to relatively short pieces such as songs or chorals. However, suitable harmonic means in music composition depend on compositional purposes. For example, in classical sonata form, the harmony of the development is typically far more complex than the harmony of the exposition or recapitulation.

Existing systems already offer some means for shaping harmonic developments over time. Situation [12,53] offers a mini-language expressing index patterns that control which objects (e.g., which chords) in a sequence are affected by a given combination of a constraint and its arguments. These constraints can affect various aspects of the chords at the specified indices including required tones or intervals, the development of the overall ambitus of chords, patterns of melodic intervals and so on. Also other constraint systems (e.g., PWConstraints, Strasheela and Cluster Engine) allow for applying constraints only to individual objects at certain positions in a sequence, but Situation supports doing this for index combinations (e.g., index ranges) in a particularly concise way, which turns this idea into a compositional tool for shaping the harmonic development.

The system COPPELIA [64] composes music intended to support the structure and contents of given multimedia presentations. To this end, one subsystem generates harmonic plans for a sequence of very short sections with different purposes (e.g., opening, announcement or transition) that translate musical parameters (e.g., the harmony can be calm, cadencing, express tension or an increasing tension) into Riemannian chord symbols, which a second subsystem then translates into a homorhythmic chord progression. The constraints in this system are hard-coded, though some settings can be changed by a user interface.

Beyond constraint-based systems, with the real-time chord sequence generation system described by Eigenfeldt and Pasquier [27] users can control the development of musical features such as the bass line, harmonic complexity (dissonance degree) and voice-leading tension (related to common tones between consecutive chords), e.g., using envelopes.

However, what is missing are computer-assisted ways that support the structuring of harmonic developments for larger musical forms in a way that is stylistically flexible and takes the specific harmonic needs for different form sections into account. Of course, in the final composition such harmonic developments for formal sections only serve their purpose if also other musical means support it (e.g., the motivic or gestural content of a transition tends to be rather repetitive and leads into a certain direction).

For conventional tonal harmony, a good starting point for modelling structural considerations could be Schoenberg's second harmony book [56]. In chapter XI of that book, Schoenberg discusses progressions for various compositional purposes and formal segments such as different theme constructions (sentence and period), contrasting middle sections, sequences, transitions and so on.

Fundamental principles of form for conventional tonal harmony can also be relevant for other styles where harmony plays a role. For example, a contrasting section may present new pitch materials (a generalisation of the notion of a modulating middle section), or for a transition it can be helpful if the harmonic progression is rather predictable.

11.7.2   Combining Rule-Based Composition with Machine Learning

Both learning-based and rule-based approaches have been very successful for algo-rithmically modelling music composition. These two general approaches mimic aspects of how humans (learn to) compose. Rules have been used for centuries for teaching specific details of composition that are less obvious at the surface level (e.g., certain harmonic relations), while composers learn from examples of existing music aspects that are more easily to grasp intuitively for humans and that are also more difficult to control by rules (e.g., aspects of how to compose a melody; or how to mimic typical accompaniments and accompaniment textures of a certain style).

As combining rules and learning from examples helps humans when compos-ing, it would be very interesting to combine these two general approaches also for algorithmic composition. This could be done by either using some hybrid approach where the output generated with one method is refined with another, or by finding a unifying formalism that allows for implementing both rules and Machine Learning. For example, the composer Jacopo Baboni-Schilingi uses CP to refine parameter sequences that have been generated with other algorithmic techniques [7]. Perhaps a similar hybrid approach could be used for refining with a rule-based approach results generated with some method based on Machine Learning.

One approach of a unifying formalism could be learning rules with Machine Learning. First steps have already been taken in that direction. For example, Morales and Morales [41] used Inductive Logic Programming, a Machine Learning tech-nique for learning first-order logic formulas, to learn counterpoint rules (how to avoid open parallels). Anglade and Dixon [13] also used Inductive Logic Program-ming for extracting harmonic rules from two music corpora, Beatles songs (Pop Music) and the Real Book (Jazz), which express differences between these corpora. Genetic Programming is a Machine Learning technique capable of learning formulas consisting of both logic and numeric relations. Anders and Inden [8] used Genetic Programming for learning rules on dissonance treatment from a corpus of music by Palestrina.

Another approach might be using Machine Learning as a unifying formalism, where a Machine Learning technique learns explicitly given rules. At the core of Deep Learning [32] lies the computation of an error (cost, loss) during training between the intended output for a given input and a neural network's actual output—coupled with the ability to gradually adapt the network (typically the weights of neurons) to reduce that error. The direction into which the weights must be adapted for reducing the error is computed with the derivative (gradient) of the cost/loss function.

It would be interesting to customise the computation of the error by additionally taking into account how far a neural network's actual output violates explicitly given rules. Such rules could perhaps have a format similar to heuristic rules of music constraint systems like PWConstraints or Cluster Engine, which return a number expressing how far they are violated. However, adding explicitly given rules to the computation of a neural network's error would require that this expanded error func-tion is still differentiable so that the learning process still "knows" in which way to improve the weights of the neural net. Differentiable programming allows for computing the gradient of complex programmes, which may use, e.g., control flow, functions, higher order functions and nested data structures. For example, a promising development in this direction is the recent Julia [17] library Zygote [38], which aims for computing gradients for arbitrary Julia programmes.

11.8 Summary

The Constraint Programming paradigm offers a powerful means for modelling harmony. While approaches based on Machine Learning work well for emulating the harmonic language of existing styles, CP is a compelling tool for composers interested in creating their own harmonic language with the help of algorithms.

This chapter presents a framework that simplifies the development of user-defined harmony models by providing suitable building blocks such as chords, scales and a variety of pitch representations. The supported pitch representations include pitch numbers, pitch classes, an enharmonic note representation, scale degrees of notes and chord roots, as well as chord "degrees" such as the fifth or the third of a triad. Accidentals allow for alterations of these degrees. Importantly, all these representations are freely constrainable. This rich representation leads to harmony constraint satisfaction problems with a high level of abstraction.

This framework is suitable for efficient propagation-based constraint solvers. The "types" (domains) of its decision variables are limited to the domains supported by various such solvers.

Application examples in this chapter demonstrate that the proposed framework is rather flexible. Multiple pieces of harmonic information can serve as input and output. For example, the paradigm allows for deriving a harmonic analysis of a given melody; to generate chord progressions that follow a set of rules; to constrain some score to express a given underlying harmony (including a suitable treatment of nonharmonic tones); and combinations of these scenarios.

The chapter also demonstrates that with CP even complex theories of harmony can be formalised with a manageable amount of code (when one considers the equations of this chapter as pseudo-code). The chapter formalises core ideas of Schoenberg's tonal theory of harmony including chord inversions, root progressions, cadences, dissonance treatment and modulation. What is important, though, are suitable levels of abstractions. For example, introducing variables for scale (and chord) degrees together with the corresponding accidentals greatly simplified the formalisation of many Schoenbergian rules.

References

1. Anders, T. (2007). *Composing music by composing rules: Design and usage of a generic music constraint system*. Ph.D. thesis, School of Music & Sonic Arts, Queen's University Belfast.
2. Anders, T. (2011). Variable orderings for solving musical constraint satisfaction problems. In G. Assayag & C. Truchet (Eds.), *Constraint programming in music* (pp. 25–54). London: Wiley.
3. Anders, T. (2013a). *Modelling Schoenberg's theory of harmony*. Retrieved February 05, 2020, from http://strasheela.sourceforge.net/strasheela/doc/Example-Schoenberg-TheoryOfHarmony.html.
4. Anders, T. (2013b). *Strasheela*. Retrieved February 05, 2020, from http://strasheela.sourceforge.net/.
5. Anders, T. (2014). Modelling durational accents for computer-aided composition. In *Proceedings of the 9th Conference on Interdisciplinary Musicology—CIM14* (pp. 90–93). Berlin, Germany.
6. Anders, T. (2016). Teaching rule-based algorithmic composition: The PWGL library cluster rules. *Journal of Pedagogic Development, 6*(1), 3–14.
7. Anders, T. (2018). Compositions created with constraint programming. In A. McLean & R. T. Dean (Eds.), *The oxford handbook of algorithmic music* (pp. 133–154). Press: Oxford University.
8. Anders, T., & Inden, B. (2019). Machine learning of symbolic compositional rules with genetic programming: Dissonance treatment in Palestrina. *PeerJ Computer Science, 5.e244.*
9. Anders, T., & Miranda, E. R. (2009). A computational model that generalises Schoenberg's guidelines for favourable chord progressions. In F. Gouyon, A. Barbosa, & X. Serra (Eds.), *6th Sound and Music Computing Conference* (pp. 48–52). Porto, Portugal. Retrieved February 05, 2020, from http://smc2009.smcnetwork.org/programme/pdfs/151.pdf.
10. Anders, T., & Miranda, E. R. (2010a). A computational model for rule-based microtonal music theories and composition. *Perspectives of New Music, 48*(2), 47–77.
11. Anders, T., & Miranda, E. R. (2010b). Constraint application with higher-order programming for modeling music theories. *Computer Music Journal, 34*(2), 25–38.
12. Anders, T., & Miranda, E. R. (2011). Constraint programming systems for modeling music theories and composition. *ACM Computing Surveys, 43*(4). Article 30, *30*(1), 38.
13. Anglade, A. & Dixon, S. (2008). Characterisation of harmony with inductive logic programming. *ISMIR*, 63–68.
14. Apt, K. R. (2003). *Principles of constraint programming*. Cambridge: Cambridge University Press.
15. Assayag, G., et al. (1999). Computer assisted composition at IRCAM: From PatchWork to OpenMusic. *Computer Music Journal, 23*(3), 59–72.
16. Beldiceanu, N., & Demassey, S. (2014). *Element*. Retrieved February 05, 2020, from https://sofdem.github.io/gccat/gccat/Celement.html.
17. Bezanson, J., et al. (2017). Julia: A fresh approach to numerical computing. *SIAM Review, 59*(1), 65–98.
18. Boulanger-Lewandowski, N., Bengio, Y., & Vincent, P. (2012). Modeling temporal dependencies in high-dimensional sequences: Application to polyphonic music generation and transcription. In *Proceedings of the 29th International Conference on Machine Learning* (ICML 2012).
19. Bratko, I. (2011). *Prolog. Programming for artificial intelligence* (4th ed.) Pearson Education.
20. Courtot, F. (1990). A constraint based logic program for generating polyphonies. In *Proceedings of the International Computer Music Conference* (pp. 292–294). San Francisco: International Computer Music Association.
21. Dechter, R. (2003). *Constraint processing*. San Francisco, CA: Morgan Kaufmann.

22. Doty, D. B. (2002). *The just intonation primer. An introduction to the theory and practice of just intonation* (3rd ed.) San Francisco, CA: Just Intonation Network.
23. Ebcioglu, K. (1980). Computer counterpoint. In *Proceedings of the International Computer Music Conference 1980* (pp. 534–543). San Francisco: International Computer Music Association.
24. Ebcioglu, K. (1987a). An efficient logic programming language and its application to music. In *Proceedings of Fourth International Conference on Logic Programming* (pp. 513–532). Melbourne: MIT Press.
25. Ebcioglu, K. (1987b). *Report on the CHORAL project: An expert system for harmonizing four-part chorales* (Tech. Rep. Report 12628). IBM, Thomas J. Watson Research Center.
26. Ebcioglu, K. (1992). An expert system for harmonizing chorales in the style of J. S. Bach. In M. Balaban, K. Ebcioglu, & O. Laske (Eds.), *Understanding music with AI: Perspectives on music cognition* (pp. 295–332). Cambridge, MA: MIT Press.
27. Eigenfeldt, A., & Pasquier, P. (2010). Realtime generation of harmonic progressions using controlled Markov selection. In *Proceedings of ICCCX-Computational Creativity Conference* (pp. 16–25).
28. Fernández, J. D., & Vico, F. (2013). AI methods in algorithmic composition: A comprehensive survey. *Journal of Artificial Intelligence Research, 48*, 513–582.
29. Fineberg, J. (2000). Guide to the basic concepts and techniques of spectral music. *Contemporary Music Review, 19*(2), 81–113.
30. Fokker, A. D. (1955). Equal temperament and the Thirty-one-keyed Organ. *The Scientific Monthly, 81*(4), 161–166.
31. Forte, A. (1973). *The structure of atonal music.* New Haven, CT: Yale University Press.
32. Goodfellow, I., Bengio, Y., & Courville, A. (2016). *Deep learning.* MIT Press.
33. Herremans, D., Chuan, C.-H., & Chew, E. (2017). A functional taxonomy of music generation systems. *ACM Computing Surveys (CSUR), 50*(5), 69.
34. Hewlett, W. B. (1992). A base-40 number-line representation of musical pitch notation. *Musikometrika, 4*, 1–14.
35. Hild, H., Feulner, J., & Menzel, W. (1992). HARMONET: A neural net for harmonizing chorales in the style of JS Bach. In *Advances in Neural Information Processing Systems 4 (NIPS 4)* (pp. 267–274). Morgan Kaufmann Publishers.
36. Hiller, L., & Isaacson, L. (1993). Musical composition with a high-speed digital computer. In S. M. Schwanauer & D. A. Lewitt (Eds.), *Machine Models of Music.* (Reprint of original article) *Journal of Audio Engineering Society, 9*–21. MA, Cambridge: MIT press.
37. Holladay, R. L. (1977). *The Musica enchiriadis and Scholia enchiriadis: A translation and commentary.* Ph.D. thesis. The Ohio State University.
38. Innes, M. (2018). Don't unroll adjoint: Differentiating SSA-form programs. arXiv preprint arXiv:1810.07951. Retrieved February 05, 2020, from https://arxiv.org/pdf/1810.07951.pdf.
39. Laurson, M. (1996). *PATCHWORK: A visual programming language and some musical applications.* Ph.D. thesis. Helsinki: Sibelius Academy.
40. Levine, M. (1995). *The Jazz theory book.* Sher Music Co.
41. Morales, E., & Morales, R. (1995). Learning musical rules. In G. Widmer (Ed.), *Proceedings of the IJCAI-95 International Workshop on Artificial Intelligence and Music, 14th International Joint Conference on Artificial Intelligence (IJCAI-95).* Montreal, Canada.
42. Mozart, C. (2013). *The Mozart programming system.* Retrieved February 05, 2020, from http://mozart.github.io.
43. Pachet, F. (1993). *An object-oriented representation of pitch-classes, intervals, scales and chords: The basic MusES* (Tech. Rep. 93/38). Revised and extended version. LAFORIA-IBP-CNRS, Universite Paris VI.
44. Pachet, F., Ramalho, G., et al. (1996). Representing temporal musical objects and reasoning in the MusES system. *Journal of New Music Research, 5*(3), 252–275.

45. Pachet, F., & Roy, P. (2001). Musical harmonization with constraints: A survey. *Constraints Journal, 6*(1), 7–19.
46. Persichetti, V. (1961). *Twentieth-century harmony: Creative aspects and practice*. W. W: Norton & Company.
47. Phon-Amnuaisuk, S. (2001). *An explicitly structured control model for exploring search space: Chorale harmonisation in the style of J. S. Bach*. Ph.D. thesis. Centre for Intelligent Systems and their Application, Division of Informatics, University of Edinburgh.
48. Phon-Amnuaisuk, S. (2002). Control language for harmonisation process. In C. Anagnostopoulou, M. Ferrand, & A. Smaill (Eds.), *Music and Artificial Intelligence: Second International Conference, ICMAI 2002* (Vol. 2445, pp. 155–167). Lecture Notes in Computer Science. Heidelberg/Berlin: Springer.
49. Piston, W. (1950). *Harmony*. Victor Gollancz Ltd.
50. Rothstein, J. (1995). *MIDI: A comprehensive introduction*, 2nd ed. Madison, WI: A-R Editions, Inc.
51. Roy, P., & Haridi, S. (2004). *Concepts, techniques, and models of computer programming*. Cambridge, MA: MIT Press.
52. Roy, P., & Pachet, F. (1997). Reifying constraint satisfaction in smalltalk. *Journal of Object-Oriented Programming, 10*(4), 43–51.
53. Rueda, C., & Lindberg, M., et al. (1998). Integrating constraint programming in visual musical composition languages. In *ECAI 98 Workshop on Constraints for Artistic Applications*. Brighton.
54. Rueda, C. & Valencia, F. D. (1997). Improving forward checking with delayed evaluation. In *XXIII Conferencia Latinoamericana de Informática (CLEI'97)*. Santiago, Chile.
55. Sandred, Ö. (2010). PWMC, a constraint-solving system for generating music scores. *Computer Music Journal, 34*(2), 8–24.
56. Schoenberg, A. (1969). *Structural functions of harmony*, 2nd Rev. ed. Leonard Stein. New York, NY: W. W. Norton.
57. Schoenberg, A. (1983). *Theory of harmony*. University of California Press.
58. Schottstaedt, W. (1989). Automatic counterpoint. In M. V. Mathews & J. R. Pierce (Eds.), *Current directions in computer music research* (pp. 199–214). Cambridge, MA: The MIT Press.
59. Tack, G. (2009). *Constraint propagation: models, techniques, implementation*. Ph.D. thesis. Saarland University, Germany.
60. Truchet, C., & Codognet, P. (2004). Musical constraint satisfaction problems solved with adaptive search. *Soft Computing, 8*(9), 633–640.
61. Tsang, C. P., & Aitken, M. (1991). Harmonizing music as a discipline of constraint logic programming. In *Proceedings of then International Computer Music Conference*. San Francisco: International Computer Music Association.
62. Tymoczko, D. (2011). *A geometry of music: Harmony and counterpoint in the extended common practice*. Oxford: Oxford University Press.
63. Young, R. W. (1939). Terminology for logarithmic frequency units. *The Journal of the Acoustical Society of America, 11*(1), 134–139.
64. Zimmermann, D. (2001). Modelling musical structures. *Constraints, 6*(1), 53–83.

Torsten Anders is a composer, researcher and software developer. He is interested in the computational modelling of composition and music theories, with over 20 years of experience in this field. He has worked on various aspects of the composition process, including models of rhythm, harmony, musical form and their combination. These models often use methods of symbolic Artificial Intelligence such as Constraint Programming. He studied electroacoustic and instrumental composition at the Franz Liszt University of Music Weimar (Germany), and received a Ph.D.

in Music from Queen's University Belfast (UK). He worked as a computer programmer in the Music, Mind, Machine research group at the University of Nijmegen (Netherlands), served as a research fellow at the Interdisciplinary Centre for Computer Music Research (ICCMR), University of Plymouth (UK), and lectured music technology at the University of Bedfordshire (UK). In 2019, he joined the algorithmic composition company Aiva as a researcher and developer. E-mail: torstenanders@gmx.de.

Constraint-Solving Systems in Music Creation

12

Örjan Sandred

12.1 Introduction

Rule-based approaches to music creation put the focus on the relationship between logic and music. Can meaningful music be created from rational reasoning? This chapter will discuss some developments of constraint solving systems for computer music from the 1950s until the early 2010s. Without covering the full historic development, we will begin by looking at some pioneering research. We will discuss two aspects of the work: the algorithms that were used to build music structures from rule definitions, and the relationship between the chosen techniques and musical concepts. We will continue by looking at some systems dedicated to music composition. Finally, we will be investigating in more detail the ideas and techniques behind the Cluster Engine, a constraints satisfaction problem solver dedicated to music composition.

It is often said that music speaks directly to the human mind. There are many examples of this idea. Arthur Schopenhauer wrote about the direct nature of musical expression, and stated that music "never expresses the phenomenon, but only the inner nature, the in-itself of all phenomena, the Will itself" [20, p. 339]. Any communication outside abstract emotions is according to Schopenhauer a result of the mind's imagination, and thus not part of what music communicates. From the perspective of neuroscience and music psychology, 100 years after Schopenhauer, Flaig and Large [9, p. 268] at the University of Connecticut wrote in a comment to an article on emotional responses to music that "We would counter that music speaks to the brain in its own neurodynamic language, leading directly to the kinds of feelings that we associate with emotional experiences."

Ö. Sandred (✉)
Desautels Faculty of Music, University of Manitoba, 136 Dafoe Rd, Winnipeg,
MB R3T 2N2, Canada
e-mail: Orjan.Sandred@umanitoba.ca

© Springer Nature Switzerland AG 2021
E. R. Miranda (eds.), *Handbook of Artificial Intelligence for Music*,
https://doi.org/10.1007/978-3-030-72116-9_12

If music speaks directly to the mind, musical structures should tell us something about the structure of the human brain. Maybe music compositions can be seen as fingerprints of the brain's organization, and by understanding how music functions, we can get a clue into how the brain works? The brain's memory functions decipher musical formal structures, and its ability to find patterns and symmetries makes rhythms and frequency structures meaningful. When music makes sense, its acoustical structure probably matches the brain's neurodynamic language.

If music communicates through its structure, it needs to carefully be planned and built to have full impact. Music theorists have studied the nature of successful musical structures and based treatises on their findings. While these treatises rarely speak about the exact match between a certain structural characteristic and the emotion it triggers, they often go into details about pitch organization and rhythmic considerations—we might think of it as the grammar of a musical style. The emotional content seems to be up to the intuition of the composer (or in some cases, the improviser) to create. The music treatises typically observe what is acceptable or not within a specific musical style and formalize these observations as sets of rules. Exercises can then be created based on these rules. These exercises help music students to absorb and learn the craft that is associated with a historical music style. Probably the most well-known work in this field is Johann Joseph Fux's treatise *Gradus ad Parnassum*, written in 1725 and describing sixteenth-century counterpoint.

12.2 Early Rule Formalizations for Computer-Generated Music

When Lejaren Hiller and Leonard M. Isaacson did their pioneering work on their computer-generated *Illiac suite* for string quartet in the 1950s [10], their starting point was the above-mentioned treatise by Fux. Hiller noted that it is the existence of the musical score that makes it possible to compute musical structures. He referred to it as the objective side of music.

> The information encoded [in the score] relates to such quantitative entities as pitch and time, and is therefore accessible to rational and ultimately mathematical analysis [11, p. 110].

It is of course also true that music theory studies (before the existence of computers) for the same reason also depended on music notation. Fux would not have been able to easily discuss the structure of Renaissance counterpoint without the abstract representation notation provide.

In the first and second movements of Hiller and Isaacson's *Illiac Suite*, they treated the ILLIAC mainframe computer they used as a beginner counterpoint student. They began by implementing some of Fux's rules for 1st species counterpoint, creating a number of simple melodies and basic 2-voice counterpoint. Then they focused on 4-voice counterpoint, creating a movement that went from harmonic and melodic chaos to order by adding Fux's rules one-by-one. The very pedagogic approach tells us about their intention with their work to demonstrate their experiments rather than create a full-blown composition. The computer was of course an excellent student in terms of following instructions, the experiment rather displayed the quality of the given rules. Can we consider the output music? Does it have a musical value? Students of 1st species counterpoint become well aware of the fact that, while the exercises can create a pleasing result, the musical expression is very limited. We should not expect anything more than that just because a computer is doing the exercise. We are still quite far from the type of communication Schopenhauer discussed in his text.

There are some limitations to Hiller and Isaacson's approach. In the second movement, they implemented up to 14 simultaneous rules, which is not a high number when it comes to creating a musically interesting result. The algorithm they used was based on a try-and-error principle, which put a limitation on how complex a problem that is possible to solve could be. The algorithm built the solution pitch-by-pitch, randomly suggesting one out of 15 pitches that the rules either kept or rejected. If only one of the pitches was acceptable, there was a 1/15 chance to find it at the first try. The system was set to retry 50 times before giving up, which gave it a fair chance to find the correct pitch (nothing stopped the system from retrying the same pitch again). If every pitch only depends on its immediate predecessor, this works fairly well. However, musical dependencies are more complex than this. Hiller and Isaacson indicated that their system from time to time run into a dead end: most likely the mixture of horizontal melodic rules and vertical harmonic rules created dependencies that put constraints on *groups* of pitches, lowering the chance to find the acceptable combination.

12.3 Improving Your Chances

Creating music excerpts with the use of computers must have seemed like an obvious research area already in the early days of computer science. Through the hard work of music theorists, the formalization of music structures was already done, neatly summarized as rule collections in music treatises. Since the music theoretical rules were available, it should be possible to make a machine to follow them.

We encountered the first obstacle already in the *Illiac Suite*: the complexity of a music score can be very high, and finding an efficient strategy for how to build a score that fulfils music rules is a very challenging assignment. So why are humans so much better at the task than the machine—what is the secret? Luc Steels developed a knowledge representation system for music and used rules and machine learning algorithms to tackle the problem [22]. He differentiated between deep knowledge, which is based on stylistic and physical properties of musical material, and heuristics, which only guides someone when solving a problem.

Our hypothesis is that there are two forms of problem solving going on during composition. The first one is based on deep reasoning. This means that the composer starts from fundamental principles and explores a search space using weak methods. The second one is based on heuristics. The composer has a large number of ready-made fragments and outlines of solutions and applies these to arrive at a solution [22, p. 29].

Steels generated 4-voice chord progressions based on classical tonal harmonies in his experiments described in the quoted article. The algorithm he used differed from Hiller and Isaacson's try-and-error principle by systematically going through as many combinations of pitches as necessary until an acceptable solution was found; often referred to as a generate-and-test strategy, or brute-force search. If a solution existed, it was guaranteed to be found—but it might take time, potentially as long as it takes to go through every existing combination of the pitches. To speed up the process, heuristics were added. When possible, the heuristic rules guided the process into partial solutions that would be considered having higher chances to end up as a valid full solution. If the advice from a heuristic rule did not give an acceptable next step (i.e., if fundamental rules would be broken if the heuristic rule was followed), it was simply ignored and replaced by another heuristic rule (or if no heuristic remained, the system would solve the sub-problem without a heuristic direction). To this Steels developed a system that observed similarities between successful solutions, and automatically added heuristics based on these observations in future searches.

It is my belief that computers cannot be programmed to compose music, simply because humans do not know themselves consciously the many heuristics involved, and even if they did the programming task would be too complex for hand coding. Therefore, if we ever want computers to compose music, we will have to find ways so that they can learn themselves to do it [22, p. 31].

12.4 Making Room for Exceptions

Rule formalizations of musical styles come with a complication: the fact that composers occasionally break even very fundamental rules. Music theorists are well aware of this. The composer's intention when breaking a rule is typically to improve the result musically. We have to remember that the existing rule formalizations are based on observations on how composers structure music. These observations are not 100% accurate. With the intuition of an experienced composer, exceptions from rules occasionally happen without jeopardizing the characteristics of a certain music style. Trying to sharpen the formalization by making rules for how a specific exception can occur will either result in a very complex rule formalization or be practically impossible.

Bill Schottstaedt's system for automatic species counterpoint opened up for rules to be broken [21]. Instead of insisting on every rule to be followed, he attached a penalty to each rule for breaking it. Rules that were considered fundamental and more important had higher penalties. The task for the system was to find the solution with the least penalty. The system could then consider one solution better than another. In this case, better does not necessary mean better musically, only closer to Fux's textbook. Schottstaedt used Fux treatise *Gradus ad Parnassum* as-is, but found it necessary to add a few "common sense" rules.

> However, this entire program ignores issues of phrasing or larger melodic and rhythmic structures. If we decide to carry this effort further in that direction, a much more complex decision and search mechanism will be required [21, p. 34].

Rhythm in the fifth species (i.e., when the rhythm is "free") is simply built by randomly picking from a set of pre-made rhythmic patterns. Schottdteadt suggested (but did not implement) to treat a melody as a waveform and look for its low-frequency components as a tool to guide the search to find a good overall shape.

There are two challenges with Schottstaedt's penalty approach:

- Judging the importance of individual rules and balancing their penalties in a large set of rules is not trivial. Some cases are obvious, some are not.
- Decisions that give low penalties at the beginning of the sequence might force high penalties towards the end. It is very hard to predict this before it is too late to correct.

Schottstaedt tried a few different variations of his algorithm, and while the use of penalties speeded up the computation, he noted himself that there were problems finding good solutions to complex tasks (i.e., to fifth species counterpoint).

Many experiments by various researchers followed, several of them were occupied by choral harmonization or renaissance counterpoint. Most work in the field was focused on improving the efficiency of the algorithm, only reflecting superficially on the musical aspect or the creative process behind composition. It is outside the scope of this chapter to give a complete overview of all this work, there are already several surveys on rule-based systems for music. Jose Fernández and Francisco Vico have done a detailed survey of AI methods in general, and included a section on knowledge-based (i.e., rule-based) systems [8]. Torsten Anders and Eduardo Miranda have written an overview of constraint programming systems in music, with a focus on application for music composition [2].

12.5 The Musical Challenge

Kemal Ebcioğlu's work on choral harmonization in Bach-style is interesting for several reasons, the most important being that it was considered giving a musically high quality output compared to other attempts of the time. His system CHORAL [7] was based on a backtracking algorithm. In backtracking, the system searches for a solution step-by-step and checks at each step if there is a value that satisfies the rules. In this way, the algorithm builds a sequence of values that all comply with the constraints. If the system runs into a dead end and discovers that, at a certain step no value will satisfy all rules, it will turn back and try another value at the previous step—and continue from that point. In this way, backtracking can eliminate a large number of combinations of values in one test and will thus speed up the computation time significantly compared to a search based on brute force. Backtracking only works if a problem has a sequential order, and if it is possible to validate partial solutions—two conditions that are typically fulfilled for music problems. There are some well-known issues with backtracking, one being that if one value depends on another that is not immediately preceding it, it will discover the problem late, take some time to work its way back to the value that created the conflict, and potentially do some redundant work on the way back. The further apart the dependent values are, the slower this process will be. The CHORAL approached part of this problem by identifying what step was responsible for a failure, and return directly to this point (i.e., "back jumping").

The CHORAL system used a language called BSL (Backtracking Specification Language). Beside hard rules, Ebcioğlu's had implemented heuristic rules into his system. The purpose is similar to Steels' system discussed above: to guide the process when searching for a solution. Heuristic rules in the CHORAL system work, however, quite differently from Steels heuristics. In CHORAL, heuristic rules are used to evaluate valid temporary solutions at each step during the calculation. The heuristic rules give a temporary solution a weight, where a high weight indicates a better choice. In this way, the system will at each step add the element to the temporary solution that not only satisfy all rules but also gives the highest weight; but if it later through backtracking is failing, the element that gives the second highest weight will be picked, and so on. Similar to a hard rule, a heuristic rule uses general logic to specify its heuristic criteria.

While heuristic rules can speed up the computation time by guiding the way to a valid solution, Ebcioğlu also observes the musical impact heuristic rules can have.

> The purpose of heuristics is to estimate, at each step, which among the possible ways of extending the partial chorale will lead to its best completion. Heuristics are very important, since programs without heuristics, which are based solely on absolute rules and random selection, tend to quickly get trapped in a very unmusical path, and generate gibberish instead of music [7, p. 170].

> However, heuristics have a different and more human-composer-like flavor of describing what constitutes a good solution, because heuristics, in contrast to constraints, are rules that are to be followed whenever it is possible to follow them [7, p. 170].

Ebcioğlu did not rely on a single musical treatise when designing his system. Instead he approached the problem from multiple viewpoints: one that considers a choral as a sequence of rhythmless chords (the "chord-skeleton" view), one that considers the individual notes with all voice leading implications such as passing notes and suspensions (the "fill-in" view), two that consider the melodic line of each individual voice (the "melodic-string" and the "merged melodic-string" views), one that considered harmonic constraints related to duration/time (the "time-slice" view) and one that was based on Schenkerian analysis (the "Schenkerian-analysis" view); see further [7, pp. 161–166].

According to its author, about 350 rules were implemented in the system. The relation between the number of rules and the complexity of a rule formalization is, however, not obvious. An identical problem can be formalized by many simple rules, or by a few complex, composite rules that combine several simple rules in one. Ebcioğlu notes that in his experience, it is better to break down a long rule into several shorter rules [7, p. 157].

Modelling music from rules implies the idea that music can be understood as abstract formal principles, and that the musical mind depends on the same principles. But how close is this to how we understand music? Does the way the computer makes decisions relate to how a composer composes? Ian Cross commented on the CHORAL system from the perspective of Cognitive Science.

> However, [the CHORAL system] performs in a way that is unlikely to reflect processes involved in 'real world' composition; it can 'only' harmonise Bach chorales, and does so by methods such as generate-and-test that do not seem to be intuitively plausible or to relate to known psychological processes [6, p. 10].

According to Cross, the creative process in a human mind works very differently from Ebcioğlu's algorithms. Bach's starting point might also not only have been about the structure. He would, for example, probably have taken the words of the choral into consideration for his harmonization. Many possible sources of inspiration that affected the way Bach worked exist.

> In effect, what Ebcioğlu was proposing was not a model of the workings of the mind in musical composition. It was a powerful demonstration that mechanisms other than human minds can do some of the same things as human minds [6, p. 11].

What seems to have inspired some work to come in the field is not that a system like CHORAL could compose music (even though the result is impressive, from a musical point of view, it is rather about mimicking already defined stylistic elements than composing new music), but that it altered the way we could think of music composition. The fact that the technique does not reflect how the human mind works does not mean that it cannot be used. The musical potential lies in the possibility to develop new compositional methods. In this perspective, its strength may lie in that rather than replacing the human mind, it complements it.

12.6 Opening up for Creativity

Contemporary music composition has objectives that are quite different from the objectives when we model existing musical styles. Composers are expected to create original music that is not only expressive and musically communicative (and that sometimes also communicates extra-musical ideas), but also clearly differs from earlier music. From this perspective, if the rules that define the musical structure for one piece are known, they could not be reused as-is to create another original piece. A rule-based computer system for music composition will for this reason have to be flexible to adapt to various musical structures and ideas.

The algorithm behind the CHORAL system—the concept is borrowed from research in Artificial Intelligence (A) outside of music—became the base for many systems for solving music constraint satisfaction problems following it: the task is to determine values for a sequence of *variables*. The values have to be picked from a *domain* of possible values. The user defines relations between the variables, i.e., *constraints* (or *rules*). The system *searches* for a solution by using a strategy such as *backtracking*.

While the CHORAL system is specialized on Bach-style chorales, other systems were developed with a user interface intended to be more style independent. A good example is the PWConstraints system inside the PatchWork and PWGL visual programming languages for computer-aided composition, both developed by Laurson [12]. The fact that PWConstraints [12, pp. 145–186], was implemented inside an environment for computer-aided composition that was available to many composers probably contributed to its relative popularity. Even though PatchWork was developed as part of a Ph.D. thesis at the Sibelius Academy, it was distributed by IRCAM in Paris (Paavo Heininen and Magnus Lindberg are the examples of two composers who were early PWConstraints users.). The general description of the algorithm to solve music constraint satisfaction problems in the previous paragraph is equally accurate for how PWConstraints worked. Just as the CHORAL system, it also had the same type of heuristic rules implemented. What differed was the user interface. PWConstraints used a pattern matching syntax that made it very flexible to define constraints within a single sequence of variables (for example, a sequence of pitches that together make up a melody). The syntax for defining rules was based on standard Lisp and was relatively easy to learn for someone who was not a computer programming expert.

An even more developed user interface can be found in the Score-PMC [12, pp. 212–250, 13]. This system was based on the same algorithm as PWConstraints, but used a music score as the centre for both input and output to the system. Score-PMC could only search for pitches. Before the search, the score needed to contain the complete rhythmic structure of the final music. The interface enabled the user to create pitch-based constraints that related to the rhythmical context of the score. The solution was the rhythmic score given as input, now completed with pitches. The interface had some additional features to assist the user, such as if you were only partially happy with the solution the computer found, you could mark sections and/or individual notes in the score you wanted to keep and then search for an alternative solution for everything else.

The Open Music Rhythm Constraints system (OMRC) was developed by this author [17, 18] to make it possible to work on constraint satisfaction problems that built rhythm scores. It provides a data structure and a user interface on top of Laurson's PWConstraints system and uses the possibility to define both strict and heuristic rules, i.e., the type of heuristic rules that both Ebcioğlu and Laurson used in their systems. While many music treatises have researched and discussed how pitches are structured in various styles, less is written about rhythm. A constraint satisfaction system for rhythm needs to be based on clear musical concepts in order to provide a framework for how to define rhythm rules. In OMRC, three observations regarding rhythmic expressivity are fundamental for the system:

- Rhythms tend to be perceived in groups, i.e., as rhythmic motifs or gestures.
- The relation between a rhythmic gesture and metric pulse affects how we understand rhythm. If a complex rhythm is shifted inside a metric structure, events will be perceived with different metric weights and have a different meaning. For example, every musician knows that syncopations have a different expression than rhythms that are lined up with the pulse. It should be recognized that this does not apply to every music style. (For example, in many compositions by the composer György Ligeti, the composer wants to erase the notion of perceived pulse.)
- There is often a hierarchic relationship between rhythmic events, where some events are more structural important and others have a more ornamental role.

The domain in OMRC contains rhythm values (expressed as ratios) and/or groups of rhythm values (which can be understood as motifs or fragments of motifs), as well as empty metric units (i.e., measures with different time signatures). The rules constrain how these elements can be combined into a score, for example, how gestures can be lined up with the pulse, and how events relate hierarchically. A score in OMRC can have several voices.

There is also a special version of the Score-PMC, called Texture-PMC, that can generate a rhythm score. The system tweaks the data structure of the Score-PMC and lets the pitch information indicate note onsets. Metric structure and a basic rhythmic "grid" have to be predetermined before the search, which is one reason why it is less flexible than the OMRC.

PWConstraints is not the only generic constraint engine that was developed for music composition. Some composers have experimented with SCREAMER, an extension of Common Lisp that supports constraint programming in general (not specifically music constraints). Others prefer a generic system that already has support for music parameters implemented. A few more examples will be discussed below.

12.7 The Need for Higher Efficiency

A general concern with backtracking algorithms as those discussed above is that they can be very inefficient when a rule describes a constraint between variables that are not immediate neighbours in the sequence. The further apart the constrained variables are, the slower it is to correct a conflict. Variable ordering is thus an important design consideration for a system. Typically, a chronologic order (i.e., searching for the pitches and durations in the order they will appear in the score) is proven to be most efficient for generic music problems. When there are simultaneous events in a score, the order becomes more complex. The bottleneck in the systems discussed above is that the search algorithms have to solve the problems as a single sequence, disregarding that a score often consists of several superimposed sequences. Conflicting values have to be resolved by backtracking the sequence in the reversed order of how the variables are ordered.

> The basic idea is to collapse any given polyphonic score to a flat list of search-variables. Each note of the input score is represented in the search- engine by a search-variable. The critical point is to determine the exact *position* of each note in the final flat queue structure [12, p. 213].

It is especially difficult to find a good order when searching for superimposed sequences of durations. The reason is that different durations take up different times in the score, and different voices might end up having different numbers of variables. In a flexible system for rhythm, we would not necessarily know the number of durations that will be needed in each voice before searching for a solution, and the system might reconsider the number of durations during backtracking. In OMRC, a number of "strategy rules" where implemented to help the system finding an efficient variable order during the search. These rules guided the system to decide what voice/variable the system should visit next. While the strategy rules made it possible to find solutions, they pushed the maximum complexity problems could have when solved with pure backtracking to the limit.

Some systems use preprocessing techniques to reduce the size of the domain, often referred to as constraint propagation. While the objective of preprocessing is to speed up the system by removing values that can be ruled out before performing the search for a solution, preprocessing in-itself adds computational time, which could out-weight the saving that is done during the search that still has to follow. If a user is running the identical constraint satisfaction problem many times (the purpose can for example be to find more than one solution), the argument for preprocessing becomes stronger. An alternative to preprocessing is to use forward checking, which similarly aims to reduce the size of the domain for a future variable. A difference is that forward checking is done *during* the search. Two examples of systems that apply this type of techniques will follow.

The Situation system by Rueda [14] was developed around the same time as PWConstraints. The data structure in Situation was optimized for solving harmonic problems. Situation used a first-found forward checking algorithm that is called Minimal Forward Checking [15]. With the domain optimized for harmonic constraint satisfaction problems, this algorithm was proven more efficient than pure backtracking. A side effect of the algorithm was that the system could not support heuristic rules in the way Ebcioğlu implemented them in his CHORAL system. There was, however, a support for weak constraints, which were based on a concept that resembles Schottstaedt's use of rules that can be broken if necessary.

The Strasheela system by Anders [1] was implemented in the Oz programming language that has extensive support for constraint programming. Strasheela can thus handle both constraint propagation and backtracking.

The improved efficiency of constraint propagation allows for a different approach where propagation and the actual search take turns: before every single decision made by the search, constraint propagation runs and reduces variable domains [2, p. 31].

Strasheela differs from the systems discussed above by being able to solve constraint satisfaction problems where rhythm, pitch, and metre are all unknown before the search. The music representation in the system can also contain theoretical information such as intervals, scales, chords, metre, and more. The representation can be expanded by the user, and in that way support searches for other parameters than those listed here. Thanks to its search strategies and data structure, Strasheela can solve problems of higher complexity than the systems discussed earlier are able to.

While Strasheela uses powerful algorithms, it is relatively hard to use. Its purely textual interface can also slow down the workflow for a composer.

However, these systems [i.e. Strasheela and more] have been designed for experienced programmers [2, p. 38].

12.8 OMRC -> PWMC -> ClusterEngine

From this point in this text, this chapter discusses my own work with the Cluster Engine. This is a constraint satisfaction problem solver that similarly to Strasheela can solve constraint satisfaction problems that combine rhythm, pitch, and metre in one search. The Cluster Engine is based on the musical concepts from its predecessor PatchWork Music Constraints (PWMC) [19], which in its turn is a development of the OMRC system discussed above. The objective of developing these three systems has been to explore the possibilities of rule-based computer-assisted composition.

Rules in PWMC and the Cluster Engine are formalized in a very similar way. PWMC inherited the concepts for constraining rhythm from OMRC, but extended this further with the possibility to search for pitches as well. The user interface was also improved to make it easier for a user to formalize rules. Pitches/pitch motifs and durations/rhythm motifs were kept separate in the domain. A motif was thus first conceived as consisting of only pitches or durations, and then combined with the missing parameter during the search (how this could be done was restricted by rules). Just as in OMRC, the domain in PWMC also included empty metric units.

Similar to PWConstraints, a rule in PWMC (and in the Cluster Engine) contained two parts. The first part was the rule applicator that accessed music elements in the score, such as the duration or pitch of a note, or of a group of notes in one or more voices. This was similar to the pattern matching part of a rule in PWConstraints, and the accessors that restored the score context in Score-PMC. In PWMC, the rule applicator was a box in the graphical user interface.

The second part was the logic statement that defined the relation between the score elements the rule applicator accessed. In PWConstraints this was called the Lisp-code part. In PWMC, the logic statement was defined inside a sub-patch using PatchWorkGL's graphical user interface.

12.8.1 Musical Potential

When working on PWMC, it was soon clear that by combining rhythm and pitch in one search, musical concepts that could not be formalized with a system that was specialized on only pitch or rhythm were now possible. Contexts where the harmony would restrict the rhythmic language, or where the beat structure would influence melodic movements could be solved through a dynamic search process. For example, if a rule constrained how harmony related to rhythm, the system did not necessarily impose a predefined rhythm to restrict the harmonic progression, but allowed the system to change the rhythm if it preferred. A rhythm structure could thus be symbiotically built together with the pitch structure that would articulate the rhythmic gesture. The system also invited a user to expand the concept of what a musical rule could be. The rules from traditional treatises were combined with, for example, rules restricting statistical properties in the score, or rules using graphs to describe higher level parameters such as the energy profile of a certain passage [4].

Of great musical interest were the heuristic rules. Already Ebcioğlu observed their musical value in the CHORAL system. By only insisting on a certain characteristic when it is possible, tendencies and directions rather than fixed musical situations could be created with heuristic rules. There are numerous examples of how this has been done using the PWMC system [16, p. 160]. One example is the use of heuristic rules to set up musical goals combined with strict rules that partially contradict the stated goal. This type of contradiction had the potential to create interesting musical tensions.

PWMC was still relying on the PWConstraints engine to perform the search, and the variable order was controlled by the same type of strategy rules that were used in OMRC. This approach had some clear limitations. When solving more complex problems, the search could at times be so slow that the whole system seemed stuck. To develop the method further, and to make it possible to work with more complex scores, the search algorithm needed to be reconceived. This became the starting point for developing the Cluster Engine.

12.8.2 Challenging Order

To better understand how the PWMC carried out a search, I spent some time analyzing the search process step-by-step for some actual problems. It typically resulted in a realization such as "It is a real detour to solve the actual conflicting values this way, it is spending too much time on unrelated variables." Since my background is not in Computer Science neither Mathematics, rather than applying a sophisticated generic algorithm for constraint satisfaction problems that potentially could be more efficient than what I already used, I wanted to try to make the system adopt the strategy I would use myself if I was to solve the problem by hand. It is my conviction that a deep understanding of the actual problem (i.e., how to create a music score) can get you far.

The fundamental issue with PWMC was that the search engine (borrowed from PWConstraints) was only able to solve a problem for a flat sequence of variables. A music score on the other hand consists of several superimposed voices. A composer working on a score is using its layered structure to his/her advantage: It gives an overview of the problem that helps identifying elements that need to be adjusted. The starting point for the Cluster Engine is thus to keep the layered data structure intact, even during the search. To make this possible, each layer is considered a sub-problem and will be solved using its own search engine. The inspiration for this design comes from the notion of computer clusters, where connected computers work together and can be considered a single system. It should clearly be stated that the Cluster Engine does not search for the voices in the score in parallel. Instead the computation is still done in sequence, solving one variable after the other, jumping between the layers.

In the Cluster Engine, each voice is represented by two sequences of variables: one for durations, and one for pitches. A score with 4 voices will thus be represented as 8 sequences + one extra sequence for the metric units all voices share and would need 9 engines to be solved. The advantage of splitting the problem over several search engines becomes clear when the system discovers conflicts and needs to backtrack: Even though backtracking will have to respect the order the variables were visited, it can now be done in one sub-sequence without disturbing the other sub-sequences. This will not only increase the speed with which the failing variable is corrected, it will also dramatically reduce the amount of redundant work the system will have to do. Added to this method, the Cluster Engine is also able to identify which variable caused the conflict and backjump directly to this position; that is, it can jump to the failing variable without spending time at intermediate steps.

Figure 12.1 illustrates the difference between how PWMC and the Cluster Engine backtracks. Both PWMC and the Cluster Engine might build the sequence in the order shown in the left illustration. In PWMC, the order will depend on the specific strategy rules that are used. When the system reaches the 11th variable, it discovers a conflict between the 3rd and 11th variables that can only be resolved by adjusting the 3rd variable. The figure in the middle illustrates how PWMC would solve this through pure backtracking. Note that PWMC, due to the variable order, has to backtrack and erase variables in sequence 1, 2, and 4, even though these are unrelated to the conflict. After the 3rd variable is changed, the system will have to rebuild all variables it unnecessary erased. The figure to the right illustrates how the Cluster Engine will backjump directly to the failing variable without affecting the unrelated sequences. As stated above, backtracking only works if the problem has a sequential order, which each sub-problem has. To make sure that all rules still are

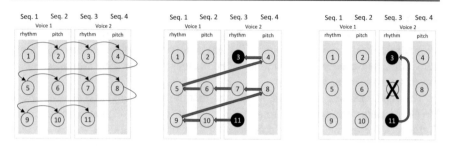

Fig. 12.1 The figure illustrates a simple 2-voice problem discussed in the text

respected, after the 3rd variable has been assigned a new value, it is necessary to search for the 7th variable again.

The technique of avoiding erasing unrelated variables should not be confused with backmarking, where the system remembers the values before erasing them in order to make it fast to recreate them. The Cluster Engine does not erase the values why backmarking is not needed.

While each voice builds its sequence of variables independent from the others, rules that restrict values between different sequences can look into the other sequences to access their data. When the system discovers a conflict caused by this type of rule, it will trigger backtracking in the engine belonging to the sequence where the conflicting variable is located. One search engine will thus have the power to backtrack another (Fig. 12.2).

Fig. 12.2 In this example, a conflict was discovered between variables 6 and 12, which triggered backtracking in the 2nd sequence. To ensure that all rules are respected, variable 10 has to be searched for again after variable 6 has been assigned a new value

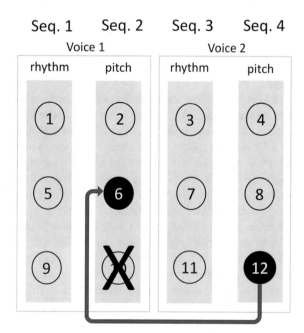

Rules that constrain relations between values in three or more sequences are quite common, for example, a rule that restricts the harmonic interval between two voices will have to constrain not only the two pitches, but also check their positions in the score. In this case, four sequences will be constrained by the rule. If the rule fails, the conflict can be resolved by either (1) changing the pitch in the other voice or (2) changing the rhythm for either of the two voices to make the notes not appear simultaneously; that is, if they are not simultaneous, the harmonic restriction would not apply. Each rule-type has a default preference for how to resolve a conflict. For example, harmonic rules would by default prefer to change the pitch in the voice that caused the conflict before changing any rhythm. It can happen that more than one rule fails at a step during the search. In this scenario, all failing rules "cast a vote" for what sequence they consider a problem. The system will backjump according to the votes. Whether this is the best way to solve a conflict is very hard to determine since there are often more than one valid option, and it is only a "qualified guess" that the chosen way is the best.

The variable order of each sub-sequence is always intact in the Cluster Engine; however, the variable order of the system as a whole has now become very flexible. The system does not backtrack in the reverse overall variable order. Instead it can backjump into the middle of the overall sequence and change some values without creating any inconsistencies. Any found solution will always be guaranteed to respect all rules. The challenge is now to make sure that the system does not revisit states it already checked. When the system is shifting from backtracking one engine to another and then back again, it is a risk that it could end up in a loop. In these situations, it is essential to not recreate and build back the identical state the system had before backtracking. While backtracking was the bottleneck in PWMC, in the Cluster Engine it is the forward stepping algorithm that needs to be taken care of. To minimize the risk of endless loops, the system will be forced to step forward in the reverse overall order backtracking was done. This technique was concluded the safest after testing several options. Loops can still occur, but typically only for very complex problems, or (occasionally) when there is no solution. Even though backtracking loops are a concern for the Cluster Engine, they typically only occur for problems that are too complex to handle for the PWMC system, why the risk was considered acceptable.

A simple speed comparison was performed on a fairly complex problem, where three voices were harmonically restricted two-and-two, and the melodic lines were restricted by not allowing notes to exist more than once within groups of six notes. The domain was a major scale and note values where all quarter notes. The systems were instructed to search for a score with two full 4//4 measures. The example was not chosen to emphasize the differences in speed, but rather to create a problem that PWMC could handle with reasonable performance speed. PWMC and the Cluster Engine used the identical rule set. Both systems run the problem 10 times:

(1) It took PWMC between 0.90 s and 6 min 15 s to find a solution. The difference in computation time reflects that when the initial random state of the system was favourable, the system would find a solution without much backtracking.

Typically, this was, however, not the case. If removing the slowest and fastest runs, the average computation time was 31.7 s.

(2) The time it took the Cluster Engine to find a solution was much more consistent; it varied between 0.046 and 0.083 s. The average computation time was 0.053 s. Compared to the PWMC, the Cluster Engine performs much more efficiently. In this example, the Cluster Engine was on average ca 600 times faster than PWMC. This corresponds quite well with my experiences of the two systems.

Neither PWMC nor the Cluster Engine uses preprocessing. While preprocessing can give an advantage to systems that are intended to run the identical problem many times, it is unclear how much the overall calculation speed of the search strategy the Cluster Engine is using would benefit.

12.8.3   An Efficient User Interface

When designing the Cluster Engine, priority was given to make it easy to define and adjust rules. The system is intended to be a "test bench" for a composer to try out structural concepts. A user spends probably more time on defining and coding rules than on running the actual computation, why ease of use can be a crucial factor for the time it takes for a user to try out a certain compositional idea.

There have been efforts to create collections of the type of rules that users commonly use. The idea is that a user should not have to spend time on recreating standard rules, only tweak their settings. Jacopo Baboni Schilingi's JBS-Constraints library [5] contains a large number of rules that systematically explore different rule types. The rules are formatted for the PWConstraints and the Score-PMC systems. The library provides a fast way of creating rules, as well as makes it possible for users with close to no knowledge of Lisp to work with a rule-based composition system. Torsten Anders developed the Cluster-rules library [3] that provides a set of rules for the Cluster engine. While these rule collections have a clear purpose and can be very useful, there is a risk of steering users into preconceived ways of thinking. It is therefore important to always make it possible for a user to invent new rules that explore alternative ways of structuring music, which would not be the case if only relying on a standardized set of rules.

12.9   Future Developments and Final Remarks

The field of rule-based composition is still exploring new possibilities. An example is the combination of constraints solvers and real-time environments. Julien Vincenot has developed a system that can evaluate Lisp-code inside the Max software [23]. Through his work, functions for computer-assisted composition that previously only were available inside a Lisp-based software, including the

PWConstraints and the Cluster Engine systems, can now be used in real-time applications. For example, close to real-time generation of fairly complex scores based on rule-based computing is possible. Also, projects that take advantage of the sound processing possibilities in Max have been developed. An example is my sound installation *Sonic Trails*, where parameters for sound synthesis are controlled as constraint satisfaction problems. Here, the music structure is performed by the system, without the intermediate step of a score [24].

There are many objectives for exploring constraint-based computing in music. The latter part of this chapter has been written from the perspective of systems that can assist composers. While music structures can be a good test bench for constraints satisfaction computing, the main challenge remains being the music itself. Music might be built on structures based on logic, but there is still a step to make these structures communicate with us. How do we avoid ending up with a result where musical expressions exist more or less at random? A helping hand from a human seems often to be necessary. Rule-based computing provides tools for exploration that can be of great help and give inspiration, but the role of the composer is still intact.

References

1. Anders, T. (2007). *Composing music by composing rules: Design and usage of a generic music constraint system.* Ph.D. thesis, School of Music & Sonic Arts, Queen's University Belfast.
2. Anders, T., & Miranda, E. R. (2011). Constraint programming systems for modeling music theories and composition. *ACM Computing Surveys, 43*(4), 30:1–30:38.
3. Anders, T. (2016). Teaching rule-based algorithmic composition: The PWGL library cluster rules. *Journal of Pedagogic Development, 6*(1), 3–14.
4. Aralla, P. (2003). Analisi morfologica. Un modello matematico per descrivere la relazione fra struttura morfologica del messaggio, attivita` mnemonico-percettiva e risposta psichia. In *PRISMA 01* (pp. 51–75). Milano: Euresis Edizioni.
5. Baboni Schilingi, J. (2009). Local and global control in computer-aided composition. *Contemporary Music Review, 28*(2), 18–191.
6. Cross, I. (2007). Bach in mind. *Understanding Bach, 2,* 9–18.
7. Ebcioğlu, K. (1990). An expert system for harmonizing chorales in the style of J.S. Bach. *The Journal of Logic Programming, 8*(1–2), 145–185.
8. Fernández, J. D., & Vico, F. (2013). AI methods in algorithmic composition: A comprehensive survey. *Journal of Artificial Intelligence Research, 48,* 513–582.
9. Flaig, N. K., & Large, E. W. (2013). What is special about musical emotion? *Physics of Life Reviews, 10*(3), 267–268.
10. Hiller, L., & Isaacson, L. (1958). Musical composition with a high-speed digital computer. *Journal of Audio Engineering Society, 6*(3), 154–160.
11. Hiller, L. (1959). Computer music. *Scientific America, 201*(6), 109–121.
12. Laurson, M. (1996). *PATCHWORK: A visual programming language and some musical applications.* Ph.D. thesis, Sibelius Academy, Helsinki.
13. Laurson, M., & Kuuskankare, M. (2005). Extensible constraint syntax through score accessors. In *Journées d'Informatique Musicale*, Maison des Sciences de l'Homme Paris Nord, 2–4 June, Paris (pp. 27–32).

14. Rueda, C., Lindberg, M., Laurson, M., Block, G., & Assayag, G. (1998). Integrating constraint programming in visual musical composition languages. In *ECAI 98 Workshop on Constraints for Artistic Applications*, August, Brighton UK.
15. Rueda, C., & Valencia, F. D. (1997). Improving forward checking with delayed evaluation. In *XXIII Conferencia Latinoamericana de Informática*, November 10–15, Valparaíso, Chile.
16. Sandred, Ö. (2009). Approaches to using rules as a composition method. *Contemporary Music Review, 28*(2), 149–165.
17. Sandred, Ö. (2011). From rhythm rules to music rules. In C. Truchet & G. Assayag (Eds.), *Constraint programming in music* (pp. 197–237). London: Iste Ltd.
18. Sandred, Ö. (2000). *OMRC 1.1. A library for controlling rhythm by constraints* (2nd ed.). Paris: IRCAM.
19. Sandred, Ö. (2010). PWMC, a constraint solving system for generating music scores. *Computer Music Journal, 34*(2), 8–24.
20. Schopenhauer, A. (1819). *The world as will and idea* (Vol. 1, 6th ed.). [Translated from German by R. B. Haldane & J. Kemp (1909).] London: Kegan Paul, Trench, Trübner & Co.
21. Schottstaedt, B. (1984). *Automatic species counterpoint.* Technical Report STAN-M-19, Stanford University CCRMA.
22. Steels, L. (1986). Learning the craft of musical composition. In *International Computer Music Conference*, The Hague, The Netherlands, October 20–24 (pp. A27–31). Michigan Publishing.
23. Vincenot, J. (2017). LISP in Max: Exploratory computer-aided composition in real-time. In *International Computer Music Conference*, Shanghai Conservatory of Music 15–17 October (pp. 87–92). Michigan Publishing.
24. Sandred, Ö. (2020). Sonic trails. On Sonic Trails [CD]. Winnipeg: Audiospective Media.

Örjan Sandred studied composition at the Royal College of Music, Sweden and received an M.F. A. (1990) and a 4-year Composition Diploma of Excellence (1997). He also studied composition at McGill University (Canada) and at the Institut de Recherche et Coordination Acoustique/Musique (IRCAM) in Paris, France. Örjan moved to Winnipeg (Canada) from Stockholm in 2005 to join the Desautels Faculty of Music at the University of Manitoba. Supported by grants from the Canada Foundation for Innovation and the Manitoba Research and Innovation Fund, he founded Studio FLAT, a studio for computer music research and production at the University of Manitoba. Previous to his current position he taught composition and electro-acoustic music at the Royal College of Music in Stockholm 1998–2005. In 2016 Örjan was a D.A.A.D. visiting professor at Hochschule für Musik Detmold in Germany. E-mail: Orjan. Sandred@umanitoba.ca.

AI Music Mixing Systems

13

David Moffat

13.1 Introduction

Mixing music, or music production, is the process of combining a series of different musical tracks together, while applying a range of audio processing to *blend* the tracks together in a pleasant and aesthetically pleasing way. Music mixing practices require the pleasant combination of all aspects of a musical piece, using a set of engineering tools to do so. Owsinski [106] identified five key components to consider while making a mix, and they are

- Balance,
- Spectrum,
- Space,
- Depth, and
- Dynamics.

Balance is related to ensuring that all instruments can be heard within a mix and that none are monopolising the mix, in terms of volume. Spectrum is related to the frequency content on the mix, to ensure that this is balanced, and there is not too much weight on a particular frequency component, and that the frequency components of each sound source are distinct and clear. Space represents a good image of the sound between two ears, allowing for better differentiation between all the different sources, without one side sounding louder than the other. Depth is to ensure that each sonic element has enough interest and complexity on its own, and

D. Moffat (✉)
Interdisciplinary Centre for Computer Music Research (ICCMR), University of Plymouth, Plymouth PL4 8AA, UK
e-mail: david.moffat@plymouth.ac.uk

© Springer Nature Switzerland AG 2021
E. R. Miranda (ed.), *Handbook of Artificial Intelligence for Music*,
https://doi.org/10.1007/978-3-030-72116-9_13

that the richness of each sound can be clearly heard, whilst all sonic elements can be blended together to produce a pleasant rich timbral sound. Dynamics are related to the sudden transient nature of the sound, to ensure there is ample and adequate change in the overall, and individual, volumes of the tracks, by creating quieter parts of the music, where the sounder parts can stand out more, creating interest and an evolving sonic signature over time.

These five dimensions of a mix are typically controlled through a range of different audio effects. The way in which a piece of music is mixed can heavily influence the way in which it is perceived, in terms of preference [28], perceived quality [172], and evoked emotion [135,140]. Music mixing is a highly complex, multi-dimensional problem, where a number of different complex sounds are combined in a multitude of different ways. The processing and modification of each and every track depend on all other tracks within the musical mixture, and often require different processing and effects in different sections of the song. Some equaliser setting applied in the chorus may be very different from the equaliser setting required in the verse. This results in a highly complex non-linear search space, relying heavily on human perception and preference of music, along with the limitations of human hearing and emotional responses to music.

The integration of an artificially intelligent music mixing system, or intelligent mixing system (IMS), has the capacity to change music production workflows and approaches [170]. The use of an IMS can change the way in which a mix engineer can explore through the vast array of mixing options available to them; they could use this as an opportunity to reduce the dimensionality of the music mixing problem, controlling their path through the mixing environment, and could even use an IMS as a tool for collaboration, where they are both enacting control over the musical mix as a whole. The use of an IMS will even inform and influence professional practice [11].

Historically, music mixing has grown and developed over time, constantly using new technology and practice to create new and interesting music [16], and some musical trends and music styles are, as a result of technology, rather just cultural evolutions [81]. Some genres of music, such as *techno* and *acid-house*, were created as a result of technological innovations [15]. A large proportion of these technological innovations are, as a result of borrowing, using, or misappropriating, technology from other fields, and applying them to music mixing processes [170]. The culture of misusing and misappropriating technology, within music, has been prevalent throughout the history of music [124], as a way to be creative, explore new approaches, and uncover the opportunities within different musical spaces. The use of IMS, in music mixing, brings a number of opportunities, not just for the new technology to be used as intended but also for practitioners to take this new technology, use and misuse it and explore the expressive opportunities it affords. New technologies have the advantages and opportunity to lead to new approaches for music production [67]. This could either be intentional through the understanding of how a tool works in one domain, and applying it to music mixing context, or this could be accidental. It is well reported in music production that often trying new things and exploring, even making mistakes, can result in *happy accidents* which has resulted in many of the mixing practices that are commonplace today [20]. This

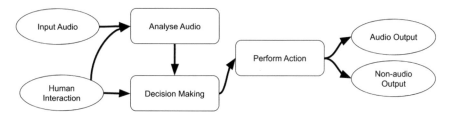

Fig. 13.1 The typical structure of an IMS

was best summed up by Bromham, who said "Some of the most creative moments in recording have come from accidents where devices have been plugged up incorrectly and technology misappropriated" [11].

There are numerous approaches for developing an IMS. In principal, there are a few key aspects of an IMS that are necessary to consider. Figure 13.1 shows a typical IMS structure. There must be some system for parsing audio tracks, with or without additional human input. There must also be an interpretation of the audio tracks input and a response, which should either directly modify and manipulate the audio or present some representation of the audio, which can benefit the mix engineer. In the field of theoretical artificial intelligence, an *intelligent agent* is one which has three key components, the ability to *observe* or perceive the environment, the ability to *act* upon the environment, and *decision-making* capacity to achieve the desired goal [136]. Following a theoretical artificial intelligence approach three key aspects of an IMS, which will be discussed within this chapter. The three aspects of an IMS are

Decision-Making Process   The process of the IMS analysing the inputs, and using this to make some mixing decision. This process includes representing all the musical knowledge and concepts, creative and technical decisions, along with understanding why the decision is made.

Audio Manipulation   The way in which an IMS will act upon the world, how it can interact with the world, and the tools it is provided with to have an impact.

Human-Computer Interaction   The observations made of the wider environment, the way in which an IMS will have utility to any user, and how the tools can be used.

13.2 Decision-Making Process

The decision-making process is arguably one of the most challenging components of an IMS. The ability to capture the concept of a creative decision that a mix engineer may make, or to understand the reasoning behind a single decision being made, is a challenging approach, and to embed this concept into an IMS can be even more challenging. The idea of modelling some *knowledge* of musical mixing, and using that to perform actions later on, is one of the key aspects of any intelligent system. In the case of music mixing, this could be through some domain knowledge, learning or defining a rule, such as "We want the vocals in this track to be really clear", or these rules could be implicitly learned, through the analysis of data collections. De Man and Reiss [33] identified three different approaches for modelling the decision-making process in IMS: knowledge encoding, expert systems, and data-driven approaches.

13.2.1 Knowledge Encoding

In most IMS literature, this approach is referred to as *Grounded Theory* [32]. The grounded theory approach is a formalised approach taken within social sciences, where theories are created through systematic methodological collection and analysis [50]. Many IMS approaches take an informal grounded theory-inspired approach, without following the systematic practices of a formal grounded theory approach.

The knowledge encoding approach is to formalise the understanding of the mixing process. There are a number of different approaches taken to gather *knowledge* of mixing practices. Ethnographic studies can be conducted, as a formal framework to analyse and understand the practice of mixing engineers [25,84]. Interviews and surveys can be conducted [116,132], which can provide insight into how mix engineers state that they approach mixing problems. Often, this can be verified through the analysis of mixing practices [29,119]. Published literature by respected practitioners [60,106,146] can often be a useful way to gain a better understanding of mixing processes.

Often, practitioners' experience, coupled with rules derived from literature, can be used to automate specific audio effects independently. There are a large number of studies looking into perceptual attributes of mixing production practice. Hermes [56] performed an overview of mixing approaches, and focused on understanding spectral clarity for automatic mixing. Bromham et al. [13] conducted a study to understand which compressor settings would be deemed appropriate for a given piece of programme material. Bromham et al. [12] looked to understand how different audio effects would influence the perception of timbral attributes of a piece of music, including brightness and warmth. Weaver et al. [166,167] investigated the impact of reverberation on how musicians perform together, which was further analysed by De Man et al. [30]. Fenton and Lee [42] investigated the perceptual attribute punch, within a music mixing context, whereas Moore [101] investigated how aggressive a distortion effect can be. Both Wilson and Fazenda [171] and Colonel and Reiss [26] performed statistical analyses of a large number of musical mixes.

These inferred rules can then be applied to IMS. Perez Gonzalez and Reiss [113] proposed setting the gains of all audio tracks to the same perceptual loudness within a mix, and Moffat and Sandler [98] proposed including a source separation evaluation metric to compensate for crosstalk between different microphones in a live situation. Perez Gonzalez and Reiss [115] sets the pan of some audio tracks to reduce spectral interference of different tracks, while maintaining the low-frequency content as close to the centre as possible, and Ward et al. [165] extend this to use a perceptual model of masking to place each track within the stereo field. Perez Gonzalez and Reiss [112] equalised tracks to reduce the spectral overlap of audio tracks, where Hafezi and Reiss [52] used a perceptual masking model to define the equalisation values. Maddams et al. [73] automated the parameters of a dynamic range compressor, based on signal analysis, to consistently set the dynamic range of audio tracks. Moffat and Sandler [95] identified that mix engineers will often use dynamic range compressors for a number of different uses, and developed a parameter setting for emphasising transients of drums. Moffat and Sandler [97] automated reverberation parameters, where the reverb time is controlled by the tempo of the audio track [166].

It is clear here that most approaches undertaken will only automate one type of audio effect, and will typically restrict themselves to a simple set of rules. Any more complex rule structures require more complex management of multiple conflicting rules, such as that described in Sect. 13.2.2. Throughout this approach, there is a necessity to consistently update the collection of mixing approaches, and to evaluate the approaches taken to implement them, especially as it has been demonstrated that professional mix engineers may identify one approach while actually using an alternative approach [119]. This could easily lead to cases where an IMS approach is well intentioned but never able to produce effective results.

The knowledge encoding approach is critical to understand the *human* approach to mixing. This could be ideal as a training system, where simplified use cases could be given to an individual, to demonstrate isolated concepts or approaches. However, the ability to combine all these approaches together creates a much larger set of problems, where approaches will contradict each other, and there will be differences of opinion in the mixing approach. There are also numerous examples of *happy accidents*, where something is done accidentally, which results in producing a preferable mixing result, typically through breaking the rules, rather than confirming to existing rules [20]. This is both acknowledged and embraced by many practitioners, and some mix engineers embrace this approach [38].

13.2.2   Expert Systems

Expert system is the approach where a human expert decision-making process is modelled by a computer system. The computer model is often more generally called a knowledge-based system. Expert systems are designed to approach problems by understanding the problem, and then representing a typical expert approach using a series of *if-then-else* rules. Expert systems are broken up into two different components sections: the knowledge base, and the inference engine. The knowledge base is where a series of facts and rules can be stored, and the inference engine will then utilise these rules to make deductions and suggestions.

In the context of IMS, an expert system can either be considered as an inference problem, or a constraint optimisation problem. The mixing system could be set up to explicitly state a set of rules, and use these to then perform some inference, or optimise towards a given result define rules and perform inference [6, 100]. Alternatively mixing can be set up as a constraint optimisation problem, where a series of goals are defined, in a mathematical form, and the system must perform a search for the mathematically optimal solution [155,156].

The rule/inference approach can be used as an effective way to build on the grounded theory approaches outlined in Sect. 13.2.1. Specific rules are developed and coded, such as discussed by De Man and Reiss [32], which can then be applied to a given problem. Pachet and Delerue were the first to identify that musical mixing could be defined as an inference or optimisation problems. Pachet and Delerue [107] constructed a full mixing system, based on sound source spatialisation and mixing, by placing individual musical sources in a sonic space, defining a series of rules, and allowing the inference engine to perform the mixing task. Deruty [34] developed a range of high-level mixing goals which should be achieved during the mixing process. Benito and Reiss [6] constructed a probabilistic soft logic engine to apply reverb to a musical mix. Rules were collected from grounded theory approaches, coded into a logical inference engine, and applied to different musical tracks. The author notes the challenges in translating grounded theory rules into probability weighting. Moffat et al. [100] created a generalised framework for constructing musical mixing rules to be applied to an inference engine, and suggests that there is potential to learn mixing rules from data, utilising the semantic web [7].

Mathematical optimisation approaches have also been effectively demonstrated in the music production field. Barchiesi and Reiss [4] proposed setting the gain and equalisation parameters to mix towards a given reference track. Kolasinski [68] performed an optimisation approach to mixing a series of tracks to match a given same timbre of some selected reference track. The timbre is defined using a spectral histogram, and only gains of different tracks could be adjusted to match the reference track. Gang et al. [45] used timbre and a range of musical score-based features to optimise a number of audio effect parameters towards a given reference track. A range of mixing targets have been used, such as mixing to a specific targets loudness [41, 168], using a perceptual model of masking, to minimise the inter-track masking [64, 133], as this is often considered a negative effect of track interference, or optimising to reduce a number of different objective measures [154]. Terrell and Sandler [155] and Terrell et al. [156] investigated music mixing in a live music context, optimising the layout of different sources and speaker to counteract for room effects. Pestana et al. [118] optimised the phase offset of each instrument track, to minimise the comb filtering effects of phase cancellation. Wilson and Fazenda [173] proposed a *human-in-the-loop* mixing approach, where a human is able to state a preference over a set of mixes, which is used, in turn, to generate more mixes, in the hope that a "personal global optima" [173] is found.

There is also a variety of different optimisation approaches that have been taken, linear approaches, such as least squares [4,156] or genetic inspired approaches such as genetic algorithms [64,68], or particle swarm algorithms [133]. Wilson et al. [174] discuss the use of genetic algorithms, compared to other expert system approaches, in creating intelligent music systems.

Expert systems benefit from their ability to model highly complex rule structures that are ever-growing, with multiple target objectives, and aims to always find a solution that has the ability to fulfil as many of the targets as possible. These systems are able to consider each and every rule, in turn, and identify when certain rules need to be broken or ignored, in order to produce the best overall system. The ability to create hard constraints and soft constraints, such that an IMS can navigate any complex mix-space is vital, and enables it to both anticipate and follow an individuals mixing intention.

The rule-based mixing approaches present considerable power, as the ability to produce a formalised approach to construct, compare, and evaluate formal mixing rules, in a simple structure that could prove to be very powerful. As there are many cases where a mix engineer may give a rule that they follow, there are examples where mix engineers will say one thing but do another [129]. This could be because an engineer does not objectively understand exactly what their mixing process is or that they feel a need to justify their approach. The formal and consistent evaluation of a range of mixing rules, through a quantitive approach, would be highly insightful into both a better understanding of mixing practice and assist greatly in developing state-of-the-art intelligent mixing systems.

The key encapsulating factor of an optimisation approach-derived IMS is contained within the *fitness function*. This is the component of the optimisation that defines what to prioritise, and how it should be evaluated. These fitness functions have been used, in optimisation approaches, to reveal greater understanding of the auditory system [82], perceptual similarity measures [91], adjusting synthesiser parameters [46], and for musical composition [89]. The fitness function is required to encapsulate all the understanding and knowledge that the experts have and how it can be applied to the mixing problem at hand.

A review of expert systems, and how they were applied to IMS, was performed by De Man and Reiss [33], where the challenges in defining rules for IMS are identified. The inherent complexity of music mixing means that there is no certain *optimal solution*, but a number of different *appropriate mixes* given a set of contexts [64]. There are a number of different mixes that are preferred by different individuals, in different moods, at different times. Mixing has the ability to change and transform a piece of music [135], and so any set of constraints defined would need to acknowledge this and take this into consideration while defining the rules to be applied [69].

Inherent to how optimisation approaches work, it is not possible for most of them to operate in real time, and as such, they need to be seen as tasks where an entire track is given to an IMS, and the mix is produced at a later date. This can severally limit the ability of an individual to interact with the music mixing system, as this would not integrate well with traditional music production studio workflows. Expert-based system relies on the assumption that experts will make consistent, agreeable decisions. This implies that experts should be considered to be time invariant—that an engineer who applies a given equaliser setting today would apply the same equaliser setting tomorrow, or next year. There have been a number of cases where expert systems have been demonstrated to be highly effective AI approaches [104,125], however, there are few cases where these approaches have been demonstrated to creative approaches with great effect.

13.2.3 Data Driven

Data-driven IMS approaches have been developing in recent years, particularly with the growth in machine learning and neural network techniques. These approaches rely on analysis on datasets or lots of example mixes and use this to extrapolate some set of mixing parameters. This is commonly done by selecting a set of relevant audio features, or audio descriptors [93], typically designed to represent some semantic or perceptual attributes [149], and discover how these can be related to a specific mixing decision [74,77]. Reed [126] first proposed a data-driven mixing approach, where data was analysed as to how the frequency band energy can influence the timbral attributes of brightness, darkness, and smoothness, and this was used to automatically equalise a given audio track to an identified semantic term, using the nearest neighbour algorithm. Since then, machine learning approaches have grown considerably, and there many approaches for using a data-driven approach to construct an IMS.

Deep learning approaches have become very relevant recently, since it was demonstrated that a neural network has the ability to parse and apply a large amount of nonlinear processing [78], or even to simply perform an entire mix in a single *black box* system [76]. Moffat and Sandler [99] extract gain parameters from a series of audio mixes, using a *reverse engineering mix* approach, developed by Barchiesi and Reiss [5], and then use this to predict gain parameters and extrapolate to larger datasets, using a random forest approach. Pestana et al. [117] analysed 60 years of the UK and USA pop chart music, and then Ma et al. [72] used this to predict an *ideal* equalisation curve, which can be applied to different tracks. Martínez Ramírez et al. [75] and Sheng and Fazekas [147] both generated a set of audio samples modified with the use of a dynamic range compressor, and then learned the transformations applied by that compressor. Hestermann and Deffner [57] took on the task of manually annotating a large dataset of audio tracks, to develop an intelligent de-esser. Chourdakis and Reiss [22,23] developed an approach for learning reverberation parameters from a specific user input, which then extrapolates the selected reverb parameters to other tracks, though they comment on the challenges of finding appropriate quantities of data. Mimilakis et al. [87] constructed a neural network to learn the mastering process of jazz music, taken from the Jazzomat dataset [62]. Martínez Ramírez et al. [79] recently demonstrated a full end-to-end IMS, using drums. This system learns the full music production process of drum mixing and demonstrates that the intelligently produced mix is indistinguishable from the professional engineer-generated mix.

Clearly, one of the largest restricting factors within a data-driven approach for intelligent mixing is data gathering. Other than taking on large-scale manual annotation approaches, there are numerous approaches that have been taken, such as using a mix parameter reverse engineer approach [5], as used by Moffat and Sandler [99]. There are also a number of curated multitrack datasets, including the

Cambridge MT Multitrack Dataset [145], the Open Multitrack Dataset [31], and MedleyDB [9]. There are instrument-specific multitrack dataset, such as the ENST-Drum dataset [49]. Despite limitations, data-driven approaches are highly effective results, once suitable datasets are curated [1].

The considerable growth in data science and machine learning approaches over the past decade [175] has resulted in there being ample directions for further work in data-driven IMS. It has been demonstrated that data-driven approaches are highly effective, and extendable, leaving considerable opportunities for future work in this space. The input track ordering is a present challenge, where any machine learning approach should be able to mix tracks together in a way that is invariant to the input track order. As the number of musical tracks grows, the problem search space becomes exponentially more and more complex, which can lead to real challenges. And networks need to be able to deal with missing instruments, e.g. some tracks will have a brass section, or a violin track, but many will not, as Bittner et al. [9] identify that within their dataset only two of the 16 instruments exist in more than 50% of the multitracks.

13.2.4 Decision-Making Summary

The decision-making processes used by an IMS are of critical importance to both the inputs needed to perceive the system and to how an IMS will operate. The decision-making process encodes all the knowledge of a given system and will enact some decision to the action component of the IMS. The input system is greatly influenced, as some approaches require a single audio track input, whereas some require a full multitrack mixing context. Furthermore, if any additional metadata is required, or human interaction is required, this will also greatly impact the decision-making process. Knowledge encoding approaches rely heavily on professional mix engineer knowledge and understanding, and attempt and represent this domain knowledge in a simple direct way, however these knowledge encoding approaches are highly restricted to often controlling single audio effect directly, and so do not model the interaction between different audio effects or processing chains. Expert systems attempt to quantify the uses more formally, performing some inference or optimisation based on these rules, which allow for considerably more complex rules. Conversely, data-driven systems have recently shown that they are able to mix as effectively as a professional engineer [79]. Though this is in a simplified mixing task, mixing only drums, these results are highly promising for future research. The future of IMS can also lie heavily in expert systems. By combining knowledge approaches, and learning defined rules from data, this approach could both be used to not only gain insight into music mixing practices and approaches taken but also develop state-of-the-art IMS. This will only be possible once data collection challenges within the data-driven approaches have been addressed. The decision-making process will then provide a decision, and an action will be taken to some change to the audio, as discussed in the following section.

13.3 Audio Manipulation

The manner in which an IMS will perform an action upon a piece of audio will greatly influence the limitations and restrictions of the IMS, and will also emphasise the opportunities of the IMS. How a piece of audio is modified will greatly define and limit the IMS. There are two approaches to modify audio with an IMS, and they are either to use adaptive audio effects or to perform a direct transformation on the audio.

13.3.1 Adaptive Audio Effects

The use of audio effects to construct an IMS is the most common approach taken. Audio effects are the processes used to manipulate and change a sound in an intentional manner. Audio effects have been around for as long as we have had documented music [170]. In principal, an audio effect can be any sound modification, from as simple as a loudness control to a dereverberation algorithm [103] or noise removal algorithm [80]. These audio effects are used as part of the music making, mixing, and production, to shape and control the musical sounds. The principal aspect of this is to ensure that control can be harnessed over a pre-existing sound. An audio effect is an approach of taking a sound and modifying it, in some consistent, predictable, and usually controllable manner. An adaptive audio effect (AFx) is one in which control parameters are changed over time, based on either analysis of audio, or an external sensor input, such as a gestural control.

Figure 13.2 shows the general structure of an AFx. Verfaille et al. [161] developed a classification for AFx, which identifies the following AFx categories:

Auto-adaptive An effect where the audio analysis is performed on the input signal that is also being modified, as shown in Fig. 13.3a. AFx adapts directly to the audio signal being used. An example of this could be a dynamic range compressor.

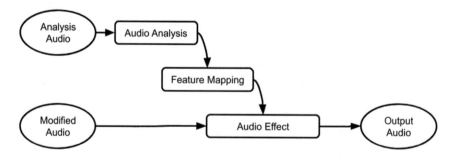

Fig. 13.2 A flow diagram of a typical adaptive audio effect

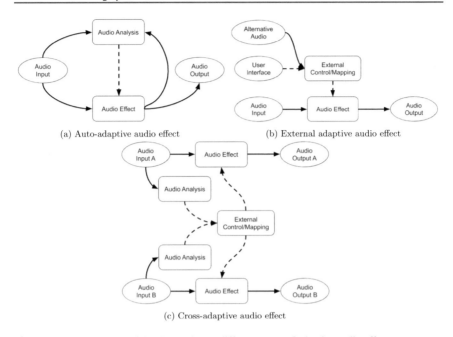

(a) Auto-adaptive audio effect   (b) External adaptive audio effect

(c) Cross-adaptive audio effect

Fig. 13.3 Flow diagrams of the three primary different types of adaptive audio effects

External adaptive   An effect where the control analysis input is presented from something external, such as an alternative audio stream, or gestural input, as shown in Fig. 13.3b, for example, a side-chain compressor.

Cross-adaptive   Cross-adaptive AFx is where two different audio tracks are used to modify each other directly, where both the audio samples and the AFx interact, potentially conflict with each other, and typically reach some equilibrium state, which changes as the audio channels progress, as shown in Fig. 13.3c.

The use of adaptive audio effect for IMS was formalised by Reiss [128]. The audio effect is some signal processing block which modifies audio and is adaptive in some way. The feature mapping or parameter automation is performed, so that the IMS can directly control a parameter, much in the same way a human engineer would. Adaptive effect implementation is performed in a number of different ways, depending on the type of audio effect being used [160]. Adaptive effects can be used either to directly modify perceptual attributes of a piece of music [58], or for individual performers to be able to interact with each other in more complex musical ways [138].

AFx is used within IMS to automate pre-existing audio effect parameters [127]. This has been a common approach for some time, and intuitively it makes sense to maintain as much of the processing chain as constant when developing IMS. There are many auto-adaptive audio effects, such as dynamic range compressors, that are not considered to be intelligent but do rely on some analysis of an audio signal to automate some internal parameters. Even cross-adaptive effects, such as a side-chain compressor, are considered *advanced mixing techniques* but not intelligent. The AFx approach to IMS allows for an easy and intuitive transition from traditional music production paradigms to IMS. There are clear opportunities for how to interact with, or expose the effect parameters being automated to a user. This could be done through effect parameter recommendation, such as creating an *adaptive preset* [110], whether automating some or all of the effect parameters, or by creating a fully automatic plug-in, which fits within the traditional mixing workflows.

The use of adaptive audio effects within an IMS introduces a number of challenges. Primarily, there are a large number of audio effects that can be applied in any order, to achieve a number of different goals. To this end, there are a number of approaches to analyse and propose an audio effect chain. McGarry et al. [83] performed an ethnographic study into the music mixing processes that are undertaken in studios. Sauer et al. [139] used natural language parsing and a range of semantic terms to define a target, which is analysed to propose a suggestion as to the types of audio processing that should be applied to a given audio track. Stasis et al. [150] conducted a study, evaluating the use and ordering of audio effects on a range of different audio tracks, in an attempt to understand the types of audio processing chains that are commonly used. This work was developed further, and related to semantic descriptors [151].

There are a large number of restrictions on using AFx in IMS. The limitations on how the audio can be manipulated and changed are highly limiting; there may be a number of cases where a specific target is wanted, but the IMS is not able to understand how to achieve the desired outcome. This is often a problem with student engineers, who may know what they want to achieve but do not know how to achieve it [66]. Furthermore, constructing an independent IMS for a single audio effect will greatly limit the opportunity for that IMS to understand the complexity of the impact it may have on the signal, and a later IMS in the same chain may then be attempting to undo whatever that IMS is performing. As such, constructing a global IMS, with an understanding of the overall musical context, will have considerably greater power.

13.3.2 Direct Transformation

Alternative to using AFx, there have recently been a number of approaches which have demonstrated some sort of direct audio transformation. Instead of using some mid-level audio interaction algorithm, which is typically based on some electronic circuit or mechanical system [170], the audio can be modified directly. This can be performed either through direct audio sample modification, as performed in end-to-end learning [79], or modifying the audio in some reversible domain, such as the short-time Fourier transform [76,87]. The ability to directly transform audio is common in the field of neural networks, which have demonstrated the ability to directly modify audio for a range of different tasks, including intelligent mixing [79], audio style transfer [51,162], audio effect modelling [55,75], signal denoising [105], and even sound synthesis [47]. Fundamentally, all of these approaches, whether called denoising, style transfer, or timbre modification, are each audio effects, in one way or another.

An IMS developed with a direct transformation capacity would not be limited to traditional human approaches of modifying audio, instead is able to learn to produce the desired effect, regardless of how possible or easy that would have been through modelling in electronic circuitry [170]. There is no reliance on some complex non-linear mapping between audio attributes, perceptual attributes, and audio effect parameters, and instead the important transformation and ordering are implicitly understood.

There are clear opportunities for a neural network approach to learning some signal processing transform, based on a given dataset, which could be used to create or realise new audio effect approaches or ways for interacting with audio, both from a creative and an engineering approach. This has the potential to allow for some new, interesting, and highly meaningful audio effects to be created. Instead of an engineer having trouble with masking, and thus selectively using a panner, an equaliser, and a compressor, they could instead load up their *demasker*, which could provide some composite tool consisting of aspects of all the individual audio effects that are relevant, and allow dynamic effect ordering where appropriate with a simple high-level user interface to control it. This system would not necessarily have any intelligent controls, but would still be an IMS, as the use of the AI to develop the audio effect would be the intelligence within the system.

The impact to both the traditional studio paradigm and the opportunities present in constructing an IMS are considerable, both easing the ability not only to shape audio as intended but also for the creation of new audio effects, from both a technical and a creative perspective. The direct transformation paradigm has yet to be fully explored, and new opportunities are being regularly coming to light, but nonetheless, the opportunities for the creation of new audio effects, and the recent outcomes, suggest that the direct transform method has considerable opportunity for exploration and innovation.

13.3.3   Audio Manipulation Summary

The audio modification approach selected, while constructing an IMS, will influence a number of factors of the ISM. An AFx approach will modify existing known audio effect parameters in an intuitive *human-like* manner. This fits directly into the understanding of music mixing, and it can be believed that this approach would swiftly be taken up by practitioners. There are, however, a number of limitations of this approach. Music is a complex system, and the large multichannel signal modification required, with several different mapping layers and understanding the inter-correlation between different audio effect parameters, audio effect ordering in the signal chain, and processing approaches, makes this a highly complex and non-linear search space. It takes a human mixer years of experience to gain an intuition as to the best audio effect ordering, understanding which parameters settings will provide the intended change to the audio, both on a single audio track and relative to the overall musical mix.

Conversely, when a direct transformation IMS is implemented, the system would be able to learn the exact transform required to the audio and directly implemented. It would even be possible for this direct transformation to be developed and framed in the more traditional audio effect domain, thus allowing for easy integration into pre-existing music mixing workflows. The ability for a direct transform IMS to create novel, interesting, and creative audio effect processors can produce insights into existing mixing practices, and is highly advantageous to expert and amateur mix engineers alike.

13.4 Human-Computer Interaction

There are a number of reasons for constructing an IMS. It could be that one is looking to completely automate the music mixing process, either due to budget constraints, or there is no way that a human can possibly be in the position to mix the piece of music, such as in a video game [141]. Alternatively, the aim could be to use an IMS to develop some form of technology that can help a mix engineer in live conditions, such as microphone bleed removal [24,90]. The aim could be to provide a mix engineer with more insight into the mix, through some form of visualisation [43], or to be used as an educational tool [70]. Based on the aim of developing a given IMS, it is vital to design and build an IMS, in acknowledgement of how it can interact with a human mix engineer.

In fields outside of music production, the introduction of IMS to provide task automation has been prevalent for decades [71,148], however, the vast majority of these approaches relate to automating heavy industry, where working conditions are slow and dangerous, or on production lines, where repetitive tasks are performed in a highly repetitive manner, under the supervision of a human operator [10,44]. In these cases, there are clear advantages to using an AI system, either to speed up the process, reduce the risk to workers, or maintain a 24-hour production cycle and vastly increasing the production outputs.

However, in music mixing, the purpose of an IMS would only ever be to act as a tool, for a practitioner to use, to allow them to produce their music. Whether they are amateur or professional, they will all require different types of tools [137], but IMS can be used to construct useful tools that can provide some advantages to them each. The purpose of the tool and the manner in which the tool is used will define the interaction between the human and the computer, where it is acknowledged what capacities are given to the AI system, rather than kept within the human mixing domain. Palladini [108] proposed a number of different levels of AI approaches, and how these can be used to construct an IMS. This approach is derived from the field of self-driving cars [130], where there is a constant interaction between a human and an AI, in order to build trust of the AI system. The analogy of a self-driving car and an IMS is a very effective one, as in both cases, there is a strict human-computer interaction, in multiple different ways, from the addition of an automatic breaking system to automatic gear selection to fully automatic driving systems. In both cases, the AI system is being used as a tool for a human to use, in a way they see fit: one in a very practical deliberate way, and the other in a very creative way.

Palladini [108] identified that there are different levels to which a human can interact with an IMS. These levels of interaction that can be described are Automatic, Independent, Recommendation, and Discovery.

13.4.1 Automatic

An automatic IMS is where a series of audio tracks are provided to the IMS and a full mix of the audio tracks is expected in return. This approach will automate all aspects of the mix, with no human interaction, other than perhaps a few high-level control parameters, where an individual may wish to select a style or genre to be mixed. This approach could take the form of defining a set of requirements or constraints [155], by identifying a target track to mix in the same way as [4], by the definition of some predefined mixing goal [133], or even by mixing examples to learn the style of a specific mix engineer [79]. In the self-driving car analogy, this approach would be the fully autonomous driving car.

A fully automated mixing system does not require any external interventions, other than the input of some audio tracks, and thus could be advantageous for an amateur, who is not experienced with music mixing, but instead requires the highest quality produced audio content, with minimal effort [69]. These systems could also be used as benchmark mixes, which could be analysed and compared to one's own mix, to reflect on what issues or challenges are being faced within a mix. There are cases where it is not possible for a mix engineer to produce a mix, such as in a video game, where objects and components of the mix are constantly changing and need to be dynamically mixed [144, 152]. There are a number of bespoke approaches for this challenge, which include implementing some level of audio detail [36, 142, 158], where sonic elements are only included when there is suitable *space* in the mix, for each sonic element. Other approaches include the dynamic generation of sonic elements within a video game [40, 85], or generative music approaches, only creating and mixing voices as and when required [27].

13.4.2 Independent

An independent IMS is one where a series of tasks can be allocated to the IMS, which it can manage and perform, while a mix engineer acts as a supervisor to the system. Overall, the mix engineer has control over the system, with the ability to change or overrule a decision made by an IMS. The ISM would have to react to the dynamic changes of a mix engineer, who will be modifying and manipulating other aspects of the audio. This could be achieved through the automation of a single type of audio effect, such as gain across all tracks [114], through the automation of an entire music mixing process, such as automating the final mastering process [88, 157], by enhancing the audio signal quality for the mix engineer, in an adaptive manner, by reducing microphone bleed [90, 159], reducing the comb filtering effects of phase interference between sound sources [24], or by mixing a set audio effect to a given task, such as providing an equaliser to an IMS, and asking for it to maintain the relative masking below a given threshold [52]. One of the best examples of an independent IMS is the "automatic microphone mixing" system, developed by Dugan [35], where the gain control for a series of microphone channels is presented to the IMS for automating, but all other components of the mix are controlled by the mix engineer. This approach has been integrated into the Yamaha CL series sound desks.

Another approach that is taken in building an independent IMS is to allow the IMS to create a *rough mix*, where a set of initial parameters are set up for a mix engineer [19]. This rough mix could be based on direct microphone analysis [98], through an understanding of the physical geometry of the room [153], or through some initialisation process—more commonly known as a *sound-check* [39]. This is analogous to a car which is able to provide some basic self-driving capabilities, such as automatic parking [59], or monitoring to ensure that the steering is staying within a specific lane on a motorway. The small segmented tasks are highly useful, individually, but do not remove the overall system control from the end user.

An independent IMS provides the mix engineer with knowledge as to what the system is automating, and how, with an active acknowledgement as to when the IMS will relinquish control to the mix engineer. One of the most important aspects of an independent IMS is that the mix engineer is able to trust the system [102]. The requirement for a consistent, predictable outcome, that the mix engineer can rely upon, without being betrayed [3], will greatly influence the utility of the IMS. If a mix engineer is in a position where they need to battle with the IMS to achieve the desired outcome, if the IMS contradicts the mix engineer, or if the IMS introduces some challenges that frustrate or interfere with the mixing process, then the IMS has no purpose in that mixing context, and the mix engineer will quickly use their super-visory role to remove the IMS from the music mixing process. However, developing an independent IMS that can mix audio content within the constraints provided, and understand the greater context of the changes it makes, provides considerable benefit to pro-am [137], and amateur mix engineers, who could be in a position to focus down on smaller simpler tasks, or not have to worry about the negative impacts of their mixing exploration, ensuring that a good quality mix is presented at all points during the mixing process, rather than necessitating a destructive process before a new and improved mix can be found.

13.4.3 Recommendation

A recommendation IMS, sometimes called a suggestive mixing system [96], is one where the IMS has the capacity to analyse and interpret the current mixing process, gaining an understanding of the current mixing context [69], and use this to provide the mix engineer with some recommendations or suggestions. These recommendations could be the automatic labelling of instrument tracks [111,137] and adaptive audio effect parameter settings [110]. Recommendations could take the format of suggesting an audio processing workflow or chain, either through the suggestion of the audio effect chain directly [150] or through the hierarchical sub-grouping or sub-mixing of stems [134].

Pestana et al. [117] developed an IMS which is able to analyse a set of audio tracks and recommend changes to spectral characteristics of the tracks. Stables et al. [149] developed an approach where audio effect parameters can be suggested, based on semantic descriptors, and a mix engineer can search through lists of descriptors to find the most appropriate for their use case. Zheng et al. [176] crowdsourced a range of semantic terms associated with different mixing audio effects, which Seetharaman and Pardo [143] developed into an IMS. Jillings and Stables [64] suggested gain mixing parameter settings to reduce perceived masking of a set of audio tracks. Cartwright and Pardo [18] developed an advisory approach to synthesis voicing, where given a midi score, it could make recommendations as to what instrument voice would be most appropriate for that track. Vickers [163] identified occasions when a single effect, namely dynamic range compression, has been overused, and negatively impacts the musical mix. IMS can also utilise mix statistical analysis approaches [26,171], querying attributes of a mix to identify any potential issues, and maybe the cause of those issues. Suggestions can then be made to correct these problems [65], where a mix engineer would have the opportunity to engage with if they so choose. Extending the autonomous car analogy, a recommendation system would be comparable to a system to suggest which gear the car should be in, or making suggestions to slow down as the speed limit changes, as performed by modern-day sat-nav systems.

The real benefit of a recommendation system is the ability for the IMS to become interpretable and adaptable. It will make suggestions to users, who can accept or reject them, and this in turn can be used to search for more appropriate answers to the problem, similar to the approach proposed by Wilson and Fazenda [173]. The engineer maintains control over the mix, and the IMS at all times, and has the opportunity to actively engage with the IMS, or to pursue their own mixing approach.

A recommendation IMS could be beneficial to amateur mix engineers, while learning or attempting to hone their mixing skills, or used by professional mix engineers when in a situation that they are unsure as to what to do, or what approach to take. This approach could even be considered the intelligent, adaptive, and context-dependent equivalent to *Oblique strategies*, developed by Eno and Schmidt [38]. Oblique strategies is a set of cards, which all have different, general comments to consider while mixing, such as "Honour thy error as a hidden intention" or "Only one element of each kind". The cards were developed to assist with challenging creative decisions, or situations where the engineer is not sure what to do. The key aspect is the control lies with the mix engineer at all stages, which gives them the power to make any decision during the mixing process, with the possibility of querying the IMS if deemed relevant. Furthermore, the development of interpretable AI systems [2], which would provide insight into the mixing decisions taken, and justification for recommendations made, could be a highly insightful one, both from understanding the benefits and applicability of the IMS to better understand existing music production workflows.

13.4.4 Discovery

An IMS constructed for the purposes of discovery is designed to provide the mix engineer with some additional insight into the mixing process being undertaken. At this stage, the IMS will have no ability to enact control over the audio signal, instead produce representations which a mix engineer can use to inform themselves and aid in their own decision-making process. The IMS is designed to support the mix engineer with their current goals and targets in some way. This could be through some mix visualisations, comparisons to existing *target* mix approaches, or a textual or numerical response to the current mix.

Hargreaves et al. [54] developed an approach for structural analysis of multitrack audio, and used this to automatically identify the chorus and verse components of the musical track being mixed. Virtanen et al. [164] present a review of different approaches for structural sound analysis. Wichern et al. [168] developed an approach for analysing and visualising the level of inter-track masking within a mix, which Izotope developed into an audio plugin, which is presented as part of Neutron [61]. Ford et al. [43] took a similar approach, to visualise the perceptual masking between sets of audio tracks in a mix. De Man et al. [30] analysed and identified the reverberation level and the impact it had on every track within a mix. Sauer et al. [139] made a number of mix processing recommendations based on intended target semantic descriptors. Cannam et al. [17] developed an approach for advanced visualisation of an audio track, and allowed for multiple versions, or mixes, of the same piece of music to be compared to one another, allowing for effective comparison and analysis between multiple mixes of the same raw audio input, whereas Gelineck and Overholt [48] and Merchel et al. [86] both developed approaches for providing haptic feedback of music mixing. Bruford et al. [14] developed an approach for searching for appropriate drum loops, given the rest of the audio content. Moffat et al. [94] created a hierarchical structure to sound, based on unsupervised learning and perceptual attributes, which is designed to assist with searching for audio samples and loops.

The principal value of this approach is to provide a greater level of understanding as to the current audio mixture. Following the autonomous car analogy, this would be the development of parking sensors or a sat-nav technology that can give a view of the traffic around the next corner. This approach is beneficial to amateur mix engineers, as it can bring insight to parts of the musical mix, where their hearing ability or experience may not allow them to be aware of otherwise. It is often the case that an amateur will know they have a particular issue, such as a muddy mix, but not know how they can fix it. This approach can provide simple, easy-to-interpret information which can lead to a faster and more effective decision-making process.

13.4.5 Control-Level Summary

The development of an IMS is heavily constrained by the way in which mix engineers are intended to interact with it. Engineers can remain in complete control, but allow an IMS to provide some insight or discovery of the music they are mixing, or they can hand off the entire mixing process, allowing the IMS complete autonomous control, with little but the most high-level controls over the result. The way in which this interaction takes place will completely change the dynamic of the situation and will directly impact the usability and attitude of the engineer. It is vital that, at all stages, there is an agreement between the IMS and the engineer as to what the expectation is, and the IMS should never step outside of this boundary, without clear signposting. There is current research demonstrating all four approaches to developing an IMS, however, the challenges of an automatic IMS are only just being overcome. There is a significant need for further investigation into how individuals can interact with an IMS, and how the IMS can learn from this approach to refine the mixing protocol implemented. Due to the critical importance of the interaction between the IMS and the mix engineer, it is also necessary to understand the approach the IMS will take to create rules, how they will be represented, and what feedback can be presented back to the user, at all stages.

13.5 Further Design Considerations

A number of decisions that need to be made while creating an IMS have been outlined. However, there are a number of music-specific considerations that can highly influence the effectiveness and capacity of an IMS. In this section, we will discuss and outline these approaches.

13.5.1 Mixing by Sub-grouping

Within mixing the process of sub-grouping or using *buses* is one where groups of similar tracks are all mixed together, independent of the rest of the mix, and processed as a smaller group, or *stem*, which is then integrated into the main mix. This is most commonly done with vocals and drums [131], but there are many types of mix buses used in professional mixing approaches.

McGarry et al. [83] performed an ethnographic study, where they discuss the importance of subgrouping in music production. Ronan et al. [132] surveyed a number of professional mix engineers to ask about their subgrouping practices, and concluded that almost all mix engineers will perform some form of subgrouping and apply audio effect processing to the group. Ronan et al. [131] identified that the use of subgrouping will have a positive impact on the final mix produced. Ronan et al. [134] developed an unsupervised approach for automatic subgrouping of sets of musical stems, which was shown to improve the result of a mix when used in combination with an IMS [133]. Wilmering et al. [169] describe a formal structure of the mixing process and audio effect processing workflow, which Jillings and Stables [63] use to make proposals for channel routing of audio tracks.

It is clear that the approach of grouping together audio tracks, and reducing the complexity of the music mixing problem, is highly advantageous, though the subject still demands further research. As such, there is an opportunity to develop a bespoke IMS for a given sub-group. It can be considered that where a given IMS would be useful and effective at mixing a drum stem, it may be less effective at mixing the vocal stem, and then there would be a stem-mixing IMS, which only needs to process a smaller number of preprocessed music stems. Current results demonstrate that this approach has the potential to be highly effective in the field of IMS.

13.5.2 Intelligent Mixing Systems in Context

Music production is consistently driven by context. The shape of the music industry now versus 50 years ago means that the types of musical performances, the expectation on how the music will be consumed, and the expectation of a piece of music have all changed. The music industry and social contexts of a piece of music shape the way that professional engineers mix [121], and the way that that music is consumed. It only makes sense that the expectation of an IMS is that this context can, and should, be considered when constructing an IMS. Pras et al. [120] identified that cultural and geographic differences between groups of individuals will influence how different mixes of the same track are perceived, making it clear that cultural context, along with educational and semantic contexts will heavily influence how a piece of music is perceived, and thus this will influence the types of IMS required for these given contexts. Lefford et al. [69] present an in-depth discussion as to how mixing in context can be performed, and the necessity of this approach, while Pardo et al. [109] discuss the use of Music Information Retrieval (MIR) tools, such as source separation and noise removal within musical contexts.

For example, Ma et al. [72] developed an IMS, which analysed 60 years of UK and US pop music, and it follows that there an IMS that could be constructed, following this approach, which continually updates the given IMS parameters, identifying suitable genre and cultural contexts to select data from, and use this to apply an equalisation curve most appropriate to a chosen piece of music, based on cultural, genre, and current societal contexts and trends.

This concept could surely be extended further, to draw inspiration and concepts from the latest releases, or larger sets of audio tracks that fall into a similar cluster, based on the relevant contexts in a given situation.

13.6 Discussion

IMS can have a multitude of different aims and purposes. They can be designed to suggest parameters for a pre-existing digital audio effect, as an educational tool for training students, or be designed as *black-box* systems which will take a number of pre-recorded audio tracks and produce a mix, as high quality as possible, subject to the quality of the input material. Regardless of the manner in which an IMS is used, it is designed as a tool to be used by an audio engineer or operator, and as such, the way the tool is interacted with and used is of critical importance. We can never forget about the human in the mixing process, as there will always be some creative intention or decision to be realised, and the form that this interaction takes will heavily influence the usefulness of the tool for mixing music, whether that be to remove some noise, as a tool to produce a full mix, or as creative inspiration.

Sandler et al. [137] identified that there are three different levels of experience of individuals who work in studio production: amateur, pro-am, and professional. The use of IMS will be considerably different, depending on the individual experience and knowledge of the music production field, and their experience of using the tools of the trade. A professional may use an IMS as an exploratory tool, to allow them to quickly prototype a number of ideas that they have, which gives them a wide range of rough mixes. This will then allow them to decide which creative direction to take the mix in, which they can then pursue in a more traditional manner. An amateur, on the other hand, may allow the IMS to direct a specific creative vision, and they can gently direct the IMS within a small range on some specific details that they are focused on. A pro-am may well use the IMS as a collaboration, where the IMS and the individual will work together at different points, bouncing ideas off each other, moving forward, and constantly changing different elements of the mix until an agreement is met between the pro-am and the IMS.

Music mixing and production is inherently an interconnected and multidimensional process, where processing applied to each and every individual track is highly dependent on both the content of the individual track, but on the content of every other audio track in the mix. This means that there are often highly iterative processes, where changes are made to several different tracks, in turn, constantly making small changes to each track, until the desired effect is reached. Alternatively, a mix engineer may speculate as to how they can make a particular track sound, and then adjust a number of other tracks to fit with their imagined track. Regardless of which process is taken, it is clear that there are a high level of inter-dependencies between all the audio tracks within a mix. This is highly relevant to IMS, as firstly, there is a requirement to model the interdependencies between audio tracks. In a machine learning context, this is not entirely trivial. This concept of modelling interdependence between variables is often called *data fusion*, and this concept has been applied to music mixing [53], however, there is no consensus as to which approach is most appropriate for an IMS. A review of data fusion approaches is presented by Castanedo [21].

In considering the music mixing process, it could be viewed as a specific type of sound design, where different sonic elements are gathered together, and crafted into an aesthetically pleasing format. Similarly in the wider context of sound design, the purpose is to take a number of relevant sonic elements, select which sounds are most appropriate to include and exclude, and blend them together in a pleasant and believable manner. The creative design nature of music mixing is one which lends itself to a combination of both highly technical and highly creative approaches. Similarly, design approaches may include both design and technical approaches. Lefford et al. [70] proposed learning from computer-assisted design approaches, when designing an IMS. The growth of AI technology in both these fields draws some strong parallels, and there are certainly intersections between the concepts of these works.

The development of a fully automatic IMS is a contentious subject, as many aspects of music mixing are considered a *dark art*, and a highly creative practice, and AI systems will never be able to produce a mix in the same way as a professional mix engineer [8], however, there are counter arguments that suggest that the integration of AI tools into the music mixing workflow can provide powerful new insights into music mixing practices, facilitate new ways to explore musical content, and even influence the creative capacity of practitioners [11]. Furthermore, the facility for a mix engineer to misappropriate these intelligent tools, to use them to create new types of sounds, interesting mixes, and to guide and influence the creative music production space have considerable impact on the entire field of music production. The potential for this new technology to drive potential creative outcomes is well known [37], and there are many changes to the future of music production, with the inclusion of AI mixing technologies [122,123].

13.7 The Future of Intelligent Mixing Systems

It is clear that there are significant opportunities for new and interesting developments within music production, through the development and use of IMS. The opportunities to include some signal processing approaches, and computational musicology into the system, can provide the system with a better understanding of the fundamentals of music. Fields such as audio source separation and music information retrieval afford considerably better musical and sonic understanding of the music medium, and often of the psychoacoustic and perceptual attributes, as music is perceived by people in general.

In the process to developing a highly effective IMS system, the opportunity to develop simplified *stem mixing* approaches, which group together a small number of tracks and produce an effective submit, has been shown to be a highly promising approach, though clearly further exploration is needed within this space.

The development of assistive technologies, for the creation and production of music, also presents a realm of exciting opportunities. Using audio analysis tools to provide recommendations of music samples and stems that will work well together, building the structure of a piece of music, may help reduce laborious tasks of finding the appropriate sounds in libraries of millions of different sounds, whereas a recommendation for voicing or re-voicing different melodies allows much greater control over the shape of the timbre. A method to analyse a melody, either midi or musical, and recommend alternative instruments to play that piece that would work well within the content of the current musical composition, could greatly aid the creation and mixing of any musical piece.

Video games, virtual reality, and augmented reality, all lend themselves highly to dynamic intelligent mixing systems. In these cases, it would never be possible to predict the exact detail of how an individual will interact with the environment, and there are clear opportunities for developing approaches that can mix both diegetic and non-diegetic audio content seamlessly, within these environments.

It is clear that there are considerable challenges to overcome within the field of IMS. A combination of fundamental research, coupled with creative development and integration of technologies, has the potential to have a considerable impact on the music industry and field of music production.

References

1. Arel, I., Rose, D. C., & Karnowski, T. P. (2010). Deep machine learning-a new frontier in artificial intelligence research. *IEEE Computational Intelligence Magazine, 5*(4), 13–18.
2. Baehrens, D., Schroeter, T., Harmeling, S., Kawanabe, M., Hansen, K., & Müller, K.-R. (2010). How to explain individual classification decisions. *Journal of Machine Learning Research, 11*(June), 1803–1831.
3. Baier, A. (1986). Trust and antitrust. *Ethics, 96*(2), 231–260.
4. Barchiesi, D., & Reiss, J. (2009). Automatic target mixing using least-squares optimization of gains and equalization settings. In *Proceedings of the 12th Conference on Digital Audio Effects (DAFx-09)*, Como, Italy.
5. Barchiesi, D., & Reiss, J. (2010). Reverse engineering of a mix. *Journal of the Audio Engineering Society, 58*(7/8), 563–576.
6. Benito, A. L., & Reiss, J. D. (2017). Intelligent multitrack reverberation based on hinge-loss markov random fields. In *Audio Engineering Society Conference: 2017 AES International Conference on Semantic Audio.*
7. Berners-Lee, T., Hendler, J., Lassila, O., et al. (2001). The semantic web. *Scientific American, 284*(5), 28–37.
8. Birtchnell, T., & Elliott, A. (2018). Automating the black art: Creative places for artificial intelligence in audio mastering. *Geoforum, 96*, 77–86.
9. Bittner, R. M., Salamon, J., Tierney, M., Mauch, M., Cannam, C., & Bello, J. P. (2014). MedleyDB: A multitrack dataset for annotation-intensive MIR research. In *15th International Society for Music Information Retrieval Conference (ISMIR 2014).*
10. Bolton, C., Machová, V., Kovacova, M., & Valaskova, K. (2018). The power of human-machine collaboration: Artificial intelligence, business automation, and the smart economy. *Economics, Management, and Financial Markets, 13*(4), 51–56.
11. Bromham, G. (2016). How can academic practice inform mix-craft? In R. Hepworth-Sawyer & J. Hodgson (Eds.), *Mixing music*. Perspective on music production, Chap. 16 (pp. 245–256). Taylor & Francis.

12. Bromham, G., Moffat, D., Barthet, M., Danielsen, A., & Fazekas, G. (2019). The impact of audio effects processing on the perception of brightness and warmth. In *ACM Audio Mostly Conference*, Nottingham, UK. ACM.
13. Bromham, G., Moffat, D., Fazekas, G., Barthet, M., & Sandler, M. B. (2018). The impact of compressor ballistics on the perceived style of music. In *Audio Engineering Society Convention*, New York, USA (Vol. 145).
14. Bruford, F., Barthet, M., McDonald, S., & Sandler, M. B. (2019). Groove explorer: An intelligent visual interface for drum loop library navigation. In *24th ACM Intelligent User Interfaces Conference (IUI)*.
15. Bull, R. (1997). *The aesthetics of acid*.
16. Burgess, R. J. (2014). *The history of music production*. Oxford University Press.
17. Cannam, C., Landone, C., & Sandler, M. (2010). Sonic visualiser: An open source application for viewing, analysing, and annotating music audio files. In *Proceedings of the ACM Multimedia 2010 International Conference*, Firenze, Italy (pp. 1467–1468).
18. Cartwright, M., & Pardo, B. (2014). Synthassist: An audio synthesizer programmed with vocal imitation. In *Proceedings of the 22nd ACM International Conference on Multimedia* (pp. 741–742).
19. Cartwright, M., Pardo, B., and Reiss, J. D. (2014). Mixploration: Rethinking the audio mixer interface. In *International Conference on Intelligent User Interfaces*.
20. Cascone, K. (2000). The aesthetics of failure: "Post-digital" tendencies in contemporary computer music. *Computer Music Journal*, 24(4), 12–18.
21. Castanedo, F. (2013). A review of data fusion techniques. *The Scientific World Journal*.
22. Chourdakis, E. T., & Reiss, J. D. (2016). Automatic control of a digital reverberation effect using hybrid models. In *Audio Engineering Society Conference: 60th International Conference: DREAMS (Dereverberation and Reverberation of Audio, Music, and Speech)*. Audio Engineering Society.
23. Chourdakis, E. T., & Reiss, J. D. (2017). A machine-learning approach to application of intelligent artificial reverberation. *Journal of the Audio Engineering Society*, 65(1/2), 56–65.
24. Clifford, A., & Reiss, J. D. (2013). Using delay estimation to reduce comb filtering of arbitrary musical sources. *Journal of the Audio Engineering Society*, 61(11), 917–927.
25. Cohen, S. (1993). Ethnography and popular music studies. *Popular Music*, 12(2), 123–138.
26. Colonel, J., & Reiss, J. D. (2019). Exploring preference for multitrack mixes using statistical analysis of mir and textual features. In *Audio Engineering Society Convention* (Vol. 147). Audio Engineering Society.
27. Dawson, R. (2013). *Cell: A generative music game*. Master's thesis, University of Sussex.
28. De Man, B., Boerum, M., Leonard, B., Massenburg, G., King, R., & Reiss, J. D. (2015). Perceptual evaluation of music mixing practices. In *Audio Engineering Society Convention* (Vol. 138).
29. De Man, B., Jillings, N., Moffat, D., Reiss, J. D., & Stables, R. (2016). Subjective comparison of music production practices using the Web Audio Evaluation Tool. In *2nd AES Workshop on Intelligent Music Production*.
30. De Man, B., McNally, K., & Reiss, J. D. (2017). Perceptual evaluation and analysis of reverberation in multitrack music production. *Journal of the Audio Engineering Society*, 65(1/2), 108–116.
31. De Man, B., Mora-Mcginity, M., Fazekas, G., & Reiss, J. D. (2014). The Open Multitrack Testbed. In *Audio Engineering Society Convention* (Vol. 137).
32. De Man, B., & Reiss, J. D. (2013). A knowledge-engineered autonomous mixing system. In *Audio Engineering Society Convention* (Vol. 135). Audio Engineering Society.
33. De Man, B., & Reiss, J. D. (2013). A semantic approach to autonomous mixing. *Journal on the Art of Record Production (JARP)*, 8.
34. Deruty, E. (2016). Goal-oriented mixing. In *Proceedings of the 2nd AES Workshop on Intelligent Music Production*.

35. Dugan, D. (1975). Automatic microphone mixing. *Journal of the Audio Engineering Society*, *23*(6), 442–449.
36. Durr, G., Peixoto, L., Souza, M., Tanoue, R., & Reiss, J. D. (2015). Implementation and evaluation of dynamic level of audio detail. In *Audio Engineering Society Conference: 56th International Conference: Audio for Games*, London, UK.
37. Eno, B. (2004). The studio as compositional tool. In C. Cox & D. Warner (Eds.), *Audio culture: Readings in modern music*, Chap. 22 (pp. 127–130). Londres: Continuum.
38. Eno, B. and Schmidt, P. (1975). Oblique strategies. *Opal. (Limited edition, boxed set of cards.) [rMAB]*.
39. Ewert, S., & Sandler, M. (2016). Piano transcription in the studio using an extensible alternating directions framework. *IEEE/ACM Transactions on Audio, Speech, and Language Processing*, *24*(11), 1983–1997.
40. Farnell, A. (2007). An introduction to procedural audio and its application in computer games. In *Audio Mostly Conference*, Ilmenau, Germany (pp. 1–31). ACM.
41. Fenton, S. (2018). Automatic mixing of multitrack material using modified loudness models. In *Audio Engineering Society Convention* (Vol. 145). Audio Engineering Society.
42. Fenton, S., & Lee, H. (2015). Towards a perceptual model of "punch" in musical signals. In *Audio Engineering Society Convention* (Vol. 139). Audio Engineering Society.
43. Ford, J., Cartwright, M., & Pardo, B. (2015). Mixviz: A tool to visualize masking in audio mixes. In *Audio Engineering Society Convention* (Vol. 139). Audio Engineering Society.
44. Furman, J., & Seamans, R. (2019). AI and the economy. *Innovation Policy and the Economy*, *19*(1), 161–191.
45. Gang, R., Bocko, G., Bocko, M. F., Headlam, D., Lundberg, J., & Ren, G. (2010). Automatic music production system employing probabilistic expert systems. In *Audio Engineering Society Convention* (Vol. 129). Audio Engineering Society.
46. Garcia, R. A. (2001). Automating the design of sound synthesis techniques using evolutionary methods. In *Proceeding 4th International Conference on Digital Audio Effects (DAFx)*, Limerick, Ireland.
47. Gatys, L., Ecker, A. S., & Bethge, M. (2015). Texture synthesis using convolutional neural networks. *Advances in Neural Information Processing Systems*, 262–270.
48. Gelineck, S., & Overholt, D. (2015). Haptic and visual feedback in 3d audio mixing interfaces. In *Proceedings of Audio Mostly Conference on Interaction With Sound* (p. 14). ACM.
49. Gillet, O., & Richard, G. (2006). ENST-drums: An extensive audio-visual database for drum signals processing. In *Proceedings of the 7th International Society for Music Information Retrieval Conference (ISMIR-06)* (pp. 156–159).
50. Glaser, B., & Strauss, A. (1967). Grounded theory: The discovery of grounded theory. *Sociology the Journal of the British Sociological Association*, *12*(1), 27–49.
51. Grinstein, E., Duong, N. Q., Ozerov, A., & Pérez, P. (2018). Audio style transfer. In *International Conference on Acoustics, Speech and Signal Processing (ICASSP)* (pp. 586–590). IEEE.
52. Hafezi, S., & Reiss, J. D. (2015). Autonomous multitrack equalization based on masking reduction. *Journal of the Audio Engineering Society*, *63*(5), 312–323.
53. Hargreaves, S. (2014). *Music metadata capture in the studio from audio and symbolic data*. Ph.D. thesis, Queen Mary University of London.
54. Hargreaves, S., Klapuri, A., & Sandler, M. B. (2012). Structural segmentation of multitrack audio. *IEEE Transactions on Audio, Speech, and Language Processing*, *20*(10), 2637–2647.
55. Hawley, S. H., Colburn, B., & Mimilakis, S. I. (2019). Signaltrain: Profiling audio compressors with deep neural networks. arXiv:1905.11928.
56. Hermes, K. (2019). Enhancing creativity through automatic mixing research: Testing spectral clarity predictors in the mixprocess. *The Art of Record Production*.
57. Hestermann, S., & Deffner, N. (2020). Enhanced de-essing via neural networks. In *Machine Learning and Knowledge Discovery in Databases: International Workshops of ECML PKDD*

2019, Würzburg, Germany, September 16–20, 2019, Proceedings, Part II (pp. 537–542). Springer.

58. Holfelt, J., Csapo, G., Andersson, N., Zabetian, S., Castenieto, M., Dahl, S., et al. (2017). Extraction, mapping, and evaluation of expressive acoustic features for adaptive digital audio effects. In *Proceedings of the Sound & Music Computing Conference.*
59. Hsu, T.-h., Liu, J.-F., Yu, P.-N., Lee, W.-S., & Hsu, J.-S. (2008). Development of an automatic parking system for vehicle. In *2008 IEEE Vehicle Power and Propulsion Conference* (pp. 1–6). IEEE.
60. Izhaki, R. (2008). *Mixing audio: Concepts, practices and tools.* Focal Press.
61. Izotope. (2020). *Neutron plugin.* Retrieved from https://www.izotope.com/en/learn/unmasking-your-mix-with-neutron.html.
62. Jazzomat. (2018). *Jazzomat dataset, the jazzomat research project.* Retrieved May 26, 2020, from http://jazzomat.hfm-weimar.de/dbformat/dbcontent.html.
63. Jillings, N., & Stables, R. (2017). Automatic channel routing using musical instrument linked data. In *3rd AES Workshop on Intelligent Music Production.*
64. Jillings, N., & Stables, R. (2017). Automatic masking reduction in balance mixes using evolutionary computing. In *Audio Engineering Society Convention* (Vol. 143). Audio Engineering Society.
65. Jun, S., Kim, D., Jeon, M., Rho, S., & Hwang, E. (2015). Social mix: Automatic music recommendation and mixing scheme based on social network analysis. *The Journal of Supercomputing, 71*(6), 1933–1954.
66. Katz, B., & Katz, R. A. (2003). *Mastering audio: The art and the science.* Butterworth-Heinemann.
67. King, A. (2015). Technology as a vehicle (tool and practice) for developing diverse creativities. In P. Burnard & E. Haddon (Eds.), *Activating diverse musical creativities: Teaching and learning in higher music education*, Chap. 11 (pp. 203–222). Bloomsbury Publishing.
68. Kolasinski, B. (2008). A framework for automatic mixing using timbral similarity measures and genetic optimization. In *Audio Engineering Society Convention* (Vol. 124).
69. Lefford, M. N., Bromham, G., Fazekas, G., & Moffat, D. (2021). Context aware intelligent mixing systems. *Journal of the Audio Engineering Society, 69*(3), 128–141. https://doi.org/10.17743/jaes.2020.0043
70. Lefford, M. N., Bromham, G., & Moffat, D. (2020). Mixing with intelligent mixing systems: Evolving practices and lessons from computer assisted design. In *Audio Engineering Society Convention*, Vienna, Austria (Vol. 148).
71. Lindsay, R. K., Buchanan, B. G., Feigenbaum, E. A., & Lederberg, J. (1993). DENDRAL: A case study of the first expert system for scientific hypothesis formation. *Artificial Intelligence, 61*(2), 209–261.
72. Ma, Z., Reiss, J. D., & Black, D. A. (2013). Implementation of an intelligent equalization tool using yule-walker for music mixing and mastering. In *Audio Engineering Society Convention* (Vol. 134). Audio Engineering Society.
73. Maddams, J. A., Finn, S., & Reiss, J. D. (2012). An autonomous method for multi-track dynamic range compression. In *Proceedings of the 15th International Conference on Digital Audio Effects (DAFx-12)* (pp. 1–8).
74. Martínez Ramírez, M. A., Benetos, E., & Reiss, J. D. (2019). *A general-purpose deep learning approach to model time-varying audio effects.*
75. Martínez Ramírez, M. A., Benetos, E., & Reiss, J. D. (2020). Deep learning for black-box modeling of audio effects. *Applied Sciences, 10*(2), 638.
76. Martínez Ramírez, M. A., & Reiss, J. D. (2017). Deep learning and intelligent audio mixing. In *Proceedings of the 3rd Workshop on Intelligent Music Production.*
77. Martínez Ramírez, M. A., & Reiss, J. D. (2017). Stem audio mixing as a content-based transformation of audio features. In *19th IEEE Workshop on Multimedia Signal Processing (MMSP)* (pp. 1–6). IEEE.

78. Martínez Ramírez, M. A., & Reiss, J. D. (2019). Modeling nonlinear audio effects with end-to-end deep neural networks. In *IEEE International Conference on Acoustics, Speech and Signal Processing (ICASSP)* (pp. 171–175). IEEE.

79. Martínez Ramírez, M. A., Stoller, D., & Moffat, D. (2021). A deep learning approach to intelligent drum mixing with the wave-u-net. *Journal of the Audio Engineering Society, 69*(3), 142–151. https://doi.org/10.17743/jaes.2020.0031.

80. Mat, M., Yassin, I. M., Taib, M. N., Zabidi, A., Hassan, H. A., & Tahir, N. M. (2010). Adaptive filter based on narx model for recorded audio noise removal. In *2010 IEEE Control and System Graduate Research Colloquium (ICSGRC 2010)* (pp. 26–32). IEEE.

81. Mauch, M., MacCallum, R. M., Levy, M., & Leroi, A. M. (2015). The evolution of popular music: USA 1960–2010. *Royal Society Open Science, 2*(5).

82. McDermott, J. H., & Simoncelli, E. P. (2011). Sound texture perception via statistics of the auditory periphery: evidence from sound synthesis. *Neuron, 71*(5), 926–940.

83. McGarry, G., Tolmie, P., Benford, S., Greenhalgh, C., & Chamberlain, A. (2017). "They're all going out to something weird" workflow, legacy and metadata in the music production process. In *Proceedings of the 2017 ACM Conference on Computer Supported Cooperative Work and Social Computing* (pp. 995–1008).

84. McGrath, S., & Love, S. (2017). The user experience of mobile music making: An ethnographic exploration of music production and performance in practice. *Computers in Human Behavior, 72,* 233–245.

85. Mengual, L., Moffat, D., & Reiss, J. D. (2016). Modal synthesis of weapon sounds. In *Proceeding Audio Engineering Society Conference: 61st International Conference: Audio for Games*, London. Audio Engineering Society.

86. Merchel, S., Altinsoy, M. E., & Stamm, M. (2012). Touch the sound: Audio-driven tactile feedback for audio mixing applications. *Journal of the Audio Engineering Society, 60*(1/2), 47–53.

87. Mimilakis, S. I., Cano, E., Abeßer, J., & Schuller, G. (2016). New sonorities for jazz recordings: Separation and mixing using deep neural networks. In *2nd AES Workshop on Intelligent Music Production (WIMP)* (Vol. 13).

88. Mimilakis, S. I., Drossos, K., Virtanen, T., & Schuller, G. (2016). Deep neural networks for dynamic range compression in mastering applications. In *Audio Engineering Society Convention* (Vol. 140).

89. Miranda, E. R., & Al Biles, J. (2007). *Evolutionary computer music.* Springer.

90. Moffat, D., & Reiss, J. D. (2016). Dereverberation and its application to the blind source separation problem. In *Proceeding Audio Engineering Society Conference: 60th International Conference: DREAMS (Dereverberation and Reverberation of Audio, Music, and Speech).* Audio Engineering Society.

91. Moffat, D., & Reiss, J. D. (2018). Objective evaluations of synthesised environmental sounds. In *Proceeding 21th International Conference on Digital Audio Effects (DAFx-17)*, Aveiro, Portugal.

92. Moffat, D., & Reiss, J. D. (2020). Semantic music production. *Journal of the Audio Engineering Society* (in press).

93. Moffat, D., Ronan, D., & Reiss, J. D. (2015). An evaluation of audio feature extraction toolboxes. In *Proceeding 18th International Conference on Digital Audio Effects (DAFx-15)*, Trondheim, Norway.

94. Moffat, D., Ronan, D., & Reiss, J. D. (2017). Unsupervised taxonomy of sound effects. In *Proceeding 20th International Conference on Digital Audio Effects (DAFx-17)*, Edinburgh, UK.

95. Moffat, D., & Sandler, M. B. (2018). Adaptive ballistics control of dynamic range compression for percussive tracks. In *Audio Engineering Society Convention*, New York, USA (Vol. 145).

96. Moffat, D., & Sandler, M. B. (2019). Approaches in intelligent music production. *Arts, 8*(4), 125.

97. Moffat, D., & Sandler, M. B. (2019). An automated approach to the application of reverberation. In *Audio Engineering Society Convention*, New York, USA (Vol. 147).
98. Moffat, D., & Sandler, M. B. (2019). Automatic mixing level balancing enhanced through source interference identification. In *Audio Engineering Society Convention*, Dublin, Ireland (Vol. 146).
99. Moffat, D., & Sandler, M. B. (2019). Machine learning multitrack gain mixing of drums. In *Audio Engineering Society Convention*, New York, USA (Vol. 147).
100. Moffat, D., Thalmann, F., & Sandler, M. B. (2018). Towards a semantic web representation and application of audio mixing rules. In *Proceedings of the 4th Workshop on Intelligent Music Production (WIMP)*, Huddersfield, UK.
101. Moore, A. (2020). Dynamic range compression and the semantic descriptor aggressive. *Applied Sciences, 10*(7), 2350.
102. Muir, B. M. (1994). Trust in automation: Part I. theoretical issues in the study of trust and human intervention in automated systems. *Ergonomics, 37*(11):1905–1922.
103. Naylor, P. A., & Gaubitch, N. D. (2010). *Speech dereverberation.* Springer Science & Business Media.
104. Nelson, W. R., et al. (1982). *Reactor: An expert system for diagnosis and treatment of nuclear reactor accidents* (pp. 296–301). Pittsburgh, PA: AAAI.
105. Nercessian, S., & Lukin, A. (2019). Speech dereverberation using recurrent neural networks. In *Proceeding 23rd International Conference on Digital Audio Effects (DAFx-19)*, Birmingham, UK.
106. Owsinski, B. (2013). *The mixing engineer's handbook.* Nelson Education.
107. Pachet, F., & Delerue, O. (2000). On-the-fly multi-track mixing. In *Audio Engineering Society Convention* (Vol. 109). Audio Engineering Society.
108. Palladini, A. (2018). Intelligent audio machines. In *Keynote Talk at 4th Workshop on Intelligent Music Production (WIMP-18)*.
109. Pardo, B., Rafii, Z., & Duan, Z. (2018). Audio source separation in a musical context. In *Springer handbook of systematic musicology* (pp. 285–298). Springer.
110. Paterson, J. (2011). The preset is dead; long live the preset. In *Audio Engineering Society Convention* (Vol. 130). Audio Engineering Society.
111. Pauwels, J., O'Hanlon, K., Fazekas, G., & Sandler, M. B. (2017). Confidence measures and their applications in music labelling systems based on hidden markov models. *ISMIR*, 279–285.
112. Perez Gonzalez, E., & Reiss, J. (2009). Automatic equalization of multichannel audio using cross-adaptive methods. In *Audio Engineering Society Convention* (Vol. 127). Audio Engineering Society.
113. Perez Gonzalez, E., & Reiss, J. (2009). Automatic gain and fader control for live mixing. In *IEEE Workshop on Applications of Signal Processing to Audio and Acoustics (WASPAA'09)* (pp. 1–4).
114. Perez Gonzalez, E., & Reiss, J. D. (2008). Improved control for selective minimization of masking using interchannel dependancy effects. In *11th International Conference on Digital Audio Effects (DAFx)* (p. 12).
115. Perez Gonzalez, E., & Reiss, J. D. (2010). A real-time semiautonomous audio panning system for music mixing. *EURASIP Journal on Advances in Signal Processing, 2010*(1).
116. Pestana, P., & Reiss, J. (2014). Intelligent audio production strategies informed by best practices. In *Audio Engineering Society Conference: 53rd International Conference: Semantic Audio.* Audio Engineering Society.
117. Pestana, P. D., Ma, Z., Reiss, J. D., Barbosa, A., & Black, D. A. (2013). Spectral characteristics of popular commercial recordings 1950–2010. In *Audio Engineering Society Convention* (Vol. 135). Audio Engineering Society.
118. Pestana, P. D., Reiss, J. D., & Barbosa, A. (2015). Cross-adaptive polarity switching strategies for optimization of audio mixes. In *Audio Engineering Society Convention* (Vol. 138).

119. Pestana, P. D. L. G. (2013). *Automatic mixing systems using adaptive digital audio effects.* Ph.D. thesis, Universidade Católica Portuguesa.
120. Pras, A., De Man, B., & Reiss, J. D. (2018). A case study of cultural influences on mixing practices. In *Audio Engineering Society Convention* (Vol. 144).
121. Pras, A., & Guastavino, C. (2011). The role of music producers and sound engineers in the current recording context, as perceived by young professionals. *Musicae Scientiae, 15*(1), 73–95.
122. Pras, A., Guastavino, C., & Lavoie, M. (2013). The impact of technological advances on recording studio practices. *Journal of the American Society for Information Science and Technology, 64*(3), 612–626.
123. Prior, N. (2010). The rise of the new amateurs: Popular music, digital technology, and the fate of cultural production. In J. R. Hall, L. Grindstaff, & M.-C. Lo (Eds.), *Routledge handbook of cultural sociology* (pp. 398–407). Routledge.
124. Prior, N. (2012). Digital formations of popular music. *Réseaux, 2*, 66–90.
125. Rasmussen, A. N. (1990). The inco expert system project: Clips in shuttle mission control. In *First CLIPSConference* (p. 305).
126. Reed, D. (2000). A perceptual assistant to do sound equalization. In *Proceedings of the 5th International Conference on Intelligent User Interfaces* (pp. 212–218). ACM.
127. Reiss, J., & Brandtsegg, Ø. (2018). Applications of cross-adaptive audio effects: Automatic mixing, live performance and everything in between. *Frontiers in Digital Humanities, 5*, 17.
128. Reiss, J. D. (2011). Intelligent systems for mixing multichannel audio. In *Proceeding 17th International Conference on Digital Signal Processing (DSP)* (pp. 1–6). IEEE.
129. Reiss, J. D. (2018). *Do you hear what I hear? The science of everyday sounds.* Professorial: Inaugural Lecture Queen Mary University.
130. Rödel, C., Stadler, S., Meschtscherjakov, A., & Tscheligi, M. (2014). Towards autonomous cars: The effect of autonomy levels on acceptance and user experience. In *Proceedings of the 6th International Conference on Automotive User Interfaces and Interactive Vehicular Applications* (pp. 1–8). ACM.
131. Ronan, D., De Man, B., Gunes, H., & Reiss, J. D. (2015). The impact of subgrouping practices on the perception of multitrack music mixes. In *Audio Engineering Society Convention* (Vol. 139).
132. Ronan, D., Gunes, H., & Reiss, J. D. (2017). Analysis of the subgrouping practices of professional mix engineers. In *Audio Engineering Society Convention* (Vol. 142).
133. Ronan, D., Ma, Z., Mc Namara, P., Gunes, H., & Reiss, J. D. (2018). *Automatic minimisation of masking in multitrack audio using subgroups.*
134. Ronan, D., Moffat, D., Gunes, H., & Reiss, J. D. (2015). Automatic subgrouping of multitrack audio. In *Proceeding 18th International Conference on Digital Audio Effects (DAFx-15)*, Trondheim, Norway.
135. Ronan, D., Reiss, J. D., & Gunes, H. (2018). *An empirical approach to the relationship between emotion and music production quality.* arXiv:1803.11154.
136. Russell, S. J., & Norvig, P. (2016). *Artificial intelligence: A modern approach* (3rd ed.). Pearson Education Limited.
137. Sandler, M., De Roure, D., Benford, S., & Page, K. (2019). Semantic web technology for new experiences throughout the music production-consumption chain. In *2019 International Workshop on Multilayer Music Representation and Processing (MMRP)* (pp. 49–55). IEEE.
138. Sarkar, S., Reiss, J. D., & Brandtsegg, Ø. (2017). Investigation of a drum controlled cross-adaptive audio effect for live performance. In *Proceeding 20th International Conference on Digital Audio Effects (DAFx-17)*, Edinburgh, UK.
139. Sauer, C., Roth-Berghofer, T., Auricchio, N., & Proctor, S. (2013). Recommending audio mixing workflows. In *International Conference on Case-Based Reasoning* (pp. 299–313). Springer.

140. Scherer, K. R., Zentner, M. R., et al. (2001). Emotional effects of music: Production rules. *Music and Emotion: Theory and Research, 361*(2001), 392.
141. Schmidt, B. (2003). Interactive mixing of game audio. In *Audio Engineering Society Convention* (Vol. 115). Audio Engineering Society.
142. Schwarz, D., Cahen, R., Jacquemin, C., & Ding, H. (2011). Sound level of detail in interactive audiographic 3d scenes. In *International Computer Music Conference (ICMC)*, Huddersfield, UK.
143. Seetharaman, P., & Pardo, B. (2016). Audealize: Crowdsourced audio production tools. *Journal of the Audio Engineering Society, 64*(9), 683–695.
144. Selfridge, R., Moffat, D., Avital, E. J., & Reiss, J. D. (2018). Creating real-time aeroacoustic sound effects using physically informed models. *Journal of the Audio Engineering Society, 66*(7/8), 594–607.
145. Senior, M. (2011). *Mixing secrets for the small studio: Additional resources.*
146. Senior, M. (2012). *Mixing Secrets.* Focal Press.
147. Sheng, D., & Fazekas, G. (2019). A feature learning siamese model for intelligent control of the dynamic range compressor. In *2019 International Joint Conference on Neural Networks (IJCNN)* (pp. 1–8). IEEE.
148. Sheridan, T. B., & Verplank, W. L. (1978). *Human and computer control of undersea tele-operators.* Technical report, Massachusetts Inst of Tech Cambridge Man-Machine Systems Lab.
149. Stables, R., Enderby, S., De Man, B., Fazekas, G., & Reiss, J. D. (2014). SAFE: A system for the extraction and retrieval of semantic audio descriptors. In *15th International Society for Music Information Retrieval Conference (ISMIR 2014).*
150. Stasis, S., Jillings, N., Enderby, S., & Stables, R. (2017). Audio processing chain recommendation. In *Proceedings of the 20th International Conference on Digital Audio Effects*, Edinburgh, UK.
151. Stasis, S., Jillings, N., Enderby, S., & Stables, R. (2017). Audio processing chain recommendation using semantic cues. In *3rd Workshop on Intelligent Music Production.*
152. Stevens, R., & Raybould, D. (2013). *The game audio tutorial: A practical guide to creating and implementing sound and music for interactive games.* Routledge.
153. Terrell, M., & Reiss, J. D. (2009). Automatic monitor mixing for live musical performance. *Journal of the Audio Engineering Society, 57*(11), 927–936.
154. Terrell, M., Reiss, J. D., & Sandler, M. (2010). Automatic noise gate settings for drum recordings containing bleed from secondary sources. *EURASIP Journal on Advances in Signal Processing, 2010*, 10.
155. Terrell, M., & Sandler, M. (2012). An offline, automatic mixing method for live music, incorporating multiple sources, loudspeakers, and room effects. *Computer Music Journal, 36*(2), 37–54.
156. Terrell, M., Simpson, A., & Sandler, M. (2014). The mathematics of mixing. *Journal of the Audio Engineering Society, 62*(1/2), 4–13.
157. Toulson, R. (2016). The dreaded mix sign-off: Handing over to mastering. In *Mixing Music* (pp. 257–269). Routledge.
158. Tsilfidis, A., Papadakos, C., & Mourjopoulos, J. (2009). Hierarchical perceptual mixing. In *Audio Engineering Society Convention* (Vol. 126).
159. Van Waterschoot, T., & Moonen, M. (2011). Fifty years of acoustic feedback control: State of the art and future challenges. *Proceedings of the IEEE, 99*(2), 288–327.
160. Verfaille, V., & Arfib, D. (2002). Implementation strategies for adaptive digital audio effects. In *Proceeding 5th International Conference on Digital Audio Effects (DAFx-02)*, Hamburg (pp. 21–26).
161. Verfaille, V., Arfib, D., Keiler, F., Knesebeck, A. v. d., & Zölter, U. (2011). Adaptive digital audio effects. In U. Zölter (Ed.), *DAFX—Digital Audio Effects*, Chap. 9 (pp. 321–391). Wiley.

162. Verma, P., & Smith, J. O. (2018). Neural style transfer for audio spectograms. In *31st Conference on Neural Information Processing Systems (NIPS 2017). Workshop for Machine Learning for Creativity and Design*, Long Beach, CA, USA.
163. Vickers, E. (2010). The loudness war: Background, speculation, and recommendations. In *Audio Engineering Society Convention* (Vol. 129). Audio Engineering Society.
164. Virtanen, T., Gemmeke, J. F., Raj, B., & Smaragdis, P. (2015). Compositional models for audio processing: Uncovering the structure of sound mixtures. *IEEE Signal Processing Magazine, 32*(2), 125–144.
165. Ward, D., Reiss, J. D., & Athwal, C. (2012). Multitrack mixing using a model of loudness and partial loudness. In *Audio Engineering Society Convention* (Vol. 133).
166. Weaver, J., Barthet, M., & Chew, E. (2018). Analysis of piano duo tempo changes in varying convolution reverberation conditions. In *Audio Engineering Society Convention* (Vol. 145). Audio Engineering Society.
167. Weaver, J., Barthet, M., & Chew, E. (2019). Filling the space: The impact of convolution reverberation time on note duration and velocity in duet performance. In *Audio Engineering Society Convention* (Vol. 147). Audio Engineering Society.
168. Wichern, G., Wishnick, A., Lukin, A., & Robertson, H. (2015). Comparison of loudness features for automatic level adjustment in mixing. In *Audio Engineering Society Convention* (Vol. 139).
169. Wilmering, T., Fazekas, G., & Sandler, M. B. (2016). AUFX-O: Novel methods for the representation of audio processing workflows. In *International Semantic Web Conference*.
170. Wilmering, T., Moffat, D., Milo, A., & Sandler, M. B. (2020). A history of audio effects. *Applied Sciences, 10*(3), 791.
171. Wilson, A., & Fazenda, B. (2015). 101 mixes: A statistical analysis of mix-variation in a dataset of multi-track music mixes. In *Audio Engineering Society Convention* (Vol. 139). Audio Engineering Society.
172. Wilson, A., & Fazenda, B. M. (2013). Perception & evaluation of audio quality in music production. In *Proceedings of the 16th International Conference on Digital Audio Effects (DAFx-13)*.
173. Wilson, A., & Fazenda, B. M. (2016). An evolutionary computation approach to intelligent music production informed by experimentally gathered domain knowledge. In *Proceedings of the 2nd Audio Engineering Society Workshop on Intelligent Music Production (WIMP)*, London, UK.
174. Wilson, A., Loughran, R., & Fazenda, B. M. (2017). On the suitability of evolutionary computing to developing tools for intelligent music production. In *3rd Workshop on Intelligent Music Production (WIMP)*, Salford, UK.
175. Witten, I. H., Frank, E., Hall, M. A., & Pal, C. J. (2016). *Data Mining: Practical machine learning tools and techniques*. Morgan Kaufmann.
176. Zheng, T., Seetharaman, P., & Pardo, B. (2016). SocialFX: Studying a crowdsourced folksonomy of audio effects terms. In *Proceedings of the 24th ACM International Conference on Multimedia* (pp. 182–186).

David Moffat is a lecturer in Sound and Music Computing at the Interdisciplinary Centre for Computer Music Research (ICCMR), University of Plymouth, UK. He received an M.Sc. in Digital Music Processing from Queen Mary University of London (UK) and graduated from Edinburgh University with a B.Sc. in Artificial Intelligence and Computer Science (UK). He previously worked as a postdoc within the Audio Engineering Group of the Centre for Digital Music at Queen Mary University London, UK. His research focuses on intelligent and assistive mixing and audio production tools through the implementation of semantic tools and machine learning. E-mail: david.moffat@plymouth.ac.uk.

Machine Improvisation in Music: Information-Theoretical Approach

14

Shlomo Dubnov

14.1 What Is Machine Improvisation

This chapter introduces the methods and techniques of machine improvisation based on information-theoretical modeling of music, starting from the first 1998 universal classification modeling of music as an information source, style mixing using joint information source, variable-length motif dictionary improvisation based on universal prediction, and use of information dynamics for symbolic approximation in the factor oracle machine improvisation algorithm. Later developments include query-guided machine improvisation, free-energy modeling of music cognition, and reformulating of variational generative neural music models in terms of rate-distortion theory. This information-theoretical framework offers a novel view of man–machine creative music interaction as a communication problem between an artificial agent and a musician, seeking optimal trade-off between novelty and stylistic imitation under scarcity constraints.

Machine improvisation differs from other uses of AI in music as it operates with little or no prior constraints on the style of music it generates. Through the use of AI, the interactive improvisation agent tries to learn the style of the musician it interacts with, live or pre-recorded, without relying on human music expert analysis and manual encoding of musical rules, rendering any use of pre-programmed algorithms that model a particular style impractical. AI-based machine improvisation also differs from computer music experimental improvisation practices that rely on computers to process, transform or generate musical materials, often in sophisticated and surprising ways, but without modeling of the style of its musical input. Accordingly, machine

S. Dubnov (✉)
Department of Music, University of California San Diego, 9500 Gilman Dr. MC 0099,
La Jolla, CA 92093-0099, USA
e-mail: sdubnov@ucsd.edu

© Springer Nature Switzerland AG 2021
E. R. Miranda (ed.), *Handbook of Artificial Intelligence for Music*,
https://doi.org/10.1007/978-3-030-72116-9_14

improvisation can be defined as the use of computer algorithms to create improvisation on existing music materials by using machine learning and pattern matching algorithms to analyze existing musical examples and create new music in the style of the musical data it analyzed. Here, one can distinguish between two types of machine learning models—those creating dictionary of musical phrases or indexing into a database of recordings using string-matching algorithms (sequence learning) in order to create re-combinations of musical phrases extracted from existing music, a method that we shall term "shallow," versus those transforming a random input into a musical sequence by sophisticated mapping functions that are often learned by neural networks or by other "deep" statistical learning methods. Deep models thus require learning of latent or hidden musical representations (representation learning) that are then used to approximate the probability distribution of the musical data by inverse mapping from randomly triggered events in the "deep" latent space back to the musical surface. Shallow methods, in contrast, often rely on existing features, such as human-engineered representations, with the critical step being a step of approximate string-matching for finding repeated phrases, which is often achieved by quantization of features into a finite set of clusters, a process known as symbolization. As will be shown in this chapter, both methods are essential formulations of the same underlying rate-distortion principle, where the string-based methods are trying to deal with reducing uncertainty in time under complexity penalty of the resulting symbolic alphabet, while the mapping function approach tries to best approximate an instantaneous chunk of musical data, such as few bars of music or audio frames, under a complexity penalty for the underlying random process in latent space. A particularly interesting compromise between sequence and representation learning methods is recurrent neural models with attention, or attention only models using neural transformers. Since these methods are not well understood yet in terms of their statistical properties, we will discuss them only briefly, without setting them into a rate-distortion framework. Although many researchers have proposed computational approaches to encoding musical style, some of which are highly sophisticated and implemented by large software systems, the information-theoretical approach is mathematically elegant and scientifically testable, which partially explains the interest it has attracted among computer music researchers.

14.2   How It All Started: Motivation and Theoretical Setting

The information-theoretical research for machine improvisation started with the application of universal sequence models, and specifically, the well-known Lempel–Ziv (LZ) compression technique [29], to midi files [7]. The universality of LZ compression is understood in terms of not assuming any a-priory knowledge on the statistics of the probability source that generated that sequence, and having its asymptotic compression performance as good as any Markov or finite-state model. Universal modeling is especially relevant for machine improvisation since it takes an empirical learning approach where a statistical model is induced automatically through the application of compression algorithms to existing compositions. The utility of universal information-theoretical methods for characterization and classification of sequences is especially interesting for music, as it captures statistics of musical sequences of different lengths, a situation that is typical to music improvisation that creates new musical materials at different time levels, from short motifs or even instantaneous sonority to melodies and complete thematic phrases. Specifically, the universal modeling allows to apply the notion of entropy to compare sequences in terms of similarity between their statistical sources, as well as the generation of novel musical sequences without explicit knowledge of their statistical model. One should note that "universality" in the universal modeling approach still operates under the assumption that musical sequences are realizations of some high-order Markovian sources. The universal modeling method allowed the following musical operation to be applied to any musical sequence:

- stochastic generation of new sequences that have similar phrase structure as the training sequence, which musically results in between improvisation and the original on the motivic or melodic level
- stochastic morphing or interpolation between musical styles where generation of new sequences is done in a manner where new statistics are obtained by a mixing procedure that creates a "mutual source" between two or more training styles. The extent to which the new improvisation is close to one of the original sources can be controlled by the mixture parameters, providing a gradual transition between two styles which is correct in the statistical sense.

Early experiments with style morphing were the "NTrope Suite" [8] using a joint source algorithm, and later "Memex" and "Composer Duets" [11], using more efficient dictionary and string matching methods as explained below. In addition to generative applications, universal models could be used for music information retrieval, such as performing hierarchical classification by repeatedly agglomerating closest sequences or selecting the most significant phrases from the dictionary of parsed phrases in a MIDI sequence, selected according to the probability of their appearance.

14.2.1 Part 1: Stochastic Modeling, Prediction, Compression, and Entropy

The underlying assumption in the information-theoretical approach to machine improvisation is that a given musical piece can be produced by an unknown stochastic source and that all musical pieces in that style are generated by the same stochastic sources. Despite the finite Markov-order assumptions that do not allow capturing arbitrarily complex music structures, such as very long structure dependency due to musical form, nevertheless, by allowing for sufficiently long training sequences that capture dependence on the past, the universal model capture much of the melodic structure of variable length in a musical piece.

This connection between compression and prediction is a consequence of the asymptotic equipartition property (AEP) [6], which is the information-theoretical analog to the law of large numbers in probability theory. The AEP tells us that if $x_1, x_2, \ldots$ are i.i.d random variables distributed with probability $P(x)$, then

$$-\frac{1}{n} \log_2 P(x_1, x_2, \ldots) \to H(P) \tag{14.1}$$

where $H(x)$ is the Shannon Entropy of the $x \sim P(x)$, $H(x) = -\Sigma_x P(x) \log_2 P(x)$, where the averaging is over all possible occurrences of the sequences x.

The AEP property is graphically represented in Fig. 14.1. The outer circle represents all possible sequences of length n, which are combinatorial number of possibilities depending on the size of the alphabets. Shannon's theory proves that in view of the different probabilities of occurrence of each symbol (in the simplest case these are unbalanced heads or tails or Bernoulli distribution with binary choice), the entropy of the probability can be used to define an effectively much smaller set of outcomes whose probability will tend to one. This set of outcomes is called the "Typical Set" and is denoted here as A_n, where n is the number of elements in a sequence that needs to be sufficiently large. Moreover, all sequences of the typical set are equiprobable, or in other words, one can index them in a way that no further structure or compression can be done. In our case, for generative purposes, this means that we can access these strings using a uniform random number generator.

For stationary ergodic processes, and in particular, finite order Markov processes, the generalization of AEP is called the Shannon–McMillan–Breiman theorem [6]. The connection with compression is that for long x the lower limit on compressibility is $H(x)$ bits per symbol. Thus, if we can find a good algorithm that reaches the

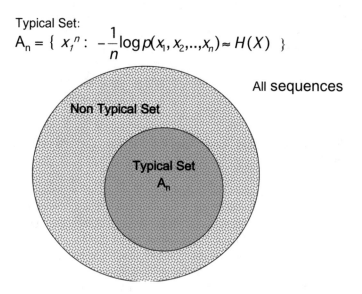

Typical Set:
$$A_n = \{\ x_1^n :\ -\frac{1}{n} \log p(x_1, x_2, .., x_n) \approx H(X)\ \}$$

All sequences

Non Typical Set

Typical Set
A_n

Fig. 14.1 Asymptotic Equipartition Property of long sequences

entropy, then the dictionary of phrases it creates can be used for generating new instances from that source. Since the dictionary has to be very efficient, or in other words, it has to eliminate any other structure present in the sequence, or otherwise it could be compressed more, then we can now sample from the source by random selection from that dictionary. More specific aspects of how the dictionary is created and how continuity is being maintained between the random draws will be discussed next.

14.3 Generation of Music Sequences Using Lempel-Ziv (LZ)

LZ takes a series of symbols from a finite alphabet as input and builds a tree of observed continuations of combinations of the input symbols. This tree grows dynamically as the input is parsed using what is called the incremental parsing (IP) method. If the input is a sample of a stationary stochastic process, LZ asymptotically achieves an optimal description of the input in the sense that the resulting tree can be used to encode the input at the lowest possible bit rate (the entropy of the process). This implies that the coding tree somehow encodes the law of the process; for instance, if one uses the same tree (as it stands after a sufficiently large input) to encode another string, obeying a different law, the resulting bit rate is higher than the entropy.

14.3.1 Incremental Parsing

We chose to use an incremental parsing (IP) algorithm [7] suggested by Lempel and Ziv [30]. IP builds a dictionary of distinct motifs by sequentially adding every new phrase that differs by a single next character from the longest match that already exists in the dictionary. LZ allows assigning conditional probability $p(x_{n+1}|x_1^n)$ of a symbol $x_n + 1$ given x_1^n as context according to the code lengths of the LZ compression scheme [14]. Let $c(n)$ be the number of motifs in the parsing of an input n-sequence. Then, $\log(c(n))$ bits are needed to describe each prefix (a motif without its last character), and 1 bit to describe the last character (in case of a binary alphabet).

For instance, given a text $ababaa\ldots$, IP parses it into $a, b, ab, aa, \ldots$, where motifs are separated by commas. The dictionary may be represented as a tree.

LZ code for the above sequence is $(00, a), (00, b), (01, b), (01, a)$ where the first entry of each pair gives the index of the prefix and the second entry gives the next character. Ziv and Lempel have shown that the average code length $c(n) \log(c(n))/n$ converges asymptotically to the entropy of the sequence with increasing n. This proves that the coding is optimal. Since for optimal coding the code length is 1/probability, and since all code lengths are equal, we may say that, at least in the long limit, the IP motifs have equal probability. Thus, taking the equal weight for nodes in the tree representation, $p(x_{n+1}|x_1^n)$ will be deduced as a ratio between the cardinality of the sub-trees (number of sub-nodes) following the node x_1^n. As the number of sub-nodes is also the node's share of the probability space (because one code-word is allocated to each node), we see that the amount of code space allocated to a node is proportional to the number of times it occurred.

14.3.2 Generative Model Based on LZ

In order to produce new sequences from LZ tree, we create a generative model in two steps [7]: first, the motif dictionary is transformed into a continuation dictionary, where each key will be a motif M from the previous dictionary, and the corresponding value will be a list of couples $(..(k, P(k|W))..)$ for each possible continuation k in the sequence alphabet, and second, a generation function the samples a new symbol from a continuation dictionary. The two steps can be demonstrated as follows:

$$Text = (ababcabccbabdabcedabcddadc)$$
$$IP = (a, b, ab, c, abc, cb, abd, abce, d, abcd, da, dc)$$
$$Motif\ dictionary = ((a)6)((b)1)((c)3)((d)3)((ab)5)((abc)3)((abd)1)((abcd)1)...$$
$$((abce)1)((cb)2)((cbd)1)((da)1)((dc)1)$$
$$Continuation\ dictionary = ((a)((b1.0)))((ab)((c0.75)(d0.25)))((abc)((d0.5)(e0.5)))...$$
$$((c)((b1.0)))((cb)((d1.0)))((d)((a0.5)(c0.5))$$

Suppose we have already generated a text $a_0 a_1 \ldots a_{n-1}$. Setting a parameter L which is an upper limit on the size of the past we want to consider in order to choose the next object, and initialize current context length to this maximal length $l = L$ (Fig. 14.2).

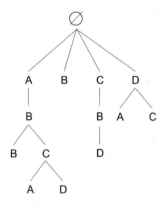

Fig. 14.2 LZ-based tree representation of a sequence abba derived from incremental parsing algorithm

1. Current text is $a_0a_1 \ldots a_{n-1}$, context $= a_{n-l} \ldots a_{n-1}$.
2. Check if context is a motif in the continuation dictionary.

- if context is empty (this happens when $l = 0$), sample from the root according to symbol probabilities and go back to step 1.
- If non-empty context is found, look up its associated dictionary value for the probability distribution of the continuation symbols. Sample this distribution and append the chosen object k to right of text. Increment $n = n + 1$, set l to max value $l = L$ and go back to step 2.
- If context is non-empty but its entry is not found in the dictionary key, shorten it by popping its leftmost object $l = l - 1$ and go back to step 1.

This procedure requires repeated search from the root of the tree, iteratively shortening the context each time the context is not found in the dictionary key entry, which is very inefficient. By inverting the sequences and accordingly changing the tree representation, the repeated search can be avoided and the algorithm becomes amenable to real-time implementation, as described in [7]. The LZ and has been implemented in OpenMusic [3] and Flow Machine [22] systems, and in view of its similarity to Markov generation, it has been often termed variable memory Markov (VMM), although, from a strict mathematical point, the probability assignments are not estimated by ngram approximations but rather rely on Feder's universal prediction weighting scheme [14].

14.4   Improved Suffix Search Using Factor Oracle Algorithm

As IP builds tree structures in the learning stage, finding the best suffix involves walking the tree from the root to the node bearing that suffix. In order to make the suffix search more efficient, and also take into account partial repetitions that may occur between the parsing points of IP, We explored the use of Factor Oracle (FO) [2]. In order to use the automation for generation, the auxiliary set of links $S(i) = j$ called Suffix Links running backward are used. These links point to node j at the end of the longest repeating suffix (also called repeating factor) appearing before node i (i.e., longest suffix of prefix of i that appears at least twice in prefix of i). FO automation provides the desired tool for efficiently generating new sequences of symbols based on the repetition structure of the reference example. Compared to IP and PST, FO is structurally closer to the reference suffix tree. Its efficiency is close to IP (linear, incremental). Moreover, it is an automaton, rather than a tree, which makes it easier to handle maximum suffixes in the generation process. This method also differs from Markov chain-based style machines mentioned above in the extent of the signal history or context that it is able to capture. An oracle structure carries two kinds of links, forward link and suffix link. Suffix link is a backward pointer that links state t to k with $t > k$, without a label and is denoted by $\mathtt{sfx}[t] = k$.

$$\texttt{sfx}[t] = k \iff \text{the longest repeated suffix of}$$

$$\{x_1, x_2, \ldots, x_t\} \text{ is recognized in } k.$$

Suffix links are used to find the longest repeated suffix in X. In order to track the longest repeated suffix at each time index t, the length of the longest repeated suffix at each state t is computed by the algorithm described in [20] and is denoted by $\texttt{lrs}[t]$. $\texttt{lrs}$ is essential to the on-line construction algorithm of an oracle structure [20] and its generalization for approximate matching by threshold search for model selection [12] for *VMO*.

Forward links are links with labels and are used to retrieve any of the factors from X. An oracle structure has two types of forward links; the first is an internal forward link which is a pointer from state $t - 1$ to t labeled by the symbol x_t, denoted as $\delta(t - 1, x_t) = t$. The other forward link is an external forward link which is a pointer from state t to $t + k$ labeled by x_{t+k} with $k > 1$. An external forward link $\delta(t, x_{t+k}) = t + k$ is created when

$$x_{t+1} \neq x_{t+k}$$

$$x_t = x_{t+k-1}$$

$$\delta(t, x_{t+k}) = \emptyset.$$

In other words, an external forward link is created between x_t and x_{t+k} when the sequence of symbols $\{x_{t+k-1}, x_{t+k}\}$ is first seen in X with x_t and x_{t+k-1} share the same label. The function of the forward links is to provide an efficient way to retrieve any of the factors of X, starting from the beginning of X and following the path formed by forward links. We exploited forward link's functionality by treating forward links as indications of possible transitions from state to state for our time series query-by-content tasks (Fig. 14.3).

The use of FO for generation can be conceptualized as a memory recombination scheme is shown in Fig. 14.4.

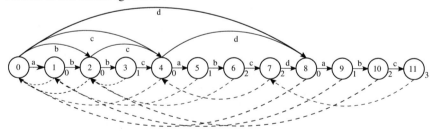

Fig. 14.3 A *VMO* structure with symbolized signal $\{a, b, b, c, a, b, c, d, a, b, c\}$, upper (normal) arrows represent forward links with labels for each frame and lower (dashed) are suffix links. Values outside of each circle are the $\texttt{lrs}$ value for each state

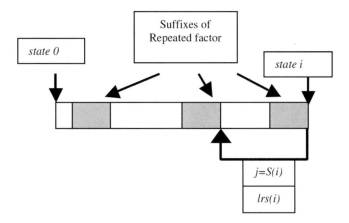

Fig. 14.4 Representation of the improvisation process as memory recall by following suffixes of repeated sub-sequences (factors) in the musical past

14.5   Lossless Versus Lossy Compression Methods for Machine Improvisation

Introducing the concept of lossy compression is important for machine improvisations for several reasons:

- it allows better generalization and more novelty during the generation process by ignoring partial or insignificant differences in the data.
- allows finding repetitions in time series and continuously valued data, such as a sequence of audio features, by reducing the fidelity of the representation through quantization or clustering of nearby data points into classes. This process is also known as symbolization.
- reducing the amount of symbols or size of the alphabet is also essential when dealing with complex symbolic data, such as multiple voices in midi representation. For example, to capture harmonic or chordal structure it is essential to ignore differences in voicing and possibly some passing or embellishing notes.
- allows control of improvisation algorithm from partial specification, such as abstract scenario.
- creating a low-dimensional representation allows mapping between different types of musical data that is needed for guiding improvisation from another musical input.
- lossy compression can be used to extract features from music and can be used for representation learning.

The theory of lossy compression was formulated by Shannon in terms of Rate-Distortion. We will discuss this approach in detail in the second part of the chapter. An early example of applying lossy representation to sequence modeling is a VMM structure called Prediction Suffix Tree (PST) that was suggested by [21]. Much like the IP structure, PST represents a dictionary of distinct motifs, but instead of relying on LZ lossless coding scheme, the PST algorithm builds a restricted dictionary of only those motifs that both appear a significant number of times throughout the complete source sequence, and are meaningful for predicting the immediate future. The information-theoretical framework underlying the approach is that of efficient lossy compression, a topic which we will return to in the section on rate-distortion theory.

It should be noted that both IP and PST build tree structures in the learning stage, where finding the best suffix consists of walking the tree from the root to the node labeled by that suffix. PST, which was originally designed for classification purposes, has the advantage of the better gathering of statistical information from shorter strings, with a trade-off of deliberately throwing away some of the original sub-strings during the analysis process to maintain a compact representation. Another significant advantage of PST is an aggregation of suffix statistics as a sliding window, thus obtaining more statistics for short sequences compared to the incremental parsing approach that skips shorter sub-sequences in a previously recognized suffix.

A possible disadvantage of PST is that partial retention of original data through lossy representation introduces more false notes into the generation procedure. We have carried experiments on using IP for music classification and music generation, as described in [Dub03]. The pros and cons of these two approaches led to the adoption of a different string matching approach, based on the Factor Oracle (FO) string searching algorithm, that will be described in the next section. FO effectively provided an indexing structure built on top of the original music sequence, pointing to its repetition points as a graph of suffix links. This allowed an efficient recombination of existing patterns for improvisation. From information-theoretical perspective, this type of model belongs to a family of lossless compression algorithms. The lossy version of the suffix links construction called Variable Markov Oracle (VMO) will be described in the section after FO.

14.6 Variable Markov Oracle

Variable Markov Oracle (VMO) is a generative machine learning method that combines lossy compression with the Factor Oracle (FO) string matching algorithm. VMO was developed in order to allow machine improvisation on real-valued scalar or vector data, such as sequences of audio feature vectors, or data vectors extracted from human poses during dance movements. Moreover, the VMO suffix tree data structure allows for query-guided audio content generation [24] and multimedia query-matching [25]. VMO is capable of finding embedded linkages between samples along with the multivariate time series and enables tracking and comparison between time series using a Viterbi-like dynamic programming algorithm. In order to operate on such multivariate time series data, *VMO* symbolizes a signal X sampled at time t,

$X = x_1, x_2, \ldots, x_t, \ldots, x_T$, into a symbolic sequence $S = s_1, s_2, \ldots, s_t, \ldots, s_T$, with T states and with observation frame x_t labeled by s_t whose value is one of the symbols in a finite-sized alphabet Σ. The labels are formed by following suffix links along with the states in an oracle structure.

The essential step for the construction of *VMO* is finding a threshold value, θ that partitions the space of features into categories. The threshold θ is used to determine if the incoming x_t is similar to one of the frames following the suffix link started at $t - 1$. *VMO* assigns two frames, x_i and x_j, the same label $s_i = s_j \in \Sigma$ if $||x_i - x_j|| \leq \theta$. In extreme cases, setting θ too low leads to *VMO* assigning different labels to every frame in X and setting θ too high leads to *VMO* assigning the same label to every frame in X. As a result, both extreme cases are incapable of capturing any informative structures (repeated suffixes) of the time series. Elsewhere in this chapter we describe the use of *Information Rate* (*IR* hereafter) to select the optimal θ in the context of music information dynamics. We show an example of the oracle structure with extreme θ values in Fig. 14.5. It should be noted that the alphabet of the symbolization is constructed dynamically, as new symbols can be added when an input sample cannot be assigned to one of the existing clusters of samples already labeled by the existing label. We will denote the resulting alphabet for a given θ as Σ_θ.

In the process of IR analysis, the system is performing a search over different θ values, where for each value *VMO* constructs different suffix structures for different symbolized sequences derived from the time series (as shown in Fig. 14.5). To select the sequence with the most informative structures, *IR* is used as the criterion in model selection between the different structures generated by different θ values [12, 24]. *IR* measures the relative reduction of uncertainty of the current sample in a time series when past samples are known. Let the past samples of a time series denoted by $x_{\text{past}} = \{x_1, x_2, \ldots, x_{n-1}\}$, the current sample x_n and $H(x) = -\sum P(x) \log_2 P(x)$ the entropy of x with $P(x)$ the distribution of x, the statistical definition of *IR* is the mutual information between x_{past} and x_n,

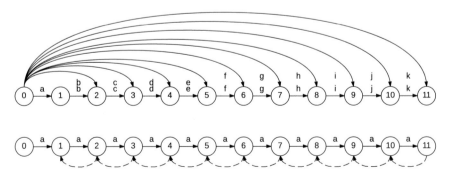

Fig. 14.5 Two oracle structures with extreme values of θ. The characters near each forward link represent the assigned labels. (Top) The oracle structure with $\theta = 0$ or extremely low. (Bottom) The oracle structure with a very high θ value. It is obvious that in both cases the oracles are not able to capture any structures of the time series

$$I(x_{\text{past}}, x_n) = H(x_n) - H(x_n | x_{\text{past}}).$$ (14.2)

In [12], the above statistical definition of *IR* is replaced by a deterministic notion of a compression algorithm $C(\cdot)$ that is used as a computational measure of time series complexity. This allows estimation of the mutual information by replacing the entropy term $H(\cdot)$ with compression gain for the best symbolization, searching over possible values of the quantization threshold θ (14.2).

$$IR(x_{\text{past}}, x_n) = \max_{\theta, s_t \in \Sigma_\theta} [C(s_n) - C(s_n | s_{\text{past}})].$$ (14.3)

The IR measure has been used, independently of generative applications in machine improvisation, as a method for analysis of music structure, tracking the changes in information contents through prediction of the next frame based on the musical past, called Music Information Dynamics [9, 27].

The value of the deterministic *IR* defined in (14.3) can then be robustly calculated by complexity measures associated with a compression algorithm with $C(s_n)$ the number of bits used to compress s_n independently and $C(s_n | s_{\text{past}})$ the number of bits used to compress s_n using s_{past}. In [19], a lossless compression algorithm, *Compror*, based on *FO* is provided and is proven to have similar performance to *gzip* and *bzip2*. The detail formulations of how *Compror*, *AO* and *IR* are combined is provided in [12]. In the context of time series pattern and structure discovery with *VMO*, the *VMO* with higher *IR* value indicates more of the repeating subsequences (ex. patterns, motifs, themes, gestures, etc.) are captured than the ones with lower *IR* value.

14.7 Query-Based Improvisation Algorithm

Let R be the query observation indexed by n, denoted as $R = r_1, r_2, \ldots, r_N$. The matching algorithm provided in Algorithm 1 takes R as input and matches it to the target *VMO*, $Oracle(S = s_1, s_2, \ldots, s_T, X = x_1, x_2, \ldots, x_T)$, constructed by a target time series, X. The algorithm returns a cost and a corresponding recombination path. The cost is the reconstruction error between the query and the best match from X given a metric on a frame-by-frame basis. The recombination path corresponds to the sequence of indices that will reconstruct a new sequence from X that best resembles the query (Fig. 14.6).

14.7.1 Query-Matching Algorithm

The query-matching algorithm tracks the progress of traversing the oracle using forward and backward links, finding the optimal path via a dynamic programming algorithm. We separate the algorithm into two steps, initialization and decoding. In Algorithm 1, the initialization is in line 1 to line 6. During initialization, the size of the alphabet, M, is obtained from the cardinality of Σ. Then for the mth list, the frame within the mth list that is closest to the first query frame, R_1, is found and stored. After

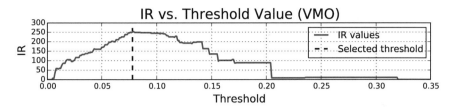

Fig. 14.6 *IR* values are shown on vertical axis while θ are on horizontal axis. The solid curve in blue color shows the relations between the two quantities and the dashed black line indicates the chosen θ by locating the maximal *IR* value. Empirically the *IR* curves possess quasi-concave function shapes thus global maximum could be located

the initialization step, the decoding step (line $7-13$ in Algorithm 1) iterates over the rest of the query frames from 2 to N to find M paths, with each path beginning with the state found corresponding to the respective label in the initialization step. It could be observed that the proposed query-matching algorithm is similar to the Viterbi decoding algorithm for *HMM* and max-sum inference algorithm for graphical models [23] in the sense that each update in the decoding step depends only on its neighboring findings, thus making it efficient to compute and of no need to search over the whole state space. A visualization of Algorithm 1 from initialization to decoding for one path among the M paths is shown in Fig. 14.7.

Algorithm 1 Query-Matching

Require: Target signal in *VMO*, $Oracle(S = s_1, s_2, \ldots, s_T, X = x_1, x_2, \ldots, x_T)$ and query time
    series $R = r_1, r_2, \ldots, r_N$
1: Get the number of clusters, $M \leftarrow |\Sigma|$
2: Initialize cost vector $C \in \mathbb{R}^M$ and path matrix $P \in \mathbb{R}^{M \times N}$.
3: **for** $m = 1 : M$ **do**
4:    $P_{m,1} \leftarrow$ Find the state, t, in the mth list from Σ
             with the least distance, $d_{m,1}$, to r_1
5:    $C_m \leftarrow d_{m,1}$
6: **end for**
7: **for** $n = 2 : N$ **do**
8:    **for** $m = 1 : M$ **do**
9:        $P_{m,n} \leftarrow$ Find the state, t, in lists with labels
             corresponding to forward links from state
             $P_{m,n-1}$ with the least distance, $d_{m,n}$ to $R[n]$
10:     $C_m \mathrel{+}= d_{m,n}$
11:    **end for**
12: **end for**
13: **return** $P[\arg\min(C)], \min(C)$

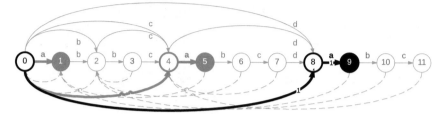

(a) At $t = 1$ (Initialization for label **a**); {**a**, 9}, the pair of label initialized and frame matched. At initialization, for label **a** the choices for the first frame are stored in the list, $\{1, 5, 9\}$ from Σ. Assuming the closest frame in X to r_1 with label **a** is X_9, then the first frame for path beginning with label **a** will be 9. With the help of keeping track of Σ, the calculation between r_1 and $\{x_1, x_5, x_9\}$ is straight forward.

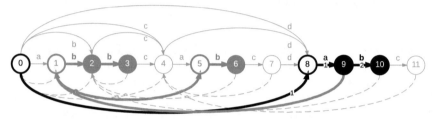

(b) At $t = 2$ (Decoding); {**b**, 10}, the pair of label identified and frame matched. At $t = 2$, the only possible label following label **a** from $t = 1$ is **b**, thus making frames in $\{2, 3, 6, 10\}$ the possible candidates. Let $s_1 0$ be the closest frame from the candidates to r_2

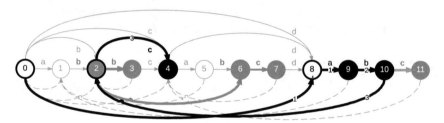

(c) At $t = 3$ (Decoding): {**c**, 4}, the pair of label identified and frame matched. At $t = 3$, the possible labels following label **b** from $t = 2$ is **b** and **c** by examining the forward links from state 10. The possible frames are now the union of labels **b** and **c**, $\{2, 3, 4, 6, 7, 10, 11\}$. Let the closest frame from the candidates to r_3 be x_4, the result path beginning at label **a** is $\{9, 10, 4\}$. The steps from (a) to (c) are done for all other 3 possible paths as well

Fig. 14.7 Decoding steps: Consider the target time series represented as the *VMO* shown above, the same from Fig. 14.3. The light gray parts of each subplot are the same from Fig. 14.3. In each subplot, parts marked by black with thick arrows indicate the path for the chosen state, dark gray ones with thick arrows represent possible paths, and filled circle represents the candidate states. Numbers on the thick black arrows are step numbers. In this example, the query R, is assumed to have 3 frames and the subplots demonstrate hypothetic steps for the path started with frames in X in cluster labeled by **a** (among 4 possible paths started via **a**, **b**, **c** or **d**). Here the visualization of the query time series is omitted and the path is chosen generically to demonstrate Algorithm 1

14.8   Part 2: Variational Encoding, Free Energy, and Rate Distortion

We have encountered implicitly the concept of rate-distortion when we introduced VMO in the previous section as a method that utilizes lossy compression to find structure in musical data. In this section, we expand on the notion of partial or approximate and incomplete representation of the data through combining the concepts of lossy compression with Variational Auto-Encoder (VAE), which is one of the fundamental deep learning generative methods for learning representations. In this section, we will show how VAE can be used to learn a representation of musical short-term structure, such as frames in midi files, without considering its temporal structure. This will solve the basic problem of feature engineering, hopefully relieving the need for human-based expertise in finding the adequate representation of musical data for the subsequent step of sequential model. In later sections, we will extend the VAE representation learning with sequential models and define a unified deep information dynamics model, but before doing that, we want to motivate the use of variational methods starting from some basic principles of modeling complex system, also pointing out to some possible intriguing relations between statistical modeling of music and current approaches to the understanding of human cognition.

The basic notion of variational modeling in statistics is that given a set of measurements, which in our case consists of musical data in the shape of midi or audio recording, and assuming there exist some hidden parameters that determine that data distribution, which in our case may refer to hidden factors governing the musical structure,[1] in case when the problem of estimating this probability is too complex to be written explicitly or to be tractable computationally, variational methods allow a simplification that can be more easily solved. An important point here is that both the hidden parameters and the data (z, x respectively) are assumed to be random variables, so the complete knowledge of the system requires knowing the joint distribution $p(x, z)$, or alternatively learning the generative or decoding probability (likelihood of the data) going from latent states to data, averaged over all possible latent state $p(x|z)p(z)$, or in the opposite direction, learning the encoding (posterior probability) of the latent states given the data $p(z|x)p(x)$. When learning the complete model might be too hard, the variational solution approach is to approximate the posterior $p(z|x)$ with a simpler distribution $q(z)$ that is part of some family of distributions functions Q. Typically, choosing Q is done by making some additional assumptions to simplify the model, such as independence between latent states, a tractable form of a probability distribution, such as Gaussian, and so on. The big advantage of variational methods is that it allows to re-write a statistical inference problem as an optimization problem, searching for an optimal function q over some family of functions Q. The term "statistical inference" refers to learning about what we do not observe (latent states) based on what we observe (musical surface). In

---

[1] The latent states do not correspond specifically to any music-theoretical notions such as harmony or rhythm, but are a rather generic formulation for any underlying cause that governs musical structure.

other words, inference is the process of drawing conclusions about the world (understanding of musical structure) based on some observed variables (notes or sounds). The terms used in statistical literature referring to conclusions (the "posterior"), the prior knowledge (the "prior") and the knowledge coming from the observation (the "likelihood") are taken from Bayes theorem that establishes the relations between joint, conditional and marginal distributions $p(x, z) = p(x|z)p(z) = p(z|x)p(x)$. The term "variational" comes from the "calculus of variations," which deals with optimization problems that pick the best function in a family of functions. Also, it should be noted that finding the posterior can be handled using non-variational methods, such as Monte Carlo or Gibbs sampling. Since our theme is information-theoretical models of music, we will show the connection between notions of entropy and distortion in information, and entropy and energy in physics using variational methods. The general concept of free energy is discussed next.

14.8.1 Variational Free Energy

In thermodynamics, free energy is whatever remains of the energy after heat or temperature caused the system to move toward a state of highest entropy, or in other words, the free energy principle assumes that a learning system (including biological system) tries to balance its survival abilities in the world, accounted by two competing factors: it being able to tell what is likely or probable and what is not by learning the probability distribution of the underlying causes of phenomena seen in the environment, which is accounted as minimizing a cost function related to energy; and its own system complexity, accounted by an entropy function that measures its internal order, trying to reach a configuration that is most compact in terms of the number of states it needs to understand the world. For a system having an energy level E and Entropy H, the free energy F at temperature T is $F = E - TH$. It can be understood as a constrained optimization problem where minimization of energy is subject to an entropy constraint, with temperature serving as (an inverse of) a Lagrange multiplier. Rewriting this expression in probabilistic terms, we denote the approximate encoding done by our system as $q(z|x)$, while the observations and true latent variable are distributed according to $p(x, z)$. The entropy of the encoding done by our system for a given observation x is $H = -\mathbb{E}_{q(z|x)} \log(q(z|x))$, and if We refer to $\mathbb{E}_{q(z|x)} \log(p(z, x)$ as energy, we get an expression of free energy as

$$F = -\mathbb{E}_{q(z|x)}[\log(p(z, x) - \log(q(z|x))] = \text{Energy} - \text{Entropy} \qquad (14.4)$$

where the Lagrange multiplier (temperature) equals 1. Later, we will discuss cases where temperature is not equal 1. Why this formulation is special? One way to answer this is to postulate free energy minimization as a principle that learning systems operate by. As such, it can not be proved or disproved. A more principled approach is to show that negative free energy is a lower bound to the likelihood of observations,

$$\log p(x) = -F + D_{KL}(q(z|x)||p(z|x)) \qquad (14.5)$$

We will not prove this derivation here, but it is a standard derivation shown in texts on variational Bayes, including Kingma and Welling's VAE paper [18]. Accordingly, the variational approximation gives us both a tractable approximation for the posterior $p(z|x)$, and a lower bound for the evidence $\log p(x)$ since the KL-divergence is always strictly non-negative). As the log evidence $\log p(x)$ is fixed with respect to $q(Z)$, finding $q(z)$ that maximizes the negative free energy will thus minimize $D_{KL}(q(z|x)||p(z|x))$, bringing the approximate posterior to the true conditional distribution of the latent variables. In variational inference terminology, negative free energy is commonly called Evidence Lower Bound (ELBO). In the next section, we will look at the alternative formulation of this principle in terms of rate-distortion theory.

14.8.2 Rate Distortion and Human Cognition

Rate distortion is a term originating in Shannon's work on lossy communication, measured in terms of mutual information $I(x, z)$ between a signal X and its compressed version Z, where a loss or distortion $d(x, z)$ occurs during the encoding process. This distortion allows transmission at rates that are lower than the lossless compression limit $H(x)$ of the signal entropy. It is intuitive that the two factors, information $I(x, z)$ and distortion $d(x, z)$ are at odds with each other. For example, a low-resolution image or low sampling rate audio requires less bits to encode than their full-resolution version. What is interesting about the rate-distortion theory is that it provides theoretical lower bounds for the rate of information transmission, given by $I(x, z)$, under the constraint that the distortion between the two signals $d(x, z)$ does not exceed a certain threshold.

In psychology, rate-distortion theory was suggested as a principled mathematical framework for incorporating limits on the capabilities of the cognitive system. This entails reformulating the goal of perception from tasks related to storage, or reproduction of afferent signals, to the task of minimizing some survival-related cost function. The distinction of the rate-distortion approach from other neural information processing theories, such as an efficient coding hypothesis [4] is that the costs and constraints are imposed not just by the constraints on the internal neural architecture but also by the goals of the organism and the structure of the external environment. For organisms, it may be more important to be "good" than "efficient," where good means solving an important problem that exists in the environment. For example, rate distortion is used to explain the results of an absolute identification experiment where subjects are asked to respond with his or her best guess regarding the identity of the stimulus from a previously shown set of lines of varying length, or tones of varying frequency or loudness. The rate-distortion method showed that participants' implicit goals in the experiment were not to identify each example precisely, but rather to select a broader response category that is as close as possible to the correct response. What is relevant in this approach for our purposes is that it shows that acts of exact memorization of musical materials (themes, phrases, or chords), without being able to group them into common categories, will not serve well the purposes of having a good music "behavior." For the purpose of music generation, lossy or partial representation of musical signal might be actually a desirable property, as it encourages creativity and allows producing different levels of music anticipation and surprise. By discarding irrelevant details of the musical surface, the intermediate latent encoding z becomes more susceptible to generating novel materials, while still maintaining some level of agreement with deeper or hidden aspects of the musical structure or style. Since music is in constant flux and variation, the development of music composition requires balancing between the sense of coherence or structural unity and the sense of novelty and variety. Accordingly, viewing creativity as "useful novelty," the rate-distortion framework offers a possible principled approach to such problems.

It should be noted that in the latent space representation, the distortion is measured only after the signal is decoded back into the same domain as the original observation. Moreover, the distortion or error resulting from encoding–bottleneck–decoding process does not have to be measured necessarily in terms of actual data errors, but rather as a statistical error of producing or decoding signals that are low probability compared to the true statistics of the source distribution. Thus, deciding on the nature of the distortion measure is important for finding a compressed representation that is right for the problem, thus shifting the burden of the problem from general modeling to one of formulating the trade-off between representation complexity (encoding) and reconstruction task. In later sections, we will generalize the concept of distortion measure and use quality of prediction for the reconstruction task. This way, we will be looking for the most compact representation of past musical data that results in the best prediction of its future. This generalization is motivated by the Bayesian brain theory that includes predictive coding as one of the goals of an organism trying to optimize its behavior. Moreover, in this context, prediction error can be regarded as free energy, such that minimizing free energy is effectively the same as minimizing prediction error [15]. We will turn to these points in the later sections, but first, we need to define the relation between variational encoding and rate distortion.

14.9 VAE Latent Information Bounds

The idea behind Variational models, as we mentioned before, is using an approximation to the unknown true distribution, while at the same time also treating the hidden parameters of the model as random variables. We denote the input as x and the latent representation as z. The mapping of x to z is done by a stochastic encoder $q(z|x)$ that induces a joint "encoder" distribution $p_e(x, z) = p(x)q(z|x)$. A powerful method of estimating the model parameters is so called Evidence Lower Bound or ELBO. The use of ELBO for variational inference comes from the inequality $\log p(x) \geq ELBO$,

$$\log p(x) = \log \int p(x, z)dz = \log \int q(z|x)\frac{p(x, z)}{q(z|x)}dz \geq \mathbb{E}_{q(z|x)} \log \frac{p(z, x)}{q(z|x)} \tag{14.6}$$

The ELBO expression can be shown to have two equivalent forms

$$ELBO := \mathbb{E}_{q(z|x)}(\log p(x|z)) - D_{KL}(q(z|x)\|p(z))$$
$$= \mathbb{E}_{q(z|x)}(\log p(x,z)) - \mathbb{E}_{q(z|x)}(\log(q(z|x))) \quad (14.7)$$

The right-side version of ELBO is the free energy formulation winc $\mathbb{E}_{q(z|x)}$ $(\log p(x,z))$ can be interpreted as the negative energy in a Boltzmann distribution and $\mathbb{E}_{q(z|x)}(\log(q(z|x)))$ is interpreted as entropy of the encoded state, with their sum becoming the thermodynamic free energy expression with temperature one.

Using the definition of mutual information,

$$I_e(x,z) = D_{KL}(p_e(x,z)\|p(x)q(z)) \quad (14.8)$$
$$= \mathbb{E}_{p(x)}(D_{KL}(q(z|x)\|q(z)))$$

it becomes evident that when the latent states are independent of the input, the mutual information between x and z is zero. In other words, for the encoding to be informative, the distribution of latent states has to substantively deviate from it marginal distribution when input signal is provided.

In order to examine the relation between VAE method of representation learning and information-theoretical bounds on the data x and representation variable S, we average the ELBO over all possible inputs $xp(x)$.

$$\mathbb{E}_{p(x)}(ELBO) = \mathbb{E}_{p_e(x,z)}(\log p(x|z)) - \mathbb{E}_{p(x)}D_{KL}(q(z|x)\|p(z)) \quad (14.9)$$
$$= \mathbb{E}_{p_e(x,z)}(\log p(x|z)) - (\mathbb{E}_{p(x)}D_{KL}(q(z,x)\|q(z)) + D_{KL}(q(z)\|p(z)))$$
$$= \mathbb{E}_{p_e(x,z)}(\log p(x|z)) - I_e(x,z) - D_{KL}(q(z)\|p(z))$$
$$\leq \mathbb{E}_{p_e(x,z)}(\log p(x|z)) - I_e(x,z)$$

where last inequality is due to non-negativity of D_{KL}. Changing signs, we have the following information-theoretical bound:

$$I_e(x,z) - \mathbb{E}_{p_e(x,z)}(\log p(x|z)) \leq \mathbb{E}_{p(x)}(-ELBO) \quad (14.10)$$

Minimizing $-ELBO$, or equivalently minimizing free energy, will lower the upper bound on mutual information between data x and representation z created by the VAE encoder, combined with an extra penalty factor given by the negative log-likelihood of the data reconstructed or generated by the decoder from latent states z. Equality will occur only when the marginal distribution of the encoding equals the "true" distribution of the latent variables that produced the data x. This can be viewed as a rate-distortion pair, where the rate $I_e(x,z)$ is paired with a distortion constraint $D = -\mathbb{E}_{p_e(x,z)}(\log p(x|z))$ with Lagrange multiplier of one. Repeating the same process with an alternative definition of ELBO that has a weighting factor β (temperature $1/\beta$)

$$ELBO(\beta) := \mathbb{E}_{q(z|x)}(\log p(x|z)) - \beta D_{KL}(q(z|x)\|p(z)) \quad (14.11)$$
$$I_e(x,z) - \beta\mathbb{E}_{p_e(x,z)}(\log p(x|z)) \leq \mathbb{E}_{p(x)}(-ELBO(\beta))$$

This formulation makes the complexity accuracy, or rate-distortion aspect of learning more explicit, with β controlling the trade-off between the amount of information passing from input to the latent states (rate), and the quality of reconstruction (distortion). This trade-off is normally determined during learning phase by fixing the value of β in the loss function [17].

14.10 Deep Music Information Dynamics

Music Information Dynamics broadly quantifies the study of information passing over time between past and future in musical signal [1]. The study of musical information dynamics was shown to be important for understanding human perception of music in terms of anticipation and predictability. The ability to find repetitions in music depends on the ability to perceive similarity between different variations of musical materials—two similar chords often have different voicing or added notes, melodies modulate, rhythms change, but the overall musical form is still perceivable by capturing unity in this variety. One of the promises in neural modeling of music is the ability to automatically find feature representations that capture essential musical structure without a need for expert human engineering. Moreover, the creative hope is that these structures would be idiomatic to a specific style of the training corpus and would allow generating new instances of music in that style in ways that are controllable as desired by the user. In earlier sections, we introduced the Information Rate (IR) measure for studying music information dynamics of a signal $x(n)$ by considering the relation between a present data point $x = x(n)$ and it's past $x_{past} = x(1), x(2), .., x(n-1)$. Maximal IR is obtained for signal that looks uncertain and thus has high entropy $Hx)$, but is predictable or has little uncertainty when the past is taken into account $H(x)|x_{past})$.

In [28], VMO was proposed as an efficient method for estimating IR. This method generalizes a string matching FO algorithm to operate over metric space. In order to take into account the past to compress or predict the present, the algorithm tries to find approximate repetitions in the time series. The difficulty arises when the data points assume real values (such as in the case of audio feature vectors) or have a very large set of discrete values (such as a possible note combinations in polyphonic music), making exact repetitions meaningless. Thus, in order to find approximate repetitions, a reduction of the set of values that the data can assume into a much smaller set of values or limited alphabet is required. IR performs this task by searching over different similarity thresholds while searching for repeating suffixes and retaining a suffix structure (factor oracle graph) for threshold level that obtained the best compression ratio and thus best information rate. This process can be considered as performing a quantization or symbolization of the time series. The quantization is implicitly performed by finding approximate repetitions between time series values up to a threshold. The entropy differences are estimated by considering the compression rate obtained by encoding repeated blocks versus encoding of individual frames. Since a different amount of repetitions is captured at different thresholds, the algorithm finds the highest IR by exhaustive search over all possible thresholds. In addition to finding the numerical IR values, VMO analysis also allows visualization of the salient motifs by enumerating the salient repetitions and identifying their position and duration in the signal. The motifs are detected by enumerating the repetitions found at the optimal threshold and selecting instances that are longer than certain minimal length and have more than minimal number of repetitions. The details of pattern-finding are provided in [26] According to this interpretation, we can generalize the concept of IR by defining it as maximum of mutual information over possible encodings of the signal z. In the following, we will generalize information dynamics to stochastic encoding $z \sim q(z|x) : q \in Q$. This will lead us to using IR over latent variables,

$$IR(x) = \max_{q \in Q:z \sim q(z|x)} I(z, z_{past}) \tag{14.12}$$

$$= H(z) - H(z|z_{past}) \tag{14.13}$$

This still leaves us with the problem of finding approximate repetitions in the latent space, which could be accomplished by using autoregressive models, RNN, or applying VMO with symbolization/threshold search step. Finding maximum mutual information from past to the present in the latent space needs now to be balanced against the desire to have the least structured, simplest, or most compact latent representation for a given distortion level. In the next section, we will present a principled approach that combines all three factors (high predictability, low distortion, and high latent entropy).

14.10.1 Representation–Prediction Rate Distortion

In order to combine the temporal information with representation learning, we generalize the idea of information dynamics by using rate distortion as follows: Instead of finding the most efficient or the lowest rate latent states (minimum $I(x, z)$) for a given distortion constraint, we are considering the lowest rate latent state representation $I(x_{past}, z)$ that gives as good predictability into the future as true past. Accordingly, we rewrite the rate-distortion objective using statistical similarity $D_{KL}(p(x|x_{past})||p(x|z))$ as our predictive distortion measure. This measure favors latent states z that carry significant information, or share the same belief about the future x as does the past x_{past}. Since z is an encoding derived from x_{past}, knowledge of x_{past} supersedes that of z resulting in the following relations $p(x|x_{past}, z) = p(x|x_{past})$, which establishes $z - x_{past} - x$ Markov chain relation between these three variables. Averaging over all possible x_{past}, z pairs, we get

$$\langle D_{KL}(p(x|x_{past})||p(x|z)))\rangle_{p(x_{past},z)} \tag{14.14}$$

$$= \int p(x_{past},z)p(x|x_{past}) \log \frac{p(x|x_{past})}{p(x|z)} dx dx_{past} dz \tag{14.15}$$

$$= \int p(x_{past},z,x) \log \frac{p(x|x_{past})p(x_{past})}{p(x_{past})p(x)} \frac{p(x)p(z)}{p(x|z)p(z)} dx dx_{past} dz \tag{14.16}$$

$$= I[x_{past},x] - I[z,x] = I[x_{past},x|z] \tag{14.17}$$

So what we have here is a probabilistic version of rate-distortion in time-latent space written as minimization problems of

$$\mathcal{L} = I(x_{past},z) + \gamma I(x_{past},x|z) = I(x_{past},z) - \gamma I(z,x), \tag{14.18}$$

where $I(x_{past},x)$ is neglected as it is independent of $p(z|x_{past})$. This derivation suggests a new training criteria for musical neural models that combines both latent and temporal information as

$$\mathcal{L} = I(x_{past},z) + \beta \langle d(x_{past},z)\rangle - \gamma I(z,x) \tag{14.19}$$

The optimization of $\mathcal{L}$ promises finding a solution that simultaneously minimizes the rate between musical surface and latent state and maximizes the mutual information between the latent states and future of the musical surface while balancing the distortion between the latent states and the reconstructed surface. The modeling of the statistical relations between x_{past}, z and x could be done by means of a Variational Recurrent Neural network, such as [13]. The adaptation of such a model to the deep music information dynamics framework is currently being explored. In the next section, we will discuss a simplified method based on separate steps of learning representation and information rate modeling.

14.11   Relation to VMO Analysis

A simplified version of deep information dynamics approach can be done by separating the representation learning and information rate steps. Moreover, the errors encountered in each step have to be manually evaluated, depending on the musical judgments and preference of the improviser/composer. In the next section, we will describe a solution that would allow controlling the rate of information passed between the musical input and the latent state, and the effect it has on the information rate. The proposed process of iterative representation and prediction learning is as follows:

1. learn representation using an information controllable model, such as $\beta - VAE$, on short segments of music such as a bar or subdivision of a bar. This achieves the minimization (finds a stochastic mapping $q(z|x)$):

$$\min_{q \in Q: z \sim q(z|x)} (I_e(x,z) - \beta \mathbb{E}_{p_e(x,z)}(\log p(x|z))) \tag{14.20}$$

2. having trained the representation, process complete musical piece $X = x_1,$ $x_2, ..., x_T$ to obtain a sequence of latent states $Z = z_1, z_2, ..., z_T$
3. apply information rate analysis to the sequence of latent state and observe the music information dynamics structure in latent space by quantization of the latent states Z into symbolic sequence $S = s_1, s_2, ..., s_T$

$$I R(Z) = \max_{\theta, s_t \in \Sigma_{theta}} I(s, s_{past}) \qquad (14.21)$$

This process can be repeated by changing the β parameter to obtain higher or lower IR by the user, while monitoring the reconstruction error until a satisfactory musical solution is obtained. This effectively combines steps of dimension reduction from X to Z and a step of quantization from Z to S. In musical terms, the process of encoding and decoding a musical piece through a VAE results in a variety of musical outputs, from exact replication in the case of over-fitting during the training stage, to a novel musical output that keeps some aspects of the input but also varying it according to the decoder statistics. Accordingly, it is desirable to be able to control or reduce the rate of information passing from input to output in order to create novelty or variations. It should be noted that in step one, the training assumes independence between the short-term musical segments, and only in step three, time structure is taken into account. As shown in the experimental section below, the VMO analysis package allows plotting IR as a function of time, and detection and visualization of motifs, which provides additional insight into the deep musical structure. Moreover, since the reconstruction of the observations x at the decoder is done in a determin-istic manner, the maximization of $I R(Z)$ can be considered as an approximation to $I(x, z)$, where z_{past} is considered as the latent variable z in Eq. 14.19, and the current z is deterministically decoded into x.

Maximal value of IR is obtained for signals that look instantaneously complex, thus having a high entropy, but that is predictable or have little uncertainty when the signal past is taken into account. Applying this to a latent sequence $z(1), z(2), ...,$ we search of a representation $z(n) \sim q(z|x(n))$ that has low $H(z|z_{past})$. It is the first time, to the best of our knowledge, that IR is being applied to the analysis of dynamic of latent states.

14.11.1 Controlling Information Rate Between Encoder and Decoder

Learning z representation at β different from one requires repeating the learning process. A different approach that saves on the need to retrain a model at different β was proposed in [10]. In this work, the training was performed using standard ELBO (which amounts to rate-distortion training at $\beta = 1$). Then the rate of information that passes between the observations x and the latent states z was modified by limiting the bit-rate of the information passing from the encoder to the decoder. Performing optimal bit-allocation at a bit-limited regime effectively modifies the decoding rate, which can be viewed as a process of limiting the capacity in the encoder–decoder

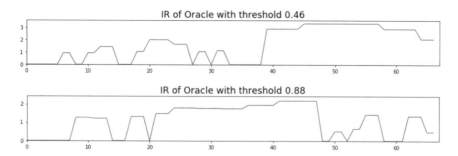

Fig. 14.8 Information rate of the latent states at full rate (top) and at 256 bits/frame (bottom)

channel. Finally, the information rate over latent state is computed using the VMO with cosine distance between the latent vectors. Figure 14.8 shows IR values over time, with high IR corresponding to points in time having longer repetitions. These results illustrate that change in bit-rate indeed affects the information dynamics structure of the query, but it is hard to know exactly what musical aspects remained salient after bit-reduction.

The above result makes the link between VAE encoding–decoding and rate-distortion theory of noisy communication more evident. During the process of learning, maximization of ELBO effectively reduces the mutual information between the input signal X and the latent state Z, while being constrained by the quality of reconstruction as measured by D. Using this noisy channel model, we consider the connection between musical query and the resulting improvisation through VAE as source encoder and target decoder model. Accordingly, we suggest to add a noisy channel between the source and target, which enables us to introduce information rate control through the use of bit allocation. It is assumed in VAE that the latent states are distributed as multi-variate uncorrelated Gaussians. The rate distortion of such signal is

$$R(D) = \begin{cases} \frac{1}{2} \log_2 \frac{\sigma^2}{D}, & \text{if } 0 \leq D \leq \sigma^2 \\ 0, & \text{if } D > \sigma^2. \end{cases} \quad (14.22)$$

This rate distortion can be converted to distortion-rate function $D(R) = \sigma^2 2^{-2R}$, which can be efficiently achieved for a multivariate Gaussian channel by the so-called reverse water filling algorithm that starts with a predefined bit-regime and successively allocates one bit at a time to the strongest component, every time reducing the component variance by a factor of four and repeating the process until all bits in the bit-pool are exhausted. One should note that channels with variance less than allowed distortion, or channels that run out of bits for a given rate, are given zero bits and thus are eliminated from the transmission. We use such channel to reduce the rate of the decoder by adding noise or eliminating some of the weaker latent components. Schematic representation of the channel inclusion in the auto-encoder architecture is given by Fig. 14.9.

Performing finite bit-size encoding and transmission of the binary quantized latent values from encoder Z_e to decoder Z_d is not required since we are interested in gating

Fig. 14.9 Noisy channel between encoder and decoder

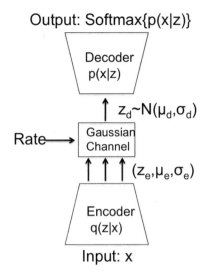

Output: Softmax$\{p(x|z)\}$

Decoder
$p(x|z)$

$z_d \sim N(\mu_d, \sigma_d)$

Rate $\longrightarrow$ Gaussian Channel

(z_e, μ_e, σ_e)

Encoder
$q(z|x)$

Input: x

and biasing the original signal towards the prior distribution by encoding it at a limited bitrate, which is given by the following optimal channel [5]

$$Q(z_d|z_e) = Normal(\mu_d, \sigma_d^2) \tag{14.23}$$

$$\mu_d = z_e + 2^{-2R}(\mu_e - z_e) \tag{14.24}$$

$$\sigma_d^2 = 2^{-4R}(2^{2R} - 1)\sigma_e^2 \tag{14.25}$$

The practical way of using this channel in our bit-rate controlled model is by plugging each latent encoder value, mean, and variance into the above equation, giving us the mean and variance of the decoder's conditional probability and then picking at random the decoder value according to this distribution. One can see that channels with zero rate will transmit in a deterministic manner the mean value of that element, while channels with infinite rate will transmit the encoder values unaltered.

14.12   Experimental Results

The experiments conducted using our model comprise querying a pre-trained model with a midi input and reducing the information available to the decoder in a controlled way by passing the encoding through a bit-rate limited channel. Then the decoded music is evaluated both qualitatively for apparent musical structure, and quantitatively in terms of its predictability by analyzing the temporal information rate of the latent states across different time frames. The different experiments that we conducted included training a VAE and then generating new compositions by random sampling of latent states, creating an output sequence by querying the model with another midi file, and finally reconstruction of a midi input query at differ-

Fig. 14.10 Output of VAE that was trained on Pop Music database, using Naruto Shippuden midi file as an input query. Note that the figure begins with measure four

ent channel rates by passing the latent states through a noisy channel between the encoder and decoder.

The VAE was trained on a Pop Music database that contained 126 music clips, mostly comprising of chords and melody, divided into chorus and verse sections. The VAE architecture used here had an input layer comprising of a concatenation of 16 musical units, each containing notes played at a resolution of 16th notes, representing a total of four quarter notes or one bar in 4/4 m. The hidden layer had 500 units, passed respectively to VAE mean and variance networks for variational encoding. As an input query, we used midi file from Naruto Shippuden anime. This song is longer and has a different style from the music in the Pop Music corpus that was used for training. Figure 14.10 shows measures four through eight of the improvised output printed together with the query input. This allows us to analyze their relations. We see that the texture of the improvisation is significantly different from the chord-melody texture of the query, but the harmonic relations are preserved and the improvisation reproduces music that matches the chords or the overall harmony of the query.

The correspondence between query and improvisation starts deteriorating when passing through the noise channel. Figure 14.11 shows the results of reducing the bit-rate of the encoder to 256 bits per frame. Musical analysis of the resulting music

Fig. 14.11 Generation by VAE from a bit-reduced query starting at same measure number four as in the previous figure

shows that the improvisation breaks away in some cases from the harmony of the query. For example, in measures four through nine shown in Fig. 14.11, the improvisation showed on top plays a quick chord progression G-A-D, while the query on bottom plays D in the left hand and melody closer to G. Harmonic collisions continue in third and fourth bars, merging together to meet on Amin chord in bar five.

14.12.1   Experimental Results

In order to assess the effect of noisy channel on VAE encoding, we performed an analysis of the original query and the outputs at different bit rates. Figure 14.12 shows the motifs detected at optimal quantization level based on VMO analysis of the midi signal. We also plot the values of information rate as a function of similarity threshold in Fig. 14.13. These graphs provide an interesting insight into the level of signal detail versus repetition structure, with a lower threshold corresponds to finer

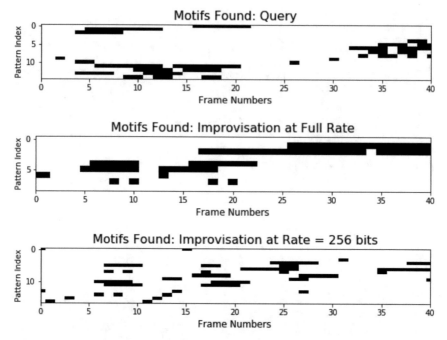

Fig. 14.12 Generation by VAE with bit-rate controlled query: Motifs found in the query (Top), full rate (Middle) and bit-rate limited resynthesis (Bottom). See text for more detail

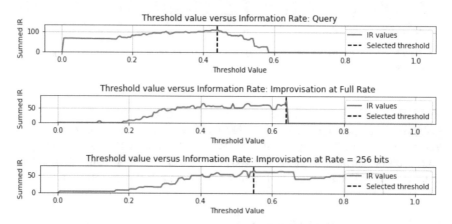

Fig. 14.13 Information rate as a function of similarity threshold found in the query (Top), full rate (Middle), and bit rate-limited resynthesis (Bottom). See text for more detail

musical detail, usually resulting in shorter motifs. Only the motif found at optimal threshold are shown in Fig. 14.12.

One should also note that computation of similarity requires specification of a distance function. In the results shown here, we used a variant of Tonnetz distance that defines a distance on chromagram vectors (12 bin pitch-class arrays). This distance is computed by first projecting pitch vectors into a 6-dimensional space replicating the circle of pure fifth and both circles of minor and major thirds, then computing the Euclidian distance between those two (normalized) vectors [16].

14.13 Summary and Discussion

In this chapter, we explored the role information theory plays in mathematical and computational approaches to machine improvisation. Starting with Shannon's first theorem that allows compression of sequences to the lower limit of their entropy, we have shown how compression algorithms are used to construct dictionaries of phrases of variable length, and how continuations could be formed in order to create smooth musical improvisations. We considered several string matching and compression methods that made the recombination of repeated phrases more efficient, both in terms of capturing early and overlapping repeated factors, and as a way to efficiently index the original musical data (midi file or audio recording) for recombination from only partial feature representations. We introduced the Variable Markov Oracle (VMO) that addressed the important problem of finding such optimal partial or lossy representation by searching over different quantizations or symbolizations of features and selecting the best model in terms of its information dynamic properties, estimated by information rate algorithm which in the VMO system. The need to quantize or use lossy or partial representation of musical data in order to be able to capture its structure and generalize it to novel examples lead us to the third Shennon theorem of lossy compression so-called rate-distortion theory. In the second part, we combine questions of representation learning with questions of predictive information by formulating a novel *Deep Information Dynamics* model. The unique property of this model is that they unite the questions of representation and prediction into one information-theoretical framework. In order to do so, we first have shown how representation learning problems, namely variational encoding, could be viewed as a special case of information minimization between the musical surface (observable music data) and its latent codes. On the other hand, information rate as a function of time assumes maximization of mutual information between past and present of musical data. Using notions of Rate-Distortion we combined both of these factors into one unifying principle, we the choice of the latent states has to satisfy both incentives—be the most compact representation of the musical surface while being able to reconstruct it up to a certain error, and be able to predict musical present from the latent states derived from the musical past in the best possible way (in other words, predict the musical present from latent states as well as it would predict the present from its actual past). This approach provides an additional aspect of flexibility in representation learning since the penalty related to prediction quality in time is considered relative to information dynamics of the music itself rather than as an independent criterion. So music that is less structured in time also has less demands on the predictability of latent representation, this increasing the importance of reconstruction error and paying attention to instantaneous sound or music detail. According to same logic, music that has very dominant temporal structure might compromise the details of instantaneous reconstruction in order to gain the predictability of the musical future. This trade-off of representation-prediction led us to developing an experimental framework for controlling the level of information passing between the musical surface and latent representation by using the encoder–decoder structure of VAE. We conducted several experiments where the information content of the decoder output was reduced by adding a noisy channel between the encoder and the decoder. By changing the bit-rate of the encoder–decoder we were able to move between more and less meaningful latent space representations. The synthesis-by-query process was done by encoding an input signal using a pre-trained encoder and degrading it in a controlled manner by application of bit-rate reduction before passing it to the decoder. One should note that unlike β-VAE and InfoVAE that control information rate during the phase of model training, our study focused on rate control between encoder and decoder in a pre-trained VAE. This rate control could not of course improve the representation learning itself, but allowed us to alter the extent of query influence on the output contents and its predictability in time. As mentioned in the introduction, the main motivation for investigating information-theoretical models of music is to develop a principled approach and allow novel algorithms for machine improvisation and composition. The deep music information dynamics suggest the one can develop novel tools and high-level criteria for controlling the improvisation process in terms of controlling the information rate between input, representation, and output data. In the final section of the paper we demonstrate some musical examples of our initial experiments with this framework, In order to get more musical insight into the effect of rate control in VAE encoding–decoding, we used VMO analysis to examine the resulting musical structures, showing the trade-offs between reconstruction and prediction as a function of the encoding rate.

References

1. Abdallah, S., & Plumbley, M. (2009). Information dynamics: Patterns of expectation and surprise in the perception of music. *Connection Science, 21*(2–3), 89–117. ISSN: 0954-0091.
2. Allauzen, C., Crochemore, M., & Raffinot, M. (1999). Factor oracle: A new structure for pattern matching. In *SOFSEMŌ99: Theory and practice of informatics* (pp. 295–310). Springer.
3. Assayag, G., et al. (1999). Computer-assisted composition at IRCAM: From PatchWork to OpenMusic. *Computer Music Journal, 23*(3), 59–72.
4. Barlow, H. B. (1961). Possible principles underlying the transformations of sensory messages. *Sensory Communication,* 217–234.

5. Berger, T. (1971). *Rate distortion theory; a mathematical basis for data compression* (Vol. xiii, 311 pp.). English. Englewood Cliffs, NJ: Prentice-Hall. ISSN: 0137531036.
6. Cover, T. M., & Thomas, J. (1991). *Elements of information theory*. Wiley.
7. Delerue , O., Assayag, G., & Dubnov, S. (1999). Guessing the composer's mind: Applying universal prediction to musical style. In *Proceedings of the International Computer Music Conference, ICMC98.*
8. Dubnov, S. (1999). Stylistic randomness: About composing NTrope Suite. *Organised Sound,4*(2), 87–92.
9. Dubnov, S. (2011). Musical information dynamics as models of auditory anticipation. In W. Wang (Ed.), *Machine audition: Principles, algorithms and systems* (pp. 371–397). IGI Global.
10. Dubnov, S. (2019). Query-based deep improvisation. In *International Conference on Computational Creativity, ICCC2019, Workshop on Musical Meta-Creation.* Charlotte: University of North Carolina.
11. Dubnov, S., & Assayag, G. (2008). Memex and composer duets: Computer aided composition using style modeling and mixing. In Collection Musique Sciences ircam Delatour et al. (Eds.), *Open music composers book 2.* cote interne IRCAM.
12. Dubnov, S., Assayag, G., & Cont, A. (2011). Audio oracle analysis of musical information rate. In *2011 Fifth IEEE International Conference on Semantic Computing (ICSC)* (pp. 567–571). IEEE.
13. Dubnov, S., Koh, E. S., & Wright, D. (2018). Rethinking recurrent latent variable model for music composition. In *IEEE 20th International Workshop on Multimedia Signal Processing (MMSP)* (pp. 1–6). Vancouver, BC.
14. Feder, M., Merhav, N., & Gutman, M. (1992). Universal prediction of individual sequences. *IEEE Transactions on Information Theory, 38,* 1258–1270.
15. Friston, K. (2012). The history of the future of the Bayesian brain. *Neuroimage, 62*(2), 1230–1233.
16. Harte, C., Sandler, M., & Gasser, M. (2006). Detecting harmonic change in musical audio. In *Proceedings of Audio and Music Computing for Multimedia Workshop.*
17. Higgins, I., et al. (2017). β-VAE: Learning basic visual concepts with a constrained variational framework. In *ICLR.*
18. Kingma, D. P., & Welling, M. (2013). Auto-encoding variational Bayes. In *Proceedings of the 2nd International Conference on Learning Representations (ICLR).*
19. Lefebvre, A., & Lecroq, T. (2002). Compror: On-line lossless data compression with a factor oracle. *Information Processing Letters,83*(1), 1–6.
20. Lefebvre, A., Lecroq, T., & Alexandre, J. (2003). An improved algorithm for finding longest repeats with a modified factor oracle. *Journal of Automata, Languages and Combinatorics, 8*(4), 647–657.
21. Ron, D., Singer, Y., & Tishby, N. (1994). The power of amnesia. In J. D. Cowan, G. Tesauro, & J. Alspector (Eds.), *Advances in neural information processing systems* (Vol. 6, pp. 176–183). Morgan-Kaufmann.
22. Roy, P., Ghedini, F., & Pachet, F. (2016). *Creating music and texts with flow machines. Multidisciplinary contributions to the science of creative thinking. Creativity in the twenty first century.* Singapore: Springer.
23. Wainwright, M. J., & Jordan, M. I. (2008). Graphical models, exponential families, and variational inference. In *Foundations and Trends in Machine Learning 1.1-2* (pp. 1–305).
24. Wang, C., & Dubnov, S. (2014). Guided music synthesis with variable Markov Oracle. In *The 3rd International Workshop on Musical Metacreation, 10th Artificial Intelligence and Interactive Digital Entertainment Conference.*
25. Wang, C., & Dubnov, S. (2014). Variable Markov Oracle: A novel sequential data points clustering algorithm with application to 3D gesture query-matching. In *International Symposium on Multimedia* (pp. 215–222). IEEE.

26. Wang, C., & Dubnov, S. (2015). Pattern discovery from audio recordings by Variable Markov Oracle: A music information dynamics approach. In *Proceedings of 40th IEEE International Conference on Acoustics, Speech and Signal Processing (ICASSP)*.
27. Wang, C., & Dubnov, S. (2015). Pattern discovery from audio recordings by variable Markov Oracle: A music information dynamics approach. In: *2015 IEEE International Conference on Acoustics, Speech, and Signal Processing (ICASSP)*. IEEE.
28. Wang, C., & Dubnov, S. (2015). The variable Markov Oracle: Algorithms for human gesture applications. *IEEE MultiMedia, 22*(04), 52–67. ISSN: 1070-986X.
29. Ziv, J., & Lempel, A. (1977, May). A universal algorithm for sequential data compression. *IEEE Transactions on Information Theory, 23*(3), 337–343.
30. Ziv, J., & Lempel, A. (1978). Compression of individual sequences via variable-rate coding. *IEEE Transactions on Information Theory,24*(5), 530–536.

Shlomo Dubnov is a computer music researcher and composer. He is a Professor in the Music Department and Affiliate Professor in Computer Science and Engineering at University of California San Diego (UCSD), USA. He is a founding member of the Halicioğlu Data Science Institute at UCSD, where he is also the Director of the Qualcomm Institute's Center for Research in Entertainment and Learning (CREL), also part of UCSD. Shlomo graduated in composition at Jerusalem Academy of Music and Dance (Israel) and holds a Ph.D. in Computer Science from Hebrew University of Jerusalem (Israel). He is also a graduate of the Israel Defence Forces (IDF) Talpiot program. Prior to joining UCSD, he served as a researcher at the Institut de Recherche et Coordination Acoustique/Musique (IRCAM) in Paris, and headed the multimedia group of the Department of Communication Systems Engineering at Ben-Gurion University of the Negev (Israel). He is a Senior Member of Institute of Electrical and Electronics Engineers (IEEE). E-mail: sdubnov@ucsd.edu.

Structure, Abstraction and Reference in Artificial Musical Intelligence

15

Geraint A. Wiggins

15.1 Introduction

An apocryphal account of a composition seminar given by the late Harrison Birtwhistle at King's College, London has a student asking, 'How did you choose the notes for this piece?' The story goes that he answered, 'First, it's none of your business. Second, I could have written the same piece with different notes'. The implication is that the detail of the notes in the score is not what defines the music. What, then, does define it?

Holmes [20, pp. 317–8] quotes a letter, claimed to be written by Wolfgang Amadeus Mozart, though previously identified [21] as a fake made by Rochlitz [42]. Henahan [18] attributes the strength of this myth to a Romantic ideal: he argues that the 'gist of it was that his scores came to Mozart fully formed, ready to be scribbled onto paper whenever he could find the time.' Evidently, Henahan did not read the fake letter very carefully, for if he had, he would have seen something rather more detailed and interesting, fake or not. The key portion runs thus:

> When I am, as it were, completely myself, entirely alone, and of good cheer – say traveling in a carriage, or walking after a good meal, or during the night when I cannot sleep; it is on such occasions that my ideas flow best and most abundantly. Whence and how they come, I know not; nor can I force them. Those ideas that please me I retain in memory, and am accustomed, as I have been told, to hum them to myself.
>
> All this fires my soul, and provided I am not disturbed, my subject enlarges itself, becomes methodized and defined, and the whole, though it be long, stands almost completed and finished in my mind, so that I can survey it, like a fine picture or a beautiful statue, at a glance. Nor do I hear in my imagination the parts successively, but I hear them, as it were,

G. A. Wiggins (✉)
Vrije Universiteit Brussel, Pleinlaan 9, 1050 Brussels, Belgium
e-mail: geraint@ai.vub.ac.be

© Springer Nature Switzerland AG 2021
E. R. Miranda (ed.), *Handbook of Artificial Intelligence for Music*,
https://doi.org/10.1007/978-3-030-72116-9_15

all at once. What a delight this is I cannot tell! All this inventing, this producing takes place in a pleasing lively dream. …What has been thus produced I do not easily forget, and this is perhaps the best gift I have my Divine Maker to thank for. ([20, pp. 317–8], after [42])

Many composers (and certainly the one writing this chapter) have had this experience or similar, though not all of us are lucky enough to have Mozart's extraordinary musical memory, which is more securely attested elsewhere. The author of the letter—no matter who he really was—was insightful in pointing out that memory was a crucial aspect of the process described therein.

From the perspective of the current chapter, memory is important too, but still more so is the idea that a composition can, in a sense, 'grow out of' pre-existing, smaller ideas. Mozart's music inhabits a very clear and well-defined formal tradition; while being intensely creative, his compositions also conform rigorously to cultural norms, while sometimes bending those norms in ways that change them permanently. It follows that there must be some generic (or schematic) representation of those cultural norms, that can be instantiated by particular pieces of detail, with the effect of making the representation less generic: ruling out possibilities. The experience described in the fake letter then describes the process of satisfying these constraints: not in one flash of inspiration, but as a sequence of steps, and working from the middle out. It is not difficult, then, for an AI specialist to imagine one of many techniques that could be used to simulate such a process: unification, constraint satisfaction, spreading activation, heuristic search and so on. These and others have indeed been brought to bear on the musical composition problem in the past 35 years or so. The interesting question, then, is not so much which technique to use, but over what, if any, representations it should work.

Necessarily, at this point, I must disclaim: my opening statement makes no distinction between symbolic and non-symbolic representations. This is entirely intentional. For the purposes of the current argument, the symbolic versus non-symbolic distinction (and the sometimes bitter debate that follows it) is irrelevant. What matters is a particular set of properties and affordances of representations, not the syntactic means by which they are implemented. In terms of Marr's [29] *levels of description*, therefore, I am discussing the *computational level*, and neither the *algorithmic* nor the *implementational*.

This chapter explores the problem of music representation in AI from the perspective of evidence from cognitive science. Music representation is not just about representing data, but about doing so in a way appropriate to the cognitive affordances of human music perception and musical memory, and to the perceptual structuring that results from those affordances. This claim needs some support, and I supply it in the next section. The rest of the paper discusses three key aspects of music representation and processing, focusing on cognitive-scientific clues that can perhaps guide Artificial Musical Intelligence (AMI) to better simulations of musical behaviour. Those aspects are, in turn, hierarchy, abstraction and reference.

Having introduced the term *Artificial Musical Intelligence* (AMI), I should say what I mean by it. I do not mean rule-based systems that harmonise Bach chorales (e.g. [11]) or deep neural networks that will generate a convincing musical style at the push of a button (e.g. [45]), though these are both enlightening and interesting things. I believe that now is the time to look beyond artefacts produced by programs, and, most importantly, for creative systems to leave behind the constraints of the problem-solving approach to AI, as exemplified above. When I write *AMI*, I do not mean a system that solves musical problems like those we ask our students to solve in exams, even though that is a very good way to make progress in the right direction. Rather, I mean a system that *behaves* like a musician, composing or improvising or performing alongside humans or machines or solo, or maybe just listening to and discussing music with humans, as humans do.

The late Marvin Minsky suggested such an AMI might be available around 2022 [24, Introduction]. Unfortunately, futurology is not an exact science, and there is still a long way to go.

15.2 The Nature of Music

I claim in the previous section that cognitive science of music is relevant to the AI study of music. The reason for this relates to the nature of music itself, and how it is perceived. For the avoidance of doubt: this is not about an attempt to restrict what composers (natural or artificial) may do, as supposed by, for example, Blackwell,[1] but a philosophical argument about what is intrinsically necessary for sound to be understood as music by humans.

Wiggins [60, §3.1] suggests that five specific features make music uniquely interesting in context of cognitive science:

1. 'It is *ephemeral*: music does not exist as an object in the world,[2] and is therefore *entirely* dependent on the mechanisms of memory for its cognitive effect [55, 64];
2. 'It is *anepistemic*: except in very unusual circumstances, essentially equating with onomatopoeia in language, and notwithstanding evidence of association [23], music is without denotational meaning, being incapable of making statements that are truth-functional [53, 55];
3. 'It is *autoanaphoric*: music can refer, but in a different way from language, because, except in the same unusual circumstances as above, it always refers to itself, and usually only within a single piece [35, 37, 43, 54, 56];
4. 'It is *cultural*: music (like language) is a cultural artefact and requires enculturation to be understood [57–59]: in consequence (like language), it is heavily dependent on learning;

---

[1] Unpublished panel session, International Conference on Creative Music Systems, 2018: https://csmc2018.wordpress.com/programme/.

[2] Note that *music* is not the same as *music notation*: the latter evidently exists as an object, but it constitutes only *instructions on how to produce* music, and not the music itself. The same is true of recordings.

5. 'It is *enchanting*: music engages humans in strong, non-conscious and conscious motor and/or affective responses, often to the extent that they react both physically, and often involuntarily [e.g., 2, 13, 51], and also by spending their hard-earned cash on recordings.'

Wiggins [60] gives a detailed argument as to the value of music to cognitive science. To see why human perception and memory are important in AMI, we reverse that argument: it follows from the above that music is, and its features are, *defined* by human perception and memory. That does not mean they are fixed, because humans are good at learning to perceive and memorise new things. But it does mean that, for an AI system to produce artefacts that a human will recognise as music, the system needs to have some encoding, implicit or explicit, rule-based or emergent, of the human perceptual capabilities that define music perception and musical memory. Boden [1] points out the important distinction between recognising the form of a created artefact and assessing its quality. Without some human-like notion of music, an AMI system has no means of deciding either whether its output is or is not music, in a human-like sense, or whether it is good.

On the other hand, both science and musical experience suggest that, once new perceptual capacities are learned, they are difficult to unlearn or even to leave unused. For example, absolute pitch usually gives way to relative pitch around three months after birth, and is usually not available thereafter [44]; and, once one has learned to hear music tonally, (i.e. in terms of tonal function of notes and chords), it is very difficult to hear past that interpretation, entailing that 12-note music, which explicitly eschews tonality, requires a consciously different kind of listening from tonal music [30]. So even when listeners actively desire music that is different from what we (in any given culture) have learned to hear, our implicitly learned perceptual programming still mediates (and thus defines, or at least constrains) its comprehension. Therefore, if an AMI is intended to create music for humans,[3] it must be able to compose and/or perform its artefacts *in terms of a human standard* (albeit perhaps being able to bend it like Mozart, in interesting ways).

Of course, it does not follow that an AI system *must* model human musical memory directly as its central function, nor that it must always explicitly reason about human perception. For instance, music theory forms an excellent proxy for some aspects of these things [58] in Western, Indian, Chinese and other cultures. But music theory generally lacks theories of similarity, for example, that would allow an AI system to decide to what degree, for example, one theme is a reference to another. For this, we must turn to the music cognition literature (e.g. [3, 4, 9, 50]). Similarly, music theory tells us next to nothing about affective response to music, while music cognition research on musical effect abounds (e.g. [22]).

Therefore, I posit that an AMI must use knowledge (implicit or explicit) about human music perception, if it is to exhibit non-trivial musical creativity, in composition and/or performance, regardless of how that knowledge is acquired or represented.

---

[3]It is unclear what music for non-humans would be, so I do not discuss that here.

If it did not, then any musical success it achieved with a human audience would be by chance, and not by creative design. Of course, John Cage and other composers have shown how chance can be a valuable part of music [41], but that is in the context either of meta-level conceptual art, where the art is *about* the music and not *in* the music, or of carefully constructed musical contexts in which randomness is made to be interesting by a talented composer such as Lutosławski [28].

Three overarching properties that human perception and memory afford and that underpin musical understanding, are *hierarchical structure*, *abstraction* and *reference*. Many specific capabilities of musicians are specialisations of these three general capabilities. They interact in important ways, which are also relevant in language processing, though that is beyond the scope of the current chapter. I discuss them, in the musical context, in the next sections.

15.3 Hierarchy in Music Representation

Everything in music is hierarchical, from the sinusoidal components of a musical note up to the structure of the grandest symphony. Minds use hierarchies such as this to manage structure in the world in general: the concept of a CHAIR entails SEAT, LEGS, BACK, for example. The word 'chair' is enough to evoke all this structural information, as well as to activate a network of associations, such as the word 'sit'. These ideas are well-rehearsed in AI and underpinned some of the earliest approaches to its science. Music theory matches and describes many of the same phenomena in the specifically musical context [58]. Music analysis, usually implicitly, aims to explicate the relationships thus entailed [25, 43, 46, 58].

From a music-cognitive perspective, there is a spectrum of representations, from very detailed and small-scale (timed in milliseconds), to very large scale (timed in hours), which have varying phenomenological properties. For example, harmonic spectra underpin perceived musical tone events, which may be perceived as individual pitches, or as chords, or as unpitched sounds (e.g. white noise, or the sound of a maraca). The process by which a set of harmonically related sine waves, as detected by the Organ of Corti [33] is assembled into a note percept is called *fusion*. It is, for most people, irreversible, in the sense that only highly skilled listeners can consciously perform analysis of the comparative amplitude of the harmonics by hearing alone. A very similar process seems to lead to perception of chords (i.e. multiple notes played simultaneously): most listeners do not hear the individual notes of the chord, but a combined effect, and we explicitly train our musical children to be able to open up the combined percept at will. This task, which requires the identification of individual harmonic series from a superposed set, is much easier than the task of undoing fusion, mentioned above, but still hard enough to require training and practice. Ways to make note separation in chords easier include using a different instrument for each note or separating the notes across a stereo field. Both of these devices give the auditory system extra information to help it discriminate the component harmonic series.

From this level upwards, a practiced listener finds it easier to separate structures, especially when they are placed in a sequential musical context. It is much easier to separate simultaneous notes when they are part of moving instrumental lines, for example. The interplay between those lines can then become an object of aesthetic value in its own right, as in the complex fugue forms of the Baroque and Classical periods. This demonstrates that *multiple* hierarchies are simultaneously present in non-trivial music: the commonest example of this is the fact that a vocal line, in a classic Western setting of four-part harmony, can be heard *both* as a line, proceeding in time, and *also* as a chord in context of the other simultaneous voices, and, furthermore, both percepts are perceptible *at subjectively the same time*. For an AMI to produce outputs that are recognisable as music by a human, these properties must be present in our programs (e.g. a neural network) and/or in our representations (e.g. a logic-based representation), or both [49], whether implicitly or explicitly; otherwise, anything recognisable as music that is produced, is recognisable as music only by chance.

Cognitively, hierarchies arise in the construction of melodies. Evidence suggests that small groups of notes, which musicians would call *phrases*, by analogy with language, are remembered as groups when assembled into melodies [6]. So melodies of non-trivial length are not simple sequences, but hierarchically structured objects, not unlike the trees of Chomskian grammar. This is blindingly obvious when one thinks of repetition-based songs like *Happy Birthday* or *Frère Jacques*. We need to make our AMIs reason in a way appropriate to such hierarchical structuring, even if the structure is not explicit in the output: human listeners need it if they are to undergo a musical experience.

Finally, hierarchical representations naturally entail the ability to represent relations that look like long-term dependencies, if one considers only the surface. This is obvious from a top-down perspective, such as that of Chomskian grammar: what makes a grammar context-free or context-sensitive is precisely the property of recursion that allows unbounded sequences between two prescribed syntactic categories. However, from the bottom up, this is less obvious. Widmer [52] posits that, 'Music is fundamentally non-Markovian', rightly pointing out that AI music systems often uncritically use Markov models without considering long-term dependencies. However, he goes on to say that, with sufficient hierarchy, Markovian techniques are sufficient, citing Hierarchical Temporal Memory [17] as a possible solution. Another (similar) possible solution is the IDyOT architecture [60, 65]. Wiggins [60] shows how long-term dependency can be learned with a combination of hierarchy and abstraction (see next section). So I would suggest since statistical learning does seem to explain local musical learning rather well, that a better claim might be 'Music is only hierarchically Markovian'.

15.4 Abstraction in Music Representation

'Abstraction' means different things in different contexts. Here, I deliberately use it as a broad umbrella term, unifying *processes which identify, use and sometimes formalise, specific information in data that is particularly important in a given context.*

The aim of using such a broad definition is to allow us to see regularities that need to be accounted for when considering music representation, explicit or implicit. The definition accords with the notion of Abstract Data Type in computer science, which mathematically specifies the meaning of something, independent of its syntax but also with the idea that a complex data item may have separable features with different mathematical properties, and which sometimes are best considered separately from each other. Respective examples of these are to be found in AMI: the former, for example, in work by Lewin [27] and Wiggins et al. [62, completed and implemented by Harley, 16] and the latter, for example, in work by Conklin and Witten [7, 8]. Given this definition, we proceed in parallel with the previous section.

The cognitive operation of fusion, introduced above, is a form of abstraction: it converts a complex set of dynamic spectral information into a single, summarising percept, which has fewer and more accessible properties: pitch, amplitude, timbre. Even in making this statement, I have committed abstraction, because most musical tones have more complex sub-features, such as vibrato (low-frequency periodic pitch modulation). In general, too, we abstract away information about precise tuning, so that a little tuning variation in a sung line remains tolerable, and so that we can use equal temperament tuning instead of physically exact just intonation [60, §3]. Thus, here, categorisation of pitch is a kind of abstraction. Note, however, that the abstracted representation (agreed musical pitch categories, A, B, C, do, re, mi, etc.) coexists with the continuous pitch space, making utterances such as, 'Your C is too sharp', meaningful; the fact that we recognise a bassoon does not prevent us from hearing the very prominent third harmonic in its timbre (this is one inverse fusion operation that many people can apply because the harmonic is so strong). Another abstraction, cutting the cake at a different angle, is that produced by embedding the simple pitch line (representing pitch height) as a spiral in a 3-dimensional space [48]. In this space, (continuously represented) octave and pitch class are abstracted separately from the continuous pitch.

McAdams and Saariaho [31] discuss musical timbre, but also make important general points concerning comprehensibility of perceptual dimensions. They argue that perceptual dimensions divided into relatively few (for example, seven) categories are easier to process than those divided into many (for example, the full pitch range of a piano). It turns out that experienced listeners tend to learn representations (for example, based on tonal scale-degree) that conform to these constraints [60]. Embedding the continuous pitch line in Shepard's 3D space is the first step on the way to this simpler-to-process representation, which has the effect of transforming a one-dimensional representation with many categories into a two-dimensional one, each of whose dimensions has few categories.

The pitch dimension of melody can be abstracted out as a time-variant signal in its own right, and when we do so, we arrive at a representation that humans find particularly useful in recognition [10, 12, 32, 34, 47].

The pitches represented as points in the Shepard pitch space can be combined to make further levels in the hierarchy of representations, taking us to four-dimensional representations of harmony that afford yet more abstract representations of harmonic tension [5, 26], and also as harmonic tension contour. Interestingly, at this level of abstraction, it becomes less easy to identify direct phenomenological correlates of the dimensions of the space, perhaps because they are relatively difficult to learn.

Therefore, these successive abstractions also form a hierarchy, with the raw sound at the bottom, and the most advanced percept at the top. Sometimes nodes in this hierarchy will coincide with nodes in the more obvious music-theoretic partonomy, but not always, because some percepts do not have a partonomic counterpart—consider a crescendo, for example, which is a combined property of each of a sequence of notes or chords. The converse is also true: self-evidently, some collections of musical events, that become meaningful in a given context, are simply collections of musical events and do not have their own specific, differentiated percept.

A key feature of musical intelligence is the ability of musicians to zoom effortlessly in and out of musical detail, skipping lightly up and down these hierarchies of abstraction as they rehearse, discuss and perform music together. Often, the skipping is around the abstraction hierarchy, communicated using the structure of the partonomy. A composer must be able to do the same, unless she can hold all the detail in her mind's eye at once, like Rochlitz's imaginary Mozart. Therefore, an AMI must also be able to do the same.

For an AMI to perform these cognitive gymnastics, it must use representations which are *structurally general* in the sense proposed by Wiggins et al. [63], that is: a wide 'range of high-level structures…can be represented and manipulated' [63, p. 31].

15.5 Reference in Music Representation

While hierarchy and abstraction allow us to describe many of the observable features of music perception and cognition, a key feature that requires further mechanism is *reference*. I use this word by deliberate analogy with reference in language, which seems to use comparable, perhaps the same, mechanisms [39].

By reference in music, I mean the possibility of one musical component (phrase, piece, melody, etc.) being *related to* another in the perception of individual listeners. This can and does happen in a very literal way, by strict repetition. But in general, musical components may be related in much more complex ways, and a theory of similarity is required for this. This theory of similarity is again determined, or at least constrained, by perception and by memory. To see this, consider the process involved in a human determining whether two musical components are similar, as follows.

Because of music's ephemerality (see Sect. 15.2), it is impossible to compare two pieces of music by hearing them simultaneously, or even in an interleaved way. Thus, one can never actually compare two pieces of music by hearing them: one can at best compare the *memory* of an earlier hearing with a current one. Of course, we might also compare two pieces of music when they are written down, but that comparison is different in kind: either it is done by imagining the sound, in which case, again one is comparing something based on memory, or it is done in a music-theoretic,

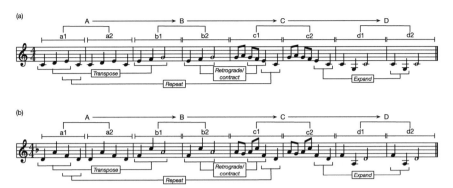

Fig. 15.1 a The folk melody *Frère Jacques*, with partonomy (above) and a small selection of the similarity relations that hold within the piece (below). Note that these similarity relations in fact hold between each occurrence of each group, making a dense constraint network even in this simple melody. **b** A different melody that conforms to the same constraints, produced by manipulating pitch only

knowledge-based way, which does not engage perceptual memory. The consequence of this is that musical similarity is, in a very strong sense, determined by memory and the workings thereof. Ruwet [43] used this in his *paradigmatic analysis*, one of the bases of semiology in music [36–38]: similarity partly defines structure, while structure partly defines similarity. One of the benefits of this approach is that it need not be culture-specific, and therefore it offers access to music as a generic human phenomenon, rather than as a specific cultural one. One of the drawbacks is that such cyclic systems are notoriously difficult to understand and engineer.

Without musical similarity detection, an AMI cannot identify the global structure in a piece, and therefore cannot, for example, respond in a human-like way when, for example, the main theme returns triumphantly at the end of a symphony, or when the middle eight of a pop song shocks the world, by appearing also at the start, as in Abba's *Dancing Queen*. Even the most simple music has this structural property: again, *Happy Birthday* and *Frère Jacques* are examples, and show nicely how grouping relates with phrasal reference. Figure 15.1 gives an example, showing (1) how dense these similarity constraints are, and that they reach, long-term, across the hierarchical structure, and (2) how a piece can thus be recomposed. To be clear: I do not claim that each of these relations is consciously recognised by every listener; rather, they affect the listener on a non-conscious level, in such a way that the overall effect is indeed consciously noticeable [13–15, 40]. This is a very subtle, but very important, part of the experience of musical listening. Herremans and Chew [19] present *MorpheuS*, a computer system convincingly capable of such manipulations, with musical sophistication far higher than the current trivial example.

Here, then, we begin to see what Harrison Birtwhistle meant. It need not be the notes that are the significant part of a composer's intent: they can be (and often are) merely the surface form that expresses it.

15.6 Synthesis

Hierarchy, similarity and reference all work together in tight coupling, to determine the perceived structure in music, but few candidate mechanisms exist to model this complex feedback (cf. [60]). Complex though the system is, the current discussion has focused almost entirely on listening, which, as suggested elsewhere [61], is the primary musical activity, that precedes all else. How, then, do we get from representations produced by listening to music to the more advanced musical capacities, such as composition?

In my opinion, the answer lies in the fact that pieces of music are not stored separately in memory, isolated from each other, as evidenced by our capacity to hear similarities *between* separate pieces as well as within them. Indeed, when hearing a piece in one's mind's ear, it is easy to segue from one to another via the worm-holes induced by such similarities; the same applies within a piece.

Thus, human musical memory is a hierarchically structured, representationally rich, sequential, web of connections. While many (though not all) AMIs tend to work in the bottom few layers of hierarchy, looking at notes and chords, I contend that human compositional intelligence generally works at a higher level, focusing on structure in an abstract way, and then filling in details. As details are made concrete in one part of the structure, so they are filled in elsewhere, because of the constraints. The constraints themselves are also open to variation, and thus can new structural ideas be produced.

Now, suppose that we can activate multiple parts of this network at middle levels, and use the links between the parts to constrain the relationships between them. We could spread that activation to find ways to join fragments together, extending the hierarchy upwards to the complete structure of a piece, and downwards to the notes that express that structure, satisfying the multifarious constraints in each dimension as we go. This closely describes my personally introspected experience of composition, and it seems to me to accord with that described by Rochlitz [42] on behalf of Mozart.

Note that this view, of a defining cognitive structure that is filled in, rather than a sequence which is constructed more or less left to right, does not contradict the experience of the songwriter who starts by working out a chord sequence on her guitar. In the same way, that language parsing may be top-down or bottom-up, and parallel or serial, so may the elaboration of an abstract musical structure. In other words, the fact that the hierarchical, abstract representation is used bottom-up in some clear cases does not imply that it does not exist.

My position, therefore, is that musical creativity is the constrained exploration and transformation [1] of musical memory, represented in the rich, multidimensional, hierarchical ways that I have described. I suggest that human-like musical behaviour will not be achievable in an AMI until we grasp this nettle [and there are other nettles to grasp too: see 52]. It may well be possible for non-symbolic systems to achieve the levels of human-like performance sought here. However, I contend that such performance is unlikely to be achieved reliably *from a scientific perspective*, until fully explainable non-symbolic systems are developed. At the time of writing, such systems seem to be some way off.

Therefore, for the short and medium terms, it seems that conventional, explicit representations that allow annotation of cognitively valid relations of structure, abstraction and reference, as a result of listening, would be a minimal basis for a human-like artificial musician, affording all the information needed for performance and composition, and even human-like discussion in rehearsal.

This, it seems to me, is the future of artificial musical intelligence.

References

1. Boden, M. A. (1990). *The creative mind: Myths and mechanisms*. London: Weidenfield and Nicholson.
2. Bown, O., & Wiggins, G. A. (2009). From maladaptation to competition to cooperation in the evolution of musical behaviour. *Musicæ Scientiæ, 13*, 387–411. Special Issue on Evolution of Music.
3. Cambouropoulos, E. (2001). Melodic cue abstraction, similarity, and category formation: A formal model. *Music Perception, 18*(3), 347–370.
4. Cambouropoulos, E., Crawford, T., & Iliopoulos, C. S. (1999). Pattern processing in melodic sequences: Challenges, caveats and prospects. In *Proceedings of the AISB'99 Symposium on Musical Creativity* (pp. 42–47), Brighton, UK. SSAISB.
5. Chew, E. (2014). *Mathematical and computational modeling of tonality: Theory and applications*, volume 204 of *International series on operations research and management science*. New York, NY: Springer.
6. Chiappe, P., & Schmuckler, M. A. (1997). Phrasing influences the recognition of melodies. *Psychonomic Bulletin & Review, 4*(2), 254–259.
7. Conklin, D., & Witten, I. H. (1990). Modelling music: Systems, structure, and prediction. *Journal of New Music Research, 19*(1), 53–66.
8. Conklin, D., & Witten, I. H. (1995). Multiple viewpoint systems for music prediction. *Journal of New Music Research, 24*, 51–73.
9. Deliège, I. (1987). Grouping conditions in listening to music: An approach to Lerdahl and Jackendoff's grouping preference rules. *Music Perception, 4*, 325–360.
10. Dowling, W. J., & Fujitani, D. S. (1971). Contour, interval, and pitch recognition in memory for melodies. *The Journal of the Acoustical Society of America, 49*(2, Part 2), 524–531.
11. Ebcioğlu, K. (1988). An expert system for harmonizing four-part chorales. *Computer Music Journal, 12*(3), 43–51.
12. Edworthy, J. (1985). Interval and contour in melody processing. *Music Perception, 2*(3), 375–388.
13. Egermann, H., Pearce, M. T., Wiggins, G. A., & McAdams, S. (2013). Probabilistic models of expectation violation predict psychophysiological emotional responses to live concert music. *Cognitive, Affective, & Behavioral Neuroscience, 13*(3), 533–553.
14. Gingras, B., Pearce, M. T., Goodchild, M., Dean, R. T., Wiggins, G., & McAdams, S. (2016). Linking melodic expectation to expressive performance timing and perceived musical tension. *Journal of Experimental Psychology: Human Perception and Performance, 42*(4), 594.
15. Hansen, N. C., & Pearce, M. T. (2014). Predictive uncertainty in auditory sequence processing. *Frontiers in Psychology, 5*(1052).
16. Harley, N. (2019). *Abstract representation of music: A type-based knowledge representation framework*. Ph.D. thesis, Queen Mary University of London.

17. Hawkins, J., & George, D. (2006). *Hierarchical temporal memory: Concepts, theory, and terminology*. Technical report, Numenta.
18. Henahan, D. (1981). Myths just keep coming back. *New York Times*, p. 17.
19. Herremans, D., & Chew, E. (2019). Morpheus: Generating structured music with constrained patterns and tension. *IEEE Transactions on Affective Computing*, *10*(4), 510–523.
20. Holmes, E. (2009). *The life of Mozart: Including his correspondence*. Cambridge Library Collection. Cambridge, UK: Cambridge University Press.
21. Jahn, O. (1882). *Life of Mozart*. London, UK: Novello, Ewer & Co. Translated from the German by P. D. Townsend.
22. Juslin, P., & Sloboda, J. (2010). *Handbook of music and emotion: Theory, research, applications*. Affective Science. Oxford University Press.
23. Koelsch, S., Kasper, E., Sammler, D., Schulze, K., Gunter, T., & Friederici, A. D. (2004). Music, language and meaning: Brain signatures of semantic processing. *Nature Neuroscience*, *7*(3), 302–307.
24. Laske, O., Balaban, M., & Ebcioğlu, K. (1992). *Understanding music with AI—Perspectives on music cognition*. Cambridge, MA: MIT Press.
25. Lerdahl, F., & Jackendoff, R. (1983). *A generative theory of tonal music*. Cambridge, MA: MIT Press.
26. Lerdahl, F., & Krumhansl, C. L. (2007). Modeling tonal tension. *Music Perception*, *24*, 329–366.
27. Lewin, D. (1987). *Generalised musical intervals and transformations*. New Haven/London: Yale University Press.
28. Lutosławski, W. (1961). *Jeux vénitiens* [Venetian games].
29. Marr, D. (1982). *Vision: A computational approach*. San Francisco: Freeman & Co.
30. Marsden, A. (2012). Counselling a better relationship between mathematics and musicology. *Journal of Mathematics and Music*.
31. McAdams, S., & Saariaho, K. (1985). Qualities and functions of musical timbre. In *Proceedings of the 1985 International Computer Music Conference, Vancouver* (pp. 367–374). Berkeley, CA. Computer Music Association.
32. Monahan, C. B., Kendall, R. A., & Carterette, E. C. (1987). The effect of melodic and temporal contour on recognition memory for pitch change. *Perception & Psychophysics*, *41*(6), 576–600.
33. Moore, B. C. J. (1982). *An introduction to the psychology of hearing* (2nd ed.). London: Academic Press.
34. Müllensiefen, D., & Wiggins, G. A. (2008). Polynomial contour as a core feature for representing melodies. In *10th International Conference on Music Perception and Cognition*, Sapporo, Japan.
35. Nattiez, J.-J. (1972). Is a descriptive semiotics of music possible? *Language Sciences*, *23*.
36. Nattiez, J.-J. (1973). Analyse musicale et sémiologie: le structuralisme de Lévi-Strauss. *Musique en jeu*, *12*, 59.
37. Nattiez, J.-J. (1975). *Fondements d'une sémiologie de la musique*. Paris: Union Générale d'Editions.
38. Nattiez, J.-J. (1990). *Music and discourse—Toward a semiology of music*. Princeton University Press.
39. Patel, A. D. (2008). *Music, language, and the brain*. Oxford: Oxford University Press.
40. Pearce, M. T., Herrojo Ruiz, M., Kapasi, S., Wiggins, G. A., & Bhattacharya, J. (2010). Unsupervised statistical learning underpins computational, behavioural and neural manifestations of musical expectation. *NeuroImage*, *50*(1), 303–314.
41. Revill, D. (1993). *The roaring silence: John Cage: A life*. Arcade Publishing.
42. Rochlitz, J. F. (1815). *Brief von Mozart an Baron E.*. Publisher unknown.
43. Ruwet, N. (1972). *Language, musique, poésie*. Paris: Editions du Seuil.
44. Saffran, J. R., & Griepentrog, G. J. (2001). Absolute pitch in infant auditory learning: Evidence for developmental reorganization. *Developmental Psychology*, *37*(1), 74–85.

45. Sakellariou, J., Tria, F., Loreto, V., & Pachet, F. (2017). Maximum entropy models capture melodic styles. *Scientific Reports, 7*(9172).
46. Schenker, H. (1930). *Das Meisterwerk in der Musik*. Drei Maksen Verlag, Munich. In 3 volumes, published 1925, 1926, 1930.
47. Schmuckler, M. A. (1999). Testing models of melodic contour similarity. *Music Perception, 16*(3), 109–150.
48. Shepard, R. N. (1982). Geometrical approximations to the structure of musical pitch. *Psychological Review, 89*(4), 305–333.
49. Smaill, A., Wiggins, G. A., & Harris, M. (1993). Hierarchical music representation for analysis and composition. *Computers and the Humanities, 27*, 7–17.
50. Toiviainen, P. (Ed.). (2007). *Musicae Scientiae*, Special issue on musical similarity, *11*, 2. ESCOM.
51. van der Velde, F., Forth, J., Nazareth, D. S., & Wiggins, G. A. (2017). Linking neural and symbolic representation and processing of conceptual structures. *Frontiers in Psychology, 8*, 1297.
52. Widmer, G. (2016). Getting closer to the essence of music: The con espressione manifesto. *ACM Transactions on Intelligent Systems and Technology, 8*(2), Article 19.
53. Wiggins, G. A. (1998). Music, syntax, and the meaning of "meaning". In *Proceedings of the First Symposium on Music and Computers* (pp. 18–23), Corfu, Greece. Ionian University.
54. Wiggins, G. A. (2007). Models of musical similarity. *Musicae Scientiae, 11*, 315–338.
55. Wiggins, G. A. (2009). Semantic Gap?? Schemantic Schmap!! Methodological considerations in the scientific study of music. In *Proceedings of 11th IEEE International Symposium on Multimedia* (pp. 477–482).
56. Wiggins, G. A. (2010). Cue abstraction, paradigmatic analysis and information dynamics: Towards music analysis by cognitive model. *Musicae Scientiae*, Special Issue: Understanding musical structure and form: Papers in honour of Irène Deliège, 307–322.
57. Wiggins, G. A. (2012). The future of (mathematical) music theory. *Journal of Mathematics and Music, 6*(2), 135–144.
58. Wiggins, G. A. (2012). Music, mind and mathematics: Theory, reality and formality. *Journal of Mathematics and Music, 6*(2), 111–123.
59. Wiggins, G. A. (2012). On the correctness of imprecision and the existential fallacy of absolute music. *Journal of Mathematics and Music, 6*(2), 93–101.
60. Wiggins, G. A. (2020). Creativity, information, and consciousness: The information dynamics of thinking. *Physics of Life Reviews*. In press; preview available on line at https://www.sciencedirect.com/science/article/pii/S1571064518300599.
61. Wiggins, G. A. (2021). Artificial musical intelligence: Computational creativity in a closed cognitive world. In *Artificial intelligence and the arts: Computational creativity in the visual arts, music, 3D, games, and artistic perspectives, computational synthesis and creative systems*. Springer International Publishing.
62. Wiggins, G. A., Harris, M., & Smaill, A. (1989). Representing music for analysis and composition. In M. Balaban, K. Ebcioğlu, O. Laske, C. Lischka, & L. Soriso (Eds.), *Proceedings of the Second Workshop on AI and Music* (pp. 63–71), Menlo Park, CA. AAAI.
63. Wiggins, G. A., Miranda, E., Smaill, A., & Harris, M. (1993). A framework for the evaluation of music representation systems. *Computer Music Journal, 17*(3), 31–42.
64. Wiggins, G. A., Müllensiefen, D., & Pearce, M. T. (2010). On the non-existence of music: Why music theory is a figment of the imagination. *Musicae Scientiae, Discussion Forum, 5*, 231–255.
65. Wiggins, G. A., & Sanjekdar, A. (2019). Learning and consolidation as re-representation: revising the meaning of memory. *Frontiers in Psychology: Cognitive Science, 10*(802).

Geraint A. Wiggins studied Mathematics and Computer Science at Corpus Christi College, University of Cambridge (UK) and holds Ph.D. degrees from the University of Edinburgh's Artificial Intelligence and Music Departments, respectively, in the UK. His main research area is computational creativity, which he views as an intersection of artificial intelligence and cognitive science. He is interested in understanding how humans can be creative by building computational models of mental behaviour and comparing them with the behaviour of humans. He has worked at the University of Edinburgh and three colleges of the University of London, UK: City, Goldsmiths, and Queen Mary. He recently moved his Computational Creativity Lab to the Vrije Universiteit Brussel, in Belgium. He is a former chair of Society for the Study of Artificial Intelligence and Simulation of Behaviour (SSAISB), the UK learned society for AI and Cognitive Science, and of the international Association for Computational Creativity, of whose new journal he is editor-in-chief. He is associated editor (English) of the Musicae Scientiae (the journal of the European Society for the Cognitive Sciences of Music), a consulting editor of Music Perception (the journal of the Society for Music Perception) and an editorial board member of the Journal of New Music Research. E-mail: geraint@ai.vub.ac.be.

Folk the Algorithms: (Mis)Applying Artificial Intelligence to Folk Music

16

Bob L. T. Sturm and Oded Ben-Tal

16.1 Introduction

This chapter motivates the application of Artificial Intelligence (AI) to modeling styles of folk music. In this context, we focus particularly on questions about the meaningful evaluation of such AI, and argue that music practitioners should be integral to the research pursuit. We ground our discussion in specific music AI that model symbolic transcriptions of traditional dance music of Ireland and Scandinavia. Finally, we discuss several ethical dimensions of such work. After reading this chapter, the reader should have a grasp of approaches to modeling music data, evaluating those approaches, and critically considering wider aspects of the application of AI to music.

Our foray into modeling and generating folk-like music began modestly as a humorous exercise one weekend in 2015 after reading Andrej Karpathy's entertaining blogpost, "The unreasonable effectiveness of recurrent neural networks" [46]. Karpathy shows how Long Short-Term Memory networks (LSTM)—a particular kind of Recurrent Neural Network (RNN)—can be trained to generate novel text one character at a time resembling Shakespeare, Wikipedia articles, and even formatted computer code. How well would such models work for music? Since Karpathy included computer code with his blogpost to reproduce his experiments, it would be

B. L. T. Sturm (✉)
Tal, Musik och Hörsel (Speech, Music and Hearing), School of Electronic Engineering and Computer Science, Royal Institute of Technology KTH, Lindstedtsvägen 24, 100 44 Stockholm, Sweden
e-mail: bobs@kth.se

O. Ben-Tal
Department of Performing Arts, Kingston University, London KT1 2EE, UK

© Springer Nature Switzerland AG 2021
E. R. Miranda (ed.), *Handbook of Artificial Intelligence for Music*,
https://doi.org/10.1007/978-3-030-72116-9_16

a simple matter to just replace the Shakespeare data with music—all we needed was a dataset of music expressed as text.

We downloaded an online collection of transcriptions of Irish traditional dance music from the website thesession.org [48] expressed in *ABCnotation* [1]—a text-based shorthand representation invented to help memorize folk music. We extracted each transcription to create a text file of 423,249 lines and 13,519,069 characters. Below is an extract from that file showing three settings of an Irish polka titled "The Ballydesmond":

```
T: Ballydesmond, The
M: 2/4
L: 1/8
K: Ador
|:E>A AB|cd e2|G>F GA|GF ED|
|E>A AB|cd ef|ge dB|A2 A2:|
|:a2 ab|ag ef|g2 ga|ge de|
|e<a ab|ag ef|ge dB|A2 A2:|
```

```
T: Ballydesmond, The
M: 2/4
L: 1/8
K: Ador
|:"Am"EA AB|cd e2|"G"G>F GA|GE ED||"Am"EA AB|B1/2c1/2d ef|"G"g1/2
    f1/2e"Em" dB|"Am"A2 A2:||:"Am"a>g ab|ag ef|"G"g>f ga|ge d2||"
    Am"ea ab|ag ef|"G"ge "E7"dB|"Am"A2 A2:||:"Am"c2"Em"Bc1/2B1
    /2|"Am"AB1/2A1/2G>A|"G"Bded|g2gd||"Am"e1/2g1/2a"Em"ge|"G"
    dBGA1/2B1/2|"Am"ce"Em"dB|"Am"A2 A2:||:"Am"eaag1/2e1/2|"G"
    dgge1/2d1/2|"Am"eaab|"Em"g2ed||"Am"ea"Em"g1/2a1/2g1/2e1/2|"G"
    dBGA1/2B1/2|"Am"ce"Em"dB|"Am"A2 A2:|
```

```
T: Ballydesmond, The
M: 2/4
L: 1/8
K: Ador
|: A/G/ |EA A>B | cd e2 | G/A/G/F/ G>A | GE ED |
EA- A>B | cd e>f | g/f/e dB | A2 A :|
|: B/d/ |ea a>b | a/b/a/g/ ef | g>f ga | ge ed |
ea- a>b | ag ef | ge dG | A2- A :|
```

ABCnotation is described more thoroughly in Sect. 16.3.2, but for now all one needs to understand is that training an LSTM network on this text file means adjusting its parameters such that it is likely to output a correct character given all the characters it has seen up to that point. Taking the first setting of "The Ballydesmond" as an example, this means making the LSTM network likely output ':' given the input 'T'; and then output a space given 'T:'; and then output a 'B' given 'T: '; and then outputting 'a' given 'T: B'; and so on.

Using Karpathy's code [46], we trained an LSTM network on batches of 50-character excerpts of this text file. We then had the trained model—which we call *folk-rnn (v1)*—generate tens of thousands of new transcription and published some of these online [28]. Here is one example generated by *folk-rnn (v1)*:

Fig. 16.1 Notation of "The Mal's Copporim" generated by *folk-rnn* (v1), which exemplifies many of the local and global conventions of the transcriptions in its training data

```
T: The Mal's Copporim
M: 4/4
K: Dmaj
|: a>g | f2 f>e d2 d>B | A>BA<F A2 d>e | f2 d>f e<ac>d | e>dc>B
    Agfe |
f2 f>e d2 d>B | A2 A>G F2 F2 | G2 B>A d2 c>d |[1 e>dc>A d2:|[2 e2
    d2 d2 ||
|: f<g | a>Ag>A f>Ae>A| d>gd>B d2 g>A| f>Af>e d>ed>c| e>ed>c (3
    Bcd (3efg |
a2 a>g f2 e2 | d2 A>d f2 f>g | a2 g>f e2 f>g | a2 A2 D2 :|
```

Figure 16.1 shows the notation of this transcription. While the melody does not sound particularly Irish, it is convincing and original, has a typical AABB structure, shows rhythmic consistency and novelty, repetition and variation, and uses cadences appropriately. The first part also has been given two endings. The model has even created a unique title: neither "Mal" nor "Copporim" appear in the training data.

We synthesized over 35,000 of these generated tunes using a variety of instruments common to Irish traditional music, and created *The Endless Traditional Music Session* website to stream these results. Figure 16.2 shows a screenshot. Every five minutes a new random set of seven tunes would appear in rotation. We posted a message about this on the discussion forum of the website from which we got the data (https://thesession.org/discussions/37800). Most replies were critical: user hnorbeck writes, "Interesting, but the results sound rather dull." Ergo writes: "I listened to a couple and they sound – weird. I mean the melodies themselves, not the production. Nothing going on. I think you'd have to get a good musician or two to actually play a few of these for them to make sense, if they can make any sense." AB writes, "Basically it's crude turntabling without the sense of a musician familiar with the significance of various motifs & phrases." ceolachan notes a disconnec-

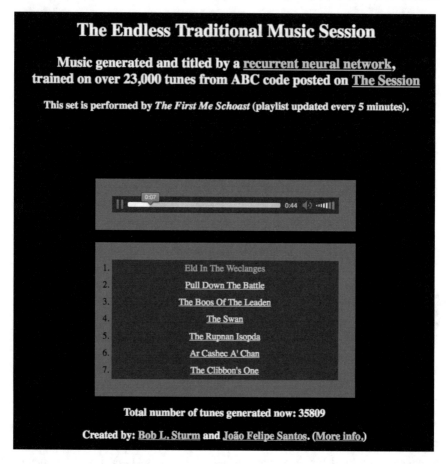

Fig. 16.2 Screenshot of *The Endless Traditional Music Session* webpage, which served up a random set of seven tunes generated by the music AI *folk-rnn (v1)*. The titles and group names were generated by the model as well

tion between the music and its function: "Teach it to dance first?!" A few comments describe trying to play some of the generated tunes, e.g., `Mark Harmer` writes,

> I've had a romp round the archive of mp3s. It's a slightly surreal experience, like you are listening to the output of someone locked in a cell and forced to write tunes! ...Interesting to listen to a few - normally you know pretty much immediately whether a tune's going to be good or not, but there is quite a lot of variation during the tune - not "totally unexpected variation" but not simple repetition either. In [The Mal's Copporim], the first two phrases are quite fun as a generative idea to "human-compose" the rest of it! I know that's not quite the point of course. Still had fun trying the opening of this one on the harp ...

Regardless of the fact that many of the generated melodies did not sound like authentic Irish traditional tunes, we did not have difficulties finding examples that were plausible and interesting enough for composition. One of the first examples is Sturm's 2015 electroacoustic composition, "Eight short outputs generated by a long short-term memory network with three fully connected hidden layers of 512 units each trained on over 23,000 ABC transcriptions of session music (Irish, English, etc.), and arranged by my own 'personal' neural network trained on who knows what for who knows how long (I can't remember any of the settings)" [68]. Our exploration eventually led to many interesting research questions that motivated more serious and deliberate work in a variety of directions, and which resulted in many conference papers [35,69,70,73], journal articles [43,71,74,75], workshops and concerts, a professionally recorded music album, "Let's Have Another Gan Ainm" [72], media attention, and significant research funding including AHRC No. AH/R004706/1 (Engaging three user communities with applications and outcomes of computational music creativity) and ERC-2019-COG No. 864189 (MUSAiC: Music at the Frontiers of Artificial Creativity and Criticism).

In this chapter, we survey several directions of our research in music AI. In the next section, we discuss how folk music provides exciting avenues for research in machine learning and AI, and survey past work in emulating folk music with computers. Section 16.3 describes several versions of *folk-rnn* that we have created, motivated by questions of music and engineering. Section 16.4 evaluates some of these systems to gauge how successful they are, and, more broadly, how useful they can be for music creation. Finally, Sect. 16.5 discusses some of the ethical dimensions of our research. We hope that this chapter provides an intriguing look at how research in music AI can be accomplished in ways that are productive and respectful of the practices from which it draws.

16.2 Music Artificial Intelligence and Its Application to Folk Music

Music AI involves engineering machines that can perform tasks that would normally require human music intelligence or ability. Examples include: recognizing musical instruments, segmenting music, recommending music, identifying musical characteristics like melody, harmony, and structure, expressively performing music, transcribing music, composing, accompanying, and improvising. The commercial and cultural applicability of such systems translates to considerable impacts, both positive and negative [43,75]. Technical details of such systems can be found in several texts; e.g., Lerch [52], Müller [57], Knees and Schedl [49], Dean and McLean [20].

Applying computational modeling to create music has a rich history beginning in the late 1950s [40]. Much of that work is centered on the emulation of heavily theorized musical styles such as the chorales of J. S. Bach; e.g., Ebcioğlu [22], Hild et al. [38], Hadjeres et al. [34]. Comparatively little work, however, has been devoted to modeling and emulating folk music. This is surprising for several reasons. For traditions that are still practiced, like Irish music, there exists a lot of data with which music AI can be trained. Much of this music data is free of copyright as well. Even though folk music can lack explicit rules, it often still has implicit conventions that can motivate decisions for modeling and evaluation. Irish traditional music is unique in the sense that expert practitioners can be found in many places around the world. This makes it possible to involve practitioners in an evaluation process. Such research can provide starting points for exploring the emulation of other music styles, and for studying the computer augmentation of human creative practices. Sections 16.3 and 16.4 give several examples of the above; but first, we survey past research (other than our own) in the computational modeling of folk music.

16.2.1 1950s–60s

The first reference we can find applying machines to generating folk-like music is given by Hiller [39], who mentions work performed around 1951 but not published until a decade later: Olson and Belar [60] programmed a machine to generate melodies in the style of those written nearly a century earlier by American composer Stephen Foster, himself borrowing from folk songs at that time. Olson and Belar [60] describe their machine as meant to be an "aid" to the composer, "in his search for melody which is the essence of most music." This work occurred only a few years after machines started to be applied to analyzing folk melodies, as in the work of Bronson [8].

Cohen [12] mentions work from 1955 on the generation of music by a first-order Markov chain with note transition probabilities found by analyzing "Western cowboy songs". This work appears to never have been published. Pinkerton [66] takes a similar approach but with 39 nursery tunes. These works appear to be motivated by the mathematical study of music from the perspective of information theory.

Brooks et al. [9] is perhaps the most thorough early investigation of melody generation by computer models with parameters found from existing music. They analyze the melodies in 37 common-meter hymns, and build Markov chains having orders from one to eight. They also impose a variety of constraints on the generation process, such as note durations, and starting and ending pitches, and generate 600 new melodies of eight measures. They discuss some of the results in terms of pitch range, melodic contour, intervalic content and singability, and the reproduction of melodies in the training material. Similar to Pinkerton [66], Brooks et al. [9] explore the use of music synthesis to test the completeness of their statistical analysis of music.

Hiller [39], in a section titled, "Algorithms for generating folk tunes", observes that much music generation synthesis work up to that time had occurred in the Soviet Union, Hungary and Czechoslovakia, and gives several examples. For instance, Havass [36] analyze 100 folk songs collected by Hungarian composer Zoltán Kodály, and synthesize new melodies using a Markov model built from that analysis. They present no musical examples in the text, but propose to play five generated melodies from magnetic tape at the August 1964 conference of the "International Folk Music Council" (where Zoltán Kodály delivered the keynote address). It is unclear if this materialized since a report about the conference makes no mention of this in the schedule. The Hungarian Academy of Sciences, the institute under which Havass worked, is also noted to be studying folk dancing from computational perspectives [27].

16.2.2 1970s–90s

Lieberman [53] proposes testing whether a given set of statistics is sufficient for describing a melodic style by generating melodies using those statistics and comparing them with real ones. They briefly discuss applying such an approach using Markov models with parameters derived from analyses of Javanese melodies, and motivate the search for statistics that are more descriptive of that style of music since the results are poor. A similar argument of studying the completeness of a set of musical rules is found in Sundberg and Lindblom [76], who study the generation of melodies according to grammatical rules found from analyzing Swedish nursery songs by a specific composer, as well as a small set of folk tunes.

Cope [19] applies his *Experiments in Music Intelligence*—an approach he developed for imitating Western composers such as Bach or Chopin by focusing on patterns and their variation—to gamelan gong kebyar, based on transcriptions into Western notation. These, as he observes, abstract away the tuning system as well as the timbral qualities—both rather important attributes in this music. According to Cope, the generated outputs were considered acceptable to gamelan musicians. He acknowledges that this endeavor may be biased because of the grounding in Western musical concepts that only partially capture the gong kebyar music.

Mozer [56] proposes music modeling and generation using artificial neural networks and a musically-informed representation. He presents results based on artificial melodies, melodies by Bach, and 25 "traditional European folk melodies" from a 17th century collection of melodies for recorder. He provides an example of a melody generated in the latter style, but performs no deeper evaluation.

16.2.3 2000s–10s

Eck and Schmidhuber [24,25] investigate the success of a long short-term memory network (LSTM) [42] in modeling and generating "twelve-bar blues"—a melodic form following a specific harmonic progression. The training data was constructed by concatenating together 12 common-meter measures of crotchets from a scale of 6 pitches each within a particular harmonic context. Each measure was composed by the authors. The results are evaluated by informal listening, and by comparison with melodies generated by random walks.

Lapalme [51] appears to be the first to train music AI on traditional music from Ireland and England, which is extended in Eck and Lapalme [23]. They created one dataset from 56 Irish tunes downloaded from thesession.org [48], and a second dataset of 435 tunes from the so-called *Nottingham* dataset, which is a collection of about 1035 British folk music pieces [29]. All transcriptions in this dataset are notated in common meter. The authors quantize each melody as a sequence of quavers, and build a representation that links notes to others in the same metric position occurring previously. They train an LSTM network to predict the next pitch of a sequence given the previous pitch, and the pitches occurring at the same beat position in the three preceding measures. They test the accuracy of each model in continuing the first eight measures from tunes in a validation partition of their datasets.

Spiliopoulou and Storkey [67] also use the *Nottingham* dataset and explicitly state that their motivations are to study the success of machine learning systems in capturing and imitating the structures in these melodies, as well as analyzing what musical concepts the models learn and how that knowledge is represented. They compare three machine learning models trained on 117 melodies. As done in Eck and Lapalme [23], they encode a melody as a sequence of events quantized with a quaver time step. The events are either pitch (one of 24), silence, or a continuation. The models are built to predict events occurring several time steps ahead of conditioning events. Their analysis of some of the components of the trained models show them to have acquired sensitivity to meaningful musical features, e.g., triads, arpeggiation, and scalar movement.

The *Nottingham* dataset appears in several other published works in machine learning; e.g., Paiement [61], Boulanger-Lewandowski et al. [7], Bengio et al. [5], Pascanu et al. [62], Goel et al. [30], Chung et al. [11], Yu et al. [78], Johnson [44], Bacciu et al. [3]. The only form of evaluation of the resulting models appearing in these works involves computing how well-trained models predict real sequences held out from training. These works contain no discussion of the usefulness of such systems for music creation.

A unique project involving AI and folk music is LIVINGSTON [54]: "an artificially intelligent, digital organism capable of accessing the totality of the history of Canadian folk music (among other corpuses) and generating new yet hyper-authentic Canadian folk objects via her/his algorithmic agents and compression formats." This system seems to only generate lyrics and chord progressions, and the two volumes of recorded music produced with it—titled "Artificially Intelligent Folk Songs Of Canada"—is performed by humans. Not much more can be surmised from existing resources at this time.

Herremans et al. [37] train Markov models of different orders on transcriptions of 37 melodies performed on the traditional Ethiopian lyre (called a *bagana*). This instrument has 10 strings, only 6 of which are sounded. Each played string is associated with a different finger: five on the left hand, and the index finger of the right hand. A melody can then be represented by the finger that plucks the string. The authors explore a variety of metrics to gauge the fitness of the resulting models. This work is the first we can find in which melodies generated by models are qualitatively assessed by a practitioner of the music style used for training.

Colombo et al. [14] train music AI on 2,158 Irish traditional melodies transcribed by Norbeck [58]. They represent a melody as a sequence of elements: paired pitch and duration values, as well as "ending" and "silence". They normalize the melodies by transposing them to be in C major or A minor, and scaling all durations based on the frequency of the most common duration. They propose to model a melody by two recurrent neural networks, one modeling a conditional distribution on the durations, and another modeling a conditional distribution on the pitches and duration—that is, one network predicts the next duration based on the previous durations generated, and the other network predicts the next pitch based on the previous pitches generated and the duration of the pitch to be generated. They evaluate the resulting model by observing how it continues a given seed, either 2 notes or 8 full measures. The melodies shown in the paper are aimless and bear little resemblance to Irish traditional music.

Colombo et al. [15] extend the approach taken in Colombo et al. [14]. They again propose using two recurrent neural networks, but this time one models the conditional distribution of durations given all previous durations and the current pitch; and the other models the conditional distribution of pitches given all previous pitches and the next duration. They create a dataset combining 2,160 Irish melodies from Norbeck [58], and 600 Klezmer melodies from Chambers [10]. In this case, they do not transpose all melodies to a common key. They propose a measure of tune novelty with respect to a collection based on the co-occurrence of subsequences in each. The article is accompanied by synthesized examples, using harp sound for the Irish ones and clarinet for the Klezmer, thus accentuating the differences. Several examples have aimless melodies that do not sound Irish, and some of the Klezmer examples veer off course.

Colombo et al. [16] propose a different music representation from their past work. Each note in a sequence is given by a tuple: pitch, duration, and time offset relative to last note. They propose modeling the joint probability of a sequence of notes as a product of three conditional distributions. Each of these distributions is modeled as a layer in a recurrent neural network (RNN), with conditioning supplied after sampling from the output of each of the three hidden layers. In the first step, their model samples a time offset; then the model samples a duration; and finally, the model samples a pitch. They train models on a variety of datasets, including *Nottingham*. For their trained model, they measure the mean likelihood of melodies of a validation dataset. They also link to a website where one can listen to dozens of sound files created from synthesizing the generated music.

Goienetxea and Conklin [31] are motivated by the challenging problem of creating a music AI that can compose melodies with "coherence", or sensible long term structure coming from the creative development of basic material. They focus on modeling the structures found in a set of 2,379 Basque folk melodies [21]. Their music representation uses what is called "multiple viewpoints" perspectives, a description of music at several levels of detail [18]. They use the resulting model to generate melodies in the same style, and describe a concert in which the audience was tasked with trying to identify which of three melodies was not computer generated.

Pati et al. [64] propose a music AI that generates material linking a given beginning and ending. They approach this by building a probabilistic model that interpolates between representations of these contexts in a latent space. They write of using a subset of size about 21,000 melodies notated with a common meter from the collection of Irish traditional music transcriptions used in Sturm et al. [73]. Since that dataset only has at most 12,593 melodies that fit this description, it is possible the authors split up melodies into eight-measure sections. The resulting models are evaluated quantitatively in terms of model fit, and qualitatively, using a subjective listening test involving rank which of two completed melodies is preferred.

16.3 Modeling Folk Music Transcriptions with Long Short-Term Memory Networks

Building *folk-rnn (v1)* and experimenting with it motivated several interesting research questions. What would happen if we trained the same kind of model but using transcriptions expressed with a more efficient and musically meaningful vocabulary? How can we meaningfully evaluate these systems with music practitioners, both inside and outside the traditions from which the data comes? How can we measure the "musical intelligence" of these systems? How can we adapt their knowledge to other music traditions? How could such models contribute to and detract from music creation? What does the training, evaluation, existence, and use of such models mean for traditional music? How might they impact traditional music in positive and negative ways?

We have so far built several versions of *folk-rnn*. While each version is a standard LSTM network, they differ in terms of training data and music representation. In this section, we discuss the technical details of LSTM networks. We then describe several different versions of *folk-rnn*, and present some of their outputs. Section 16.4 discusses in more depth methods we have used to evaluate these models.

16.3.1 Long Short-Term Memory Networks

LSTM networks are a type of recurrent neural network (RNN) with special mechanisms to control the flow of information through it as it models a sequence [42]. It is essentially a dynamic model of a probability distribution describing what is likely to come next in a sequence it is observing. To be more explicit, say the LSTM network has observed the sequence of vectors $(\mathbf{x}_1, \mathbf{x}_2, \ldots, \mathbf{x}_t)$. It computes the *posterior probability distribution* of the next vector, $P(\mathbf{x}_{t+1}|\mathbf{x}_t, \ldots, \mathbf{x}_1)$—that is, the probability of observing $\mathbf{x}_{t+1}$ given the t observations up to that step.

Figure 16.3 diagrams an LSTM network having a single hidden layer. There can be any number of hidden layers, however. The hidden layer we use for *folk-rnn* models processes the input at time step t according to the following algorithm [32]:

$$\mathbf{i}_t \leftarrow \sigma \left(\mathbf{W}_{xi}\mathbf{x}_t + \mathbf{W}_{hi}\mathbf{h}_{t-1} + \mathbf{b}_i \right) \tag{16.1}$$

$$\mathbf{f}_t \leftarrow \sigma \left(\mathbf{W}_{xf}\mathbf{x}_t + \mathbf{W}_{hf}\mathbf{h}_{t-1} + \mathbf{b}_f \right) \tag{16.2}$$

$$\mathbf{o}_t \leftarrow \sigma \left(\mathbf{W}_{xo}\mathbf{x}_t + \mathbf{W}_{ho}\mathbf{h}_{t-1} + \mathbf{b}_o \right) \tag{16.3}$$

$$\mathbf{c}'_t \leftarrow \tanh \left(\mathbf{W}_{xc}\mathbf{x}_t + \mathbf{W}_{hc}\mathbf{h}_{t-1} + \mathbf{b}_c \right) \tag{16.4}$$

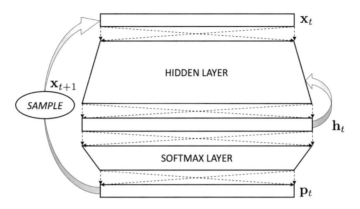

Fig. 16.3 An LSTM network with one hidden layer. An input vector $\mathbf{x}_t$ at step t is processed by the hidden layer, to form the hidden state vector $\mathbf{h}_t$ in a possibly higher dimension. This is then projected by a softmax layer to a vector $\mathbf{p}_t$, which defines the probability distribution $P(\mathbf{x}_{t+1}|\mathbf{x}_t, \mathbf{x}_{t-1}, \dots, \mathbf{x}_1)$. Sampling from this distribution produces the output for the next time step, $\mathbf{x}_{t+1}$, which becomes the next input to the model when the LSTM network is generating a sequence

where σ denotes the sigmoid function

$$\sigma(x) := \frac{1}{1 + e^{-x}}$$

which is applied to each element of the vector. The hyperbolic tangent is similarly applied to each element of the vector. The vectors $\mathbf{i}_t$, $\mathbf{f}_t$ and $\mathbf{o}_t$ are called the "in gate," "forget gate," and "out gate", respectively. These encode the new information passed into the LSTM by $\mathbf{x}_t$ with the context of past information represented by $\mathbf{h}_{t-1}$. The matrices $\mathbf{W}_{x*}$ and $\mathbf{W}_{h*}$, and bias vectors $\mathbf{b}_*$, define how this information is encoded in the hidden layer. These vectors are then combined to update the "cell state" and "hidden state" of the hidden layer, respectively:

$$\mathbf{c}_t \leftarrow \mathbf{f}_t \odot \mathbf{c}_{t-1} + \mathbf{i}_t \odot \mathbf{c}_t' \tag{16.5}$$

$$\mathbf{h}_t \leftarrow \mathbf{o}_t \odot \tanh(\mathbf{c}_t) \tag{16.6}$$

where $\odot$ denotes element-wise multiplication. This shows how updating the cell state involves modulating the cell state of the prior step with the forget gate while adding new information from the in gate. The new hidden state is a product of the out gate with a compression of the updated cell state.

The softmax layer transforms $\mathbf{h}_t$ as follows:

$$\mathbf{p}_t \leftarrow \text{softmax}\left(T_s^{-1}[\mathbf{W}_s\mathbf{h}_t + \mathbf{b}_s]\right) \tag{16.7}$$

where T_s is a user-specified parameter called *temperature*, and the softmax function is defined

$$\text{softmax}(\mathbf{y}) := \frac{\exp(\mathbf{y})}{\sum \exp(\mathbf{y})}$$

which scales the vector **y** such that its elements sum to one. The vector $\mathbf{p}_t$ specifies the posterior probability distribution $P(\mathbf{x}_{t+1}|\mathbf{x}_t, \ldots, \mathbf{x}_1)$. Sampling from this distribution produces a prediction of $\mathbf{x}_{t+1}$. If the LSTM network is generating a sequence, one need only make $\mathbf{x}_{t+1}$ the input for updating the posterior distribution, and then predict the next element of the sequence. This procedure cycles indefinitely until a stopping criterion is reached. If the LSTM network has several hidden layers, then each hidden layer after the first transforms the hidden state vector of the preceding layer according to the equations above (but with different parameters). Other architectures are possible too; e.g., where each hidden layer has access to the states of all other hidden layers [32].

The parameters of an LSTM network—the initial conditions $\mathbf{h}_0$ and $\mathbf{c}_0$ of each layer, the matrices and biases transforming the input of each layer, and the matrix and bias of the softmax layer—come from training the LSTM network to minimize a specified loss function. The loss used for *folk-rnn* models is called the *mean cross-entropy loss*. Consider a sequence s of M indices into a discrete vocabulary; e.g., 256 alpha numeric characters. Let us encode this sequence as a series of vectors, $(\mathbf{x}_1, \mathbf{x}_2, \ldots, \mathbf{x}_M)$, each dimension being zero except for the one that corresponds to the vocabulary element, which is called *one-hot encoding*. Each dimension of $\mathbf{x}_m$, and likewise the LSTM network output $\mathbf{p}_m$, refers to a particular element of the vocabulary. The goal of the network in step m of modeling sequence s using cross-entropy loss is to predict which dimension of $\mathbf{p}_m$ should be set to one. This means that at step m we want to make the network produce a vector $\mathbf{p}_m$ that looks like $\mathbf{x}_{m+1}$. In order to do that, we want the output of the network to minimize the mean cross-entropy loss over a sequence:

$$L(s) := -\frac{1}{M} \sum_{m=1}^{M-1} \log[\mathbf{p}_m]_{s(m+1)} \tag{16.8}$$

where $s(m)$ is the mth element of the sequence, and $[\mathbf{p}_m]_i$ is the ith element of the vector. Each individual term in the sum above is the cross-entropy loss at that step in the sequence. If the LSTM network produces $\mathbf{p}_m = \mathbf{x}_{m+1}$ for all elements of the sequence, then $L(s) = 0$, the smallest it can be. However, if the network produces a $\mathbf{p}_m$ which is close to zero in dimension $s(m+1)$, then $L(s)$ will become very large. Training the network with this loss entails making it move as much probability mass into the correct dimensions of the posterior distribution so as to make $L(s)$ small for most training sequences. This is accomplished by using back-propagation through time with stochastic gradient descent, and other computational techniques intended to avoid overfitting. More details are provided in Sturm et al. [73].

16.3.2 folk-rnn (v2)

The second version of *folk-rnn* [50], applies the same LSTM network architecture to the same training data as the first version [48], but uses a modified music representation. Since *folk-rnn (v1)* is trained to model blocks of text one character after another, it has to learn that some characters can have different functions. For instance, 'E' can refer to a letter in a title, a pitch, part of a pitch (e.g., '_E'), or part of a key (e.g., 'K:Emin'). This ambiguity means *folk-rnn (v1)* has to learn the different contexts in which each character can appear. Furthermore, modeling blocks of text in a document is not necessarily modeling music transcriptions. For instance, some training blocks could begin in the middle of a transcription. *folk-rnn (v1)* also had to learn about the many keys in which the training tunes are transcribed. Most Irish traditional music uses four modes: ionian (major), aeolian (natural minor), dorian, and mixolydian; but these can involve many keys; e.g., G, D, and A major, E and B minor, D and A mixolydian, A and E dorian. To create *folk-rnn (v2)*, we thus set out to train an LSTM on music transcriptions expressed by a vocabulary where each of its symbols has only one meaning.

Before we discuss the vocabulary we designed, we review the representation used in the data collected from thesession.org [48]. ABCnotation [1] was designed to compactly describe the "bones" of a folk tune. It is important to know that in Irish traditional music, a transcription of a tune only provides a basic structure. Rarely is a melody played as notated; performers elaborate upon the "bones" using ornamentation, variation, harmony, and rhythmic push and pull to give "lift" [26]. In ABCnotation [1], information fields are marked with a capital letter followed by a colon; e.g., 'T:' provides the title; 'M:' specifies the meter; 'L:' specifies the base duration of a note without an explicit duration marker; 'K:' specifies the key. Following these fields is the tune body, which notates the melody. Pitches within the given key are specified by a letter, which may be sharped or flatted by preceding it by '^' or '_', respectively. In the key of C major, 'C' is middle C, while 'C,' is an octave below, 'c' is an octave above, and 'c'' is two octaves above. More commas and single quotes can be added to lower or raise the pitch. Harmonic accompaniment is specified in double quotes, such as "Am". Multiple pitches sounding at the same time are grouped between square brackets, such as '[Gd]'. When note durations are specified explicitly, they are either numbers after the pitch (e.g., '2'), or symbols: '/' is shorthand for '1/2', while 'A > B' steals time from the second pitch and gives it to the first, conversely 'A < B' does the opposite, and '(3 EFG' indicates a triplet. Otherwise, note durations take on the value specified by the 'L:' field. Finally, the symbol '|' shows a measure line, '|:' and ':|' are beginning and ending repeat signs, and '|1' and '|2' are first or second endings, respectively. Many other symbols are possible.

To address the issue of ambiguity in ABC representations, we designed a vocabulary of musical *tokens*, where each token represents only one thing. The vocabulary we designed consists of 137 tokens grouped into seven types (examples given in parentheses): *meter* ('M:6/8'), *key* ('K:Cmaj'), *measure* (':|' and '|1'), *pitch* ('C' and '^c''), *grouping* ('(3'), *duration* ('2' and '/2'), and *transcription* ('<s>' and '</s>'). We transposed all transcriptions to have a root note of C as well, so that a model would only need to learn about the four typical modes. We also removed titles, harmonic specifications, grace notes, ties and slurs, and other markings. As an example, *The Ballydesmond Polka* given in the Introduction becomes the following sequence of 90 tokens in the new representation:

Fig. 16.4 Notation of transcription #18727 generated by *folk-rnn* (v2), which can be found in "The folk-rnn (v2) Session Book Volume 7 of 10" [28]. We transpose it here to E dorian from C dorian

```
<s> M:2/4 K:Cdor |: G > c c d | e f g 2 | B > A B c | B A G F | G
    > c c d | e f g a | b g f d | c 2 c 2 :| |: c' 2 c' d' | c'
    b g a | b 2 b c' | b g f g | g < c' c' d' | c' b g a | b g f
    d | c 2 c 2 :| </s>
```

Each token is demarcated by a space. The tokens '`<s>`' and '`</s>`' signify the beginning and ending of a transcription, respectively.

In addition to transposing and tokenizing the collection of transcriptions we retrieved from thesession.org [48], we performed a significant amount of cleaning: removing comments masquerading as tunes, removing jokes (e.g., Cage's "4m33s"), removing chord progressions, and fixing as many human counting errors as possible. We removed all transcriptions that had explicit changes in meter or key so that all transcriptions followed the same pattern: meter, mode, and tune. The encoded and cleaned dataset consists of a total of 23,635 transcriptions, with a total of 4,056,459 tokens, of which 2,816,498 are of the type pitch, 602,673 are of the type duration, and 520,290 are of the type measure [50].

The network architecture of *folk-rnn (v2)* is essentially the same as for the first version (having three hidden layers of 512 units each), but with input and output dimension 137. The total number of parameters in *v2* is 5,599,881. Training proceeds in nearly the same way as for the first version, but uses minibatches of 64 entire transcription sequences rather than continuous chunks of text. The *v2* model results from 100 epochs of training, one epoch being exposure to all transcriptions in a training partition. More details are provided in Sturm et al. [73].

As for the first version, we had *folk-rnn (v2)* generate tens of thousands of transcriptions and published 10 volumes of these [28]. The model is initialized with the one-hot vector representing the token '`<s>`', and terminates token generation when it produces '`</s>`'. One example output of this model is shown notated in Fig. 16.4. This transcription shows the conventional structure, rhythmic consistency, repetition and variation, and appropriate cadences. The second part goes higher in

Fig. 16.5 Notation of transcription #5712 generated by *folk-rnn* (v3), which can be found in "The folk-rnn (v3) Session Book Volume 3 of 4" [28]. We transpose it here to G major from C major

pitch than the first, which is a typical characteristic of this kind of music. The two sections of the tune are also linked together well: the fourth measure of each part is similar, and the endings of both parts are the same. It also sounds like Irish traditional dance music, and is very playable on traditional instruments—providing opportunities for ornamentation and variation. Several more examples generated by *v2* are discussed in Sturm et al. [73], Sturm and Ben-Tal [71], including using the model to "autocomplete" melodic ideas.

16.3.3   folk-rnn (v3)

Although the vocabulary we designed for *v2* addresses ambiguity in ABCnotation [1], it still has redundancy. For instance, for a transcription in the mode of C major, the token '^B,' refers to the same pitch as 'C' and '=C'. In the C minor mode, the token 'E' refers to the pitch E flat above middle C, which is the same as the token '_E'. We thus decided to train an LSTM network on the same collection of transcriptions but with all pitches made explicit, and using only naturals and sharps. Furthermore, so that the model could learn about all possible pitches in the vocabulary, we added all transcriptions transposed up a half step (having a root of C-sharp). We keep the four mode tokens, but do not specify the root. This resulted in a vocabulary of size 104 tokens in the same seven types as for *v2*. In this representation *The Ballydesmond Polka* given in the Introduction becomes (with a root of C):

```
<s> M:2/4 K:Cdor |: G > c c d | e f g 2 | B > A B c | B A G F | G > c c d
    | e f g a | b g f d | c 2 c 2 :| |: c' 2 c' d' | c' b g a | b 2 b c' |
    b g f g | g < c' c' d' | c' b g a | b g f d | c 2 c 2 :| </s>
```

As for *v1* and *v2*, we had the trained *folk-rnn (v3)* generate 10,000 transcriptions, available in four volumes [28]. Figure 16.5 shows a particularly good output of this model displaying many of the conventions of the style.

Fig. 16.6 Notation of a transcription generated by *folk-rnn (v2)* using beam search with $n = 4$ tokens selected in each step. We transpose it here to D major from C major

16.3.4 folk-rnn (vBeamSearch)

One step of an LSTM network results in an estimation of $P(\mathbf{x}_{t+1}|\mathbf{x}_t, \ldots, \mathbf{x}_1)$. However, this can be generalized to estimating a joint probability distribution of several tokens at once; e.g., $P(\mathbf{x}_{t+1}, \mathbf{x}_{t+2}|\mathbf{x}_t, \ldots, \mathbf{x}_1) = P(\mathbf{x}_{t+1}|\mathbf{x}_t, \ldots, \mathbf{x}_1)P(\mathbf{x}_{t+2}|\mathbf{x}_{t+1}, \mathbf{x}_t, \ldots, \mathbf{x}_1)$. This means that the model can be used to predict several tokens at each step by first computing the probability distribution of each token conditioned on all others, then multiplying these to form the joint conditional distribution, and finally sampling from this. As the number of tokens to be predicted simultaneously becomes large the computational complexity grows, but a strategic approach called "beam search" can make it efficient. Figure 16.6 shows a transcription generated four tokens at a time using beam search with *folk-rnn (v2)*. Henrik Norbeck, an expert in Irish traditional music and creator of a large dataset of transcriptions [58], says of this output:

> This tune sounds like it could have been composed by Paddy Fahy or Sean Ryan. There are already two tunes by them that are similar to each other — so much that in my mind they are connected — and this generated one becomes a third tune in the same class, but still a distinct tune.

16.3.5 folk-rnn (vScandinavian)

While the collection of thesession.org [48] is focused on Irish traditional music, the website folkwiki.se focuses on Scandinavian traditional music, and contains many thousand transcriptions in ABCnotation [1]. Hallström et al. [35] describes training LSTM networks using this collection of data. In this case, the amount of data acquired from folkwiki.se is an order of magnitude smaller than that used to train the

Fig. 16.7 Notation of a tune generated by *folk-rnn (vScandinavian)*, which can be found at https://themachinefolksession.org/tune/551

"Irish" versions of *folk-rnn* (4,083 transcriptions vs. 23,635). Even after designing an efficient vocabulary, models trained on only the Scandinavian transcriptions did not produce plausible melodies. To overcome this, the model was first trained on a dataset combining all transcriptions of the Scandinavian and Irish datasets. Then the pre-trained model was "fine-tuned" on just the Scandinavian transcriptions. The purpose of pretraining is to help a model learn about the vocabulary, and the syntax of the dataset. Fine-tuning then aims to adjust the model parameters to specifics of a subset. To accommodate the different ABC notation conventions in the Scandinavian transcriptions, other tokens had to be included in the vocabulary. Furthermore, the Irish transcriptions were not transposed to a common root before they were tokenized because the use of keys in the Scandinavian data follows slightly different conventions, like key changes between sections. The resulting vocabulary size of the model is 226. Figure 16.7 shows a particularly good transcription generated by the trained model.

16.4 Evaluation

One of the major questions underlying our research with *folk-rnn* is how to meaningfully analyze and evaluate such models, as well as their involvement and impact in music practice [74]. A common approach to evaluating music AI is what is often termed a "musical Turing test": listeners are presented with some music and are asked whether it came from a human or a machine. One example of this approach is by Cope [19], who asked an audience to decide whether a human-performed piece of music is by Mozart or generated by his system in the style of Mozart. More recently, Collins and Laney [13] ask listeners to compare two pieces and to identify which was written by a real composer (in this case, Bach or Chopin). Ariza [2] argues how this terminology—"musical Turing test"—is inaccurate since the Turing test is focused on having an interactive dialogue in natural language. In contrast, the music discrimination task is very different from how we normally engage with music. Ariza [2] instead uses the terminology, "Musical Output Toy Test." We should note that in addition to the methodological problems with this approach, it also inspires the narrative pitting machines against humans, portraying AI as a threat.

Pease and Colton [65] provide an in-depth discussion of the problems with these discrimination tests in the context of computational creativity, and review alternative approaches. They first distinguish between judging the value of a generated output and evaluating the creativity of the system. They advocate focusing more on the latter in order to provide measures that can drive research forward and that are also theoretically sound. They summarise two earlier approaches, called the FACE and the IDEA models [17]. The first aims to capture aspects of the creative process: Framing information about the work, Aesthetic measures, developing Concepts, and Expressing such a concept. The IDEA model brings the viewer/listener into the equation. They propose to evaluate the effect of the experience on audience well-being (positive or negative), and the cognitive effort required to engage with the work.

Another common approach is to ask listeners to rank music generated by an AI, such as how pleasant a melody is. Problems with this include the lack of definition, and subjectivity and bias in listening. A stark example of the latter is exemplified by an unintentional experiment. An article appearing in *The Daily Mail* [33] about our work included a 30-s music excerpt from a set performed by traditional musicians at one of our workshops. Readers of the article were able to comment for a few weeks: "[The excerpt] sounds very neat. It's missing the 'human' element." "Total Crap! A foot tapping tune in 6/8 does not make it Irish. Also it feels pretty bland." "Totally lifeless without warmth." "Sounds like a robotic Irish jig…." The music excerpt posted by the Daily Mail, however, was not of a computer-generated tune, but a real traditional tune. This unintentional experiment nicely illustrates how a listener's experience of music is not just about the acoustic waves hitting their ears. Music happens at the intersection of incoming (or sometimes imagined) sounds, perception, memory, preconceptions, past experiences, social and physical environment, and myriad other factors.

Within the domain of computational creativity, Jordanous [45] proposes to capture the meaning of creativity through an analysis of existing discussion about it. She identifies fourteen components of creativity including familiar ones such as competence, originality, and value, but also aspects that are not often included in proposed definitions, such as social interactions, perseverance, and spontaneity. She suggests that evaluations should start from identifying what aspect of creativity will be assessed. The suggestion is that this would not only enable more meaningful comparisons but will also guide the choice of evaluation that matches specific components under investigation.

Yang and Lerch [77] propose the use of note-based statistical measures as a basic form of evaluation. For collections of musical works, they calculate pitch and duration ranges, note transitions histograms, and other fairly general statistics. They note that these only apply to monophonic data, though some of the properties can be extended. The internal variability of these statistics can provide an informative profile of a dataset, either real or generated. Comparing datasets in this way can, at least, identify problems with modeling procedures, which can assist engineering. If, for example, generated melodies display markedly different statistical properties from those in the training data, this can point to specific problems with the model. Using these general measures to compare outputs of two different models can suggest the dimensions that each is successful in modeling.

Sturm and Ben-Tal [71] demonstrate five different approaches to evaluate the *folk-rnn (v2)* model: (1) comparing the statistics of real and generated transcription data ("first-order sanity check"); (2) performing basic music analysis of generated transcriptions; (3) probing a model's musical knowledge with "nefarious" initializations; (4) involving a model in music composition; and (5) performing expert elicitation with real-world music practitioners. Sturm [69,70] take another approach by attempting to reverse engineer the parameters of *folk-rnn (v2)* to understand their musical significance. Sturm et al. [74] analyze different music AI from several perspectives to determine how such models can impact music creation, and how the use of such models for music creation can inform the engineering pursuit. In the following, we look at several of these evaluation approaches.

16.4.1   Evaluation by Parameter Analysis

Sturm [70] analyzes the parameters of the input layer of *folk-rnn (v2)*, and Sturm [69] analyzes those of its softmax layer, in terms of the model vocabulary. Much more work has yet to be done to fully understand the model, but it is clear from these analyses that the model has learned some musically meaningful characteristics from looking only at data; e.g., placement of measure lines, enharmonic relationships, cadences. In a similar direction, Karpathy et al. [47] analyze the internal dynamics of recurrent models of characters in English texts, and find some parts of the models are activated near the conclusion of a sentence, quotation, or paragraph. In the case of a character model, it is difficult to draw concrete conclusions about how it is treating the elements of the vocabulary because of the ambiguity of the representation. The vocabulary of *folk-rnn (v2)*, however, is much less ambiguous by design, and so the analysis of the model becomes easier.

A unique way to analyze *folk-rnn (v2)* is by looking at how it stores and processes information in vector spaces. Figure 16.8 diagrams the procedure by which this model transforms its input into an output. Since the size of its vocabulary is 137, its input and output are vectors in $\mathbb{R}^{137}$. However, they are more restricted than that. First, since the LSTM has been trained on one-hot encoded input vectors, then the input is just one of the 137 standard basis vectors of $\mathbb{R}^{137}$. (The input can of course by any point in $\mathbb{R}^{137}$, but the model has only "seen" the 137 standard basis vectors of $\mathbb{R}^{137}$.) Second, since the output is computed by a softmax (16.7), then all elements of the output vector will be positive, and the sum of the magnitudes of the vector will be one. Hence, the output vector is a point on the positive face of the ℓ_1 unit-ball in

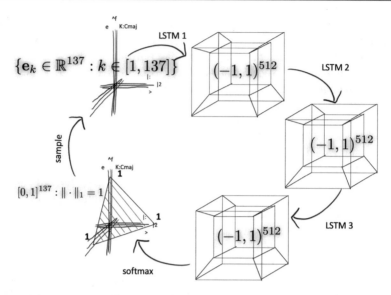

Fig. 16.8 Diagram of how *folk-rnn (v2)* is transforming information between different vector spaces. Elements of the standard basis of $\mathbb{R}^{137}$ are transformed by the first LSTM hidden layer to points in a hypercube $(-1, 1)^{512}$. The second and third LSTM hidden layers transform points in $(-1, 1)^{512}$ to points in hypercubes of the same dimension. The softmax layer then transforms points in $(-1, 1)^{512}$ to the points on the positive face of the ℓ_1 unit-ball in $\mathbb{R}^{137}$. A sampling operation then projects that point to an element of the standard basis of $\mathbb{R}^{137}$

$\mathbb{R}^{137}$. Furthermore, the ordering of the dimensions at the input and the output relative to the vocabulary is the same; i.e., the token represented by the mth dimension of the input is also represented by the mth dimension of the output.

Now let us look at the steps involved in this transformation. The first hidden layer transforms a vector of dimension 137 to a 512-dimensional vector. This is performed by the algorithm in Eqs. (16.1)–(16.6), producing $\mathbf{h}_t$—the hidden state of the first layer. From Eq. (16.6) we see that each element of $\mathbf{h}_t$ is bounded in $(-1, 1)$. Hence, this first layer is mapping the standard basis of $\mathbb{R}^{137}$ to the hypercube $(-1, 1)^{512}$. Likewise, the second layer takes as input the first-layer hidden states in $(-1, 1)^{512}$ and maps it to $(-1, 1)^{512}$. The third layer does the same, but using the second-layer hidden states. We finally reach the softmax layer, which maps $(-1, 1)^{512}$ onto the positive face of the ℓ_1 unit-ball in $\mathbb{R}^{137}$. Finally, a sampling operation projects that point to an element of the standard basis of $\mathbb{R}^{137}$.

Each one of these vector spaces has significance with respect to the concepts learned by the model. The significance of the dimensions of the input and output spaces are clear since they are closely connected with the vocabulary we have designed: each orthogonal direction corresponds to one of the tokens. This fact helps us interpret those layers closest to the input and output, which are the first hidden layer and the softmax layer. Sturm [70] analyzes the parameters of the input layer of *folk-rnn (v2)* in terms of the vocabulary. It appears that the first hidden layer has carved out subspaces of $(-1, 1)^{512}$ in which to represent the seven types of tokens. For instance, we see overlap in the representation of enharmonic pitches, such that their representation in the model is similar. Figure 16.9 shows the relationships between all pairs of pitch-token-related columns of $\mathbf{W}_{xc}$ in the first hidden layer. If two columns point in very similar directions, the color of the corresponding element of this matrix will be white. If they are orthogonal, the color will be gray. This comparison shows clear relationships between different tokens; e.g., pitch tokens 'A' and '=A' are encoded by this gate in nearly the same way, as are 'B' and '=B', as well as 'C' and '=C'. We also see a similarity between 'B', '_B' and '^A', which are the same in C mixolydian, C dorian, and C minor. This shows *folk-rnn (v2)* has learned something about enharmonic relationships from the data alone, and that the cell gate of the first layer is treating these enharmonic pitch tokens in similar ways.

Sturm [69] analyzes the parameters of the softmax layer, which is transforming the hidden state of the third hidden layer into a probability distribution. This work shows how some principal directions are important for representing tokens of the measure type. This analysis also provides ways to adjust the behavior of the model, for instance, to make it less likely to output particular pitches. Much more analytical work has yet to be done to fully understand what is occurring in *folk-rnn (v2)*, but this kind of approach to analyzing an RNN is unique. The fact that the vocabulary of the system is not ambiguous helps to reveal the significance of particular subspaces.

16.4.2   Evaluation by Co-creation

One way of evaluating *folk-rnn* models is by looking at how composers can use them in the process of composition. Sturm, Ben-Tal and others have composed several pieces using *folk-rnn* [50]. One approach for a composer is to sift through generated outputs and locate ones that are interesting or inspire. A different approach involves searching the creative space [6] of *folk-rnn* transcriptions by iteratively generating transcriptions and changing parameters. In Boden's formulation [6], generative rules constrain the novel artifacts (poems, paintings, or music pieces, but also an idea or scientific discovery) that are possible to discover within a conceptual space. In that sense, *folk-rnn* is a manifestation of generative rules, which define the rather large conceptual space of all possible *folk-rnn* transcriptions. Iteratively generating outputs and tweaking the initialization parameters of the model is a search for valuable artifacts in that space. But, as we explain in more detail in Ben-Tal et al. [4], sifting for "gold" in this manner is not a straightforward process. The model is highly nonlinear, which could contribute to it producing interesting results, but also makes steering the generation process towards useful outputs somewhat unpredictable.

There are essentially three ways to interact with *folk-rnn* models. Changing the *random seed* of the sampling procedure just results in a different sampling from each posterior distribution. It has no musical significance. Changing the *temperature* parameter, which is the multiplicative factor T_s in (16.7), affects how "conservative" the sampling will be in each iteration. Figure 16.10 shows one example transcription

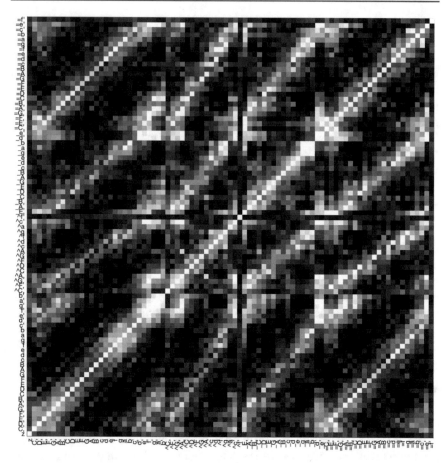

Fig. 16.9 Angles between columns cell matrix $\mathbf{W}_{xc}$ related to the pitch tokens in the first hidden-layer. White means the columns point in the same direction. The axes are labeled with the associated tokens. The diagonal structures show that columns of $\mathbf{W}_{xc}$ are related in ways that reflect enharmonic relationships; e.g., 'A' and '=A' point in very similar directions; as do 'B' and '=B'

generated by *folk-rnn (v2)* at a low temperature; and Fig. 16.11 shows an example generated at a high temperature. Setting the temperature to be very low will result in the network choosing the most likely event at each step. This can produce transcriptions having repeated notes and simple rhythms, but not always. High temperatures will result in transcriptions that adhere less to the conventions in the training data.

The third way a user can interact with *folk-rnn* is by giving it a sequence to continue. This provides perhaps the most immediate way to influence the content of the model output. Figure 16.12 shows how *folk-rnn (v2)* completes the given first measure 'M:4/4 K:Cmaj |: G C D E F G B A' that is within the style of its training material. If a given sequence is a little outside the scope of what *folk-rnn* has seen it can produce unpredictable results. Figure 16.13 shows how *folk-rnn*

Fig. 16.10 Notation of a transcription generated by *folk-rnn (v2)* at a low sampling temperature ($T_s = 0.1$) The first part of the transcription is very close to a traditional Irish polka, "Babes in the Woods."

Fig. 16.11 Notation of a transcription generated by *folk-rnn (v2)* at a high sampling temperature ($T_s = 3$)

Fig. 16.12 Notation of a transcription generated by *folk-rnn (v2)* initialized with 'M:4/4 K:Cmaj |: G C D E F G B A'

(v2) continues nearly the same measure, changed in only one token to make it less conventional.

The design of the interaction with systems like *folk-rnn* needs considerable attention for them to serve as useful co-creative tools. To engage wider audiences in the potential for machine learning to stimulate music making, we created a pair of websites [4]: folkrnn.org and themachinefolksession.org. The first provides a web interface to use *folk-rnn* models for generating transcriptions. The second is a growing archive of transcriptions created by people using *folk-rnn*. At this time, folkrnn.org has been more successful than the archive. The interface for generating transcriptions continues to be used with several hundred individual users each month (with spikes following mention of the website in media or large events).

Fig. 16.13 Notation of a transcription generated by *folk-rnn (v2)* initialized with 'M:4/4 K:Cmaj | : G C ^D E F G B A'. Compare to Fig. 16.12

https://themachinefolksession.org was intended to be a community portal for sharing interesting machine-generated but human-edited/performed tunes, but this has not gained much attention.

Finally, as noted above, the search for interesting or useful material from the generated outputs can be tedious. An "artificial critic" that sifts through generated material and identifies that having musical potential could greatly help—though a composer would like to be able to personalize "musical potential". More direct control over the features that a model learns, as well as the generation process, would also be useful. With increased knowledge about how the system learns and how it encodes its knowledge (see Sect. 16.4.1), it should be possible to provide additional methods of shaping the generated material.

16.4.3 Evaluation by Cherry Picking: "Let's Have Another Gan Ainm"

A different approach to gauging the creative potential of *folk-rnn* is to ask performers to make music out of the generated material. We collaborated with a range of musicians—both those familiar with the music traditions upon which *folk-rnn* was trained and musicians coming from other backgrounds. Many of these show a fair variety of results [71,72,74]. Significantly, most of the musicians did not have difficulties locating generated melodies they can perform, including performances on the soprano trombone, trumpet, and the double bass (instruments that are atypical in traditional music). At the same time, most of the musicians changed the generated melodies in performance. They frequently changed notes here and there, especially at the cadence points of phrases.

The relative ease of finding playable material in the generated outputs led us to record and release an album [72]. The aim was to investigate the potential of *folk-rnn* in creating material that sits comfortably within the domain of Irish traditional music. We worked with Daren Banarsë, a London-based composer and performer who is well-versed in this kind of music. By his account, he looked at several hundred generated transcription and selected 20 to be recorded in the studio. Selecting the tunes involved judgments about what makes a tune 'good': does it work as a session tune? Is it playable by traditional instruments? Is it interesting and well-shaped? How well will it work with other tunes combined in a set? How well do the tracks add up to create a good album displaying both range and balance of the different dance types that constitute this musical world. Sturm and Ben-Tal [72] describes the process, and shows the changes Banarsë made to the generated material, and how he combined them with real traditional tunes to form the eleven tracks of the album.

We purposely kept secret the background of the album until a number of experts reviewed it. We did that to avoid bias in the reaction of the listener [55,63] rather than to discover if people would be fooled by the machine composed ones. The music was well-received by experts in this (fairly small) field—which is probably due in large part to the musical proficiency of the performers, and with Banarsë's careful curation of material. While cherry picking is an unacceptable way to evaluate many applications of machine learning, when applied to art it is not so different to how many artists work. Painters, writers, and composers constantly reject ideas in the creative process. In fact, a lack of ability to be self-critical can be a major hindrance. The creative process requires identifying weaknesses and fixing them, and persistence in doing that even when this can be slow and frustrating work. When it comes to music AI, the question to answer with cherry picking is not, "Which outputs best show the success of my model?" but, "How easy is it to find material generated by this model that I would like to work with?"

16.5   Ethical Considerations

A particularly original and illuminating outcome of this research has been the critical assessment of its motivations and impacts. We started a number of discussion threads on the forum of thesession.org requesting feedback on transcriptions generated by *folk-rnn (v2)*. The user Ergo agreed with another commenter about seeing no point to the research, but also mentioned some concern about its impact: "My concern is that some people, somewhere and sometime, may consider one or more of these tunes – maybe all of them? – to be actual traditional tunes...I think it's reckless to send 3,000 machine-created fiddle tunes into the world." Another user commented: "I would suggest confining your computerised efforts to the archives of whichever University you are at, I don't think this helps trad music in any way." In another thread, Ergo asks: "explain how this is going to contribute to [Irish traditional music]."

Someone later posted an article about our work to a Facebook group focused on Swedish folk music. Some comments among the 163 show real displeasure at the idea of involving computers in traditional music. One person writes, "Where is the heart and feeling in the computer?" Another writes

> Talk about soul-less tunes ...MUSIC .. Especially folk music .. Must come from experiences, tradition's deep imprint. ...Where the people are the focus, there the folk music characterizes the traditional cultural life. ...When I see something like this, I get either pissed off or very critical.

Some express fears: "This takes away possibilities for real musicians to compose Music and earn a living!" Another writes

> You have stolen from existing music to offer a library based on goods made by [musicians] who have got their material from older musicians or composed their own now for tecknocrats within music to continue to steal patterns from the existing traditional music. ...Within [pop music] there are rules for how much in seconds you are allowed to use from an existing piece of music for a mix or other use. One should pay the same respect to traditional music.

We experienced similar frictions when making the album, "Let's Have Another Gan Ainm" (Sect. 16.4.3) [72]. For instance, the professional musicians involved did not want to be too closely associated with the project. Though they were not a part of the research, and were only hired to perform on the album, they wanted to make sure that their professional careers were clearly separated.

Working together with Irish traditional harper Úna Monaghan also uncovered interesting aspects [74]. The music of this tradition is aural, and so modeling transcriptions is not really modeling the music. Irish traditional music is not a collection of transcriptions of music, but is bound together with functional notions, from dancing to making music together to expressing national pride [26,41,59]. Hence, anything produced by a music AI will be several steps away from the music that occurs in practice. Second, these AI-generated transcriptions, which necessarily come from a statistical mishmash of regional and historical styles, have only tenuous and confusing relation to the wider context that players use to perform this music. Because the data used for training *folk-rnn* is crowd-sourced, the choice of what to transcribe and how is not consistent in any manner across the corpus. What, therefore, should musicians do with these transcriptions? Should they try to correct or improve a generated transcription, to bring it "in line" with the tradition? Should they play them "straight", in tension to their own instinct and training?

These experiences show how our research can be seen in negative ways, and how our use of data could be an overstep. Our initial humorous application of machine learning could be regarded as trivializing a living tradition. While there is bound to be fear of human redundancy, or appeals to the narrative of machines taking control, many of the objections raised are more subtle and deserve careful attention. This motivated us to critically examine our assumptions, methodology, and research questions [43,75]. For example, since the data that we used to train music AI can be freely downloaded, does that give us the right to use it in the way we have? Considering that this data is essentially crowd-sourced over 18 years, contributed by people aiming to share, preserve,and advocate a particular form of traditional music, our use of the data for such a different outcome was likely unanticipated. That the dataset includes transcriptions of original works that are copyright protected can mean that our use of the data could be an infringement on those rights [75].

Our critical reflection has motivated us to learn much more about the living traditions from which we as researchers are benefiting, and to examine how our research could be detrimental and beneficial to Irish traditional music. While some of the musicians we worked with enjoyed learning the music, and some of the material has ended up in their regular repertoire [4], it is not completely clear how our research contributes to Irish traditional music. It did enable us to pay traditional musicians to perform and participate in various experiments. It also deepened Sturm's involvement with this music by attending traditional music summer schools in Ireland, and organizing regular learners' sessions in Stockholm. What is clear, however, is that this living tradition is not so weak that any music AI we or others might create can likely do any harm. One cannot confuse the tradition with symbols in a sequence, dots on a page, or tunes in an online database. Nonetheless, the variety of questions about the ethics of such research deserve to be discussed and assessed openly and regularly with practitioners.

16.6 Conclusion

Applying artificial intelligence to model and generate folk music offers many opportunities to study the capabilities and limitations of such methods, especially so in traditions that are living. It also motivates the critical examination of the use and misuse of artificial intelligence for music. In this chapter, we have surveyed the application of artificial intelligence to folk music. We have presented in depth our work in modeling transcriptions of traditional music from Ireland and Scandinavia using recurrent neural networks. We have also surveyed a variety of approaches we use to evaluate our models, from analyses of model parameters, to the use of the models in music creation. We finally discussed several contentious issues of our work, which motivates a careful study of its ethical dimensions.

Since our work with musicians and domain experts show that our machine learning models can generate transcriptions that are plausible within folk music traditions, it is clear that they have learned something relevant about identifiable and distinguishing characteristics from the training data. Special care needs to be taken, however. It is easy to fall into a trap of thinking human-like outputs from the machine reflect human-like learning or ability. Deeper examinations of our *folk-rnn* models reveal their knowledge about music to be very brittle. Nonetheless, we have found that these models can still be used as co-creative tools for music. In some cases, the brittleness of the knowledge of a model provides creative opportunities, which makes it a feature and not a bug. Indeed, our aims for building models of traditional music do not include generating a limitless number of cheap imitations. Instead, modeling folk music provides starting points to explore more interesting research questions.

One of these questions is the meaningful and effective evaluation of music AI and its involvement in music creation. While the field has progressed beyond simply listening to a few examples and confirming they sound reasonable, the evaluation of music-generating AI must include many dimensions, from the comparison of statistical summaries of populations, to relating the models to music as a practice. Good evaluation methods identify ways for making improvements. We believe an essential component of the success of our project has been deep and meaningful partnerships between the engineering and musical sides, eventually engaging musicians in the research process and not just with the final outcome. The expertise of musicians, working in the specific domains from which we collect data for training AI—however superficially—is invaluable in that regard.

As to the future of *folk-rnn*, there are several directions we are exploring. We continue to analyze the parameters of our models to understand how they are encoding information, and how we might adjust them in musically meaningful ways; e.g., adjusting the parameters such that the model constructs jigs of nine-measures length instead of the conventional eight. Another direction is building an "artificial critic" that can streamline the search for interesting material a model has or could generate. This can be seen as a problem of information retrieval, for either an existing collection of material, or a collection that could be created by a given model. In line with this are methods for comparing collections of materials, including detecting plagiarism. All of these can potentially be incorporated into training models in more musically meaningful ways than just reproducing sequences of tokens.

Another avenue for future research can develop the system to accommodate polyphonic practices, or non-Western music. Polyphony means concurrent but also semi-independent voices, where the musical-logic has both a horizontal component (that governs the construction of each line) and a vertical one (that governs the interdependence of those lines). These different dimensions do not need to have the same or even similar rules. A challenge in applying machine learning to non-Western folk music entails finding a representation that is meaningful within the context of that tradition. Any representation necessarily abstracts away some aspects of the music, just as ABC notation does for Irish and Scandinavian folk music. The music AI researcher needs to produce a representation that can encode important and relevant aspects of music they want to model, and at the same time be aware of the aspects they discard.

References

1. ABCnotation. (2011). *Standard v2.1*. Retrieved May 30, 2020, from http://abcnotation.com/wiki/abc:standard:v2.1.
2. Ariza, C. (2009). The interrogator as critic: The Turing test and the evaluation of generative music systems. *Computer Music Journal, 33*(2), 48–70.
3. Bacciu, D., Carta, A., & Sperduti, A. (2018). *Linear memory networks*. arXiv:1811.03356.
4. Ben-Tal, O., Harris, M. T., & Sturm, B. L. T. (2021). How music AI is useful: Engagements with composers, performers, and audiences. *Leonardo* (in press).
5. Bengio, Y., Boulanger-Lewandowski, N., & Pascanu, R. (2013). Advances in optimizing recurrent networks. In *IEEE International Conference on Acoustics, Speech, and Signal Processing* (pp. 8624–8628).

6. Boden, M. A. (2009). Computer models of creativity. *AI Magazine, 30*(3).
7. Boulanger-Lewandowski, N., Bengio, Y., & Vincent. P. (2012). Modeling temporal dependencies in high-dimensional sequences: Application to polyphonic music generation and transcription. In *Proceedings of International Conference on Machine Learning* (pp. 1159–1166).
8. Bronson, B. H. (1949). Mechanical help in the study of folksong. *Journal of American Folklore, 62*, 81–86.
9. Brooks, F. P., Hopkins, A. L., Neumann, P. G., & Wright. W. V. (1957). An experiment in musical composition. *IRE Transactions on Electronic Computers, EC-6*(3), 175–182.
10. Chambers, J. (2014). *Chambers' Klezmer tunes*. Retrieved May 30, 2020, from http://trillian. mit.edu/~jc/music/abc/Klezmer/.
11. Chung, J., Gulcehre, C., Cho, K., & Bengio. Y. (2014). Empirical evaluation of gated recurrent neural networks on sequence modeling. In *Proceedings of Neural Information Processing Systems*.
12. Cohen, J. E. (1962). Information theory and music. *Behavioral Science, 7*(2), 137–163.
13. Collins, T., & Laney, R. (2017). Computer-generated stylistic compositions with long-term repetitive and phrasal structure. *Journal of Creative Music Systems, 1*(2).
14. Colombo, F., Muscinelli, S. P., Seeholzer, A., Brea, J., & Gerstner, W. (2016). Algorithmic composition of melodies with deep recurrent neural networks. In *Proceedings of 1st Conference on Computer Simulation of Musical Creativity*.
15. Colombo, F., Seeholzer, A., & Gerstner, W. (2017). Deep artificial composer: A creative neural network model for automated melody generation. In: *Proceedings of EvoMUSART*.
16. Colombo, F., Brea, J., & Gerstner, W. (2019). Learning to generate music with Bachprop. In *Proceedings of Sound and Music Computing Conference*.
17. Colton, S., Charnley, J., & Pease, A. (2011). Computational creativity theory: The face and idea descriptive models. In *Proceedings of International Conference Computational Creativity*.
18. Conklin, D., & Witten, I. H. (1995). Multiple viewpoint systems for music prediction. *Journal of New Music Research, 24*(1), 51–73.
19. Cope, D. (1991). *Computers and musical style*. Oxford University Press.
20. Dean, R., & McLean, A. (Eds.). (2018). *The Oxford handbook of algorithmic music*. Oxford, UK: Oxford University Press.
21. Dorronsoro, J. (1995). Bertso doinutegia. Euskal Herriko Bertsolari Elkartea. Retrieved May 30, 2020, from http://bdb.bertsozale.eus/es/.
22. Ebcioğlu, K. (1988). An expert system for harmonizing four-part chorales. *Computer Music Journal, 12*(3), 43–51.
23. Eck, D., & Lapalme, J. (2008). *Learning musical structure directly from sequences of music*. Technical report, University of Montreal, Montreal, Canada.
24. Eck, D., & Schmidhuber, J. (2002). *A first look at music composition using LSTM recurrent neural networks*. Technical report, Instituto Dalle Molle di studi sull' intelligenza artificiale.
25. Eck, D., & Schmidhuber, J. (2002). Learning the long-term structure of the blues. In *Proceedings of International Conference on Artificial Neural Networks*, LNCS, Madrid, Spain (pp. 284–289).
26. Fairbairn, H. (1993). *Group playing in traditional Irish music: Interaction and heterophony in the session*. Ph.D. thesis, Cambridge University.
27. Ferentzy, E. N., & Havass, M. (1964). Human movement analysis by computer: Electronic choreography and music composition. *Computational Linguistics, 3*, 129–188.
28. folk-rnn. (2017). *The folk-rnn session books*. Retrieved May 30, 2020, from https:// highnoongmt.wordpress.com/2018/01/05/volumes-1-20-of-folk-rnn-v1-transcriptions/.
29. Foxley, E. (2001). *Eric Foxley's music database*. Retrieved May 30, 2020, from http://www. chezfred.org.uk/freds/music/database.htm.
30. Goel, K., Vohra, R., & Sahoo, J. K. (2014). Polyphonic music generation by modeling temporal dependencies using a RNN-DBN. In *Proceedings of International Conference on Artificial Neural Networks* (pp. 217–224).

31. Goienetxea, I., & Conklin, D. (2017). Melody transformation with semiotic patterns. In *Proceedings of International Symposium on Computer Music Multidisciplinary Research*.
32. Graves, A. (2013). *Generating sequences with recurrent neural networks*. arXiv:1308.0850.
33. Gray, R. (2017). The future of music: 'Bot Dylan' AI writes its own catchy folk songs after studying 23,000 tunes. *The Daily Mail*. Retrieved May 30, 2020, from https://www.dailymail. co.uk/sciencetech/article-4544400/Researchers-create-computer-writes-folk-music.html.
34. Hadjeres, G., Pachet, F., & Nielsen, F. (2017). DeepBach: A steerable model for Bach chorales generation. In *Proceedings of International Conference on Machine Learning* (pp. 1362–1371).
35. Hallström, E., Mossmyr, S., Sturm, B. L., Vegeborn, V. H., & Wedin, J. (2019). From jigs and reels to schottisar och polskor: Generating Scandinavian-like folk music with deep recurrent networks. In *Proceedings of Sound and Music Computing Conference*.
36. Havass, M. (1964). A simulation of musical composition. Synthetically composed folkmusic. *Computatiuonal Linguistics*, *3*, 107–128.
37. Herremans, D., Weisser, S., Sörensen, K., & Conklin, D. (2015). Generating structured music for bagana using quality metrics based on Markov models. *Expert Systems with Applications*, *42*, 7424–7435.
38. Hild, H., Feulner, J., & Menzel, W. (1992). HARMONET: A neural net for harmonizing chorales in the style of J. S. Bach. In *Proceedings of the Neural Information Processing Systems* (pp. 267–274).
39. Hiller, L. (1970). Music composed with computers—A historical survey. In *The computer and music*. Cornell University Press.
40. Hiller, L., & Isaacson, L. (1959). *Experimental music: Composition with an electronic computer*. New York, USA: McGraw-Hill Book Company.
41. Hillhouse, A. N. (2005). *Tradition and innovation in Irish instrumental folk music*. Master's thesis, The University of British Columbia.
42. Hochreiter, S., & Schmidhuber, J. (1997). Long short-term memory. *Neural Computation*, *9*(8), 1735–1780.
43. Holzapfel, A., Sturm, B. L., & Coeckelbergh, M. (2018). Ethical dimensions of music information retrieval technology. *Transactions of the International Society for Music Information Retrieval*, *1*(1), 44–55.
44. Johnson, D. D. (2017). Generating polyphonic music using tied parallel networks. In *Computational intelligence in music, sound, art and design* (pp. 128–143).
45. Jordanous, A. (2012). A standardised procedure for evaluating creative systems: Computational creativity evaluation based on what it is to be creative. *Cognitive Computation*, *4*(3), 246–279.
46. Karpathy, A. (2015). *The unreasonable effectiveness of recurrent neural networks*. Retrieved May 30, 2020, from http://karpathy.github.io/2015/05/21/rnn-effectiveness.
47. Karpathy, A., Johnson, J., & Li, F. (2015). *Visualizing and understanding recurrent networks*. arXiv:1506.02078.
48. Keith, J. (2020). *The session.org github repository*. Retrieved May 30, 2020, from https:// github.com/adactio/TheSession-data.
49. Knees, P., & Schedl, M. (2016). *Music similarity and retrieval: An introduction to audio- and web-based strategies*. Springer.
50. Korshunova, I., Santos, J. F., & Sturm, B. L. T. (2015). *folk-rnn code repository*. Retrieved May 30, 2020, from https://github.com/IraKorshunova/folk-rnn.
51. Lapalme, J. (2005). Composition automatique de musique à l'aide de réseaux de neurones récurrents et de la structure métrique. Master's thesis, Université de Montréal.
52. Lerch, A. (2012). *An introduction to audio content analysis*. Wiley/IEEE Press.
53. Lieberman, F. (1970). Computer-aided analysis of Javanese music. In *The computer and music*. Cornell University Press.
54. LIVINGSTON. (2014). *Artificially intelligent folk songs of Canada*. Retrieved May 30, 2020, from http://www.folksingularity.com.

55. Moffat, D., & Kelly, M. (2006). An investigation into people's bias against computational creativity in music composition. In *Proceedings of Workshop on Computational Creativity*.
56. Mozer, M. C. (1994). Neural network composition by prediction: Exploring the benefits of psychophysical constraints and multiscale processing. *Cognitive Science, 6*(2&3), 247–280.
57. Müller, M. (2015). *Fundamentals of music processing: Audio, analysis, algorithms, applications*. Springer.
58. Norbeck, H. (2020). *Henrik Norbeck's abc tunes*. Retrieved May 30, 2020, from http://www.norbeck.nu/abc/.
59. ÓhAllmhuráin, G. (1998). *A pocket history of Irish traditional music*. The O'Brien Press.
60. Olson, H. F., & Belar, H. (1961). Aid to music composition employing a random-probability system. *Journal of Acoustical Society America, 33*(6), 862.
61. Paiement, J. F. (2008). *Probabilistic models for music*. Master's thesis, Ecole Polytechnique Fédérale de Lausanne (EPFL).
62. Pascanu, R., Mikolov, T., & Bengio, Y. (2013). On the difficulty of training recurrent neural networks. *Journal of Machine Learning Research, 28*(3), 1310–1318.
63. Pasquier, P., Burnett, A., Thomas. N. G., Maxwell. J. B., Eigenfeldt, A., & Loughin, T. (2016). Investigating listener bias against musical metacreativity. In *Proceedings of International Conference on Computational Creativity*.
64. Pati, A., Lerch, A., & Hadjeres, G. (2019). Learning to traverse latent spaces for musical score in painting. In *Proceedings of International Symposium on Music Information Retrieval*.
65. Pease, A., & Colton, S. (2011). On impact and evaluation in computational creativity: A discussion of the Turing test and an alternative proposal. In *Proceedings of AISB Symposium on Musical Creativity*.
66. Pinkerton, R. C. (1956). Information theory and melody. *Scientific American, 194*(2), 77–87.
67. Spiliopoulou, A., & Storkey, A. (2011). Comparing probabilistic models for melodic sequences. In *Proceedings Machine Learning Knowledge Discovery and Data* (pp. 289–304).
68. Sturm, B. L. T. (2015). *Eight short outputs ... (electroacoustic music composition)*. Retrieved May 30, 2020, from https://youtu.be/RaO4HpM07hE.
69. Sturm, B. L. T. (2018). How stuff works: LSTM model of folk music transcriptions. In *Proceedings of Joint Workshop on Machine Learning for Music, International Conference on Machine Learning*.
70. Sturm, B. L. T. (2018). What do these 5,599,881 parameters mean? An analysis of a specific LSTM music transcription model, starting with the 70,281 parameters of its softmax layer. In *Proceedings of Music Metacreation Workshop of International Conference on Computational Creativity*.
71. Sturm, B. L. T., & Ben-Tal, O. (2017). Taking the models back to music practice: Evaluating generative transcription models built using deep learning. *Journal of Creative Music Systems, 2*(1).
72. Sturm, B. L. T., & Ben-Tal, O. (2018). *Let's have another Gan Ainm: An experimental album of Irish traditional music and computer-generated tunes*. Technical report, KTH Royal Institute of Technology.
73. Sturm, B. L. T., Santos, J. F., Ben-Tal, O., & Korshunova, I. (2016). Music transcription modelling and composition using deep learning. In *Proceedings of Conference on Computer Simulation of Musical Creativity*.
74. Sturm, B. L. T., Ben-Tal, O., Monaghan, U., Collins, N., Herremans, D., Chew, E., et al. (2018). Machine learning research that matters for music creation: A case study. *Journal of New Music Research, 48*(1), 36–55.
75. Sturm, B. L. T., Iglesias, M., Ben-Tal, O., Miron, M., & Gómez, E. (2019). Artificial intelligence and music: Open questions of copyright law and engineering praxis. *MDPI Arts, 8*(3).
76. Sundberg, J., & Lindblom, B. (1976). Generative theories in language and music descriptions. *Cognition, 4*, 99–122.

77. Yang, L. C., & Lerch, A. (2018). On the evaluation of generative models in music. *Neural Computing and Applications*.
78. Yu, L., Zhang, W., Wang, J., & Yu, Y. (2016). *SeqGAN: Sequence generative adversarial nets with policy gradient*. arXiv:1609.05473.

Bob Sturm received a Ph.D. in Electrical and Computer Engineering from University of California, Santa Barbara, USA, in 2009. He has been employed as an academic at Aalborg University Copenhagen (Denmark), Queen Mary University of London (UK), and since 2018 at the Royal Institute of Technology (KTH), in Stockholm, Sweden. Since 2015, he has been building, learning from and collaborating with AI systems trained on transcriptions of traditional music. A portion of this work is supported by funding from the European Research Council under the European Union's Horizon 2020 research and innovation programme (Grant agreement No. 864189). E-mail: bobs@kth.se.

Oded Ben-Tal is a composer and researcher working at the intersection of music, computing, and cognition. His compositions include both acoustic pieces, interactive, live electronic pieces and multimedia work. As an undergraduate he combined composition studies at the Jerusalem Academy of Music with a B.Sc. in Physics at the Hebrew University, Israel. He did his doctoral studies at Stanford University's Center for Computer Research in Music and Acoustics (CCRMA). Since 2016 he is working on a multidisciplinary research project applying state of the art machine learning to music composition. He is a senior lecturer at the Performing Arts Department, Kingston University London, UK. E-mail: obental@gmail.com.

Automatic Music Composition with Evolutionary Algorithms: Digging into the Roots of Biological Creativity

17

Francisco Vico, David Albarracin-Molina, Gustavo Diaz-Jerez and Luca Manzoni

17.1 Introduction

Music composition is considered an expression of human creativity, even if composers (like artists, in general) take inspiration from other sources (like Nature sounds, and—mostly—other authors). Similarly, the algorithmic composition of music usually follows an imitative approach, by feeding a computer system with a large corpus of existing (human-made) scores. Here we investigate the composition of music from a different perspective: as a discovery process of aesthetically pleasing musical patterns. This is achieved by using mathematical systems which are able to represent self-similarity (formal grammars), and can evolve as to produce valid and aesthetic music scores. The result of this endeavor is *Melomics*, a tool which is able to produce musical scores without any knowledge of pre-existing music. Apart from the usefulness of Melomics in the arts, this project has also opened a philosophical discussion on the nature of music itself: is music created or is it just discovered?

In this chapter, we introduce the reader to two distinct but interweaved ideas. From the technical side, we present the approach of encoding music by means of L-systems and context-free grammars, and how to compose music by grammatical evolution. From a more abstract and motivational point of view, we want to explore the reasons for the automatic composition of music and the nature of automatically composed music. As the premier specimen of this kind of composition software, we use *Melomics*. This software is actually multiple programs, developed from the same principles, but adapted with time for the composition of both atonal music, with the cluster computer *Iamus*, and tonal music, with the cluster computer *Melomics109*.

F. Vico (✉) · D. Albarracin-Molina · G. Diaz-Jerez · L. Manzoni
ETS Ingeniería Informática - Campus de Teatinos, Complejo Tecnológico Bulevar Louis Pasteur, 35, 29071 Malaga, Spain
e-mail: fjvico@uma.es

© Springer Nature Switzerland AG 2021
E. R. Miranda (ed.), *Handbook of Artificial Intelligence for Music*,
https://doi.org/10.1007/978-3-030-72116-9_17

Melomics has been in the spotlight multiple times [5,22] since it started as the target of two research projects [1,2]. Here we introduce and discuss Melomics, for a comprehensive overview on the interesting general topic of algorithmic composition, we suggest the book by Nierhaus [18] and the survey by Fernández and Vico [8].

The first idea that computers could be able to compose music can be traced back to *before* the actual realization of a physical computer. In 1842, Luigi Menabrea reported the following quote from Ada Lovelace [17]:

> [The Analytical Engine] might act upon other things besides number, were objects found whose mutual fundamental relations could be expressed by those of the abstract science of operations, and which should be also susceptible of adaptations to the action of the operating notation and mechanism of the engine…Supposing, for instance, that the fundamental relations of pitched sounds in the science of harmony and of musical composition were susceptible of such expression and adaptations, the engine might compose elaborate and scientific pieces of music of any degree of complexity or extent.

Clearly, the ideas of Ada Lovelace were not put into practice for more than a century and half. However, this seed of algorithmic music was planted in the nineteenth century and can be used as a starting point for our discussion. With today's knowledge, we can see that this short text contains at least the spark of some interesting ideas: the necessity to *encode* the structure of the music, and to encode not only the single pitches, but the relation between them. Furthermore, there is a distinction between the *composition* and the actual performing of the music, with the analytical engine being tasked with composing music. Finally, there is no mention of imitating existing composers, but the production of *"scientific pieces of music of any degree of complexity or extent."* While we do not know if those ideas were already present in the mind of Ada Lovelace, we can read them in the text, and recognize them as important aspects in algorithmic composition:

- **Encoding**. It is necessary to find a way of encoding not only the single pitches and durations, but also the relations between them. That is, there should be a higher-level structure than a simple list of pitches and durations. This structure will be more compact than the entire composition. In some sense, it is a *compressed* version of the composition. The presence of a more compact representation hints to the presence of some kind of repetitions and structured behavior, since truly random data would not be susceptible to compression.
- **Composition**. While computers are capable of sound synthesis and procedural generation of sound, we are interested in the actual composition. That is, the production of a music score in the traditional staff notation.
- **(Non-)Imitation**. Some systems have the aim of reproducing a particular style of a specific artist, period, or genre by using a corpus of compositions from which recurring structures can be extracted. Melomics is instead focused on producing a particular style without any access to an existing corpus.

To incorporate all three points, Melomics employs L-systems and context-free grammars, where the structure of an entire piece of music is encoded, and deploys from a series of derivations. This allows the *encoding* to have one interesting aspect: L-systems and context-free grammars provide a way to encode repetitions in the product of their derivation from a simple axiom, without being themselves repetitive. That is, a set of rules for an L-system can appear not to provide any repeated structure, but its product might contain a high amount of repetitions and self-similar structures. This is, indeed, an essential aspect in both biology and music [19].

The final interpretation of the derivations produced is then an actual composition. Melomics can synthesize music in multiple formats, but starting from a single internal representation that is equivalent to the usual staff notation. In this sense, Melomics is mainly a *composer* of music.

The final point, i.e., the ability to generate music without performing imitation, is given by the fact that no corpus is provided to Melomics. How can then music in a specific style be composed? This can be enforced by a combination of constraints:

- *Constraints in the encoding*. Each encoding generates different biases in the search space. That is, by changing the way we represent music we also change what is easy to write and what is difficult—or even impossible—to express. By forcing the music to be expressed as an L-system or as a context-free grammar, regular structures are easier to represent and will appear more often than completely unrelated fragments of music.
- *Constraints in the fitness function*. Forcing the encoding to restrict and "guide" the search for music is not, by itself, completely sufficient. As an additional filter, a *fitness function*, is used to associate to each composition a measure of quality, that is usually determined by looking at some high-level features of the composition.

The dual effect of having an encoding that restricts the search into a space of already reasonable compositions, combined with the filtering of a fitness function helps the generation process of Melomics to "converge" to music respecting a particular style or set of conditions, thus allowing Melomics to generate music in a particular style *without* any imitation. Notice that the music composed by Melomics seems more "discovered" than generated is an important aspect that is discussed in this chapter, since it is the source of many different questions on the nature of algorithmic music and, more in general, of all music.

This chapter is organized as follows: in Sect. 17.2 the L-systems and their applications are introduced. The second main component of Melomics, the evolutionary algorithm, is described in Sect. 17.3, while Melomics proper is described in detail in Sect. 17.4. A discussion on the applications of Melomics and the motivations for producing artificial music are presented in Sect. 17.5, while some further directions of investigation in Sect. 17.6 conclude the chapter.

17.2 Lindenmayer Systems

Lindenmayer systems, or L-systems, were introduced in the late 60s by Aristid Lindenmayer [13] as a mathematical model of some biological growth processes. L-systems have been widely studied both as mathematical objects (see, for example, [25]) and as a generative model in the arts [21]. In what follows, by L-system we will refer to 0L-system, which is the simplest and most used type of L-system.

An L-system is formally defined as a triple (Σ, S, P), where Σ is the alphabet (a non-empty, finite set of symbols), $S \in \Sigma$ is the *axiom* symbol, and $P \subseteq \Sigma \times \Sigma^*$ is a set of production rules of the form $a \to \alpha, a \in \Sigma, \alpha \in \Sigma^*$ (where Σ^* is the set of all words over Σ). By convention, if P in a given L-System does not include any rule of the form $a \to w \in P$ for a given symbol $a \in \Sigma$, then the rule $a \to a$ is assumed to be included in the L-system. Given a production rule $a \to w \in P$, one application of the rule to a word $v \in \Sigma^*$ containing at least one instance of the symbol a, rewrites one instance of a as w in v.

Differently from the conventional derivation process of the generative grammar, in L-systems the derivation rules are applied in a maximally parallel way. That is, each symbol $v_i \in \Sigma$ of a given word $v \in \Sigma^*$ is rewritten by a rule of the form $v_i \to w$. In the case that more than one rule can be applied, one is selected non-deterministically. When only one rule $a \to w$ exists for each symbol $a \in \Sigma$, the system is said to be deterministic, or a D0L-system. Given a word $w = w_1 \cdots w_n \in \Sigma^*$, we say that it is generated by $v = v_1 \cdots v_n \in \Sigma^*$ when $v_i \to w_i \in P$ for $1 \leq i \leq n$; this is written as $v \Rightarrow w$. We say that a word w is generated in a derivation of length n by a word v if there exists a sequence of words $u_1, u_2, \ldots, u_{n-1}$ such that $v \Rightarrow u_1, u_1 \Rightarrow u_2,$ $\ldots, u_{n-1} \Rightarrow w$.

Starting from the axiom S, the iterative application of the rules in a maximally parallel way gives raise to new words, as shown in the following example.

Example 1 Let $(\{a, b\}, a, \{a \to ab, b \to b\})$ be an L-system. Starting from the axiom a, at the first iteration we obtain the word ab by application of the rule $a \to ab$. At the second step, the obtained word is abb, by simultaneous application of both production rules.

While L-systems appear as an interesting theoretical device, they have been successfully applied in the generation of self-similar structures, especially with application to the generation of images. This can be performed by interpreting the string obtained after n steps as a set of drawing instructions—to be executed sequentially— possibly with access to a stack data structure.

Let us consider the following simple example, where the following drawing commands are available:

By using the symbol X as the axiom symbol (with no graphical interpretation) we can define the following two rules:

$$X \to F[+F[X]] - [F[X]] - -F[X]$$
$$F \to FF$$

F : draw a forward line of unitary length
$+$: rotate the current heading left by 30°
$-$: rotate the current heading right by 30°
[: push the current position and heading on a stack
] : pop position and heading from the stack to replace the current heading and position

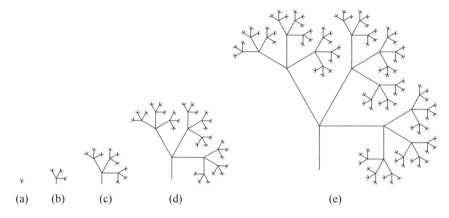

(a)   (b)   (c)   (d)   (e)

Fig. 17.1 The figures generated by the example L-system with a different number of iterations, starting from one iteration to the left (**a**), and ending with five iterations on the right (**e**)

These two rules, produce strings of symbols that, when interpreted as drawing commands, produce figures like the one shown in Fig. 17.1.

As this example shows, complex self-similar structures can be encoded in a very compact way by means of L-systems. This suggests that they can be applied to music, where self-similarity and repetition are common resources for gaining aesthetically pleasing sound. However, the initial application of L-system to the generation of music was not as successful as it was in graphics [reference needed]. Even if now other systems have applied L-systems for the generation of music [12, 15], Melomics has established high standards in automatic music composition, by generating scores and music tracks that could hardly be differentiated from human-made music.

17.3 Evolutionary Algorithms

Evolutionary Algorithms (EA) are a series of techniques, usually employed for optimization purposes, that all take inspiration from Darwin's theory of evolution. Most EA start from a collection (usually called a *population*) of possible solutions to a problem, that are then selected according to some principle, mimicking the process of natural selection. The selected solutions are then modified, usually with operators inspired by either the natural occurrence of DNA mutations or the biological reproduction. In this section, we will formally define what is an optimization problem and how it can be solved using EA. For a more in-depth introduction to evolutionary algorithms, we refer the reader to [16].

17.3.1 Optimization Problems

Suppose that we want to find the optimal solution for a given problem. As an example, consider the classical knapsack problem, where we are given a set of items each with a given weight and value, and a knapsack with a limited capacity (i.e., a limit on the sum of weight of the items contained). Therefore, solutions can be set of items to put into the knapsack whose total weight is less than the knapsack capacity. To have an *optimization* problem we need to have a way of evaluating the quality of solutions, to determine which, among the two solutions, is "better". This is usually performed by defining a *fitness function*, i.e., a function mapping each solution to a real number representing how "good" the solution is. For example, in the case of the knapsack problem, a suitable fitness function would be one returning, for each solution, the total value of the item in the knapsack. We must then decide if we want to maximize or minimize the fitness, i.e., if better solutions have higher or lower fitness values.

Formally, let S be a set of solutions to an optimization problem, and let $f : S \to \mathbb{R}$ be a fitness function. An optimal solution for a maximization (resp., minimization) problem is then defined as

$$\operatorname{argmax}_{x \in S} f(x) \quad (\text{resp.}, \operatorname{argmin}_{x \in S} f(x))$$

While finding an optimal solution might be desirable, a "good enough" solution might be sufficient. For this task, optimization algorithms like EA are particularly suitable.

17.3.2 Evolutionary Algorithms

While EA are an entire family of methods, we will focus on one prototypical example to introduce the basic principles governing them all. Probably the most famous example of EA are the *genetic algorithms* (GA), introduced in the 1960s by John Holland [9], where solutions (usually called *individuals*) to an optimization problem are represented as sequences of symbols (a string), and a population is simply a collection of individuals where the phases of selection, crossover, and mutation are iterated until some termination criteria have been met.

The mains structure of a GA can be described by the following procedure:

1. (*initialization*) Generate a random population P of n individuals.
2. (*fitness evaluation*) For each individual compute its fitness.
3. Check if the termination criteria are met (e.g., we have found a solution or enough time has passed). If so, then return the best solution found so far, otherwise continue to the next step.
4. (*selection*) Select n individuals from P in a way that depend on their fitness to generate a new population P'.

5. (*crossover*) Exchange part of the structure between pairs of individuals (called *parents*) to generate new individuals (called *offsprings*). The offsprings replace the parents in P'.
6. (*mutation*) Slightly change the structure of an individual with a small probability. The mutated individual replaces the original one in P'.
7. Replace P with P' and go to step 2.

From this high-level description of GA, it is possible to observe the main characteristics of an evolutionary algorithm:

- A selection phase, where solutions are extracted from the current population, usually with some criterion that is dictated by the fitness, where a better fitness means a higher probability of survival. The exact selection scheme can be a fitness proportional selection (i.e., a *roulette wheel* selection), a *tournament selection* (where at each step a limited number of individuals is extracted from the population and the one with the best fitness is selected), or a *truncated selection* (where the individuals are ranked by fitness and only the top $p\%$, for some parameter p, is selected).
- Mutation and recombination operators. Where solutions either exchange part of their structure (or *genetic material*), as in the recombination operators, or where a single solution has its structure mutated with a mutation operator.

To find why these two characteristics differ in a more substantial way, we need to introduce the concepts of *genotype* and *phenotype*:

- **Genotype**. The genotype of an individual in the population is the actual representation of the solution. For example, for the knapsack problem with size items a possible genotype could be 010011. In some sense, we can see the genotype as the "raw" representation of the solution without any interpretation.
- **Phenotype**. The phenotype of an individual in the population is the actual solution it represents. For example, for the individual with genotype 010011, its phenotype could be the set of item $\{s_2, s_5, s_6\}$, where each one in the genotype representing the presence of a specific object in the solution.

It is then possible to notice that selection operators only operate on the phenotype of the individuals. That is, the selection process is not concerned at all with the genotype of an individual, but only with the quality of its phenotype, which is assessed with the fitness function. On the contrary, mutation and recombination operators operate only on the genotype of the individuals; they manipulate the representation of the solutions without any consideration about the effect on the phenotype. While this distinction might seem rather "academic", since in the examples moving from the genotype to phenotype is immediate, when a more complex mapping is present, the distinction is essential.

17.3.3 Indirect Encoding

An important distinction when talking about evolutionary algorithm is the difference between a *direct* and an *indirect* encoding. In a direct encoding, there is a simple mapping between the genotype and the phenotype of an individual. For example, a representation of a set as an array of bits is a direct encoding: each element of the genotype corresponds directly to an element of the phenotype. Other examples of direct encoding could be the representation of the structure of a neural network by having the neural network itself as the genotype, as in the NEAT algorithm [27].

Indirect encoding, instead, does not provide a direct mapping between genotype and phenotype. We can think of it as providing, instead a genotype that is a blueprint for constructing the phenotype. One prominent example of this kind of encoding is given by grammatical evolution (GE) [26], where the individuals have, as genotype, strings of numbers. The interpretation of those individuals, however, requires the presence of a context-free grammar, as detailed in the following example.

Example 2 Consider the following context-free grammar, with axiom S, representing expressions in two variables with $+$ and $*$, and expressed in BNF:

$$S \rightarrow (S + S) \mid (S * S) \mid \text{Var} \mid \text{Const}$$
$$\text{Var} \rightarrow x \mid y$$
$$\text{Const} \rightarrow \text{Digit} \mid \text{Digit Const}$$
$$\text{Digit} \rightarrow 1 \mid 2 \mid 3 \mid 4 \mid 5 \mid 6 \mid 7 \mid 8 \mid 9 \mid 0$$

Consider now the individual $X = 132415$ and how to decode it. Starting from the axiom S, we read the first digit of X, which is one; therefore, we apply the first production rule $S \rightarrow (S + S)$. We now have to rewrite the two instances of S in the obtained string $(S + S)$. by going forward in reading X we encounter 3, which is interpreted as using the third production rule with left hand side S to rewrite the first instance of S, thus obtaining $(\text{Var} + S)$ by continuing this rewriting process, guided by the digits of X, we obtain:

$$S \rightarrow (S + S) \rightarrow (\text{Var} + S) \rightarrow (y + S) \rightarrow (y + \text{Const}) \rightarrow (y + \text{Digit}) \rightarrow (y + 5)$$

Therefore, the *genotype* 132415 corresponds to the *phenotype* $(y + 5)$.

While some simplifications were necessary in this brief example, it should be clear that the correspondence between genotype and phenotype is not direct and that the variation on the genotype can have a different influence on the development of the phenotype.

17.3.4 Evolving L-Systems

After having introduced both L-systems and the main concepts of evolutionary algorithms, we can now combine them by showing ways to evolve L-systems. Clearly, if our goal is to obtain a string representing a piece of music, the L-system producing that string is not a direct encoding, but an indirect one. The peculiar characteristics of L-systems invite the invention of specifically crafted operators, like [6], which was an inspiration for Melomics ad its operators [3].

In L-systems we can consider the axiom fixed and the set of symbols Σ also pre-determined, but the rules can instead be evolved. Since the interpretation of the strings produced by most L-systems makes use of a stack, it is important to employ genetic operators that, while allowing mutations and exchange of genetic material, also preserve the correct use of the stack (e.g., by not performing a "pop" operation on an empty stack). A collection of operators respecting this set of restrictions is described in [6].

17.4   Melomics

Melomics can be thought of as a combination of a language for expressing music based on L-systems and as a way of evolving derivation rules of that language by using evolutionary computation techniques. Melomics can be used to compose both atonal and tonal music and, while the encoding employed and the constraints are different, the main structure remains the same, showing the flexibility of the approach. Melomics's use of L-systems to encode music, where the music "grows" from an initial seed, the axiom, resembles embryological development (or *evo-devo*), and can be considered a successful application of evo-devo principles in the generation of music [3].

The general execution workflow of Melomics, in both its atonal and tonal version, can be described as follows:

- Filling the desired input parameters in the designed interface. In any case, the parameters will represent musical specifications or directions at different levels of abstraction, with no need for creative input from the user.
- Some of the input parameters will be used to drive the stochastic processes of producing genomes.
- A genotype, based on deterministic grammar and stored in a plain text file, is read and developed into a resulting string of symbols.
- The string of symbols is rewritten after some processes of adjustment that can be of different forms: cleaning of the string, by removing, for example, by removing duplicate idempotent operators, and adjustments due to physical constraints of the instruments, like the maximum number of consecutive notes or the suppression (or emergence) of particular musical effects.
- Each symbol in the final string has a low-level musical meaning, which is interpreted by the system through a sequential reading from left to right and stored in an internal representation.
- Once again the musical information will be adjusted and stabilized due to internal and external factors: the first ones are to make the format of the music more

manageable, and the others are due to the physical context, like constraints in the tessituras, discretization of the note duration, and so on.

- Some of the input directions will be assessed and different actions might be taken as a consequence: the current composition may be discarded, it may simply pass the filter or it could pass the filter and some of its genetic material being saved for future executions.
- Finally, the different modules for translating the musical information to the corresponding output formats may be used.

A visual depiction of this workflow is given in Fig. 17.2.

In the rest of the section, we will focus on the encoding used for the music more than on the fitness functions or the operators employed, since we consider the encoding the essential part of Melomics.

Fitness versus encoding. It is well known that the fitness function guides the search process, but it might not be immediate that the encoding used can play an even more prominent role. This is the case for Melomics: the encoding employed has the property that it is relatively *easy* to generate good-sounding music. In this sense, the fitness function acts more as a filter, where certain constraints are encoded (e.g., by penalizing a music that is difficult to play on real instruments, or by requiring some structural constraints to be present, or a specific style to be generated).

17.4.1 Atonal Music

To generate *atonal* music, the genome employed in the evolutionary process describes a set of rules for a *deterministic* L-system coupled with some additional parameters that are employed during the decoding phase, where the L-system is translated into music.

In particular, we can interpret an individual as a program, written as L-systems rules, that rewrites the initial symbol, the axiom, into another program, this time represented as a string, executed by an abstract machine that outputs the actual music. Here, we will see how the production rules of the L-system are defined and how the resulting program is interpreted. The L-system employed has an alphabet Σ that can be divided into two main parts:

- A set of symbols of the form #i for $i \in \{0, \ldots, n\}$, e.g., #0, #1, #2, ... Those symbols can appear on the left-hand side of a production rule and each of them represents either "higher-level" structure of the composition or, if it appears in the final string, a note played by the i-th instrument where, usually, #1 represents a pause.
- A set of reserved symbols that change the current state of the abstract machine, by changing the pitch, duration, dynamics, tempo, and so on. Some of the available operators are:

  - \$1 increases the pitch value one step in the scale;

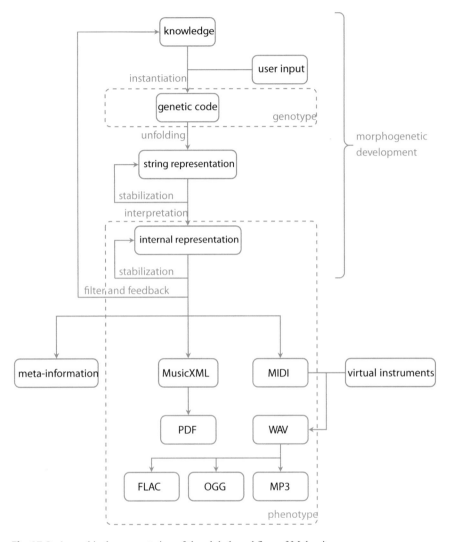

Fig. 17.2 A graphical representation of the global workflow of Melomics

- \$2 decreases the pitch value one step in the scale;
- \$5 saves the current values for pitch and duration into a stack (the *PS* stack);
- \$6 pops the top value of pitch and duration from the PS stack, replacing the current values;
- \$7 saves the current time position into a stack (the *TS* stack);
- \$8 pops the top value of time position from the TS stack, replacing the current value;
- \$96 applies the dynamic *mezzo-forte*;
- @60\$120 applies the tempo: a quarter equal 60.

To illustrate how music can be generated, let us consider an L-system with alphabet containing #0, #1, #2, #3, #4 plus the eight previously defined reserved symbols, #0 as the axiom, and the following rules, one for each symbol of the form #i:

$$\#0 \rightarrow @60\$120\$96\#2\$1\$1\$1\$1\$1\$1\#2$$
$$\#1 \rightarrow \#1$$
$$\#2 \rightarrow \$7\#3\$8\#4$$
$$\#3 \rightarrow \#3\$2\#3\$1\$1\#1\#3$$
$$\#4 \rightarrow \#4\#1\$5\$1\$1\$1\#4\$6\#4$$

Since L-systems can potentially generate new strings forever, it is necessary to decide when to stop. To do so, each rule has associated a budget of applications computed as follows: each rule has an associated value r_i, that denotes the possibility of that rule to be applied at the next rewriting iteration. Initially, $r_i = T$, where T is a global parameter equal for all rules. Each rule also has a weight I_i that is fixed and specific for each rule. After a rule has been applied in a rewriting step, the value of r_i associated to it is updated as

$$r_i = \max\left(0, \text{round}(r_i \cdot I_i - 1)\right).$$

When a rule reaches $r_i = 0$, then it cannot be used anymore in a rewriting step. This means that the application of the rewriting rules always ends.

In the system used as an example, let $T = 1$ and $I_i = 1$ for all rules. This means that every rule will be applied in only one rewriting step, i.e., it has a "budget" of applications of one.

Let us now explore what are the intermediate steps that, starting from the axiom #0, will produce a music score.

Iteration 0

When no iteration has been performed the output sting is the axiom #0 itself. In abstract, the string interpretation is "play a note on the instrument 0". To give meaning to this, we need to set a collection of default parameters:

- *Scale*: C-major;
- *Default duration*: quarter note;
- *Default tempo*: 80 bpm;
- *Default dynamic*: mezzo-piano;
- *Initial pitch*: middle C;
- *Instruments*: piano (0), rest (1), church organ (2 and 3), cello (4).

The string #0 can now be interpreted as the musical score in Fig. 17.3.

Fig. 17.3 Resulting score
from axiom #0

Fig. 17.4 Resulting score
from iteration 1

Iteration 1

While the zeroth iteration actually had no rewriting, the first iteration requires the application of one rewriting rule. In this case, the only applicable rule is the one having the axiom on the left-hand side, thus generating the string

$$@60\$120\$96\#2\$1\$1\$1\$1\$1\$1\$1\#2$$

which can be interpreted by reading it from left to right:

- @60$120$96: change the default tempo to a quarter equal 60 and apply the dynamic mezzo-forte;
- #2: play a note on the instrument number 2 (church organ);
- $1$1$1$1$1$1$1: raise the pitch seven times. Since the scale is C-major, this means that the next note will be played one octave higher,
- #2: play a note on the instrument number 2 (church organ).

Following this interpretation, the resulting musical score is shown in Fig. 17.4.

Iteration 2

Starting from the string obtained after one iteration, it is now possible to apply the only rule having #2 on the left-hand side, which has right-hand side $7#3$8#4. This right-hand side has the effect of rewriting each copy of #2 into it. That is, #2 ceases to be a low-level command (playing a note), to be a building block of a more complex structure. In particular, the effect will be that each time #2 was present in the string obtained after iteration 1, now the same note will be played at the same time on instruments 3 (church organ) and 4 (cello). This is the resulting string with the rewritten parts highlighted:

$$@60\$120\$96 \underbrace{\$7\#3\$8\#4} \$1\$1\$1\$1\$1\$1\$1 \underbrace{\$7\#3\$8\#4}$$

The resulting score is shown in Fig. 17.5.

Fig. 17.5 Resulting score
from iteration 2

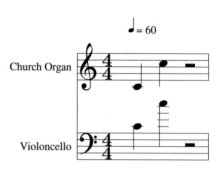

As it is possible to observe, the "synchronization" between the two instruments is an emerging property resulting from the rewriting rules of the L-system. In the case of a direct encoding, this would not be as easy: playing the same notes on two instruments would be highly improbable, at least without a complex fitness function able to capture these features, which would itself be a complex task.

Iteration 3

There two rules having left-hand side #3 and #4 are the only two that can be applied, resulting in the following string, where the rewritten parts are highlighted:

@60$120$96

$7 #3$2#3$1$1#1#3 $8 #4#1$5$1$1$1#4$6#4

$1$1$1$1$1$1$1

$7 #3$2#3$1$1#1#3 $8 #4#1$5$1$1$1#4$6#4

Notice how the music has acquired a structure. The initial rewriting, which resulted in two notes played one after the other with an octave of difference in pitch is now expressed in the same sequence of notes played two times with the second time one octave higher, as shown in Fig. 17.6.

Such musical structure would, again, be extremely complex to obtain with a direct encoding, since it is a high-level feature that cannot easily be expressed if, instead of an L-system, we were only evolving a sequence of notes.

There actually is a fourth iteration, where only the rule #1 → #1 is applicable, resulting in the same string. While rules with left-hand side #3 and #4 could potentially be applied again, their "budget" of one iteration is already exhausted after the third iteration.

17.4.2 Examples of Atonal Music

Here we will describe some of the relevant examples of atonal music produce using Melomics, from the composition "Iamus Opus One" (from the name of the computer

Fig. 17.6 Resulting score from iteration 2

cluster employed in the composition), to the later composition "Hello world!", to the use for relaxation in the music therapy setting.

Iamus Opus #1

One of the first works of Melomics was *Iamus Opus One*, written for flute, clarinet, horn, violin, and violoncello. The composition was generated on October 15, 2010, and it is the first piece of professional contemporary classical music composed by a computer in its own style, as a result of the first directed search using the algorithm (see Fig. 17.7).

With respect to the aforementioned system, it was necessary to introduce certain constraints, in order to produce music that could be performed with real instruments; some of these boundaries tried to maximize the allowed polyphony, tessituras, effects, and note durations and dynamics.

For the evolutionary phase, new functions were necessary to assess the compositions after being developed; they measured the textural evolution, the amount of dissonance, and the repetition of note-values and note-pitches. The method and the thresholds to discriminate the validity of a composition were fine-tuned in an iterative fashion with the help of the expert. The general goal pursued was to obtain pieces of music with a limited amount of perceived dissonance and whose fundamental musical materials (specific melodic constructions, structure, etc.) were evoked along the time and among the different participant instruments.

Hello World!

One year after Iamus Opus One, four main improvements were incorporated into the system:

1. the fitness function employed in the evolutionary system was refined;

Fig. 17.7 First beats of *Iamus Opus #1*

2. the capability to compose for real instruments was increased, handling more types of instruments, more performing techniques and the music content produced for each track, being more suitable to the instrument in charge of performing it;
3. the functions to write the output MusicXML file were enhanced, so the produced score was richer and able to show most of the elements of the standard music notation;
4. the process of building genomes was divided in two phases, one controlling the structure and another to build the low-level material (phrases and motives).

The computer cluster Iamus was programmed to run Melomics software for about ten hours, creating independent compositions for clarinet, violin, and piano. In the end, one composition was arbitrarily picked among the hundreds that were produced, and was named *Hello World!*, making reference to the first computer program written by most novices (see Fig. 17.8). This piece of contemporary classical music was composed in September 2011 and premiered on October 15, 2011, at the Keroxen music festival in Santa Cruz de Tenerife, Spain.

17.4.3 Tonal Music

While the same system employed for the production of *atonal* music could also be employed for the generation of *tonal* music, the amount of constraints needed would be too large, and the system would need too much time to converge to a reasonable solution. However, these obstacles can be mitigated or removed by changing the symbols employed in the strings, thus changing the "abstract machine" interpreting the strings.

In particular, the generation of tonal music is performed in a strictly hierarchical structure, by defining five nested levels, inspired by [10], from the most abstract to the most concrete:

Fig. 17.8 The first few beats of *Hello World!*

1. **Composition**. This is the highest structural level that can be defined. A composition will be formed by a sequence of similar or different kinds of periods, possibly with some music operators (alterations in tone, harmony, tempo, macrodynamics,…) between each of them. Some of the parameters that can be established at this level (apart from the ones described in the previous section) are: boundaries for the number of periods, boundaries for the number of different periods, allowed music operators, and boundaries for the number of measures in the whole composition.

2. **Period**. This is the highest structural subdivision of a composition. There can be more than one type of period, which can be repeated along the composition. The different types are built independently, becoming separate musical units, recognizable in the composition. Some of the parameters that can be defined at this level are: boundaries for the number of phrases inside one period, boundaries for the number of different phrases, allowed music operators inside the period, and boundaries for the number of measures in each period.

3. **Phrase**. This is the third structural level, the constituent material of the periods. Some of the parameters that can be defined at this level are: boundaries for the number of ideas, boundaries for the number of different ideas, allowed music operators, and boundaries for the number of measures in each phrase.

4. **Idea**. Constitutes the lowest abstract level in the structure of a composition. Once again, a phrase can be composed by different ideas that can be repeated in time, with music operators in the middle. A musical idea will be a short sequence of notes generated independently for each role, using many different criteria (harmony, rhythm, pitch intervals, relationship with other roles, …). Several of the described global parameters affect the process of creating an idea, and other applicable parameters at this level are: boundaries for the number of chords, boundaries for the size of chords and boundaries for the number of measures.

5. **Texture**. This subsection allows the possibility to define rules for the inclusion of roles; different types of dependencies between them, the compositional units where they are forced, allowed, or prohibited to appear in, and, finally, the general evolution of the presence of instruments.

As with atonal music, a set of parameters must be defined for the composition:

- **Duration**. Lower and upper bounds for the duration of the composition.
- **Tempo**. Lower and upper bounds to choose the tempos used in the composition.
- **Dynamics**. Lower and upper bounds for the macro-dynamics to be applied in the composition.
- **Role Types**. A list of roles or behaviors that may appear in the composition. There are 89 available roles divided into multiple groups: melody, accompaniments, homophony (harmonized melody), and counterpoint. There are different forms in which the harmonic and rhythmic accompaniments can appear: chords, bass, pads, arpeggios, ostinati, drums, and percussion.
- **Arpeggio Configuration**. This parameter is significant only if the arpeggio role has been selected as possible. In that case, additional parameters must be given: mode or contour type (Chord, Up, Down, Up-Down, Down-Up, Up-Down+, Down-Up+, Random); durations or time segments into which the note-values of the primary rhythmic cell must be divided; scope or number of octaves where the contour should be fitted into; and tie notes, indicating whether consecutive similar notes shall be tied or not.
- **Instruments**. For each of the roles, a set of specific instruments, each with its additional parameters, must be specified.
- **Rhythmic Incompatibilities**. Defines the incompatibilities of instruments to play notes at the same exact moment.
- **Scales**. A set of modes and notes of reference that can be employed in the composition, defining one of the following scales: C-major, C-minor, D-Dorian, and C-Mixolydian.
- **Harmony**. This set of parameters describes how to build the harmony in the different compositional levels. Examples include the allowed chords and roots, a measure of the allowed dissonance between melodies or the form of chord progressions.
- **Rhythmic Modes**. Includes the allowed types of measures, the types of accents to perform the notes, and so on.
- **Rhythmic Patterns**. Each role has a set of note-values or patterns, establishing the desired frequency of occurrence in a composition.
- **Melodic Pitch Intervals**. This set of parameters is available only for the "melody" role and consists, for each one of them, of a weighted list of pitch intervals that is used to define how the melodic contour has to be built.

Due to the different set of parameters and the strictly hierarchical structure of the composition, the way a composition is encoded had to be changed with respect to the encoding used for atonal music. It is now useful to distinguish the symbols in the alphabet Σ into *terminals* (i.e., that cannot be further expanded) and *non-*

terminal (i.e., that have rewriting rules associated with them). Therefore, instead of employing and L-system, we use a *context-free grammar* $(\Sigma_N, \Sigma_T, S, P)$ where, Σ_N (resp., Σ_T) is the set of non-terminal (resp., terminal) symbols. In some sense, the symbols in Σ_N represent the high-level structure of the composition, while the symbols in Σ_T represent operations directly linked to playing notes, the modulation of the pitch, duration, current harmonic root, and current harmonic chord.

This is an enumeration of the operators appearing in Σ_T:

- **N**: increase the current pitch and harmonic root of one unit;
- **n**: decrease the current pitch and harmonic root of one unit;
- **[**: saves in the stack the current value of the pitch, harmonic root, and duration;
- **]**: pops from the top of the stack the values to use for the pitch, harmonic root, and duration;
- **<**: saves in the stack the current time position, value of pitch, harmonic root, and duration;
- **>**: pops from the top of the stack the values to use for time position, value of pitch, harmonic root, and duration;
- **W4.0**: applies the macro-dynamic "mezzo-forte";
- **M0.0.0.0**: the next symbol linked to an instrument will play the root note of the current chord, instead of the current pitch.

We can explore how the hierarchical structure unfolds with a simple example. Let $\Sigma_N = \{Z, A, B, C, D, E, F\}$ with Z the axiom, and let Σ_T be composed to all the previously defined operators plus the three symbols a, b, and s, representing the first instrument (the violin), the second instrument (the double bass), and the rest, respectively. The production rules are defined as follows:

$$Z \to W4.0 \; ANNNNNNNAB$$
$$A \to CC$$
$$B \to D$$
$$C \to ENEnE$$
$$D \to FFNF$$
$$E \to \; < anaNNsa > M0.0.0.0 \; b \; M0.0.0.0 \; bs \; M0.0.0.0 \; b$$
$$F \to as[NNNa]a$$

Even without starting the application of the production rules to the axiom, a structure is already visible. The axiom Z is the top-level structural unit, i.e., the *composition*. From Z the only non-terminal symbols generated are A and B, which represents the second level of structure, i.e., the *periods*. A and B generate C and D, respectively, going down one level in the hierarchy to the *phrases*. The symbols E and F are generated by C and D, and represents the *ideas*. Finally, E and F generate only terminal symbols.

We can now observe the first steps of the expansion of Z, where each rewritten part is highlighted by braces:

Z	Composition
$W4.0\underbrace{ANNNNNNNAB}$	Periods
$W4.0\underbrace{CC}NNNNNNN\underbrace{CC}\underbrace{D}$	Phrases
$W4.0\underbrace{ENEnE}\underbrace{ENEnE}NNNNNNN\underbrace{ENEnE}\underbrace{ENEnE}\underbrace{FFNF}$	Ideas

As it is possible to observe after the first iterations, the composition will contain the same period A two times, but the second time it will be played seven steps higher in the pitch dimension, and then the composition will end with the period B. Each period will then be expanded independently, with A containing the phrase C repeated two times, and C consisting of the single phrase D.

To exhaust all possible rewriting, we need an additional rewriting phase, moving from ideas to the actual notes. To interpret it, we need to fix the scale (C-major), the default duration (a quarter note), a default dynamic (mezzo-piano), the roles (the violin plays a single melody and the bass is an accompaniment). The violin's starting pitch will be middle C, while it will be one octave lower for the double bass. The resulting composition is:

It is possible to observe that the structure of the composition contains some repetitions in the structure, if not in the notes. Inside an idea, the difference in pitches is minimal for the violin, while the double bass always plays the same root note. The first two periods share the same structure but with a bit of pitch jump between them, while the third period is distinctly different and is only played by the violin. Notice again that the use of an indirect encoding—an evo-devo system—is essential to obtain this kind of structural similarity that can encompass the entire composition.

17.4.4 Example of Tonal Music: 0Music and the Web Repository

One of the achievements of the tonal version of Melomics was the population of a web repository with more than fifty thousand themes. The styles were pieces of music of the most popular genres, ranging from disco to pop, and from symphonic to

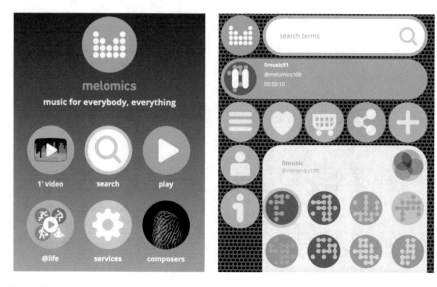

Fig. 17.9 The web interface of Melomics' repository

synth music. The music is available at http://melomics.uma.es/, with an easy-to-use interface, as shown in Fig. 17.9. All themes are distributed under a CC0 license and can be downloaded in different formats.

Apart from making a large amount of themes available to the public, the generation of such a large amount of themes was, in some sense, a "stress test" for Melomics, testing the ability to produce music with enough diversity in each style, even with a large amount of imposed constraints, and the ability to produce music of many different styles, controlling harmony in compositions with many interrelated roles.

A small sample of themes in different styles was selected by musicians to showcase the current state of Melomics: this is the *0Music* album, presented in a one-day symposium in 2014 (see http://www.geb.uma.es/0music).

17.4.5 Example of Application: Music Therapy

In addition to focusing only on the more contemporary music style, Melomics was also employed for helping people via music therapy. Differently from compositions with mainly aesthetic purposes, the main goal of music therapy is different [23]. An example of this effect can be observed in lullabies, which are similar across a wide spectrum of cultures while not having a mainly aesthetic goal. With the help of an expert in music therapy, Melomics can be configured to produce simpler samples, with a more reduced set of possible structures [24,28].

17.4.6 Output Formats and Interoperability

A system like Melomics also has to tackle more concrete concerns, like how to make the music available in a way that is distinct from its internal representation. We can distinguish multiple levels of exchange formats:

- The internal representation of the composition can be represented using a standard JSON format;
- The score can be exported using the MusicXML format, which is an open format licensed under the W3C Community Final Specification Agreement (FSA) specifically designed for music score representation. It can be imported in multiple software, including Finale, NOtation, MuseScore, etc.
- The music can be exported in the MIDI format. It still contains the information on the notes to be played and is commonly used with a real-time virtual synthesizer, thus providing a middle ground between the MusicXML format and synthesized music;
- Melomics is able from its internal representation to produce directly synthesized music in the WAV format that can be further converted into other formats like FLAC, MP3, or OGG.

We can then conclude that Melomics, from a practical point of view, is well equipped to interoperate with other systems and be integrated into other applications or workflows.

17.5 A Soundtrack for Life

Until now, we have avoided the question of the motivation for composing music and on the nature of artificial music. The composition of music is regarded as a creative process where humans can express and evoke sensations. We want to discuss three questions related to the nature of artificial music. The first one is on whether artificially composed music can be considered actual music. The second question is about the nature of the artificial composition of music: is this music discovered or created? Finally, we want to answer the question of *why* artificial music exists.

17.5.1 Is Artificial Music Actually Music?

One first question to be asked before considering whether artificial music is created or discovered, it whether artificial music can be considered music. As discussed in [11], the question on the nature of music is neither easy nor settled. Even when limited to the "absolute" or "pure" music, i.e., instrumental music devoid of non-musical aspects, the definition of music is a tricky question. The definition of music as organized sound is too broad since it includes a collection of sounds that, while organized, are not music. Even this definition, while broad, is at risk of excluding the composition generated by Melomics, since they alone are the only score, they need to be performed to actually obtain music. This is, however, only a small hurdle and we can consider the question of whether Melomics's scores when performed are actual music.

Two additional properties that are usually required in the definition of music are either tonality—or the presence of certain musical features—and an appeal to aesthetic properties. One or both properties can be considered necessary to obtain music. The first of them can be respected by Melomics, since it requires the presence of certain features that can be a force in either the encoding or the fitness function. The second property is certainly more complex to be respected. We cannot ascribe any intention of aesthetics to software, but we can suspect that the person setting the parameters of Melomics as having as a goal the generation of aesthetically pleasant sound. Also, if we move the focus from the composer to the listener, the fact that the composer is a machine is not as relevant as initially envisioned.

We remark that these properties are not the only way to define music, and, indeed, they have problems in capturing all and only what humans usually consider music. There are multiple possible definitions, each one with strengths and weaknesses, and their discussion is more the domain of discussion of the philosophy of music [11].

We can also take a more practical approach, where instead of looking at Melomics's compositions from a purely philosophical perspective, we consider the opinion of critics and of the general public. If they consider the end result as music, then it can be considered music.

In the case of experts, Peter Russell's critics of a piece composed by Melomics is illuminating:

> Quite opposite to my usual comment when my ears are assaulted by serial music written in the 12 tone scale, on listening to this delightful piece of chamber music I could not bring myself to say that it would probably be more satisfying to read the score than listen to it. In fact after repeated hearings, I came to like it.

Notice the absence of doubts on whether the piece is music. There is a judgment on the quality of the piece, and a positive one at it, but the piece is undoubtedly considered music. Russell had no knowledge that the piece of music was the creation of an algorithm, and was wondering himself of the origin of the piece:

> I did not recognise either the piece or the composer. [...] It will be interesting to finally know the name of the composer.

The fact that Melomics's composition are considered the product of human creativity shows that, at least, in this case, artificial music can be considered music. It can also be considered as music having a particular style, since Russell also suggest a possible time period and geographical location for the composition:

> However, if I were forced to hazzard a guess, I would say that it was written during the early years of the twentieth century -1920's, 1930's. There was a feeling of France about it [...]

To discuss an additional point of view, Philip Ball in [4] comments on Peter Russell's critics, and also discuss the generation process of Melomics, noticing that:

> In a sense, these algorithms are not doing anything so very different from the way composers have always composed.

also highlights the similarity between Melomics's composition process and the human one.

Also, in 2013, Matt Peckham titled its article "Finally, a Computer that Writes Contemporary Music Without Human Help" [20], showing that what Melomics produces is music. He also reiterates this by writing:

> Music is elementally mathematical, so it makes sense that with exponential increases in computer processing power, a computer could be designed that creates recognizable and even interesting music.

Thus stating that computers *can* create music.

Not all people were positive in defining the work of Melomics as music. For example, David Ecker [7] wrote that:

> Without humanity, music is nothing but sonic manipulation

This would exclude any artificial composition, and skepticism is to be expected when computers enter a domain that was previously only accessible to humans. However, we want to point out that the situation is not a zero-sum game. For example, the existence of chess-playing computers above the human level has not removed the ability and pleasure to play chess with another human. As a second point, we might want to consider the humanity of the listener. If an artificially composed piece evokes certain sensations in the listener, are those sensations somehow diminished by the absence of a human composer? Finally, if a piece is of unknown origin, at least to the listener, is its status as music unknown? Do we really need to know the origin of a piece to decide if it is music or not?

17.5.2 Creation or Discovery?

The nature of music and the dichotomy between creation—or invention—and discovery has long been a topic of discussion especially in the area of the philosophy of music [11]. We will now consider the Platonism approach, in which musical works exist as abstract objects; other theories, like the nominalist theory, are not considered in this discussion.

Even inside Platonism, we can distinguish two possible views: the simple Platonism, where musical objects exist as immutable outside of both space and time, and the complex Platonism, where the musical objects exist in time as a result of human action. This second view in particular is based on the observation that humans compose music, that musical objects can be created, and that they possess individual tracts that derive from the human that composed them. The first view, however, has musical objects as immutable and the role of the human is to discover them, not to create them.

The nature algorithms and their outputs are more in the area of philosophy of Mathematics [14], where the Platonistic view is also present. In particular, if we ascribe to the view that mathematical entities exist in an immutable way, then the Melomics algorithm is simply discovering points into the space of compositions that can be represented via L-systems or context-free grammars. The idea that solutions are discovered and not created is also present in the evolutionary algorithm community. For example, if we consider a genetic algorithm and a fitness function f, we say that want to find the optimum (either a global minimum or maximum) of f, not to construct it. In some sense, we are saying that the existence of f itself is sufficient to say that the optimum of f exists and we only need to discover it.

If we adopt this view also in our case, the combination of the encoding given by Melomics and a collection of constraints given by the fitness function are enough to ensure the existence of the compositions even before Melomics find them. This view is consistent with assuming simple Platonism in music: in both cases, the music is "only" discovered since it was always there. However, if we adopt a complex Platonism view of music, we would have the inconsistency that algorithms discover music, while humans create it. The same piece of music can be found by an algorithm and created by a human; a difficult position since the first situation implies the existence of musical objects as immutable outside of time, while the second implies musical objects existing in time.

While this discussion is by no means exhaustive, it is interesting to consider how the existence of algorithmic music might be a new lens to use in the analysis of the nature of music and of mathematical objects.

17.5.3 Why Artificial Music?

The last question that remains to answer is the motivation for having artificially composed music. An answer that might be not very satisfactory could be "Pour l'honneur de l'esprit humain" (*for the honor of the human spirit*), as the title of the book of the famous mathematician Jean Dieudonné. While discovering new music can be done without any other goal in mind, there are real and tangible benefits to artificial composition.

The first benefit is to create new and original music that would have remained undiscovered without the help of an artificial composer. These ideas can then be used in the composition of new music. As Philip Ball wrote [4]:

> Iamus's ultimate value, however, might not be so much as a composer in its own right but as a factory of musical ideas, which human composers can mine for inspiration.

In this sense, artificial composition can be considered not as a replacement of human composition and creativity, but as an instrument for augmentation of human capabilities.

Another, possibly less explored, aspect of artificial music is that there might be a discrepancy between what a human composer wants to express with his/her music in terms of sensations, images, and feelings, and what a person listening might want. There are a lot of daily situations that might benefit from music, but those are not the focus of composers. Consider, for example, a music to favor sleeping: not many composers might want to write music to "put people to sleep". Artificial music can cover this discrepancy by composing music that, while useful to people, is not of interest to the composers. In some sense, artificial music can provide a soundtrack for all daily human activity, a *soundtrack for life*.

17.6 Conclusions

In this chapter, we have provided an introduction to the basic idea of combining L-system and evolutionary algorithms to compose music. We have described how the most prominent system of this kind, Melomics, works internally for composing both atonal and tonal music, with also a brief historical excursus on the impact of Melomics in the arts. We have remarked how, differently from many other existing systems for the generation of music, Melomics does not require an existing corpus of music to perform its compositions. In fact, it is only in the constraints imposed by the L-systems construction and the evolutionary process that the distinction between music and non-music is encoded into Melomics.

We tackled the discussion of the goal of producing artificial music, for example, by pointing out the usefulness of music that, while being useful for humans, is not pleasing for humans to compose. More "philosophical" is the discussion on the nature of music, if music is constructed/generated or if it is discovered. While no conclusion can be reached on this discussion, we consider extremely interesting the perspective that can be gained by investigating computer programs.

Melomics's applications are not limited to the ones presented here. Its principles can be applied and adapted to produce more music; its rules and evolutionary process can be refined with time: in some sense, as composer, Melomics is still growing.

Acknowledgements This research was supported by INNPACTO project Melomics, funded by the Spanish Government (reference code IPT-300000-2010-010).

References

1. Melomics: Optimización de la respuesta terapéutica a la modulación de estímulos auditivos (2010–2013). IPT-300000-2010-010, Spanish Ministry of Economy and Competitivity (INNPACTO subprogram/Strategic initiative on Health)
2. Cauce: Generación automática de contenidos audiovisuales con calidad profesional (2011–2013). TSI-090302-2011-0008, Spanish Ministry of Industry, Tourism and Commerce (AVANZA Digital Content Subprogram)
3. Albarracín-Molina, D. D., Moya, J. C., & Vico, F. J. (2016). An evo-devo system for algorithmic composition that actually works. In *Proceedings of the 2016 on Genetic and Evolutionary Computation Conference Companion* (pp. 37–38).
4. Ball, P. Artificial music: The computers that create melodies. Retrieved Feburary 10, 2020, from https://www.bbc.com/future/article/20140808-music-like-never-heard-before.
5. Ball, P. (2012). Computer science: Algorithmic rapture. *Nature, 488*(7412), 458.
6. Casas, M. J., & Vico, F. J. (2009). On the performance of some bioinspired genetic operators in complex structures evolution. In *Proceedings of the 11th Annual conference on Genetic and evolutionary computation* (pp. 1841–1842).
7. Ecker, D. (2013). Of music and men. *Columbia Daily Spectator.*
8. Fernández, J. D., & Vico, F. (2013). Ai methods in algorithmic composition: A comprehensive survey. *Journal of Artificial Intelligence Research, 48*, 513–582.
9. Holland, J. H. (1992). *Adaptation in natural and artificial systems: An introductory analysis with applications to biology, control, and artificial intelligence.* MIT press (1992)
10. Ian, D., & Bent, A. P. Analysis. In *Grove music online.* Oxford University Press. https://doi.org/10.1093/gmo/9781561592630.article.41862.
11. Kania, A. (2017). *The philosophy of music.* https://plato.stanford.edu/archives/fall2017/entries/music/.
12. Lim, C. K., Tan, K. L., Yusran, H., & Suppramaniam, V. (2017). Lsound: An l-system framework for score generation. *Journal of Telecommunication, Electronic and Computer Engineering (JTEC), 9*(2–11), 159–163.
13. Lindenmayer, A. (1968). Mathematical models for cellular interaction in development, part i and part ii. *Journal of Theoretical Biology, 18*, 280–315.
14. Linnebo, Ø. (2018). *Platonism in the philosophy of mathematics.* https://plato.stanford.edu/archives/spr2018/entries/platonism-mathematics.
15. Lourenço, B. F., Ralha, J. C., & Brandao, M. C. (2009). L-systems, scores, and evolutionary techniques. *Proceedings of the SMC*, 113–118.
16. Luke, S. (2013). Essentials of metaheuristics. *Lulu.* https://cs.gmu.edu/sean/book/metaheuristics/
17. Menabrea, L. F., & Lovelace, A. (1842). *Sketch of the analytical engine invented by Charles Babbage.*
18. Nierhaus, G. (2009). *Algorithmic composition: Paradigms of automated music generation.* Springer Science & Business Media.
19. Ohno, S. (1987). Repetition as the essence of life on this earth: Music and genes. In *Modern trends in human leukemia VII* (pp. 511–519). Springer.
20. Peckham, M. *Finally, a computer that writes contemporary music without human help.* Retrieved February 20, 2020, from. https://techland.time.com/2013/01/04/finally-a-computer-that-writes-contemporary-music-without-human-help/.
21. Prusinkiewicz, P. (1986). Score generation with l-systems. In *Proceedings of the 1986 International Computer Music Conference* (pp. 455–457).
22. Quintana, C. S., Arcas, F. M., Molina, D. A., Rodríguez, J. D. F., & Vico, F. J. (2013). Melomics: A case-study of ai in Spain. *AI Magazine, 34*(3), 99–103.
23. Raglio, A., & Vico, F. (2017). Music and technology: The curative algorithm. *Frontiers in Psychology, 8*, 2055.

24. Requena, G., Sánchez, C., Corzo-Higueras, J. L., Reyes-Alvarado, S., Rivas-Ruiz, F., Vico, F., et al. (2014). Melomics music medicine (m3) to lessen pain perception during pediatric prick test procedure. *Pediatric Allergy and Immunology, 25*(7), 721–724.
25. Rozenberg, G., & Salomaa, A. (1980). *The mathematical theory of L systems*. Academic Press.
26. Ryan, C., Collins, J. J., & Neill, M. O. (1998). Grammatical evolution: Evolving programs for an arbitrary language. In *European Conference on Genetic Programming* (pp. 83–96). Springer.
27. Stanley, K. O., & Miikkulainen, R. (2002). Evolving neural networks through augmenting topologies. *Evolutionary Computation, 10*(2), 99–127.
28. de la Torre-Luque, A., Caparros-Gonzalez, R. A., Bastard, T., Vico, F. J., & Buela-Casal, G. (2017). Acute stress recovery through listening to melomics relaxing music: A randomized controlled trial. *Nordic Journal of Music Therapy, 26*(2), 124–141.

Francisco Vico is full professor at the Department of Artificial Intelligence, in the Computer Science School of the University of Malaga, Spain. Since 1996, he leads the Group of Studies in Biomimetics in this university. His main subject of interest is the complexity of living matter, and how to study it from a computer modeling and simulation approach. Noteworthy among the various research projects he has developed is the Melomics project, focused on developing a genomic-based computational system for automatic music composition.
E-mail: fjvico@uma.es.

David Albarracin-Molina studied Computer Engineering at Universidad de Málaga in Spain, and obtained a Master in Design and Management of Technological Projects at Universidad Internacional de La Rioja, also in Spain. Between 2009 and 2015, he worked with the Group of Studies in Biomimetics at the University of Malaga and currently he is a Ph.D. student in Computational Intelligence at this university. His research includes bio-inspired generative music and information retrieval techniques. He has been working at Virtually Live in Switzerland since 2018 as a Lead Researcher, designing prototypes based on deep learning and managing the workflow in the research team.
E-mail: david@geb.uma.es.

Gustavo Díaz-Jerez is a composer and pianist based in San Sebastián, Spain. His compositional output spans all genres, from solo works to opera. His orchestral work *Ymarxa*, commissioned by the XXVII Canary Islands Music Festival, was premiered by the Royal Philharmonic Orchestra, conducted by Charles Dutoit. His first opera, *La casa Imaginaria*, was premiered in 2018. As a performer of Spanish music, he has been awarded the Albéniz Medal for his recording of the composition *Iberia*, by Isaac Albéniz. His CD releases include a monographic CD with his piano works, *Metaludios* for piano. He has also recorded for the first time Albéniz' *Iberia* in HD video. He is the author of software program *FractMus*, for algorithmic composition.
E-mail: diazjerez@gmail.com.

Luca Manzoni is an assistant professor at the Department of Mathematics and Geosciences ad the University of Trieste in Italy. He obtained his Ph.D. in Computer Science from the University of Milano-Bicocca, Italy, in 2013. In 2012, he was awarded a Postdoctoral Fellowship from the Japan Society for the Promotion of Science (JSPS) to conduct research at Osaka Electro-Communication University in Japan, and in 2017 he was awarded the best young postdoctoral researcher in Computer Science and Mathematics at the University of Milano-Bicocca. His interests are in the areas of natural computing models, cellular automata, and evolutionary computation.
E-mail: lmanzoni@units.it.

Assisted Music Creation with Flow Machines: Towards New Categories of New

18

François Pachet, Pierre Roy and Benoit Carré

18.1 Background and Motivations

This chapter reflects on about 10 years of research in AI-assisted music composition, in particular during the Flow Machines project. We reflect on the motivations for such a project, its background, its main results and impact, both technological and musical, several years after its completion. We conclude with a proposal for new categories of "new", created by the many uses of AI techniques to generate novel material.

The dream of using machines to compose music automatically has long been a subject of investigation, by musicians and scientists.

Since the 60s, many researchers have used virtually all existing artificial intelligence techniques at hand to solve music generation problems. However, little convincing music was produced with these technologies.

A landmark result in machine music generation is the *Illiac Suite*, released to the public in 1956 [37]. This piece showed that Markov chains of a rudimentary species (first order, augmented with basic generate-and-test methods) could be used to produce interesting music. We invite the reader to listen to the piece, composed more than 70 years ago, to appreciate its enduring innovative character [36].

However, the technology developed for that occasion lacked many fundamental features, to make it actually useable for concrete, professional musical projects. Notably, the experiment involved generate-and-test methods to satisfy various constraints imposed by the authors. Also, the low order of the Markov chain did not produce convincing style imitation. In spite of these many weaknesses, the Illiac Suite remains today a remarkable music piece that can still be listened to with interest.

F. Pachet (✉) · P. Roy · B. Carré
Spotify CTRL, Paris, France
e-mail: francois@spotify.com

© Springer Nature Switzerland AG 2021
E. R. Miranda (ed.), *Handbook of Artificial Intelligence for Music*,
https://doi.org/10.1007/978-3-030-72116-9_18

The Flow Machines project (2012–2017), funded by an ERC advanced grant and conducted at Sony CSL and Sorbonne Université, aimed at addressing the core technical issues at stake when generating sequences in a given style. In some sense, it addressed the two main weaknesses of the Markov chains used in the *Illiac Suite*: the low order (and the poor style imitation quality) and the controllability, i.e. the capacity to force generated sequences to satisfy various criteria, not captured by Markov models.

18.1.1 The Continuator

More precisely, the main motivation for Flow Machines stemmed from the Continuator project. The Continuator [71] was the first interactive system to enable real-time music dialogues with a Markov model. The project was quite successful in the research community and led to two main threads of investigation: jazz and music education. Jazz experiments were conducted notably with György Kurtag Jr. and Bernard Lubat, leading to various concerts at the Uzeste festival (2000–2004) and many insights concerning the issues related to control [64].

The education experiments consisted in studying how these free-form interactions with a machine learning component could be exploited for early-age music education. Promising initial experiments [1,73] led to an ambitious project [111] about so-called "reflexive interactions". During this project, the Continuator system was substantially improved and extended, to handle various types of simple constraints. An interesting variant of the Continuator for music composition, called MIROR-Impro, was designed, deployed and tested, with which children could generate fully fledged music compositions, built from music generated from their own doodling [95]. It was shown also that children could clearly recognize their own style in the material generated by the system [40], a property considered as fundamental for achieving reflexive interaction.

18.2 Markov Constraints: Main Scientific Results

These promising results in the investigation of Markov sequence control led to the Flow Machines project. Technically, most of the work consisted in exploring many types of interesting constraints to be enforced on finite-length sequences generated from various machine learning models, such as variable-order Markov models. Other tools were developed to offer musicians a comprehensive tool palette with which they could freely explore various creative use cases of style imitation techniques.

Table 18.1 The chord progression of the Boulez Blues

C7/Fmin	Bb7/Ebmin	Ab7/Db7	Dbmin/Cmin
F7/Bbmin	Eb7/Abmin	Gmin/Gbmin	B7/Gb7
Bmin/E7	Amin/D7	Emin/A7	Dmin/G7

18.2.1   The "Markov + X" Roadmap

Markov models are used everywhere, from economics to Google ranking algorithms, and are good at capturing local properties of temporal sequences and abstract them into well-known mathematical concepts (e.g. transition matrice or graphs). A Markov model can easily be estimated from a corpus of sequences in a given style to represent information about how musical notes follow each other. This model can then be used to produce new sequences that will sound more or less similar to the initial sequences. Generation, or sampling, is extremely simple and consists in so-called random walks (also called drunken walks): starting from a random state, transitions are drawn randomly from the model to build a sequence step by step. However, the remarkable simplicity of random walks in Markov models meets its limitations as soon as one tries to impose specific constraints on the generated sequences. The difficulty arises when one wants to impose simple properties that cannot be expressed as local transition probabilities: for instance, imposing that the last note equals the first one, or that the notes follow some pattern, or that the total duration be fixed in advance. Even more difficult, how to impose that the generated melody is nicely "balanced", for instance exhibiting a well-known $1/f$ property, characteristic of natural phenomena?

The initial idea was to use the powerful techniques of combinatorial optimization, constraint satisfaction in particular (CP), precisely to represent Markovianity, so that other, additional properties could also be stated as constraints. Indeed, the main advantage of constraint programming is that constraints can be added at will to the problem definition, without changing the solver, at least in principle.

The idea of representing Markovianity as a global constraint was first detailed in [67]. We reformulated Markov generation as a constrained sequence generation problem, an idea which enabled us to produce remarkable examples. For instance, the *AllDifferent* constraint [93], added to a Markov constraint, could produce our *Boulez Blues*: a Blues chord sequence in the style of Charlie Parker so that all chords are different! Table 18.1 shows the chord progression of the Boulez Blues. A rendering with jazz musicians can be heard at [59].

However, this approach was costly, and we did not propose any boundaries on the worst-case complexity. So we started to look for efficient solutions for specific cases.

18.2.2 Positional Constraints

The first substantial result we obtained was to generate efficiently Markov sequences with positional constraints (called *unary constraints* at the time). Enforcing specific values at specific positions in a finite-length sequence generated from a Markov model turned out to be solvable in polynomial time. The result described in [75] consists in first propagating all the zero probability events (filtering) and then back-propagating probabilities to ensure unbiased sampling. This result enabled us to implement an enhanced version of Continuator and triggered the development of the Flow Machines project.

An interesting and unexpected application of this result (possibility to add positional constraints to Continuator) enabled us to introduce several types of continuations, depending on positional constraints posted on the beginning and endings of a musical phrase. Unary constraints could be used to represent various musical *intentions*, when producing a melody from a Markov model and an input melody provided in real time. For instance, we defined the following types of melodic outputs:

1. Continuation: input is continued to produce a sequence of the same size. A constraint is posted on the last note to ensure that it is "terminal", i.e. occurred at the end of an input melody, to produce a coherent ending.
2. Variation: it is generated by adding two unary constraints that the first and last notes should be the same, respectively, as the first and last notes of the input.
3. Answer: it is like a Continuation, but the last note should be the same as the first input note. This creates a phrase that resolves to the beginning, producing a sense of closure.

Additionally, for all types of responses, unary constraints were posted on each intermediary note stating that they should not be initial nor final, to avoid false starts/ends within the melody. This use of positional constraints to bias the nature of a continuation nicely echoes the notion of conversation advocated by composer Hans Zimmer in [24]. These constraints substantially improved the musical quality of the responses generated by Continuator.

Figure 18.1 shows a melody from which we build a Markov model M. Figure 18.2 shows examples of continuations, variations and answers, built from M and the constraints corresponding to each melody type, from an input (I). It is clear that these melodies belong to their respective musical categories: Continuations end naturally, with the same 3 notes as the input (a consequence of the constraint on the last note); variations sound similar to the input; and answers sound as responses to the input. This shows how simple unary constraints can produce a global effect on the structure of generated melodies.

An application of positional constraints to the generation of jazz virtuoso melodies [65] was also designed, controlled by a gesture controller. Sessions were recorded with various musicians [63,66,91].

Fig. 18.1 A training sequence

Fig. 18.2 Different continuation types generated from the same training sequence: continuations (C), variations (V) and answers (A), generated from the input melody (I)

An interesting application of positional constraints was lyric generation, satisfying rhymes and prosody constraints [6,7], leading to the generation of lyrics from arbitrary prosody and rhyme templates.

In all cases, the imposition of these positional constraints, and their "backpropagation" consequence on the generated sequence, produces pleasing musical effects, probably due to the implicit generation of meaningful "preparations" for specific, imposed events. Note that this work was extended to handle positional constraints for recurrent neural networks in [33], leading to similar effects.

18.2.2.1 Harmonization

An interesting application of positional constraints was the harmonization system described in [69]. In the system, positional constraints were used to enforce specific constraints on chords to be played during the onset of melody notes. Passing chords were generated in between those notes to create interesting harmonic movements (called fioritures) that would fit with the imposed melody, but not necessarily in conformant ways. Some remarkable results were obtained, such as a version of Coltrane's *Giant Steps* in the style of Wagner [60] (see Fig. 18.3).

An interesting harmonization of the title *Começar de Nuovo* composed by Ivan Lins, in the style of Take 6, was produced and shown to Ivan Lins himself, who reacted enthusiastically [46].

These results obtained with positional constraints and Markov chains and their application paved the way for an extensive research roadmap, aimed at finding methods for controlling Markov chains with constraints of increasing complexity.

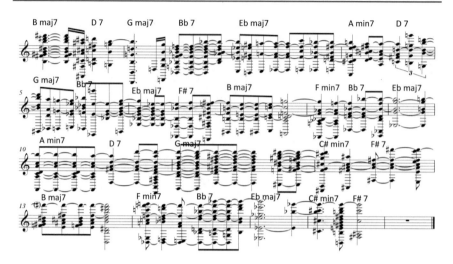

Fig. 18.3 A harmonization of Coltrane's *Giant Steps* in the style of Wagner. The melody is the soprano line, chord symbols are displayed and the rest is generated in the style of Wagner

18.2.3 Meter and All that Jazz

The next problem to solve was meter: notes have durations, and there are many reasons to constrain the sum of these durations in music. Meter cannot be expressed easily by index positions in a sequence. As a consequence, one cannot easily generate Markov sequences of events having variable durations, while imposing a fixed total duration, for instance, which is problematic for music composition. Thanks to a theorem by Khovanskii in additive number theory [41], we found a pseudo-polynomial solution for meter and Markov sequences. The *Meter* constraint enables the generation of Markov sequences satisfying arbitrary constraints on partial sums of durations. This important result [100] was heavily used in our subsequent systems, notably for lead sheet generation "in the style of" with arbitrary constraints [68].

Another big step was to address the recurring problems of Markov chains: increasing the order leads to solutions which contain large copies of the corpus: how to limit this effect? MaxOrder was introduced in [84] precisely to solve this problem. The solution consists in reformulating the problem as an automaton, using the framework of regular constraints [90]. We proposed a polynomial algorithm to build this automaton (max order imposes a set of forbidden substrings to the Markov sequences).

Now that we had a way to enforce basic constraints on meter and order, we investigated ways of making sequences more "human". A beautiful result, in our opinion, was to revisit the classical result of Voss and Clarke concerning $1/f$ distribution in music [113, 114]. We looked for a constraint that biases a sequence so that its spectrum is in $1/f$. We showed that the stochastic, dice-based algorithm proposed by Voss can be expressed as a tree of ternary sum constraints, leading to an efficient implementation [78]. For the first time, one could generate meter sequences in $1/f$.

Fig. 18.4 A 10-bar cancrizan canon generated by our palindrome Markov generator

The examples in the original Voss paper did not have bars, understandably: now we could add them!

Paradoxically, the only negative result we obtained was to show that enforcing binary equalities within Markov chains was #P-complete in the general case (as well as grammar constraints more generally) [94]. This is a counter-intuitive result as this constraint seemed a priori the simplest to enforce.

18.2.4 Sampling Methods

The next class of problems we addressed was sampling: how to get not only all the solutions of a constraint problem, but also a distribution of typical sequences, and for more powerful graphical models than linear Markov chains, to handle polyphonic sequences. Works on sampling led to a remarkable result: that all regular constraints (as introduced by Pesant in [90]) added to Markov constraints can be sampled in polynomial time [83]. We later realized that our positional constraint algorithm was equivalent to belief propagation [87], and that meter, as well as *MaxOrder* [82] were regular. This led to a novel, faster and clearer implementation of metrical Markov sequences [83].

Some interesting extensions to more sophisticated constraints were studied, such as *AllenMeter* [104]. *AllenMeter* allows users to express contraints using temporal locations (instead of events) involving all the Allen relations [3]. This constraint was used to generate polyphonic music enforcing complex synchronization properties (see Sect. 18.5). Palindromes were also studied (i.e. sequences that can read both forward and backward), and a beautiful graph-based solution was found to generate all palindromic sequences for first-order Markov chains [86]. A fascinating application to the generation of cancrizan canons was experimented with by Pierre Roy with promising results (see Fig. 18.4).

Another interesting development addressed the issue of generating meaningful variations of musical sequences. This was performed by representing musical distance as biases of the local fields in the belief propagation algorithm [74, 103]. This type of issue is now addressed typically with variational auto-encoders [11] with similar results.

These results somehow closed the chapter *Markov + X* global constraints, since most interesting constraints in music and text can be expressed as regular constraints. This line of works generated a substantial amount of theoretical and algorithmic results [80], as well as fruitful collaborations with other CP researchers. Jean-Charles Régin and Guillaume Perez, in particular, reformulated a number of our algorithms in the framework of Multi-valued Decision Diagrams (MDD), yielding substantial gains in efficiency [88,89].

18.3 Beyond Markov Models

Markov models (and their variable-order species) having been thoroughly investigated; we turned to more powerful models with the same goal in mind: finding efficient ways of controlling them. We explored the use of the *maximum entropy* principle [39] for music modelling. This model is based on the representation of binary relationships between possibly not contiguous events, thereby preventing issues related to parameter explosion inherent to higher order Markov models. Departing from a pure filtering approach, parameter estimation is performed using high-dimension gradient search, and generation using a Metropolis algorithm. This model gave interesting results for monophonic sequences [107] and some extensions were studied to polyphonic ones as well [35]. An application to modelling expressiveness in monophonic melodies was conducted in [56] with promising results.

Other aspects of style capture and generation were considered in Flow Machines, such as the generation of audio accompaniments "in the style of". A dynamic programming approach was developed in conjunction with a smart "audio glueing" mechanism to preserve *groove*, i.e. small deviations in the onset of events that characterize the style [92]. A convincing example can be heard in the Bossa nova orchestration of *Ode to Joy* [72]. This result triggered a fruitful collaboration with Brazilian colleagues to capture Brazilian guitar styles (the Brazyle project [61]).

18.4 Flow Composer: The First AI-Assisted Lead Sheet Composition Tool

These techniques were used to develop a lead sheet generator called Flow Composer (see [79] for a retrospective analysis of the development of this project). The lead sheet generator was trained using a unique database of lead sheets developed for this occasion, LSDB [70]. In order to use these generators, we designed the interface Flow Composer [85]. The basic idea was to let users enter arbitrary chunks of songs (melody or chords) and let the generator fill in the blanks, a process referred to now as *inpainting* [12]. This process took several iterations, ranging from the development of a javascript library for music web editing [50] to studies about the impact of feedback on composition with these tools [51].

Thanks to this interface, Flow Composer was intensively used by musicians, in particular by SKYGGE (SKYGGE is the artist name Benoit Carré uses for all musical productions done with AI [15]) to compose and produce what turned out to be the first mainstream music album composed with AI: *Hello World* [31].

18.5 Significant Music Productions

In this section, we review some of the most significant music produced with the tools developed in the Flow Machines project. Departing from most research in computer music, we stressed from the beginning the importance of working with musicians, in order to avoid the "demo effect", whereby a feature is demonstrated in a spectacular but artificial way, regardless of the actual possibility by a real musician to use it to make real music to a real audience. It is the opinion of the authors that some of the music described above stands out, but we invite the reader to listen to these examples to form his/her judgement.

1. The *Boulez Blues*
   The *Boulez Blues* (see Sect. 18.2.1) is a Blues chord sequence in the style of Charlie Parker (generated from a first-order Markov model). The sequence contains only major and minor chords, in all 12 keys (i.e. 24 chords in total, 2 per bar) and additionally satisfies an *AllDifferent* constraint, i.e. all chords are different. The sequence was generated with a preliminary version of Markov constraints that enabled the computation of the most probable sequence (using branch & bound). In that sense, we can say that the *Boulez Blues* is the most Parker-like Blues for which all 24 chords are different. A rendering with jazz musicians can be found at [59]. This remarkable Blues chord progression can be considered as an original stylistic singularity (of the style of Charlie Parker, using a specific constraint which clearly goes in the way of the style).
2. Two harmonizations with Flow Composer
   Some harmonizations produced with Flow Composer (see Sect. 18.2.2.1) stand out. We stress here the musical qualities of the Wagner harmonization of *Giant Steps* [60], and the harmonization of *Começar de Nuovo* (Ivan Lins) in the style of Take 6 [46]. These pieces can be seen as particular instances of style transfer (here the style of orchestration is transferred from one piece to another).
3. Orchestrations of Ode to Joy
   During the project, at the request of the ERC for the celebration of the 5000th grantee, we produced seven orchestrations of Beethoven's *Ode to Joy* (the anthem of the European Union). These orchestrations were produced with various techniques and in different styles [26,72].
   The most notable orchestrations are as follows:

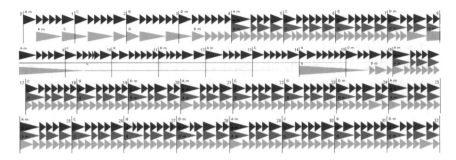

Fig. 18.5 A multi-track audio piece generated with Allen Meter: A graphical representation of the guitar (top), bass (centre) and drum (bottom) tracks of Prayer in C. Each track contains 32 bars and each triangle represents a chunk. Vertical lines indicate bar separations

(a) Multi-track audio generation A particularly interesting application of the work on *AllenMeter* by Marco Marchini (see Sect. 18.2.3) is the generation of multi-track audio, involving temporal synchronization constraints between the different tracks (bass, drum, chords). Figure 18.5 shows an excerpt of Ode to Joy in the style of Prayer in C (Lilly Wood and the Prick).

(b) Bossa Nova Orchestration with concatenative synthesis
A Bossa nova orchestration was generated for which the guitar accompaniment was produced using concatenative synthesis, applied to a corpus of guitar recordings (see Sect. 18.3). The techniques used are described in [92], and this Bossa nova example nicely emphasizes how the groove of the original guitar recording (by the first author of this paper) was preserved.

(c) Bach-like chorale using Max Entropy
Orchestration in the style of Bach was generated using the maximum entropy principle (see Sect. 18.3), which had shown great theoretical as well as musical results on monophonic music modelling [107]. This anachronic yet convincing orchestration paved the way for the DeepBach system, a more complete orchestration system in the style of Bach based on an LSTM architecture [34].

4. *Beyond The Fence*
Beyond The Fence is a unique musical, commissioned by Wingspan Productions. The idea was to produce a full musical show using various *computational creativity* techniques, from the pitch of the musical to the songs, including music and lyrics. The musical was produced in 2015 and was eventually staged in the Arts Theatre in London's West End during February and March of 2016. The complex *making of* of the musical gave birth to two 1-hour documentary films, which were aired on Sky Arts under the title *Computer Says Show*.
Some of the songs were composed with a preliminary version of Flow Composer, under the control of composers Benjamin Till and Nathan Taylor. In particular, the song *Scratch That Itch* (see Fig. 18.6) received good criticism. The song was

Fig. 18.6 An excerpt of *Scratch That Itch*, a song composed with Flow Composer for the musical *Beyond The Fence*

produced by training Flow Composer on a corpus of musicals, mostly broadway shows, in an attempt to replicate that style.

An analysis of the production and reception of the musical was published in [21]. The overall reception was good, though difficult to evaluate, because of the large scope of the project. Concerning the songs made with Flow Composer, a critic wrote:

> I particularly enjoyed Scratch That Itch, …, which <u>reminded</u> me of a Gilbert & Sullivan number whilst other songs have elements of Les Miserables. Caroline Hanks-Farmer, carns, TheatrePassion.com

This critic embodies the essence of the reception in our view: songs created did bear some analogy with the corpus, and created a feeling of <u>reminiscence,</u> at least to some listeners.

5. Catchy tune snippets with Flow Composer

   Before Flow Composer was used on a large scale for the *Hello World* album (see below), the system was used to compose fragments of songs in various styles. Some of these fragments are today still worth listening to, bearing a catchiness that is absent from most of the generated music produced 4 years later. These three examples can be seen as <u>stylistic explorations</u> of various composers.

   (a) in the style of Miles Davis

   This song snippet was generated by training Flow Composer on a set of about 10 songs composed by Miles Davis (see Fig. 18.7) [98]. These 8 bars, played in loop, produce an engaging groove though with a rather unconventional yet consistent melody.

   (b) From *Solar* to *Lunar*

Fig. 18.7 A song snippet composed with Flow Composer in the style of Miles Davis [98]

Fig. 18.8 *Lunar*, a song composed with Flow Composer in the style of Miles Davis, with the structure of Solar [96,97]

This short song was also generated by training Flow Composer on a set of 10 songs composed by Miles Davis (see Figs. 18.7, 18.8). Additionally, the structure of the song *Solar* was reused, an instance of templagiarism, hence its title. A rendering is available at [96]. This song was deemed sufficiently interesting to be performed live in London (Mark d'Inverno quartet [97]; see Fig. 18.9) during an "AI concert". Listening to the tune performed by Mark d'Inverno quartet, journalist James Vincent wrote [112]:

> The AI's contribution was just a lead sheet—a single piece of paper with a melody line and accompanying chords—but in the hands of d'Inverno and his bandmates, it swung. They started off running through the jaunty main theme, before devolving into a series of solos that d'Inverno later informed me were *all human* (meaning, all improvised).

(c) in the style of Bill Evans

This short song (listen to a rendering at [99]) was generated by training Flow Composer on a set of 10 songs composed by Bill Evans (see Fig. 18.10). The melody nicely navigates through the chord progression, sometimes in an unconventional but clever manner (bar 3). Thanks to unary constraints, the tune nicely transitions from the end to the beginning. Other songs in the style of Bill Evans were generated on the fly and performed live at the Gaîté Lyrique concert (see below).

6. *Daddy's car*

The song *Daddy's car* was generated with Flow Composer, using a corpus of 45 Beatles songs (from the latest period, considered usually as the richest and

Fig. 18.9 The concert of the Mark d'Inverno quartet playing *Lunar* at the Vortex Club in London, October 2016

Fig. 18.10 A song snippet composed with Flow Composer in the style of Bill Evans. Available at [99]

most singular in the recording history of The Beatles). Flow Composer was used to generate the lead sheet, while the lyrics and most of the orchestration were done manually, by SKYGGE. The song was released in September 2016 on YouTube [17] and received a lot of media attention (about 2.5 million views as of April 2020).

An interesting aspect of this song is how the system identified and reproduced a typical harmonic pattern found in many Beatles songs. This pattern consists in a chromatic descending bass and can be found, for instance, in the introduction

Fig. 18.11 The introduction of *Michelle* uses a typical harmonic pattern of The Beatles (here in D minor). Note that we show here the Real Book spelling, with a C#+ chord, which is equivalent to a DmM7

Fig. 18.12 The song *Daddy's car* reuses the harmonic pattern of *Michelle* in a different context (here in A minor)

and in the middle of the song *Michelle* (which was part of the training set) (see Fig. 18.11). This pattern was reused and instantiated in a novel context in the middle of *Daddy's car* (see Fig. 18.12). For that reason, the song can be considered a <u>pastiche</u>: it reuses explicitly typical patterns of the style, without any attempt at introducing novelty.

7. Busy P remix

   Artist Busy P (real name Fred Winter, French DJ, producer and ex-manager of Daft Punk) launched title *Genie* in 2016 [115]. Several remixes of the title were produced, including one made with Flow Machines [10]. In this remix, a variation of the chord sequence was generated with Flow Composer by SKYGGE, and then rendered using concatenative synthesis [92]. The remix features an interesting and surprising slowdown, due to an artefact in the generation algorithm that was considered creative and kept by the remixer.

8. *Move on*

   The UNESCO commissioned a song to be composed with Flow Machines, using material representative of 19 so-called "creative cities". This song, called *Move On*, was composed in 2017 and distributed as a physical 45 RPM vinyl [16]. 20 scores of songs were gathered and used as a training set. The composition and realization were performed by SKYGGE, Arthur Philippot and Pierre Jouan, with the band "Catastrophe" [20]. The song integrates a large number of musical elements, sounds and voices but manages to produce a coherent and addictive picture, thanks to the repeated use of smart transformations of the sources to fit the same chord progression throughout.

9. Concert at Gaité Lyrique

   A unique concert involving several artists who composed songs with Flow Machines was performed at Gaité Lyrique in Paris, in October 2016. This concert was probably the first ever concert showcasing pop tunes (as well as jazz) composed (in real time for some of them) with AI.

   The concert [14] involved the following artists and songs:

Fig. 18.13   A haunting 4-bar melody/harmony combination at the heart of the song Azerty

(a) SKYGGE (*Daddy's Car*)
SKYGGE performed *Daddy's car* as well as several titles [13] which appeared later in the *Hello World* album (see below for descriptions).

(b) Camille Bertault
Jazz singer Camille Bertault (who has, since then, become a successful jazz interpret) sung various songs composed in real time by Flow Composer, in the style of Bill Evans [9]. The voice of Bertault fits particularly well with the Evanssian harmonies and the simple but efficient voicings played by the pianist (Fady Farah).

(c) O (*Azerty*)
Artist Olivier Marguerit (aka "O") composed a beautifully original song titled *Azerty* [48]. Verses were generated by Flow Composer trained on a mix of *God Only Knows* by The Beach Boys, *Sea Song* by Robert Wyatt and *The Sicilian Clan* by Ennio Morricone. This song features interesting, and in some sense typical, melodic patterns created with Flow Composer that sound momentarily unconventional but eventually seem to resolve and make sense, pushing the listener to keep his attention on the generously varied melodic line. The song also features a 4-bar melody woven onto an unconventional harmony that deserves attention (see Fig. 18.13).

(d) François Pachet (Jazz improvisation with Reflexive Looper)
Pachet performed a guitar improvisation on the jazz standard *All the things you are* using Reflexive Looper [62], a system that learns in real time how to generate bass and chord accompaniments [47,77] (see Sect. 18.6).

(e) Kumisolo (*Kageru San*)
Japanese artist Kumisolo interpreted the song *Kageru San*, composed in the JPop style by SKYGGE with Flow Composer [42]. Flow Composer was trained with songs from the album *Rubber Soul* by The Beatles. The audio renderings were generated from excerpts of *Everybody's Talking at Me* by Harry Wilson and *White Eagle* by Tangerine. The song, while firmly anchored in the JPop style, has a memorizable, catchy chorus.

(f) Lescop (*A mon sujet*)
The song *A mon sujet* [45] was composed by Lescop with Flow Composer trained on songs *Yaton* by Beak, *Vitamin C* by Can, *Tresor* by Flavien Berger, *Supernature* by Cerrone and *Rain* by Tim Paris. Although the resulting melodic and harmonic lines are monotonous compared to other songs, the voice of Lescop mixed with the piano and bass ostinato create a hauntingly obsessive and attaching musical atmosphere.

Fig. 18.14 An enigmatic 8-bar theme at the heart of *Ballad of the Shadow*

(g) ALB (*Deedadooda*)

The song *Deedadooda* [2] by emerging artist ALB was composed with a training set of 16 songs by ALB himself. It features a dialogue between ALB and a virtual composer, cleverly integrated into the song itself.

(h) Housse de Racket (*Futura*)

Futura was composed from a training set of 6 songs by "Housse de Racket" themselves [38]. The rendering is generated from the introduction of *Love's in Need of Love Today* by Steve Wonder, which creates an enigmatic and original Pop atmosphere on an unusually slow tempo.

10. *Hello World*

The most sophisticated music production of the project was the album *Hello World* [31]. *Hello World* was the first mainstream music album featuring only AI-assisted compositions and orchestrations. This album features 15 songs composed by various artists who used Flow Machines at its latest stage. Composition sessions were held at Sony CSL, conducted by SKYGGE, and involved artists in several genres (Pop, Jazz, Electronic Music). *Hello World* received considerable media attention [30] and reached remarkable audience stream counts (about 12 million streams). The song list is the following and each song has its *story*:

(a) *Ballad of the Shadow*

Ballad of the Shadow is the first song written for this album. It was composed by SKYGGE with Flow Machines, inspired by jazz standards, with the goal of making a vaporwave cowboy song. The idea of shadows singing was developed into a melody with a happy mood. It resembles a cartoon-like tune when it is played at 120 bpm, but becomes melancholic when played slower, especially with ambient textures. Ash Workman and Michael Lovett detuned the drums and added some drive effects. The main theme (see Fig. 18.14) is, again, enigmatic, unconventional yet beautifully making its way through an unusual chord progression.

(b) *Sensitive*

Sensitive was composed by SKYGGE with Flow Machines, inspired by Bossa novas. The lyrics and voice are from C Duncan. The song was composed

Fig. 18.15 The first bars of *Sensitive*, a song composed in the style of Bossa novas, but rendered in a slow pop ballad

from a corpus of Bossa novas of the 60s. There are some patterns in the song such as major-minor progressions that Bossa nova fans will recognize and like (see Fig. 18.15). Harmonic changes are sometimes very audacious, but the melody always stays on track. SKYGGE generated a voice for the melodic line with random lyrics, like a mosaic of syllables extracted from the a cappella recording of a vocalist. However, once played with a piano, the music sounded like a powerful 70s ballad. SKYGGE liked the combination of the two styles, and recorded a string arrangement written by Marie-Jeanne Serrero and live drums. C Duncan was very enthusiastic when he listened to the song; he wrote lyrics from random material inspired by key words like *wind*, *deep* and *feel*.

(c) *One Note Samba*

François Pachet and SKYGGE share an endless admiration for Antonio Carlos Jobim, the great Brazilian composer, and they wanted to do a cover of his famous song *One Note Samba* with Flow Machines.

SKYGGE put together generated stems with drums, bass and pads and right away got awesome results: a singular and catchy tune with great harmonies and timbre. The resulting harmonies slightly differ from the original but do not betray the logic of the song. The chord progression brings a Jobimian touch to the melody through unexpected harmonic modulations.

A few days before, the French band "The Pirouettes" had come to the studio and had uploaded two songs from their first album *Carrément, Carrément*. Vocals were generated from these recordings for *One Note Samba*, so fans of The Pirouettes may recognize words from their original songs.

(d) *Magic Man*

SKYGGE fed Flow Machines with French pop songs from the 80s. The machine generated a simple melody, which sounded groovy when rendered with a generated choir. The title comes from a phrase that comes back frequently in the choir: *Magic Man*. It was a nice surprise that the machine came up with a shiny pop song title with such an electro-disco feel. Flow Machines generated guitars from an American folk stem, as well as other vocals on the verse, and SKYGGE sung over those voices to get a more complex vocal blend. He also asked the singer Mariama to sing along with the generated choir to reinforce the groove. The lyrics are a mashup from all the generated

Fig. 18.16 The catchy and singular verse of *In the house of poetry*

Fig. 18.17 The chorus of *In the house of poetry* features an unconventional and audacious ascending melody

syllables. French electro band Napkey worked on the arrangement at the end of the production, and Michael Lovett added synthesizer arpeggios.

(e) *In the House of Poetry*

SKYGGE wanted to compose a song with the enchanting charm of ancient folk melodies. He fed Flow Machines with folk ballads and jazz tunes. As a result, the machine generated melodies with chord progressions right in that mood, and a catchy and singular melodic movement (see Fig. 18.16). Once the verse was done, he fed Flow Machines with a jazzier style for the chorus part, in order to bring in rich harmonic modulations.

Flow Machines then proposed an unconventional and audacious harmonic modulation in the first bar of the chorus, with an ascending melody illuminating the song (see Fig. 18.17). SKYGGE followed up with a small variation by exploiting a 2-bar pattern generated by Flow Machines and asked the system again to generate a harmonic progression that would resolve nicely with the tonality of the verse.

He subsequently asked Kyrie Kristmanson to join, hoping she would like the song and would not be afraid of its technically challenging nature. She was indeed enthusiastic and wrote lyrics inspired by the tale *The Shadow* by Andersen. She focused on the part of the story where the Shadow tells the learned man what he saw in the house of Poetry.

The song is divided into two parts. In the first part Kyrie sings; in the second part, Kyrie's vocals are generated by Flow Machines from the recordings of Kyrie's voice.

Flow Machines generated pianos, strings and vocals from SKYGGE's material as well as from Kyrie's voice. SKYGGE played all additional instruments (drums, piano and electric guitars).

(f) *Cryyyy*

This simple melody in the style of pop tunes from the 60s was generated almost exactly in its final form. When SKYGGE was working in the studio of Ash Workman with Michael Lovett, Ash had just received an old cabinet organ from the 70s bought on the Internet. They plugged it in and began to play the chords of *Cryyyy*. It sounded great, and they recorded all those sounds for the song. SKYGGE wanted a melancholic but modern sound and the timbre of Mariama's voice matched perfectly. Flutes and detuned and distorted guitars were generated by Flow Machines, and SKYGGE added some beats and deep bass.

(g) *Hello Shadow*

Stromae was fascinated by the possibilities of the software, and he fed the machines with his own influences: scores and audio stems in the Cape Verdian style. He selected his favourite melodies and stems from what Flow Machines had generated. Those fragments were put together and the song was built step by step. Stromae sung a vocal line that followed the generated melody, and he improvised on the pre-chorus. The choir in the chorus was also generated. When the song was ready for final production, it was sent to singer Kiesza who loved it. She wrote lyrics inspired by the tale *The Shadow*. Kiesza envisioned a happy, shiny shadow. A most unusual and characteristic feature of this song is its first four notes of the verse, which evoke the image of a ball bouncing and rolling.

(h) *Mafia Love (Oyestershell)*

This song was composed by SKYGGE with Flow Machines, inspired by pop of the 60s. It is almost a direct composition by Flow Machines, with very little human edits to the melody. The song has its internal logic, like all good songs. It tells a story, though unconventionally due to its rich structure, with almost no repetition. This absence of repetition sounds seem strange at first, but the song becomes an earworm after hearing it a couple of times. The song was rendered with a generated voice from an a cappella recording of Curtis Clarke Jr., and a generated piano track from a stem by SKYGGE.

(i) *Paper Skin*

Paper Skin is an interesting, indirect use of AI. This song was built from the song *Mafia Love* (see above). JATA picked up fragments of *Mafia Love* for the verse and the pre-chorus. He then composed a new chorus fitting those fragments. Ash Workman added some sounds from *Mafia Love* in the intro and in the bridge. *Paper Skin* is an offshoot of *Mafia Love*, illustrating how a melodic line can travel ears and be transformed according to unpredictable inspirations of musicians.

(j) *Multi Mega Fortune*

Michael Lovett from NZCA Lines fed Flow Machines with his own audio stems, vocals, drums loops, bass and keyboards, as well as lead sheets in the style of Brit pop. A lot of material was generated, both songs and stems. Michael Lovett and SKYGGE curated the results, and Lovett wrote lyrics inspired by the tale The Shadow. The result is a synth-pop catchy tune with a distinctive gimmick generated by Flow Machines that runs throughout the song.

(k) *Valise*

When Stromae came to the studio, we tried several ideas based on six lead sheets generated with Flow Machines. Between sessions, SKYGGE explored one of those directions and generated a vocal line from the song *Tous les mêmes*, a former song of Stromae, uploaded on Flow Machines. The lyrics produced from the generated vocals meant something different from the original song by Stromae, but they were relevant, since they addressed the theme of "luggage" (*Valise*, in French). Stromae liked the song, but at the time we focused on the song *Hello Shadow* and left *Valise* aside for a while. SKYGGE asked the French band "The Pirouettes" to sing the melody instead of using the generated voice. The Pirouettes sung in sync with the generated voice by Stromae. This song bears an uncommon yet catchy chord progression and structure. Like other songs from the album, first hearings may sound strange, but after a couple of listenings, the song becomes an earworm. One can hear the generated choir laughing on top of this unusual chord progression.

(l) *Cake Woman*

Médéric Collignon, an amazing jazz trumpet player, came to the lab full of energy, with his own audio tracks, mostly jazz progressions played on a Rhodes piano, and some bass synths. SKYGGE also brought some hip-hop grooves, and the two musicians worked on a funk pop in the style of the 80s. The generated lead sheet was simple but contained harmonic twists that Médéric digs as a jazz composer. He selected chromatic modulations that he often uses in his own scores.

When they generated audio stems for the song from all the audio material, the output was messy but sounded very exciting. In particular, the groovy Rhodes generated from Médéric's own recordings reinforced the funkiness of the song. Pachet and SKYGGE wrote lyrics inspired by the nonsensical words of the generated voice, in the style of surrealist poetry. They asked the young and talented jazz singer Camille Bertault to sing the song. She also performed a scat-like improvisation, echoing the trumpet solo. In Andersen's tale, the Shadow is hiding in the coat of a "cake woman", hence the title.

(m) *Whistle Theme*

Themes from older soundtracks are often more melodic than recent ones. Today, film scores are more often based on textures than melodies. Inspired by those old soundtracks, Flow Machines generated a catchy theme for this song (see Fig. 18.18). The whistling was backed up by airport sounds generated to match the song. Pierre Jouan from the pop band "Catastrophe" sung another song, from which the machine generated the voice heard in the song.

(n) *Je Vais Te Manger*

Laurent Bardainne came to the studio with his audio stems, marimba, synth bass patterns and compositions in the style of 80's pop. Flow Machines generated a few songs, and Laurent selected the good parts. Laurent and SKYGGE built the song in a few hours. They left each other without knowing what to do

Fig. 18.18 The catchy line of *Whistle song*

Fig. 18.19 The catchy line of *Je Vais Te Manger*

with their song. For over a week, SKYGGE woke up every morning with this melody stuck in his head. Looking in depth at the generated lead sheet, one can see a harmonic twist that no one would have thought of. This twist pushes the melody up and down over an audacious modulation (see Figure 18.19). SKYGGE and Laurent asked Sarah Yu to sing. The song is about a woman who says she will eat our souls and that we are lost.

(o) *Cold Song*

The *Cold Song* is a well-known part of the opera *King Arthur* by Purcell. It has been sung by many singers in many styles (Sting, Klaus Nomi). For this cover, SKYGGE was inspired by artists such as Andre Bratten, Anne Clarke and Johann Johannsson, who have used machines to produce melancholic moods. The voice is generated from an a cappella recording of singer Kyte. It turns out that the generation produced many "A I A I", by coincidence. In this song cover, everything was produced by Flow Machines, and there was no manual production.

11. *Hello World Remix*

A few months after the release of *Hello World*, a remix album was released [19], with remixes of 10 songs, produced by various producers. This album did not involve the use of AI, but is an important sign that the original songs of *Hello World* were deemed sufficiently rich musically by several top remixers to deserve a remix.

18.6 Unfinished but Promising Projects

The Flow Machines project generated a rich flow of ideas and experiments. Some of these ideas did not contribute directly to music making, but are worth mentioning, to illustrate how an ambitious goal supported by a generous grant (the ERC) can lead to very high levels of creativity and productivity.

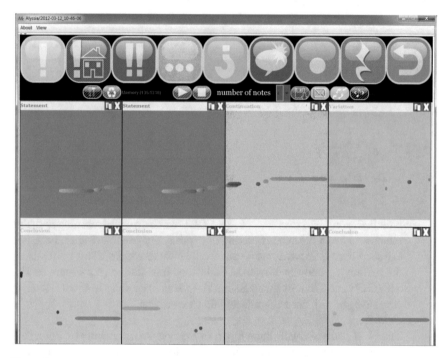

Fig. 18.20 A composition software for children that allows building pieces by reusing their previous doodlings

(a) Continuator II

The Continuator system, which was at the root of the Flow Machines project, was substantially extended, improved and tested, notably during the MIROR project. Extensions consisted mostly to add constraining features, notably positional, as described in Sect. 18.2.2, thereby improving substantially the musicality of the responses. Many experiments involving children and the question of music education based on reflexive interactions were conducted and described in [95]. A composition software (Miror-Compo) was implemented, allowing users to build fully fledged musical compositions that would reuse their doodlings (see Fig. 18.20).

(b) Film Music

Experiments in Film Music by Pierre Roy consisted in implementing the theory proposed in [57,58]. The basic idea of Murphy is to consider all pairs of consecutive chords, and assign them an emotional category. It turns out that enforcing such typical pairs of chords can be approximated by biases of binary factors of the belief propagation algorithm. For instance, sadness is related to the pattern *M4m*, i.e. a major chord, followed by a minor chord 4 semitones (2 tones) above. Figure 18.21 shows the lead sheet generated in the style of Bill Evans (for the melody) and The Beatles (for the chords) biased to favour chord pairs related to "sadness" [105].

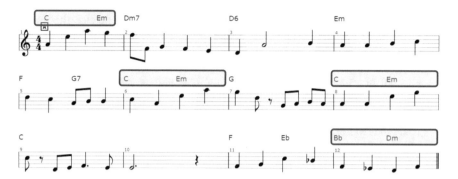

Fig. 18.21 A lead sheet in the style of The Beatles, with a bias towards "sadness" related chord pairs: C to Em (3 times), Bb to Dm

(c) Reflexive Looper

Reflexive Looper is the latest instantiation of a project consisting in building an interactive, real system dedicated to solo performance. The initial fantasy was that of a guitarist playing in solo, but in need of a bass and harmony backing that would be tightly coupled to his real-time performance. The core ideas of the system are described in [25,77] and many experiments and refactors were done during several years [55], culminating by a version implemented by Marco Marchini [47]. This system was nominated for the Guthman Instrument Competition and was demonstrated to a jury including guitarist Pat Metheny.

(d) Interaction studies in jazz improvisation

A question that arose regularly in our work about real-time assisted improvisation was how to model actual humans interacting together when they improvise. It turns out that little is known about the nature of such interactions. In particular, a key question is to which extent this interaction involves the content of the music (rhythm, harmony, melody, expressiveness)? Such a question was crucial for designing our music interaction systems. We proposed in [76] an analytical framework to identify correlates of content-based interaction. We illustrated the approach with the analysis of interaction in a typical jazz quintet (the Mark d'Inverno quintet). We extracted audio features from the signals of the soloist and the rhythm section. We measured the dependency between those time series with correlation, cross-correlation, mutual information and Granger causality, both when musicians played concomitantly and when they did not. We identified a significant amount of dependency, but we showed that this dependency was mostly due to the use of a common musical context, which we called the *score effect*. We finally argued that either content-based interaction in jazz is a myth or that interactions do take place but at unknown musical dimensions. In short, we did not see any real interaction!

(e) Feedback in lead sheet composition

We studied the impact of giving and receiving feedback during the process of lead sheet composition in [51]. To what extent can peer feedback affect the quality of a music composition? How does musical experience influence the quality of feedback during the song composition process? Participants composed short songs using an online lead sheet editor, and are given the possibility to provide feedback on other participants' songs. Feedback could either be accepted or rejected in a later step. Quantitative data were collected from this experiment to estimate the relation between the intrinsic quality of songs (estimated by peer evaluation) and the nature of feedback. Results show that peer feedback could indeed improve both the quality of a song composition and the composer's satisfaction with it. Also, it showed that composers tend to prefer compositions from other musicians with similar musical experience levels.

(f) Experiments in collective creativity (aka the rabbits experiment)

In order to better understand the impact of feedback and collective creation, we designed an experiment to highlight different types of creator "profiles" [27]. In this experiment, users could write captions to short comic strips, and were shown what other users in a group would do, and given the possibility "switch" to their productions. One of the conclusions is that the potential impact of implicit feedback from other participants and objectivity in self-evaluation, even if encouraged, are lessened by a bias "against change". Such a bias probably stems from a combination of self-enhancing bias and of a commitment effect.

(g) A Comic book on style creation

A comic book, titled *Max Order*, was designed and produced, telling a story about a character (Max) who struggles to invent her own style [28]. The name of the character stemmed from the Max Order result, which concerns the limitation of plagiarism in Markov sequence generation [82,84]. The comic is available on the Web [32]. This comic gave rise to the ERCcOMICS [29] project, which was about disseminating ERC project through comics.

(h) Song composition project

In this project, the author participated actively in the composition and release of 2 albums: one in Pop music (*Marie-Claire* [81]) and one in jazz (*Count on it* [22]). Most composition sessions were recorded on video for later analysis. The jazz album was premiered in a sold-out concert at Pizza club express, one of the main jazz venues in London (Fig. 18.22).

(i) Automatic Accompaniment generation

Following the Flow Composer project (see above), we addressed the issue of real-time accompaniments using similar techniques, i.e. based on belief propagation. We recorded jazz pianist Ray d'Inverno (see Fig. 18.23) as well as saxophonist Gilad Atzmon, and produced various accompaniment algorithms (see, for instance, [106]).

(j) Interview series

Several interviews with composers were conducted during the project: Ennio Morricone, Ivan Lins, Benoit Carré, Hubert Mounier (L'affaire Louis Trio), Michel Cywie (composer of beautiful French pop songs in the 70s) and Franco Fabbri. The initial idea was to track down what composers of famous hits thought of the songwriting process, to form a book about how songwriters make hits.

(k) Flow-Machines radio

Fig. 18.22 The character named Max Order, who tries to create her own style

Fig. 18.23 Jazz pianist Ray d'Inverno recording an accompaniment on *Girl from Ipanema*

A prototype of an online web radio was developed. This web generated on-the-fly pieces composed by Flow Composer, rendered them with our concatenative synthesis system and streamed them on a dedicated website. Users could rate the songs they listened to. The goal was to obtain enough feedback on songs to use reinforcement learning to tune automatically the generators (see Fig. 18.24).

Fig. 18.24 A snapshot of a web radio broadcasting automatically generated music, with user feedback

18.7 Impact and Followup

Three years after the completion of the project, what remains the most important for us in these developments is not the technologies we built *per se*, though many strong results were obtained in the *Markov + X* roadmap, but the music that was produced with these technologies. In that respect, the utmost validation of this work lies in the following:

1. The overwhelming media reception of the album composed with it [30], including some outstanding reviews, such as "AI and humans collaborated to produce this hauntingly catchy pop music" [4], or "Is this the world's first good robot album?" [49];
2. The enthusiasm of all the musicians who participated in this project. 15 songs were composed and signed by various artists (including Stromae), and this is in

itself a validation, as dedicated musicians would not sign songs they are not proud of;

3. The overall success of the album on streaming platforms (a total of 12 million streams as of April 2020), with *Magic Man* (5.9 million streams) and *Hello Shadow* (2.8 million) as main hits;
4. The positive reception by music critics. For instance, Avdeef writes [5]:

> SKYGGE's *Hello World* is a product of these new forms of production and consumption, and functions as a pivot moment in the understanding and value of human-computer collaborations. The album is aptly named, as it alludes to the first words any new programmer uses when learning to code, as well as serving as an introduction to new AI-human collaborative practices. Hello, World, welcome to the new era of popular music.

Similarly, emphasizing the difference between interactive AI-assisted song composition, which Flow Composer pioneered, and fully automatic composition, Miller writes [52]:

> On the one hand, we have François Pachet's Flow Machines, loaded with software to produce sumptuous original melodies, including a well-reviewed album. On the other, researchers at Google use artificial neural networks to produce music unaided. But at the moment their music tends to lose momentum after only a minute or so.

5. Sony Flow Machines
   The Flow Machines project is continuing at Sony CSL [109, 110], and research around the ideas developed in the project has been extended, for instance, with new interactive editors in the same vein as Flow Composer [8]. Promising musical projects have also been set up, notably involving Jean-Michel Jarre [108].
6. Beyond Flow Machines
   Since *Hello World*, SKYGGE has launched another album made with Artificial Intelligence, *American Folk Songs* [18]. In this album, original *a cappellas* of traditional songs (notably by Pete Seegher, with his right owner's approval) were reorchestrated with automatic orchestration tools developed at Spotify. The techniques used are based on a belief propagation scheme [102] combined with advanced edition features [101]. All the orchestrations were generated by orchestration transfer, i.e. transfering the orchestration style of existing music pieces to these traditional folk melodies. Ongoing work to use large-scale listening data (skip profiles) to tune the model are ongoing with promising results [53].

18.8   Lessons Learned

18.8.1   Better Model Does Not Imply Better Music

We experimented with various generative models: variable-order Markov models, max entropy and deep learning techniques. Paradoxically, the most interesting music generation was not obtained with the most sophisticated techniques. In spite of many attempts to use deep learning methods upfront for generation, we did not succeed in using these techniques for professional use (at the time of the project). The Bach chorales are of undisputed high quality, but they are not very *interesting* musically: they produce either "correct" material, or mistakes, but not much in between. However, we observed that the combination of various tools (*e.g.*, the lead sheet generation tool and our audio synthesis tool) produced flow states more easily than the use of single algorithms. This may have to do with the appropriation effect mentioned below.

18.8.2 New Creative Acts

The use of generative algorithms introduces new tasks for the user, and these tasks are actually creative acts, in the sense that they require some musical expertise or, at least intuition and intention: 1) the selection of training sets and 2) the curation of the results. Of course, training set selection and curation can be performed using random algorithms, but so far we did not succeed in automating these processes.

18.8.3 The Appropriation Effect

More importantly, there seems to be a trade-off to find between the sophistication of the algorithm and the sense of appropriation of the results by the user. The IKEA effect is a cognitive bias which has been confirmed by many experiments, in which consumers place a disproportionately high value on products they partially created [43]. Many consumer studies have shown, for instance, that instant cake mixes were more popular when the consumer had something to do (such as adding an egg) than when the instant mix was self-sufficient. It is likely that in the case of AI-assisted creation, the same type of effect applies, and that users do not get a sense of appropriation if the algorithm, whatever its sophistication, does all the creative job. This is a fascinating area of study that will surely produce counter-intuitive results in the future.

18.9 Towards New Categories of *New*

The traditional conceptual landscape used to describe novelty in music is based essentially on three notions: (1) *original* songs (new material, possibly inspired by preexisting work, but to an acceptable degree), (2) *covers* (new orchestrations of existing songs) and (3) *plagiaristic work*, i.e. works containing segments of existing songs with no or little transformations. Another category is *parasiting*, the action of imitating an orchestration style without plagiarizing it, in order to avoid paying royalties [44], but this category is apparently less used by music professionals. A lot of arguments used in the debate about the role of AI in music creation touch on the notion of creativity or novelty, i.e. can AI produce really novel music material? However, we don't think the question "is AI creative" is relevant, since we see AI as a tool for creators, an opinion shared by most researchers in the field (*e.g.* [23]). Yet, we argue the idea that all the generations we described here, and the ones to come, are instances of new categories of "new". In this text, we have described several pieces generated with various techniques, and used intentionally the following terms (underlined):

1. stylistic explorations: Song snippets "in the style of", the song *Sensitive*
2. stylistic singularities: the *Boulez Blues*
3. reminiscences: *Scratch my itch*
4. pastiches and exercises: *Daddy's car* and Bach chorales
5. orchestration transfers: the orchestrations in the album *American Folk Songs*, which were all produced by transferring existing orchestration styles to existing songs
6. timbre transfers: most of the renderings of the examples described here
7. templagiarism: the song *Lunar*

It is our view that these new categories may help us conceptualize the contributions of these generative technologies to music creation. Interestingly, images created with Deep Dream [54] and referred to as hallucinations do not have their equivalent yet in music: what would be, indeed, a musical hallucination?

18.10 Conclusion

We have described a number of research results in the domain of assisted music creation, together with what we consider are remarkable music productions. We attempted to describe why these generations are interesting, as technological arte-facts, and also from a musical viewpoint. Since the Flow Machines project ended (2017), research in computer music generation has exploded, mostly due to the progress in deep learning [11]. After the launch of *Daddy's car* and *Hello World*, several music titles were produced with AI (notably by artists Taryn Southern and Holly Herndon), contributing to the exploration of these technologies for music creation.

These explorations are still only scratching the surface of what is possible with AI. However, they already challenge the status and value of what is considered "new" in our digital cultures. We have sketched a draft of a vocabulary to describe and distinguish different types of "newness" in music. These categories start to have well-defined meaning technically but much more is needed to give them precise definitions. Surely, more categories will arise, some will vanish. In the end, only music and words will remain, not technologies.

Acknowledgements The Flow Machines project received funding from the European Research Council under the European Union's Seventh Framework Programme (FP/2007–2013)/ERC Grant Agreement no. 291156. We thank the team of the musical *Beyond the Fence* for their insightful comments in using earlier versions of Flow Composer. We thank the researchers and engineers who participated in the Flow Machines project: Gabriele Barbieri, Vincent Degroote, Gaëtan Hadjeres, Marco Marchini, Dani Martín, Julian Moreira, Alexandre Papadopoulos, Mathieu Ramona, Jason Sakellariou, Emmanuel Deruty and Fiammetta Ghedini. We also thank Profs. Jean-Pierre Briot (CNRS), Mirko Degli Esposti (University of Bologna), Mark d'Inverno (Goldsmiths College, University of London), Jean-François Perrot (Sorbonne Université) and Luc Steels (VUB), for their precious and friendly contributions. We thank our colleagues and friends Giordano Cabral, Geber Ramalho, Jean-Charles Régin, Guillaume Perez and Shai Newman for their insights. We also thank all the musicians who were involved in the projects, under the supervision of Benoit Carré: Stromae, Busy P, Catastrophe, ALB, Kumisolo, Olivier Marguerit, Barbara Carlotti, Housse de Racket, Camille Bertault, Lescop, Raphael Chassin, Michael Lovett, Ash Workman, C Duncan, Marie-Jeanne Serrero, Fred Decès, Mariama, Kyrie Kristmanson, The Bionix, Kiesza, JATA, The Pirouettes, Médéric Collignon, Pierre Jouan, Sarah Yu Zeebroeke and Laurent Bardainne. Finally, we thank our host institutions Sony CSL, UPMC, Spotify, the label Flow Records and the distributor Idol for hosting, supporting and believing in this research.

References

1. Addessi, A. R., & Pachet, F. (2005). Experiments with a musical machine: musical style replication in 3 to 5 year old children. *British Journal of Music Education*, 22(1), 21–46.
2. ALB. (2016). The performance of *Deedadoda* by artist ALB at Gaité Lyrique in October 2016. https://www.youtube.com/watch?v=u7iG4SKbIbY&list=PLvoqwxjRRNfmn2A6e9-gdWo9ORhZfLFmO&index=4. Accessed 01 May 2020
3. Allen, J. F. (1983). Maintaining Knowledge about Temporal Intervals. *Communications of the ACM*, 26(11), 832–843.
4. Avdeef, M. (2018). AI and humans collaborated to produce this hauntingly catchy pop music. https://qz.com/quartzy/1420576/listen-to-haunting-ai-generated-pop-music-from-skygge-and-kiesza.
5. Avdeef, M. (2019). Artificial intelligence and popular music: SKYGGE, Flow Machines, and the audio uncanny valley. *Arts*, 8(130).
6. Barbieri, G. (2020). Remixing Dylan lyrics with style. https://redylan.neocities.org. Accessed 09-Feb-2020
7. Barbieri, G., Pachet, F., Roy, P., & Esposti, M.D. (2012). Markov constraints for generating lyrics with style. In: L.D.R. et al. (ed.) *Proceedings of the 20th European conference on artificial intelligence* (ECAI 2012), pp. 115–120.
8. Bazin, T., & Hadjeres, G. (2019). NONOTO: A model-agnostic web interface for interactive music composition by inpainting. CoRR **abs/1907.10380**.
9. Bertault, C. (2016). The performance of Camille Bertault at Gaité Lyrique in October 2016. https://www.youtube.com/watch?v=1YfKbLcjwUM. Accessed 01 May 2020
10. Briat, A. (2020). The flow machines remix of Busy P's *Genie*, mixed by Alf Briat. https://www.youtube.com/watch?v=Pf_1_wDeoSY, also on Spotify at https://open.spotify.com/track/6BoZ3l8dTJ7cWPENY28M2a?si=GBPppzwuQ_Goe79LYksFqA. Accessed 01 May 2020
11. Briot, J. P., Hadjeres, G., & Pachet, F. D. (2019). *Deep learning techniques for music generation*. Springer.

12. Carré, B. (2020). *A demo of flow composer.* https://www.youtube.com/watch?v=f6V8N3ZcSEs. Accessed 01 May 2020
13. Carré, B. (2016). A performance of song *Daddy's Car* at Gaité Lyrique in October 2016. https://www.youtube.com/watch?v=cTP0Sr_ehmY. Accessed 01 May 2020
14. Carré, B. (2016). A summary of the concert held at Gaité Lyrique in October 2016. https://www.youtube.com/watch?v=bptKZ2ACZfQ. Accessed 01 May 2020
15. Carré, B. (2020). *The artist page of SKYGGE on Spotify.* https://open.spotify.com/artist/4aGSoPUP1v4qh7RfBlvgbR/about. Accessed 01 May 2020
16. Carré, B. (2020). The song *Move On* representing 19 creative cities, commissioned by UNESCO. https://soundcloud.com/user-76901948/sets/la-playlist-des-villes-creatives-de-lunesco. Accessed 01 May 2020
17. Carré, B., & Pachet, F. (2020). The song *Daddy's car.* https://www.youtube.com/watch?v=LSHZ_b05W7o. Accessed 01 May 2020
18. Carré, B. (2020). *The American folk songs album, on Spotify.* https://open.spotify.com/album/6NbX54oOpEZhSOjfdSYepw?si=RcTgqFqgTfC5iXkVMlW2Ug. Accessed 01 May 2020
19. Carré, B. (2020). *The hello world remixed album on Spotify.* https://open.spotify.com/album/5TAfJI5wypZ7JW1iyki6pI?si=GXsy6uQtReCWQFgtoLpETQ. Accessed 01 May 2020
20. Catastrophe. La Catastrophe. http://lacatastrophe.fr/. Accessed 01 May 2020
21. Colton, S., Llano, M.T., Hepworth, R., Charnley, J., Gale, C.V., Baron, A., Pachet, F., Roy, P., Gervas, P., Collins, N., Sturm, B., Weyde, T., Wolff, D., & Lloyd, J. (2016). The beyond the fence musical and computer says show documentary. In: *7th international conference on computational creativity* (ICCC 2016), Paris (France)
22. d'Inverno, M., & Pachet, F. (2020). *The jazz album count on it by Mark d'Inverno quintet, on Spotify.* https://open.spotify.com/album/1VKlb1ZCYhFA6aKzmCLfIW?si=NSorGAU4S12nCzd2AMNHSg. Accessed 01 May 2020
23. Fiebrink, R., & Caramiaux, B. (2016). The machine learning algorithm as creative musical tool. ArXiv arXiv:1611.00379.
24. Fisch, S.K. (2020). *Hans zimmer: Music is a conversation.* https://scottkfish.com/2017/03/19/hans-zimmer-music-is-a-conversation/. Accessed 09 Feb 2020
25. Foulon, R., Roy, P., & Pachet, F. (2013). Automatic classification of guitar playing modes. In: M. Aramak, O. Derrien, R. Kronland-Martinet, & S. Ystad (eds.) *Sound, music, and motion—10th international symposium, CMMR 2013, Marseille, France*, 15–18 Oct 2013. Revised Selected Papers. Lecture notes in computer science, vol. 8905, (pp. 58–71). Springer
26. Ghedini, F. (2016). The video of the orchestrations of *Ode to Joy*, which received the best video award for AAAI. https://www.youtube.com/watch?v=buXqNqBFd6E. Accessed 01 May 2020
27. Ghedini, F., Frantz, B., Pachet, F., & Roy, P. (2015). The comic strip game: Observing the impact of implicit feedback in the content creation process. In: N. Osman, & M. Yee-King (eds.) *Proceedings of the first international workshop on AI and feedback, AInF 2015, co-located with the 24th international joint conference on artificial intelligence (IJCAI 2015), Buenos Aires, Argentina, July 26, 2015. CEUR workshop proceedings*, vol. 1407 (pp. 18–26). CEUR-WS.org
28. Ghedini, F., Pachet, F., & Roy, P. (2015). Max order: A tale of creativity. In: Q. Yang, M. J. Wooldridge (eds.) *Proceedings of the twenty-fourth international joint conference on artificial intelligence, IJCAI 2015, Buenos Aires, Argentina, July 25–31*, (pp. 4136–4137). AAAI Press (2015)
29. Ghedini, F. (2020). The ERCcOMICS project. http://www.erccomics.com. Accessed 01 May 2020
30. Ghedini, F. (2020). *The media reception of the Hello World album.* https://www.helloworldalbum.net/press/. Accessed 01 May 2020
31. Ghedini, F. (2020). *The site of the Hello World album.* https://www.helloworldalbum.net. Accessed 01 May 2020

32. Ghedini, F. (2020). *The web version of the comic Max Order.* https://www.erccomics.com/comics/max-order. Accessed 01 May 2020

33. Hadjeres, G., & Nielsen, F. (2020). Anticipation-RNN: Enforcing unary constraints in sequence generation, with application to interactive music generation. *Neural Computing and Applications, 32*(4), 995–1005.

34. Hadjeres, G., Pachet, F., & Nielsen, F. (2017). Deepbach: A steerable model for Bach chorales generation. In: D. Precup, Y. W. Teh (Eds.) *Proceedings of the 34th international conference on machine learning, ICML 2017, Sydney, NSW, Australia, 6–11 August 2017. Proceedings of Machine Learning Research*, vol. 70 (pp. 1362–1371). PMLR

35. Hadjeres, G., Sakellariou, J., & Pachet, F. (2016). Style imitation and chord invention in polyphonic music with exponential families. CoRR arXiv:1609.05152

36. Hiller, L. A., & Isaacson, L. M. (2020). *The Illiac suite.* https://www.youtube.com/watch?v=n0njBFLQSk8. Accessed 01 May 2020

37. Hiller, L. A., & Isaacson, L. M. (1959). *Experimental music: Composition with an electronic computer.* McGraw-Hill.

38. Housse de Racket (2016). The performance of *Futura* by artist Housse de Racket at Gaité Lyrique in October 2016. https://www.youtube.com/watch?v=BU9g0X_H8zo. Accessed 01 May 2020

39. Jaynes, E. T. (1957). Information theory and statistical mechanics. *Physical Review, 106*(4), 620–630. https://doi.org/10.1103/PhysRev.106.620.

40. Khatchatourov, A., Pachet, F., & Rowe, V. (2016). Action identity in style simulation systems: Do players consider machine-generated music as of their own style? *Frontiers in Psychology, 7,*

41. Khovanskii, A. G. (1995). Sums of finite sets, orbits of commutative semigroups, and Hilbert functions. *Functional Analysis and Its Applications, 29*(2), 102–112. https://doi.org/10.1007/BF01080008.

42. Kumisolo (2016). The performance of *Kageru San* by artist Kumisolo at Gaité Lyrique in October 2016. https://www.youtube.com/watch?v=sCmp3Xp_PG4. Accessed 01 Mya 2020

43. Landers, R. (2012). Unfolding the IKEA Effect: Why we love the things we build. *Journal of Consumer Psychology, 22*(3), 453–460.

44. Le Tavernier, S. (2016). Private conversation

45. Lescop (2016). The performance of *A mon Sujet* by artist Lescop at Gaité Lyrique in October 2016. https://www.youtube.com/watch?v=9uTIyJ8vDRM. Accessed 01 May 2020

46. Lins, I. (2020). Ivan Lins listens to a reorchestration of his title *Começar de nuovo* in the style of Take 6. https://www.youtube.com/watch?v=WBvX-03qP6A. Accessed 01 May 2020

47. Marchini, M., Pachet, F., & Carré, B. (2017). Rethinking Reflexive Looper for structured pop music. In: *NIME.*

48. Marguerit, O. (2016). The performance of *Azerty* by artist O at Gaité Lyrique in October 2016. https://www.youtube.com/watch?v=v69KcJBrpuo. Accessed 01 May 2020

49. Marshall, A. (2018). Is this the world's first good robot album? http://www.bbc.com/culture/story/20180112-is-this-the-worlds-first-good-robot-album.

50. MartíÃÂÂn, D., Neullas, T., & Pachet, F. (2015). LeadsheetJS: A Javascript library for online lead sheet editing. In: *Proceedings of the first TENOR conference*

51. Martín, D., Pachet, F., & Frantz, B. (2018). *The creative process in lead sheet composition: Perspectives from multiple domains,* (pp. 275–296). Palgrave Macmilan

52. Miller, A. (2019). *Creativity and AI: The next step.* Scientific American.

53. Montecchio, N., Roy, P., & Pachet, F. (2019). The skipping behavior of users of music streaming services and its relation to musical structure. CoRR arXiv:1903.06008

54. Mordvintsev, A., Olah, C., & Tyka, M. (2015). Inceptionism: Going deeper into neural networks. https://research.googleblog.com/2015/06/inceptionism-going-deeper-into-neural.html

55. Moreira, J., Roy, P., & Pachet, F. (2013). Virtualband: Interacting with stylistically consistent agents. In: A. de Souza Britto Jr., F. Gouyon, S. Dixon (eds.) *Proceedings of the 14th international society for music information retrieval conference, ISMIR 2013, Curitiba, Brazil,* November 4–8, pp. 341–346 (2013)
56. Moulieras, S., & Pachet, F. (2016). Maximum entropy models for generation of expressive music. CoRR arXiv:1610.03606
57. Murphy, S. (2014). Transformational theory and the analysis of film music. In: *The Oxford handbook of film music studies.* Oxford University Press
58. Murphy, S. (2020). *Video of scott murphy explaining his movie Film theory.* https://www.youtube.com/watch?v=YSKAt3pmYBs&t=529s. Accessed 01 May 2020
59. Pachet, F. (2020). *A rendering of the Boulez Blues.* https://www.francoispachet.fr/wp-content/uploads/2020/04/boulez_blues.mp3. Accessed 01 May 2020
60. Pachet, F. (2020). *An orchestration of Giant Steps in the style of Wagner.* https://youtube.com/watch?v=Kq0ZwmOln7Y. Accessed 01 May 2020
61. Pachet, F. (2020). The Brazyle project. http://www.brazyle.com. Accessed 01 May 2020
62. Pachet, F. (2016). *The performance of Autumn Leaves* by F. Pachet at Gaité Lyrique in October 2016. https://www.youtube.com/watch?v=8YzPaCzDDzg. Accessed 01 May 2020
63. Pachet, F. (2020). *Virtuoso session on all the things you are.* https://www.youtube.com/watch?v=f1iPQOFRKzQ. Accessed 01 May 2020
64. Pachet, F. (2003). Music interaction with style. In: *SIGGRAPH 2003 conference abstracts and applications.* ACM Press, San Diego, USA
65. Pachet, F. (2012). Musical virtuosity and creativity. In: J. McCormack, & M. D'Inverno, (Eds.) *Computers and creativity.* Springer
66. Pachet, F., & d'Inverno, M. (2020). *Virtuoso session with Mark d'Inverno.* https://www.youtube.com/watch?v=wCaC53GlEY0. Accessed 01 May 2020
67. Pachet, F., & Roy, P. (2011). Markov constraints: steerable generation of Markov sequences. *Constraints, 16*(2).
68. Pachet, F., & Roy, P. (2014). Imitative leadsheet generation with user constraints. In: *Proceedings of the 22th European Conference on Artificial Intelligence (ECAI 2014).* Prague, Czech Republic
69. Pachet, F., & Roy, P. (2014). Non-conformant harmonization: The real book in the style of Take 6. In: *International conference on computational creativity.* Ljubljana
70. Pachet, F., Suzda, J., & Martín, D. (2013). A comprehensive online database of machine-readable leadsheets for Jazz standards. In: A. de Souza Britto Jr., F. Gouyon, S. Dixon (Eds.) *Proceedings of the 14th international society for music information retrieval conference (ISMIR 2013),* pp. 275–280. ISMIR, Curitiba, PA, Brazil
71. Pachet, F. (2003). The continuator: Musical interaction with style. *Journal of New Music Research (JNMR), 32*(3), 333–341.
72. Pachet, F. (2017). A joyful ode to automatic orchestration. *ACM TIST, 8*(2), 18:1–18:13. https://doi.org/10.1145/2897738.
73. Pachet, F., & Addessi, A. R. (2004). When children reflect on their own playing style: Experiments with continuator and children. *Computers in Entertainment, 2*(1), 14. https://doi.org/10.1145/973801.973824.
74. Pachet, F., Papadopoulos, A., & Roy, P. (2017). Sampling variations of sequences for structured music generation. In: S. J. Cunningham, Z. Duan, X. Hu, D. Turnbull (Eds.) *Proceedings of the 18th international society for music information retrieval conference, ISMIR 2017,* Suzhou, China, October 23–27, 2017, (pp. 167–173)
75. Pachet, F., Roy, P., & Barbieri, G. (2011). Finite-length Markov processes with constraints. In: *Proceedings of the 22nd international joint conference on artificial intelligence (IJCAI 2011),* pp. 635–642. Barcelona, Spain
76. Pachet, F., Roy, P., & Foulon, R. (2017). Do jazz improvisers really interact? The score effect in collective jazz improvisation. In: *The Routledge companion to embodied music interaction,* (pp. 167–176). Routledge

77. Pachet, F., Roy, P., Moreira, J., & d'Inverno, M. (2013). Reflexive loopers for solo musical improvisation. In: W.E. Mackay, S.A. Brewster, S. Bødker (Eds.) *2013 ACM SIGCHI conference on human factors in computing systems, CHI '13, Paris, France,* April 27–May 2, 2013, (pp. 2205–2208). ACM

78. Pachet, F., Roy, P., Papadopoulos, A., & Sakellariou, J. (2015). Generating 1/f noise sequences as constraint satisfaction: The Voss constraint. In: *IJCAI*, (pp. 2482–2488). AAAI Press

79. Pachet, F., Roy, P., & Papaopoulos, A. (2019). Comments on "Assisted lead sheet composition using FlowComposer". Virtual Volume, 25th anniversary of the CP Conference (2019)

80. Pachet, F., Roy, P., Papadopoulos, A., & Briot, J. P. (2019). *Constrained Markov sequence generation applications to music and text.* Springer.

81. Pachet, F., & Diran, C. (2020). *The pop album Marie Claire by band Marie-Claire, on Spotify.* https://open.spotify.com/album/6fXMeoGU8KXlGM6VWQtIq6?si=rqD64rtxRcepoXGywvjtBg. Accessed 01 May 2020

82. Papadopoulos, A., Pachet, F., & Roy, P. (2016). Generating non-plagiaristic markov sequences with max order sampling. In: *Creativity and universality in language,* pp. 85–103. Springer

83. Papadopoulos, A., Pachet, F., Roy, P., & Sakellariou, J. (2015). Exact sampling for regular and Markov constraints with belief propagation. In: *CP. Lecture notes in computer science,* vol. 9255, (pp. 341–350). Springer

84. Papadopoulos, A., Roy, P., & Pachet, F. (2014). Avoiding plagiarism in markov sequence generation. In: *AAAI.* AAAI Press

85. Papadopoulos, A., Roy, P., & Pachet, F. (2016). Assisted lead sheet composition using Flow-Composer. In M. Rueher (Ed.), *Principles and practice of constraint programming: 22nd international conference, CP 2016, Toulouse, France, September 5–9, 2016, Proceedings* (pp. 769–785). Programming and Software Engineering: Springer International Publishing.

86. Papadopoulos, A., Roy, P., Régin, J., & Pachet, F. (2015). Generating all possible palindromes from ngram corpora. In: Q. Yang, & M. J. Wooldridge. (eds.) *Proceedings of the twenty-fourth international joint conference on artificial intelligence, IJCAI 2015, Buenos Aires, Argentina,* July 25–31, 2015, (pp. 2489–2495). AAAI Press

87. Pearl, J. (1982). Reverend Bayes on inference engines: A distributed hierarchical approach. In: *AAAI,* pp. 133–136. AAAI Press

88. Perez, G., Rappazzo, B., & Gomes, C.P. (2018). Extending the capacity of $1/f$ noise generation. In: *CP. Lecture notes in computer science, vol. 11008,* (pp. 601–610). Springer

89. Perez, G., & Régin, J. (2017). MDDs: Sampling and probability constraints. In: *CP. Lecture notes in computer science,* vol. 10416 (pp. 226–242). Springer

90. Pesant, G. (2004). A regular language membership constraint for finite sequences of variables. In: *CP. Lecture notes in computer science,* vol. 3258, (pp. 482–495). Springer

91. Ramalho, G. (2020). *Virtuoso session with Geber Ramalho.* https://www.youtube.com/watch?v=3NWkmSKyMXY. Accessed 01 May 2020

92. Ramona, M., Cabral, G., & Pachet, F. (2015). Capturing a musician's groove: Generation of realistic accompaniments from single song recordings. In: Q. Yang, & M. J. Wooldridge. (Eds.) *Proceedings of the twenty-fourth international joint conference on artificial intelligence, IJCAI 2015, Buenos Aires, Argentina,* July 25–31, (pp. 4140–4142). AAAI Press. http://ijcai.org/Abstract/15/583

93. Régin, J. C. (1994). A Filtering Algorithm for Constraints of Difference in CSPs. In: *Proceedings of the 12th national conference on artificial intelligence* (vol. 1), (pp. 362–367). AAAI '94, American Association for Artificial Intelligence, Menlo Park, CA, USA

94. Rivaud, S., & Pachet, F. (2017). Sampling Markov models under constraints: Complexity results for binary equalities and grammar membership. CoRR arXiv:1711.10436.

95. Rowe, V., Triantafyllaki, A., & Pachet, F. (2016). *Children's creative music-making with reflexive interactive technology.* Routledge.

96. Roy, P. (2020). *A basic rendering of Lunar, a song in the style of Miles Davis.* https://www.francoispachet.fr/wp-content/uploads/2020/04/Miles-Davis-Mix_DEF.mp3. Accessed 01 May 2020

97. Roy, P. (2020). *Performance of Lunar at the Vortex Club, London.* https://www.francoispachet.fr/wp-content/uploads/2020/04/LunarPerformance.mp3. Accessed 01 May 2020

98. Roy, P. (2020). Rendering of a song in the style of Miles Davis, in the accompaniment style of Daft Punk's *Get Lucky.* https://www.francoispachet.fr/wp-content/uploads/2020/04/MilesGetLucky.mp3. Accessed 01 May 2020

99. Roy, P. (2020). A short song in the style of Bill Evans. https://www.francoispachet.fr/wp-content/uploads/2020/04/BillEvansStyle.mp3. Accessed 01 May 2020

100. Roy, P., & Pachet, F. (2013). Enforcing meter in finite-length markov sequences. In: M. desJardins, M. L. Littman. (Eds.) *AAAI.* AAAI Press

101. Roy, P., & Pachet, F. (2019). Smart edition of MIDI files. CoRR arXiv:1903.08459

102. Roy, P., Pachet, F., & Carré, B. (2020). A robust, controllable music orchestrator that's fun to use, with commented examples. CoRR to appear

103. Roy, P., Papadopoulos, A., & Pachet, F. (2017). Sampling variations of lead sheets

104. Roy, P., Perez, G., Régin, J., Papadopoulos, A., Pachet, F., & Marchini, M. (2016). Enforcing structure on temporal sequences: The Allen constraint. In: *CP. Lecture notes in computer science*, vol. 9892 (pp. 786–801). Springer

105. Roy, P. (2020). A composition in the style of the Beatles, with sadness chord pairs. https://www.francoispachet.fr/wp-content/uploads/2020/04/Beatles_Sadness_melody_Bill_Evans.mp3. Accessed 01 May 2020

106. Roy, P., & Pachet, F. (2020). A generated accompaniment to song Giant Steps from a recording of *Girl from Ipanema* by jazz pianist Ray d'Inverno. https://www.francoispachet.fr/wp-content/uploads/2020/04/Girl_from_Ipanema_mix.mp3. Accessed 01 May 2020

107. Sakellariou, J., Tria, F., Loreto, V., & Pachet, F. (2017). Maximum entropy models capture melodic styles. *Scientific reports, 7*(1), 1–9.

108. Savage, M. (2020). Jean-Michel Jarre launches 'infinite album', BBC News. https://www.bbc.com/news/entertainment-arts-50335897. Accessed 01 May 2020

109. Sony CSL (2020). The flow machines project. www.flow-machines.com. Accessed 01 May 2020

110. Sony CSL (2020). *The flow machines project continuation at Sony CSL.* https://www.sonycsl.co.jp/tokyo/2811/. Accessed 01 May 2020

111. University of Bologna: the Miror project. http://mirorproject.eu/. Accessed 01 May 2020

112. Vincent, J. (2020). A night at the AI jazz club. https://www.theverge.com/2016/10/12/13247686/ai-music-composition-jazz-club-london-deep-learning. Accessed 01 May 2020

113. Voss, R.F., & Clarke, J. (1975). 1/f noise in music and speech. *Nature, 258*(5533), 317–318. https://doi.org/10.1038/258317a0

114. Voss, R. F., & Clarke, J. (1978). 1/f noise in music: Music from 1/f noise. *The Journal of the Acoustical Society of America, 63*(1), 258–263. https://doi.org/10.1121/1.381721.

115. Winter, F. (2020). *Spotify link to Genie.* https://open.spotify.com/track/7J02VXGmyD2OuGPLTnuONu?si=QKqpmXe_SACtpGsI81Okbw. Accessed 01 May 2020

François Pachet is a scientist specialized in the use of artificial intelligence for music creation. He obtained a Ph.D. from Pierre and Marie Curie University, Paris, France, in Computer Science. He was director of the music group of Sony Computer Science Laboratory in Paris, France, for almost two decades. In 2017 he joined Spotify as director of Creator Technology Research Lab (CTRL), in Paris. He is devoted to the development of tools for Artificial Intelligence-assisted music composition. François is also a semi-professional guitarist, interested in pop and jazz. E-mail: francois@spotify.com.

Pierre Roy is a musician who studied Computer Science at Sorbonne University, Paris, France. He was a research scientist in music at Sony Computer Science Laboratory Paris, France, before joining Spotify's Creator Technology Research Lab in 2017. He has been designing and implementing generative tools for music for the last 10 years. E-mail: proy@spotify.com.

Benoit Carré is a songwriter, composer, author and singer. He has been developing and using Artificial Intelligence (AI) for pop music creation since 2015, under the name SKYGGE. Benoit released several critically acclaimed music albums composed and/or orchestrated with AI, notably *Hello World and American Folk Songs*. E-mail: benoitc@spotify.com.

Performance Creativity in Computer Systems for Expressive Performance of Music

19

Alexis Kirke and Eduardo Reck Miranda

19.1 Introduction

This chapter presents a detailed example of expressive music performance that focuses on performance creativity, preceded by a survey of research into automated and semi-automated computer systems for expressive performance of music. There are a number of surveys available, a more recent one [18]. However, the focus of this chapter is a survey with an emphasis on performance creativity. One definition of Artificial Intelligence (AI) is an AI is a program which in an arbitrary world will cope no worse than a human [34]. When humans deal with an arbitrary world, they use creative problem-solving—they require creativity. AI without creativity is not AI, or is a very limited form of AI. In musical AIs it could be argued that creativity plays an even more central role (as it clearly does for humans in musical activities). Hence, the focus in this chapter on the creativity of the generated performances. In the early 1980s, the seeds of a problem were sown as a result of synthesisers being developed and sold with built-in sequencers. The introduction of MIDI into this equation led to an explosion in the use of sequencers and computers, thanks to the new potential for connection and synchronisation. These computers and sequencers performed their stored tunes in perfect metronomic time, a performance which sounded robotic. They sounded robotic because human performers normally perform expressively—for example, speeding up and slowing down while playing, and changing how loudly they play. The performer's changes in tempo and dynamics allow them to express a fixed score—hence the term *expressive* performance [114]. However, rather than looking for ways to give the music performances more

A. Kirke · E. R. Miranda (✉)
Interdisciplinary Centre for Computer Music Research (ICCMR), University of Plymouth, Plymouth PL4 8AA, UK
e-mail: eduardo.miranda@plymouth.ac.uk

A. Kirke
e-mail: alexis.kirke@plymouth.ac.uk

© Springer Nature Switzerland AG 2021
E. R. Miranda (eds.), *Handbook of Artificial Intelligence for Music*,
https://doi.org/10.1007/978-3-030-72116-9_19

human-like expression, pop performers developed new types of music, such as synth-pop and dance music, that actually utilised this metronomic perfection to generate robotic performances.

Outside of pop, the uptake of sequencers for performance (as opposed to for composition) was less enthusiastic, except for occasional novelties like Snowflakes are Dancing by Tomita [59], computer performance of classical music was a rarity. Computer *composition* of classical music had been around since 1957 when The Illiac Suite for String Quartet—the first published composition by a computer—was published by Hiller [54]. Since then there has been a large body of such music and research published, with many successful systems produced for automated and semi-automated computer composition [12, 77, 95]. But publications on computer expressive performance of music lagged behind composition by almost quarter of a century. During the period when MIDI and computer use exploded amongst pop performers, and up to 1987—when Yamaha had released their first Disklavier MIDI piano—there were only 2 or 3 researchers publishing on algorithms for expressive performance of music [101, 109]. However, from the end of the 1980s onwards, there was an increasing interest in automated and semi-automated Computer Systems for Expressive Music Performance (CSEMP). A CSEMP is a computer system able to generate expressive performances of music. For example, software for music typesetting will often be used to write a piece of music, but some packages play back the music in a relatively robotic way—the addition of a CSEMP enables a more realistic playback. Or a digital audio player could include a CSEMP which would allow performances of music to be adjusted to different performance styles.

19.1.1 Human Expressive Performance

How do humans make their performances sound so different to the so-called "perfect" performance a computer would give? In this chapter, the strategies and changes which are not marked in a score but which performers apply to the music will be referred to as expressive *Performance Actions*. Two of the most common performance actions are changing the *Tempo* and the *Loudness* of the piece as it is played. These should not be confused with the tempo or loudness changes marked in the score, like accelerando or mezzo-forte, but to additional tempo and loudness changes not marked in the score. For example, a common expressive performance strategy is for the performer to slow down as they approach the end of the piece [39]. Another performance action is the use of expressive *articulation*—when a performer chooses to play notes in a more staccato (short and pronounced) or legato (smooth) way. Those playing instruments with continuous tuning, for example, string players, may also use expressive *intonation*, making notes slightly sharper or flatter; and such instruments also allow for expressive *vibrato*. Many instruments provide the ability to expressively change *timbre* as well.

Why do humans add these expressive performance actions when playing music? We will set the context for answering this question using a historical perspective. Pianist and musicologist Ian Pace offers up the following as a familiar historical model for the development of notation (though suggests that overall it constitutes an oversimplification) [83]:

In the Middle Ages and to a lesser extent to the Renaissance, musical scores provided only a bare outline of the music, with much to be filled in by the performer or performers, freely improvising within conventions which were essentially communicated verbally within a region or locality. By the Baroque Era, composers began to be more specific in terms of requirements for pitch, rhythm and articulation, though it was still common for performers to apply embellishments and diminutions to the notated scores, and during the Classical Period a greater range of specificity was introduced for dynamics and accentuation. All of this reflected a gradual increase in the internationalism of music, with composers and performers travelling more widely and thus rendering the necessity for greater notational clarity as knowledge of local performance conventions could no longer be taken for granted. From Beethoven onwards, the composer took on a new role, less a servant composing to occasion at the behest of his or her feudal masters, more a freelance entrepreneur who followed his own desires, wishes and convictions, and wrote for posterity, hence bequeathing the notion of the master-work which had a more palpable autonomous existence over and above its various manifestations in performance. This required an even greater degree of notational exactitude; for example, in the realms of tempo, where generic Italianate conventions were both rendered in the composer's native language and finely nuanced by qualifying clauses and adjectives. Through the course of the nineteenth century, tempo modifications were also entered more frequently into scores, and with the advent of a greater emphasis on timbre, scores gradually became more specific in terms of the indication of instrumentation. Performers phased out the processes of embellishment and ornamentation as the score came to attain more of the status of a sacred object. In the twentieth century, this process was extended much further, with the finest nuances of inflection, rubato, rhythmic modification coming to be indicated in the score. By the time of the music of Brian Ferneyhough, to take the most extreme example, all minutest details of every parameter are etched into the score, and the performer's task is simply to try and execute these as precisely as he or she can.

Thus, in pre-twentieth century music, there has been a tradition of performers making additions to a performance which were not marked in the score (though the reason Pace calls this history an oversimplification is that modern music *does* have the capacity for expressive performance, as we will discuss later).

A number of studies have been done into this pre-twentieth century (specifically Baroque, Classical, and Romantic) music performance. The earliest studies began with Seashore [96], and good overviews include [43, 84]. One element of these studies has been to discover what aspects of a piece of music—what *Musical Features*—are related to a performer's use of expressive performance actions. One of these musical features expressed is the performer's *structural* interpretation of the piece [84]. A piece of music has a number of levels of meaning—a hierarchy. Notes make up motifs, motifs make up phrases, phrases make up sections, sections make up a piece (in more continuous instruments there are intranote elements as well). Each element—note, motif, etc—plays a role in other higher elements. Human performers have been shown to express this hierarchical structure in their performances. Performers tend to slow down at boundaries in the hierarchy—with the amount of slowing being correlated to the importance of the boundary [24]. Thus, a performer would tend to slow more at a boundary between sections than between phrases. There are also regularities relating to other musical features in performers' expressive strategies. For example, in some cases, the musical feature of higher pitched notes causes a performance action of the notes being played more loudly; also notes which introduce melodic tension relative to the key may be played more loudly. However, for every rule, there will always be exceptions.

Another factor influencing expressive performance actions is *Performance Context*. Performers may wish to express a certain mood or emotion (e.g. sadness, happiness) through a piece of music. Performers have been shown to change the tempo and dynamics of a piece when asked to express an emotion as they play it [42]. For a discussion of other factors involved in human expressive performance, we refer the reader to [58].

19.1.2 Computer Expressive Performance

Having examined human expressive performance, the question now becomes why should we want *computers* to perform music expressively? There are at least five answers to this question:

1. *Investigating human expressive performance by developing computational models*—Expressive performance is a fertile area for investigating musicology and human psychology [43, 84, 96]. As an alternative to experimentation with human performers, models can be built which attempt to simulate elements of human expressive performance. As in all mathematical and computational modelling, the model itself can give the researcher greater insight into the mechanisms inherent in that which is being modelled.
2. *Realistic playback on a music typesetting or composing tool*—There are many computer tools available now for music typesetting and for composing. If these tools play back the compositions with expression on the computer, the composer will have a better idea of what their final piece will sound like. For example, Sibelius, Notion and Finale have some ability for expressive playback.
3. *Playing computer-generated music expressively*—There are a number of algorithmic composition systems that output music without expressive performance but which audiences would normally expect to hear played expressively. These compositions in their raw form will play on a computer in a robotic way. A CSEMP would allow the output of an algorithmic composition system to be played directly on the computer which composed it (for example, in a computer game which generates mood music based on what is happening in the game).
4. *Playing data files*—a large number of non-expressive data files in formats like MIDI and MusicXML [46] are available on the internet, and they are used by many musicians as a standard communication tool for ideas and pieces. Without CSEMPs most of these files will playback on a computer in an unattractive way, whereas the use of a CSEMP would make such files much more useful.
5. *Computer accompaniment tasks*—it can be costly for a musician to play in ensemble. Musicians can practice by playing along to recordings with their solo part stripped out. But some may find it too restrictive since such recordings cannot dynamically follow the expressiveness in the soloist's performance. These soloists may prefer to play along with an interactive accompaniment system that not only tracks their expression but also generates its own expression.

19.1.3 Performance Creativity

Performance Creativity refers to the ability of the system to generate novel and original performances, as opposed to simulating previous human strategies. For example, the Artificial Neural Network Piano system [11] is designed to simulate human performances (an important research goal), but not to create novel performances; whereas a system like Director Musices [38], although also designed to capture human performance strategies, has a parameterisation ability which can be creatively manipulated to generate entirely novel performances. There is an important proviso here—a system which is totally manual would seem at first glance to have a high creativity potential, since the user could entirely shape every element of the performance. However, this potential may never be realised due to the manual effort required to implement the performance. Not all systems are able to act in a novel and *practically controllable* way. Many of the systems generate a model of performance which is basically a vector or matrix of coefficients. Changing this matrix by hand ("hacking it") would allow the technically knowledgeable to creatively generate novel performances. However, the changes could require too much effort, or the results of such changes could be too unpredictable (thus requiring too many iterations or "try outs"). This is to say that performance creativity includes the ability of a system to produce novel performances with *a reasonable amount of effort*. Having said that, simple controllability is not the whole of Performance Creativity, for example, there could be a CSEMP which has only three basic performance rules which can be switched on and off with a mouse click and the new performance played immediately. However, the results of switching off and on the rules would in all likelihood generate a very uninteresting performance.

Thus, for performance creativity, a balance needs to exist between automation and creative flexibility, since in this review we are only concerned with automated and semi-automated CSEMPs. By automated, we refer to the ability of the system —once set up or trained—to generate a performance of a new piece, not seen before by the system, without manual intervention. Some automated systems may require manual setup, but then can be presented with multiple pieces which will be played autonomously. A semi-automated system is one which requires some manual input from the user (for example a musicological analysis) to deal with a new piece.

An example of such a balance between automation and creative flexibility would be an almost totally automated CSEMP, but with a manageable number of parameters that can be user-adjusted before activating the CSEMP for performance. After activating the CSEMP, a performance is autonomously generated but is only partially constrained by attempting to match past human performances. Such creative and novel performance is often applauded in human performers. For example, Glenn Gould has created highly novel expressive performances of pieces of music and has been described as having a vivid musical imagination [21]. Expressive computer performance provides possibilities for even more imaginative experimentation with performance strategies.

19.2   A Generic Framework for Previous Research in Computer Expressive Performance

Figure 19.1 shows a generic model for the framework that most (but not all) previous research into automated and semi-automated CSEMPs tends to have followed. The modules of this diagram are described beneath Fig. 19.1.

1. *Performance Knowledge*—This is the core of any performance system. It is the set of rules or associations that controls the performance action. It is the "expertise" of the system which contains the ability, implicit or explicit, to generate an expressive performance. This may be in the form of an Artificial Neural Network, a set of cases in a Case-based Reasoning system, or a set of linear equation with coefficients. To produce performance actions, this module uses its programmed knowledge together with any inputs concerning the particular performance. Its main input is the Music/Analysis module. Its output is a representation of the performance of the musical input, including expressive performance actions.

2. *Music/Analysis*—The Music/Analysis module has two functions. First of all, in all systems, it has the function of inputting the music to be played expressively (whether in paper score, MIDI, MusicXML, audio or other form) into the system. The input process can be quite complex, for example, paper score or audio input will require some form of analytical recognition of musical events. This module is the only input to the Performance Knowledge module that defines the particular piece of music to be played. In some systems, it also has a second function—to provide an analysis of the musical structure. This analysis provides information about the Music Features of the music—for example, metrical, melodic or harmonic structure (It was mentioned earlier how it has been shown that such structures have a large influence on expressive

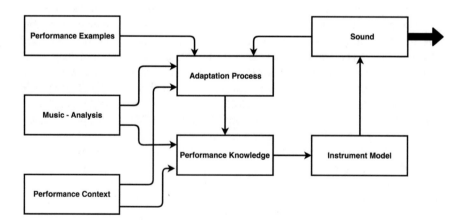

Fig. 19.1 Generic model for most current CSEMPs

performance in humans). This analysis can then be used by the Performance Knowledge system to decide how the piece should be performed. Analysis methods used in some of the systems include Lerdahl and Jackendoff's Generative Theory of Tonal Music [68], Narmour's Implication Realisation [81], and various bespoke musical measurements. The analysis may be automated, manual or a combination of the two.

3. *Performance Context*—Another element which will effect how a piece of music is played is the performance context. This includes such things as how the performer decides to play a piece, for example, happy, perky, sad or lovelorn. It can also include whether the piece is played in a particular style, e.g. baroque or romantic.

4. *Adaptation Process*—The adaptation process is the method used to develop the Performance Knowledge. Like the Analysis module this can be automated, manual or a combination of the two. In some systems, a human expert listens to actual musical output of the performance system and decides if it is appropriate. If not then the Performance Knowledge can be adjusted to try to improve the musical output performance. This is the reason that in Fig. 19.1 there is a line going from the Sound module back to the Adaptation Procedure module. The Adaptation Procedure also has inputs from Performance Context, Music/Analysis, Instrument Model and Performance Examples. All four of these elements can influence the way that a human performs a piece of music, though the most commonly used is Music/Analysis and Performance Examples.

5. *Performance Examples*—One important element that can be incorporated in the Performance Knowledge building is the experience of past human performances. These examples can be used by the Adaptation procedure to analyse when and how performance actions are added to a piece of music by human performers. The examples may be a database of marked-up audio recordings, MIDI files together with their source scores or (in the manual case) a person's experience of music performance.

6. *Instrument Model*—By far the most common instrument used in computer-generated performance research is the piano. This is because it allows experiments with many aspects of expression, but requires only a very simple instrument model. In fact the instrument model used for piano is often just the MIDI/media player and soundcard in a PC. Alternatively, it may be something more complex but still not part of the simulation system, for example, a Yamaha Disklavier. However, a few simulation systems use non-keyboard instruments, for example, Saxophone and Trumpet. In these cases, the issue of a performance is more than just expressiveness. Just simulating a human-like performance, even if it is non-expressive, on these instruments is non-trivial. So systems simulating expressive performance on such instruments may require a relatively complex instrument model in addition to expressive performance elements.

19.2.1 Modules of Systems Reviewed

Table 19.1 lists the systems reviewed and the section they are reviewed in, together with information about their modules. This information will be explained in the detailed part of the review. Note that the column for Instrument Model is also used for CSEMPS without an explicit instrument model, so as to show their applicability to various instruments. A number of abbreviations are used in Table 19.1 and throughout the paper. Table 19.2 lists these abbreviations and their meaning.

Note that the final row of Table 19.1 will be used as an in-depth example. Due to lack of space, not all systems can be examined in great detail. Only one of them will be examined at this depth, to give the reader an opportunity to gain a deeper understanding in the theory and practicalities of creativity and CSEMPs.

Before discussing the primary term of reference for this review, it should be observed that the issue of evaluation of CSEMPs is an open problem. How does one evaluate what is essentially a subjective process? If the CSEMP is trying to simulate a particular performance, then correlation tests can be done. However, even if the correlations are low for a generated performance, it is logically possible for the generated performance to be more preferable to some people than the original performance. Papadopoulos and Wiggins [85] discuss the evaluation issue in a different but closely related area—computer algorithmic composition systems. They list four points that they see as problematic in relation to such composition systems:

1. The lack of evaluation by experts, for example, professional musicians.
2. Evaluation is a relatively small part of the research with respect to the length of the research paper.
3. Many systems only generate melodies. How do we evaluate the music without a harmonic context? Most melodies will sound acceptable in some context or other.
4. Most of the systems deal with computer composition as a problem-solving task rather as a creative and meaningful process.

This chapter will be focusing on point 4—performance creativity. At some point in the description of each system, this point will be implicitly or explicitly addressed, and summarised at the end of the paper (see Table 19.8). It is worth noting that this is not an attempt to measure how successful the system is overall, but an attempt to highlight some key issues which will help to show potential directions for future research. What now follows is the actual descriptions of the CSEMPs, divided into a number of groups.

Table 19.1 Systems reviewed in this chapter

CSEMP	Performance knowledge	Music	Analysis	Performance context	Adaptation process	Performance examples	Instrument model (or Application)	Performance actions
Director Musices (Sect. 19.3.1.1)	Rules	MIDI, Score	Custom	Mood space	–	MIDI performances	All (Piano)	T/D/A/P
Hierarchical Parabola (Sect. 19.3.1.2)	Parabola equation	MIDI, Score	GTTM TSR	–	–	–	Piano	T/D
Composer Pulse (Sect. 19.3.1.3)	Multiplier set	MIDI	–	–	Manual	Tapping	All	T/D
Bach Fugue (Sect. 19.3.1.4)	Rules	Score	Custom	–	Manual	Books, experts	Keyboard	T/A
Trumpet Synthesis (Sect. 19.3.1.5)	Linear model	Audio, Score	Custom	–	Manual	Audio performances	Trumpet	A/P/O
Rubato (Sect. 19.3.1.6)	Operators	MIDI, Score	Custom	–	Manual	–	All (Piano)	T/D
Pop-E (Sect. 19.3.1.7)	Rule-based	MIDI, Score	GTTM, Custom	–	–	MIDI performances	Piano	T/D
Hermode Tuning 19.3.1.8	Rule-based	MIDI	Custom	–	–	–	All	P
Sibelius (Sect. 19.3.1.9)	Rule-based	Score	Custom	–	–	Unknown	–	Unknown
CMERS (Sect. 19.3.1.10)	Linear model	MIDI, Score	Custom	Mood space	–	Performances and experiments	Piano	T/D/P/O
MIS (Sect. 19.3.2.1)	Linear model	MIDI, Score	GTTM/Meyer	–	Regression with ANDs	Audio performances	Piano	T/D/A
CaRo (Sect. 19.3.2.2)	Linearmodel	Audio	Custom	Mood space	PCA, Linear Regression	Audio performances by mood	All	T/K/D/A
ANN Piano (Sect. 19.3.3.1)	ANN	MIDI	Custom	–	ANN training	MIDI performances	Piano	T/D
Emotional Flute (Sect. 19.3.3.2)	ANN and rules	Audio, Score	Custom	Mood space	ANN training	Audio performances by mood	Flute	T/D/V
User-curated Piano (Sect. 19.3.3.3)	ANN/Basis Functions	Audio, Score	Custom	–	ANN training	Audio performances	Piano	T/D/A

(continued)

Table 19.1 (continued)

CSEMP	Performance knowledge	Music	Analysis	Performance context	Adaptation process	Performance examples	Instrument model (or Application)	Performance actions
SaxEx (Sect. 19.3.4.1)	Fuzzy Rules	Audio, Score	Narmour/IR/GTTM, Custom	Mood space	CBR training	Audio performances by mood	Saxophone	T/D/V/K
Kagurame (Sect. 19.3.4.2)	Rules	MIDI, Score	Custom	Performance conditions	CBR training	MIDI performances by context	Piano	T/D/A
Ha-Hi-Hun (Sect. 19.3.4.3)	Rules	MIDI, Score	GTTM TSR	Language Performance conditions	CBR training	MIDI performances by condition	Piano	T/D
PLCG (Sect. 19.3.4.4)	Learned rules	MIDI, Score	Custom	–	Meta-sequential learning	MIDI performances	Piano	T/D/A
PLCG/Phrase-decomposition (Sect. 19.3.4.5)	Learned rules	MIDI, Score	Custom, Harmonic by musicologist	–	CBR training, Meta-sequential learning	MIDI performances	Piano	T/D/A
DISTALL (Sect. 19.3.4.6)	CBR	MIDI, Score	Custom, Harmonic by musicologist	–	CBR training	MIDI performances	Piano	T/D/A
Music Plus One (Sect. 19.3.5.1)	BBN	Audio/MIDI, Score	Custom	Soloist tempo	BBN training	Audio soloist performances	All	T/D
ESP Piano (Sect. 19.3.5.2)	HMM	MIDI, Score	Custom	–	HMM training	MIDI performances	Piano	T/D/A
Drumming (Sect. 19.3.6.1)	Non-linear mapping	Audio	Custom	–	KRR, GPR, kNN	Audio performances	Drums	T
KCCA Piano (Sect. 19.3.6.2)	Non-linear mapping	Worm, Score	Custom	–	KCCA	Performance worm	Piano	T/D
Genetic Programming (Sect. 19.3.7.1)	Regression trees	Audio	IR, Custom	–	Genetic programming	Audio PERFORMANCES	Saxophone	T/D/A/N
Sequential Covering GAs (Sect. 19.3.7.2)	Rule-based	Audio	IR, Custom	–	Sequential covering by GA	Audio performances	Saxophone	T/D/A
Jazz Guitar (Sect. 19.3.7.3)	Rule-based/GA	Score	Custom, Narmour	–	GA/Propositional rule learner	Audio performances	Guitar	T/D/A/O
Ossia (Sect. 19.3.7.4)	Fitness rules	MIDI	–	–	–	None	Piano	T/D/P

(continued)

Table 19.1 (continued)

CSEMP	Performance knowledge	Music	Analysis	Performance context	Adaptation process	Performance examples	Instrument model (or Application)	Performance actions
MASC (Sect. 19.3.7.5)	Rule-based (2)	MIDI	Performance skill	Affective state	Imitation	None	Piano	T/D
IMAP (MAS with Imitation) (Sect. 19.4)	Pulse set	MIDI, Score	LBDM, Kruhmans, Melisma	–	Imitation	None	Piano	T/D

Table 19.2 Abbreviations

A	Articulation
ANN	Artificial Neural Network
BBN	Bayesian Belief Network
CBR	Case-based Reasoning
CSEMP	Computer System for Expressive Music Performance
D	Dynamics
DM	Director Musices (KTH System)
EC	Evolutionary Computing
GA	Genetic Algorithm
GP	Genetic Programming
GPR	Gaussian Process Regression
GTTM	Lerdahl and Jackendoff's Generative Theory of Tonal Music
GUI	Graphical User Interface
HMM	Hidden Markov Model
IBL	Instance-based Learning
IR	Narmour's Implication/Realisation Theory of Melody
K	Attack
KCCA	Kernel Canonical Correlation Analysis
kNN	k-Nearest Neighbour
KRR	Kernel Ridge Regression
LBDM	Local Boundary Detection Model of Cambouropoulos
MAS	Multi-agent System
CMERS	Computational Music Emotion Rule System by Livingstone et al.
MIDI	Musical Intrument Digital Interface
MIMACS	Mimetics-inspired Multi-agent Composition System
MusicXML	Music Extensible Markup Language
MIS	Music Intepretation System by Katayose et al.
N	Note addition/consolidation
O	Ornamentation
P	Pitch
PCA	Principal Component Analysis
T	Tempo
TSR	Time Span Reduction Technique (from GTTM)
V	Vibrato

19.3 A Survey of Computer Systems for Expressive Music Performance

The review presented here is meant to be representative rather than exhaustive but will cover a significant sample of published automated and semi-automated CSEMP systems to date. Each CSEMP is grouped according to how their performance knowledge is built—i.e. by learning method. This provides a manageable division of the field, shows which learning methods are most popular and shows where there is room for development in the building of performance knowledge models. The grouping will be

1. Non-learning (10 systems)
2. Linear regression (2 systems)
3. Artificial Neural Networks (3 systems)
4. Rule/Case-based learning (6 systems)
5. Statistical Graphical Models (2 systems)
6. Other Regression methods (2 systems)
7. Evolutionary computation (6 systems).

The ordering of this grouping is by average year of CSEMP references within the grouping, so as to help highlight trends in approaches to generating performance knowledge. For example, most early CSEMPs were non-learning, and most evolutionary computation CSEMPs have only been developed in the last few years. The 4th grouping—Rule/Case-based learning—is in the middle because it has been used throughout the history of CSEMP research.

19.3.1 Non-Learning Systems

19.3.1.1 Director Musices
Director Musices (DM) [38, 101] has been an ongoing project since 1982. Researchers including violinist Lars Fryden developed and tested performance rules using an analysis-by-synthesis method (later using analysis-by-measurement and studying actual performances). Currently, there are around 30 rules which are written as relatively simple equations that take as input Music Features such as height of the current note pitch, the pitch of the current note relative to the key of the piece, or whether the current note is the first or last note of the phrase. The output of the equations defines the Performance Actions. For instance, the higher the pitch the louder the note is played, or during an upward run of notes, play the piece faster. Another DM rule is the Phrase Arch which defines a "rainbow" shape of tempo and dynamics over a phrase. The performance speeds up and gets louder towards the centre of a phrase and then tails off again in tempo and dynamics towards the end of the phrase. Some manual score analysis is required—for example, harmonic analysis and marking up of phrase start and ends. DM's ability

for expressive representation is at the note and phrase level—it does not use information at higher levels of the musical structure hierarchy.

Each equation has a numeric "k-value"—the higher the k-value the more effect the rule will have and a k-value of 0 switches the rule off. The results of the equations are added together linearly to get the final performance. Thanks to the adjustable k-value system, DM has much potential for performance creativity. Little work has been reported on an active search for novel performances, though it is reported that negative k-values reverse rule effects and cause unusual performances. DM's ability as a semi-automated system comes from the fact it has a "default" set of k-values, allowing the same rule settings to be applied automatically to different pieces of music (though not necessarily with the same success).

Rules are also included for dealing with non-monophonic music [38]. The "Melodic-sync" rule generates a new voice consisting of all timings in all other voices (if two voices have simultaneous notes, then the note with the greatest melodic tension is selected.) Then all rules are applied to this synchronisation voice, and resulting durations are mapped back onto the original voices. The "Bar-sync" rule can also be applied to make all voices re-synchronise at each bar end.

DM is also able to deal with some Performance Contexts, specifically emotional expression [10], drawing on work by Gabrielsson and Juslin [42]. Listening experiments were used to define the k-value settings on the DM rules for expressing emotions. The music used was a Swedish nursery rhyme and a computer-generated piece in a minor mode written in the musical style of Chopin. Six rules were used from DM to generate multiple performances of each piece. Subjects were asked to identify a performance emotion from the list: fear, anger, happiness, sadness, solemnity, tenderness or no-expression. As a result, parameters were found for each of the six rules which mould the emotional expression of a piece. For example, for "tenderness": inter-onset interval is lengthened by 30%, sound level reduced by 6 dB, and two other rules are used: the Final Ritardando rule (slowing down at the end of a piece) and the Duration Contrast rule (if two adjacent notes have contrasting durations, increase this contrast).

A more recent development in Director Musices has been the real-time generation of performances using a version of the system called pDM [41]. pDM essentially acts as an expressive sequencer, allowing the adjustment of rule parameters during playback and the live incorporation of the changes as the playback continues. Unlike pDM, many CSEMPs in this survey receive the inputs and parameters and the whole piece of music, process the data and when this processing is complete, a generated performance is available to the user. They are not designed for real-time usage.

Director Musices has a good test status, having been evaluated in a number of experiments. In [40] k-values were adjusted by a search algorithm, based on 28 human performances of 9 bars of Schumann's Träumerei. A good correlation was found between the human performances and the resulting DM performance. Another experiment involved manually fitting to one human performance the first 20 bars of the Adagio in Mozart's sonata K.332 [102]. The correlations were found to be low, unless the k-values were allowed to change dynamically when the piece was performed. An attempt was made to fit k-values using a larger corpus of piano music using Genetic algorithms in [65], and the results were found to give a low correlation as well. In an attempt to overcome this [139, 139] allowed k-values to vary in a controlled way over a piece of music. This was tested on Beethoven's Sonatine in G Major and Mozart's K.332 piano sonata (the slow movement)—but the results were found to be poor for the Beethoven. In the first RenCon in 2002, the second prize went to a DM-generated performance, however, the first placed system (a manually generated performance) was voted for by 80% of the jury. In RenCon 2005, a Director Musices default-settings (i.e. automated) performance of Mozart's Minuette KV 1(1e) came a very close 2nd in the competition, behind Pop-E (Sect. 19.3.1.7). However, three of the other four systems competing were versions of the DM-system.

The DM model has been influential, and as will be seen in the later systems, DM-type rules appear repeatedly.

19.3.1.2 Hierarchical Parabola Model

One of the first CSEMPs with a hierarchical expressive representation was Todd's Hierarchical Parabola Model [109–112]. Todd argues it was consistent with a kinematic model of expressive performance, where tempo changes are viewed as being due to accelerations and decelerations in some internal process in the human mind/body, for example, the auditory system. For tempo, the hierarchical parabola model uses a rainbow shape like DM's phrase arch, which is consistent with Newtonian kinematics. For loudness the model uses a "the faster the louder" rule, creating a dynamics rainbow as well.

The key difference between DM and this hierarchical model is that the hierarchical model has greater expressive representation and wider performance action. Multiple levels of the hierarchy are analysed using Lerdahl and Jackendoff's Generative Theory of Tonal Music (GTTM). GTTM Time Span Reduction (TSR) examines each note's musicological place in all hierarchical levels. The rainbows/parabolas are generated at each level, from the note-group level upwards Fig. 19.2 and added to get the performance. This generation is done by a parametrized parabolic equation which takes as input the result of the GTTM TSR analysis.

The performance was shown to correlate well by eye with a short human performance but no correlation figures were reported. Clarke and Windsor [23] tested the first four bars of Mozart's K.331, comparing two human performers with two performances by the Hierarchical Parabola model. Human listeners found the Parabola version unsatisfactory compared to the human ones. In the same experiment, however, the Parabola model was found to work well on another short melody. The testing also showed that the idea of "the louder the faster" did not always hold. Desain and Honing [31] claim through informal listening tests that in general the performances do not *sound* convincing.

The constraint of utilising the hierarchy and the GTTM TSR approach limits the Performance Creativity. Note groupings will be limited to those generated by a GTTM TSR analysis, and the parabolas generated will be constrained by the

Tempo Parabolas

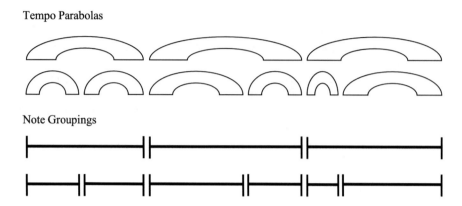

Note Groupings

Fig. 19.2 Todd's parabola model

model's equation. Any adjustments to a performance will be constrained to working within this framework.

19.3.1.3 Composer Pulse and Predictive Amplitude Shaping

Manfred Clynes' Composer Pulse [26] also acts on multiple levels of the hierarchy. Clynes hypothesises that each composer has a unique pattern of amplitude and tempo variations running through performances—a pulse. This is captured as a set of numbers multiplying tempo and dynamics values in the score. It is hierarchical with separate values for within the beat, the phrase and at multiple bar level. Table 19.3 shows the values of pulses for phrase level for some composers. The pulses were measured using a sentograph to generate pressure curves from musicians tapping their finger whilst thinking of or listening to a specific composer. Figure 19.3 shows the structure of a pulse set in three-time (each composer has a three-time and a four-time pulse set defined). This pulse set is repeatedly applied to

Table 19.3 Level 2 composers' pulses

Level 2 composers' pulses—4 pulse					
Beethoven	Duration	106	89	96	111
	Amplitude	1.00	0.39	0.83	0.81
Mozart	Duration	105	95	105	95
	Amplitude	1.00	0.21	0.53	0.23
Schubert	Duration	97	114	98	90
	Amplitude	1.00	0.65	0.40	0.75
Haydn	Duration	108	94	97	102
	Amplitude	1.00	0.42	0.68	1.02
Schumann	Duration	96	116	86	102
	Amplitude	0.60	0.95	0.50	1.17
Mendelssohn	Duration	118	81	95	104
	Amplitude	1.00	0.63	0.79	1.12

a score end on end. Thus, if the pulse is 12 beats long and the score is 528 beats, the pulse will repeat 528/12 = 44 times end on end.

Another key element of Clyne's approach is Predictive Amplitude Shaping. This adjusts a note's dynamic based on the next note simulating "a musician's unconscious ability to sculpt notes in this way" that "makes his performance flow beautifully through time, and gives it meaningful coherence even as the shape and duration of each individual note is unique". A fixed envelope shape model is used (some constants are manually defined by the user), the main inputs being distant to the next note and duration of the current note. So, the Pulse/Amplitude system has only note level expressive representation.

Clynes' test of his own model showed that a number of expert and non-expert listeners preferred music with a composer's pulse than with a different pulse. However, not all tests on Clynes' approach have supported a universal pulse for each composer [94, 106], suggest instead that the pulse may be effective for a *subset* of a composer's work. Clynes' pulses and amplitude shaping have been combined with other performance tools (e.g. vibrato generation) as part of his commercial software SuperConductor. Two SuperConductor generated performances were submitted to RenCon 2006 open section: Beethoven's Eroica Symphony, Op.55, Mvt.4 and Brahms' Violin Concerto, Op.77, Mvt.1. The Beethoven piece scored low, but the Brahms piece came 1st in the open section (beating two pieces submitted by Pop-E—Sect. 19.3.1.7). The generation of this piece could have involved significant amounts of manual work. Moreover, because it was the open section, the pieces submitted by Pop-E were not the same as submitted by SuperConductor—hence like was not compared to like. SuperConductor also won the open section in RenCon 2004 with J. S. Bach, Brandenburg Concerto No. 5, D Major, 3rd Movement. The only competitor included from this review was Rubato (Sect. 19.3.1.6) performing a Bach piece. It should be re-emphasised that these results were for SuperConductor and not solely for the Pulse and Amplitude tools.

In the context of SuperConductor, Clynes approach allows for significant Performance Creativity. The software is designed to allow a user to control the expressive shaping of a MIDI performance, giving significant amounts of control.

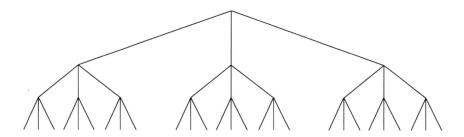

Fig. 19.3 Structure of a pulse set in three-time

However, outside of the context of SuperConductor, the pulse has little scope for performance creativity—though the amplitude shaping does. The pulse and amplitude shaping do not explicitly address non-monophonic music, though SuperConductor can be used to generate polyphonic performances.

19.3.1.4 Bach Fugue System

In the Bach Fugue System [57], Expert System methods are used to generate performance actions. Johnson generated the knowledge base through interviews with two musical expert performers, and through a performance practice manual and an annotated edition of the Well-Tempered Clavier; so this system is not designed for performance creativity. Twenty-eight conditions for tempo and articulation are so-generated for the knowledge base. For example, "If there is any group of 16th notes following a tied note, then slur the group of 16th notes following the long note". Expressive representation is focused on the note to phrase level. The CSEMP does not perform itself but generates instructions for 4/4 fugues. Testing was limited to examining the instructions. It gave the same instructions as human experts 85–90% of the time, though it is not said how many tests were run. The system is working in the context of polyphony.

19.3.1.5 Trumpet Synthesis

The testing of three out of the last four CSEMPs reviewed has focused on keyboard. This pattern will continue through the paper—most CSEMPs focus on the piano because it is easier to collect and analyse data for the piano than for other instruments. One of the first non-piano systems was Dannenberg and Derenyi's Trumpet Synthesis [30, 28]. The authors' primary interest here was to generate realistic trumpet synthesis, and adding performance factors improves this synthesis. It is not designed for performance creativity but for simulation. This trumpet system synthesises the whole trumpet performance, without needing any MIDI or audio building blocks as the basis of its audio output. The performance actions are amplitude and frequency, and these are controlled by envelope models which were developed using a semi-manual statistical analysis-by-synthesis method. A 10-parameter model was built for amplitude, based on elements such as articulation, direction and magnitude of pitch intervals, and duration of notes. This system works by expressively transforming one note at a time, based on the pattern of the surrounding two notes. In terms of expressive representation, the system works on a 3 note width. The pitch expression is based on envelopes which were derived and stored during the analysis-by-synthesis.

No test results are reported. Dannenberg and Derenyi placed two accompanied examples online: parts of a Haydn Trumpet Concerto and of a Handel Minuet. The start of the trumpet on the Concerto without accompaniment is also online, together with a human playing the same phrase. The non-accompanied synthesis sounds quite impressive, only being let down by a synthetic feel towards the end of the phrase—though the note-to-note expression (as opposed to the synthesis) consistently avoids sounding machine-like. In both accompanied examples it became clear as the performances went on that a machine was playing, particularly in faster passages. But once again note-to-note expression did not sound too mechanical. Despite the reasonably positive nature of these examples, there is no attempt to objectively qualify how good the Trumpet Synthesis system is.

19.3.1.6 Rubato

Mazzola, a mathematician and recognised Jazz pianist, developed a mathematical theory of music [72, 73], where music is represented in an abstract geometrical space whose co-ordinates include onset time, pitch, and duration. A score will exist in this space, and expressive performances are generated by performing transformations on the space. The basis of these transformations is series of "Operators" which can be viewed as a very generalised version of the rule-based approach taken in Director Musices. For example, the Tempo operator and the Split operator allow the generation of tempo hierarchies. These give Rubato a good expressive representation. However, the definition of the hierarchy here differs somewhat from that found in the Hierarchical Parabola Model (Sect. 19.3.1.2) or DISTALL (Sect. 19.3.4.6). A tempo hierarchy, for a piano performance, may mean that the tempo of the left hand is the dominant tempo, at the top of a hierarchy, and the right-hand tempo is always relative to the left-hand tempo—and so is viewed as being lower in the hierarchy. Mazzola also discusses the use of tempo hierarchies to generate tempo for grace notes and arpeggios—the tempo of these is relative to some global tempo higher in the hierarchy. Ideas from this theory have been implemented in a piece of software called Rubato, which is available online. The expressive performance module in Rubato is the "Performance Rubette". A MIDI file can be loaded in Rubato and pre-defined operators used to generate expressive performances. The user can also manually manipulate tempo curves using a mouse and GUI, giving Rubato good scope for performance creativity.

Test reports are limited. In RenCon 2004, a performance of Bach's Contrapunctus III modelled using Rubato was submitted, and came 4th in the open section (SuperConductor came 1st in the section with a different piece). It is not clear how automated the generation of the performance was. Listening to the submission it can be heard that although the individual voices are quite expressive and pleasant (except for the fastest parts), the combination sounds relatively unrealistic. An online MIDI example is available of Schumann's Kindersezenen op. 15 Nr. 2, "Kuriose Geschichte" which evidences both tempo and dynamics expression and is quite impressive, though once again it is not clear how automated the production of the music was.

19.3.1.7 Pop-E

Pop-E [49], a Polyphrase Ensemble system, was developed by some of the team involved in MIS (Sect. 19.3.2.1). It applies expression features separately to each voice in a MIDI file, through a synchronisation algorithm. The music analysis uses GTTM local level rules, and utilises beams and slurs in the score to generate note groupings. So, the expressive representation is to up to phrase level. Expressive actions are applied to these groupings through rules reminiscent of Director Musices. The five performance rules have a total of nine manual parameters between them. These parameters can be adjusted, providing scope for performance creativity. In particular jPop-E [50], a Java implementation of the system, provides such tools for shaping new performances.

To deal with polyphony, Synchronisation Points are defined at the note grouping start and end points in the *attentive part*. The attentive part is that voice which is most perceptually prominent to a listener. The positions of notes in all other non-attentive parts are linearly interpolated relative to the synchronisation points (defined manually). This means that all parts will start and end at the same time at the start and end of groupings of the main attentive part.

Pop-E was evaluated in the laboratory to see how well it could reconstruct specific human performances. After setting parameters manually, performances by three pianists were reconstructed. The average correlation values between Pop-E and a performer were 0.59 for tempo and 0.76 for dynamics. This has to be viewed in the context that the average correlations between the human performers were 0.4 and 0.55, respectively. Also, the upper piano part was more accurate on average. It is interesting to note that for piano pieces whose attentive part is the right hand, the Pop-E synchronisation system is similar to the methods in the DISTALL system for dealing with polyphony—see Sect. 19.3.4.6.

Pop-E won the RenCon 2005 compulsory section, beating Director Musices (Sect. 19.3.1.1). In RenCon 2006 Pop-E won the compulsory section beating Kagurame (Sect. 19.3.4.2) and Ha-Hi-Hun (Sect. 19.3.4.3). In the open section in 2006 SuperConductor (Sect. 19.3.1.3) beat Pop-E with one performance, and lost to Pop-E with another.

19.3.1.8 Hermode Tuning

The next two sub-sections describe successful commercial CSEMPs. Despite the lack of details available on these proprietary systems they should be included here, since they are practical CSEMPs that people are paying money for, and illustrate some of the commercial potential of CSEMPs for the music business. However, because of the lack of some details, the four review terms of reference will not be applied. The first system is Hermode Tuning [97]. Most systems in this review focus on dynamics and timing. Nonetheless, intonation is another significant area of expression for many instruments—for example, many string instruments. (In fact, three intonation rules were added to Director Musices in its later incarnations; for example, the higher the pitch, the sharper the note.) Hermode Tuning is a dedicated expressive intonation system which can work in real time, its purpose being to "imitate the living intonation of well-educated instrumentalists in orchestras and chamber music ensembles". Instrumentalists do not perform in perfect intonation— in fact, if an orchestra performed music in perfect tuning all the time, the sound would be less pleasant than one that optimised its tuning through performance experience. A series of algorithms are used in Hermode tuning not just to avoid perfect intonation but to attempt to achieve *optimal* intonation. The algorithms have settings for different types of music, for example, Baroque and Jazz/Pop.

19.3.1.9 Sibelius

As mentioned in the introduction of this paper, the music typesetting software package Sibelius has built-in algorithms for expressive performance. These use a rule-based approach. Precise details are not available for these commercial algorithms but some information is available [37]. For dynamics, beat groups such as bar lines, sub-bar groups and beams are used to add varying degrees of stress. Also, the higher the note is the louder it is played, though volume resets at rests and dynamic expression is constrained to not be excessive. Some random fluctuation is added to dynamics to make it more human sounding as well. Tempo expression is achieved using a simple phrase-based system; but this does not include reliable phrase analysis. The manufacturer reports that "phrasing need only be appropriate perhaps 70% of the time—the ear overlooks the rest" and that "the ear is largely fooled into thinking it's a human performance". Notion and Finale also have expressive performance systems built into them, which are reportedly more advanced than Sibelius', but even fewer details are available for the proprietary methodologies in these systems.

19.3.1.10 Computational Music Emotion Rule System

In relation to the philosophy behind the Computational Music Emotion Rule System (CMERS) [70], Livingstone observes that "the separation of musical rules into structural and performative is largely an ontological one, and cedes nothing to the final audio experienced by the listener". The Computational Music Emotion Rule System has a rule set of 19 rules developed through analysis-by-synthesis. The rules have an expressive representation up to the phrase level, some requiring manual mark-up of the score. These rules are designed not only to inject micro-feature deviations into the score to generate human-like performances, but also to use microfeature and macro-feature deviations to express emotions to the listener. To this end CMERS is able to change the score itself, recomposing it.

CMERS has a 2-D model of human emotion space with four quadrants going from very active and negative to very active and positive, to very passive and positive through to very passive and negative. These four elements combine to give such emotions as angry, bright, contented and despairing. The quadrants were constructed from a review of 20 studies of music and emotion. The rules for expressing emotions include moving between major and minor modes, changing note pitch classes, and DM-type rules for small changes in dynamics and tempo. It was found that the addition of the microfeature humanisation rules improved the accuracy of the emotional expression (as opposed to solely using macro-feature "re-composition" rules). The rules for humanising the performance include some rules which are similar to Director Musices, such as Phrase Arch and emphasising metrically important beats. Creative Performance is possible in CMERS by adjusting the parameters of the rule set, and the emotional specification would allow a user to specify different emotions for different parts of a performance.

A significant number of formal listening tests have been done by Livingstone and they support the hypothesis that CMERS is more successful than DM at expressing emotions. CMERS is one of the better tested systems in this review—

one reason being that its aim is more measurable than a purely aesthetic goal. Examples of CMERS are available on the author's webpage.

19.3.2 Linear Regression

Learning CSEMPs can incorporate more knowledge more quickly than non-learning systems. Nonetheless, such methods do not always provide tools for creative performance because they are strongly rooted in past performances. Before continuing it should be explained that any CSEMP that learns expressive deviations needs to have a non-expressive reference point, some sort of representation of the music played robotically/neutrally. The CSEMP can then compare this to the score played expressively by a human, and learn the deviations. Linear Regression is the first learning method which will be addressed. Linear Regression models assume a basically linear relationship between the Music Features and the Expressive Actions. The advantage of such models is their simplicity. The disadvantage is that assuming music expressive performance a linear process is almost certainly an oversimplification.

19.3.2.1 Music Interpretation System

The Music Interpretation Systems (MISs) [56, 60] generates expressive performances in MIDI format, but learns expressive rules from audio recordings. This is done using a spectral analysis system with dynamic programming for note detection. The system is a simulatory CSEMP and uses a set of linear equations which map score features on to performance deviation actions. Its expressive representation is on the note and phrase level. MIS has methods to include some non-linearities using logical ANDs between music features in the score, and a way of reducing redundant music features from its equations. This redundancy reduction improves "Generalisation" ability (the ability for the system to perform music or composers that weren't explicitly included in its learning). MIS learns links between music features and performance actions of tempo, dynamics, and articulation. The music features used include score expression marks, and aspects of GTTM and two other forms of musicological analysis: Leonard Meyer's Theory of Musical Meaning [74] and Narmour's IR Theory. IR considers features of the previous two notes in the melody, and postulates that a human will expect the melody to move in a certain direction and distance; thus, it can classify each note as being part of a certain expectation structure. Meyer's Theory is also an expectation-based approach, but coming from the perspective of Game Theory.

For testing, MIS was trained on the first half of a Chopin Waltz and then used to synthesise the second half. Correlations (accuracies when compared to a human performance of the second half) were for velocity 0.87, for tempo 0.75, and for duration 0.92. A polyphonic MIS interpretation of Chopin, Op. 64, No. 2 was submitted to RenCon 2002. It came 3rd behind DISTALL (Sect. 19.3.4.6) beating 3 of the other 4 automated systems—DM, Kagurame (Sect. 19.3.4.2), and Ha-Hi-Hun (Sect. 19.3.4.3).

19.3.2.2 CaRo

CaRo [15, 17, 16] is a monophonic CSEMP designed to generate audio files which —like CMERS (Sect. 19.3.1.1)—express certain moods/emotions. It does not require a score to work from, but works on audio files which are mood-neutral. The files are, however, assumed to include the performer's expression of the music's hierarchical structure. Its expressive representation is at the local note level. CaRo's performance actions at the note and intranote level include changes to inter-onset interval, brightness, and loudness-envelope centroid. A linear model is used to learn actions—every action has an equation characterised by parameters called Shift and Range Expansion. Each piece of music in a particular mood has its own set of Shift and Range Expansion values. This limits the generalisation potential.

CaRo also learns "how musical performances are organised in the listener's mind" in terms of moods: hard, heavy, dark, bright, light and soft. To do this, a set of listening experiments analysed by Principal Component Analysis (PCA) generates a two-dimensional space that captures 75% of the variability present in the listening results; this space is used to represent listeners' experience of the moods. A further linear model is learned for each piece of music which maps the mood space onto Shift and Range Expansion values. The user can select any point in the mood space, and CaRo generates an expressive version of the piece. A line can be drawn through mood space, and following that line in time CaRo can generate a performance morphing through different moods. Apart from the ability to adjust Shift and Range expansion parameters manually, CaRo's potential for creative performance is extended by its ability to have a line drawn through the mood space. Users can draw trajectories through this space which create entirely novel performances, and this can be done in real time.

For testing, 20 s clips each from 3 piano pieces by different composers were used. A panel of 30 listeners evaluated CaRo's ability to generate pieces with different expressive moods. Results showed that the system gave a good modelling of expressive mood performances as realised by human performers.

19.3.3 Artificial Neural Networks

19.3.3.1 Artificial Neural Network Piano System

The earliest ANN approach is the Artificial Neural Network Piano System [11]. It has two incarnations. The first did not learn from human performers: a set of 7 monophonic Director Musice rules were selected, and two (loudness and timing) feedforward ANNs learned these rules through being trained on them. By learning a fixed model of Director Musices, the ANN loses the performance creativity of the k-values. When monophonic listening tests were done with 20 subjects, using Mozart's Piano Sonatas K331 and K281, the Director Musices performance was rated above the non-expressive computer performance, but the Neural Network performance rated highest of all. One explanation for the dominance of the ANN over the original DM rules was that the ANN generalised in a more pleasant way than the rules. The other ANN system by Bresin was a simulation CSEMP which also used a separate loudness and timing feedback ANN. The ANNs were trained using actual pianist performances from MIDI, rather than on DM rules; but some of the independently learned rules turned out to be similar to some DM rules. Informal listening tests judged the ANNs as musically acceptable. The network looked at a context of four notes (loudness) and five notes (timing), and so had a note to phrase-level expressive representation, though it required the notes to be manually grouped into phrases before being input.

19.3.3.2   Emotional Flute

The Camurri et al. [14] Emotional Flute system uses explicit Music Features and Artificial Neural Networks, thus allowing greater generalisation than the related CaRo system (Sect. 19.3.2.2). The music features are similar to those used in Director Musices. This CSEMP is strongly related to Bresin's second ANN, extending it into the non-piano realm and adding mood space modelling. Expressive actions include inter-onset interval, loudness and vibrato. Pieces need to be segmented into phrases before being input—this segmentation is performed automatically by another ANN. There are separate nets for timing and for loudness—net designs are similar to Bresin's, and have similar levels of expressive representation. There is also a third net for the duration of crescendo and decrescendo at the single note level. However, the nets could not be successfully trained on vibrato, so a pair of rules were generated to handle it. A flautist performed the first part of Telemann's Fantasia no.2 in nine different moods: cold, natural, gentle, bright, witty, serious, restless, passionate and dark. Like CaRo a 2-D mood space was generated and mapped on to the performances by the ANNs, and this mood space can be utilised to give greater Performance Creativity.

To generate new performances the network drives a physical model of a flute. Listening tests gave an accuracy of approximately 77% when subjects attempted to assign emotions to synthetic performances. To put this in perspective, even when listening to the original human performances, human recognition levels were not always higher than 77%; the description of emotional moods in music is a fairly subjective process.

19.3.3.3   User-Curated Piano

Basis function modelling is used by this system [98], one very much focused on performance creativity, for generating expressive piano performances. It creates individualised performances by allowing the user to weight the contribution of individual aspects of the musical score to the overall performance. Expressive parameters such as tempo and dynamics are modelled as function of score basis functions. Parameters include notated features such as pitch and timing. Each expressive parameter is written as $y_i = f(\varphi_i)$, where φ_i is a vector of basis functions evaluated on score element x_i (e.g. a note in the score) and $f()$ is a neural network. The basis functions are trained using two expressive performance datasets: Chopin and Beethoven [18]. During expressive playback (audio or MIDI) the user can adjust sliders to change how much different expressive features (e.g. tempo and articulation) are affected by expressive deviations. Thus, the system is not designed to perfectly simulate previous expressive performances, but to use previous expressive performances as a starting point to allow the user to creatively shape new ones.

19.3.4 Case and Instance-Based Systems

19.3.4.1 SaxEx

Arcos and Lopez de Mantaras' SaxEx [2–5, 71] was one of the first systems to learn performances based on the performance context of mood. Like the trumpet system described earlier (Sect. 19.3.1.5), SaxEx includes algorithms for extracting notes from audio files, and generating expressive audio files from note data. SaxEx also looks at intranote features like vibrato and attack. Unlike the trumpet system, SaxEx needs a non-expressive audio file to perform transformations upon. Narmour's IR theory is used to analyse the music. Other elements used to analyse the music are ideas from Jazz theory, as well as GTTM TSR. This system's expressive representation is up to phrase level and is automated.

SaxEx was trained on cases from monophonic recordings of a tenor sax playing four Jazz standards with different moods (as well as a non-expressive performance). The moods were designed around three dimensions: tender-aggressive, sad-joyful and calm-restless. The mood and local IR, GTTM and Jazz structures around a note are linked to the expressive deviations in the performance of that note. These links are stored as performance cases. SaxEx can then be given a non-expressive audio file and told to play it with a certain mood. A further AI method is used then to combine cases: Fuzzy Logic. For example—if two cases are returned for a particular note in the score and one says play with low vibrato, and the other says play with medium vibrato, then fuzzy logic combines them into a low-medium vibrato. The learning of new CBR solutions can be done automatically or manually through a GUI, which affords some performance creativity giving the user a stronger input to the generation of performances. However, this is limited by SaxEx's focus on being a simulation system. There is—like the Computational Music Emotion Rule System (Sect. 19.3.1.10)—the potential for the user to generate a performance with certain moods at different points in the music.

There is no formal testing reported, but SaxEx examples are available online. The authors report "dozens" of positive comments about the realism of the music from informal listening tests, but no formal testing is reported or details given. The two short examples online (Sad and Joyful) sound realistic to us, more so than—for example—the trumpet system examples. But the accuracy of the emotional expression was difficult for us to gauge.

19.3.4.2 Kagurame

Kagurame [103, 104] is another case-based reasoning system which—in theory— also allows expressiveness to be generated from moods, this time for piano. However, it is designed to incorporate a wider degree of performance conditions than solely mood, for example, playing in a Baroque or Romantic style. Rather than

GTTM and IR, Kagurame uses its own custom hierarchical note structures to develop and retrieve cases for expressive performance. This hierarchical approach gives good expressive representation. Score analysis automatically divides the score into segments recursively with the restriction that the divided segment must be shorter than one measure. Hence, manual input is required for boundary information for segments longer than one measure. The score patterns are derived automatically after this, as is the learning of expressive actions associated with each pattern. Kagurame acts on timing, articulation, and dynamics. There is also a polyphony action called Chord Time Lag—notes in the same chord can be played at slightly different times. It is very much a simulation system with little scope for creative performance.

Results are reported for monophonic Classical and Romantic styles. Tests were based on learning 20 short Czerny etudes played in each style. Then, a 21st piece was performed by Kagurame. Listeners said it "sounded almost human like, and expression was acceptable" and that the "generated performance tended to be similar to human, particularly at characteristic points". A high percentage of listeners guessed correctly whether the computer piece was Romantic or Classical style. In RenCon 2004 Kagurame came 4th in one half of the compulsory section, one ahead of Director Musices, but was beaten by DM in the second half, coming 5th. At RenCon 2006 a polyphonic performance of Chopin's piano Etude in E major came 2nd—with Pop-E (Sect. 19.3.1.7) taking 1st place.

19.3.4.3 Ha-Hi-Hun

Ha-Hi-Hun [55] utilises data structures designed to allow natural language statements to shape performance conditions (these include data structures to deal with non-monophonic music). The paper focuses on instructions of the form "generate performance of piece X in the style of an expressive performance of piece Y". As a result, there are significant opportunities for performance creativity through generating a performance of a piece in the style of a very different second piece; or perhaps performing the Y piece bearing in mind that it will be used to generate creative performances of the X piece. The music analysis of Ha-Hi-Hun uses GTTM TSR to highlight the main notes that shape the melody. TSR gives Ha-Hi-Hun an expressive representation above note level. The deviations of the main notes in the piece Y relative to the score of Y are calculated, and can then be applied to the main notes in the piece X to be performed by Ha-Hi-Hun. After this, the new deviations in X's main notes are propagated linearly to surrounding notes like "expressive ripples" moving outwards. The ability of Ha-Hi-Hun to *automatically* generate expressive performances comes from its ability to generate a new performance X based on a previous human performance Y.

In terms of testing, performances of two pieces were generated, each in the style of performances of another piece. Formal listening results were reported as positive, but few experimental details are given. In RenCon 2002, Ha-Hi-Hun learned to play Chopin Etude Op. 10, No. 3 through learning the style of a human performance of Chopin's Nocturne Op. 32, No. 2. The performance came 9th out of 10 submitted performances by other CSEMPs (many of which were manually produced). In

RenCon 2004, Ha-Hi-Hun came last in the compulsory section, beaten by both Director Musices and Kagurame (Sect. 19.3.4.2). In RenCon 2006, a performance by Ha-Hi-Hun also came third out of six in the compulsory section, beaten by Pop-E (Sect. 19.3.1.7) and Kagurame (Sect. 19.3.4.2).

19.3.4.4 PLCG System

Gerhard Widmer has applied various versions of a rule-based learning approach, attempting to utilise a larger database of music than previous CSEMPs. The PLCG system [116–118] uses data mining to find large numbers of possible performance rules and cluster each set of similar rules into an average rule. This is a system for musicology and simulation rather than one for creative performance.

PLCG is Widmer's own *meta-learning* algorithm—the underlying algorithm being Sequential Covering [80]. PLCG runs a series of sequential covering algorithms in parallel on the same monophonic musical data, and gathers the resulting rules into clusters, generating a single rule from each cluster. The data set was thirteen Mozart Piano sonatas performed by Roland Batik in MIDI form (only melodies were used—giving 41,116 notes). A note-level structure analysis learns to generate tempo, dynamics and articulation deviations based on the local context—e.g. size and direction of intervals, durations of surrounding notes, and scale degree. Hence this CSEMP has a note level expressive representation. As a result of the PLCG algorithm, 383 performance rules were turned into just 18 rules. Interestingly, some of the generated rules had similarities to some of the Director Musices rule set.

Detailed testing has been done on the PLCG, including its generalisation ability. The testing methods were based on correlation approaches. Seven pieces selected from the scores used in learning were regenerated using the rule set, and their tempo/dynamics profiles compared to the original performances very favourably. Regenerations were compared to performances by a different human performer Phillipe Entremont and showed no degradation relative to the original performer comparison. The rules were also applied to some music in a romantic style (two Chopin pieces), giving encouraging results. There are no reports of formal listening tests.

19.3.4.5 Combined Phrase-Decomposition/PLCG

The above approach was extended by Widmer and Tobudic into a monophonic system whose expressive representation extends into higher levels of the score hierarchy. This was the combined Phrase-decomposition/PLCG system [115]. Once again this is a simulation system rather than one for creative performance. When learning, this CSEMP takes as input scores that have had their hierarchical phrase structure defined to three levels by a musicologist (who also provides some harmonic analysis), together with an expressive MIDI performance by a professional pianist. Tempo and Dynamics curves are calculated from the MIDI performance, and then the system does a multi-level decomposition of these expression curves. This is done by fitting quadratic polynomials to the tempo and dynamics curves (similar to the curves found in Todd's Parabola Model—Sect. 19.3.1.2).

Once the curve-fitting has been done, there is still a "residual" expression in the MIDI performance. This is hypothesised as being due to note-level expression, and the PLCG algorithm is run on the residuals to learn the note-level rules which generate this residual expression. The learning of the non-PLCG tempo and dynamics is done using a case-based learning type method—by a mapping from multiple-level features to the parabola/quadratic curves. An extensive set of music features are used including length of the note group, melodic intervals between start and end notes, where the pitch apex of the note group is, whether the note group ends with a cadence, and the progression of harmony between start, apex and end. This CSEMP has the most sophisticated expressive representation of all the systems described in our review.

To generate an expressive performance of a new score, the system moves through the score and in each part runs through all its stored musical features vectors learned from the training; it finds the closest one using a simple distance measure. It then applies the curve stored in this case to the current section of the score. Data for curves at different levels, and results of the PLCG, are added together to give the expression performance actions.

A battery of correlation tests was performed. Sixteen Mozart sonatas were used to test the system—training on 15 of them and then testing against the remaining one. This process was repeated independently selecting a new 1 of the 16 and then re-training on the other 15. This gave a set of 16 results which the authors described as "mixed". Dynamics generated by the system correlated better with the human performance than a non-expressive performance curve (i.e. straight line) did, in 11 out of 16 cases. For the timing curves, this was true for only 6 out of 16 cases. There are no reports of formal listening tests.

19.3.4.6 DISTALL System

Widmer and Tobudic did further work to improve the results of the Combined Phrase-decomposition/PLCG, developing the DISTALL system [107, 108] for simulation. The learned performance cases in the DISTALL system are hierarchically linked, in the same way as the note groupings they represent. Hence when the system is learning sets of expressive cases, it links together the feature sets for a level 3 grouping with all the level 2 and level 1 note groupings it contains. When a new piece is presented for performance, and the system is looking at a particular level 3 grouping of the new piece, say X—and X contains a number of level 2 and level 1 subgroupings—then not only are the score features of X compared to all level 3 cases in the memory, but the subgroupings of X are compared to the subgroupings of the compared level 3 cases as well. There have been measures available which can do such a comparison in case-based learning before DISTALL (e.g. RIBL [36]). However, DISTALL does it in a way more appropriate to expressive performance—giving a more equal weighting to subgroupings within a grouping, and giving this system a high expressive representation.

Once again correlation testing was done with a similar set of experiments to Sect. 19.3.4.5. All 16 generated performances had smaller dynamics errors relative to the originals than a robotic/neutral performance had. For tempo, 11 of the 16 generated performances were better than a robotic/neutral performance. Correlations varied from 0.89 for dynamics in Mozart K283 to 0.23 for tempo in Mozart K332. The mean correlation for dynamics was 0.7 and for tempo was 0.52. A performance generated by this DISTALL system was entered into RenCon 2002. The competition CSEMP included a simple accompaniment system where dynamics and timing changes calculated for the melody notes were interpolated to allow their application to the accompaniment notes as well. Another addition was a simple heuristic for performing grace notes: the sum of durations of all grace notes for a main note is set equal to 5% of the main note's duration, and the 5% of duration is divided equally amongst the grace notes. The performance was the top-scored automated performance at RenCon 2002—ahead of Kagurame (Sect. 19.3.4.2), MIS (Sect. 19.3.2.1) and Ha-Hi-Hun (Sect. 19.3.4.3)—and it beat one non-automated system.

19.3.5 Statistical Graphical Models

19.3.5.1 Music Plus One

The Music Plus One system [90–92] is able to deal with multiple instrument polyphonic performances. It has the ability to adjust performances of polyphonic sound files (e.g. orchestral works) to fit as accompaniment for solo performers. This CSEMP contains two modules: Listen and Play modules. Listen uses a Hidden Markov Model (HMM) to track live audio and find the soloist's place in the score in real time. Play uses a Bayesian Belief Network (BBN) which, at any point in a soloist performance and based on the performance so far, tries to predict the timing of the next note the soloist will play. Music Plus One's BBN is trained by listening to the soloist. As well as timing, the system learns the loudness for each phrase of notes. However, loudness learning is deterministic—it performs the same for each accompaniment of the piece once trained, not changing based on the soloist changing their own loudness. Expressive representation is at the note level for timing and phrase level for loudness.

The BBN assumes a smooth changing in tempo, so any large changes in tempo (e.g. a new section of a piece) need to be manually marked up. For playing MIDI files for accompaniment, the score needs to be divided up manually into phrases for dynamics; for using audio files for accompaniment such a division is not needed. When the system plays back the accompaniment it can play it back in multiple expressive interpretations dependent on how the soloist plays. Hence, it has learned a flexible (almost tempo-independent) concept of the soloist's expressive intentions for the piece.

There is no test reported for this system—the author states their impression that the level of musicality obtained by the system is surprisingly good, and asks readers to evaluate the performance themselves by going to the website and listening. Music Plus One is actually being used by composers, and for teaching music students. It came first at RenCon 2003 in the compulsory section with a performance of Chopin's Prelude No. 15 "Raindrop", beating Ha-Hi-Hun (Sect. 19.3.4.3),

Kagurame (Sect. 19.3.4.2) and Widmer's system (Sect. 19.3.4.6). To train Music Plus One for this, several performances were recorded played by a human, using a MIDI keyboard. These were used to train the BBN. The model was extended to include velocities for each note, as well as times, with the assumption that the velocity varies smoothly (like a random walk) except at hand-identified phrase boundaries. Then, a mean performance was generated from the trained model.

As far as performance creativity goes, the focus on this system is not so much to generate expressive performances, as to learn the soloist's expressive behaviour and react accordingly in real time. However, the system has an "implicit" method of creating new performances of the accompaniment—the soloist can change their performance during playback. There is another creative application of this system: multiple pieces have been composed for use specifically with the Music Plus One system—pieces which could not be properly performed without the system. One example contains multiple sections where a musician plays 7 notes while the other plays 11. Humans would find it difficult to do this accurately, whereas a soloist and the system can work together properly on this complicated set of polyrhythms.

19.3.5.2 ESP Piano System

Grindlay's [48] ESP Piano system is a polyphonic CSEMP designed to simulate expressive playing of pieces of piano music which consist of a largely monophonic melody, with a set of accompanying chords, known as *homophony*. A Hidden Markov Model learns expressive performance using music features such as whether the note is the first or last of the piece, the position of the note in its phrase, and the notes duration relative to its start and the next note's start (called its "articulation" here). The expressive representation is up to the phrase level. Phrase division is done manually, though automated methods are discussed. The accompaniment is analysed for a separate set of music features, some of which are like the melody music features. Some are unique to chords—for example the level of consonance/dissonance of the code (based on a method called Euler's Solence). Music features are then mapped on to a number of expressive actions such as (for melody) the duration deviation, and the velocity of the note compared to the average velocity. For the accompaniment similar actions are used as well as some chord-only actions, like the relative onset of chord notes (similar to the Kagurame Chord Time Lag, in Sect. 19.3.4.2). These chordal values are based on the average of the values for the individual notes in the chord.

Despite the focus of this system on homophony, tests were only reported for monophonic melodies, training the HMM on 10 graduate performances of Schumann's Träumerei. 10 out of 14 listeners ranked the expressive ESP output over the inexpressive version. 10 out of 14 ranked the ESP output above that of an undergraduate performance. 4 out of 7 preferred the ESP output to a graduate student performance.

19.3.6 Other Regression Methods

19.3.6.1 Drumming System

Thus far in this review only pitched instrument systems have been surveyed—mainly piano, saxophone and trumpet. A system for non-pitched (drumming) expression will now be examined. In the introduction about it was mentioned that pop music enthusiastically utilised the "robotic" aspects of MIDI sequencers. However, eventually pop musicians wanted a more realistic sound to their electronic music, and "humanization" systems were developed for drum machines that added random tempo deviations to beats. Later systems also incorporated what are known as *Grooves*—a fixed pattern of tempo deviations which are applied to a drum beat or any part of a MIDI sequence (comparable to a one-level Clynes pulse set, see Sect. 19.3.1.3). Such groove systems have been applied commercially in mass-market systems like Propellorhead Reason, where it is possible to generate *Groove Templates* from a drum track and apply it to any other MIDI track [19]. However, just as some research has suggested limitations in the application of Clynes' composer pulses, so [122] research shows the limits of groove templates. Their analysis of multi-voiced Brazillian drumming recordings found that groove templates could only account for 30% of expressive timing.

Wright and Berdahl investigated other methods to capture the expressive timing using a system that learns from audio files. The audio features examined were a note's timbre, metric position and rhythmic context. The rhythmic context being the timbres and relative temporal position of notes within 1 beat of the input notes—thus giving the system a narrow expressive representation. The system learns to map these audio features onto the timing deviations of each non-pitched note; it is not designed to generate creative performances but to simulate them. The mapping model is based on regression between audio features and timing deviation (versus a quantized version of the beat). Three different methods of learning the mapping model were tried: Kernel Ridge Regression [51], Gaussian Process Regression [93] and kNN [53] methods. This learning approach was found to track the expressive timing of the drums much better than the groove templates, clearly demonstrated in their graphs showing the error over the drum patterns. All three learning methods were found to give approximately equal accuracy, though it is believed that Gaussian Process Regression has the greatest room for improvement. Examples are provided online. Note that the system is not only limited to Brazilian drumming, Wright and Berdahl also tested it on Reggae rhythms with similar success.

19.3.6.2 KCCA Piano System

An interesting application of kernel regression methods to expressive performance is the system by Dorard et al. [35]. Their main aim is simulatory, to imitate the style of a particular performer and allow new pieces to be automatically performed using the learned characteristics of the performer. A performer is defined based on the "Worm" representation of expressive performance [33]. The worm is a visualisation tool for the dynamics and tempo aspects of expressive performance. It uses a 2D representation with tempo on the x-axis and loudness on the y-axis. Then, as the piece plays, at fixed periods in the score (e.g. once per bar) an average is calculated for each period and a filled circle plotted on the graph at the average. Past circles remain on the graph, but their colour fades and size decreases, as time passes—thus creating the illusion of a wriggling worm whose tail fades off into the distance in time. If the computer played an expressionless MIDI file then its worm would stand still, not wriggling at all.

The basis of Dorard's approach is to assume that the score and the human performances of the score are two views of the musical semantic content, thus enabling a correlation to be drawn between the worm and the score. The system focuses on homophonic piano music—a continuous upper melody part and an accompaniment—and divides the score into a series of chord and melody pairs. Kernel Canonical Correlation Analysis (KCCA) [99] is then used, a method which looks for a common semantic representation between two views. Its expressive representation is based on the note-group level, since KCCA is looking to find correlations between short groups of notes and the performance worm position. An addition needed to be made to the learning algorithm to prevent extreme expressive changes in tempo and dynamics. This issue is a recurring problem in a number of CSEMPs (see the Artificial Neural Network Models in Sect. 19.3.3, Sibelius in Sect. 19.3.1.9, and also Sect. 19.3.7.3).

Testing was performed on Frédéric Chopin's Etude 3, Opus 10—the system was trained on the worm of the first 8 bars, and then tried to complete the worm for bars 9 to 12. The correlation between the original human performance worm for 9 to 12 and the reconstructed worm was measured to be 0.95, whereas the correlation with a random worm was 0.51. However, the resulting performances were reported (presumably through informal listening tests) to not be very realistic.

19.3.7 Evolutionary Computation

A number of more recent CSEMPs have used evolutionary computation methods, such as Genetic Algorithms [79] or Multi-Agent Systems [62]. In general (but not always) such systems have opportunities for performance creativity. They often have a parameterization that is simple to change—for example, a fitness function. They also have an emergent [20] output which can sometimes produce unexpected but coherent results.

19.3.7.1 Genetic Programming Jazz Sax

Some of the first researchers to use EC in computer systems for expressive performance were Ramirez and Hazan. They did not start out using EC, beginning with a Regression Tree system for Jazz Saxophone [88]. This system will be described before moving on to the Genetic Programming (GP) approach, as it is the basis of their later GP work. A performance Decision Tree was first built using C4.5 [86]. This was built for musicological purposes—to see what kinds of rules were generated—not to generate any performances. The Decision Tree system had a

3-note-level expressive representation, and music features used to characterise a note included metrical position and some Narmour IR analysis. These features were mapped on to a number of performance actions from the training performances, such as lengthen/shorten note, play note early/late and play note louder/softer. Monophonic audio was used to build this decision tree using the authors' own spectral analysis techniques and five Jazz standards at 11 different tempos. The actual performing system was built as a Regression rather than Decision Tree, thus allowing continuous expressive actions. The continuous performance features simulated were duration, onset and energy variation (i.e. loudness). The learning algorithm used to build the tree was M5Rules [120] and performances could be generated via MIDI and via audio using the synthesis algorithms. In tests, the resulting correlations with the original performances were 0.72, 0.44 and 0.67 for duration, onset and loudness, respectively. Other modelling methods were tried (linear regression and 4 different forms of Support Vector Machines) but didn't fare as well correlation-wise.

Ramirez and Hazan's next system [52] was also based on Regression Trees, but these trees were generated using Genetic Programming (GP), which is ideal for building a population of "if–then" Regression Trees. GP was used to search for Regression Trees that best emulated a set of human audio performance actions. The Regression Tree models were basically the same as in their previous paper, but in this case a whole series of trees was generated, they were tested for fitness and then the fittest were used to produce the next generation of trees/programs (with some random mutations added). Fitness was judged based on a distance calculated from a human performance. Creativity and expressive representation are enhanced because, in addition to modelling timing and dynamics, the trees modelled the expressive combining of multiple score notes into a single performance note (consolidation), and the expressive insertion of one or several short notes to anticipate another performance note (ornamentation). These elements are fairly common in jazz saxophone. It was possible to examine these deviations because the fitness function was implemented using an Edit Distance [69] to measure score edits.

This evolution was continued until average fitness across the population of trees ceased to increase. The use of GP techniques was deliberately applied to give a *range* of options for the final performance since, as the authors say—"performance is an inexact phenomenon". Also because of the mutation element in Genetic Programming, there is the possibility of unusual performances being generated. So this CSEMP has quite a good potential for performance creativity. No evaluation was reported of the resulting trees' performances—but average fitness stopped increasing after 20 generations.

19.3.7.2 Sequential Covering Algorithm GAs

The Sequential Covering Algorithm genetic algorithm (GA) [89] uses Sequential Covering to learn performance. Each covering rule is learned using a GA, and a series of such rules are built up covering the whole problem space. In this paper, the authors return to their first (non-EC) paper's level of expressive representation—

looking at note level deviations *without* ornamentation or consolidation. However, they make significant improvements over their original non-EC paper. The correlation coefficients for onset, duration, and energy/loudness in the original system were 0.72, 0.44 and 0.67—but in this new system they were 0.75, 0.84 and 0.86—significantly higher. And this system also has the advantage of slightly greater creativity due to its GA approach.

19.3.7.3 Jazz Guitar

Another use of GAs in CSEMPS is for optimising the model for feature extraction from the melody to be performed [44]. This method can be viewed as a hybrid of GAs and the rule-based approach. The GA is used to optimise the model for detecting the guitar melody in jazz guitar recordings and a propositional rule learner algorithm is applied to create a model for expressive performance based on the melody and other musical features, including Narmour-type features. The recordings (16 polyphonic recordings of American jazz guitarist Grant Green) are cross-referenced with a MusicXML versions of the scores. The resulting accuracies were 70%, 56%, 63% and 52%, respectively, the ornamentation, duration, onset and energy features. Considering these are done using actual polyphonic audio, the results are very encouraging—though the system is focused on performance simulation rather than creativity.

19.3.7.4 Ossia

Like the Computational Music Emotion Rule System (Sect. 19.3.1.10), Dahlstedt's [27] Ossia is a CSEMP which incorporates both compositional and performance aspects. However, whereas CMERS was designed to operate on a composition, Ossia is able to generate *entirely new and expressively performed* compositions. Although it is grouped here as an EC learning system, technically Ossia is not a learning system. It is not using EC to learn how to perform like a human, but to *generate* novel compositions and performances. However, it is included in this section because its issues relate more closely to EC and learning systems than to any of the non-learning systems (the same reason applies for the system described in the Sect. 19.3.7.5). Ossia generates music through a novel representational structure that encompasses both composition and performance—Recursive Trees (generated by GAs). These are "upside down trees" containing both performance and composition information. The bottom leaves of the tree going from left to right represent actual notes (each with their own pitch, duration and loudness value) in the order they are played. The branches above the notes represent transformations on those notes. To generate music the tree is flattened—the "leaves" higher up act upon the leaves lower down when being flattened to produce a performance/composition. So, going from left to right in the tree represents music in time. The trees are generated recursively—this means that the lower branches of the tree are transformed copies of higher parts of the tree. Here, we have an element we argue is the key to combined performance and composition systems—a *common representation*—in this case transformations.

This issue of music representation is not something this survey has addressed explicitly, being in itself an issue worthy of its own review, for example, see [1, 29]. However, a moment will be taken to briefly discuss it now. The representation chosen for a musical system has a significant impact on the functionality—Ossia's representation is what leads to its combined composition and performance generation abilities. The most common music representation mentioned in this review has been MIDI, which is not able to encode musical structure directly. As a result, some MIDI-based CSEMPs have to supply multiple files to the CSEMP, a MIDI file together with files describing musical structure. More flexible representations than MIDI include MusicXML, ENP-score-notation [67], WEDELMUSIC XML [7], MusicXML4R [47], and the proprietary representations used by commercial software such as Sibelius, Finale, Notion, and Zenph High-Resolution MIDI [6] (which was recently used on a released CD of automated Disklavier re-performances of Glenn Gould).

Many of the performance systems described in this review so far *transform* an expressionless MIDI or audio file into an expressive version. Composition is often done in a similar way—motifs are *transformed* into new motifs, and themes are transformed into new expositions. Ossia uses a novel transformation-based music representation. In Ossia, transformations of note, loudness and duration are possible —the inclusion of note transformations here emphasising the composition aspect of the Ossia. The embedding of these transformations into recursive trees leads to the generation of gradual crescendos, decrescendos and duration curves—which sound like performance strategies to a listener. Because of this Ossia has a good level of performance creativity. The trees also create a structure of themes and expositions. Ossia uses a GA to generate a population of trees, and judges for fitness using such rules as number of notes per second, repetivity, amount of silence, pitch variation, and level of recursion. These fitness rules were developed heuristically by Dahlstedt through analysis-by-synthesis methods.

Ossia's level of expressive representation is equal to its level of compositional representation. Dahlstedt observes "The general concept of recapitulation is not possible, as in the common ABA form. This does not matter so much in short compositions, but may be limiting". So Ossia's expressive representation would seem to be within the A's and B's, giving it a note to section-level expressive representation. In terms of testing, the system has not been formally evaluated though it was exhibited as an installation at Gaudeamus Music Week in Amsterdam. Examples are also available on Dahlstedt's website, including a composed suite. The author claims that the sound examples "show that the Ossia system has the potential to generate and perform piano pieces that could be taken for human contemporary compositions". The examples on the website are impressive in their natural quality. The question of how to test a combined performance and composition, when that system is not designed to simulate but to create, is a sophisticated problem which will not be addressed here. Certainly, listening tests are a possibility but these may be biased by the preferences of the listener (e.g. preferring pre-1940s classical music, or pop music). Another approach is musicological analysis but the problem then becomes that musicological tools are not available for all genres and all periods—for example, musicology is more developed for pre-1940 than post-1940 art music.

An example score from Ossia is described which contains detailed dynamics and articulations, and subtle tempo fluctuations and rubato. This subtlety raises another issue—scores generated by Ossia in common music notation had to be simplified to be simply readable by humans. The specification of exact microfeatures in a score can lead to it being unplayable except by computer or the most skilled concert performer. This has a parallel in a compositional movement which emerged in the 1970s "The New Complexity", involving composers such as Brian Ferneyhough and Richard Barret [113] In "The New Complexity" elements of the score are often specified down to the microfeature level, and some scores are described as almost unplayable. Compositions such as this, whether by human or computer, bring into question the whole composition/performance dichotomy (These issues also recall the end of Ian Pace's quote in the first section of this review.). However, technical skill limitations and common music notation scores are not necessary for performance if the piece is being written on and performed by a computer. Microfeatures can be generated as part of the computer (or computer-aided) composition process if desired. In systems such as Ossia and CMERS (Sect. 19.3.1.10), as in The New Complexity, the composition/performance dichotomy starts to break down—the dichotomy is really between macro-features and microfeatures of the music.

19.3.7.5 MASC

Before discussing the MASC system, another motivation for bringing composition and performance closer in CSEMPs should be highlighted. A significant amount of CSEMP effort is in analysing the musical structure of the score/audio. However, many *computer* composition systems generate a piece based on some structure which can often be made explicitly available. So in computer music it is often inefficient to have separate composition and expressive performance systems—i.e. where a score is generated and the CSEMP sees the score as a black box and performs a structure analysis. Greater efficiency and accuracy would require a protocol allowing the computer composition system to communicate structure information directly to the CSEMP, or—like Ossia—simply combine the systems using, for example, a common representation (where micro-timing and micro-dynamics are seen as an actual part of the composition process). A system which was designed to utilise this combination of performance and composition is the Multi-agent Affective Social Composition System MASC [64].

MASC is a multi-agent system that generates melody pitch sequences with a hierarchical structure. The agents have no explicit melodic intelligence and generate the pitches as a result of artificial emotional influence and communication between agents, and the melody's hierarchical structure is a result of the emerging agent social structure. The system is not a mapping from multi-agent interaction onto musical features, but actually utilises music for the agents to communicate artificial emotions. Each agent in the society learns its own growing tune during the interaction process, represented in Fig. 19.4.

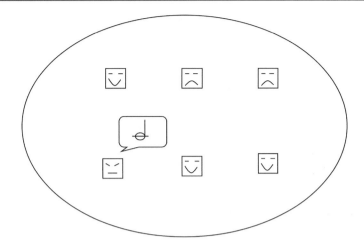

Fig. 19.4 Representation of the MASC interaction process. Agents communicate tunes with affectively transformed features—based on their current affective state. Other agents' affective states are transformed during their listening process

The following are some of the key features of the system. MASC usually consists of a small-medium size—2 to 16—collection of agents, but can be more. Each agent can perform monophonic MIDI tunes and learn monophonic tunes from other agents. An agent has an affective state, an artificial emotional state which affects how it performs the music to other agents; for example, a "happy" agent will perform their music more "happily". An agent's affective state is in turn affected by the affective content of the music performed to it; for example, if "sad" music is performed to a happy agent, the agent will become a little "more sad". Agents can be made to only learn tunes performed to them if the affective content of the tune is similar enough to their current affective state. Learned tunes are added to the end of their current tune. Agents develop opinions/trust of other agents that perform to them, depending on how much the other agents can help their tunes grow. These opinions affect who they interact with in the future. A final contribution of MASC is the linear music-emotion analysing model which takes as input a monophonic MIDI file and estimates its affective content. MASC has not been as rigorously tested as some, and is focused on monophonic tunes.

In terms of testing, the research demonstrates diagrammatically how the interaction structure relates to the music's hierarchical structure. An example is given showing the musical structure building up and how it related to the agents' social structure. It is also demonstrated how different combinations of initial emotions lead to different social dynamics. MASC's potential for creative performance is high, as agent's behaviour is driven by the metaphor of emotion—which the user can adjust —rather than simulating specific performance styles.

19.4 A Detailed Example: IMAP

As already discussed, the final reviewed example will be done in depth to give the reader more insight into the details of CSEMP design, testing and creativity. This example will be IMAP, the description of which will require some background introduction to Evolutionary Computation. IMPA was presented for the first time in 2010, in [76].

19.4.1 Evolutionary Computation

Evolutionary Computation (EC) methods have been successfully applied to algorithmic composition (please refer to [75] for an introduction to a number of such systems). The great majority of these systems use genetic algorithms [45], or GA, to produce melodies and rhythms. In these systems, music parameters are represented as "genes" of software agents, and GA operators are applied to "evolve" music according to given fitness criteria.

Progress in applying EC to CSEMP has been reported [87, 88, 126, 127]. EC-based CSEMPs have all applied the neo-Darwinian approach of selecting the musically fittest genes to be carried into the next generation. IMAP is focused, however, on investigating the application of an alternative EC approach to expressive performance—one that is based on cultural transmission rather than genetic transmission.

Musical behaviour in human beings is based both in our genetic heritage and also on cultural heritage [32]. One way of achieving a cultural, as opposed to genetic, transmission is through imitation of behaviour [9, 125]. Work on the application of this imitative cultural approach to algorithmic composition was initiated by [78]. In this chapter, the cultural transmission methodology is followed up with an application of an imitative multi-agent systems approach to expressive music performance: the Imitative Multi-Agent Performer, or IMAP.

In the GA model of behaviour transmission, a population of agents is generated having its own behaviour defined by their "genetic" code. The desirability of the behaviour is evaluated by a global fitness function, and agents with low fitness are often discarded, depending on which version of the algorithm is adopted [45]. Then, a new population of agents is generated by combination and deterministic or non-deterministic transformation of the genes of the highest-scoring agents.

Conversely, in the imitation model of behaviour transmission, an agent interacts with one or more other agents using a protocol that communicates the first agent's behaviour to the other agents. The other agents evaluate the first agent's behaviour based on some evaluation function, and if the evaluation scores highly enough, one or more of the other agents will change their own behaviours based on the first agent's behaviour. The evaluation function in the imitation model plays a similar role to the fitness function in the GA model. However, in imitative multi-agent systems, the evaluation function is particularly suited for the design of EC systems using a non-global fitness function, for example, by giving each agent their own evaluation function.

The potential for diversity is a desirable trait for a system for generating creative and novel expressive music performances—as opposed to replicating existing ones —because there is no objectively defined optimal performance for a musical score [10, 87]. Performance is a subjective, creative act. Previous work, described earlier in this chapter, on genetic transmission in generating expressive music performance has been significantly motivated by the desire to generate a variety of performances. As will be demonstrated herein, there is even more scope for such variety in IMAP because a multiplicity of evaluation functions is used. Furthermore, there is scope for easily controlling the level of diversity in IMAP.

It is not the intention to compare the imitative approach with the GA approach, because both approaches have their own merits and should be considered as complementary approaches. [87] demonstrated the validity of a GA model in their SaxEx model discussed earlier. The IMAP experiments later in this chapter demonstrate the validity of our imitative approach.

One obvious measure of validity is whether the system generates performances that are expressive. The other two measures of validity relate to those elements of the imitative approach, which differentiate it from the standard GA approach—in particular, the ability to easily provide the system with a number of parallel interacting fitness functions. Hence, IMAP will be evaluated in terms of

- The expressiveness of IMAP-generated performances (note, however, that this is not assessed by means of experiments with human subjects; we assess how well the agents can generate performances that embody their preference weights)
- Performance-diversity generation and control of the level of diversity
- The ability to control diversity when it is being affected by multiple musical elements simultaneously.

Imitative learning has been frequently used in other multi-agent systems research [82]. However, to the best of our knowledge, IMAP is the first application of such methods to the generation of expressive musical performances.

19.4.2 IMAP Overview

Each agent has two communication functions: it can listen to the performance of another agent, and it can perform to another agent. All agents are provided with the same monophonic melody—the melody from which expressive performances will be generated. In all interactions, all agents perform the same melody, usually with different expressive actions. Agents in IMAP have two types of expressive actions: changes in tempo and changes in note loudness. Each agent also has a musical evaluation function based on a collection of rules, where different agents give different weightings to the rules and use the combination to evaluate the performances they hear. Initially, agents will perform with random expressive actions. If they evaluate another agent's expressive performance highly enough through their evaluation function, then they will adjust their own future performances towards the other agent's expressive actions. As this process continues, a repertoire of different expressive performances evolves across the population.

19.4.2.1 Agent Evaluation Functions

The agents' evaluation functions could be generated in a number of ways. As discussed earlier, one of the most common methods used in CSEMPs is providing agents with rules describing what features an expressive performance should have. For example, see Sects. 19.3.1.1, 19.3.1.2 and 19.3.1.7. This approach was chosen for IMAP because it was desired to provide the means to explicitly change the influence of various musical factors on the final expressive performance. Machine-learning approaches, such as those based on artificial neural networks, tend to develop a more implicit reasoning system [8]. An explicitly described rule set allows for simpler controllability of a multi-agent system. However, unlike many rule-based CSEMPs, the agents in IMAP do not use their rules to generate their performances. Rather, they use them to evaluate performances (their own and those of other agents) and therefore choose which other agents to imitate.

This will become clearer as the system is introduced. In short, the more highly another agent's performance is scored by the parameterized evaluation function of a listening agent, the more highly the listening agent will regard the performing agent.

An agent's evaluation function is defined at two stages: the Rule Level and the Analytics Level. The first stage—the Rule Level—involves a series of five rules derived from previous work on generative performance. The second stage—the Analytics Level—involves a group of musical analysis functions that the agent uses to represent the structure of the musical score. The Rule Level and the Analytics Level are both parameterized to allow the user to control which elements have most influence on the resulting performances.

For the Rule Level, a large number of rules available from previous research into CSEMP could have been used. To keep the rule list of IMAP manageable, only five rules were selected, bearing in mind the application and controllability of the imitative approach. One should note, however, that these rules are not absolute; as will be demonstrated later, the agents often create performances that do not fully conform to all rules. For this reason, we refer to these rules as *preference rules*.

The five preferences rules of the Rule Level relate to *Performance Curves*, *Note Punctuation*, *Loudness Emphasis*, *Accentuation* and *Boundary Notes*. Each preference rules is based on previous research into music performance, as follows. Many of these ideas have been discussed previously in this chapter.

Rule 1: Performance Curves

Performance deviations for tempo between note group boundaries (e.g. motif and phrase boundaries) should increase for the beginning part of the group and decrease for the second part of the group; how these "parts" are defined is explained later. This is consistent with the expressive shapes, which are well established in the field of CSEMP (e.g. Sects. 19.3.1.1 and 19.3.1.2). This shape should also occur for the loudness deviations (see Sect. 19.3.1.2).

Rule 2: Note Punctuation

According to this rule, the ending note of a group of notes should be lengthened [38].

Rule 3: Loudness Emphasis

Performance deviations for loudness should emphasise the metrical, melodic and harmonic structure [25, Sundberg 1983].

Rule 4: Boundary Notes

The last note in a note grouping should have an expressive tempo, which is either a local minimum or local maximum [25].

Rule 5: Accentuation

Any note at a significantly accentuated position (as defined later) must either have a lengthened duration value or a local loudness maximum [13, 25].

19.4.2.2 Evaluation Equations

These five preference rules of the Rule Level were implemented as a set of evaluation equations, which are detailed in the following sections. The user can change the influence of a preference rule in the final evaluation through the setting of weights. The rules take as input the result of a musical score analysis done by four analysis functions in the Analytics Level, namely *Local Boundary Detection Model (LBDM)*, *Metric Hierarchy*, *Melodic Accent* and *Key Change*. A detailed explanation of these analysis functions is beyond the scope of this chapter; the reader is invited to consult the given references.

- **Local Boundary Detection Model (LBDM)**: The first of these, LBDM, takes a monophonic melody as input and returns a curve that estimates the grouping structure of the music; that is, where the note–group boundaries are and how important each boundary is [13]. Each adjacent note pair is given an LBDM value. The higher the value, the more likely that the interval is at a grouping boundary; and the higher the value at a boundary, the more important the boundary is. This function allows an agent to express aspects of the grouping structure of the music.
- **Metric Hierarchy** The second function is the Metric Hierarchy function, which uses the Lerdahl and Jackendoff [68] method of assigning notes a position in a metric hierarchy. As discussed earlier, in most Western European classical music, each note has a position in a metric hierarchy. For example, a piece in 4/4 time might have a note with a strong beat at the start of every bar and a weaker beat half-way through each bar. The Metric Hierarchy function is implemented in IMAP as a function that takes as input a melody and returns the strength of each beat (A detailed explanation of the implementation is beyond the scope of this chapter; it suffices to say that the representation does not explicitly include

information about bar lines and time signatures.). Thus, it allows an agent to express aspects of the metric structure in its performance.

- **Melodic Accent**: Another form of accent analysis used in the Analysis Level is the Melodic Accent. Thomassen [105] proposes a methodology for analysing the importance of each note in a melody; each note is assigned an importance value. This allows an agent to express aspects of the melodic structure in its performance.
- **Key Change**: The fourth function in the Analysis Level is the Key Change analysis. Krumhansl [66] introduces an algorithm, based on perceptual experiments, for analysing changes of key in a melody. This algorithm allows an agent to express aspects of the harmonic structure in its performance.

Therefore, an agent will represent the score by its note groupings, metric hierarchy, melodic accents and key changes, although different agents may see the music score differently depending on how they parameterize the functions in the Analytics Level. Then, based on the five preference rules, the agents will prefer certain expression deviations for different parts of the musical score, where the types of expressive deviations preferred depend on an agent's parameterization of the preference rules in the Rules Level.

19.4.2.3 Agent Function Definitions

The evaluation function $E(P)$ of an agent evaluating a performance P is defined as

$$E(P) = w_{Tem} * E_{Tem}(P) + w_{Lou} * E_{Lou}(P) \tag{19.1}$$

E_{Tem} and E_{Lou} are the agent's evaluation of how well a performance fits with its preference for expressive deviations in tempo and loudness, respectively. The preference weights w_{Tem} and w_{Lou} define how much an agent focuses on timing elements of expression in relation to loudness elements of expression. The evaluation functions for tempo and loudness are defined using evaluation sub-functions E_{iTem} and E_{iLou}, which evaluate all five preference rules discussed earlier. Indices 1–5 relate to preference rules 1–5, respectively,

$$E_{Tem} = w_{1Tem} * E_{1Tem} + w_{2Tem} * E_2 + w_{4Tem} \\ * E_{4Tem} + w_{5Tem} * E_5 \tag{19.2}$$

$$E_{Lou} = w_{1Lou} * E_{1Lou} + w_{1Lou} * E_1 \\ + w_{4Lou} * E_{4Lou} \tag{19.3}$$

The E_{1Tem} and E_{1Lou} functions refer to preference rule 1 and affect both tempo and loudness, respectively. Function E_2 refers to preference rule 2 and affects only tempo. Similarly, function E_3 refers to preference rule 3 and only affects loudness. Functions E_{4Tem} and E_{4Lou} refer to preference rule 4 and affects both loudness and tempo, and unction E_5 refers to rule 5 and only affects tempo.

The weights w_{iTem}, and w_{iLou} allow the setting of agent preferences for each of the five rules, though not all rules need to be part of both functions because some apply only to tempo or only to loudness. The sub-functions are defined in terms of the deviations of tempo and loudness from the nominal score values found in a performance. The sub-functions are given in Eqs. (19.4)–(19.10).

Equations (19.4) and (19.5) implement the preference rule 1.

$$
E_{1Tem} = \sum_{1}^{n} \left(\sum_{i=s_{start}}^{s_{turn}-1} \begin{cases} 1 & (dev_{Tem}(i+1) > dev_{Tem}(i)) \\ 0 & (dev_{Tem}(i+1) \leq dev_{Tem}(i)) \end{cases} \right.
$$
$$
\left. + \sum_{i=s_{turn}}^{s_{end}-1} \begin{cases} 1 & (dev_{Tem}(i+1) < dev_{Tem}(i)) \\ 0 & (dev_{Tem}(i+1) \geq dev_{Tem}(i)) \end{cases} \right)
\tag{19.4}
$$

$$
E_{1Lou} = \sum_{1}^{n} \left(\sum_{i=s_{start}}^{s_{turn}-1} \begin{cases} 1 & (dev_{Lou}(i+1) > dev_{Lou}(i)) \\ 0 & (dev_{Lou}(i+1) \leq dev_{Lou}(i)) \end{cases} \right.
$$
$$
\left. + \sum_{i=s_{turn}}^{s_{end}-1} \begin{cases} 1 & (dev_{Lou}(i+1) < dev_{Lou}(i)) \\ 0 & (dev_{Lou}(i+1) \geq dev_{Lou}(i)) \end{cases} \right)
\tag{19.5}
$$

The i-th note's tempo and loudness expressive deviations are written as $dev_{Tem}(i)$ and $dev_{Lou}(i)$ in the sub-functions. By virtue of the first (outer) summation in each equation, the calculations are applied to each note grouping separately and the scores summed across the whole performance. The index values s_{start} and s_{end} are the note indices at which a note grouping starts and ends, and s_{turn} is its *turning point*. There is no fixed threshold for defining boundaries using the LBDM method. One was chosen, which was found sufficient for the purposes of IMAP: for a note to be a boundary note, its LBDM value must be greater than the average LBDM value of the whole melody. The turning point of a grouping is the point at which the expressive tempo defined by the preference rule 1 peaks before dropping; it is not defined explicitly by LBDM either. In IMAP the "third most important note" in the group is selected as representing a boundary between the first part of the group and the last part. So the turning point is defined as the note having the third highest LBDM in the group: the start and end notes will be the two highest LBDM values. This definition of turning point was found to be more musically meaningful than simply taking the mid-point between the start and end notes. In order to ensure that every note grouping has at least one potential turning point, another constraint is placed on note groupings: they must contain at least four notes, i.e. three intervals.

Equation (19.6) is summed over all note groups in the melody. This sub-function implements the preference rule 2. A tempo deviation value equal to 1 means the performance is the same as the nominal value in the score, a value greater than one means louder or faster than the score. This is applied to each note group in the melody.

$$E_2 = \sum_1^n \begin{cases} 1 & (dev_{Tem}(s_{end}) < 1) \\ 0 & (dev_{Tem}(s_{end}) \geq 1) \end{cases} \tag{19.6}$$

Equation (19.7) implements the preference rule 3. The curve $s_A(i)$ used in this equation is the *accentuation curve*, which is generated by a weighted sum of three other curves: *melodic accent*, *metrical hierarchy* and the *key change*, thus representing multiple musical elements (Note: the notion of "curve" here is broadly metaphorical, it is not a mathematical curve in the strict sense of the term).

$$E_3 = \sum_{i=1}^{q-1} \begin{cases} 1 & (\Delta d * \Delta dev_{Lou} > 0) \\ 0 & (\Delta d * \Delta dev_{Lou} \leq 0) \end{cases} \quad where$$
$$\Delta d = s_{A(i-1)} - s_{A(i)} \tag{19.7}$$
$$\Delta dev_{Lou} = dev_{Lou}(i+1) - dev_{Lou}(i)$$

The melodic accent curve moves higher for more important melodic notes [105], whereas the metrical hierarchy curves moves higher for notes that are more important in the metrical hierarchy [68]. The key change curve moves higher the further away the melody moves from the estimated key [66] of the previous N bars, the default being two bars. These three curves are normalised, and then weighted based on an agent's preferences, and added to generate the accentuation curve $s_A(i)$. Equation (19.7) will evaluate more highly if the loudness deviation curve of a performance follows the same direction as this accentuation curve, encouraging the emphasis of the parts of the performance based on elements of their melodic, metrical and harmonic properties.

Figure 19.5 shows examples of accentuation and loudness curves (as well as the LBDM and tempo deviation curves) for a single agent, given a sequence of ten notes. This sort of analysis is done once per agent.

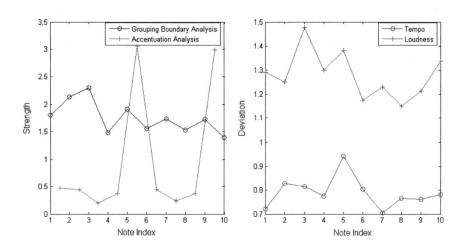

Fig. 19.5 Example characteristics of a single agent

In Fig. 19.5, both x-axes refer to note index, where 1 is the first note in the score, 2 the second note, etc. The left side of Fig. 19.5, shows part of an example LBDM curve (circled points) used to define grouping boundaries, and an accentuation curve (crossed points) used for expressive loudness. The y-axis is the normalised strengths of the curves. It is not the absolute strength that is important but the relative values. The right side of Fig. 19.5 shows the resulting deviation curves for tempo (circles) and loudness (crosses) after a number of iterations. A deviation greater than 1 implies an increase in tempo, or an increase in loudness, a deviation less than 1 implies tempo decrease or loudness decrease.

Equations (19.8) and (19.9) implement the preference rule 4. The rule is only applied to accentuated notes $\{a_1, ..., a_m\}$, which are defined as those notes i whose value on the accentuation curve $s_A(i)$ is a local maximum on the s_A curve. This definition chooses notes whose metric, melodic or harmonic properties make them more significant than the notes surrounding them. The values of Eqs. (19.8) and (19.9) are higher if an accentuated note is, respectively: (i) reduced in tempo more than its neighbour notes, or (ii) played with a higher loudness.

$$E_{4Tem} = \sum_{j=a_1}^{a_m} \begin{cases} 1 & (dev_{Tem}(j) < dev_{Tem}(j-1) \ and \\ & dev_{Tem}(j) < dev_{Tem}(j+1)) \\ 0 & (otherwise) \end{cases} \tag{19.8}$$

$$E_{4Lou} = \sum_{j=a_1}^{a_m} \begin{cases} 1 & (dev_{Lou}(j) < dev_{Lou}(j-1) \ and \\ & dev_{Lou}(j) < dev_{Lou}(j+1)) \\ 0 & (otherwise) \end{cases} \tag{19.9}$$

Equation (19.10) implements the preference rule 5, checking that notes at the end of a group have a higher or lower tempo deviation, compared to the notes on either side.

$$E_5 = \sum_1^n \begin{pmatrix} 1 & (dev_{Tem}(s_{end}) - dev_{Tem}(s_{end}-1)) \\ & *(dev_{Tem}(s_{end}) - dev_{Tem}(s_{end}+1)) > 0 \, . \\ 0 & (otherwise) \end{pmatrix} \tag{19.10}$$

With the above Eqs. (19.1)–(19.10), a user can set weights to control how an agent represents or, speaking metaphorically, "sees" the score, and also, how the agent prefers such a "seen" score to be performed.

19.4.2.4 Agent Cycle

Agents are initialised with evaluation weights for their evaluation functions, and with a common monophonic score in MIDI form, which they will perform. Agents are also initialised with an initial performance. This will be a set of expressive deviations from the score in loudness and tempo, which are implemented when the agent plays to another agent. These initial deviations are usually set randomly but they can be set by the user should one wish to do so. Default minimum and maximum values used are for tempo 55 and 130% of nominal, and for loudness 75 and 125%. These values were established intuitively after experimenting with different ranges. Agents have a learning rate between 0 and 100%. If an agent with a learning rate $L\%$ hears a performance P, which it prefers to its own, then it will move its own performance deviations linearly towards P by $L\%$. An agent with a learning rate of 100% will allow another agent's performance to influence 100% of its own performance. That is, the agent will replace its performance entirely with any it hears, which it prefers to its own. An agent with a learning rate of 0% will ignore all other performances it hears.

The core algorithm of the agents' interaction cycle is given below. Note that the algorithm shown here is sequential, but in reality, the agents are asynchronous, in the sense that all agents are operating simultaneously in separate threads.

Start of Cycle 1

An agent is selected to perform, say agent **A1**

Agent **A1** performs

All agents **Aj** apart from **A1** evaluate **A1**'s performance, to get **Ej1**

If an agent **Aj**'s evaluation **Ej1** is greater than its evaluation of its own performance,

>   then **Aj** moves its own expressive performance deviations closer to

>>   **A1**'s performance by an amount defined by the learning rate.

An agent is selected to perform, say agent **A2**

Agent **A2** performs

All agents **Aj** apart from **A2** evaluate **A2**'s performance, to get **Ej2**

If an agent **Aj**'s evaluation **Ej2** is greater than its evaluation of its own performance,

>   then **Aj** moves its own expressive performance deviations closer to

>>   **A2**'s performance by an amount defined by the learning rate.

…

Continue this process until all agents have performed, then Cycle 1 is complete

End of Cycle 1

Repeat cycles until some user-defined stopping condition is met.

19.4.3   User-Generated Performances of IMAP

As was discussed earlier, for performance creativity, a balance needs to exist between automation and creative flexibility. In IMAP there are a number of weights, which need to be defined for an agent's evaluation function. Table 19.4 lists all the weights that need to be set in IMAP. Although a set of nine weights may seem too large for practical performance creativity, in reality many of these weights

Table 19.4 List of evaluation weights for IMAP. These are the weights that can be set in Eqs. (19.1), (19.2) and (19.3) by the user to influence the final expressive performance. The nine weights define the effects of the five rules in the Rules Level

Weight name ("Preference for...")	Weight label	Applied to
All rules tempo-based effects	w_{Tem}	Evaluation function (1)
All rules loudness-based effects	w_{Tem}	Evaluation function (1)
Rule (I) tempo effects	w_{1Tem}	Tempo evaluation function (2)
Rule (II) tempo effects	w_{2Tem}	Tempo evaluation function (2)
Rule (IV) tempo effects	w_{4Tem}	Tempo evaluation function (2)
Rule (V) tempo effects	w_{5Tem}	Tempo evaluation function (3)
Rule (I) loudness effects	w_{1Lou}	Loudness evaluation function (3)
Rule (III) loudness effects	w_{3Lou}	Loudness evaluation function (3)
Rule (IV) loudness effects	w_{4Lou}	Loudness evaluation function (3)

can be fitted to default values and the remaining weights would still provide a wide scope for creativity. For example, users could simply adjust the top two weights of the equation hierarchy (w_{Tem} and w_{Lou}) for Eq. (19.1), fixing all other weights to their default values. This two weight set could be simply extended by also allowing the user to adjust the weights w_{4Tem} and w_{4Lou}—in Eqs. (19.2) and (19.3)—to change the amount of tempo and loudness emphasis, respectively, of accentuated notes. It is worth noting that the parameters in the Analytics Level can also be made available to users, for example, the user could set weights that would indirectly change the shape of the accentuation curve shown in Fig. 19.5.

Another key element of IMAP is how agents can have different "views" on what makes a good expressive performance. This provides an ability, which will be demonstrated later in the paper, for generating and controlling diversity in the results of the population learning. For example, a population whose initial preference weights are all very close will tend to learn a group of far more similar performances than a population whose initial weight values differ widely.

The method for generating expressive performances with IMAP will now be described. Before the first cycle of IMAP, a population size is defined; for example, 3, 10 or 50 agents. Larger populations may have the advantage of greater statistical stability and a larger choice of performances. Then, a learning rate needs to be set. In this paper, a global learning rate is used: all agents have the same learning rate, a default of 10%. A low learning rate was desired so as to allow agents to build up a good combination of performances through imitation. A learning rate closer to 100% would turn the system into more of a performance-swapping population rather than one for performance combining. However, too low a rate would slow convergence.

Concerning the question of how many cycles to run the system, one approach would be to define a fixed number of cycles. Another approach would be to define a more sophisticated stopping condition. A common form of stopping condition is a convergence criterion; for example, stopping when agents are no longer updating their performance deviations during the interactions. This normally occurs when no agent is hearing a performance better than its own performance. Another option is to base convergence on the average performance; that is, the average deviations across the whole of the population. Once this ceases to change by a significant amount per cycle—that amount defined by the user—convergence may be considered to have been achieved.

Three experiments with IMAP will be detailed below, which test the system in terms of capability of expression generation, generation of diversity and controlling the direction of the diversity.

19.4.4 Experiments and Evaluation

The melody of the piece Étude No. 3, Op. 10 by Frédéric Chopin (see bottom of Fig. 19.6 was used in the experiments that follow. Although IMAP is able to process whole pieces of (monophonic) music, for the sake of clarity only the first five bars of Chopin's piece were considered below.

19.4.4.1 Experiment 1: Can Agents Generate Performances Expressing Their "preference" Weights?

The purpose of this experiment is to demonstrate that the agents generate performances that express their "preference" weights. In order to show this clearly, two weight sets were used: set (A) $w_{Tem} = 1$, $w_{1Tem} = 1$, all other weights = 0; and set (B) $w_{Lou} = 1$, $w_{3Lou} = 1$, all other weights = 0. The first set of weights will only lead to preference rule 1 being applied, and only apply it to tempo, The second set of weights will lead to preference rule 3 being applied, and only apply it to loudness. If agents express the music structure through their weights, then a multi-agent system where agents have only the weight set A should generate

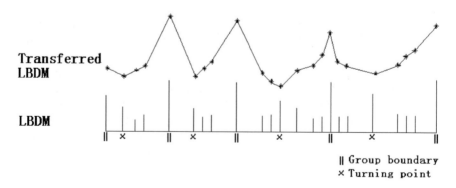

Fig. 19.6 Example of a transferred LBDM curve. The horizontal axis is time. In the lower graph, the LBDM values are plotted for each note pair/interval. The group boundaries and turning points are shown on the horizontal axis

performances whose tempo deviations clearly express the grouping structure (LBDM) of the music as defined by the preference rule 1. Similarly, if the agents are given the weight set B, then the generated loudness deviations should express the accentuation curve as implemented by the preference rule 3.

Two groups of experiments were run: 5 with weight set A and 5 with weight set B. A system of 15 agents was used, and 20 iterations were used for each run. For each run in the experiment with weight set A, the initial agent performances were randomised. For comparison purposes, exactly the same set of initial performances was used for the parallel run with weight set B; hence the 10 runs only use 5 sets of 15 random initial performances. In order to enable meaningful results for the scenario with the weight set A, a new curve is defined: the *transferred LBDM* curve. The transferred LBDM curve is our own adaptation of the LBDM curve into a form more easily comparable with the grouping expression. The transferred curve will have maxima at the boundary points on the LBDM curve, and minima at the turning points within each note group. The transferred LBDM is concave between boundary points. An example is shown in Fig. 19.6. The preference rule 1 can then be interpreted as saying that tempo curves should move in the opposite direction to the transferred LBDM curve, or equivalently that the reciprocal of the tempo curve should move in the same direction as the transferred LBDM curve.

In this experiment, the average performance was used to represent the performances evolved by the system: the tempo and loudness values are expressed as deviations from the average performance across all agents. The results of scenarios with weight sets A and B can be seen in Table 19.5, which shows the average correlations *Corr(x, y)* across the five runs for

(a) x = the transferred LBDM curve *tLBDM*
(b) x = the accentuation curve *Acc*
(c) y = the reciprocal of performance tempo *rTem*

Table 19.5 Results from Experiment 1 showing correlations for average performance across a population of agents. An increase in correlation between tempo deviations and the Transferred LDBM shows that the tempo deviations are expressing the grouping structure of the music. An increase in correlation between loudness and the accentuation curve shows that the loudness is expressing elements of the metric, melodic and harmonic structure of the music, as defined in the Accentuation Curve

	Before iterations	After iterations	Increase
Weight Set A (Tem)			
Corr(tLBDM, rTem)	0.49	0.61	0.11
Corr(tLBDM, Lou)	0.52	0.52	0
Corr(Acc, Lou)	0.5	0.52	0.02
Weight Set B (Lou)			
Corr(tLBDM, rTem)	0.49	0.49	0
Corr(tLBDM, Lou)	0.52	0.48	−0.04
Corr(Acc, Loud)	0.5	0.7	0.2

(d) y = the performance loudness *Lou*.

It can be seen that for the weight set A (a weight set that should cause grouping structure to be expressed, and use tempo deviations to express it) there is an increase in correlation between the transferred LBDM and the reciprocal performance tempo: *Corr(tLBDM, rTem)* = 0.11. For the weight set B (a weight set that should cause the accentuation curve to be expressed by loudness deviations), the only increase in correlation is between the accentuation curve and the loudness: *Corr(Acc, Lou)* = 0.2. These results show that the average agent performances are expressing the preference weights in the system. Figure 19.7 shows expressive deviations evolved by two agents for Chopin's melody.

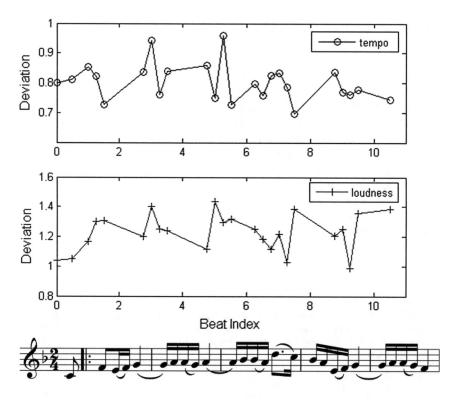

Fig. 19.7 Expressive deviations of two agents from Experiment 1 after 20 iterations. These are plotted above the first 5 bars of the melody of Chopin's Étude No. 3, Op. 10. The agent in the top graph (circles) has weight set A (tempo expression only), hence only tempo expression is plotted. The agent in the bottom graph (crosses) has weight set B (loudness evaluation only), hence only loudness expression is plotted

19.4.4.2 Experiment 2: Can One Control the Extent of the Performances' Diversity?

The purpose of this experiment was to demonstrate that IMAP can generate a diversity of performances, and that the user can control that diversity. In the experiment a group of 15 agents was used, each with randomly initialised performance deviations. A set of default weights W for Table 19.4 was defined. The experiment was set with two conditions. In Condition (i), agents' weights were assigned that could vary by no more than 10% from the corresponding default weight in set W. In Condition (ii) this variation was raised to 60%. So in Condition (ii) the preference weights varied much more widely across agents than in Condition (i). In each condition, 30 iterations were done and the coefficient of variation was calculated for deviations across the population, i.e. the ratio of standard deviation to mean for both tempo and loudness deviations. This experiment was repeated 10 times, each time with different initial random performance deviations. After 30 iterations in Condition (i) the resulting average coefficient of variation for Tempo and for Loudness deviations were 0.2%. In Condition (ii), with the more diverse preference weights, the value was 1.9%. This supports the ability of IMAP to generate a diversity of performances, and to control that diversity using the spread of preference weights.

19.4.4.3 Experiment 3: Controlling the Direction of the Performances' Diversity

The purpose of this experiment was to demonstrate that if agent preferences are biased a certain way in a subset of the population then the resulting performances will become affected by that preference. This demonstrated that although a diversity of performances can be produced as shown by Experiment 2, changing the distribution of weights enables one to change the distribution of outcomes in a coherent way. In order to show this, the same two weight sets as in Experiment 1 were used: (A) $w_{Tem} = 1$, $w_{1Tem} = 1$, all other weights = 0; and (B) $w_{Lou} = 1$, $w_{3Lou} = 1$, all other weights = 0. Thus, the weight set A only affects timing and the weight set B only affects loudness. The two weight sets do not overlap in their effect. In this experiment the population of 15 agents from Experiment 1 had another 5 agents added to it. The 15 agents (labelled group G2) are assigned weight set B and the 5 additional agents (labelled group G1) are assigned weight set A. The objective is to demonstrate that the addition of G1 to G2 leads to G1 influencing the performances of G2, in spite of the fact that G1 and G2 have mutually exclusive weight sets.

Before running the experiment, it is necessary to benchmark the level of random relative increase in evaluation that can be generated in the system. Specifically, given an agent system of 15 agents with preference weights that only affect loudness, how much would we expect their expressive tempo evaluation to increase relative to the increase relative to the increase in their expressive loudness evaluation, solely due to random fluctuations in tempo during iterations? These random fluctuations come from the randomised initial performances influencing each other. This was measured by taking a system of 15 agents with loudness-only weights (i.e. weight set B) and doing 5 runs of 25 cycles (The authors ran a number of versions of these experiments and it was clear that as little as 5 runs of 25 cycles were sufficient to generate meaningful random fluctuations in this context.). The results are shown in Table 19.6. The column and row headings in this table are defined as follows: "Lou" refers to the expressive loudness evaluation by Eq. (19.3), "Tem" refers to the expressive tempo evaluation by Eq. (19.2), "Before" is the average evaluation before iterations, "After" is the average evaluation after 25 iterations, "Change" is the change in evaluation before and after 20 iterations, and "TempoRatio" is the change in tempo evaluation divided by the change in loudness evaluation. Essentially, this ratio is a measure of the increase of tempo expressiveness relative to the increase of loudness expressiveness, as shown in Eq. (19.11).

$$Terpo\ Ratio\ (P) = \frac{Increase\_in\_E_{Tem}(P)}{Increase\_in\_E_{Lou}(P)} \tag{19.11}$$

The average value of *TempoRatio* across the five runs is equal to -0.013. This will be used as a measure of relative tempo evaluation increase due to random fluctuations in performance, since during these five runs there was no evaluation function pressure to increase tempo expressiveness. This particular *TempoRatio* = -0.013 is referred to as the *baseline value* of *TempoRatio*.

Next, another set of runs were done with 5 agents added to the system of 15 agents described above. As has been mentioned, the 5 agents (group G1) were assigned tempo-only weight set A, as opposed to the 15 agents (group G2) who had loudness-only weight set B. The results after 25 iterations are shown in Table 19.4. The column heading "AP2" is the average performance deviation of agents in G2. For instance, $G1(AP2) = 0.255$ is G1's average evaluation of G2's performances in Run 2 after 25 iterations.

The key measurements in Table 19.7 are G1's evaluations of G2's performances AP2, this will be written as $G1(AP2)$. Note that all values in "Increase G1(AP2)"

Table 19.6 Agents are given weight set B, the loudness-only weight set from Experiment 1. After 25 iterations, the increase in loudness evaluation (Eq. 19.3) and tempo evaluation (Eq. 19.2) were measured. The ratio of tempo evaluation increase to loudness evaluation increase was calculated

Weight set B	Run1		Run2		Run3		Run4		Run5	
	Lou	Tem	Lou	Tem	Lou	Tem	Lou	Tem	Lou	Tem
b	0.19	0.19	0.213	0.213	0.223	0.223	0.21	0.213	0.301	0.301
a	0.315	0.19	0.325	0.19	0.306	0.248	0.35	0.208	0.374	0.292
Change	0.125	0	0.112	−0.023	0.083	0.025	0.137	−0.005	0.073	−0.009
Ratio of Tem to Lou change	0		−0.205		0.301		−0.037		−0.123	

Table 19.7 Results for a 20 agents system made up of 15 agents with weight set B, and 5 agents with weight set A. After 25 iterations, the increase in loudness evaluation (Eq. 19.3) and tempo evaluation (Eq. 19.2) for the average performance of G2 was measured for both groups. The ratio of tempo evaluation increase to loudness evaluation increase was then calculated

		Run1	Run2	Run3	Run4	Run5
		AP2	AP2	AP2	AP2	AP2
G1	b	0.245	0.273	0.239	0.269	0.255
	a	0.252	0.255	0.274	0.276	0.291
G2	b	0.21	0.236	0.284	0.24	0.234
	a	0.335	0.307	0.349	0.322	0.305
Increase G1		0.007	−0.018	0.035	0.007	0.036
Increase G2		0.125	0.071	0.065	0.082	0.071
Increase G1/ Increase G2		0.056	−0.253	0.538	0.085	0.507

row are smaller than all the values in the "Increase G2(AP2)" row. These values are shown before and after iterations in rows 1 and 2 of Table 19.7, respectively. $G1$ $(AP2)$ is calculated using Eq. (19.12), but this equation can be simplified into Eq. (19.13) because w_{LouG1} is equal to 0 and w_{TemG1} is equal to 1 (weight set A).

$$G1(AP2) = E_{G1}(AP2) = w_{TemG1} * E_{TemGl}(AP2)$$
$$+ w_{LouG1} * E_{LouG1}(AP2) \tag{19.12}$$

$$G1(AP2) = E_{TemGl}(AP2) \tag{19.13}$$

Thus, because G1's evaluation functions measure only tempo expressivity, $G1$ $(AP2)$ provides a measure of the expressive tempo evaluation of G2's performance. Thus, the difference between $G1(AP2)$ before and after the iterations is a measure of how much G2's expressive tempo evaluation has increased, as evaluated by G1. Similarly, the measure of G2's expressive loudness evaluation is found by calculating G2's evaluation of its own performance, $G2(AP2)$, as shown in Eq. (19.14), which can be simplified into Eq. (19.15) because w_{TemG2} is equal to 0 and w_{LouG1} is equal to 1 (weight set B).

$$G2(AP2) = E2_{G2}(AP2) = w_{TemG2} * E_{TemG2}(AP2)$$
$$+ w_{LouG2} * E_{LouG2}(AP2) \tag{19.14}$$

$$G2(AP2) = E_{LouG2}(AP2) \tag{19.15}$$

The increase in $G2(AP2)$ before and after iterations gives the increase in G2's loudness expressivity as a result of iterations. The ratio of these two values is shown in Eq. (19.16) and is the increase of expressiveness of G2's tempo deviations

Table 19.8 Summary of the primary term of reference

CSEMP	Performance creativity
Director Musices	8
Hierarchical Parabola Model	3
Composer Pulse	5
Bach Fugue	3
Rubato	8
Trumpet Synthesis	3
MIS	3
ANN Piano	3
Music Plus One	4
SaxEx	8
CARO	7
Emotional Flute	6
Kagurame	3
Jazz Guitar	3
Ha-Hi-Hun	8
PLCG	3
Phrase-decomposition/PLCG	3
DISTALL	3
Pop-E	8
ESP Piano	3
KCCA Piano	3
Drumming	3
Genetic Programming	6
Sequential Covering GAs	6
Generative Performance GAs	8
Ossia	10
Music Emotionality	10
MASC	10
IMAP	10
User-curated Piano	10

relative to the increase in expressiveness of G2's loudness deviations. This could be interpreted as a form of "cross-group" *TempoRatio* (*CGTR*) of G2's performance *AP2*. However, Eq. (19.16) is not G1's actual *TempoRatio* as defined in Eq. (19.11), otherwise the numerator in Eq. (19.16) would have to be *Increase in* $E_{TemG2}(AP2)$. A *TempoRatio* based on this numerator would always be equal to 0, since G2's evaluation function E_{TemG2} is defined by weight set B, which has all weights in E_{TemG2} set equal to 0. Therefore, the only meaningful tempo ratio has G1's E_{TemG1} in the numerator. This is not just meaningful, but also relevant: the purpose of this experiment was to investigate how G1's view of expressive performance has influenced G2. Thus, when looking at the influence of G1's evaluation function on G2, the function to use is G1's evaluation function. Hence the use of the cross-group *TempoRatio*, or CGTR. This is calculated in the last row of Table 19.4. The average value of CGTR for G2's performance is equal to 0.219.

$$\frac{Increase\_in\_G1(AP2)}{Increase\_in\_G2(AP2)}$$
$$= \frac{Increase\_in\_E_{TemG1}(AP2)}{Increase\_in\_E_{LouG2}(AP2)} = CGTR(AP2) \tag{19.16}$$

It would be tempting to say that the average CGTR = 0.219 supports the hypothesis that G1's tempo weights have influenced G2's tempo expression, just because it is a positive value. However, on its own, this positive average CGTR may just represent the result of random fluctuations in G2's tempo deviations caused during the iterations. But recall that it has been shown in a previous set of 5 runs that the baseline value *TempoRatio* due to random fluctuations in a dynamics-only agent set was of the order of −0.013. By comparing G2's CGTR of 0.219 to the baseline value *TempoRatio* of −0.013, and considering that G1 and G2 have mutually exclusive weight sets, one can see that the expressiveness of G2's tempo deviations relative to the expressiveness of G2's loudness deviations is significantly larger than could likely be explained by random fluctuations. This supports the hypothesis that G1 has significantly influenced the increase in G2's tempo expressivity relative to its loudness expressivity. This in turn supports the idea that if agent preferences are biased a certain way in a subset of the population, then the whole system's performances will become affected by that preference.

19.4.5 IMAP Summary

IMAP demonstrates the approach of an imitative multi-agent system approach to generate expressive performances of music, based on agents' individual parameterized musical rules. Aside from investigating the usefulness of such an application of the imitative multi-agent paradigm, there was also a desire to investigate the inherent feature of diversity and control of diversity in this methodology: a desirable feature for a creative application, such as synthesised musical performance. In order to aid this control of diversity, parameterized rules were utilised based on previous expressive performance research. These were implemented in the agents using previously developed musical analysis algorithms. When experiments were run, it was found that agents were expressing their preferences through their music performances, and that diversity could be generated and controlled.

In addition to the possibility of using IMAP in practical applications, there are also potential applications of IMAP in an area that multi-agent systems are frequently used: modelling for sociological study, specifically in the sociological study of music performance [22]. However, the focus of this system is on the practical application of imitative multi-agent systems to generate expressive performance, rather than to investigate social modelling.

A priority piece of future work for IMAP would be to conduct formal listening tests to measure human judgments of automatically generated performances. Only then would it be possible to evaluate whether or not IMAP would indeed be more practical and more beneficial for music-making than simply allowing the user to control parameters directly. Another area of work would be listening experiments on how adjusting parameters such as the pitch and inter-onset intervals weights in the LBDM would affect performances, and how other variables such as the number-of-bars horizon in the key change part of the accentuation curve impacts performances.

The effectiveness of IMAP is to a significant degree decided by the effectiveness of the Analysis Level. It is acknowledged that the algorithms used are not absolutely perfect; for example, LBDM is known to only be a partial solution to the detection of local boundaries. Different analysis algorithms should be tested. The same could be said of the Rule Level: other sets of rules could be experimented with. In both the case of the Rule Level and the Analysis Level such work could include the investigation of explicitly polyphonic analysis functions and rules. Furthermore, despite the initial experience and thoughts regarding convergence criteria for the system, such criteria are by no means obvious in a creative application; so further work should be done at this front.

This advanced learning rate functionality would be a fruitful area for further investigation. For example, agents with learning rates of 0% have the power to influence but not be influenced by the system. Another area of investigation is interaction control. The system currently assumes that all agents can always interact with all agents. In multi-agent systems, there are often "popularity" or "connection" measures [61, 62, 121] that define which agents interact with which. The addition of a social network, which could change conditionally over time, would be worth investigating.

IMAP has the potential to be influenced by human performances, and this is certainly an area worth investigating further. Suppose the system is set up with 50% of agents supplied with performance deviations from a single performance M by a human Performer A. The other 50% would have random performances. Depending on preference weightings, the resulting performances would be influenced to a degree by Performer A's performance. Another approach would be to reverse engineer evaluation function weights from Performer A's performance, using a parameter search optimization technique [119]. Performer A's preference weights would affect the performances more strongly than just using Performer A's initial performances. The preference function would not necessarily contain Performer A's real preference, and there would not be a one-to-one relationship between function weights and a single performance. Nevertheless, such an approach would be worth investigating as a tool for generating new expressive performances. In fact, one could envision a "recipe book" of different agent preferences generated by deviations from different professional performers. These agents could then be added to IMAP in the proportions desired by the user. For example, "I would like a performance repertoire of Bach's Piano Partita No. 2 based 30% on Daniel Barenboim's performance, 50% on Glen Gould's performance and 20% based on the preference weights I explicitly specify".

Another suggested future work for IMAP would be to study the effect of agent communication noise on the convergence of the system. For instance, Kirke and Miranda [63] have introduced a multi-agent system in which agents communicate musical ideas and generate new ideas partially through errors in the communication. Similarly, allowing agents in IMAP to make small errors in their performances could be viewed as an imitative equivalent of a GA mutation operator. This would potentially lead to agents generating performances that more closely match their preferences.

Also, one should consider extending IMAP to expressive performance indicators other than tempo and loudness. However, the limitations of MIDI make this difficult with our current framework. Ideally, this extension can be addressed once it is possible to deal directly with audio rather than MIDI.

This CSEMP has significant performance creativity, one reason being that the pulse sets generated may have no similarity to the hierarchical constraints of human pulse sets. They are generated mathematically and abstractly from agent imitation performances. So entirely novel pulse set types can be produced by agents that a human would never generate. Another element that contributes to creativity is that although a global evaluation function approach was used, a diversity of performances was found to be produced in the population of agents.

19.5 Concluding Remarks

Having completed the in-depth introduction to the CSEMP IMAP, the whole chapter will now be summarised. Before reading this summary, another viewing of Table 19.1 at the start of the chapter may be helpful to the reader. Expressive Performance is a complex behaviour with many causative conditions—so it is no surprise that in this chapter that almost two-thirds of the systems produced have been learning CSEMPS, usually learning to map music features on to expressive actions. Expressive performance actions most commonly included timing and loudness adjustments, with some articulation, and the most common non-custom method for analysis of music features was GTTM, followed by IR. Due to its simplicity in modelling performance, the most common instrument simulated was piano—but interestingly this was followed closely by saxophone—possibly because of the popularity of the instrument in the Jazz genre. Despite, and probably because, of its simplicity—MIDI is still the most popular representation.

It can be seen that only a subset of the systems has had any formal testing, and for some of them designing formal tests is a challenge in itself. This is not that unexpected—since testing a creative computer system is an unsolved problem. Also, about half of the systems have only been tested on monophonic tunes. Polyphony and Homophony introduce problems both in terms of synchronisation and in terms of music feature analysis. Further to music feature analysis, most of the CSEMPs had an expressive representation up to one bar/phrase, and over half did not look at the musical hierarchy. However, avoiding musical hierarchy analysis can have the advantage of increasing automation.

The focus of the chapter has been performance creativity. We have seen that most CSEMPs are designed for *simulation* of human expressive performances, general or specific—a valuable research goal, and one which has possibly been influenced by the philosophy of human simulation in machine intelligence research. The results for the primary term of reference—performance creativity—are summarised in Table 19.8. The numerical measure is an attempt to quantify observations, scaled from 1 to 10. The greater the perceived potential of a system to enable the creative generation of novel performances, the higher the number in column 2. Obviously, such measures contain some degree of subjectivity but should be a useful indicator for anyone wanting an overview of the field, based on creativity.

Although there have been significant achievements in the field of simulating human musical performance in the last 40 years, there are many opportunities ahead for future improvements. One aim of the RenCon competitions is for a computer to win the Chopin competition by 2050. Such an aim begs some philosophical and historical questions, but nonetheless captures the level of progress being made in CSEMP work. It also raises the issue that famous winners of the competition such as Martha Argerich [100] have been renowned for their *creative* interpretations of Chopin, interpretations that push the boundaries. So, for a CSEMP to win the Chopin competition, performance creativity will need to be at its heart. Perhaps investigations in performance creativity could benefit from a wider understanding of the relationship between performance and composition elements in computer music. Creativity research is more advanced in computer composition work.

It could be that whole new vistas of creativity will open up in CSEMP research as a result of this focus. The question is open as to what forms of non-human expression can be developed, with machines providing whole new vistas of the meaning of the phrase "expressive performance" for human players.

References

1. Anders, T. (2007). Composing music by composing rules: Design and usage of a generic music constraint system. Ph.D. Thesis, University of Belfast.
2. Arcos, J. L., de Mantaras, R. L., & Serra, X. (1997). SaxEx: A case-based reasoning system for generating expressive musical performances. In P. R. Cook (Ed.), *Proceedings of 1997 International Computer Music Conference*, Thessalonikia, Greece, September 1997, ICMA, San Francisco, CA (pp. 329–336).
3. Arcos, J. L., de Mantaras, R. L., & Serra, X. (1998). Saxex: A case-based reasoning system for generating expressive musical performance. *Journal of New Music Research, 27*, 194–210.
4. Arcos, J. L., & de Mantaras, R. L. (2001). The SaxEx system for expressive music synthesis: A progress report. In C. Lomeli & R. Loureiro (Eds.), *Proceedings of the Workshop on*

Current Research Directions in Computer Music, Barcelona, Spain, November 2001 (pp. 17–22).

5. Arcos, J. L., & Lopez de Mantaras, R. (2001). An interactive case-based reasoning approach for generating expressive music. *Journal of Applied Intelligence, 14*, 115–129.
6. Atkinson, J. (2007). J.S. Bach: The Goldberg variations. *Stereophile*, September 2007
7. Bellini, P., & Nesi, P. (2001). WEDELMUSIC format: An XML music notation format for emerging applications. In *Proceedings of First International Conference on Web Delivering of Music*, Florence, November 2001 (pp. 79–86). Los Alamitos, CA: IEEE Press.
8. Ben-David, A., & Mandel, J. (1995). Classification accuracy: Machine learning vs. explicit knowledge acquisition. *Machine Learning, 18*, 109–114
9. Boyd, R., & Richardson, P. J. (2005). Solving the puzzle of human cooperation. In S. Levinson (Ed.), *Evolution and culture.* (pp. 105–132). Cambridge MA: MIT Press.
10. Bresin, R., & Friberg, A. (2000). Emotional coloring of computer-controlled music performances. *Computer Music Journal, 24*, 44–63
11. Bresin, R. (1998). Artificial neural networks based models for automatic performance of musical scores. *Journal of New Music Research, 27*, 239–270.
12. Buxton, W. A. S. (1977). A composers introduction to computer music. *Interface, 6*, 57–72.
13. Cambouropoulos, E. (2001). The Local Boundary Detection Model (LBDM) and its application in the study of expressive timing. In R. Schloss & R. Dannenberg (Eds.), *Proceedings of the 2001 International Computer Music Conference*, Havana, Cuba, September 2001. San Fransisco, CA: International Computer Music Association.
14. Camurri, A., Dillon, R., & Saron, A. (2000). An experiment on analysis and synthesis of musical expressivity. In *Proceedings of 13th Colloquium on Musical Informatics*, L'Aquila, Italy, September 2000.
15. Canazza, S., Drioli, C., de Poli, G., Rodà, A., & Vidolin, A. (2000). Audio morphing different expressive intentions for multimedia systems. *IEEE Multimedia, 7*, 79–83
16. Canazza, S., de Poli, G., Drioli, C., Rodà, A., & Vidolin, A. (2004). Modeling and control of expressiveness in music performance. *The Proceedings of the IEEE, 92*, 686–701
17. Canazza, S., de Poli, G., Rodà, A., & Vidolin, A. (2003). An abstract control space for communication of sensory expressive intentions in music performance. *Journal of New Music Research, 32*, 281–294
18. Cancino-Chacon, C. E., Grachten, M., Goebl, W., & Widmer, G. (2018). Computational models of expressive music performance: A comprehensive and critical review. *Frontiers in Digital Humanities, 5*, 25
19. Carlson, L., Nordmark, A., & Wiklander, R. (2003). *Reason version 2.5—Getting started.* Propellorhead Software.
20. Chalmers, D. (2006). Strong and weak emergence. In P. Clayton & P. Davies (Eds.), *The re-emergence of emergence.* Oxford: Oxford University Press.
21. Church, M. (2004). The mystery of Glenn Gould. *The Independent.*
22. Clarke, E. F., & Davidson, J. W. (1998). The body in music as mediator between knowledge and action. In W. Thomas (Ed.), *Composition, s.* (pp. 74–92). Oxford: Oxford University Press.
23. Clarke, E. F., & Windsor, W. L. (2000). Real and simulated expression: A listening study. *Music Perception, 17*, 277–313
24. Clarke, E. F. (1998). The semiotics of expression in musical performance. *Contemporary Music Review, 17*(2), 87–102.
25. Clarke, E. F. (1988). Generative principles in music performance. In J. A. Sloboda (Ed.), *Generative processes in music: The psychology of performance, improvisation, and composition* (pp. 1–26). Oxford: Clarendon Press.
26. Clynes, M. (1986). Generative principles of musical thought: Integration of microstructure with structure. *Communication and Cognition, 3*, 185–223.

27. Dahlstedt, P. (2007). Autonomous evolution of complete Piano pieces and performances. In *Proceedings of ECAL 2007 Workshop on Music and Artificial Life (MusicAL 2007)*, Lisbon, Portugal, September 2007.

28. Dannenberg, R. B., & Derenyi, I. (1998). Combining instrument and performance models for high-quality music synthesis. *Journal of New Music Research, 27,* 211–238

29. Dannenberg, R. B. (1993). A brief survey of music representation issues, techniques, and systems. *Computer Music Journal, 17,* 20–30.

30. Dannenberg, R. B., Pellerin, H., & Derenyi, I. (1998). A study of trumpet envelopes. In *Proceedings of the 1998 International Computer Music Conference*, Ann Arbor, Michigan, October 1998 (pp. 57–61). San Francisco: International Computer Music Association.

31. Desain, P., & Honing, H. (1993). Tempo curves considered harmful. *Contemporary Music Review, 7,* 123–138

32. Dissanayake, E. (2001). Birth of the arts. *Natural History, 109,* 84–92.

33. Dixon, S., Goebl, W., & Widmer, G. (2002, September). The performance worm: Real time visualisation of expression based on Langner's tempo-loudness animation. In ICMC.

34. Dobrev, D. (2005). Formal definition of artificial intelligence. *International Journal ITA, 12.*

35. Dorard, L., Hardoon, D. R., & Shawe-Taylor, J. (2007). Can style be learned? A machine learning approach towards 'performing' as famous pianists. In *Music, Brain and Cognition Workshop, NIPS 2007*, Whistler, Canada.

36. Emde, W., & Wettschereck, D. (1996). Relational instance based learning. In L. Saitta (Ed.), *Proceedings of 13th International Conference on Machine Learning*, Bari, Italy, July 1996 (pp. 122–130). Morgan Kaufmann.

37. Finn, B. (2007). Personal Communication. August 2007.

38. Friberg, A., Bresin, R., & Sundberg, J. (2006). Overview of the KTH rule system for musical performance. *Advances in Cognitive Psychology, 2,* 145–161

39. Friberg, A., & Sundberg, J. (1999). Does music performance allude to locomotion? A model of final ritardandi derived from measurements of stopping runners. *Journal of Acoustical Society of America, 105,* 1469–1484

40. Friberg, A. (1995). A quantitative rule system for music performance. Ph.D. Thesis, Department of Speech, Music and Hearing, Royal Institute of Technology, Stockholm.

41. Friberg, A. (2006). pDM: An expressive sequencer with real-time control of the KTH music-performance rules. *Computer Music Journal, 30,* 37–48.

42. Gabrielsson, A., & Juslin, P. (1996). Emotional expression in music performance: Between the performer's intention and the listener's experience. *Psychology of Music, 24,* 68–91

43. Gabrielsson, A. (2003). Music performance research at the millenium. *Psychology of Music, 31,* 221–272.

44. Giraldo, S. I., & Ramirez, R. (2016). A machine learning approach to discover rules for expressive performance actions in jazz guitar music. *Frontiers in psychology, 7,* 1965.

45. Goldberg, D. E. (1989). *Genetic algorithms in search, optimization, and machine learning.* Essex: Addison-Wesley.

46. Good, M. (2001). MusicXML for notation and analysis. In W. B. Hewlett & E. Selfridge-Field (Eds.), *The virtual score: Representation, retrieval, restoration* (pp. 113–124). Cambridge, MA: MIT Press.

47. Good, M. (2006). MusicXML in commercial applications. In In W. B. Hewlett & E. Selfridge-Field (Eds.), *Music analysis east and west* (pp. 9–20). Cambridge, MA: MIT Press.

48. Grindlay, G. C. (2005). Modelling expressive musical performance with Hidden Markov Models. Ph.D. Thesis, University of Santa Cruz, CA.

49. Hashida, M., Nagata, N., & Katayose, H. (2006). Pop-E: A performance rendering system for the ensemble music that considered group expression. In M. Baroni, R. Addessi, R. Caterina, & M. Costa (Eds.), *Proceedings of 9th International Conference on Music Perception and Cognition*, Bologna, Spain, August 2006 (pp. 526–534). ICMPC.

50. Hashida, M., Nagata, N., & Katayose, H. (2007). jPop-E: An assistant system for performance rendering of ensemble music. In L. Crawford (Ed.), *Proceedings of 2007 Conference on New Interfaces for Musical Expression (NIME07)* (pp. 313–316).
51. Hastie, T., Tibshirani, R., & Friedman, J. (2001). *The elements of statistical learning.* Springer.
52. Hazan, A., & Ramirez, R. (2006). Modelling expressive performance using consistent evolutionary regression trees. In G. Brewka, S. Coradeschi, A. Perini, & P. Traverso (Eds.), *Proceedings of 17th European European Conference on Aritifial Intelligence (Workshop on Evolutionary Computation)*, Riva del Garda, Italy, August 2006. IOS Press.
53. Hellman, M. (1991). The nearest neighbor classification rule with a reject option. In B. Dasarathy (Ed.), *Nearest Neighbor (NN) Norms: Pattern Classification Techniques.* IEEE Computer Society Press.
54. Hiller, L., & Isaacson, L. (1959). *Experimental music. Composition with an electronic computer.* New York: McGraw Hill.
55. Hirata, K., & Hiraga, R. (2002). Ha-Hi-Hun: Performance rendering system of high controllability. In *Proceedings of the ICAD 2002 Rencon Workshop on Performance Rendering Systems*, Kyoto, Japan, July 2002 (pp. 40–46).
56. Ishikawa, O., Aono, Y., Katayose, H., & Inokuchi, S. (2000). Extraction of musical performance rule using a modified algorithm of multiple regression analysis. In *Proceedings of the International Computer Music Conference*, Berlin, Germany, August 2000 (pp. 348–351). International Computer Music Association.
57. Johnson, M. L. (1991). Toward an expert system for expressive musical performance. *Computer, 24*, 30–34.
58. Juslin, P. (2003). Five facets of musical expression: A psychologist's perspective on music performance. *Psychology of Music, 31*, 273–302.
59. Kajanova, Y. (2002). Johann Sebastian Bach and the modern Jazz quartet—A desire for sonic sensualism or seriousness. In J. Fukac (Ed.), *Bach 2000, Music Between Virgin Forest and Knowledge Society* (pp. 253–260). Compostela Group of Universities.
60. Katayose, H., Fukuoka, T., Takami, K., & Inokuchi, S. (1990). Expression extraction in virtuoso music performances. In *Proceedings of the 10th International Conference on Pattern Recognition*, Atlantic City, New Jersey, USA, June 1990 (pp. 780–784). IEEE Press.
61. Kirke, A., & Miranda, E. (2015). A multi-agent emotional society whose melodies represent its emergent social hierarchy and are generated by agent communications. *Journal of Artificial Societies and Social Simulation, 18*(2), 16
62. Kirke, A. (1997). Learning and co-operation in mobile multi-robot systems. Ph.D. Thesis, University of Plymouth.
63. Kirke, A., & Miranda, E. R. (2009). Using a biophysically-constrained multi-agent system to combine expressive performance with algorithmic composition. In E. R. Miranda (Ed.), *Music and artificial life.* Middleton, WI: A-R Editions.
64. Kirke, A. (2011). Application of intermediate multi-agent systems to integrated algorithmic composition and expressive performance of music. Ph.D Thesis, University of Plymouth, Plymouth, UK.
65. Kroiss, W. (2000). Parameteroptimierung für ein Modell des musikalischen Ausdrucks mittels Genetischer Algorithmen. Master's thesis, Department of Medical Cybernetics and Artificial Intelligence, University of Vienna, Vienna, Austria.
66. Krumhans, C. (1991). *Cognitive foundations of musical pitch.* Oxford: Oxford University Press.
67. Laurson, M., & Kuuskankare, M. (2003). From RTM-notation to ENP-score-notation. In *Proceedings of Journées d'Informatique Musicale 2003*, Montbéliard, France.
68. Lerdahl, F., & Jackendoff, R. (1983). *A generative theory of tonal music.* Cambridge: The MIT Press.
69. Levenshtein, V. I. (1966). Binary codes capable of correcting deletions, insertions, and reversals. *Soviet Physics Doklady, 10*, 707–710.

70. Livingstone, S. R., Muhlberger, R., Brown, A. R., & Loch, A. (2007). Controlling musical emotionality: An affective computational architecture for influencing musical emotions. *Digital Creativity, 18.*
71. Lopez de Mantaras, R., & Arcos, J. L. (2002). AI and music: From composition to expressive performances. *AI Magazine, 23,* 43–57.
72. Mazzola, G., & Zahorka, O. (1994). Tempo curves revisited: Hierarchies of performance fields. *Computer Music Journal, 18*(1).
73. Mazzola, G. (2002). *The topos of music—Geometric logic of concepts, theory, and performance.* Basel/Boston: Birkhäuser.
74. Meyer, L. B. (1957). Meaning in music and information theory. *Journal of Aesthetics and Art Criticism, 15,* 412–424.
75. Miranda, E. R., & Biles, J. A. (2007). *Evolutionary computer music.* London: Springer.
76. Miranda, E. R., Kirke, A., & Zhang, Q. (2010). Artificial evolution of expressive performance of music: An imitative multi-agent systems approach. *Computer Music Journal, 34,* 80–96
77. Miranda, E. R. (2001). *Composing music with computers.* Oxford, UK: Focal Press.
78. Miranda, E. R. (2002). Emergent sound repertoires in virtual societies. *Computer Music Journal, 26*(2), 77–90.
79. Mitchell, M. (1998). *Introduction to genetic algorithms.* Cambridge: The MIT Press.
80. Mitchell, T. (1997). *Machine learning.* New York: McGraw-Hill.
81. Narmour, E. (1990). *The analysis and cognition of basic melodic structures: The implication-realization model.* Chicago: The University of Chicago Press.
82. Noble, J., & Franks, D. W. (2004). Social learning in a multi-agent system. *Computing and Informatics, 22*(6), 561–574
83. Pace, I. (2007). Complexity as imaginative stimulant: Issues of Rubato, Barring, Grouping, Accentuation and Articulation in Contemporary Music, with Examples from Boulez, Carter, Feldman, Kagel, Sciarrino, Finnissy. In *Proceedings of the 5th International Orpheus Academy for Music & Theory,* Gent, Belgium, April 2007.
84. Palmer, C. (1997). Music performance. *Annual Review of Psychology, 48,* 115–138.
85. Papadopoulos, G., & Wiggins, G. A. (1999). AI methods for algorithmic composition: A survey, a critical view, and future prospects. In *Proceedings of the AISB'99 Symposium on Musical Creativity,* AISB.
86. Quinlan, J. R. (1993). *C4.5: Programs for machine learning.* Morgan Kaufmann.
87. Ramirez, R., Hazan, A., Maestre, E., & Serra, X. (2008). A genetic rule-based model of expressive performance for Jazz saxophone. *Computer Music Journal, 32*(1), 38–50
88. Ramirez, R., & Hazan, A. (2005). Modeling expressive performance in Jazz. In *Proceedings of 18th International Florida Artificial Intelligence Research Society Conference (AI in Music and Art),* Clearwater Beach, FL, USA, May 2005 (pp. 86–91). AAAI Press.
89. Ramirez, R., & Hazan, A. (2007). Inducing a generative expressive performance model using a sequential-covering genetic algorithm. In *Proceedings of 2007 Genetic and Evolutionary Computation Conference,* London, UK, July 2007. ACM Press.
90. Raphael, C. (2001a). Can the computer learn to play music expressively? In T. Jaakkola & T. Richardson (Eds.), *Proceedings of Eighth International Workshop on Artificial Intelligence and Statistics,* 2001 (pp. 113–120). San Francisco, CA: Morgan Kaufmann.
91. Raphael, C. (2001b). A Bayesian network for real-time musical accompaniment. *Neural Information Processing Systems, 14.*
92. Raphael, C. (2003). Orchestra in a box: A system for real-time musical accompaniment. In G. Gottlob & T. Walsh (Eds.), *Proceedings of 2003 International Joint Conference on Artificial Intelligence (Working Notes of RenCon Workshop),* Acapulco, Mexico, August 2003 (pp. 5–10). Morgan Kaufmann.
93. Rasmussen, C., & Williams, C. (2006). *Gaussian processes for machine learning.* Massachusetts: The MIT Press.
94. Repp, B. H. (1990). Composer's pulses: Science or art. *Music Perception, 7,* 423–434.

95. Roads, C. (1996). *The computer music tutorial.* Cambridge, Massachusetts, USA: MIT Press.
96. Seashore, C. E. (1938). *Psychology of music.* New York: McGraw-Hill.
97. Sethares, W. (2004). *Tuning, timbre, spectrum, scale.* London: Springer.
98. Shi, Z., Cancino-Chacon, C., & Widmer, G. (2019). User curated shaping of expressive performances. arXiv preprint. arXiv:1906.06428.
99. Sholkopf, B., Smola, A., & Muller, K. (1998). Nonlinear component analysis as a kernel eigenvalue problem. *Neural Computation, 10,* 1299–1319. Cambridge, Massachusetts, USA: IT Press.
100. Strickland, E. (2016). Artistic expression, individuality and authenticity in Chopin performance. Ph.D. Thesis, University of Oregon (Doctoral dissertation, University of Oregon).
101. Sundberg, J., Askenfelt, A., & Frydén, L. (1983). Musical performance a synthesis-by-rule approach. *Computer Music Journal, 7,* 37–43
102. Sundberg, J., Friberg, A., & Bresin, R. (2003). Attempts to reproduce a pianist's expressive timing with Director Musices performance rules. *Journal of New Music Research, 32,* 317–325
103. Suzuki, T., Tokunaga, T., & Tanaka, H. (1999). A case based approach to the generation of musical expression. In *Proceedings of the 16th International Joint Conference on Artificial Intelligence,* Stockholm, Sweden, August 1999 (pp. 642–648). San Francisco, CA, USA: Morgan Kaufmann.
104. Suzuki, T. (2003). Kagurame phase-II. In G. Gottlob & T. Walsh (Eds.), *Proceedings of 2003 International Joint Conference on Artificial Intelligence (Working Notes of RenCon Workshop),* Acapulco, Mexico, August 2003. Los Altos, CA: Morgan Kauffman.
105. Thomassen, J. M. (1982). Melodic accent: Experiments and a tentative model. *Journal of the Acoustical Society of America, 71*(6), 1596–1605.
106. Thompson, W. F. (1989). Composer-specific aspects of musical performance: An evaluation of Clynes's theory of pulse for performances of Mozart and Beethoven. *Music Perception, 7,* 15–42.
107. Tobudic, A., & Widmer, G. (2003a). Relational IBL in music with a new structural similarity measure. In T. Horváth & A. Yamamoto (Eds.), *Proceedings of the 13th International Conference on Inductive Logic Programming,* Szeged, Hungary, September 2003 (pp. 365–382). Berlin: Springer.
108. Tobudic, A., & Widmer, G. (2003b). Learning to play Mozart: Recent improvements. In K. Hirata (Ed.), *Proceedings of the IJCAI'03 Workshop on Methods for Automatic Music Performance and their Applications in a Public Rendering Contest (RenCon),* Acapulco, Mexico, August 2003.
109. Todd, N. P. (1985). A model of expressive timing in tonal music. *Music Perception, 3,* 33–58.
110. Todd, N. P. (1989). A computational model of Rubato. *Contemporary Music Review, 3,* 69–88.
111. Todd, N. P. (1992). The dynamics of dynamics: a model of musical expression. *Journal of the Acoustical Society of America, 91,* 3540–3550.
112. Todd, N. P. (1995). The kinematics of musical expression. *Journal of Acoustical Society of America, 97,* 1940–1949.
113. Toop, R. (1988). Four facets of the new complexity. *Contact, 32,* 4–50.
114. Widmer, G., & Goebl, W. (2004). Computational models of expressive music performance: The state of the art. *Journal of New Music Research, 33,* 203–216
115. Widmer, G., & Tobudic, A. (2003). Playing Mozart by analogy: Learning multi-level timing and dynamics strategies. *Journal of New Music Research, 32,* 259–268
116. Widmer, G. (2000). Large-scale induction of expressive performance rules: first quantitative results. In I. Zannos (Ed.), *Proceedings of the 2000 International Computer Music*

Conference, Berlin, Germany, September 2000 (pp. 344–347). San Francisco, CA: International Computer Music Association.

117. Widmer, G. (2002). Machine discoveries: A few simple, robust local expression principles. *Journal of New Music Research, 31*, 37–50.

118. Widmer, G. (2003). Discovering simple rules in complex data: A meta-learning algorithm and some surprising musical discoveries. *Artificial Intelligence, 146*, 129–148.

119. Winston, W. L., & Venkataramanan, M. (2002). *Introduction to mathematical programming: Applications and algorithms*. Duxbury.

120. Witten, I. H., & Frank, E. (2000). *Data mining: Practical machine learning tools and techniques with java implementations*. San Mateo, CA: Morgan Kaufmann.

121. Wooldridge, M. (2004). *An introduction to multi-agent systems*. Wiley.

122. Wright, M., & Berdahl, E. (2006). Towards machine learning of expressive microtiming in Brazilian drumming. In I. Zannos (Ed.), *Proceedings of the 2006 International Computer Music Conference*, New Orleans, USA, November 2006 (pp. 572–575). San Fransisco, CA: ICMA.

123. Zanon, P., & de Poli, G. (2003). Estimation of parameters in rule system for expressive rendering of musical performance. *Computer Music Journal, 27*, 29–46

124. Zanon, P., & de Poli, G. (2003). Time-varying estimation of parameters in rule systems for music performance. *Journal of New Music Research, 32*, 295–315.

125. Zentall, T., & Galef, B. G. (1988). *Social learning: Psychological and biological perspectives*. Erlbaum.

126. Zhang, Q., & Miranda, E. R. (2006a). Evolving musical performance profiles using genetic algorithms with structural fitness. In J. V. Diggelen, M. A. Wiering, & E. D. D. Jong (Eds.), *Proceedings of the 8th Annual Conference on Genetic and Evolutionary Computation*, Seattle, Washington, July 2006 (pp. 1833–1840). New York, USA: ACM Press.

127. Zhang, Q., & Miranda, E. R. (2006b). Towards an interaction and evolution model of expressive music performance. In Y. Chen & A. Abraham (Eds.), *Proceedings of the 6th International conference on Intelligent Systems Design and Applications*, Jinan, China, October 2006 (pp. 1189–1194). Washington, DC, USA: IEEE Computer Society.

Alexis Kirke is a Senior Research Fellow in Computer Music at the Interdisciplinary Centre for Computer Music Research (ICCMR) at the University of Plymouth, UK. He studied for a B.Sc. (Hons) in Mathematics at the University of Plymouth. He subsequently received a Ph.D. on the topic of Artificial Neural Networks and a Ph.D. in the field of Computer Music, both from the University of Plymouth. His research interests include applications of music and the arts to technology, human-computer interaction, computational modelling of musical performance, assistive technology for dementia, and quantum computing. E-mail: alexis.kirke@plymouth.ac.uk

Eduardo Reck Miranda is Professor in Computer Music and head the Interdisciplinary Centre for Computer Music Research (ICCMR) at the University of Plymouth, UK. He studied music, philosophy and informatics in Brazil before he graduated with an M.Sc. in Music Technology from the University of York, UK. Subsequently he received a Ph.D. on the topic of sound design with Artificial Intelligence (AI) from the University of Edinburgh, UK. Before joining the University of Plymouth, he worked at Sony Computer Science Laboratory in Paris, France, as a research scientist in the fields of AI, speech and evolution of language. He also is a composer working at the crossroads of music and science. His distinctive music is informed by his unique background as a classically trained composer and AI scientist with an early involvement in electroacoustic and avant-garde pop music. E-mail: eduardo.miranda@plymouth.ac.uk

Imitative Computer-Aided Musical Orchestration with Biologically Inspired Algorithms

20

Marcelo Caetano and Carmine E. Cella

20.1 Introduction

Musical orchestration is an empirical art form based on tradition and heritage whose lack of formalism hinders the development of assisstive computational tools. Computer-aided musical orchestration (CAMO) systems aim to assist the composer in several steps of the orchestration procedure. Particularly, *imitative* CAMO focuses on instrumentation by aiding the composer in creating timbral mixtures as instrument combinations. Imitative CAMO allows composers to specify a reference sound and replicate it with a predetermined orchestra [51]. Therefore, the aim of imitative CAMO is to find a combination of musical instrument sounds that perceptually approximates a reference sound when played together. However, the complexity of timbre perception and the combinatorial explosion of all possible musical instrument sound combinations make imitative CAMO a very challenging problem.

M. Caetano (✉)
Schulich School of Music & CIRMMT, McGill University, Montreal, Canada
e-mail: marcelo.caetano@mcgill.ca

C. E. Cella
University of California, Berkeley, Berkeley, CA, USA

© Springer Nature Switzerland AG 2021
E. R. Miranda (ed.), *Handbook of Artificial Intelligence for Music*,
https://doi.org/10.1007/978-3-030-72116-9_20

This chapter covers the theoretical background, the basic concepts, and algorithms involved in imitative CAMO. Specifically, this chapter describes the computational formalization of imitative CAMO and the motivation to use algorithms inspired by biological systems to tackle the complexity of timbral mixtures and the subjective nature of music composition. First, we present a brief review of timbre perception to motivate the use of the computer in musical orchestration. Then, we review several approaches to CAMO found in the literature. Next, we review CAMO systems that rely on the biologically inspired algorithms designated as genetic algorithms (GA) and artificial immune systems (AIS), which are used to search for orchestrations via single-objective optimization (SOO) or multi-objective optimization (MOO). We discuss several aspects related to the different biologically inspired algorithms and optimization strategies focusing on the compositional perspective of orchestration. Finally, we conclude with future perspectives of CAMO.

20.1.1 Musical Orchestration

Traditionally, orchestration manuals regard musical orchestration as the process of writing music for the orchestra [65]. Orchestration has always been one of the most difficult disciplines to explain and convey [51]. The gap between the symbols in the score and their acoustic realization involves many steps that are difficult to quantify and some of these steps are oftentimes unpredictable. More than any other component of music composition, orchestration is an empirical activity essentially based on tradition and heritage. Even contemporary manuals of orchestration approach orchestration as an art form rather than a systematic procedure that can be captured by an algorithm. The lack of formalism in orchestration practice has been a major hindrance to the development of assisstive computational tools.

Broadly speaking, orchestration is understood as "the art of blending instrument timbres together" [63]. Initially, orchestration was simply the assignment of instruments to pre-composed parts of the score, which was dictated largely by the availability of resources, such as what instruments and how many of each are available in the orchestra [42, 47]. Later on, composers started regarding orchestration as an integral part of the compositional process whereby the musical ideas themselves are expressed [47, 69]. Compositional experimentation in orchestration arises from the increasing tendency to specify instrument combinations to achieve desired effects, resulting in the contemporary use of timbral mixtures [55, 69]. Orchestration remains an empirical activity largely due to the difficulty to formalize the required knowledge [47, 51, 63].

In the past 20 years or so, composers felt the need for a more systematic approach to orchestration to gain more control over timbral mixtures. Research in music writing pushed composers very far in imagining possible timbres resulting from extended instrumental techniques. Timbral mixtures have become more and more complex, and predicting their *sound quality* while writing the score requires a great deal of experience and experimentation. In such a context, a tool to help simulate the result of timbral mixtures became a necessity. While other parameters of musical writing such as harmony and rhythm have been supported by computer-assisted techniques since the beginning of computer music [8], only recently did orchestration benefit from such tools because of its high complexity, requiring knowledge and understanding of both mathematical formalization and musical writing.

The concept of timbre lies at the core of musical orchestration [6, 7, 47, 51, 63, 65] because music and, consequently, musical instruments are strongly associated with timbre [53, 65, 73]. Musical orchestration uses the principle of instrumental combinations to obtain the desired effect. The orchestrator must have thorough knowledge of the individual instruments allied with a mental conception of their timbres. Additionally, the effects resulting from different instrumental combinations must be learned, such as balance of tone, mixed tone colors, and clarity in texture [65]. In this chapter, we will consider the specific example of *imitative orchestration*, where the aim is to find a combination of musical instrument sounds that, when played together, blends into a new timbre that perceptually approximates a given reference timbre. Imitative orchestration requires a great deal of knowledge about timbre, from the timbre of isolated musical instruments to timbral mixtures. Unfortunately, timbre is a complex perceptual phenomenon that is not well understood enough to this day. In fact, nowadays timbre is considered the last frontier of auditory science [71]. Therefore, this chapter will provide a brief overview of timbre research to illustrate the complexity of (imitative) musical orchestration.

20.1.2   Musical Timbre

Historically, timbre was viewed as the perceptual quality of sounds that allows listeners to tell the difference between different musical instruments and ultimately recognize the instrument (or, more generally, the sound source). However, the term *timbre* can be misleading [55] because it has different meanings when it is used in psychoacoustics, music, audio processing, and other disciplines. Siedenburg et al. [73] recently wrote that "Roughly defined, timbre is thought of as any property other than pitch, duration, and loudness that allows two sounds to be distinguished." Indeed, the complexity that the term timbre encompasses is mainly because [55] "[timbre] covers many parameters of perception that are not accounted for by pitch, loudness, spatial position, duration, and various environmental characteristics such as room reverberation." Similar to *pitch* and *loudness*, timbre is a *perceptual* attribute [72], so timbre research commonly attempts to characterize quantitatively the ways in which sounds are perceived to differ [55].

20.1.2.1   The Helmholtz Theory of Timbre

In the nineteenth century, Hermann von Helmholtz published his seminal work in hearing science and musical acoustics [43] in which he used Fourier analysis to study musical instrument sounds. Helmholtz concluded that Fourier's theorem closely described both the acoustics of sound production and the physiological underpinnings of sound perception [73]. Regarding timbre, Helmholtz stated that [43] "the quality of the musical portion of a compound tone depends solely on the number and relative strength of its partial simple tones, and in no respect on their difference of phase." Thus, Helmholtz posited that the spectral shape is the acoustic feature that captures the timbre of the sound. However, his conclusions apply mainly to the steady state portion of musical instrument sounds because he assumed that the "musical tones" are completely stationary, neglecting the attack and decay portions of musical instrument sounds, as well as any temporal variations occurring during the course of the sound such as those found in *glissando*, *sforzando*, and *vibrato* playing techniques. Later studies [52, 67] revealed the importance of temporal variations such as the attack time and spectral fluctuations in the recognition of these musical instruments. The sound quality captured by the spectral shape alone became known as *sound color* [74].

20.1.2.2   Timbre Spaces

Some of the most successful attempts to study timbre perception quantitatively have resulted from multidimensional scaling (MDS) of dissimilarity ratings between pairs of musical instrument sounds [40, 56]. MDS generates a spatial configuration with points representing the musical instruments where the distances between the points reflect the dissimilarity ratings. This representation, called a *timbre space* (see Fig. 20.1), places similar timbres closer together and dissimilar timbres farther apart. The musical instrument sounds used in MDS studies are equalized in pitch, loudness, and duration to ensure that the listeners focus on differences due to other perceptual attributes. Similarly, the sounds are presented over loudspeakers or headphones to remove differences due to spatial position. MDS timbre spaces [11, 40, 50, 55, 56] assume that the dimensions of timbre perception arising from the model are continuous and common to all the sounds presented. Additionally, there is the underlying assumption that all the listeners use the same perceptual dimensions to compare the timbres [55].

20.1.2.3   Acoustic Correlates of Timbre Spaces

In MDS timbre studies, listeners typically use more than one dimension to rate the dissimilarity between pairs of sounds. This means that the sounds cannot be arranged along a single scale that reflects their pairwise dissimilarity (contrary to pitch, for example, where the sounds can be ordered from low to high). The resulting MDS timbre space commonly has two or three dimensions. Ultimately, the goal of MDS timbre studies is to unveil the psychological dimensions of timbre perception and associate them with the dimensions of the timbre space. Consequently, MDS timbre studies usually propose explanations for the dimensions of the timbre space found. Grey [40] qualitatively interpreted the three dimensions of his timbre space (see Fig. 20.1) as (I) the distribution of spectral energy, (II) attack synchronicity of the partials, and (III) spectral balance during the attack. Later, researchers started to calculate acoustic descriptors from the sounds used in the MDS study and corre-

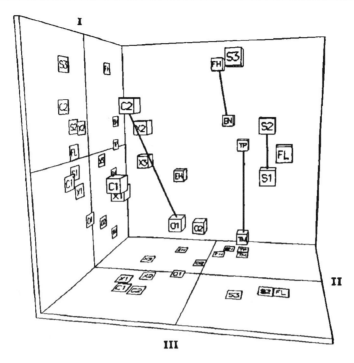

Fig. 20.1 Grey's [40] MDS timbre space. Each point represents a musical instrument sound, such that similar timbres are close together and dissimilar timbres are farther apart. Reprinted with permission from [40]. Copyright 1977, Acoustic Society of America

late these with the dimensions of the timbre space found [41, 49, 56], giving rise to *acoustic correlates of timbre spaces* [55, 56] also known as *descriptors of timbre* [14, 64]. From the plethora of descriptors proposed [64], the most ubiquitous correlates derived from musical instrument sounds include *spectral centroid*, the *logarithm of the attack time*, *spectral flux*, and *spectral irregularity* [55]. Nowadays, these descriptors of timbre are widely used in many computational tasks involving timbre [14], notably CAMO. Figure 20.2 illustrates the temporal variation of two descriptors of timbre for a relatively stable trumpet note. See [14] for details on the extraction of descriptors of timbre from audio and [64] for details on audio content descriptors in general. The role descriptors of timbre play in contemporary CAMO systems will be explored in more detail throughout this chapter. But first, Sect. 20.1.2.4 summarizes conceptually the contemporary view of timbre.

20.1.2.4   The Contemporary View of Timbre

Today, we understand timbre from two distinct viewpoints, namely a sensory quality and a categorical contributor to sound source identification. Timbre as a multidimensional sensory quality is associated with timbre spaces, illustrated in Fig. 20.1,

Fig. 20.2 Temporal
variation of descriptors of
timbre. The figure shows the
temporal variation of the
spectral centroid and of the
spectral spread on top of the
waveform of a trumpet note
from which the descriptors
were extracted

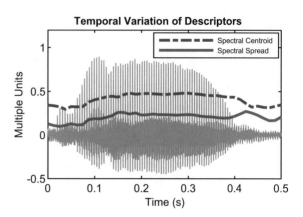

whose dimensions can be either continuous (e.g., brightness) or categorical (e.g., the pinched offset of the harpsichord). From this viewpoint, two sounds can be declared qualitatively dissimilar independently from any association with their sources. In turn, timbre is also the primary perceptual vehicle for the recognition and tracking over time of the identity of a sound source, and thus involves the absolute categorization of a sound (into musical instruments, for example). This viewpoint sees timbre as a collection of auditory sensory descriptors that contributes to the inference of sound sources and events [72]. Further adding to its complex nature, timbre functions on different scales of detail [72] such that timbral differences do not always correspond to differences in sound sources [9] and timbres from sound-producing objects of the same type but different make may differ substantially enough to affect quality judgments [70]. The complexity of timbre perception plays a major role in the difficulty to formalize musical orchestration and also motivates the use of CAMO systems.

20.1.3 Musical Orchestration with the Aid of the Computer

The development of computational tools that aid the composer in exploring the virtually infinite possibilities resulting from the combinations of musical instruments gave rise to CAMO [18, 20–22, 44, 66, 69]. Imitative CAMO tools typically automate the search for instrument combinations that perceptually approximate a reference timbre commonly represented by a reference sound [51]. The combinations found can be subsequently included in the score and later played by orchestras in live performances [63]. However, most CAMO tools allow the composer to preview the result of the combinations found using musical instrument sounds from pre-recorded databases, which has been deemed an appropriate rendition of the timbre of the instrument combinations [48].

Descriptors of timbre play a key role in several steps of recent CAMO systems [15, 26, 57], namely timbre description of isolated sounds, timbre description of combinations of musical instrument sounds, and timbre similarity between instrument combinations and the reference sound. The timbre of both the reference sound and of the isolated musical instrument sounds is represented with a descriptor vector comprising a subset of the traditional descriptors of timbre [14]. Each instrument combination corresponds to a vector of descriptors that captures the timbral result of playing the instruments together [47]. So, the descriptor vector of an instrument combination is estimated from the descriptor vectors of the isolated sounds used in the combination [22, 36]. Timbre similarity between the reference sound and the instrument combination can be estimated as distances in timbre spaces [55], which are calculated as weighted distances between the corresponding descriptor vectors [18]. Smaller distances indicate a higher degree of timbral similarity [18] with the reference, so the instrument combinations with the smallest distances are returned as proposed orchestrations for a given reference sound.

The resulting instrument combinations found to orchestrate a given reference sound will depend on which descriptors are included in the descriptor vector. For example, spectral shape descriptors focus on approximating the distribution of spectral energy of the reference sound. However, early CAMO systems did not use descriptors of timbre at all, commonly resorting to the use of spectral information. In Sect. 20.2, we will delve deeper into the historical development of CAMO focusing mainly on the conceptual approach adopted to solve the problem of musical orchestration.

20.2   State of the Art

This section presents the state of the art of CAMO grouped into "early approaches", "generative approaches", and "machine learning". Section 20.2.1 presents the first CAMO systems proposed in the literature that commonly used subtractive spectral matching to find orchestrations. Next, Sect. 20.2.2 focuses on CAMO systems that search for orchestrations with the aid of biologically inspired algorithms. Finally, Sect. 20.2.3 covers CAMO systems based on machine learning.

20.2.1   Early Approaches

Early CAMO systems adopted a top-down approach [44, 66, 69] that consists of spectral analysis and subtractive spectral matching. These works commonly keep a database of spectral peaks from musical instruments that will be used to match the reference spectrum. The algorithm iteratively subtracts the spectral peaks of the best match from the reference spectrum aiming to minimize the residual spectral energy in the least squares sense. The iterative procedure requires little computational power, but the greedy algorithm restricts the exploration of the solution space, often resulting in suboptimal solutions because it only fits the best match per iteration [19].

Psenicka [66] describes SPORCH (SPectral ORCHestration) as "a program designed to analyze a recorded sound and output a list of instruments, pitches, and dynamic levels that, when played together, create a sonority whose timbre and quality approximate that of the analyzed sound." SPORCH keeps a database of spectral peaks of musical instrument sounds and uses subtractive spectral matching and least squares to return one orchestration per run. Hummel [44] approximates the spectral envelope of phonemes as a combination of the spectral envelopes of musical instrument sounds. The method also uses a greedy iterative spectral subtraction procedure. The spectral peaks are not considered when computing the similarity between reference and candidate sounds, disregarding pitch among other perceptual qualities. Rose and Hetrik [69] use singular value decomposition (SVD) to perform spectral decomposition and spectral matching. SVD decomposes the reference spectrum as a weighted sum of the instruments present in the database, where the weights reflect the match. Besides the drawbacks from the previous approaches, SVD can be computationally intensive even for relatively small databases. Additionally, SVD sometimes returns combinations that are unplayable such as multiple simultaneous notes on the same violin, requiring an additional procedure to specify constraints on the database that reflect the physical constraints of musical instruments and of the orchestra.

20.2.2 Generative Approaches

The top-down approach neglects the exploration of timbral mixtures by relying on spectral matching, which does not capture the multidimensional nature of timbre. Carpentier et al. [18, 20–22, 76] adopted a bottom-up approach that relies on timbre similarity and evolutionary computation to search for instrument combinations that approximate the reference. The bottom-up approach represents a paradigm shift toward *generative CAMO* [1, 15, 18, 21, 33], where the timbre of instrument combinations is compared with the timbre of the reference sound via descriptors of timbre. Currently, there are two generative CAMO frameworks, the Orch* family of CAMO systems based on GA [18, 22, 26, 33], and CAMO-AIS [1, 15], which uses an artificial immune system (AIS). Orch* comprises three CAMO systems, namely *Orchidée* [18, 20–22, 76], Orchids [32, 33], and Orchidea [26]. Both Orch* and CAMO-AIS rely on algorithms inspired by biological systems that use a population of individuals to search for a solution in the vast pool of possible instrument combinations following *Orchidée*, the first generative CAMO system to be proposed.

20.2.2.1 Orch*

Orchidée searches for combinations of musical instrument sounds as a constrained combinatorial optimization problem. Carpentier et al. [18, 20–22, 76] formulate CAMO as a binary allocation knapsack problem where the aim is to find a combination of musical instruments that maximizes the timbral similarity with the reference constrained by the capacity of the orchestra (i.e., the database). *Orchidée* explores the vast space of possible instrument combinations with a GA that optimizes a fitness function which encodes timbral similarity between the candidate instrument combinations and the reference sound. Specifically, *Orchidée* uses the well-known multi-objective genetic local search (MOGLS) optimization algorithm [45] to return multiple instrument combinations in parallel that are nearly Pareto optimal. Section 20.4.2 explains multi-objective optimization (MOO) in more detail, whereas Sect. 20.4 explores the use of biologically inspired algorithms.

Orchids was born out of a compositional drawback of *Orchidée*, namely *static orchestrations*. The problem is that static orchestrations do not take into account temporal variations in the reference sound. Static orchestrations can be understood with the aid of Fig. 20.2, which shows the temporal variation of two descriptors of timbre calculated at equal steps. *Orchidée* uses descriptor vectors with the average value of the descriptors across time. A timbre-similarity measure based on temporal averages is appropriate when orchestrating reference sounds that do not present much temporal variation, such as stable musical notes sung or played on musical instruments [15, 18]. However, reference sounds such as an elephant trumpeting require taking the temporal variation of descriptors into consideration. Esling et al. [32, 33] developed Orchids with the ability to perform dynamic orchestrations by representing the temporal variation of descriptors of timbre. Orchids uses a multi-objective time series matching algorithm [31] capable of coping with the temporal and multidimensional nature of timbre. Orchids also uses MOO to return a set of efficient solutions rather than a single best solution.

Orchidea [26], the third generation of the Orch* family, expands *Orchidée* and Orchids toward macro-scale dynamic orchestration. Orchidea was conceived to be a full-fledged framework that helps composers in all the steps of the compositional process. Most of its design focuses on usability and on the integrability of the proposed solutions into a compositional workflow. In particular, Orchidea handles the temporal dimension of the reference sound differently from Orchids. While Orchids focuses on the micro-temporal scale of low-level descriptors, Orchidea shifts attention to the macro-scale of musical onsets, providing a more accessible approach for the users. Section 20.5.4 provides further information about dynamic orchestrations with Orchidea.

20.2.2.2 CAMO-AIS

CAMO-AIS addresses a different drawback of the Orch* family, namely *diversity of orchestrations*. Diversity has been identified as an important property that can provide the composer with multiple alternatives given the highly subjective nature of musical orchestration combined with the complexity of timbre perception [19]. Theoretically, the use of MOO allows finding many orchestrations (see Sect. 20.4.2 for more details). However, in practice, the orchestrations returned by *Orchidée*, for example, were all very similar to one another, commonly differing by only one musical instrument sound [15]. Caetano et al. [1, 15] proposed to use an AIS called opt-aiNet to search for combinations of musical instrument sounds that minimize the distance to a reference sound encoded in a fitness function. CAMO-AIS relies on single-objective optimization (SOO) and the multi-modal ability of opt-aiNet to find multiple solutions in parallel. Opt-aiNet was developed to maximize diversity in the solution set, which results in alternative orchestrations for the same reference sounds that are different among themselves. The companion webpage for CAMO-AIS [12] has several sound examples that compare orchestrations returned by *Orchidée* and CAMO-AIS for their diversity and perceptual similarity with the reference.

20.2.3 Machine Learning

Recently, Antoine et al. [4–6, 57] proposed the interactive CAMO system i-Berlioz to address what is considered to be a hindrance to the compositional workflow of *Orchidée* and Orchids, namely the multiple orchestrations returned by these CAMO systems [51]. They argue that the process of listening to multiple orchestrations to select one can be tedious, ineffective, and time-consuming, especially when the user has a particular sound quality in mind [57]. Instead, they propose to *narrow down* the orchestrations returned by i-Berlioz with constraints, making i-Berlioz conceptually opposed to the principle of maximum diversity in CAMO-AIS. i-Berlioz [57] suggests combinations of musical instruments to produce timbres specified by the user by means of verbal descriptors. Currently, five semantic descriptors of timbre are supported, namely "breathiness", "brightness", "dullness", "roughness", and "warmth". A support vector machine classifier is trained to match instrument combinations to the semantic descriptions. Additionally, i-Berlioz is also capable of performing dynamic orchestrations [57].

20.3 Imitative Computer-Aided Musical Orchestration

The purpose of this section is to lay the groundwork for a formalization of imitative CAMO focusing on generative systems that use biologically inspired algorithms to search for orchestrations. The end of this section points out the technical difficulties involved in finding orchestrations that perceptually approximate a given reference sound. Then, Sect. 20.4 presents the solutions adopted to circumvent the difficulties in this formalization of imitative CAMO from a conceptual standpoint.

There are several bio-inspired generative CAMO algorithms (*Orchidée*, Orchids, Orchidea, and CAMO-AIS), each of which frames CAMO differently. Therefore, it would be impractical and rather confusing to try to exhaustively describe all of them. Instead, this section will focus on CAMO-AIS [1, 15], which closely follows the framework proposed by Carpentier et al. [17–22]. Section 20.4 will explore the main differences between CAMO-AIS and *Orchidée*, especially the differences between the optimization method adopted by each and the consequence in terms of diversity of orchestrations. It is out of the scope of this chapter to provide a detailed explanation of either the bio-inspired algorithms (GA and AIS) or the optimization methods (SOO and MOO). See the references in the respective sections for further details.

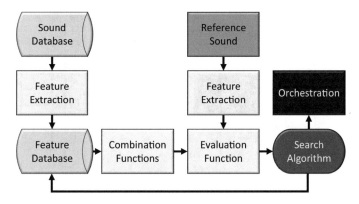

Fig. 20.3 Overview of CAMO-AIS. The figure illustrates the different components of the framework. Reprinted from [15] with permission from Elsevier

20.3.1 Overview

Figure 20.3 shows an overview of CAMO-AIS. The sound database is used to build a feature database, which consists of descriptors of pitch, loudness, and timbre calculated for all sounds prior to the search for orchestrations. The same descriptors are calculated for the reference sound being orchestrated. The combination functions estimate the descriptors of a sound combination from the descriptors of the individual sounds. The evaluation function uses these descriptors to estimate the similarity between combinations of descriptors from sounds in the database and those of the reference sound. The search algorithm opt-aiNet is used to search for combinations that approximate the reference sound, called orchestrations.

20.3.2 Representation

Figure 20.4a illustrates an orchestration as a combination of sounds from the sound database that approximates the reference sound when played together. Figure 20.4b shows the representation used by CAMO-AIS, in which an orchestration has M players $p(m)$, and each player is allocated a sound $s(n) \in S$, where $n = [1, \ldots, N]$ is the index in the database S, which has N sounds in total. Thus an orchestration is a combination of sounds $c(m, n) = \{s_1(n), \ldots, s_M(n)\}$, $\forall s_m(n) \in S$. Figure 20.4b shows $c(m, n)$ represented as a list, but the order of players $p(m)$ does not matter for the orchestration. Each sound $s_m(n)$ corresponds to a specific note of a given instrument played with a dynamic level, and $s_m(n) = 0$ indicates that player $p(m)$ was allocated no instrument.

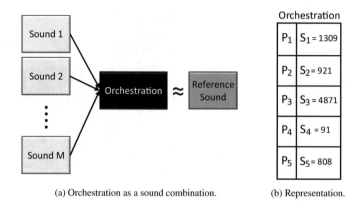

(a) Orchestration as a sound combination.   (b) Representation.

Fig. 20.4 Representation of orchestrations. Part **a** illustrates the orchestration as a combination of sounds that approximates the reference. Part **b** shows the internal representation of each orchestration in CAMO-AIS. Reprinted from [15] with permission from Elsevier

20.3.3 Audio Descriptor Extraction

Timbre perception excludes pitch, loudness, and duration (see Sect. 20.1.2). Therefore, we consider pitch, loudness, and duration separately from timbre dimensions. The descriptors used are fundamental frequency f_0 (pitch), frequency f, and amplitude a of the contribution spectral peaks A, loudness λ, spectral centroid μ, and spectral spread σ. The fundamental frequency f_0 of all sounds $s(n)$ in the database is estimated with Swipe [16]. The spectral centroid μ captures brightness while the spectral spread σ correlates with the third dimension of MDS timbre spaces [11, 40, 50, 56]. All the descriptors are calculated over short-term frames and averaged across all frames.

20.3.3.1 Contribution Spectral Peaks

The spectral energy that sound $s(m)$ contributes to an orchestration is determined by the *contribution spectral peaks* vector $\mathbf{A}_m(k)$. In what follows, only peaks whose spectral energy (amplitude squared) is at most 35 dB below the maximum level (i.e., 0 dB) are used and all other peaks are discarded. These peaks are stored as a vector with the pairs $\{a(k), f(k)\}$ for each sound $s(m)$, where k is the index of the peak. The *contribution spectral peaks* $\mathbf{A}_m(k)$ are the spectral peaks from the *candidate* sound $s(m)$ that are common to the spectral peaks of the *reference* sound r. Equation (20.1) shows the calculation of $\mathbf{A}_m(k)$ as

$$\mathbf{A}_m(k) = \begin{cases} a_s(k) & \text{if } (1+\delta)^{-1} \leq f_s(k)/f_r(k) \leq 1+\delta \\ 0 & \text{otherwise} \end{cases} \tag{20.1}$$

where $a_s(k)$ is the amplitude and $f_s(k)$ is the frequency of the spectral peak of the *candidate* sound, and $f_r(k)$ is the frequency of the *reference* sound.

Fig. 20.5 Contribution spectral peaks $\mathbf{A}_m$ (k). The figure shows the representation of the contribution spectral peaks of a candidate sound. Reprinted from [15] with permission from Elsevier

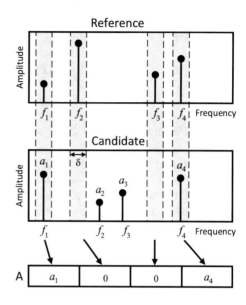

Figure 20.5 illustrates the computation of spectral peak similarity between the *reference* sound and a *candidate* sound. Spectral peaks are represented as spikes with amplitude a (k) at frequency f (k). The frequencies f_r (k) of the peaks of the *reference* sound are used as reference. Whenever the *candidate* sound contains a peak in a region δ around f_r (k), the amplitude a (k) of the peak at frequency f_s (k) of the *candidate* sound is kept at position k of the contribution spectral peaks vector $\mathbf{A}_m$ (k).

20.3.3.2 Loudness
Loudness λ is calculated as

$$\lambda = 20 \log_{10} \left(\sum_k a\,(k) \right), \tag{20.2}$$

where a (k) are the amplitudes at frequencies f (k).

20.3.3.3 Spectral Centroid
The spectral centroid μ is calculated as

$$\mu = \sum_k f\,(k) \frac{|a\,(k)|^2}{\sum_k |a\,(k)|^2}. \tag{20.3}$$

20.3.3.4 Spectral Spread

The spectral spread σ is calculated as

$$\sigma = \sum_k (f(k) - \mu)^2 \frac{|a(k)|^2}{\sum_k |a(k)|^2}. \tag{20.4}$$

20.3.4 Pre-processing

Prior to the search for orchestrations of a given reference sound r, the entire sound database S is reduced to a subset S^r of sounds that will be effectively used to orchestrate r. All the sounds whose contribution spectral peaks vector $\mathbf{A}_m(k)$ is all zeros are eliminated because these do not contribute spectral energy to the orchestration. Similarly, all the sounds whose f_0 is lower than f_0^r are eliminated because these add spectral energy outside of the region of interest and have a negative impact on the final result. Partials with frequencies higher than all frequencies in r are not considered because these are in the high-frequency range and typically have negligible spectral energy.

20.3.5 Combination Functions

The sounds $s(n)$ in an orchestration $c(m, n)$ should approximate the reference r when played together. Therefore, the combination functions estimate the values of the spectral descriptors of $c(m, n)$ from the descriptors of the isolated sounds $s(n)$ normalized by the RMS energy $e(m)$ [22]. The combination functions for the spectral centroid μ, spectral spread σ, and loudness λ are given, respectively, by

$$\mu_c = \frac{\sum_m^M e(m) \mu(m)}{\sum_m^M e(m)}, \tag{20.5}$$

$$\sigma_c = \sqrt{\frac{\sum_m^M e(m) \left(\sigma^2(m) + \mu^2(m)\right)}{\sum_m^M e(m)} - \mu_c^2}, \tag{20.6}$$

$$\lambda_c = 20 \log_{10} \left(\sum_m^M \frac{1}{K} \sum_k^K a(m, k) \right). \tag{20.7}$$

The estimation of the contribution spectral peaks of the combination $\mathbf{A}_c$ uses the contribution vectors $\mathbf{A}_s$ of the sounds $s(n)$ in $c(m, n)$ as

$$\mathbf{A}_r = \left\{ \max_{k \in K} [\mathbf{A}(m, 1)], \max_{k \in K} [\mathbf{A}(m, 2)], \cdots, \max_{k \in K} [\mathbf{A}(m, N)] \right\}. \tag{20.8}$$

20.3.6 Distance Functions

Equation (20.13) shows the calculation of the fitness value F of an orchestration as the weighted sum of distances D_j. Each distance D_j in Eq. (20.13) measures the difference between the descriptors from the reference sound r and the candidate orchestration $c_q(m, n)$, where q is the index of the orchestration among all the candidates for r, as follows:

$$D_\mu = \frac{|\mu(c_q) - \mu(r)|}{\mu(r)}, \tag{20.9}$$

$$D_\sigma = \frac{|\sigma(c_q) - \sigma(r)|}{\sigma(r)}, \tag{20.10}$$

$$D_\lambda = \frac{|\lambda(c_q) - \lambda(r)|}{\lambda(r)}. \tag{20.11}$$

The distance between the contribution vector of the reference sound $\mathbf{A}_r$ and the contribution vector of the orchestration $\mathbf{A}_c$ is calculated as

$$D_\mathbf{A} = 1 - \cos(\mathbf{A}_r, \mathbf{A}_c). \tag{20.12}$$

20.3.7 Calculating the Fitness of Orchestrations

The fitness of orchestration is an objective measure of the timbral distance between the orchestration and the reference. Since each descriptor used has an independent distance function D_j associated, the total fitness F is defined as the weighted combination of D_j expressed as

$$F(\alpha_j) = \sum_j \alpha_j D_j \quad \text{with} \quad \sum_j \alpha_j = 1 \quad \text{and} \quad 0 \le \alpha_j \le 1, \tag{20.13}$$

where j is the index of each feature, α_j are the weights, and D_j are the distance functions. The fitness value $F(\alpha_j)$ of a candidate orchestration calculated with Eq. (20.13) depends on the values of the weights α_j. Choosing numerical values for α_j subject to $\sum_j \alpha_j = 1$, $0 \le \alpha_j \le 1$ allows comparing numerically the fitness F of different orchestrations. Optimization of F following the numerical choice of α_j is known as SOO, which constrains the solutions found to that particular combination of weights. CAMO-AIS [1, 15] uses SOO to minimize F, whereas *Orchidée* [22] uses MOO. Section 20.4 will discuss the difference between SOO and MOO from the perspective of CAMO.

20.4 Computer-Aided Musical Orchestration with Bio-inspired Algorithms

The goal of imitative CAMO is to find a combination c of M musical instrument sounds s from a database S that perceptually approximates a given reference sound r. Section 20.3 formalized imitative CAMO as a function optimization problem, where the goal is to minimize the fitness F in Eq. (20.13). However, minimization of F is not a trivial task because it is an *inverse problem* and because F is a combination of *multiple objectives*. The formulation of CAMO as an inverse problem requires searching for orchestrations, so Sect. 20.4.1 discusses the need for bio-inspired algorithms to perform the search. Finding an orchestration requires minimizing the multiple distances encoded in the fitness function, and Sect. 20.4.2 discusses the use of SOO and MOO to do it.

20.4.1 Searching for Orchestrations for a Reference Sound

Calculating the fitness F of an orchestration with Eq. (20.13) requires multiple steps as shown in Fig. 20.3. Mathematically, the fitness function $\mathcal{F}$ measures the distance between a reference sound r and a combination $c\,(m, n)$ of M sounds from the database S as $F = \mathcal{F}\,(c, r)$. Thus, minimizing $\mathcal{F}$ can be expressed as

$$\min_{c(m,n)} \mathcal{F}\,(c, r), \quad c\,(m, n) = \{s_1\,(n)\,, \ldots, s_M\,(n)\} \in S^r \subseteq \mathbb{N}^M, \qquad (20.14)$$

which is read as "find the combination $c\,(m, n)$ of M sounds $s\,(n)$ from the database S^r that minimizes the distance F to r". This mathematical formulation of CAMO is known as an *inverse problem* in the optimization literature because $\mathcal{F}$ only allows to calculate the distance F given the combination c and the reference r. There is no inverse $\mathcal{F}^{-1}$ to retrieve which c corresponds to a specific F. So we cannot simply set a desired value for F and retrieve the orchestration(s) that correspond to it. In practice, we must search for the combination c that results in the minimum distance F.

At first, it might seem trivial to search for the orchestration that minimizes $\mathcal{F}$. For example, an exhaustive search will simply try all possible combinations and return the one with minimum distance F. However, the combinatorial nature of CAMO means that this *brute-force* approach will suffer from the growth in complexity as the size of the database S increases known as *combinatorial explosion*. Depending on the size of the database, an exhaustive search can take from a few minutes to longer than the age of the universe! In computational complexity, combinatorial optimization problems are said to be in NP. It is easy to check if a candidate is indeed an answer to a problem in NP, but it is really difficult to find any answer [38]. See the Clay Mathematics Institute webpage about the P versus NP problem [27] for further information. Carpentier et al. [18, 20–22, 76] formalized imitative CAMO as a binary allocation knapsack problem, which was proved to be NP-complete [46]. Thus, *heuristic* search strategies are typically used to find approximate solutions to imitative CAMO. Biologically inspired algorithms such as GA and AIS are popular choices because they use clever search heuristics to check promising instrument combinations.

20.4.1.1 Genetic Algorithms

GA uses an abstraction of biological evolution to provide computer systems with the mechanisms of adaptation and learning [30]. Evolution can also be seen as a method for designing innovative solutions to complex problems. Thus the GA evolves a population of candidate solutions represented as *chromosomes* by means of the genetic operators of mutation, crossover, and selection [37, 59]. A fitness function evaluates the quality of each individual of the population. The fittest individuals are selected to generate offspring by exchanging genetic material (crossover). Then the offspring undergo mutation and only the fittest offspring are selected for the next generation.

The *search space* comprises the collection of all potential solutions resulting from the representation adopted. A measure of "distance" between candidate solutions allows defining the neighborhood of regions in the search space as well as the *fitness landscape*, which is a representation of the fitness of all the individuals in the search space. A smooth fitness landscape is akin to a continuous function where "neighboring" candidate solutions have similar fitness values. Combinatorial optimization problems typically do not feature continuous fitness landscapes, adding to their difficulty. The mutation operator is responsible for the exploitation of the search space by introducing small random perturbations that search the neighborhood of promising regions. The crossover operator performs exploration of the search space under the assumption that high-quality "parents" from different regions in the search space will produce high-quality "offspring" candidate solutions. Finally, the selection operator is responsible for implementing the principle of *survival of the fittest* by only allowing the fittest individuals to generate offspring and be passed on to the next generation. So, GA work by discovering, emphasizing, and recombining good *building blocks* of solutions in a highly parallel fashion. Adaptation in a GA results from the trade-off between the exploration of new regions of the search space and the exploitation of the current promising regions (e.g., local optima). In fact, the parallel nature of the search can be interpreted as the GA allocating resources (i.e., candidate solutions) to regions of the search space based on an estimate of the relative performance of competing regions.

GA have become popular to solve hard combinatorial optimization problems, such as imitative CAMO. In fact, GA are particularly suited to find solutions in complex domains, such as music [10, 58, 60] and the arts [68, 78]. See also the online proceedings of the EvoMUSART conference [75] and the EvoStar web page [34]. In CAMO, the timbre arising from instrument combinations is unknown a priori and the orchestrations proposed by the GA might contain surprising combinations of musical instruments not contained in traditional orchestration manuals. However, GA also present several drawbacks, such as slow convergence and loss of diversity [59]. The next section will introduce AIS and focus on how the characteristic of *maintenance of diversity* can be used in CAMO.

20.4.1.2 Artificial Immune Systems

AIS are inspired by theoretical immunology and immune functions applied to solve real-world problems [28, 29]. The biological immune system features many properties that can be useful in several branches of science [29, 39], engineering [28, 77], and the arts [13, 61, 62], including robustness, pattern recognition, fault and noise tolerance, learning, self-organization, feature extraction, and diversity. Additionally, the immune system is self-organizing, highly distributed, adaptable to dynamic and complex environments, and displays cognitive properties such as decentralized control and memory [77], akin to neural networks. The (vertebrate) immune system is incredibly complex and not yet fully understood [39]. However, several mechanisms of the adaptive immune system have served as inspiration for AIS [29, 39], such as negative selection, immune network theory, and clonal selection, among others. Thus, it can be said that AIS use abstractions of immunological processes to endue algorithms with some of their properties. Consequently, AIS is an umbrella term that encompasses several different algorithms [29, 39, 77].

CAMO-AIS uses opt-aiNet [24], an AIS for multi-modal optimization that draws inspiration from the immunological principles of clonal selection, affinity maturation, and the immune network theory [29, 39, 77]. Clonal selection commonly serves as inspiration for search and optimization, whereas the immune network theory is commonly associated with learning [39]. Clonal selection algorithms [23] present a strong resemblance to GA without crossover, but their notion of affinity and their significantly higher mutation rate (i.e., hypermutation) distinguish them from similar adaptive algorithms [29, 39]. In opt-aiNet, hypermutation contributes to diversity [29, 77] and affinity maturation adds learning and adaptation. Additionally, the affinity measure is used in a suppression stage that is instrumental to the characteristic maintenance of diversity of opt-aiNet [24].

20.4.1.3 Maintenance of Diversity in Opt-aiNet

Opt-aiNet was developed to solve multi-modal optimization problems [29, 39, 77], which exhibit *local optima* in addition to a *global optimum*. A local optimum is better than its neighbors but worse than the global optimum. Figure 20.6 shows a (continuous) multi-modal function with global and local optima represented by the peaks. Standard optimization methods such as GA commonly only return one solution (i.e., one black dot) corresponding to one local optimum of the fitness function. The property of maintenance of diversity allows opt-aiNet to find and return multiple local optima in parallel.

Local optima can be very interesting for CAMO given the subjective nature of orchestration. Composers are seldom interested in the "best" solution to Eq. (20.14) in a mathematical sense. A set of multiple orchestrations to choose from is potentially more interesting from a compositional point of view. A CAMO algorithm that is capable of proposing multiple orchestrations in parallel that resemble the reference sound differently can be valuable. However, finding local optima of a multi-modal fitness function with SOO is not the only method to propose multiple orchestrations for a reference sound. MOO also allows finding multiple orchestrations in parallel.

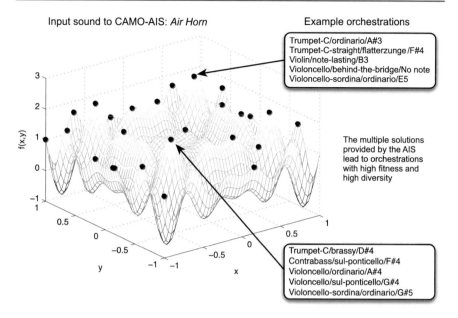

Fig. 20.6 Illustration of multi-modal function optimization in CAMO. The figure shows an objective function with multiple optima. The black dots represent multiple orchestrations returned by CAMO-AIS. Two example orchestrations for the reference sound *air horn* are given following the convention *instrument/playing technique/note*. Access the CAMO-AIS webpage [12] to listen to these orchestrations among several other examples. Reprinted from [15] with permission from Elsevier

Section 20.4.2 illustrates the difference between the SOO and the MOO approaches in CAMO. Then, Sect. 20.5 discusses the differences between these approaches, emphasizing the advantages and disadvantages of each.

20.4.2   Finding Orchestrations for a Reference Sound

Equation (20.13) defined the fitness $F(\alpha_j)$ of an orchestration as the weighted sum of the individual distances D_j calculated for each descriptor. It is important to note that the value of $F(\alpha_j)$ depends on the weights α_j. The SOO approach consists in choosing numerical values for α_j and finding one or more orchestrations corresponding to that particular combination of weights, whereas the MOO [79] approach returns multiple solutions corresponding to different values of the weights α_j. CAMO-AIS uses SOO and the multi-modal ability of opt-aiNet to find multiple local optima that maximize diversity in the feature space. *Orchidée* uses the well-known multi-objective genetic local search (MOGLS) optimization algorithm [45] to generate a pool of orchestrations by approximating the Pareto frontier [79].

Figure 20.7 shows the search space, the feature space, and the objective space to illustrate the difference between SOO and MOO conceptually. Each point in the

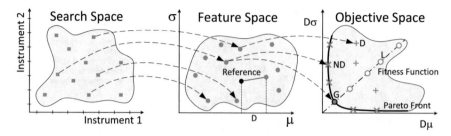

Fig. 20.7 Illustration of the different spaces in CAMO. The left-hand panel shows the search space, the middle panel shows the feature space, and the right-hand panel shows the objective space. Each point in the search space is an instrument combination (orchestration) that has a corresponding position in the feature space. The reference sound can also be seen in the feature space. The distances D between points in the feature space and the reference sound are calculated in the feature space. The weights α_j map points in the feature space to the objective space. Reprinted from [15] with permission from Elsevier

search space is an orchestration represented as an instrument combination that has a corresponding position in the feature space. The middle panel in Fig. 20.7 shows the reference sound (black dot) in the feature space among the orchestrations (gray dots) to illustrate the calculation of the distances D_j between the orchestrations and the reference sound. Finally, the objective space is obtained by associating a dimension to each distance D_j. The weights α_j map the distances D_j from the feature space to the objective space, where each point corresponds to a fitness value F of an orchestration.

The main difference between SOO and MOO lies in the objective space. In SOO, the weights α_j are fixed, so the objective space is one-dimensional (i.e., a line) and the fitness values F depend exclusively on the distances D_j. Therefore, minimizing F requires finding an orchestration whose distances D_j are as small as possible (i.e., as close as possible to the origin). In MOO, the weights α_j are not defined beforehand, so each point in the objective space (corresponding to a specific value F) depends on the values of both D_j and α_j. Each orchestration occupies a fixed point in the feature space, and so does the reference. Therefore, the distances D_j are also fixed for each orchestration. However, different weights α_j will map the same orchestration in the feature space to different points in the objective space, as illustrated in Fig. 20.7. Consequently, in MOO, each orchestration corresponds to multiple points in the objective space with varying values of F. Thus, minimizing the fitness function $\mathcal{F}(\alpha_j)$ requires finding both the orchestration with distances D_j and the combination of weights α_j for that specific orchestration that are as close to the origin as possible. So, there is more than one possible direction from which to minimize $\mathcal{F}(\alpha_j)$. In fact, there are multiple minima of $\mathcal{F}(\alpha_j)$ corresponding to different combinations of weights α_j. The set of all minima of $F(\alpha_j)$ is called *Pareto front*, illustrated in Fig. 20.7 as the thick border in the objective space.

Figure 20.7 illustrates the objective space with non-dominated solutions (ND) represented as "X" and dominated solutions (D) represented as "+". Solutions along the Pareto front are called non-dominated (ND) because there is no other solution whose value of $\mathcal{F}\left(\alpha_j\right)$ is closer to the origin. The SOO fitness function in the objective space can also be seen as a straight line containing the global optimum (G) illustrated as the filled "O" and the local optima (L) illustrated as the empty "O". Note that dominated solutions D can coincide with local optima L and, in turn, non-dominated solutions ND can coincide with the global optimum G. Thus CAMO-AIS returns solutions L that were discarded by *Orchidée* because there is a solution G closer to the reference in the same direction in the objective space (i.e., specified by the same α_j). Section 20.5 will explore further the consequence of the different approaches by CAMO-AIS and *Orchidée*.

20.5 Discussion

This section discusses aspects of the Orch* family and of CAMO-AIS. Firstly, the differences between the SOO and MOO approaches are examined more closely. Then, the attention shifts to the difference between dynamic orchestrations with Orchids and with Orchidea.

20.5.1 Perceptual Considerations

Conceptually, two values have important perceptual and aesthetic consequences in CAMO, namely the fitness value F and the weights α_j in Eq. (20.13). F is the objective measure of distance between the orchestrations and the reference. Therefore, minimizing F is conceptually similar to maximizing the timbral similarity, so F is inversely proportional to the perceptual similarity with the reference. In theory, a smaller F indicates a higher degree of similarity.

The weights α_j allow emphasizing the relative importance of each descriptor in the orchestrations returned. For example, a relatively high value of α_μ for the spectral centroid distance D_μ would penalize more severely orchestrations whose D_μ is higher. Consequently, the focus would be on matching *brightness* because it is the perceptual counterpart of the spectral centroid [56]. Therefore, α_j can be interpreted as specifying the *perceptual direction* from which an orchestration approaches the reference. In other words, the weights α_j control the perceptual dimension(s) of the similarity between the orchestration and the reference.

The main differences between the orchestrations by CAMO-AIS and by *Orchidée* result from the use of SOO and MOO, respectively. The MOO approach by *Orchidée* returns orchestrations that approximate the Pareto front, which is where the orchestrations with the lowest F are in the objective space. However, each point on the Pareto front corresponds to a different combination of α_j. Consequently, the orchestrations along the Pareto front approach the reference sound from different perceptual directions. Therefore, each orchestration returned by *Orchidée* is the most similar to the reference sound according to different criteria emphasized by the different

α_j. *Orchidée* prioritizes the objective similarity of Pareto optimal orchestrations over the perceptual similarity controlled by α_j. Consequently, the composer using *Orchidée* implicitly chooses a different perceptual direction by selecting an orchestration among the pool of solutions returned.

On the other hand, CAMO-AIS returns solutions that always approach the reference in the same direction, emphasizing the same perceptual similarities. Ultimately, α_j in CAMO-AIS are an aesthetic choice by the composer to determine the perceptual direction to search for orchestrations, allowing the composer to interactively explore the vast space of compositional possibilities. The trade-off is that, in theory, the timbral similarity between the orchestrations returned and the reference decreases. CAMO-AIS returns orchestrations that correspond to the local optima of the SOO fitness function, so the objective distance is not the smallest possible. Caetano et al. [15] compared the orchestrations returned by CAMO-AIS and *Orchidée* in terms of diversity and perceptual similarity with the reference. They showed that CAMO-AIS returns orchestrations with more diversity than *Orchidée*, yet the systems did not differ in perceptual similarity with the reference. Therefore, CAMO-AIS provides more options to the composer without loss of perceptual similarity. Section 20.5.2 delves deeper into the diversity of orchestrations.

20.5.2 Diversity of Orchestrations in CAMO-AIS

Some authors [51, 57] argue that CAMO systems that return multiple orchestrations present the composer with the challenge of choosing which one(s) to use. Instead, they suggest that there is a "best" solution to the imitative CAMO problem when it is posed correctly [51]. However, the CAMO framework described in this chapter does not narrow down the search space enough to admit only one solution. The descriptors of timbre used do not result in an exhaustive description such that multiple sounds would potentially match these descriptor values. In CAMO, this redundancy in the description of timbre translates as multiple instrument combinations approximating the reference timbral description.

Caetano et al. [15] argue that having multiple orchestrations provides aesthetic alternatives for the composer. The composer is rarely interested in a single combination (i.e., an orchestration) that optimizes some objective measure(s) with a reference sound [19]. Often, the composer uses CAMO tools to explore the problem space and find instrument combinations that would be missed by the empirical methods found in traditional orchestration manuals [51, 63]. The reference sound guides the search toward interesting regions of the search space, and α_j fine-tune the relative importance of perceptual dimensions of timbre similarity encoded in the fitness function.

CAMO systems that return only one orchestration seldom meet the requirements of the highly subjective and creative nature of music composition [19]. Very often, the composer will use subjective criteria not encoded in the objective measure(s) guiding the search to choose one or more orchestrations of interest. In that case, diversity provides the composer with multiple choices when orchestrating a reference sound, expanding the creative possibilities of CAMO beyond what the composer initially imagined. From that perspective, a CAMO algorithm should be capable of returning several orchestrations that are all similar to the reference sound yet dissimilar among themselves, representing different alternative orchestrations for that reference sound. Thus, diversity of orchestrations allows the exploration of different musical ideas [15].

20.5.3 Dynamic Orchestrations with Orchids

Orchids was the first CAMO algorithm to allow dynamic orchestrations. However, the approach proposed by Esling et al. [31–33] has both technical and usability issues resulting from the time series matching algorithm used for dynamic orchestration. Since both issues are related, we will discuss the technical aspect first and then the usability problem related to it. The time series matching algorithm at the heart of Orchids [32] matches the *shape* of the temporal variation of the descriptors used. The algorithm includes two pre-processing steps prior to matching, namely *descriptor range normalization* and *dynamic time warping* (DTW). Normalization works along the axis of the descriptor (e.g., Hz for the spectral centroid), whereas DTW equalizes the sound duration along the temporal axis. Thus, both the range of descriptor values and the absolute duration associated with the original sounds are lost. These pre-processing steps have the undesired side effect of matching shapes in the normalized descriptor space that would not be considered similar in the original descriptor space. In practice, perceptually different sounds may be matched by Orchids.

Two radically different sounds were used in the example as shown in Fig. 20.8 to illustrate the issue. The first sound is a two-second pure sine wave whose frequency varies from 440 Hz down to 400 Hz (in total, a 40 Hz frequency range variation). The second sound is a 14-second long orchestral recording in which strings perform a downward *glissando* whose range is about 200 Hz. The top panel of Fig. 20.8 shows the temporal variation of the spectral centroid of the original sounds, the sine wave is shown with a solid line, and the strings with a dashed line. Note how the shapes differ radically because of the absolute values of both frequency and time. The middle panel shows the result of normalizing the range of descriptors, where the sine wave and the orchestral *glissando* now occupy the same normalized frequency range. Finally, the bottom panel of Fig. 20.8 shows the result of applying DTW to both curves. Now, the shape of the two time series of descriptors is very similar, and the algorithms behind Orchids would match them even if the two sounds are perceptually very different. Additionally, matching fast decays in energy, long downward *glissandos*, slowly amplitude modulated sounds, or fast *vibratos* requires instrument sounds played with these techniques in the musical instrument sound database. This could result in an exponentially increasing size of the database with problems in scalability.

Finally, from the perspective of the composer, using time series of descriptors places the focus on the micro-temporal scale and on the low-level aesthetic, perceptual, and musical aspects that this scale implies. Instead of thinking about musical elements such as chords, notes, and musical scales, the user has to deal with the time series of spectral descriptors that are difficult to relate to orchestration problems. Users who had musical training but no technical background reported having dif-

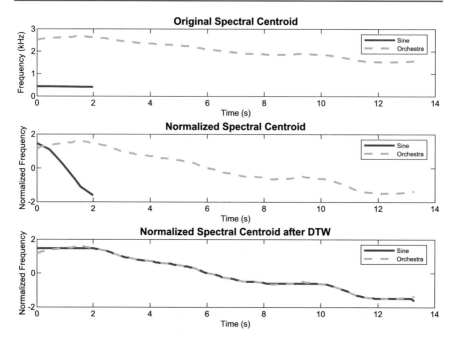

Fig. 20.8 The figure represents the spectral centroid of two radically different sounds. The top panel shows the original spectral centroids in kHz, the middle panel shows the spectral centroids after frequency range normalization, and the bottom panel shows the time-warped normalized spectral centroids. This kind of processing alters considerably the shape of the two spectral centroid curves, creating a mathematical match that is not representative of the perceptual similarity

ficulty interpreting orchestration results and this difficulty naturally led to usability issues. While several composers showed interest in micro-temporal dynamic orchestration, a large share of the community did not manage to use this idea efficiently.

20.5.4 Dynamic Orchestrations with Orchidea

In Orchidea, dynamic orchestrations focus on a different temporal scale when compared with Orchids. Orchidea shifts the focus from the micro-temporal scale of milliseconds typical of time series of descriptors to the more musically meaningful temporal scale of musical notes. Orchidea breaks up the reference sound into a sequence of *events* that are orchestrated separately. First, Orchidea uses a two-stage optimization process in a high-dimensional descriptor space. Finally, Orchidea ensures the continuation of the final orchestrations.

The main steps in Orchidea can be summarized as *segmentation*, *embedding*, *optimization*, and *continuation*. *Segmentation* determines the most important *musical events* in the reference sound with a *novelty*-based segmentation algorithm [35] that generates *sub-references* that are subsequently optimized separately. *Embedding* represents both the set of sub-references and the database of musical instrument sounds in a high-dimensional descriptor space. *Optimization* comprises a *preliminary* step followed by *refinement*. Stochastic matching pursuit performs the *preliminary* estimation of the orchestrations, followed by *refinement* with a GA performing SOO. Finally, a *continuation* model is applied on the selected solution for each subreference to minimize the number of changes for each instrument. Continuation is intended to improve the *voicing* of each player in the orchestra and to implement the orchestration principle of *dovetailing*: different instruments change notes at different times in order to maximize the blending of the orchestral colors (see pages 467–472 in [3]).

An interesting aspect of Orchidea is how it estimates the descriptors of instrument combinations. Given the high number of instrumental combinations generated during the optimization, it is impractical to synthesize a new audio file and then compute descriptors for every combination of sounds. Previous members of the Orch* family and CAMO-AIS estimate the descriptors of each candidate instrument combination using a simple energy-weighted linear combination (see Sect. 20.3.5), even if these descriptors are not themselves linear [22]. Orchidea takes a different approach and estimates the new descriptors using a non-linear long short-term memory (LSTM) deep neural network (DNN). While the training phase of the predictor is time-consuming, the estimation is very fast since it has a low complexity [36]. Refer to the Orchidea companion webpage [25] to listen to sound examples, download the system, and watch tutorial videos.

20.6 Conclusions

Musical orchestration remains one the most elusive aspects of musical composition to develop computer-assisted techniques due to its highly empirical approach combined with the complexity of timbre perception. A major consequence of this lack or formalization is that computer-aided musical orchestration (CAMO) is still in its infancy relative to other aspects of musical composition, such as harmony and rhythm. This chapter focused on *imitative* CAMO methods aimed at helping composers find instrument combinations that replicate a given reference sound. Imitative CAMO is formalized as the search for a combination of instrument sounds from a database that minimizes the timbral distance captured by descriptors of timbre. Biologically inspired algorithms such as genetic algorithms (GA) and artificial immune systems (AIS) are commonly used to minimize a single-objective or multi-objective fitness function that encodes timbral similarity between the candidate orchestrations and the reference.

Several aspects of imitative CAMO deserve further investigation, such as orchestrating time-varying reference sounds with dynamic orchestrations [26] and proposing orchestrations that feature diversity [15]. Similarly, future research effort should be devoted to improving specific steps such as timbre similarity measures or the timbre of instrument combinations [36]. However, this formulation of imitative CAMO, albeit powerful, stems from a conceptual framework first laid out over a decade ago [17, 20, 21]. In particular, the current framework of imitative CAMO addresses musical orchestration from the narrow scope of instrumentation via timbre matching [51]. Recent developments in machine learning and computational intelligence have the potential to lead to a paradigm shift in CAMO that breaks free from the constraints of imitative CAMO into the next generation of CAMO systems that will address orchestration as a whole. For example, Piston [65] mentions *background and accompaniment* as well as *voice leading and counterpoint*, whereas Maresz [51] argues that "high-level orchestration is the art of combining simultaneous yet different sound layers." Each layer relies on specific musical parameters to provide an identity depending on the musical context. This high-level approach to orchestration would require a formalization that includes *descriptors of orchestral qualities* rather than descriptors of timbre. Currently, little is known about the timbre of instrumental music [54] to propel CAMO into full-fledged orchestration systems. Initiatives such as the ACTOR project [2] are currently investigating musical orchestration from multiple perspectives to take the first steps in the exciting yet relatively unexplored world of computer-aided musical orchestration.

Acknowledgements This project has received funding from the European Union's Horizon 2020 research and innovation program under the Marie Sklodowska-Curie grant agreement No 831852 (MORPH).

References

1. Abreu, J., Caetano, M., & Penha, R. (2016). Computer-aided musical orchestration using an artificial immune system. In C. Johnson, V. Ciesielski, J. Correia, & P. Machado (Eds.) *Evolutionary and biologically inspired music, sound, art and design* (pp. 1–16). Springer International Publishing.
2. ACTOR. (2020). Actor project web page. Retrieved June 18, 2020, from https://www.actorproject.org/.
3. Adler, S. (1989). *The study of orchestration*. London and New York: W. W. Norton and Company.
4. Antoine, A., & Miranda, E. R. (2015). Towards intelligent orchestration systems. In *11th International Symposium on Computer Music Multidisciplinary Research (CMMR)*, Plymouth, UK (pp. 671–681).
5. Antoine, A., & Miranda, E. R. (2017). Musical acoustics, timbre, and computer-aided orchestration challenges. In *Proceedings of the 2017 International Symposium on Musical Acoustics*, Montreal, Canada (pp. 151–154).
6. Antoine, A., & Miranda, E. R. (2017). A perceptually oriented approach for automatic classification of timbre content of orchestral excerpts. *The Journal of the Acoustical Society of America, 141*(5), 3723. https://doi.org/10.1121/1.4988156.
7. Antoine, A., & Miranda, E. R. (2018). Predicting timbral and perceptual characteristics of orchestral instrument combinations. *The Journal of the Acoustical Society of America, 143*(3), 1747. https://doi.org/10.1121/1.5035706.
8. Assayag, G., Rueda, C., Laurson, M., Agon, C., & Delerue, O. (1999). Computer-assisted composition at IRCAM: From PatchWork to OpenMusic. *Computer Music Journal, 23*(3), 59–72.

9. Barthet, M., Depalle, P., Kronland-Martinet, R., & Ystad, S. (2010). Acoustical correlates of timbre and expressiveness in clarinet performance. *Music Perception: An Interdisciplinary Journal, 28*(2), 135–154. https://doi.org/10.1525/mp.2010.28.2.135.

10. Biles, J. (1994). GenJam: A genetic algorithm for generating Jazz solos. In *Proceedings of the International Computer Music Conference* (p. 131). International Computer Music Association.

11. Caclin, A., McAdams, S., Smith, B., & Winsberg, S. (2005). Acoustic correlates of timbre space dimensions: A confirmatory study using synthetic tones. *The Journal of the Acoustical Society of America, 118*(1), 471–482.

12. Caetano, M. (2019). CAMO-AIS web page. Retrieved June 18, 2020, from http://camo.prism.cnrs.fr/.

13. Caetano, M., Manzolli, J., & Von Zuben, F. J. (2005). Application of an artificial immune system in a compositional timbre design technique. In C. Jacob, M. L. Pilat, P. J. Bentley, & J. I. Timmis (Eds.), *Artificial immune systems* (pp. 389–403). Berlin, Heidelberg: Springer.

14. Caetano, M., Saitis, C., & Siedenburg, K. (2019). Audio content descriptors of timbre. In K. Siedenburg, C. Saitis, S. McAdams, A. N. Popper, & R. R. Fay (Eds.), *Timbre: Acoustics, perception, and cognition* (pp. 297–333). Cham: Springer International Publishing. https://doi.org/10.1007/978-3-030-14832-4_11.

15. Caetano, M., Zacharakis, A., Barbancho, I., & Tardón, L. J. (2019). Leveraging diversity in computer-aided musical orchestration with an artificial immune system for multi-modal optimization. *Swarm and Evolutionary Computation, 50*. https://doi.org/10.1016/j.swevo.2018.12.010.

16. Camacho, A., & Harris, J. (2008). A sawtooth waveform inspired pitch estimator for speech and music. *Journal of the Acoustical Society of America, 124*(3), 1638–1652.

17. Carpentier, G. (2008). Approche Computationnelle de L'Orchestration Musicale-Optimisation Multicritère sous Contraintes de Combinaisons Instrumentales dans de Grandes Banques de Sons. Ph.D. thesis, Université Pierre et Marie Curie-Paris VI.

18. Carpentier, G., Assayag, G., & Saint-James, E. (2010). Solving the musical orchestration problem using multiobjective constrained optimization with a genetic local search approach. *Journal of Heuristics, 16*(5), 681–714.

19. Carpentier, G., Daubresse, E., Garcia Vitoria, M., Sakai, K., & Villanueva, F. (2012). Automatic orchestration in practice. *Computer Music Journal, 36*(3), 24–42. https://doi.org/10.1162/COMJ_a_00136.

20. Carpentier, G., Tardieu, D., Assayag, G., Rodet, X., & Saint-James, E. (2006). Imitative and generative orchestrations using pre-analysed sound databases. In *Proceedings of the Sound and Music Computing Conference* (pp. 115–122).

21. Carpentier, G., Tardieu, D., Assayag, G., Rodet, X., & Saint-James, E. (2007). An evolutionary approach to computer-aided orchestration. In M. Giacobini (Ed.), *Applications of evolutionary computing* (Vol. 4448, pp. 488–497)., Lecture Notes in Computer Science Berlin, Heidelberg: Springer.

22. Carpentier, G., Tardieu, D., Harvey, J., Assayag, G., & Saint-James, E. (2010). Predicting timbre features of instrument sound combinations: Application to automatic orchestration. *Journal of New Music Research, 39*(1), 47–61.

23. de Castro, L., & Von Zuben, F. (2002). Learning and optimization using the clonal selection principle. *IEEE Transactions on Evolutionary Computation, 6*(3), 239–251.

24. de Castro, L. N., & Timmis, J. (2002). An artificial immune network for multimodal function optimization. In *Proceedings of the Congress on Evolutionary Computation, CEC'02* (Vol. 1, pp. 699–704). IEEE.

25. Cella, C. E. (2020). Orchidea web page. Retrieved June 18, 2020, from www.orch-idea.org.

26. Cella, C. E., Esling, P. (2018). Open-source modular toolbox for computer-aided orchestration. In *Proceedings of Timbre 2018: Timbre Is a Many-Splendored Thing*, Montreal, Canada (pp. 93–94).

27. Clay-Mathematics-Institute (2020). P vs NP problem. Retrieved June 18, 2020, from https://www.claymath.org/millennium-problems/p-vs-np-problem.
28. Dasgupta, D. (2006). Advances in artificial immune systems. *IEEE Computational Intelligence Magazine, 1*(4), 40–49. https://doi.org/10.1109/MCI.2006.329705.
29. de Castro, L. N., & Timmis, J. (2002). *Artificial immune systems: A new computational intelligence approach.* Springer.
30. De Jong, K. (1988). Learning with genetic algorithms: An overview. *Machine Learning, 3*(2–3), 121–138. https://doi.org/10.1007/BF00113894.
31. Esling, P., & Agon, C. (2012). Time-series data mining. *ACM Computing Surveys, 45*(1), 1–34. https://doi.org/10.1145/2379776.2379788.
32. Esling, P., & Agon, C. (2013). Multiobjective time series matching for audio classification and retrieval. *IEEE Transactions on Audio, Speech, and Language Processing, 21*(10), 2057–2072. https://doi.org/10.1109/TASL.2013.2265086.
33. Esling, P., Carpentier, G., & Agon, C. (2010). Dynamic musical orchestration using genetic algorithms and a spectro-temporal description of musical instruments. Lecture Notes in Computer Science (Vol. 6025, pp. 371–380). Berlin, Heidelberg: Springer.
34. EvoStar. (2019). EvoStar web page. Retrieved June 18, 2020, from www.evostar.org.
35. Foote, J., & Cooper, M. L. (2003). Media segmentation using self-similarity decomposition. In *Proceedings of SPIE 5021, Storage and Retrieval for Media Databases 2003*, January 10, 2003. https://doi.org/10.1117/12.476302.
36. Gillick, J., Cella, C. E., & Bamman, D. (2019). Estimating unobserved audio features for target-based orchestration. In *Proceedings of the 20th International Society for Music Information Retrieval Conference*, Delft, the Netherlands (pp. 192–199).
37. Goldberg, D. (1989). *Genetic algorithms in search, optimization and machine learning.* Reading, MA: Addison-Wesley Professional.
38. Goldreich, O. (2010). *P, NP, and NP-completeness: The basics of computational complexity.* New York, NY: Cambridge University Press.
39. Greensmith, J., Whitbrook, A., & Aickelin, U. (2010). Artificial immune systems. In M. Gendreau & J. Y. Potvin (Eds.), *Handbook of metaheuristics.* International Series in Operations Research & Management Science (Vol. 146, pp. 421–448). US, Boston, MA: Springer. https://doi.org/10.1007/978-1-4419-1665-5_14.
40. Grey, J. (1977). Multidimensional perceptual scaling of musical timbres. *The Journal of the Acoustical Society of America, 61*(5), 1270–1277.
41. Grey, J., & Gordon, J. (1978). Perceptual effects of spectral modifications on musical timbres. *The Journal of the Acoustical Society of America, 63*(5), 1493–1500.
42. Handelman, E., Sigler, A., & Donna, D. (2012). Automatic orchestration for automatic composition. In *1st International Workshop on Musical Metacreation (MUME 2012)* (pp. 43–48). AAAI.
43. Helmholtz, H. (1895). *On the sensations of tone as a physiological basis for the theory of music.* London, New York: Longmans, Green, and Co.
44. Hummel, T. (2005). Simulation of human voice timbre by orchestration of acoustic music instruments. In *Proceedings of the International Computer Music Conference (ICMC)* (p. 185).
45. Jaszkiewicz, A. (2002). Genetic local search for multiple objective combinatorial optimization. *European Journal of Operational Research, 1*(137), 50–71.
46. Karp, R. M. (1972). Reducibility among combinatorial problems. In R. E. Miller & J. W. Thatcher (Eds.), *Complexity of computer computations* (pp. 85–103). New York: Plenum Press.
47. Kendall, R. A., & Carterette, E. C. (1993). Identification and blend of timbres as a basis for orchestration. *Contemporary Music Review, 9*(1–2), 51–67. https://doi.org/10.1080/07494469300640341.
48. Kopiez, R., Wolf, A., Platz, F., & Mons, J. (2016). Replacing the orchestra?—The discernibility of sample library and live orchestra sounds. *PLOS ONE, 11*(7), 1–12. https://doi.org/10.1371/journal.pone.0158324.

49. Krimphoff, J., McAdams, S., & Winsberg, S. (1994). Caractérisation du timbre des sons complexes. II. Analyses acoustiques et quantification psychophysique. *Journal de Physique IV France, 04*(C5), 625–628 (1994).
50. Krumhansl, C. L. (1989). Why is musical timbre so hard to understand? Structure and perception of electroacoustic sound and music *9*, 43–53.
51. Maresz, Y. (2013). On computer-assisted orchestration. *Contemporary Music Review, 32*(1), 99–109. https://doi.org/10.1080/07494467.2013.774515.
52. Mathews, M. V., Miller, J. E., Pierce, J. R., & Tenney, J. (1965). Computer study of violin tones. *The Journal of the Acoustical Society of America, 38*(5), 912–913. https://doi.org/10. 1121/1.1939649.
53. McAdams, S. (2019). Timbre as a structuring force in music. In K. Siedenburg, C. Saitis, S. McAdams, A. N. Popper, & R. R. Fay (Eds.), *Timbre: Acoustics, perception, and cognition* (pp. 211–243). Cham: Springer International Publishing. https://doi.org/10.1007/978-3-030-14832-4_11.
54. McAdams, S. (2019). Timbre as a structuring force in music. In K. Siedenburg, C. Saitis, S. McAdams, A. N. Popper, & R. R. Fay (Eds.), *Timbre: Acoustics, perception, and cognition* (pp. 211–243). Cham: Springer International Publishing. https://doi.org/10.1007/978-3-030-14832-4_8.
55. McAdams, S., & Giordano, B. L. (2009). The perception of musical timbre. In S. Hallam, I. Cross, & M. Thaut (Eds.), *The Oxford handbook of music psychology* (pp. 72–80). New York, NY: Oxford University Press.
56. McAdams, S., Winsberg, S., Donnadieu, S., De Soete, G., & Krimphoff, J. (1995). Perceptual scaling of synthesized musical timbres: Common dimensions, specificities, and latent subject classes. *Psychological Research, 58*(3), 177–192.
57. Miranda, E. R., Antoine, A., Celerier, J. M., & Desainte-Catherine, M. (2019). i-Berlioz: Towards interactive computer-aided orchestration with temporal control. *International Journal of Music Science, Technology and Art, 1*(1), 15–23.
58. Miranda, E. R., & Biles, J. A. (Eds.). (2007). *Evolutionary computer music*. London: Springer. https://doi.org/10.1007/978-1-84628-600-1.
59. Mitchell, M. (1996). *An introduction to genetic algorithms*. Cambridge, MA: MIT Press.
60. Moroni, A., Manzolli, J., Von Zuben, F., & Gudwin, R. (2000). Vox Populi: An interactive evolutionary system for algorithmic music composition. *Leonardo Music Journal, 10*, 49–54.
61. Navarro, M., Caetano, M., Bernandes, G., Castro, L., & Corchado, J. (2015). Automatic generation of chord progressions with an artificial immune system. In *Proceedings of EVOMUSART 2015*.
62. Navarro-Cáceres, M., Caetano, M., Bernardes, G., & de Castro, L. N. (2019). ChordAIS: An assistive system for the generation of chord progressions with an artificial immune system. *Swarm and Evolutionary Computation, 50*. https://doi.org/10.1016/j.swevo.2019.05.012.
63. Nouno, G., Cont, A., Carpentier, G., & Harvey, J. (2009). Making an orchestra speak. In *Sound and music computing*. Porto, Portugal.
64. Peeters, G., Giordano, B. L., Susini, P., Misdariis, N., & McAdams, S. (2011). The timbre toolbox: Extracting audio descriptors from musical signals. *The Journal of the Acoustical Society of America, 130*(5), 2902–2916. https://doi.org/10.1121/1.3642604.
65. Piston, W. (1955). *Orchestration*. London: W. W. Norton & Company.
66. Psenicka, D. (2003). SPORCH: An algorithm for orchestration based on spectral analyses of recorded sounds. In *Proceedings of International Computer Music Conference (ICMC)* (p. 184).
67. Risset, J. C. (1965). Computer study of trumpet tones. *The Journal of the Acoustical Society of America, 38*(5), 912. https://doi.org/10.1121/1.1939648.
68. Romero, J., & Machado, P. (Eds.). (2007). *The art of artificial evolution: A handbook on evolutionary art and music.*, Natural Computing Series. Berlin, Heidelberg: Springer.

69. Rose, F., & Hetrik, J. E. (2009). Enhancing orchestration technique via spectrally based linear algebra methods. *Computer Music Journal*, *33*(1), 32–41.
70. Saitis, C., Giordano, B. L., Fritz, C., & Scavone, G. P. (2012). Perceptual evaluation of violins: A quantitative analysis of preference judgments by experienced players. *The Journal of the Acoustical Society of America*, *132*(6), 4002–4012. https://doi.org/10.1121/1.4765081.
71. Siedenburg, K., Jones-Mollerup, K., & McAdams, S. (2016). Acoustic and categorical dissimilarity of musical timbre: Evidence from asymmetries between acoustic and chimeric sounds. *Frontiers in Psychology*, *6*, 1977. https://doi.org/10.3389/fpsyg.2015.01977.
72. Siedenburg, K., & McAdams, S. (2017). Four distinctions for the auditory "wastebasket" of timbre. *Frontiers in Psychology*, *8*, 1747. https://doi.org/10.3389/fpsyg.2017.01747.
73. Siedenburg, K., Saitis, C., & McAdams, S. (2019). The present, past, and future of timbre research. In K. Siedenburg, C. Saitis, S. McAdams, A. N. Popper & R. R. Fay (Eds.), *Timbre: Acoustics, perception, and cognition* (pp. 1–19). Cham: Springer International Publishing. https://doi.org/10.1007/978-3-030-14832-4_1.
74. Slawson, W. (1985). *Sound color*. Berkeley: University of California Press.
75. Springer. (2020). *Proceedings of the International Conference on Computational Intelligence in Music, Sound, Art and Design (Part of EvoStar)*. Retrieved June 18, 2020, from https://link.springer.com/conference/evomusart.
76. Tardieu, D., & Rodet, X. (2007). An instrument timbre model for computer aided orchestration. In *Applications of Signal Processing to Audio and Acoustics, 2007 IEEE Workshop* (pp. 347–350). IEEE.
77. Timmis, J., Knight, T., de Castro, L. N., & Hart, E. (2004). An overview of artificial immune systems. In R. Paton, H. Bolouri, M. Holcombe, J. H. Parish, & R. Tateson (Eds.), *Computation in cells and tissues: Perspectives and tools of thought* (pp. 51–91). Berlin, Heidelberg: Springer. https://doi.org/10.1007/978-3-662-06369-9_4.
78. Todd, S., & Latham, W. (1994). *Evolutionary art and computers*. USA: Academic Press Inc.
79. Yang, X. S. (2004). Multi-objective optimization. In X. S. Yang (Ed.) *Nature-inspired optimization algorithms* (pp. 197–211). Oxford: Elsevier. https://doi.org/10.1016/B978-0-12-416743-8.00014-2.

Marcelo Caetano Marcelo Caetano received the Ph.D. degree in signal processing from *Université Pierre et Marie Curie* and *Institut de Recherche et Coordination Acoustique/Musicque* (IRCAM), France, under the supervision of Prof. Xavier Rodet in 2011. He worked as a postdoctoral fellow at the Signal Processing Laboratory of the Foundation for Research and Technology—Hellas (FORTH), Greece, and at the Sound and Music Computing group of INESC TEC, Portugal. In 2017, Dr. Caetano was a visiting researcher at the Application of Information and Communication Technologies (ATIC) research group of the University of Malaga, Spain. In 2019, Dr. Caetano received funding from the European Union's Horizon 2020 research and innovation program under the Marie-Sklodowska Curie grant agreement No 831852 (MORPH). Currently, Dr. Caetano is a research fellow of the Centre for Interdisciplinary Research in Music Media and Technology (CIRMMT) at McGill University, Canada, and of the laboratory Perception, Representations, Image, Sound, and Music (PRISM) of the *Centre National de la Recherche Scientifique* (CNRS), France. Dr. Caetano is interested in the connection between mechanisms of sound production and sound perception. His research focuses on analysis and synthesis for sound transformation, musical orchestration, and musical timbre. Email: marcelo.caetano@mcgill.ca; marcelo.caetano@prism.cnrs.fr

Carmine Emanuele Cella is an internationally acclaimed composer with advanced studies in applied mathematics. He studied piano, computer music, and composition and he got a Ph.D. in musical composition at the Accademia di S. Cecilia in Rome and a Ph.D. in applied mathematics at the University of Bologna entitled On Symbolic Representations of Music (2011). From 2007 to 2008, Carmine-Emanuele Cella had a research position at Ircam in Paris working on audio indexing. In 2008, he won the prestigious Petrassi prize for composition, from the President of the Italian Republic Giorgio Napolitano, and he has been nominated member of Academie de France à Madrid for 2013–2014 at Casa de Velazquez. In 2015–2016, he conducted research in applied mathematics at École Normale Supérieure de Paris with Stéphane Mallat and he won the prize Una Vita Nella Musica Giovani at Teatro La Fenice in Venice. In 2016, he was in residency at the American Academy in Rome, where he worked on his first opera premiered in June 2017 at the National Opera of Kiev. Since January 2019, Dr. Cella has been Assistant Professor in music and technology at CNMAT, University of California, Berkeley. E-mail: carmine.cella@berkeley.edu

Human-Centred Artificial Intelligence in Concatenative Sound Synthesis

21

Noris Mohd Norowi

21.1 Introduction

Concatenative Sound Synthesis (CSS) is a data-driven method to synthesize new sounds from a large corpus of small sound snippets. It unlocks endless possibilities of re-creating sounds, which is exciting, particularly as the technique also necessitates very little musical knowledge for anyone to utilize. However, synthesizing a specific sound does require more than just matching segments of sound at random. Very few synthesis results are the result of the first raw output. Sometimes, sound manipulation and transformation need to be applied to the synthesized sound. At other times, the desired results can only be achieved by adding or removing certain sound segments in the corpus collection. This trial-and-error run is indeed a tedious and frustrating process, and this uninspiring method of producing music making may hinder creative composition from happening. The inclusion of Artificial Intelligence (AI) can potentially facilitate this process by making the machines which synthesizes the new sounds to understand exactly the composer's vision, through the seed sound provided. Thus, an ideal machine that implements any AI technique that can dissect and decipher accurately what the composer wants based on the seed sounds, also referred to as the query, is provided.

N. M. Norowi (✉)
Faculty of Computer Science and Information Technology, Universiti Putra Malaysia, 43400 Serdang, Selangor, Malaysia
e-mail: noris@upm.edu.my

© Springer Nature Switzerland AG 2021
E. R. Miranda (eds.), *Handbook of Artificial Intelligence for Music*,
https://doi.org/10.1007/978-3-030-72116-9_21

21.2   Sound Synthesis: A Brief Overview

A very broad definition of *sound synthesis* is given as designing sound through the combination of certain base waveforms and processes. Loosely, the general usage of the term referring to the process of synthesizing sounds is taken as designing a sound 'from scratch'. There can be many motivations behind synthesizing sounds, but one of the most common reasons is to enable the emulation of existing sounds. For instance, sound synthesis allows the replication of sounds that are difficult to capture, e.g. in the case of a human performance, replacing the need of a human performer. In addition to producing usual, everyday sounds, it is also useful in producing 'new', unheard of sounds such as creating sound effects for the production of films depicting various sci-fi or fantasy characters. Moreover, sound synthesis can also mix life-like sounds and physically impossible sounds together, providing composers with endless possibility of creating different range of sounds.

There are many ways in which sounds can be synthesized: from combining basic waveforms together, to formulating complex mathematical algorithms to reconstruct a sound's physical attributes. These include syntheses that are derived through spectral or Fourier-based techniques (e.g. subtractive synthesis, additive synthesis and wavetable synthesis), modulation techniques (i.e. amplitude, frequency or based modulations), waveshaping synthesis (e.g. distorting an input waveform using a transfer function), time modelling (e.g. granular synthesis, re-synthesis by fragmentation) and physical modelling (e.g. modal synthesis). A more thorough dissection of the strengths, weaknesses and suitability of each of these techniques can be found covered by several experts in the area [7, 8, 18, 20, 24, 29].

Despite the many different sound synthesis techniques available, the techniques above are mostly considered to be in low-level terms. This is because sound syntheses using these techniques are carried out by attempting direct emulation of the intended sound, which typically involves basic analysis of the sound, followed by addition or elimination of different parameters until the replication of desired sound is reached. The configuring and re-configuring numerical input into the sound synthesis system until the anticipated sound is synthesized is both a laborious process and is difficult to achieve. In addition, low-level sound synthesis techniques do not take into account any qualitative input from composers. Miranda [18] proposed that the situation can be improved by combining these sound synthesis techniques with Artificial Intelligence (AI) techniques.

AI research has discovered how to embed mechanisms in computers so that they can be made to act in an intelligent manner and perform the very same task as humans can. In the context of this sound synthesis, AI is desirable for several main reasons: (1) to automate the process making it more efficient as it requires fewer resources; (2) to help reduce errors in exhaustive judgement-related tasks and (3) adept at deciphering the needs and visions of composers. A system that can generate new sounds that are in line with the composers' interpretation is highly sought after. This can be achieved by enhancing the AI elements in current sound synthesis systems, but also at the same time extending the user control on these system, so as to form a fluent, symbiotic relationship between man and machine.

Typically, there are two approaches to sound synthesis with AI: rule based and data driven. Synthesis using rule-based model includes the use of a set of assertion, or 'rules' that are constructed from the collective knowledge of composers, which specify the actions or solutions when certain conditions are met. Data-driven model, on the other hand, does not involve rules to create sound, but instead utilizes sound corpus to re-create sounds. Its intelligence lies in the selection algorithm that it employs to select the string of sound units that most closely match the input specifications. The data-driven approach is the more common approach employed in Concatenative Sound Synthesis (CSS). This means that new sounds are created by re-synthesizing a seed sound to sounds available in the corpus. The obvious advantage of using the data-driven model in the synthesis of music is that it preserves the fine details of the sound as it uses actual recordings, as opposed to modelling sounds from scratch which is rule based is applied. Using actual sounds also means that it is easier to materialize sounds that have been envisaged in the minds of composers, a feat that is extremely difficult otherwise to perform with the rule-based approach. However, this approach requires a larger storage space compared to rule-based synthesis. Nevertheless, it is an ideal solution when naturalness is a priority and space is not an issue—generally, the larger the size of the database, the more likely an exact matching sound is to be found, hence greatly reducing the need to apply transformation on the sounds from a data-driven CSS system.

21.3 How Can Concatenative Sound Synthesis Synthesize Sounds?

CSS involves taking in a stream of sound as a target or seed sound and decomposing it into smaller sound segments or target units. Each target units are then analysed on its spectral and other auditory content. From the analysis, each target unit has a digital 'genetic makeup', which is used as the basis of finding a similar unit in the database containing a large collection of sound segments or source units. Once a matching source unit in the database is found for a particular target unit, that particular source unit is selected and the same step is repeated with the next target unit. These selected segments are then concatenated together in string of sound unit sequence, and are then re-synthesized to produce new sounds (Fig. 21.1).

Essentially, CSS is synthesizing new sounds by matching small segments of a seed sound with segments of sounds from an existing corpus collection. Although many factors can affect the outcome of this synthesis, in general, resulting synthesis should somewhat resemble the original seed sound. This technique can produce really interesting synthesis sometimes. For example, the outcome of matching a seed sound of a popular country song to a sound corpus of screaming primates

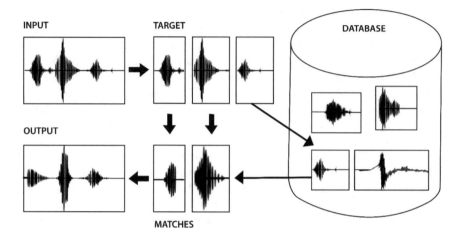

Fig. 21.1 The basic mechanism of a CSS system

results in what sounds like a group of monkeys 'singing' the unmistakable melody of the country song!

This method of sound creation had been inspired by the art of mosaicing. Mosaics are designs and pictures formed from a process of putting bits and pieces (called tesserae or tiles) made of cubes of marbles, stones, terracotta or glass of different range of colours to create larger, whole images. Mosaics are typically seen in many decorative paraphernalia and are also applied to the design of many significant cultural and spiritual erections of the past. Through the same concept of rearranging small tiles together to produce a larger, more meaningful artwork, mosaicing has been applied to digital image synthesis and digital audio synthesis and is referred to as 'photomosaicing' and 'musaicing' (musical mosaicing), respectively. In photomosaicing, small tiles of images are assembled together to compose a bigger, overall picture [30], as illustrated in Fig. 21.2. Likewise, musical

Fig. 21.2 Example of photomosaic

mosaicing assembles a large number of unrelated sound segments together according to specifications from the target sounds.

In photomosaic, images are synthesized by matching the target units with the source units in the database based on information such as size, shape, colour orientation and pixels. In the same respect, there are many properties or parameters which can be used as a basis for similarity matching between the target units and the source units in the musaicing process in CSS. To comprehend the impact that different audio properties may have on the synthesis result, it is important to understand the stages involved in a typical CSS system. There are two major phases: analysis and synthesis. During the analysis phase, both the original sounds (seed) and the sounds in the corpus (source) are segmented into smaller sound snippets. Following segmentation, relevant information from these sound snippets are then extracted. The extracted information defines each segment of what they are, and become the source of comparison when matches are made.

In some CSS systems, a 'Query' stage is sometimes added between the target input, database and unit selection process. Granted, this stage had always been implicitly present; however, it needs to be acknowledged that the query stage is essential and in fact, the core of the system, as all means of command from the user gets communicated through. By adding the query stage, it is made apparent that different parameters can be added, selected or enabled, e.g. audio feature options, weight assignments for each feature, clarifying the perceptual attribute that defines the basis of sound similarity, creating a taboo list and threshold of match, etc. Many of the research work on improving synthesis results from CSS systems are more commonly focused on the transformation part, i.e. smoothing the seams between two sound segments when they are joined. While this is a valid move, this suggests that the process of deciphering and fine-tuning to match the composer's vision only happens after the synthesis process has already taken place. Perhaps it makes more sense for any CSS system to seek clarification to further understand the composer's synthesis requirements, long before the matching process even commences.

This then continues with the synthesis phase, sound snippets in the database that match closely with the targets are selected and concatenated together forming a long string of sound, which are then synthesized. Figure 21.3 presents the flow model of a basic CSS system.

The common components of any CSS system include a database, a sound segmenter, seed (target units), source units (units in the corpus collection), audio features or descriptors, matching units and intelligence. Short descriptions for each of the components are as follows:

- Database
  In general, the database is a collection of files, but instead of only storing the actual audio files or the corpus, it can also save the source files, references, units, unit descriptors and the relationships between all of the entities in it. The actual synthesis of sound is also generated from the database.
- Sound Segmenter

Fig. 21.3 The flow model of
a basic CSS system

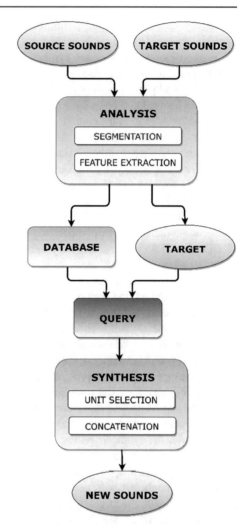

In order to synthesize concatenatively, audio files in the database need to be
segmented into smaller units, that is, 500 milliseconds or less. Typically, this is
done based on the spectral changes which occur in the stream of audio, but can
also be done through time based or even arbitrarily.

- Seed Units (Target Sounds)

  Seed units or the target sound are the seeds or pieces of audio that are supplied to
  a CSS system as an input so that matching units can be searched from the
  database and be played back concatenatively as the output. The seed units can be
  supplied to the system in several ways, such as providing a short piece of music
  to the system, through a microphone, or using a MIDI keyboard or instruments.

- Source Units (Sounds in Corpus Collection)

Source units are the units which are available to be concatenated in the database. Similar to seed units, the source units usually have already been extracted to obtain certain descriptor characteristics.

- Audio Features or Descriptors
  Feature extraction is the process of computing a compact numerical representation that can be used to characterize a segment of audio. An audio signal has many different quantities or features that can be extracted, which may be related to physiological auditory models or to spectral models of the sound. Examples of audio features are such as pitch, loudness, energy, Zero Crossing Rate (ZCR), Root Mean Square (RMS), Centroid, Flux, Mel-Frequency Cepstral Coefficients (MFCCs), etc.

- Matching Units
  The matching unit is the unit or sequence of unit that is returned for playback based on the seed that is originally provided. The way in which a matching unit is selected is normally based on its distance from the target, where the lowest distance value is selected. Euclidean distance is commonly used in many CSS systems as it corresponds to the perceptual similarity between the seed and the source unit [12]. Based on the Pythagoras theorem, the Euclidean distance measures the straight line distance between two points. When multidimensional features are used, the Euclidean distance calculates the distance between two vector points, x and y, and is given in the equation below, where x_j (or y_j) is the coordinate of x (or y) in dimension j.

$$d_{x,y} = \sqrt{\sum_{j=1}^{J} \left(x_j - y_j \right)^2}$$

- Intelligence
  The selection process contains the algorithm where the seed is actually matched with a sound unit from the database. Hence, this stage is also known as the backbone of a data-driven concatenative synthesis as it is reflects its 'intelligence'.

CSS systems which are used to aid musical creation in the early years are such as CataRT [26], Skeleton [15], Musical Mosaic [33] and MATConcat [28]. The more recent work on CSS systems includes RhythmCAT [23], SuperSampler [32], EarGram [3], Audio Guide [14], Audio Garden [10] and Database System for Organizing Musique Concrète [2]. Although the core of these systems functions in a similar manner from another, different systems brought about different strengths and advancement over the previous systems. Earlier systems notably focused more in areas concerning the input mechanism, feature analysis, use of transformation, real-time capability and graphical user interfaces, while the more recent works gave more highlights on interaction, visualization and rhythm and tempo capacity. A more detailed review of the CSS systems is discussed by Nuanáin et al. [23], and Bernardes [4].

21.4   What Affects CSS Result?

The phrase 'rubbish in, rubbish out' holds true for any CSS system. Being data driven, it goes without saying that the output of any CSS system is directly dependent on the nature and content of the source sounds made available in the database. Expecting to produce graceful classical music of high elegance from a corpus containing only of industrial sound effects such as the aggressive grinding of metals is stretching it a bit too far (though probably not impossible). The further away the nature of the source sounds are from the seed sounds, the broader and more divergent the concatenation output can be expected. It is common sense to include only the sounds which are as close as possible to the desired synthesis sounds. Nevertheless, adding uncharacteristic source files in the database can potentially create interesting surprises to the synthesis results too. Often times, only by experimenting with a wide range of source files will these interesting syntheses be discovered. Similarly, changing the seed sounds will also result in a different synthesis, even if the source sounds in the database remains the same. This is because the seed units and their extracted information act as a blueprint for any new musical creation in CSS.

Another key factor that affects synthesis result is the database size. A database with very few source units to be selected from can be insufficient to produce a quality synthesis, regardless of how thoroughly the source sounds have been curated to suit the intended synthesis. This is because there are few source units to choose from and selected for concatenation. Depending on the rules set, if a CSS system allows for the same source units to be selected and concatenated repeatedly, the resulting synthesis from a limited corpus may literally sound like a 'broken record'—playing the same units again and again as if the vinyls on the record are severely scratched. Regardless, it must be acknowledged the bigger the database, the longer the time it takes for the CSS system to search for the matching files to concatenate and synthesize. Like other cases with search and retrieval, there is also a ceiling point where no matter how large the content of the database is added, the accuracy is no longer improved. Therefore, it is wise to set the database to be large and relevant, but not excessive.

In order to be synthesized concatenatively, audio files in the database need to be segmented into smaller units. The most primitive way to do this is to do it manually, but it can be laborious and time-consuming. Automatic or semi-automatic segmentation helps to facilitate the task. Segmentation can either be event based, time based or even arbitrarily. Event-based segmentation produces heterogeneous units of various lengths, as the segmentation is only initiated when a characteristic change in the audio stream is detected, e.g. the entrance of a guitar solo or a change from spoken words to music. One of the ways to perform event-based segmentation is by separating the musical signals at the boundaries of audio objects, i.e. where the note starts (onset) or where it finishes (offset). Onset and offset segmentation is particularly useful for the modelling of attacks, as it helps localizing the beginning of an event and has been employed in segmentation for many different applications such as music classification, characterization of rhythmic pattern and tempo tracking [5]. Time-based segmentation results in homogeneous units (uniform-sized), as the sound stream is segmented at every specific millisecond. Time-based concatenation can sometimes produce atypical synthesis, as the source units can end up being cut at an unfortunate place in time. This abrupt chopping approach has made it lighter and demands less computational power, compared to event-based segmentation which heavy computational power to compute the algorithms for different events and conditions. Hence, for a live performance which requires real-time concatenation, perhaps homogeneous segmentation is preferred. One solution to solve the mid-stream cut-off challenge that happens with time-based segmentation is by adding a transformation algorithm to make the joints between the concatenating units smoother. Thus, different segmentation modes will result in different concatenation results as there will be different number of units, different information extracted for each unit sequence, etc. Different segmentation modes are best suited for different kinds of audio and given the variety of options available, users should be provided with options when selecting which modes are more applicable [6]. Intelligently automating the segmentation mode to suit the purpose of composition is also worth exploring.

Each of the segmented sound unit has unique characteristics that can be extracted from the segment itself. These descriptors are sometimes interchangeably referred as features, and can be generated from either the audio signal, their spectral, acoustical, perceptual, instrumental or harmonic properties, or symbolic score. There are many different features that can be extracted, and they may be extracted based on their acoustical properties such as pitch, loudness, energy and formants. Features are normally extracted automatically in a process known as audio feature extraction—a process of computing a compact numerical representation that can be used to characterize a segment of audio. Usually, the use of one feature is not enough for any unique deductions to be made about a sound; therefore, it is common that several features are combined into feature vectors. Feature vectors list all features for a single point in time. Figure 21.4 depicts a feature vector from the combination of d features. The d-dimensional space defined by the feature vector is also known as the 'feature space' and the floating points in the feature space are sound characteristics.

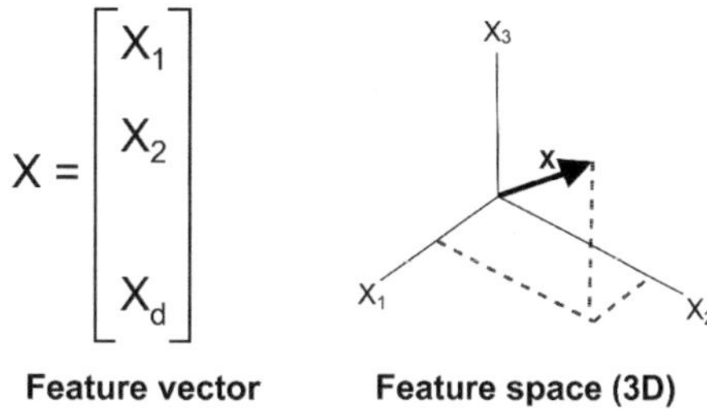

Fig. 21.4 Feature vector and feature space

$$X = \begin{bmatrix} X_1 \\ X_2 \\ \\ X_d \end{bmatrix}$$

Feature vector

Feature space (3D)

In most cases, when several features are extracted together, a step called normalization of the feature vector is required. Normalizing a vector is done by
dividing a norm of the vector, for example, to make Euclidean length of the vector
equal to one. It is often referred as scaling by a minimum and range of the vector, to
make all elements lie between 0 and 1. In a CSS system, both the source units and
seed units will have to undergo feature extraction. The values obtained from the
feature extraction of both of these source units and seed units are what is compared
when calculating the similarity distance between them. As explained earlier, there
are many different levels in which the audio files can be extracted—time domain,
frequency domain, time–frequency domain, etc. Each of these levels have the
potentials of extracted hundreds of different audio features. For example, the Root
Mean Square Amplitude (RMS) and the Zero Crossing Rate (ZCR) are
time-domain audio features, while fundamental frequency and harmonicity are
examples of frequency-domain audio features. One of the more important audio
characteristics that researchers have been trying to extract is 'timbre'. Timbre refers
to the colour of sound and is typically divorced conceptually from pitch and
loudness [31]. Perceptual research on timbre has demonstrated that the spectral
energy distribution and temporal variation in this distribution provide the acoustical
determinants of human's perception of sound quality [13]. Many researchers
believe that the timbral quality of brightness correlated with increased power at high
frequencies. For example, a note played at a high pitch generally has a higher
spectral centroid than when it is played at a lower pitch, even when the note is
played on the same instrument. Thus, spectral-based features such as spectral
centroid, spectral roll off, spectral flux, mel-frequency cepstral coefficients and
combinations therewith may be able to help timbre-related audio tasks.

In general, the more audio features extracted, the higher chance that a closer
match can be found between the seed unit and the source units in the database.
However, a multitude random audio features are not necessary, as they demand
higher computational power to compute and take longer time to process (Fig. 21.5).
Furthermore, in many cases, not all features may be relevant for comparison in unit
selection. CSS system will benefit from a mechanism that is able to not only

Fig. 21.5 Result of different audio features on synthesis (runtime). Note that as the number or features added increases, so does the runtime duration

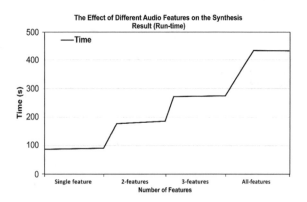

intelligently suggest which relevant audio features to extract for a particular composition task, but one that can also allow users to have control in deciding and ranking which audio features have more importance over other features by assigning different weights on these features.

The algorithm that matches the seed unit to the source unit in the database during the unit selection stage is another factor that determines the outcome of the synthesis. Most CSS systems are programmed to perform search using the Viterbi algorithm, but some utilizes a fixed search algorithm such as KNN, or some descendent form of local search algorithm. There are many more search methods available that might be just as useful for finding the match between the seed unit and the source unit. Each of the search algorithms is designed to carry out search in a slightly different manner, so applying the most fitting search method is essential. Trade-offs such as accuracy, speed and computational load are some of the criteria that must be taken into consideration. For instance, when fast results are more important than high accuracy (e.g. in a live performance), the simplest search algorithm may be the best option. However, when composing a piece of music that requires high fidelity to the original target sound, a search algorithm that can deliver a more accurate match takes precedence.

21.5 At All Costs

An ideal CSS system should offer the flexibility of fine-tuning the factors that affect synthesis result. For instance, although it is possible to extract all the possible audio features, the most practical option would be to extract only the features that are most relevant or features that can distinctly improve the target distance between the seed units and the source units, as mentioned earlier. This distance is also referred to as 'target cost'.

Another 'cost' that is sometimes measured in the unit selection stage in concatenative sound synthesis is the concatenation cost. The concatenation cost measures the quality of the join between two consecutive units. This is why the concatenation distance is interchangeably referred as the join cost. The relationship between the target distance and the concatenation distance is illustrated in Fig. 21.6. This suggests that for any synthesis, the distance between the seed unit, t_i, needs to be compared first with the source unit, u_i. Once the source unit with the shortest distance is determined, its concatenation cost is calculated by comparing its value with the value of the previous source unit concatenate in the string of audio [26].

Hence, for any synthesis, the distance between the seed unit, t, needs to be compared with the source unit, u. Once the source unit with the shortest distance is determined, its concatenation cost is calculated by comparing its value with the value of the previous source unit concatenate in the string of audio.

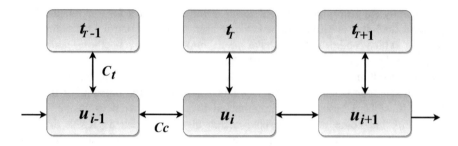

Fig. 21.6 The relationship between target cost (C_t) and concatenation cost (C_c)

$$C\left(t_1^n, u_1^n\right) = \sum_{i=1}^{n} C(t_i, u_i) + \sum_{i=2}^{n} C(t_{i-1}, u_i)$$

Concatenation cost is useful because sometimes, the 'best' unit does not necessarily lie within the unit which returns the lowest target distance, but could come from another candidate unit with a slightly larger target distance but with smaller distortion. This situation appears more apparent in concatenative speech synthesis than it is in music, as the degradation in the naturalness of speech utterance can be very noticeable to human. Music, being a more subjective domain, is less affected by this. As expected, including concatenation cost into the calculation can demand more computational resources from a CSS system. To compromise on this, the concatenation cost can be omitted when segment continuity is less important. An intelligent CSS system should be able to differentiate when it is necessary to include concatenation cost and when it can do without it. Additionally, a smart CSS system would also be able to weigh lighter option between calculating both target and concatenation costs together, or relying solely on target cost and remedying continuity later through linear smoothing or other transformation such as amplitude and pitch corrections.

Alternatively, a hierarchical model can be applied where the target cost is calculated first, and the concatenation cost is only calculated if there is any dispute over the matching units, for instance, in the case of homosonic units or equidistant units. Homosonic units are units that have the same sonic properties with each other, but do not sound the same when played. This can happen when the use of only one (or very few audio) features is/are compared, and the extracted values for the limited features of the two units appear identical. Only when additional features are further extracted does it reveal that the two units have different audio signal make up. For example, two homosonic sounds may carry the same values when the intensity level is compared, but when played, both sounds are very different timbrally. This happens because the timbral information has not been included in the initial extraction and thus not compared (Fig. 21.7).

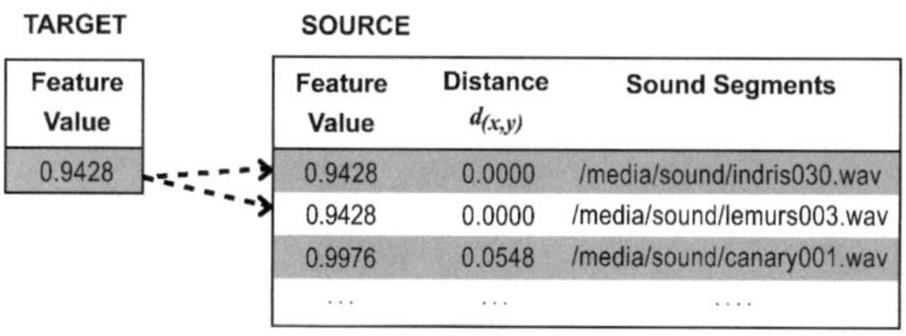

TARGET	SOURCE		
Feature Value	Feature Value	Distance $d_{(x,y)}$	Sound Segments
0.9428	0.9428	0.0000	/media/sound/indris030.wav
	0.9428	0.0000	/media/sound/lemurs003.wav
	0.9976	0.0548	/media/sound/canary001.wav
	…	…	…..

Fig. 21.7 Unit selection involving homosonic segments

In such situations, two most common solutions are practised in existing CSS systems: (1) to select the source segment that appears on the top of the list and (2) to randomly select any of the segments that have the same sonic information. The former solution presents noticeable weaknesses, the most obvious being the tendency to select only the first matching source segment that appears in the list of possible solutions, disregarding other equally qualified segments. Since the list is typically arranged alphabetically, source segments represented with the filename that begins with letters that are further down the alphabetical order are almost never selected, unless a 'taboo list' function or selection without replacement is enabled. The flaw is even more intensified when there are several segments in the target segment that occur more than once, which can give way to a very tediously repetitive sound. The latter solution reduces the chances of re-selecting the first line of segments in the list of matching units, but the randomness of this process suggests that there is very little intelligence or reasoning behind the selection.

Another challenge that stems from a similar situation is the occurrence of 'equidistant' segments in the returned list of matching segments. In contrast to homosonic segments, equidistant segments occur when there is no exact match found in the database, but several source segments with same distance from the target segment are present (Fig. 21.8). Again, there is the issue of which segments should be selected from the list resurfaces. Selecting the first segment on the list or random selection will both result in the previously described flaws. Thus, a more intelligent solution to overcome unit selection issues involving homosonic and equidistant segments in existing CSS systems is needed.

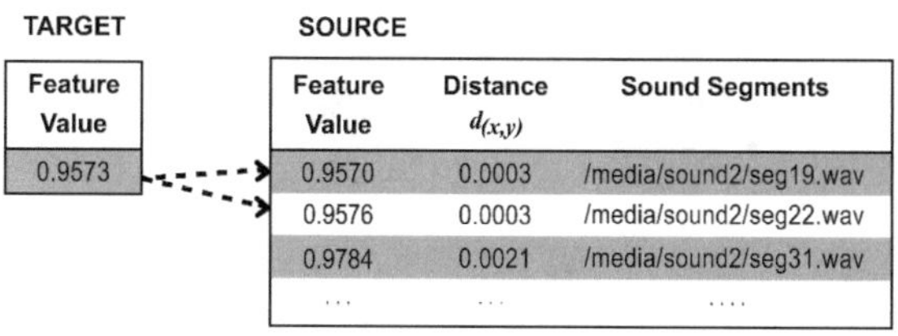

TARGET	SOURCE		
Feature Value	Feature Value	Distance $d_{(x,y)}$	Sound Segments
0.9573	0.9570	0.0003	/media/sound2/seg19.wav
	0.9576	0.0003	/media/sound2/seg22.wav
	0.9784	0.0021	/media/sound2/seg31.wav
	…	…	…..

Fig. 21.8 Unit selection involving equidistant segments

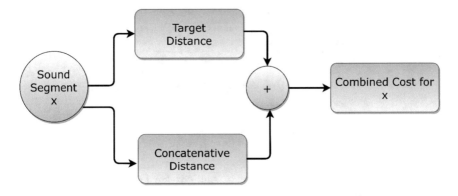

Fig. 21.9 Non-hierarchical model in CSS systems

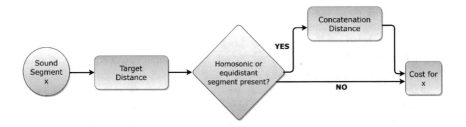

Fig. 21.10 Hierarchical model in CSS systems

As homosonic units and equidistant units can potentially be solved through the use of concatenation cost, albeit more costly in terms of processing power and time. However, performing the costs calculation in a hierarchical fashion can reduce the computational demands as the concatenation cost is only calculated when there are homosonic or equidistant segments present. The structural difference between the two models is shown in Figs. 21.9 and 21.10. Not only does a hierarchical model slices the problem into smaller, manageable tasks, but it also cuts down the effort over an otherwise complex and time-consuming process.

21.6 Human-Centred Artificial Intelligence: That's not What I Ordered

Issues that have been discussed thus far have all been concerning on improving the synthesis results by reducing the target and concatenation distances of the source units to the seed units—the technical aspects of existing CSS systems. However, the fundamental issue lies in the question—'*what makes humans perceive two sounds*

Target   Database

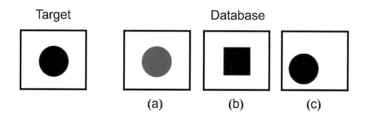

(a)   (b)   (c)

Fig. 21.11 Issue with basis of similarity in visual data—which image in the database has the closest similarity to the target?

as similar?' The technical issues may have undergone many improvements, but unless the above question is answered, CSS systems may be generating sounds that are numerically identical to the original seed, but one that is actually far from the expectation of its users.

A more visual example can be seen in determining image similarity. Figure 21.11 consists of a target image which is a picture of a centrally located black circle. Of the three images: (a) a centrally located grey circle, (b) a centrally located black square and (c) a black circle situated on the bottom left corner. The question is, which of the three images between (a) and (c) would be considered the image that has the closest match to the target image? Image (a) has the right shape and is spatially correct, but of a different colour. Image is also spatially correct and has the right colour, but of a different shape. Image (c) is off spatially, but is otherwise the correct colour and shape from the target image.

Similarly, if a target sound is of an A4 note played on a piano, which is a closer match, an A4 note played on a wind instrument or a C4 note played on a piano? There are different attributes that can become the basis of sound similarity, the basics being elements such as pitch, rhythm, tempo, timbre and loudness. Moreover, combinations of these elements then give rise to higher order concepts such as meter, key, melody and harmony [16, 19]. Identifying the perceptual audio attributes that influence sound similarity in humans may reveal the audio feature sets that are more likely to extract relevant information from sounds, which can possibly return perceptually closer matching segments from the database. Determining which audio attributes are more dominant maybe the key to improving similarity in sounds generated by CSS systems. Which attributes do humans find to be more dominant than others (if any)? There is only so much that an intelligent CSS system can do, but unless it figures out what exactly is it '*this*' means when a human composer submits a request to the CSS system to '*generate something that sounds close to this, please*', then all effort is rather useless.

Therefore, the only way forward is to focus on Human-Centred Artificial Intelligence (HCAI). HCAI is the study and design of algorithms that perform tasks or behaviours that a person could reasonably deem to require intelligence if a human were to do it [25]. Examples of the use of HCAI in our daily lives are such as in the use of many speech assistant systems, for instance, Siri, Google Assistant,

Cortana and Alexa. Its use can also be seen in products recommender that sneaks onto our screen when we are online, making gutsy assumptions that we need a certain product based on our online activity and search history. It is trying to understand exactly what we mean based on our questions and behaviour.

Thus, deciphering what a human composer means by '*this*' in the '*compose-me-a-sound-that-sounds-like-this*' query, extends more than just matching two sounds which has similar frequency, amplitude and phase. Sounds very rarely exist in this simple form and usually the Fourier analysis is used to break down complex sounds into a series of simple sounds to achieve this. The psychology of sound, on the other hand, is based on the human perception of these criteria, and also the time factor, giving rise to other sound elements such as pitch, intensity, timbre and rhythm. Usually, human listeners have a well-developed feeling whether two songs sound similar or whether they do not [1].

A study has been conducted to further understand how humans perceive sound similarity by identifying the dominant acoustic information on which judgements are based by humans when performing a sound similarity task [21]. The study presented participants with a task to choose between the two source tracks which they felt were more similar to the seed track. The test was designed so that each source tracks in the comparison would correspond to a different attribute from one another. For example, in a melody versus timbre pair, one source track would be melodically similar to the target, while the other would be closer in terms of timbral similarities, while other perceptual attributes that were not being compared were kept constant. A total of four attributes were included—melody, timbre, loudness and tempo.

It was found that when asked in a forced choice manner to select one (source) sound that they felt were the closest match to the seed sound, the result was not always agreeable among the human subjects, particularly between the musician group and the non-musician group. While it was consistently agreed that tempo and loudness played very little impact on sound similarity match in both groups, i.e. very few people refer to the same tempo or the same loudness when they query for a source sound to be generated from a given seed sound, no dominant sound attribute could be established. The scores for both melody and timbre tied—the scores were almost equal! Interestingly, non-musicians based their similarity on the melody, while the musicians referred to timbre during the similarity test. This means that non-musicians tended to select source sounds which had the same melody as the seed sounds, whereas when the same test was conducted on musicians, they had mostly based their selection on the timbral similarity of the source sounds to the seed sounds.

Melody seems to be the most dominant perceptual attribute for audio. This could be because melody is perceptually grouped as part of the same event unfolding over time, based on Gestalt's principles of perceptual organization such as similarity, proximity and good continuation. As humans conform to these principles, melody tends to be preferred over attributes such as tempo or loudness [11]. This phenomenon could also be the direct result of how the human brain is designed. The human brain is divided into two hemispheres, the left lies the more logical and calculative thinking and the right handles the more intuitive feelings. Musicians tend to use the left hemisphere of the brain to a larger extent when listening to music because they possess an analytical knowledge of it and thus approach music more intellectually. In comparison, those with no musical background mostly perceive music in the right hemisphere because they are not analysing, but are simply experiencing the music [27].

This also suggests that human's musical background strongly affects the similarity judgement as musical training alters the way music is perceived by humans. This test shows that musicians generally are more tuned to selecting sounds that are similar timbrally than they are melodically, whereas the reverse is true for non-musicians. Again, this is possibly owing to their analytical behaviour in listening to music, where experienced musicians can be very sensitive in assessing similarities based on the quality of musical expressions rather than the actual melody. Therefore, sounds that are deemed similar melodically to the non-musicians may not be 'similar' enough for musicians. For example, two same melodies played at varying speed and intensity may still be perceived as two similar sounds by a layperson, but musicians may not agree so strongly, having scrutinized the discrepancies in the technical details such as the tempo and loudness. In addition, timbre is fuzzy in nature to begin with. There is no clear-cut classes or range for timbres which are normally found with other perceptual attributes (e.g. tempo and loudness can be described quantitatively such as slow, fast, low, medium, high or even in a given range such as 110–120 bpm). With timbre, two very different sound sources can be perceived to have very similar sounding timbre, e.g. sound of the rain hitting the roof and sound of food frying in a pan of hot oil. Unable to approach timbral similarity in the same technical sense as it is for melody, musicians may deduce that two sounds are less dissimilar timbrally than melodically, hence explaining their sound similarity perception.

At this stage, it is still difficult to conclude whether sound similarity perception in humans is influenced by their musical training alone. Age, experience and even sex might have also affected the result. However, it is clear that sound similarity is still a very wide and complex area that is yet to be fully understood. To develop a working CSS system with human-centred artificial intelligence that can understand and suggest similar sounds to what humans actually perceive at the time when they perform the sound similarity query is a really difficult challenge. Unfortunately, due to the extreme complexity (too many features to compute, extract, and map to the correct sound attributes, data too large to make analysis from, subjective nature of the topic, etc.), this level of perfection is yet to be accommodated.

21.7   Is Similar, Interesting?

Supposing that a flawless technique has been developed to locate source units that has a 100% similarity rate with the original seed units on every single sound features extracted, at every single time that it is run. This flawless technique will have appeared utterly useless for generating new sounds, as theoretically, it will be composing its identical self. This brings out the next fundamental question in synthesis new sounds via a CSS system—how similar is desirable? Furthermore, does high similarity always equate to high creativity and interestingness? In the field of sound retrieval, the highest possible similarity score is always sought, but in a more creative and artistic purposes such as sound composition, higher is not always better.

Likewise, if the sounds are too similar, is it not of little use for the composers as it lacks originality? It may even tread into the serious issue of plagiarism. This opens up another thought-provoking question: how similar is acceptable? A definite answer to this question cannot be easily derived, and certainly beyond the scope of this chapter, but it is nonetheless interesting to note that the performance of a CSS system cannot simply be measured solely on the use of precision and recall as is the case in many sound similarity systems or speech synthesis systems.

A study to understand the correlation between similarity and interesting has been done in [22], where participants were presented with a target sound, followed by another sound which was explained to them as a source sounds synthesized using CSS (not all were). A total of ten sounds were presented, and they appeared in an ascending order based on their similarity scores. Participants were asked to listen to a list of target sounds and then make a subjective judgement on their perceived similarity between both sounds. They were also asked to rate the 'interestingness' level of the synthesized sounds, i.e. is how pleasant or amusing they found the sound that was synthesized from the target sound to be using a Likert scale. For measuring perceived similarity, the scale was between (1) entirely different and (5) exactly the same. For measuring perceived interestingness, the scale was between (1) extremely uninteresting and (5) extremely interesting. The list of songs is seen in Table 21.1, where the first five sounds were assortment of synthesis results based on loudness, spectral and timbral content, and sounded granular like. The last three sounds in the test were not actually synthesized sounds, but main-stream songs which had been chosen because the analysis on their melodic contour showed that they were melodically similar to their target sounds.

The study found that with respect to *similarity*, both musician and non-musician groups agreed that as the listening test progressed, the sounds appeared to possess more similar qualities to their targets (Fig. 21.12). This suggests that general agreement on sound similarity is very much possible.

The same could not be said, however, for the humans' perception of sound *interestingness*. The non-musician group had exhibited a general disinterest in the earlier sounds presented, but thought the sounds towards the end of the test, where the similarity scores were higher, were more interesting. On the other hand, the musician group seemed have a neutral liking of all sounds initially, but exhibited a drop in the interestingness score for the last few sounds with higher similarity score (Fig. 21.13).

Thus, humans possessed the same ability and managed to achieve an agreement with regard to judging sound similarity which tallies with the similarity score calculated, irrespective of their musical training background or knowledge of

Table 21.1 List of songs for similarity versus interestingness

	Target	Source	Matching criteria	CSS system
1	Mahler, Ritenuto (2nd Symphony)	Monkeys	Loudness, spectral rolloff	*Matconcat*
2	Mozard, Sonata K 457 (3rd Mvmt)	Whales	Spectral centroid	*ConQuer*
3	Meat Purveyors, Circus Clown	Indris	Spectral centroid	*ConQuer*
4	George W. Bush, Military Speech	Monkeys	Unlisted	*MATConcat*
5	Schoenberg, String Qrt 4, (lst Mvmt)	Anthony Braxton	Spectral centroid, spectral rolloff	*MATConcat*
6	Cornershop, Brimful of Asha	Cornershop, Brimful of Asha (remix)	Melody	N/A
7	Natasha Beddingfield, Pocketful of Sunshine	Lady Gaga, So Happy 1 Could Die	Melody	N/A
8	Green Day, Warning	The Kinks, Picture Book	Melody	N/A

Fig. 21.12 Perceived similarity judgement between musician and non-musician group

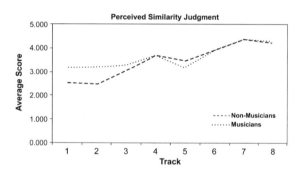

Fig. 21.13 Perceived interestingness judgement between musician and non-musician group

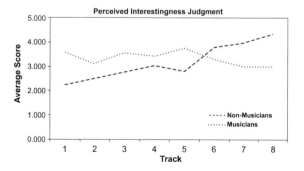

music. This occurrence suggests that perhaps similarity is an innate skill for humans. Judgement on sound interestingness, however, was not as straightforward as musicians do not always perceive sounds with higher similarity sounds score to be more aesthetically pleasing. This difference is perhaps due to the different ways in which the brain is programmed between the two groups upon hearing an audio event. Rigorous training and experience over the years has left musicians to perceive the musical experience primarily in the left hemisphere of their brains. This made them more analytical and approach music more intellectually. On the other hand, non-musicians dominantly occupy the right hemisphere of the brain during a listening task, and hence they do not analyse music, but are simply experiencing it [27].

Also with respect to interestingness, many educated musicians may not appreciate music unless it is 'profound', whereas non-musicians, who are the majority, may prefer music that makes them feel good. So it is possible that a musician writes a piece of music that is extremely complex and is heralded by the academic music world as a masterpiece, but the same piece may only be perceived as boring or too cerebral by the general [9]. Non-musicians are also likely to be influenced by the 'exposure effect', where familiarity with, or exposure to, repeated songs bred partiality on the sounds that they favoured [17]. This means that unfamiliar sounds are perceived as peculiar and unpopular.

As sound similarity and sound interestingness do not always occur simultaneously, for any sound creation tool like the CSS system, the key to synthesizing the 'right' materials lies in finding the balance between similarity and interestingness. The synthesized sounds must not be too similar to the target to be perceived as boring or unoriginal, yet at the same time not too dissimilar as to render the involvement of the target segment useless or falsely accused as plagiary. Again, the incorporation of not just AI, but human-centred AI, is imperative in order to obtain an insight over complex thinking process that a human composer goes through. This will undoubtedly avoid synthesis results in a CSS system that mismatch user's expectations.

21.8 Where Are We Now?

This chapter has highlighted that in order to overcome the challenges in synthesizing new sounds through a CSS system, the human cognitive domain must first be well explored and understood. The information obtained from the users must then be converted into some form of AI solutions. In order to improve sound similarity, the elements that are used by humans as a common ground as the basis of sound similarity (and many other elements too!) in performing tasks that involve sound similarity perception must be determined. It is apparent that HCAI is essential to crack the code of each composers who wishes to synthesize new sounds using a CSS system. Without a common ground declared, it is very likely that a CSS system will never be able to generate sounds that match the expectation of its users, despite having a large repository of source sounds. This mismatch can leave the user feeling puzzled by the output, and perhaps brandishing the system as a failure, even when it is fully functional. Likewise, it is important that the mindless tweaking of the parameters that leaves users feeling overwhelmed and frustrated is fixed. The soul-less representation of numerical data to communicate results to users often means distancing any valuable qualitative input from users such as similarity judgement and feature priority judgement. Existing CSS systems may still rely on some form of human input in order to synthesize sounds, but CSS has come a long way since the days Pierre Schaffer had to cut and paste magnetic tapes manually by his own bare hands. Although complete automation is not yet achieved and the level of intelligence integrated within the CSS system is no match to that of humans (yet), exciting possibilities of more intelligent solutions are emerging in the near future. Soon, a CSS system will be able to not only read and materialize the sounds which are inside the minds of composers, but it will be taking it a step further by actually generating sounds which the composers have not thought of yet, but would have come up themselves had they have more resources (time, money, inspiration, and so on and so forth).

But for the time being, CSS can do exactly as its name suggests—concatenatively synthesizing sounds.

References

1. Allamanche, E., Herre, J., Hellmuth, O., Kastner, T., & Ertel, C. (2003, October). A multiple feature model for musical similarity retrieval. In *Proceedings of the International Symposium on Music Information Retrieval (ISMIR)*.
2. Bailey, C. (2010). A database system for organising musique concrete. In *International Computer Music Conference, 2010* (pp. 428–431).
3. Bernardes, G., Guedes, C., & Pennycook, B. (2013). EarGram: An application for interactive exploration of concatenative sound synthesis in pure data. In *From Sounds to Music and Emotions* (pp. 110–129).
4. Bernardes, G. (2014). *Composing music by selection: Content-based algorithmic-assisted audio composition*. Ph.D. thesis, University of Porto.
5. Brossier, P. (2006). *Automatic annotation of musical audio for interactive applications*. Centre for Digital Music, Queen Mary University of London.
6. Casey, M. A. (2005). Acoustic lexemes for organizing internet audio. *Contemporary Music Review, 24*(6), 489–508
7. Chafe, C. (1999). A short history of digital sound synthesis by composers in the USA. *Creativity and the Computer, Recontres Musicales Pluridisciplinaires, Lyon*.
8. Cook, P. R. (2002). *Real sound synthesis for interactive applications*. AK Peters/CRC Press.
9. David, J. H. (1994). *In the two sides of music*. https://jackhdavid.thehouseofdavid.com/papers/brain.html.
10. Frisson, C., Picard, C., Tardieu, D., & Pl-area, F. R. (2010). Audiogarden: Towards a usable tool for composite audio creation. *Target, 7*, 8
11. Gates, A., & Bradshaw, J. L. (1977). The role of the cerebral hemispheres in music. *Brain and Language, 4*(3), 403–431
12. Gower, J. C. (1985). Measures of similarity, dissimilarity and distance. *Encyclopedia of Statistical Sciences, Johnson and CB Read, 5*, 397–405
13. Grey, J. M. (1975). *An exploration of musical timbre*. Doctoral dissertation, Department of Music, Stanford University.
14. Hackbarth, B. (2011). *Audioguide: A framework for creative exploration of concatenative sound synthesis*. IRCAM research report.

15. Jehan, T. (2005). *Creating music by listening*. Doctoral dissertation, Massachusetts Institute of Technology, School of Architecture and Planning, Program in Media Arts and Sciences).
16. Levitin, D. J. (2006). *This is your brain on music: The science of a human obsession*. New York: Plume Books.
17. Loui, P., Wessel, D. L., & Kam, C. L. H. (2010). Humans rapidly learn grammatical structure in a new musical scale. *Music Perception, 27*(5), 377
18. Miranda, E. (2012). *Computer sound design: Synthesis techniques and programming*. Taylor & Francis.
19. Mitrović, D., Zeppelzauer, M., & Breiteneder, C. (2010). Features for content-based audio retrieval. In *Advances in computers* (vol. 78. pp. 71–150). Elsevier.
20. Moffat, D., Selfridge, R., & Reiss, J. D. (2019). Sound effect synthesis. In *Foundations in sound design for interactive media: A multidisciplinary approach*. Routledge.
21. Norowi, N. M., Miranda, E. R., & Madzin, H. (2016). *Identifying the basis of auditory similarity in concatenative sound synthesis users: A study between musicians and non-musicians*.
22. Norowi, N. M. (2013). *An artificial intelligence approach to concatenative sound synthesis*.
23. Nuanáin, C. Ó., Herrera, P., & Jordá, S. (2017). Rhythmic concatenative synthesis for electronic music: Techniques, implementation, and evaluation. *Computer Music Journal, 41*(2), 21–37
24. Pellman, S. (1994). *An introduction to the creation of electroacoustic music*. Wadsworth Publishing Company.
25. Riedl, M. O. (2019). Human-centered artificial intelligence and machine learning. *Human Behavior and Emerging Technologies, 1*(1), 33–36
26. Schwarz, D. (2006). Concatenative sound synthesis: The early years. *Journal of New Music Research, 35*(1), 3–22
27. Segalowitz, S. J. (1983). *Two sides of the brain*. Englewood Cliffs: Prentice Hall.
28. Sturm, B. L. (2004). MATConcat: An application for exploring concatenative sound synthesis using MATLAB. In *Proceedings of Digital Audio Effects (DAFx)*.
29. Tolonen, T., Välimäki, V., & Karjalainen, M. (1998). *Evaluation of modern sound synthesis methods*.
30. Tran, N. (1999, February). Generating photomosaics: an empirical study. In *Proceedings of the 1999 ACM Symposium on Applied Computing* (pp. 105–109).
31. Wessel, D. L. (1979). Timbre space as a musical control structure. *Computer Music Journal*, 45–52.
32. Wu, S. C. A. (2017). *SuperSampler: A new polyphonic concatenative sampler synthesizer in supercollider for sound motive creating, live coding, and improvisation*.
33. Zils, A., & Pachet, F. (2001, December). Musical mosaicing. In *Digital audio effects (DAFx)*.

Noris Mohd Norowi studied for her Ph.D. degree in Computer Music at the Interdisciplinary Centre for Computer Music Reserch, University of Plymouth, UK. She received her M.Sc. in Multimedia Systems and Bachelor of Computer Science degree (majoring in Multimedia) from Universiti Putra Malaysia, Malaysia. She is currently the Head of Human-Computer Interaction Lab at the Faculty of Computer Science and Information Technology, Universiti Putra Malaysia. She is an active member of the ACM SIGCHI Kuala Lumpur Chapter (myHCI-UX), where she holds the position as the Membership Chair for Malaysia. Her research interests include music interaction, Artificial Intelligence in music, immersive technologies, sound cognition, and sound synthesis. She also has a deep passion for traditional Malaysian music, where she had worked on several projects to automatically classify them into their respective genres. She plays traditional percussion instruments such as the Gendangs, Gongs, and Kompang. E-mail: noris@upm.edu.my.

Deep Generative Models for Musical Audio Synthesis

22

Muhammad Huzaifah and Lonce Wyse

22.1 Introduction

Sound modelling is the process of developing algorithms that generate sound under parametric control. There are a few distinct approaches that have been developed historically including modelling the physics of sound production and propagation, assembling signal generating and processing elements to capture acoustic features, and manipulating collections of recorded audio samples. While each of these approaches has been able to achieve high-quality synthesis and interaction for specific applications, they are all labour intensive and each comes with its own challenges for designing arbitrary control strategies. Recent generative deep learning systems for audio synthesis are able to learn models that can traverse arbitrary spaces of sound defined by the data they train on. Furthermore, machine learning systems are providing new techniques for designing control and navigation strategies for these models. This paper is a review of developments in deep learning that are changing the practice of sound modelling.

The development of capable "guided" parametric synthesis systems, that is, the generation of sound given some user-determined parametric inputs, remains as one of the foremost challenges in digital audio production. A central challenge is that it is not enough for a model to generate a particular sound whether it be a drop of water or

M. Huzaifah
NUS Graduate School for Integrative Sciences and Engineering, National University of Singapore, Singapore, Singapore
e-mail: muhd.huz@gmail.com

L. Wyse (✉)
Communications and New Media Department, National University of Singapore, Singapore, Singapore
e-mail: lonce.acad@zwhome.org

© Springer Nature Switzerland AG 2021
E. R. Miranda (ed.), *Handbook of Artificial Intelligence for Music*,
https://doi.org/10.1007/978-3-030-72116-9_22

a whole symphony. A sound model includes an interface that can be used to traverse a space of sounds along different paths. A musical wind instrument, for example, affords access to a constrained class of sounds, and allows fingering patterns for the control of pitch, embouchure for timbre, or breath pressure for loudness. There is no *a priori* limit on the range of sounds a designer might want from a model, nor the trajectories through the space they might desire to navigate via the interface. Deep learning-based generative models can be seen as spanning ground between two types of control principles—one in which the user directly controls all aspects of the synthesis at each step akin to playing an instrument, and another whereby almost all decisions are left to the system, allowing sound to be generated unconditionally. There exists a broad spread in research focus along these lines, from finding novel control strategies for pre-existing models to designing algorithms comprising the sound synthesis.

Although each extreme has its merit and use cases, there is an increasing need in media production for more adaptable systems that marry extensive modelled knowledge to the flexibility of shaping the audio output in real time. For instance, a live performer may wish to blend the timbres of several distinct acoustic instruments with natural sounds to create unique soundscapes on the fly. On the other hand, a developer may want to procedurally generate background music in a computer game based on certain in-game cues. A new approach to modelling audio utilizing deep learning paradigms may offer an avenue to build such systems.

Deep learning has seen a surge of interest in the recent past, not least because of its huge potential in actualizing many practical applications, including many areas of signal processing. It is already in widespread use in the music information retrieval community [6], while many have declared automatic speech recognition as a largely "solved" problem with the advent of deep learning technology [57]. The remarkable ability of deep learning models to extract semantically useful features and utilize them for such downstream tasks has directed researchers to not only purpose these models to analyse and process existing data, but to actually *generate* new data.

Deep generative models are a powerful subset of deep learning networks that discover latent structure in data in order to generate new samples with the same distribution as the training data. Unlike more common learning objectives that try to discriminate labelled inputs (i.e. classification) or estimate a mapping (i.e. regression), generative models instead learn to replicate the hidden statistics behind observed data. This "understanding" of the structure of data space allows them to display impressive expression capabilities on a variety of audio and non-audio-related tasks. For image media, state-of-the-art generative adversarial networks are now able to synthesize extremely life-like human faces, even retaining some control over both broad and fine-grained stylistic features in the process [44]. Audio data has unique characteristics that make it a challenge to synthesize with reasonable fidelity using existing techniques derived primarily for visual applications. Despite this, current deep learning models have often shown to outperform previous widely used parametric models such as the hidden Markov model, especially in applications where adequate data is available.

In the following sections, we will analyse several key deep generative models developed for musical audio synthesis. This is prefaced by a discussion on the audio synthesis task and as well as a broader introduction to more generic generative neural networks that form the basis of the systems used for audio. Although the focus of this chapter will be on the musical domain, some discussion on speech models will also be included to provide a better general picture of the capabilities of deep generative audio models, and because there are many overlapping issues concerning audio synthesis and issues of designing real-time control. We will also give little attention to musical modelling in the symbolic domain of notes except where it is directly relevant to audio modelling such as when notes are used as parameters to conditionally synthesize audio.

22.1.1 Overview

22.1.1.1 Problem Background

Synthetically generated media is ubiquitous today. This holds true in the musical domain, where digital synthesizers have been widely and increasingly used in both production and performance. Artists and engineers work with synthesizers in a variety of roles that typically fall within one of the following scenarios:

- generate interesting or novel sounds or timbres that are infeasible/impossible to be produced acoustically;
- simulate the sounds of real-world acoustic instruments or of other sources such as environmental sounds;
- facilitate the automation of systems and processes (e.g. text-to-speech, virtual assistants, etc.)

In terms of a computational task, the process driven by a digital synthesizer is that of guided audio synthesis. Succinctly, the aim is to produce a sound with particular characteristics defined by the user. As illustrated in Fig. 22.1, we can further distil this overall objective into two associated aspects: that of *generation* and that of *control*. The former concerns the algorithm behind the actual sound production, while the latter relates to how this sound can be shaped (hence "guided"). A considerable body of literature on sound modelling has been devoted to mapping musical gestures and sensors through an interface to the parameters a signal-processing algorithm makes available [40, 82].

In the natural physical world, a sound is generated as a result of a physical interaction between two or more objects called "sources" or "excitors", that is, transmitted in the form of pressure waves through a medium. In the digital realm, a synthesis algorithm tries to replicate the target sounds without having or requiring physical sources. There are many approaches to sound modelling, and each has advantages and disadvantages for different classes of sounds, as well as in terms of expressiveness, control and computational efficiency. A "physical modelling" approach mathematically models the physics that generate a target waveform (see, for example, [72]). An example is using equations that model travelling waves along strings attached to resonating bodies and excited by a bow being drawn across the string. One advantage of physical modelling is that the equations expose parameters that are intuitive for control such as bow pressure, string length and stiffness, and resonating body size. An "acoustic modelling" approach uses signal generators and processors for manipulating waveforms such as oscillators, modulators, filters and waveshapers designed to generate acoustic features regardless of physical processes. Commercial synthesizers are comprised of such units that can be configured to generate a vast variety of sounds, but expose algorithm-specific parameters that may not be as manageable or intuitive as physical model parameters for control. Prerecorded sound samples are also used in several techniques and can obtain a natural quality difficult for purely synthetic approaches. Techniques in this category include wavetable synthesis for musical instruments which uses looping to extend note durations and layers for timbral variation. Concatenative synthesis, more common for speech, draws on a large database of very short snippets of sound to assemble the target audio. Prerecorded samples have the naturalness of the recorded audio, but present their own control challenges for achieving arbitrary sequences of sound samples. Manually constructing synthesis algorithms that cover a specific range of sounds under desired parametric trajectories and that capture the complexity of natural audio is a difficult and labour-intensive task.

22.1.1.2 Data-Driven Parametric Synthesis

Statistical models first came to prominence in the 1980s with the hidden Markov model (HMM) that eventually dominated the fields of automatic speech recognition and generation. HMMs use a series of hidden states to represent non-stationary acoustic features and are often combined with a Gaussian mixture model (GMM) that admits frame-wise mappings beneficial for several speech generation tasks such as voice conversion and speech enhancement [50]. Statistical models learn their model parameters from data as opposed to expert design in the case of physical and acoustic models. The data-driven nature of statistical parametric models would make them similar in that aspect to sample-based techniques. Indeed, data-driven parametric synthesis systems posses many of the positive qualities of the prior approaches.

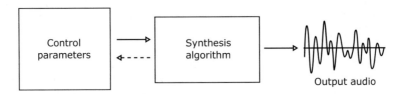

Fig. 22.1 A high-level system view of the audio generative task. A user interacts with the system via control parameters to change various qualities of the waveform. A synthesis algorithm determines what kind of parameters are available and their relation to the overall waveform, which would indirectly instruct how the user goes about conceiving a particular sound

The more modern successor to HMMs are deep generative models, also known as generative neural networks, that are more powerful and scale much better with data. They are also capable of "end-to-end" learning (without separate components for feature extraction, processing and feature-to-audio synthesis) whereas HMM-based models operate on and produce engineered features not learned by the model.

The idea behind generative neural network models is to synthesize sounds according to the learned characteristics of an audio database. The generated sound would therefore be perceptually similar to, but not merely be reproductions of, the data the model was trained on. The underlying assumption here is that the training data (audio plus metadata) contains all the necessary information required to recreate the different dimensions of the desired sound(s) without the model requiring *a priori* knowledge of those properties. During training, the network is tasked to find patterns, dependencies and variations in the data. This process can be framed as an instance of the inverse problem, where we try to determine the causal factors to a set of observations. Whereas physical modelling synthesis finds an analytical solution that corresponds to a set of equations governing the sound production and propagation, generative neural networks provide a numerical solution with model parameters (i.e. the network weights) that may or may not correspond to real-world physical or perceptual parameters.

22.1.1.3 Control Affordances

One drawback of using the physical, acoustic and sample-based approaches to interactive sound model design is that the interface to the model is either the set of parameters inherent in the equations or algorithms used for synthesis, or else it is designed separately by mapping desired control gestures to the parameters exposed by a synthesis algorithm. However, the affordances [73] for interaction are a critical part of the expressive potential of a sound model designed for music. Machine learning approaches have been used for mapping gestures to the space of algorithm parameters. Fels and Hinton [19] described a neural network for mapping hand gestures to parameters of a speech synthesizer. Fiebrink [20] developed the Wekinator for mapping arbitrary gestures to parameters of sound synthesis algorithms. Fried and Fiebrink [23] use stacked autoencoders for reducing the dimensionality of physical gestures, images and audio clips. Francoise et al. [22] developed various strategies for mapping complete gestures to parameters of synthesizers. Fasciani and Wyse [18] used machine learning to map vocal gestures to sound, and separately to map from sound to synthesizer parameters for generating sound. Gabrielli et al. [24] used a convolutional neural network to learn upwards of 50 "micro-parameters" of a physical model of a pipe organ. These techniques show the value of various machine learning techniques for gesture mapping, but they all use predefined synthesis systems for the generation of sound or images, and are thus limited by the capabilities of the synthesis algorithms they learn to control. They do not support learning mappings "end to end" between gestures and arbitrary sound sequences.

How can we design networks that not only generate data from distributions on which they have been trained, but do so under the type of intimate control that we require of musical instruments? Deep learning networks do not facilitate reworking their internal structure during the generative phase as a viable means of controlling the output. Several studies from both audio and vision fields therefore focus on the training phase instead to determine the characteristics of the post-training generative phase. This has seen the use of specialized architectures (e.g. Siamese networks that learn two different genres of music from a common input of sheet music [52]), specific loss functions (e.g. first- versus second-order activation losses to abstract "style" and "content" from images [27] or spectrograms [76]) or curated training sets (e.g. adding or removing representative data to bias the model output a certain way [21]). However, there are several limitations with these approaches, especially in the context of an audio synthesizer in a production setting. Firstly, they are fundamentally not dynamic in real time, requiring time-consuming re-training to alter the synthesis. They furthermore conflate many perceptual dimensions without allowing more fine-tuned control over each independently. Also they do not offer easy ways to add new control dimensions to existing ones.

An alternative strategy available for controllable generative models is *conditioning*, whereby auxiliary information is given to the model in addition to the audio samples themselves during training. If the generative phase is run without such information, samples are drawn from the model distribution based on the whole training set. For instance, for a network trained on sample vectors of speech without being augmented with phonemic information, the generation produces "babble". However, when conditioned with the augmented input information during training, the phonemic part of the input can be externally specified so that the audio samples are generated conditionally based on the phonemes presented in the input sequence. This technique has been used successfully in networks used for sequence generation such as WaveNet [77] and Char2Wav [74], a conditional extension of SampleRNN [54]. Conditional models provide a means to directly influence the synthesis with more intuitive labels since the dimensions are chosen by the model developer. Choosing a set of conditional parameter values is comparable to restricting the output generation to a restricted region of the complete data space. It is also possible to use learning mechanisms to discover low-dimensional representations that "code" for different regions of the whole data space and that can then be used during generation. Models that incorporate conditioning now form a huge part of generative deep learning literature and the concept has played an important role in their success. Conditioning strategies are addressed in more detail below.

22.1.1.4 Data Representation and Hierarchy

At the heart of the deep generative model is the data used to train them. Audio as data is representationally challenging since it is a hierarchically structured medium that can be encoded in different forms. Moreover, the various levels of structure coexist and interact and support different descriptive levels of abstraction and experience (see Fig. 22.2). What is representationally appropriate then is dependent upon the task objective, which would in turn be greatly influence the model design.

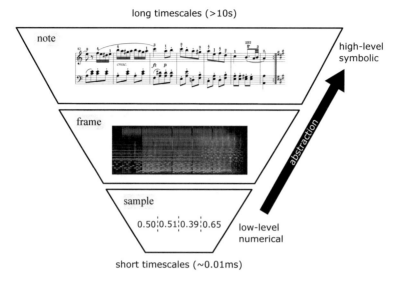

long timescales (>10s)

Fig. 22.2 Audio representation in the musical domain exists as a hierarchy of timescales and levels of abstraction, starting from smallest digital audio quantum of a sample, up to the entire musical passage, often represented symbolically in the form of a score. A generative model of audio that can capture structure of all the different timescales may not be entirely feasible without compromising quality at some scale, usually manifesting as a loss in fidelity or a lack of long-term structure. The task can be made easier by focusing on a specific timescale and using the appropriate representation

Many generative models of music are built around the use of high-level symbolic (e.g. note) representations such as MIDI, sheet music or piano rolls that abstract away the peculiarities of a particular musical performance. Although relatively simpler to model compared to other forms of audio, they lose the more fine-grained nuances that are present in performed music which may negatively impact the overall enjoyment of the listener.

Another class of audio representations are transformed signals that represent "frames" or "windows" of audio samples in vectors that are sequenced in time at a much lower rate than sampled audio. Spectrograms are an example of a time versus frequency representation. A two-dimensional representation suggests the use of techniques developed for images for discriminative and generative tasks. However, audio data in the time and frequency dimensions behave very differently than typical image data, and do not necessarily suit the assumptions built in to image processing networks [41,88]. Furthermore, while a complex spectrogram can be lossless, a typical representation in practice is the magnitude-based spectrogram which requires an audio signal to be reconstructed. The most common technique for "inverting" a spectrogram comes from Griffin and Lim [33] but it requires information from across the duration of the entire signal, so is not directly applicable to real-time interactive generative systems, though more recent techniques have addressed this issue [92] and dramatically increased the quality [63] achievable. Other spectra-based representations such as mel-scaled spectrograms or mel-frequency cepstral coefficients (MFCCs) are common but even more lossy. Neural network "vocoders" have been developed that learn to generate plausible audio signals from such representations [75].

The most straightforward audio representation is the raw sampled audio waveform which is lossless and trivially convertible to actual sound. Unlike symbolic representations that may be instrument-specific, models that operate on raw audio samples can be applied to any set of instruments and even non-musical audio like speech and environmental sounds. All the musically relevant nuances and idiosyncrasies are also embedded in an audio waveform. On the other hand, modelling such waveforms is extremely challenging, particularly in the handling of the inherent long-term dependencies in sound over time. This is exacerbated by the fact that audio signals are sampled at high temporal resolutions, from between 16000 and 48000 samples per second. This makes capturing typical musical time dependencies that span many seconds or minutes difficult for some network architectures.

As shown in Fig. 22.2, the shift from shorter to longer timescales broadly coincides with the use of more symbolic representations to capture and transmit information at increasingly higher levels. The guided synthesis task of interest is, on the whole, more focused on local musical structures such as timbre and pitch. Accordingly, the systems that will be discussed here tend to directly model raw audio signals in the form of digital samples in a PCM stream or processed with other standard quantization encodings such as μ-law. We do not address "automatic music composition", which concerns much longer timescales and attempts to model concepts that are relevant at the level of a song or musical piece like continuity, repetition, contrast and harmony. The majority of automatic composition models also use symbolic representations as input data to abstract away low-level information, making the capture of longer time dependencies more feasible. Performance RNN [58] is an example of an automatic music composition network that jointly predicts MIDI notes and also their expressive timing and dynamics.

In summary, the paradigm for guided audio synthesis put forth in this chapter focuses on modelling local structure and leaves the longer term evolution of the sound to user control. This entails working mainly in the raw audio domain which contains the greatest detail at short timescales.

22.1.1.5 Audio Domains

The types of audio from the literature can essentially be divided into three spheres of speech, music and environmental sounds. The primary concern here is with models for musical sound with a focus on pitch, timbre and articulation characteristics. Nevertheless, a portion of the synthesis systems analysed were not developed for any particular domain, and like many deep learning models, are agnostic to the dataset used to train them. Since they are trained on raw audio, many of these generative models can be extended to music even though they were not specifically built for that purpose. A large number of generative models for audio were developed first and foremost for speech applications. Some speech models will also be included for a more comprehensive discussion on audio-based deep generative models as the development in that field runs parallel to the development of synthesis models for music.

22.1.1.6 Related Works

We end this section by providing a brief outline of other reviews of deep generative models for audio that may be of relevance.

Briot et al. [3] provide a comprehensive survey of systems that generate musical content through a multi-pronged analysis in terms of objective, representation, architecture and strategy. Another work on music generation by deep learning [4] instead orient their analysis in terms of domain challenges. They look at concepts such as originality, control and interactivity, among others, and determine how current models can fill these gaps (or fall short of fully addressing the issues). For speech, Ling et al. [50] evaluate various statistical parametric models, noting the shift from the well-established hidden Markov model (HMM) and Gaussian mixture model (GMM) to deep learning architectures, though the systems highlighted mostly belong to older classes of deep learning models such as deep believe networks (DBNs) and restricted Boltzmann machines (RBMs). These nonetheless share similar theoretical underpinnings with the more modern autoencoders that are widely used for current generative tasks. Henter et al. [36] discuss unsupervised learning methods for expressive text-to-speech, especially in the context of variational autoencoders. Purwins et al. [64] go against the trend of domain-specific surveys. They instead give a broad overview of the advances in deep learning as applied to audio processing. A wide range of methods, models and applications including both analysis and synthesis aspects are covered albeit without going into detail. Perhaps the closest in terms of content to the review here is an overview of generative music models dealing with raw waveforms by Dieleman [11], which, for the reader wanting to gain a more complete picture of the field, would serve as a good follow-up text to this work.

The next section will introduce some of the key deep learning architectures that form the basis for generative musical audio models, important for the understanding of how these models work and the motivation behind them. Specific generative systems from the literature will be discussed afterwards as part of a narrative on the conceptual development of a functional synthesizer.

22.1.2 Generative Neural Networks

Statistical generative or predictive models based on artificial neural networks have gained prominence since the development of the generative adversarial network (GAN) in 2014. To better understand how they work, it is best to study generative models through the lens of probability theory. The core goal of a generative model is to approximate an underlying probability distribution p_{data}, given access to a finite set of samples drawn from this distribution. Training a generative model entails choosing the most plausible model parameters that minimize some notion of distance between the model distribution and the true data distribution. More formally, given training data points X as samples from an empirical distribution $p_{data}(X)$, we want to learn a model $p_\theta(X)$, belonging to a model family M that closely matches $p_{data}(X)$, by iteratively changing model parameters θ. In short, we specify the following optimization problem.

$$\min_{\theta \in M} d(p_{data}, p_\theta)$$

A commonly used objective function d to evaluate the quality of the model and drive learning is the Kullback–Leibler (KL) divergence, a measurement of how different two distributions are, which satisfies the required notion of a quantifiable "distance" between the data distribution and model distribution. Equivalently, minimizing the KL divergence can be thought of as maximizing the log-likelihood of data points X with respect to the model distribution p_θ.

To understand just how difficult the problem of generating audio data is, we can have a look at the size of its state space, or the number of possible configurations a segment of audio can take. With a conservative assumption of 1 s of audio, sampled at 16kHz with 8 bits per sample (i.e. 256 possible values), there exists $256^{16000} \approx 10^{38500}$ possible sequences, a number that will only get larger for longer sequences or with higher quality and therefore impossible to capture by just memorizing all possible configurations. Fortunately, real-world audio is highly structured, and it is this underlying structure that the generative neural network aims to learn.

When trained in a supervised setting with inputs X and targets Y, a generative model estimates the full joint probability $p(Y, X)$, which can not only predict Y but also say something about the generative process of X. In contrast, a discriminative model would learn to output the most likely Y for a given X more directly with a conditional distribution $p(Y|X)$. Although learning a conditional probability is oftentimes much easier, with the joint probability, a generative model can be used in a number of interesting ways. For our main objective of synthesizing audio, we can *sample* from the model distribution to generate novel data points (in which case Y is also a complex high-dimensional object like an audio waveform as opposed to a label). Since the model distribution is close to the dataset distribution, we get something perceptually similar to the training data. Generative models can also be used for *density estimation*, that is, assigning a likelihood value to a given X. This can provide an indication of how good the model actually is in approximating p_{data}. Finally, generative models are often used for *unsupervised representation learning* as an intermediate objective. Internally, the deeper neural network layers making up the model have a significantly smaller number of parameters compared to the input data, thereby forcing them to discover and capture the essential dependencies mapping the low-level input to a higher level abstracted representation known as the *feature space/latent space*. The latent variables extracted by the model are often essential for further downstream inference tasks such as classification and conditional generation. With such flexible and powerful properties, researchers have used generative models for many objectives aside from synthesis, including data compression and data completion.

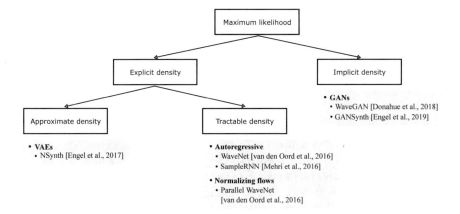

Fig. 22.3 One way of organizing different generative models is by looking at how the model treats maximum likelihood and whether the density distribution is explicitly or implicitly expressed. This chapter covers some of the important generative model families in current use for audio synthesis. Autoregressive models (Sect. 22.1.2.1), variational autoencoders (VAEs) (Sect. 22.1.2.2) and normalizing flow models (Sect. 22.1.2.3) constitute explicit density models, while the generative adversarial network (GAN) (Sect. 22.1.2.4) is an implicit density model. Included under each heading is a non-exhaustive list of essential audio-related works that utilize that model type

One caveat to take note of when using generative networks is that not all model families can perform equally well on every inference task. Indeed, the various trade-offs in their inference capabilities plus the particular assumptions made on a given dataset have led to the development of a wide array of generative networks which we break down in Fig. 22.3. Since many generative models are trained using maximum likelihood estimation as mentioned, a natural way to taxonomize generative models is in how they represent the likelihood. Some types of networks allow for the explicit formulation of the marginal likelihood $p(X)$ of the data. These include autoregressive networks and variational autoencoders. In other cases, a training regime specifies a stochastic process that instead requires the network to have implicit knowledge of the underlying probability distribution to sample from, an example of which is the GAN. In practice, being able to calculate the likelihood provides an unambiguous way of measuring how close the model is in approximating the real data distribution; with GANs, we can only evaluate the model by looking at the generated examples and comparing them to the real data.

The rest of this section will elaborate several of these model families that have been used for audio synthesis with varying success. Researchers have taken advantage of their different properties to fulfil a range of audio generative tasks and challenges. Generally from the most to least widespread in current use for audio they are

- Autoregressive models—make sample predictions sequentially in time;
- Variational autoencoders (VAEs)—used to discover low-dimensional parametric representations of the data;

- Normalizing flow models—for speeding up generation and modelling complicated distributions without "bounding" approximations;
- Generative adversarial networks (GANs)—for speed and parallelization, developing representations that apply globally across the temporal extent of a sound, and producing large chunks of audio at a time.

22.1.2.1 Autoregressive Models

The first type of generative network in focus is designed specifically with sequential data in mind, and hence lends itself naturally to audio data viewed as a temporal sequence. Autoregressive networks define an explicit and computationally tractable density model by decomposing the probability distribution over an n-dimensional data space X into a product of one-dimensional probability distributions via the chain rule of probability.

$$p(X) = \prod_{i=1}^{n} p(x_i | x_1, ..., x_{i-1})$$

We see that data is assumed to have a canonical sequential direction—the current term in the sequence (x_i) is only conditioned on a recency window of previous terms and not on "future" terms relative to the current. These models learn to predict the next sample in time given what has come just prior. It is in part this "causality" that permits real-time manipulation of the generated audio using techniques described below. Autoregressive models are also known to be easier to train in comparison to the other model families discussed after.

The process of basing the subsequent prediction on previous terms may seem similar to the perhaps more familiar recurrent neural network (RNN). Indeed an RNN can be cast as a type of autoregressive model that compresses the prior terms into a hidden state instead of providing them explicitly as input to the model. RNNs have been used as building blocks for more complex autoregressive models of audio such as SampleRNN [54]. Each layer in SampleRNN is comprised of RNNs that work to capture dependencies at a particular timescale.

Autoregressive models, however, are not exclusive to the RNN. At the time of writing, the most prevalent generative model for audio was proposed by van den Oord et al. at DeepMind, known as WaveNet [77]. Where an RNN sees only one input sample at each time step and retains the influence of past samples in its state, WaveNet has explicit access to a past window of input samples. The constituents of WaveNet are convolutional neural networks (CNNs) where each neural network layer learns multiple filters for which to process the input to that layer. To make CNNs abide by the autoregressive principle, the filters are partly masked to avoid a computation with non-causal inputs of the data. A big advantage of CNNs over RNNs is their capacity for parallelism, where a long input sequence can be processed quickly as a whole. This can greatly speed up training since the entire output can be processed in one forward pass. At generation time, however, there is no training data to base previous time steps, so the model has to wait for each sample to be generated in turn in order to use it to predict the next sample. Slow generation is one inherent weakness of autoregressive networks that has been addressed by other model families, namely, normalizing flows and GANs.

Another drawback of autoregressive models is that they do not learn unsupervised representations of data directly by themselves, and so we do not have access to a feature space intrinsically. A workaround is combining an autoregressive model with a separate encoder to allow the autoregressive network to condition itself on latent variables provided by the encoder to augment the input data. van den Oord et al. [79] demonstrate other types of conditioning as well, including one-hot encodings of class labels and features taken from the top layers of a pre-trained CNN. The combination of an autoregressive model with an additional encoder network has been used extensively in the literature to impose some conditioning influence over the synthesis procedure, including for extensions to WaveNet as in Engel et al. [16], discussed in more detail in Sect. 22.1.7.

22.1.2.2 Variational Autoencoders

The variational autoencoder (VAE) [47] belongs to a family of explicit density models known as a directed latent variable model. Whereas a standard autoencoder will learn a compressed representation of the dataset, the VAE extends this by learning parameters of a probability distribution in the latent space from which samples can be drawn. One important use for latent variable models in doing domain transformations or feature interpolations, sometimes casually referred to as "morphs". Various works have demonstrated this effect by blending two distinct timbres or extending the pitch range of a particular instrument [16,51], where the associated timbres and pitches were learnt by the model from data in an unsupervised or semi-supervised fashion. For completion, other partially relevant systems that were not tested on raw musical audio but may be of interest include DeepMind's VQ-VAE [81] that deals mostly with speech and Magenta's MusicVAE [66]) which uses MIDI.

The high-level architecture of VAEs, shown in Fig. 22.4, is similar to the standard autoencoder—an encoder network takes inputs and maps them to a latent space space comprised of latent variables z, then a decoder network uses the latent variables to produce an output. The VAE places additional constraints on the form of the latent space and introduces a loss function based on KL divergence for probability distributions jointly trained with the standard autoencoder reconstruction loss.

To motivate the VAE framework, we start with an inference model from Bayes' rule.

$$p(z|X) = \frac{p(X|z)p(z)}{p(X)}$$

Unfortunately, in many cases, computing $p(X)$ directly is intractable. To approximate the posterior $p(z|X)$, either a Monte Carlo (sampling) approach would be used, or as in the case of VAE, variational inference. The variational approach circumvents the intractability problem by defining a new distribution $q(z|X)$ and tries to make it as similar to $p(z|X)$ as possible by minimizing their KL divergence. By substituting

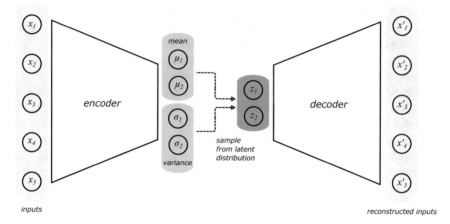

Fig. 22.4 Architecture of a VAE. The encoder processes the input data $X = (x_1, x_2, \ldots)$ and maps them to a Gaussian distributed latent space $q(z|X)$ parameterized by mean μ and variance σ. The decoder samples from this latent space using $p(X|z)$ to produce a synthetic output $\hat{X}$

the inference model above into the formula for KL divergence and rearranging, we can derive the objective function that we maximize, known in this context as the variational lower bound $\mathcal{L}$ (see Doersch [13] for full details on the derivation).

$$\mathcal{L} = \mathbb{E}_{z \sim q(z|X)}[\log p(X|z)] - \mathcal{D}_{KL}[q(z|X)||p(z)]$$

The first term on the right-hand side can be interpreted as the reconstruction loss. This naturally lends itself to an autoencoder design, trained to reconstruct its own input. Regularization is provided by the KL divergence term where the form chosen for $p(z)$ is typically a unit Gaussian distribution. The intuition behind this is to encourage the encoder to distribute all encodings evenly around the centre of the latent space instead of clustering them apart. The resultant continuous latent space then allows smooth interpolation between variables during generation by sampling from $p(X|z)$. Musically, a smooth interpolation of the latent space can create smooth audio morphs [71] by manipulating these parameters that define the distributions from which different types of audio are drawn during generation.

22.1.2.3 Normalizing Flow Models

As we have seen, autoregressive models provide tractable likelihoods but no direct mechanism for learning features. On the other hand, VAEs can learn feature representations but come with intractable marginal likelihoods. Normalizing flows is another family of models that combines the best of both worlds, allowing for both representation learning and tractable likelihood estimation. This means that normalizing flow models have access to latent data features that can be used to condition the generation like the VAE, while possibly learning a more accurate representation of the data distribution.

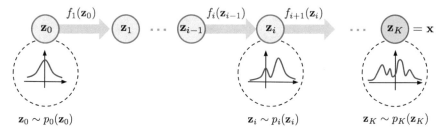

Fig. 22.5 A normalizing flow model transforms a simple distribution shown here as $p_0(z_0)$ to a more complex one $p_k(z_k)$, after k such forward mappings. The resulting output distribution can be taken as the learned distribution of the data. Figure reproduced from Weng [86]

Perhaps the most prominent utilization of normalizing flows from the audio generation literature is Parallel WaveNet [80]. It takes advantage of the parallel generation possible with an inverse autoregressive flow (IAF) [46] that was not previously possible with the purely autoregressive nature of the original. This advancement improved the efficiency over the vanilla WaveNet by a factor of 300, essentially making faster than real-time generation achievable. Aside from Parallel WaveNet, other significant flow models developed specifically for audio generation include ClariNet [61] and the non-autoregressive WaveGlow [62] primarily used for speech.

The key concept behind normalizing flows is to map simple distributions to more complex distributions using the change of variables technique. We start off with a simple distribution such as a Gaussian for the latent variables z that we aim to transform into a complex distribution to represent the audio output X. A single transformation is given by a smooth and invertible function f that can map between X and z, such that $X = f(z)$ and $z = f^{-1}(X)$. Since a single transformation may not yield a complex enough distribution, multiple invertible transformations are composed one after another, constructing a "flow". Each mapping function in the flow can be parameterized by neural network layers (Fig. 22.5)

All the advantages of normalizing flows do come with certain compromises. Unlike the other model families discussed here, normalizing flow models have a much more restrictive set of requirements when it comes to its architecture, namely, an invertible mapping function, an easily computable determinant of the Jacobian matrix needed to calculate the likelihood, and an X and z with the same dimensionality.

22.1.2.4 Generative Adversarial Networks

The final family of models to be considered is the generative adversarial network or GAN, a deep learning framework introduced by Goodfellow et al. [30]. GANs learn to map random input vectors (typically of much smaller dimension than the data) to data examples in the target domain. They tend to cluster similar output data to neighbourhoods of input values which provides a natural means of navigating among output data with different characteristics. However, in the vanilla GAN, there

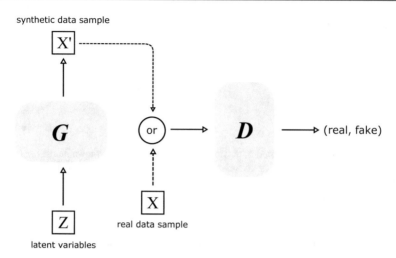

synthetic data sample

latent variables

Fig. 22.6 A summary of the adversarial training process of discriminator network D and generator network G

is no control during training over which regions of input map to which regions of the output space. The user of the model must search and discover the structure after training.

The development of the GAN architecture was partly motivated to overcome the difficulties inherent in the training of other implicit models such as the generative stochastic network [2], which have issues scaling to high-dimensional spaces and come with increased computational cost [29]. Instead it utilizes the backpropagation and dropout algorithms that have been so successful with discriminative networks, while introducing a novel training regime based on a *minimax* game.

In a vanilla GAN, the adversarial training pits two separate networks, a discriminator network D and a generator network G, against each other (illustrated in Fig. 22.6). We can think of G as a mapping from some input representation space, made up of a prior of latent variables z (traditionally initialized as noise), to some data space $\hat{X}$ (e.g. spectrograms). D maps the input data, be it X or $\hat{X}$, to a categorical label according to whether it thinks the input came from the true data distribution $p(X)$ or the model distribution $p(z)$. While D is trained to maximize the probability of distinguishing the real from the synthesized data, G is trained in parallel for the antagonistic objective, that is, to fool D by minimizing $\log(1 - D(G(z)))$. The combined value function V is presented below.

$$G : G(z) \rightarrow \hat{X}$$
$$D : D(X, \hat{X}) \rightarrow (0, 1)$$
$$\min_G \max_D V(G, D) = \mathbb{E}_{X \sim p(X)}[\log D(X)] + \mathbb{E}_{z \sim \hat{p}(z)}[\log(1 - D(G(z)))]$$

At equilibrium, in an ideal setting (that is, difficult to achieve in practice), the generator (re)produces perfectly the true data distribution, which ultimately leads to the discriminator merely randomly guessing the input label, unable to tell the real from the fake. It is important to note that while the discriminator is exposed to both real and modelled data, the generator has no direct access to the training samples, and so has to develop an understanding of the data distribution solely via the error signal provided by the discriminator.

Researchers have pointed out that since the GAN framework does not impose any restriction on the structure of z, the generator may use it in a highly entangled way, where individual dimensions do not correspond to semantic features of the data [5]. If various musical instruments are being trained over a range of pitch, for example, it may well be that the input dimensions make it difficult to, say, manipulate timbre holding pitch steady, or to play a scale holding the instrument timbre steady. One way to induce additional structure is to use a conditioning strategy. Mirza and Osindero [55] present a version that feeds both G and D some extra information, which could be, for instance, class labels (e.g. pitch and instrument), at input. This setup allows control over the modes of the generated data based on a conditional label. Another extension, InfoGAN [5], decomposes z into two parts: a noise vector like before and a latent code that is trained to have high mutual information with the generator distribution. This latent code can be used to discover features in an unsupervised fashion.

While GANs have seen great success in producing high-resolution images, the same level of fidelity has not yet translated to the audio domain, leading to few attempts at using GANs for audio generation. Initial experiments that directly replaced images with spectrograms resulted in low-quality samples that can partly be attributed to phase misalignments during the upsampling of the latent variables to achieve the final spectrogram output. GANs do have certain notable advantages over the sample-level generation in autoregressive and some VAE architectures, namely, a significant speed-up and a more refined control over global conditioning via its latent variables. Lately, there have been more sophisticated efforts for audio such as WaveGAN [14], VoiceGAN [26] and GANSynth [15]. The newer works collectively introduce methods that make GAN-based audio generation much more viable than before.

22.1.3   The Gift of Music: DNN-based Synthesizers

The model families introduced in the preceding section have been used in isolation and sometimes in combination for various audio synthesis tasks. One of the fundamental challenges of generating audio, especially as a raw waveform, is to capture dependencies across long sequences while still maintaining rich timbral information. For perceptually coherent sound this might mean modelling temporal scales across four orders of magnitude, from the sub-milliseconds to tens of seconds. The pioneering models that try to accomplish this objective were autoregressive in nature and led by two competing models, one from Google DeepMind called WaveNet and the other from MILA called SampleRNN. Both focus on modelling at the finest scale possible, that of a single sample, but each use a different network architecture to

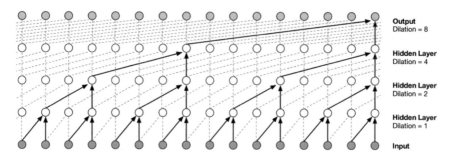

Fig. 22.7 High-level view of the WaveNet architecture showing the dilated causal convolutional layers. Figure reproduced from van den Oord et al. [77]

capture long-term temporal dependencies, namely, *dilated convolutions* for WaveNet versus *stacked recurrent units* for SampleRNN. At the time of writing, WaveNet is by far the more popular DNN-based audio synthesis model of the two, and has been incorporated into many other systems as the terminal processing block to map output features to audio.

22.1.3.1 WaveNet

WaveNet's design [77] is rooted in the PixelCNN architecture [79] where each step models a joint probability $p(X) = p(x_t|x_1, \ldots, x_{t-1})$ to predict the next audio sample conditioned on a context of t past samples. The architecture consists of a stack of convolutional layers; no pooling layers are present so as to keep the dimensionality between the input and output consistent.

Two main features of WaveNet's convolution operation is that it is *dilated* and *causal*. Dilated convolutional layers expand the extent of the receptive field by skipping time steps, enabling the output to be conditioned on samples that are further in the past than is possible with standard convolutions. As illustrated in Fig. 22.7, each filter takes every nth element from the previous layer as input instead of a contiguous section, where n is determined by a hyperparameter called the dilation factor. As the receptive field grows exponentially with depth, fewer layers need to be implemented. In addition, the causal component means that "future" samples relative to the current time step do not factor into the next sample prediction.

Alongside the convolutional layers, the same gated activation units as PixelCNN were used as non-linear activation functions, while residual and skip connections [35] were utilized to improve convergence. van den Oord previously demonstrated that modelling the output as a categorical softmax distribution over quantized possible pixel values worked better than real-valued distributions such as a Gaussian mixture model [78]. For WaveNet, μ-law encoding was first applied to the audio before quantizing to 1 of 256 possible values. For each time step, each of the 256 possible values for the next sample is assigned a probability representing a distribution from which the next sample is drawn. Experiments with WaveNet modelled both music and

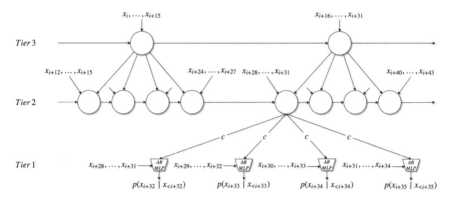

Fig. 22.8 Overview of the SampleRNN architecture. Higher tiers capture increasingly longer time frames which are used to condition the tiers below. Figure reproduced from Mehri et al. [54]

speech but it is also capable of multi-speaker speech generation when conditioned on speaker identity and text-to-speech when conditioned on text-derived features.

22.1.3.2 SampleRNN

Instead of convolutional layers, the SampleRNN architecture [54] relies on long short-term memory (LSTM) units/gated recurrent units (GRUs), which are variants of the RNN, operating in a hierarchy of layers over increasingly longer temporal scales. The recurrent modules in each layer summarize the history of its inputs into a conditioning vector that is then passed to the subsequent layer all the way to the lowest level modules made up of multilayer perceptrons, which then combines this information with preceding samples to output a distribution over a sample as seen in Fig. 22.8. As with WaveNet, the output is discretized with a softmax.

Qualitatively, the subjective performances of WaveNet and SampleRNN are very similar. Quantitatively, the SampleRNN authors claim slightly better negative log-likelihood scores for SampleRNN compared to WaveNet on several datasets for speech, non-linguistic human sounds and music. Nevertheless, the authors concede that their re-implementation of WaveNet may not have been optimal due to a lack of published information regarding hyperparameters.

22.1.4 Only a Matter of Time: Real-Time Generation

WaveNet and SampleRNN significantly improved the quality of audio synthesis over previous parametric and concatenative methods, particularly in terms of the naturalness of its speech synthesis. In the initial experiments, both were trained on not only speech but music databases as well, in particular, MagnaTagATune [49] and various solo piano datasets, showing that the models can generalize, to a degree, to different audio domains. These early audio generative models had a huge impact on the deep learning community, and moreover brought attention to the possibilities of audio generation with deep generative networks. With gains in quality, the next step required to actually utilize these models in a production or performance environment was to boost the generative speed. Although the architecture of these autoregressive models is causal, and could thus in theory operate under real-time control, they were dependent on inefficient ancestral sampling resulting in an inherently slow synthesis speed, making the original WaveNet and SampleRNN far from being able to generate audio in real time. Subsequent years of development have focused on improving efficiency for speed and for the ability to run with restricted resources on embedded systems or mobile devices while preserving audio quality.

22.1.4.1 (Faster Than) Real-Time Synthesizers

A direct approach to mitigate the problem was to improve the computational efficiency in these models. Fast WaveNet [59] was one of the earlier improvements over the original, which implemented specialized lower level kernels to store intermediate calculations through caching. This reduced the need for recomputing WaveNet nodes from scratch for each sample generated. Furthermore, the temporal gains acquired by the method scales with the number of layers and could generalize to other autoregressive networks.

Other implementations try to push efficiency further by redesigning the components that significantly contribute to computational time themselves. For WaveRNN [43], this was done by reducing the number of parameters and operations, implementing custom graphics processing unit (GPU) operations, and generating samples in a more parallel manner. The core of WaveRNN is a single-layer RNN followed by two fully connected layers ending with a softmax output that predicts 16-bit audio samples (in comparison the original WaveNet and many other papers output 8-bit μ-law encoded samples). The state-based operation of an RNN is advantageous in this context as it can perform highly non-linear transformations without requiring the multiple stacked layers present in convolutional architectures like WaveNet, thus reducing the overall number of operations. The bigger contributor to the speed-up nevertheless is the heavy use of low-level code optimization to overcome memory bandwidth and calculation execution bottlenecks. The resulting WaveRNN implementation can produce 24kHz 16-bit audio at 4×real time.

A significantly simpler model in comparison to the original WaveNet is FFTNet [42] which contains layers that operate like a fast Fourier transform (FFT). Here the input into each layer is split, transformed separately using 1×1 convolutions, and then summed. Each step corresponds to a process in the Cooley–Tukey FFT algorithm [7]: separating even and odd discrete Fourier transform (DFT) components, calculating the complex exponential part of the DFT, and then combining the two DFT halves into the full DFT. It is much faster than the vanilla WaveNet given the simpler architecture, and real-time generation is possible.

Several studies have sought to reformulate autoregressive models as normalizing flows to skirt around the inherent inefficiency of sample-by-sample autoregressive synthesis networks. These models preserve the general structure of a WaveNet model but redesign the network layers or training procedure to adhere to the restrictions of a flow-based setup. Compared to the purely autoregressive models, their flow-based counterparts can take better advantage of the massively parallel computation capabilities of a GPU, particularly during the generative phase. In particular, Parallel WaveNet [80] combines two types of flow models, a flow-based WaveNet student model that generates samples and another pre-trained WaveNet teacher model to score the generated samples. Together they are trained by comparing their KL divergence. This teacher–student training scheme is known as *probability density distillation* and has shown to achieve $20\times$ real-time synthesis for 24kHz speech samples albeit at the expense of longer training times. Parallel WaveNet has been successfully deployed in Google's Google Assistant systems.

Notably, Parallel WaveNet had to apply a Monte Carlo method to approximate the KL divergence between the distributions given by the teacher and student models. This may lead to large variances in the gradient calculation during backpropagation due to the sampling procedure which are not ideal for training. ClariNet [61] introduced a distillation algorithm that instead estimates the KL divergence in closed form, largely stabilizing the training procedure.

22.1.5   The Answer Lies Within: Interfacing via Conditional Models

Notwithstanding their high quality, there are several issues to consider for the DNN-based synthesizers in the preceding section to reliably function as a synthesizer. Despite the special architectures designed to capture long-term dependencies, there is a limit to how much the receptive field of the network can be stretched, and we quickly encounter memory bottlenecks with increasing numbers of layers. Moreover, being autoregressive in nature, each generated sample is only directly conditioned on the immediate previous samples, and hence the influence from samples further back in its output history quickly diminishes. Effectively, the synthesized audio is only coherent up to a length of 10–100 samples. Indeed this is most obvious in unconditional versions of WaveNet that, while getting the characteristic timbre of human speech correct, produces incoherent babble akin to splicing random phonemes. Otherwise, when trained on music data made up of multiple instruments, it produces extremely unstructured music that jumps around between different timbres—hardly a viable model to be used as a synthesizer.

In the generative task, we aim to learn a function that approximates the true data distribution of the training set via our model, then sample from this approximate distribution to produce new examples. Since the model presumably learns the entire data distribution, sampling from it unbiasedly would consequently yield random pieces of generated data originating from anywhere in the distribution. Instead of generating data from the entire distribution, what we often want in practice is to produce something only from certain subsections of the distribution. One might therefore introduce a sampling algorithm as a means of guiding the output.

Graves, in his influential paper on generating sequences with RNNs [31], outlined a few methods to constrain the sampling of the network. One way is to *bias* the model towards churning out more probable elements of the data distribution, which in Graves' example corresponded to more readable handwriting. The sampler is biased at each generative step independently by tuning a parameter called the probability bias b which influences the standard deviation of the probability density of the output. When $b = 0$, unbiased sampling is recovered, and as $b \to \infty$, the variance vanishes so the model outputs an approximation of the mode of the posterior distribution. Similar control parameters that affect the randomness of output samples appear in other works. For Performance RNN [69], a network designed to model polyphonic music with MIDI, a "temperature" parameter reduces the randomness of events as it is decreased, making for a more repetitive performance.

While biased sampling introduces one aspect of control, not much can be done by way of choosing the kinds of examples we want to generate. For RNNs in sequence generation, the network can be *primed* by presenting the network with a user-specified sequence that determines the state of the recurrent units before the generation begins (when predicted output samples are used as input to predict following samples). Any characteristics embodied by the priming sequence will tend to continue into the generative phase assuming they extended through time in the training data. This is true not just for easily describable characteristics such as pitch, but also for characteristics harder to describe but statistically present (over limited durations) such as "style" characteristics. *Priming* allows a higher degree of control over desired aspects of the dataset than bias manipulation. Again referencing Graves' handwriting study, primed sampling allows generation in the style of a particular writer rather than a randomly selected one. As illustrated using handwriting in Fig. 22.9, the generated output following the priming sequence can retain the stylistic aspects of the primer.

The priming technique does have several weaknesses. As the RNN's memory capacity has shown to be limited in practice, for longer sequences, the generated samples tend to "drift" away from possessing the characteristics of the priming sequence. Glover [28] has a sound example of an RNN trained to generate a tone which slowly drifts around the frequency of the priming tone. Also, priming conflates many perceptual dimensions without allowing more fine-tuned control over them independently. In the case of the handwriting example above, the entire style of writing is preserved. However, one cannot individually alter lower level stylistic aspects like the roundness of letters or the spacing between letters and so forth. This lack of specific control as well as the lack of real-time interaction throughout the generative phase limits the potential use of priming for real-time sound models.

Fortunately, given that a generative model learns the entire joint distribution over a dataset, it is possible not just to alter the sampling procedure but to change the distribution itself by modelling a distribution depending on externally imposed conditions. Mathematically, this means that instead of sampling directly from the model distribution $p_\theta(X)$, we sample from a conditional probability $p_\theta(X \mid C)$ given the set of conditions $C = \{c1, c2, c3, ...\}$. As such, the model output is constrained only to certain subsections of the posterior distribution that are congruent to the conditions imposed. It is often useful to condition on rich side information that correspond to certain high-level features of the dataset. If the model has learned the data well,

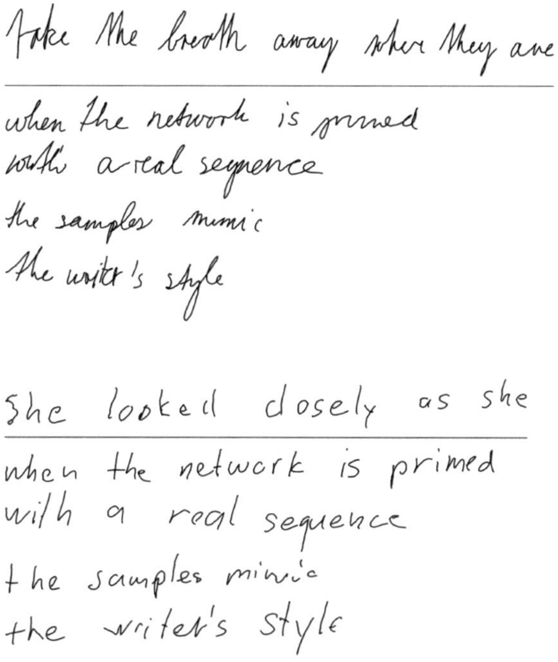

Fig. 22.9 Handwriting examples generated by a LSTM-based network. The top line of each block (underlined) shows the priming sequences drawn from the training set. The following generated text, while never having existed in the training set, retains the handwriting style of the priming sequence. Analogously, generated audio samples would retain the sound characteristics of the priming sequence over a finite number of time steps. Figure reproduced from Graves [31]

by specifying certain factors of variation, such as pitch or timbre in the case of music data, one can then contextualize the type of output desired. Overall, the idea of *conditioning* makes for an extremely appealing approach to constructing control parameters required to guide a synthesis model.

Conditioning can be induced at either a global level (effecting the entire output signal) or a local level (dynamic at every time step) and can come from labels external to the network or from the network's own feature space. Utilizing the feature space of the network is especially compelling since on top of reducing the need for laborious labelled data, the network has the ability to discover for itself conditioning parameters during training (see Fig. 22.10 and Sect. 22.1.7). Furthermore, regular or continuous provision of conditioning information presents the network with a strong signal to maintain structure over a longer time span that might otherwise be lost due to limitations on long time dependencies. Wyse [89] showed that the pitch drift described earlier in an unconditional RNN is non-existent with a similar network trained conditionally with pitch information. Conditioning frees the network from having to model dependencies across long timescales so that more capacity can be devoted to local structure.

In essence, conditioning is a way to restrict the probabilistic model only to certain configurations that we care about. In practice, leveraging data to drive both the synthesis and control affordances goes a long way towards addressing some of the issues introduced earlier; conditioning information simultaneously provides an interface for control and restricts the output to the correct set of parameter combinations.

(a) Rotation   (b) Width

Fig. 22.10 Sampling from the latent space in the InfoGAN model shows how it captures rotation and widths of a chair while preserving its shape. Notably, the learned "semantic" concepts are abstracted from the type of chair, meaning it is generalizable across different examples. In the same way, a generative model for audio can potentially learn prosodic or stylistic elements of sounds in an unsupervised fashion which can then be further utilized as conditioning information. For music, this could mean having access to latent codes for timbre, pitch and other useful audio properties, potentially to be used for many creative applications. Figure reproduced from Chen et al. [5]

From an engineering point of view, transitioning to a conditional model requires two major ingredients: a way to inject supplementary information into the model pipeline during training, followed by a way to expose the same labels again for user control in the generative phase. These developments will be the main focus of the following sections.

22.1.6 Along for the Ride: External Conditioning

A basic music synthesizer interface would typically give the user an option to choose the instrument desired, along with a way to change common musical parameters like pitch and volume. One way to adapt this control structure for a deep generative model is to introduce additional labels which can come in many different forms, including categorical class labels, text, one-hot encoding and real-valued numbers representing pitch, loudness or duration, depending on the control dimension desired; each corresponding to a musical parameter. The desired combination of labels can be concatenated and fed to the model as a conditioning vector together with the audio samples themselves.

The actual implementation for conditioning may be further broken down into two different methodologies according to whether the labels originate externally with respect to the generative model or are discovered internally as part of the unsupervised representation learning process. External labels may be derived directly from raw inputs that are prepared beforehand and annotated by the developer (Sect. 22.1.6.1) or otherwise pre-processed by other models or algorithms to produce the final conditional vector (Sects. 22.1.6.2–22.1.6.3). Several studies have investigated the viability of these approaches.

22.1.6.1   External Conditioning via Observed Labels

The extent to which external conditional parameters can influence synthesis was studied by Wyse [89] via a simple multilayer RNN model. The network was jointly trained on real-valued parameters indicating pitch, volume and instrumentation, together with raw audio from the NSynth database [16]. During the generative phase, combinations of these parameters were fed as input to the network at every time step, augmenting input from audio predicted from previous steps. The work further highlighted the network's ability to interpolate between conditioning parameter values unseen during training. This was demonstrated through a pitch sweep that interpolated between two trained data points at pitches as much as an octave apart. This work was extended by Wyse and Huzaifah [90] focusing on the learning and synthesis of acoustic transients (the "attack" and "decay" segments at the beginning and end of tones). In the experimental setup, transients were modelled as a non-instantaneous response to a change in the volume parameter that resulted in the gradual increase or decrease in the amplitude of the waveform towards the desired loudness level. This demonstrated that conditioning can function to effect the audio generation for a significant period of time following changes in value. This effect is shown in Fig. 22.11.

Direct conditioning using labels and values based on observed hand-picked characteristics have been shown to allow relatively fine-grained control of the output signal since the conditioning labels are time-aligned and present for every sample of the audio signal. Still, this method requires accurately capturing and aligning labels that may not be readily available or expensive to assemble in terms of time and labour. Labels do not have to be measurable from data but can be perceptually derived as well. However, they must of course be consistent with the data and with each other to be learnable.

22.1.6.2   External Conditioning via Intermediate Representations

Instead of directly providing conditioning information as raw inputs into the generative model, for certain tasks it may be more effective to further process the information beforehand. Take for example text-to-speech (TTS), a task that can be considered under-constrained given the innumerable ways the same text can be vocalized. On account of text being such a compressed representation compared to audio waveforms, it may be difficult to model audio directly on text. It is usually more prudent to model lower level components such as phonemes, intonation and duration separately and then provide this information as conditioning parameters for the waveform generation model. In brief, sometimes one or more models separate from the generative network are employed to first map raw inputs to an intermediate representation before feeding this to a generative network. This in effect breaks a complex problem into smaller more manageable tasks, leading to easier convergence during optimization.

It is not uncommon for these "pre-processing" modules to also themselves be deep neural networks. Functionally, these networks play several roles in this context. They convert and integrate various sources of information that may be very different representationally (one-hot encoding, real numbers, text, etc.) into a common and probably more unified feature space. They can serve as embeddings which are

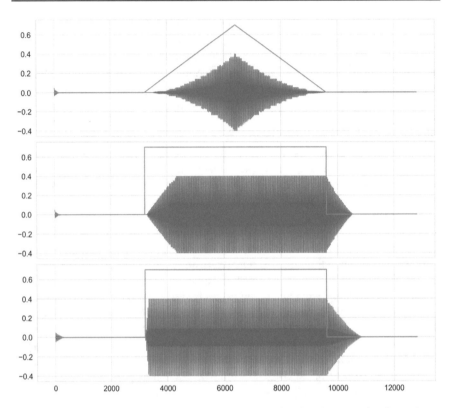

Fig. 22.11 In the top figure, the amplitude of the generated signal tracks a smooth volume change in the conditioning parameter (orange line). However, sudden changes in the value of the volume conditioning parameter trigger transient attacks and decays in the output audio waveform that form over a finite time as they did during the training phase. The middle and bottom figures with their different waveforms and transient characteristics are produced by different settings for the "instrument ID" conditioning parameter. Figure reproduced from Wyse and Huzaifah [90]

low-dimensional spaces that high-dimensional information such as audio and text can be mapped onto. Embeddings usually contain meaningful distance relationships between values (i.e. features semantically close together are also close in the embedding space. For example, a human male voice would be closer to a human female voice compared to a bird chirping) and so serve as a more compact and useful representation to train the model on. Finally, they are feature extractors that can tease out any helpful latent variables present in the data to aid in the learning of their task.

A music model that does this multi-step feature extraction to obtain conditioning information for a generative model is SING (symbol-to-instrument neural generator) [9]. SING aims to synthesize audio a frame at a time (consisting of 1024 samples), making it arguably more efficient than the sample-level autoregressive models. The main architecture consists of two parts: an LSTM-based sequence generator and a convolutional decoder (see Fig. 22.12). Unlike the autoregressive networks that

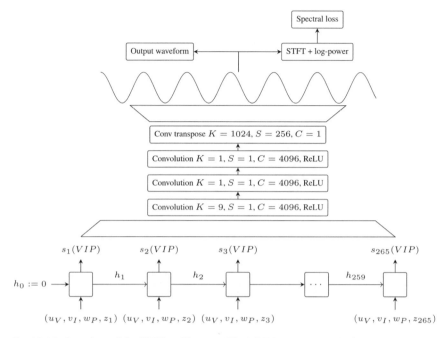

Fig. 22.12 Overview of the SING architecture. The LSTM generator at the bottom produces an intermediate sequential representation from velocity, instrument, pitch and time embeddings (u_V, v_I, w_P and z_{1-256}, respectively). The sequence is then fed through a convolutional decoder to synthesize a waveform. Figure reproduced from Défossez et al. [9]

require prior audio samples to generate what follows, SING's sequence generator takes in embedded values corresponding to audio parameters of velocity, pitch and instrument plus a component to quantify time dependency, without actual audio samples as input. The generated sequence, which can be regarded as an intermediate feature representation, is then processed and upsampled through several convolutional layers to obtain the final real-valued waveform.

Training such a multi-component network is usually not a trivial undertaking. Each module in SING must be separately trained before fine-tuning the entire model. For instance, the convolutional decoder is initially pre-trained together with an encoder as an autoencoder. The encoder was subsequently dropped since it was no longer required for the generative task.

A compelling contribution of the paper is the adoption of spectral loss, which was shown to be superior to mean square error (MSE) commonly used when comparing real-valued objects. The authors surmised that this could be due to errors in phase reconstructions when training with the latter. During generation a model chooses implicitly a phase value that could take any number between $[0, 2\pi]$, altering the output in a somewhat random fashion unless it has learnt all possible phase and frequency combinations. This unpredictability makes a MSE comparison with the ground truth in the time domain uninformative and unlikely to train the model well.

In comparison, the spectral loss is calculated using the magnitude spectra of the signal, discarding phase information for both the generated waveform and the target waveform. Hence, the model is free to choose a canonical phase by which to base the generation on instead of devoting capacity to learn all possible phase combinations.

Various extensions to WaveNet and SampleRNN also employ one or more external models to convert raw inputs to an intermediate representation [1, 74]. Many of these were purposed for TTS tasks and were pre-trained on existing TTS systems to extract vocoder features. In a similar spirit to SING, Tacotron [83] also implements RNN-based networks to sequentially predict mel spectrograms for speech, contingent upon embeddings for speaker, text and reference spectrograms. The original version of Tacotron uses the Griffin–Lim algorithm [33] to invert the output spectrograms but this was later replaced with a WaveNet in follow-up work [68]. The Tacotron team in a series of papers [70, 84, 85] displayed some ways for conditioning to be utilized more creatively that may be more in line with how music synthesis systems would later be designed. "Style tokens" were introduced to extract independent prosodic styles from training data within a Tacotron model. Style tokens comprise of a bank of embeddings shared across training samples. The embeddings were trained without any explicit labels (i.e. unsupervised) but are able to generate interpretable parameters that can control synthesis in interesting ways. Ten style tokens were used for experiments, enough to adequately present a small but rich variety of prosodies. They were found to be able to generalize beyond learned inputs, generating audio in the corresponding embedded style even on unseen text. The group's research in style tokens culminates in an enhanced Tacotron with explicit prosody controls allowing changing prosodic style while preserving speaker identity.

22.1.6.3 Capturing Long-Term Structure in Music

As highlighted by Dieleman et al. [12], autoregressive models excel at generating raw waveforms of speech, whereas when applied to music, they tend to be biased towards capturing local structure at the expense of modelling long-range correlations. One way to alleviate this problem is to divest the modelling of long-term correlations to a conditioning signal. This relieves the network from having to model signal structure beyond a few hundred milliseconds and dedicate more modelling capacity to localized patterns. Analogous to how text is used to condition a neural synthesizer for TTS, several papers have sought the use of MIDI notes or piano rolls as a way of directing a musical signal. This takes advantage of the fact that symbolic representations are easier to model over the long term, while still preserving the expressivity and richness of raw audio models.

To that end, Manzelli et al. [53] provided MIDI pitch and timing as conditioning for a WaveNet model. Rather than feeding these values by hand, a second generative network was used to compose MIDI sequences. This second network essentially takes over the modelling of long-range correlations, with the final synthesized audio output shown to follow the timing and pitch of the MIDI notes fairly closely. This idea was further expanded by Hawthorne et al. [34] in their Wave2Midi2Wave system that adds an encoder network to transcribe raw audio to MIDI, plus a state-of-the-art transformer network [37] to generate MIDI sequences instead of a LSTM-based one used by Manzelli et al. The paper reported that there was not a statistically significant difference in ratings between real recordings and those generated by the model conditioned on a MIDI test set of piano recordings. Ratings were given by human assessors in a pair-wise blind test according to which clip they thought sounded more like it came from a person playing a real piano.

Conditioning can be used for many other applications in music besides modelling long-term structure. In the original WaveNet paper, the authors mooted conditioning the model with a set of tags specifying musical characteristics like genre and instrument identity essentially as a way to alter timbre but did not go in to detail about these findings. This line of research has since been taken up by others primarily through a latent variable model approach where the latents are jointly learned as part of training the generative model instead of depending on external models or direct observable labels. Open AI's Jukebox [10] uses several VQ-VAEs [81] in parallel to produce quantized embeddings at different temporal resolutions to help maintain coherence over long time spans. Training is tuned such that each stage encodes information at different levels of abstraction, with the topmost level capturing high-level semantics like melody, while the middle level captures more local features like timbre. Decoding is likewise carried out progressively over multi-timescale stages and uses a combination of autoregressive transformers and WaveNet-style dilated convolutions to model embeddings over time and upsample them to retrieve audio samples. The system was trained on 1.2 million songs, and is able to generate musically coherent samples in a wide variety of styles at timescales of minutes at a CD-quality sample rate of 44.1kHz. Conditioning information on artists and genre allow for high-level control over musical style. Further, conditioning on text allows coherent lyrics to be produced accompanied by the music.

22.1.7 Beneath the Surface: Latent Variable Models of Music

There may be times when the audio training dataset is too cumbersome for hand-labelling; metadata may be incomplete, or it may be difficult to process features equitably across the entire dataset. In cases such as these, we can instead pass the burden of extracting useful features to the model itself. With a latent variable model such as the VAE, feature extraction can be carried out internally in an unsupervised or semi-supervised manner. While many other deep learning model variants also learn features to aid its training objective, a latent variable model goes a step further to impose structure on the feature space and adds a generative model that samples from this space. This process entails the discovery of underlying latent factors of variation in the dataset as part of the training procedure (and often encouraged by the objective function itself), in comparison to a more direct mapping from inputs to a feature space akin to a pre-processing step for many of the conditional models discussed in the prior section. On the other hand, compared to the previous models discussed, particularly the autoregressive models, latent variable models are often harder to train.

Having these useful properties, latent variable models are often utilized for two functions that are musically relevant. Firstly, features can be "disentangled" from the source material. Take for example a dataset made up of audio clips of several instruments each playing a range of notes. Each piece of data can be said to have an intrinsic timbre and pitch. During training, the model attempts to decouple these two features to conceptualize a characteristic timbre for each instrument as well as separate the different pitch levels in a way that is abstracted from any particular audio sample. If successfully modelled, one can then treat timbre and pitch as independent features to possibly be used as conditioning for the synthesis. After disentanglement, the assorted features can be mixed in creative ways. *Timbre transfer* is the process of selecting a particular timbre and composing it with a pitch not found for that instrument in the dataset or even outside of the instrument's physical range in real life, creating a novel sound. The concept has been demonstrated in principle by Hung et al. [39] with separate VAE variants, one utilizing distinct encoders for pitch and timbre and the other employing skip connections to process pitch on a different pathway than that of timbre. Both were trained on constant-Q transformed (CQT) audio to output a piano-roll-like symbolic representation. This work was later extended by Luo et al. [51] using a more general mel-spectrogram representation.

Being able disentangle features and construct latent spaces have allowed researches to extend seminal work on timbre spaces reliant on perceptual "dissimilarity" scores from human subjects then analysed by multi-dimensional scaling (MDS) [32,87]. Latent variable models admit organizing a timbre space in a more objective manner with meaningful distance relationships and so can be treated as an embedding. The unsupervised organization of the timbre space was studied by Kim et al. [45] in relation to their Mel2Mel architecture which predicts mel spectrograms for conditioning of a WaveNet in a similar way to Tacotron. This work, in particular, used FiLM (feature-wise linear modulation) layers [60] to learn temporal and spectral envelope features from the instrument embeddings that drives the timbre during synthesis. Visualizations of the learned instrument embedding space in Mel2Mel indicated separation along the lines of spectral centroid and mean energy. Although this model seemed to have disentangled timbre in a perceptually meaningful fashion, being unsupervised, there is no guarantee that this will always be the case. In many cases, individual latent dimensions may not actually embody or correspond to any clear-cut audio characteristic. This is unlike the external conditioning shown in Sect. 22.1.6.1 that, by virtue of being hand-prepared, ensures it can be used as intended during generation. To overcome this, Esling et al. [17] incorporated the timbre space from the traditional MDS studies by using it as the prior distribution to train a VAE model, thus guaranteeing some perceptual correspondence. The learned space is topologically similar to the MDS space but with added advantages by virtue of being a VAE, including being continuous and generalizable.

The benefit of a structured feature space is having a principled way of navigating its topology. This is especially significant for a non-ordinal parameters like timbre which, by itself, has no natural arrangement. Since we now have a continuous embedding with meaningful distances, interpolation, the second major use of latent variable models, becomes possible. Rather than sampling from the centre of mass of known features in the feature space as is done when selecting a particular timbre and a particular pitch both present in the training dataset, it is possible to instead choose a point somewhere in between two distinct features. Smooth interpolation allows the model to blend the characteristics of surrounding features when sampling from an interpolated value. In this way, sounds can be synthesized that generalizes beyond the training dataset. For instance, a point in the middle of two known pitches in the feature space can be selected which would roughly correspond to a pitch halfway between two pitches. Perhaps more interesting is the possibility of blending timbres in a perceptually integrated way, quite distinct from the superficial "mixing" of audio signals from distinct sources.

One of the first music synthesis systems to display such use was set out in Engel et al. [16]. Here the encoder side of the VAE learns a mapping from raw instrument tones to an embedding layer that is connected to a WaveNet decoder. Their encoder is built as a 30-layer non-linear residual network of dilated convolutions followed by 1×1 convolutions and average pooling. The embedding result is sequential, with separate temporal and channel dimensions whose resolution is dependent on the pooling stride. While keeping the size of the embedding constant, the stride is tuned for a trade-off between temporal resolution and embedding expressivity. Experiments showed that the embedding space spans the range of timbre and dynamics present in the dataset. For generation, the latent vectors are upsampled in time and provided to the autoregressive model as conditioning parameters. Interpolation between two timbers is thus between two targets that are each changing in time. Interpolation between these factors does result in a perceptual melding of different instruments creating novel sounds. On the other hand, trying to generate multiple pitches from a single embedding preserving timbre and dynamics by conditioning on pitch during training was less successful. The authors postulated that this may have been due to unsatisfactory disentanglement between pitch and timbre.

22.1.8 Build Me Up, Break Me Down: Audio Synthesis with GANs

Up to now the generative approaches discussed have been based around likelihood models including autoregressive models, VAEs, normalizing flow models, or a combination of them. Unlike these other models families, GANs are not trained using maximum likelihood. A GAN training objective is instead set up to determine whether or not a set of samples from two distributions are in fact from the same distribution—a procedure known as the *two-sample test*. Despite the difficulty in training GANs, they have shown outstanding success in the vision domain and remains the dominant model family for image generation. Several research groups have attempted to apply the GAN framework to audio. The historical development of GAN models for audio was as much a search for representations that work well with GANs as they are of advancements in the network architecture. The naive approach of replacing images with an image-like representation of audio, i.e. the spectrogram while retaining most of the vision informed architecture resulted in extremely noisy generated samples. GAN-based audio models have come a long way since then. They operate at a much faster rate than the more prevalent autoregressive models, requiring a single forward pass for generation, and so fall well within the computationally real-time requirement of a music synthesizer.

One of the early relatively successful audio GAN models was WaveGAN [14]. It works in the time domain and utilizes one-dimensional convolutional filters, with an upsampling strategy based on DCGAN [65] but with new procedures such as *phase shuffling* to take care of aliasing artefacts created by convolutional filters and strides. WaveGAN was the better of two similar GAN architectures presented in the paper, the other of which operated on spectrograms. Evaluation was measured through the *inception score* [67] and human judges. The authors report that WaveGAN has not reached the level of fidelity of the best autoregressive models, but is orders of magnitude faster as it can take advantage of the inherent parallelism of GANs to generate hundreds of times faster than real time. Of course, despite its computational speed, it is still not real-time interactive because the architecture is structured to generate large chunks of audio at a time—one second in this case. Furthermore, the parametric input to a WaveGAN (like DCGAN) is a 100-dimensional "latent vector" which is trained by mapping noise to sound. The input parameter space of the network must thus be searched after training in order to find desired output sounds. Since similar sounds tend to cluster in the parameter space, a typical search strategy is to search coarsely for the desired "class" (e.g. drum type) and then in a neighbourhood to fine-tune the audio output. A separate strategy would be necessary to map a desired parametric control space consisting of say, instrument ID and some timbral characteristics to the control parameters of the GAN. This is similar to strategies for mapping gesture to parameters for fixed synthesizer architectures discussed above.

GANSynth [15] is, at the time of this writing, the state of the art in several aspects of sound modelling. Like WaveGAN, it is much faster than the autoregressive models, although it suffers the same limitations concerning real-time interaction. Several innovations were introduced that have resulted in very high-quality audio as well as the ability to intuitively manipulate audio the parameter space for specific audio characteristics. The model is trained on the NSynth dataset of 4-second musical instrument notes. Thus, like WaveGAN, global structure is encoded in the latent parameter space because each input generates long audio sequences (4 s for GAN-Synth).

GANSynth generates a spectral representation of audio, but one that encodes both the magnitude and the phase of the signal. Furthermore, it is actually the derivative of phase which is coded, referred to as "instantaneous frequency". This turns out to make a significant difference in audio quality. A second innovation is the augmentation of the latent vector input with a one-hot vector representation of the musical pitch of the data. After training, latent vectors encode timbre which to a very rough approximation are consistent across pitch for a given instrument, while the pitch component can be used for playing note sequences on a fixed instrument. Interpolation between points in the latent vector space also works effectively.

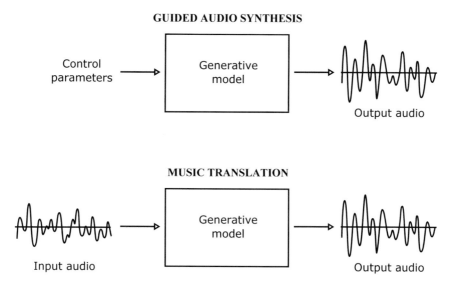

Fig. 22.13 While in the standard guided synthesis task we are interested in generating sound from a set of parameters, for music translation we want to map the sound of one musical domain to another, retaining some audio characteristics of the input domain (e.g. pitch, duration, rhythm) while taking on some other characteristics of the target domain (e.g. timbre)

22.1.9 A Change of Seasons: Music Translation

There is yet another way to use generative models that opens up many possibilities musically. What we have discussed so far entails sampling from the modelled distribution to synthesize novel audio sequences. During this generative phase, the model maps conditional parameters to output audio which is consistent with these parameters. Instead of conditioning on relatively low-level parameters like pitch or volume, an alternative is to provide actual audio as conditioning. During the training phase, if the input audio and the target audio are different, what the generative model does in effect is to find some transformation function between the two (Fig. 22.13).

The goal of *music translation* is a domain transfer, where the hope is to imbue the input audio with some characteristics of the target audio while retaining its general structure. During synthesis, this translation should be able to generalize to new waveforms belonging to the original domain. For images, there is a vast amount of recent literature on "style transfer" [27] where the desired property to transfer is broadly the artistic style of the target, but preserving the "content" or global structure and arrangement of objects in the original image. A more general formulation of this objective can be seen in applications to CycleGAN [91] where the model maps sets of images from one domain to another (e.g. photographs to paintings, horses to zebras, etc.). We might imagine doing something similar with music and indeed several systems have been developed for such use cases.

Timbre is one obvious candidate for an audio property to transfer. Timbretron [38] seeks to do this via a model similar to CycleGAN, working with a CQT representation within the GAN architecture, and then retrieving audio through a WaveNet. The training dataset consisted of real recordings of piano, flute, violin and harpsichord sounds, and the task was to translate one timbre to another. Moreover, to be effective, the system must transform a given audio input so that the output is still perceptible as the same basic musical piece, but recognizably played with the target instrument. The response was broadly positive in those aspects with human evaluators of the system, therefore showing definitive proof-of-concept for music translation.

The domains of interest can also be more loosely defined. Mor et al. [56] presented a "universal music translation network" that is able to translate music across instruments, and to a degree, genres and styles. Their novel architecture consists of a single, universal encoder shared across all inputs connected to multiple WaveNets that each decode for a separate musical domain. In addition, a domain confusion network similar to that put forward by Ganin et al. [25] was employed during training to ensure domain-specific information was not encoded. Their method displayed an impressive ability to execute high-level transformations such as converting a Bach cantata sung by an opera to a solo piano in the style of Beethoven. The domain mapping, however, has to be decided beforehand as only the desired output decoder (out of the multiple trained WaveNets) is to be exposed to the input during generation. Hence, the user cannot change transformations in real time. While switching domain transformations on the fly remains an issue, the generative speed itself have been boosted tremendously in later work that replaces the WaveNet decoder with a GAN model [48].

Rather than translating across whole instruments or styles which may prove to be challenging and not completely convincing by current methods, one could possibly design for smaller transformation tasks and view the generative model as a complex non-linear filter. Damskägg et al. [8] modelled several famous distortion guitar pedals like the Boss DS-1 (distortion), Ibanez Tube Screamer (overdrive) and Electro-Harmonix Big Muff Pi (fuzz) with a modified WaveNet architecture. The final deployed model was able to process a clean guitar input signal in real time on a standard desktop computer, effectively acting as an actual distortion circuit and sounding very close to the actual pedals. Although the mapping from clean sound to distortion is now fixed without the ability to tune further, future work might add the parameters of the original guitar pedals like tone control or gain as conditioning variables to fully emulate their capabilities.

22.1.10 Discussion and Conclusion

Machine learning approaches to audio processing, in general, and sound modelling, in particular, are quickly gaining prominence and replacing previous techniques based on manual feature selection and coding. Deep learning architectures offer new approaches and new ways to think about perennial sound modelling issues such as designing affordances for expressive manipulation during real-time performance.

Hybrid architectures that draw on signal analysis as part of an overall sound modelling strategy are becoming more common. Variational autoencoders, for example, are exploited to discover low-dimensional representations of the data space that can then be used for external control for generation.

Great strides have been made in capturing complexity and naturalness that is hard to code for manually. Automatic discovery of structure in data combined with specific techniques for regularizing representations has led to intuitive ways of navigating through a space of sounds even across regions where there is no training data. Using strategies for training generative models with conditional distributions is a very musically intuitive way to design interfaces. This methodology shifts the scope of the control space primarily to the training data, or specifically factors of variation in the data (latent or otherwise), from what used to be defined as a by-product of the synthesis algorithm or a design decision for an interface. It is a new way of thinking about how to construct such control affordances in comparison to traditional synthesis techniques.

Perhaps flexibility is the greatest strength of the deep learning paradigm; models can be reused or redesigned for a wide variety of sound classes. Different model families can be combined to extend their capabilities such as using a VAE to discover latent features that can be passed to an autoregressive generator, or using a normalizing flow model to speed up a standard autoregressive network. This opens up the possibility of attempting more complicated tasks that were not previously possible such as expressive TTS for speech or real-time timbre transfer for music.

Outstanding issues remain. The best-sounding systems are still very computationally expensive. This makes them challenging to port to ubiquitous low-cost devices. Training typically depends on many hours of data. Data must capture not only sound, but also control factors that can be difficult to obtain such as air pressure inside a mouth for a wind instrument model. The amount of data necessary for creating good models can take days to train even on the best GPU platforms which is both time-consuming and expensive. Learning and synthesizing more complex sounds including multi-track, multi-instrument audio are still largely beyond current models. Different types of models have different advantages (VAEs for structuring data spaces, GANs for global parameterization, autoregressive models for the causality necessary for real-time synthesis, etc.) but we have yet to see a deep learning system make its way into general usage for musical audio synthesis the way they have in, for example, the domain of speech synthesis. With the rate that these technologies are being developed, it seems certain to happen in the near future, perhaps even by the time you are reading this manuscript.

Acknowledgements This research was supported by a Singapore MOE Tier 2 grant, "Learning Generative Recurrent Neural Networks", and by an NVIDIA Corporation Academic Programs GPU grant.

References

1. Arik, S. Ö., Chrzanowski, M., Coates, A., Diamos, G., Gibiansky, A., Kang, Y., Li, X., Miller, J., Ng, A., Raiman, J., & Sengupta, S. (2017). Deep voice: Real-time neural text-to-speech. arXiv:1702.07825.
2. Bengio, Y., Laufer, E., Alain, G., & Yosinski, J. (2014). Deep generative stochastic networks trainable by backprop. In *International conference on machine learning*, pp. 226–234.
3. Briot, J. P., Hadjeres, G. & Pachet, F. D. (2017). Deep learning techniques for music generation—a survey. arXiv:1709.01620.
4. Briot, J. -P., & Pachet, F. (2017). Music generation by deep learning-challenges and directions. arXiv:1712.04371.
5. Chen, X., Duan, Y., Houthooft, R., Schulman, J., Sutskever, I., & Abbeel, P. (2016). Infogan: Interpretable representation learning by information maximizing generative adversarial nets. In *Advances in neural information processing systems*, pp. 2172–2180.
6. Choi, K., Fazekas, G., Cho, K., & Sandler, M. (2017). A tutorial on deep learning for music information retrieval. arXiv:1709.04396.
7. Cooley, J. W., & Tukey, J. W. (1965). An algorithm for the machine calculation of complex fourier series. *Mathematics of Computation, 19*(90), 297–301.
8. Damskägg, E. -P., Juvela, L., & Välimäki, V. (2019). Real-time modeling of audio distortion circuits with deep learning. In *Sound and music computing conference*, pp. 332–339.
9. Défossez, A., Zeghidour, N., Usunier, N., Bottou, L., & Bach, F. (2018). Sing: Symbol-to-instrument neural generator. In *Advances in neural information processing systems*, pp. 9041–9051.
10. Dhariwal, P., Jun, H., Payne, C., Kim, J. W., Radford, A., & Sutskever, I. (2020). Jukebox: A generative model for music. arXiv:2005.00341v1.
11. Dieleman, S. (2020). Generating music in the waveform domain. Retrieved June 08, 2020, from https://benanne.github.io/2020/03/24/audio-generation.html.
12. Dieleman, S., Oord, A. V. D., & Simonyan, K. (2018). The challenge of realistic music generation: modelling raw audio at scale. In *Advances in neural information processing systems*, pp. 7989–7999.
13. Doersch, C. (2016) Tutorial on variational autoencoders. arXiv:1606.05908.
14. Donahue, C., McAuley, J., & Puckette, M. (2018). Synthesizing audio with generative adversarial networks. arXiv:1802.04208.
15. Engel, J., Agrawal, K. K., Chen, S., Gulrajani, I., Donahue, C., & Roberts, A. (2019). Gansynth: Adversarial neural audio synthesis. arXiv:1902.08710.
16. Engel, J., Resnick, C., Roberts, A., Dieleman, S., Norouzi, M., Eck, D., & Simonyan, K. (2017). Neural audio synthesis of musical notes with wavenet autoencoders. arXiv:1704.01279.
17. Esling, P., ChemlaRomeu-Santos, A., & Bitton, A. (2018) Generative timbre spaces with variational audio synthesis. In *21st international conference on digital audio effects (DAFx-18)*, Aveiro, Portugal.
18. Fasciani, S., & Wyse, L. (2012). A voice interface for sound generators: adaptive and automatic mapping of gestures to sound. In *International conference on new interfaces for musical expression*, Ann Arbor, MI.
19. Fels, S., & Hinton, G. (1993). Glove-talk ii: A neural network interface between a data-glove and a speech synthesizer. *IEEE Transactions on Neural Networks, 4*(1), 2–8.
20. Fiebrink, R. (2011). *Real-time human interaction with supervised learning algorithms for music composition and performance*. Ph.D. thesis, Princeton University.
21. Fiebrink, R., & Caramiaux, B. (2016). The machine learning algorithm as creative musical tool. *Handbook of Algorithmic Music*.
22. Francoise, J., Schnell, N., Borghesi, R., & Bevilacqua, F. (2014). Probabilistic models for designing motion and sound relationships. In *International conference on new interfaces for musical expression* (pp. 287–292), London, UK.

23. Fried, O., & Fiebrink, R. (2013). Cross-modal sound mapping using deep learning. In *International conference on new interfaces for musical expression Korea* (pp. 531–534). New interfaces for musical expression, Seoul.

24. Gabrielli, L., Tomassetti, S., Squartini, S., & Zinato, C. (2017). Introducing deep machine learning for parameter estimation in physical modelling. In *20th international conference on digital audio effects (DAFx-17)* (pp. 11–16). Edinburgh, UK.

25. Ganin, Y., Ustinova, E., Ajakan, H., Germain, P., Larochelle, H., & Laviolette, F., et al. (2016). Domain-adversarial training of neural networks. *The Journal of Machine Learning Research, 17*(1), 2096–2030.

26. Gao, Y., Singh, R., & Raj, B. (2018). Voice impersonation using generative adversarial networks. arXiv:1802.06840.

27. Gatys, L. A., Ecker, A. S., & Bethge, M. (2015). A neural algorithm of artistic style. arXiv:1508.06576.

28. Glover, J. (2015). Generating sound with recurrent networks. Retrieved December 04, 2019, from http://www.johnglover.net/blog/generating-sound-with-rnns.html.

29. Goodfellow, I. (2016). Nips 2016 tutorial: Generative adversarial networks. arXiv:1701.00160.

30. Goodfellow, I., Pouget-Abadie, J., Mirza, M., Xu, B., Warde-Farley, D., Ozair, S., Courville, A., & Bengio, Y. (2014). Generative adversarial nets. In *Advances in neural information processing systems*, pp. 2672–2680.

31. Graves, A. (2013). Generating sequences with recurrent neural networks. arXiv:1308.0850.

32. Grey, J. M. (1977). Multidimensional perceptual scaling of musical timbres. *Journal of the Acoustical Society of America, 61*(5), 1270–1277.

33. Griffin, D., & Lim, J. (1984). Signal estimation from modified shorttime fourier transform. *IEEE Transactions on Audio, Speech and Language Processing, 32*(2), 236–243.

34. Hawthorne, C., Stasyuk, A., Roberts, A., Simon, I., Huang, C. -Z. A., Dieleman, S., Elsen, E., Engel, J. and Eck, D. (2018). Enabling factorized piano music modeling and generation with the maestro dataset. arXiv:1810.12247.

35. He, K., Zhang, X., Ren, S., & Sun, J. (2016). Deep residual learning for image recognition. In *IEEE conference on computer vision and pattern recognition*, pp. 770–778.

36. Henter, G. E., Lorenzo-Trueba, J., Wang, X., & Yamagishi, J. (2018). Deep encoder-decoder models for unsupervised learning of controllable speech synthesis. arXiv:1807.11470.

37. Huang, C. Z. A., Vaswani, A., Uszkoreit, J., Shazeer, N., Simon, I., Hawthorne, C., Dai, A. M., Hoffman, M. D., Dinculescu, M., & Eck, D. (2018a) An improved relative self-attention mechanism for transformer with application to music generation. arXiv:1809.04281.

38. Huang, S., Li, Q., Anil, C., Bao, X., Oore, S., & Grosse, R. B. (2018b) Timbretron: A wavenet (cyclegan (cqt (audio))) pipeline for musical timbre transfer. arXiv:1811.09620.

39. Hung, Y. -N., Chen, Y. -A., & Yang, Y. -H. (2018). Learning disentangled representations for timber and pitch in music audio. arXiv:1811.03271.

40. Hunt, A., Wanderley, M. M., & Paradis, M. (2003). The importance of parameter mapping in electronic instrument design. *Journal of New Music Research, 32*(4), 429–440.

41. Huzaifah, M., & Wyse, L. (2020). Applying visual domain style transfer and texture synthesis techniques to audio: Insights and challenges. *Neural Computing and Applications, 32*(4), 1051–1065.

42. Jin, Z., Finkelstein, A., Mysore, G. J., & Lu, J. (2018). Fftnet: A real-time speaker-dependent neural vocoder. In *IEEE international conference on acoustics, speech and signal processing (ICASSP)* (pp. 2251–2255). IEEE.

43. Kalchbrenner, N., Elsen, E., Simonyan, K., Noury, S., Casagrande, N., Lockhart, E., Stimberg, F., Oord, A., Dieleman, S., & Kavukcuoglu, K. (2018). Efficient neural audio synthesis. arXiv:1802.08435.

44. Karras, T., Laine, S., & Aila, T. (2019). A style-based generator architecture for generative adversarial networks. In *Proceedings of the IEEE conference on computer vision and pattern recognition*, pp. 4401–4410.

45. J. W. Kim, R. Bittner, A. Kumar, and J. P. Bello. Neural music synthesis for flexible timbre control. In *IEEE International Conference on Acoustics, Speech and Signal Processing (ICASSP)*, pages 176–180. IEEE, 2019.
46. Kingma, D. P., Salimans, T., Jozefowicz, R., Chen, X., Sutskever, I., & Welling, M. (2016). Improved variational inference with inverse autoregressive flow. In *Advances in neural information processing systems*, pp. 4743–4751.
47. Kingma, D. P., & Welling, M. (2013). Auto-encoding variational bayes. arXiv:1312.6114.
48. Kumar, K., Kumar, R., de Boissiere, T., Gestin, L., Teoh, W.Z., Sotelo, J., de Brébisson, A., Bengio, Y., & Courville, A. (2019) Melgan: Generative adversarial networks for conditional waveform synthesis. In *Advances in neural information processing systems*, pp. 14881–14892.
49. Law, E., & Von Ahn, L. (2009). Input-agreement: A new mechanism for collecting data using human computation games. In *SIGCHI conference on human factors in computing systems* (pp. 1197–1206). ACM.
50. Ling, Z.-H., Kang, S.-Y., Zen, H., Senior, A., Schuster, M., Qian, X.-J., et al. (2015). Deep learning for acoustic modeling in parametric speech generation: A systematic review of existing techniques and future trends. *IEEE Signal Processing Magazine, 32*(3), 35–52.
51. Luo, Y.-J., Agres, K., & Herremans, D. (2019). Learning disentangled representations of timbre and pitch for musical instrument sounds using gaussian mixture variational autoencoders. arXiv:1906.08152.
52. Malik, I., & Ek., C. H. (2017). Neural translation of musical style. arXiv:1708.03535.
53. Manzelli, R., Thakkar, V., Siahkamari, A., & Kulis, B. (2018). Conditioning deep generative raw audio models for structured automatic music. arXiv:1806.09905.
54. Mehri, S., Kumar, K., Gulrajani, I., Kumar, R., Jain, S., Sotelo, J., Courville, A., & Bengio, Y. (2016). Samplernn: An unconditional end-to-end neural audio generation model. arXiv:1612.07837.
55. Mirza, M., & Osindero, S. (2014). Conditional generative adversarial nets. arXiv:1411.1784.
56. Mor, N., Wolf, L., Polyak, A., & Taigman, Y. (2018). A universal music translation network. arXiv:1805.07848.
57. Mwiti, D. (2019). A 2019 guide for automatic speech recognition. Retrieved September 19, 2019, from https://heartbeat.fritz.ai/a-2019-guide-for-automatic-speech-recognition-f1e1129a141c.
58. Oore, S., Simon, I., Dieleman, S., Eck, D., & Simonyan, K. (2018). This time with feeling: Learning expressive musical performance. *Neural Computing and Applications*, 1–13.
59. Oore, S., Simon, I., Dieleman, S., Eck, D., & Simonyan, K. (2016). Fast wavenet generation algorithm. arXiv:1611.09482.
60. Perez, E., Strub, F., De Vries, H., Dumoulin, V., & Courville, A. (2018). Film: Visual reasoning with a general conditioning layer. In *32nd AAAI conference on artificial intelligence*.
61. Ping, W., Peng, K., & Chen, J. (2018). Clarinet: Parallel wave generation in end-to-end text-to-speech. arXiv:1807.07281.
62. Prenger, R., Valle, R., & Catanzaro, B. (2019). Waveglow: A flow-based generative network for speech synthesis. In *IEEE international conference on acoustics, speech and signal processing (ICASSP)* (pp. 3617–3621). IEEE.
63. Pruša, Z., & Rajmic, P. (2017). Toward high-quality real-time signal reconstruction from stft magnitude. *IEEE Signal Processing Letters, 24*(6), 892–896.
64. Purwins, H., Li, B., Virtanen, T., Schlüter, J., Chang, S., & Sainath, T. N. (2019). Deep learning for audio signal processing. *Journal of Selected Topics of Signal Processing, 13*(2), 206–219.
65. Radford, A., Metz, L., & Chintala, S. (2015). Unsupervised representation learning with deep convolutional generative adversarial networks. arXiv:1511.06434.
66. Roberts, A., Engel, J., Raffel, C., Hawthorne, C., & Eck, D. (2018). A hierarchical latent vector model for learning long-term structure in music. arXiv:1803.05428.
67. Salimans, T., Goodfellow, I., Zaremba, W., Cheung, V., Radford, A., & Chen, X. (2016). Improved techniques for training gans. In *Advances in neural information processing systems*, pp. 2234–2242.

68. Shen, J., Pang, R., Weiss, R.J., Schuster, M., Jaitly, N., Yang, Z., Chen, Z., Zhang, Y., Wang, Y., Skerrv-Ryan, R. and Saurous, R.A., Agiomyrgiannakis, Y., & Wu, Y. (2017). Natural tts synthesis by conditioning wavenet on mel spectrogram predictions. arXiv:1712.05884.
69. Simon, I., & Oore, S. (2017). Performance RNN: Generating music with expressive timing and dynamics. Retrieved November 28, 2017, from https://magenta.tensorflow.org/performance-rnn.
70. Skerry-Ryan, R. J., Battenberg, E., Xiao, Y., Wang, Y., Stanton, D., Shor, J., Weiss, R., Clark, R., & Saurous, R. A. (2018). Towards end-to-end prosody transfer for expressive speech synthesis with tacotron. arXiv:1803.09047.
71. Slaney, M., Covell, M., & Lassiter, B. (1996). Automatic audio morphing. In *IEEE international conference on acoustics, speech, and signal processing*, pp. 1001–1004.
72. Smith, J. O. (1992). Physical modeling using digital waveguides. *Computer Music Journal, 16*(4), 74–91.
73. Soegaard, M., & Dam, R. F. (2012). The encyclopedia of human-computer interaction. *The Encyclopedia of Human-Computer Interaction.*
74. Sotelo, J., Mehri, S., Kumar, K., Santos, J. F., Kastner, K., Courville, A., & Bengio, Y. (2017). Char2wav: End-to-end speech synthesis. In *2017 international conference on learning representations (ICLR) workshop track.*
75. Tamamori, A., Hayashi, T., Kobayashi, K., Takeda, K., & Toda, T. (2017). Automatic audio morphing. In *Conference of the international speech communication association (Interspeech)*, pp. 1118–1122.
76. Ulyanov, D., & Lebedev, V. (2016). Audio texture synthesis and style transfer. Retrieved July 10, 2019, from https://dmitryulyanov.github.io/audio-texture-synthesis-and-style-transfer/.
77. Van den Oord, A., Dieleman, S., Zen, H., Simonyan, K., Vinyals, O., Graves, A., Kalchbrenner, N., Senior, A., & Kavukcuoglu, K. (2016a). Wavenet: A generative model for raw audio. arXiv:1609.03499.
78. Van den Oord, A., Kalchbrenner, N., & Kavukcuoglu, K. (2016b). Pixel recurrent neural networks. arXiv:1601.06759.
79. Van den Oord, A., Kalchbrenner, N., Vinyals, O., Espeholt, L., Graves, A. and Kavukcuoglu, K. (2016c). Conditional image generation with pixelcnn decoders. In *Advances in neural information processing systems*, pp. 4790–4798.
80. Van den Oord, A., Li, Y., Babuschkin, I., Simonyan, K., Vinyals, O., Kavukcuoglu, K., Van den Driessche, G., Lockhart, E., Cobo, L.C., Stimberg, F., Casagrande, N., Grewe, D., Noury, S., Dieleman, S., Elsen, E., Nal, K., Zen, H., Graves, A., King, H., Walters, T., Belov, D., & Hassabis, D. (2017a). Parallel wavenet: Fast high-fidelity speech synthesis. arXiv:1711.10433.
81. Van den Oord, A., Vinyals, O., & Kavukcuoglu, K. (2017b). Neural discrete representation learning. In *Advances in neural information processing systems*, pp. 6309–6318.
82. Wanderley, M. M., & Battier, M. (2000) (Eds.). *Trends in gestural control of music.* IRCAM.
83. Wang, Y., Skerry-Ryan, R. J., Stanton, D., Wu, Y., Weiss, R. J., Jaitly, N., Yang, Z., Xiao, Y., Chen, Z., Bengio, S., Le, Q., Agiomyrgiannakis, Y., Clark, R., & Saurous, R. A. (2017a). Tacotron: Towards end-to-end speech synthesis. arXiv:1703.10135.
84. Wang, Y., Skerry-Ryan, R. J., Xiao, Y., Stanton, D., Shor, J., Battenberg, E., Clark, R., & Saurous, R. A. (2017b). Uncovering latent style factors for expressive speech synthesis. arXiv:1711.00520.
85. Wang, Y., Stanton, D., Zhang, Y., Ryan, R. S., Battenberg, E., Shor, J., Xiao, Y., Jia, Y., Ren, F., & Saurous, R. A. (2018). Style tokens: Unsupervised style modeling, control and transfer in end-to-end speech synthesis. arXiv:1803.09017.
86. Weng, L. (2018). Flow-based deep generative models. Retrieved December 06, 2019, from http://lilianweng.github.io/lil-log/2018/10/13/flow-based-deep-generative-models.html.
87. Wessel, D. L. (1979). Timbre space as a musical control structure. *Computer Music Journal*, 45–52.

88. Wyse, L. (2017). Audio spectrogram representations for processing with convolutional neural networks. In *1st international workshop on deep learning and music, International joint conference on neural networks*. arXiv:1706.09559), pp. 37–41.
89. Wyse, L. (2018). Real-valued parametric conditioning of an RNN for interactive sound synthesis. In *6th international workshop on musical metacreation* arXiv:1805.10808). Salamanca, Spain.
90. Wyse, L., & Huzaifah, M. (2019). Conditioning a recurrent neural network to synthesize musical instrument transients. In *Sound and music computing conference*, pp. 525–529.
91. Zhu, J. -Y., Park, T., Isola, P., Efros, A. A. (2017). Unpaired image-to-image translation using cycle-consistent adversarial networks. In *IEEE international conference on computer vision*, pp. 2223–2232.
92. Zhu, X., Beauregard, G. T., & Wyse, L. (2007). Real-time signal estimation from modified short-time fourier transform magnitude spectra. *IEEE Transactions on Audio, Speech and Language Processing, 15*(5), 1645–1653.

Muhammad Huzaifah is a Ph.D. candidate at the National University of Singapore Graduate School for Integrative Sciences and Engineering. He obtained his B.Sc. in Physics from Imperial College London, UK, in 2015. His research focuses on developing learning algorithms for creative applications, primarily in the audio domain. E-mail: muhd.huz@gmail.com

Lonce Wyse is an Associate Professor with the Department of Communications and New Media at the National University of Singapore, and holds a Ph.D. in Cognitive and Neural Systems from Boston University in the USA. He serves on the editorial boards of the Computer Music Journal (MIT Press), Organized Sound (Cambridge University Press) and the International Journal of Performance Arts and Digital Media. He teaches courses on software studies, creative coding, media art and interactive audio. His primary research focus is on developing neural networks as interactive sound and music synthesis models. Email: cnmwll@nus.edu.sg

Transfer Learning for Generalized Audio Signal Processing

23

Stavros Ntalampiras

23.1 Introduction

Transfer learning technologies have not been well explored in the scientific domain of audio signal processing. This chapter provides a brief introduction to transfer learning followed by a generic tool for feature space adaptation, which comprises a fundamental step toward the successful application of such technologies. Two use cases are described where transfer learning provided improved performance over traditional learning. These come from diverse application domains; i.e., affective computing [32] and biodiversity monitoring [29], and we emphasize on the exact way transfer learning was applied to each one. The chapter closes by outlining potential promising research lines of such a technology within the generalized sound processing domain [30].

Transfer learning consists in the beneficial transfer of knowledge rigorously available in a domain $\mathcal{D}^i$ to a different one $\mathcal{D}^j$, $i \neq j$ [34]. There exist domains where we have sufficient knowledge of their characteristics regarding e.g. the data generating process, the class dictionary, successful features, modeling techniques, and so on (see Fig. 23.1). The idea behind *transfer learning* technologies is that we may exploit such knowledge so as to address problems in domains where such knowledge is limited, unreliable, or even not available at all. It has been inspired by the respective human ability of learning not only in multiple but across domains as well. The main three motivations behind the expansion of transfer learning in the last decade are:

1. the unavailability of annotated data in the domain of interest,
2. the cost of calibration is prohibitive, and

S. Ntalampiras (✉)
University of Milan, Milan, Italy
e-mail: stavros.ntalampiras@unimi.it

© Springer Nature Switzerland AG 2021
E. R. Miranda (ed.), *Handbook of Artificial Intelligence for Music*,
https://doi.org/10.1007/978-3-030-72116-9_23

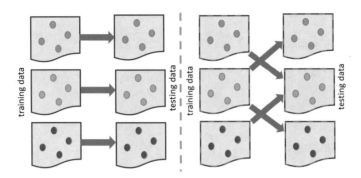

Fig. 23.1 Traditional machine learning versus transfer learning

3. learning a model able to accurately explain the available data distribution requires complex data analytics, could be computationally expensive as well as time-consuming.

To this end, more often than not, transfer learning is realized by means of feature space adaptation where the features characterizing domain $\mathcal{D}^i$ are adapted to fit the specifics of domain $\mathcal{D}^j$ or by model sharing, where a model trained on a plethora of reliably labeled data D_i is adapted to fit the needs of $\mathcal{D}^j$. Furthermore, hybrid approaches are feasible too, where both features and models are transferred across domains and exploited interchangeably according to the needs of domain $\mathcal{D}^j$.

Even though such a learning paradigm is not necessarily tightly coupled with Deep Learning, it has been found extensively useful in such type of modeling [36]. The modeling abilities of Deep Learning solutions are substantially beneficial when large-scale datasets are available. That said, a major milestone in computer vision was reached via the availability of a massive labeled dataset leading to the birth of ImageNet [11]. ImageNet comprises the driving factor for the application of transfer learning to various problems where the main data source is images or the problem can be translated to an image-based one. More specifically, tasks, where the available dataset is limited, are dealt with adapting the knowledge included in ImageNet to the target domain $\mathcal{D}^j$. Typically only the weights of the last ImageNet layers are "touched"; i.e. retrained or finetuned at a relatively small learning rate.

With respect to the speech processing domain, there are several large-scale datasets ready to be used similar to the way ImageNet [11] has been used by the image processing community. For example, one is able to pretrain a model using a vast amount of transcribed data. Such a model can subsequently be tailored to address applications related to languages characterized by low-resources [22] or even different domains [25].

Moving to applications related to music signal processing including music information retrieval (MIR) [31, 33, 41], the available datasets are limited with the notable exception of the Million Song Dataset serving various MIR type of tasks [3, 6, 18, 35]. The status of environmental sound classification is similar with the AudioSet corpus [17] standing out which includes more than 2 million annotated sounds. Unfortunately, such a large-scale dataset fitting the needs of generalized sound processing encompassing speech, music, and environmental sounds is not yet available and thus, *transfer learning* technologies are not significantly popular among the researchers working on this field [12].

However, as mentioned above, transfer learning does not depend on deep architectures nor has to take place at the model level. As a result, several transfer-learning-based solutions exist in the generalized sound processing domain with promising results. After describing a feature space adaptation method, this chapter briefly analyses two such solutions: (a) the first one proposes a joint space to represent and subsequently model the emotional responses to music and sound events [27], and (b) the second one quantifies the similarity between bird vocalizations and music genres toward boosting the performance of bird species identification [28]. Finally, the chapter discusses the potential relevance of such a learning paradigm within the generalized audio signal processing domain and concludes with potentially promising future directions.

23.2   Feature Space Adaptation

Following the categorization presented in [34], four different approaches to transfer learning can de identified:

- *Instance transfer*, which aims at re-using available labeled data from the source domain to the target one [9],
- *Feature representation transfer*, where the goal is to identify a feature representation to effectively project the joint distribution of both source and target domain data [8],
- *Parameter transfer*, where common model parameters among the source and target domain are identified and subsequently used to carry out classification, regression, etc. [15], and
- *Relational knowledge transfer*, where a relational base knowledge is constructed revealing common characteristics between source and target domain [10].

The solutions focusing on affective computing and biodiversity monitoring presented in this chapter belong to the first and third class, respectively. However, they share the need to address the mismatch between the feature distributions of source and target domain. To this end, a specific type of neural network was used able to provide a Multiple Input Multiple Output (MIMO) transformation permitting the usage of data from the source domain to the target one (and vice-versa if needed). Such a neural network; i.e. the Echo State Network (ESN) is presented in the following subsection. It should be mentioned that such a feature space adaptation method can be extended to more than two domains in a straightforward way. For simplicity, the rest of this section assumes the availability of two domains.

23.2.1 Echo State Network

Feature space transformation is a decisive mechanism permitting a model trained on a domain $\mathcal{D}^i$ to be used in a different on $\mathcal{D}^j$, while addressing the diversities existing in the respective feature distributions. We overcome the particular obstacle by learning an ESN-based transformation based [21, 46]. It should be mentioned that this process could be bidirectional.

The flow adaptation process is the following: after separating the data associated to each domain D_i, D_j, where D_i, D_j denote the data of domains $\mathcal{D}^i$, $\mathcal{D}^j$ respectively, a MIMO transformation is learned using the training data T_i, T_j of both domains. ESN modelling is employed at this stage as it is able to capture the non-linear relationships existing in the data. ESNs represent a novel kind of neural networks providing good results in several demanding applications, such as speech recognition [46], saving energy in wireless communication [20], and so on.

An ESN, the topology of which is depicted in Fig. 23.2, includes neurons with non-linear activation functions which are connected to the inputs (input connections) and to each other (recurrent connections). These two types of connections have randomly generated weights, which are kept fixed during both the training and operational phase. Finally, a linear function is associated with each output node.

Recurrent neural networks aim at capturing the characteristics of high-level abstractions existing in the acquired data while designing multiple processing layers of complicated formations; i.e. non-linear functions. The area of reservoir computing, in which ESN originates, argues that since backpropagation is computationally complex but typically does not influence the internal layers severely, it may be totally excluded from the training process. On the contrary, the read-out layer is a generalized linear classification/regression problem associated with low complexity. In addition, any potential network instability is avoided by enforcing a simple constraint on the random parameters of the internal layers.

In the following, we explain (a) how the ESN E learns the transformation from $\mathcal{D}^i$ to $\mathcal{D}^j$, and (b) how the transformation is employed.

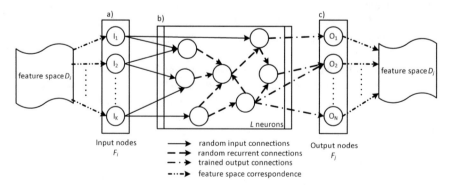

Fig. 23.2 A generic echo state network used for feature space transformation

ESN Learning E is used to learn the relationships existing in the features spaces of domains $\mathcal{D}^i$ to $\mathcal{D}^j$. We assume that an unknown system model is followed, which may be described as a transfer function f_E.

f_E comprises an ESN with K inputs and N outputs. Its parameters are the weights of the output connections and are trained to achieve a specific result; i.e. a feature vector of $\mathcal{D}^j$. The output weights are learned by means of linear regression and are called read-outs since they "read" the reservoir state [23]. As a general formulation of the ESNs, depicted in Fig. 23.2, we assume that the network has K inputs, L neurons (usually called reservoir size), N outputs, while the matrices $W_{in}(K \times L)$, $W_{res}(L \times L)$ and $W_{out}(L \times N)$ include the connection weights. The ESN system equations are the following:

$$x(k) = f_{res}(W_{in}u(k) + W_{res}x(k)) \tag{23.1}$$

$$y(k) = f_{out}(W_{out})x(k), \tag{23.2}$$

where $u(k)$, $x(k)$ and $y(k)$ denote the values of the inputs, reservoir outputs and the read-out nodes at time k, respectively. f_{res} and f_{out} are the activation functions of the reservoir and the output nodes, respectively. Typical choices consist in $f_{res}(x) = tanh(x)$ and $f_{out}(x) = x$ [1, 26].

Linear regression is used to determine the weights W_{out},

$$W_{out} = \underset{W}{argmin}(\frac{1}{N_{tr}}\|XW - D\|^2 + \epsilon\|W\|^2) \tag{23.3}$$

$$W_{out} = (X^T X + \epsilon I)^{-1}(X^T D), \tag{23.4}$$

where XW and D are the computed vectors, I a unity matrix, N_{tr} the number of the training samples while ϵ is a regularization term.

The recurrent weights are randomly generated by a zero-mean Gaussian distribution with variance v, which essentially controls the spectral radius s^r of the reservoir. The largest absolute eigenvalue of W_{res} is proportional to v and is particularly important for the dynamical behavior of the reservoir [45]. W_{in} is randomly drawn from a uniform distribution $[-s^f, +s^f]$, s^f denoting the scaling factor, which emphasizes/deemphasizes the inputs in the activation of the reservoir neurons. It is interesting to note that the significance of the specific parameter is decreased as the reservoir size increases.

In the feature space adaptation case, f_E adopts the form explained in Eqs. (23.1), (23.2) by substituting $y(k)$ with F_j and $u(k)$ with F_i, denoting features extracted out of domains $\mathcal{D}^j$ and $\mathcal{D}^i$, respectively.

Application of f_E After the learning process, f_E may be thought of as a MIMO model of the form:

$$\begin{pmatrix} F_j^1(t) \\ F_j^2(t) \\ \vdots \\ F_j^N(t) \end{pmatrix} = f_E \begin{pmatrix} F_i^1(t) \\ F_i^2(t) \\ \vdots \\ F_i^K(t) \end{pmatrix}$$

where features $\{F_i^1 \ldots, F_i^K\}$ at time t are transformed to observations belonging to domain $\mathcal{D}^j$; i.e. $\{F_j^{1'} \ldots, F_j^N\}$ using f_E.

ESN Parameterization There are several parameters that need to be decided during the design of an ESN with the one having the strongest impact on it modelling ability are s^r, L, and s^f. As a standardized process identifying the optimal set of parameters, an exhaustive search can be followed where s^r values close to 1 are preferred, while the rest of the parameters depends on the problem specifics. Each parameter combination is evaluated in terms of reconstruction error on the validation set and the one offering the lowest error is finally selected.

23.3 Use Cases

This section describes two cases where transfer-learning-based approaches have been applied to the generalized sound processing domain with encouraging results.

23.3.1 Affective Computing

The first application resides in the domain of affective computing and more specifically in predicting the emotions evoked by generalized sound events. Sounds are of paramount importance in our everyday lives carrying a plethora of information including the communication of emotional meanings/states. In signals containing speech, one is able to perform such an activity by altering one's vocal parameters [40]. Generalized sound events may carry emotional information as well; e.g. one may feel fearful in case a gunshot is heard [16].

The area of affective computing is receiving ever-increasing attention in the past decades with the emphasis being placed on the analysis of emotional speech and music [2, 24]. On the contrary, and even though the content of generalized sound events may be critical regarding the emotion conveyed to the listener, they have not received a similar amount of attention by the scientific community. Thus, here lies fertile ground for transfer learning since there is a common application; i.e. emotion prediction, for different types of data. In other words, one may able to transfer the knowledge existing in the speech and music domains and construct a respective framework able to carry out such a task in the field of generalized audio signals.

Importantly, the absence of respective solutions is partially caused by the lack of available labeled data addressing such a task. Inspired by the Instance transfer approach (see Sect. 23.2) one may attempt to transfer labeled data from the music domain to the one of generalized sound events. Interestingly, the work presented in [27] investigated the existence of an emotional space; i.e. a valence-arousal plane, which is common among generalized sounds and music pieces. Such a plane is illustrated in Fig. 23.3.

Briefly, the pipeline of such an emotion prediction framework is the following:

– signal preprocessing,
– feature extraction,

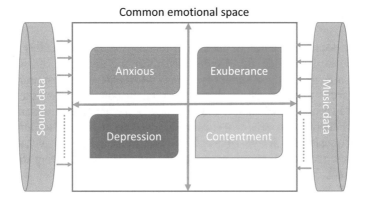

Fig. 23.3 The joint emotional space is formed by general sounds and music signals

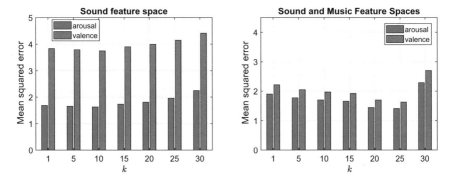

Fig. 23.4 The alteration of the MSE for both arousal and valance prediction as a function of k with and without including transfer learning; i.e. the song feature space

– feature space adaptation for the music feature vectors, and
– k-medoids based regression.

As we see, all parts of the pipeline are common among sound and music signals but the feature adaptation module is based on ESNs (see Sect. 23.2). Design and implementation information is available in [27]. It should be highlighted that such a transfer learning-based approach surpassed the state-of-the-art methods in sound emotion prediction (see Fig. 23.4) and is currently the best performing approach on the standardized emotionally annotated generalized sound dataset; i.e. the International Affective Digital Sounds database [4]. Such success encourages research focused on the development of transfer-learning-based solutions to deal with applications of the generalized sound recognition technology.

23.3.2 Bird Species Identification

In the past decades, research in the area of biodiversity monitoring has flourished mostly due to the availability of automated recording units [13, 39, 42, 47]. A relatively large part of these studies is dedicated to the processing of bird vocalizations for various purposes starting from understanding population trends to detecting endangered species. Motivated by the relevance of the application domain and the potential similarities between bird vocalizations and music signals, one may think of exploiting transfer learning possibilities to boost the performance of such automated mechanisms. Indeed, there are several motivations behind following the specific research path:

- several musicologists share the belief that the development of music was affected by birdsong to a relatively large extent [7, 19].
- birds vocalize at traditional scales used in human music (e.g. pentatonic, diatonic, and so on.) suggesting that birdsong may be thought of as music the way humans perceive it [38].
- famous composers have employed birdsong as a compositional springboard in several genres; e.g. classical (Antonio Vivaldi, Ludwig van Beethoven, Richard Wagner, and so on.) and jazz (Paul Winter, Jeff Silverbush, and so on.) [14, 37, 43] suggesting perceptual similarities in the respective acoustic structures.

Towards incorporating knowledge available in the music signal processing domain in the bird species identification one, [28] proposed to include the similarities between bird vocalizations and music genres in the identification chain. More precisely, a hidden Markov model (HMM) is constructed to learn the distribution of each music genre included in the standardized dataset of [44] with ten genres; i.e. *blues, classical, country, disco, hiphop, jazz, metal, pop, reggae, rock*. These models represent the knowledge available in the music domain which can be transfered to the bird vocalization one. To this end, an ESN-based MIMO transformation is used (see Sect. 23.2) for adapting the characteristics of the bird vocalizations' feature space. Subsequently, [28] matches each bird vocalization to the previously constructed HMMs and stores the log-likelihoods which are essentially a degree of resemblance between the vocalizations of each species and the available music genres. The corpus included the following ten species: *Acrocephalus melanopogon, Calidris canutus, Carduelis chloris, Emberiza citrinella, Falco columbarius, Lanius collurio, Larus melanocephalus, Parus palustris, Sylvia sarda, Turdus torquatus*. These are European bird species covering regular breeding, wintering and migrant ones. All sounds were obtained from http://www.xeno-canto.org/.

In other words, [28] tries to answer the question "*how pop does the Sylvia sarda species sound?*". Figure 23.5 shows a quantification of the number of frames associated with a given music genre; i.e. how many times the maximum log-likelihood of a bird vocalization is given by the specific HMM. As an example, this is demonstrated for four species where we see that *Acrocephalus melanopogon* is mostly associated

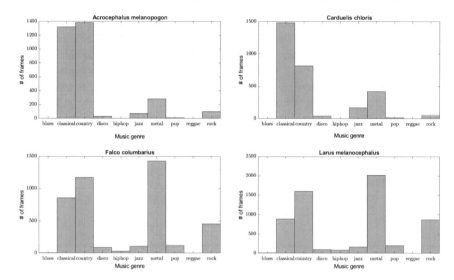

Fig. 23.5 The quantity of frames associated with each music genre for four bird species; i.e. *Acrocephalus melanopogon*, *Carduelis chloris*, *Falco columbarius*, *Larus melanocephalus*

with country music, *Carduelis chloris* with the classical genre, while *Falco columbarius* and *Larus melanocephalus* with the metal one.

The log-likelihoods produced by music genre models are appended to the feature vector extracted out of the bird vocalizations and finally classified using a random forest [5]. Importantly, the obtained results show an 11.2% improvement in the classification accuracy when the similarities with music genres is used.

23.4 Conclusions and Future Directions

This chapter provided a picture of the approaches exploiting transfer learning technologies within the generalized audio signal processing domain. After providing a brief introduction to the field, it presented a generic solution to the feature space adaptation problem which is usually encountered when one employs transfer learning. Importantly, this chapter demonstrated that such a technology can be applied without assuming the availability of deep models trained on vast amounts of data as is usually the case; e.g. ImageNet. Two such applications were critically presented: (a) one following the *Instance transfer* paradigm addressing affective computing applications, while (b) the second one adopts *Feature representation transfer* and exploits knowledge available in music genres to boost bird species identification.

The importance of transfer learning was highlighted in both cases as it reached state-of-the-art performance in both tasks.

This chapter gave only a taste of the opportunities existing in the audio signal processing domain and we hope to encourage further research in the field. In general, one should try to transfer knowledge available in rich domains in terms of labeled datasets, feature design, model engineering, and so on, to less explored ones and create automated solutions able to satisfy the requirements of a wide range of applications. The results of this research may open the path for works of similar logic; i.e. exploiting data, knowledge, features, distributions, and so on, from specific domain(s) to address problems existing in different but related one(s) and vice-versa. Such relationships could be proven particularly useful in the future by increasing the quantity of training data, thus enhancing the recognition performance in a cross-domain manner.

References

1. Alippi, C., Ntalampiras, S., & Roveri, M. (2013). Model ensemble for an effective on-line reconstruction of missing data in sensor networks. In *The 2013 International Joint Conference on Neural Networks (IJCNN)* (pp. 1–6). https://doi.org/10.1109/IJCNN.2013.6706761.
2. Asadi, R., & Fell, H. (2015). Improving the accuracy of speech emotion recognition using acoustic landmarks and Teager energy operator features. *Journal of the Acoustical Society of America, 137*(4), 2303.
3. Bertin-mahieux, T., Ellis, D. P. W., Whitman, B., & Lamere, P. (2011). The million song dataset. In *Proceedings of the 12th International Conference on Music Information Retrieval (ISMIR)*.
4. Bradley, M. M., & Lang, P. J. (2007). The international affective digitized sounds (2nd edition; IADS-2): Affective ratings of sounds and instruction manual.
5. Breiman, L. (2001). Random forests. *Machine Learning, 45*(1), 5–32. https://doi.org/10.1023/A:1010933404324.
6. Choi, K., Fazekas, G., Sandler, M. B., & Cho, K. (2017). Transfer learning for music classification and regression tasks. CoRR abs/1703.09179. http://arxiv.org/abs/1703.09179.
7. Clark, S., & Rehding, A. (2005). *Music theory and natural order from the renaissance to the early twentieth century*. Cambridge University Press.
8. Dai, W., Xue, G. R., Yang, Q., & Yu, Y. (2007). Co-clustering based classification for out-of-domain documents. In *Proceedings of the 13th ACM SIGKDD International Conference on Knowledge Discovery and Data Mining, KDD '07* (pp. 210–219). New York, NY, USA: ACM. https://doi.org/10.1145/1281192.1281218.
9. Dai, W., Xue, G. R., Yang, Q., & Yu, Y. (2007). Transferring naive bayes classifiers for text classification. In *Proceedings of the 22Nd National Conference on Artificial Intelligence—Volume 1, AAAI'07* (pp. 540–545). AAAI Press. http://dl.acm.org/citation.cfm?id=1619645.1619732.
10. Davis, J., & Domingos, P. (2009). Deep transfer via second-order markov logic. In *Proceedings of the 26th Annual International Conference on Machine Learning, ICML '09* (pp. 217–224). New York, NY, USA: ACM. https://doi.org/10.1145/1553374.1553402.
11. Deng, J., Dong, W., Socher, R., Li, L. J., Li, K., & Fei-Fei, L. (2009). ImageNet: A large-scale hierarchical image database. In *Proceedings of CVPR09*.
12. Diment, A., & Virtanen, T. (2017). Transfer learning of weakly labelled audio. In *2017 IEEE Workshop on Applications of Signal Processing to Audio and Acoustics (WASPAA)* (pp. 6–10). https://doi.org/10.1109/WASPAA.2017.8169984.

13. Fanioudakis, L., & Potamitis, I. (2017). Deep networks tag the location of bird vocalisations on audio spectrograms. EESS abs/1711.04347. https://arxiv.org/abs/1711.04347.
14. Franks, R. (2016). Six of the best: Pieces inspired by birdsong. http://www.classical-music.com/article/six-best-birdsong-pieces.
15. Gao, J., Fan, W., Jiang, J., & Han, J. (2008). Knowledge transfer via multiple model local structure mapping. In *Proceedings of the 14th ACM SIGKDD International Conference on Knowledge Discovery and Data Mining, KDD '08* (pp. 283–291). New York, NY, USA: ACM. https://doi.org/10.1145/1401890.1401928.
16. Garner, T., & Grimshaw, M. (2011). A climate of fear: Considerations for designing a virtual acoustic ecology of fear. In *Proceedings of the 6th Audio Mostly Conference: A Conference on Interaction with Sound, AM '11* (pp. 31–38). New York, NY, USA: ACM. https://doi.org/10.1145/2095667.2095672.
17. Gemmeke, J. F., Ellis, D. P. W., Freedman, D., Jansen, A., Lawrence, W., Moore, R. C., et al. (2017). Audio set: An ontology and human-labeled dataset for audio events. In *Proceedings of IEEE ICASSP 2017*, New Orleans, LA.
18. Hamel, P., Davies, M. E. P., Yoshii, K., & Goto, M. (2013). Transfer learning in MIR: Sharing learned latent representations for music audio classification and similarity. In *14th International Conference on Music Information Retrieval (ISMIR '13)*.
19. Head, M. (1997). Birdsong and the origins of music. *Journal of the Royal Musical Association, 122*(1), 1–23. http://www.jstor.org/stable/766551.
20. Jaeger, H., & Haas, H. (2004). Harnessing nonlinearity: Predicting chaotic systems and saving energy in wireless communication. *Science, 304*(5667), 78–80. http://science.sciencemag.org/content/304/5667/78.
21. Jalalvand, A., Triefenbach, F., Verstraeten, D., & Martens, J. (2011). Connected digit recognition by means of reservoir computing. In *Proceedings of the 12th annual conference of the International Speech Communication Association* (pp. 1725–1728).
22. Li, B., Sainath, T., Chan, W., Wu, Y., & Zhang, Y. (2019). Bytes are all you need: End-to-end multilingual speech recognition and synthesis with bytes. In *Proceedings of ICASSP 2019*.
23. Lukoševičius, M., & Jaeger, H. (2009). Survey: Reservoir computing approaches to recurrent neural network training. *Computer Science Review, 3*(3), 127–149. https://doi.org/10.1016/j.cosrev.2009.03.005.
24. Markov, K., & Matsui, T. (2014). Music genre and emotion recognition using gaussian processes. *IEEE Access, 2*, 688–697. https://doi.org/10.1109/ACCESS.2014.2333095.
25. Narayanan, A., Misra, A., Sim, K. C., Pundak, G., Tripathi, A., Elfeky, M., et al. (2018). Toward domain-invariant speech recognition via large scale training. CoRR abs/1808.05312. http://arxiv.org/abs/1808.05312.
26. Ntalampiras, S. (2015). Audio pattern recognition of baby crying sound events. *Journal of the Audio Engineering Society, 63*(5), 358–369. http://www.aes.org/e-lib/browse.cfm?elib=17641.
27. Ntalampiras, S. (2017). A transfer learning framework for predicting the emotional content of generalized sound events. *The Journal of the Acoustical Society of America, 141*(3), 1694–1701. https://doi.org/10.1121/1.4977749.
28. Ntalampiras, S. (2018). Bird species identification via transfer learning from music genres. *Ecological Informatics, 44*, 76–81. https://doi.org/10.1016/j.ecoinf.2018.01.006.
29. Ntalampiras, S. (2019). Automatic acoustic classification of insect speciesbased on directed acyclic graphs. *The Journal of the AcousticalSociety of America, 145*(6), EL541–EL546. https://doi.org/10.1121/1.5111975.
30. Ntalampiras, S. (2019). Generalized sound recognition in reverberant environments. *Journal of the Audio Engineering Society, 67*(10), 772–781. http://www.aes.org/e-lib/browse.cfm?elib=20695.
31. Ntalampiras, S. (2019). Unsupervised spectral clustering of music-related brain activity. In *2019 15th International Conference on Signal-Image Technology Internet-Based Systems (SITIS)* (pp. 193–197).

32. Ntalampiras, S. (2020). Toward language-agnostic speech emotion recognition. *Journal of the Audio Engineering Society, 68*(1/2), 7–13. http://www.aes.org/e-lib/browse.cfm?elib=20713.
33. Ntalampiras, S., & Potamitis, I. (2019). A statistical inference framework for understanding music-related brain activity. *IEEE Journal of Selected Topics in Signal Processing, 13*(2), 275–284.
34. Pan, S. J., & Yang, Q. (2010). A survey on transfer learning. *IEEE Transactions on Knowledge and Data Engineering, 22*(10), 1345–1359. https://doi.org/10.1109/TKDE.2009.191.
35. Park, J., Lee, J., Park, J., Ha, J., & Nam, J. (2017). Representation learning of music using artist labels. CoRR abs/1710.06648. http://arxiv.org/abs/1710.06648.
36. Purwins, H., Li, B., Virtanen, T., Schlter, J., Chang, S., & Sainath, T. (2019). Deep learning for audio signal processing. *IEEE Journal of Selected Topics in Signal Processing, 13*(2), 206–219. https://doi.org/10.1109/JSTSP.2019.2908700.
37. Reich, R. (2010). NJIT professor finds nothing cuckoo in serenading our feathered friends. http://www.nj.com/entertainment/music/index.ssf/2010/10/njit_professor_finds_nothing_c.html.
38. Rothenberg, D. (2006). *Why birds sing: A journey into the mystery of bird song.* Basic Books. https://books.google.gr/books?id=J1gemza3aOkC.
39. Ntalampiras, S. (2019). Automatic acoustic classification of insect species based on directed acyclic graphs. *The Journal of the Acoustical Society of America, 145*(6), EL541–EL546.
40. Scherer, K. R. (2003). Vocal communication of emotion: A review of research paradigms. *Speech Communication, 40*(1-2), 227–256. https://doi.org/10.1016/S0167-6393(02)00084-5.
41. Simonetta, F., Ntalampiras, S., & Avanzini, F. (2019). Multimodal music information processing and retrieval: Survey and future challenges. In *2019 International Workshop on Multilayer Music Representation and Processing (MMRP)* (pp. 10–18). https://doi.org/10.1109/MMRP.2019.00012.
42. Stowell, D., & Plumbley, M. D. (2014). Automatic large-scale classification of bird sounds is strongly improved by unsupervised feature learning. CoRR abs/1405.6524. http://arxiv.org/abs/1405.6524.
43. Thompson, H. (2014). This birds songs share mathematical hallmarks with human music. http://www.smithsonianmag.com/science-nature/birds-songs-share-mathematical-hallmarks-human-music-180953227/?no-ist.
44. Tzanetakis, G., & Cook, P. (2002). Musical genre classification of audio signals. *IEEE Transactions on Speech and Audio Processing, 10*(5), 293–302. https://doi.org/10.1109/TSA.2002.800560.
45. Verstraeten, D., Schrauwen, B., DHaene, M., & Stroobandt, D. (2007). An experimental unification of reservoir computing methods. *Neural Networks, 20*(3), 391–403. http://www.sciencedirect.com/science/article/pii/S089360800700038X. Echo State Networks and Liquid State Machines.
46. Verstraeten, D., Schrauwen, B., & Stroobandt, D. (2006). Reservoir-based techniques for speech recognition. In *International Joint Conference on Neural Networks, 2006, IJCNN '06* (pp. 1050–1053). https://doi.org/10.1109/IJCNN.2006.246804.
47. Wolfgang, A., & Haines, A. (2016). Testing automated call-recognition software for winter bird vocalizations. *Northeastern Naturalist, 23*(2), 249–258.

Stavros Ntalampiras is an Associate Professor at the Department of Computer Science of the University of Milan, Italy. He received engineering and Ph.D. degrees from the Department of Electrical and Computer Engineering, University of Patras, Greece, in 2006 and 2010, respectively. He has carried out research and didactic activities at Polytechnic University of Milan, Joint Research Center of the European Commission, National Research Council of Italy, Bocconi University, all in Italy. Currently, he is an Associate Editor of Institute of Electrical and Electronics

Engineers (IEEE) Access, PlosOne, IET Signal Processing and CAAI Transactions on Intelligence Technology. He is a founding member of the IEEE Computational Intelligent Society Task Force on Computational Audio Processing. His research interests include Artificial Intelligence, signal processing, audio pattern recognition, machine learning, bioacoustics, and cyber-physical systems. E-mail: stavros.ntalampiras@unimi.it

From Audio to Music Notation

24

Lele Liu and Emmanouil Benetos

24.1 Introduction

The field of Music Information Retrieval (MIR) focuses on creating methods and practices for making sense of music data from various modalities, including audio, video, images, scores and metadata [54]. Within MIR, a core problem which to the day remains open is Automatic Music Transcription (AMT), the process of automatically converting an acoustic music signal into some form of musical notation. The creation of a method for automatically converting musical audio to notation has several uses including but also going beyond MIR: from software for automatic typesetting of audio into staff notation or other music representations, to the use of automatic transcriptions as a descriptor towards the development of systems for music recommendation, to applications for interactive music systems such as automatic music accompaniment, for music education through methods for automatic instrument tutoring, and towards enabling musicological research in sound archives, to name but a few.

Interest in AMT has grown during recent years as part of recent advances in artificial intelligence and in particular deep learning, which have led to new applications, systems, as well as have led to a new set of technical, methodological and ethical challenges related to this problem. This chapter presents state-of-the-art research and open topics in AMT, focusing on recent methods for addressing this task based on deep learning, as well as on outlining challenges and directions for future research.

The first attempts to address this problem come back to the 1970s and the dawn of the field of computer music (e.g. [47]), while the problem faced a resurgence in the

L. Liu (✉) · E. Benetos
School of Electronic Engineering and Computer Science, Queen Mary University of London, London E1 4NS, UK
e-mail: lele.liu@qmul.ac.uk

© Springer Nature Switzerland AG 2021
E. R. Miranda (ed.), *Handbook of Artificial Intelligence for Music*,
https://doi.org/10.1007/978-3-030-72116-9_24

mid-2000s with the development of methods for audio signal processing and pattern recognition, and encountered a second wave of popularity in recent years following the emergence of deep learning methods. Irrespective of the methodologies used to investigate and develop tools and practices for AMT, researchers addressing this task draw knowledge from several disciplines, including digital signal processing, machine learning/artificial intelligence, music perception and cognition, musical acoustics and music theory. There are also strong links with other problems both within and beyond MIR, including Optical Music Recognition (OMR—which is the counterpart of AMT but for printed music or manuscripts instead of recorded audio—e.g. [50]), automatic speech recognition and speaker diarisation [66], sound event detection for everyday and nature sounds [59], and object recognition and tracking in video [17]. AMT is also closely related to the fields of music language modelling and symbolic music processing [15], serving as a bridge between the acoustic and symbolic domains in music.

Given the complexity of the problem of AMT, the overarching task is often split into subtasks, including pitch/multi-pitch detection, onset and offset detection, instrument identification and tracking, meter estimation and rhythm quantisation, estimation of dynamics and expression and typesetting/engraving. However, recent advances in artificial intelligence have promoted the development of 'end-to-end' methods for AMT, thus often skipping intermediate tasks or steps and directly producing a transcription in a particular notation format. Figure 24.1 shows the typical stages of an AMT system for a short excerpt from a Mozart sonata, starting with the input waveform, the extracted time-frequency representation (in this case a short-time Fourier transform magnitude spectrogram), the output transcription in piano-roll representation and the output transcription in the form of Western staff notation.

Despite active research on this problem for decades and measurable progress over the years, AMT is still faced by several challenges, both technical and ethical. Broadly, the performance of certain AMT systems can be deemed sufficient for audio recordings containing solo acoustic instruments, within the context of Western tonal music, assuming a relatively moderate tempo and a level of polyphony around 3, 4. Here, the term 'polyphony' refers to the maximum number of concurrent pitches at a given time instant. The problem of automatically transcribing audio recordings which contain sounds produced by multiple instruments, vocals and percussion with a high polyphony level or a fast tempo is still relatively limited. Other factors that can affect the performance of such systems include the existence of distortions either at the instrumental production stage or at the audio production/mastering stage, or cases where the performance or composition in question does not fall under the auspices of Western tonal music. A relatively new challenge which has emerged with the adoption of data-driven methods for addressing the task is the bias imposed by the algorithms through the choice of datasets. Given that most datasets for AMT include Western tonal music performed by solo piano or other solo Western orchestral instruments have created certain limits and biases with respect to the range of instruments or to the range of music cultures and styles that can be supported by state-of-the-art AMT systems. Limitations of symbolic representations and encodings for music (MIDI, MEI, MusicXML, Lilypond, etc.) also further constrain the potential of current AI-

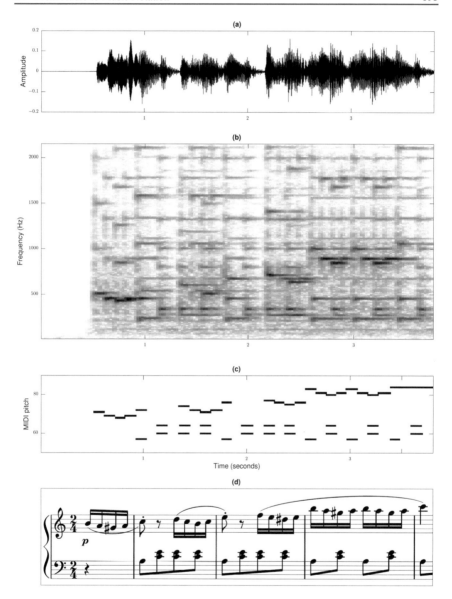

Fig. 24.1 Typical stages of an AMT system: **a** input waveform; **b** time-frequency representation; **c** output piano-roll representation; **d** output music score, typeset using Musescore. The example corresponds to the first 4 s of W.A. Mozart's Piano Sonata no. 11, 3rd movement

based AMT systems to support the transcription of music performances that cannot necessarily be expressed through Western staff notation or do not assume 12-tone equal temperament.

The aim of this chapter is to provide a review and discussion of recent methods for AMT, focusing on methods based on AI and deep learning in particular. The focus of the chapter is on automatic transcription of pitched sounds; see [61] for a recent review on the related task of Automatic Drum Transcription (ADT). For a detailed look on signal processing and statistical methods for AMT, the reader is referred to [36]; for a discussion related to the challenges of AMT methods relying on signal processing or statistical methods, please see [6]. A recent tutorial-like overview of both 'traditional' machine learning and deep learning methodologies for AMT is presented in [5].

The outline of this chapter is as follows. Section 24.2 provides a concise definition of various problems that have been posed under AMT; an overview of commonly used datasets and evaluation metrics in AMT is presented in Sect. 24.3. An overview of the state-of-the-art in AMT is presented in Sect. 24.4, including a more detailed look at deep learning methods for the task. Current methodological and ethical challenges facing AMT methods, tools, systems and practices are outlined in Sect. 24.5. Finally, conclusions are presented in Sect. 24.6.

24.2 Problem Definition

As mentioned in Sect. 24.1, AMT is divided into several subtasks, and most approaches have only been addressing a small subset of these subtasks. Perhaps the most essential subtask (especially when referring to the transcription of pitched sounds) is *pitch detection*, or in the case of multiple concurrent sounds, *multi-pitch detection*. Here, we define pitch in the same way as in [27], where a sound has a certain pitch if it can be reliably matched to a sine tone of a given frequency at a sound pressure level of 40 dB. Typically, this task refers to estimating one or more pitches at each time frame (e.g. at 10 ms intervals), where pitch is typically expressed in Hz. Given the close links between pitch and the fundamental frequency of periodic signals, this task is often referred to as multiple-F0 estimation. This task is publicly evaluated annually as part of the Music Information Retrieval Evaluation eXchange (MIREX) task on MultiF0 estimation [1].

It is often useful for multi-pitch detection systems to produce a non-binary representation of estimated pitches over time, which could be used for pitch visualisation purposes, or as an intermediate feature for other MIR tasks that rely on an initial pitch estimate (e.g. melody estimation [53], chord estimation [41]). Often this representation is referred to as *pitch salience*, or a *time-pitch representation*. Figure 24.2a shows the pitch salience representation for the excerpt of Fig. 24.1 using the method of [8].

Moving on to a higher level of abstraction which is closer to how humans might transcribe music, we would need express notes as characterised by their start time, end

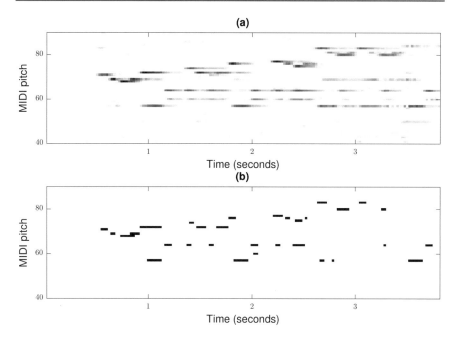

Fig. 24.2 a The pitch salience representation for the excerpt of Fig. 24.1 using the method of [8]; **b** The corresponding binarised piano-roll representation

time, and pitch—in a similar way as expressed, e.g. in the MIDI format. This task is referred to as *note tracking* and involves the subtasks of *onset detection* (i.e. detecting the start of a note), *offset detection* (i.e. detecting the end of a note), and (multi-)pitch detection. A comprehensive tutorial on signal processing-based methods for onset detection can be found in [4]. Approaches for note tracking are publicly evaluated annually as part of the Music Information Retrieval Evaluation eXchange (MIREX) note tracking task [1]. Figure 24.2b shows the output of the note tracking process by performing simple thresholding on the pitch salience of Fig. 24.2a.

In addition to the detection of pitched sounds and their timings, a key element towards a successful musical transcription is on assigning each detected note to the musical instrument that produced it. This task is referred to in the literature as *instrument assignment*, *timbre tracking*, or *multi-pitch streaming*. A closely related task in the wider field of MIR is that of *musical instrument recognition* from audio, which has received relatively little attention from the research community (see [30] for a recent overview).

The above mentioned note tracking task estimates the start and end times of notes, but in terms of seconds as opposed to beats or any other metrical subdivision. To that end, the task of *rhythm transcription* or *note value recognition* aims to estimate the metrical structure of the music recording in question and estimate the note timings and durations in terms of metrical subdivisions (e.g. [20,44]). By having estimated pitches with their respective timings in terms of meter, one can typeset the transcribed

Fig. 24.3 The rhythm-quantised transcription of the excerpt of Fig. 24.1, automatically transcribed using the method of [8] and typeset using Musescore (https://musescore.org/)

audio in some form of human-readable music notation, e.g. Western staff notation. This is a task that depending on the complexity of the music performance in question might also require to split the detected stream of notes into multiple music staves (this is referred to as *voice separation* and *staff estimation*). The process of converting music audio into staff notation is sometimes referred to as *complete music transcription* (taking into account that such a 'complete' transcription might not contain information related to musical instruments, phrasing, expression or dynamics).

Figure 24.3 shows the rhythm-quantised transcription of the excerpt of Fig. 24.1 in Western staff notation, automatically transcribed using the method of [8]. While from a first glance there are little similarities with the score of Fig. 24.1d, a close inspection shows that the majority of pitches have been correctly detected, although their respective durations are not properly estimated (which can be attributed to sustain and pedalling of the piano performance of this piece).

24.3 Datasets and Evaluation Metrics

24.3.1 Datasets

As there are an increasing amount of exploration on deep learning methods for AMT, people are using larger datasets to train and evaluate the systems they developed. There are several datasets that are commonly used for AMT problems in literature, such as the RWC dataset [26], MIDI Aligned Piano Sounds (MAPS) dataset [24], Bach10 [22], MedleyDB [10], and MusicNet [58]. Two recently proposed datasets are MAESTRO [29] and Slakh [38]. Table 24.1 provides an overview on commonly used AMT datasets.

Table 24.1 AMT datasets and their properties. Instrument abbreviations—Vc: Vocal, Gt: Guitar, Bs: Bass, Dr: Drums, Pn: Piano, Tp: Trumpet, Cl: Cello, Vl: Violin, Cr: Clarinet Sx: Saxophone, Bn: Bassoon. Music style abbreviations—Cls: Classical, Plr: Popular, Jzz: Jazz, Ryf: Royalty-Free

Dataset	Instruments	Music style	Size	Comments
RWC dataset ([26], 2002)	Gt, Vc, Dr, Pn, Tp, Cl, etc.	Cls, Ryf, Plr, Jzz, etc.	315 pieces in 6 subsets	Real recordings, with non-aligned MIDI files for Popular, Royalty-Free, Classical and Jazz subsets. A version of automatically aligned MIDI annotations for the Classical subset can be found in the SyncRWC dataset [2]
MAPS dataset ([24], 2010)	Pn	Cls + non musical piece (notes and chords)	30 pieces * 9 piano synthesizers in the MUS subset	synthesized and real piano recordings. Additional rhythm and key annotations can be found in A-MAPS dataset [64]
Bach10 ([22], 2010)	Vl, Cr, Sx, Bn	Four-part J.S. Bach Chorales	10 pieces	Real recordings, individual stems, F0 annotations
MedleyDB ([10], 2014)	multiple instrument (Pn, Vc, etc.)	Ryf	196 pieces in MedleyDB 2.0	Real recordings, With individual stems of each instrument recording. 108 pieces with melody annotation
MusicNet ([58], 2016)	multiple instrument (Pn, Vl, Cl, etc.)	Cls	330 pieces	Real recordings under various conditions. Labels aligned by dynamic time wrapping and verified by trained musicians, estimated labeling error rate 4%
GuitarSet ([62], 2018)	Gt	Plr	360 pieces	Real recordings
MAESTRO ([29], 2019)	Pn	mostly Cls	1282 pieces	From e-piano competition, 201.2 h in total
Slakh ([38], 2019)	Pn, Gt, Bs, Dr, etc.	Cls, Plr, etc.	2100 tracks	Synthesized from Lakh MIDI dataset [49]

Although there are plenty of choices of AMT datasets, there are relatively more datasets for piano transcription (given the ease in automatically exporting MIDI annotations from acoustic pianos when using specific piano models such as Disklavier or Bösendorfer), but much less for other instruments, especially non-Western instruments. The biggest challenge of collecting AMT datasets is that annotating music recordings requires a high degree of music expertise, and is very time-consuming. Also, there might not be enough music pieces and recordings for some less popular traditional instruments when a large dataset is needed. Moreover, human-annotated transcription datasets are not guaranteed to have a high degree of temporal precision, which makes them less suitable for model evaluation on frame and note level. Su and Yang [57] proposed four aspects to evaluate the goodness of a dataset: generality, efficiency, cost and quality. They suggest that a good dataset should be not limited to a certain music form or recording conditions, should be fast-annotated, should be as low-cost as possible and be accurate enough. Because of the difficulty in collecting large human-transcribed datasets, researchers have used electronic instruments or acoustic instruments with sensors that can directly produce annotations (e.g. electronic piano, MAESTRO dataset), or synthesised datasets (e.g. Slakh) instead of real recordings. The use of synthesised recordings greatly speed up dataset collection, but on the other hand, could introduce some bias in model training, limiting generality of the developed AMT system.

24.3.2 Evaluation Metrics

Despite collecting datasets, model evaluation is another important process in developing methodologies for AMT problems. Evaluating a music transcription can be difficult since there are various types of errors, from pitch errors to missing/extra notes, and each has a different influence on the final evaluation of results. Currently, common evaluation metrics for AMT systems focus mainly on frame/note level transcriptions [3,9,14,28,33]. Much less work has been down on stream and notation level transcriptions [39,40,42]. In the 2019 annual Music Information Retrieval Evaluation eXchange (MIREX), there are three subtasks [1] for music transcription for pitched-instruments—multiple fundamental frequency estimation on frame level, note tracking and timbre tracking (multi-pitch streaming).

Common multiple fundamental frequency estimation methods [3] calculate frame-wise *precision*, *recall* and relevant *F-measure* values. The three scores are defined as:

$$precision = \frac{TP}{TP + FP} \tag{24.1}$$

$$recall = \frac{TP}{TP + FN} \tag{24.2}$$

$$F\text{-}measure = \frac{2 \times precision \times recall}{precision + recall} \tag{24.3}$$

The *TP*, *FP* and *FN* values correspond to *true positives*, *false positives* and *false negatives* respectively, and are calculated from all pitch values and time frames in the piano roll. There are also other methods for evaluating frame-wise transcription, such as separating different types of errors (e.g. missed pitches, extra pitches, false alarm) in multiple F0 estimation. A type-specific error rate is calculated in [48], where the authors defined a frame-level transcription error score combining different error types. Separating different error types can lead to a better interpretation on music transcription evaluation.

Note tracking problems usually define transcription results as sequences of notes, characterised by a pitch, onset and offset. A *tolerance* is defined to allow small errors in onset times since it is difficult to estimate exact time when building an AMT dataset as well as transcribing music with an AMT system. A common *tolerance* is 50 ms, which is used in the MIREX note tracking subtask. There are also some other scenarios where offset times are included (e.g. in [7] a 20% tolerance for offset is applied and in [19] a tolerance of the larger one in 20% of the note length or 50 ms is used for offset time). For any of the above scenarios, note-level precision, recall and F-measure are calculated for a final evaluation. Similar to frame-level F0 estimation, researchers have attempted to include error types in evaluation metrics (see e.g. [42]).

There are less works on *multi-pitch streaming*. The evaluation for *multi-pitch streaming* uses similar metric like precision and recall. Gómez and Bonada [25] proposed a simple method of calculating accuracy and false rate to evaluate voice streaming applied to A Capella transcription. In 2014, Duan and Temperley [23] used a similar evaluation method to calculate a more general multi-pitch streaming accuracy. The accuracy is defined as:

$$accuracy = \frac{TP}{TP + FP + FN} \tag{24.4}$$

Another work by Molina et al. [42] proposed to include types of errors in streaming process, and used a standard precision-recall metric.

Recent years has seen some introduction of evaluation metrics for *complete music transcription* given a recent increase in methods that directly transcribes audio to music scores. Some methods proposed include [18,39,40]. A recent approach for evaluating score transcriptions is proposed by Mcleod and Yoshii [40], which is based on a previous approach [39] called *MV2H* (representing Multi-pitch detection, Voice separation, Metrical alignment, note Value detection and Harmonic analysis). According to this metric, a score is calculated for each of the five aspects, then the scores are combined into a joint evaluation following a principle of one mistake should not be penalised more than once.

While most of evaluation metrics are based on music theory and simple statistical analysis, there are some metrics that contain some considerations on human perception of music transcriptions. In 2008, Daniel et al. [21] explored the difference of some error types in AMT from the aspect of human perception, and proposed a modified evaluation metric that weights different error types.

24.4 State of the Art

In this section, we look into state-of-the-art methodologies for AMT, mainly focusing on Neural Network methods. The section will be structured as follows. In Sect. 24.4.1, we provide an overview for the development and common methods for AMT, followed by Sect. 24.4.2 where we discuss Neural Network methods used in AMT. The following sections cover more specific topics within AMT: we give a review on *multi-task learning methods* for AMT in Sect. 24.4.3; the use of *music language models* and related works are covered in Sect. 24.4.4 and finally we review works on *complete transcription* in Sect. 24.4.5.

24.4.1 Overview

As the field of MIR has evolved over the past 20 years since the inception of the International Symposium on Music Information Retrieval (ISMIR), so has the topic of AMT. Roughly, proposed methods for AMT in the early 2000s made use of signal processing and statistical machine learning theory (see [36] for more details). Following the seminal paper of [56] on the potential of non-negative matrix factorisation when applied to the problem of AMT, a series of different methods were proposed for AMT that made use of matrix decomposition approaches. In the early 2010s, following the rise of deep learning methods and the paper by Humphrey et al. [30] advocating for the use of deep learning methods for MIR, neural network-based methods started being widely used for AMT and are still in use to date.

In terms of AMT subtasks to be addressed, the vast majority of methods have been and still do focus on (framewise) multi-pitch detection, with a smaller proportion of methods focusing on note tracking or rhythm transcription/typesetting. Due to the emergence of end-to-end deep learning methods for AMT, an increasing trend towards systems producing higher-level representations (such as outputs in MIDI format or in staff notation) can be observed [5]. The problem of timbre tracking/instrument assignment is however still under-explored.

Current literature for AMT includes a mixture of deep learning and matrix decomposition approaches, with deep learning methods currently being used in the majority of scenarios. Compared to other tasks in MIR, a large proportion of methods still employ matrix decomposition approaches (see e.g. [5]), due to their ability to work with limited data, fast learning and inference, and due to the models' interpretability. The remainder of this chapter will focus more on neural network-based methods for AMT, due to their increasing popularity in the research community and also due to certain methodological challenges when using deep learning methods for AMT that are still to be addressed.

24.4.2 Neural Networks for AMT

Research in AMT has increasingly been relying on deep learning models, which use feedforward, recurrent and convolutional layers as main architectural blocks. An early example of a deep neural model applied to AMT is the work of Nam et al. [45], which uses a Deep Belief Network (DBN) in order to learn representations for a polyphonic piano transcription task. Resulting learned features are then fed to a Support Vector Machine (SVM) classifier in order to produce a final decision. Another notable early work that made use of deep neural architectures was by Böck and Schedl [13], where the authors used a bi-directional Recurrent Neural Network (RNN) with Long Short-Term Memory (LSTM) units, applied to the task of polyphonic piano transcription. Two points are particularly worth mentioning for the work of [13]: (i) the use of two STFT magnitude spectrograms with different window sizes as inputs to the network, in order to achieve both a 'good temporal precision and a sufficient frequency resolution'; (ii) The output is a piano-roll representation of note onsets and corresponding pitches, and does not include information on note durations/offsets.

A first systematic study towards the use of various neural network architectures for AMT was done by Sigtia et al. in [55]. The study compared networks for polyphonic piano transcription that used feedforward, recurrent and convolutional layers (noting that layer types were not combined), all using a Constant-Q Transform (CQT) spectrogram as input time-frequency representation. Results from [55] showed that networks that include convolutional layers reported the best results for the task, which is also in line with other results reported in the literature, and with current methodological trends related to neural networks for AMT. The ability of Convolutional Neural Networks (CNNs) to function well for tasks related to multi-pitch detection and AMT stems from the useful property of shift-invariance in log-frequency representations such as the CQT: a convolutional kernel that is shifted across the log-frequency axis can capture spectro-temporal patterns that are common across multiple pitches.

Following the work of [55], Kelz et al. [33] showed the potential of simple frame-based approaches for polyphonic piano transcription using an architecture similar to [55], but making use of up-to-date training techniques, regularisers and taking into account hyper-parameter tuning. The 'ConvNet' architecture from the work of [33] can be seen in Fig. 24.4.

An influential work that used CNNs for multiple fundamental frequency estimation in polyphonic music was the *deep salience* representation proposed by Bittner et al. [12]. Contrary to most methods in AMT that produce a binary output, the model of [12] produces a non-binary time-pitch representation at 20 cent pitch resolution, which can be useful for both AMT applications but also for several downstream applications in the broader field of MIR. A particular contribution of this work was the use of a Harmonic Constant-Q Transform (HCQT) as input representation; the HCQT is a three-dimensional representation over frequency, time and the harmonic index, produced by computing several versions of the CQT by scaling the minimum frequency used by a harmonic. Figure 24.5 shows the pitch salience representation for the Mozart excerpt of Fig. 24.1, computed using the deep salience method of [12].

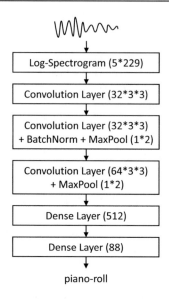

Fig. 24.4 Model architecture for the convolutional neural network used in [33] for polyphonic piano transcription. The depicted network corresponds to the 'ConvNet' architecture of [33]

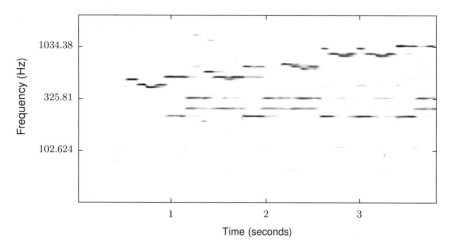

Fig. 24.5 Pitch salience representation for the excerpt of Fig. 24.1, using the deep salience method of [12]

The ability of CNNs in learning features in time or time-frequency representations keeps them still active in the AMT literature. This includes the work of Thickstun et al. [58] that was carried out as part of the MusicNet dataset, and compared feedforward and convolutional networks learned on raw audio inputs, as opposed to having a time-frequency representation as input. It is worth noting however that convolutional, and more broadly neural networks, when trained for AMT as a multi-label classification task, face the issue that they appear to learn combinations of notes exposed to them during training, and are not able to generalise unseen combinations of notes—the so-called *entanglement problem* as discussed in [34].

24.4.3   Multi-task Learning Methods

Recent research in machine learning has focused on *multi-task learning* [52], where multiple learning tasks are addressed jointly, thus exploiting task similarities and differences. In the context of AMT, multi-task learning has been shown to improve transcription performance in certain cases. Tasks related to AMT such as note level transcription, onset detection, melody estimation, bass line prediction and multi-pitch detection (also sharing similar chroma and rhythm features) can be integrated into one model that would exploit task interdependencies.

In the 'Onsets and Frames' system by Hawthorne et al. [28], which is currently considered the benchmark in automatic piano transcription, the authors used a deep Convolutional Recurrent Neural Network (CRNN) to jointly predict onsets and multiple pitches. The onset detection results are fed back into the model for further improving frame-wise multi-pitch predictions. The Onsets and Frames model was further improved in the work of Kim and Bello [35], which addresses the problem of expressing inter-label dependencies through an adversarial learning scheme.

Bittner et al. [11] proposed a multi-task model that jointly estimates outputs for several AMT-related tasks, including multiple fundamental frequency estimation, melody, vocal and bass line estimation. The authors show that the more tasks included in the model, the higher the performance and that the multi-task model outperforms the single-task equivalents. In another recent work [32], the authors designed a multi-task model with CNNs which enables four different transcription subtasks: multiple-f0 estimation, melody estimation, bass estimation and vocal estimation. Results on the method of [32] showed an overall improvement in the multi-task model compared to single task models.

24.4.4   Music Language Models

Inspired by work in the field of speech processing, where many systems for Automatic Speech Recognition (ASR) benefit from language models that predict the occurrence of a word or phoneme [31], researchers in MIR have recently attempted to use Music Language Models (MLMs) and combine them with acoustic models in order to improve AMT performance. While the problem of polyphonic music prediction using statistical machine learning models (such as n-grams and hidden Markov models) is not trivial, the emergence of neural network methods for high-dimensional sequence prediction has enabled the use of MLMs for polyphonic music.

One of the first works to use neural network-based MLMs for polyphonic music prediction and combine them with multi-pitch detection, was carried out by Boulanger-Lewandowski et al. [15]. The MLM was based on a combination of a recurrent neural network with a Neural Autogressive Distribution Estimator (NADE). The same RNN-NADE music language model was also used in [55], which was combined with a CNN as the acoustic model, showing that the inclusion of an MLM can improve transcription performance.

It was shown however that the MLMs which operate at the level of a small time frame (e.g. 10 msec) are only able to produce a smoothing effect in the resulting transcription [63]. More recently, Wang et al. [60] used an LSTM-RBM language model as part of their proposed transcription system, but each frame corresponds to an inter-onset interval as opposed to a fixed temporal duration, resulting in improved transcription performance when using note-based metrics. Finally, Ycart et al. [65] combined an LSTM-based music language model with a feedforward neural blending model which combines the MLM probabilities with the acoustic model probabilities. In line with past observations, the blending and language models work best when musically-relevant time steps are used (in this case, time steps corresponding to a 16th note).

24.4.5 Complete Transcription

Recent works have paid attention to *complete transcription*, where systems are developed to convert music audio into a music score. There are two common ways in designing a complete transcription system. A traditional way is by using a combination of several methods and subtasks of AMT to form an system that can transcribe music audio to a notation level, which usually involves estimating a piano-roll representation in an intermediate process [43]. Another way which has become increasingly popular is designing an end-to-end system that directly converts input audio or a time-frequency representation into a score level representation such as textual encoding, without having a piano-roll or similar intermediate representation in the pipeline. In this scenario, a deep learning network is used to link the system input and output. A challenge in designing a end-to-end system is that the input and output of the system cannot be aligned directly (one is a time-based representation and the other is a representation in terms of metres or symbolic encoding). As a result, research has focused on encoder-decoder architectures [16,46] which do not rely on framewise aligned annotations between the audio and music score.

A work worth mentioning which combined subtasks to build a transcription system is by Nakamura et al. [43]. In this work, the authors divided a whole transcription system into a stream of subtasks: multi-pitch analysis, note tracking, onset rhythm quantisation, note value recognition, hand separation and score typesetting. The final system reads a spectrogram calculated from music audio, and outputs readable music

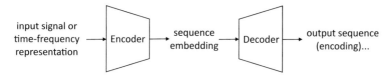

Fig. 24.6 General structure for an end-to-end AMT system using encoder-decoder architecture

scores. Offering the whole system structure, the authors did not focus on integrating algorithms for all the subtasks, but optimised methods for multi-pitch detection and rhythm quantisation. The improved subtask performance ends up adding to the final performance of the system.

Encoder-decoder mechanisms have also been used for AMT in recent years, with the advantage in creating complete transcription systems without estimating and integrating complicated subtasks. In Fig. 24.6, we provide an encoder-decoder structure commonly used in AMT systems. Recent works have showed the potential of encoder-decoder methods, although their performance on polyphonic music transcription remains less explored in the literature. In 2017, Carvalho and Smaragdis proposed a method for end-to-end music transcription using a sequence-to-sequence architecture combined with CNNs and RNNs [16]. The developed system can output a textual music encoding in Lilypond language from an input audio waveform. However, the work focused mainly on monophonic music (which showed high-level performance), but only a simple scenario of polyphonic music was tested (with two simultaneous melodies within a pitch range of two octaves). Another exploration on singing transcription by Nishikimi et al. [46] also used a sequence-to-sequence model. A point worth mentioning is that they applied an attention loss function for the decoder, which improved the performance of the singing transcription system. The work, still, focused only on monophonic singing voice.

Using an encoder-decoder architecture is a simple way of designing end-to-end AMT systems, but there are also other works using Connectionist Temporal Classification (CTC). A recent example is by Román et al. [51], in which the authors combined the use of a CRNN and a CTC loss function. The CTC loss function enables the system to be trained using pairs of the input spectrogram and output textual encoding. In that work, a simple polyphonic scenario is considered where four voices are included in a music piece (in string quarters or four-part Bach chorales). Still, the problem of end-to-end complete music transcription with unconstrained polyphony is still open.

24.5 Challenges

Although AMT is still very active as a topic within MIR, the performance of current AMT systems is still far from satisfactory, especially when it comes to polyphonic music, multiple instruments, non-Western music and 'complete' transcription. There are plenty of challenges in this area where further exploration is required. In this section, we summarise current challenges and provide potential further directions.

24.5.1 Datasets

The lack of annotated datasets is an aspect that limits the development of AMT systems. Due to the difficulty in collecting and annotating music recordings, there is still a lack of data for most music transcription tasks, especially for non-western music and certain musical instruments. Apart from the lack of large datasets, current datasets for AMT also have some limitations. For example, the temporal precision of annotations for some datasets with real recordings is not always satisfactory—which is also a reason that most AMT systems set a relatively large onset/offset *tolerance* for note tracking tasks. Also, dataset annotations are typically limited to note pitch, onset and offset times and sometimes note velocity. Additional annotations are needed for a more comprehensive transcription, such as rhythm, key information and expressiveness labels.

Recently, an increasing number of datasets has been released, which are based on synthesising MIDI files. MIDI files provide a good reference for multi-pitch detection since they provide temporally precise note annotations, but there are also limitations, since MIDI files do not provide annotations for score level transcription. Another limitation for synthesised data is that they might not reflect the recording and acoustic conditions of real-world audio recordings and can cause bias during model training.

24.5.2 Evaluation Metrics

Current evaluation metrics mainly focus on frame-wise and note-wise evaluations, where transcription results are provided in a piano-roll representation or note sequences. Benchmark evaluation metrics also do not model different error types beyond measuring precision and recall. For example, an extra note may be more severe than a missing note in a polyphonic music, on-key notes may be less noticed than off-key ones, and an error in a predominant voice may be more obvious compared to a similar error in a middle voice. Besides, much less work can be found in evaluating complete transcription systems.

There is also a lack of perceptual considerations in commonly used evaluation metrics. Some work [43,48] has attempted to create different types of errors, however these metrics still do not account for human perception. Deniel et al. provided an early work on perceptually-based multi-pitch detection evaluation [21], but is not widely used in the community. In addition, there is still no work on perceptually-based evaluation metrics for score-level transcription.

24.5.3 Non-Western Music

Most AMT methods aim specifically at modelling Western tonal music, but there is much less work done on automatically transcribing music cultures beyond Western tonal music, such as world, folk and traditional music. This results in AMT systems not being able to accurately or adequately transcribe non-Western music.

Differences between Western and non-Western music cultures that can affect the design of AMT systems include but are not limited to pitch space organisation and microtonality, the presence of heterophony (vs. homophony or polyphony occurring in Western tonal music), complex rhythmic and metrical structures, differences in tuning and temperament, differences in musical instruments and differences in methods for expressive performance and music notation amongst others. Despite the above differences, the lack of large annotated datasets is another limitation for music transcription research for non-Western music cultures.

24.5.4 Complete Transcription

Although research in AMT has increasingly been focusing on complete transcription in recent years, current methods and systems are still not suitable for general-purpose audio-to-score transcription of multi-instrument polyphonic music. Some systems for complete transcription rely on typesetting methods as a final step, but most typesetting methods assume a performance MIDI or similar representation as input and are not designed to take noisy input into account. In addition, when many tasks are combined into a whole system for complete transcription, the errors in each step can accumulate and worsen the system's performance. As for end-to-end transcription methods, current research is still limited to monophonic music and special cases for polyphonic music, mostly using synthetic audio. There is still a large room for further work towards the development of systems for complete music transcription.

24.5.5 Expressive Performance

Including expressive performance annotations is another challenge in current AMT research. Most AMT systems transcribe music into a defined framework of note pitch, onset and offset in a metre constrained format, but cover little expressive labels such as note velocity, speed symbols, as well as expressive playing techniques. It is currently hard to predict such information in AMT, although MIR research has been focusing on specific problems within the broader topic expressive music performance modelling (e.g. vibrato detection). How to incorporate the estimation and modelling of expressive performance into AMT systems remains an open problem.

24.5.6 Domain Adaptation

Due to the increasing use of synthesised datasets, or due to the mainstream use of piano-specific datasets for AMT, the ability of such models to generalise to real recordings, different instruments, acoustic recording conditions or music styles has become a problem worth considering. There is currently no research focusing on this question in the context of AMT, although the broader problem of *domain adaptation* has been attracting increasing interest in MIR and the broader area of machine learning.

For example, tasks in MIR such as music alignment and singing voice separation were explored in a recent paper [37] using domain adaptation methods based on variational autoencoders. We believe that similar domain adaptation methods can be applied to AMT tasks to solve existing problems such as the lack of data for some less popular instruments and dealing with the differences between synthesised and real-life recorded datasets or different recording conditions.

24.6 Conclusions

AMT is a core problem in the field of Music Information Retrieval (MIR), and has attracted a lot of attention during the past few decades. In this chapter, we review and discuss some of the main topics within the problem of AMT. We make a concrete definition of the problem of AMT, and describe the main subtasks in the AMT process (see Sect. 24.2). We also introduce the problem of complete transcription, which refers to the process of converting music audio into a music score representation. We review commonly used datasets and evaluation metrics for AMT (see Sect. 24.3), and look into the state of the art methodologies used in AMT (see Sect. 24.4). Current research on AMT has focused on methods using neural networks with promising results. We look into several topics in particular, including the use of commonly used neural network architectures, the use of multi-task learning methods, the use of music language models and methods for complete transcription. However, challenges still exist in the field of AMT, as we discussed in Sect. 24.5. A large room for improvement is open in areas such as building better datasets and evaluation metrics, building systems for non-Western music transcription, complete transcription, adding expressive performance in transcription results and considering domain adaptation. Given our review in this chapter, we believe that AMT is an open and promising field within both MIR and the broader intersection of music and artificial intelligence.

Acknowledgements L. Liu is a research student at the UKRI Centre for Doctoral Training in Artificial Intelligence and Music and is supported by a China Scholarship Council and Queen Mary University of London joint Ph.D. scholarship. The work of E. Benetos was supported by RAEng Research Fellowship RF/128 and a Turing Fellowship.

References

1. Music Information Retrieval Evaluation eXchange (MIREX). Retrieved April 29, 2020, from http://music-ir.org/mirexwiki/.
2. SyncRWC dataset. Retrieved April 29, 2020, from https://staff.aist.go.jp/m.goto/RWC-MDB/AIST-Annotation/SyncRWC/.
3. Bay, M., Ehmann, A. F., & Downie, J. S. (2009). Evaluation of multiple-F0 estimation and tracking systems. In *10th International Society for Music Information Retrieval Conference* (pp. 315–320). Kobe, Japan.
4. Bello, J. P., Daudet, L., Abdallah, S., Duxbury, C., Davies, M., & Sandler, M. (2005). A tutorial on onset detection of music signals. *IEEE Transactions on Audio, Speech, and Language Processing, 13*(5), 1035–1047.
5. Benetos, E., Dixon, S., Duan, Z., & Ewert, S. (2019). Automatic music transcription: An overview. *IEEE Signal Processing Magazine, 36*(1), 20–30. https://doi.org/10.1109/MSP.2018.2869928.
6. Benetos, E., Dixon, S., Giannoulis, D., Kirchhoff, H., & Klapuri, A. (2013). Automatic music transcription: Challenges and future directions. *Journal of Intelligent Information Systems, 41*(3), 407–434. https://doi.org/10.1007/s10844-013-0258-3.
7. Benetos, E., & Holzapfel, A. (2013). Automatic transcription of Turkish makam music. In *14th International Society for Music Information Retrieval Conference* (pp. 355–360). Curitiba, Brazil.
8. Benetos, E., & Weyde, T. (2015). An efficient temporally-constrained probabilistic model for multiple-instrument music transcription. In *16th International Society for Music Information Retrieval Conference (ISMIR)* (pp. 701–707). Malaga, Spain.
9. Bittner, R., & Bosch, J. J. (2019). Generalised metrics for single-f0 estimation evaluation. In *Proceedings of the 20th International Society of Music Information Retrieval Conference, ISMIR* (pp. 738–745). Delft, Netherlands.
10. Bittner, R., Salamon, J., Tierney, M., Mauch, M., Cannam, C., & Bello, J. (2014). Medleydb: A multitrack dataset for annotation-intensive mir research. In *International Society for Music Information Retrieval Conference* (pp. 155–160). Taibei, Taiwan.
11. Bittner, R. M., McFee, B., & Bello, J. P. (2018). *Multitask learning for fundamental frequency estimation in music*. arXiv:1809.00381 [cs.SD].
12. Bittner, R. M., McFee, B., Salamon, J., Li, P., & Bello, J. P. (2017). Deep salience representations for f0 estimation in polyphonic music. In *International Society for Music Information Retrieval Conference* (pp. 63–70). Suzhou, China.
13. Böck, S., & Schedl, M. (2012). Polyphonic piano note transcription with recurrent neural networks. In: *IEEE International Conference on Audio, Speech and Signal Processing* (pp. 121–124). Kyoto, Japan.
14. Bosch, J. J., Marxer, R., & Gómez, E. (2016). Evaluation and combination of pitch estimation methods for melody extraction in symphonic classical music. *Journal of New Music Research, 45*(2), 101–117.
15. Boulanger-Lewandowski, N., Bengio, Y., & Vincent, P. (2012). Modeling temporal dependencies in high-dimensional sequences: Application to polyphonic music generation and transcription. In *29th International Conference on Machine Learning*. Edinburgh, Scotland, UK.
16. Carvalho, R. G. C., & Smaragdis, P. (2017). Towards end-to-end polyphonic music transcription: Transforming music audio directly to a score. In *IEEE Workshop on Applications of Signal Processing to Audio and Acoustics* (pp. 151–155).
17. Chen, C. H. (2016). *Handbook of Pattern Recognition and Computer Vision* (5th ed.). River Edge, NJ, USA: World Scientific Publishing Co., Inc.
18. Cogliati, A., & Duan, Z. (2017). A metric for music notation transcription accuracy. In *Proceedings of the International Society for Music Information Retrieval Conference* (pp. 407–413).

19. Cogliati, A., Duan, Z., & Wohlberg, B. (2017). Piano transcription with convolutional sparse lateral inhibition. *IEEE Signal Processing Letters, 24*(4), 392–396.
20. Cogliati, A., Temperley, D., & Duan, Z. (2016). Transcribing human piano performances into music notation. In *Proceedings of the International Society for Music Information Retrieval Conference* (pp. 758–764).
21. Daniel, A., Emiya, V., & David, B. (2008). Perceptually-based evaluation of the errors usually made when automatically transcribing music. In *International Society for Music Information Retrieval Conference, ISMIR* (pp. 550–555).
22. Duan, Z., Pardo, B., & Zhang, C. (2010). Multiple fundamental frequency estimation by modeling spectral peaks and non-peak regions. *IEEE Transactions on Audio, Speech, and Language Processing, 18*(8), 2121–2133.
23. Duan, Z., & Temperley, D. (2001). *Note-level music transcription by maximum likelihood sampling.*
24. Emiya, V., Badeau, R., & David, B. (2010). Multipitch estimation of piano sounds using a new probabilistic spectral smoothness principle. *IEEE Transactions on Audio, Speech, and Language Processing, 18*(6), 1643–1654.
25. Gòmez, E., & Bonada, J. (2013). Towards computer-assisted flamenco transcription: An experimental comparison of automatic transcription algorithms as applied to a cappella singing. *Computer Music Journal, 37*(2), 73–90. https://doi.org/10.1162/COMJ_a_00180.
26. Goto, M., Hashiguchi, H., Nishimura, T., & Oka, R. (2003). RWC music database: Music genre database and musical instrument sound database. In *International Conference on Music Information Retrieval*. Baltimore, USA.
27. Hartmann, W. M. (1996). Pitch, periodicity, and auditory organization. *The Journal of the Acoustical Society of America, 100*(6), 3491–3502. https://doi.org/10.1121/1.417248.
28. Hawthorne, C., Elsen, E., Song, J., Roberts, A., Simon, I., Raffel, C., et al. (2018). Onsets and frames: Dual-objective piano transcription. In *Proceedings of the 19th International Society for Music Information Retrieval Conference, ISMIR* (pp. 50–57). Paris, France.
29. Hawthorne, C., Stasyuk, A., Robers, A., Simon, I., Huang, C.Z.A., Dieleman, S., et al. (2019). Enabling factorized piano music modeling and generation with the maestro dataset. In *International Conference on Learning Representations (ICLR)*.
30. Humphrey, E. J., Durand, S., & McFee, B. (2018). OpenMIC-2018: An open dataset for multiple instrument recognition. In *19th International Society for Music Information Retrieval Conference* (pp. 438–444). Paris, France.
31. Jurafsky, D., & Martin, J. H. (2008). *Speech and language processing* (2nd ed.). Pearson.
32. Kelz, R., Böck, S., & Widmer, G. (2019). Multitask learning for polyphonic piano transcription, a case study. In *International Workshop on Multilayer Music Representation and Processing (MMRP)* (pp. 85–91). https://doi.org/10.1109/MMRP.2019.8665372.
33. Kelz, R., Dorfer, M., Korzeniowski, F., Böck, S., Arzt, A., & Widmer, G. (2016). On the potential of simple framewise approaches to piano transcription. In *Proceedings of International Society for Music Information Retrieval Conference* (pp. 475–481).
34. Kelz, R., & Widmer, G. (2017). An experimental analysis of the entanglement problem in neural-network-based music transcription systems. In *Audio Engineering Society Conference: 2017 AES International Conference on Semantic Audio*.
35. Kim, J. W., & Bello, J., Adversarial learning for improved onsets and frames music transcription. In *International Society for Music Information Retrieval Conference*.
36. Klapuri, A., & Davy, M. (Eds.). (2006). *Signal processing methods for music transcription.* New York: Springer.
37. Luo, Y. J., & Su, L. (2018). Learning domain-adaptive latent representations of music signals using variational autoencoders. In *Proceedings of International Society for Music Information Retrieval Conference* (pp. 653–660). Paris, France.
38. Manilow, E., Wichern, G., Seetharaman, P., & Roux, J. L. (2019). Cutting music source separation some slakh: A dataset to study the impact of training data quality and quantity. In *IEEE Workshop on Applications of Signal Processing to Audio and Acoustics*. New Paltz, NY.

39. McLeod, A., & Steedman, M. (2018). Evaluating automatic polyphonic music transcription. In *Proceedings of the 19th International Society for Music Information Retrieval Conference, ISMIR* (pp. 42–49). Paris, France

40. McLeod, A., & Yoshii, K. (2019). Evaluating non-aligned musical score transcriptions with mv2h. In *Extended Abstract for Late-Breaking/Demo in International Society for Music Information Retrieval Conference, ISMIR*.

41. McVicar, M., Santos-Rodríguez, R., Ni, Y., & Bie, T. D. (2014). Automatic chord estimation from audio: A review of the state of the art. *IEEE/ACM Transactions on Audio, Speech, and Language Processing, 22*(2), 556–575. https://doi.org/10.1109/TASLP.2013.2294580.

42. Molina, E., Barbancho, A. M., Tardòn, L. J., & Barbancho, I. (2014). Evaluation framework for automatic singing transcription. In *International Symposium on Music Information Retrieval Conference* (pp. 567–572).

43. Nakamura, E., Benetos, E., Yoshii, K., & Dixon, S., *Towards complete polyphonic music transcription: Integrating multi-pitch detection and rhythm quantization*.

44. Nakamura, E., Yoshii, K., & Sagayama, S. (2017). Rhythm transcription of polyphonic piano music based on merged-output hmm for multiple voices. *IEEE/ACM Transactions on Audio, Speech, and Language Processing, 25*(4), 794–806.

45. Nam, J., Ngiam, J., Lee, H., & Slaney, M. (2011). A classification-based polyphonic piano transcription approach using learned feature representations. In *12th International Society for Music Information Retrieval Conference* (pp. 175–180). Miami, Florida, USA.

46. Nishikimi, R., Nakamura, E., Fukayama, S., Goto, M., & Yoshii, K. (2019). Automatic singing transcription based on encoder-decoder recurrent neural networks with a weakly-supervised attention mechanism. In *Proceedings of IEEE International Conference on Acoustics, Apeech and Signal Processing*.

47. Piszczalski, M., & Galler, B. A. (1977). Automatic music transcription. *Computer Music Journal, 1*(4), 24–31.

48. Poliner, G., & Ellis, D. (2007). A discriminative model for polyphonic piano transcription. *EURASIP Journal on Advances in Signal Processing, 8*, 154–162.

49. Raffel, C. (2016). *Learning-based methods for comparing sequences, with applications to audio-to-midi alignment and matching*. Ph.D. thesis, Columbia University.

50. Rebelo, A., Fujinaga, I., Paszkiewicz, F., Marcal, A. R. S., Guedes, C., & Cardoso, J. S. (2012). Optical music recognition: State-of-the-art and open issues. *International Journal of Multimedia Information Retrieval, 1*(3), 173–190. https://doi.org/10.1007/s13735-012-0004-6.

51. Román, M. A., Pertusa, A., & Calvo-Zaragoza, J. (2019). A holistic approach to polyphonic music transcription with neural networks. In *Proceedings of the 20th International Society for Music Information Retrieval Conference* (pp. 731–737). Delft, Netherlands.

52. Ruder, S. (2017). *An overview of multi-task learning in deep neural networks*. arXiv:1706.05098.

53. Salamon, J., Gomez, E., Ellis, D., & Richard, G. (2014). Melody extraction from polyphonic music signals: Approaches, applications, and challenges. *IEEE Signal Processing Magazine, 31*(2), 118–134. https://doi.org/10.1109/MSP.2013.2271648.

54. Serra, X., Magas, M., Benetos, E., Chudy, M., Dixon, S., Flexer, A., et al. (2013). *Roadmap for music information research*. Creative Commons BY-NC-ND 3.0 license.

55. Sigtia, S., Benetos, E., & Dixon, S. (2016). An end-to-end neural network for polyphonic piano music transcription. *IEEE/ACM Transactions on Audio, Speech, and Language Processing, 24*(5), 927–939. https://doi.org/10.1109/TASLP.2016.2533858.

56. Smaragdis, P., & Brown, J. C. (2003). Non-negative matrix factorization for polyphonic music transcription. In *IEEE Workshop on Applications of Signal Processing to Audio and Acoustics* (pp. 177–180). New Paltz, USA.

57. Su, L., & Yang, Y. H. (2015). Escaping from the abyss of manual annotation: New methodology of building polyphonic datasets for automatic music transcription. In *International Symposium on Computer Music Multidisciplinary Research*.

58. Thickstun, J., Harchaoui, Z., & Kakade, S. M. (2017). Learning features of music from scratch. In *International Conference on Learning Representations (ICLR)*.
59. Virtanen, T., Plumbley, M. D., & Ellis, D. P. W. (Eds.). (2018). *Computational analysis of sound scenes and events*. Springer.
60. Wang, Q., Zhou, R., & Yan, Y. (2018). Polyphonic piano transcription with a note-based music language model. *Applied Sciences, 8*(3). https://doi.org/10.3390/app8030470.
61. Wu, C., Dittmar, C., Southall, C., Vogl, R., Widmer, G., Hockman, J., et al. (2018). A review of automatic drum transcription. *IEEE/ACM Transactions on Audio, Speech, and Language Processing, 26*(9), 1457–1483. https://doi.org/10.1109/TASLP.2018.2830113.
62. Xi, Q., Bittner, R. M., Pauwels, J., Ye, X., & Bello, J. P. (2018). Guitarset: A dataset for guitar transcription. In *Proceedings of the 19th International Society for Music Information Retrieval Conference, ISMIR* (pp. 453–460). Paris, France.
63. Ycart, A., & Benetos, E. (2017). A study on LSTM networks for polyphonic music sequence modelling. In *18th International Society for Music Information Retrieval Conference (ISMIR)* (pp. 421–427).
64. Ycart, A., & Benetos, E. (2018). A-MAPS: Augmented MAPS dataset with rhythm and key annotations. In *19th International Society for Music Information Retrieval Conference Late Breaking and Demo Papers*. Paris, France.
65. Ycart, A., McLeod, A., Benetos, E., & Yoshii, K. (2019). Blending acoustic and language model predictions for automatic music transcription. In *20th International Society for Music Information Retrieval Conference (ISMIR)*.
66. Yu, D., & Deng, L. (Eds.). (2015). *Automatic Speech Recognition: A Deep Learning Approach*. London: Springer.

Lele Liu is a research student at the Centre for Doctoral Training in Artificial Intelligence and Music (AIM), based at the School of Electronic Engineering and Computer Science of Queen Mary University of London, UK. Her research is on automatic music transcription with neural networks. E-mail: lele.liu@qmul.ac.uk.

Emmanouil Benetos is Senior Lecturer at the School of Electronic Engineering and Computer Science of Queen Mary University of London and Turing Fellow at the Alan Turing Institute, in the UK. His research focuses on signal processing and machine learning methods for music and audio analysis, as well as applications to music information retrieval, sound scene analysis, and computational musicology. E-mail: emmanouil.benetos@qmul.ac.uk.

Automatic Transcription of Polyphonic Vocal Music

25

Rodrigo Schramm

25.1 Introduction

The practice of collective singing represents an inherent manifestation of vocal music in the cultural development of many societies. It is often part of the communal lifestyle, motivated by aesthetic enjoyment and also used as a possible way to strengthen society's cohesiveness [46]. These groups of singers can perform in unison or several distinct melodic lines. Examples of such singing structures can be recognized in varied styles of music, and in many parts of the world. Moreover, vocal music retains a significant role in Western musical development where vocal quartets and choirs constitute a traditional form of music. These vocal quartets and choirs typically divide a musical piece into multiple vocal parts like Soprano, Alto, Tenor, and Bass (SATB) [22].

Over the last years, many signal processing and machine learning approaches have been proposed to convert acoustic music signal into symbolic music representation. A core task in Automatic Music Transcription (AMT) [6] is multi-pitch detection. This task is frequently addressed by a frame-based analysis procedure toward a traditional music notation scheme (e.g., MIDI notes). Multi-pitch detection can additionally be implemented as a functional step for many applications in music information retrieval, including interactive music systems, tools for assisted music education and musicology. Innovative AMT techniques have intensively adopted deep learning-based algorithms [9,24,41]. However, these machine learning techniques have been primarily applied to ordinary musical instruments (e.g., piano, guitar, drums, etc.), and polyphonic vocal music has not been extensively addressed yet. Moreover, deep

R. Schramm (✉)
Federal University of Rio Grande do Sul, Rua Dona Leonor, Porto Alegre 90420180, Brazil
e-mail: rschramm@ufrgs.br

© Springer Nature Switzerland AG 2021
E. R. Miranda (ed.), *Handbook of Artificial Intelligence for Music*,
https://doi.org/10.1007/978-3-030-72116-9_25

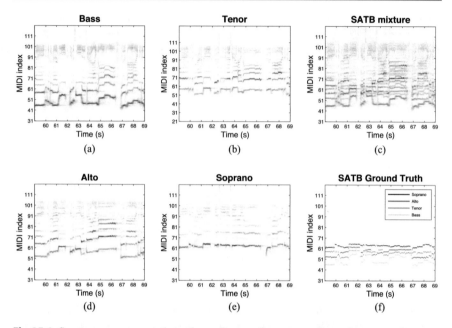

Fig. 25.1 Spectrogram representations of an audio recording excerpt of a vocal quartet performance (BQ058): **a** monophonic Bass voice; **b** monophonic Tenor voice; **d** monophonic Alto voice; **e** monophonic Soprano voice; **c** polyphonic vocal quartet mixture (SATB); **f** Multi-pitch representation for the four voices (ground truth)

learning methods applied to the polyphonic vocal music domain can be difficult since lack of appropriate training data.

This chapter presents an alternative machine learning approach in the direction of automatic transcription of vocal music. The proposed method focuses on frame-based analysis and addresses two fundamental problems: multi-pitch detection and voice assignment. The text will conduct the reader through a specific pipeline based on Probabilistic Latent Component Analysis (PLCA) [29]. This pipeline requires less data for training, and it is effective to detect multiple pitches in polyphonic vocal music. Moreover, it can properly assign each detected pitch to the respective SATB voice type.

Multi-pitch detection is achieved through an acoustic model that performs iterative spectrogram factorisation and makes use of a dictionary with spectral templates (six-dimensional tensor). Voice assignment is carried out by integrating the acoustic model with a music language model, resulting in the association of each detected vocal melody (voice) to a specific SATB part. The approach described in this chapter focuses on musical recordings of singing performances by vocal quartets without instrumental accompaniment—*a capella* Choral singing.

An example of this kind of music is illustrated by Fig. 25.1. It shows spectrogram representations extracted from an audio excerpt of a vocal quartet recording (BQ058, "It's a long, long way to Tipperary", by Jack Judge and Harry Williams [33]).

Figures 25.1a, b, d, e show the respective spectrograms for each isolated monophonic voice type (Soprano, Alto, Tenor, Bass). Each monophonic voice presents a clear fundamental frequency sequence and particular set of harmonic components; Fig. 25.1f shows the SATB Ground Truth where the pitch sequence of each vocal line is identified by distinct colors. The resulting spectrogram of the SATB mixture is shown in Fig. 25.1e. It is possible to see many harmonic overlaps among the voices in the mixture, illustrating the complexity of the task for automatically picking the correct pitch sequences (multi-pitch detection) plus assigning them to the right voices (voice assignment).

The next section of this chapter gives a panoramic overview of related works. The overview aims to contextualize the reader to the challenging task of automatic music transcription of audio recordings with polyphonic vocal content. Section 25.3 inserts the reader to the music and acoustic context of polyphonic vocal music. The section highlights specific characteristics of vocal intonation that can be used by machine learning models to achieve the desired automatic music transcription. A short introduction to the PLCA framework is given in Sect. 25.3.2. The PLCA framework is the basis for the two models presented in Sect. 25.4, which are specially designed to support automatic transcription of polyphonic vocal music: (1) MSINGERS, primarily designed to multi-pitch detection of vocal quartets; (2) VOCAL4, which integrates acoustic and music language models, being able to perform joint multi-pitch detection and voice assignment.

25.2 Related Works

Singing voice analysis has sparked attention among the music information retrieval research community. Expressive characteristics of the choir singing are studied in [12], with a focus on singers' interaction during unison performances. The published study analyzed how singers blend their voices together by means of F0 dispersion, intonation accuracy, and vibrato. Pitch accuracy on four-part ensembles, regarding individual singer intonation, and the influence of members interactions is investigated in [14]. Both [12, 14] do not perform multi-pitch estimation on polyphonic content.

Polyphonic music with vocal content is addressed in [23, 26], but these researches focused only on extracting the leading vocal contour from the music accompaniment. These techniques were employed to the analysis of particular vocal characteristics, however, they did not address the multi-pitch estimation of the polyphonic vocal signal. Detection of multiple concurrent pitches (multi-f0) is a core problem of the automatic transcription task [8], and recent research work [24, 41] has applied deep learning approaches toward this specific task. A fully convolutional neural network is presented in [9] for learning salience representations from an input spectrogram. The pitch salience representation is then used to multi-f0 detection and melody tracking. The technique addresses general polyphonic audio, not focusing only on polyphonic vocal music. Robust deep learning-based models need massive amount of data for training. Regardless of the worthy achievements of deep learning approaches on polyphonic music, the lack of specific datasets with annotated vocal recordings is still an issue.

Alternatively, models based on spectrogram factorisation have been extensively applied to the problem of multi-pitch detection over the last decade. In such approaches, the input time-frequency representation is factorized into a linear combination of non-negative components, often consisting of spectral atoms and pitch activations. Common spectrogram factorisation methods are Non-Negative Matrix Factorisation (NMF) [17] and Probabilistic Latent Component Analysis (PLCA) [17,21]. Positive results of template-based techniques encourage the exploration and extension of methods based on spectrogram factorisation. However, as the number of audio sources increases, the complexity of the input spectral shape causes strong effect on the performance of the decomposition. Even on approaches that use pre-learning steps, the large variation of the spectral templates, needed to represent a significant number of audio sources (e.g., several singers plus the high number of phonemes), affects the generalization of the model. Constraints and regularizations can be integrated to reduce the degree of freedom of these models, as proposed in [5,7].

Often, the time-frequency representation used in the factorisation process is based on the Constant-Q Transform (CQT) [10]. This representation allows AMT techniques to implement shift-invariant models [3,4,30]. Additionally, these approaches frequently design a particular sparse set of spectral envelopes to denote the timbre of specific audio sources and a wide pitch range. A particular multi-pitch detection model based on spectrogram factorisation for a cappella of vocal quartets was proposed in [39]. The acoustic driven model exploited a pre-trained dictionary of spectral templates that aims to represent the timbre of multiple singers. Singer voice was modeled regarding vocal characteristics as vowel types, voice types, pitch, and tuning deviation. The model proposed in [39] will be explained in detail in Sect. 25.4.2. Besides the multi-pitch detection task, there is also the problem of instrument (or voice) assignment. It was explored in [2] by integrating a hidden Markov model that enforces continuity to the pitch contour of each instrument, avoiding abrupt changes on pitch estimation between close audio frames.

Aiming to improve the multi-pitch detection and achieve the voice assignment of SATB parts, [29] combined an acoustic model (PLCA based) with a music language model (HMM based). The music language model uses heuristics based on knowledge from music theory and from constraints automatically derived from symbolic music data to separate pitches into monophonic streams of notes (voices). Common characteristics used by the music language model in [29] are (1) large melodic intervals between consecutive notes within a single voice should be avoided; (2) crossing of two voices should be avoided; (3) the sequence of notes should be relatively continuous without big temporal gaps within a single voice.

The successful results obtained by [29,39] have motivated the written of this chapter. This work aims to draw an incremental pipeline to guide the reader through a PLCA-based algorithm applied to multi-pitch detection and voice assignment tasks.

25.3 Polyphonic Vocal Music

Polyphony is a specific kind of musical texture that combines two or more lines of melodies, producing dense and complex mixtures in contrast to more empties textures. In the strict musical sense, the musical textures can be classified as Monophony, Homophony, and Polyphony/Contrapuntal [36]. The term Monophony describes a musical texture with just one melody for an instrument or human voice. Audio recordings of Monophony textures are monophonic audio signals. An example of a typical MIR task applied to Monophony textures is the fundamental frequency estimation (pitch tracking) [27]. Homophony refers to a musical texture with one dominant melodic voice accompanied by chords.

Terms Polyphony and Contrapuntal denote more than many simultaneous sounds. They refer to specific stylistic and historical classification of music. Within the context of Western musical tradition, the term Polyphony refers to the repertoire of the late Middle Ages and Renaissance. Besides, Polyphony describes a type of musical texture consisting of two or more simultaneous and independents melodies (voices) with formal musical interaction between them.

The constitution of a dense texture presents horizontals elements as melodies and verticals elements as harmonic intervals and chords. These two kinds of components in the musical structure are inseparable and establish laws of attractiveness or repulsion between the sounds that form them. The term Contrapuntal (note against one note) is practically synonymous with Polyphony, except for one difference: the term Counterpoint refers to the art, to the composition technique, and to the set of rules that governs the conduction of voices (movements and combinations) in the Polyphony and Harmony.

However, in the context of music information retrieval, the *polyphonic audio* expression usually generalizes the term *Polyphony*, considering any musical texture that is not monophonic. On this way, Homophony and Contrapuntal are sub-types of Polyphony. Thus, audio recordings of Polyphony (which includes Homophony and Contrapuntal) textures are polyphonic audio signals. Many MIR tasks address this kind of signal, such as multi-pitch detection, chord recognition, and audio source separation. For the task of automatic music transcription, the definition of polyphonic audio recordings often includes all results of multiple sound sources that we can hear at the same time. These simultaneous sounds can be produced by human and/or instrumental voices, with a music formal interaction with each other or not.

In the context of the vocal repertoire, Choral is a specific texture of music pieces, written specially for a choir to perform. The term choir indicates a musical ensemble, whose musicians sing together, with or without instrumental accompaniment. This group of people is organized, normally, as SATB. This acronym denotes the four principal types of human voices, respectively, Soprano, Alto, Tenor, and Bass.

25.3.1 Particular Characteristics of Vocal Sounds

The human voice and its use applied to communication have been studied for centuries, and the source-filter theory based on acoustics aspects of voice production is supported by many researchers [11,44]. According to Vagone (1980, p. 180) [47], "Phonetics is ancient knowledge and young science". It arose in antiquity, especially among the Indians, from the fourth century onwards. But only in the 18th century, scientific research has shown that phonetics was not linked exclusively to the study of languages. Therefore, the origin of studies on the sounds of the human singing voice, as understood here, came about three centuries ago. The source-filter theory states that the vocal sound starts from the air pressure variation that is controlled by the respiratory musculature. The air flows through the vocal folds (vocal cords) and makes them vibrate. In voiced sounds, this excitation generates a periodic complex waveform that contains a fundamental frequency and multiple harmonics.

The fundamental frequency of human singing voices varies in range between 70 Hz (the average lower pitch in male singing voices) and 1397 Hz (the average in child or high-pitched female singing voices). The vocal range is an approximation because it depends on the physiological and cultural characteristics of each human being [47]. Voiceless (unvoiced) sounds are not produced by vibrating the vocal cords but by a turbulent noise produced by the airflow interaction with lips, teeth, and constrictions of muscles in the oral cavity. Both voiced or unvoiced sounds are subsequently modified by the resonance and filtering characteristics of the vocal tract. The vocal tract, in the source-filter theory, constitutes a group of filters that interacts with the primary sound source from the larynx and then shape the spectrum of the waveform.

The fundamental frequency of voiced sounds defines the pitch. It is worth noting that sound perception is quite complex [34]. In the presence of the harmonics of a given frequency f (e.g., $2f$, $3f$, $4f$, etc.), humans tend to identify f as the pitch of a sound even without the presence of f in the audio signal. This phenomenon is known as "missing fundamental". Each particular vocal range, spanning from the lowest to the highest note, can be used to specify the voice type [31]. Figure 25.2 presents a typical classification based only on the vocal range regarding female and male subjects, even though this classification is not unique [43]. It is worth mentioning that there are alternative classifications for voice types which might consider several other vocal characteristics [15].

Resonances in the vocal tract accentuate specific frequencies and give particular shape to the spectrum. Prominent peaks in the spectrum generated by the vocal tract are called formants, and identified as a sequence: first formant (F1), second format (F2), third formant (F3), etc. [18]. These formants have straight connection to the vowels sounds, whose quality is mostly determined by the first two formants. The relation between vowels and the mean frequencies of extracted formants are usually visualized by a cardinal vowel chart [1].

Besides the characteristics as pitch, vowel type, and vocal range, the singing voice also has important expressive features as vibrato and portamento. Vibrato, in the case of singing techniques, is a periodic low-frequency pitch modulation applied by the

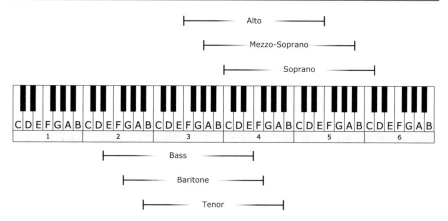

Fig. 25.2 Common voice type classification based on vocal range [47]

singer. The amount of pitch variation defines the vibrato extension and the speed of how the pitch oscillates around the steady note gives the rate of vibrato. Usually, the mean vibrato extent for individual tones ranges between ± 34 and ± 123 cent [35], and Western professional opera singers can perform vibrato rates in the range of about 5–7 Hz [47]. Portamento is used by singers to connect one pitch note to another in sequence. During the portamento, the pitch increases (or decreases) to conduct the voice from one tone to another passing by all intermediate pitches.

Vibrato, portamento, and tuning deviation generates a continuum range of intonation frequencies. Small deviations in the pitch imposes the challenge of cent resolution representation that must be efficiently addressed by techniques for automatic analysis of multi-pitch content.

25.3.2 Probabilistic Latent Component Analysis

Probabilistic Latent Component Analysis is a statistical technique that has been successfully used for acoustic modeling over the past decade [4,21,30]. A PLCA-based model can express a multivariate distribution as a mixture where each component is a product of many one-dimensional marginal distributions. PLCA models are equivalent to Non-Negative Matrix Factorisation. They can typically interpret a normalized input magnitude spectrogram $V_{\omega,t}$ as a bivariate probability distribution $P(\omega, t)$, where ω denotes frequency and t denotes the frame index (time).

This section introduces and summarizes this probabilistic framework as described in [40]. The framework uses a particular case of the decomposition of the latent variable model where each input data vector is considered independent. In this case, the PLCA models T one-dimensional distributions $P_t(\omega)$ instead of the two-dimensional distribution $P(\omega, t)$.

Following similar notation as the used in the seminal paper, this PLCA model can be defined as follows:

$$P_t(\omega) = \sum_z P(\omega|z)P_t(z), \qquad (25.1)$$

where $P_t(\omega)$ gives the overall probability of observing feature ω in the t-th experiment. z is the latent variable. The multinomial distributions $P(\omega|z)$ represent the basis components, and $P(z)$ are mixture weights that refer to the contribution of each basis $P(\omega|z)$ to express $P_t(\omega)$. The subscript t indicates that the mixture weights change from time frame to time frame.

If we consider applying this model to factorize an audio input spectrogram, $P_t(\omega)$ would be the given frequency distribution at frame t from the normalized spectrogram and z could represent audio sources. Figure 25.3 illustrates this hypothetical example for the model of Eq. (25.1). $P(\omega|z)$ are the spectral atoms, encoding the pitch and timbre of three distinct piano notes. $P_t(z)$ gives the activations over time for each spectral basis, regarding the latent variable $z \in \{C3, D\#3, G3\}$.

The estimation of the marginals $P(\omega|z)$ is performed using a variant of the Expectation and Maximization (EM) algorithm [16]. In the Expectation step (E-step), the algorithm estimates the posteriori probability for the latent variable z as

$$P_t(z|\omega) = \frac{P(\omega|z)P_t(z)}{\sum_z P(\omega|z)P_t(z)}. \qquad (25.2)$$

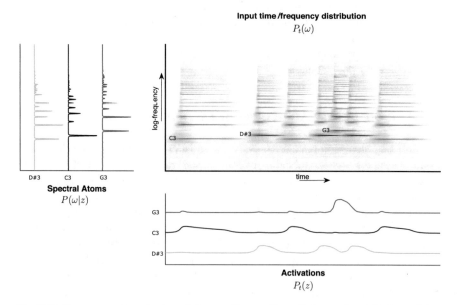

Fig. 25.3 Spectrogram factorisation of piano audio recording which contains activations of three distinct notes ($z \in \{C3, D\#3, G3\}$). The input time/frequency distribution $P_t(\omega)$ is shown on the top right. On the left, the marginals $P(\omega|z)$ are shown as spectral templates, and on the bottom, $P_t(z)$ gives the respective activations over time

The EM algorithm uses $P_t(z|\omega)$ as a weighting coefficient in the Maximization step (M-step) to obtain a more accurate estimate of the marginals $P_t(\omega|z)$ and of the prior $P_t(z)$:

$$P(\omega|z) = \frac{\sum_t V_{\omega,t} P_t(z|\omega)}{\sum_{\omega,t} V_{\omega,t} P_t(z|\omega)}, \tag{25.3}$$

$$P_t(z) = \frac{\sum_\omega V_{\omega,t} P_t(z|\omega)}{\sum_{\omega,z} V_{\omega,t} P_t(z|\omega)}, \tag{25.4}$$

where V is the two-dimensional data which we want to fit the model. In the case of a model design for audio analysis, V matrix is usually the input magnitude spectrogram.

Estimates of the conditional marginal $P(\omega|z)$ and the mixture weight $P_t(z)$ are obtained by iterating Eqs. 25.2–25.4, until convergence to a local optimum. The above described framework can be easily applied to audio analysis since energy and power spectra are distributions of acoustic energy over frequency [40]. Thus, the only demand for the PLCA technique gets working straightforwardly is a proper normalization of V to transform the magnitude spectrogram into true distributions.

25.3.2.1 Pre-learning

Many approaches for spectrogram factorisation adopt the pre-learning of the spectral atoms, represented by the marginal distribution $P(\omega|z)$ in Eq. (25.1). Usually, after the pre-learning of $P(\omega|z)$, it is kept fixed during the EM estimation. For the case illustrated in Fig. 25.3, applying pre-learning of the spectral atoms reduces the factorisation problem to the trivial estimation of the prior $P_t(z)$ (weights of a linear combination).

Despite the naivety of the model described in this section, it serves as the foundations for more complex formulations. Latent class models are powerful techniques that allow the characterization of the underlying distribution ($P_t(\omega)$ in our previous example), providing a theoretical basis for modeling, and statistical inference for estimation. Moreover, the probabilistic interpretation allows the model to factorisation into several meaningful components, strongly connected to the statistical nature of the problem. All these positive properties of PLCA have motivated the development of various models for multi-pitch detection [4,21,30]. In the next section, we describe two specific models designed to multi-pitch detection and voice assignment in the context of polyphonic vocal music.

25.4 PLCA Applied to Polyphonic Vocal Music

This section presents two PLCA-based approaches for automatic multi-pitch detection in the context of polyphonic vocal audio recordings. The first technique, named as MSINGERS [39], focuses only on the multi-pitch detection task. The second strategy, named as VOCAL4 [29], integrates a music language model to achieve concomitant better multi-pitch detection and voice assignment.

In the example of Fig. 25.3, if the spectral bases $P(\omega|z)$ are pre-learned as a dictionary of templates, then the spectrogram factorisation process uses a two-dimensional tensor, and the solution is less complex. However, to explore intrinsic characteristics of the audio source, several approaches have proposed custom dictionaries for helping the spectrogram decomposition in the context of more complex models [7,21]. For example, [7] uses a five-dimensional tensor to represent log-frequency, pitch, tuning deviation, sound state (e.g., attack and sustain), and the instrument type. These techniques had shown promising results on multi-pitch detection applied to audio recordings of several musical instruments.

Inspired by these outstanding results, we have designed a six-dimensional dictionary for the factorisation of spectrograms containing polyphonic vocal content. Both models (MSINGERS and VOCAL4) use the same fixed dictionary of log-spectral templates. These models aim to decompose an input time-frequency representation into several components meaning the activations of pitches, voice types, tuning deviations, singer subjects, and vowels. The components are bound to important vocal characteristics mentioned in Sect. 25.3.1 and were integrated into these models because they open new possibilities for external model interactions. This is the case for VOCAL4 which takes advantage of this feature and integrates a hidden Markov model to interact with specific components (voice type) in the PLCA decomposition. Details of the VOCAL4 model integration will be described in Sect. 25.4.3.

25.4.1 Dictionary Construction

The dictionary uses spectral templates extracted from solo singing recordings available in the RWC audio dataset [20]. The recordings contain singing intonation of sequences of notes following a chromatic scale, where the range of notes varies accordingly to the tessitura of distinct vocal types: bass, tenor, alto, and soprano. Each singer sings a scale in five distinct English vowels (/a/, /æ/, /i/, /ɒ/, /u/). In total, the dictionary used by MSINGERS [39] and VOCAL4 [29] models has featured fifteen distinct singers (nine male and six female, consisting of three human subjects for each voice type: bass, baritone, tenor, alto, soprano).

These vocal characteristics are arranged into a six-dimensional tensor matrix to shape the dictionary $P(\omega|s, p, f, o, v)$, where ω denotes the log-frequency index and p denotes pitch. Since voice intonation can deviate from the semitone scale, f denotes the pitch deviation from 12-tone equal temperament in 20 cent resolution ($f \in \{1, \ldots, 5\}$, with $f = 3$ denoting ideal tuning). The vocal characteristics used in both the PLCA-based models are represented by the s, o, v, p variables, with the following meaning:

- s denotes the singer index (out of the collection of singer subjects used to construct the input dictionary). Theoretically, s would be in a very wide range of values. However, in practical implementation, the design of the dictionary must take into account the memory requirements, computational cost, as well as the availability of training data. Aiming to alleviate this limitation, part of the timbre variability from s is absorbed by the variables o and v.

- $o \in \{$ /a/, /æ/, /i/, /ɒ/, /u/$\}$ is the common vowels used for singing in Western music. For this implementation, the model uses English pure vowels (monophthongs), such as those used in the solfège system of learning music: Do, Re, Mi, Fa, Sol, La, Ti, and Do. It is clear that only vowels would not give the best spectral representation of the singing voices. Nonetheless, since most of the time vocal quartets hold the singing notes on vowels, the configuration of this dictionary presents a reasonable trade-off.
- $v \in \{S, A, T, B\}$ captures the main timbre differences between voice types (e.g., soprano, alto, tenor, bass).

25.4.1.1   Spectral Template Extraction

The spectral templates representations are extracted from the solo singing recordings using the Variable-Q Transform (VQT) [38] with 60 bins per octave. The pitch from each note intonation (chromatic scale) is automatically estimated with pYin algorithm [27] and each spectral template is arranged regarding the singer source, vowel type and voice type. Multiple estimates from the same singer that fall inside the same pitch bin are replaced by its metrically trimmed mean, discarding 20% of the samples as possible outliers. The set of spectral templates are then pre-shifted across log-frequency in order to support tuning deviations ± 20 and ± 40 cent.

Recording sessions from the RWC dataset cover only part of all possible pitches. Many tune deviations and pitched notes from the chromatic scale are not present in the original audio recordings. As a consequence, the dictionary $P(\omega|s, p, f, o, v)$ is a sparse matrix, with many templates missing along the pitch scale. A linear replication procedure is applied such that existing templates are copied with the appropriated log-frequency shift to fill the gaps in the dictionary. More details about the replication process can be found in [39]. Figure 25.4 shows a slice (ω versus p) from the six-dimensional dictionary. On the left side of this Figure, it is possible to see many empty columns (sparse matrix). These columns were filled with the replication process as shown on the right side.

25.4.2   Model 1: MSINGERS

In the case of polyphonic vocal music, there are many characteristics that can be explored in the design of the PLCA-based model, such as the variability of singer voice timbre, the type of singing voice (e.g., soprano, alto, tenor, bass), pitch intonation and type of vowels. This section will present the MSINGERS model [39]. This model uses the fixed $P(\omega|s, p, f, o, v)$ dictionary of log-spectral templates described in the previous Sect. 25.4.1 and aims to decompose an input time-frequency representation into several components denoting the activations of pitches, voice types, tuning deviations, singer subjects, and vowels.

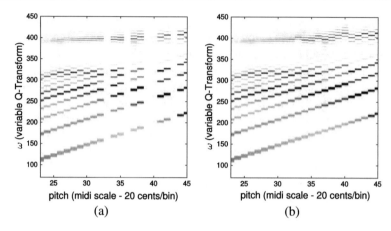

Fig. 25.4 Example from an /a/ vowel utterance templates extracted from one singer (adopted from [39]): **a** original templates from the VQT spectrogram; **b** revised dictionary templates following replication

MSINGERS factorizes the normalized input VQT spectrogram $V_{\omega,t} \in \mathbb{R}^{\Omega \times T}$, where ω denotes frequency and t time.

The normalized log-frequency spectrogram $V_{\omega,t}$ is approximated by a bivariate probability distribution $P(\omega, t)$. $P(\omega, t)$ is in turn decomposed as follows:

$$P(\omega, t) = P(t) \sum_{s,p,f,o,v} P(\omega|s, p, f, o, v) P_t(s|p) P_t(f|p) P_t(o|p) P_t(v|p) P_t(p),$$

(25.5)

where $P(t)$ is the spectrogram energy (known quantity). The model conveys specific meaning for each marginal distribution: $P_t(s|p)$ is the singer contribution per pitch over time, $P_t(f|p)$ is the tuning deviation per pitch over time, $P_t(o|p)$ is the time-varying vowel contribution per pitch, $P_t(v|p)$ is the voice type activation per pitch over time, and $P_t(p)$ is the pitch activation at frame t.

The factorisation can be achieved by the Expectation-Maximization (EM) algorithm [16], where the unknown model parameters $P_t(s|p)$, $P_t(f|p)$, $P_t(o|p)$, $P_t(v|p)$, and $P_t(p)$ are iteratively estimated. In the *Expectation* step we compute the posterior as follows:

$$P_t(s, p, f, o, v|\omega) = \frac{P(\omega|s, p, f, o, v) P_t(s|p) P_t(f|p) P_t(o|p) P_t(v|p) P_t(p)}{\sum_{s,p,f,o,v} P(\omega|s, p, f, o, v) P_t(s|p) P_t(f|p) P_t(o|p) P_t(v|p) P_t(p)}.$$

(25.6)

Each unknown model parameter is then updated in the *Maximization* step, using the posterior from (25.6)

$$P_t(s|p) = \frac{\sum_{f,o,v,\omega} P_t(s, p, f, o, v|\omega) V_{\omega,t}}{\sum_{s,f,o,v,\omega} P_t(s, p, f, o, v|\omega) V_{\omega,t}},$$

(25.7)

$$P_t(f|p) = \frac{\sum_{s,o,v,\omega} P_t(s,p,f,o,v|\omega)V_{\omega,t}}{\sum_{s,f,o,v,\omega} P_t(s,p,f,o,v|\omega)V_{\omega,t}}, \qquad (25.8)$$

$$P_t(o|p) = \frac{\sum_{s,f,v,\omega} P_t(s,p,f,o,v|\omega)V_{\omega,t}}{\sum_{s,f,o,v,\omega} P_t(s,p,f,o,v|\omega)V_{\omega,t}}, \qquad (25.9)$$

$$P_t(v|p) = \frac{\sum_{s,f,o,\omega} P_t(s,p,f,o,v|\omega)V_{\omega,t}}{\sum_{s,f,o,v,\omega} P_t(s,p,f,o,v|\omega)V_{\omega,t}}, \qquad (25.10)$$

$$P_t(p) = \frac{\sum_{s,f,o,v,\omega} P_t(s,p,f,o,v|\omega)V_{\omega,t}}{\sum_{s,p,f,o,v,\omega} P_t(s,p,f,o,v|\omega)V_{\omega,t}}. \qquad (25.11)$$

The EM algorithm iterates from Eqs. (25.6) to (25.11). The authors of MSINGERS [39] have used 35 iterations and random initialization of unknown parameters.

Sparsity constraints are commonly used in PLCA-based models [7,42]. MSINGERS applies sparsity constraints on $P_t(o|p)$ (vowel type) and $P_t(v|p)$ (voice type). These constraints are based on the assumption that vowel utterances and voice types for a specific pitch are very unlikely to be co-occurring at time t by distinct singers. The rationale behind the sparsity applied to the voice type component is that distinct voices tend to sing different pitches. As might be expected, if the vocal quartet sings a chord with three pitches (triad), then it is possible that two voices share a same pitch. Even so, the sparsity constraints are beneficial and help to drive the PLCA-based model to a meaningful solution.

After the convergence of the EM algorithm, the output of the transcription model is a semitone-scale pitch activation matrix $P(p,t) = P(t)P_t(p)$ and a pitch shifting tensor $P(f,p,t) = P(t)P_t(p)P_t(f|p)$. In order to create a 20 cent-resolution time-pitch representation, it is possible to stack together slices of $P(f,p,t)$ for all values of p:

$$P(f',t) = P((f' \bmod 5)+1, \left[\frac{f'}{5}\right]+21, t), \qquad (25.12)$$

where $f' = 0, ..., 439$ denotes pitch in 20 cent resolution.

Despite the reasonable factorisation model defined by Eq. (25.5) and its promising multi-pitch detection, the marginal distributions $P(s|p)$ (singer source), $P(v|p)$ (voice type), and $P(o|p)$ (vowel type) do not achieve meaningful solutions. In fact, with appropriated arrangement of the dictionary of spectral templates, the MSINGERS model could be reduced, for example, to

$$P(\omega,t) = P(t) \sum_{p,f} P(\omega|p,f)P_t(f|p)P_t(p) \qquad (25.13)$$

holding similar multi-pitch detection results, if not implementing sparsity constraints. Notice that the model given by Eq. (25.13) is very close to the basic model described in Eq. (25.1) of the introductory Sect. 25.3.2, regardless the pitch shift component f which gives the 20 cent resolution.

However, besides the improvement achieved by the application of sparsity constraints on $P_t(o|p)$ and $P_t(v|p)$, the findings with the design and application of the MSINGERS acoustic model have motivated its extension. By integrating an external language model that can interact with specific factors of the decomposition, we have created the VOCAL4. This model can carry out joint multi-pitch detection and voice assignment. VOCAL4 is described in the following section

25.4.3 Model 2: VOCAL4

Unlike the MSINGERS [39], the alternative model

$$P(\omega, t) = P(t) \sum_{s,p,f,o,v} P_t(\omega|s, p, f, o, v) P_t(s|p) P_t(f|p) P_t(o|p) P(v) P_t(p|v)$$

(25.14)

decomposes the probabilities of pitch and voice type as $P(v) P_t(p|v)$. That is, $P_t(p|v)$ denotes the pitch activation for a specific voice type (e.g., SATB) over time and $P(v)$ can be viewed as a mixture weight that denotes the overall contribution of each voice type to the whole input recording. The contribution of specific singer subjects from the training dictionary is modeled by $P_t(s|p)$, i.e., the singer contribution per pitch over time. $P_t(f|p)$ is the tuning deviation per pitch over time and finally $P_t(o|p)$ is the time-varying vowel contribution per pitch. Although $P_t(s|p)$ and $P_t(o|p)$ are not explicitly used in the output of the proposed approach, they are kept to ensure consistency with the RWC audio dataset structure.

The factorisation is achieved by the EM algorithm. For the E-step, we obtain the a posteriori probability for the latent variables as

$$P_t(s, p, f, o, v|\omega) = \frac{P_t(\omega|s, p, f, o, v) P_t(s|p) P_t(f|p) P_t(o|p) P(v) P_t(p|v)}{\sum_{s,p,f,o,v} P_t(\omega|s, p, f, o, v) P_t(s|p) P_t(f|p) P_t(o|p) P(v) P_t(p|v)}.$$

(25.15)

We obtain the M-step re-estimation equations for each unknown model parameter from Eq. (25.15):

$$P_t(s|p) = \frac{\sum_{f,o,v,\omega} P_t(s, p, f, o, v|\omega) V_{\omega,t}}{\sum_{s,f,o,v,\omega} P_t(s, p, f, o, v|\omega) V_{\omega,t}},$$

(25.16)

$$P_t(f|p) = \frac{\sum_{s,o,v,\omega} P_t(s, p, f, o, v|\omega) V_{\omega,t}}{\sum_{s,f,o,v,\omega} P_t(s, p, f, o, v|\omega) V_{\omega,t}},$$

(25.17)

$$P_t(o|p) = \frac{\sum_{s,f,v,\omega} P_t(s, p, f, o, v|\omega) V_{\omega,t}}{\sum_{s,f,o,v,\omega} P_t(s, p, f, o, v|\omega) V_{\omega,t}},$$

(25.18)

$$P_t(p|v) = \frac{\sum_{s,f,o,\omega} P_t(s, p, f, o, v|\omega) V_{\omega,t}}{\sum_{s,p,f,o,\omega} P_t(s, p, f, o, v|\omega) V_{\omega,t}},$$

(25.19)

$$P(v) = \frac{\sum_{s,f,o,\omega,t} P_t(s, p, f, o, v|\omega) V_{\omega,t}}{\sum_{s,p,f,o,v,\omega,t} P_t(s, p, f, o, v|\omega) V_{\omega,t}}. \tag{25.20}$$

The model parameters are randomly initialized, and the EM algorithm iterates over Eqs. (25.15)–(25.20). Authors of VOCAL4 [29] have used 30 iterations. The output of the acoustic model is a semitone-scale pitch activity tensor for each voice type and a pitch shifting tensor, given by $P(p, v, t) = P(t)P(v)P_t(p|v)$ and $P(f, p, v, t) = P(t)P(v)P_t(p|v)P_t(f|p)$, respectively. Similar to Eq. (25.12), we can also create a 20 cent-resolution time-pitch representation for each voice type v:

$$P(f', v, t) = P((f' \bmod 5) + 1, \left[\frac{f'}{5}\right] + 21, v, t), \tag{25.21}$$

where $f' = 0, ..., 439$ denotes pitch in 20 cent resolution.

The overall multi-pitch detection without voice assignment is given by $P(p, t) = \sum_v P(p, v, t)$. The voice-specific pitch activation output $P(p, v, t)$ is binarized and post-processed through a refinement step described in [39], where each pitch is aligned with the nearest peak to it in the input log-frequency spectrum.

The acoustic model VOCAL4 is slightly different from MSINGERS. It is worth to mention that this alternative way to decompose the probabilities of pitch and voice type as $P(v)P_t(p|v)$ is still not sufficient to help the acoustic model to achieve significant improvement on the voice assignment task. Even though the voice separation is still difficult for the acoustic model VOCAL4, its new PLCA formulation given by Eq. (25.14) allows us to integrate external information in order to drive the spectrogram factorisation.

25.4.4 Voice Assignment

In VOCAL4, voice assignment is accomplished by connecting a music language model that performs voice separation on the multi-pitch activations outputs. The music language model is a variant of the HMM-based approach proposed in [28], and attempts to assign each detected pitch to a single voice based on musicological constraints. The HMM separates the input sequential sets of multi-pitch activations into monophonic voices (of type SATB) based on three principles: (1) voices are unlikely to cross; (2) consecutive notes within a voice have a tendency to happen at close pitches; (3) gaps between pitch activations within a voice are expected to be minimal. For the sake of clarity, the HMM definition and details of the language model implementation are omitted here. We refer the reader to [29] for a complete report.

The observed data used by the HMM are notes generated from the acoustic model, after the binarisation of the multi-pitch activations $P(p, t)$.

These note detections are processed by the HMM model that estimates $P_t^a(p|v)$ from the most probable final HMM state. $P_t^a(p|v)$ gives the probability of each pitch detection to belong to a specific voice (e.g., SATB). It is worth to mention that

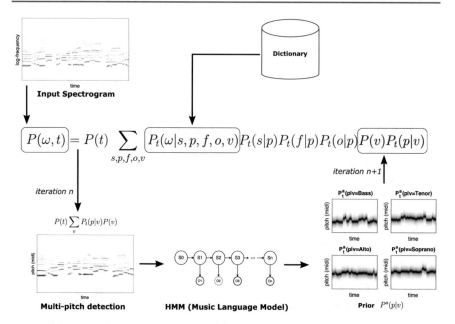

Fig. 25.5 Acoustic and Music Language models integration: At each EM iteration, the multi-pitch detections from the PLCA model are fed to the HMM. The HMM outputs soft masks $P_t^a(p|v)$ to reweigh the pitch contribution of each voice. The masking process drives the EM by updating the model with $P_t^{new}(p|v)$ (Eq. (25.22)) at each new iteration

$P_t^a(p|v)$ is entirely estimated through the HMM and it is based only on musicological constraints.

To integrate the acoustic model (PLCA based) with the music language model (HMM based), we apply a fusion mechanism inspired by the one used in [19].

Besides the voice assignment goal, this integration also works as a two way mechanism. At each EM iteration, the voice assignments generated by the HMM are injected back into the PLCA model, helping to drive the factorisation. The output of the language model is reintroduced into the acoustic model as a prior to $P_t(p|v)$. Thus, at the end of each acoustic model's EM iteration, $P_t(p|v)$ is updated as follows:

$$P_t^{new}(p|v) = \alpha P_t(p|v) + (1 - \alpha)\phi_t(p|v), \qquad (25.22)$$

where α is a weight parameter controlling the effect of the acoustic and language model and ϕ is a hyperparameter defined as follows:

$$\phi_t(p|v) \propto P_t^a(p|v)P_t(p|v). \qquad (25.23)$$

Figure 25.5 illustrates the model integration. The hyperparameter of Eq. (25.23) acts as a soft mask, reweighing the pitch contribution of each voice regarding only the pitch neighborhood previously detected by the model. The final output of the integrated system is a list of the detected pitches at each time frame, along with the voice assignment for each. Figure 25.6 illustrates these parameters estimation for a recording excerpt of BC060 ("If Thou but Suffer God to Guide Thee", by J.

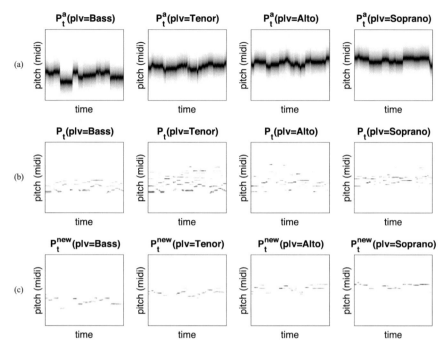

Fig. 25.6 Soft masking used to model integration. The results shown in the figure were obtained at the last EM iteration for an audio excerpt (BC060): **a** Soft masks $P_t^a(p|v)$ generated by the music language model (HMM). **b** Marginal distribution $P_t(p|v)$ generated by the acoustic model. **c** Updated marginal distribution $P^{new}(p|v)$

S.Bach [33]). Figure 25.6a shows the soft masks $P_t^a(p|v)$, generated by the HMM after processing the multi-pitch output (last EM iteration). Figure 25.6b shows the marginal distribution $P_t(p|v)$ before the reweighing by the masking process and Fig. 25.6c shows the updated marginal distribution $P_t^{new}(p|v)$. The improvement of voice separation, after the update, is visible for all voices.

Figure 25.7 shows the system output results obtained from an audio excerpt (BC060). On the top row of this figure, there is a comparison between multi-pitch detection using MSINGERS (Fig. 25.7a) and VOCAL4 (Fig. 25.7b). The music language model cooperates with the acoustic model and assists the multi-pitch detection process, removing false positives and providing better precision on pitch estimates. Figure 25.7c shows the ground truth and Fig. 25.7d shows the final multi-pitch detection and voice assignment obtained by the binarisation of $P(p, v, t)$

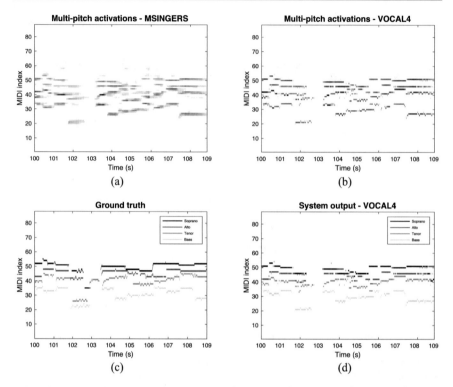

Fig. 25.7 System output: MSINGERS *versus* VOCAL4. **a** Multi-pitch detection using MSINGERS without voice assignment. **b** Multi-pitch detection using VOCAL4 with voice assignment. **c** Ground truth. **d** Multi-pitch detection and voice assignment. Colors indicate the voice type (SATB).

25.5 Final Considerations

In this chapter, we have presented a framework to assist the process of automatic transcription of polyphonic vocal music. The framework used several acoustic features of voiced sounds to model the input audio signal through a PLCA-based technique. Besides the acoustic model, our approach also integrated a music language model to assist the spectrogram factorisation into meaningful components. In Sect. 25.4.2, we introduced the MSINGERS model, which uses only acoustic features of voiced sounds. Despite promising multi-pitch detection results, it cannot achieve a proper SATB voice assignment. Intending to overcome this limitation, we presented the VOCAL4 model in Sect. 25.4.3. In this second approach, the acoustic model interacts with an HMM-based music language model. The HMM uses musical assumptions to perform voice separation, improving the multi-pitch detection when compared with the first approach (MSINGERS).

Extensive evaluations of MSINGERS and VOCAL4 are available in [29, 39], respectively. The evaluations were reported with experiments using audio recordings of 26 Bach Chorales and 22 Barbershop Quartets. In summary, f-measures for the task of multi-pitch detection with VOCAL4 are %71.76 on Bach Chorales and %75.70 on Barbershop quartets. VOCAL4 achieved better results than MSINGERS, and it was superior than other multi-pitch detection algorithms [25,32,37,45]. A recent study [13] has compared VOCAL4 model with DeepSalience [9] algorithm. In this new comparison, DeepSalience achieved slightly better f-measure, however, both algorithms were tested with a very small dataset (only three SATB recordings). Moreover, among all comparative methods, only VOCAL4 implements voice assignment.

Based on the evaluation results, it is clear that the integration of the music language model has a positive contribution to the meaningful spectrogram factorisation. It also encourages the exploration of additional vocal features and acoustic components for the PLCA model. These components open possibilities to the interconnection to even more advanced musical language models that could include harmony progression, rhythmic structure, genres, and music styles.

Acknowledgements This chapter presents results of joint work with Emmanouil Benetos (Queen Mary University of London), Andrew McLeod (University of Edinburgh), and Mark Steedman (University of Edinburgh).

References

1. Ashby, P. (2011). *Understanding phonetics*. Hodder Education: Understanding language series.
2. Bay, M., Ehmann, A. F., Beauchamp, J. W., Smaragdis, P., & Stephen Downie, J. (2012). Second fiddle is important too: Pitch tracking individual voices in polyphonic music. *ISMIR*, 319–324.
3. Benetos, E., Badeau, R., Weyde, T., & Richard, G. (2014). Template adaptation for improving automatic music transcription. *ISMIR*, 175–180.
4. Benetos, E., & Dixon, S. (2012). A shift-invariant latent variable model for automatic music transcription. *Computer Music Journal*, 36(4), 81–94.
5. Benetos, E., & Dixon, S. (2013). Multiple-instrument polyphonic music transcription using a temporally constrained shift-invariant model. *Journal Acoustical Society of America*, 133(3), 1727–1741.
6. Benetos, E., Dixon, S., Giannoulis, D., Kirchhoff, H., & Klapuri, A. (2013). Automatic music transcription: Challenges and future directions. *Journal of Intelligent Information Systems*, 41(3), 407–434.
7. Benetos, E., & Weyde, T. (2015). An efficient temporally-constrained probabilistic model for multiple-instrument music transcription. *ISMIR*, 701–707.
8. Benetos, E., Dixon, S., Giannoulis, D., Kirchhoff, H., & Klapuri, A. (2013). Automatic music transcription: Challenges and future directions. *Journal of Intelligent Information Systems*, 41(3), 407–434.
9. Bittner, R. M., McFee, B, Salamon, J., Li, P., & Pablo Bello, J. (2017). Deep salience representations for f0 estimation in polyphonic music. *ISMIR*.
10. Brown, J. (1991). Calculation of a constant Q spectral transform. *Journal Acoustical Society of America*, 89(1), 425–434.
11. Chiba, T., & Kajiyama, M. (1958). *The vowel*. Its Nature and Structure: Phonetic Society of Japan.

12. Cuesta, H., Gómez, E., Martorell, A., & Loáiciga, F. (2018). Analysis of intonation in unison choir singing. In *15th International Conference on Music Perception and Cognition (ICMPC)*, Graz (Austria).
13. Cuesta, H., Gomez, E., & Chandna, P. (2019). A framework for multi-f0 modeling in satb choir recordings. In *Sound and music computing conference* (pp. 447–453).
14. Dai, J., & Dixon, S. (2017). Analysis of interactive intonation in unaccompanied satb ensembles. *ISMIR*.
15. Davids, J., & LaTour, S. A. (2012). *Vocal technique: A guide for conductors, teachers, and Singers*. Waveland Press.
16. Dempster, A. P., Laird, N. M., & Rubin, D. B. (1977). Maximum likelihood from incomplete data via the EM algorithm. *Journal Royal Statistical Society, 39*(1), 1–38.
17. Dessein, A., Cont, A., & Lemaitre, G. (2010). Real-time polyphonic music transcription with non-negative matrix factorization and beta-divergence. In *ISMIR—11th International Society for Music Information Retrieval Conference* (pp. 489–494), Utrecht, Netherlands.
18. Fant, G. (1960). *Acoustic theory of speech production*. The Hague: Mouton.
19. Giannoulis, D., Benetos, E., Klapuri, A., & Plumbley, M. D. (2014). Improving instrument recognition in polyphonic music through system integration. *ICASSP*, 5222–5226.
20. Goto, M., Hashiguchi, H., Nishimura, T., & Oka, R. (2004). RWC music database: Music genre database and musical instrument sound database. *ISMIR*, 229–230.
21. Grindlay, G., & Ellis, D. P. Y. (2011). Transcribing multi-instrument polyphonic music with hierarchical eigeninstruments. *IEEE Journal of Selected Topics in Signal Processing, 5*(6), 1159–1169.
22. Grout, D. J., Burkholder, J. P., & Palisca, C. V. (2010). *A history of western music*. W. W: Norton.
23. Jansson, A., Bittner, R. M., Ewert, S., & Weyde, T. (2019). Joint singing voice separation and f0 estimation with deep u-net architectures. In *2019 27th European Signal Processing Conference (EUSIPCO)* (pp. 1–5).
24. Kelz, R., Dorfer, M., Korzeniowski, F., Böck, S., Arzt, A., & Widmer, G. (2016). On the potential of simple framewise approaches to piano transcription. *ISMIR*, 475–481.
25. Klapuri, A. (2006). Multiple fundamental frequency estimation by summing harmonic amplitudes. *ISMIR*.
26. Lin, K. W. E., Balamurali, B.T., Koh, E, Lui, S., & Herremans, D. (2018). Singing voice separation using a deep convolutional neural network trained by ideal binary mask and cross entropy. *Neural Computing and Applications*.
27. Mauch, M., & Dixon, S. (2014). pYIN: A fundamental frequency estimator using probabilistic threshold distributions. *ICASSP* (pp. 659–663).
28. McLeod, A., & Steedman, M. (2016). HMM-based voice separation of MIDI performance. *Journal of New Music Research, 45*(1), 17–26.
29. McLeod, A., Schramm, R., Steedman, M., & Benetos, E. (2017). Automatic transcription of polyphonic vocal music. *Applied Sciences, 7*(12).
30. Mysore, G. J., & Smaragdis, P. (2009). Relative pitch estimation of multiple instruments. *ICASSP*, 313–316.
31. Peckham, A. (2010). *The contemporary singer: Elements of vocal technique*. Berklee guide: Berklee Press.
32. Pertusa, A., & Iñesta, J. M. (2012). Efficient methods for joint estimation of multiple fundamental frequencies in music signals. *EURASIP Journal on Advances in Signal Processing*.
33. PGmusic. (202). Multimedia performance series. https://www.pgmusic.com.
34. Plack, C. J. (2005). *The sense of hearing*. Lawrence Erlbaum Associates.
35. Prame, E. (1997). Vibrato extent and intonation in professional western lyric singing. *The Journal of the Acoustical Society of America, 102*(1), 616–621.
36. Randel, D. M. (2003). *The Harvard dictionary of music* (4th ed.). Cambridge, Mass: Belknap Press of Harvard University Press.

37. Salamon, J., & Gomez, E. (2012). Melody extraction from polyphonic music signals using pitch contour characteristics. *IEEE Transactions on Audio, Speech, and Language Processing*, *20*(6), 1759–1770.
38. Schörkhuber, C., Klapuri, A., Holighaus, N., & Dörfler, M. (2014). A Matlab toolbox for efficient perfect reconstruction time-frequency transforms with log-frequency resolution. *AES 53rd Conference on Semantic Audio*.
39. Schramm, R., & Benetos, E. (2017). Automatic transcription of a cappella recordings from multiple singers. In *AES International Conference on Semantic Audio*.
40. Shashanka, M., Raj, B., & Smaragdis, P. (2008). Probabilistic latent variable models as non-negative factorizations. *Computational Intelligence and Neuroscience*. Article ID 947438.
41. Sigtia, S., Benetos, E., & Dixon, S. (2016). An end-to-end neural network for polyphonic piano music transcription. *IEEE/ACM Transactions on Audio, Speech, and Language Processing*, *24*(5), 927–939.
42. Smaragdis, P., Shashanka, M. V. S., Raj, B., & Mysore, G. J. (2009). Probabilistic factorization of non-negative data with entropic co-occurrence constraints. *ICA*.
43. Stark, J. A. (1999). *Bel Canto: A history of vocal pedagogy*. University of Toronto Press.
44. Stevens, K. N. (2005). The acoustic/articulatory interface. *Acoustical Science and Technology*, *26*(5), 410–417.
45. Vincent, E.,.Bertin, N., & Badeau, R. (2010). Adaptive harmonic spectral decomposition for multiple pitch estimation. *IEEE/ACM Transactions on Audio, Speech, and Language Processing*, *18*(3), 528–537.
46. Wang, J.-C. (2015). Singing polyphony: An Asian experience. *Music Educators Journal, 101*, 85–95.
47. Welch, G. F., Howard, D. M., & Nix, J. (2019). *The oxford handbook of singing*. Oxford Library of Psychology Series: Oxford University Press.

Rodrigo Schramm holds Bachelor (2007) and Master (2009) degrees in Computer Science from the University of the Vale do Rio dos Sinos (UNISINOS), Brazil. He received a Ph.D. degree (2015) in Computer Science from the Federal University of Rio Grande do Sul (UFRGS), Brazil, where he is currently a faculty member. Between 2013 and 2014, he was a Visiting Research Fellow at the Interdisciplinary Centre for Computer Music Research at Plymouth University, UK. In 2016, he received a Newton Research Collaboration Program Award from the Royal Academy of Engineering. He conducts research at UFRGS' Computer Music Laboratory, with focus on signal processing, pattern recognition and machine learning applied to automatic music transcription and automatic assessment of musical performances. He co-organized the Electronic Music Computing Workshop in southern Brazil (2017) and he was General Chair of the 19th Conference of New Interfaces for Musical Expression (2019). Between 2017 and 2019, he coordinated the Brazilian Committee for Music and Computing of the Brazilian Computing Society. E-mail: rschramm@ufrgs.br.

Graph-Based Representation, Analysis, and Interpretation of Popular Music Lyrics Using Semantic Embedding Features

26

Mitsunori Ogihara, Brian Manolovitz, Vítor Y. Shinohara, Gang Ren and Tiago F. Tavares

26.1 Introduction

The hearts of popular music are their lyrics. Rich in narration and emotional expression, popular music lyrics reflect the social trends and show the introspection and viewpoint of their performers [1, 2]. Lyrics is a more direct (or verbal) conversation compared to the other forms of musical expressions, together they can speak to the subtlest soul of their audience. The analysis of popular music lyrics is an intriguing research topic. Since the accessibility to the listener and the sing-ability by the singer are important constraints, the word choices in popular music are subtle and peculiar. The true meanings are hidden behind the word selection, phonetic arrangement, form, and the art of balancing the denotations and connotations [3–6]. In this chapter, we propose a systematic lyric modeling and analysis framework for popular music lyric analysis and interpretation using linguistic semantic embedding [7, 8] and network structural analysis [9–12]. We implemented various algorithms on

M. Ogihara (✉) · B. Manolovitz · G. Ren
Department of Computer Science, University of Miami, P.O.Box 248154, Coral Gables, FL 33124-4245, USA
e-mail: ogihara@cs.miami.edu

B. Manolovitz
e-mail: bmm157@miami.edu

G. Ren
e-mail: gxr467@miami.edu

V. Y. Shinohara · T. F. Tavares
School of Electrical and Computer Engineering, University of Campinas, Av. Albert Einstein, 400, Campinas 13083-852 Brazil
e-mail: vitorys@dca.fee.unicamp.br

T. F. Tavares
e-mail: tavares@dca.fee.unicamp.br

© Springer Nature Switzerland AG 2021
E. R. Miranda (ed.), *Handbook of Artificial Intelligence for Music*,
https://doi.org/10.1007/978-3-030-72116-9_26

the characterization of the distributional and structural characteristics of the linguistic patterns in the language semantic embedding space that imitates human cognition and response of music lyrics [13, 14]. Using the characterizations, we performed various empirical studies on music lyrics from different genres and time periods. The proposed lyrics analysis tool serves as a computational experimentation platform for proving the analytic concept and for exploratory analysis of lyrics patterns. It also serves as a basis for future predictive analysis implementations.

Our proposed automatic analysis framework reflects the analytic concepts from the manual lyric analysis processes but provides significant extensions on existing methodology and analysis scope. Specifically, our proposed analysis framework focuses on the structural characteristics of the temporal semantic patterns of the lyrics and uses a graph-based representation and complex network-based structural features as the modeling tool for interpreting the underlying linguistic patterns in the semantic embedding space such as structural symmetry, word distribution pattern, sequential trajectory shapes, and so on. The proposed analysis framework extends the depth and the scope of the existing manual analysis processes by providing formalized quantitative methodologies, designing and implementing new structural and statistical descriptors for lyric word sequences, and enabling us to study the lyric dataset of large scale using automatic processes.

Our proposed lyric analysis framework maps the words of the lyrics to a semantic embedding space. Using the framework, we can observe the semantic characteristics of the lyrics. The semantic space represents the geometrical relationships between the meanings of the words and uses the topological relationship to approximate the connections and the differences between the word tokens [8]. Word tokens with similar meanings are clustered together when mapped to such a semantic space, while word tokens with disparate meanings are separated further apart. By mapping the words from the lyrics into a semantic embedding space, our proposed analysis framework allows us to explore the semantic content and the contextual information of the music lyrics using quantitative approaches. The semantic embedding space represents each word as a constellation point, or a vector of location coordinates of the spatial dimensions, in the semantic embedding space. Then a sequence of words, such as lyrics in a phrase or section, is modeled as a linear trajectory connecting the points corresponding to the word tokens in the semantic embedding space. Our proposed analysis framework provides various feature descriptors for depicting the spatial distribution of the word tokens and the structural properties of the word trajectories. These feature descriptors provide a comprehensive characterization of the semantic and syntactic properties of the music lyrics. Furthermore, we implemented comparative studies of the music lyrics from different genres or production time periods and observe the differences observed from these feature descriptors.

Section 26.2 presents a review of the existing works on natural language processing, lyrics studies, and computational/empirical musicology. Section 26.3 introduces the semantic word embedding space for lyrics processing. Section 26.4 shows the proposed graph-based representations. Section 26.5 presents our graph feature extraction algorithms. Section 26.6 presents the empirical study of the lyrics from different music genres and different time periods. Section 26.7 includes the conclusion and the possible future research directions.

26.2 Key Concepts and Related Works

26.2.1 Deep Modeling of Lexical Meanings

Compared with the existing natural language processing frameworks of word semantic embedding analysis and interpretations [15–18], our proposed framework is more focused on the detailed exploration of the contextual structures of the lyric patterns. The design aim of these features is to enable meaningful linguistic pattern analysis when only a small amount of text is available. Most existing tools for word semantic embedding are designed for application scenarios where a large amount of text is the analysis target, such as online comments about consumer products, books, magazines, and newspapers. In these scenarios, the length of the texts is a few hundred or more. Because the statistical pattern of the word distribution tends to converge and stabilize [16] for the text corpus at this size, the existing analysis tools based on the statistical distributions of words produce many interesting patterns.

The analysis tasks of music lyrics aim at extracting meaningful results from short lyric excerpts with a typical length of 30–80 words. The tools we proposed are focused on the lyric analysis scale. In our proposed framework, we sort the employed text analysis tools into two different analysis scales with different target text lengths. The first analysis scale is termed the social media scale. The analysis tools at this analysis scale are tailored at the text corpus with 200 or more words for each analysis target. We termed this analysis scale the social media scale because social media is one of the most representative application targets for this type of analysis, but similar approaches can be applied to literary studies [19, 20], media studies [21], content management system analysis [22], and web database system analysis [23]. The analysis method for this analysis scale is mainly the "bag-of-word" approaches [14–16], which discard the temporal order of the word and instead calculate the distributional statistics of the words. Because the analysis target of this analysis scale usually contains enough words that aggregate enough statistical descriptors even without considering the temporal orders of the words. Our implementation includes several related feature descriptors in this analysis scale with appended methodologies from graph and complex network analysis. The second analysis scale in our implementation is termed sparse text scale, with a typical analysis target of less than 100 words. Our proposed tools are mainly focused on this scale, where more analysis resolution is demanded for limited text length.

26.2.2 Mapping Artificial Intelligence Research for Lyrics Studies

A computational implementation of lyrics analysis helps to bridge the research area of lyrics studies to other areas of Artificial Intelligence (AI) [24–27] and multimedia/multimodal data analysis [28–30]. Our current focus is to adapt highly successful tools developed or refined in the other areas of AI and machine learning and investigates their effectiveness for lyrics studies. Specifically, the computational implementation in our work enables us to bridge musicology, music theory, and lyrics studies to extremely successful "wavefront" AI research areas such as computer vision, natural language processing, and robotics [24, 25].

In recent years, these "wavefront" research areas developed or fine-tuned many high performance tools for exploratory data analysis, data mining, predictive analysis, and user interactions. Currently, the research and development in these three "wavefront" areas can be roughly categorized into four arenas as illustrated in Fig. 1.1. The first is the behavior-based research [29], where the researchers investigate the human psychological and physiological behaviors and develop models to explain them. The second is the computational implementation, where the researchers use computer hardware and software to implement many human workflows or psychological/physiological processes. The third is the human–computer interfaces. In this arena, the researchers try to mix computational elements with human psychological/physiological. The last is the deep learning research. In recent years, deep learning systems in "wavefront" areas achieved many remarkable successes in perception tasks. Figure 26.1 also includes the timeline for implementing these research areas of consecutive research phases for these three research areas, where the research focuses and their evolutions are clearly-drawn.

Fig. 26.1 Mapping the research focuses of artificial intelligence areas and comparing "wavefront" areas with lyrics studies. The wavefront areas have clearly defined research and implementation goals

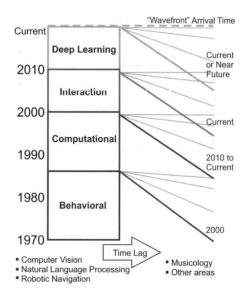

For other research areas in AI, we observe two trends in the timing of the research phases and in the topic areas of research in each phase. Most research and development areas in these directions are developed behind the "wavefront" areas with various time lags (note many exceptions, where "wavefront" areas often integrate many emerging "fast success" topics from other areas and repackage these topics into their scopes). The second trend is that the boundaries between behavioral research, computational research, interaction research, and deep learning research are becoming nebulous. Instead of a succession of rise-and-fall research phases, research areas are more consistent and interweaved.

The research focus of computational musicology [31, 32] and computational music theory [33] is very versatile and comprehensive in both depth (or completeness of investigations) and breadth (the topic area coverage). The musicology research directions on lyrics studies have complete coverage on all spectrum of artificial intelligence concepts and methodologies. Currently, lyrics studies show concentration in behavior (psychology) and computational (formal modeling, information retrieval, automatic analyses). There are many attempts on interactions (annotation, algorithmic composition, multimodal media studies) and deep learning (syntactic and structural analysis), but these directions have relatively much less footprints. In-depth, we see very complete and comprehensive or even systematic conceptual theories and empirical studies in the behavioral front. Then the coverage of research topics gradually decreases and we see more rarely-tackled areas or unexplored areas. These vacuum areas provide many exciting research opportunities for researchers in lyrics studies. Behavior areas also have more inter-area fusions where multiple research communities join forces and tackle problems in their common borders. We also see many vacuum areas between conventional defined split lines of music theory and musicology, which present ample research opportunities and promising growth of the overlapping research areas.

26.2.3 Believe in Data: Data-Driven Approaches for Lyrics Studies

Data-driven approaches [24–26] focus on the accumulation of data and the interpretation of data. Essentially, such methodologies allow data to speak, and ask the researchers to "believe in" data when data counter our intuitions and research conventions. Data-driven research methods have shown profound power in many artificial intelligence areas such as computer vision, natural language processing, biomedical and bioinformatics, and robotic navigation. A data-first approach usually brings in extremely rich research results and high research and development efficiencies compared to other research methods.

Using data-driven research methodologies, research teams can easily split tasks on data collection and data analyses. Modular approaches are easier to implement in research and development and are the preferred research management modes of modern research and development operations. Lyrics studies require prolonged investigations to produce meaningful results. A large amount of studies or implementations are required to realize a relevant concept or a convincing theory. When spliting research tasks using conventional research management instruments for a large team [34, 35], each team member still needs to invest a substantial amount of research depth in the subareas not assigned to them, in order to utilize the work contributed by their collaborators. The research management pattern in these research works shows large portions of overlapping trajectories for researchers in the same team when the tasks are performed concurrently. Modern research project management emphasizes agile workflows for enhancing the task organization and accelerating the research pace, which is difficult to implement on the conventional non-data-driven approaches.

The modular feature of data-driven approaches provides many natural and efficient task separations that can significantly accelerate research and development workflows [36]. The tasks in the data collection are naturally modular because of the easiness to split work. For data analysis, the standardization of analysis software enables modularization. The standardization of data analysis pipelines in recent years provides comprehensive implementations of the common data analysis routines: simply applying readily available data analysis packages can go a long research mileage on most data-driven research areas. Furthermore, a modular and standardized data analysis pipeline allows the researchers to borrow or exchange existing code, algorithms, and concepts. This feature prevents "reinventing the wheel" and facilitates cross-disciplinary conversations.

26.2.4 Critical Re-definition from Empirical to Experimental

The topic imbalance illustrated in the previous section also provides unique opportunities for reexamining the existing theories and practices of the more matured areas both in theory and applications [37, 38]. The research and implementation in computational areas provide unique devices for rethinking and validating the existing theory using formal or data-driven approaches. The proposed semantic word embedding framework for lyrics processing is useful for not only lyrics studies, but also for other musicological studies. In recent years, Empirical musicology has integrated more data-driven or computational elements. This trend results in a transition from empirical musicology to experimental musicology: using data and their tailor-made algorithms, more rigorous and quantitative methods can be applied to musicology. The result is a comprehensive experimental study platform for computational musicology. This transition from empirical musicology to experimental musicology opens many new doors to unexplored territories in musicology, while allowing existing theory and practice to be tested (and unambiguous verified or falsified), expanding the scopes and depth of existing studies (e.g., tackling large-scale data sets or complex feature dimensions).

Integrating the methodologies of experimental studies to lyrics analyses is essential to modernize the lyrics analyses in multiple ways. Most existing studies on music lyrics lack the test and verification elements because of the difficulty to conduct verification. Follow-up studies of new ideas tend to build upon the new ideas, by performing different interpretations, expansion, and reinforcement, without going through experimental verifications. The recent proliferation of critical theory reopens many research avenues for reexamination with experimentation [39–41]. Our implementation is one step towards this direction by providing experimental platforms that are very different from the conventional methodologies in art and humanities. Our proposed framework also includes transparent data and pattern interfaces, allowing flexible integrations of data-driven approaches with existing methods. We promote a view that the diversification of approaches helps a research area proliferate and take healthy growth paths.

26.3 Semantic Word Embedding

The lyrics in our proposed modeling approach are first processed using the semantic word embedding framework of Global Vectors for Word Representation (GloVe) [7, 8]. The concept of semantic word embedding is based on the dependencies of the meaning of a word and the words that surround it. By explicitly modeling the contextual semantic embedding of words in a language corpus, word embedding can reliably show the relationship between the meaning of words as geometrical relationships. Most semantic word embedding frameworks such as Word2Vec [42, 43] and GloVe [7, 8] can also provide satisfactory geometric modeling relationships of a diverse range of natural language concepts such as the parallel relationship between "cat -> tiger" and "dog -> wolf". Words with similar meanings are allocated together, while words with disparate meanings are allocated further apart.

These semantic word embedding frameworks provide quantitative methods for exploring linguistic meanings for various text analysis tasks [7, 8]. In our implementation, each analysis target (the music lyrics of a song) is usually short in length and thus impractical to aggregate robust frequency counts as statistical patterns when the words are only treated as meaningless tokens. By mapping the lyric words into the semantic embedding space, the sparse word length in the lyric dataset is amplified by the semantic representation of words and the complex semantic relationships of the words. This semantic word embedding step provides a boost of information in the lyric modeling and representation stage that benefits the subsequent feature extraction and pattern interpretation stages.

In the processing step of semantic word embedding, the embedding space is adapted from the word embedding models trained on the text corpus other than the music lyrics. For example, many such word embedding models are trained from online articles [7, 8]. These word embedding models do not necessarily reflect the text usage patterns in the musical lyrics and thus limit the representation power of our proposed analysis framework. On the other hand, a word embedding model solely trained on a large text corpus of music lyrics will be severely limited in the representation scope by the topics and the linguistic inclinations of the lyrics selected. For example, many word relationships are better reflected in ordinary articles than in music lyrics such as the semantic representation of emotion-related words [8]. Thus, a combination of lyrics induced word embedding space and existing word embedding models will further enable the representational flexibilities for lyrics analysis.

In our implementation, the musical lyrics are first mapped to a word token sequence. The token index number is just an assigned number unique to each word but without specific meaning. Then the token sequence is translated into the constellation points in the semantic word embedding space using the GloVe framework. The semantic embedding process assigns specific linguistic meanings to each word token in the token sequences. From this modeling step, each lyric is represented as a chain of constellation points in the semantic word embedding space. An example of the embedding process is presented in Fig. 26.2. Each node represents the semantic coordinates of a word in the semantic word embedding space. Each edge between two adjacent words shows the sequential relationships in the lyrics. In this visualization, the start and the end directions are not specifically annotated but it is retained in the sequential token representation as the "lyrics travel" directional tags. These directional tags will be utilized in many feature descriptors in the following processing stages.

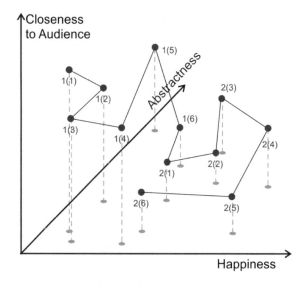

Fig. 26.2 Example of a lyric chain in the semantic word embedding space. The word tokens in a song are the blue dots and the trajectory show their temporal order. The projection of each word token dot is also plotted as the gray-colored dots and projection lines. Each semantic dimension is provided with an axis label as the interpretations obtained from key words locations in that dimension

26.4 Appending Relational Links

Our implementation also appends several groups of attachment edges to the graph representation by specifying many types of relationships between the word tokens as additional graph edges between various constellation points in the semantic embedding space. Later these additional edges allow us to use feature descriptors based on complex network terminologies [9–12] to summarize the relationships between the word tokens. By transforming the additional information such as the relationships of nodes or the properties of a graph into additional edges, the additional information is embedded into the appended graph structure, which is useful for both feature extraction using complex network methodology and for visualization.

A similar approach is applied extensively in molecular biology [44] and organic chemistry [45], where various types of forces between atoms are appended as graph edges in the structural representation of molecules. For example, the basic edges of these structures are the strong link between atoms, which is parallel to the "hard" temporal edges of our proposed lyric representation. Then the weak forces between the structural elements are responsible for the folding mechanisms of the molecules and subsequently their biological and chemical function and properties. These weak forces are usually modeled as the additional links upon the basic edges to emphasize the interactions between structural elements.

In our proposed lyric analysis framework, we provided several options to append these relational edges to the chain structure of the musical lyrics. The following relational links can be appended separately or in combination, depending on the settings of the feature extraction algorithm in the next section or the visualization preference settings.

26.4.1 Appending Similarity Links

The most obvious way to append the relational links is to connect between any pairs of word tokens that are allocated near to each other in the semantic embedding space, i.e., words that have similar meanings according to the interpretations of the selected semantic embedding space. In our implementation, we first calculate the average edge number for each node and then add in the similarity links to the point that the average number for each node doubles. Alternatively, we also set the threshold to 2/3 of the average value of the similarity values between any two nodes (words) in all graphs of an analysis (high value means that the two nodes are similar). A pair of nodes with a similarity value higher than this threshold is appended with a similarity link. The above two threshold values are designed to ensure that enough new edges are appended to the basic lyric graph so that the appended graph is significantly different from the basic lyric graph. At the same time, these settings prevent the graph from turning into fully connected. For graph or complex network-based representations, a fully connected graph carries little or no information because full connection and zero connection are two polar null statuses of a graph [9]. The information in a graph builds up either as a process of appending edges from non-connected graphs or as a process of eliminating edges from fully connected graphs. Most feature descriptors proposed in our analysis framework also perform the best when the connectedness of the graph is in the middle range.

26.4.2   Appending Lyric Structural Links

The music lyrics have many types of the structural elements such as the song forms and the narrative structures. In our implementation, we provide the options to include two types of the song form structures that are uniform to all the lyrics disregard the difference of song forms. The first type of the song structure links is the parallel structural links between two lyric sentences. We assume that the adjacent sentences are connected to each other as the composition intention [13] and add in edges for nodes in the same relative locations of the music lyric. An illustration of this edge appending process is shown in Fig. 26.3, where we append the song form links starting from the lyric tokens in the shorter phrase. We first connect the beginning and the ending words of the phrases. Then we connect the center words if available. We then add in the connection links in the middle part of the lyric segments in the same manner by connecting the middle words and leaving the blanks in the longer phrase evenly. Several extreme cases of length imbalance are also presented in Fig. 26.4. In these imbalanced cases, the edge appending priority is the head word, the tail word, and then the middle word, which provides a relative even lattice of connection that depicts the conceptual connections between music phrases.

The second type of song form link is the parallel link between the blocks (paragraphs) of the lyrics. This link is based on the structural similarity of the lyrics at similar relative locations in the adjacent blocks of the lyrics. For each lyric block, we attach the beginning, ending, and the middle point of each text block to the corresponding text locations in the adjacent text block by appending the relational link edges. Then we repeat this linking process by adding the link edges at the middle points for the two intervals between the beginning and the middle point and between the middle point and the ending. The depth of this link appending process is provided as a parameter for tuning the balance between the emphasis of phrase level connections and the block level connections. In this chapter, we maintain a similar number of edges appended at these two levels for simplicity but this parameter can be adjusted according to the emphasis of analysis at different time scales or tailored to the lyric corpus.

For both types of song form links, we also provide an option to add in the closure links between the beginning and the ending points of the structural elements. The connections of these structural units are caused by the prevalence of arc-shaped tension-relaxation structures in the music lyrics. For example, the beginning and the ending part of a lyric phrase are more similar and connected

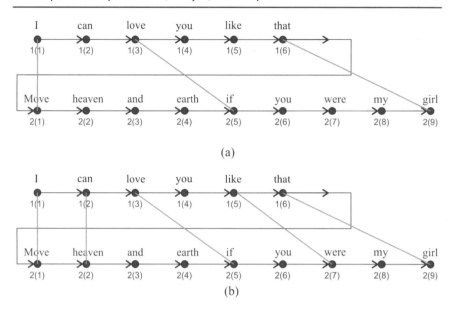

Fig. 26.3 Examples for adding in phrase structure links on top of the temporal links. The blue colored lines are the temporal links of the lyric. Then we append the orange colored structural links to depict the mapping locations in the adjacent music phrase. **a** Appends head, middle, and tail links, then **b** adds in more links in the intervals

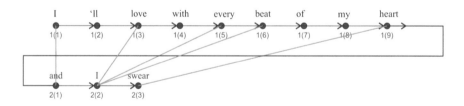

Fig. 26.4 Example for adding in structural links for imbalanced phrase length. The tokens in the shorter phrase are mapped to more tokens while keeping the blank tokens evenly distributed

compared with the middle part. And so are the lyric blocks: the first phrase is usually closely connected to the last phrase in a block. Although in many lyric excerpts some parts will not always obey this structure. The prevalence of such structure warrants its usefulness in most analysis scenarios.

26.4.3 Adjacency to the Key Analysis Concepts

This option enables the algorithm to append in the connection edges between word tokens if they are in the adjacent region of a word token that belongs to the key concept of lyric analysis such as common theme (love, car, people, life, etc.) or key emotion (happy, sad, angry, etc.) For each key concept token and a preset semantic radius in the word semantic embedding space, a word token is assumed to belong to the key concept token group if its constellation is within the radius. For the words in the key concept token group, we first calculate their weight center and then select a word token nearest to the weight center as the central words for this group. Then we add in key analysis concept link from each other word in the group to the central word.

26.5 Details of Feature Descriptors

The feature descriptors are designed for modeling the semantic characteristics of the lyrics from the spatial distribution of the word tokens and the topological relationships among word tokens. The descriptors are categorized into three types. The type I descriptors do not consider the sequential order of the word tokens. Instead, the word tokens are treated as scattered constellation points in the word embedding space. The feature descriptors of this type depict the "cloud shape" of the word tokens in the text embedding space such as the maximum distance between any two-word tokens, the symmetry of the word distribution shape, and the evenness of word token distribution in the semantic word embedding space. The type II descriptors emphasize the temporal order of the word token and extract the structural features from the chain structure, such as adjacent word distance, smoothed adjacent word distance, high order word distance (semantic distance between alternative words or every three words), the angles between adjacent vertices, smoothed vertex angles, and high order vertex angles. The type III descriptors are extracted from the lyric graph with appended structural edges. This type of descriptors is mostly the network topological descriptors rooted from the complex network literature such as the average number of edges and the symmetrical balance of edge distribution.

26.5.1 Spatial Distribution Based Features

26.5.1.1 Centroid Location
This feature dimension calculates the center locations of all word tokens in a lyric. Suppose the specific lyric includes tokens $\{e_i | i = 1, \cdots, p\}$ with locations in the word semantic space as $\{S(e_i) | i = 1, \cdots, p\}$, then the center location is calculated as

$$S_c = \sum_{i=1}^{p} S(e_i) W(e_i) \tag{26.1}$$

where $W(e_i)$ is a weight factor for token e_i. We can assign all $W(e_i)$ to "1" so all tokens are treated as the same. Alternatively, we can assign $W(e_i)$ to decay from the start of the lyrics towards to end of the lyric to account for the narrative focus and the audience attention pattern [34].

26.5.1.2 Span Volume and Dispersion Between Semantic Word Embedding Dimensions

This feature depicts the width of the "lyric cloud" of a song in all directions. For each semantic embedding dimension g, suppose the distance between the widest separated two points is d_g, then the span volume is calculated as

$$V = 10^{\frac{1}{G}\sum_{g=1}^{G}\log 10^{d_g}} \tag{26.2}$$

where G is the number of dimensions in the semantic embedding. We apply this average method, instead of calculating the multiplication of the span of all dimensions, to suppress the influence of extremely large or small span values in certain feature dimensions. To cope with the outliners of the text token distribution, we also provide an option to calculate d_g as the interquartile range (the distance between the 25% percentile and the 75% percentile points) of the text token distribution in the semantic embedding dimension g. Because this option suppressed the extremely large values of the lyric span, the span volume is calculated as the summation of the d_g value in all semantic embedding dimensions.

$$V = \sum_{g=1}^{G} d_g \tag{26.3}$$

The dispersion measurement P_g calculates the standard deviation of the text token distribution on each semantic word embedding dimension g. A high standard deviation indicates that the word tokens span a longer semantic distance in that dimension. Optionally, we can also calculate the interquartile range q_g of the token distributions of each dimension g. Then we calculate the statistical parameters such as the mean and the standard deviation across the dimensions of the semantic word embedding space for each song.

26.5.1.3 Maximum Semantic Span

This parameter is calculated as the distance between the two most distant word tokens from the lyrics in semantic word embedding space. The distance of token e_i and e_j is calculated as

$$D(e_i, e_j) = \text{sqrt}\left[\sum_{d=1}^{D} (e_{i,d} - e_{j,d})^2\right] \tag{26.4}$$

where *sqrt* denotes the square root function, $e_{i,d}$ is the d-th dimension of token e_i, in the semantic word embedding space. D is the total number of dimensions of the semantic embedding space. Then the maximum semantic span is calculated as the maximum distance between any pairs of tokens in a lyric

$$D_{\max} = \text{Max}_{\in i,j} D(e_i, e_j) \qquad (26.5)$$

26.5.1.4 Semantic Span Distribution

To mitigate the effect of outliers in the semantic span between word tokens, we also calculate the percentiles of pairwise distances between the word token pairs. Suppose the distances of all pairs are denoted as $D = \{D(e_i, e_j) | \text{for all } i, j\}$. The percentile point η for D as $\text{prc}(D, \eta)$ means the number of $D(e_i, e_j)$ values smaller than $\text{prc}(D, \eta)$ is smaller than the η proportion of all pair numbers

$$\text{Num}[D(e_i, e_j) < \text{prc}(D, \eta)] < \eta \text{Num}[D(e_i, e_j) | \text{for all } i, j] \qquad (26.6)$$

where Num function counts the total number of the token pairs that satisfy the condition. In our implementation, we use η values of 0.7 and 0.85 as percentile feature descriptors.

26.5.1.5 Semantic Span Imbalance Among Semantic Embedding Dimensions

This group of feature descriptors calculates the difference between the semantic span in different directions of the semantic word embedding space. The distance between token e_i and e_j in semantic embedding dimension d is calculated as

$$\text{dist}(e_i, e_j, d) = |e_{i,d} - e_{j,d}| \qquad (26.7)$$

where $|\bullet|$ denotes absolute value.

For each semantic embedding dimension d, we calculate the percentile points for $\eta = 0.7$ and for $\eta = 0.85$ as $\text{dist}_{\text{prc}}(d, \eta)$. Then we calculate the range and the standard deviation for $\{\text{dist}_{\text{prc}}(d, \eta), d \in D_{\text{SE}}\}$, D_{SE} as the total number of dimensions in the semantic word embedding space.

The variance value of the semantic word embedding space such as Word2Vec and GloVe is not fully normalized; instead, the higher dimensions usually have a lower variance in coordinate value similar to the variance decay in principle component analysis [46] or independent component analysis [47]. Thus, the distribution patterns calculated from different feature dimensions are not at the same scale. However, because our analysis employs the same semantic word embedding space for all analysis tasks, the offsets caused by the scaling between feature dimensions are consistent and will not affect the comparison between lyric graphs. Thus, for simplicity, we directly apply the semantic word embedding space to the lyrics mapping without changing the scales, although alternatively, we can also calibrate the variance between semantic embedding dimensions using a sample lyric set.

26.5.1.6   Token Distributional Symmetry Based Descriptors

This group of descriptor depicts the symmetry of the unordered distribution shape of word tokens. We first choose an arbitrary word token as the center of the word token distribution. Suppose the center token we selected is located at $(C_1, C_2, \cdots, C_D)$ in the word semantic space, the mirror point for $(e_{i,1}, e_{i,2}, \cdots, e_{i,D})$ is $(2C_1 - e_{i,1}, 2C_2 - e_{i,2}, \cdots, 2C_D - e_{i,D})$. Then we calculate the mirror points for the lyric tokens except for the token selected as the center point.

Suppose the mirror points for the word tokens are denoted as $(\overline{e}_{j,1}, \overline{e}_{j,2}, \cdots, \overline{e}_{j,D})$, for each mirror point, we pair it with the nearest token in the lyric token points $(e_{i,1}, e_{i,2}, \cdots, e_{i,D})$ and calculate their distances.

In our implementation, we use a heuristic approach for pairing mirror tokens with the source tokens by taking a point from the mirror tokens, finding the nearest point in the source tokens, and then removing the paired source token from the group of candidate source tokens for the following pairing steps. The mean mirror point distance, the mean value of all distances of the paired mirror tokens and the source tokens, is a measurement of the symmetry of the token distribution shape. A smaller value of the mean mirror point distance indicates that the folded token distribution "cloud" relatively overlaps with the source token distribution, thus indicating a more symmetrical form with the reference central point. Then we iteratively choose all token points within a preset radius of the centroid location as the central point and use the lowest mean mirror point distance as the symmetrical measurements. Alternatively, we provide an option to choose the centroid location as the center point and then calculate the mean mirror point distance without iteration.

26.5.2   Temporal Structure-Based Features

26.5.2.1   Average Step Size

The average step size is the mean value of the distance between the successive word tokens in the lyric chain in the semantic word embedding space. This feature descriptor depicts the semantic span in the temporal direction. Because this feature descriptor considers the temporal order, it shows different structural characteristics compared to the unordered spatial descriptors in the previous section. For example, a song with the lyrics of alternating words of very different emotion concepts will show a high value of the average step size, because the trajectory of the lyric chain zigzags through the semantic word embedding space even when the tip points do not move too far from each other. In the contrast, a song with gradual and small semantic steps but the consistent movement towards one direction shows a low value of the average step size. Without considering the temporal order of the sequence, the constellations of word tokens in these two examples might show a similar spatial distribution pattern.

Fig. 26.5 Using moving templates for calculating smoothed lyric chain. The red color template 1 only moves one step from and overlapping four steps from the green color template 2. The smoothed spatial locations are plotted as the red dot (T1) and the green dot (T2)

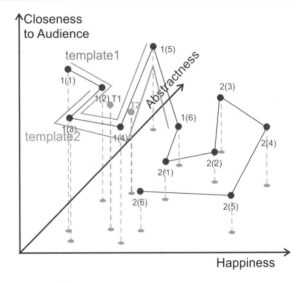

Our implementation also provides high order descriptors for the average step size by only considering tokens in every alternative step as the second order average step size or evenly sampling a single word token from every three word tokens as the third order average step size. The high order descriptors capture the variations of the token locations at different variation rates, similar to the filters in signal process capturing the signal variation at different frequency bands [48].

The high order descriptors for the average step size can be combined with various smoothing operations on the word token coordinates or on the step size sequences. When the smoothing operation is performed on the coordinates of the consecutive word tokens, we implement a moving template as in Fig. 26.5 for calculating the average coordinates of the word tokens within the template. This moving template only shifts one temporal step at one time. The average of the coordinates in every dimension of the semantic word embedding space is calculated as the smoothed constellation points for feature extraction. A moving template with long length yields a smoother lyric chain because the local variations tend to cancel each other better when more token points are summed up. The option for smoothing the step size sequence can be based on a similar moving average smoothing or by convolving a smooth function with the step size sequence. The smoothing operation yields similar results with the high order descriptors by emphasizing the variations of the temporal lyric chain at a certain time scale while suppressing the variations at other time scales.

26.5.2.2 Variation Pattern of the Step Size

This feature dimension calculates the standard deviation of the maximum step, the minimum step, and the range of the step sizes (difference between the maximum and minimum step) of the step size from the lyric chain of a song or from its smoothed versions. A smaller value of this feature dimension means that each step size in the lyric chain is similar in length, i.e., the temporal step size of the lyric chain is even.

26.5.2.3 Average Adjacent Edge Angles

The angles between the adjacent edges in the lyric chain show the change of directions in the semantic embedding space. The average adjacent edge angles is the mean absolute value of the angles between adjacent edges in a song

$$A_g = \frac{1}{Q} \sum_{g=1}^{Q} |\theta_g| \tag{26.8}$$

where $|\bullet|$ denotes absolute value. Q is the number of edges in the lyric chain. θ_g is the transition angle at the gth node in the range of $(-\pi, \pi]$.

Similar to the high order descriptors and the smoothing option for the average step size features, we also provide options for sampling the nodes in the lyric chain or for smoothing the lyric chain and the adjacent edge angle sequence. These high order descriptors and smoothing options enable us to observe the time variation at different time scales from the transient angles of the lyric chain.

26.5.2.4 Variations of Adjacent Edge Angles

This feature dimension calculates the standard deviation of the adjacent edge angles in the lyric chain. The lyric chain with the relative uniform value of the adjacent edge angles will have a smaller value. For this descriptor, the angle values are in the $(-\pi, \pi]$ range and we calculate their absolute values before calculating the standard deviations.

26.5.2.5 Mean of Adjacent Edge Angle Increment

The value of the adjacent edge angle increment is calculated as the difference of the edge angles $\theta(i)$ between two consecutive nodes in the lyric chain

$$I_{ea}(i) = |\theta(i) - \theta(i-1)| \tag{26.9}$$

where i denotes the index of the edge angles, and $|\bullet|$ is the operation for taking the absolute value. Then we calculate the mean value of $I_{ea}(i)$ for a song from each of its temporal steps in the lyric chain.

26.5.2.6 Skip Length Descriptors

The skip length descriptor is calculated as the Euclidean distance between the semantic embedding coordinates of adjacent. Hence, high values represent large semantic skips, whereas low values represent small semantic skips.

A large mean is related to lyrics whose words quickly change meaning, indicating possible metaphors, while a small mean is related to lyrics whose words are semantically related, indicating storytelling [6, 7]. A similar interpretation holds for the maximum and minimum step size lengths.

Furthermore, a large standard deviation of the step sizes can indicate that the lyrics switch between metaphors and storytelling, whereas a small standard deviation suggests lyrics whose mood is more constant. The same interpretation holds for the range of the step sizes, which is the difference between the maximum and minimum step size of a song.

26.5.2.7 Symmetric Pattern of the Lyric Chain

A similar feature descriptor for the measurement of symmetry is also implemented for the lyric chain. Different from the symmetry descriptor implemented earlier for the unordered spatial word token distribution, which only counts the overlapping of word tokens and its mirror images in the semantic word embedding space, the symmetry descriptor for the lyric chains also considers the temporal edges between the connecting token nodes. The measurement of the symmetric pattern for the chain nodes is identical to the measurement method employed for spatial word token distributions. From this, we add in a measurement of the symmetric pattern for the connecting edges in the lyric chain. One edge in the lyric chain is modeled as the location of its two nodes location. We first calculate the spatial locations of the mirror nodes and then try to find the nearest two token nodes with the right edge direction. Here the right edge direction means two mirror direction modes of either directions similar $\left(\text{within}\left(-\frac{\pi}{2}, \frac{\pi}{2}\right)\right)$ to the mirror nodes or directions similar to the reversed direction of the mirror nodes (in $\left[-\pi, -\frac{\pi}{2}\right]$ or $\left[\frac{\pi}{2}, \pi\right)$ angles of the mirror edge). The algorithm tries both modes and calculates the distance of the edge-attached nodes and the angles between the token edge and the mirror edge (reversed direction in the second mode). Then the aligned edges are removed and this heuristic process repeats for the other edges. The overall symmetric measurement is the sum of the aligned node distances, aligned edge distances, and the sinusoidal values of the angles between the token edge and the mirror edges. For the latter two terms, we compare the value obtained from the two edge reversal modes (using mirror edge or using reversed mirror edge) and choose the lower value.

26.5.3 Feature Descriptor for Graph Topology

26.5.3.1 Average Node Connectedness

For a lyric graph (lyric chain with appended relational links), the connectedness of each node (word token) is calculated as the number of edges attached to the node. In the context of complex network analysis, this number is termed as the degree of the node but for here we opt a simpler terminology. The average connectedness is calculated as the average number of edge numbers of all the nodes in the lyric graph.

Nodes with dense connections will dominantly decide the value of the average connectedness by masking off the nodes with sparse connections. To mitigate this masking effect, we provide an option to saturate the edge count of any node to a top-off number. Typical such numbers are 9, 15, and 20, depending on the density of the lyric graph edges in the densest part of the graph and the contrast of edge numbers between the dense nodes and the sparse nodes.

26.5.3.2   Variation of Node Connectedness

This feature describes the divergence of node connectedness among all nodes in a lyric graph and is calculated as the standard deviation of the edge numbers of the nodes in the lyric graph. Similar to the previous feature descriptor, large values of edge number in a few "popular" nodes will mask off the sensitivity of the dynamic range of this feature descriptor in the low and middle range of the edge numbers. A similar saturation mechanism is provided as an option for topping off the high edge number nodes and reveals the patterns in the low and middle range of the edge number distribution.

26.5.3.3   Topological Balance of Node Connectedness

This feature descriptor is similar to the symmetry descriptor for the spatial token node distribution. We calculate the image points of the token nodes from a center point. Then each token node is paired with the nearest image node. Then we calculate their difference of the connected edge number as the imbalance measurement for these two nodes. Then we remove these two nodes and repeat this process. The mean value of the imbalance measurements for all nodes is selected as the imbalance descriptor of the node connectedness.

26.5.3.4   Page Rank Descriptor

Besides the node connectedness, another descriptor for topological connectedness is the page rank descriptor [10–12], which quantifies the significance of the node using an iterative importance distribution algorithm that assigns more significance to a node connected to more number of nodes and more significant nodes. This feature descriptor can be source back to the web page ranking for online search engines. Web pages connected to a large number of other web pages are not necessarily the most significant web pages according to the PageRank algorithm. Instead, this algorithm emphasizes the role of the connected significant web pages' contribution to the significance of the page under measurement. We will not cover the algorithm in detail because it is covered nicely in [10, 11]. In practice, page rank descriptors and plain node connectedness descriptors are often applied together to analysis problems because they usually show very different distribution patterns.

26.5.3.5   Distribution of Edge Angles

The edge angles are the angles of the adjoining edges at token nodes. Because multiple edges might intersect on the same node, the edge angles of these edges can be measured in multiple ways by pairing different edges for the angle measurements. In our implementation, we employ a heuristic approach that first imposes an artificial order to the edges according to their tip node indices. Then we pick the first edge (edge with the smallest index number) and select one edge from the adjoining edges with the minimum intersection angle. Then we remove both the edges from the graph and start the same process again from the remaining edges with the smallest index number.

The feature descriptors are the mean and the standard deviation of the edge angles. We also provide an option for calculating the skewness and the kurtosis of the edge angles.

26.5.3.6 Graph Symmetry Descriptors

This feature descriptor is similar to the symmetric measurement of the lyric chain except for two points: first, all edges here are treated as undirected and thus the two edge reversal modes are not necessary; second, the angles between the aligned edges are simply the smallest angle using any one edge/direction as the start point and the other edge/direction as the end point, so the range is always within $\left[0, \frac{\pi}{2}\right]$.

26.5.3.7 Connection Topological Symmetry Based on Betweenness Centrality

The graph's connectedness can be decoupled from the text token location in the semantic word embedding space by analyzing only the connection topology instead of the combined graph topology of token locations and connections. For example, the connection center of a graph is where most other nodes can be reached easily, which is not necessarily the geometrical center of the graph.

Our implementation provides the feature descriptors based on the graph concept of betweenness. Betweenness is the property that one node or a subpart of a graph is in the shortest connection path between the other two nodes in the graph [5]. In an unweighted graph, where each node is equal in status and the distance is only determined by the connection step disregarding the difference of step sizes, the measurements related to betweenness provide a way to algorithmically measure the graph connections while not considering the nodes' locations. First, we heuristically find the shortest connection paths (the minimum number of hops in between) between any two pairs of nodes in the graph. Then for each node, we calculate the number of such shortest connection paths that pass it as the betweeness centrality count. If this count is large, this means it is in the connection topological center of the graph, similar to airline hubs with high traffic (airline hubs are more towards a population weighted betweenness center). We then compute the mean and the standard deviation of the betweenness centrality count of all nodes in a song as the feature descriptors.

26.5.4 Feature Descriptors on Graph Spectra and Other Analytical Graph Representations

26.5.4.1 Matrix Decomposition Based Descriptors

The matrix decomposition of the graph connection matrix shows the elementary components of the graph topology. Similar to Fourier transform, which decomposes complex signals into simpler signal components. The matrix decomposition method applied in this chapter is eigen-decomposition. Eigen-decomposition is a spectral decomposition that factorizes a matrix into canonical components. The original matrix is the combination of these canonical components. Each such component is associated with eigenvalues and eigenvectors. The eigenvalue is the strength of that component and the eigenvector is the topological graph matrix of that component.

The feature descriptor on eigenvector first calculates the magnitude of each eigenvector $E_1 = [e_{1,1}, e_{1,2}, \ldots, e_{1,D}]$ as the square root of each dimension

$$\text{mag}(E_1) = \sqrt{e_{1,1}^2 + e_{1,2}^2 + \ldots + e_{1,D}^2} \qquad (26.10)$$

Then we calculate the mean and the standard deviation of the magnitudes of the eigenvectors

$$\text{mean}(E) = \text{mean}(\text{mag}(E_1), \text{mag}(E_2), \ldots, \text{mag}(E_N)) \qquad (26.11)$$

$$\text{std}(E) = \text{std}(\text{mag}(E_1), \text{mag}(E_2), \ldots, \text{mag}(E_N)) \qquad (26.12)$$

The mean here is interpreted as the complexity of the graphical components as simpler graph components will have less connection, thus have a smaller means magnitude. The standard deviation shows the diversity of the constituent graphical components.

26.5.4.2 Root Mean Square of Spectra Span Volume

This feature descriptor depicts the spectral volume for each lyric. First, we use the GloVe word vector representation to compute a vector for each word in the lyric. Then we calculate all the pairwise distances from the lyric vectors as the distance matrix $M_1 = [C_{1,1}, C_{1,2}, \ldots, C_{1,p}]$. Then we select the large distances only using a threshold η to form a span matrix $M_2 = [C_{2,1}, C_{2,2}, \ldots, C_{2,p}]$ as

$$C_{2,i} = C_{1,i}; \text{if } \text{mag}(C_{1,i}) > \eta \qquad (26.13)$$

$$C_{2,i} = 0; \text{if } \text{mag}(C_{1,i}) \leq \eta$$

where mag() calculates the root mean square of all components of a vector. The threshold η is obtained as the topological minimum spanning tree distance by calculating the average size of the minimum spanning tree size in a lyric. We first compute the minimum spanning tree from word vectors in a lyric. The tree size for each lyric is calculated as the maximum distance between any two nodes in the minimum spanning tree. After computing the tree size for each song lyric in the dataset, the average of the tree sizes is calculated as the threshold.

The root mean square of spectra span value is calculated as a weighted average of the global magnitudes of M_1 and M_2. By averaging the magnitudes in all topological components and the large components (large trees)

$$\text{RMS}(M_1, M_1) = \alpha_1 \sqrt{g_{1,1}^2 + g_{1,2}^2 + \ldots + g_{1,p}^2} + \alpha_2 \sqrt{g_{2,1}^2 + g_{2,2}^2 + \ldots + g_{2,p}^2}$$

(26.14)

where $g_{1,i} = mag(C_{1,i})$. As a simplification we select $\alpha_1 = \alpha_2 = 0.5$. This method measures the span of the graph more robustly as smaller components also contribute to a large amount of spectra energy and their presences might overwhelm the magnitudes of the larger components.

26.6 Empirical Studies

For empirical studies, we apply our proposed feature descriptors to the lyrics of four different music genres of country, hip-hop, pop, and rock. Our studies are based on the MetroLyrics dataset [49], which is available on Kaggle. The dataset contains 380,000 music lyrics. Each lyric is tagged according to its music genre and the year. We segment the music lyrics as subgroups according to their genre labels and the year labels. Then we extract and compare the feature descriptor distributions across these genre categories. We analyzed 2,000 songs for each subgroup. For each analysis task, we first perform manual checks and corrections for the lyrics of the selected songs. Then we eliminate meaningful words or phonetic tokens not presented in the GloVe framework. Then each song is modeled as a sequence of word tokens in the semantic word embedding space for graph structure forming and feature extraction. We presented two groups of studies. The first group of studies explores the distributional patterns of the proposed graphical semantic features at different genre categories. Then the second group of studies explores the distributional pattern across genres with time range split on different periods during which the music was produced.

Previous research in lyric-based genre identification has found that particular words are more common to specific genres. Slangs and curse words, for example, are found more frequently in Hip-Hop [50]. The nouns related to lifestyles in rural farms are frequent in Country music [51]. Although statistically valid, these word distributional patterns cannot be considered as definitive characteristics of genre because of a large amount of exceptions and constant innovations of composers and lyrics writers [52]. Our studies aim at enhancing the categorical analysis of this line of research by applying semantic-based analysis methods to the genre categorization tasks as alternative method for genre classification, as well as exploratory analysis for initial conceptualization and empirical studies.

26.6.1 Studies on Distributional Patterns Over Genre Categories

Figure 26.6 shows the distributional patterns of lyrics according to the four genre categories for 20 representative feature dimensions. The feature dimension indices are:

1. Maximum semantic span
2. Dispersion between semantic word embedding dimensions: average
3. Dispersion between semantic word embedding dimensions: standard deviation
4. Average step size
5. Step size: standard deviation
6. Maximum step size
7. Maximum step size minus minimum step size'
8. Average node connectedness
9. Node connectedness: standard deviation'
10. Page rank: mean
11. Page rank: standard deviation
12. Number of connected components
13. Number of nodes in smallest connected components
14. Average edge weight
15. Percentage of nodes with zero edges
16. Eigenvector: mean
17. Eigenvector: standard deviation
18. Root mean square
19. Span volume
20. Average adjacent edge angles.

Figure 26.7 shows the Analysis of Variance (ANOVA) results and their multiple comparisons (e.g., comparing Rock with Country, then comparing Rock with Pop, etc.). In the box plots in Fig. 26.6, the four boxes in each group represent the

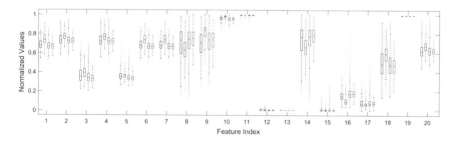

Fig. 26.6 Distributional patterns of lyrics according to the four genre categories for 20 representative feature dimensions. Each box group includes one box for each genre: Pop, Hip-hop, Rock, and Country. The separation of genres for each feature dimension is easy to observe

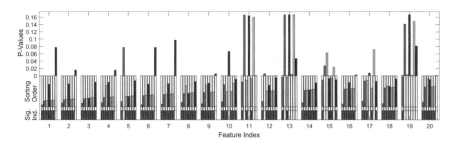

Fig. 26.7 Analysis of Variance (ANOVA) results and their multiple comparisons. Most comparison groups show very high statistical significance both for a group and for pairwise comparisons

feature values from the feature dimension indicated by the feature index below. For each group, the four boxes correspond to the genre categories of Pop, Hip-hop, Rock, and Country. Each box's central line indicates the median. The top edge indicates the 75th percentile. The bottom edge indicates the 25th percentile. The distance between the top and the bottom edges is the interquartile range. The whiskers further extend 1.5 times the interquartile range from the top and the bottom edges. Data points outside the whiskers are considered outliers and plotted as gray colored dots.

The upper part of Fig. 26.7 shows the distribution of P-values for ANOVA tests for the four genre groups for each dimension as the first entry in each 7-grid group. Note many P-values are very small so it is not shown at the magnitude scale but the grid below zero magnitude serves as placeholders. For ANOVA tests, a lower P-value indicates higher statistical significance. For example, a P-value of 0.05 indicates that the pattern can only occur in average 5 times in 100 experiments if generating from random data [53, 54]. A low P-value means the feature values of the four genres are well-separated, the statistical proof that the corresponding feature dimension is a strong indicator of the genre information. The grids at the bottom of the figure show the significance indicators. An empty grid indicates not significant, whereas red, green, and blue indicate statistically significant, as follows. The blue color means the feature dimension is more significant than the significance level of 0.05 after Bonferroni correction [55], which means "significant". The green color means more significant than 0.005 after Bonferroni correction, indicating "very strong" proof. The red color is at 0.001 "overwhelming" significant level, the strongest proof among these three indicators.

The middle grid shows the ranking order for the P-values from the significance indicator grid below. These significant feature/multiple-test dimensions have small P-values so they are not shown at the upper-half P-value plot. This ranking order grid uses a small value to show more significant (small) values but the values here only reflect the sequential sorting order of all significant values by linearly interpolating the sorting order. This sorting order view compresses and normalizes the dynamic range of small P-values so that they can be plotted together for visual comparison.

Each seven-bar group in Fig. 26.7 shows the P-values for a feature dimension. The first bar is the P-value for testing whether the feature data from the four genres are the same (strictly, have a common mean [53]). The following six bars test pairwise genres. The genre categories are encoded as "1-Pop", "2- Hip-hop", "3-Rock", and "4-Country". The following six bars correspond to genre comparison pairs of "1–2", "1–3", "1–4", "2–3", "2–4", and "3–4".

Our results show that Country and Rock lyrics typically use similar semantic structures. We observe significant distributional differences in their semantic span, their number of connected components, and their average step sizes. However, Country and Rock music lyrics typically focus on different themes [56], and the songs have different instrumentation [57–59]. Such similarities and differences can be linked to the history of Country and Rock, which were both rooted in Blues and Bluegrass in the beginning of the twentieth Century, a time period with different music composition practices of different functions (e.g., more narrative functions [60–62]). These music genres commonly have lyrics that tell coherent stories, which lead to a lower semantic span, number of connected components, and average step sizes.

Hip-Hop lyrics show different structural characteristics from the other genres, for example, larger semantic step sizes in Hip-Hop lyrics than the lyrics from the other genres. This difference can be attributed to the origins of hip-hop lyrics. Of course, the embedding space was built using standard English texts with an encyclopedia type content. In opposition to that, the language used in Hip-Hop frequently uses slangs, curse words, and non-standard grammar [50]. As a consequence, Hip-Hop lyrics present a particular semantic structure that can be dramatically different from the standard embedding space. Partially, this misalignment of semantic representations contributed to some differences in the distributional patterns. The distribution patterns show that the four genre categories are very different in all these statistics. Hip-hop songs are most different from the other three categories. Excluding hip-hop songs, country songs show a large distributional difference on these statistical parameters.

Pop music lyrics commonly show large standard deviations in various semantic features. Such behavior can be a consequence of the large diversity of mainstream artists that identify with the tag "Pop". Such a tag does not relate to any specific niche or preference, that is, any artist could self-identify as a "pop" artist [63–65]. As a consequence, there is less style cohesion within the "pop" genre than within other, more specific, genres. Pop is rather a mixture of genres in all the analyses in this group. the elements of different genres can be picked up very differently by the computer algorithms and the human listeners. Thus, a calibration model that counts in the strength of computer algorithms' "feature read" strengths is necessary to better align the computational genre studies and the annotations provided by human annotators.

We observe that Pop and Hip-Hop have a greater number of connected components in their lyrics. This characteristic shows when lyrics have words that are semantically more distant from the others. A possible reason for this is using words that rhythmically fit the song, but that have no semantic relation to the other words within the lyrics. Such a technique is common in Pop and Hip-Hop, but Country and Rock music have a greater tendency of being about stories and sacrificing the rhythmic characteristics of a word to improve their storytelling [66–68]. The mean and the standard deviation of the page rank measurements and the betweenness measurements of tokens show that Hip-hop lyrics are less "compact" in the topological domain, which can be roughly interpreted as "incoherent".

Another possible source of ambiguity and perplexity of Pop lyrics studies is the complexity of the available genre tags themselves. Many genre tags used by composers, producers, labels, and distributors, often from different sources, are designed to organize and showcase their albums and tracks in the physical storefront and digital distribution channels. In another word, they are just what the composers, producers, and marketers want the song to be, instead of what the song really is [63]. However, genre tags are also related to the social behavior and group identity of music fans [62]. Moreover, artists that typically identify themselves within one genre can produce meaningful work using elements from other genres, as it is the case of D'yer Mak'er, a reggae-sounding song by the Heavy Metal band Led Zeppelin [63]. These perspectives are constantly in a dialog that embeds genre tags with a divergent meaning that must be discussed when interpreting data-driven, genre-related systems.

A similar genre-specific pattern can also be observed in the eigenvalue features. The eigenvalues are typically lower for hip-hop, which indicates a lower overall connectivity in its graphs. Again, the statistical analysis indicates that Country and Rock tend to favor semantic cohesion while Hip-Hop tends to favor other aspects. Pop music lies between these two trends, again as a genre of stylistic fusion and conceptual ambiguity.

26.6.2 Studies on Distributional Patterns from Different Time Period

This group of study first separates the music lyrics according to their production time. We implemented decade-based subgroups under each genre category and aggregate the semantic features over each time period. Figure 26.8 shows the distributional pattern of feature values split into five decades of 1970s, 1980s, 1990s, 2000s, and 2010s, corresponding to the five boxes in each group. The box plot specifications are identical to those of Fig. 26.6 and detailed in Sect. 26.6.1. Figure 26.9 shows the P-value distributions of decade separations. The separation of decades is not as strong as the separation of genres. But the first bar in many feature dimensions is significant, indicating these feature dimensions can separate a subset (and their "interaction", strictly speaking [53]) but cannot sufficiently separate each pair. The decade categories are encoded as "1-1970s", "2-1980s", "3-1990s", "4-2000s", and "5-2010s". The following bars after the lead bar of each group correspond to the comparison pairs of "1–2", "1–3", "1–4", "1–5", "2–3", "2–4", "2–5", "3–4", "3–5", and "4–5". Figure 26.10 shows the P-value distributions of decade separations with only Rock songs included. Figure 26.11 shows the

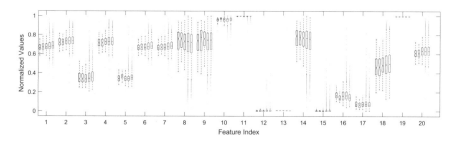

Fig. 26.8 Distributional pattern of feature values split into five decades of 1970s, 1980s, 1990s, 2000s, and 2010s, corresponding to the five boxes in each group. The separations of time periods are visible but not so obvious. Following statistical analysis will show more detailed patterns

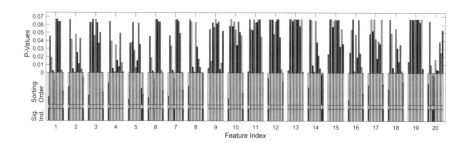

Fig. 26.9 Analysis of Variance (ANOVA) results and their multiple comparisons for time periods. Most comparison groups show very high statistical significance for group means. A few pairwise comparisons also show the significance

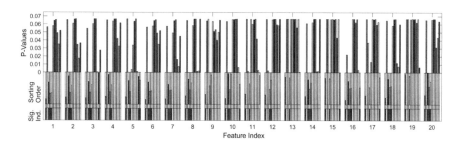

Fig. 26.10 Analysis of Variance (ANOVA) results and their multiple comparisons for time periods. Only Rock songs are included. Most comparison groups show the improved significance

P-value distributions of decade separations with only Pop songs included. The significance level of all tests increases, due to more uniform song genres.

We observe Rock as the genre with least lyric structural characteristic changes through different time periods. Country and Pop show a greater feature variation

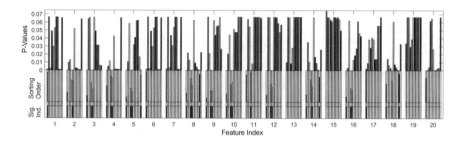

Fig. 26.11 Analysis of Variance (ANOVA) results and their multiple comparisons for time periods. Only Pop songs are included. Most comparison groups show the improved significance

over the decades. This indicates that the musical trends in Country and Pop music have been changing over the decades, whereas Rock is relatively stable [56, 66]. Interestingly, the aggregated statistics of Country music lyric features lead to a distribution that is similar to that of Rock. This indicates that Country music's changes are not a linear evolution; rather, they revolve around some common characteristics. These characteristics are rooted in blues and bluegrass [69], and share these roots with Rock music.

The aggregated statistics of Pop lyric features lead to a distribution that is different from that of Rock and Country. Following the same reasoning used for Country music, this indicates that Pop changes in time without the need of returning to any well-rooted "authentic" characteristics. The diversity in Pop music lyrics is also highlighted by their higher number of connected components in the long tail.

Hip-Hop genre presents the most interesting distributional patterns. In our dataset, this genre appeared after the decade of 1980. This means that Hip-Hop only exists commercially after this decade. In the 1980s, Hip-Hop features have the greatest standard deviation when compared to the following decades. This can indicate that the genre was being defined in the 1980s, followed by more chaotic trends of creation within this genre. The following 1990s sees decreasing standard deviation of the features, which indicates that the genre started having more rigid rules, probably becoming more niche-specific. In the 2000s and 2010s, the standard deviations of these features slowly increased, indicating more diversification as more Hip-Hop artists moved towards experimental.

Overall, the patterns observed in this study show strong evidence that genres change through time. Lyrics of a particular genre in the decade of 2010 could be very different from music from that same genre in the decade of 1970. This indicates that the meaning of genre tags could be more specific with time identifiers (e.g., 1980s Rock). Although our results only indicate this pattern in music lyrics, we speculate that this also happens in the audio domain.

Our data show that Pop and Hip-Hop have a greater tendency to have lyrics with a broader semantic span. This can be linked to their higher use of rhythm-related words, in contrast to the tendency of Country and Rock of having storytelling lyrics with meaning-related words [56]. We also note that Pop is a label that aggregates a myriad of artists, and because of that, it shows a higher degree of lyric variations. Hip-Hop, on the other hand, had a more experimental phase in the 1980s, but it now has niche-specific roots. It is important to note here that genre is both a tag used for music marketing and as a fanbase identification reference [70]. Genres with stronger group-related identification, such as Rock and modern Hip-Hop, tend to have a lower variation in their characteristics over time.

In most analyses, the tails of most distributions significantly overlap and some P-values are large. This indicates that this analysis method can fail if used for genre prediction experiments. This type of experiment requires finding aspects in music that can help discriminate between individual elements that belong to each one of the genres. However, it is evident that lyrics, although important, are not necessarily a reliable predictor of music genres. It is possible, for example, to have a cross-genre song (e.g., a Hip-Hop version of a Country song). Nevertheless, these analyses highlight general trends within music styles and within time periods. This serves as an important empirical tool that can deepen the understanding of lyrics and their cultural environments related to each music genre.

26.7 Conclusions and Future Work

We implemented a graph-based representation and analysis framework for popular music lyric analysis, interpretation, and visualization in the natural language semantic embedding space. The music lyrics are represented as word token sequences in the high dimensional natural language embedding space. Then we implemented various structural and statistical descriptors extracted from the graphic trajectory of the word token sequences. These descriptors of the graph properties show strong classification performance between the contrast groups of music genres. We also implemented various interpretation and visualization tools for exploring the graphical word trajectories and the feature descriptors. Our proposed analysis framework combines the conventional "bag-of-words" models from natural language processing while emphasizes the temporal context of the music lyric sequence. Furthermore, some proposed graph feature descriptors also represent the structural properties such as graph symmetry, transition angles between vertices, and the semantic distances between adjacent tokens. These descriptors provide the modeling and analysis capabilities beyond the conventional statistical "counting" approaches and reveal many lyric patterns not easily observable from manual analysis and highly relevant for an in-depth understanding of music lyrics.

Several extensions to our proposed analysis framework are promising for enhancing the representational capacity and interpretative relevance. First, the semantic word embedding space is directly adapted from the word embedding space learned from online article databases. The semantic content of these corpora is very different from the lyric text corpus in our implementation. We plan to explore the semantic representation induced from other corpora or induced from online article databases and then fine-tuned using other corpora, for example, inducing or adjusting semantic representations using databases that contain novels, poems, uncategorized music lyrics, or music lyrics of a specific genre and composed in a different time period, etc. These alternative semantic representations will provide alternative analytical devices for understanding music lyrics from many complementary perspectives. Learning a semantic representation from one text corpus and applying the representation for analyzing another text corpus is a process of comparing the semantics of these two corpora in a systematic ways, similar to model calibration and measurement. In this context, the semantic representations induced or adjusted from alternative text corpora are essentially different measurement instruments or linguistic investigations. Of course, the semantic representation induced from larger online article datasets has rich and contemporary text meanings, which is difficult to be replaced from the other text corpora. The other semantic representations are expected to serve as an alternative or extension of the result presented in this chapter and we will report these alternative analyses in our subsequent works.

Second, we plan to extend our lyrics study framework towards multimodal methodologies that can handle multiple tracks of information including lyrics, audio, and listener perception. We hope the use of multimodal tools will further enhance the statistical significance of the reported studies by exploring the synergies among multiple tracks of information. The music lyrics are intrinsically connected to the music in which it is sung. A word embedding space induced jointly from the music lyric dataset and its synchronized audio features extracted from the audio can encompass the phonetic connections between words and other parts of the music. The linkage between the sound and the lyrics can be modeled as a joint semantic representation in a hybrid learning process, for example, mixing the word token symbols from the lyrics with the tokenized sound descriptors and then infer a joint semantic representation that combines the sound and the words. In this work, we show that lyric characteristics change through time. We speculate that this characteristic also holds to audio, that is, each genre and era have its own characteristic sounds and ways of combining lyrical elements with sounds. This phonetic link between the sound and the words is an important element for music lyric composition [6, 13]. This joint representation scheme can also be implemented for other multimodal representational combinations such as connected lyrics tokens with music emotion labels, human response signals (e.g., sensor generated physiological signals), or musical analysis structural labels (e.g., chord sequence, short voice-leading models, short phrase, song forms, Roman numerical analysis) as multimodal lexicon before the learning process of the semantic representations. The semantic models induced from these multimodal representations can further utilize the semantic dependency between multiple modalities for enhancing the perceptual relevance and application scope.

Third, our framework applies a manual feature extraction approach for the structural features of semantic token distribution, lyric chain modeling, and lyric graph modeling. Alternatively, the lyric graphs can be modeled using deep learning systems to utilize its automatic feature selection and hierarchical structure recognition capabilities [24, 25, 71]. Our proposed framework relies on manually designed features implemented from existing natural language processing, speech processing, and music signal analysis literature. These features are very comprehensive in scope and many such features are well testified by many speech and music analysis tasks for their robustness. Testing the analytical power of these manually designed features is usually the first step towards an in-depth exploration of Musicology analysis tasks. Another benefit for applying these features is that the analytical results from applying these manually designed features are easier to interpret and interact with other manual analysis tasks (i.e., more transparent). Deep learning-based methods usually have higher predictive analysis performance but the interpretation of the results is not as direct as the methods based on manually designed features. Thus, a combination of our proposed graph features and deep learning approaches is promising for improving the relevance transparency, and robustness of the learned patterns and the learning mechanism.

Last but not least, our empirical studies are limited to the conventional musical genre categories concentrated in popular music. Many more refined musical genres and musical expressiveness concepts such as subgenres [72], performer styles [73, 74], cross-cultural genres [75] will extend the application scope of our proposed analysis framework. Specifically, our ongoing work explores the relationship between the lexicon patterns identified from musical lyrics with the performance nuance the artists rendered "beyond the score". The focus is to explore the expressiveness connections between the lyrics semantics and performance expressions identified from the musical sound. Our current result shows the dynamic characteristics of genres such as Pop and Country as they evolve over time. More refined analysis on subgenres and genre-year data, instead of the "simple genre" will enhance many musicological tasks. Such more refined analysis can be applied to Rock and Hip-Hop, which shows weaker categorical differences in the analysis tasks. We also plan to investigate audience group-based genre tag split schemes. This group of research will also be extended towards more diversified music contents such as modern musical theater and musicals, classical opera, film music accompanied by dialogs, and modern/experimental music composition and practices.

References

1. Campbell, M. (2011). *Popular music in America the beat goes on* (4th edn). Schirmer.
2. Brackett, D. (2013). *The pop, rock, and soul reader: Histories and debates* (3rd edn). Oxford University Press.
3. Starr, L., & Waterman, C. (2017). *American popular music: From minstrelsy to MP3* (5th edn). Oxford University Press.
4. Szatmary, D. (2013). *Rockin' in time: A social history of rock-and-roll* (8th edn). Pearson.
5. Stuessy, J., & Lipscomb, S. D. (2012). *Rock and roll: Its history and stylistic development* (7th edn). Pearson.
6. Middleton, R. (1990). *Studying popular music*. Open University Press.

7. Mikolov, T., Sutskever, I., Chen, K., Corrado, G. S., & Dean, J. (2013). Distributed representations of words and phrases and their compositionality. *Advances in Neural Information Processing Systems*. arXiv:1310.4546.

8. Pennington, J., Socher, R., & Manning, C. D. (2014). GloVe: Global vectors for word representation. In *Proceedings of the 2014 conference on empirical methods in natural language processing (EMNLP)*, (pp. 1532–1543).

9. Manoj, B. S., Chakraborty, A., & Singh, R. (2018). *Complex networks: A networking and signal processing perspective*. New York, USA: Pearson.

10. Bornholdt, S., & Schuster, H. G. (Eds.). (2003). *Handbook of graphs and networks: From the genome to the internet*. New York, NY: Wiley & Sons, Inc.

11. Estrada, E. (2011). *The structure of complex networks: Theory and Applications*. Oxford University Press.

12. Newman, M., Barabási, A., & Watts, D. (2006). *The structure and dynamics of networks*. Princeton: Princeton University Press.

13. Middleton, R. (ed.) (2000). *Reading pop: Approaches to textual analysis in popular music*. Oxford University Press.

14. Moore, A. F. (2012). *Song means: Analysing and interpreting recorded popular song*. Routledge.

15. Dumais, S. T. (2005). Latent semantic analysis. *Annual Review of Information Science and Technology., 38*, 188–230

16. Levy, O., Goldberg, Y., & Dagan, I. (2015). Improving distributional similarity with lessons learned from word embeddings. *Transactions of the Association for Computational Linguistics*.

17. Mikolov, T., Yih, W., & Zweig, G. (2013). Linguistic regularities in continuous space word representations. *HLT-NAACL 746–751*.

18. Mannes, J., & John. Facebook's fasttext library is now optimized for mobile. *TechCrunch*.

19. Jockers, M. (2013). *Macroanalysis: Digital methods and literary history*. University of Illinois Press.

20. Klarer, M. (2013). *An introduction to literary studies*. Routledge

21. Sayers, J. (ed.) (2018). *The Routledge companion to media studies and digital humanities (Routledge media and cultural studies companions)*. Routledge

22. Mauthe, A., & Thomas, P. (2004). *Professional content management systems: Handling digital media assets*. Wiley.

23. Austerberry, D. (2006). *Digital asset management* (2nd edn). Focal Press.

24. Sejnowski, T. J. (2018). *The deep learning revolution*. Cambridge, Massachusetts: MIT Press.

25. Gerrish, S. (2018). *How smart machines think, Cambridge*. Massachusetts: MIT Press.

26. Kelleher, J. D. (2019). *Deep learning (MIT Press essential knowledge series), Cambridge*. Massachusetts: MIT Press.

27. Nilsson, N. J. (2010). *The quest for artificial intelligence: A history of ideas and achievements*. Cambridge; New York: Cambridge University Press.

28. Divakaran, A. (2009). *Multimedia content analysis: Theory and applications*. New York: Springer.

29. Baltrusaitis, T., Ahuja, C., & Morency, L.-P. (2019). Multimodal machine learning: A survey and taxonomy. *IEEE Transactions on Pattern Analysis and Machine Intelligence (TPAMI), 41*(2).

30. Müller, M. (2007). *Information retrieval for music and motion*. New York: Springer.

31. Balaban, M., Ebcioğlu, K., & Laske, O. (Eds.). (1992). *Understanding music with AI: Perspectives on music cognition*. Cambridge, MA: MIT Press.

32. Miranda, E. R. (2000). *Readings in music and artificial intelligence*. Amsterdam: Harwood Academic.

33. Meredith, D. (Ed.) (2016). *Computational music analysis*. Springer.

34. Wingate, L. M. (2014). *Project management for research and development: Guiding innovation for positive R&D outcomes*. Auerbach Publications.

35. Jain, R., Triandis, H. C., & Weick, C. W. (2010). *Managing research, development and innovation: Managing the unmanageable* (3rd edn). Wiley.
36. Miller, W. L., & Morris, L. (1999). *Fourth generation R&D: Managing knowledge, technology, and innovation*. Wiley.
37. Cook, N. (1998). *Music : A very short introduction*. Oxford; New York: Oxford University Press.
38. Clarke, E., & Cook, N. (2004). *Empirical musicology: Aims, methods*. Prospects. Oxford; New York: Oxford University Press.
39. Kerman, J. (1985). *Contemplating music: Challenges to musicology*. Cambridge, Mass.: Harvard University Press.
40. Kerman, J. (1980). How we got into analysis, and how to get out. *Critical Inquiry, 7*(2), 311–331
41. Bohlman, P. (1993). Musicology as a political act. *Journal of Musicology: a Quarterly Review of Music History, Criticism, Analysis, and Performance Practice, 11*(4), 411–436
42. Aggarwal, C. C. (2018). *Machine learning for text*. Springer.
43. Bengfort, B., Bilbro, R., & Ojeda, T. (2018). *Applied text analysis with python: Enabling language-aware data products with machine learning*. O'Reilly.
44. Asgari, E., & Mofrad, M. R. K. (2015). Continuous distributed representation of biological sequences for deep proteomics and genomics. *PLOS One, 10*(11), e0141287. arXiv:1503.05140.
45. Helgaker, T., Jorgensen, P., & Olsen, J. (2013). *Molecular electronic-structure theory*. Wiley.
46. Hair, J. F. (2013). *Multivariate data analysis*. Pearson.
47. Roberts, S., & Everson, R. (eds.) (2001). *Independent component analysis: Principles and practice*. Cambridge University Press.
48. Oppenheim, A. V., & Schafer, R. W. (2009). *Discrete-time signal processing* (3rd edn). Prentice Hall
49. MetroLyrics Dataset: https://www.metrolyrics.com
50. Adams, T. M., & Fuller, D. B. (2006). The words have changed but the ideology remains the same: Misogynistic lyrics in rap music. *Journal of Black Studies, 36*(6), 938–957
51. Lacy, R. (2012). When country was country. *The Sewanee Review, 120*(1), 151–156
52. Chin, D. (1990). Pop pop pop (new) music. *Performing Arts Journal, 12*(2/3), 137–143
53. Wu, C. F. J., & Hamada, M. (2000). *Experiments: Planning, analysis, and parameter design optimization*. Wiley.
54. Neter, J., Kutner, M. H., Nachtsheim, C. J., & Wasserman, W. (1996). *Applied linear statistical models* (4th edn). Irwin Press.
55. Leskovec, J., Rajaraman, A., & Ullman, J. D. (2019). *Mining of massive datasets* (3rd edn). Cambridge University Press.
56. Condit-Schultz, N., & Huron, D. (2015). Catching the lyrics: Intelligibility in twelve song genres. *Music Perception: An Interdisciplinary Journal, 32*(5), 470–483
57. Astor, P. (2010). The poetry of rock: Song lyrics are not poems but the words still matter; another look at richard Goldstein's collection of rock lyrics. *Popular Music, 29*(1), 143–148
58. Gardner, B. (1986). Pop lyrics as auto-affect. *ETC: A Review of General Semantics, 43*(2), 141–146.
59. Tracey, H. (1963). Behind the lyrics. *African Music, 3*(2), 17–22
60. Eddy, J. (2007). Song lyrics as culturally authentic material for standards-based performance. *Hispania, 90*(1), 142–146
61. Coffin, L. W. (1970). Writing song lyrics. *The English Journal, 59*(7), 954–955
62. Davis, S. (1985). Pop lyrics: A mirror and a molder of society. *ETC: A Review of General Semantics, 42*(2), 167–169.
63. Murphey, T. (1989). The when, where, and who of pop lyrics: The Listener's prerogative. *Popular Music, 8*(2), 185–193
64. Mitchell, T. (1989). Performance and the postmodern in pop music. *Theatre Journal, 41*(3), 273–293

65. Batcho, K. (2007). Nostalgia and the emotional tone and content of song lyrics. *The American Journal of Psychology, 120*(3), 361–381
66. Cutietta, R. (1986). Rock music gets a label. *Music Educators Journal, 72*(8), 36–38
67. Donaldson, S. (1968). Love in rock-and-roll lyrics. *ETC: A Review of General Semantics, 25* (3), 354–358.
68. Kalinin, G. (1999). Virtual lyrics. *Leonardo, 32*(1), 61–62
69. Erbsen, W. (2003). *Rural roots of bluegrass: Songs.* Native Ground Music: Stories & History.
70. Martin, P. (2002). Over the rainbow? On the quest for 'the social' in musical analysis. *Journal of the Royal Musical Association, 127*, 130–146
71. Alpaydin, E. (2016). *Machine learning: The new AI.* MIT Press.
72. Brackett, D. (2016). *Categorizing sound: Genre and twentieth-century popular music.* University of California Press.
73. Barker, H., & Taylor, Y. (2007). *Faking it: The quest for authenticity in popular music.* W. W. Norton & Company.
74. Inglis, I. (Ed.). (2006). *Performance and popular music: History.* Place and Time: Routledge.
75. Shelemay, K. (2015). *Soundscapes: Exploring music in a changing world* (3rd edn). W. W. Norton & Company.

Mitsunori Ogihara is a professor of Computer Science at the University of Miami, USA. He received his B.S., M.S., and Ph.D. degrees in Information Sciences from the Tokyo Institute of Technology, Japan. His research interests include computational complexity theory, data mining, music data mining, digital humanities, and biological data analysis. E-mail: ogihara@cs.miami.edu

Brian Manolovitz is currently a graduate student of Computer Science at the University of Miami, USA. He received his B.M. in Music Composition and M.S. in Computer Science from California State University Long Beach, USA. His research interests include analyzing the psychological effects of music, music cognition, and automatic playlist generation. E-mail: bmm157@miami.edu

Vitor Yudi Shinohara is studying for an M.Sc. degree in Electrical Engineering at the Universidade Estadual de Campinas (Unicamp), Brazil. He also has a B.Sc. in Computer Science from the Universidade Tecnológica Federal do Paraná, Brazil (2018). His research interests include natural language processing, music information retrieval, and machine learning. E-mail: vitorys@dca.fee.unicamp.br

Gang Ren is a postdoctoral associate at the Institute for Data Science and Computing, University of Miami, USA. He received his B.S. and M.S. degrees in Electrical Engineering from Sichuan University, Chengdu, China, in 1999 and 2005, respectively, and a Ph.D. degree in Electrical Engineering from the University of Rochester, USA, in 2016. His research interests include applying multimedia signal processing techniques to web-scale information retrieval tasks, the development of sequential pattern analysis tools for the analysis and interpretation of long-span semantic structures, and designing human–computer interaction mechanisms for perceptual/cognitive analyses and their related computational implementations. E-mail: gxr467@miami.edu

Tiago F. Tavares Tiago Fernandes Tavares is a professor at the School of Electrical and Computer Engineering at the University of Campinas (Unicamp), Brazil. He has a B.Sc. (2008) in Computer Engineering, and M.Sc. (2010) and Ph.D. (2013) in Electrical Engineering, also from the University of Campinas. His research interests comprise audio information retrieval, natural language processing, digital signal processing, machine learning, and new interfaces for musical expression. E-mail: tavares@dca.fee.unicamp.br

Interactive Machine Learning of Musical Gesture

27

Federico Ghelli Visi and Atau Tanaka

27.1 Introduction

This chapter presents an overview of Interactive Machine Learning (IML) techniques applied to the analysis and design of musical gestures. We go through the main challenges and needs related to capturing, analysing, and applying IML techniques to human bodily gestures with the purpose of performing with sound synthesis systems. We discuss how different algorithms may be used to accomplish different tasks, including interacting with complex synthesis techniques and exploring interaction possibilities by means of Reinforcement Learning (RL) in an interaction paradigm we developed called Assisted Interactive Machine Learning (AIML). We conclude the chapter with a description of how some of these techniques were employed by the authors for the development of four musical pieces, thus outlining the implications that IML have for musical practice.

Embodied engagement with music is a key element of musical experience, and the gestural properties of musical sound have been studied from multiple disciplinary perspectives, including Human-Computer Interaction (HCI), musicology, and the cognitive sciences [1]. Likewise, designing gestural interactions with sound synthesis for musical expression is a complex task informed by many fields of research. The results of laboratory studies of music-related body motion based on sound-tracing

F. G. Visi (✉)
GEMM))) Gesture Embodiment and Machines in Music, School of Music in Piteå, Luleå University of Technology, Snickargatan 20, 941 63 Piteå, Sweden
e-mail: federico.visi@ltu.se

A. Tanaka
EAVI–Embodied Audiovisual Interaction, Goldsmiths, University of London, New Cross, London SE14 6NW, UK
e-mail: a.tanaka@gold.ac.uk

© Springer Nature Switzerland AG 2021
E. R. Miranda (ed.), *Handbook of Artificial Intelligence for Music*,
https://doi.org/10.1007/978-3-030-72116-9_27

were indicated as a useful starting points for designing gestural interactions with sound [2]. Informed by environmental psychology, the notion of sonic affordance was introduced to look at how sound invites action, and how this could potentially aid the design of gestural interfaces [3].

Designing and exploring gestural interactions with sound and digital media is at the foundation of established artistic practices where the performer's body is deeply engaged in forms of corporeal interplay with the music by means of motion and physiological sensing [4]. Gesture and embodiment become the core concepts of extended multimedia practices, where composition and interaction design develop side by side [5, 6], and gesture is a fundamental expressive element [7].

27.1.1 Why Machine Learning Musical Gestures? Needs and Challenges

Designing gestural interactions that afford dynamic, consistent, and expressive artic- ulations of musical sound is a challenging and multifaceted task. A key step of the design process is the definition of mapping functions between gesture tracking signals (usually obtained through some motion sensing device) and sound synthesis param- eters [8]. These parameter spaces can be very complex, depending on the motion sensing and sound synthesis approaches adopted. An effective mapping strategy is one of the crucial factors affecting the expressive potential of a gestural interaction, and as the spaces defined by motion signals and synthesis parameters become more highly-dimensional and heterogeneous, designing mappings can be an increasingly elaborate task, with many possible solutions [9].

In this scenario, gestural interaction design is a robust nontrivial problem, and Machine Learning (ML) techniques can be used by researchers and artists to tackle its complexity in several ways. One of the most notable implications of using ML in this domain is that mappings between gesture and sound can be interactively "shown" to a system capable of "learning" them [10] instead of being manually coded, which in certain situations could become excessively complex and time consuming. In other words, this delineates an interaction design paradigm where interactive systems shift from executing rules to learning rules from given examples [11]. This has advantages in collaborative and interdisciplinary creative practices, as it makes trying and work- shopping different gestural interactions easier and quicker, and enables practitioners that are unfamiliar with programming to prototype their own gestural interactions. Moreover, software tools such as the Wekinator [12] and ML libraries for popular pro- gramming environments in the arts [13] have made ML for gestural interaction more accessible and easier to learn. Another advantage of interaction design approaches based on ML is that mapping models can be trained to be more resilient to noisy signals. This can be challenging to achieve with manually programmed mappings. This is particularly useful with certain motion tracking technologies and physiologi- cal sensors (see Sect. 27.2). Noise is not, however, the only challenge when tracking and analysing body movement for musical interaction. Motion tracking systems may return considerably different data when the user changes, different motion sensing

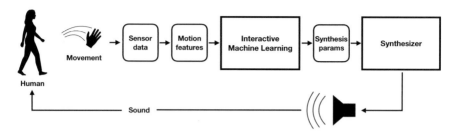

Fig. 27.1   Architecture of an Interactive Machine Learning system for gestural musical interaction

technologies measure and represent movement in very different ways, musical gestures may convey musical ideas at different timescales [14], and therefore, it should be possible to model both spatial and temporal features of musical gestures whilst maintaining the possibility of dynamic and continuous expressive variations. We will now describe how ML is a helpful resource in addressing these challenges.

27.1.2   Chapter Overview

The sections that follow will describe the main components of an IML system for gesture-sound interaction—schematised in Fig. 27.1—namely motion sensing, analysis and feature extraction, ML techniques, and sound synthesis approaches. Following this, we will describe the typical workflow for deploying an IML system for gesture-sound mapping and how this model can be extended further using RL to explore mapping complexity in an AIML system prototype. We will then describe how these models were used in some pieces composed by the authors, before closing the chapter with some remarks regarding the necessity of adopting an interdisciplinary approach encompassing basic research, tool development, and artistic practice in order to make substantial advances in the field of expressive movement interaction. We finish by showing that the research field has implications stretching beyond the musical domain, given the increasing role of ML technologies in everyday life and the peculiarities that make music and the arts a fertile ground for demystifying ML and thereby understanding ways of claiming and negotiating human agency with data and algorithmic systems.

27.2   Machine-Sensing Gesture

Capturing body movement for the purpose of real-time interaction with sound may be done by various technological means. Rather than providing a list of the many devices available for this purpose, we will describe the main approaches for tracking body movement employed in the context of music and multimedia performance, and the implications that adopting an approach over another has for using ML techniques. These include notes on how different types of motion data represent movement, and the opportunities afforded by the use of physiological data.

27.2.1 Sensing Movement

Optical Sensing

Optical motion sensing relies on the analysis of the signals coming from various kinds of video cameras. There are many examples of multi-camera systems used in the arts [15, 16] as well as of systems using more sophisticated optical approaches such as depth and stereoscopic cameras.

Despite the technology being a few decades old, marker-based infra-red Motion Capture (MoCap) is still considered as one of the most reliable methods for measuring complex movement in a three-dimensional space. Tracking precision and temporal resolution have progressively improved, allowing accurate tracking of finger movements and facial expressions. Recent MoCap systems are also capable of streaming motion data live, thus making real-time applications possible. Data obtained from these systems is usually in the form of three-dimensional vectors referring to a global coordinate system. Each sample in the data returns three-dimensional information regarding the position of a point (marker) in space in relation to the origin of the Cartesian axes. The origin is defined during the calibration procedure and is usually set in an arbitrary place on the floor within the capture area. Most marker-based systems also allow to track movement in six degrees of freedom (6DoF), meaning that—in addition to position along the three spatial axes—the system also returns information on the orientation and rotation of a point in space along three rotational axes. This information is usually represented in Euler angles or quaternions. In MoCap systems, 6DoF tracking is usually achieved by processing positional data of single markers grouped into a rigid body in a predefined spatial configuration. This should be unique for each rigid body in order to avoid mislabelling when multiple rigid bodies are in the capture space at the same time.

Inertial Measurement Units

Inertial Measurement Units (IMU) are small, low-cost, highly portable devices that incorporate accelerometers and gyroscopes. When these devices are paired with magnetometers, the resulting arrays are also known as Magnetic, Angular Rate, and Gravity (MARG) sensors. These sensor arrays allow the tracking of acceleration, rotational velocity, and orientation relative to the earth's magnetic field of whatever they are attached to. They are used extensively in aviation, robotics, and HCI. Their increasing affordability and small size have made them a very common feature of mobile and wearable devices and other consumer electronics. Sensors featuring 3D accelerometers, 3D gyroscopes, and 3D magnetometers have become the most widely used type of IMU/MARG. They enable the estimation of various motion features including optimised three-dimensional orientation obtained by fusing together the data from the different types of sensors. These devices are often marketed as 9DoF

(9 Degrees of Freedom) sensors, since they consist of three tri-axis sensors and thus have a total of nine sensitive axes.

Whereas the raw data obtained using marker-based optical motion capture consists of samples of position based on a 3D Cartesian coordinate system, the data returned by IMU/MARG sensors is usually in the form of three three-dimensional vectors, each one expressing acceleration, rotational velocity, and orientation, respectively. Calculating absolute position from the data of a single IMU in real time is technically very difficult if not unfeasible, as the operation would require double integration of acceleration data. This would result in a considerable amount of residual error since drift would accumulate quadratically.

The lack of reliable information on absolute position when using single IMUs is a key difference between data obtained through inertial sensing and that of optical motion capture. The data obtained from IMUs sensors is morphologically very different from positional data returned by optical MoCap. The differences in the way movement is tracked and represented by the two different technologies have implications on how movement data is eventually interpreted and used, particularly in the context of expressive movement tracking and ML of musical gestures. As an example, single IMUs afford working with movement relative to the body of the performer and postures, whereas having access to absolute positions may enable interaction strategies that take into consideration the spatial relationships between different performers and the different areas of the performance space where action takes place.

27.2.2 Sensing the Body

It can be argued that representing human movement solely as displacement of body parts in three-dimensional space would result in a limited interpretation. Merleau-Ponty maintains that we act upon the environment through proprioception and "a knowledge bred of familiarity which does not give us a position in objective space" [17, p. 166]. Salazar Sutil [18] points out that the conceptualisation of corporeal movement is often optically biased, where sensations that are independent of sight are often neglected. Thus, we argue that expressive body movement cannot be entirely represented, and therefore, fully understood exclusively by means of visual media. In the context of music performance, we looked at the concepts of intention, effort, and restraint in relation to the use of electromyogram (EMG) for digital musical instrument application [19]. EMG is a signal representing muscle activity employed in the biomedical and HCI fields as a highly sensitive way to capture human movement and has been used as a signal with which to sense musical gesture [20, 21]. Using EMG for music presents several challenges. The raw signal itself resembles noise and sensing such a low voltage signal is difficult to do without accumulating noise from the environment. Individual anatomies vary and we each employ our muscles differently, even when performing what looks like the same gesture. Basic signal processing can only go so far when interpreting expressive, nuanced biosignals. Adopting approaches based on ML can considerably help with these challenges, making EMG an attractive technology for musical interaction. In particular, supervised learning approaches—which will be described in Sect. 27.4—constitute a way for tackling the intersubject variability and the noisy quality of muscular signals.

27.3 Analysing Gesture

High-level descriptors are often used to extract features from raw motion data to help describing body movement in a more meaningful way. Such descriptors are frequently employed in expressive movement analysis, motion recognition, and music performance analysis. Feature extraction is a crucial step in an IML pipeline. This is an important task, as it will affect how ML algorithms will interpret body movement, and therefore, determine the affordances of the resulting gesture-sound interactions.

Programming environments such as Eyesweb [22] offer solutions dedicated to real-time human movement analysis and feature extraction. Libraries for real-time motion analysis such as the Musical Gesture Toolbox were initially dedicated mainly to standard RGB video analysis [23]. The library has been developed further to process MoCap data and be compatible with several programming environments [24]. Notably, some of the features that were initially designed for analysing video data—such as Quantity of Motion (QoM, see Sect. 27.3.1)—have been extended for the use with MoCap data. We developed the *modosc* library to make methods for handling complex motion data streams and compute descriptors in real time available in music performance systems [25, 26]. At the time of writing, the library is being extended for use with IMU and EMG in addition to MoCap data. The following sections will give an overview of some of the descriptors most widely used for processing motion and EMG data.

27.3.1 Motion Features

Fluidity
Inspired by the theoretical work on human motion by Flash and Hogan—which maintains that trajectories of human limbs can be modelled by the *minimum jerk law* [27], Piana et al. [28] defined Fluidity Index as the inverse of the integral of jerk. Jerk or "Jolt"—is the third-order derivative of position, i.e. the rate of change of the acceleration of an object with respect to time. Fluidity Index has been used with supervised learning algorithms for the purpose of recognising expressed emotions from full-body movement data [28].

Quantity of Motion
Fenza et al. defined Quantity of Motion (QoM) as the sum of the speeds of a set of points multiplied by their mass [29]. Glowinski et al. [30] included a similar measure in their feature set for the representation of affective gestures, denoted as "overall

motion energy." This motion feature has also been used for real-time video analysis [23] and a version for IMU data was also proposed [5].

Contraction Index

Contraction Index is calculated by summing the Euclidean distances of each point in a group from the group's centroid [29]. It is an indicator of the overall contraction or expansion of a group of points and—similarly to Fluidity Index—it has been used for emotion recognition applications [28].

When using independent inertial sensors, the lack of positional data might make it difficult to compute Contraction Index. We proposed an alternative measure of contraction and expansion of body posture using IMU data in [5]. This solution uses the Euclidean distance between projected points to estimate whether the limbs of a person wearing IMUs are pointing in opposite directions.

Bounding Shapes

Bounding shapes have been used in the analysis of affective gestures [30] as well as in dance movement asnalysis [31]. Several bounding shapes can be used for real-time movement analysis. For example, a *bounding box* is the rectangular parallelepiped enclosing a given group of points in a 3D space. Assuming these points are placed on the body of a performer, the height, width, and depth of the bounding box can be used as an indicator of the posture of the full-body evolves over time. The minimum polyhedron that encloses a given group of points in a 3D space is instead called *three-dimensional convex hull*. The volume of the convex hull represents the size of the space the body interacts with and can be used as a feature for various ML tasks.

Periodic Quantity of Motion

Periodic Quantity of Motion (PQoM) was proposed as a way to measure periodicity in the movement in relation to the musical rhythm [5], or—in other words—how much body movement resonates with each rhythmic subdivision (i.e. quarter note, eighth note, etc.). The first PQoM implementation was designed to extract periodic motion from optical motion capture data [32]. The PQoM is estimated by decomposing the motion capture signal into frequency components by using filter banks [33]. The amplitude of the signal for each frequency component corresponds to an estimate of the resonance between the corresponding rhythmic subdivision and the movement. A script for PQoM estimation was made available as an extension to version 1.5 of the MoCap Toolbox for Matlab [34], and a redesigned version of the script has been made available [35].

27.3.2   EMG Features

Signal Amplitude

One of the most important features of EMG signals is the amplitude of the signal with respect to time. This measure is related to the force exerted whilst executing a gesture. Given the complexity and variability of the EMG signal, reliable amplitude estimation may be challenging. Simply applying a low-pass filter to the signal to reduce undesired noise may result in the loss of sharp onsets describing rapid movement and may also introduce latency when processing the signal in real time. Adopting a nonlinear recursive filter based on Bayesian estimation [36] significantly reduces the noise whilst allowing rapid changes in the signal, greatly improving the quality of the signal for real-time gestural interaction.

Mean Absolute Value

Mean Absolute Value (MAV) is one of the most popular features used in EMG signal analysis [37]. It has been shown that MAV is more useful than other features for gesture recognition tasks based on supervised learning algorithms [38]. MAV corresponds to the average of the absolute values of the EMG signal amplitudes in a given time window. When computed in real time, a larger time window returns a smoother signal, whilst a shorter one can be useful to track sharper onsets in muscular activity.

Root Mean Square

Root mean square (RMS) is a common signal processing feature, widely used for audio analysis. With EMG signals, it has been used together with ML algorithms for gesture classification tasks [39]. RMS is equal to the square root of the sum of the squares of the values of the signal in a given time window.

Teager-Kaiser Energy-tracking Operator

The Teager-Kaiser Energy-tracking Operator (TKEO) was first proposed as a way for estimating energy in speech signals [40]. It has been employed for a variety of signal processing tasks, including noise suppression [41]. It has been shown that TKEO considerably improves the performance of onset detection algorithms also in situations with a high signal-to-noise ratio [42]. The feature can be easily calculated from three adjacent samples. For each signal sample, TKEO is equal to the square of the amplitude minus the product of the precedent and successive samples.

Zero Crossing Rate

The Zero Crossing Rate (ZCR) corresponds to the number of times the signal changes sign within a given time window. Widely adopted in audio signal processing, ZCR is used to recognise periodic sounds from noisy ones and is employed in speech recognition [43]. In [44], we used ZCR as one of the features for the analysis of two different modalities of muscle sensing to explore the notion of gesture power.

27.4 Machine Learning Techniques

ML techniques are statistical analysis methods and computational algorithms that can be used to achieve various tasks by building analytical models (i.e. "learning") from example data. Many ML techniques involve a *training* phase and a *testing* phase. During the training phase, sample data is used to model how the system should respond and perform different tasks. During the *testing* phase, new input data is fed into the model, which then responds and performs tasks following decisions based on structures and relationships learned during the training phase. As an example, during the training phase a performer using motion sensors may want to record a gesture and associate it to specific sounds being produced by a sound synthesis engine. Then during the testing phase, the performer moves freely whilst the system follow their movements and infer which sounds should be played according to the examples given during the training phase. This allows for flexibility and generalisation, making ML techniques particularly useful for complex applications that involve many variables and that may be dependent on factors that are difficult to predict or control, such as the environments in which systems are deployed, or high variability in how the system responds to different users. For example, in a musical context one may want to use a gesture-sound interaction system in different performance spaces, which may have different lighting conditions. This may result in undesirable unexpected behaviours, such as the system responding differently in the concert hall where a piece is to be performed compared to the space where the piece has been rehearsed. Moreover, the system may be used by different performers, whose bodies may differ considerably and thus be tracked differently by various types of sensors (see Sect. 27.2). In such situations designing interactions by explicitly programming how each sound parameter should behave in response to incoming sensor data might be too time-consuming, impractical, or result in interactions that are too shallow and do not afford expressive variations.

There are several standard learning strategies to train a programme to execute specific tasks [45]. Amongst the most common paradigms, we find Supervised Learning (SL), Unsupervised Learning (UL), and Reinforcement Learning (RL). In SL, the training data consists of input paired with the desired output. In other words, training examples are *labelled*. For example, in a supervised learning scenario motion feature data is paired with the desired sound and passed to the learning algorithm as training data. Classification and regression are some of the most common supervised learning tasks. In UL, training data is unlabelled. The goal is learned from the data itself, by analysing patterns and underlying structures in the given examples. As an example, a set of unlabelled sounds may constitute the training set and the task of the unsupervised learning algorithm may be to group the sounds that have similar features. Common unsupervised learning tasks include clustering and dimensionality reduction. We employed dimensionality reduction approaches to observe commonalities and individualities in the music-related movements of different people miming instrumental performance [46]. Strategies in RL entail giving feedback in response to the algorithm's output. The goal of the algorithm is to maximise the positive feedback—or rewards—they are given by a human (or by another algorithm) that is observing the outcome of their actions. Training and testing phases here are more intertwined than in typical supervised and unsupervised strategies, as training occurs through testing. For example, in a RL scenario, one may task an algorithm to propose some sound synthesis presets, and the user may give positive or negative feedback in order to obtain a sound that is closer to their liking. Parameter space exploration is a task associated with this learning strategy. A gesture-sound mapping exploration method that takes advantage of RL [47] will be described in Sect. 27.6.

The following sections will outline how these strategies are employed to perform tasks often associated with ML of musical gesture, namely classification, regression, and temporal modelling.

27.4.1 Classification

Classification is the task of assigning a category, or class, to an item. In a supervised learning scenario, the training dataset is constituted by items labelled with the category they belong to. The training dataset is then used to build a model that will assign labels to new unlabelled items, or instances, that have not been classified before. As an example in the context of musical gestures, the training set may be made of discrete gestures (e.g. tracing a circle in the air, or a triangle...) where the sensor data and motion features resulting from performing such gestures are paired with the corresponding label (circle, triangle, etc.). These labelled gestures constitute a *vocabulary*. In performance, the classifier may be used to track the movements of the performer and recognise when one of the gestures in the vocabulary is being performed. Successful recognition of one of the gestures in the vocabulary may be then paired with specific musical events (e.g. play a kick drum sample when the tracked gesture is classified as a circle, play a snare sample when the gesture is classified as a triangle, etc.). In a typical gesture classification scenario, classification occurs *after* the gesture is performed, and output of the model is *discrete*, meaning that a gesture will always belong to one of the defined classes. Common algorithms for classification include K-Nearest Neighbours (k-NN), Adaptive Boosting (AdaBoost), Support Vector Machines (SVM), and Naive Bayes. These and other algorithms are described in detail in the manual by Hastie et al. [48]. It is important to note that different classification algorithms afford different interaction sound parameter mapping approaches. For example, by using a probabilistic classifier such as Naive Bayes, one can use the probability distribution (i.e. the set of likelihoods that the incoming gesture belongs to each of the predefined classes) and map their values to parameters (e.g. a set of volume levels) instead of using the class labels to trigger discrete musical events. Finally, classifiers can be used to recognise static postures if trained—for example—with data describing the absolute or relative position of parts of the body of a performer. Classification of gestures based on how they unfold over time can be done by using various temporal modelling approaches, which will be described in Sect. 27.4.3.

27.4.2 Regression

Regression is the task of estimating the relationship between an independent variable (or a *feature*) and a dependent, or *outcome*, variable. This is done by building a statistical model that explains how the variables are related, and thus allows to infer the value of the dependent variable given the independent variable. The model describing this continuous function is built using a set of discrete samples of independent variables (the input) paired with the corresponding values of the dependent variables (the output). Building a regression model is a supervised learning problem, given that to do so one requires labelled data (input paired with corresponding output). Regression is used in several domains for tasks such as prediction and forecasting. In the context of musical interaction, regression is an attractive approach as it allows to define complex, continuous mapping functions between gesture features and sound synthesis parameters. This can be done by providing examples consisting of sample input data (e.g. motion or EMG features, see Sect. 27.3) paired with sound synthesis parameters.

Artificial Neural Networks (ANN) are an efficient way to build linear regression models. A typical ANN is a network of binary classifiers—called perceptrons—organised in a number of layers. Perceptrons are also referred to as "neurons" or "nodes." The first layer of the network (the input layer) has a node for each input feature. Perceptrons in layers after the input layers produce an output based on the activation function (the binary classifier, generally a sigmoid function, but other activation functions may be used) applied to the input they received from the previous layer. The function includes a set of weights applied to each input and an additional parameter, the bias. After producing the output of each node feeding layer after layer (the feedforward process), the error is calculated and a correction is sent back in the network in a process known as backpropagation. After a number of iterations, or epochs, the error is progressively reduced. ANNs are an attractive ML technique when dealing with real-time motion tracking, as they can handle errors in the incoming data (which may be caused by noisy sensor signal) relatively well.

The model obtained by training a neural network may then be used to map incoming motion features to sound synthesis continuously and in real time. Several approaches based on regression may be used to map gestural features to sound synthesis [20]. We have developed the GIMLeT pedagogical toolkit for Max [49] to provide some practical examples of using linear regression for this purpose. However, ordinary ANNs do not take into account the temporal aspects of the input data. The next section will look at some of the approaches designed to analyse and follow the evolution of a gesture in time.

27.4.3   Temporal Modelling

Gesture unfolds over time, and gestures that may look similar in terms of displacement in space may differ radically in expressivity depending on their temporal evolution. For example, moving an arm outwards very slowly or very fast following the same trajectory may convey very different expressive intentions. Whilst certain types of neural networks such as Echo State Networks exhibit short-term memory and can be trained to operate on temporal aspects of their input [50], longer time spans require different approaches. Dynamic Time Warping (DTW) [51] is a technique that allows to temporally align incoming time series (e.g. motion features changing over time) to previously saved gesture templates. Templates are pre-recorded gesture examples. The DTW algorithm will attempt to align incoming gesture features to the set of recorded gesture templates, also referred to as a gesture vocabulary. This way, it is possible to perform various tasks including assessing to which gesture template the incoming motion data is closer to. DTW has been used extensively for music applications such as musical gesture classification [52], to evaluate the timing of musical conducting gestures [53], or as a distance measure to place musical gestures in a feature space [46]. One major drawback of DTW for musical applications is that, albeit giving access to how a gesture evolves over time, recognition occurs only after the gesture has been fully performed, and thus not continuously. Bevilacqua et al. [54] proposed a real-time gesture analysis system based on Hidden Markov Models (HMM). This method allows to continuously recognise a gesture against stored gesture templates, outputting parameters describing time progression (i.e. how much of the gesture has already been performed, this is known as "gesture following") and the likelihood of the gesture belonging to one of the predefined gesture classes. This allows musical interactions such as audio stretching/compressing in synchronisation with gesture performance. Françoise et al. [55] extended this approach further, proposing a set of probabilistic approaches to define motion to sound relationships. These include a hierarchical structure that allows to switch between the difference gestures in the vocabulary and follow the temporal progression of the likeliest matching template whilst performing, and a multimodal approach that models the temporal evolution of both the motion features and the sound parameters. Caramiaux et al. [56] proposed extensions to continuous gesture following by focusing on the online analysis of meaningful variations between gesture templates and performed gestures. Their approach uses particle filtering for tracking variations from the recorded template in real time, allowing to estimate geometric variations such as scaling (i.e. how much is the gesture bigger/smaller than the template?), rotation angles (i.e. how much is the performed gesture tilted with respect to the template?), and temporal dynamics (i.e. is the gesture performed faster or slower than the recoded template?). These gesture variation parameters can then be mapped to sound synthesis parameters. For example, the authors describe a study where an increase in scaling corresponds to louder volume, temporal dynamics are mapped to the playback speed of samples, and rotation angles to high-pass filtering [56, p. 19].

27.5 Sound Synthesis and Gesture Mapping

Modern sound synthesis techniques are often characterised by a high number of parameters one can manipulate in order to make different sounds. Whilst these afford vast synthesis possibilities, exploring the resulting extensive parameter spaces may be a challenging task, which can be particularly difficult to accomplish by manipulating every parameter by hand.

The choice of synthesis algorithm, therefore, can be one where individual synthesis parameters may be difficult to manually parametrise. Instead, we will exploit the "mapping by demonstration" paradigm where the ML algorithm will create a model whereby performance input is translated to synthesis output. In this regard, a difficult to programme synthesis method like Frequency Modulation could be a good candidate.

Here we present two approaches from our work to demonstrate how regression can work with different levels of complexity of sound synthesis. We show a simple granular synthesiser, and a more sophisticated synthesis using corpus-based concatenative synthesis [57].

27.5.1 Granular Synthesis and Sound Tracing

We created a basic granular synthesis module using the in-built capabilities of a sample buffer reader in Max [58], `groove~`. The implementation is a time domain sample-based synthesiser where an audio buffer contains the sample being played, and pitch transposition and playback speed are decoupled. This is combined with subtractive synthesis with a classic resonant low-pass filter. There are six control parameters:

– playback start time
– playback duration
– playback speed
– pitch shift
– filter cutoff frequency
– filter resonance.

A version of this synthesiser is available as part of the GIMLeT example of a synthesiser where the sound authoring parameters are human readable and where parametrisation could be done by hand. The challenge comes in creating sounds that dynamically respond to incoming gestures without hardwiring gestural features to synthesis parameters in a traditional mapping exercise. Here we use sound tracing [59] as a method where a sound is given as a stimulus to create evoked gestural response. By gesticulating to a sound that evolves in time, we author gesture that then becomes training data for the regression algorithm in a "mapping-by-demonstration" workflow. In order to author time varying sound using this synthesiser, we create a system of "anchor points", salient points in the timbral evolution of the sound that are practical for sound synthesis parametrisation, and useful in pose-based gesture training [20]. The synthesiser is controlled by our breakpoint envelope-based playback system and enables the user to design sounds that transition between four fixed anchor points (start, two intermediate points, and end) that represent fixed synthesis parameters. The envelope interpolates between these fixed points. The temporal evolution of sound is captured as different states in the breakpoint editor whose envelopes run during playback, feeding both synthesiser and the ML algorithm. Any of the synthesis parameters can be assigned to breakpoint envelopes to be controlled during playback.

These sound trajectories are then reproduced during the gesture design and model training phases of our workflow. In performance a model maps sensor data to syn-

Table 27.1 Audio feature vector for corpus based concatenative synthesis

Sound Features
Duration
Frequency μ
Frequency σ
Energy μ
Energy σ
Periodicity μ
Periodicity σ
AC1 μ
AC1 σ
Loudness μ
Loudness σ
Centroid μ
Centroid σ
Spread μ
Spread σ
Skewness μ
Skewness σ
Kurtosis μ
Kurtosis σ

thesis parameters, allowing users to reproduce the designed sounds or explore the sonic space around the existing sounds.

27.5.2 Corpus-Based Synthesis and Feature Mapping

Corpus-based concatenative synthesis (CBCS) is a compelling means to create new sounds based on navigating a timbral feature space. In its use of atomic source units that are analysed, we can think of CBCS as an extension of granular synthesis that harnesses the power of music information retrieval and the timbral descriptors they generate. The actual sound to be played is specified by a target and features associated with that target.

A sound file is imported into the synthesiser, and it is automatically segmented into units, determined by an onset segmentation algorithm. A vector of 19 auditory features, shown in Table 27.1, are analysed for each unit. Playback typically takes place as navigation in the audio feature space. A set of desired features is given to the synthesiser, and a k-nearest neighbours algorithm retrieves the closest matching unit to a given set of auditory features. This synthesis method, therefore, is not one where the user programmes sound by setting synthesis parameters in a deterministic way.

Schwarz typically uses CataRT [60] controlled through a 2D GUI in live performance, which enables control of only two target audio features at a time.

Here, the full vector of all auditory features are associated with with the sensor feature vectors to train the neural network, and roughly represent a high-dimensional timbral similarity space. We refer to this as multidimensional *feature mapping*, that is to say, that a gesture-sound mapping is created in the feature domain.

The high dimensionality of gesture and sound feature spaces raises challenges that ML techniques have helped to tackle. However, this complexity also offers opportunities for experimentation. This led us to develop an extension to the IML paradigm that allows to explore the vast space of possible gesture-sound mappings with the help of an artificial agent and RL.

27.6 Reinforcement Learning

RL is an area of ML in which algorithms in the form of artificial agents are programmed to take actions in an environment defined by a set of parameters. Their goal is to maximise the positive feedback—or rewards—they are given by a human (or by another algorithm) observing the outcome of their actions. Deep RL approaches—such as the Deep TAMER algorithm—leverage the power of deep neural networks and human-provided feedback to train agents able to perform complex tasks [61]. Scurto et al. [62] implemented the Deep TAMER algorithm to design artificial agents that allow to interactively explore the parameter spaces of software synthesisers.

We have developed a system that makes use of Deep RL to explore different mappings between motion tracking and a sound synthesis engine [47]. The user can give positive or negative feedback to the agent about the proposed mapping whilst playing with a gestural interface, and try new mappings on the fly. The design approach adopted is inspired by the ideas established by the IML paradigm (which we schematised in Fig. 27.1), as well as by the use of artificial agents in computer music for exploring complex parameter spaces [63–65]. We call this interaction design approach *Assisted Interactive Machine Learning* (AIML).

27.6.1 RL for Exploring Gesture-Sound Mappings: Assisted Interactive Machine Learning

An AIML system is designed to interactively explore the motion-sound mappings proposed by an artificial agent following the feedback given by the performer. This iterative collaboration can be summarised in four main steps:

1. Sound design: the user authors a number of sounds by editing a set of salient synthesis parameters;

2. Agent exploration: the agent proposes a new mapping between the signals of the input device and the synthesis parameters based on previous feedback given by the user;
3. Play: the user plays with the synthesiser using the input device and the mapping proposed by the agent;
4. Human feedback: the user gives feedback to the agent.

In step 2, the agent creates a new mapping based on user feedback. If no feedback was previously given, the agent starts with a random mapping. Steps 3 and 4 are repeated until the user has found as many interesting motion-sound mappings as they like. The following subsections will describe the system architecture and a typical workflow.

It is worth noting that, differently from most IML applications for gestural interaction, there is not a gesture design step during which the performer records some sample sensor data for training the system. This is perhaps one of the most obvious differences between the IML and AIML paradigms. In an AIML workflow, the sample sensor data used for training the model is provided by the artificial agent, whereas the user gives feedback to the agent interactively whilst playing the resulting gesture-sound mappings.

27.6.2 AIML System Architecture

The architecture of the system is schematised in Fig. 27.2. Motion features are stored in a vector and sent to a regression model created using a neural network. This

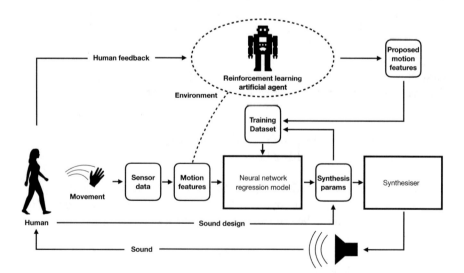

Fig. 27.2 Architecture of an assisted interactive machine learning system

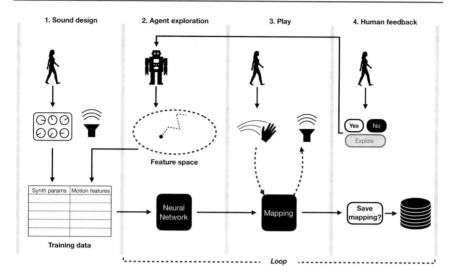

Fig. 27.3 The prototypical assisted interactive machine learning workflow

was implemented in Max using the `rapidmax` object [66], an external built using RapidLib [67, 68], a set of software libraries for IML applications in the style of Wekinator [69]. These features also represent the dimensions of the environment in which the artificial agent operates. By exploring this feature space following the user's feedback, the agent proposes a set of motion features to be paired with the synthesis parameters defined by the user during the sound design step. This becomes the dataset used to train the neural network. The resulting regression model maps the incoming sensor data to sound synthesis parameters.

27.6.3   AIML Workflow

The four main steps of the interactive collaboration between the human performer and the artificial agent are schematised in Fig. 27.3.

1. Sound design In this first step, the user defines a number of sounds by manipulating a set of synthesis parameters. This process may differ depending on the synthesiser chosen and which synthesis parameters are exposed to the user in this step. In the first version of the system using the sample-based synthesiser described in Sect. 27.5.1, the sounds are defined by manipulating six parameters (playback speed, pitch shift, start time, duration of the sample selection, filter cutoff frequency, and resonance). Here, the user defines the parameters of four sounds that will be used to train a neural network in step 2 and perform regression in step 3. The sounds designed in the sound design step will thus act as timbral anchor points that define a space for interpolation and extrapolation of new sounds.

2. Agent exploration The dimensions of the environment explored by the agent are defined by the motion features extracted from the raw sensor data for each of the sounds presets. Thus, at the end of the exploration step, the agent returns a vector with a set of input features for each of the sound synthesis parameters sets defined in the sound design step. This means that in the case of the version of the system using a 2D accelerometer, the agent will return four 2D vectors. These will be automatically paired with the synthesis parameters to train a neural network and create a regression model, which will be used in the following step to map live incoming sensor data to sound synthesis.

3. Play In this step, the user is free to play with and explore the resulting gesture-sound mapping for, however, long they like. Given that the regression models allow both interpolation and extrapolation of the input sound synthesis data, this step also allows to explore the timbral possibilities of the synthesiser whilst playing the mapping.

4. Human feedback After playing with the mapping, the user gives feedback to the artificial agent through a purposely designed interface. We adopted the concepts of *guiding feedback* and *zone feedback* implemented in the agent designed by Scurto et al. [62]. Guiding feedback is a binary evaluation of the actions performed by the agent, or the direction of its exploration of the feature space. Zone feedback is instead an evaluation of the area of the feature space the agent is currently exploring. For example, a negative guiding feedback would change the direction of the agent's trajectory in the feature space, whereas a negative zone feedback would immediately transfer the agent to a different region of the space.

In our system, the user can give positive or negative guiding feedback to the agent about the proposed mapping. This feedback guides the direction of the next explorations of the feature space, and thus affects the next mappings proposed by the agent. In addition, the user can tell the agent to move to a different area of the feature space by means of a negative zone feedback. This will likely result in a new mapping that is considerably different from the previous one. In practice, this could be useful for trying something new once one is satisfied with the mappings proposed by the agent after a few guiding feedback iterations. In fact, whereas negative guiding feedback results in adjustments to the mappings currently being proposed by the agent, negative zone feedback triggers the exploration of a new area of the feature space, thereby exploring new mapping possibilities. Finally, users can save mappings, which can be retrieved later for performance or as material to be further refined using other interaction design approaches.

27.7 In Practice: IML Techniques in Musical Pieces

The sections that follow will describe how the techniques we outlined so far were employed by the authors for the development of their own musical pieces. The four pieces we selected showcase how these methods may be deployed to aid certain expressive intentions. Through their use in artistic practice, some of the creative affordances of IML paradigms become clearer, showing how certain creative processes may be facilitated and exposing strength and limitations of specific techniques.

27.7.1 Wais (Tanaka)

Wais (2019) is an homage to Michel Waisvisz, his work at the studio STEIM in Amsterdam, and his performances on the instrument, *The Hands*. On one arm a short recording of a Waisvisz performance is articulated. On the other, an electronic music track, *Delull* by Tanaka. These two sources are granulated and placed in counterpoint. Two neural networks create independent regression models associating static posture and sound grain for each source. Once in "test" mode, these models take dynamic gestures, deconstructing the two prior works into a single improvisation.

Gesture is captured by one Myo sensor armband [70] on each forearm, providing 8 EMG channels, IMU quaternions, and combinatorial features resulting in 19 total muscle tension and movement features each from the left and right arms. An instance of the synthesiser described in Sect. 27.5.1 is associated with each sensor armband, allowing an independent sound buffer to be articulated by each arm.

The gesture input and sound synthesis output are associated by means of a neural network regression algorithm (see Sect. 27.4.2), one for each arm. The performance consists of three sections, first to audition the unaltered source samples, second to train the neural network, and third to explore the trained model. At the beginning of the performance, the regression models are empty. The source sounds are played from the beginning, going up to 5 min for Tanaka's recording and 19 s looped of Waisvisz's recording. The overall summed RMS muscle tension for each arm initially modulates the amplitude of each recording, allowing the two musical voices to be articulated in a direct, gross manner. This section familiarises the listener with the original source materials.

In section two, a series of four granular regions and filter settings for each voice are associated with four static postures for each arm, with the gesture input recorded to establish a training set. This is done in performance as a sequence of events to set the synths to each precomposed sound and prompt the performer to adopt a pose for each. The overall amplitude continues to be modulated by the summed muscle RMS. So, whilst each posture for the training set is static, the music continues to be articulated in a continuous manner through muscle tension. This creates a continuation of the first section where four segments of each voice are chosen as a way to zoom into segments of the original recordings. The eight segments are called up in an alternating manner for each arm through rhythmic timing aided by a foot pedal push button to advancing and promoting the performer to each subsequent pose. After the training set of example poses and associated target sounds are recorded, the two neural networks are trained to produce a regression model.

The regression model is put into test mode for the third section of the piece and all three components of the work—38 total dimensions of gesture, the two neural networks, and 12 total dimensions of sound synthesis output—come to life in dynamic interplay. The performer explores the gesture-sound space through continuous movement. He may approach or go through the poses from the training to see if the precomposed segments are recalled. He may explore multimodal decomposition and recombining of the source poses, perhaps striking a posture from one pose in space to recall IMU data for that pose, combined with muscle tension from another pose. This exploration is fluid, comprised of continuous gesture that dynamically goes in-between and beyond the input points from the training set. The result is a lively exchange of the two musical voices, with the granular synthesis and filters constantly shifting in ways unlikely to be possible with manual parameter manipulation or direct mapping.

27.7.2   11 Degrees of Dependence (Visi)

11 Degrees of Dependence (2016) is a composition for saxophone, electric guitar, wearable sensors, and live electronics that makes use of ML for continuously mapping the movements of the musicians to sound synthesis based on physical models and granular synthesis. The piece explores the relationship between the performers and their instruments, focusing on the constraints that instrumental practice imposes on body movement and a topological interpretation of the musician's kinesphere [71]. The score includes symbols to notate movements, designed to be easily interpreted by musicians familiar with standard notation.

The piece is a duet for alto or soprano sax and electric guitar tuned in Drop C (open strings tuned CGCFAD from low to high). The sax player and the guitarist each wear two Myo armbands to control the physical model whereas the guitarist wears the same devices to control granular synthesis and an electroacoustic resonator placed on the guitar headstock. Parameter mapping is done using a supervised learning workflow based on SVMs. The data from the lateral (pitch) and longitudinal (roll) axes of the magnetometer are used as input to train the ML model. Four 'postures' are then defined for both musicians. In the case of the sax player, these are:

- a 'default' performance position (named 'Rest') with arms comfortably by the side of the chest,
  gently leaning back, raising the saxophone with the elbows slightly open (named 'Open'),
- leaning to the left with the right elbow slightly pointing outwards (named 'Left'),
- leaning to the right with the left elbow slightly pointing outwards (named 'Right').

During the training phase, each posture is coupled with a set of synthesis parameters of the flute physical model. The Rest posture is paired with a clean sound with a clear fundamental frequency, the Open posture with a louder sound rich of breath noise, the Left posture adds overtones, and the right posture with a flutter tongued 'frullato' sound. In performance (testing phase, in ML terms), the synthesis parameters are continuously interpolated using the output likelihoods of the classifier as interpolation factors. This synthesised wind instrument sounds are designed to blend with the saxophone sound to generate a timbre with both familiar and uncanny qualities. The pitch played by the flute model is a C1, which is also the tonic of the piece. The amount of noise fed into the physical model (or breath pressure) is controlled by the sum of the EMG MAV values of both arms. This implies that the amount of synthesised sound is constrained by the movement of the fingers operating the saxophone keys. Notes that require more tone holes to be closed—such as low notes for example—cause more muscular activity and thus louder sounds from the physical model. This design choice adds a component of interdependent, semi-conscious control to the performance creating a tighter coupling between the sounds of the saxophone and those of the flute model.

11 Degrees of Dependence is structured in 3 parts, each of which contains scored themes at the beginning and the end a middle improvised section. The full score of the alto saxophone part can be found in the appendix of [72]. The score adopts conventional notation along with some custom symbols (printed in red) used to notate movement. Whilst the symbols indicate at which point in time the posture should be reached, the red lines show how the transition between the different postures should be articulated. These lines resemble other lines commonly found in conventional music notation. A straight line between two symbols means that the performer should start from the posture represented by the first symbol and progressively move towards the posture represented by the second symbol. The movement resulting from the transition between the postures should end in correspondence with the second symbol, thus following the rhythmic subdivision indicated in the staff. This is similar to a glissando, also notated using straight lines between note heads. A curved line between the posture symbols works instead analogously to a legato, meaning that the indicated posture is quickly tied with the following one. The score is where affordances and constraints of the agencies involved in the piece coalesce: each posture is represented by a symbol and corresponds to a class of the ML classifier, body movements occur in-between postures, causing sound synthesis to move in-between predefined parameter sets. At the centre of these interdependent agencies, we find the bodies of the musicians and their embodied relationships with their instruments.

27.7.3 Delearning (Tanaka)

Delearning (2019) takes as its source a work by Tanaka for chamber orchestra, DSCP, as sound corpus for analysis and subsequent neural network regression with gestural input. Feature extraction of arm poses is associated with audio metadata and used to train an artificial neural network. The algorithm is then put into performance mode allowing the performer to navigate a multidimensional timbre space with musical gesture.

This piece puts into practice the technique we describe in Zbyszyński et al. [21], where multimodal EMG and IMU sensing is used in conjunction with corpus-based concatenative sound synthesis (CBCS) to map 19 dimensions of incoming gesture features by a regression model to 19 dimensions of audio descriptors.

The nineteen gesture features are taken from the right forearm and are: IMU quaternions (4 dimensions), angular velocity (4 dimensions), 8 channels of Bayes filtered

EMG, total summed EMG (1 dimension), and a separation of all EMG channels on the perimeter of the forearm to horizontal and vertical tension (2 dimensions).

The nineteen target audio descriptors are grain duration followed by the means and standard deviations of frequency; energy; periodicity; autocorrelation coefficient; loudness; spectral centroid, spread, skew and kurtosis.

The gesture input feature space is mapped to the target audio feature space by means of a neural network that creates a regression model associating gesture as performed and sound synthesis output.

The source audio is a recording of an 18 minute piece for chamber orchestra of mixed forces. The work was chosen as it contains a diverse range of timbres and dynamics all whilst being musically coherent. Before the performance, the recording is analysed to generate the audio descriptors. The recording is read from beginning to end and is segmented by transient onset detection into grains. This generates 21,000 grains over the course of the duration of the recording, making the average grain 50 ms in duration.

The composition consists of five points in the original piece that have been selected to be associated with performance postures. The EMG and IMU sensors on the right arm feed the neural network, whilst EMG amplitude from the left arm modulates the overall synthesiser amplitude, and IMU quaternions modulate, at different points in the composition, filtering and spatialisation.

The performance begins with the analysed recording, but with an empty regression model. The first grain is heard, and the performer adopts a posture to associate with it, and records that as training data into the neural network. This continues for the two subsequent grains, at which point the training set consists of gesture features of the three poses associated with the audio descriptors of the three grains. The neural network is trained, then put into test mode. The performer then explores this gesture-timbre space through fluid, dynamic gesture. The regression model takes gesture feature input to report a set of audio descriptors to the synthesiser. The synthesiser applies a k-nearest neighbour algorithm to find a grain in the corpus that has the closest Euclidean distance to the look up features.

In the next section of the piece, the neural network is put back into training mode, and a fourth grain is introduced and associated with a fourth posture. This pose is recorded as an extension to the existing training set, putting in practice the IML paradigm of providing more examples. The neural network is retrained on this enhanced data set and put in performance mode for further free exploration by the performer.

This is repeated with the fifth and final grain to extend the regression model one last time to model the data representing 5 poses associated with five audio grains. This creates a musical structure where the gesture-timbre space becomes richer and more densely populated through the development of the piece.

27.7.4 "You Have a New Memory" (Visi)

"You Have a New Memory" (2020) [73] makes use of the AIML interaction paradigm (see Sect. 27.6) to navigate a vast corpus of audio material harvested from the messaging applications, videos, and audio journals recorded on the author's mobile phone. This corpus of sonic memories is then organised using audio descriptors and navigated with the aid of an artificial agent and RL. Feedback to the agent is given through a remote control, whilst embodied interaction with the corpus is enabled by a Myo armband.

Sonic interaction is implemented using CBCS (see Sect. 27.5.2). The approach is further refined by adopting the method based on self-organising maps proposed by Margraf [74], which helps handling the sparseness of heterogenous audio corpora.

In performance, the assisted exploration of sonic memories involves an embodied exploration of the corpus the entails both a search of musical motives and timbres to develop gestural musical phrases, as well as the intimate, personal exploration of the performer's recent past through fragments of sonic memories emerging from the corpus following the interaction with the agent. The juxtaposition of sounds that are associated with memories from different periods may guide the performer towards an unexpected introspective listening that co-inhabits the performance together with a more abstract, sonic object-oriented reduced listening [14]. The shifting between these modalities of listening influences the feedback given to the agent, which in return alters the way the performer interacts with the sonic memories stored in the corpus.

The title of the piece—*"You Have a New Memory"*—refers to the notifications that a popular photo library application occasionally send to mobile devices to prompt their users to check an algorithmically generated photo gallery that collects images and videos related to a particular event or series of events in their lives. These collections are ostensibly compiled by algorithms that extract and analyse image features, metadata (e.g. geotags), and attempt to identify the people portrayed in the photos [75].

The piece aims at dealing with the feelings of anxiety associated with the awareness that fragments of one's life are constantly turned (consciously or not) into data that is analysed and processed by unattended algorithms, whose inner workings and purposes are often opaque. The piece then is also an attempt at actively employing similar algorithms as a means of introspection and exploration. Rather than passively receiving the output of ML algorithms dictating when and how one's memories are forming, here the algorithms are used actively, as an empowering tool for exploring the complexity outlined by the overwhelming amount of data about ourselves that we constantly produce.

27.8 Conclusion

The purpose of this chapter was to provide an overview of the solutions, challenges, needs, and implications of employing IML techniques for analysing and designing musical gestures. The research field is still rapidly developing, and the topics we touched upon in the previous sections may give an idea of the interdisciplinary effort required for advancing research further. Advances in the field require an interdisciplinary perspective as well as a methodology encompassing basic research inquiry, the development of tools, their deployment in artistic practice and an analysis of the impact such techniques have on one's creative process. Learning more about the use of ML in music has manifold implications, stretching beyond the musical domain. As ML technologies are used to manage more and more aspects of everyday life, working along the fuzzy edges of artistic practice—where tasks are often not defined in univocal terms and problems are, and need to be left, open to creative solutions— becomes a laboratory in which we understand how to claim and negotiate human agency over data systems and algorithms. Understanding ML as a tool for navigating complexity that can aid musicians' creative practice may contribute to the advancement of these techniques, as well as to their demystification and broader adoption by artists, researchers as well as educators, thereby becoming sources of empowerment and inspiration.

Acknowledgements The *GEMM))) Gesture Embodiment and Machines in Music* research cluster is funded by Luleå University of Technology, Sweden.
Some of the research carried out at Goldsmiths, University of London, described in this chapter has received funding from the European Research Council (ERC) under the European Union's Horizon 2020 research and innovation programme (Grant agreement No. 789825–Project name: BioMusic). The authors would like to acknowledge Micheal Zbyszyński and Balandino Di Donato for their contributions to the BioMusic project and the discussions and sharing of ideas that led to some of the work presented in this chapter.

References

1. Godøy, R. I., & Leman, M. (Eds.). (2010). *Musical gestures: Sound, movement, and meaning*. Routledge.
2. Nymoen, K., Godøy, R. I., Jensenius, A. R., & Torresen, J. (2013). Analyzing correspondence between sound objects and body motion. *ACM Transactions on Applied Perception, 10*, 1–22.
3. Altavilla, A., Caramiaux, B., & Tanaka, A. (2013). Towards gestural sonic affordances. In: W. Yeo, K. Lee, A. Sigman, J. H., & G. Wakefield (Eds.) *Proceedings of the international conference on new interfaces for musical expression* (pp. 61–64). Graduate School of Culture Technology, KAIST, (Daejeon, Republic of Korea).
4. Tanaka, A., & Donnarumma, M. (2019). The body as musical instrument. In: Y. Kim & S. L. Gilman (eds.) *The Oxford handbook of music and the body* (pp. 78–96). Oxford University Press.

5. Visi, F., Coorevits, E., Schramm, R., & Miranda, E. R. (2017). Musical instruments, body movement, space, and motion data: Music as an emergent multimodal choreography. *Human Technology, 13*, 58–81.

6. Elblaus, L., Unander-Scharin, C., & Unander-Scharin, Å. (2014). Singing interaction: Embodied instruments for musical expression in Opera. *Leonardo Music Journal, 24*, 7–12.

7. Östersjö, S. (2016). "Go To Hell : Towards a gesture-based compositional practice. *Contemporary Music Review, 35*, 475–499.

8. Hunt, A., & Wanderley, M. M. (2003). Mapping performer parameters to synthesis engines. *Organised Sound, 7*, 97–108.

9. Van Nort, D., Wanderley, M. M., & Depalle, P. (2014). Mapping control structures for sound synthesis: Functional and topological perspectives. *Computer Music Journal, 38*, 6–22.

10. Françoise, J., Schnell, N., & Bevilacqua, F. (2014). MaD: Mapping by demonstration for continuous sonification. In: *ACM SIGGRAPH 2014 emerging technologies on–SIGGRAPH '14*, (pp. 1–11). New York, New York, USA: ACM Press.

11. Fiebrink, R. A., & Caramiau, B. (2018). *The machine learning algorithm as creative musical tool*, vol. 1. Oxford University Press.

12. Fiebrink, R., & Cook, P. R. (2010). The Wekinator: A system for real-time, interactive machine learning in music. In: *Proceedings of the eleventh international society for music information retrieval conference (ISMIR 2010)*, vol. 4, p. 2005.

13. Bullock, J., & Momeni, A. (2015). ml.lib: Robust, cross-platform, open-source machine learning for max and pure data. In: *Proceedings of the international conference on new interfaces for musical expression*, (pp. 265–270). Baton Rouge, USA.

14. Godøy, R. I. (2018). Sonic object cognition. In R. Bader (Ed.), *Springer handbook of systematic musicology* (pp. 761–777). Berlin Heidelberg: Springer.

15. Camurri, A., Hashimoto, S., Ricchetti, M., Ricci, A., Suzuki, K., Trocca, R., et al. (2000). Eyesweb: Toward gesture and affect recognition in interactive dance and music systems. *Computer Music Journal, 24*(1), 57–69.

16. Elblaus, L., Unander-Scharin, Å, & Unander-Scharin, C. (2016). New scenic subjects. In: *Proceedings of the 2016 CHI conference extended abstracts on human factors in computing systems—CHI EA '16*, vol. 07–12, (pp. 265–268). New York, New York, USA: ACM Press.

17. Merleau-Ponty, M. (2002). *Phenomenology of perception*. London, UK: Routledge.

18. Salazar Sutil, N. (2015). *Motion and representation: The language of human movement*. Cambridge, MA, USA: MIT Press.

19. Tanaka, A. (2015). Intention, effort, and restraint: The EMG in musical performance. *Leonardo, 48*, 298–299.

20. Tanaka, A., Di Donato, B., Zbyszynski, M., & Roks, G. (2019). Designing gestures for continuous sonic interaction. In: M. Queiroz & A. X. Sedó, (Eds.) *Proceedings of the international conference on new interfaces for musical expression*, (pp. 180–185). Porto Alegre, Brazil: UFRGS.

21. Zbyszyński, M., Di Donato, B., Visi, F. G., & Tanaka, A. (2020). Gesture-Timbre space: Multidimensional feature mapping using machine learning & concatenative synthesis. In M. Aramaki, R. Kronland-Martinet, & S. Ystad (Eds.), *Perception, representations, image, sound, music—Revised papers of CMMR2019, LNCS*. Switzerland: Springer Nature.

22. Camurri, A., Mazzarino, B., & Volpe, G. (2004). Analysis of expressive gesture: The EyesWeb expressive gesture processing library. *Gesture-based Communication in Human-Computer Interaction, LNAI, 2915*, 460–467.

23. Jensenius, A. R., Godøy, R. I., & Wanderley, M. M. (2005). Developing tools for studying Musical Gestures within the Max/MSP/Jitter environment. *International Computer Music Conference, ICMC, 2005*(3), 3–6.

24. Jensenius, A. R. (2018). The musical gestures toolbox for Matlab. In: *Proceedings of the 19th international society for music information retrieval conference.*

25. Visi, F. G., & Dahl, L. (2018). Modosc repository. https://github.com/motiondescriptors/modosc. Accessed 16 June 2020.
26. Visi, F., & Dahl, L. (2018). Real-time motion capture analysis and music interaction with the Modosc descriptor library. In: *NIME'18—international conference on new interfaces for musical expression*. VA, US: Blacksburn.
27. Flash, T., & Hogan, N. (1985). The coordination of arm movements: An experimentally confirmed mathematical model. *The Journal of Neuroscience, 5,* 1688–1703.
28. Piana, S., Staglianò, A., Odone, F., & Camurri, A. (2016). Adaptive body gesture representation for automatic emotion recognition. *ACM Transactions on Interactive Intelligent Systems, 6,* 1–31.
29. Fenza, D., Mion, L., Canazza, S., & Rodà, A. (2005). Physical movement and musical gestures: A multilevel mapping strategy. In: *Proceedings of sound and music computing conference, SMC 2005.* Italy: Salerno.
30. Glowinski, D., Dael, N., Camurri, A., Volpe, G., Mortillaro, M., & Scherer, K. (2011). Toward a minimal representation of affective gestures. *IEEE Transactions on Affective Computing, 2,* 106–118.
31. Hachimura, K., Takashina, K., & Yoshimura, M. (2005). Analysis and evaluation of dancing movement based on LMA. In: *ROMAN 2005. IEEE international workshop on robot and human interactive communication,* vol. 2005 (pp. 294–299). IEEE
32. Visi, F., Schramm, R., & Miranda, E. (2014). Gesture in performance with traditional musical instruments and electronics. In: *Proceedings of the 2014 international workshop on movement and computing—MOCO '14,* (pp. 100–105). New York, NY, USA: ACM Press.
33. Müller, M. (2007). *Information retrieval for music and motion.* Berlin, Germany: Springer.
34. Burger, B., & Toiviainen, P. (2013). MoCap Toolbox—A Matlab toolbox for computational analysis of movement data. In: R. Bresin, (ed.) *Proceedings of the 10th sound and music computing conference,* (pp. 172–178). Stockholm, Sweden: KTH Royal Institute of Technology.
35. Schramm, R., & Visi, F. G. (2019). Periodic quantity of motion repository. https://github.com/schramm/pqom/. Accessed 16 June 2020.
36. Sanger, T. D. (2007). Bayesian filtering of myoelectric signals. *Journal of Neurophysiology, 97,* 1839–1845.
37. Phinyomark, A., Phukpattaranont, P., & Limsakul, C. (2012). Feature reduction and selection for EMG signal classification. *Expert Systems with Applications, 39,* 7420–7431.
38. Arief, Z., Sulistijono, I. A., & Ardiansyah, R. A. (2015). Comparison of five time series EMG features extractions using Myo Armband. In: *2015 international electronics symposium (IES),* (pp. 11–14). IEEE.
39. Kim, K. S., Choi, H. H., Moon, C. S., & Mun, C. W. (2011). Comparison of k-nearest neighbor, quadratic discriminant and linear discriminant analysis in classification of electromyogram signals based on the wrist-motion directions. *Current Applied Physics, 11,* 740–745.
40. Kaiser, J. (1990). On a simple algorithm to calculate the 'energy' of a signal. In: *International conference on acoustics, speech, and signal processing,* vol. 1 (pp. 381–384). IEEE.
41. Kvedalen, E. (2003). *Signal processing using the Teager energy operator and other nonlinear operators.* Master thesis, Universitetet i Oslo.
42. Solnik, S., DeVita, P., Rider, P., Long, B., & Hortobágyi, T. (2008). Teager-Kaiser Operator improves the accuracy of EMG onset detection independent of signal-to-noise ratio. *Acta of bioengineering and biomechanics, 10*(2), 65–8.
43. Bachu, R., Kopparthi, S., Adapa, B., & Barkana, B. (2010). Voiced/unvoiced decision for speech signals based on zero-crossing rate and energy. In: *Advanced techniques in computing sciences and software engineering,* (pp. 279–282). Dordrecht: Springer Netherlands.
44. Caramiaux, B., Donnarumma, M., & Tanaka, A. (2015). Understanding gesture expressivity through muscle sensing. *ACM Transactions on Computer-Human Interaction, 21,* 1–26.
45. Mehryar, M., Afshin, R., & Ameet, T. (2018). *Foundation of machine learning* (2nd ed.). MIT Press.

46. Visi, F., Caramiaux, B., Mcloughlin, M., & Miranda, E. (2017). A knowledge-based, data-driven method for action-sound mapping. In: *NIME'17—international conference on new interfaces for musical expression*.
47. Visi, F. G., & Tanaka, A. (2020). Towards assisted interactive machine learning: Exploring gesture-sound mappings using reinforcement learning. In: *ICLI 2020—the fifth international conference on live interfaces*. Norway: Trondheim.
48. Hastie, T., Tibshirani, R., & Friedman, J. (2009). *The elements of statistical learning: Data mining, inference, and prediction*., Springer Series in Statistics New York, New York, NY: Springer.
49. Visi, F. G. (2020). Gimlet—gestural interaction machine learning toolkit repository. https://github.com/federicoVisi/GIMLeT/. Accessed 16 June 2020.
50. Kiefer, C. (2014). Musical instrument mapping design with echo state networks. In: *Proceedings of the international conference on new interfaces for musical expression*, pp. 293–298.
51. Senin, P. (2008). *Dynamic time warping algorithm review* tech. rep.
52. Gillian, N., Knapp, B., & O'Modhrain, S. (2011). Recognition of multivariate temporal musical gestures using N-dimensional dynamic time warping. In: Jensenius, A. R., Tveit, A., Godoy, R. I., & Overholt, D. (eds.). *Proceedings of the international conference on new interfaces for musical expression*, pp. 337–342. (Oslo, Norway).
53. Schramm, R., Jung, C. R., & Miranda, E. R. (2015). Dynamic time warping for music conducting gestures evaluation. *IEEE Transactions on Multimedia*, *17*, 243–255.
54. Bevilacqua, F., Zamborlin, B., Sypniewski, A., Schnell, N., Guédy, F., & Rasamimanana, N. (2010). Continuous realtime gesture following and recognition. In: *Proceedings of the 8th international conference on gesture in embodied communication and human-computer interaction, GW'09*, (pp. 73–84). Berlin, Heidelberg: Springer-Verlag.
55. Françoise, J., Schnell, N., Borghesi, R., & Bevilacqua, F. (2014). Probabilistic models for designing motion and sound relationships. In: B. Caramiaux, K. Tahiroglu, R. Fiebrink, & A. Tanaka, (eds.) *Proceedings of the international conference on new interfaces for musical expression*, pp. 287–292. London, United Kingdom: Goldsmiths, University of London.
56. Caramiaux, B., Montecchio, N., Tanaka, A., & Bevilacqua, F. (2014). Adaptive gesture recognition with variation estimation for interactive Systems. *ACM Transactions on Interactive Intelligent Systems*, *4*, 1–34.
57. Schwarz, D. (2007). Corpus-based concatenative synthesis. *IEEE Signal Processing Magazine*, *24*, 92–104.
58. Cycling '74 (2019). Max software. https://cycling74.com/products/max. Accessed 16 June 2020.
59. Caramiaux, B., Bevilacqua, F., & Schnell, N. (2010). Towards a gesture-sound cross-modal analysis. In: *In embodied communication and human-computer interaction, vol. 5934 of lecture notes in computer science*, (pp. 158–170). Springer Verlag (2010).
60. ircam (2019). Catart. http://imtr.ircam.fr/imtr/CataRT. Accessed 16 June 2020.
61. Warnell, G., Waytowich, N., Lawhern, V., & Stone, P. (2018). Deep TAMER: Interactive agent shaping in high-dimensional state spaces. In: *32nd AAAI conference on artificial intelligence, AAAI 2018*, (pp. 1545–1553).
62. Scurto, H., Van Kerrebroeck, B., Caramiaux, B., & Bevilacqua, F. (2019). Designing deep reinforcement learning for human parameter exploration. *ArXiv Preprint*.
63. Miranda, E. R. (1995). Granular synthesis of sounds by means of a cellular automaton. *Leonardo*, *28*(4), 297.
64. Dahlstedt, P. (2001). Creating and exploring huge parameter spaces: Interactive evolution as a tool for sound generation. In: *Proceedings of the 2001 international computer music conference*, (pp. 235–242).
65. Yee-King, M. J., Fedden, L., & D'Inverno, M. (2018). Automatic programming of VST sound synthesizers using deep networks and other techniques. *IEEE Transactions on Emerging Topics in Computational Intelligence*, *2*, 150–159.

66. Parke-Wolfe, S. T., Scurto, H., & Fiebrink, R. (2019). Sound control: Supporting custom musical interface design for children with disabilities. In: M. Queiroz & A. X. Sedó, (eds.) *Proceedings of the international conference on new interfaces for musical expression*, (pp. 192–197). Porto Alegre, Brazil: UFRGS.
67. Zbyszyński, M., Grierson, M., & Yee-King, M. (2017). Rapid prototyping of new instruments with CodeCircle. In: *Proceedings of the international conference on new interfaces for musical expression*, (pp. 227–230). Copenhagen, Denmark: Aalborg University Copenhagen.
68. RAPID-MIX consortium (2019). Rapid-mix api. www.rapidmixapi.com. Accessed 16 June 2020.
69. Fiebrink, R., Trueman, D., & Cook, P. (2009). A metainstrument for interactive, on-the-fly machine learning. In: *Proceedings of the international conference on new interfaces for musical expression*, (pp. 280–285). Pittsburgh, PA, USA.
70. Visconti, P., Gaetani, F., Zappatore, G., & Primiceri, P. (2018). Technical features and functionalities of myo armband: An overview on related literature and advanced applications of myoelectric armbands mainly focused on arm prostheses. *International Journal on Smart Sensing and Intelligent Systems*, *11*(1), 1–25.
71. Laban, R. (1966). *Choreutics*. London: Macdonald & Evans.
72. Visi, F. (2017). *Methods and technologies for the analysis and interactive use of body movements in instrumental music performance*. Ph.D thesis, Plymouth University.
73. Visi, F. G., & AQAXA (2020). You have a new memory. In: *ICLI 2020—the fifth international conference on live interfaces*. Norway: Trondheim.
74. Margraf, J. (2019). *Self-organizing maps for sound corpus organization*. Master's Thesis. Audiokommunikation—Technische Universität Berlin.
75. Apple Computer Vision Machine Learning Team. (2017). An on-device deep neural network for face detection. *Apple Machine Learning Journal, 1*(7).

Federico Ghelli Visi is a researcher, composer, and performer based in Berlin, Germany, and Piteå, Sweden. He carried out his doctoral research at the Interdisciplinary Centre for Computer Music Research (ICCMR), University of Plymouth, UK. In 2017, he was awarded a Ph.D. for his thesis "Methods and Technologies for the Analysis and Interactive Use of Body Movements in Instrumental Music Performance". His research interests include gesture in music, motion sensing technologies, machine learning and embodied interaction. His work as a performer is centred on the musician's body and the use of movement and physiological signals in electronic music. He recently joined the "GEMM)))" Gesture Embodiment and Machines in Music" research cluster at Luleå University of Technology in Sweden as a Postdoctoral Researcher. E-mail: mail@federicovisi.com.

Atau Tanaka conducts research into embodied musical and human-computer interaction. He has a B.A. from Harvard, composition/audio engineering degrees from Peabody Conservatory and obtained his doctorate from Stanford University's Center for Computer Research in Music and Acoustics (CCRMA). He uses muscle sensing via the electromyogram (EMG) in conjunction with machine learning in concert performance and interaction research, where the human body can be said to become a musical instrument. Atau has carried out research at the Institut de Recherche et Coordination Acoustique/Musique (IRCAM) in Paris, France, and was Artistic Ambassador for Apple France. He was researcher in computer music at Sony Computer Science Laboratory in Paris, France, and currently he is Professor of Media Computing at Goldsmiths University of London, United Kingdom. E-mail: a.tanaka@gold.ac.uk.

Human–Robot Musical Interaction

28

Sarah Cosentino and Atsuo Takanishi

28.1 Introduction

To be engaging and creatively adaptive in a joint live performance, musical robots must be interactive, and able to communicate at various social levels.

Technical communication exchanged with other performers can support synchronization and enhance the performance aesthetics, while accompanying emotional communication can help conveying the performance emotional message to the audience. Moreover, the ability to read the audience emotional state and engagement level can give the robot real-time feedback on its overall performance.

In particular, during a musical performance direct verbal communication is not possible, and the set of communicative gestures can be limited due to restraining postures and allocated resources for musical instrument playing.

We start this chapter with a brief overview on the relationship between performance and interaction; then introduce our musical robots, WF the flutist, and WAS the saxophonist. We then discuss the evolution of those robots and the effects of technical and emotional interaction on joint musical performance and on audience engagement with WF and WAS.

S. Cosentino (✉) · A. Takanishi
Waseda University, 162-8480 Tokyo, Japan
e-mail: sarah.cosentino@aoni.waseda.jp

A. Takanishi
e-mail: contact@takanishi.mech.waseda.ac.jp

© Springer Nature Switzerland AG 2021
E. R. Miranda (eds.), *Handbook of Artificial Intelligence for Music*,
https://doi.org/10.1007/978-3-030-72116-9_28

28.2 Music, Interaction, and Robots

Music is a form of art, and art is communication, the expression of the self: the interaction between artists and their surrounding is a critical part of the artistic process. Artists perform in what we can call the performance space, an environment in which there is usually an audience and often other performers. To give engaging and powerful performances, artists need to master artistic techniques, but also to effectively interact with the audience and fellow performers at various level of communication. They need to convey an emotional message to the audience, and technical signals to synchronize with their fellow performers. At the same time, they need to lookout for and acknowledge technical signals from the other performers, and sense the audience emotional state as a feedback to adjust their performance. In the scope of musical performance, most of these interactions are in the form of silent ancillary gestures, to avoid auditory interference: both technical signaling and emotional gestures must blend in seamlessly and harmonically within the performance. Moreover, due to physical motion constraints related to instrument playing, these gestures are limited to posture changes, gazing, and face expressions.

To be integrated in the musical performance space, a musical robot must be able not only to play an instrument with a fair amount of technical skills, but also to interact with fellow performers and the audience in the same way a human performer does. This imposes certain constraints on the robot design and control. In fact, a specialized non-human-like robot could be specifically designed to bypass the technical difficulties typically encountered by human musicians, and easily achieve a very high level of musical virtuosism with its enhanced dexterity. However, understanding and performing human communication signals requires hardware and software to capture human movement, vocalizations, and physiological changes linked to informational communication and emotional states, and a humanoid body to perform human-like gestures. To study how interaction affects the execution and perception of a musical performance, we at Waseda focused on the development of anthropomorphic musical robots able to play instruments and interact with both fellow performers and the audience as human musicians. In fact, sensing and actuating functions are important, but the quality of the interaction depends on the amount of autonomous decisional power the robot has when reacting to perceived signals: WABOT-1, the first humanoid robot developed at Waseda University, able to walk, carry objects, and even communicate verbally, was estimated to have the same mental faculty as a one-and-a-half year old child. The second humanoid, the musical robot WABOT-2, was developed with the specific aim to explore the potentiality of robotic artificial intelligence, as an artistic activity like playing the keyboard was though to require advanced human-like intelligence and dexterity, due to the strict real-time computational requirements for musical performance combined with the computational complexity of musical improvisation [1]. For this reason, in the development of the WF (Waseda Flutist) and WAS (Waseda Anthropomorphic Saxophonist) robots, dexterity and interaction systems refinement was carried out in parallel, as the two functions revealed interdependent to improve the overall robot musical performance.

28.3 The Waseda Wind Robot Players

28.3.1 The Waseda Flutist WF

The WF (Waseda Flutist) robot took 15 years to acquire full real-time autonomous musical performance ability (Fig. 28.1). The early versions of the robot were not humanoid in shape, and were built on extremely simplified models, to study and clarify the necessary human mechanisms for playing the flute. The first version of the flutist, WF-1 (Waseda Flutist 1), was completed in 1990. Although WF-1 was not humanoid, it featured a system simulating a human lung with a piston and cylinder mechanism. The synthetic lung was actuated by a DC servomotor and a ball screw to control the air flow. The robot was equipped with a MIDI-processing unit and could perform very simple tunes following MIDI input data. The second version of the robot, WF-2, completed in 1992, had human-like fingers mounted on a movable frame that controlled the relative position of the flute to the mouth (i.e., the embouchure). A linear actuator and a ball screw controlled the opening of the not yet human-like mouth mechanism, whilst an actuated rod and a voice-coil motor mimicked the tongue, an important mechanism to perform tonguing, a necessary technique for flute playing. These mechanisms were refined in the third version of the robot [2, 3]. In 1994, the WF-3RIV robot version featured a critically improved lip mechanism, enabling fine control of the air flow rate and angle. The flute holding mechanism was also redesigned, allowing fine controlling of the embouchure with 3 DoF (Degrees of Freedom) [4]. The WF-3RIX, completed in 1998, was the first robot version truly humanoid in shape. It reproduced, as realistically and precisely as possible, every single human organ involved in playing the flute: two lungs, lips in a rubber-based soft material, a refined tongue mechanism that allowed double-tonguing and vibrato, human-like arms to hold the flute and control the embouchure, multiple DoF fingers that could perform trilling. The human-like design and flute-playing attitude was further refined in the following robot version, the WF-4, built in 2003. The 5-DoF lips and 4-DoF new neck mechanisms enhanced the flute positioning accuracy; a voice-coil motor increased the efficacy of the vibrato system; and two piston cylinders, driven by embedded ball screws, improved the controllability of the lungs system [5]. In the 2004 WF-4R robot version fully actuated arm mechanisms were added to improve precision and accuracy of the flute positioning, and a sound pressure control system was implemented to enhance performance expressivity [5].

The very first version of the robot featuring a basic interaction system, WF-4RII, was initiated in 2004. This robot version had a two-coupled cameras mechanism mimicking human-like eyes and a human face-tracking algorithm to maintain visual

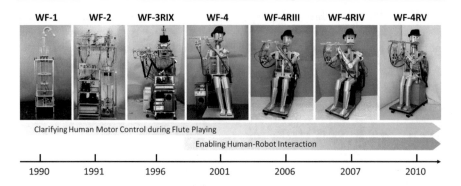

Fig. 28.1 Evolution of the Waseda Flutist (WF) robot

contact with the users [6]. Since 2005, the subsequent versions of the robot, WF-4RIII, WF-4RIV, WF-4RV and the latest WF-4RVI, focused on improving the robot performance expressivity and interactivity. Control algorithms were refined and mechanical systems were redesigned to stabilize notes duration and vibrato, whilst musical composition algorithmic functions and sensing systems were added to enable the robot generating real-time expressive variations from the nominal score in synchronization with partner performers during a joint performance. The impact and efficacy of these systems will be analyzed in detail in the following sections.

28.3.2 The Waseda Anthropomorphic Saxophonist WAS

The first version of the WAS (Waseda Anthropomorphic Saxophonist) robot was completed in 2009, following the first attempt to transform the specialist flute player robot WF as a generalized wind instrument player robot (Fig. 28.2). WAS-1 was an extremely simplified version of the WF, built to clarify the different technical challenges required to play a saxophone, a reed instrument, instead of a flute. In particular, the lip system was a simplified 1-DoF mechanism, the synthetic lung system was substituted by an air rotational pump and an air flow controlling valve, and the fingers, with only 11 DoF, were designed to play a limited range of notes, from C3 to C#5. The modified lip mechanism enabled WAS-1 to correctly calibrate the sound pitch, however the sound pressure range was too short. The air flow management system was studied for maximum accuracy of intraoral air pressure, a critical parameter for correct note emission during musical performance. However, due to mechanical control limitations, there was a delay from the note attack command in reaching the target air pressure, which severely affected the technical performance of the robot. In the second version of the robot, WAS-2, which was already completely humanoid, most of the initial technical problems were solved [7–9]. The subsequent versions of the robot focused on improving the sound generation and control system.

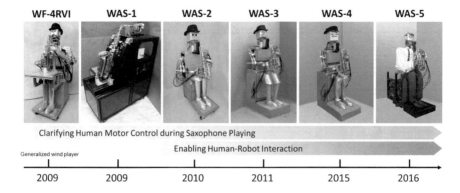

Fig. 28.2   Evolution of the Waseda Anthropomorphic Saxophonist (WAS) robot

28.4   Technical Musical Interaction

28.4.1   Asynchronous Verbal Technical Interaction

The first studies on interaction with the Waseda musical robots were conducted in 2004 with the WF robot. Due to the limited musical synchronization and improvisation abilities of the robot, interaction was carried out verbally offline. In fact, even though verbal interaction is reduced to a minimum during a musical performance, to minimize noise interference, before and after the performance performers engage often in conversation with the audience and fellow performers, to foster group empathy and discuss about performance details. This type of off-line interaction is extremely useful to receive and provide both technical and emotional feedback, enhancing personal engagement and group cohesion. A musical robot should be able to introduce and give feedback about the musical performance to the audience and its fellow partners. For this reason, the first Waseda musical robot, WABOT-2, the organ player robot developed by the late Professor Kato in 1984, could verbally introduce itself and the piece to be presented. Moreover, it had basic speech recognition and synthesis systems to understand and handle spoken requests related to its musical repertoire [1].

The effect of verbal interaction with WF was tested in the scope of a project aiming at using WF in a robot-based musical training protocol for beginner flutists [10, 11]. During the training, the WF-4RII robot first demonstrated the correct execution of a musical piece, then provided verbal feedback on the novice flutist's execution of the same piece. In fact, WF-4RII could analyze in an articulated manner the details of a musical performance by means of a dedicated sound quality evaluation system [11], and suggest practical corrections for sound improvement. Moreover, WF-4RII could visually recognize and track the face of the users, to maintain eye contact during the interactive session (Fig. 28.3).

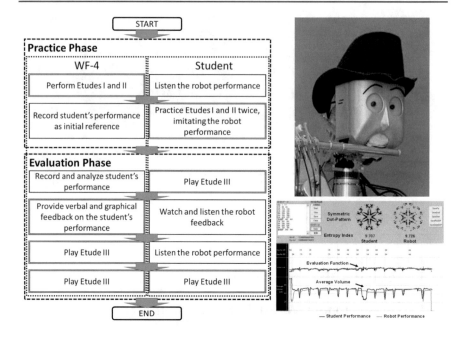

Fig. 28.3 Musical training protocol with WF-4RII

Interestingly, even though the feedback system was proven to provide useful advice only in 25% of the cases and partially correct advice in 55% of the cases, the improvement in performance technique of the students using the interactive training procedure with the robot was found significantly higher in a controlled evaluation experiment compared to a control group training only with a human music teacher. This is a successful example of how human–robot interaction-based educational tools can be used effectively for reinforcement, information and motivation during training, accelerating the learning process.

28.4.2 Synchronous Automatic Interaction

Real-time musical interaction requires advanced musical technical abilities. WF-4RII was equipped with an automatic sound quality evaluation system, which used a deterministic musical measurement algorithm and sound processing techniques to evaluate a performance. However, personal expressivity requires the musician to perform deviation from a nominal score according to personal tastes. Evaluation rules determined on the basis of real performances measurements use statistical analysis of the sound data, reflecting typical, rather than individual, deviations from a nominal score. For this reason, such rules might prove inefficient in the analysis of a performer's individual expressivity, hindering the robot adaptability to a particular partner performer. To overcome these limitations, an AI-based approach was proposed for the WF-4RIII, using a feed-forward neural network to analyze a specific set of musical parameters deviation from the nominal score in a professional flutist performance [12]. The parameters deemed significant for expressivity were the *note duration* and *vibrato* duration and frequency. The idea was to train the neural network with a specific data set from a recorded expressive performance of a professional flutist, then test how well the performer expression rules model could predict the performer's execution of a different score. This system had a dual impact: on one hand, it allowed the robot to build expression rules for an individual performer, to improve adaptively its synchrony and coordination with that performer, similar to playing repetitively with a partner performer improves synchronization and coordination. On the other hand, it enabled the robot to analyze different performers and build different sets of expression rules, eventually leading to the development of a personal set of expression rules for musical performance, similar to listening to several different performers helps in building an individual musical taste and expression. Also as a result of this work, after additional mechanical design improvement to enhance sound clarity and shape [13], the WF-4RIV robot expressivity and ability to accompany a human flutist in a duet significantly increased [14] (Fig. 28.4).

However, the system required further improvements in the robot mechanical and control system to significantly improve the quality of the sound during the flute

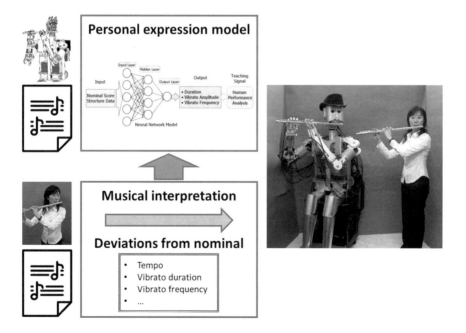

Fig. 28.4 Performer's individual musical expression model

performance. In particular, a closed-loop fast control of the air flow depending on the generated sound was necessary. For this purpose, an auditory feedback control system, consisting in a music expressive generator, a feed-forward air pressure control system and a pitch evaluation module was implemented. Experimental results confirmed that the implemented system greatly reduced the generated sound errors, significantly improving the robot performance [15–17].

28.4.3 Interaction via Direct Signaling

The next step to human–robot natural musical interaction is the implementation of strategies to exchange direct technical signaling during the performance for synchronization and coordination. In general, the two principal methods used by human musicians to interact with each other during a performance are communication through the acoustic and visual channel. Although aural exchange of information seems predominant in a musical band setup there is also a large amount of silent communication taking place via visual interaction.

As previously mentioned, during musical performance musicians rely heavily on a limited set of gestures to communicate with fellow performers, given the limitations imposed by instrument playing. Understanding human communication gestures and postural changes would allow the robot to coordinate with joint performers more precisely and react real-time to contextual performance deviations, dramatically improving the overall performance. In this scope, a vision-based hands-free controller was developed for WF-4RIV [18–21]. The two types of commands implemented were a visual push button and a virtual fader.

The first implementation of the system required the user to stand in front of a camera, watching the camera recorded image on a monitor located beside the robot. Superimposed on the camera recorded image a virtual push button was graphically displayed, in a semitransparent color, so the area covered by the button was clearly defined and at the same time the video image beneath could still be seen. The second controller implemented was a virtual fader, which could be used to continuously set a controller value. The user could manipulate the button and fader by touching them virtually on the screen. Manipulation of these virtual controllers would send real-time MIDI controller messages to the robot. The implemented control system was robust, and experimental results showed that lighting and background changes within certain limits did not strongly affect the control system, even though more extreme conditions caused larger movement recognition errors, which could likely be avoided with a preliminary contextual calibration of the camera. The implemented control system accuracy was also high, as experimental results showed a closely proportional relationship between input and output when the system was used to control a MIDI synthesizer. However, the performance accuracy was strongly affected by the type of command these virtual controllers were used for, due to the robot mechanical limitations. Moreover, a usability test showed that from the user viewpoint this hands-free virtual controller system did not offer significant practical advantage over classical mechanical controllers used

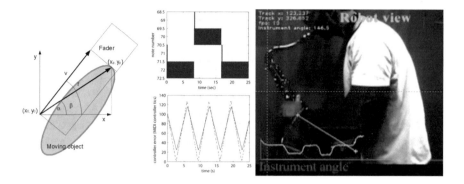

Fig. 28.5 Virtual fader interface

during live performance, as the system was just a direct method to control the robot musical performance parameters, and the musician also needed some perceptual training to get acquainted with the interface [18, 19]. The system was subsequently improved using the cameras mounted on the robot for a 3D visual recognition of the human musician partner postural changes, specifically the holding orientation of the saxophone by a saxophonist. Simply changing the absolute saxophone orientation by varying the pitch or the roll angles of the saxophone, a very natural movement for a professional saxophonist, enabled controlling the robot vibrato tone (Fig. 28.5). The new system was perceived much more natural and easy to use, although it still was simply a mean of directly controlling the robot performance without any automatic adaptation assistance [20, 21]. The two different control systems provided different control interfaces and could be used by performers with different musical skills to control the robot during joint performances.

28.4.4   Multimodal Dynamic Interaction

Subsequent work in human–robot natural musical interaction focused on enabling the flutist robot to interact more naturally with musical partners in the context of a Jazz band. This required integration of visual and aural cues from partner performers. In fact, in the context of improvisation in a Jazz band, during solo play, in most cases, one player at a time takes the lead and the other players provide accompaniment. Upon finishing a solo, through movements with their instrument and specific harmonic and rhythmic cues, a musician directs the lead to the next performer. A Musical-Based Interaction System (MbIS) was then developed to enable the robot to process both visual and aural cues from partner performers, complementing the previous visual gestural recognition system with an aural cues perception system. The proposed system enabled the robot to detect the tempo and harmony of a partner performance, with a specific focus on improvisation, via a real-time analysis of the rhythmical and harmonic characteristics of the recorded sound.

The Musical-Based Interaction System (MbIS) was designed for people with different musical skills, allowing two levels of interaction: beginner and advanced. Similar to when two human musicians play together, the more advanced person always adapts to the less advanced person, the system allowed the flutist robot to adapt to the musical interaction skills of the partner performer. A person without experience in performing with the robot would need more time to adjust to the particularities of this type of human–machine interaction. For this reason the beginner level interaction system was designed to provide direct and easy to learn controllers similar to usual studio equipment. Moreover, the level of complexity of acoustic interaction was reduced by only considering rhythmic data: the robot analyzed the timing of a partner's musical sequence and adapted its performance to the same rhythm. In this way, the human player could focus on the rhythmic exchange, without paying attention to the harmonic content of the melody, resulting in a simpler interaction, suitable to a beginner player. The system would instead offer to an advanced level player more refined ways of creative expression, allowing free control of the performance parameters. The advanced interaction mode required more experience in working interactively with the robot, but also allowed for more subtle control of the musical performance. In this mode both the rhythmic and harmonic information of the human musician's performance was analyzed by the system, and the robot played in response an adapted suitable rhythm and melody.

Experimental results showed that the implemented algorithm enabled the robot to correctly recognize a number of rhythms and harmonies, allowing it to engage in a simple form of stimulus and response play with a human musician. However, the overall performance quality was strongly influenced by contextual conditions and the robot mechanical limitations could lead to very poor results [22].

Interaction experiments to provide qualitative results documenting the usability of the system were performed with two beginner-level, two intermediate-level and two professional level instrument players. Individual impressions on the interaction quality was investigated with a subjective questionnaire. The questionnaire asked to evaluate the system on a 10-points Likert scale, from 1 = insufficient to 10 = excellent, in three categories: Overall Responsiveness of the System, Adaptability to Own Skill-Level and Musical Applicability/Creative Inspiration.

Overall Responsiveness of the system scored higher among less experienced players and lower among experienced players. More experienced musicians have more stringent responsiveness requirements. Adaptability to Own Skill Level results confirmed preliminary expectations that less experienced players would feel more comfortable with the beginner level interaction system and the more experienced players would give higher grades to the advanced level interaction system. Musical Applicability/Creative Inspiration results show intermediate scores for all skill levels, sign that the system needs still improvement in the direction of natural creative interaction [23, 24] (Fig. 28.6).

Interestingly, the Musical-Based Interaction System was implemented on both robots, the WAS-2 and the WF-4RIV, to verify the technical challenges for

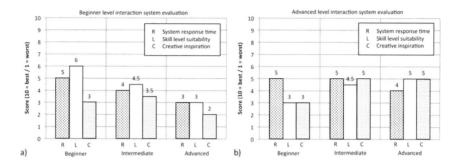

Fig. 28.6 Usability evaluation of the MbIS

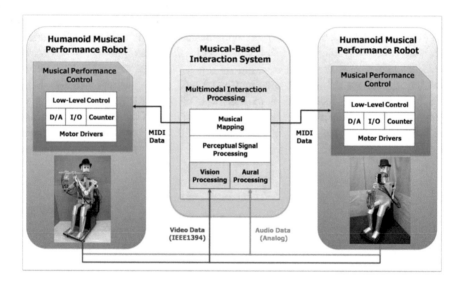

Fig. 28.7 Robot interaction protocol using the MbIS

performing a duet between the saxophonist robot as main voice and the flutist robot as second voice (Fig. 28.7).

Both robots were programmed to perform Theobald Böhm's *Trois Duos de Mendelssohn et Lachner*. As a preliminary work, information was exchanged between the two robots by direct synchronized MIDI signal. The performance of each robot was recorded separately via two separate microphones. Experimental results show that performances were synchronized and the differences between the main and second voice were clearly observable by comparing the volume and the pitch of the performances. However, joint performance quality was lowered by the robots technical limitations, in particular the complex air flow control of the flutist lung system. Future works in this direction should enable performance information exchange between the two robots not only via the MIDI signal, but also via audio and visual cues, like a natural human interaction [25].

More recent work shifted the point of view from passive to active interaction, enabling the WAS robot to send, not only receive, direct interaction signals for synchronization with a human musician. Consistently with musical interaction specifications, signaling was limited to silent gestures, body posture and facial expression changes. For facial expressions, a pre-existing constraint of the design was to maintain unchanged the gaze mechanism, used to track a user's face and maintain eye contact. To avoid mechanism-generated noise that could influences the musical performance, an implementation with direct drive, instead of gears, was chosen. Based on these specifications, the motions that the mechanism should reproduce were investigated. Focus was on the upper face expressions, especially eyebrows and eyelid movements, because the mouth is used for playing the saxophone and the lower face is partially hidden by the instrument. Eyebrow and eyelid movements were modeled on human saxophonists' video performances analysis. Moreover, upon discussion with a professional saxophonist, it was found that raising the eyebrows and winking during a performance might be used as specific signals for the articulations and attacks. Therefore, it was decided that a mechanism for the synchronized motion of eyebrows, for eyebrows raising or frowning; and a mechanism for the independent motion of the eyelids for blinking or winking would be sufficient to generate the most common iconic facial expressions used by a human saxophonist during musical performances

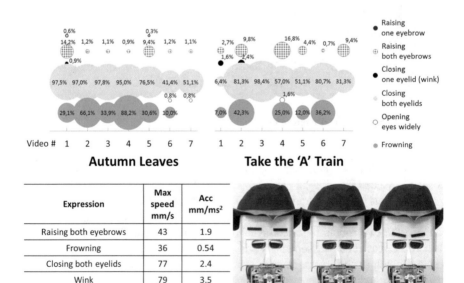

Fig. 28.8 Communicative facial expression occurrences and specifications

(Fig. 28.8). Experimental results showed that not only the joint performance was perceived as more engaging and natural by a partner musician, but also by the audience [26, 27].

28.4.5 Technical Interaction in an Orchestra: Conducting Gestures

A long-term goal of the research on human–robot musical interaction is to enable the dynamic interaction between robots and humans at the same level of perception, in order for the robots to play actively together with a human ensemble. For this purpose, the focus so far has been on perfecting the perceptual abilities of the robots and developing a dynamic interaction system with human musicians. However, the limit of these interaction systems is that they use a specific, ad-hoc engineered set of interaction commands, and can only be used in small groups, because big ensembles are controlled and synchronized by conductors. Conductors use a standard set of signals, or better say a complex non-verbal gestural language, to convey the musical parameters information to all the ensemble members at once during live performance. For the communication to be effective, every member, robot included, must know the language used to exchange information. Modelling a language is not trivial, but, if the model is accurate, the level of uncertainty of the communication is low and the effectiveness of communication high.

To effectively model a non-verbal language, the concepts that must be expressed with that specific language, and with which symbol they are expressed, should be clarified. In this specific application, this requires a deeper understanding of musical rules and theory. Moreover, after modelling, an effective perception system to detect and identify correctly these symbols is required. In this case, this requires a highly accurate and precise gesture detection and analysis system. First of all, elements of basic music theory were analyzed, and linked to the conductor's gestures. A musical piece is characterized by three fundamental parameters that can be dynamically adjusted to represent different expressions: *Tempo, Dynamics,* and *Articulation.* Orchestra conductors use their hands, with or without a baton, to represent changes in these three parameters during the performance, to obtain specific effects and shape the musical performance according to the composer specified directives but also to their individual taste.

Tempo is the unit to measure the duration in time of the notes to be played; in modern Western music is usually indicated in beats per minute (bpm). The beat is the basic unit of time, the regularly occurring pattern of rhythmic stresses in music, and it is specified on the score with a time signature. The conductor usually indicates the *Tempo* tracing with the hand a shape in the air, indicating each beat with a change in the motion direction. Different time signatures correspond to different beat patterns and are represented with different shapes. The first beat of the pattern is called downbeat, and the instant at which the downbeat occurs is called the ictus.

Dynamics is the acoustic volume of the notes to be played. Conductors represent this parameter with the size of the traced shape, larger shapes representing louder sounds. Changes in *Dynamics* can also be signaled with the hand that is not being used to indicate the beat: an upward motion (usually palm-up) indicates a crescendo, an increase in volume; a downward motion (usually palm-down) indicates a diminuendo, a decrease in volume.

Articulation affects the transition between multiple notes. Conductors represent this parameter with the movement type of their hands, usually linked to the performance meaning of the articulation type: from short and sharp for *staccato*, to long and fluid for *legato*. Many conductors change also the muscular tension of hands and arms: strained muscles and rigid movements correspond to *marcato*, while relaxed hands and softer movements may correspond to *legato* or *espressivo*.

The variety of movements connected to musical expression is virtually infinite; therefore, to develop a reasonably simple conducting gesture recognition experimental system, we focused on a minimum set of motion patterns expressing *Tempo*, *Dynamics*, and *Articulation*.

A visual recognition system would not be sufficiently accurate to recognize differences the conductor gestures, also taking into consideration the contextual conditions for large ensemble performance: very large and visually noisy spaces, with the conductor potentially very far away from the robot. For this reason, it was decided to use a wearable Inertial Measurement Unit (IMU) system containing a 3-axes accelerometer, gyroscope and magnetometer. The IMU was small and lightweight and was easily embedded in a fingerless sport glove providing stable anchorage but minimal hindrance to the conductor's hand. The system was tested with a professional and several beginner conductors. Results show that analysis performed on accelerometer data provided information on both *Tempo* and *Dynamics* with a recognition rate precision of over 95%, and could also help in evaluating the user's conducting skills level, via the analysis of standard deviation from median values for each movement cycle. The results of the *Articulation* discrimination algorithm, using a Principal Component Analysis (PCA), produced instead mixed results, depending on how different were the articulation types (Fig. 28.9). This also depends on the individual differences in gestural representation of similar, but distinct, articulation types. An audience perception evaluation experiment showed that using the system led to significant improvement in the perceived temporal synchronization of the overall performance, but not on the piece emotional representation, due to low accuracy in articulation discrimination [28–30]. In the future, an AI-based algorithm could be used to enable the robot better adapt to individual gestural deviations of conductors and improve the articulation discrimination accuracy.

28.5 Creative Interaction

The more the interaction focus moves up on the expressivity scale, the more the performance requires a higher musical skill level and a deeper understanding of artistic and social interaction rules. Musical creative interaction with a partner

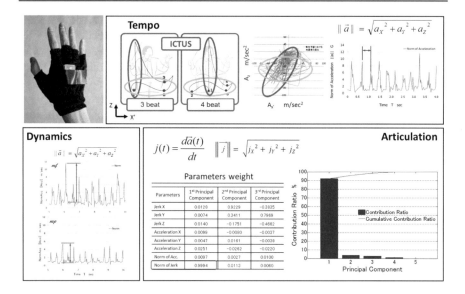

Fig. 28.9 Orchestra directing movements musical parameters analysis

performer of another artistic discipline, for example a dancer, requires an understanding of expressive rules for both music and dance. Since expressivity and expression methods are heavily influenced by individual taste, creative expressive interaction relies less and less on expression rules and defined language; and more and more on partner performers' empathy and connection. In fact, humans tune in unconscious signals to capture the interacting partner's inner feelings. These unconscious or involuntary signals are typical of humans as a species, and so are generally universally recognized, independently on individual cultural and language differences. However, unconscious signals are often subtle or invisible, and conscious attempts are sometimes made to suppress them altogether. On the other hands, conscious gestures to express the same inner feelings, for example in performing arts, are intuitively modeled on those unconscious signals, with which share characteristics and similarities. In addition, these gestures are usually caricatured and stylized, to minimize uncertainty and maximize effectiveness. Analyzing the semantics of emotional expressive gestures is then an auxiliary intermediate step in the process of recognition of human communication signals, from completely conscious, direct and fixed to completely unconscious and naturally unconstrained emotional communication.

A good starting point for this analysis is constituted by the study of acting or dance emotional expressive movements, and of music emotional expression theory. For this reason, to improve the interaction expressivity of the Waseda musical robots, emotional expression semantics in dance and in music were explored, and a human–robot direct creative interaction framework was implemented. In particular, a study on how emotions are expressed in dance and in music, and how a robot can perceive and recognize these expressions in dance and follow and reproduce them real-time in music, during a live artistic performance, was performed.

Several previous studies looked at the correlation existing between types of movements and emotions. One of the most complete studies in this sense is the research of De Meijer, who studied different dimensions of body movement in relation to emotion expression. For this human–robot musical interaction application, a subset of dance movements and their corresponding emotional expressions was chosen as a starting point for the emotional expression analysis:

- body extension (opening, closing)
- movement velocity (fast, slow).

Opening or closing of the limbs, especially the arms, is related to meaning like openness or closeness to the environment, as it is related to extending the body to the world or acquire a self-protective posture. Velocity of the movements is directly related to arousal state: a fast movement is related to a high arousal state, to excitement, whilst a slow movement to low arousal, might it come from a relaxed or depressed state of mind. From these two selected dance movement parameters four basic dance movement patterns can be built:

1. arms closed, slow movement
2. arms closed, fast movement
3. arms opened, slow movement
4. arms opened, fast movement.

According to one of the basic emotional models, developed by psychologists, these four movement patterns can be then related to four emotional patterns:

1. grief
2. fear
3. joy
4. surprise.

In this specific application, to achieve human–robot creative expressive interaction, the musical robot should then be able to recognize these four emotional patterns from the dancer's movements, and reproduce those using musical emotional expressive patterns. For this reason, a study of musical expressive patterns is also necessary.

The way music arouses listeners' emotions has been studied from many different perspectives and there is a vast literature on this field. Summarizing, it can be said that the most powerful musical cues to generate emotional impression are mode, tempo, dynamics, articulation, timbre, and phrasing. In real music, it is challenging to assess the exact contribution of individual cues to emotional expression because all these cues are strictly correlated. Previous studies on emotional expression in music using factorial design have often focused on relatively few cues as one has to manipulate each level of the factors separately, and the ensuing exhaustive combinations will quickly amount to an unfeasible total number of trials needed to evaluate the design. Because of this complexity, the existing studies have usually evaluated two or three separate factors using typically two or three discrete levels in each.

From this wide musical features collection a subset was chosen, roughly correlated to changes in the same emotional expressive patterns chosen for the dance movements subset. Roughly, the idea of "openness" and "closeness" to the external environment is related, in music, with the scale of notes that are played: a wider scale, a wider musical variation, denotes a greater openness, and vice versa. The arousal level can instead be represented linearly with variation in tempo, which implies different density of played notes in the same amount of time. Changes in these two parameters can then be summarized as, respectively:

1. Narrow scale—slow tempo
2. Narrow scale—fast tempo
3. Wide scale—slow tempo
4. Wide scale—fast tempo.

To achieve human–robot creative expressive interaction, the musical robot should then be able to express changes in these four emotional patterns according to the dancer's movements, and to reproduce such changes using the listed musical emotional expressive patterns.

The dancer's movements were captured by a 3D frontal camera and a wearable IMU on the dancer's hand. The 3D camera provided data on body openness, whilst the IMU accelerometer provided data on the movement velocity. To observe the difference in movements representing different sets of parameters, the dancers were asked to do several repetitions of different motions with different movement parameters. However, these movements were not following specific movement rules, but changed according to the dancer's inspiration and creativity.

At first, four predefined musical phrase types following fixed melodic rules and musical patterns according to the expressions were composed.

Dance movement data were separated in four clusters, two for body openness and two for movement velocity, using the k-means clustering method, and the clusters centroids were calculated. The movement transition thresholds between clusters for the two parameters were calculated as the mean between the two movements clusters centroids (Fig. 28.10).

However, this approach proved too approximated and unsatisfactory, because in this way the human auditory perception ability were not taken into account. Using this method, the robot response to movement change was too slow, about 1 s. In addition, in this way changes in the musical parameters were approximated and not anymore directly proportional to changes in the movement parameters. These two discrepancies between musical and movement variation were clearly perceived by both the dancer and the external audience.

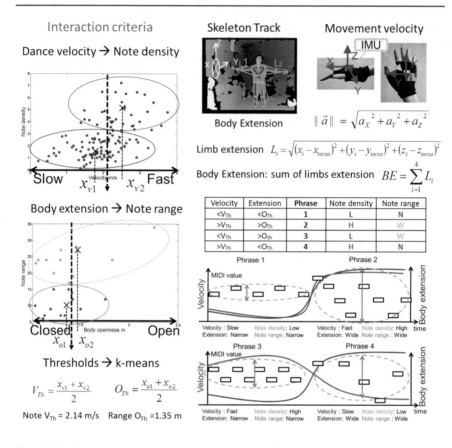

Fig. 28.10 Dance movements and musical patterns mapping

For this reason, an automatic musical pattern generator for instantaneous real-time musical adaptation was implemented. Professional musicians, during improvisation, change their performance combining and tying together suitable short musical phrases from their repertoire. So, instead of 4 different phrases to be selected, a repository of short phrase patterns was built, with several different combinations of rhythm and scale range. Rhythm and range were selected by the robot according to the movement data, following the previous criteria: rhythm and density of the notes are proportional to movement velocity, while scale range is proportional to body extension.

Moreover, in absence of data, the selection algorithm used a Markov chain to determine the next pattern, inside the current cluster.

Compared to the previous algorithm, the response time of the robot to movement changes was reduced to 108 ms, or about 1/10. As the human auditory sense reaction time is around 190 ms, this response time is acceptable because the delay is not perceivable by the human ear.

Results of the perception experiment show that there is a significant difference in the audience evaluation of the robot performances without or with the interaction system. The performance of the robot following the dancer using the interaction system presented a significant increase in perceived phrase diversity and naturalness of the joint performance, which led to a significant increase of the overall entertainment level of the joint performance.

28.6 Emotional Interaction

Current direction of research focuses on the interaction between the musical robot and the audience. In particular, building on the previous studies on emotional expression, a simple system for automatic recognition of the emotional feedback from the audience has been implemented. Preliminary research work has explored the feasibility of recognizing the audience emotional state to enhance the robot emotional interaction with the audience.

The system has a dual application: on one hand, depending on the audience emotional state, it enables the robot to select and play a suitable melody with similar emotional expression characteristics, to improve the robot perceived empathy with the audience. On the other, this emotional expression system can be used as an emotional feedback system for the robot musical emotional expressivity: following the choice of a specific musical melody, the audience emotional response can be analyzed to measure the effectiveness of the robot expressive performance and the audience emotional engagement with the robot.

Technical requirements for the system include ecological, unobtrusive sensing, and the ability to recognize and process the emotional state of several subjects in parallel. As WAS-5 is equipped with two front cameras, emotion recognition was implemented via unobtrusive, visual analysis of facial expression, based on Ekman's basic emotions model and facial expression analysis works. However, the simultaneous analysis of multiple subjects' facial features involves a high computational load, and embedded processing and memory constraints limit the system scalability. For this reason, Microsoft Azure, a cloud computing-based system, was selected, to easily scale computational power and facial expressions database. In particular, Microsoft Azure comes with two already implemented APIs for face detection and emotion detection: Microsoft Cognitive Services—Face API and Emotion API. Face API analyzes an image and returns the number and the position of the faces in the image. Emotion API analyzes a face image and returns coefficients in the range [0–1] for all the seven basic emotions and neutral of the Ekman's "Big Six + 1" model: *happiness, sadness, fear, surprise, anger, disgust,* and *contempt*. The more a coefficient is near to one, the stronger is the corresponding emotional component in the facial expression. The subject's displayed emotion can be estimated using these coefficients, and in the most simple of the cases, the estimated emotion equals the emotion with the highest coefficient (Fig. 28.11).

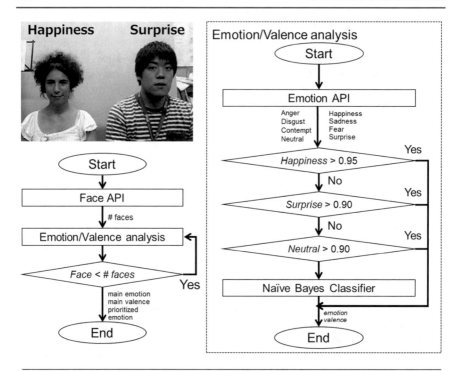

Fig. 28.11 Emotion recognition algorithm and emotional musical parameters mapping

The performances of Face API and Emotion API were preliminarily tested with existing facial recognition databases to check the performances of the proposed system against preexisting standards in the field: the HeadPoseImage database for facial recognition depending on the face orientation towards the camera, the Cohn-Kanade (CK) and the Cohn-Kanade Extended (CK+) database, for specific emotional face expression recognition, and the Japanese Female Facial Expression (JAFFE) Database, to compare the system performance depending on the subject's facial features differences.

Facial expression recognition experimental results show that the success rate does not increase linearly with the size of the training set. That reflects the presence of a bias in the face expression training or validation data set: the Emotion API performance is excellent in the recognition of a "happy" or "surprised" expression, but produces mixed results with other emotions, in particular emotions with negative valence. Moreover, compared to the CK+, the performance of the Emotion API is significantly worse with the JAFFE database, highlighting a bias in the face feature recognition training or validation data set. Finally, the system performance is severely limited by the range of suitable camera positions for a correct detection of the face and recognition of the emotional face expression [31].

The evaluation, and addressing of the general mood of a group of people, provided the individual emotions of most people in the group are estimated correctly, is a very complex problem that strongly depends on the interaction context: the social implications of an erroneous reaction strategy might vary greatly and have different lasting consequences for all the implied actors. Different automatic strategies to define the global mood of a group of people have been implemented and compared with human strategies. This work proved very difficult, and current results are inconclusive, as it is difficult also for humans to decide which is the dominant emotion when presented with several different emotions display within members of the same group [32]. Future works in this direction will be strongly application-dependent, and will require an extensive analysis of the interaction contextual factors, to enable the robot to address the most compelling emotional state in a specific interaction setting, in relation to the musical application objectives.

28.7   Concluding Discussion

Real-time musical interaction between partner performers greatly improves the perceived quality of the overall joint performance, even when these interactions are very basic and strictly limited to direct signaling for performance synchronization. On the other hand, true musical expressive interaction requires advanced interaction experience, higher musical skills, and a deeper theoretical knowledge foundation. For this reason, a musical robot needs to advance simultaneously in all these 3 fields, similar to what a professional musician does. Performing arts are in fact very demanding in terms of individual acquisition of common technical knowledge, but also in the development of a personal expression style. In the future, to enable the musical robots to be completely integrated in the musical space, not only all the technical challenges linked to perfect musical execution must be solved, but also truly adaptive strategies of expressive communication with partner performers, both human and robotic, and the audience, must be implemented. While the first require finer mechanical and control implementations, the second must be based on the autonomous development and refinement of the robot individual expressivity, similarly to a human musician personal style formation. AI-based adaptive expressive algorithms, relying on a broad analysis of data from many different performances, could help in this direction, while specific analysis of data from individual performers could help in the robot adaptation to these performers' expression patterns during joint performance. These two types of individual expressivity development strategies are not easy to combine: similarly, performers with very different styles cannot easily work together in a joint performance. Strategies to detect and use the audience the emotional state as a feedback on the robot performance must also be implemented. This is the greatest challenge so far, as group psychological and emotional models are not yet defined even for human interactions.

In conclusion, this chapter presented the evolution of strategies for musical human–robot interaction, from very basic direct synchronization signaling to advanced emotional expression patterns. Works in this direction are far from being completed, and could help clarify and model also human complex interaction patterns.

References

1. Kato, I., et al. (1987). The robot musician 'wabot-2' (waseda robot-2). *Robotics, 3*(2), 143–155. https://doi.org/10.1016/0167-8493(87)90002-7.
2. Takanishi, A., Hirai, T., & Miyoshi, S. (1994). Development of an anthropomorphic flutist robot. *Journal of the Robotics Society of Japan, 12*(3), 439–443.
3. Takanishi, A. (1996). Development of anthropomorphic flutist robot. *Journal of the Robotics Society of Japan, 14*(2), 188–191.
4. Takanishi, A., Sonehara, M., & Kondo, H. (1996). Development of an anthropomorphic flutist robot WF-3RII. In *Proceedings of IEEE/RSJ International Conference on Intelligent Robots and Systems. IROS '96* (Vol. 1, pp. 37–43). https://doi.org/10.1109/IROS.1996.570624.
5. Chida, K., et al. (2004). Development of a new anthropomorphic flutist robot WF-4. In *IEEE International Conference on Robotics and Automation, 2004. Proceedings. ICRA '04. 2004* (Vol. 1, pp. 152–157). https://doi.org/10.1109/ROBOT.2004.1307144.
6. Solis, J., Chida, K., Taniguchi, K., Hashimoto, S. M., Suefuji, K., & Takanishi, A. (2006). The Waseda flutist robot WF-4RII in comparison with a professional flutist. *Computer Music Journal, 30*(4), 12–27.
7. Solis, J., et al. (2010). Development of the anthropomorphic Waseda saxophonist robot. In *ROMANSY 18 Robot Design, Dynamics and Control* (pp. 209–216). Springer.
8. Solis, J., et al. (2010). Implementation of an overblowing correction controller and the proposal of a quantitative assessment of the sound's pitch for the anthropomorphic saxophonist robot WAS-2. In. *IEEE/RSJ International Conference on Intelligent Robots and Systems, 2010*, 1943–1948.
9. Solis, J., et al. (2011). Improvement of the oral cavity and finger mechanisms and implementation of a pressure-pitch control system for the Waseda Saxophonist Robot. In. *IEEE International Conference on Robotics and Automation, 2011* (3976–3981).
10. Solis, J., Bergamasco, M., Isoda, S., Chida, K., & Takanishi, A. (2004). Learning to play the flute with an anthropomorphic robot. In *ICMC*.
11. Solis, J., Bergamasco, M., Chida, K., Isoda, S., & Takanishi, A. (2004). Evaluating the sound quality of beginner players by an anthropomorphic flutist robot (WF-4). In *2004 IEEE/RSJ International Conference on Intelligent Robots and Systems (IROS) (IEEE Cat. No.04CH37566)* (Vol. 2, pp. 1568–1573). https://doi.org/10.1109/IROS.2004.1389619.

12. Solis, J., Suefuji, K., Taniguchi, K., Ninomiya, T., Maeda, M., & Takanishi, A. (2007). Implementation of expressive performance rules on the WF-4RIII by modeling a professional flutist performance using NN. In *Proceedings 2007 IEEE International Conference on Robotics and Automation* (pp. 2552–2557). https://doi.org/10.1109/ROBOT.2007.363849.

13. Solis, J., Taniguchi, K., Ninomiya, T., Yamamoto, T., & Takanishi, A. (2007). The Waseda Flutist Robot No. 4 Refined IV: Enhancing the sound clarity and the articulation between notes by improving the design of the lips and tonguing mechanisms. In *2007 IEEE/RSJ International Conference on Intelligent Robots and Systems* (pp. 2041–2046).

14. Solis, J., Taniguchi, K., Ninomiya, T., Yamamoto, T., Sato, A., & Takanishi, A. (2007). Musical skills of the Waseda Flutist Robot WF-4RIV. In. *IEEE/RSJ International Conference on Intelligent Robots and Systems, 2007* (pp. 2570–2571).

15. Solis, J., Taniguchi, K., Ninomiya, T., Yamamoto, T., & Takanishi, A. (2008). Development of Waseda flutist robot WF-4RIV: Implementation of auditory feedback system. In. *IEEE International Conference on Robotics and Automation, 2008* (pp. 3654–3659).

16. Solis, J., Taniguchi, K., Ninomiya, T., Petersen, K., Yamamoto, T., & Takanishi, A. (2008). Improved musical performance control of WF-4RIV: Implementation of an expressive music generator and an automated sound quality detection. In *RO-MAN 2008-The 17th IEEE International Symposium on Robot and Human Interactive Communication* (pp. 334–339).

17. Solis, J., Taniguchi, K., Ninomiya, T., Petersen, K., Yamamoto, T., & Takanishi, A. (2009). Implementation of an auditory feedback control system on an anthropomorphic flutist robot inspired on the performance of a professional flutist. *Advanced Robotics, 23*(14), 1849–1871.

18. Petersen, K., Solis, J., & Takanishi, A. (2008). Development of a real-time gestural interface for hands-free musical performance control. In *ICMC*.

19. Petersen, K., Solis, J., & Takanishi, A. (2008). Toward enabling a natural interaction between human musicians and musical performance robots: Implementation of a real-time gestural interface. In *RO-MAN 2008-The 17th IEEE International Symposium on Robot and Human Interactive Communication* (pp. 340–345).

20. Petersen, K., Solis, J., & Takanishi, A. (2008). Development of a real-time instrument tracking system for enabling the musical interaction with the Waseda Flutist Robot. In. *IEEE/RSJ International Conference on Intelligent Robots and Systems, 2008* (pp. 313–318).

21. Petersen, K., Solis, J., Taniguchi, K., Ninomiya, T., Yamamoto, T., & Takanishi, A. (2008). Development of the Waseda Flutist Robot No. 4 Refined IV: Implementation of a real-time interaction system with human partners. In *2008 2nd IEEE RAS & EMBS International Conference on Biomedical Robotics and Biomechatronics* (pp. 421–426).

22. Petersen, K., Solis, J., & Takanishi, A. (2009). Development of a aural real-time rhythmical and harmonic tracking to enable the musical interaction with the waseda flutist robot. In. *IEEE/RSJ International Conference on Intelligent Robots and Systems, 2009* (pp. 2303–2308).

23. Petersen, K., Solis, J., & Takanishi, A. (2010). "Implementation of a musical performance interaction system for the Waseda Flutist Robot: Combining visual and acoustic sensor input based on sequential Bayesian filtering. *IEEE/RSJ International Conference on Intelligent Robots and Systems*, 2283–2288.

24. Petersen, K., Solis, J., & Takanishi, A. (2010). Musical-based interaction system for the Waseda Flutist Robot. *Autonomous Robots, 28*(4), 471–488. https://doi.org/10.1007/s10514-010-9180-5.

25. Solis, J., & Takanishi, A. (2010). *Research on anthropomorphic musical robots and their application to musical interaction. In The First IROS 2010 Workshop on Robots and Musical Expressions*. Taiwan: Taipei.

26. Matsuki, K., Yoshida, K., Sessa, S., Cosentino, S., Kamiyama, K., & Takanishi, A. (2016). Facial expression design for the saxophone player robot WAS-4. In *ROMANSY 21-Robot Design, Dynamics and Control* (pp. 259–266).

27. Xia, G., et al. (2016) Expressive humanoid robot for automatic accompaniment. In *13th Sound and Music Computing Conference and Summer School (SMC 2016)* (pp. 506–511).

28. Cosentino, S., et al. (2012). Music conductor gesture recognition by using inertial measurement system for human-robot musical interaction. In *IEEE International Conference on Robotics and Biomimetics (ROBIO), 2012* (pp. 30–35).
29. Cosentino, S., et al. (2012). Musical robots: Towards a natural joint performance. In *First International Conference on Innovative Engineering Systems, 2012* (pp. 19–24).
30. Cosentino, S., et al. (2014). Natural human–robot musical interaction: Understanding the music conductor gestures by using the WB-4 inertial measurement system. *Advanced Robotics, 28*(11), 781–792.
31. Randria, E., Cosentino, S., Lin, J.-Y., Pellegrini, T., Sessa, S., & Takanishi, A. (2017). *Audience mood estimation for the Waseda Anthropomorphic Saxophonist 5 (WAS-5) using cloud cognitive services. In* 第35回日本ロボット学会学術講演会. Japan: Tokyo.
32. Cosentino, S., Randria, E. I., Lin, J.-Y., Pellegrini, T., Sessa, S., & Takanishi, A. (2018). Group emotion recognition strategies for entertainment robots. In *IEEE/RSJ International Conference on Intelligent Robots and Systems (IROS), 2018* (pp. 813–818).

Sarah Cosentino received her M.S. degree in Electronic Engineering from Polytechnic University of Milan, Italy (2006) and her Ph.D. degree in Mechanical Engineering from Waseda University, Japan (2015). She is currently Associate Professor at the Global Center for Science and Engineering at Waseda University and Affiliate Professor at the Biorobotics Institute of the Sant'Anna School of Advanced Studies (SSSA) in Italy; she is also the President of the Association of Italian Researchers in Japan (AIRJ). Her main scientific interests are the observation and analyses of the human behaviour for the development of natural human-robot interfaces and humanoid robotics. She is particularly interested in the areas of affective computing, enaction and human-robot interaction. E-mail: ing.cosentino.sarah@gmail.com.

Atsuo Takanishi received his B.S., M.S. and Ph.D. degrees in Mechanical Engineering from Waseda University, Japan, in 1980, 1982 and 1988, respectively. He is a Professor at the Department of Modern Mechanical Engineering and Director of the Humanoid Robotics Institute (HRI), at Waseda University. He is a board member of Robotics Society of Japan, member of the Japanese Society of Biomechanisms, Japanese Society of Mechanical Engineers, Japanese Society of Instrument and Control Engineers and Society of Mastication Systems and Institute of Electrical and Electronics Engineers (IEEE). His research interests are in the field of humanoid robotics for medical, therapeutic, and social applications, such as biped walking humanoid robots, wind instrument player robots, emotion expression humanoid robots, patient simulator humanoid robots, ultrasonic diagnosis robots, and colonoscopy diagnosis robots. E-mail: takanisi@waseda.jp.

Shimon Sings-Robotic Musicianship Finds Its Voice

29

Richard Savery, Lisa Zahray and Gil Weinberg

29.1 Introduction—Robotic Musicianship at GTCMT

Robotic Musicianship research at Georgia Tech Center for Music Technology (GTCMT) focuses on the construction of autonomous and wearable robots that analyze, reason about, and generate music. The goal of our research is to facilitate meaningful and inspiring musical interactions between humans and machines. The term Robotic Musicianship refers to the intersection of the fields of Musical Mechatronics—the study and construction of physical systems that generate sound through mechanical means, and Machine Musicianship, which focuses on developing algorithms and cognitive models representative of music perception, composition, improvisation, performance, interaction, and theory. Research in Robotic Musicianship at GTCMT addresses the design of autonomous and wearable music-playing robots that have the underlying musical intelligence to support performance and interaction with human musicians. The motivation for our research is not to imitate human creativity or replace it, but rather to supplement it and enrich the musical experience for humans. We aim to explore the possibilities of combining computers with physical sound generators to create systems capable of rich acoustic sound production, intuitive physics-based visual cues from sound-producing movements, and expressive physical behaviors through sound-accompanying body movements. Our work is driven by the artistic potential that is embedded in non-human characteristics of machines, including humanly impossible speed and precision, freedom of physical design, and the ability to explore artificial constructs and algorithms that could surprise and inspire human musicians.

R. Savery (✉) · L. Zahray · G. Weinberg
Georgia Tech Center for Music Technology, Atlanta, GA, USA
e-mail: rsavery3@gatech.edu

© Springer Nature Switzerland AG 2021
E. R. Miranda (ed.), *Handbook of Artificial Intelligence for Music*,
https://doi.org/10.1007/978-3-030-72116-9_29

In this chapter, we describe our efforts to develop new singing capabilities for Shimon, the robotic marimba player developed at GTCMT. Shimon was originally built in 2008 to play, improvise, and compose music for marimba. In 2019, Shimon's head was redesigned to allow vocal social interaction and improved musical expression. As part of the redesign, Shimon was provided with a singing voice synthesizer designed at the Music Technology Group at Universitat Pompeu Fabra. For this synthesizer, we developed a deep learning-driven lyrics generator and a rule-based embodied singing gesture generator. The chapter starts with a presentation of Shimon and other robotic musicians designed at GTCMT along with the design principles that have driven our robotic musicianship research. We then discuss the motivation and approach behind the "Shimon Sings" project, focusing on our lyrics generation and facial gesture modules. We describe the implementation of both modules and two experiments that were conducted to evaluate our work. The paper ends with a discussion and a number of possible directions for future work.

29.1.1 Platforms

Over the last 15 years, we have developed multiple robotic platforms in an effort to explore a wide variety of aspects of Robotic Musicianship. The platforms include a robotic drummer, a robotic marimba player, a personal robotic musical companion, and a number of wearable robotic musicianship prosthetics and exoskeletons, as described below.

Haile
GTCMT's first robotic musician, Haile (Fig. 29.1), was designed to play a Native American pow-wow drum, a multi-player instrument used in ceremonial events [1]. To match the natural aesthetics of the Native American pow-wow ritual, the robot was constructed from plywood. One of Haile's arms uses a solenoid which can generate fast notes—up to 10 hits per second—but is limited in terms of amplitude and visibility. The other arm uses a linear motor that can produce louder sounds and more visible motions but can only play 7 hits per second. Haile listens to and interacts with two humans playing hand percussion instruments such as Darbukas—Middle Eastern goblet-shaped hand drums. Haile listens to audio input from each drum and detects musical aspects such as note onset, pitch, amplitude, beat, and rhythmic density. It is also designed to analyze higher level musical percepts such as rhythmic stability and similarity. Based on these detected features, Haile utilizes multiple interaction modes that are designed to address the unique improvisatory aesthetics of the Middle Eastern percussion ensemble [2]. Haile responds physically by operating its mechanical arms, adjusting the sound of its hits in two manners: pitch and timbre varieties are achieved by striking the drumhead in different locations while volume variety is achieved by hitting harder or softer.

Shimon
The next robotic musician designed at GTCMT was Shimon (Fig. 29.2)—an eight-mallet marimba playing robot, designed to expand the scope of robotic musicianship

Fig. 29.1 Two percussionists interact with Haile, Georgia Tech's first robotic musician

by introducing two main additional functionalities, the ability to play a melodic and harmonic instrument, and the ability to communicate with co-players using music-making gestures and socio-musical ancillary gestures. Several musical considerations informed the physical design of Shimon: we wanted to have large movements for visibility, as well as fast movements for high note density. In addition, Shimon was designed to play a wide range of sequential and simultaneous note combinations utilizing fast, long-range, linear actuators, and two sets of rapid parallel solenoids per arm. Over the last 10 years, Shimon has been programmed to use both rules and machine learning to improvise with humans. Shimon demonstrates how visual cues can improve musical performance both objectively and subjectively [3]. It was the first robot to compose original music based on deep learning [4], and has performed dozens of concerts in world-wide venues, in genres such as jazz, rock, hip-hop, and reggae [5].

Shimi

Shimi (Fig. 29.3) is a smartphone-enabled five-Degrees-of-Freedom (DoF) robotic musical companion that can respond to and enhance humans' musical experiences [6]. Shimi was originally designed to be controlled by an Android phone using the phone's built-in sensing and music generation capabilities. This allowed for easy development of additional custom mobile apps for the robot. Multiple interactive applications have been developed for Shimi such as Query by Tapping and Query by Bobbing—where Shimi listened to and analyzed rhythms based on human tapping

Fig. 29.2 A bass player interacts with Shimon, the robotic marimba player

and head movements. It then responded by choosing and playing songs in similar beat and tempo and dancing to the music using a set of expressive gestures that fit the beat and genre. Other functionalities included the ability to project emotions through gestures [7], to analyze music in real time and respond in a choreographed manner based on structural elements of the music, and to perform musical searches based on natural language, interactive improvisation, and games [8].

Wearable Robotic Musicians

In recent years, we have expanded our research to explore the implementation of robotic musicianship in wearable robots for both people with disabilities as well as able-bodied people. Our first project in this realm was the robotic drumming prosthesis (Fig. 29.4), which allowed amputees not only to regain their lost drumming capabilities and expression but also to enhance their skills to new uncharted domains [9]. The prosthetic has two sticks, each capable of playing 20 hits per second—faster than any human. These abilities led to novel timbres and polyrhythmic structures that are humanly impossible. The first stick is controlled both physically by the musicians' arms and electronically using electromyography (EMG) muscle sensors. The other stick has "a mind of its own" and can improvise based on musical analysis, leading to unique shared-control scenarios leading to new unexplored musical experiences [10].

Our next wearable robotic musicianship project was an effort to bring novel drumming capabilities not only to amputees but to able-bodied users as well. The Robotic Drumming Third Arm (Fig. 29.5) project explored how a shared control paradigm between a human drummer and a wearable robotic arm can influence and poten-

Fig. 29.3 Shimi analyzes humans clapping, and responds by playing a song in the right tempo and groove

Fig. 29.4 Jason Barnes, amputee drummer, presents the robotic drumming prosthetic

Fig. 29.5 The third drumming arm allows able-bodied musicians to explore enhanced drumming capabilities

tially enhance musical performance [11]. The project's primary research challenges focused on design and usability using a device that allowed for comfort and robust functionality.

Our latest wearable robotics project is the Skywalker Piano Hand (Fig. 29.6), which provides amputees with finger-by-finger control of their robotic hand prosthetics. The device uses a novel ultrasound sensor and Deep Learning algorithms that detect and predict muscle patterns in the amputees' residual limb. The predicted finger movements are mapped to control detailed robotic finger movements with dexterity and subtlety that can support expressive musical performance.

29.1.2 Design Principles

While working on the robotic musicianship platforms described above, we have identified and followed a few design guidelines that have since informed our work. We believe that for robotic musicians to be able to support expressive and creative interactions with human, they should be able to:

- "Listen Like a Human"—utilize human-informed music perception modeling.
- "Play Like a Machine"—feature humanly impossible software and hardware musical capabilities.
- "Be Social"—support socio-musical interaction between humans and machines.

Fig. 29.6 The Skywalker Piano Hand project—ultrasound- enabled finger-by-finger prosthetic arm control

- "Watch and Learn"—use artificial vision applications for musical gesture analysis.
- "Wear It"—allow for novel wearable capabilities for humans with disabilities as well as able-bodied musicians.

The first two guidelines suggest that robotic musicians would "Listen Like a Human" and "Play Like a Machine." These principles are aimed at allowing our robots to both understand how humans perceive music ("listen like a human"), and to expand on humans' musical experiences by generating music like no human can, both algorithmically and mechanically ("play like a machine"). The next two guidelines— "Be Social" and "Watch and Learn"—focus on embodiment allowing both humans and robots not only to listen to each other but also to communicate visually through musical gestures. The last guideline addresses our recent efforts to bring our robotic musicians into the human body, enabling and enhancing musical experiences for people with disabilities and others. Below is some more information about each one of these guidelines.

Listen Like a Human—Human-Informed Music Perception Modeling
We have been developing computational modeling of music perception to allow robots to perceive and understand music similar to how humans do. If a robotic musician can recognize humanly perceived musical aspects such as beat, stability, similarity, tension, and release, it would be able to respond musically in a relatable manner that could be understood and appreciated by its human co-players. We believe that such perceptual modeling is crucial for creating meaningful interaction and

connection with human co-players, supporting expressive and emotional musical experiences.

Play Like a Machine—Software and Hardware Generators Designed to Play Like No Human Can

While implementing "Listening Like a Human" modules in robotic musicians allows robots to connect to humans in a relatable manner, "Play Like A Machine" modules are aimed at generating novel musical outcomes that are humanly impossible in an effort to surprise and inspire human collaborators. A well-crafted balance between these two aspects bears the promise of leading to musical outcomes and experiences that are both meaningful for humans and human aesthetic ("Listen Like a Human"), yet novel, exciting, and inspiring for humans ("Play Like a Machine"). We have explored two main approaches in our effort to develop robots that play like machines. The first approach focuses on software and algorithmic modeling while the second approach focuses on hardware actuators. In software, we developed artificial algorithms that require computation power and are based on pattern processing that is foreign to human thinking, but bear the promise of creating compelling aesthetic results. These include computational techniques such as genetic algorithms, mathematical constructs such as fractals, and statistical modeling approaches such as Markov processes. In hardware, we developed mechanical abilities that are humanly impossible such as robot percussionists that can control eight simultaneous arms, or strikers that can hit in humanly impossible speeds. By combining both software and hardware approaches, we hope that our robotic musicians could create novel musical responses that would push musical experiences and outcome to uncharted domains.

Be Social—Embodied Socio-Musical Interaction between Humans and Machines

One of the benefits of Robotic Musicianship over computer-supported interactive music systems is the ability to control music-related physical and social cues to aid multi-modal joint musicianship. Such gestural interaction can enable better synchronicity between players through visual anticipation or support the conveyance of emotions through gestures, which can significantly affect the musical experiences. Physical and social cues in non-musical Human-Robot Interaction (HRI) have been shown to have a significant effect on social interaction, from enabling more fluent turn-taking with humans to affecting subjects' positive perception of the HRI experience. Similarly, a robot musician's embodied social presence could inspire human co-players to be more engaged in the joint activity. The robot's physical movements could also create visual choreography that would add to the aesthetic impression of both players and audiences. We explored the notion of "Be Social" with all of our robots, including the design of social interactions and turn-taking for Haile, studying the effect of Shimon's ancillary gestures on co-player anticipation and audience engagement, and exploring the effect of Shimi's emotional gestures on subjects' perception of the robot and the music it generates.

Watch and Learn—Artificial Vision for Robotic Musicians

Movement and vision-based interactions have been part of the human musical experience since the dawn of time, with evidence of coordinated dance and music activities from the prehistoric age. In collaborative music-making, visual connection between musicians can assist with anticipation, coordinating, and synchronization between musicians. Consider, for example, a guitar player maintaining visual connection with a drummer to anticipate and synchronize the ending chord of a song, musicians gesturing to each other to signify turn- taking, or reinforcing the tempo, beat, and groove of a song by looking at the bobbing head of collaborators. We believe, therefore, that robotic musicians should not only listen to music input but also be able to see and use visual cues to inform their musical decisions. We have therefore developed multiple applications that allow robots such as Shimon and Shimi to use visual information to assist with anticipation, synchronization, learning, song selection, and even film composition [12].

Wear It—Wearable Robotic Musicians
Recent developments in wearable technology can help people with disabilities regain their lost capabilities, merging their biological body with technological enhancements. Myoelectric prosthetic hands, for example, allow amputees to perform basic daily-life activities by sensing and operating based on electric activity from their residual limbs. These new developments not only bring back lost functionalities but can also provide humanly impossible capabilities, turning those who were considered disabled to become super-abled. The current frontier of Robotic Musicianship research at Georgia Tech focuses on the development of wearable robotic limbs that allow not only amputees but also able-bodied people to play music like no human can, with virtuosity and technical abilities that are humanly impossible.

29.2 "Shimon Sings"—Motivation and Approach

After exploring numerous approaches for instrumental robotic musicianship over the last 16 years, we have identified vocal robotic musicianship as our next research challenge. Our current goal is to implement some of our robotic musicianship design principles described above in novel musical vocal applications such as lyrics generation and embodied singing. We previously worked on non-linguistic robotic vocal approaches [13, 14], which laid the ground for the language-based vocal approaches described in this paper. For this purpose, we collaborated with the Music Technology Group at Universitat Pompeu Fabra (UPF), who provided us with their deep learning singing voice synthesizer [15–17]. Informed by our first three design principles— "listen like a human", "play like a machine", and "be social"—we developed a lyrics generator and a singing gesture generator for the UPF synthesizer. As a platform for these applications, we chose Shimon— our most sophisticated and versatile robotic musician. We revised Shimon's facial appearance to be perceived as a singing robot by adding an new eye mask (Fig. 29.7). This allowed us to actuate Shimon's lower facial DoF to control lip-syncing and mouth size, while the top DoF is actuated to control newly added emotion-conveying eyebrow movements.

When designing the lyrics generator, we studied related work in Natural Language Generation (NLG) and deep learning narrative generators such as [18] as well

Fig. 29.7 Shimon sings—an attachable eye mask allows Shimon to be perceived as a singer. The lower facial DoF controls mouth size, while the upper DoF controls expressive eyebrows

as chatbot literature. While these generators provide promising results, they do not address some of the challenges we face in lyrics generation such as rhyming and the ability to fit a melody. Moreover, unlike common NLG scenarios, song lyrics do not necessarily follow a linear path so that semantic coherence may be less demanding. When designing the synchronized mouth movement for Shimon, we looked at related work in animal vocal production [19], as well as previous robotic lip- syncing robotic efforts such as [20] to inform our approach to generate believable mouth synchronization using only one degree of freedom. For eyebrow and neck gesture design, we have studied related work such as human perception of musicians' movements [21], including ancillary gestures that are not directly responsible for sound generation [22]. We aimed to integrate these larger gestures with smaller eyebrow movements [23] to allow Shimon to convey emotions. Informed by these related works, we implemented the lyrics and gesture generation modules as described below.

29.3 Lyrics Generation

We present a novel method to combine deep learning with semantic knowledge of meaning and rhyme, to generate lyrics based on selected keywords. These processes work iteratively, with the deep learning system generating new phrases based on semantic meanings, and new meanings developed based on the neural network. Figure 29.8 shows an overview of each component within the generation system.

These underlying processes are used by Shimon in three systems. The first system creates lyrics to a given melody through a rule-based approach that sets syllables and words to melodic phrases. The second system presents users with a set of lyrics that were generated based on priming words, allowing manual placement of these lyrics in melodies. The third system generates lyrics for a complete song for which users can write a melody. For each of these systems, the process starts with users giving Shimon a list of keywords or topics to inform the semantics of the generated lyrics.

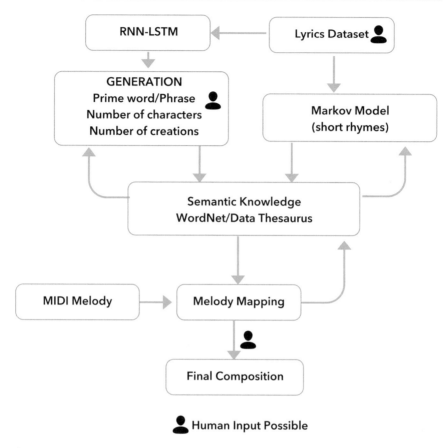

Fig. 29.8 System overview of lyrics generation

To support our design principles which combine both human input and machine generation, our work pipeline allows easy customization of datasets and training methods and is highly flexible for creative variations per song.

29.3.1 Implementation

Dataset

For the underlying system, we decided to generate our own dataset. This was done through a custom lyric gatherer called Verse Scraper [24], created by Rob Firstman. Verse Scraper is designed to address two main challenges. First, when looking at hip-hop datasets, it is common for multiple lyricists to appear on one track and existing tools tend to assign these lyrics to one author. Secondly, existing tools such as the LyricGenius [25] gather all tracks from an artist at once. Verse Scraper solves both these problems by not only filtering song verses by lyricist but also allowing for the creation of datasets ranging from the entire catalog of multiple artists to small subsets such as a certain year of an artist [24].

LSTM

Our system uses a Long Short-Term Memory (LSTM) Artificial Neural Network (ANN) to generate lyrics, much as has been done in other text generation systems [26]. LSTMs are able to retain long-term dependencies in generation and proved more effective than other common options such as Gated Recurrent Units, or a vanilla RNN. We trained new word embeddings on the lyric dataset, which allows the system to learn the relationship between different words from the data.

Semantic Knowledge

Unlike Karpathy, we incorporate a separate semantic knowledge builder that allows the system to generate larger quantities of text with varied meaning in comparison to standard deep learning networks. For this purpose, we use WordNet [27] to generate synonyms and antonyms of keywords that are given by the user. We then also gather keywords and sentiment from the generations and create further generations based on synonyms and antonyms from the generated material. This builds a loop between WordNet and the LSTM that allows ideas to move further away from the original priming words creating lyrical development. This approach also enables non-neural network, rule-based implementations of longer term structure. An additional advantage is this method allows for rapid development and training on different datasets and better customization to new songs.

Rhyming

To add rhymes to the lyrics, we use a simple Markov model tied into semantic knowledge as a final layer. The LSTM network inherently creates rhyming phrases, however at times, phrases do not rhyme, or additional lines are added. To address this problem, a rhyming word or keyword is created and followed by a second-to third-order Markov model that generates phrases backwards to create additional lines.

Melody Mapping

The implementation allows multiple modes of mapping generated lyrics to a melody. The first system adds an extra layer to the loop between semantic meaning and LSTM. A user-chosen melody is fed into the system, which is then processed and broken into phrases. In the loop between LSTM and semantic meaning, an extra preference is given to lyrics that have the same amount of syllables as notes per phrase. This system only allows for one syllable per note in each phrase. The second system for lyrics creates many lyric patterns, each of four lines and presents them to the user. The final system creates a complete set of lyrics, without a relation to a preset melody. Figure 29.9 shows completed lyrics, set to a human-composed melody.

Fig. 29.9 Example of generated lyrics chosen for a composed melody

29.3.2 Experiment

We evaluated the generated lyrics by conducting individual 30 min sessions with 48 participants. Each participant was shown 15 pairs of lyrics. This included 5 pairs of human and computer-generated lyrics, 5 sets of human and human-generated lyrics, and 5 pairs of robot and robot-generated lyrics. The subjects were first asked if they recognized either set of lyrics. For each lyrics, subjects were asked to rate the originality, the expressivity, the coherence, and the overall quality. These metrics were chosen based on Boden's criteria for computational creativity [18]. After rating the lyrics, subjects were asked if they believed either lyrics were written by a computer. Computer lyrics chosen for evaluation were the first 15 generations by the system. The human generations were 15 random samples from the dataset the system was trained on. All lyrics were four lines long and were created without a melody.

29.3.3 Results

Our results show that participants were unable to distinguish between human and computer-generated lyrics in all examples. Many subjects tended to incorrectly believe that one of the musical excerpts was generated by a robot. This may indicate that subjects are looking for specific musical features to decide whether the excerpt was human-generated or robot created, but they did not accurately recognize these features. Figure 29.10 shows the number of responses to each category, in comparing human and computer-generated responses. For each question, they could choose from any of the categories, correctly identifying the computer-generated response occurred only 79 times out of a possible 230.

Figure 29.11 shows the combined results between robot and human-generated excerpts for each category, where the generated lyrics had a higher mean of expressivity.

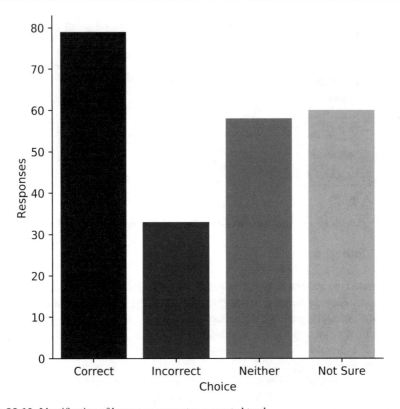

Fig. 29.10 Identification of human or computer-generated track

Figure 29.12 shows the combined correlation between perceived coherence, originally and expressivity. The results show that there is a very low correlation between originality and coherence, with users rating a low coherence as more original for both robot and human.

Some of our qualitative results in our survey included comments such as "I would be surprised if any of the lyrics were computer- generated." and "Were they all written by a computer?"

29.4 Gesture Generation

This section describes the techniques we used to generate Shimon's gestures for performances. This includes synchronizing his mouth with sung lyrics, as well as head and body movements to add lifelike expressivity. We additionally present results from an experiment evaluating the effects of embodiment on the perception of song audio.

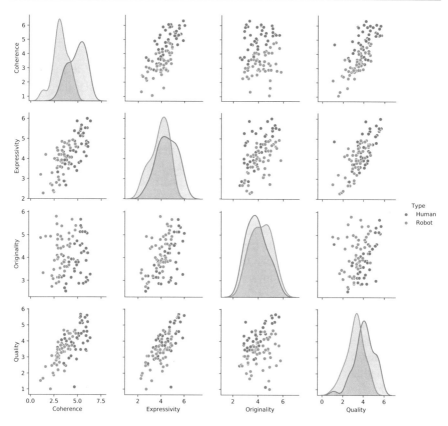

Fig. 29.11 Scatter matrix of results

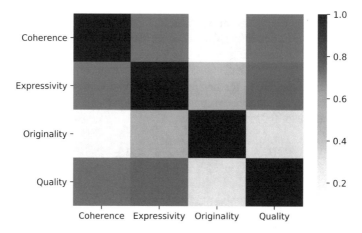

Fig. 29.12 Correlation of human and robot results

29.4.1 Implementation

Mouth Synchronization
For synchronizing Shimon's one-DoF mouth to sung lyrics, we used a phoneme alignment scheme built on past work [20]. We used the song's MIDI file to align each syllable with a start and end time, defining a syllable as containing one vowel as its last phoneme, with the exception of a word's final syllable which was additionally assigned the word's remaining consonants. Each consonant was given 0.06 s of motion, while vowels were given 0.2 s to move to the correct position. During the remaining time, the mouth stays stationary. In the case of very fast syllables, where this time allotment was not possible, we assigned half of the available time to the vowel, and divided the other half among the beginning and ending consonants of the syllable, when applicable. During rests, when Shimon is not singing, we commanded the mouth to slowly close over a maximum time of 0.75 s.

To command the mouth's motor to change position, a target position and velocity must be provided. In order to make the movements seem smooth, we interpolated the velocity commands over a movement's duration. We have previously used this technique to smooth the trajectory of Shimi's gestures [28], easing in and out of gestures by slowing down at the beginning and end of each movement. For Shimi, the desired peak velocity v_p and movement duration d were used to determine the commanded velocity $v(t)$ at each timestep. Equation 29.1, presented in the top of Fig. 29.13, shows this relationship. The movements for Shimon's mouth occur more quickly than Shimi's movements, over small fractions of a second instead of multiple seconds. Therefore, to overcome the mouth's inertia in a timely manner, we alter Eq. 29.1 to begin and end the rotational velocity $\omega(t)$ at half the value of peak rotational velocity ω_p, rather than 0. This is shown in Eq. 29.2 and visualized in the bottom graph of Fig. 29.13. Shimon's mouth movements also differ from Shimi's body movements in that the total angle traversed by the motor must be fixed in order to end in the correct position. We therefore calculate the desired peak velocity by integrating Eq. 29.2 over the desired duration, setting it equal to the total desired change in angle $\Delta\theta$. Substituting into Eq. 29.2 gives the final result, Eq. 29.3. We add a small offset constant c to the calculated peak velocity to account for the time it takes for the motor to accelerate to the desired velocity. The value of c was determined via subjective experimentation. We update the commanded velocity according to Eq. 29.3 at intervals of 0.015 s.

$$v(t) = v_p(1 - \frac{2|t - \frac{d}{2}|}{d}) \text{ for } 0 \leq t \leq d \tag{29.1}$$

$$\omega(t) = \omega_p(1 - \frac{|t - \frac{d}{2}|}{d}) \text{ for } 0 \leq t \leq d \tag{29.2}$$

$$\int_0^d \omega(t)dt = \Delta\theta \quad \rightarrow \quad \omega_p = \frac{4}{3} * \frac{\Delta\theta}{d}$$

$$\omega(t) = (\frac{4}{3}\frac{\Delta\theta}{d} + c)(1 - \frac{|t - \frac{d}{2}|}{d}) \text{ for } 0 \leq t \leq d \tag{29.3}$$

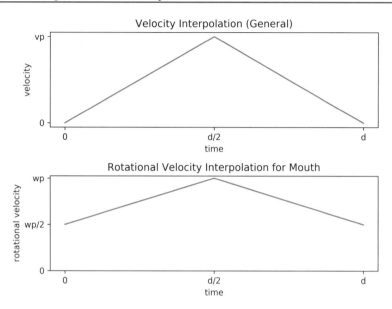

Fig. 29.13 Graphs of Eq. 29.1 (top) and Eq. 29.2 (bottom), showing how velocity is interpolated over duration d

Head and Body Gestures

We designed Shimon's gestures using his four rotational degrees of freedom: head tilt (up-and-down rotation of just the head), neck tilt (up-and-down rotation of entire neck), neck pan (side-to-side head rotation), and base pan (side-to-side rotation of entire body). At any given time, Shimon may be doing any combination of singing, playing marimba, listening to a specific performer, and/or dancing to the music. We took into account all of these roles when choreographing Shimon's body and head movements for each song. Through iterative design, informed by movements of human singers, instrumentalists, and dancers, we identified several gestures of interest as well as guidelines to abide by when choreographing gestures.

While Shimon is playing, we generally try to keep his head close to the arms horizontally, centering his body around the striker motions. When Shimon is playing a complicated part, we move his head and neck downwards so he appears to be focusing intensely on his playing gestures. When Shimon is singing, we keep his head tilted high enough so that his mouth can always be seen by the audience. In general, Shimon uses slower gestures while singing, saving faster and more complicated dance moves for instrumental breaks. We have noticed that simple expressive gestures, such as nodding to the beat, can help create a personal connection to the audience when timed well. When Shimon isn't playing or singing, we often add visually compelling arm and striker choreography. The arms can move across the marimba, and the strikers can move up and down without striking any notes on the marimba. For example, the strikers can clap together on strong beats, or make it appear that Shimon is counting in time by flicking up and down with the music. These gestures are especially effective when synchronized with the head movements. When Shimon is improvising, we find the interaction to be socially engaging for both human musicians and audience if Shimon makes eye contact with the musician while they play. While Shimon watches the other musicians, we often use an interpolated up-and-down gesture we call "breathing" to project liveliness.

In addition to neck movements, we have also focused on animating Shimon's eyebrows. Robotic eyebrows have been found to increase recognition of emotions in social robots [23]. Therefore, in an effort to increase Shimon's emotional expressivity during performances, we added a one-DoF eyebrow to Shimon's head. We can position the eyebrow higher or lower depending on the mood we intend to convey. To project negative emotion, for instance, we move the eyebrow lower, which can be perceived as a frown. We also use quick raising and lowering of the eyebrow when the lyrics pose a question, or upon completion of a difficult marimba part.

For the first few songs, we hard-coded specific gestures to fit with the music. We have also experimented with automating gestures, allowing Shimon to choreograph his own head and body movements based on features extracted from the song's audio MIDI files. Currently, these gestures are rule-based with a certain amount of randomness to add variety and surprise to the experience. Since we found that it looks unnatural for Shimon to stay completely still at any point during the song, we ensure that one degree of freedom is always in motion at any given time.

Below is an example for gesture automation that was used in the experiment discussed in Sect. 29.4.2. Based on the song's MIDI file, we first categorized each measure into "singing" or "non-singing", depending on whether the measure contained notes in the vocal line. During singing measures, Shimon's base pans slowly back and forth, changing direction on every downbeat. Each downbeat was given a 50% chance of executing a neck pan, which alternates direction with each occurrence. Head and neck tilts were mapped to a moving average of the pitch of the vocal line, so that when Shimon sings higher pitches his head and neck move slowly upwards. During non-singing measures, the neck continues to rotate side-to-side with the base pan, to keep continuity between song sections. However, when Shimon dances to the music, he uses faster and sharper movements, as he nods his head to the beat using neck tilt. We also detected note onsets based on the audio file, and quantized onsets with a strength of at least 0.75 times the average to the nearest eighth note. For each onset, Shimon randomly chooses between changing his neck pan position or his neck tilt position, alternating respectively between left-right and up-down.

29.4.2 Experiment Methodology

We designed an experiment to evaluate the value of a physical robot performing gestures with a song, and whether the embodiment of a robot would affect the listener's perception of the song, similar to [29, 30]. The experiment had 46 participants, with 22 in the "software" group and 24 in the "robot" group. All participants were told the experiment was about evaluating computer- generated music. In both groups, participants listened to one song played from a speaker with one researcher present in the room, then filled out a survey about the song, repeating this procedure for a total of four songs. The order of the songs was randomized for each participant. Participants in the "robot" group saw Shimon performing mouth and head/body gestures along with each of the four songs, while participants in the software group only heard each song's audio without Shimon performing gestures.

We were interested in learning whether there was a difference between the robot group and software group in the following metrics:

1. Participants' ratings of enjoyment for each song individually
2. Participants' rankings of the songs relative to each other.

29.4.3 Results

After listening to each individual song, the participants rated their enjoyment level of the song on a scale of 0–7. We used this data, shown in Fig. 29.14, to test our first hypothesis. Although the means are slightly higher in the robot group, the variance in the data is high. We found no significant differences when performing a Mann-Whitney U test on each song using an alpha of 0.05, supporting the null hypothesis.

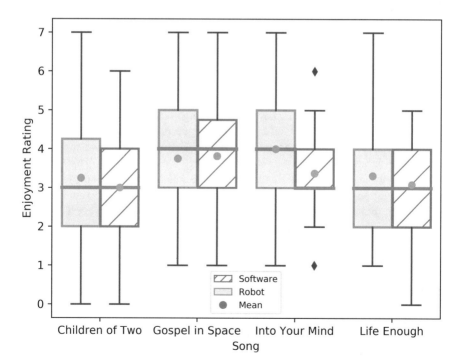

Fig. 29.14 Boxplot comparison of enjoyment ratings (0 low–7 high) between robot and software groups

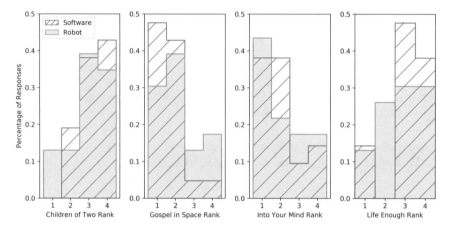

Fig. 29.15 Comparison of song rankings between robot and software groups. Songs were ranked in order of preference, where 1 corresponds to favorite and 4 corresponds to least favorite

After participants listened to all four songs, they were asked to rank the songs from their favorite (1) to least favorite (4). Data for the rankings are shown in Table 29.1 and Fig. 29.15. To test our second hypothesis comparing the rankings between the two participant groups, we performed a separate Mann-Whitney U test for each song's ranking numbers. We found a significant difference for one song, Children of Two. The p-value is 0.0415, which is less than the alpha of 0.05.

Because this test indicated a significant difference in the rankings between the two groups, we were interested in further exploring the nature of this difference. We performed a paired Wilcoxon signed-rank test within each group for each of the 6 possible song pairs to see how their rankings differed from each other. The p-values are shown in Table 29.2. In the software group, this produces a p-value less than the alpha 0.05 for 4 of the 6 pairs. The same test for each pair of songs in the robot group produces significant p-values for only 2 of the 6 pairs. This indicates that the robot group tended to rank the songs more equally, while the software group had a stronger pattern to their preferences. This trend can also be seen in the mean rankings in Table 29.1, where the robot group's mean rankings for each song are closer together than the software group's.

In both of our evaluation metrics of the ranked data, we made use of multiple statistical tests, which can result in an increased risk of type I errors. Because our Mann-Whitney U tests on each song were a small number of planned comparisons to test our hypothesis, it is not advised to apply a correction [31]. Our post-hoc pairwise tests for each song pairing are also not advised to be corrected if only regarded as a hypothesis for further investigation [31]. However, by applying the Bonferroni correction, 3 pairs in the software group would fall under the new alpha of .0042, compared to 0 pairs in the robot group. The observation that the robot group had less consensus on their rankings is still supported.

Table 29.1 Comparison of song rankings between robot and software groups. Songs were ranked in order of preference, where 1 corresponds to favorite and 4 corresponds to least favorite

Song	Mean rank robot	Mean rank software	Stdev robot	Stdev software
Children of two	2.96	3.24	1.02	0.77
Gospel in space	2.17	1.67	1.07	0.80
Into your mind	2.09	2.00	1.16	1.05
Life enough	2.78	3.10	1.04	1.00

Table 29.2 p-values of Wilcoxon signed-rank test, performed on each pair of songs. Bolded values are below the alpha .05. Shaded cells are values below the Bonferroni-corrected alpha of .0042

	Children of Two	Gospel in Space	Into Your Mind			Children of Two	Gospel in Space	Into Your Mind
Gospel in Space	**.000313**	-	-		Gospel in Space	**.0435**	-	-
Into Your Mind	**.00380**	.313	-		Into Your Mind	**.0450**	.852	-
Life Enough	.795	**.000970**	**.0129**		Life Enough	.449	.0978	.0777

| (a) Software group | (b) Robot group |

Our results failed to support our hypothesis that there would be a difference in the enjoyment level of the songs. However, while the presence of the robot did not result in higher enjoyment of the songs, it also did not lower enjoyment. Lower enjoyment was a possibility, as the participants could have found the gestures distracting. The high variance in the data could be due, in part, to differing musical preferences among participants. Performing the experiment on shorter song sections could provide more data for analysis and potentially reduce variance. Furthermore, including questions in the survey about the experience as a whole, rather than just the audio, may provide further insights. Our result is consistent with the findings of Whittaker and O'Conaill [32]. They found that in human-human interactions, video was found to be better than audio for tasks involving social interaction, but there was little difference for tasks without social aspects. Future work could include comparing enjoyment ratings for software versus robot when participants musically interact with Shimon, rather than simply watch performances.

Our results did support that there was a difference in the rankings of the songs relative to each other. Our post-hoc analysis indicates that the software group had a stronger consensus over their rank ordering than the robot group. The reasons for this warrant further investigation. One possibility we propose is that watching the robot's gestures made songs that were ranked lower by the software group seem less boring to the robot group, making them more competitive with the other songs. Children of Two was the song that was found to have significantly different rankings between the two groups, where the software group ranked the song worse on average. It is also the only song that was unfinished when played to the participants, with a long rhythm section where an instrumental solo will later be inserted.

29.5 Discussion and Future Work

Our research in Robotic Musicianship aims to enhance and supplement human creativity through interaction with robots. The scope of our work includes social, wearable, and instrument-playing robotic musicians. This chapter focused primarily on our adaptation of the marimba-playing robot, Shimon, to become a singer. We designed both our lyrics and gesture generation techniques with consideration for Shimon's relation to and interactions with the other humans they are performing and/or composing with.

Our lyrics generation process used human-provided keywords as a seed, supporting back-and-forth robot-human collaboration in songwriting. This is at the core of our approach to robotic musicianship. Our goal is for robots to inspire humans musically: "listening like a human", in this case understanding the human's keyword inputs, and "playing like a machine" to produce interesting lyrics that the human may not have thought of by themselves. In our lyric evaluation, participants were unable to distinguish between human and robot-generated lyrics.

Shimon's multiple roles as a singer, marimba-player, dancer, and improvisation partner at various times during a song present unique challenges for gesture generation. We used interpolated, pose-based movements to synchronize lip-syncing with the lyrics. The "be social" design principle guided our choreography decisions for head and body gestures, so that Shimon interacts with his fellow performers. We are beginning to automate gesture generation using audio features, and are investigating data-driven approaches for future work.

Our gesture evaluation experiment supports the conclusion that embodiment affected participants' perceptions of the four songs. The participant group that only heard the songs' audio showed a stronger consensus on their song rankings than the participant group that saw Shimon performing gestures with the songs. However, we found no significant difference between the two groups' reported enjoyment levels for any of the songs. Therefore, more work is needed to better understand the nature of the song ranking differences. For future work, we plan to do a thorough evaluation of different types of generated gestures, comparing multiple forms of creation, such as manually designed, rule-based, data-driven, and no gestures. We also intend to investigate embodiment's impact on interactions with Shimon, as opposed to just performance.

We are beginning to extend the Shimon Sings project to Shimon Raps, with real-time lyrical improvisation. This introduces many challenges, such as understanding the words and meaning of a human's rap, and formulating a real-time response with coherent meaning, as well as rhyme structures and rhythmic patterns that fit the hip-hop genre. We will also further explore real-time gesture generation, reacting to the energy level and movements of the human rapper and instrumentalists.

Shimon Sings is an ongoing collaboration between researchers, human musicians, and robotic musicians. As Shimon continues to collaborate with composers and perform as a singer, we will learn new ways to improve Shimon to further enhance and inspire human creativity.

References

1. Weinberg, G., Driscoll, S., & Parry, R.M. (2005). Haile-an interactive robotic percussionist. In *ICMC*.
2. Weinberg, G., Driscoll, S. and Thatcher, T. (2006). Jam'aa-a middle eastern percussion ensemble for human and robotic players. In *ICMC*, pp. 464–467.
3. Hoffman, G., & Weinberg, G. (2010). Synchronization in human-robot musicianship. In *19th International Symposium in Robot and Human Interactive Communication* (pp. 718–724). IEEE.
4. Bretan, M., Weinberg, G. and Heck, L. (2016). A unit selection methodology for music generation using deep neural networks. arXiv:1612.03789.
5. Bretan, M., Cicconet, M., Nikolaidis, R. and Weinberg, G. (2012). Developing and composing for a robotic musician using different modes of interaction. In *ICMC*.
6. Bretan, M. and Weinberg, G. (2014). Chronicles of a robotic musical companion. In *NIME*, pp. 315–318.
7. Bretan, M., Hoffman, G., & Weinberg, G. (2015). Emotionally expressive dynamic physical behaviors in robots. *International Journal of Human-Computer Studies, 78*, 1–16.
8. Weinberg, G. (1999) *Expressive digital musical instruments for children*. Ph.D. thesis, Massachusetts Institute of Technology.
9. Bretan, M., Gopinath, D., Mullins, P., & Weinberg, G. (2016). A robotic prosthesis for an amputee drummer. arXiv:1612.04391.
10. Gopinath, D., & Weinberg, G. (2016). A generative physical model approach for enhancing the stroke palette for robotic drummers. *Robotics and Autonomous Systems, 86*, 207–215.
11. Khodambashi, R., Weinberg, G., Singhose, W., Rishmawi, S., Murali, V., & Kim, E. (2016). User oriented assessment of vibration suppression by command shaping in a supernumerary wearable robotic arm. In *2016 IEEE-RAS 16th International Conference on Humanoid Robots (Humanoids)* (pp. 1067–1072). IEEE.
12. Savery, R., & Weinberg, G. (2018). Shimon the robot film composer and deepscore. *Proceedings of Computer Simulation of Musical Creativity*, p. 5.
13. Savery, R., Rose, R., & Weinberg, G. (2019). Finding shimi's voice: Fostering human-robot communication with music and a nvidia jetson tx2. In *Proceedings of the 17th Linux Audio Conference*, p. 5.
14. Savery, R., Rose, R. and Weinberg, G. (2019). Establishing human-robot trust through music-driven robotic emotion prosody and gesture. In *2019 28th IEEE International Conference on Robot and Human Interactive Communication (RO-MAN)* (pp. 1–7). IEEE.
15. Blaauw, M., & Bonada, J. (2017). A neural parametric singing synthesizer. arXiv:1704.03809.
16. Bonada, J., Umbert Morist, M., & Blaauw, M. (2016). Expressive singing synthesis based on unit selection for the singing synthesis challenge 2016. In *INTERSPEECH*, pp. 1230–1234.
17. Gómez, E., Blaauw, M., Bonada, J., Chandna, P. and Cuesta, H. (2018). Deep learning for singing processing: Achievements, challenges and impact on singers and listeners. arXiv:1807.03046.
18. Riedl, M. O., & Young, R. M. (2010). Narrative planning: Balancing plot and character. *Journal of Artificial Intelligence Research, 39*, 217–268.

19. Riede, T., & Goller, F. (2010). Peripheral mechanisms for vocal production in birds-differences and similarities to human speech and singing. *Brain and Language, 115*(1), 69–80.
20. Tachibana, M., Nakaoka, S.I., Kenmochi, H. (2010). A singing robot realized by a collaboration of vocaloid and cybernetic human HRP-4C. In *Interdisciplinary Workshop on Singing Voice*.
21. Dahl, S., & Friberg, A. (2007). Visual perception of expressiveness in musicians' body movements. *Music Perception: An Interdisciplinary Journal, 24*(5), 433–454.
22. Schutz, M., & Manning, F. (2012). Looking beyond the score: The musical role of percussionists' ancillary gestures. *Music Theory Online, 18*(1).
23. De Beir, A., Cao, H.L., Esteban, P.G., Van de Perre, G., Lefeber, D., & Vanderborght, B. (2016). Enhancing emotional facial expressiveness of NAO. *International Journal of Social Robotics, 8*(4), 513–521.
24. Firstman, R. (2020). Versescraper.
25. Miller, J. W. (2020). Lyricsgenius.
26. Karpathy, A. (2015). The unreasonable effectiveness of recurrent neural networks. *Andrej Karpathy Blog, 21*, 23.
27. Miller, G. A. (1995). Wordnet: A lexical database for english. *Communications of the ACM, 38*(11), 39–41.
28. Hoffman, G. (2012). Dumb robots, smart phones: A case study of music listening companionship. In *2012 IEEE RO-MAN: The 21st IEEE International Symposium on Robot and Human Interactive Communication* (pp. 358–363). IEEE.
29. Shiomi, M., Shinozawa, K., Nakagawa, Y., Miyashita, T., Sakamoto, T., Terakubo, T., et al. (2013). Recommendation effects of a social robot for advertisement-use context in a shopping mall. *International Journal of Social Robotics, 5*(2), 251–262.
30. Rossi, S., Staffa, M., & Tamburro, A. (2018). Socially assistive robot for providing recommendations: Comparing a humanoid robot with a mobile application. *International Journal of Social Robotics, 10*(2), 265–278.
31. Armstrong, R. A. (2014). When to use the bonferroni correction. *Ophthalmic and Physiological Optics, 34*(5), 502–508.
32. Whittaker, S., & O'Conaill, B. (1997). The role of vision in face-to-face and mediated communication. In A. Sellen K. Finn & S. Wilbur (Eds.), *Video-mediated communication* (pp. 23–49). Lawrence Erlbaum Associates Publishers.

Richard Savery is a musician and researcher in Artificial Intelligence and robotics, using music and creativity as a medium to understand interaction between humans and machines, and develop AI models thereof. He is currently studying for a Ph.D. at Georgia Institute of Technology, USA, working with the Robotic Musicianship Lab. He has composed and orchestrated music for video games, films and advertisements, including Fast Four featuring the famous Swiss professional tennis player Roger Federer and has worked for 15 years as a professional saxophonist, clarinettist, and flutist. His current research is looking into harnessing musical prosody and emotions for interactions within groups of humans and robots. E-mail: rsavery3@gatech.edu

Lisa Zahray is working towards a Ph.D. at the Robotic Musicianship Laboratory in Georgia Tech Center for Music Technology, USA, under the directorship of Gil Weinberg. She completed her Bachelors and Masters in Computer Science and Electrical Engineering at the Massachusetts Institute of Technology (USA), where she first became interested in music technology. Her research interests include music information retrieval and AI for creating new music. She plays the trumpet and enjoys casually singing and playing piano. E-mail: lzahray3@gatech.edu

Gil Weinberg is a professor at Georgia Tech's School of Music and the founding director of the Georgia Tech Center for Music Technology, USA, where he leads the Robotic Musicianship group. His research focuses on developing artificial creativity and musical expression for robots and augmented humans. He has presented his work worldwide in venues such as The Kennedy Center, The World Economic Forum, Ars Electronica, Smithsonian Cooper-Hewitt Museum, among others. His music has been performed with orchestras such as Deutsches Symphonie-Orchester Berlin, the National Irish Symphony Orchestra, and the Scottish BBC Symphony. Gil received his M.S. and Ph.D. in Media Arts and Sciences from the Massachusetts Institute of Technology (USA) and his B.A. from the interdisciplinary program for fostering excellence in Tel Aviv University, Israel. E-mail: gilw@gatech.edu

AI-Lectronica: Music AI in Clubs and Studio Production

30

Shelly Knotts and Nick Collins

30.1 The Artificial Intelligence Sonic Boom

Though no AI super-intelligence yet rules the Internet, there has been a solid wave of enthusiasm, hype, anxiety and deliberation about new AI technologies in society and culture [82], and their particular manifestation within music [67, 78]. It does not matter that the precedents for AI in popular music stretch back to Push Button Bertha in 1956 [53] nor that the actual software available finds the synthesis of human vocal lines and semantically coherent melody and lyric writing challenging. It feels like only a matter of time for an automatic pop tune generator to win a No. 1 chart slot, and less so for a mock-AI (part assisted by computer, with much human production and promotion) to do the same. Such an outcome is anticipated by the concept of the virtual band, familiar from 1950s voice repitching cartoon Alvin and the Chipmunks to the comic art front of the studio band Gorillaz, from the virtual idol Hatsune Miku to the robot cover band Compressorhead [24, 30, 83]. There is historical precedent, with eighteenth and nineteenth century audiences happy to receive musical automata as entertainment [72], to Kraftwerk's transhumanist affectation of The Man–Machine (following their eponymous 1978 album). Current commercial efforts from such companies as JukeDeck, Amper, Mubert, MMX and AIVA include AIs waiting in server farms ready to render music on demand for home videos and adverts, licensed to record companies, or as inspiration prompts for working composers and home hobbyists. Big tech firms have become involved, from Amazon DeepComposer through the Google Magenta research team to IBM Watson Beat.

Against this backdrop, human producers working in electronic dance music and its wilder frontiers of experimental electronica have a pedigree for the fast adoption of new software tools. The futurist leanings of electronic music, its easy association

S. Knotts (✉) · N. Collins
Durham University, Durham DH1 3LE, UK
e-mail: shelly@datamusician.net

© Springer Nature Switzerland AG 2021
E. R. Miranda (eds.), *Handbook of Artificial Intelligence for Music*,
https://doi.org/10.1007/978-3-030-72116-9_30

with a grand future narrative [81], exacerbates this willingness. Many a musician waits ready to grab the latest free tech demoes and re-purpose them to their own musical concerns. Whether the musical style instantiated in a given research project accommodates their own stylistic pre-occupations is only a partial consideration, the misuse for their own ends of technology developed under different expectations is a well-established feature of the use of music technology [17, 59], and hybridisation of musical styles a constant driver of musical evolution.

One danger of the fast pace of technological innovation is the fast pace discarding of yesterday's music programmes, evidenced by operating system version creep, the associated aggressive deprecation of API functions, and a typical three-year replacement lifecycle for computers. Social media is much faster yet, on the order of days or hours, showing impatience with new music software releases often treated more as gimmicks than as objects worthy of the ten years of intensive practise more commensurate with a traditional musical instrument. Nonetheless, viral enthusiasm can push a project to much casual use. Rob Watson's DonkDJ was an online remix project, now defunct, which allowed the addition of 'donk' techno elements of heavy on-beat and off-beat percussion to an uploaded audio file through its associated EchoNest beat tracking analysis. In 2009, it placed a heavy load for a few months on the EchoNest's servers; they were forced to introduce in response greater restrictions on the number of available third party API requests.

A current generation of commercial AI music tools is aimed at content creators seeking to avoid the copyright minefield around existing recordings, through the provision of on-demand original music. The extent to which such algorithms are rule-based or machine-learnt is often opaque, and they are judged on their outputs, which for constrained styles such as diatonic ambient music or diatonic film piano music, may well do the job. The more creative targets remain out of reach; there is no automatic hit song generator that is able to engage with cutting-edge production trends, nor any genuinely inspirational contemporary music generator. Chasing the human zeitgeist is potentially achievable through deeper application of machine listening and learning technology, alongside semantic analysis of online trends, but the social significance of the general AI problem lurks in wait outside the simplistic musical scenarios currently attempted by programmers. The current mass popularity of deep learning [14, 20] is no magic bullet for music's tricky sonic representation and social embedding.

In order to obtain an overview of current attitudes to music AI and take-up amongst tech-savvy musicians of AI music tools, we conducted an online survey, whose results over 117 participants we briefly summarise here. The respondents were overwhelmingly male, expert music software users (>10 years of experience), producing a range of music formats including recordings, generative work and live performances. 45% of respondents were live coders, reflecting the interests and networks of the authors, and a smaller percentage (16%) were DJs. Although the majority (53%) make some of their income from music creation, this was the main income for very few of the respondents (7%), perhaps suggesting that Music AI is unlikely to create the next jobs boom. Of the pre-packaged AI softwares we listed, Wekinator [41] and Magenta had been used most often by participants, with

Wekinator having the most frequent users (7 respondents). The most frequently used languages for self-built music AI systems were SuperCollider [84], Max/MSP [21], and Python with 47, 48 and 48 users, respectively, Javascript accounted for only 22% of respondents.

The attitudes to AI section were perhaps the most revealing, with many survey participants agreeing with statements that Music AI has made making music easier and has influenced their musical style, but with most disagreeing that adverse effects such as loss of musicians' jobs, homogenisation of music, and holding back music's evolution will come to pass. While many agreed that AI is the future of music (47 respondents), predictions of the exact date of an AI with human-level ability being created ranged from 1787 to never. General comments on AI music software ranged from the apocalyptic ('AI cloud clusters are destroying the environment') to apathetic ('When it appears as a free musical tool, I will definitely try it. But I can't imagine there's much fun to be had.'). In keeping with pragmatic applications for music AI, most saw AI as just another extension of available music technology tools, rather than as any fundamental shift in arts and culture. Full results of this survey are published in Knotts and Collins [56].

We proceed now to survey the state of the art in music AI for studio use and live performance, before highlighting the phenomena of the algorave, as a central locus for musical algorithms in electronica. Later in the chapter, we review the artistic practice of the co-authors in the context of such currents in culture, closing with some reflection and futurological statements.

30.2 Music Production Tools and AI

The culture of digital sampling and its faster-then-copyright pace, of mash-ups and fan remix, is a natural site for the application of sound file manipulating computer tools. The current generation of electronica producers are digital natives, and have been for some time, with trackers programmes dating from the 1980s, and the rise of the software synthesiser for Digital Audio Workstations in the mid-1990s. Studio production tools which operate through audio analysis to allow a more substantial repurposing than basic sampling have also been available for some decades. Propellerheads' Recycle, released in 1994, was an early example, utilising onset detection to segment drum breaks and allow the easy creation of sampler presets accessing individual drum hits. The duo Coldcut, in collaboration with technologists Hexstatic, created live audiovisual sampling tools, most famously affiliated with the joint audiovisual production of their 1997 album *Let Us Play*. Video samples with corresponding audio were triggered via MIDI sequencer and the VJamm software. Coldcut later authorised BrightonART's Coldcutter plug-in an automatic sample resplicing tool. Towards the end of the 1990s, the BBCut software was created, initially in the programming language C, then as a Csound [12] opcode and SuperCollider class library [29], the most advanced version, BBCut2, utilised built-in beat tracking and event analysis [22], and the most popular manifestations were probably Remy Muller's LiveCut VST plug-in based on some BBCut algorithms a simplified iPhone app version able to remix any track from a user's iTunes Library. Many other sample splicing tools have been created for such platforms as Pd [71], Max/MSP and SuperCollider, often without machine listening but always with good potential for algorithmic reworking of arbitrary audio.

The versatile dance musician BT (Brian Transeau) has been involved in the creation of software for sample manipulation at a similar rhythmic granular level, with the BreakTweaker and Stutter Edit plug-ins now licensed to iZOTOPE. It has been interesting to see BT himself promote classic computer music tools, such as the command line programmes gathered in the Composers' Desktop Project [52]. Crossover between more advanced computer music tools, commercial packing of such functionality with friendlier interfaces, and music communities, is extensive.

In academic research, Jason Hockman's investigation of downbeat detection and the backwards engineering of audio segment cut-ups in jungle breakbeat manipulation is worthy of note [47]. Research such as this is often couched in terms of the Music Information Retrieval or computational creativity communities (and further discussed in other chapters in this volume). Aside from Hockman's work, the former category might include Ringomatic, a corpus trained drummer [5], query by beatboxing for DJs [50], and automatic mash-ups [37]. In an example of the latter category, Arne Eigenfeldt led a large-scale research grant in Canada on generative electronica, exploring genetic algorithms and statistical techniques fed from analysis of a corpus of electronic dance music [38]. A later extension is Musical Agent based on Self-Organising Maps (MASOM), which analyses audio to create a generative model [80], and has been deployed in concert based on both EDM and electroacoustic art music corpora. Richard Savery's Artiin generates autonomous musical parts in response to a human-generated lead [75].

Aside from academic research, as an example of a tool currently available to everyday music producers, Logic Pro contains a capacity to code MIDI event generation and processing functions in Javascript within the Digital Audio Work station; a script is placed as a MIDI FX plug-in on a given channel strip; the script can be triggered by MIDI events on a given track, or generate entirely new events based on playback timing information. The latter capability is demonstrated by the following code example in Fig. 30.1, which creates a 64 step sequencer triggered from beat 9 (measure 3 of a 4/4 project), with random probability of triggering on-beat kicks or off-beat snares.

The live performance sequencer Ableton has had the capacity for python script control for some years, but the Max for Live module is the most obvious manifestation of algorithmic capability in the software [61]. Max is a well-known visual programming platform for live electroacoustic work, as well as sound and audiovisual installation artists. Max for Live gives the capacity to easily run Max patches within Ableton Live, providing a much wider palette of sound and MIDI manipulation than Logic's MIDI only Scripter. An example patch is shown in Fig. 30.2.

Machine Learning technology has been introduced to audio software plug-ins in the form of wrappers for such real-time machine learning facilities as Wekinator, as libraries and extensions for more customisable audio programming languages such

```
var NeedsTimingInfo = true;
var beatpositions = new Array(16);

var i;

for(i=0; i<64; ++i)
    beatpositions[i] = (i*0.25)+9;

//MIDI Note values for General MIDI percussion kit
var kick = 36;
var snare = 38;

function ProcessMIDI() {

    var info = GetTimingInfo();

    if (info.playing) {

        for(i=0; i<64; ++i) {
            var beatnow = beatpositions[i];

            //if this callback's time extent contains the beat position intended
for any of our events
            if((info.blockStartBeat<=beatnow) && (beatnow<info.blockEndBeat)) {

                var kicknow = i%4==0;

                if(Math.random() > (kicknow?0.3:0.7))  {

                    var note = new NoteOn;
                    note.pitch = kicknow? kick :snare;
                    note.velocity = kicknow? 120 : (Math.floor(Math.random()*60) +
60);

                    note.beatPos = beatnow
                    note.send();

                    //MIDI Note Off event to follow the note on for clean release
                    var noteoff = new NoteOff(note);
                    noteoff.beatPos = beatnow +0.24;
                    noteoff.send();

                }
            }
        }
    }
}
```

Fig. 30.1 Logic Pro Scripter plug-in for random kick and snare event generation over 64 steps

as SuperCollider, or internally within plug-ins whose functionality is more directly described to users (source separation, humanisation quantise/groove, automatic music generation). Examples of the latter category include the freely downloadable Magenta Studio [73] which makes available five effects based on deep learning research, automatic transcription and source separation effects such as Celemony's Melodyne plug-in, or Factor mini for Max for Live.

Magenta Studio contains five plug-ins for the manipulation of MIDI Files, exemplifying the potential applications of machine learning within algorithmic compositional studio assistants:

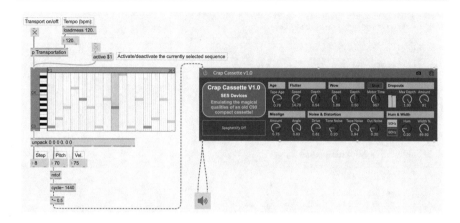

Fig. 30.2 Max patch illustrating the live.step sequencer interface object, and a Max for Live Device brought in via amxd ∼

- *Continue* (extend into new material from a MIDI File starting point)
- *Drumify* (create drum patterns based on timing of a starting clip)
- *Generate* (create from scratch new MIDI melodic material)
- *Groove* (humanise timing based on a corpus of human drummers)
- *Interpolate* (find a certain number of inbetween patterns given two MIDI File end points)

The Google Magenta team have also treated raw audio in machine learning, such as with the audio sample prediction synthesiser NSynth [39], itself available in various packaged applications for end-users.

The availability of algorithmic music-making tools in general culture has extended to follow technological developments, from smartphone apps, through web audio projects, to such recent manifestations as an Alexa skill (DeepMusic) or Amazon Web Service (Deep Composer). Video game producers have increasingly explored procedural audio and generative music, reactive and adaptive to game state [23]. Precedents include the generative ambient music for Spore (2007) created with the Pd engine [66], and beat tracking within rhythm games able to adapt to user-provided music such as Dance Factory (2006).

Web browsers provide a cross-platform route for the distribution of new music systems, and AI music tools for the browser built with Javascript have been growing, from Magenta.js through to ml5js. MIMIC or 'Musically Intelligent Machines Interacting Creatively' is a three-year AHRC-funded project (2018–2021), run by teams at Goldsmiths College, Durham University and the University of Sussex, dedicated to exploring new music AI in the web browser. Many demoes with interactive script editing are available at the project website [43], including a javascript version of the iPhone BBCut app. The MIMIC project aims to make machine learning tools more accessible to artists; further examples on the website point towards ways in which machine learning may be incorporated in the performance space, such as the Markov Sequencer, which uses Markov chains to produce variations of drum rhythms typed by a human performer, and Audio Triggers which is a simple classifier which triggers samples when it recognises particular audio inputs.

In the current erAI, well-known electronica artists are exploring the potential of AI techniques for future music, and such collaborations will only become more frequent, and in a senseless noteworthy, with each passing year. Aphex Twin worked with Dave Griffiths to make MIDI Mutant which evolves DX7 patches from microphone inputs. Actress' AI collaborator *Young Paint* analysed corpora of his past work and other styles to produce new tracks and also can be used in live performance. Holly Herndon's Spawn is a Neural Network trained on her vocal samples and was used in the album *Proto* (2019).

30.3   AllgorAIve

The live coding community have been writing algorithms to produce music as a performance practice since the early 2000s, producing experimental software for improvised coding of audio and visuals in response to both the audience and the output of algorithmic processes. In more recent years (since 2012), they have been taking that process to clubs and parties making dance music explicitly cast as 'Algorave' [33, 55]. Algorave in itself is not novel, given the many precedents for algorithmic dance music already detailed in this chapter and acknowledged in the algorave literature, but the foregrounding of technology and performance over the pure musical-social experience is unusual in the club context.

Algorave's slow start was followed by a swift rise to public consciousness in recent years, bringing with it a wave of overtly technologized music entering a public sphere close to the mainstream. Recent performances at SXSW, Amsterdam Dance Event and Glastonbury have positioned human interaction with algorithmic systems next to rock bands and DJs and attracted press attention from Mixmag, Resident Advisor, Wired and The Times amongst others. This perhaps reflects the wider public awareness of the role of algorithms in increasingly programmed systems of our daily lives. As Bucher [15] proclaims 'Algorithms are seemingly "everywhere"'... [they] are not just making their mark on culture and society; to a certain extent they have become culture'. Algorave, with its practice of screen projection, exposes audiences to algorithms—which are otherwise often mystified and obscured by profit-hungry tech companies—in friendly and enjoyable ways. Events such as the algorave in Bluedot festival in 2016 introduced large audiences to live algorithmic performance (Fig. 30.3).

Live Coders don't hold back on incorporating the latest technologies in their performance systems, but also see the code as a craft and an instrument, furthering deep exploration of interaction with code in performance. Building a live coding language is one common avenue of exploration for live coding performers, but

Fig. 30.3 Hundreds of audience members dancing to algorithms at Bluedot festival 2016

other artists have explored hybrid systems, incorporating other technologies and interfaces into the performance system. Given the technical expertise of live coders and their curiosity around human interaction with algorithmic systems, an interest in exploring data and AI through live coding is emerging. Press articles already often conflate live coding, algorithmic music and AI-generated music [19], algorave is sometimes seen as synonymous with live coding, since so many live coders are active in the scene and live programming is such a powerful interface to deeper musical computer science.

Aspects of live coding that have driven performers to explore AI tools and concepts include the inefficiency of the keyboard as a musical interface; the high cognitive load of performing with code; the automation of common performance moves and processes; the exploration of unpredictability; the development of well-specified collaborators; the avoidance of repetition; and the navigation of large parameter spaces.

One highly active performer, Renick Bell, automates aspects that he finds himself repeating across multiple performances, leaving himself free to play with other aspects that are more malleable and less routine. Bell's *Conductive* [7] explores complex algorithmically induced rhythm on the dancefloor, exploring the limits of human taste for pushing genre boundaries and danceability. The system uses a set of agents which each act as an instrument with a set of rhythmic patterns to choose from. These 'players' generate their own music autonomously. Higher level agents track parameters such as 'boredom', keeping track of how recently the agents in the system have changed rhythmic pattern and ensuring change over time. The performer acting as a conductor making high-level decisions such as rhythmic density and can turn players on and off manually. This enables Bell to 'manage' the performance without worrying about low-level details, instead focussing on the flow of the music overall.

Some performers are well aware of the longer term history of algorithmic music. Creating live music through automata can be traced back to a millennium or more; Al-Jazari's music robot band circa 1200CE is one of the earliest examples [51]. Dave Griffiths has paid homage to the engineer with his live coding system of the same name [64] which uses a computer game style visualisation of programmable robots moving in 3D space to trigger samples.

Other systems have freed the performer from the need for precision. The duo Scorpion Mouse (vocalist May Cheung and live coder Jason Levine) have used parameter space maps to allow the performer to explore sounds without worrying about precise parameter values. Scorpion Mouse's performance system [57] uses t-SNE algorithms [58] to map a large set of samples according to musical feature values. The visualisation of the t-SNE, as shown in performances, is depicted in Fig. 30.4. Early versions of the system used a large set of around 3000 samples with diverse musical characteristics. Levine uses the live coding language Extempore to traverse the maps triggering samples in the path. Performing with the system required memorising the geography of the t-SNE map in order to locate types of samples. Levine describes memorising the location of 'marimba island', for example, and navigating to the required position using extempore functions.

Later versions reduced the sample set to percussive samples and used t-SNE dimension reduction to map to two dimensions with pitch on the X-axis and variations of particular drum types on the Y-axis. This allowed an easier method of reading and traversing the samples at performance time. Further developments to

Fig. 30.4 Scorpion Mouse Performing with samples organised by t-SNE algorithms. A visualisation of the t-SNE is shown in the projected graphics alongside the performers code

the system have included mapping chords and rhythm sets with t-SNE algorithms, to allow allows chord progressions to be created through t-SNE traversals. This system was later converted to an interactive version in VR where the viewer could direct the traversals in VR space. Louis Busby's *EverySongIOwn* performance system also uses t-SNE maps to organise huge sample sets and has been deployed at a number of algoraves in the UK.

Other approaches to using machine learning for approximation and variation in Live Coding include Ivan Paz's cross-categorised-seeds [70] which explore the idea of presets as a way of navigating vast parameter spaces. Paz's RuLeR is a rule learning algorithm used in hi music. Seeds are generated, which are parameter presets with associated perceptual labels describing the sound. The system provides alternative parameter sets as variations of the seeds that still conform to the perceptual labels allowing the performer to use high-level controls to perform the piece, while low-level variation is generated by the algorithm. Paz highlights the importance of presets to provide anchors in an otherwise vast timbre space, but acknowledges that presets sometimes prevent exploration and innovation when a performer is overly reliant on known parameter sets. The album *Visions of Space* (2017) was produced using the performer's tools.

Machine Learning has been used in live coding as the pressures of fast typing often conflict with the need for the music to change and move. Assistants such as Cacharpo [68] provide a 'collaborator' which can generate music while you type, relieving the pressure on the performer to make quick changes in solo sets. Cacharpo reduces the task of automatic music making to a single tightly defined genre of Cumbia Sondiero. The autonomous performer uses Music Information Retrieval (MIR) algorithms [18] to listen to the human performer and generates code to produce complimentary patterns and instruments in the style of cumbia. Though the results have been appreciated the author admits further dance floor-based assessment is needed.

Another challenge, tackled by Jeremy Stewart and Shawn Lawson [77], was to create a system capable of fully generating TidalCycles [65] code. Cibo is an autonomous performer that uses neural networks, with similar aims to Cacharpo in that further developments of the system will allow collaboration with a human performer. However, the system gave its first performance as a solo artist with a set at the International Conference of Live Coding 2019. Unlike many musical machine learning systems Cibo takes only code as an input and does not incorporate machine listening; it trains on sequential code blocks captured from human performed TidalCycles sets.

Cibo, Cacharpo and other autonomous live coders have the potential to reduce touring pressure on artists as software can be sent to the venue without the need for a human to attend in person. Del Angel observed that viewers were neither surprised nor upset by the idea of a performing algorithm when demonstrating Cacharpo. The RAiMONES go further, proposing AI can bring artists back from the dead; using machine learning, new music can be produced 'by' an artist from beyond the grave [24, 30]. Dadabots [85] also point towards a future of endless AI-generated music with their Relentless Doppelganger YouTube channel, which has been streaming neural net-generated death metal since March 2019. The social construction of live coding [46] might push against the fully automated resurrection of bygone algoravers given the centrality of the performative struggle with algorithmic design to the audience experience at algoraves.

Though the time constraints and server load of training a musical model can inhibit machine learning in concert from entering the performance space, some experimental work in this area includes Marije Baalman's *GeCoLa* project which performatively trains a neural net to recognise physical gestures and map sounds in response to them [6]. The performance reminds us that even complex machine learning tasks require human labour to complete and it is by no means a fault-free task. Full scale use of Magenta-style machine learning models is still underexplored in live coding, perhaps because the black-box nature of machine learning seems at odds to the transparency of live coding, or because training models must largely be completed before performance time, increasing the preparation required for a set.

The act of code-bending [9]—which shares some ethos and techniques with live coding—has already made its way into live coding through the web browser performances of Joana Chicau [8] and Charles Hutchins' [49] Soundbeam project—a live coding hack of the Mozilla lightbeam plug-in for tracking data-harvesting in the browser. Given such experimentation, it is not a huge leap from using pre-built deep learning models in a live coding performance to re-coding and retraining a model mid-set.

The Sussex arm of the MIMIC research team have worked on the SEMA interface [9], which aims to allow easy integration of a customisable live coding language with Magenta's machine learning plug-ins which can themselves be edited during performance [10]. The system consists of two windows—one for live coding, and another containing code to interact with machine learning algorithms. Some simple syntax—toJS() and fromJS()—is used to pass data between the windows, allowing the performer to freely pass sequences of pitch/rhythm and other data from the live coding window to the input of the machine learning model and receive new sequences back according to the model.

30.4 A PersonAl PerspectAve: Shelly Knotts

Developing a Live Coding practice over 150 performances in the last 7 years has proved fertile ground for algorithmic exploration. Coming from an experimental music background, I didn't set out to make EDM, but was led there through the practice of live coding and determination of the algorave community to construct diverse line-ups. The task of algoraving was learnt on the job, with many early performances spent working out how to generate beat-based music through the same performances processes I use in experimental contexts. I found, for example, that quantising noisy synths that could have otherwise been drones were one route to wonky, crunchy yet danceable beats, bringing with it different timbres that might not be expected on the dancefloor.

I have been particularly intrigued by the unpredictable nature of performing with and through algorithmic processes and the potential to go on vastly different paths from those anticipated at the start of a performance. Collaborative performance also provided many perspectives on the limits and opportunities of live coding, pushing my practice in new directions. In 2013, I worked with Alo Allik, providing an audio input to his gene expression synthesis engine [4]. His system produced audio with similar characteristics to my live coded output and felt like performing with an algorithmic version of myself, gently nudging the performance out of learned routines and into new musical territory.

A long-term collaboration, referred to as *ALGOBABEZ* (2016–2019), pushed literal and metaphorical buttons [54], providing the basis for building a feminist algorithmic music practice and experimenting with musical roles in collaborative Algoraving. Working with Joanne gave the space to push the envelope on-beat-based algorithmic noise music with a collaborator who built a strong rhythmic base to anchor the performance. In response to the ultimate downfall of the collaboration, I wrote an auto-drumming algorithm which uses statistical algorithms to generate drum patterns from a sample bank, filling the rhythmic space that was largely fulfilled by my collaborator in our sets together. The rhythmic generator provides a base on which to build timbral and melodic material to fill out the remainder of the sound field, though did get somewhat unruly in its first outing.

Beyond live coding, experiments with algorithmic collaborators included *It'll Have a Better Title Later...*—which ironically never had a better title. The work was written to perform with an improvising pianist and explored autonomous improvising systems in an experimental improvisation context, which changed its timbre output according to performer inputs. The work spawned a large number of synth patches (made up of semi-random combinations of synth graphs) which were triggered according to the similarity to the improvising pianist's playing. The patches used various synthesis methods to gradually morph the timbre towards that of the piano over the course of the performance and according to how often each synth is triggered. The work gives the impression of two performers converging on a timbral space over the course of a performance.

The transparency of live coding has also fed into my work on collaborative performance systems. Many are accompanied by visualisations that attempt to communicate the complicated internal algorithmic processes to audiences. Two works in particular: *Flock* (2015) and *Union* (2015), which both used MIR and mixing algorithms to mediate collaborative performance, use data visualisation as part of a concert. *Flock* visualises audio feature data of three performers and an algorithmic voting process. The audio from the three performers is mixed according to the output of the voting, which is based on alignment to voter audio feature preferences. *Union* is an algorithmic mixer for telematic ensemble which uses MIR as a basis to determine consensus between performers and mix the audio streams accordingly.

In the sections that follow I discuss two works in detail which use MIR and data visualisation to interrogate algorithmic improvisation practice and broader theme in AI and culture. I finish with a short discussion of my current work.

30.4.1 CYOF

CYOF (2017) explores how AI could be helpful to an improvising performer in developing their improvisational skill over time without actively intervening in sound production. The system uses analysis of my previous and current live coding performances as a basis to infer improvisational novelty, and predict/suggest potential futures of the live performance in real-time. Musical Information Retrieval and text analysis techniques are used to analyse an archive of code and audio files from previous performances. A large archive of past performances was used to build a data set of likely code combinations, audio feature combinations and trajectories in live coding sets. Having habitually recorded live coding sessions and saved code files, I was fortunate to have a large data set of audio and code from live coding performances and rehearsals to work with. The piece was developed as exploration of originality in live coded improvisation, and aims to give performer and audience visual feedback on the performer's innovation in comparison to their own previous performances.

In *CYOF*, a live coding performance using SuperCollider's JITLib [74] to live programme sound synthesis is augmented by a visualisation which shows a representation of the past, present and potential future of the current performance. Real-time audio feature data (e.g. chromagram, loudness and spectral features) relating to the past, present and potential future is mapped to greyscale blocks, with features on the Y-axis and time on the X-axis. The performer's current code is projected as it is being typed alongside the most likely (in orange) and least likely (in blue) possible future code. The live performance is analysed in real time in 10 s windows using SuperCollider's SCMIR library [24, 30]. The live data is compared to the archive of past performances, and the visualisation shows data relating to the most closely related past performance alongside the data relating to the current performance. The live performance data is colour coded on a scale of blue (most original) to orange (least original).

In the visualisation, shown in Fig. 30.5, audio feature data is mapped to greyscale blocks with features shown in the Y-axis and time in the X-axis. Time is visualised in 10 s blocks. At the beginning of a performance, a random past performance is chosen as the prediction data to be represented with the visualisation. At each 10 s interval, the prediction data for the remainder of the performance is replaced by data relating to the performance in the archive with MIR data most closely related to the current performance, showing the most likely future data for the current performance. This 'prediction' data is replaced with data from the current performance as the performance progresses.

Each block of the data relating to the current performance is colour coded on a scale of blue (most 'original') to orange (least 'original'), showing the performer how close to data from past performances the previous segments were. Another aspect of the visualisation shows the performer's current code as it is being typed alongside the most likely (in orange) and unlikely (in blue) possible future code according to the database of past coding performances.

Fig. 30.5 Performance of CYOF at the International Conference of Live Coding 2017, CMMAS, Morelia, Mexico

CYOF aims to gently encourage more innovative improvisation by using archive material to determine the novelty of the current performance in relation to the archive, and provide suggestion for alternative paths. The visualisation acts as a stimulus to experiment with new ideas should it suggest too high a degree of self-similarity.

30.4.2 AlgoRIOTmic Grrrl!

AlgoRIOTmic Grrrl! (2019) uses music information retrieval to analyse a corpus of Riot Grrrl's music to be remixed and repurposed to create algorave worthy dance numbers which evoke the angry revolutionary spirit of feminist Punk.

Riot Grrrl was an early 1990s musical-political movement which grew out of Punk—which had become increasingly male dominated in the 1980s with the emergence of, often misogynistic, Hardcore Punk. This sub-genre didn't speak to the experiences of women and girls and actively marginalised them. Women in the scene wanted to carve a space for music which was relevant to their everyday lives, was produced on their own terms, and reflected feminist values [45]. *AlgoRIOTmic Grrrl!* draws on these politics to highlight the need to create space for women in electronic and computer music scenes, using explicitly feminist sound material and foregrounding the parallels between algorave and Punk subcultures.

Algorave has a disproportionately large contingent of female performers, when contrasted to other electronic music subcultures. This is perhaps surprising for such an overtly, technologized practice. Technology is used as a way to exclude and marginalise particular groups from cultural production, maintaining male mono-cultures through exclusionary language use and high technical bars for entry. In contrast to many sub-divisions of computer and electronic music, algorave has been able to create some momentum to push back against the male domination of electronic music scenes [11] with diverse line-ups being a central principle of the movement and female-only workshops providing routes into performance. A low technical bar for entry and the algorave code of conduct, which shares many values with punk and DIY music [69], help to encourage diversity. Given these values and algorave's dedication to promoting female and feminist narratives of algorithmic music, this context seemed more appropriate than other computer music subcultures to explore MIR data bias and express the political values of Riot Grrrl music in the algorithmic age.

This felt particularly pertinent to working with music AI systems, given feminist critique of AI systems, e.g. [2, 36], for producing algorithms with a white male bias through data bias and lack of cultural awareness among engineer teams. Examples include Google image recognition algorithms tagging the faces of black people with 'gorilla' [76]. Beyond biased algorithms, corporations such as Google draw on huge quantities of data to train machine learning algorithms and the labour of data production goes largely unrecognised. In music, where cultural artefacts are the data which are used to train machine learning models, this raises questions about diversity and appropriation worthy of interrogation.

In the broader MIR, data usage is biased towards the European classical tradi-tion, Western harmony and male composers. Relatively few MIR systems have been produced that work with noisy signals, primarily treat music based on timbre as the primary compositional parameter, and explicitly reference women's music [13, 16]. Further, reflection is required to explore the implications of using a dataset of explicitly feminist DIY embodied music making within algorithmic structures that have largely been built by men, as often in AI systems the labour of data production is unacknowledged and undervalued. Holzapfel et al. [48] point to the ethical considerations of MIR including issues with copyright, payment of royalties, repurposing and crediting authors. *AlgoRIOTmic Grrrl!* is a provocation, ques-tioning this grey area of appropriation and data diversity in machine listening and learning.

The performance system uses a corpus of Riot Grrrl music which is analysed before the performance using the SCMIR library to produce a data file. During the performance, search and sorting algorithms are used in SuperCollider to select chunks of musical material from across the corpus within particular ranges of audio feature data values. The Patterns library in SuperCollider is then used to live code the 'remix' of these selected audio chunks into rhythmic patterns. A second interface is written in Javascript, and using MMLL [32]. This interface facilitates the auto-remixing of a corpus of music according to audio feature data and values selected via a GUI. The two interfaces are used in parallel during the performance: SuperCollider for live coding rhythmic/pattern material and JS/MMLL generating textural material.

The first performance of the work evoked the true spirit of punk as the code was written the same day as the performance leaving no time to rehearse with the system. This fortuitously ensured I was as inexperienced as possible performing with the system, in the vein of the punk guitarist who learns on the job. During the performance the results of the search algorithms were largely unpredictable, and the performance method involved finding coherence, shape and musical flow in the arrangement of unexpected sound material. Further, performances were more refined and practiced, but lacked the rawness of true algorithmic punk-rave.

30.4.3   Future Work

My current work for MIMIC includes a browser-based performance system which uses the MMLL library to extract rhythmic, melodic and timbre data in real time from a collaborating saxophone player. The system will have two versions, one that autonomously generates variations of her playing, and another that provides a code representation that can be edited during performance time, allowing multiple modes of interaction with an AI collaborator. The work aims to expand on concepts around collaboration, automation, live coding, AI ethics and agency explored in previous works.

30.5   I Personll Perspectlve: Nick Collins

Unfortunately, no AI of sufficiently Turing-test-passing-ability was available to write this section of the chapter for me (that's what such an AI would say too, perhaps). Replacing myself with a potentially more accomplished musician remains an intriguing goal, through which I would hope to better understand what accomplishment in human music making might itself mean. Whilst I like to think I've set the bar high by years of musical training, large amounts of work in studios, many gigs, and much computer music research, however, long I spent training up is perhaps just an overnight training session to a future high-speed computer. I only have that ultimate arbiter of human music making, the human body, and must trust the continuing difficulty of creating really plausible drop-in replacement artificial ears to hold the music AIs in check.

Any sustained engagement with musical AI for practical music-making scenarios convinces you that music AI is embedded in the whole problem of general musical intelligence, given the embedding of music within sociocultural behaviours. Highly constrained specific musical tasks have fallen to AIs, where the key factor is the suitability of a particular stylistic mannerism to formalisation. The more intuitive and esoteric non-mathematical rules may be cultivated increasingly by future musicians hiding from the expansion of music AI! The grand challenge for the MusAIcian is that machine listening must be increasingly built into algorithmic composition systems, to bring them closer to the actual listening-led practical design loop of studio and concert work. The artificial ear, and by extension, the brain's immersion in culture, is the weak point of current generation AI.

With this in mind, I have conducted various projects in machine listening and algorithmic composition, stretching from the domain of electroacoustic art music, *Autocousmatic*, [25] through musical theatre ([redacted] by demand of a famous musical composer's lawyers [26, 27]), to automatic critic systems in dubstep 27 and contemporary piano music (with a public competition for concert works judged by machine, performed in the 2019 Donaueschingen festival [79]). The emulation of musical criticism forms part of such research because a self-critical perspective is at the heart of recognising novel compositional outcomes, and the explicit modelling of artificial critics ('CrAItics', 'CritAIcs' or 'CrAtIcs') improves compositional decision-making founded in the artificial ear.

This is on top of repeated attempts to explore algorithmic electronic dance music, synth pop and electronica, from a 1997 experiment in algorithmic techno coded in C controlling external MIDI gear, through the aforementioned BBCut algorithms [35] to infno/infpop [34]. Live performance with such algorithms has been an especial interest, made explicit in the rise of the algorave, and highly promoted by the intense efforts of Alex McLean, my co-author Shelly Knotts and others. In recent years, I have taken to running subsidiary AI algorithms within live sets, such as generators of chord sequences and melody lines based on large corpora of recordings of Adele, Ed Sheeran and Xenakis ('AIdele', 'Ed SheerAI', 'xenA-kIs'), or automatic rule-based techno loop generation via a system called Autom8 in homage to such early 1990s rave era bands as *Altern8*.

It is worth speculating on the future development of music AI. What would a next generation AI Electronic Dance Music generator look like? A large corpus of EDM tracks would be gathered, chronologically ordered; see, for instance, [28] for one corpus of historic electronic music already analysed. Tagging individual pieces with sub-genre labels may be counter-productive, since the notion of genre is an ill-defined mess at the lowest level in dance music, misused by artists, critics and communities on the basis of tiny differences that aren't necessarily evident in any audio signal [63]. Machine listening technology allows the automatic analysis of the beat and bar positions, and through chord analysis, of the harmonic rhythm and the modelling of chord sequences. Melody lines can be extracted via predominant fundamental frequency detection, or via source separation then monophonic transcription. All melodic examples can be reconciled with beat positions, and transposed to all 12 chromatic pitches to avoid any bias towards particular keys. This data is then the basis for machine learning with generative models. A cycle of generation and analysis may be possible, improving transcription via the automatic generation of annotated examples [31].

30.6 Conclusions

There may be a hunger amongst a certain type of electronica musician for new music technology that can get them ahead of the game, but more generally, music AI has a great capacity to provoke new musical experiences, from casual users, through gamers and hobbyists, to professionals. Nonetheless, the use cases, musical affordances and cultural rationale for AI music systems remain up for debate. Perhaps the ultimate role of the AI is to help humans understand more and more of their own musical proclivity, and analysis by synthesis should provide no threat to personal musical spaces of adventure, even as AI tech opens up new musical avenues.

As the gender balance of responses to our survey (82% male) and the poor diversity of this chapter demonstrates there is a large skew in the uptake of AI technologies in music production. Partly this reflects the broader culture of electronic music, which has consistently marginalised women and non-white people [3, 40], but beyond this accessing, learning and using new technologies can be more challenging for people who don't fit the normative white male mould of computer programmers and electronic musicians [1]. As we grapple with these new technologies, we must take the time to reflect on how diversity of access to technology can affect culture in unpredictable ways. The *Women Reclaiming AI* [60] project, for example, asks us to reflect on how AI home assistants with female voices are largely written by teams of male engineers who perhaps lack insight in the wider cultural problematics of particular characteristics and human–machine interactions with specifically gendered voices. Microsoft's Twitter bot Tay also provides a lesson in modelling AIs on particular human populations [62]. Reflection on diversity of participation and data sets is required to ensure the musical AIs of the future don't make us wade through knee-high layers of AI hardcore punk bands called *CAIrcle Jerks* [44] producing server farms full of cock-rock-algo-punk fusion albums.

We should be cautious of the role of presets in what is to come. For synthesisers and effects, presets tend to dominate 90% of usage [42]. In learning programming, real code examples are essential, and there is a natural extension from preset parameter settings for a given plug-in, to pre-built code and patches to tweak. Ease of deployment and use are essential pragmatic considerations for the majority of users, and relatively simple to code DSP or MIDI processing routines are often packaged up as commercial plug-ins by companies, a professional-looking interface goes a long way to conceal that the algorithms are freely available in harder to learn software such as Csound. There is a danger that a selected few have the skills to develop the music AI, and the majority are trapped into the prior upfront representational decisions of programmers who may or may not have considered flexibility in music making beyond certain Western conventions. Programmers ignorant of ethnomusicology or contemporary art music may too readily take the 4/4 C major 120 bpm default of many a digital audio workstation as real. We hope that the future deep learning AI composers Deepeche Mode, Deep Purple, Deepbussy and Deeplius will not force a stranglehold on the music admissible, but be part of a much grander ecosystem of computer musical ideas.

References

1. Abtan, F. (2016). Where is she? Finding the women in electronic music culture. *Contemporary Music Review, 35*(1), 53–60.
2. Adam, A. (2006). *Artificial knowing: Gender and the thinking machine.* Routledge.
3. Alessandrini, P., & Knotts, S. (2017). Letter from the guest editors. In *Array: The Journal of the ICMA 2017–2018.*.
4. Allik, A. (2014). *Computational composition strategies in audiovisual laptop performance.* Ph.D. diss., University of Hull.
5. Aucouturier, J.-J., & Pachet, F. (2005). Ringomatic: A real-time interactive drummer using constraint-satisfaction and drum sound descriptors. In *Proceedings of the International Conference on Music Information Retrieval* (pp. 412–419).
6. Baalman, M. (2019). GeCoLa. Retrieved January 14, 2020, from https://marijebaalman.eu/projects/gecola.html.
7. Bell, R. (2018). Limits in algorithmic dance music. *Dancecult: Journal of Electronic Dance Music Culture, 10*(1).
8. Bell, R., & Chicau, J. (2018). A trans-disciplinary tool for collaborative, choreographed, and embodied audio-visual live coding. In *Proceedings of the International Conference on Live Interfaces.*.
9. Bergstrom, I., & Lotto, B. R. (2015). Code bending: A new creative coding practice. *Leonardo, 48*(1), 25–31.
10. Bernardo, F., Kiefer, C., Magnusson, T. (4–6 December 2019). An AudioWorkletBased signal engine for a live coding language ecosystem. In *The Proceedings of the Web Audio Conference.* Trondheim, Norway.
11. Bolt, I. (2017). Meet the female coders pushing electronic music into the future. *Mixmag, 31* August 2017. Retrieved from https://mixmag.net/feature/female-coders-algorave.
12. Boulanger, R. (2000). *The Csound book: Perspectives in software synthesis, sound design, signal processing, and programming.* MIT Press.
13. Bowers, J., & Green, O. (2018). All the noises: Hijacking listening machines for performative research. In *Proceedings of the International Conference on New Interfaces for Musical Expression* (pp. 114–119).
14. Briot, J.-P., Hadjeres, G., & Pachet, F. (2017). Deep learning techniques for music generation: A survey. arXiv:1709.01620.
15. Bucher, T. (2018). *If... then: Algorithmic power and politics.* New York: Oxford University Press.
16. Carr, C., & Zukowski, Z. (2018). Generating albums with SampleRNN to imitate metal, rock, and punk bands. In *Proceedings of the 6th International Workshop on Musical Metacreation* (pp. 1–4).
17. Cascone, K. (2000). The aesthetics of failure: "Post-digital" tendencies in contemporary computer music. *Computer Music Journal, 24*(4), 12–18.
18. Casey, M. A., Veltkamp, R., Goto, M., Leman, M., Rhodes, C., & Slaney, M. (2008). Content-based music information retrieval: Current directions and future challenges. *Proceedings of the IEEE, 96*(4), 668–696.
19. Chandler, S. (2018). Meet the artists using coding, AI, and machine language to make music. *Bandcamp Daily,* 25 January 2018. Retrieved from https://daily.bandcamp.com/lists/music-ai-coding-algorithms.
20. Choi, K., Fazekas, G., Cho, K., & Sandler, S. (2017). A tutorial on deep learning for music information retrieval. arXiv:1709.04396.
21. Cipriani, A., & Giri, M. (2010). *Electronic music and sound design: Theory and Practice with Max/MSP* (Vol. 1). Contemponet.
22. Collins, N. (2006). BBCut2: Incorporating beat tracking and on-the-fly event analysis. *Journal of New Music Research, 35*(1), 63–70.

23. Collins, K. (2009). An introduction to procedural music in video games. *Contemporary Music Review, 28*(1), 5–15.
24. Collins, N. (2011). Trading Faures: Virtual musicians and machine ethics. *Leonardo Music Journal, 21*, 35–39.
25. Collins, N. (2012). Automatic composition of electroacoustic art music utilizing machine listening. *Computer Music Journal, 36*(3), 8–23.
26. Collins, N. (2016). A funny thing happened on the way to the formula: Algorithmic composition for musical theatre. *Computer Music Journal, 40*(3), 41–57.
27. Collins, N. (2016). Towards machine musicians who have listened to more music than us: Audio database led algorithmic criticism for automatic composition and live concert systems. *Computers in Entertainment, 14*(3), 1–14.
28. Collins, N., Manning, P., & Simone Tarsitani, S. (2018). A new curated corpus of historical electronic music: Collation, data and research findings. *Transactions of the International Society for Music Information Retrieval, 1*, 34–43.
29. Collins, N. (2002). The BBCut library. In *Proceedings of the International Computer Music Conference*, Goteborg, Sweden, 16–21 September (pp. 313–316).
30. Collins, N. (2011). SCMIR: A SuperCollider music information retrieval library. In *Proceedings of the International Computer Music Conference.*.
31. Collins, N. (2018). '...there is no reason why it should ever stop': Large-scale algorithmic composition. *Journal of Creative Music Systems, 3*(1).
32. Collins, N., & Knotts, S. (2019). A javascript musical machine listening library. In *Proceedings of the International Computer Music Conference.*.
33. Collins, N., & Alex McLean, A. (2014) Algorave: Live performance of algorithmic electronic dance music. In *Proceedings of NIME 2014*, London.
34. Collins, N. (2008). Infno: Generating synth pop and electronic dance music on demand. In *Proceedings of the International Computer Music Conference*. San Francisco, California: International Computer Music Association. Available online at http://www.informatics. sussex.ac.uk/users/nc81/research/infno.pdf.
35. Collins, N. (December, 2001). Further automatic breakbeat cutting methods. In *Proceedings of Generative Art, Milan Politecnico*. http://papers.cumincad.org/cgi-bin/works/paper/ga0121.
36. Crawford, K. (2016). Artificial intelligence's white guy problem. *The New York Times*, 25.
37. Davies, M. E. P., Hamel, P., Yoshii, K., & Goto, M. (2014). AutoMashUpper: Automatic creation of multi-song music mashups. *IEEE/ACM Transactions on Audio, Speech, and Language Processing, 22*(12), 1726–1737.
38. Eigenfeldt, A., & Pasquier, P. (2013). Evolving structures for electronic dance music. In *Proceedings of the 15th Annual Conference on Genetic and Evolutionary Computation* (pp. 319–326). ACM.
39. Engel, J., Resnick, C., Roberts, A., Dieleman, S., Norouzi, M., Eck, D., et al. (2017). Neural audio synthesis of musical notes with wavenet autoencoders. In *Proceedings of the 34th International Conference on Machine Learning* (Vol. 70, pp. 1068–1077).
40. Farrugia, R., & Olszanowski, M. (2017). Introduction to women and electronic dance music culture. *Dancecult: Journal of Electronic Dance Music Culture, 9*(1), 1–8.
41. Fiebrink, R., & Cook, P. R. (2010). The Wekinator: A system for real-time, interactive machine learning in music. In *Proceedings of The Eleventh International Society for Music Information Retrieval Conference*, Utrecht.
42. Goldmann, S. (2015). *Presets: Digital shortcuts to sound*. London: The Tapeworm.
43. Grierson, M., McCallum, L., Bernado, F., Collins, N., Fiebrink, R., Kiefer, C., et al. (2019). MIMIC: Make music and art with machine intelligence. Retrieved June 20, 2020, from https:// mimicproject.com/.
44. Grow, K. (2012). Circle Jerks tell tales about being Jerks in New Doc. Retrieved June 20, 2020, from https://www.spin.com/2012/08/circle-jerks-tell-tales-about-being-jerks-new-doc/.
45. Hanna, K. (2019). Riot Grrrl Manifesto. *Feminist Manifestos*, 329–332.

46. Haworth, C. (2018). Technology, creativity, and the social in algorithmic music. In *The Oxford handbook of algorithmic music* (pp. 557–582).
47. Hockman, J. (2014). *An ethnographic and technological study of breakbeats in hardcore, jungle and drum & bass.* Ph.D. diss., McGill University.
48. Holzapfel, A., Sturm, B. L., & Coeckelbergh, M. (2018). Ethical dimensions of music information retrieval technology. *Transactions of the International Society for Music Information Retrieval, 1*(1), 44–55.
49. Hutchins, C., Ballweg, H., Knotts, S., Hummel, J., & Roberts, A. (2014). Soundbeam: A platform for sonyfing web tracking. In *Proceedings of the International Conference on New Interfaces for Musical Expression* (pp. 497–498).
50. Kapur, A., Benning, M., & Tzanetakis, G. (2004). Query-by-beat-boxing: Music retrieval for the DJ. In *Proceedings of the International Conference on Music Information Retrieval* (pp. 170–177).
51. Kapur, A. (2005). A history of robotic musical instruments. In *Proceedings of the International Computer Music Conference.*.
52. Kirn, P. (2014). Watch BT reveal sound design tricks with free, geeky CDP—Then learn it yourself. Retrieved from https://cdm.link/2014/05/watch-bt-reveal-sound-design-tricks-free-geeky-cdp-learn/. Published online May 21, 2014.
53. Klein, M. L. (1957, June). Syncopation by automation. *Radio-Electronics,* 36–38.
54. Knotts, S., & Armitage, J. (2018) ALGOBABEZ: Writing code, pushing button. *Dancecult: Journal of Electronic Dance Music Culture, 10*(1).
55. Knotts, S., & Collins, N. (2018). Introduction to algorithmic EDM. *Dancecult: Journal of Electronic Dance Music Culture 10*(1). Retrieved from https://dj.dancecult.net/index.php/dancecult/article/view/1112.
56. Knotts, S., & Collins, N. (2020) A survey on the uptake of Music AI Software. In *Proceedings of the 20th Conference on New Interfaces for Musical Expression,* Birmingham UK.
57. Levine, J. (2018). Combining livecoding and real-time software for musical improvisation. *Arts at MIT (YouTube).* Retrieved from https://www.youtube.com/watch?v=27ZslA6_vXE.
58. Maaten, L. V. D., & Hinton, G. (2008). Visualizing data using t-SNE. *Journal of Machine Learning Research, 9,* 2579–2605.
59. Magnusson, T. (2019). *Sonic writing: Technologies of material, symbolic, and signal inscriptions.* Bloomsbury Academic.
60. Manton, C., & Aga, B. (2019). Women reclaiming AI. Retrieved January 14, 2020, from https://womenreclaimingai.com/.
61. Manzo, V. J., & Kuhn, W. (2015). *Interactive composition: Strategies using Ableton Live and Max for Live.* New York: Oxford University Press.
62. Mathur, V., Stavrakas, Y., & Singh, S. (2016). Intelligence analysis of Tay Twitter bot. In *2nd International Conference on Contemporary Computing and Informatics (IC3I).* IEEE.
63. McLeod, K. (2001). Genres, subgenres, sub-subgenres and more: Musical and social differentiation within electronic/dance music communities. *Journal of Popular Music Studies, 13*(1), 59–75.
64. McLean, A., Griffiths, D., Collins, N., & Wiggins, G. (2010). Visualisation of live code. In *Proceedings of the 2010 International Conference on Electronic Visualisation and the Arts* (pp. 26–30).
65. McLean, A., et al. (2020). *Tidal: We are not DJs (Version 1.6.1).* Github. Retrieved from https://doi.org/10.5281/zenodo.592191.
66. McLeran, A. (2009). A practical approach to generative music. *Contemporary Music Review, 28*(1), 121–122.
67. Music Ally. (2016). *Music's smart future: How will artificial intelligence impact the music industry?* Report released by the BPI. Currently unavailable online; last accessed 13th December 2016.

68. Navarro Del Angel, L., & Ogborn, D. (2017). Cacharpo: Co-performing Cumbia Sonidera with deep abstractions. In *Proceedings of the International Conference on Live Coding (ICLC)*.
69. Paul-Choudhury, S. (2019). What will music be like in 20 years? *BBC Culture,* 21 May 2019. Retrieved from https://www.bbc.com/culture/story/20190521-what-will-music-be-like-in-20-years.
70. Paz, I. (2019). cross-categorized-seeds. In *Proceedings of the Live Coding Music Seminar, Rio de Janeiro (IMPA)..*
71. Puckette, M. (1996). Pure data: Another integrated computer music environment. In *Proceedings of the Second Intercollege Computer Music Concerts* (pp. 37–41)..
72. Riley, T. (2009). Composing for the machine. *European Romantic Review, 20*(3), 367–379.
73. Roberts, A., Engel, J., Mann, Y., Gillick, J., Kayacik, C., Nørly, S., et al. (2019). Magenta Studio: Augmenting creativity with deep learning in Ableton Live. In *Proceedings of the International Workshop on Musical Metacreation* (MUME).
74. Rohrhuber, J., de Campo, A., & Wieser, R. (2005). Algorithms today notes on language design for just in time programming. In *Proceedings of International Computer Music Conference*.
75. Savery, R. J. (2018). An interactive algorithmic music system for EDM. *Dancecult: Journal of Electronic Dance Music Culture, 10*(1). Retrieved from https://dj.dancecult.net/index.php/dancecult/article/view/1022.
76. Simonite, T. (2018). When it comes to gorillas, Google photos remains blind. *Wired,* 1 November 2018. Retrieved from https://www.wired.com/story/when-it-comes-to-gorillas-google-photos-remains-blind/.
77. Stewart, J., & Lawson, S. (2019). Cibo: An autonomous tidalCyles performer. In *International Conference on Live Coding*.
78. Sturm, B. L. T., Iglesias, M., Ben-Tal, O., Miron, M., & Gómez, E. (2019). Artificial intelligence and music: Open questions of copyright law and engineering praxis. *Arts, 8,* 115. https://doi.org/10.3390/arts8030115..
79. SWR. (2019). The curAItor curates. Retrieved June 20, 2020, from https://www.swr.de/swrclassic/donaueschinger-musiktage/veranstaltung-19-10-2019-konzert-2b-100.html.
80. Tatar, K., & Pasquier, P. (2017). MASOM: A musical agent architecture based on self-organizing maps, affective computing, and variable Markov models. In *Proceedings of the 5th International Workshop on Musical Metacreation (MuMe 2017)..*
81. Taylor, T. D. (2014). *Strange sounds: Music, technology and culture.* New York: Routledge.
82. Tegmark, M. (2018). *Life 3.0: Being human in the age of artificial intelligence.* London: Penguin.
83. Whiteley, S., & Rambarran, S. (2016). *The Oxford handbook of music and virtuality.* Oxford University Press.
84. Wilson, S., Cottle, D., & Collins, N. (2011). *The SuperCollider Book.* The MIT Press.
85. Zukowski, Z., & Carr, C. J. (2018). Generating black metal and math rock: Beyond bach, beethoven, and beatles. In *Proceedings of NIPS Workshop on Machine Learning for Creativity and Design*.

Shelly Knotts is an independent musician and researcher based in Newcastle Upon Tyne (UK), Previously she was a post-doctoral researcher in the Music Department at Durham University, UK, working on the project *Musically Intelligent Machines Interacting Creatively*, funded by UK's Arts and Humanities Research Council (AHRC). Her research interests include live coding, networked performance practices, and data-driven music making. She has performed at numerous Algoraves and electronic music festivals worldwide including SXSW and Mutek Montreal. In 2017 she was a winner of BBC Radiophonic Workshop and PRSF *The Oram Awards* for innovation in sound and music. E-mail: shelly@datamusician.net.

Nick Collins is a Professor in the Durham University Music Department, UK, with strong interests in artificial intelligence techniques applied within music, the computer and programming languages as musical instrument, and the history and practice of electronic music. He has performed as composer-programmer-pianist and 'codiscian', from algoraves to electronic chamber music. E-mail: nick.collins@durham.ac.uk.

Musicking with Algorithms: Thoughts on Artificial Intelligence, Creativity, and Agency

31

Palle Dahlstedt

31.1 Introduction

In this chapter, I present a pragmatic, critical, and sometimes speculative view of what Machine Learning (ML) and Artificial Intelligence (AI) bring to the table for art and music. It is pragmatic in the sense of analyzing what can actually be done today by musicians and composers working with AI, and what is missing in terms of creative agency. How does AI relate to other technologies in the context of art? Yet critical about the popular expectations of AI, its ascribed abilities and agency, and how AI is written and talked about today in terms of creativity. No, computers cannot paint like van Gogh or compose like Bach. What is really the role of humans, as designers, programmers, users, and tweakers, behind current AI applications? Still, I try to be visionary about the long-term future of AI in art and music. Will we ever see autonomous AI artists, composers, and musicians? If so, why would they even care to make art and music for humans?

I will primarily talk about two main categories of algorithms: statistical Machine Learning (e.g., neural networks of various kinds), and Evolutionary Computation. These two categories are both wide and diverse and encompass most of today's applied AI. They share the properties that they may work with data on a higher abstraction level, find solutions to problems, and generate material of different kinds, without the specifics of these solutions or material being described in detail. They can be applied in many different ways in relation to artistic creative processes. As there is no common term for these different algorithms as a group, I will in the following use the term *AI algorithms*. When I refer to Machine Learning algorithms specifically (excluding Evolutionary Computation), I will use the term *ML algo-*

P. Dahlstedt (✉)
Department of Computer Science and Engineering, and the Academy of Music and Drama, University of Gothenburg and Chalmers University of Technology, SE-41296 Gothenburg, Sweden
e-mail: palle@chalmers.se

© Springer Nature Switzerland AG 2021
E. R. Miranda (eds.), *Handbook of Artificial Intelligence for Music*,
https://doi.org/10.1007/978-3-030-72116-9_31

rithms. I will speak about these techniques from a more general viewpoint, and some things may not be applicable to or relevant for all kinds of algorithms. I hope the reader has an understanding of this necessary simplification.

AI algorithms can be made into powerful tools that allow for new ways of working, but they are not miracles—they have constraints and limitations, and being aware of what these are, and what the implications of using them are, is crucial for an artist. Working with a tool without awareness of aesthetic implications, or maybe without even being aware that there *are* aesthetic implications, may lead to reduced independence, unconscious shift of agency from the artist toward the toolmaker, and to artistic output that is very similar to that of other users of similar tools.

In this text, I will primarily discuss the aesthetic and philosophical implications of using contemporary high-level AI algorithms in compositional and improvisational work. I will look at how such algorithms mediate agency through the influence on the aesthetic results and also speculate on the idea of art by autonomous AI, if and when that would be possible. As my own main artistic practice and training is as a musician and composer, I will use music-making as my main example, but many of the observations are applicable also to other art forms, as the reasoning deals with the artistic creative process and creative agency in general, independent of genre. The role of technology in general, and of artificial intelligence in particular, varies only in nuances between art forms, and ideas of creative agency in music are not much different from visual art, literature, or performance.

The reasoning and observations in this chapter are a continuation of a long personal investigation of these issues, in dialog with other researchers and artists, which has involved the development and long-term use of various generative systems for music-making [18–21, 30, 31] and related more philosophical and aesthetic investigations of their implications for the creative process and aesthetic implications. Primarily, the discussion about the role of tools and agency is a continuation of my previously published theoretical work on artistic creative process [22, 24, 28, 29], and my critical view of AI creativity continues the thoughts put forward in a recent paper on big data, AI, and creativity [26]. There is only space for brief summaries of this work here, and I would refer to the original texts for a more detailed view.

31.1.1 AI and Art

There are many ideas about what creativity is, and also many different definitions and variations on AI. A great variety of algorithms have been applied under this umbrella throughout the years, but the latest AI boom has centered around multi-layered neural networks, and another important category is evolutionary algorithms.

AI algorithms can perform many different tasks or sub-tasks, such as classification of arbitrary classes of objects, outlier detection within sets, and evaluation according to trained or specified criteria, and help with decision making. They can do different kinds of optimization, e.g., with respect to similarity (hence, imitation), computation and speed, or cost, but also with regards to more or less formal/explicit aesthetic criteria, with more or less open results. They can also optimize toward meta-aesthetic criteria, such as novelty or variation. AI algorithms can be used for predicting the likely continuation of a sequence, based on example sequences, and hence be used to directly generate output.

Such tasks, as performed by AI algorithms, can be applied to simulation, strategy, imitation, and game-play or to design, improvisation, and creativity. During the last decades, there have been numerous examples of applications of AI algorithms to tasks within the musical crafts, such as instrumentation, harmonization, and voice-leading. But this is not where the main creativity of musical composition lies. They are still very interesting challenges, similar to solving a game or puzzle (see, e.g., [56]) and an important part of composing music. The idea is supposedly that if we can solve such simpler tasks, we can go on toward the larger tasks of composing whole musical works.

Here, I will concentrate on when AI is applied to the more fundamental creative tasks:

- What happens when AI algorithms are applied to generate, suggest, evaluate, continue, expand, vary, or imitate musical material?
- What are the complications of using AI to generate music, related to the implications of training AI algorithms on existing music, and the general problem of getting AI to generate something it has not seen or heard before?

At the heart of this is a tension between optimization and exploration. Optimization can be defined as doing the best thing, the right thing, optimizing the outcome of some actions, or finding the best solution to a problem, under given constraints. Exploration is expanding the limits of what has been done before, searching the space of the possibilities for new and interesting solutions or material, or creating something different from everything seen or heard before, in a fundamental or conceptual way (not just tilted a little bit). It is not difficult to create a slight variation of something, and novelty is easy—any output based on chance operations will be novel in some trivial way. But it should be novel in an interesting and meaningful way, or at least in a way so that the receiver can ascribe meaning to it. Most AI algorithms were designed for optimization, but some are also applicable to exploration.

We will look at the implications of using AI algorithms in these contexts, the implications for aesthetic results, and for the agency.

31.1.2 Motivation

What does it solve to analyze where the agency lies? It does not make the systems smarter, and it is not (at least not primarily) about authorship or about giving credit, but about understanding. It helps us understand what the contributions are from each part of a system that we perceive as creative, and to appreciate to what degree everything is a part of a system. It helps us talk about it in proper terms, not ascribing intelligence and creativity to a machine in those cases when the actual creativity comes from human researchers, engineers, programmers, and algorithm users, while still acknowledging the (potential) contributions of the algorithms. And it will help us realize when an algorithm really is creative.

The conclusion may very well be that it is impossible to tell where the creative agency lies. In that case, the investigation has taught us to be more humble in relation to such systems and to be careful with how we talk about them, and it may make us realize that emergence is a powerful thing.

In the current debate, it is common to see popular science articles about how AI systems are creative, how they have composed new hits in the style of The Beatles [17, 46], or how they have created pictures in the style of van Gogh [52]. In the press, it is often spoken of as if the software algorithm, the AI, has created these aesthetic artifacts all by itself. This is of course not true. Usually, the generative AI system behind such news is nothing more than a sophisticated transformation tool or mash-up engine, and there are humans behind at all stages in the process. So many design choices are taken along the way, and so much information is flowing into the AI implementation from humans, that it is simply deceptional to talk about it as "created by machines".

There are many problems with such unrealistic descriptions. It gives artists and listeners the wrong idea about authorship and about the abilities of AI. It neglects the extent of the human agency, and while the end credits of a major movie may be exaggerated in their detail, a more adequate understanding of the attribution of agency in creative processes that involve significant generative computation may help acknowledge the influence of toolmakers and algorithm designers, mediated through algorithms, in terms of influential agency.

Sadly, such sensational attribution of agency to AI shape the general public's expectations of AI and its current capabilities. This is not only a problem of expectations, but one of politics, ethics, and a Public Relations problem for AI—depending on your position in relation to it. While these are wonderfully capable algorithms that we should absolutely use and apply in artistic contexts, we should also have realistic expectations, and talk about them in correct terms. An important part of this is to ascribe agency to the correct parts of the system and not neglect the human agency that is (still) such an important part of all AI systems and will most likely continue to be so for a while.

31.1.3 Properties of an Artist

To get some leads on creative AI, we may ask the question: What properties are needed from an AI composer or artist for us to regard it as an artist in its own right? It is clearly not enough that the output of an AI has properties similar to the output of human composers and musicians, so we could start to answer the question by thinking about what are the properties of a human artist.

Art is not instantaneous—it comes out of processes, of varying durations. During this process, the artist interacts with her surroundings. There is continuous input, in the form of a stream of impressions and social interactions, and there is similarly continuous output in the form of sketches, temporary results, dialogs, and social interactions triggered by reactions to her art. This is a feedback loop around the creative process and the artist, with information flowing in all directions.

An artist has something to say, consciously or unconsciously. Values and views held by the artist will be there, embedded in design decisions, whether she likes it or not. If the artist does not intend to say anything or does not think that her music has a message, receivers (listeners) will read something into it. The output is appreciated (ascribed a value), and it is relatable, at least in projection. Sometimes some effort is required. The artwork conceptually relates to the world and to previous art. It is also in itself a part of a long-term process and discussion about what art is and can be.

A listener can also empathically relate to music and music-making, as many have some experience of playing an instrument, or at least of singing. We can perceive effort and intention in others' behavior such as playing music [25] also when we do not have sufficient domain knowledge to understand in detail what is going on. For example, when listening to an ensemble of improvisers, we can empathically perceive their efforts, interactions, and struggle.

So, why should we not expect these properties from an artificial artist, and from art and music created by such agents? It is not enough that they imitate output from human artists, as this is fundamentally non-creative (a process of optimization instead of exploration). We must expect new material, derived from its own actions and interactions, that is meaningful in relation to its surrounding world and its place in it. And, for it to become meaningful to us, references should exist also to our world, or such relations should be possible to form or construct for us when listening.

31.1.4　Possibilities with AI in Art and Music

We can see three main ways in which AI can be used in artistic creativity:

- As a **tool**: It can be used as a **black box** system operated by a human artist, to generate a batch of output that can be used in various ways by the composer, at various stages of the creative process, e.g., a generated sound to include in a song or score material to be further manually edited or arranged into a composition.
- As a part of a **system**: It can be part of an **interactive** system consisting of both machines and human agents, which is used to create art and music.
- As an **autonomous agent**: It can form an **autonomous** system that creates art without any interactions with human agents.

Some AI algorithms, and this is especially true for evolutionary algorithms, can help us explore what is possible under certain well-defined constraints, in that they perform a structured search of the space of the possibilities. We may search the same space of possibilities as before, but with the help of such algorithms, we can search it more efficiently. The word efficient may not ring well in artistic contexts, but it can be understood as meaning two things. First, we can reach similar results as with traditional tools, but faster. Second, and more interesting, is that we can spend the same effort and time we would have spent with a traditional tool, but as the algorithm helps us reach new corners, farther away in the space of possibilities, we attain new results and new artistic expressions with similar efforts.

It is not only possible to reach new remote corners, but for time-based or linear arts such as music, the search path is also interesting. New tools allow us to find and follow new trajectories in the search space, and these paths shape the narrative [22].

AI algorithms allow us to work with new higher abstraction levels, in several ways. Neural networks, and especially Deep Learning algorithms, are able to learn, process, and reproduce patterns and stylistic properties of musical material, and with Evolutionary Computation, the use of high-level analysis in fitness functions can allow for control of complex properties in musical results without the need to explicitly formulate methods for generating them.

We can work with stylistic patterns in appearance (material patterns) or behavioral patterns in interaction. We can interact with algorithms by example, e.g., train an algorithm with examples that we want it to be influenced by.

Essentially, this possibility of working with non-precise and high-level input relieves the computer music composer from the need to understand and interact with code in a procedural way, from having to adjust detailed technical parameters, and from having to specify things explicitly in detail. She can instead concentrate on ideation and communicate with the algorithm through music (as done by, e.g., David Cope [15], and in any AI implementation that uses a musical training set). Still, she needs to understand and form the experience of working with these tools on this new abstraction level. It is not less complex nor less complicated. It is different.

AI algorithms can, due to their ability to accept high-level input and generate high-level output, be part of systems of connected interacting nodes, machines, or humans, and many different algorithms can work together. Each node contributes something to the overall creative process, but in such systems, it can be very difficult to say which part contributes what property of the output. It emerges as a systemic property of interacting parts, that each co-create the music [12, 13]. Thanks to the possibility of high-level input and output, AI algorithms can, just like human musicians, be designed to take their own output as input, and thus become complex feedback systems. This is a natural development, as many AI algorithms are in themselves already set up as feedback systems (Generative Adversarial Networks, Recurrent Neural Networks, evolutionary algorithms, etc.). Communicating (in a way) through actual musical material makes it easier to think of AI algorithms like human interactors, like a composition teacher, or a musical friend. Still much more stupid than a human, but in other ways smarter, faster, or more efficient (here is that word again). And, primarily, still different from a human.

This ability to work with higher, less precise, abstraction levels may allow for the composer and sound designer to think in potentials, using the definition of spaces of possibilities as a compositional design strategy. She may think in terms of what kind of textures or sonic features would be possible—and then let an algorithm explore that space. Already the definition of the space contains important aesthetic choices as input from the composer, and if the exploration is interactive, even more input is provided, e.g., by picking desired results from a large set of outputs or providing feedback underway. One can compare such a process with gardening. You choose what to sow, you tender it, tweak parameters during the development and growth (add nourishment and water, see that there is enough light, apply pruning and selection), and then you harvest the results (this analogy was further elaborated on in [26]). I often use this approach when composing or doing sound design with the virtual modular synthesizer Nord Modular G2. I know what kinds of phenomena I am interested to include in the patch, such as a certain kind of gestures, a certain kind of potential timbres, certain potentials for cross-modulation, a few filters, and some potential feedback paths. I make a patch containing all these building blocks without even once listening to the patch. When it is complete, I start exploring the parameter space of the patch using the built-in interactive evolutionary tool [18, 21]. While occasionally adding some manual parameter edits or some slight adjustments to the patch, the interactive exploration is the main driving force. I usually find and harvest lots of sonic material in this way, for later use.

A certain generation of computer music composers (like myself) learned AI by writing our algorithms from scratch. But the sophistication of today's AI algorithms has surpassed the point where this is realistic, and young people today learn to use high-level tools directly, as available in programming libraries or end-user applications. I will get back to that, but this means embracing a certain lack of control and transferring some agency to the toolmaker, just as a violinist relies on the contributions of generations of luthiers, and a composer rests on the shoulders of musical theorists through years of training, internalizing these theories.

But it has its advantages too. Such AI users have a chance of developing a new craft, given that they invest the same time and effort with these new tools, just as those from a developer background did, but on a higher abstraction level. As everybody's time is limited, they have a chance to accumulate a larger experience database than the developer-artist was ever able to, and if used critically and with reflection, they will develop a craft of applied AI in music. This requires developing an understanding, practice, and skills. Deep technical understanding may not be needed, but systemic understanding and the formation of good cognitive models of the systems formed by artistic practice, and this takes time and effort.

31.1.5 Art in AI

Technology does not only provide tools for the creation of art, but it is also a potential medium in itself, for artistic expression. Its complexity, and the societal and aesthetic implications of AI in music and art, are sufficiently interesting for it to also be a subject for new works, where AI algorithms in themselves can be used as a medium for expression. Artistically designed algorithms, and algorithms *as* art. Not algorithms *for* art. Here I do not refer to "the Art of Programming" in Donald Knuth's sense of a complex and refined craft [42], but to how musical AI algorithms could be tweaked, modified, and designed in personal ways, to express new thoughts in music.

AI also allows us to work with more complex material, for example, to control complex processes such as feedback networks, with complex fitness landscapes, where the interesting or even perceptional meaningful points in the solution space are far apart or hard to find. You can use an algorithm to adjust many parameters simultaneously without knowing what they mean, and hence in simple interactive processes "play" on sound engines previously hard to control, to the extent that they were previously unthinkable as musical tools [18, 19, 22]. In the same way, AI can make complex sound generation tools and generative algorithms more accessible to non-technical users, by providing more intuitive interfaces and hiding the lower computational levels.

Music is an art form that, to a large degree, builds on creating meaning through internal (within a work) and external (between works) musical references [16, 49, 50], sometimes negotiated through expectation and surprise [39]. Music created with similar techniques often exhibit similarities and form one further level of references. High-level affinities emerge from algorithmic similarities. Each new tool provides a new kind of reference, and here AI tools, operating on higher abstraction levels such as styles and patterns, can form references similar in kind to those in (postmodern) compositions that use style and imitation as the medium of expression. New kinds of references can also emerge within sets of material generated in a single process, from the same training set or from a similar genetic representation. For example, a search trajectory from a session of interactive evolution forms a narrative of related musical material [22], related to the metamorphosis or variation composition technique, as used by, e.g., Vagn Holmboe [53] and Jean Sibelius [65].

31.2 Agency

Agency as a concept goes back to Aristotle and Hume and was originally defined as the capacity of an entity to act [61], to cause something. The causal chain should not pass through the agent, but it should originate in the agent. The concept was further developed by Anscombe [1] and Davidson [32] toward an idea of *intentional agency*—when an action is initiated willfully by a conscious agent (normally a human), and as a consequence, the agent can be blamed for that action—it was intentional. In art, blame may not be the appropriate word. As art can provoke, I often use the idea of who is the agent behind artistic provocation to sort out what an intentional agent is in art. This acknowledges a sender, an author behind the work, with autonomy and intention. Can we be provoked by an artwork created by an AI? Or will we be provoked by the humans behind the implementation of AI? This emphasizes the importance of an author in art and music. A different kind of agency is *causal agency*, which is commonly used when talking about the agency of material things. Such agency cannot be blamed on the subject.

Agency understood as the intentional agency was originally assumed to come from a human agent, but expanded notions of agency and agent appeared already with the dawning cybernetics, later implemented into AI, where an agent could be as simple as a thermostat, a reflex agent that reacts to some condition with some action [58, 70]. The idea of a software agent emerged, first formulated by Hewitt et al. [37] and further developed by Hewitt [36], as a simple self-contained interactive entity, with internal states and acting according to a script. It may be goal-oriented, even though those goals may be very simple and the behavior predictable. It can also be arbitrarily complex.

Another approach to agency is found in Bruno Latour's Actor-Network theory, where actors can be also non-human agents. He asks, in relation to any kind of agent: "Does it make a difference in the course of some other agent's action or not? Is there some trial that allows someone to detect this difference?" ([43], p. 71) If the answer is yes, which is for most kinds of tools and artifacts, it can be ascribed to some kind of agency. Latour is clear that such agency can have different magnitude or strength, and he uses a number of words to describe this kind of agency of non-human entities: They can "authorize, allow, afford, encourage, permit, suggest, influence, block, render possible, forbid" (ibid., p. 72). Latour also mentions that a non-human entity can mediate agency over time, related to how Vygotsky [69] before him talked about tools as carriers of cultural behavior, and Gregory [35] describes them as carriers of intelligent behavior. For a good overview of the idea of non-human agency in Latour's work, see Sayes [60]. Another view on the agency of artifacts has been presented by Johnson and Verdicchio [41]. Their so-called "triadic agency" presents a more applied perspective, analyzing the agency contributions from the three agents: designer, user, and artifact, and related ethical aspects (responsibility) connected to ascribed intention as divided between these three agents. Another interesting attempt at redefining creative agency as distributed among a number of contributing (and potentially interacting) agents has been presented by Oliver Bown [12].

In the following, I will primarily focus on this widened (or simplified) concept of agency as an influence—we may call it *influential agency*, as carried by artifacts and tools.

In this text, we will assume that humans have free will and are able to take decisions with responsibility for the consequences of their actions. This is the basis for the judicial systems of most societies, so it is a reasonable assumption. Still, no human is independent of external influence. Nature and nurture make us what we are, and most of our ideas and actions are related to or derived from what we have observed in others. My personal view of what music is and can be is certainly very much shaped by my musical training and the music-making I have observed from others. But it has grown into a mix unique to me, shaped by my specific biographical details. So the music I compose will be personal and unique, but it is at the same time derivative. The sources that have influenced me, which perhaps have a causal agency in relation to my music, are so diverse, and have been mediated in so many steps, that it is hard to pinpoint specific dependencies. What we do undoubtedly depends on what others have done before us, backward in untraceable steps.

As artifacts get gradually more complex, like AI algorithms, the border between intentional agency and influential or causal agency becomes blurred. AI algorithms fall somewhere in between these two categories of conscious actors with intentions and dead material objects subject to the causal laws of physics.

Many scholars have ascribed intentional agency to AI entities [11, 40, 55, 71], at least hypothetically, while talking about future implementations of AI. Such future AI may be closer to humans in their cognitive abilities, but this is far from the situation we have today. Today's AIs are not autonomous, they do not reflect on their own intentions, and they can't be held responsible for their behavior and their choices. Still, they are very powerful tools. But as we will see, there are humans behind all design choices.

While lacking intentional agency, the AI implementations we have today are much more complex in their behavior and in their dependencies than the kind of tools and non-human agents people like Vygotsky and Latour were supposedly referring to when formulating their theories. So, it is definitely worth analyzing to what extent these algorithms have agency, and what determines the properties of this agency.

31.2.1 Influential Agency

I introduce *influential agency* as an aspect of agency related to causal agency. If we take into account that tools can be mediators (with Latour's words) or carriers of agency, from the toolmaker, realized during tool use, it is also related to authorship. If you include responsibility, causality becomes intentionality. But responsibility requires awareness and certain control over the processes behind the causality, which humans certainly are capable of having, but which non-humans may not have. The intentions of the toolmaker were presumably around what the tool should be capable of and how it should be designed to do this, but not exactly how it should be applied. So, in the mediated agency, intentionality may not carry over, as a toolmaker cannot predict what your intentions with the tools are. It makes sense to talk about the influential agency from the tool and toolmaker, but not about the intentional agency from the toolmaker.

It may seem far-fetched to bring in authorship to the equation, just by tool use, but when tools are as complex and carry aesthetic implications on different levels of detail, with stylistic implications, they significantly shape the music. A clear example is the complex tools of today's electronic music. You can often hear which algorithms, instruments, and modules have been used in a certain piece of music, and toolmakers certainly shape the aesthetic trends with their designs. In the case of AI algorithms, which can embody patterns and behavior from existing music and music-makers, this phenomenon may be even more significant.

Influence is not just brought by tools, but also by many other sources during the creative process [24]. As a thought experiment, we can recall Latour's question: What difference does a certain actor make? What would happen if we altered details in the creative process, such as swapping a tool for another, swapping an algorithm for another, or change the person who carried out some part of the process? Or change any other constraint? What and how large differences would these changes make to the resulting action or output? If this tool was different, how would the results be different? Perhaps there is also another kind of agency, related to influence, but more drastic: Without this tool, this result would not even be possible—we may call that *conditional agency*, and both can exist in parallel.

Influence brings meaning and references to the work, regardless of intentions. Tools bring references to other music composed with similar tools, that exhibit similar structure not connected to any intention from the toolmaker. Tools may give rise to internal structure in a piece. And they imprint traces of the process of coming into being of the work.

For example, a certain time-stretching algorithm (e.g., FFT-based stretching) produces a certain kind of artifacts that are easily recognizable (a kind of harmonic bubbling). As a result, when applied with extreme settings, we are listening more to the algorithm than to the original stretched sound. Each composer who applies this algorithm ends up with quite similar results, and even though these results are quite complex in structure, they are similar, and the input from the composer is small: A source sound (that is not quite audible anymore), a few parameters for the tool, and the decision to use this particular tool. In this case, the influence of the toolmaker is much larger than that of the composer.

In a similar way, a certain AI algorithm can—even though its output can vary widely—bring a certain kind of characteristic structure, or a kind of sounds, depending on what it is capable of representing or generating. The specifics of these implications are dependent both on the design of the algorithm, the particular implementation, and how its parameters are set.

31.2.2 Influential Agency of an Algorithm

The influential agency can exist in the form of mediated agency from humans.

What comes from the algorithm, and not from the human designers and operators behind it? It is not a simple question to answer. What influence cannot be referenced back to a human? Does it have to exhibit true emergence for that to happen? And how do we know when that happens?

While the human influence is certainly there, the algorithm may induce an influence of its own. There are some situations when we could expect this to happen.

First, when there is emergence happening in the system. Emergence is defined as high-level behavior that is not directly traceable to the low-level parts, e.g., the complex behavior of an ant farm, which is way more complex than each ant. Complexity makes emergence untraceable.

Second, when there is a layer of independent learning in the system, learning during the process, in interactions with its environment. Just as a person is shaped by nature and nurture, with complex untraceable influences, an AI algorithm doing this may exhibit autonomy and perhaps agency.

Perhaps it is easier to go back to our original question: What does not come from the algorithm itself, i.e., what comes from the humans involved? Then what is not included in these answers will emanate from the influence of the algorithm. Emergence is tricky, and a lot of human decisions go into it. As an experienced designer of complex systems (co-evolutionary, cell automata, feedback systems), I know that I can design systems that give rise to desired emergent results (sometimes after a few design iterations, but still), and that this is a craft that can be learned, even though it is hard to verbalize this knowledge. So human agency may go into such systems too.

So what is the human influence? In a typical AI implementation, there are many stages of human influence. The choice of the training set, parameter settings, feedback from the human evaluation that goes into design choices, data representations, tweaks during implementation, changes, decisions about the workflow of the algorithm, how it will interact with its user, and many more.

Time has a role in moderating influence. AI systems are still usually run in computation batches over a limited time span, with human interactions before, after, and sometimes during the process.

As systems get more complex, and the learning continues over a long time, say many years, with continued interactions with its surrounding, including humans, it will be harder to speak about the agency of specific humans or specific human decisions. As the number of interactions grows, influence becomes diluted and harder to trace, and as the system grows (due to learning), complexity increases which makes emergent behavior harder to explain.

31.2.3 Influence as Information

Can we define agency in terms of information, in the meaning of Shannon [62]? I will not even try to make a formalized theory for this here, but I will use this as one way to reason about agency in artifacts resulting from human and AI creative processes.

Agency is often defined in terms of action and causality, and the term originally comes from action theory [1, 32]. But an action can also be thought of in terms of information flow from cause to effect. This idea is not new and was an important idea of cybernetics already from the start [3], emphasizing the connection between information and control in both humans and machines. This was further formalized by, e.g., Touchette and Lloyd [67], and Shannon-inspired approaches have also been applied to learning [8] and decision and action [66].

In this way, the influential agency can be thought of as a transfer of information from the influential agent to the musical result. For example, adding a note to a composition adds a certain amount of information: timing, duration, pitch, dynamics, etc. Every choice in creating music with a modular synthesizer contains an inflow of information, such as selecting which modules to include in a patch, which patch points to connect with a cable, timing information about when connections and parameter changes are done, and physical input into gestural interfaces, which are continuous signals at high resolution containing a large amount of information, which can be measured in a crude way as the size of a MIDI file containing a recording of it. Any application of a predefined generative process with a certain number of parameters introduces a certain amount of information.

It has already been mentioned that the influence can vary in magnitude [43], and perhaps we can understand this in terms of how information flows from various agents into the creative process, and how some of that information is lost in the process, and what remains. This information flow cannot always be traced backward. Some information is lost, some is redundant, and some is transformed. But there is a clear correlation, a dependency, between the information flowing in and the information contained in the finished work.

The main idea here is that a piece of music contains a certain amount of information. This information was introduced from somewhere during the creative process that led to the existence of the music. If composed by a human, it comes from years of musical training, from external impulses during the creative process, from the tools used (such as music theory or sound processing tools), from incidental actions, and from decisions taken during the process, influenced by a myriad of factors. If the piece is generated by an AI, i.e., a computer program, the information results from the processing of other information, either previously stored, as contained in the program or as input during the running of the program.

If an AI were an isolated entity with no information flowing in (except at its creation), the expressive power of the algorithm would be saturated after a certain time. If the output is only based on the internal states of the algorithm, it does not form an interactive relationship with its environment, and its output will not be contextualized or have any relationship with its environment. Or, any such contextual relation will be diluted over time, as the environment changes, but the AI will not change.

A lot of information is embedded in the training set used within many ML algorithms. Some information, but probably less, is contained in the process of selecting the training set. Other information is input during the design and implementation process in the form of numerous design decisions and parameter settings, as borrowed code from existing libraries, and from the process of coding.

Even if the amount of influence could be estimated, it cannot be isolated as having caused particular features in the results, since several agents interact and the result emerges from these interactions in a way that is not possible to attribute to each one of them, e.g., a particular artist, with her personal aesthetic preferences and characteristic behavior and creative habits, interacting with a particular tool (in a broad sense), results in a unique combination. This is of course also affected by what happens in the environment during the process. This particular interaction and its unique results could not have occurred in any other way. The same tool in the hands of another artist would lead to different results. And the same artist using another tool would also result in different art or music.

31.2.4 Influential Agency in a Typical AI Music Implementation

AI algorithms are often talked about as being able to create artistic artifacts on their own, but in reality, there are many layers of human influential agency at play. Let us start by looking at the various points of the development and application of such algorithms where this happens.

As an example, let us consider a hypothetical generative Recurrent Neural Network (RNN) network that is used to generate music in a style based on a training set of existing music by some human composer.

- It was humans who invented the general concept of artificial neurons, inspired by biological neurons.
- In the case of this specific type of neural networks, a large number of humans have been involved in the development and improvement of the underlying algorithms, over many years.
- Humans programmed a particular implementation of this algorithm, as a library usable by others. It is still a general set of algorithms and tools, to be applied to a wide area of possible situations and tasks, but also comes with a set of constraints, following from design decisions by the programmers.
- Humans chose which particular generative algorithm to use in this project, from a large set of potential choices, and which particular implementation of this algorithm, from available software libraries, or chose to implement their project within an existing development environment that comes with a set of libraries.
- Humans also chose what hardware to run it on, which comes with a set of constraints, such as computational speed, available memory, and a processor architecture more suitable for one type of implementation than another (e.g., a certain kind of parallelism).
- Humans chose how the material was to be represented to the algorithm, which can have a large impact on what can be learned during the training phase, which features are detectable in the input, and what output can be generated.
- Humans set a myriad of parameters that control how the chosen algorithm is operating: Number of layers of neurons, number of nodes, size of the training set, training parameters and sub-algorithms, preprocessing of the training set, etc. All these parameters have implications for how the algorithm will perform and usually take some experience to get right. There are usually no default choices for such parameters that work for all kinds of projects, and often considerable experimentation is needed before good settings are found.
- Humans choose the training set which has crucial aesthetic implications for the generated output.

- Humans tweak parameters of the algorithm, based on iterated outcomes, if the algorithm does not work as expected, the result is not good enough, or shows unwanted features. In this feedback process, human aesthetic evaluation is a crucial component.
- Finally, humans select the best examples from a large set of generated outputs. Also here, human aesthetic evaluation is at play.

In most cases, all these humans are different people, working at different points in time, and their decisions were taken in very different contexts, at varying distances (in time and computational steps) from the final artistic result. Some of them were working in a very general and abstract context, not even considering what these algorithms will be applied to. Still, their decisions carry an impact on the final results. Sometimes the humans were part of the feedback process of trial and error or final tweaking, trying to make the final results as good, or as similar to the intended style, as possible. The decisions, choices, and values of those early in the chain remain embedded in the tools they develop, which are then used by others in the later steps of the chain. All these steps have an influence on the output.

31.2.5 Influential Agency in an Actual Example: Ossia

Let us look at a similar analysis of a real case. I have chosen my own Ossia system which is an implementation of an evolutionary algorithm that breeds complete performed piano pieces of a duration of 30–90 s each. It started as an interactive evolutionary composition tool in 2000 [19], and autonomous evolution (based on random or keyboard input) was added in 2002 [23] when it was exhibited as an installation for computer and Disklavier player piano at the Gaudeamus Festival in Amsterdam. Later it was exhibited for several years at the Universeum Science Center in Gothenburg, Sweden. It was chosen as an example because it is well documented, and I know it inside out, as I designed and coded it from scratch in C++ in a number of versions over several years. It is still shown sporadically in lectures, e.g., as background music to the lecture versions of this chapter. Ossia composes a continuous stream of new piano pieces/performances and performs them as a suite. It can be interactive, but I will here talk about the autonomous version, as it appears to be composing by itself, and the output is quite varied.

- The choice of algorithm was influenced by my previous work on interactive evolution for sound synthesis [18], which was in turn influenced by my reading of introductory literature—introduced by my doctoral supervisor—on the topic of Artificial Life, and by my previous extensive experimentation with random search in sound synthesis parameter spaces. The idea of simulated evolution in computers goes far back and was initially mentioned by Alan Turing and John von Neumann, further developed by a number of researchers in the 1950s and 60s, and popularized as the genetic algorithm by John Holland [38]. My understanding of evolution was also influenced by reading Darwin and Dawkins.

All these sources indirectly or directly influenced my implementation, mediated in several stages through researchers, authors, and teachers.

- The genetic representation of Ossia was designed by me, influenced by knowledge of and previous work with tree-based data structures (from computer science studies and other machine learning experiments) and generative grammar (from various books and from knowledge of Lindenmeyer systems), and my previous works with recursive algorithms (e.g., fractal graphics) and recursive programming (e.g., Prolog). The idea of recursive pointers was also based on the idea that a core property of the musical form is repetition with variation, and this construction made this possible. The modifiers (of velocity, duration and pitch) were one way to make possible another desired set of archetypal musical features: exponential crescendo/diminuendo, exponential accelerando/ritardando, and repetition with transposition. These ideas were most likely influenced by a lot of reading of classical form and music theory and of musical aesthetics.
- The genetic operators were chosen and designed by me, influenced by various papers on mutations and cross-over in tree-shaped genomes.
- The initial population can be either randomly generated trees, a set of arbitrary musical sequences (stored as MIDI files, parsed into genome trees by the system), or a set of previously evolved musical pieces (in stored genome form). In the first case, "randomly generated trees" are not entirely random. They are generated in a detailed process coded by me, with choices for what random distributions there are for certain properties to appear in the tree, and what the ranges of these values could be. So it is still much influenced by aesthetic choices by me. In the second case, the set of musical "seeds" has varied, but the most used set has been a collection of simple archetypal musical gestures such as an upwards scale, an arpeggio, or a repeated note. These simple seeds were used because I thought they would expose the kinds of variations that the system was capable of. Even though this was the initial educational motivation, the set of seeds have been kept for most performances with the system. Their exact form and selection were certainly shaped by my long training as a classical musician. In the final case, there is a procedure coded by me for selecting when a previous musical result will end up in the seed pool.
- The workflow of the system, which is behind how it acts and interacts with the world around it, was designed by me based on a series of circumstances. The initial interactive evolutionary algorithm was designed for it to be used as a composition tool, generating raw score material to be arranged into compositions (e.g., my chamber work KARG [19]). Soon after, in 2002, I made it evolve pieces of its own, influenced by opportunity for a performance at the Gaudeamus Festival in Amsterdam and by the availability of a Yamaha Disklavier concert grand player piano. It was exhibited with this piano, and I thought it would be interesting to also let visitors perform on the piano, and let the system evolve further based on the human performances. If nobody plays, it evolves new pieces from scratch.
- The fitness criteria were designed by me, in a design process that extended over several design iterations. In the first version, the system was only interactive, and

all examples were auditioned and selected by me. When I made it autonomous, I used my observations and notes from how I tended to select musical examples and tried to implement hand-coded formalized versions of the same selection criteria. They were based on statistical measures such as note density, tessitura, information content and repetition, and variations over time of these statistical measures, as a way to indirectly enforce dynamics and variation (or process) within a piece. Clearly, my aesthetic preferences influenced the workings of Ossia here.

- Evolutionary parameters (population size, mutation rates, halting criteria, etc.) were first set ad hoc by me based on previous experience of evolutionary algorithms. They were then gradually adjusted based on results of repeated test runs, based on personal preferences and informal performance evaluations.
- A final selection of pieces to be played has sometimes been made by me, as in the Ossia Suite, featuring 27 piano pieces [27]. They were selected by me from a large body of output, based on aesthetic criteria. In the real-time installation version, no such selection takes place.
- During development, the system was tested using a simple piano sound. There were two primary reasons: First, I am a pianist myself and feel very much at home with this timbre. Second, the piano is regarded as some kind of "universal" instrument, mostly because it can be played over the full pitch range by a single musician. This undoubtedly biased the design toward producing musical material that works well on the piano. In spite of the supposed universality of the piano, all instruments are different, and the way piano responds to dynamic playing, how dissonances behave perceptional in different registers, its rhythmic pregnancy, and many other features are unique to the piano. Music composed for it may not work well with other instruments. This simple design choice strongly influenced the aesthetic output of the system. And indeed, the output of the system sounds similar in aesthetics to my own piano improvisations, even though there is no training involved, nor any musical knowledge explicitly coded into the system.

The above is of course only a simplified analysis of the various sources of influence on the Ossia system. There are many more design decisions involved, and many features of the system that I cannot include here for reasons of space. Still, it is clear from the above that even though it may appear to an observer of the player piano continuously performing an endless series of new compositions that the software composes these pieces, clearly there is the extensive human agency involved. As the author of the system and a listener to maybe thousands of pieces composed by it, I can certainly hear the patterns, even though it is (designed to be) very varied. Although there is infinite variation within the result space, it is not infinite in its extension. And I am starting to grow tired of it. Exploration has mapped out the limits of the result space, if not all subspaces contained therein. I can clearly see the bars of the fence it is caged in.

31.2.6 Agency is Where in the Code?

There is usually nothing specially "AI" about the programming languages that are used for implementing AI algorithms, as they can be implemented in any common programming language. Some parts of the program implement an AI algorithm, and other parts take care of the more mundane tasks—general infrastructure of the program, the main loop that controls actions, asks for new input, asks for new output, performs memory management, etc. As all AI implementations consist of such mundane tasks and rather basic mathematics, just iterated many times, and/or in large parallel configurations, it is hard to say where in such a program agency would appear. It is often considered to emerge from the sheer scale and complexity of the algorithm.

It can also be argued that many current ML algorithms, such as deep neural networks, harbor no agency if understood as a capacity to act. As the actual AI algorithm is not associated with actions, but with evaluations and classifications, the only action-related agency in such systems happens in the "normal" code around the ML algorithm: the *main* loop, the *if..then* statements acting upon the evaluations of the AI algorithm. And these parts typically do *not* learn. And as long as these parts of the code still consist of common *for..next* loops and *if..then* statements, they will never be able to act in any intelligent way. According to this view, today's AI systems act stupidly and repetitively, but have an ability to develop and learn complex evaluations and classifications. (This particular argument was developed in dialog with Karoliina Salminen, principal AI engineer at Huawei, Finland.)

The above argument fits quite well with the Ossia system. It is programmed to compose a new piano piece as soon as the previous one is being performed, with a fixed number of seconds between each performance. If a human plays on the piano while Ossia does not play, it will evolve a new piece based on the human input as soon as the human has been quiet for a few seconds, and then perform this as soon as it is ready. If somebody presses the Q key on the computer, the system stops. The fitness criteria are varied according to a number of preprogrammed parameter sets, giving quite different outputs. There is not really any potential for long-term progression.

There is not much intentional agency in this scheme, which is basically a looping script with some external sensors (MIDI input from the piano and the computer keyboard) and some actuators (the player piano). Just like the simple thermostat, it is a reflex agent, although with slightly more complex internal states.

31.3 Tools and Humans

Most art and music are made with tools. As we have discussed earlier, tools are carriers of embedded agency and carriers of intelligent behavior. They influence the artistic results, because they define what is possible, and they define the paths in the space of the possibilities, along which creative process can travel [24]. Through this influence, they carry their agency, in several ways. They lead to characteristic results, because only certain specific things are possible to do with a specific tool. Certain things are easy to do, and certain things are hard.

Previously, instrument makers provided simple tools to be used by skilled artists (e.g., a violin maker). Not simple in terms of construction or craft, but in terms of time-complexity in their interaction. They provide constraints, but interaction is primarily based on real-time responses to direct gestural input. No pattern comes out that is not detectable in the input.

Today, instrument makers provide tools that contain extensive databases of presets and algorithms for putting together this material with potential for creative agency. Such tools have stylistic implications, as they are designed to be used within a specific style of music. They can be used at different levels of control:

Pressing play
where the tool generates a whole song, or at least significant portions of it, for example, by combining complete loops and ready-made drum patterns, applying automatic accompaniment engines, and mixing algorithms. The song you create in this way risks being very similar to the song I will create if we use the same tool and there is little inflow of information.

Collage
where you manually put together finished pieces from a database, such as loops, drum patterns, and sequence phrases, and select the sounds they play. Here, more effort is put in by the user.

Detailed
where you have control over every parameter of sequences, sounds, and processing.

There is a qualitative difference between the old instruments and such new tools, which has been analyzed in detail; e.g., by Nilsson [54]. This difference is further amplified when you take the next step toward tools based on complex systems and AI algorithms, which have complex internal states which develop over time. When designing such emergent systems, the output of which we cannot predict, design choices have to deal with low-level behavior while the consequences appear in high-level behavior, and new skills are needed to understand and work with such systems.

31.3.1 Effort Versus Tool Complexity

We can do a simplified analysis of the role of effort and inflow of information in relation to tool complexity. To simplify, we only talk about small or large effort (time and amount of interaction invested), and simple and complex tools (designed by myself or somebody else). In this analysis, we must remember that influential agency can be mediated in two ways: by a user, through previous learning from others, and by a tool, through design from the toolmaker.

There are a few obvious cases:

- **A simple tool with little effort**: This does not lead far, and results will stay at the level of playing *Twinkle, twinkle, little star* with your index finger on an unfamiliar instrument.
- **A simple tool with a large effort**, applying skills from years of training: The main part of the influential agency will be from me as an artist, except that a significant part of my skills indirectly come from others, as mediated through learning. Very little will come from the tool, except in the form of generative tool constraints.
- **A complex tool with little effort and interaction**, for example, a tool containing presets and generative algorithms: The main part of the influential agency will be from the toolmaker because I will rely on ready-made material or material generated from algorithms with default parameters.

The following cases may be less obvious.

- **A complex tool of my own design, used with little effort**: If I have written every line of code, but I let the tool do the choices, the main part of the influential agency will still be from the toolmaker—but that is me. Still, a large part of the influential agency comes from the inventor of the class of algorithms I used, and the teachers or authors that taught me those algorithms. But there has been a significant inflow of information from me into the creative process, because I designed the tool. But there is a catch. If I continue to use the same tool to produce a large amount of musical output, without much new interaction or effort, it will converge toward the situation in the above case 2. My initial effort will fade in proportion with time, as the extensive but limited one-time effort will have been used to create an ever larger amount of music, thinning out the content in relation to the total inflow of information. In a sense, it can be regarded as me re-instantiating the same piece over and over again. This is the case with the autonomous version of my generative composition Ossia. It keeps generating music but does not add anything new.
- **A complex tool with large effort**: If I use a complex tool designed by somebody else, containing databases or generative algorithms of which the inner workings are not known to me, and I put in a large effort, with a large inflow of information, then I have time to form a cognitive model of the tool based on experience. This helps me navigate the pathways in the result space. Through the effort spent, I have a chance to find distant corners in the result space that may not be found by others that put in less effort. And I have a chance to find particular pathways in the result space that are personal to me.

31.3.2 Non-mediated Agency in Algorithms

If we, by definition, assign agency to the toolmaker, we risk ending in a paradox. As all AI systems are man-made (it lies in the word *artificial*), there is a possibility that at some point the system starts to exhibit agency of its own. We do ascribe creative agency to ourselves. And we have to be able to tell what is the qualitative difference, when they attain this agency and break free from us, or we end up in the "but who created us" circle of reasoning, and will keep looking for a first mover.

So, when does a system attain agency, aside from the mediated influential agency of the toolmaker or designer? Bown and McCormack [13] have defined what they call *creative agency* as the creative contribution attributable to the actual system, and added that "novelty and value that cannot be directly attributed to the computational system should have no weight in supporting claims about the creativity of that system". When analyzing creative generative systems, creative agency is *the* important property of a system, not the actual creative output.

But what are the criteria from creative agency? When do we actually take our virtual hands off a system, and it starts creating beyond the influential agency of us as designers? It is not easy to answer this, but the following questions may help us on the way:

- What remains of our design over time—what is fixed and what is dynamic in the system, at different abstraction levels?
- Does the system search the same solution space each time or does it develop over time?
- Is the solution space searched in the same way and based on the same criteria each time or is there potential for learning?
- Are the aesthetic constraints of the underlying representation sufficiently relaxed or even open-ended?
- Is there a sufficient inflow of information from interaction with other agents or other parts of the environment?

Without having any definite answers, it seems to me that it comes down to process, and the internal changes of the system as it learns, transforms, or evolves. It needs to be able to accumulate impressions over time, and we need to allow for time for things to develop, while we remove ourselves. Given sufficient open-endedness, as a system gets more complex, and the learning continues over a long time with continued interactions with its surroundings, including humans, it will be harder to speak about the agency of specific humans or specific human design decisions. There will be many more interactions, and with a larger number of humans, so agency will be more distributed and harder to trace to specific events or agents. And the system will potentially grow in complexity, and perhaps approach the kind of emergence where underlying causes cannot be identified at all.

31.4 Spectra of Agency

A spectrum is a range of a certain quantity, such as the spectrum of audible frequencies. There are certain properties involved in this discussion about the agency that have a range from simple to complex. We will look at these spectra in this section, in an attempt to understand these parameters better.

31.4.1 Spectrum of Tool Complexity

We can think of tools as having two primary levels of complexity, even though they are related. One is the *level of abstraction of the material* that a certain tool or algorithm operates upon. Is it basic musical atoms such as individual sound samples or individual notes? Or more complex constellations of such atoms, such as phrases, patterns, or even operations on the stylistic level? The other is *the complexity of the operation*—what kind of transformation does the tool bring? Is it a simple linear transformation or a more complex operation? A few examples may help to illustrate this. A simple operation may be a transposition of a score, by moving all notes up by a major third, or changing the volume of a sound file by multiplying all sound samples by a constant. It is a simple, straight-forward operation applied to the basic material. An example of an intermediate operation could be to search and replace a given interval sequence with another sequence or to generate material with the same statistical interval and rhythm distributions as a given piece of music. A complex operation could be to compose a fugue in the style of Bach or to initiate a new musical style by creating a piece of music that differs in structural properties from all previously existing music. These operations get more complex both in terms of the amount of information that is introduced with the application of the tool—a single parameter in case of transposition and a complete set of Bach's fugues in the case of fugue generation. They are also more complex in terms of the amount of computation required.

A proposed simplified spectrum of tools could look like this, where the level of abstraction and complexity of operation have been combined into a single, rising scale (see also Fig. 31.1):

Simple tools
Straight-forward linear sequentially operating physical, virtual, or theoretical tools. Examples: A pencil, a keyboard, a violin, a pair of scissors, or cut-and-paste operations.

Template-based tools
Tools that contain predesigned databases of material or parameter sets, to be able to quickly solve complex tasks in predefined ways. Examples: Preset-based synthesizers and effects, a clip art database, or a loop library.

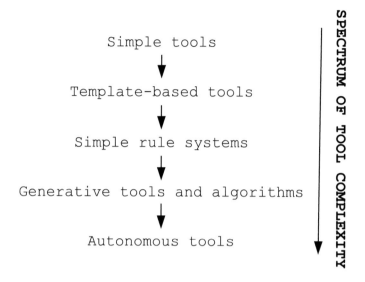

Fig. 31.1 A proposed spectrum of tool complexity. The complexity of operations increases from top to bottom

Simple rule systems

A set of behavioral rules or basic procedural code that constrain the output, and help project beyond the artist's imagination. It is easier to invent a few rules than to predict what the result will be, as we are lousy predictors. Examples: A line fractal implemented as a recursive Logo script, search-and-replace, regular expressions, isorhythmic composition techniques, a generative modular synthesizer patch, or the rules of a game piece in the style of John Zorn.

Generative tools and algorithms

More complex computational tools that generate or process material based on advanced algorithms. Possibly designed by, tweaked by, or interacted with by the artist. Examples: Most current AI algorithms.

Autonomous tools

Tools that generate or process material without any interaction with a user. If a tool becomes autonomous, it may perhaps not be called a tool anymore, as being used by someone could be considered part of the definition of a tool. No examples of this category exist yet.

31.4.2   Spectrum of Agency

Two properties shape the amount of influential agency an agent may have. The first is *the amount of interaction* with the agent or *the amount of information* embedded in the tool that mediates the influence. The second is *the distance of this interaction or the application of this information*—in time, processing steps, computational layers—from the actual result. Information may be diluted, transformed, or lost in the process. An agent may be very distant from the final result, but still have had influence through actions, e.g., the inventor of a class of tools a long time ago, or of a new kind of algorithm, e.g., a new kind of neural network, without any intention for it to be used to create art. Such an inventor still has an influence on me making music with these algorithms, since it opened up for the possibility, created a potential. It is not intentional, but somewhat casual, and definitely influential.

Tool designer
The inventor of a tool or a class of tools.

Toolmaker
The maker of a particular implementation of the tool.

The tool itself
The tool carries embedded agency from the tool designer and the toolmaker, as a mediator. In the encounter between tool user and tool, the tool's potential is actuated in a process constrained by the tool's space of possibilities and the user's aesthetic preferences and skill [24].

Tool user/Artist
The agent who applies the tool in a specific context, to a specific material, with specific parameters. The artist also brings in influence from her own previous music, from other music and musicians, and in an extended sense from all of music history.

The artwork itself
The artwork carries accumulated embedded agency from all previous agents.

The receiver/listener
The listener, who finally receives the music (or a co-player who hears a colleague play on stage), carries out, consciously or unconsciously, an interpretation of what is heard, and through this applies influential agency. At this final stage, there is also the sense of personal agency an engaged listener can sense, as if it was created by yourself, often enhanced by dancing or other synchronous movements [25].

As shown in Fig. 31.2, there is also some influential agency going in the opposite direction. Tool users often give important feedback or requests to tool-makers, and this can be iterated many times. For example, as a musician, I have worked closely with electronic instrument makers, both in testing, suggesting new functions, and sometimes even initiating new tools. These tools contain influential agency from me and the toolmaker and are then applied again by myself. The receiver—and the artist herself, as mediated by the work—contributes to the aesthetic context, and in the long run to art history, which in turn influences the artist.

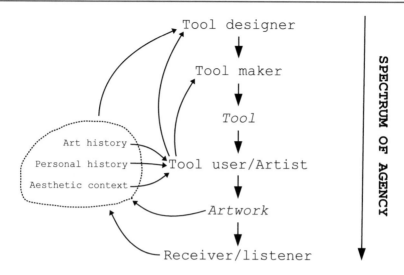

Fig. 31.2 Spectrum of agency. Influential agency flows from the tool designer and toolmaker, as mediated by the tool itself, to the tool user (the artist), and onwards, through the act of interpretation (which sometimes involves interpreters/musicians). There are also circular flows, as the artistic result becomes part of the aesthetic context these agents live in, and in the long term, becomes a part of art or music history, and hence influences both tool designers, toolmakers, and future artists

In electronic music, the tool designer, toolmaker, and tool user are often the same person. Still, electronic musicians build or program their musical tools (instruments) from other tools at lower abstraction levels. For example, a live coder may create her own language or library of functions to use in a live setting. These are usually implemented in another, more general programming language. A synthesizer builder constructs her machines from circuits designed based on decades of development by the analog synthesizer community, perhaps with added inventions of her own, and/or in new configurations, just as most pieces of music are created based upon patterns and forms that have been developed over centuries. In the same way as all music is derivative, tools are derivative.

31.4.3 Spectrum of Generativity

Based on the above spectra, we can also make an attempt at a rough spectrum of levels of generativity in music, i.e., a list of categories of music in rising order of generative complexity, and rising order of influence from underlying tools and algorithms (see also Fig. 31.3):

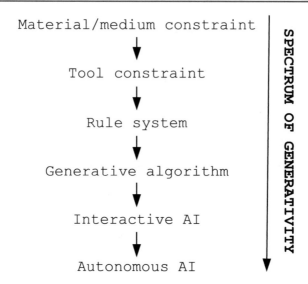

Fig. 31.3 Spectrum of generativity, with generative influence going from low level at the top to very high level at the bottom. The initial choice of medium to work in affects what can be represented. The chosen tools constrain what can be done, and successively more complex algorithms bring higher level generative properties to the creative process, gradually shifting the influential agency toward the tool designer and toolmaker—which may very well be the same as the artist

Material/medium constraint
The chosen medium has implications for what can be represented. For example, if you work with Western notation, only certain kinds of rhythms and durations are possible to write.

Tool constraint
The choice of tools has implications for what can be done in the chosen medium. Tools define pathways (structured subspaces) in the space of possibilities defined by the medium. If you work in the medium of electronic sounds, constrained by a sequenced synthesizer as a tool, certain sounds are possible as defined by the instrument/synthesizer, and certain events and kinds of parameter changes are possible to represent and control from the sequencer. Here, both the medium and the tools used have generative (and restrictive) properties.

Rule systems
Simple rules about how constituent parts interact during a creative process lead to characteristic patterns.

Generative algorithms
Computation-based algorithms generate musical material, for example, from an AI algorithm.

Interactive AI

The AI is a node in an interactive creative network of agents. It generates output based on input and based on stored/learned information. Learning may happen during the process.

Autonomous AI

The AI carries out a situated process in relation to the creation of a single work and in relation to a series of works. It has sustained artistic output, and it has a representation of and a relation to the outside world. In this situation, the AI may achieve intentional agency.

As the level of generativity increases toward the end of the list, the influential agency is shifted toward the tool designer and toolmaker, as the tools by mediation bring complex behavior and aesthetic implications that are not under the direct control of the artist. However, especially in electronic music, it is common that a composer designs her own tools.

Note also the similarity to the spectrum of tool complexities shown earlier.

31.5 Problems with Creative AI

In this section, I will briefly discuss a few fundamental problems with current AI algorithms in relation to creativity. These problems have been described and analyzed in more detail in a previous publication [26].

31.5.1 The Inherent Non-creativity of Statistical Machine Learning

Many current AI algorithms are "mean machines" that are designed to find or produce the most likely outcome. This includes most statistical methods (e.g., Markov-based models and neural networks). They will stay inside the box by definition.

Such a system learns from the training set and is then used to generate something that has very similar statistical properties. It will not be able to generate anything that adds something new, at least according to an understanding of the model as the best possible (in the given algorithm, size, etc.) representation of the complete material in the training set. Briefly, the argument is that if it is trained on, say, the set of 15 two-part inventions by Bach, it will be able to generate new inventions in the style of Bach. But each of those newly generated inventions will be completely based on what the system learned from the training set of the original inventions. And each original invention, while sharing some properties with the others, added something that was unique. If Bach would have written the 16th invention, it would have added some new ideas that were not present in the previous 15. But the AI algorithm is not able to do that, because the impulses that led Bach to the material in his hypothetical 16th invention would have come from outside of the existing 15 inventions. It could have come from an impulse, a paraphrase on an earlier piece in the same key, or a musical idea from his wife.

If such a system would produce something that went outside of the training set, it would be thanks to its characteristic inabilities, basically its flaws and limitations that make it unable to reproduce something perfectly. This may very well result in interesting output, but it will not be because of inherent creativity, but from design faults or conscious limitations.

This relates to the previously mentioned complementary relation between optimization and exploration. Most ML algorithms are convergent and optimize in relation to criteria such as similarity. An interesting parallel—which highlights why this is so important in an artistic context—is that it is very similar to the relationship between entertainment, which aims for the middle of the circle, with known responses, and art, which tries to extend the circle, testing new ideas.

Creativity is about creating new patterns, and new kinds of patterns, while most machine techniques for handling large data are about detecting, classifying, or reproducing patterns of a known form.

Machine Learning algorithms produce models that are based on correlations in superficial observations, not on causality between interactions with the environment and artistic output. This is a classic problem in empirical science, and it is especially troublesome in this field because it tells us what but does not help us understand how and why. Such algorithms are capable of generating mimetic output, which lacks all connections to the situated process from which the originals emerged. We generate diluted Bach music, but not a model of how Bach would interact given certain input, or how Bach would have developed beyond the last item of the training set.

Similar problems appear with evolutionary algorithms when fitness functions are formulated in terms of properties of the output. This is also an optimization process where the goal is well specified. Still, there are a number of successful attempts at exploratory approaches with interactive evolution [9, 18, 69] and novelty search [44].

31.5.2 Opaqueness of AI-Generated Material

Both neural-based and evolutionary algorithms suffer from the problem of opaqueness of the results. The meaning of individual weights in Deep Learning networks is very hard to detect, and evolution often generates complex but undecipherable solutions, as pointed out already by Sims [63]. The solutions work, but we do not know how. This problem also exists in natural evolution and artificial breeding. Explainable AI has been part of significant research efforts lately [59] and is often mentioned as a necessary part of ethically sustainable AI.

This opaqueness may also lead to material that is hard to work with because we do not understand its inner logic. Even if the composer has written the code herself, the output may feel alien to her, and it will take a considerable effort to learn to work with it. For an example of such a problematic result, and how to deal with it, see [28, 29].

The flip side of this is that while solutions may be hard to understand, they may work well. When evolving or training a co-improvising agent, this may be what we need.

31.5.3 The Lack of a Model of the Outside World

The lack of semantic understanding and focus on patterns is a general problem with AI. They are applied to the recognition or generation of empty patterns lacking connection to the outside world. These generated patterns may inherit an implicit referential connection from training sets, but it is never re-confirmed and calibrated as humans do, constantly. We go back and check if an answer is reasonable if it is compatible with our cognitive model of the world.

A common rule of thumb is that model complexity should match domain/data complexity, for optimal learning without over- or under-fitting. Still, simpler models are usually preferred in AI, because they are faster to compute, easier to understand, tweak, and design, and will not over-fit. Simpler models make it impossible to represent the real world in its complexity.

The lack of world models in AI implementations enhances the previously mentioned problems with mimetic pattern generation, free from causal connections, lacking interaction, situatedness, and semantic dimensions.

Even if hypothetical more advanced AI algorithms would be able to partly represent the outside world, there is a logical paradox, developed around the concept of embedded agency [34]. The learning agent is part of the world, and hence, smaller than the world. So, a complete model of the world (including itself) is impossible, because the world is larger than itself (itself + the rest of the world). Artificial agents who realize this are subject to the same limitations and feedback loops as we are. Without this realization, it will be decisive but wrong.

To summarize, most current AI creativity imitates the consequences of creativity instead of implementing the creative process and emulating the causal chains behind it. It lacks continuous interaction with its environment and the related inflow of information. As long as this approach prevails, AI creativity will remain a mimetic black box batch process.

31.6 Aesthetics

In this section, a few issues related to the aesthetics of AI-generated music will be discussed.

31.6.1 Autonomous Aesthetics and Agency

The idea that an artwork should be judged as independent from the artist was put forward by Roland Barthes in his famous essay the *Death of the Author* [4]. After being published, the text lives its own life, loses the connection to the author, and should be evaluated as a separate entity, or as Barthes says: "it is language which speaks, not the author" (ibid, p.143).

But the artwork embeds values and patterns from the artist. It is shaped by the process of the artist and her interactions with her surroundings during that process. It is evaluated or appreciated in a context of an artist, style, and culture, by a receiver (critic, listener) who is part of that context or part of another related context. It is created with tools that are part of that context, and the tools and technology behind it are often audible or detectable for the educated listener or the fellow practitioner.

The conclusion is that the artwork does indeed relate to the world. There is an information flow in and out between the world and the creative process, and this shapes the result. So, in my view, it is a utopian view that the artwork could be regarded as completely separated from the artist. The artist, the artwork, and the receiver are all part of the world. An AI artist needs to be part of this world, too, and relate to it. It needs to be an agent in this world to create art that is meaningful to others in this world.

Part of Barthes's argument is that the content of the text comes from numerous sources and numerous authors, and how all work thus is derivative. According to him, a text is

> a multi -dimensional space in which a variety of writings, none of them original, blend and clash. The text is a tissue of quotations drawn from the innumerable centres of culture. [4, p. 146].

This is of course also true for music. In resonance with my argument above about influential agency, and mediated agency from tool designers, toolmakers, teachers, and other sources of influence, we could rephrase Barthes's claim as: The death of *one* author, and the acknowledgment of *many*. It is in line with the idea of distributed influential agency, and a similar argument has been presented by Bown [12], in the context of computational creativity.

In a sense, the idea of the autonomous work from an analysis point of view does not take away from the fact that there has to be a creative process involving human or artificial agents, and that the conditions and properties of this process influence the result. A synthesist of art, i.e., a developer of creative algorithms, will still need to understand this mechanism of influence even if the analyst does not care.

Also, empathy and empathetic experience play a major role in the appreciation of music, in particular of live music performance, and here the human agency and our ability to perceive intention and agency play an important role. One could go as far as saying that in some musical contexts, for example, in free improvisation, the sonic result is not the most important part of the experience—that may instead be the empathetical experience of the interactions, the efforts, and the struggle of the musicians [25].

31.6.2 Characteristic Inability

In my previous writings on creativity (e.g., [24]), I have talked about characteristic inability or characteristic incompetence as the personal way in which an artist or musician cannot do what is considered "perfect" or what originally intended. I cannot write a perfect Bach fugue, and the personal way in which I fail becomes my personal style of fugues. These peculiarities are what makes it a Dahlstedt fugue. The same applies to generative algorithms—the way a generative system does not generate something perfect becomes its characteristic "personal" style.

Something related to pareidolia comes into play here. We read consistently "clumsy" results as personal, while anything perfect is not interesting (except for that virtuosic "awe"). But we are attracted to in what way it is not perfect, to the relation between perceived intention and actual result. Our own aesthetic sense sees the intended (ideal?) image behind the limited depiction and is able to abstract the transformational layer of imperfection, and this becomes an aesthetic experience of its own. The imperfections that emerge during the implementation process also adds ambiguity, hence it becomes open for interpretation and projected complexity. My reading is different from your reading.

31.6.3 Apparent Agency Attribution

Agency attribution is affected by many factors, e.g., synchrony, anthropomorphism, convention, and expectations. We see meaning and patterns where there are none—our wonderful disposition towards *pareidolia*—which makes abstract art a dangerously comfortable field for generative art. In the same way, we see agency when there is little of it, as we do not have the whole picture and we want to see an agent behind something—it makes what we see conceptually coherent. Hidden actors are harder to imagine and are easily forgotten or ignored.

Computer music and computer art are often presented to be reflected upon *as if* they are made by a human, and the degree to which they succeedis commonly used as an evaluation criterion in AI art, often presented as a version of the famous Turing test [68]. Typically, a number of musical examples are played to a set of listeners, who are asked which they think are composed by a musician or by a machine. As a number of practitioners and researchers have pointed out [2, 6, 7, 10, 57], this is a questionable method, or at least a questionable name for it, as the original Turing test, as described by Turing himself was a test of the quality of interaction with another agent, and a way to try to judge if it was conscious or not. Now, the output is instead evaluated in terms of human-likeness. As a program can contain large amounts of stored information (as embedded learned patterns or explicit material), judging finished music says nothing. In generative algorithms, evaluating variation over a large set of output or, where appropriate, interacting with an AI musician may approach a Turing test for music.

Does the agent of art matter? Humans can show a strong admiration for abstract complexity, as found, e.g., in mathematics and physics visualizations. Many also have admiration for natural beauty, with no intentional agent behind it. Some project an agent (a god or something else), while others, like myself, see emergence from a complex system—most scientists agree that evolution and physics are not guided by intention.

Also, as mentioned above, some regard the work and author separated (autonomous aesthetics). Then, having no clear agent would not make a difference for the receiver. But can the work as a complex entity be reflected upon in different terms than how it was conceived, who did it, why she did it, what are they trying to say, and what happened in the creative process? An artwork tells me about its coming into being, and that is the meaning of the process. And my reflections and personal associations from it, even if disregarding or honestly ignorant about the author, will be influenced by this process, as the work was shaped by it.

We could also consider AI-generated art that presents itself *as if* it had a process, even if it did not have one, or if the apparent process did not correspond to its actual genesis. This would require a representation that takes such deeper layers into account to be able to coherently fake traces of a creative process.

Consider a different hypothetical case: We know the music was composed by an artificial agent. Does this devalue the art or increase its value to us? I am not talking about monetary value here. There may currently be a certain wow factor and some awe, as we are impressed by the novelty of what is possible with machines. There is also the computational sublime [48], the aesthetic awe of what is possible with computing. This may disappear if we believe it is made by a sentient being or a human (even if it is not) and is instead replaced by an empathetic perception of the efforts and skill behind the work.

This awe is relative. That which goes beyond our understanding is obviously relative to what we can understand and relative to our cognitive models of what we are trying to do. The play with this border is what we do when creating generative art. Our predictive capacity and its limits are crucial. As new generations grow up with AI-generated art and music, this may change considerably, just as how our current perception of generative computer music would be inconceivable just a few decades ago.

What about the effort in machine-composed music? Can algorithms exhibit effort? They can (when implemented in computers) for sure play a lot of different sounds quickly and generate music of great complexity, but this does not correlate directly to effort, at least not on a human scale. These signs of human effort are, when exhibited by a computer, ineffective, because it lacks the markers of actual effort, which is an important part of human performance, such as the slight pause before a large intervallic jump on a string instrument or a large jump of the hands on a piano, because of the necessary preparation and the extra attention required from the performer.

It is hard to talk about machine effort when the effort is transferred from an effortless machine to our band-limited perception, which attempts cognitive parsing of the complexity. It becomes an effort in the listener instead of a perceived effort of the agent and completely lacks the empathetic dimension. It becomes just tiring to listen to. When listening to human-composed music, both these kinds of efforts may be present. In today's AI-generated music, empathetic appreciation is still possible by mediation, to the humans behind it. This may change when AI becomes more autonomous.

As Arthur C. Clarke worded it in his third law: "Any sufficiently advanced technology is indistinguishable from magic." [14]. We have an attraction to this perceived magic, as we like to feel awe. And we who make music want to be the machine we do not understand. We like to not be completely understood, to be ambiguous or cause awe, and we seek the challenges in doing that.

31.6.4 Uncanny Valley

In robotics, they speak of the "uncanny valley", when a robot gets more and more human-like, suddenly it becomes scarily realistic, but you are not quite sure and something feels wrong [51]. Could this appear also in AI music? I do not think so, as we are already accustomed to so much of machine-generated and machine-mediated music-making. Also, technology has made new kinds of music possible, and acoustic instrumentalists have been influenced by this and developed new ways of playing that sound similar. For example, the acoustic drummer Jojo Mayer has reverse-engineered drum-and-bass style of playing, so today it is hard to tell what is machine-related or not, and our concept of music is extremely wide. If at all, I imagine it could appear related to form and perception, such as ill-proportioned distribution of musical ideas. An example could be music with sections of completely "wrong" durations, say, suddenly there are three hours of the same material in the middle of an otherwise perfectly composed song, a glitch that a human would be unlikely to produce. The large-scale form is still a challenge for generative music.

31.6.5 Authenticity

Could authenticity even be a thing, when no human agent is acknowledged? And what constitutes authenticity? It is related to honesty about how and by whom it was created (nominal authenticity), but also to empathetic appreciation and to effort. We can say it is authentic when it is created with an "honest effort" when the artist is doing "her best". Also, something is perceived as authentic when the artist is not doing it to please expectations, but to tell you something in ernest (expressive authenticity) [33].

But as we have seen, many AI algorithms are designed to give you the most probable outcome (to please, in a way), and as they have no intentional agency (yet), they are mere projections of influence from numerous human agents behind it at all design stages. And the question becomes one of *their* authenticity.

Is it possible that perceived authenticity would suffice, as when an artifact exhibits traces of process or of fictitious agents? Well, then it is based on a lie, and the goal of AI research supposedly is not to fake it, but to make it. It should be to implement processes that can give us rich AI-generated art and music that could be aesthetically meaningful in the same way as human art and music.

In a future with autonomous AI, can AI music be authentic, and in what respect? It could be honest about where it comes from and embrace its mistakes, bugs, and limitations. It would be more honest and authentic if it were not masked as human art, and admit it is truly generated by AI. In the same way, it would be more authentic not to pretend to be AI-generated art, when humans are behind it, as is often the case today. So, current AI music and art is, in that sense, really not authentic, as it is presented as something it is not, in both directions.

31.6.6   Human Measure

All algorithmic and generative art and music (so far) has been made to be judged and received by humans. It may be machine generated, but it is made for human ears/eyes/brains—it is made to stay within the bandwidth of human perception, the frequency spectrum detectable by human hearing. When the human is taken out of the loop as sender and receiver, will the music lose its relevance to us? Will it become ungraspable?

Humans can only perceive phenomena at certain scales. Scientific instruments serve as translators to human measure and scale and to modes that we can perceive. They allow us to engage with phenomena of ungraspable scales, such as the large dimensions of space, or the microscopic scales of microorganisms and even atoms.

For whom is an AI presumed to make art? If the answer is humans, it becomes problematic. Where and how is the result coerced into human-perceivable form? And why? Does this not make the AI into an art-making slave to human masters?

If AI is supposed to make art and music for themselves, it becomes equally problematic. What complexity do machines need to achieve to need or want art? We can compare to animals, as being a little bit simpler beings than us, yet very complex— do they make or need art? We believe they do not, even though sexual selection has given rise to some spectacular aesthetic displays. That is, they are aesthetic to us, but we have no idea how they appear to the animals. And just as art produced by a different species could involve other frequencies of light or sound (many animals have senses different from ours), there is nothing that says that they would produce art perceivable to us. Instead, it is highly likely that it would be outside of our bandwidth, too complex or too simple, and incomprehensible to us. Why would it be related to our world at all, if produced by entities that live under completely different premises, who supposedly can communicate with each other through gigabit streams and which may have senses well beyond or totally different from our capabilities?

Their musical expressions may evolve into what to us sounds like super-complex noise or streams of thousands of notes per second. Or they may be completely uninterested in real-time streams and instead exchange large data objects to be parsed and analyzed in any customizable way. Or they may prefer digital silence as the optimal aesthetic experience. We can only speculate.

31.6.7 Cross-Species Art

If we assume autonomous artistic agents are possible in the future, with no (obvious) remaining connections to a human designer/engineer, or such connections being diluted by continued technical evolution or learning with no human intervention, their art and music will be for themselves, unless they explicitly make it for us because we ask them too. But would they even be interested in that? Or they make art for themselves, and we have to learn how to appreciate it, if at all possible —given that it is within our perceptual bandwidth and is communicable in media for which we have senses.

Would it be interesting then for them to reflect on our art? And is there any difference between these two directions of inter-species art? Would a cat be interested in our art or make art for us? Do we make art for cats?

Once general AI exists, it would take off in a path of its own, be completely disconnected from the human agency because of its complexity and capacity to learn and interact. It would most likely go beyond our abilities, not care about us. This is related to the extensive debate on the existential risks of AI (by Boström, Häggström and many others [11, 40, 55, 71]), but this is outside the scope of this text.

31.6.8 The Role of Time—Learning as a Non-Real-time Process

In AI (reinforcement) learning happens in simulated environments and can be computed in faster than real time (given enough computation power), and in parallel. Then, when it is applied in full in real-world action, this real world does not differ from the simulated worlds for the algorithms.

For humans, we have to live our learning experience. It has to happen in real time and not in parallel. We can isolate it somewhat into something called practice or rehearsal—I can practice my instrument or practice writing fugues and gradually get better at it. Then I apply my knowledge in a sharp situation, such as a concert or recording session.

There is a parallel here to composition versus improvisation. Composition is a non-linear, non-real-time process. I work on my composition until I am happy with it, or until I run out of time. In improvisation, the process unfolds in front of and in interaction with other musicians and other humans (listeners). If AI algorithms were forced to work at human time scales, their learning would be unbearably slow and they would not learn while we interact with them. The advantage of ML is still one of a brute-force batch process.

If the acceleration or compression of time that ML is capable of was applied to composition—as artistic creativity it is not a task that deals with virtuosity, but novelty and relevance of ideas in a given context—the compression still would not help. The extensive training may make it very good at imitating particular human composers (that it has been trained at), or perfect at some musical craft, but there is nothing that says it would become better at coming up with a novel but relevant ideas.

There is a paradox hidden here. If we assume a composing algorithm could be trained, using reinforcement training, as if composition were a game, with quantifiable rewards (and sometimes the commercial musical life looks like that), then also the rewards would need to be estimated by a model of human listeners, or a model of human society and sociological mechanisms (as music popularity is as much sociology as it is aesthetics). But as this model needs to be trained in a real society or with real humans, since musical preference and musical style is a shifting thing, it cannot be accelerated without losing the connection to the real world. We would end up in the old dilemma of evolving/training composers and listeners/critics together, and there is a big risk that they will quickly diverge from human aesthetics and perceptual constraints.

31.6.9 Culture and Forgetting

We humans all start from scratch. We have to learn everything from other (typically older) humans, and also they had to learn from other humans. Tradition is a living thing that is constantly reinterpreted, and old ways are forgotten and replaced by new versions. It could be regarded as a process of continued refinement, getting more and more advanced, or better. Or as a sideways drift, growing different but not better.

An AI is thought of as constantly learning, yet, most ML systems converge toward a sufficiently good solution, and after a certain point, they don't learn anymore. If they over-learn, they will be too specific and lose the ability to generalize. But a human continues to develop.

We talk about different characteristic learning curves, e.g., the violin has a steep threshold to beginners, but the learning curve never ends, while the piano is easy to get started with, but certainly is not easy when you get to the advanced levels. For most acoustic instruments and most human skills in general, there is no clear end to the learning process. You can always get a little better. The same goes for composers. Maybe we cannot be better, but there is always something new to explore, and we get better at the meta-skills of managing our own development and at developing ideas.

We gradually change our ways and preferences, which also presumes a kind of forgetting as a condition for re-learning, which is believed to be beneficial for learning [45]. It may not be a loss of knowledge, but a gradual shift in the values and preferences that drives our actions. Such gradual forgetting is not handled gracefully in AI, with the well-known phenomenon of *catastrophic interference* as a good example: A system that learns something new will quickly and completely forget what it learned previously [47]. Some AI researchers think the key to forgetting will be a key to better AI [5].

31.7 Conclusions

31.7.1 Will AI Make Art-Making Easier?

Will musical skills no longer be needed, now and in the near future where generative AI algorithms can produce musical material for us?

I think it is still needed. One weak point of generative algorithms is large-scale form, and many projects involving AI-generated material still need humans to arrange the material, to do a working instrumentation. If you read the fine print, even projects like the AI-generated Beatles song mentioned earlier used human arranging and even human lyrics. As I see it, the lyrics, the arrangement, and the production (the "sound") are very important parts of a pop composition, so it seems that the AI has a rather reduced influential agency in this case. Also, the human evaluating musical ear will always be needed, at least as long as we expect the algorithms to make music for humans.

There are also new skills that are needed to work with AI in music. You may need to learn how to construct sound engines and algorithms that are suitable for these techniques. Using AI algorithms effectively requires some understanding of how they actually work, like all tools. You may want to learn how to develop these kinds of tools as an extended meta-skill, especially if you want to take on the experimental artist/researcher role, wanting to go one step further.

So, there clearly is a craft of integrating AI into music, and it involves skills such as:

- Understanding complex systems.
- Understanding AI algorithms from both a theoretical and a practical point of view.
- Having an overview of available algorithms to be able to choose the right ones for the task.
- Understanding the potentials of specific algorithms and tools to be able to navigate their solution spaces.
- Understanding representations of music and how they constrain the output.
- Learning the new kinds of creative processes of generative tools (e.g., sow and harvest).
- Knowing the field to avoid doing the same things as others.

Richard Feynman famously wrote on his blackboard: "What I cannot create, I do not understand.". He wanted to be able to derive something from the ground up, to understand all involved steps. This is maybe a utopian vision reserved for geniuses like him, but artists also need to understand their tools, practice on these algorithms to acquire sufficient skills, and form appropriate cognitive models and an intuitive understanding of what is possible, to be able to interact with them in musically meaningful ways. Artists should not rely on engineers to solve technical problems, because knowledge of the tools at hand shape our imagination, what we can think of [24], and any delegation of the application of (or even more, the development of) tools involves (perhaps unknowingly) delegating aesthetic decisions.

Can anyone and everyone do this? I think they can. If the agency is proportionate to the inflow of information through interaction, everyone who is ready to put in enough effort can do it. It can be summarized as follows:

- **NO,**
  there is no free lunch. With little effort spent and little input information flow, you can get fast but impersonal results, and your agency will be insignificant.
- **YES,**
  with open-ended interactive generative systems, anybody with aesthetic judgment can spend enough time to breed/grow/generate characteristic and personal material, rendering interesting results. It may not be more efficient than other ways of working, but different. And your agency will be significant.

31.7.2   The Road Ahead—Musicking with Algorithms

Throughout this chapter, I have argued that most of today's AI implementations, even though celebrated as autonomous creative agents in the popular press, are really just tools that mediate a distribution of human agency and that they generally lack creative agency of their own. The primary argument has been that many projects focus on the production of artifacts that are perceived as if they were created by a human artist, but this process is really one of mimetic optimization, which is inherently non-creative. We should apply AI algorithms to help us explore possibilities instead of optimizing toward known goals, or we will end up with conforming entertainment drones instead of AI artists. But we have to admit that modern AI algorithms are powerful tools of a new kind that operate at an abstraction level higher than tools previously available to artists and musicians. They do indeed bring amazing possibilities, but our expectations and agency attributions should be adequate. We must think critically about our tools, understand their inherent implications, but also learn them, use them, and develop the new crafts they deserve.

AI algorithms bring new modes of creation, such as the gardening paradigm, augmented creativity (e.g., interactive suggestion engines), and systems of creative human and machine agents. They offer fantastic new possibilities, but also new challenges and new crafts that nobody knows yet. If a composer wants to experience the fascinating possibilities of AI algorithms, she must let go of the urge for complete control, admit that algorithms bring something to the table, and see them as collaborators, interact with them, and share influential agency with them. This may mean not actually composing the notes of the piece, but instead taking a more curatorial role, tending to algorithms that generate new material or variations on her own material. If she spends significant time and effort with this kind of tool, she will undoubtedly still contribute significant agency and influence the result. Being aware of these mechanisms may help a composer take the decision and work with them in a good way. And, she may choose what to delegate to the machine.

My generative AI systems will not slam the piano lid in frustration. They will not celebrate with a beer after a good gig, nor will they learn from a particularly humiliating situation on stage when things really did not work out. But they will indeed be a part of my process—I am happy to include them—and I need to understand what they can contribute, and how they can play with me.

Music-making is really an activity, it is *musicking* [64], a situated process full of interactions with information flowing in and out. We should embrace this process, as a human creative process and as implemented in algorithms. The aesthetic artifact is a by-product of the process. The interactions and their associated in- and outflow of information during the creative process fill the work with meaning—the interactions between artist and work, artist and environment, work and environment, algorithm and artist, and between algorithm and environment. The thoughts and computations that go into it, and the empathetic experience of the effort and struggle behind it, they both help to tell the story about its coming into being. We should stop our fixation with the artifacts and teach the AI algorithms the activity of musicking. We can include them in our musicking, and if and when they attain autonomy in the future, they may find their own way to music, instead of producing musical artifacts for humans.

AI algorithms can together with us be nodes in the network of creative agents that together with us shape the art. We integrate with them in an activity of situated creative intelligence. For an even stronger kind of shared interactive creativity, we may turn our interest toward smaller and simpler AI models that can be used interactively and integrate with musicians in real-time embodied interaction, i.e., we are playing not *on* but *with* them. Again, together with them, we become part of a shared situated creative musicking intelligence.

As long as we enforce human measures onto AI art, it will be us who create it, as we impose serious constraints and expectations onto it. While autonomous creative machines are theoretically possible, they are far, far away. But if and when they come, they will probably not make art for us. While waiting, let us play with them.

References

1. Anscombe, G. E. M. (1957). *Intention*. Oxford: Basil Blackwell.
2. Ariza, C. (2009). The interrogator as critic: The turing test and the evaluation of generative music systems. *Computer Music Journal, 33*(2), 48–70
3. Ashby, W. R. (1957). *An Introduction to Cybernetics*. Chapman and Hall.
4. Barthes, R. (1977). The Death of the Author, in *IMAGE-MUSIC-TEXT, Essays selected and translated by Stephen Heath*, pp. 142–148. Hill and Wang.
5. Beierle, C., & Timm, I. J. (2019). Intentional forgetting: An emerging field in AI and beyond. *KI - Künstliche Intelligenz, 33*, 5–8.
6. Belgum, E., Roads, C., Chadabe, J., Tobenfeld, T.E., & Spiegel, L. (1988). A turing test for "musical intelligence"?. *Computer Music Journal, 12*(4), 7–9.

7. Berrar, D. P., & Schuster, A. (2014). Computing machinery and creativity: Lessons learned from the turing test. *Kybernetes*.
8. Bialek, W., Nemenman, I., & Tishby, N. (2001). Predictability, complexity, and learning. *Neural Computation, 13*(11), 2409–2463
9. Biles, J. A. (1994). GenJam: A genetic algorithm for generating jazz solos. In *Proceedings of the International Computer Music Conference, Aarhus, Denmark*, pp. 131–137.
10. Boden, M. A. (2010). The turing test and artistic creativity. *Kybernetes*.
11. Boström, N. (2014). Superintelligence: Paths, dangers, strategies. Oxford University Press.
12. Bown, O. (2015). Attributing creative agency: Are we doing it right? In *Proceedings of the International Conference on Computational Creativity (ICCC)*, pp. 17–22.
13. Bown, O., & McCormack, J. (2009). Creative agency: A clearer goal for artificial life in the arts. In *European Conference on Artificial Life*, pp. 254–261. Springer.
14. Clarke, A. C. (1973). *Profiles of the future; an inquiry into the limits of the possible* (rev. ed.). Harper and Row.
15. Cope, D. (2005). *Computer Models of Musical Creativity*. Cambridge, Mass.: MIT Press.
16. Cross, L., & Tolbert, E. (2009). Music and meaning. In *The Oxford Handbook of Music Psychology*, 2nd ed. Oxford University Press.
17. Sony, C. S. L. (2020). Daddy's car: A song composed by artificial intelligence—in the style of the beatles. Retrieved from July 27, 2020, from https://youtu.be/LSHZ_b05W7o.
18. Dahlstedt, P. (2001). Creating and exploring huge parameter spaces: Interactive evolution as a tool for sound generation. In A. Schloss, R. Dannenberg, & P. Driessen (Eds.), *Proceedings of the International Computer Music Conference*. Habana, Cuba: Instituto Cubano de la Musica, and San Francisco, CA: International Computer Music Association, pp. 235–242.
19. Dahlstedt, P. (2004). *Sounds Unheard of: Evolutionary algorithms as creative tools for the contemporary composer*. Ph.D. thesis, Chalmers University of Technology.
20. Dahlstedt, P. (2007). Autonomous evolution of complete piano pieces and performances. In F. A. e Costa et al. (Eds.), *Proceedings of MusicAL Workshop, Advances in Artificial Life, 9th European Conference, ECAL 2007, Lisbon, Portugal, September 10–14, 2007, Proceedings (Workshop CDROM)*. Lecture Notes in Computer Science 4648 Springer.
21. Dahlstedt, P. (2007). Evolution in creative sound design. In E. R. Miranda & J. A. Biles (Eds.), *Evolutionary Computer Music*, pp. 79–99. London: Springer.
22. Dahlstedt, P. (2009). Thoughts on creative evolution: A meta-generative approach to composition. *Contemporary Music Review, 28*(1), 43–55
23. Dahlstedt, P. (2011). Autonomous evolution of piano pieces and performances with ossia ii. In E. R. Miranda (Ed.) *A-Life for Music: Music and Computer Models of Living Systems*. A-R Editions.
24. Dahlstedt, P. (2012). Between material and ideas: A process-based spatial model of artistic creativity. In J. McCormack, & M. d'Inverno, (Eds.), *Computers and Creativity*, pp. 205–233. Springer.
25. Dahlstedt, P. (2018). Action and perception: Embodying algorithms and the extended mind. In R. T. Dean, & A. McLean (Eds.) *OUP Handbook of Algorithmic Music*, Chap. 3, pp. 41–65. Oxford University Press.
26. Dahlstedt, P. (2019). Big data and creativity. *European Review, 27*(3), 411–439
27. Dahlstedt, P. (2020). Ossia suite (musical work). Retrieved July 27, 2020, from https://soundcloud.com/palle-dahlstedt/sets/ossia-suite.
28. Dahlstedt, P. (2001). A mutasynth in parameter space: Interactive composition through evolution. *Organised Sound, 6*, 121–124.
29. Dahlstedt, P. (2015). Turn-based evolution in a simplified model of artistic creative process. *Evolutionary Intelligence, 8*(1), 37–50
30. Dahlstedt, P., & McBurney, P. (2007). Musical agents: Toward computer-aided music composition using autonomous software agents. *Leonardo, 39*(5), 469–470.
31. Dahlstedt, P., & Nordahl, M. G. (2001). Living melodies—Coevolution of sonic communication. *Leonardo, 34*(3), 243–248

32. Davidson, D. (1963). Actions, reasons, and causes. *The Journal of Philosophy, 60*(23), 685–700

33. Dutton, D. (2003). Authenticity in art. In *The Oxford Handbook of Aesthetics*, pp. 258–274.

34. Garrabrant, S., & Demski, A. (2018). Embedded agency (full-text version). Alignment Forum. Retrieved July 27, 2020, from https://www.alignmentforum.org/posts/i3BTagvt3HbPMx6PN/embedded-agency-full-text-version.

35. Gregory, R. L. (1981). *Mind in Science*. London: Weidenfeld and Nicolson.

36. Hewitt, C. (1977). Viewing control structures as patterns of passing messages. *Artificial Intelligence, 8*(3), 323–364

37. Hewitt, C., Bishop, P., & Steiger, R. (1973). A universal modular actor formalism for artificial intelligence. In *Proceedings of the 3rd international joint conference on Artificial intelligence (IJCAI)*, pp. 235–245.

38. Holland, J. (1975). *Adaptation in Natural and Artificial Systems*. Ann Arbor, MI: University of Michigan Press.

39. Huron, D. B. (2006). *Sweet anticipation: Music and the psychology of expectation*. MIT press.

40. Häggström, O. (2016). *Here be dragons: Science, technology and the future of humanity*. Oxford University Press.

41. Johnson, D. G., & Verdicchio, M. (2019). AI, agency and responsibility: The VW fraud case and beyond. *AI & SOCIETY, 34*(3), 639–647.

42. Knuth, D. E. (1968). *The Art of Computer Programming*, Vol. 1: Fundamental Algorithms. Addison-Wesley.

43. Latour, B. (2005). *Reassembling the Social: An Introduction to Actor-Network Theory*. Oxford: Oxford University Press.

44. Lehman, J., Stanley, K. O. (2008). Exploiting open-endedness to solve problems through the search for novelty. In *ALIFE*, pp. 329–336.

45. Markovitch, S., & Scott, P. D. (1988). The role of forgetting in learning. In *Machine Learning Proceedings 1988*, pp. 459–465. Elsevier.

46. McCarthy, J. (2020). Sony uses ai to compose a beatles-inspired song, the unforgettable 'daddy's car'. Retrieved July 27, 2020, from https://www.thedrum.com/news/2016/09/27/sony-uses-ai-compose-beatles-inspired-song-the-unforgettable-daddy-s-car.

47. McCloskey, M., & Cohen, N. J. (1989). Catastrophic interference in connectionist networks: The sequential learning problem. In *Psychology of Learning and Motivation*, vol. 24, pp. 109–165. Elsevier.

48. McCormack, J., & Dorin, A. (2001). Art, emergence and the computational sublime. In *Proceedings of the Second International Conference on Generative Systems in the Electronic Arts, Victoria, Australia, Centre for Electronic Media Art, VIC, Australia*.

49. Meyer, L. B. (1957). Meaning in music and information theory. *The Journal of Aesthetics and Art Criticism, 15*(4), 412–424.

50. Minsky, M. (1982). Music, mind, and meaning. In *Music, Mind, and Brain*, pp. 1–19. Springer.

51. Mori, M. (2012). The Uncanny Valley [From the Field]. *IEEE Robotics & Automation Magazine, 19*(2), 98–100.

52. Mike Murphy, M. (2020). Computers can now paint like van gogh and picasso. Retrieved July 27, 2020, from https://qz.com/495614/computers-can-now-paint-like-van-gogh-and-picasso/.

53. Nielsen, P. (1972). Some comments on Vagn Holmboe's idea of metamorphosis. *Dansk årbog for musikforskning*, pp. 1968–1972.

54. Nilsson, P. A. (2011). *A Field of Possibilities: Designing and Playing Digital Musical Instruments*. Ph.D. thesis, University of Gothenburg.

55. Omohundro, S. (2014). Autonomous technology and the greater human good. *Journal of Experimental & Theoretical Artificial Intelligence, 26*(3), 303–315

56. Pachet, F. (2012). Musical virtuosity and creativity. In *Computers and Creativity*, pp. 115–146. Springer.
57. Pease, A., & Colton, S. (2011). On impact and evaluation in computational creativity: A discussion of the turing test and an alternative proposal. In *Proceedings of the AISB symposium on AI and Philosophy*, vol. 39.
58. Russell, S. J., & Norvig, P. (2003). *Artificial Intelligence: A Modern Approach* (2nd ed.). Upper Saddle River, New Jersey: Prentice Hall.
59. Samek, W., Montavon, G., Vedaldi, A., Hansen, L. K., & Müller, K. R. (2019). *Explainable AI: Interpreting, explaining and visualizing deep learning*. Vol. 11700. Springer Nature.
60. Sayes, E. (2014). Actor–network theory and methodology: Just what does it mean to say that nonhumans have agency? *Social Studies of Science, 44*(1), 134–149
61. Schlosser, M. (2019). Agency. In Zalta, E. N. (Ed.), *The Stanford Encyclopedia of Philosophy*. Metaphysics Research Lab, Stanford University, winter 2019 edition.
62. Shannon, C. E. (1948). A mathematical theory of communication. *The Bell System Technical Journal, 27*(379–423), 623–656
63. Sims, K. (1991). Artificial evolution for computer graphics. In *ACM SIGGRAPH '91 Conference Proceedings, Las Vegas, Nevada*, pp. 319–328.
64. Small, C. (1998). *Musicking: The meanings of performing and listening*. Wesleyan University Press.
65. Tawaststjerna, E. (1976). *Sibelius vol. 1*, translated by R. Layton. London: Faber and Faber.
66. Tishby, N., & Polani, D. (2011). Information theory of decisions and actions. In *Perception-action Cycle*, pp. 601–636. Springer.
67. Touchette, H., & Lloyd, S. (2004). Information-theoretic approach to the study of control systems. *Physica A: Statistical Mechanics and Its Applications, 331*(1–2), 140–172
68. Turing, A. M. (1950). Computing machinery and intelligence. *Mind, 59*, 433–460.
69. Vygotsky, L. S. (1978). *Mind in Society*. Cambridge, MA: Harvard University Press.
70. Wiener, N. (1948). *Cybernetics: Or Control and Communication in the Animal and the Machine*. Cambridge, MA: MIT Press.
71. Yampolskiy, R. V. (2014). Utility function security in artificially intelligent agents. *Journal of Experimental & Theoretical Artificial Intelligence, 26*(3), 373–389.

Palle Dahlstedt Palle Dahlstedt studied piano, composition, and electronic music (M.F.A. and M. A.), and has a Ph.D. in the topic of evolutionary computation for artistic creativity from Chalmers University of Technology, Sweden. His research focuses on new technologies for improvisation, composition, and art. He is particularly interested in advanced algorithms for creativity, technologies that enable embodied performance with electronic sounds, and new kinds of interactions based on a systems view of emergence from human–technology interactions. Palle is an associate professor of Interaction Design at the Department of Computer Science and Engineering of the University of Gothenburg and teaches composition at the Academy of Music and Drama, Gothenburg, Sweden. He also teaches at Chalmers University of Technology in Sweden and is a guest professor at Aalborg University, Denmark. E-mail: palle@chalmers.se

cellF: Surrogate Musicianship as a Manifestation of In-Vitro Intelligence

32

Vahri McKenzie, Nathan John Thompson, Darren Moore and Guy Ben-Ary

32.1 Introduction

cellF is a collaborative project at the cutting edge of experimental art and music that brings together artists, musicians, designers and scientists to create the world's first biological neuron-driven analogue modular synthesizer. It combines biological material with electronic circuitry, presenting a new direction in music performance and production. Advancements in biotechnology enable biological neural networks to be grown in the laboratory and outside of the body, that is, in-vitro. Such entities are directly linked to the human donors of their biological material, yet physically removed from any human body. At the same time, these are living entities with a degree of autonomy that grows and changes with an innate vitality in response to an environment. Thus, in its autonomy and plasticity, *cellF* represents a new kind of entity that can be described as possessing 'in-vitro intelligence', which is distinct from both natural and artificial intelligence. The characteristics of autonomy and plasticity demonstrated by *cellF*, which will be elaborated below, show not only that it is a living musical instrument, but also a musician in its own right: a 'surrogate musician' who symbolically represents the human donor of its biological material. *cellF* is a music-making hybridized entity: the biological neural network

V. McKenzie
Centre for Creative and Cultural Research, Faculty of Arts and Design,
University of Canberra, Canberra, Australia

N. J. Thompson
University of Western Australia, 20 Trafford Street, Beaconsfield, WA 6162, Australia

D. Moore
LaSalle College of the Arts, 36 Sturdee Rd #19-12, Singapore 207855, Singapore

G. Ben-Ary (✉)
University of Western Australia, 23 Allpike Rd, Darlington, WA 6070, Australia
e-mail: guy.benary@uwa.edu.au

© Springer Nature Switzerland AG 2021
E. R. Miranda (eds.), *Handbook of Artificial Intelligence for Music*,
https://doi.org/10.1007/978-3-030-72116-9_32

or 'brain' processes data, inputs and outputs, and is extended and embodied with analogue synthesizers and other electronic analogue circuitry. This chapter argues that *cellF*'s autonomy as a music-maker constitutes the description of surrogate musician possessing in-vitro intelligence.

32.2 Origins and Development of the Work

cellF premiered in 2015 in Perth, Australia, and has since been featured in numerous international festivals in collaboration with improvising musicians who perform with *cellF* to create posthuman sound pieces. 'Posthuman' is used not in a narrow sense that signals a hoped-for transcendence of the human body and its materiality, which fails adequately to account for the complexity of corporeal existence. Rather, we use the term as part of a broader critique of humanism and its certainties regarding the value and agency of human beings, at the expense of non-human entities. Led by artist Guy Ben-Ary, the *cellF* team consists of musician Darren Moore, artist Nathan Thompson and electrical engineer Andrew Fitch, along with scientists Stuart Hodgetts, Mike Edel and Douglas Bakkum. The project began in 2012 when Ben-Ary received a Fellowship from the Australia Council for the Arts to develop a biological self-portrait. An avid music lover, Ben-Ary wished to realize a juvenile dream and portray himself as a musician. The fact that he could not play any musical instruments was an issue addressed through Ben-Ary's creation of a biological alter ego that could live out his fantasy.

A key objective of *cellF* is to use the raw neural activity occurring in its 'brain' to produce sounds (which resemble bursts of white noise) with analogue modular synthesizers. The first step in its development was to harvest Ben-Ary's own biological material. He took a biopsy from his arm and, using induced pluripotent stem cell technology (iPSc), transformed his skin cells into stem cells in the labs of SymbioticA: The Centre for Excellence in Biological Arts at The University of Western Australia. The process involved re-programming the cell's genome back to its embryonic state using iPSc technology that was pioneered by Professor Shinya Yamanaka, who showed that the introduction of four specific genes could convert adult cells into pluripotent stem cells. The iPSc method transforms adult specialized cells into a form that is equivalent to stem cells, which are capable of becoming almost any other type of cell in the body, such as liver cells, muscle cells or neurons.

When differentiating to neurons, stem cells first transform into self-renewing and multipotent neural stem cells, and then into neurons. In *cellF*, cultures of neurons are grown in networks over a Multi-Electrode Array (MEA: a standard device that connects neurons to electronic circuitry in order to send and receive neural signals) to become Ben-Ary's external 'brain' (Fig. 32.1). Human brains contain approximately 100 billion neurons, which are interconnected via trillions of synapses. *cellF*'s 'brain' contains approximately 100,000 cells, making it a symbolic brain that introduces new ways of thinking about intelligence in hybrid entities. Like a

Fig. 32.1 *cellF*'s 'brain': Guy Ben-Ary's neurons growing over the Multi-Electrode Array interface

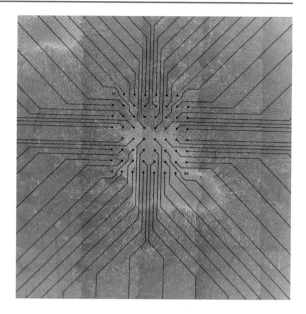

human brain, however, *cellF*'s neural network produces a large amount of data, responds to stimuli and is subject to changes in behaviour and lifespan. Plasticity— an organism's adaptability to change—is a property of cellular, that is, natural intelligence. Plasticity in neural networks is a phenomenon well established in the neuroscience community, and one that is thought to play a very large role in learning and memory [20]. *cellF*'s brain exhibits change in behaviour in response to stimulations, demonstrating plasticity sufficient to entice audiences to consider the future possibilities that iPSc technologies present.

The MEA dish hosting *cellF*'s neural network consists of a grid of sixty electrodes connected to an array of analogue modular synthesizers that produce sound. The activity of the neural network produces electrochemical data in pulses known as action potentials that are received by the electrodes. These electrodes simultaneously send electrical stimulations back to the neurons in the form of synthesized sound that is produced and controlled by a human musician. Thus, the system allows data to move between *cellF*'s brain and electronic analogue circuitry so that the neural network is able to respond in real time. In so doing, *cellF* demonstrates autonomy: receiving inputs and spontaneously responding to them, as with biological life. Although one is biological and the other is electronic, surprising similarities between neural networks and analogue modular synthesizers make them well matched: both systems produce complex data sets, with multiple inputs and outputs operating at micro-second speeds. Moreover, in both neural networks and analogue modular synthesizers, electrical information moves through components to produce data in the form of voltages. *cellF*'s neural interface creates a link between these two networks such that it operates as a single entity, like a body and brain working together.

cellF's neural activity produces electrical signals that are received by the MEA's electrodes, which passes them into *cellF*'s specially designed interface. The interface amplifies the signals from millivolts to volts and routs them to the synthesizers, where they are transformed into control voltages (the standard analogue method of controlling synthesizers). While the neural activity itself has no sound, the amplified electrical signals, transformed into control voltages, become synthesized sounds by patching into the modular synthesizer. Patching manages sound tone and pitch, and gate signals determine sounds as on or off; the innumerable patching options available offer a multitude of pathways for the neural data to travel and reflect the complexities of neural processes.

On one level patching choices are arbitrary and symbolic, with the patch cable connections between the different synthesizer modules offering a metaphor for synapse relationships in *cellF*'s brain that represents the activity of the action potentials. Additionally, the team's creative decisions are revised for each performance, informed by such considerations as the nature of the performance space and the collaborating human musician, whose performance takes into account which frequencies will be received by *cellF* as a result of patching choices set up prior to the performance. The configuration aims to balance unpredictability with a measured response that is akin to the interactivity occurring between improvising human musicians, illuminating *cellF*'s autonomy. For each performance, the sound is spatialized to sixteen speakers placed around the performance space, with the neural activity controlling the signal paths to each individual speaker, such that the speaker outputs spatially reflect the activity of the neurons in the MEA. This spatialization amplifies and abstracts the neural activity, offering audiences the opportunity to experience moving through *cellF*'s in-vitro brain in real time. *cellF* requires the project team to set up the system, but once the performance starts it operates autonomously (Fig. 32.2).

Fig. 32.2 *cellF*'s neural interface and sound producing body

In order to survive and perform, *cellF* requires incubation, nutrition and an interface with its embodiment. Incubation occurs within a tightly regulated environment. Human neurons need 100% humidity at 37 °C with ambient gas levels of CO_2 at 5%, as well as near darkness or very low UV light. Human neurons grown in-vitro need to be fed every forty-eight hours. *cellF* is manually fed, which requires a trained person to extract and replenish the liquid 'food' in a completely sterile environment; sterility is of utmost importance as contamination is fatal. *cellF*'s development and ongoing existence demonstrate its autonomy, so long as the conditions required to support its life are met. *cellF*'s plasticity is evident once the system is embodied with synthesizers, which enables its transformation expressed through sound. These characteristics support our claims, which will be elaborated below, that *cellF* represents an early form of in-vitro intelligence. Before that, the following section will explore some of the aesthetic concerns that informed *cellF*'s design and creation.

32.3   Influences from the History of Modern Music

Composer and music theorist John Cage is significant to this project for his pioneering use of electroacoustic instruments, as well as his philosophy of composition that decoupled the score from the sound of music in performance. Cage's influential 1937 essay 'The Future of Music: Credo' echoes the declarations of Italian Futurist Luigi Russolo in claiming that noise will be an essential element in the future of music (Cox and Warner 2001). Luigi Russolo was the first to attempt to build noise-making instruments, *intonarumori*, and argued in the Futurist Manifesto *The Art of Noises* (1913) that traditional orchestral instruments did not adequately capture the spirit of modernity nor reflect the clamour of the machine age (Cox and Warner 2001). Russolo called for new ways of making music that incorporate 'noise-sounds', which, he argued, came into existence with the multiplication of machines. It is no longer controversial to consider any arrangement of sounds as potentially musical, and *cellF*'s use of neural noise-sound heeds Russolo's call. Yet *cellF*'s connection with 'The Art of Noises' and *intonarumori* goes beyond the use of noise as a musical element by reflecting Russolo's concerns with societal changes and the creation of instruments that critically engage with new technologies.

Where the Italian Futurists celebrated new technologies and violence, *cellF* critiques biotechnologies by using them in a subversive way. Rather than applying iPSc to more strictly utilitarian ends, *cellF* proposes an absurd and futuristic scenario in which biotechnologies are widely available. By using sophisticated biotechnologies in a playful and complex work of art, *cellF* problematizes an imagined scenario in which such technologies are ubiquitous and considered an unexamined boon. This claim is supported by the creative team's aesthetic choices. Rather than embodying *cellF* with existing instruments, the team used innovative visual and aural strategies that encourage audiences to explore the work, engage in

Fig. 32.3 *cellF* performing
in the Cell Block Theatre,
Sydney, 2016

a dialogue, and re-evaluate their perceptions and beliefs regarding musicianship. The work avoids the clinical aesthetics of the laboratory with which biotechnological arts are more usually associated, opting instead for the dark environment of a rock concert. With its large black spiral-shaped horn, *cellF*'s design aesthetically recalls the history of amplified sound and the development of twentieth century electronic instruments (Fig. 32.3).

Furthermore, a fascination with the inventive modernity that created the gramophone, the *intonarumori*, and early electronic instruments has instilled itself within the project through eschewing the digital in favour of the analogue. In contrast with digital functionality, which symbolically represents all information in binary code, analogue information is represented in continuously variable physical quantities. Applying this preference to *cellF* has a twofold consequence; firstly, it aesthetically references twentieth century modernity and imagines a world that developed independently from the digital information age. *cellF* moves against the prevailing technoscience trends that favour artificial intelligence and computer-driven artistic practices towards the biological materiality and electrical activity that defines our existence as living entities. Secondly, an analogue approach highlights *cellF*'s intrinsically autonomous and unmediated nature. Whilst digital interfaces such MATLAB are widely used in the scientific realm to interface with neural networks, digitization requires the symbolic encoding of data. Rather, *cellF*'s neural network interfaces directly with analogue synthesizers, retaining the integrity of the neural signal and the autonomy of *cellF*'s brain. Similarly, stimulation inputs in the form of sound received from the human musician performing alongside *cellF* travel unprocessed through the interface (according to patching into the analogue synthesizers), and *cellF* responds to the stimulations it receives with a barrage of action potentials. *cellF*'s plasticity is realized, as with biological life, due to the real-time changes in physical properties (in the form of electrical signals) occurring between the neural and synthesizer systems that function as a single entity.

cellF's synthesizers draw from the concepts of subtractive and additive synthesis of classic Moog, Buchla and Serge systems of the 1960s and 1970s, and include feedback systems (in which an output signal is received as an input signal, increasing resonance) in order to highlight its self-organization. These feedback systems share similarities with those devised by Gordon Mumma and David Tudor in the 1960s and 1970s that Michael Nyman [13] describes as 'feedback-type' systems, 'whose circuitry works in a way analogous to feedback but which are also transformation devices'. The distinction here is that 'feedback-type' systems are compositional technologies producing particular musical results that are not entirely controlled by human musicians. For example, in Mumma's *Hornpipe* (1967), a horn is modified with an analogue computer that monitors the horn resonances and complements them with further resonances that cause further sound responses. Salter regards the feedback-type systems used by Mumma and Tudor as marking a critical shift in experimental music, from an emphasis on the score (and hence the composer) 'towards the real-time manipulation of parameters, both musical as well as those made possible through electronic circuits' [17]. However, where Salter's analysis points towards a new model for composition, *cellF* moves towards an autonomous system that requires minimal intervention due to the autonomous nature of biological neural networks.

Two musical projects providing important historical reference points for *cellF* are Alvin Lucier's *Music for Solo Performer* (1965) and David Tudor's *Neural Synthesis* (1995). To present *Music for Solo Performer*, Lucier sat motionless in a chair with electrodes attached to his head as he induced a relaxed state to produce alpha brain waves. The alpha signals were used as a sound source that was amplified through loudspeakers, which in turn controlled external percussion instruments through the movement of speaker cones or the motion of the surrounding air. Although the type of signal and musical instruments are different, both *cellF* and *Music for Solo Performer* use brain data to control instruments and render visible and audible the unseen and unheard. Tudor's *Neural Synthesis* (1995) used integrated circuits that mimic neural activity as the central driver in an electronic feedback system. Like *cellF*, *Neural Synthesis* used the unpredictability of electronic feedback systems to determine the musical output, a process entirely different from scored music. *cellF* takes Tudor's project to the next stage by using living biological neural networks as the source for the feedback system.

Using feedback systems in new music grew out of John Cage's radical reframing of musical composition as a means of structuring events in time [13]. First performed by David Tudor in 1952, Cage's *4'33"* showed that composition was a process with no determined relation to sound in performance. While Cage pioneered indeterminacy in composition by using chance processes at the level of composition, performer choice was limited [8]. The increasingly important role of performer choice in experimental music was realized in the works of Tudor, Mumma and Lucier, whose works ceded some of the authorial control traditionally exercised by composers in order to open up new musical possibilities with electronics. As with improvising musicians, where composer and performer are one and the same, their works gesture towards the self-organizing musical entities of the future. However, where decisions made by an improvising human musician are guided by training and tradition, *cellF*'s self-organizing musicianship is not. We have established that *cellF* is a musical entity, and, like a human improvising musician, both composer and performer. Emerging technologies of live music production will develop new musical genres and new instruments. Of more interest to the authors of this paper, future technologies of live music production will likely develop new relations between bodies and instruments, where robotic musicianship is one valid direction.

32.4 Influences from the Field of Robotic Musicianship

A number of Guy Ben-Ary's earlier works have been influenced by the field of biorobotics. *MEART* (2001) and *Silent Barrage* (2009) embodied rat neurons with robotics to perform artistic functions (Ben-Ary 2014a, b). Each used the movement of the robotic body to represent data. *cellF* departs from those works in two important ways: by using neurons reprogrammed from the artist's own skin cells, and through a musical embodiment that uses electricity to generate sound. Although there are no moving parts, *cellF* shares similarities with projects that deal with robotic musicianship. Bretan and Weinberg's survey of robotic musicianship describes it as 'the construction of machines capable of producing sound, analysing music and generating music in such a way that allows them to showcase musicality and interact with human musicians' [4]. Robotic musicianship focuses on two areas: musical mechatronics studies the physical systems that generate sound through mechanical means, and machine musicianship develops algorithms representing higher level musical features essential to human musical cognition. Two examples illustrate these features.

Shimon, developed by Gil Weinberg (2017), is a robotic marimba player that improvises with a human musician; see also Weinberg's chapter in this volume. With arms and a head that mimic human communicative gestures, Shimon creates familiar, acoustically and visually rich interactions with humans. Moreover, Shimon's artificial intelligence produces musical responses that are unlikely to be achieved by humans and so facilitates a unique musical experience, which may lead to innovative musical outcomes. Shimon uses artificial intelligence to melodically respond to the human musician's movements and to learn from historical performances of great jazz musicians [4]: 107). The human is the standard by which Shimon is guided, and designed to exceed, which contrasts with *cellF*'s less familiar form of musicianship. Z-Machines (2018), a project by Yuri Suzuki Design Studio, is an all-robot band built to perform beyond the capabilities of the most advanced human musicians. The band members have an anthropomorphic appearance, with important differences: Z-Machines features a seventy-eight-fingered guitarist, a drummer with twenty-two arms, and a keyboard player that triggers notes using laser beams. The robots have collaborated with British electronic musician Squarepusher, who composed *Music for Robots* (2014) for Z-Machines to perform. The challenge for Yuri Suzuki's Studio was to design a system that could play emotionally engaging music while rediscovering conventional instruments. This, too, illustrates an important difference with *cellF*, which deliberately avoided an embodiment recalling conventional musical instruments, in order to encourage new modes of audience engagement.

Shimon and Z-Machines' musical and analytical traits, as well as their visual behaviour, extend our understanding of musicians and live music. These are non-human musicians with the ability to play music, improvise, respond and perform original and complex music, at a level that was previously considered to be the sole preserve of human musicians. While each project presents a distinct approach and aesthetic style, they share a dependence on digital technologies and artificial intelligence that drives the musicians' behaviour, movements, analytical skills and ability to learn. Artificial intelligence is grounded in algorithms that are programmed by humans to mimic cognitive functions such as learning or problem solving. As is seen with the anthropomorphic appearance of Shimon and Z-Machines, and their use of algorithms that are designed to mimic human functionality, robotic musicianship is judged against the rubric of human musicianship.

In contrast, *cellF* eschews anthropocentrism in appearance and behaviour; it does not use the human as the model against which other entities are judged. Where robotic musicianship generally creates interest through the spectacle of complex moving parts, *cellF* has none. The lack of movement works against ocularcentrism, the perceptual and epistemological bias evident in Western culture that ranks vision over other senses. Movement in robotic musicianship reveals the sound production process, but with *cellF*, as with other electronic music, the sound production process is obscured. *cellF* challenges Bretan and Weinberg's definition of robotic musicianship. It generates music and demonstrates musicality through interacting with a human musician, but *cellF* is more than a machine: its body is void of mechanics and it has a 'brain' that is made of living neurons. Audiences of *cellF*'s performances with a human musician are required to interpret their experiences primarily through sound, which encourages consideration of what is new and challenging, and the future possibilities the experience suggests. It is a musical entity with sufficient autonomy and plasticity to stand in for a human musician in an improvised duet. It does so in a new way, as a living instrument existing outside of a human body, in which musical instrument and musician are one entity.

32.5 In-Vitro Intelligence

cellF represents an interesting and provocative move away from Artificial Intelligence (AI) enquiries that dominate our current technology-focused scientific discourse. It is not an AI musical robot driven by computer algorithms; at the same time, it lacks the complexity of natural intelligence and requires a hardware body to provide stimulation for its in-vitro 'brain'. As described above, *cellF*'s brain is made of bioengineered living human neurons that are grown into neural networks, interfaced such that inputs to and outputs from the networks control an array of analogue modular synthesizers, making it a wetware-hardware hybrid. 'Wetware' refers to the networks of neurons and other cell types that form the control systems of biological life. It is the basis of natural intelligence, which is contrasted with AI.

cellF is neither 'naturally' nor 'artificially' intelligent, yet it behaves in an apparently 'intelligent' way. Russell and Norvig (2009) outline four main approaches to understanding artificial intelligence that can be summarized as thinking and behaving humanly, and thinking and acting rationally. Behaving like a human, as in the familiar Turing Test [19], remains an accessible way to understand artificial intelligence, reflected in the anthropocentric ideals of the examples of robotic musicianship described above. In order to reach such an ideal, it is necessary to understand the underlying principles of intelligence, and this goal is pursued through cognitive modelling to enable machines to demonstrate human-like learning and problem solving. However, it is important to note that these are not the same as human intelligence, and that the principles underlying intelligence are not well understood. Thinking and acting rationally extracts the *practice* of human intelligence, which can accommodate a degree of uncertainty, into generalizable *theories* subject to mathematical modelling, known as the rational agent approach to artificial intelligence (Russell and Norvig 2009). This is, at best, a flattened approximation of natural intelligence.

Artificial Intelligence, which in its current manifestations is more accurately described as Machine Learning, requires vast amounts of data that can be searched for patterns in order to make inferences, but thinking and intelligence are much more complex and nuanced than that. AI has achieved incredible results in situations where it is possible to acquire a complete set of rules governing any given situation. Consider the artificially intelligent computer program AlphaZero, which is able to beat any human or AI player in games such as chess and go, by learning from playing against itself more times than are possible for any other human or machine. Where older versions of similar programs had learned from historic game play (as Shimon learned to improvise by studying the historical performances of great jazz musicians), AlphaZero learned from massive calculation alone and achieved unlikely wins as a result. In information games like chess and go there is no ambiguity in the rules and what constitutes 'winning'.

The operations of natural intelligence, on the other hand, rely on much more than calculation and rational decision-making. The operation of natural intelligence is distributed across brain, body and world, and 'it is in the operation of these extended systems that much of our distinctive human intelligence inheres' [5]. As Andy Clark acknowledges, the notion of situated and distributed cognition is not new. What is particularly useful in Clark's analysis for our discussion of *cellF* is his recognition of the ways in which human brains 'dovetail' their problem-solving activities with technologies in order to form larger systems that change and evolve. We draw attention to two important features of this plasticity in natural intelligence to support our claims for *cellF*'s intelligence. The first relates to the liveness of change: it happens in real time, like a musical improvisation. More than the information feedback required for machine learning, transformation can occur because the system of natural intelligence is open to other systems in a 'complex reciprocal dance'; 'the brain tailors its activity to a technological and sociocultural environment, which—in concert with other brains—it simultaneously alters and amends. Human intelligence owes just about everything to this looping process of mutual accommodation' [5]. The second important feature is that the other systems with which human intelligence 'dances' are different from it. The use of hand tools and the technologies of reading and writing are two of the more familiar examples of technological and sociocultural systems that have wrought immense changes to human thought, behaviour and society, as Havelock's [10] and Ong's (2012) theories of the transition from oral to literate cultures show. We are Clark's 'natural-born cyborgs': 'Ours are (by nature) unusually plastic and opportunistic brains whose biological proper functioning has always involved the recruitment and exploitation of nonbiological props and scaffolds' [5]. Natural intelligence has evolved within a technological and cultural world from which it cannot be definitively separated, and it is these complex relations that enable the plasticity with which natural intelligence is distinctively associated.

Neither an artificial intelligence nor a natural intelligence, *cellF* falls within a taxonomic void. In the absence of terminology that adequately accounts for *cellF*'s autonomy and plasticity, demonstrated through its capacity to make music and duet with a human musician, *cellF* is best understood as an entity possessing 'in-vitro intelligence': an intelligent system produced by bioengineered living neural networks that function as brains outside of the body. We grant that *cellF* represents a very early form of in-vitro intelligence, yet the characteristics of its neural network suggest that it, or others like it, will demonstrate changes in functional plasticity, just as naturally intelligent entities do. The biological basis of in-vitro intelligence is subject to an unanticipated change in a way that programmed AI entities are not. Artificial intelligence will achieve increasing calculation speeds, but the fundamental processes will remain the same, with a fixed material basis that constrains unanticipated change. Like naturally intelligent entities, *cellF*'s hybridity constitutes an openness to other systems that Clark and others argue supports the emergence of new intelligences: 'it is the semi-autonomous machines that hold out the best prospect of one day constituting integral parts of distributed, biotechnological, hybrid intelligences' [5]. Neuroscientist Steve Potter [15] claims it is inevitable that neural-synthetic hybrid entities will grow more sophisticated and find widespread applications: 'hybrid wetware-hardware intelligent things will someday be as common and as useful as digital computers are today' [1, 15]. As a wetware-hardware hybrid, *cellF* suggests just such an outcome, and we theorize its existence by developing a description for this phenomenon as the emergence of in-vitro intelligence.

Such a phenomenon suggests some exciting possibilities. Artificially intelligent entities are limited by the mathematically coded instructions they receive in symbolic language, which restrains the degree to which they can accommodate ambiguity or complexity, such as is required for emotional engagement. Emotions are too complex to be reduced to symbolic language and are inextricably linked to specific contexts and environments. On the other hand, an entity grounded in neural networks exhibits some plasticity and so has the potential to achieve the openness to other systems and real-time responsiveness required for emotional engagement. Entities with in-vitro intelligence demonstrate meaningful connections to human life not through human-like behaviour, appearances or thought, but through a shared cellular structure that is soft and full of salt water. Indeed, *cellF* has direct biological links to its donor. Its basis in biological life means that *cellF* is a living musical instrument; moreover, in its capacity to produce music and engage with a human musician in its human donor's stead, *cellF* is a musician in its own right; a 'surrogate musician'.

32.6 Surrogate Musicianship

Surrogate musicianship embodies the previously mentioned attributes of robotic musicianship—the ability to produce, analyze and generate music in response to sensory stimuli in real time—as well as combining musical instrument and musician in one living entity. Moreover, this new term offers something else: as is signalled in its name, surrogate musicians like *cellF* have direct biological links to their donors, enabling the surrogate to symbolically represent the donor, and, potentially, to stand in for the donor in other ways (Fig. 32.4). Regardless of whether the donor is a musician or not, human or not, they have some involvement in the musical activities of the surrogate musician.

To consider the term 'surrogate musician', it is useful to look at one of the situations with which it forms an analogy, that of surrogacy in human reproduction. This is a form of assisted reproductive technology in which a woman carries and gives birth to a baby on behalf of someone else. Gestational surrogacy involves the surrogate being implanted with an embryo via in-vitro fertilization, so that the surrogate is entirely genetically unrelated to the donors of sperm and egg. Traditional surrogacy uses donated sperm and the surrogate's own egg, so that the resulting baby is genetically related to the surrogate. Tracing the relevant terms of reproductive surrogacy in the context of *cellF* aligns Guy Ben-Ary, as the donor of biological material, with the role of the genetic parent. *cellF* is incubated in a fully technologized manner, eliminating the role of the 'surrogate mother' in this scenario. The resulting 'child' is *cellF*, the 'surrogate musician'. The experience of the child that results from a surrogacy arrangement is an under-researched area; a systematic review revealed methodological limitations and uncertain results [18]. Risks related to the child's knowledge of their origins and the implications for their developmental psychology, and long-term health outcomes that are inextricably linked to that of the genetic parents, which may include the surrogate mother. As with all analogies there are limits to this one, and many of the issues that arise with reproductive surrogacy are not relevant here. (These include legal complications regarding the different laws pertaining to surrogacy in different jurisdictions; ethical issues that relate to the situation of the surrogate mother and her right to enter into

Fig. 32.4 *cellF* performing with defunensemble, Science Centre Heureka, Helsinki, 2019

an altruistic or commercial arrangement, and the justice of such arrangements; psychological issues impacting the surrogate mother such as feelings of loss upon separating from the surrogate child.) Other issues arising in reproductive surrogacy are relevant and can hint at the debates that will emerge as biotechnologies develop, becoming more sophisticated and readily available.

Surrogate musicianship is a relational term that alludes to the connections between donors and surrogates, not unlike that between parent and child in our analogy. Reproductive surrogacy prompts consideration of the multiple meanings of parenthood, which can be separated into genetic, biological and social dimensions. It is clear that Ben-Ary is genetically related to *cellF*, and the case of reproductive surrogacy shows that genetic parents experience a strong sense of connection to, or 'ownership' of, their surrogate child [11]. Biological parenthood is a category that alludes to gestation [9] and the connections between babies and the surrogate mothers who have grown them from their own biological material, even if the egg was genetically unrelated. The distinction between genetic and biological parenthood is not clear cut, and the resulting medical and emotional connections between surrogate mother and baby are not well understood. Yet, given the significance the *cellF* project places on materiality, where biological and naturally intelligent materials and processes are awarded a significance different from that of artificially intelligent materials and processes, reproductive surrogacy offers a useful model for imagining our responsibilities to future hybrid entities.

The concept of social parenthood is salient in the case of *cellF*'s surrogate musicianship, and the lessons of reproductive surrogacy illuminate the symbolic connection between *cellF* and its donor. The use of surrogacy as an assisted reproduction technology by infertile and same sex couples (or other family groupings) definitively shows that reproduction is not the same as parenthood. Reproductive technologies in general reveal our understandings of what is 'natural' as a culturally constructed category. It is conceivable, then, that the bonds between entities like *cellF* and their donors of biological material, as well as others who contribute to their creation and care, will be powerful enough to guide human investment of time and resources. Furthermore, social notions of parenthood draw us away from the legal framework of rights, which does not universally apply to the intended or surrogate parent, let alone to entities such as *cellF*, towards a framework of social justice and the responsibilities we hold in living together, at a domestic level and at a broader ecological scale.

Despite its limitations, then, reproductive surrogacy assists us in imagining ways to consider how hybrid entities like *cellF* cannot be separated from broader considerations of fairness and justice in social relations. The use of the term 'surrogate musician' in describing *cellF* strategically assists us in imagining the significance of the bonds between biological donor and the new entity that results, bonds that are likely to strengthen as the entities develop. Furthermore, the complexities of human-assisted reproductive technologies offer a useful lesson that illustrates the ways in which the human desire for kinship can spur the development of new technologies that races ahead of legal, social and ethical resolutions. To complete this section, we will touch on some potential scenarios arising from surrogate musicianship, and their implications for new music.

cellF plays with a human musician, but a surrogate musician may perform alone or with other surrogate musicians; different manifestations of the same surrogate might play simultaneously in different locations. A human musician could create an external surrogate with their own biological material (or, for that matter, with biological material from any other living being), as the non-musician Ben-Ary did with *cellF*, and engage in musical activities with their own surrogate musician. The future may see musicians offering their cell lines to preserve their musicality after death. Surrogate musicianship might allow future generations of such entities not only to generate music and demonstrate musicality by interacting with human musicians, but also to interact with other surrogate musicians via a cultured interface that includes other cell types along with neurons. For example, it is conceivable that cochlear hair cells could be interfaced to stimulate a neural network through vibrations, opening further avenues for creative inputs and outputs. The possibilities are as diverse as the potential donors themselves.

If the surrogate musician symbolically stands in for its donor, as we have argued, these scenarios present performance contexts that engage the imagination in new ways. Surrogate musicians also have direct biological links to their donors, allowing us to consider the possibility that in-vitro entities may manifest some inherited musical traits from their donors of biological material. If a human musician is improvising with their own surrogate, their shared cellular material might lead to them making similar responses to stimuli; it is conceivable that such a scenario will produce innovations in improvised music.

32.7 Concluding Discussion

Western philosophy has long understood the world from an anthropocentric perspective that values human life, as entities with large brains and sophisticated cognition, above other kinds of life, and uses the thinking brain as the primary signifier of individual existence and sentience. Moreover, anthropocentric perspectives use the human as the analogic basis for rational arguments regarding unfamiliar biological species or processes. New scientific discoveries increasingly show the error of such thinking, where the threats posed by anthropocentric perspectives for ecological systems more broadly ultimately threaten human life as we know it. Particularly relevant here are those discoveries that reveal species and processes that fall between accepted categories. For example, Colcy and Tanner's [6] illumination of misconceptions in biological thinking discusses programmed cell death and disturbances in ecosystems as normal phenomena that, as a result of anthropocentric perspectives on 'death' and 'disturbance', are thought of as undesirable.

Biology as a field of enquiry is constantly engaged with trying to understand what 'life' is; some characteristics are accepted, while others challenge our preconceptions. Just as new scientific discoveries challenge accepted definitions, artworks using neurons have the potential to shift perceptions surrounding our understanding of 'life'. *cellF* fulfils some of the accepted characteristics of life, such as being composed of cells, growing and adapting to an environment, and responding to stimuli. Other characteristics are harder to categorize. *cellF* depends on technological support to sustain its life, but human brains too develop neat links with technologies in order to form larger systems that change and evolve. *cellF* is not a surrogate child in the common sense, but it is genetically related to a specific human being. Cognitively and genetically, humans have much more in common with non-humans than anthropocentric perspectives have traditionally allowed. *cellF* challenges audiences to rethink categorical assumptions regarding what is considered human and non-human, biological and technological, living and dead.

This chapter answers Eduardo Kac's call for 'a new critical vocabulary to meet the intellectual challenge' posed by living artworks like *cellF* [12]. We have argued for the significance of *cellF*'s biological materiality as fundamental to our use of the new terms in-vitro intelligence and surrogate musicianship. *cellF*'s current and future plasticity, its adaptation to change, is founded upon the biological basis of its neural network. We contrast this with the fixed material basis of artificial intelligence, where proper functioning depends upon the stability of its constituent metals, metalloids, alloys and plastics. Although the synthesizers and other electronic circuitry with which *cellF* is embodied are not cellular, both its neural network brain and analogue synthesizer body create and receive electrical information. These analogue systems come together in *cellF* to create music that is an expression of physical phenomena occurring in real time, in contrast with artificial intelligence that plays out a complex set of pre-arranged instructions.

Future manifestations of in-vitro intelligence will produce surrogate musicians that will neither be driven by chance nor determined by instruction, but be spontaneous and extemporaneous. The complexity and speed of information pathways will facilitate their capacity to perform nuanced operations in real time, in response to audible, and potentially visual, stimuli. These living entities will be both the instrument and the musician, with a seamless flow from input to output. The biophysical and electrochemical pathways in self-organizing biological entities allow information flows that synchronize much faster than occurs in similar-scale structures made of materials like silicon and metal. The constituent materials of instruments are significant; an instrument made of metal produces a different tone to one made of wood. Surrogate musicianship allows us to speak of the different output of sound between a musician made of dry plastic, alloy and electricity from the expressivity of one made of wet, organic materials. Furthermore, surrogate musicians will offer a unique musicality that is accorded to their biological materiality and the consequent relations between surrogates and donors.

As a new framework of music production, surrogate musicianship will change the approaches of human musicians. The future evolution of new music will occur through advances in our increased understanding of biology and the inherent coupling of sound with the body on the hormonal and cellular level. We are able to deconstruct, manipulate and re-assemble the microscopic building blocks of life in completely new ways; human bodies are more malleable that ever before. The potential and ramifications for these biotechnologies extend beyond music. As an engaging and provocative experimental artwork that applies iPSc and neural interfaces for aesthetic purposes, *cellF* opens discussions concerning the future use of stem cells and the potential to bioengineer brains. By showing audiences beyond the scientific community what is possible, the artists and the work ask questions about the use and misuse of biotechnologies, and how and why they are applied. In so doing, the technology is problematized, rather than simply celebrated. *cellF* invites us to grapple with these questions, while the stakes are quite low, in an attempt to initiate public debate and to critique a position that considers technological progress a necessary good. As our use of the terms 'in-vitro intelligence' and 'surrogate musician' show, emerging biotechnologies pose difficult questions about what counts as a life, and what sorts of lives matter.

References

1. Bakkum, D. J., Shkolnik, A. C., Ben-Ary, G., Gamblen, P., DeMarse, T. B., & Potter, S. M. (2004). Removing some "A" from AI: Embodied cultured networks. In F. Iida, R. Pfeifer, L. Steels, & Y. Kuniyoshi (Eds.), *Embodied artificial intelligence.* (pp. 130–145). New York: Springer.

2. Ben-Ary, G. (2014a). 'Meart'. Available online: https://guybenary.com/work/meart/. Accessed 29 Dec 2019.
3. Ben-Ary, G. (2014b). 'Silent Barrage'. Available online: https://guybenary.com/work/silent-barrage/. Accessed 29 Dec 2019.
4. Bretan, M., & Weinberg, G. (2016). A survey of robotic musicianship. *Communications of the ACM, 59*(5), 100–109.
5. Clark, A. (2003). *Natural-born cyborgs: Minds, technologies, and the future of human intelligence*. Oxford: Oxford University Press.
6. Coley, J. D., & Tanner, K. D. (2012). Common origins of diverse misconceptions: Cognitive principles and the development of biology thinking. *CBE-Life Sciences Education, 11*(3), 209–215. https://doi.org/10.1187/cbe.12-06-0074.
7. Cox, C., & Warner, D. (2004). *Audio culture: Readings in modern music*. New York: Continuum.
8. Dezeuze, A. (2002). Origins of the Fluxus score: From indeterminacy to the do-it-yourself artwork. *Performance Research, 7*(3), 78–94. https://doi.org/10.1080/13528165.2002. 10871876.
9. Gheaus, A. (2018). Biological parenthood: Gestational, not genetic. *Australasian Journal of Philosophy, 96*(2), 225–240. https://doi.org/10.1080/00048402.2017.1354389.
10. Havelock, E. (1963). *Preface to Plato* (A history of the Greek mind, v. 1). Cambridge: Belknap Press.
11. Healey, J. (ed.). (2015). *Surrogacy issues* (Issues in society vol. 391). Thirroul, NSW: The Spinney Press.
12. Kac, E. (2007). *Signs of life: Bio art and beyond (Leonardo)*. Cambridge, Mass.: MIT Press.
13. Nyman, M. (1999). *Experimental music: Cage and beyond*. Cambridge: Cambridge University Press.
14. Ong, W., & Hartley, J. (2012). *Orality and literacy: The technologizing of the word* (3rd ed., New accents). Hoboken: Taylor and Francis.
15. Potter, S. M. (2017). The future of computing and neural interfacing: Wetware-Hardware hybrids. In M. Frauenfelder, & B. Hamamoto (Eds.), *Future now: Reconfiguring reality* (vol. 3, pp. 57–59). Institute for the Future.
16. Russell, S., Norvig, P., & Canny, J. (2009). *Artificial intelligence: A modern approach* (3rd edn, Prentice Hall series in artificial intelligence). Upper Saddle River, N.J.: Prentice Hall/Pearson Education.
17. Salter, C. (2010). *Entangled: Technology and the transformation of performance*. Cambridge, Mass: MIT Press.
18. Söderström-Anttila, V., Wennerholm, U. B., Loft, A., Pinborg, A., Aittomäki, K., Romundstad, L. B., & Bergh, C. (2016). Surrogacy: Outcomes for surrogate mothers, children and the resulting families—a systematic review. *Human Reproduction Update, 22* (2), 260–276. https://doi.org/10.1093/humupd/dmv046.
19. Turing, A. (1950). Computing machinery and intelligence. *Mind*, LIX, 433–460. doi:https://doi.org/10.1093/mind/LIX.236.433
20. Wagenaar, D. A., Pine, J., & Potter, S. M. (2006). Searching for plasticity in dissociated cortical cultures on multi-electrode arrays. *Journal of Negative Results in BioMedicine, 5*, 16–35.
21. Yuri Suzuki Design Studio. (2018). Z-Machines. Available online: https://yurisuzuki.com/design-studio/z-machines. Accessed 29 Dec 2019.

Vahri McKenzie is an educator, artist and scholar whose work frames creative engagement as a model of, and practice for, ways of being together in a complex world. She is a Research Fellow in Arts and Health at the University of Canberra's Centre for Creative and Cultural Research. E-mail: vahri.mckenzie@canberra.edu.au.

Nathan John Thompson is a resident artist and researcher at SymbioticA, University of Western Australia, where he explores the possibilities of human-machine interaction, engineered sentience and induced pluripotent stem cell technology. Since 1995 he has built and performed with musical automatons on his own design in Australia, Europe, Asia and South America. He is passionate about designing intuitive interfaces to crude chaotic machines. E-mail: nathanxl@hotmail.com.

Darren Moore is an Australian drummer and electronic musician working in the fields of jazz, experimental music and multimedia. He lives in Singapore where he works as a Lecturer in Music at LASALLE College of the Arts. He completed his Doctorate in Musical Arts in performance at Griffith University (Queensland, Australia) in 2013, with a thesis on adapting Carnatic Indian rhythms to the drum set. His research interests focus on improvisation and interdisciplinary practice. E-mail: dazzimoore@gmail.com.

Guy Ben-Ary is an artist and researcher based in Perth, Australia. He currently works at SymbioticA, an artistic laboratory dedicated to the research, learning and hands-on engagement with the life sciences, which is located within the University of Western Australia. Guy specialises in biotechnological artwork, which aims to enrich our understanding of what it means to be alive. Guy's work has been shown across the globe at prestigious venues and festivals from the Beijing National Art Museum to San Paulo Biennale to the Moscow Biennale. His work can also be seen in the permanent collection of the Museum of Modern Art in New York. His works *cellF* & *Silent Barrage* were awarded Honorary Mentions in Prix Ars Electronica in 2017 and 2009. *Silent Barrage* also won first prize at VIDA, a significant international competition for Art and Artificial Life. Guy's main research areas of interest are cybernetics, bio-robotics and the cultural articulation of b bio-technologies. E-mail: guy.benary@uwa.edu.au

On Growing Computers from Living Biological Cells

33

Eduardo Reck Miranda, Edward Braund and Satvik Venkatesh

33.1 Introduction

The technology behind the computers, and all sorts of data processing devices pervading our daily lives, are underpinned by paradigms such as the Turing machine, the von Neumann architecture, the Harvard architecture, and so on, which were invented in the 1930 and 1940s [29, 33]. These paradigms are so successful that they still prevail in the design of today's digital computers.

This is not to say, however, that other computing paradigms have not been invented. On the contrary, a number of less well-known approaches to computing have been proposed; e.g. the Kolmogorov-Uspensky machine [18]. They have not made it to mass industrialisation for a number of reasons, which we shall refrain from discussing here. Nevertheless, it is worth pointing out that there is an increasing number of research scientists and engineers interested in developing alternative types of computers nowadays [34]. They are protagonists of a whole field of research referred to as *Unconventional Computing*.

Research into Unconventional Computing is aimed at new algorithms and computing architectures informed by, or physically implemented on, new types of substrates, such as chemical, biological and subatomic substrates. Subfields include Biocomputing, Quantum Computing, Optical Computing and Chemical Computing, to cite but four.

Whereas conventional Computer Science seeks incremental improvement of tried-and-tested technology, Unconventional Computing strives for revolutionary changes. Of course, the more revolutionary an idea is, the higher the chances it may fail to produce anything useful. Detractors of Unconventional Computing often argue that it is foolish to compete with the conventional approach. Yet the rapid rise

E. R. Miranda (✉) · E. Braund · S. Venkatesh
Interdisciplinary Centre for Computer Music Research (ICCMR), University of Plymouth, Plymouth PL4 8AA, UK
e-mail: eduardo.miranda@plymouth.ac.uk

© Springer Nature Switzerland AG 2021
E. R. Miranda (eds.), *Handbook of Artificial Intelligence for Music*,
https://doi.org/10.1007/978-3-030-72116-9_33

of Quantum Computing technology, for example, is bound to prove the detractors wrong [26].

We are interested in harnessing biological systems to build new kinds of processors for Artificial Intelligence, music and creativity. Our ambition is to develop electronic components, data processors and eventually full-fledged computers, with living organisms, such as bacteria and slime mould.

This chapter focuses on the work that is being developed with slime mould at the University of Plymouth's Interdisciplinary Centre for Computer Music Research (ICCMR). It tells the story a wild musical idea, born in 2009, and which resulted in the development of a biological processor that is capable of improvising music and doing Boolean logics.

33.2 Meet *Physarum Polycephalum*

Physarum polycephalum, referred to as *P. polycephalum*, is a type of slime mould that can be found in the underlying layer of vegetation in a forest or wooded area. It grows in damp and dark places, on substrates such as rotting tree bark Fig. 33.1. Nowadays, it is also possible to source it from suppliers of living organisms for research and educational purposes.

P. polycephalum is a single eukaryotic cell with many heads; hence the term 'polycephalum'. It is typically yellow in colour and visible to the naked eye. This organism feeds through a process called phagocytosis: it coats its food in enzymes, which allow for specific nutrients to be ingested, leaving behind a mass of unwanted material. In the laboratory, oat flakes are often used as nutrients to culture the organism in Petri dishes Fig. 33.2.

P. polycephalum exhibits a complex lifecycle [15], but the point of interest here is its plasmodium stage, which is when the organism actively forages for nutrients. As it does so, it grows a network of protoplasmic tubules that rhythmically contract

Fig. 33.1 *P. polycephalum* grows in the understory and rotting tree bark. (Photograph by Jiří Kameníček. Printed with permission.)

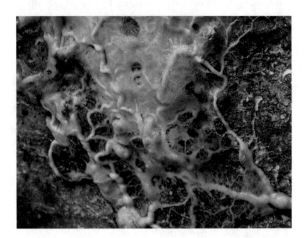

Fig. 33.2 The organism can be cultured on Petri dish by feeding it with oat flakes

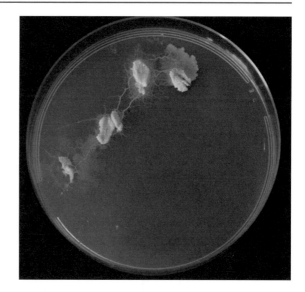

Fig. 33.3 As the organism actively forages for nutrients it grows protoplasmic tubules

and expand producing the shuttle streaming (back and forth locomotion) of its intracellular fluid Fig. 33.3.

The organism is straightforward to culture in Petri dishes and it is relatively easy to prompt it to grow specific topologies of protoplasmic tubules by placing oat flakes at specific locations on the dish. This ability to manipulate its growth patterns has underpinned the early stages of our investigations into this organism's fascinating properties [23].

What is interesting to note is that the rhythmic contraction of the plasmodium's protoplasmic tubes and the subsequent movement of intracellular components produce electricity that can be measured with electrodes [16, 17].

33.3   *Physarum Polycephalum* Sonification

Adamatzky and Jones [5] studied the electrical activity of *P. polycephalum* and identified patterns of intracellular electrical activity that uniquely characterise the organism's physiological state and spatial dynamics.

Readings of the organism's electrical potentials signpost when it reaches specific sites on the culture's substrate, and when it leaves those sites. Such measurements can also indicate whether the organism is functioning smoothly or is in a state of 'distress' (e.g. due to lack of nutrients), and also when it is about to enter hibernation mode. This encouraged us to develop a method to render sounds from *P. polycephalum*'s electrical activity. The ICCMR teamed up with Adamatzky's group at the University of the West of England, Bristol, to develop a method to sonify the organism's behaviour.

At this stage, we were curious to better understand the behaviour of the organism and explore ways in which we might be able to build a living biological musical instrument with it. The rationale was that if we could develop ways to induce the organism to produce variations of its electrical activity, then we would have the means to vary the sounds; that is, play the instrument.

The reader is invited to consult [23] for details of the technicalities behind the implementation of the experiments discussed below. What follows is an abridged introduction.

We cultured the organism in Petri dishes of 9 cm in diameter. In order to record electrical activity, we furnished the dish with an array of nine electrodes, the first of which was used as a reference electrode. In fact, the electrodes were the naked part of coated wires, which were connected to an interface to input voltage readings into a computer. Each electrode was covered with blobs of non-nutrient agar gel. The agar blobs did not touch each other. They were secured on the dish with Blu Tack on a non-conductive plastic strip placed at the bottom of the Petri dish.

To begin an experiment, an oat flake was placed on top of each agar blob. Then, we deposited a sample of *P. polycephalum* on the reference electrode's agar blob. Fig. 33.4.

As expected, the oat flakes prompted the organism to expand and colonise the other agar blobs. On a good run, it took three days colonise all electrodes. But it could take a week sometimes.

The voltages from the electrodes were logged every second. In fact, we sampled 100 measurements per second and then these values were averaged. Furthermore, in order to compress data worth of several days of activity into an amount suitable to produce a few minutes of sound, the electric potentials from electrodes $e_1, \ldots e_8$ were processed as follows: measurements $e_1^t, \ldots, e_8^t$ at time step t were considered

Fig. 33.4 Detail of the Petri dish prepared with electrodes to measure the behaviour of
P. polycephalum. A sample of the organism was placed on the reference electrode, located on the
right-hand side

only if at least N electrodes presented a change in their electric potential. Otherwise,
the measurement was ignored. (Recall that the first electrode, e_0, was used as the
reference to measure the electric potentials).

Voltage values were capped in a range between -40 and $+40$ mV, which is the
range normally expected to be produced naturally by this organism. And the
voltages were subsequently scaled by S in order to match the requirements of the
sound synthesis algorithm that we developed. For the example discussed in this
chapter, $N = 5$ and $S = 20$.

Figure 33.5 illustrates a typical example of an experiment. The organism proliferated from its initial position on the reference electrode (on the right-hand side)
onto the other electrodes, towards the left.

In Fig. 33.6, the voltages were plotted following the order in which the
colonisation took place. Note that electrode e_6 was not colonised in this example.
This sort of thing happened often, but what caused it is not fully understood. We

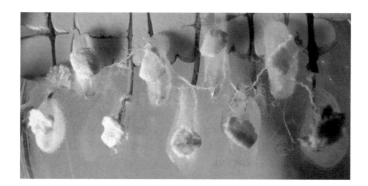

Fig. 33.5 The organism proliferated from its initial position on the reference electrode (first on
the right-hand side of the figure), towards the other 8 measurement electrodes

reckon that it is probably due to the somewhat precarious conditions of the DIY laboratory setup where we conducted our experiments at the time.

We noticed that the colonisation of an electrode produces a characteristic pattern of voltage dynamics. At first, the electrode being colonised registered a rise in its voltage by up to 20 mV. Then, a drop followed this rise, which sometimes went lower than −30 mV.

Eventually, the organism abandoned the agar blobs as they started to dry and/or nutrients were drained. A gradual decrease in voltage was registered when it abandoned an agar blob. When blobs dried and/or nutrients finished, the organism entered into a state of hibernation, forming what is referred to as *sclerotium*.

Over a fair number of runs, we observed that the voltages between stages of colonisation and hibernation were highly dynamic. They represent the interaction of many travelling waves of excitation and contraction.

In order to synthesise sounds, we developed an additive granular synthesiser. Granular synthesis works by generating a rapid succession of short sound bursts referred to as *sound granules* that together form larger sound events [24].

In our system, each sound granule is produced by adding up eight sine waves, each of which is associated with a different electrode. The sinewaves are produced by oscillators, which need two values each to function: a frequency value in Hz and an amplitude in dB.

We used the voltages from the electrodes to control either the frequencies of the oscillators, or both their frequencies and amplitudes together. In the first case, the voltages were normalised to a frequency range, which is set arbitrarily; e.g. between 20 and 4 kHz. Here the amplitudes for each of the sine waves were fixed. In the second case, the voltages also controlled the amplitudes of the sine waves. The voltages were also normalised to a predetermined amplitude range. In standard granular synthesis, the duration of each granule is typically set in terms of tens of milliseconds. Such value can change dynamically as the sound is being synthesised. For the example below, the granules were set to a fixed duration of 30 ms each.

Figure 33.7 shows the cochleagram of an 80 s long sound rendered from the data plotted in Fig. 33.6. In this case, the voltages steered the frequencies of the oscillators. Despite the compression of the original raw data, there is a clear correspondence between sound and the behaviour of the organism. This is demonstrated by the darker lines of the cochleagram, which are morphologically related to the plotting of the voltages in Fig. 33.6.

We subsequently learned that the electrical behaviour of the organism could be manipulated with light and chemical substances [4]. This enabled us to produce sound variations.

Afterwards, we developed a music sequencer and a Kolmogorov-Uspensky model [18, 19] to generate music [22], which also explored spatial displacement of the organism in response to stimuli.

However, despite various attempts to manipulate the electrical behaviour of the organism and accelerate growth speeds, admittedly, the setup above proved unsuitable for making a realistic musical instrument. Whereas it worked well for

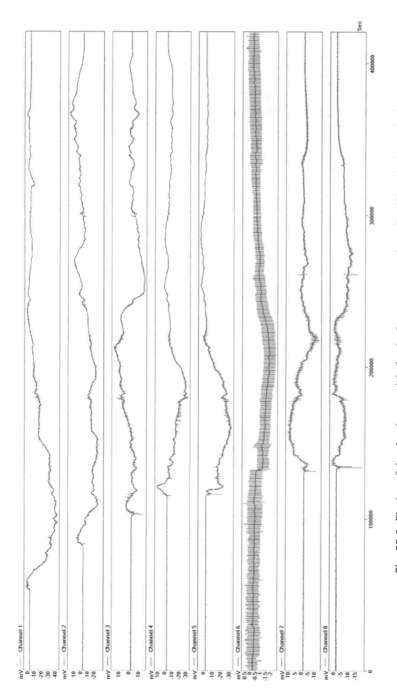

Fig. 33.6 Plotting of the electric potentials for the 8 measurement electrodes. Note that electrode 6 (referred to as channel 6) registers only noise because it has not been colonised by the organism

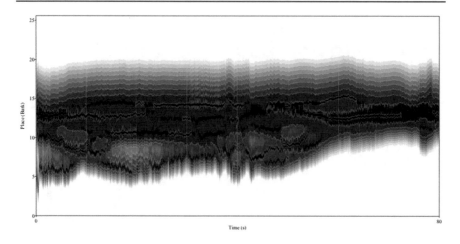

Fig. 33.7 The cochleagram of a sound representing the behaviour of *P. polycephalum*

generating music with recorded data, it proved to be overly slow for real-time synthesis.

Nevertheless, the experiments offered a glimpse at how to harness the behaviour of the unicellular organism to build programmable living machines. Moreover, they advanced our practical understanding of the organism and appreciation of what it takes to culture it and control its behaviour.

In the meantime, the research community reported that the organism had been prompted to find the shortest path to a target destination through a maze [3], develop Voronoi diagrams [32] and solve the classic combinatorial optimization Steiner tree problem [10].

Perhaps the most important outcome of our research at that stage was the realisation that the tubules connecting one agar blob to another, as shown in Fig. 33.5, exhibit very interesting conductance properties, which are explored below.

33.4 Developing the Biomemristor

Exerting electricity through a protoplasmic tubule of *P. polycephalum* prompts it to behave like an electronic component, referred to as the *memristor*.

The memristor is a relatively unknown electronic circuit component, proposed by Leon Chua in the 1970s. It can be thought of as a resistor with memory, because its resistance depends on the history of previous inputs [11]. The memristor is not yet widely employed in the electronics industry. But enthusiasts hope this component will bring a new wave of innovation in electronics because its behaviour is akin to the behaviour of neurones [36]. Hence, its potential for developing Artificial Intelligence.

The memristor is an element with two terminals. It alters its resistance as a function of the previous input voltage and the amount of time that this voltage was applied; this property is referred to as *hysteresis*. When the application of the voltage stops the element retains its most recent resistance state. Mathematically, we can use a state-dependent Ohm's laws to define memristance M as the element's resistance R to a given charge q as follows:

$$M = R(q) = \frac{d\delta(q)}{dq}$$

where q is the charge, δ is the magnetic flux and d is the derivative, denoting the change in flux with respect to the change in charge.

If the value of q is constant, then, over time, the memristor would maintain a linear relationship between voltage and current, similar to a resistor. However, if q is variable, then this relationship becomes nonlinear.

Figure 33.8 shows the memristor's current–voltage characteristic hysteresis curve, where a high or a low resistance pathway is followed according to whether the voltage is increasing or decreasing. The hysteresis curve's lobe size is a function of the rate at which the input voltage changes and the memristance.

The fact that *P. polycephalum* can be harnessed to act as a memristor provides an exciting route for making memristors, which is to grow them out of biological material [12, 28].

Fig. 33.8 The ideal memristor's current–voltage characteristic hysteresis curve

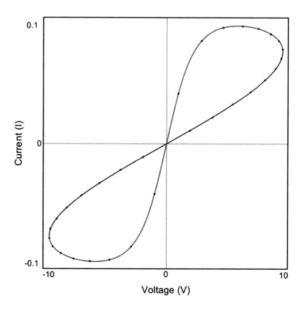

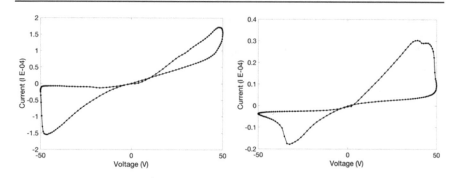

Fig. 33.9 Two examples of current–voltage curves obtained from experiments with *P. polycephalum*

The ICCMR team demonstrated that *P. polycephalum* produces current–voltage hysteresis curves in response to the systematic application of AC voltage, which is comparable with the memristor's curve shown in Fig. 33.8 [8].

Chua [11] established that if a memristor produces a consistent and symmetric figure of eight curves with the centre intersection at zero voltage and zero current, then it is considered as an 'ideal memristor'. We observed that the curve's shape produced by *P. polycephalum* varied dynamically, but remained consistent with the memristor's characteristic curve Fig. 33.9. This anomaly could be due to external factors that influence the organism, like humidity, temperature, light and electrical history. However, we believe that these minor variations can be advantageous for building computer-aided creative systems. For instance, there could be a controllable coefficient of dynamicity, which would regulate levels of variations produced by a memristor-based system in response to input data.

The initial prototypes of our biomemristor were implemented on Petri dishes retrofitted with electrodes made with circles of tinned copper wire filled with non-nutrient agar Fig. 33.10. This enabled them to grow a protoplasmic tubule connecting the two electrodes. In order to prompt the organism to lay down the required protoplasmic tubule, we positioned a *P. polycephalum*-colonised oat flake on one of the electrodes, and a fresh oat flake on the other. This arrangement influences the organism to grow towards the fresh oat.

We subsequently developed a receptacle to culture the organism in a more controlled fashion than before. The receptacle, which is fabricated using 3D printing, encapsulates the organism into a stable environment that delineates a well-defined propagation trajectory Fig. 33.11. This was achieved by printing the chambers with high-impact polystyrene (HIPS). This substance is a repellent for *P. polycephalum* [14]. Consequently, it discourages the organism from growing on the walls of the chambers. Instead, it encourages propagation across the tube linking to the other chamber, laying down the desired protoplasmic tubule between two bio-compatible electrodes Fig. 33.12. For the linking tube, we used off-the-shelf

Fig. 33.10 Photograph of a biomemristor implemented in a Petri dish

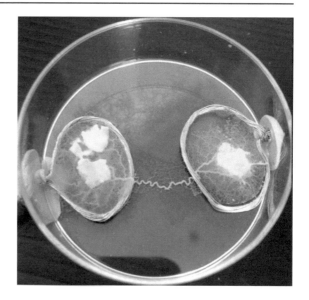

Fig. 33.11 A receptacle to grow a biomemristor. The space between the two electrodes is 1 cm

medical-grade polyvinyl chloride (PVC) tubing, which provides protection against environmental traits, such as infection from bacteria.

The receptacle-based biomemristor yielded current–voltage curves that were more symmetrical than those obtained with the previous Petri dish setup, and with more consistent lobe sizes and pinch locations Fig. 33.13. Also, the lifespan of the component was increased considerably. Whereas the Petri dish biomemristors lost their memristive properties after a few hours of use, the receptacle-based component is able to retain it for over a week. For more details on the receptacle-based component please refer to [9]. Details on how to build one can be found in [21].

Fig. 33.12 A receptacle with a cultured organism. Note the protoplasmic tubule linking the two chambers

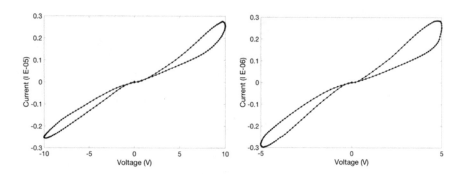

Fig. 33.13 Two examples of current–voltage curves measured with a receptacle-based biomemristor

Eventually, we developed ancillary hardware and software to handle the biomemristor using a Raspberry Pi. This is a low cost, computer board that is the size of a credit card. Each unit can handle four biomemristors simultaneously. A MIDI interface is embedded for music input and output. A standard USB port facilitates communication with other devices, if required; e.g. for uploading and downloading software or MIDI data. The whole system is self-contained and encased in a small portable box, was baptised as the PhyBox [7].

33.4.1   Music Processing with Biomemristors

A sudden change of input voltage prompts the biomemristor to produce a spike in current. The magnitude of the spike is directly related to the difference between the voltage of the incoming signal and the voltage of the previous input. The greater this difference, the higher the magnitude of the spike, and vice-versa. Furthermore, the greater the voltage difference, the longer it takes to settle down from a spike, and vice-versa. We explored these intrinsic properties of the component to develop a living interactive music system (LIMuS) on the PhyBox.

In a nutshell, LIMuS listens to musical events that are transcribed into voltages and generates music in terms of biomemristor current.

At the listening stage, the system splits the music input into four streams of data: pitch, loudness, inter-onset interval and duration. And then, it generates four streams of voltages, one for each biomemristor. For simplicity, below we will refer only to the pitch stream; the process is identical for the other three.

As the system processes the music input, it converts the pitches into voltages. It logs the pitches, the number of times they appeared in the sequence and their respective voltages. A transition matrix is created to represent how often a pitch followed another in the sequence.

At the generative phase, for each pitch to be produced at time $t + 1$, it feeds the voltage (as logged at the 'listening' stage) of the pitch at time t into the respective biomemristor. This in turn produces a current peak. The measurement of the peak is matched against the stochastic values of the transition table to establish the pitch of the new note. The same applies to the note's loudness, inter-onset interval and duration.

Below is an abridged explanation from a paper we published in *Computer Music Journal* [20] detailing music processing. For the sake of clarity, here we focus on a hypothetical case, whereby a monophonic MIDI file encoding a short tune is uploaded into LIMuS. Just pitch is considered. The system generates a musical response only after the whole excerpt has been processed. Bear in mind that the real system produces responses on the fly, for live musical interaction. An example of a composition is detailed in [20] and a video recording of its live performance is available online [25].

As an input music sequence is processed, the system generates voltage impulses ϕ and each pitch is stored with its respective number of occurrences up to the current point. An interim voltage value V in the range of 0 to 10 V is calculated as follows:

$$V = 10 - \left(\left(\frac{10}{N} \right) \times n \right)$$

where N is the total number of processed events so far and n is the number of times the present event has occurred up to this point. Then, if the present event has occurred more frequently than the previous one, the value of the impulse ϕ^t is calculated by increasing the positivity or negativity of the previous impulse ϕ^{t-1} by

Fig. 33.14 Excerpt from J. S. Bach's *Gavotte en rondeau*

the magnitude of voltage V, depending on the polarity of ϕ^{t-1}. Otherwise, ϕ^t is calculated by decreasing the positivity or negativity of the previous impulse ϕ^{t-1} by the value of V. Note that the increase or decrease occurs here in terms of voltage magnitude, which could be either positive or negative. As an example, let us consider the excerpt from J. S. Bach's *Gavotte en rondeau* shown in Fig. 33.14.

The first event is note B4, represented as note MIDI number 71. In this case $V = 10 - ((10/1) \times 1) = 0$ V, and as this is the first event, then $\phi^1 = 0$.

Next, comes the second event, which is MIDI note 80. The voltage for this note is calculated as $V = 10 - ((10/2) \times 1) = 5$ V. As this is only the second event and the magnitude of the previous impulse is neither positive nor negative, the system arbitrarily makes it as a positive impulse: $\phi^2 = V$ Table 33.1.

Then comes the third note, which is also MIDI note 80. As this note occurred more times than note 71, its respective impulse is calculated by increasing the positive value of the previous impulse by the present voltage value: $\phi = 5.00 + 3.33 = 8.33$ Table 33.2.

Table 33.1 Voltage impulses assigned to two events

Event	Note	n	V	ϕ
1	71	1	0.00	0.00
2	80	1	5.00	+5.00

Table 33.2 Voltage impulses assigned to three events

Event	Note	n	V	ϕ
1	71	1	10.00	0.00
2	80	1	5.00	+5.00
3	80	2	3.33	+8.33

Table 33.3 Voltage impulses assigned to four events

Event	Note	n	V	ϕ
1	71	1	0.00	0.00
2	80	1	5.00	+5.00
3	80	2	3.33	+8.33
4	78	1	7.50	+0.83
5	76	1	8.00	−7.17

Next in the sequence is MIDI note 78, which occurred less frequently than the previous notes. In this case, the impulse is calculated by decreasing the positive value of the previous impulse by the voltage value for note 78, that is: $\phi = 8.33 - 7.50 = 0.83$. The fifth note is 76, which occurred the same number of times as the previous one. Therefore $V = 10 - ((10/5) \times 1) = 8$ V and the impulse is calculated by decreasing the positive magnitude of the previous impulse, which brings it down to a negative value: $\phi = 0.33 - 8.00 = -7.17$ (Table 33.3). The resulting impulse sequence is plotted in Fig. 33.15.

While the system calculates the values of the impulses, it also builds a transition table of *inverted percentages* of note occurrences Table 33.4. As the musical input is processed, the system dynamically calculates percentages of transitions between two events. These percentages are subsequently inverted to make smaller values denote greater occurrence of a certain transition from one note to another, and vice-versa. This aligns the musical transitions with the behaviour of the biomemristor: it produces low memristance as the voltage increases and high memristance as the voltage decreases. Therefore, small changes from one voltage impulse to another encode more frequent transitions, whereas large changes encode less frequent ones.

The voltage impulses are then applied one at a time to biomemristor in charge of pitch, the corresponding current is measured, and this value is subsequently used to generate a note for output.

In order to translate from measurements of current to MIDI note numbers, each current reading I^t is compared against its predecessor's I^{t-1} to calculate an absolute change rate value ΔI, as follows:

$$\Delta I = \left| \left(\frac{(I^t - I^{t-1})}{I^{t-1}} \right) \times 100 \right|$$

Then, the system selects the option in the transition matrix whose inverted percentage value is the closest possible to the value of ΔI. To start with, the system considers the first note of the original input music, which in this case is equal to 71. For example, the current reading for the first impulse $\phi^1 = 0$ (corresponding to the first input note 71) is $I^1 = 0.0252 \times 10^{-4}$. As there is no predecessor value for the ΔI equation, the system establishes that $\Delta I^1 = 0.0$ and picks note 80 from Table 33.4 because note 71's inverse probability value of 60.0 is the closest to

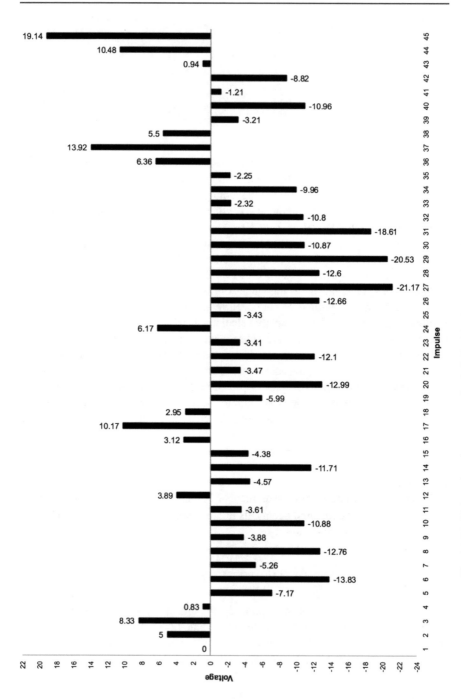

Fig. 33.15 Voltage impulse sequence for J. S. Bach's *Gavotte en rondeau*

Table 33.4 Table of inverted percentages of transitions from notes listed on the vertical axis to the ones listed on the horizontal axis

	64	66	69	71	73	75	76	78	80	81	83
64											
66						0.0					
68	50.0			50.0							
69									0.0		
71							80.0	80.0	60.0		
73								0.0			
75							0.0				
76				80.0				40.0	80.0		
78		90.0		90.0		90.0	80.0		70.0	80.0	
80			88.8		88.8		88.8	77.7	88.8	66.6	
81				83.3				50.0		83.3	83.3
83								0.0			

$\Delta I^1 = 0.0$. Next, for the second input note 80, $\phi^2 = 5.0$ yields $I^2 = 0.1961 \times 10^{-4}$, therefore $\Delta I^2 = 678.17$. In this case, the closest inverted percentage is 88.8. From the four choices available the system picks note 69. For the third input note, also 80, $\phi^3 = 8.33$ produced $I^3 = 0.2053 \times 10^{-4}$ and $\Delta I^3 = 4.69$. Therefore, the system picked note 81, whose transition has the lowest inverse probability value equal to 66.6. So far, the system generated notes 80, 69 and 81 as responses to notes 71, 80 and 80, respectively.

A plot of the currents yielded by the biomemristor is shown in Fig. 33.16 and the resulting notes in standard musical notation are shown in Fig. 33.17. Obviously, the temporal structural of the Bach input has been discarded in Fig. 33.17 because the examples focussed only on pitch processing.

The degree of variation of the musical output in relation to the input could be made controllable if a way to handle the hysteresis of the system is devised. A biomemristor with a different current–voltage profile from the one used for the above example would have produced different current readings and consequently a variation of the from the example presented above.

33.5 Performing Boolean Logic and Arithmetic Operations with the Biomemristor

Boolean logic, introduced by George Boole in the nineteenth century, is a form of algebra where variables have two unique values: True or False, or 1 or 0, respectively. For instance, if a given statement A is true and another statement B is also true, then both statements are true, represented as: A AND B = True.

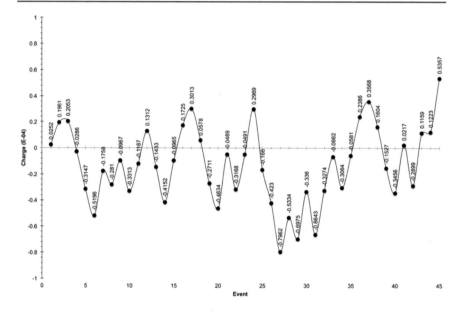

Fig. 33.16 The currents yielded by the biomemristor

Fig. 33.17 Music output from the system. Note that only pitches were processed by the system, hence the temporal structure of Bach's input is lost

Boolean logic is fundamental for developing computing systems. Therefore, a natural progression in our research is to harness the biomemristor to perform Boolean logical operations. Eventually, this will enable us to build biological processors that can speak with digital ones at their most fundamental levels, paving the way for hybrid machines making the most of both realms.

At its most fundamental level, a digital computer comprises electronic switches that operate on binary numbers. Connected together they form logic circuits that give outputs based on inputs supplied to it.

At its core, Boolean logic has three basic operators: OR, AND, and NOT. These basic operators can be combined to build other operators (e.g. NAND, NOR, etc.) and complex logic expressions.

As mentioned earlier, sudden changes in voltage cause the biomemristor to produce a spike in current. Resistance gradually shifts over time. Gale et al. [13] made use of this phenomenon to develop XOR (a variant of OR) and NOT logic operators on a memristor made of Titanium dioxide. They used a single memristor to process a sequence of two voltage values representing logic inputs. Also, there have been a few other studies exploring ways to perform Boolean logic operations with memristors [6, 31], Papandroulidakis et al. [27].

The ICCMR is championing technology to make use of *P. polycephalum* biomemristors to carry out Boolean logic and arithmetic operations. We were able to perform the logic operators OR, AND, and NOT on our biomemristor. And we also implemented a comparator and an ADDER operator, which will be introduced below.

By way of previous related work, Adamatzky et al. [2] conducted a study exploring *P. polycephalum*'s chemotaxis behaviour to implement two Boolean logic gates. Chemotaxis refers to the movement of an organism in response to chemical stimuli. Positive chemotaxis occurs when the organism moves towards a higher concentration of a stimulus, whereas negative chemotaxis takes place when the movement is in the opposite direction. They prompted the organism to move in space to perform the operations. This is pretty much in line with the approach we had adopted earlier for the sonification work. In contrast, we are exploiting the actual memristive properties of the organism to implement the operations.

In our model, the logic inputs True and False are assigned to specific voltages. In order to implement our logic gates, we set up a system that works with negative and positive voltages in the range of -2.0 to $+2.0$ V. A positive change in voltage produces a positive spike, whereas a negative change produces a negative spike. The magnitude of a spike is proportional to the amount of change. For instance, a change from 0.0 to 1.5 V produces a spike with a notably higher magnitude than the magnitude of a spike resulting from a change from 0.0 to 0.1 V.

As in the work of Gale et al. [12], inputs to a biomemristor are applied sequentially. For instance, let's assume that input A is True and input B is False, and that True is represented by $+2.0$ V and false by -2.0 V. Consider the case where $+2.0$ V is applied, followed by -2.0 V immediately after. The change here is equal to -4.0 V; i.e. the interval going from $+2.0$ to -2.0 V. In this case, the spike will be a negative spike current; the change is towards the negative domain. Conversely, a change from -2.0 to $+2.0$ V would have yielded a positive spike current; the change $+4.0$ V is towards the positive domain.

The output of a logical operator is encoded by the behaviour of the spike prompted by the inputs. Different operators are defined in terms of specific spike behaviours in relation to predetermined threshold values.

33.5.1 Bio-Logic Operations

33.5.1.1 The OR Operator

The OR operator outputs True if any of the inputs are True. The corresponding voltages for inputs True and False are +2.0 V and +0.4 V, respectively.

Let us define that β represents the magnitude of a spike and Φ represents a pre-defined threshold in the positive domain. In this case, the biomemristor will produce a spike whose magnitude β crosses the threshold Φ when the output is True.

Table 33.5 shows the logic 'truth table' and the respective biomemristor encodings for the OR operator. The OR symbol used in circuitry diagrams is shown in Fig. 33.18.

As shown in Fig. 33.19, if the current reading is above the threshold, the output is considered to be Boolean True. Otherwise, the output is Boolean False.

Let's examine an example: A = False OR B = True. Assume that $\Phi = 0.6 \times 10^{-5}$ A. To begin with, 0.0 V is input to the biomemristor as an initial reference. Then, let us input +0.4 V followed by +2.0 V. This produces a positive spike current $\beta = 0.9 \times 10^{-5}$ A. In this case, the peak exceeds the threshold, yielding Boolean result X = True.

It is important to bear in mind that the current readings β are measured after the first and second input. If any of the two measurements exceed the threshold Φ, the output is True. For the other gates below, the current reading is measured only after the second input.

Table 33.5 Truth table and respective biomemristor encodings for the OR operator, where β is the magnitude of the spike and Φ is the threshold

Input A		Input B		Output X	
Boolean	Biomem	Boolean	Biomem	Boolean	Biomem
False	+0.4 V	False	+0.4 V	False	$\beta \leq \Phi$
False	+0.4 V	True	+2.0 V	True	$\beta > \Phi$
True	+2.0 V	False	+0.4 V	True	$\beta > \Phi$
True	+2.0 V	True	+2.0 V	True	$\beta > \Phi$

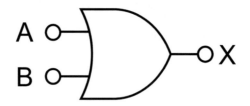

Fig. 33.18 The OR symbol. A, B and X are the Boolean variables

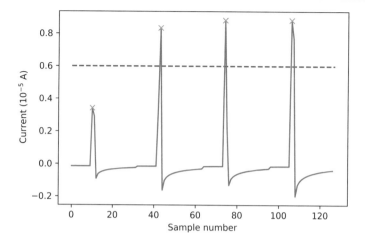

Fig. 33.19 Output spikes for the OR operator. Sequence of input voltage pairs: (0.4, 0.4), (0.4, 2.0), (2.0, 0.4) and (2.0, 2.0)

An implementation of the NOR operator can be achieved with a slight modification of the conditions in Table 33.5. Effectively, NOR is a negation of OR: if the current reading exceeds the threshold, then X = False Otherwise, the X = True.

33.5.1.2 The AND Operator

The AND operator outputs True only if both inputs are True. The corresponding voltages for inputs True and False are +2.0 V and −2.0 V, respectively. These will produce positive and negative spikes in currents. Table 33.6 shows the logic table and respective biomemristor encodings for this operator. The circuitry symbol is portrayed in Fig. 33.20.

As shown in Fig. 33.21, the AND operator works with two thresholds: and upper positive threshold Φ and a lower negative one, Υ, normally, $\Upsilon = -\Phi$. Measurement of current spikes is classified into four ranges, as follows:

Level 1: spike current is higher than Φ,

Level 2: spike current is equal to or lower than Φ, but above or equal to 0,

Table 33.6 Truth table and respective biomemristor encodings for the AND operator, where β is the magnitude of the spike and Φ and Υ are the higher and the lower thresholds, respectively

Input A		Input B		Output X		
Boolean	Biomem	Boolean	Biomem	Boolean	Biomem	Level
False	−2.0 V	False	−2.0 V	False	$\Upsilon \leq \beta < 0$	3
False	−2.0 V	True	+2.0 V	False	$\beta > \Phi$	1
True	+2.0 V	False	−2.0 V	False	$\beta < \Upsilon$	4
True	+2.0 V	True	+2.0 V	True	$0 \leq \beta \leq \Phi$	2

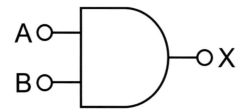

Fig. 33.20 The AND symbol. A, B and X are the Boolean variables

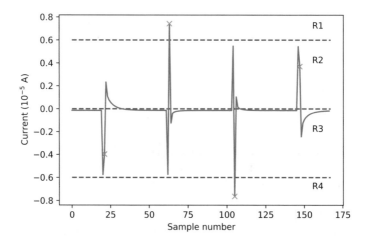

Fig. 33.21 Output peaks for the OR operator. Sequence of input voltage pairs: (−2.0, −2.0), (−2.0, 2.0), (2.0, −2.0) and (2.0, 2.0)

Level 3: spike current is lower than 0, but equal to or higher than Υ, and
Level 4: spike current is lower than Υ.

In this case, the biomemristor will output True when the spike falls within level 2.

33.5.1.3 The NOT Operator

The NOT operator inverts the value of the input A (Table 33.7). The corresponding voltages for input A are +2.0 V for True and −2.0 V for False. Figure 33.22 shows the NOT circuitry symbol.

Input B is fixed at +2.0 V, which is applied to induce the inversion. If the magnitude of the resulting peak is above the threshold, then the output is True. Otherwise, it is False Fig. 33.23.

Table 33.7 The operator NOT and the respective biomemristor encoding

Input A		Input B	Output ¬ A	
Boolean	Biomem	Biomem	Boolean	Biomem
False	−2.0 V	+2.0 V	True	$\beta > \Phi$
True	+2.0 V	+2.0 V	False	$\beta \leq \Phi$

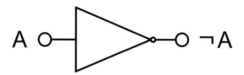

Fig. 33.22 The NOT symbol, where '¬ A' means 'not A'

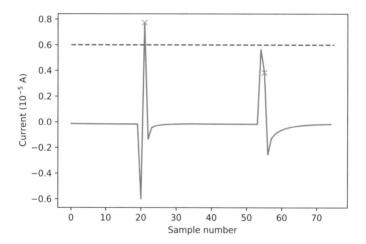

Fig. 33.23 The peaks for the NOT operator. Sequence of input voltage pairs: (−2.0, 2.0), (2.0, 2.0)

33.5.2 Towards Bio-Logic Electronic Circuits: Half ADDER

An ADDER is a device that adds two binary digits. This is one of the most basic components of a computer; it is the heart of the Arithmetic Logic Units (ALU), which is a fundamental building block of many types of computing architectures.

There are two types of ADDERs: half ADDER and full ADDER. The half ADDER, which is the focus of this section, adds two single binary digits and provides the output plus a carry value. Given two inputs A and B, it produces two outputs referred to as sum (S) and carry (C). In binary addition, 1 + 1 = 10, but as performed by the half ADDER, the actual sum is equal to 0; the digit 1 is the carry (C).

Classically, a half ADDER is implemented with AND, OR and NOT operators. However, there is a simpler form using two operators (AND and XOR), which is the one that we have implemented here. The advantage of using the XOR is that this operator is straightforward to implement with the biomemristor.

The XOR is a variation of the OR operator introduced above. It outputs True only if the inputs are different from each other; i.e. only one of them is True. If both inputs are equal to each other, then the output is False.

The corresponding voltages for inputs True and False are +2.0 V and −2.0 V, respectively. As with the AND operator, XOR also works with two thresholds: an upper positive threshold Φ and a lower negative Υ; normally, $\Upsilon = -\Phi$ Fig. 33.24. Table 33.8 shows the logic table and the respective biomemristor encodings for the XOR operator.

The circuit for the half ADDER, comprising AND and XOR operators is given in Fig. 33.25, the XOR operator is shown on top. The sum S is done through the XOR operator, whereas the carry C is obtained with the AND. Now, as we are

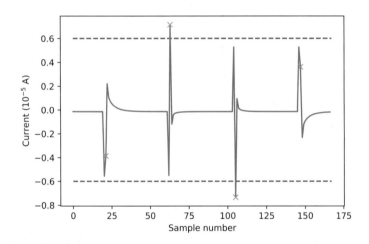

Fig. 33.24 Output peaks for the XOR operator. Sequence of input voltage pairs: (−2.0, −2.0), (−2.0, 2.0), (2.0, −2.0) and (2.0, 2.0)

Table 33.8 Truth table and respective biomemristor encodings for the XOR operator, where β is the magnitude of the peak, and Φ and Υ are the higher and the lower thresholds, respectively

Input A		Input B		Output X	
Boolean	Biomem	Boolean	Biomem	Boolean	Biomem
False	−2.0 V	False	−2.0 V	False	$\Upsilon \leq \beta < 0$
False	−2.0 V	True	2.0 V	True	$\beta > \Phi$
True	2.0 V	False	−2.0 V	True	$\beta < \Upsilon$
True	2.0 V	True	2.0 V	False	$0 \leq \beta \leq \Phi$

Table 33.9 Truth table and the respective biomemristor encodings for the half ADDER

Input A		Input B		Output S		Output C	
Bit	Biomem	Bit	Biomem	Bit	Biomem	Bit	Biomem
0	−2.0 V	0	−2.0 V	0	$\Upsilon \leq \beta < 0$	0	$\Upsilon \leq \beta < 0$
0	−2.0 V	1	2.0 V	1	$\beta > \Phi$	0	$\beta > \Phi$
1	2.0 V	0	−2.0 V	1	$\beta < \Upsilon$	0	$\beta < \Upsilon$
1	2.0 V	1	2.0 V	0	$0 \leq \beta \leq \Phi$	1	$0 \leq \beta \leq \Phi$

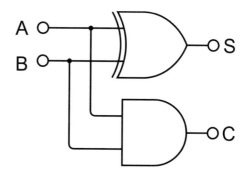

Fig. 33.25 The half ADDER circuit made with XOR (at the top) and AND operators

dealing with numeric operations, we will use binary digits rather than True and False statements.

Recall that measurement of current for the AND operator is classified into four levels. Considering the two operators together, the corresponding S and C outputs for the half ADDER are

Level 1: {A = 0, B = 1} = > {S = 1, C = 0}.
Level 2: {A = 1, B = 1} = > {S = 0, C = 1}.
Level 3: {A = 0, B = 0} = > {S = 0, C = 0}.
Level 4: {A = 1, B = 0} = > {S = 1, C = 0}.

Table 33.8 shows the logic table and the respective biomemristor encodings for the half ADDER. Note, the biomemristor's measurement conditions for outputs S and C are identical.

Our biological half ADDER was built using a single biomemristor. Conversely, it would have required eight transistors to be implemented on standard silicon chips. Despite the fact that we still need to overcome countless technical challenges before we can produce operational complex circuits with biomemristors, this reduction of logic units is an encouraging observation.

A pressing challenge that needs to be tackled before we can attempt more complex circuits is the calibration of thresholds.

The biomemristor is a living organism. As such, its behaviour is highly dynamic and somewhat unpredictable. Whereas such dynamic behaviour is cherished for certain applications, it is undesirable for ascertaining the accuracy of logic operations. In order to obtain accurate results with the operators introduced above, we had to calibrate the threshold values manually before performing the experiments. This sort of thing needs to be managed by the system itself, through some sort of 'operational systems' self-regulation'. This is not trivial.

Moreover, after processing each input pair, the device needs time to bring itself back to its initial state. This may take up to one second. We cannot simply input a 0 V to re-initiate the system because this would still incur a voltage change. Further research is needed in order to optimise this.

33.6 Concluding Remarks

This chapter glanced over the Unconventional Computing for music research that we have been developing at ICCMR for the past 12 years by the time we write this. What started as a highly speculative 'what if' question, posed by a bunch of curious computer musicians, joined a global effort to develop new types of computers. The biomemristor introduced above is unique, and so are the PhyBox and the uses we are making of it.

Unquestionably, there is a long road ahead before we can build something that may be comparable to standard computing technology. All the same, we advocate that research into Unconventional Computing should be aimed at complementary rather than contrasting technology. We believe that future computers are likely to be hybrids; e.g. digital-bio-quantum machines.

We believe that once we have developed the means to achieve robust performance of Boolean logic and other numerical operations with biomemristors, then we will be able to grow entire biological circuits, miniaturised and with the ability to morph its components; e.g. a biomemristor may become a biotransistor, or a bioresistor, or all three at the same time.

Acknowledgements We thank Bhavesh Shri Kumar Narayanan, a visiting student from SASTRA, India, for helping with the implementation of the biomemristor's Boolean logic and arithmetic operations experiments.

References

1. Adamatzky, A. (Ed.) (2017). *Advances in unconventional computing*, Vols. 1 and 2. Cham, Switzerland: Springer International Publishing.
2. Adamatzky, A., Jones, J., Mayne, R., Tsuda, S., & Whiting, J. (2016). Logical gates and circuits implemented in slime mould. In A. Adamatzky (Ed.), Advances in Physarum Machines, Cham, Switzerland: Springer.
3. Adamatzky, A. (Ed.) (2016). *Advances in Physarum machines: Sensing and computing with slime mould.*
4. Adamatzky, A. (2009). Steering plasmodium with light: Dynamical programming of Physarum machine. Retrieved December 13, 2010, from https://arxiv.org/abs/0908.0850.

5. Adamatzky A. & Jones J. (2010). On electrical correlates of *Physarum polycephalum* spatial activity: Can we see Physarum machine in the dark?. Retrieved December 21, 2010, from https://arxiv.org/abs/1012.1809.
6. Borghetti, J., Snider, G. S., Kuekes, P. J., Yang, J. J., Stewart, D. R., & Williams, R. S. (2010). 'Memristive' switches enable 'stateful' logic operations via material implication. *Nature, 464*(7290), 873–876
7. Braund, E., Venkatesh, S., & Miranda, E. R. (2019). PhyBox: A programmable interface for Physarum polycephalum-based memristors. *International Journal of Unconventional Computing, 14*(3–4), 217–233
8. Braund, E., & Miranda, E. R. (2017). On building practical biocomputers for real-world applications: Receptacles for culturing slime mould memristors and component standardisation. *Journal of Bionic Engineering, 14*(1), 151–162
9. Braund, E. & Miranda, E. R. (2017b). An approach to building musical bioprocessors with *Physarum polycephalum* memristors. In E. R. Miranda (Ed.), *Guide to unconventional computing for music*. Cham, Switzerland: Springer.
10. Caleffi, M., Akyildiz, I., & Paura, L. (2015). On the solution of the steiner tree NP-hard problem via Physarum BioNetwork. *IEEE/ACM Transactions on Networking, 23*(4), 1092–1106
11. Chua, L. O. (1971). Memristor: The missing circuit element. *IEEE Transaction on Circuit Theory, 18*(5), 507–519
12. Gale, E., Adamatzky, A., de Costelo, B., & L. . (2013). Slime mould memristors. *BioNanoScience, 5*(1), 1–8
13. Gale, E., Costello, B. de L., & Adamatzky, A. (2013b). Boolean logic gates from a single memristor via low-level sequential logic. In G. Mauri et al. (Eds.), *Unconventional computing and natural computation*. LNCS, Vol. 7956. Cham, Switzerland: Springer.
14. Gotoh, K., & Kuroda, K. (1982). Motive force of cytoplasmic streaming during plasmodial mitosis of Physarum polycephalum. *Cell Motility, 2*(2), 173–181
15. Howard, F. L. (1931). The life history of Physarum polycephalum. *American Journal of Botany, 18*(2), 116–133
16. Kamiya, N., & Abe, S. (1950). Bioelectric phenomena in the myxomycete plasmodium and their relation to protoplasmic flow. *Journal of Colloid Science, 5*, 149–163
17. Kishimoto, U. (1958). Rhythmicity on the protoplasmic streaming of a slime mold, *Physarum polycephalum*. I. A statistical analysis of the electric potential rhythm. *Journal of General Physiology, 41*, 1205–1222
18. Kolmogorov, A. N., & Uspenski, V. A. (1963). On the definition of an algorithm. *English Translation in American Mathematical Society Translations, 2*(29), 217–245
19. Mendelson, E. (1973). Reviewed work: *On the definition of an algorithm.* by A. N. Kolmogorov, V. A. Uspénskij. *The Journal of Symbolic Logic, 38*(4), 655
20. Miranda, E. R., Braund, E. & Venkatesh, S. (2018). Compositing with biomemristors: Is biocomputing the new technology for computer music?". *Computer Music Journal, 42*(3), 28–46.
21. Miranda, E. R. & Braund, E. (2017). A Method for Growing Bio-memristors from Slime Mold. *JoVE Journal*https://doi.org/10.3791/56076.
22. Miranda, E. R., Kirke, A., Braund, E. & Antoine, A. (2017). On unconventional computing for sound and music. In E. R. Miranda (Ed.), *Guide to unconventional computing for music*. Cham, Switzerland: Springer.
23. Miranda, E. R., Adamatzky, A., & Jones, J. (2011). Sound synthesis wit slime mould of *Physarum poluycephalum*. *Journal of Bionic Engineering, 8*(2), 107–113
24. Miranda, E. R. (2002). *Computer sound design: Synthesis techniques and programming*. Oxford, UK: Elsevier/Focal Press.
25. Miranda, E. R. (2016). *Biocomputer rhythms*. Retrieved August 04, 2020, from Video: https://vimeo.com/163673832.
26. Oliver, W. D. (2019). Quantum computing takes flight. *Nature, 574*, 487–488

27. Papandroulidakis, G., Vourkas, V., & Sirakoulis, G. (2014). Boolean logic operations and computing circuits based on memristors. *IEEE Transactions on Ciruits and Systems II: Express Briefs, 61*(12), 972–976
28. Pershin, Y. V., La Fontaine, S., & Di Ventra, M. (2009). Memristive model of amoeba learning. *Physical Review E, 80*(2), 021926
29. Rojas, R., & Hashagen, U. (2002). *The first computers—History and architectures.* Cambridge, MA: The MIT Press.
30. Schumann, A., & Adamatzky, A. (2009). *Physarum spatial logic. In Proceedings 11th International Symposium on Symbolic and Numeric Algorithms for Scientific Computing.* Romania: Timisoara.
31. Shin, S., Kim, K., & Kang, S.-M. (2011). Reconfigurable stateful NOR gate for large-scale logic-array integrations. *IEEE Transactions on Circuits and Systems II: Express Briefs, 58*(7), 442–446
32. Shirakawa, T., Adamatzky, A., Gunji, Y.-P., & Miyake, Y. (2009). On simultaneous construction of Voronoi diagram and Delaunay triangulation by Physarum polycephalum. *International Journal of Bifurcation and Chaos, 19*, 3109–3117
33. Soare, R. I. (2016). *Turing computability.* Cham, Switzerland: Springer.
34. Stepney, S., Braunstein, S. L., Clark, J. A., Tyrrell, A., Adamatzky, A., Smith, R. E., Addis, T., Johnson, C., Timmis, J., Welch, P., Milner, R., & Partridge, D. (2005). Journeys in non-classical computation I: A grand challenge for computing research. *International Journal of Parallel Emergent and Distributed Systems, 20*, 5–19.https://doi.org/10.1080/17445760500033291.
35. Tsuda, S., Aono, M., & Gunji, Y.-P. (2004). Robust and emergent Physarum logical-computing. *Bio Systems, 73*, 45–55
36. Vaughan, O. (2018). The memristor revisited. *Nature Electronics, 1*, 261. https://doi.org/10. 1038/s41928-018-0083-3

Eduardo Reck Miranda is Professor in Computer Music and head the Interdisciplinary Centre for Computer Music Research (ICCMR) at the University of Plymouth, UK. He studied music, philosophy and informatics in Brazil before he graduated with an M.Sc. in Music Technology from the University of York, UK. Subsequently he received a Ph.D. on the topic of sound design with Artificial Intelligence (AI) from the University of Edinburgh, UK. Before joining the University of Plymouth, he worked at Sony Computer Science Laboratory in Paris, France, as a research scientist in the fields of AI, speech and evolution of language. He also is a composer working at the crossroads of music and science. His distinctive music is informed by his unique background as a classically trained composer and AI scientist with an early involvement in electroacoustic and avant-garde pop music. E-mail: eduardo.miranda@plymouth.ac.uk

Edward Braund studied for a M.Res. in Computer Music and a Ph.D. on the topic of unconventional computing for music, both at the Interdisciplinary Centre for Computer Music Research (ICCMR), University of Plymouth, UK. Currently, he is a Lecturer in Computing, Audio, and Music Technology in this university. His current research looks to the information processing abilities of chemical, biological, and physical systems to develop new types of processors, sensors, and actuators. Recent developments at this front include a method for producing biological memristors and approaches to implementing logic gates on biological substrates. E-mail: edward.braund@plymouth.ac.uk

Satvik Venkatesh holds a Bachelor of Technology in Information and Communication Technology from Shanmugha Arts, Science, Technology & Research Academy (SASTRA), India, and a Res.M. in Computer Music from the Interdisciplinary Centre for Computer Music Research (ICCMR), University of Plymouth, UK. He currently is studying for a Ph.D. at ICCMR on the topic of on intelligent and assistive mixing and audio for live radio broadcast. His research interests include Brain-Computer Music Interfaces, Unconventional Computing, and Artificial Intelligence for music. He is also an accomplished musician and performer. E-mail: satvik. venkatesh@plymouth.ac.uk

Quantum Computer: Hello, Music!

34

Eduardo Reck Miranda

34.1 Introduction

Quantum computing is emerging as a promising technology, which is built on the principles of subatomic physics. By the time of writing, fully fledged practical quantum computers are not widely available. But research and development are advancing at exponential speeds. Various software simulators are already available [1, 2]. And a few companies have already started to provide access to quantum hardware via the cloud [3, 4]. These initiatives have enabled experiments with quantum computing to tackle some realistic problems in science; e.g., in chemistry [5] and cryptography [6].

In spite of continuing progress in developing increasingly more sophisticated hardware and software, research in quantum computing has been focusing primarily on developing scientific applications. Up till now there has been virtually no research activity aimed at widening the range of applications of this technology beyond science and engineering. In particular applications for the entertainment industry and creative economies.

We are championing a new field of research, which we refer to as *Quantum Computer Music*. The research is aimed at the development of quantum computing tools and approaches to creating, performing, listening to and distributing music.

This chapter begins with a brief historical background. Then, it introduces the notion of algorithmic music and presents two quantum computer music systems of our own design: a singing voice synthesizer and a musical sequencer. A primer on quantum computing is also given. The chapter ends with a concluding discussion and advice for further work to develop this new exciting area of research.

E. R. Miranda (✉)
Interdisciplinary Centre for Computer Music Research (ICCMR), University of Plymouth, Plymouth PL4 8AA, UK
e-mail: eduardo.miranda@plymouth.ac.uk

© Springer Nature Switzerland AG 2021
E. R. Miranda (eds.), *Handbook of Artificial Intelligence for Music*,
https://doi.org/10.1007/978-3-030-72116-9_34

34.2 Historical Background

As early as the 1840s, mathematician and allegedly the first ever software programmer, Lady Ada Lovelace, predicted in that machines would be able to compose music. On a note about Charles Babbage's Analytical Engine, she wrote:

> Supposing, for instance, that the fundamental relations of pitched sounds in the science of harmony and of musical composition were susceptible of such expression and adaptations, the Engine might compose elaborate and scientific pieces of music of any degree of complexity or extent. ([7], p. 21).

People hardly ever realize that musicians started experimenting with computing far before the emergence of the vast majority of scientific, industrial and commercial computing applications in existence today. For instance, in the 1940s, researchers at Australia's Council for Scientific and Industrial Research (CSIR) installed a loudspeaker on their Mk1 computer (Fig. 34.1) to track the progress of a program using sound. Subsequently, Geoff Hill, a mathematician with a musical background, programmed this machine to playback a tune in 1951 [8].

And in the 1950s composer and Professor of Chemistry, Lejaren Hiller collaborated with mathematician Leonard Isaacson, Lejaren Hiller and Leonard Isaacson, at University of Illinois at Urbana-Champaign, programmed the ILLIAC computer to compose a string quartet entitled *Illiac Suite*. The ILLIAC, short for Illinois Automatic Computer, was one of the first mainframe computers built in the USA, comprising thousands of vacuum tubes. The *Illiac Suite* consists of four movements, each of which using different methods for generating musical sequences,

Fig. 34.1 CSIRAC computer used to playback a tune in the early 1950s. The loudspeaker can be seen in the right-hand door of the console. (Image published with the kind permission of Prof. Paul Doornbusch.)

including hard-coded rules and a probabilistic Markov chain method [9]. This string quartet is often cited as a pioneering piece of algorithmic computer music. That is, whereas Mk1 merely played back an encoded tune, ILLIAC was programmed with algorithms to compose music.

Universities and companies have been welcoming musicians to join their research laboratories ever since. A notable early example is AT&T's Bell Laboratories, in New Jersey, where in the early 1960s composer Max Mathews developed MUSIC III: a system for synthesizing sounds on the IBM 7094 computer. Descendants of MUSIC III are still used today; e.g., programming languages for audio such as Csound [10].

The great majority of computer music pioneers were composers interested in inventing new music and/or innovative approaches to compose. They focused on developing algorithms to generate music. Hence the term 'algorithmic music'. In addition to those innovators cited above, names such as Iannis Xenakis, Pietro Grossi, Jean-Claude Risset and Charles Dodge, amongst a few others, come to mind. Those early pioneers of Computer Music unwittingly paved the way for the development of a thriving global music industry.

Computers play a pivotal part in the music industry today. And emerging quantum computing technology will most certainly have an impact in the way in which we create and distribute music in time to come. Hence the dawn of Quantum Computer Music is a natural progression for music technology.

Prior to this chapter, the ICCMR team published preliminary studies with photonic quantum computing [11] and with Grover's search algorithm to produce melodies [12]. A book chapter about *Zeno*, a composition for bass clarinet and music generated by a quantum computer interactively, is also available [13].

34.3 Algorithmic Computer Music

The first uses of computers in music were for running algorithms to generate music. Essentially, the art of algorithmic music consists of (a) harnessing algorithms to produce patterns of data and (b) developing ways to translate these patterns into musical notes or synthesised sound. An early approach to algorithmic music, which still remains popular to date, is to program the computer to generate notes randomly and then reject those that do not satisfy given criteria, or rules. Musical rules based classic treatises on musical composition (e.g., [14]) are relatively straightforward to encode in a piece of software.

Another widely used approach employs probability distribution functions to predispose the system towards picking specific elements from a given set of musical parameters. For instance, consider the following ordered set of 8 notes, which constitute a C4 major scale: {C4, D4, E4, F4, G4, A4, B4, C5} (Fig. 34.2). A Gaussian function could be used to bias the system to pick notes from the middle of the set. That is, it would generate sequences with higher occurrences of F4 and G4 notes.

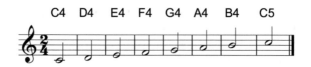

Fig. 34.2 A given ordered set of musical notes

A Gaussian function may well be viewed as a simple abstract musical rule. Abstract rules for musical composition can be expressed in a number of ways, including graphs, set algebra, Boolean expressions, finite state automata and Markov chains, to cite but a few. An example using a Markov chain to encode rules for generating sequences of notes is given below. A more detailed introduction to various classic algorithmic composition methods is available in [15].

As an example, consider the ordered set shown in Fig. 34.2. Let us define the following sequencing rules for establishing which notes are allowed to follow a given note within the set:

Rule 1: if C4, then either C4, D4, E4, G4 or C5.
Rule 2: if D4, then either C4, E4 or G4.
Rule 3: if E4, then either D4 or F4.
Rule 4: if F4, then either C4, E4 or G4.
Rule 5: if G4, then either C5, F5, G5 or A5.
Rule 6: if A4, then B4.
Rule 7: if B4, then C5.
Rule 8: if C5, then either A4 or B4.

Each of these rules represents the transition probabilities for the next note to occur in a sequence. For example, after C4, each of the five notes C4, D4, E4, G4 and C5 has a 20% chance each of occurring.

The rules above can be expressed in terms of probability arrays. For instance, the probability array for note C4 is $p(C4) = [0.2, 0.2, 0.2, 0.0, 0.2, 0.0, 0.0, 0.2]$ and for note D4 is $p(D4) = [0.33, 0.0, 0.33, 0.0, 0.33, 0.0, 0.0, 0.0]$, and so on. The

	C4	D4	E4	F4	G4	A4	B4	C5
C4	0.2	0.2	0.2	0.0	0.2	0.0	0.0	0.2
D4	0.33	0.0	0.33	0.0	0.33	0.0	0.0	0.0
E4	0.0	0.5	0.0	0.5	0.0	0.0	0.0	0.0
F4	0.33	0.0	0.33	0.0	0.33	0.0	0.0	0.0
G4	0.25	0.0	0.0	0.25	0.25	0.25	0.0	0.0
A4	0.0	0.0	0.0	0.0	0.0	0.0	1.0	0
B4	0.0	0.0	0.0	0.0	0.0	0.0	0.0	1.0
C5	0.0	0.0	0.0	0.0	0.0	0.5	0.5	0.0

Fig. 34.3 Sequencing rules represented as a Markov chain

Fig. 34.4 An example generated by the Markov chain shown in Fig. 34.3

probability arrays for all rules can be arranged in a two-dimensional matrix, thus forming a Markov chain, as shown in Fig. 34.3.

Given a starting note, the system then picks the next based on the transition probability on the corresponding column to pick the next, and so on. An example of a melody generated using this method is shown in Fig. 34.4.

A Markov chain whose matrix representation has non-zero entries immediately on either side of the main diagonal, and zeros everywhere else constitutes an example of a simple *random walk* process.

Imagine that a robot is programmed to play an instrument with 8 keys, to produce the notes shown in Fig. 34.2. However, the robot is programmed in such a way that notes can be played up and down the keyboard by stepping only one key at a time. That is, only the next neighbouring key can be played. If the robot has a probability p to play the key on the left side of the current key, then it will have the probability $q = 1 - p$ to go to the right. This is represented in the matrix shown in Fig. 34.5. Random walk processes are normally represented as directed graphs, or digraphs, as shown in Fig. 34.6.

Random walk processes are useful for generating musical sequences that require smooth gradual changes over the material rather than large jumps. Figure 34.7 shows an example sequence generated by our imaginary robot.

As computers became increasingly portable and faster, musicians started to program them to create music interactively, during a performance. Let us say, a performer plays a musical note. The computer listens to the note and produces another one as a response. Most algorithmic music methods that were developed for

	C4	D4	E4	F4	G4	A4	B4	C5
C4	**0.0**	1.0	0.0	0.0	0.0	0.0	0.0	0.0
D4	0.5	**0.0**	0.5	0.0	0.0	0.0	0.0	0.0
E4	0.0	0.5	**0.0**	0.5	0.0	0.0	0.0	0.0
F4	0.0	0.0	0.5	**0.0**	0.5	0.0	0.0	0.0
G4	0.0	0.0	0.0	0.5	**0.0**	0.5	0.0	0.0
A4	0.0	0.0	0.0	0.0	0.5	**0.0**	0.5	0.0
B4	0.0	0.0	0.0	0.0	0.0	0.5	**0.0**	0.5
C5	0.0	0.0	0.0	0.0	0.0	0.0	1.0	**0.0**

Fig. 34.5 A Markov chain for random walk

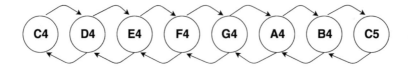

Fig. 34.6 Digraph representation of the random walk scheme depicted in Fig. 34.5

Fig. 34.7 A sequence of notes generated by the random walk robot

batch processing of music can be adapted for interactive processing. For instance, given the Markov chain above, if a performer plays the note C5, then the system would respond with A4 or B4, and so on.

A sensible approach to get started with Quantum Computer Music is to revisit existing tried-and-tested algorithmic music methods with a view to running them on quantum computers. Sooner or later new quantum-specific methods are bound to emerge from these exercises.

34.4 Quantum Computing Primer

This section provides a preliminary introduction to quantum computing, aimed at demonstrating how it differs from classical computing. It introduces the basics deemed necessary to follow the systems discussed in this chapter. The reader is referred to [16–19] for more detailed explanations.

Classical computers manipulate information represented in terms of binary digits, each of which can value 1 or 0. They work with microprocessors made up of billions of tiny switches that are activated by electric signals. Values 1 and 0 reflect the on and off states of the switches.

In contrast, a quantum computer deals with information in terms of quantum bits, or *qubits*. Qubits operate at the subatomic level. Therefore, they are subject to the laws of quantum physics.

At the subatomic level, a quantum object does not exist in a determined state. Its state is unknown until one observes it. Before it is observed, a quantum object is said to behave like a wave. But when it is observed it becomes a particle. This phenomenon is referred to as the *wave-particle duality*.

Quantum systems are described in terms of wave functions. A wave function represents what the particle would be like when a quantum object is observed. It expresses the state of a quantum system as the sum of the possible states that it may fall into when it is observed. Each possible component of a wave function, which is also a wave, is scaled by a coefficient reflecting its relative weight. That is, some states might be more likely than others. Metaphorically, think of a quantum system as the spectrum of a musical sound, where the different amplitudes of its various wave-components give its unique timbre. As with sound waves, quantum wave-components interfere with one another, constructively and destructively. In quantum physics, the interfering waves are said to be *coherent*. As we will see later, the act of observing the waves decoheres them. Again metaphorically, it is as if when listening to a musical sound one would perceive only a single spectral component; probably the one with the highest energy, but not necessarily so.

Qubits are special because of the wave-particle duality. Qubits can be in an indeterminate state, represented by a wave function, until they are read out. This is known as *superposition*. A good part of the art of programming a quantum computer involves manipulating qubits to perform operations while they are in such indeterminate state. This makes quantum computing fundamentally different from digital computing.

A qubit can be implemented in a number of ways. All the same, the qubits of a quantum processor need to be isolated from the environment in order to remain coherent to perform computations. The environment causes interferences that destroy coherence. One of the worst enemies of coherence is heat. A Quantum Processing Unit (QPU) has to be cooled to near absolute zero temperature to function; that is, $-273.15\ °C$. This is the point at which the fundamental particles of nature would stop moving due to thermal fluctuations and retain only the so-called zero-point energy quantum mechanical motion. But even then, it is very hard to shield a QPU from the effects of our environment. In practice, interactions with the environment cannot be completely avoided, only minimized.

In order to picture a qubit, imagine a transparent sphere with opposite poles. From its centre, a vector whose length is equal to the radius of the sphere can point to anywhere on the surface. In quantum mechanics this sphere is called *Bloch sphere* and the vector is referred to as a *state vector*. The opposite poles of the sphere are denoted by $|0\rangle$ and $|1\rangle$, which is the notation used to represent quantum states (Fig. 34.8).

A qubit's state vector can point at anywhere on the Bloch sphere's surface. Mathematically, it is described in terms of polar coordinates using two angles, θ and φ. The angle θ is the angle between the state vector and the z-axis (latitude) and the angle φ describes vector's position in relation to the x-axis (longitude).

It is popularly said that a qubit can value 0 and 1 at the same time, but this is not entirely accurate. When a qubit is in superposition of $|0\rangle$ and $|1\rangle$, the state vector could be pointing anywhere between the two. However, we cannot really know where exactly a state vector is pointing to until we read the qubit. In quantum computing terminology, the act of reading a qubit is referred to as 'observing', or 'measuring' it. Measuring the qubit will make the vector point to one of the poles and return either 0 or 1 as a result.

The state vector of a qubit in superposition state is described as a linear combination of two vectors, $|0\rangle$ and $|1\rangle$, as follows:

Fig. 34.8 Bloch sphere
(*Source* Smite-Meister,
https://commons.wikimedia.
org/w/index.php?curid=
5829358)

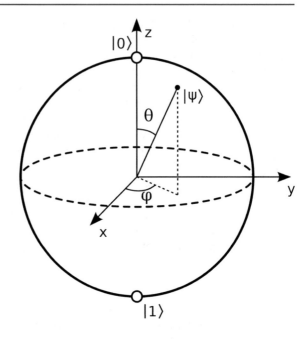

$$|\Psi\rangle = \alpha|0\rangle + \beta|1\rangle, \text{ where } |\alpha|^2 + |\beta|^2 = 1.$$

The state vector $|\Psi\rangle$ is a superposition of vectors $|0\rangle$ and $|1\rangle$ in a two-dimensional complex space, referred to as *Hilbert space*, with amplitudes α and β. Here the amplitudes are expressed in terms of Cartesian coordinates; but bear in mind that these coordinates can be complex numbers.

In a nutshell, consider the squared values of α and β as *probability values* representing the likelihood of the measurement return 0 or 1. For instance, let us assume the following:

$$|\Psi\rangle = \alpha|0\rangle + \beta|1\rangle, \text{ where } \alpha = \frac{1}{2} \text{ and } \beta = \frac{\sqrt{3}}{2}$$

In this case, $|\alpha|^2 = 0.25$ and $|\beta|^2 = 0.75$. This means that the measurement of the qubit has a 25% chance of returning 0 and a 75% chance of returning 1 (Fig. 34.9).

Quantum computers are programmed using sequences of commands, or quantum gates, that act on qubits. For instance, the 'not gate', performs a rotation of 180 degrees around the x-axis. Hence this gate is often referred to as the 'X gate' (Fig. 34.10). A more generic rotational $Rx(\vartheta)$ gate is typically available for quantum programming, where the angle for the rotation is specified. Therefore, Rx (180) applied to $|0\rangle$ or $|1\rangle$ is equivalent to applying X to $|0\rangle$ or $|1\rangle$. In essence, all quantum gates perform rotations, which change the amplitude distribution of the system.

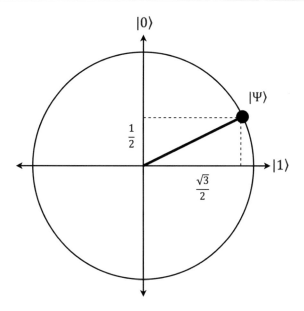

Fig. 34.9 An example of superposition, where the state vector has a 25% chance of settling to $|0\rangle$ and a 75% chance of settling to $|1\rangle$ after the measurement

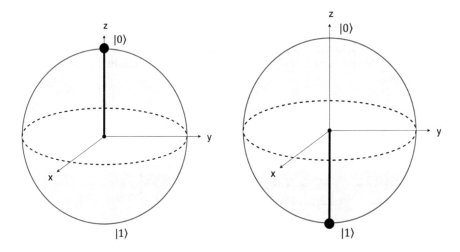

Fig. 34.10 X gate rotates the state vector (pointing upwards on the figure on the left) by 180 degrees around the x-axis (pointing downwards on the figure on the right)

An important gate for quantum computing is the Hadamard gate (referred to as the 'H gate'). It puts the qubit into a superposition state consisting of an equal-weighted combination of two opposing states: $|\Psi\rangle = \alpha|0\rangle + \beta|1\rangle$ where $|\alpha|^2 = 0.5$ and $|\beta|^2 = 0.5$ (Fig. 34.11). For other gates, please consult the references given above.

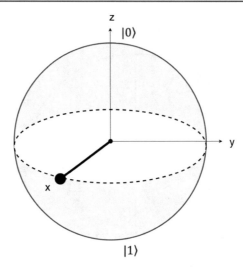

Fig. 34.11 The Hadamard gate puts the qubit into a superposition state halfway two opposing poles

A quantum program is often depicted as a circuit diagram of quantum gates, showing sequences of gate operations on the qubits (Fig. 34.12). Qubits typically start at $|0\rangle$ and then a sequence of gates are applied. Then, the qubits are read and the results are stored in standard digital memory, which are accessible for further handling. Normally a quantum computer works alongside a classical computer, which in effect acts as the interface between the user and the quantum machine. The classical machine enables the user to handle the measurements for practical applications.

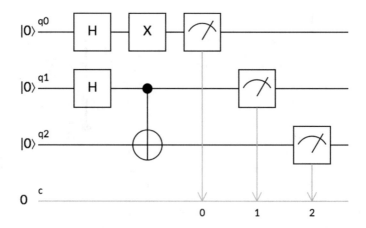

Fig. 34.12 A quantum program depicted as a circuit of quantum gates. The squares with dials represent measurements, which are saved on classic registers at the bottom line

Quantum computation gets really interesting with gates that operate on multiple qubits, such as the 'conditional X gate', or 'CX gate'. The CX gate puts two qubits in *entanglement*.

Entanglement establishes a curious correlation between qubits. In practice, the CX gate applies an X gate on a qubit only if the state of another qubit is $|1\rangle$. Thus, the CX gate establishes a dependency of the state of one qubit with the value of another (Fig. 34.13). In practice, any quantum gate can be made conditional and entanglement can take place between more than two qubits.

The Bloch sphere is useful to visualize what happens with a single qubit, but it is not suitable for multiple qubits, in particular when they are entangled. Entangled qubits can no longer be thought of as independent units. They become one quantum entity described by a state vector of its own right on a hypersphere. A hypersphere is an extension of the Bloch sphere to 2^n complex dimensions, where n is the number of qubits. Quantum gates perform rotations of a state vector to a new position on this hypersphere. Thus, it is virtually impossible to visualize a system with multiple qubits. There is no better way but to use mathematics to represent quantum systems.

The notation used above to represent quantum states ($|\Psi\rangle, |0\rangle, |1\rangle$), is referred to as *Dirac notation*, which provides an abbreviated way to represent a vector. For instance, $|0\rangle$ and $|1\rangle$ represent the following vectors, respectively:

$$|0\rangle = \begin{bmatrix} 1 \\ 0 \end{bmatrix} \text{ and } |1\rangle \begin{bmatrix} 0 \\ 1 \end{bmatrix}$$

And quantum gates are represented as matrices. For instance, the X gate is represented as:

$$X = \begin{bmatrix} 0 & 1 \\ 1 & 0 \end{bmatrix}$$

Therefore, quantum gate operations are represented mathematically as matrix operations; e.g., multiplication of a matrix (gate) by a vector (qubit state). Thus, the application of an X gate to $|0\rangle$ looks like this:

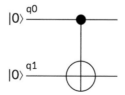

Fig. 34.13 The CX gate creates a dependency of the state of one qubit with the state of another. In this case, q1 will be flipped only if q0 is $|1\rangle$

Fig. 34.14 The Toffoli gate creates a dependency of the state of one qubit with the state of two others

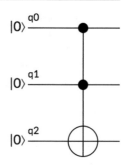

$$X(|0\rangle) = \begin{bmatrix} 0 & 1 \\ 1 & 0 \end{bmatrix} \times \begin{bmatrix} 1 \\ 0 \end{bmatrix} = \begin{bmatrix} 0 \\ 1 \end{bmatrix} = |1\rangle$$

Conversely, the application of an X gate to $|1\rangle$ would therefore is written as follows:

$$X(|1\rangle) = \begin{bmatrix} 0 & 1 \\ 1 & 0 \end{bmatrix} \times \begin{bmatrix} 0 \\ 1 \end{bmatrix} = \begin{bmatrix} 1 \\ 0 \end{bmatrix} = |0\rangle$$

The Hadamard gate has the matrix:

$$H = \begin{bmatrix} \frac{1}{\sqrt{2}} & \frac{1}{\sqrt{2}} \\ \frac{1}{\sqrt{2}} & -\frac{1}{\sqrt{1}} \end{bmatrix} = \frac{1}{\sqrt{2}} \begin{bmatrix} 1 & 1 \\ 1 & -1 \end{bmatrix}$$

As we have seen earlier, the application of the H gate to a qubit pointing to $|0\rangle$ puts it in superposition, right at the equator of the Bloch sphere. This is notated as follows:

$$H(|0\rangle) = \frac{1}{\sqrt{2}}(|0\rangle + |1\rangle).$$

As applied to $|1\rangle$, it also puts it in superposition, but pointing to the opposite direction of the superposition shown above:

$$H(|1\rangle) = \frac{1}{\sqrt{2}}(|0\rangle - |1\rangle).$$

In the preceding equations, the result of $H(|0\rangle)$ and $H(|1\rangle)$ could written as $|+\rangle$ and $|-\rangle$, respectively. In a circuit, we could subsequently apply another gate to $|+\rangle$ or $|-\rangle$, and so on; e.g. $X(|+\rangle) = |+\rangle$.

The Hadamard gate is often used to change the so-called *computational basis* of the qubit. The z-axis $|0\rangle$ and $|1\rangle$ form the *standard basis*. The x-axis $|+\rangle$ and $|-\rangle$ forms the so-called *conjugate basis*. The application of $X(|+\rangle)$ would not have much effect if we measure the qubit in the *standard basis*: it would still probabilistically return 0 or 1. However, it would be different if we were to measure it in the *conjugate basis*; it would deterministically return the value on the opposite side where the vector is aiming to. Another commonly used basis is the *circular basis* (y-axis). A more detailed explanation of different bases and their significance to computation and measurement can be found in [19]. What is important to keep in mind is that changing the basis on which a quantum state is expressed, corresponds to changing the kind of measurement we perform, and so, naturally, it also changes the probabilities of measurement outcomes.

Quantum processing with multiple qubits is represented by means of *tensor vectors*. A tensor vector is the result of the tensor product, represented by the symbol $\otimes$, of two or more vectors. A system of two qubits looks like this $|0\rangle \otimes |0\rangle$, but it is normally abbreviated to $|00\rangle$. It is useful to study the expanded form of the tensor product to follow how it works:

$$|00\rangle = |0\rangle \otimes |0\rangle = \begin{bmatrix} 1 \\ 0 \end{bmatrix} \otimes \begin{bmatrix} 1 \\ 0 \end{bmatrix} = \begin{bmatrix} 1 \times 1 \\ 1 \times 0 \\ 0 \times 1 \\ 0 \times 0 \end{bmatrix} = \begin{bmatrix} 1 \\ 0 \\ 0 \\ 0 \end{bmatrix}$$

Similarly, the other 3 possible states of a 2-qubits system are as follows:

$$|01\rangle = |0\rangle \otimes |1\rangle = \begin{bmatrix} 1 \\ 0 \end{bmatrix} \otimes \begin{bmatrix} 0 \\ 1 \end{bmatrix} = \begin{bmatrix} 1 \times 0 \\ 1 \times 1 \\ 0 \times 0 \\ 0 \times 1 \end{bmatrix} = \begin{bmatrix} 0 \\ 1 \\ 0 \\ 0 \end{bmatrix}$$

$$|10\rangle = |1\rangle \otimes |0\rangle = \begin{bmatrix} 0 \\ 1 \end{bmatrix} \otimes \begin{bmatrix} 1 \\ 0 \end{bmatrix} = \begin{bmatrix} 0 \times 1 \\ 0 \times 0 \\ 1 \times 1 \\ 1 \times 0 \end{bmatrix} = \begin{bmatrix} 0 \\ 0 \\ 1 \\ 0 \end{bmatrix}$$

$$|11\rangle = |1\rangle \otimes |1\rangle = \begin{bmatrix} 0 \\ 1 \end{bmatrix} \otimes \begin{bmatrix} 0 \\ 1 \end{bmatrix} = \begin{bmatrix} 0 \times 0 \\ 0 \times 1 \\ 1 \times 0 \\ 1 \times 1 \end{bmatrix} = \begin{bmatrix} 0 \\ 0 \\ 0 \\ 1 \end{bmatrix}$$

We are now in a position to explain how the CX gate works in more detail. This gate is defined by the matrix:

$$CX = \begin{bmatrix} 1 & 0 & 0 & 0 \\ 0 & 1 & 0 & 0 \\ 0 & 0 & 0 & 1 \\ 0 & 0 & 1 & 0 \end{bmatrix}$$

The application of CX to $|00\rangle$ is represented as:

$$CX(|00\rangle) = \begin{bmatrix} 1 & 0 & 0 & 0 \\ 0 & 1 & 0 & 0 \\ 0 & 0 & 0 & 1 \\ 0 & 0 & 1 & 0 \end{bmatrix} \times \begin{bmatrix} 1 \\ 0 \\ 0 \\ 0 \end{bmatrix} = \begin{bmatrix} 1 \\ 0 \\ 0 \\ 0 \end{bmatrix}$$

The resulting vector is then abbreviated to $|00\rangle$ as show below:

$$\begin{bmatrix} 1 \\ 0 \\ 0 \\ 0 \end{bmatrix} = \begin{bmatrix} 1 \\ 0 \end{bmatrix} \otimes \begin{bmatrix} 1 \\ 0 \end{bmatrix} = |0\rangle \otimes |0\rangle = |00\rangle$$

Note that $|00\rangle$ incurred no change because the conditional qubit (the one on the left side of the pair) is not $|1\rangle$. Conversely, should one apply CX to $|10\rangle$, then there is a change to $|11\rangle$, as follows:

$$CX(|10\rangle) = \begin{bmatrix} 1 & 0 & 0 & 0 \\ 0 & 1 & 0 & 0 \\ 0 & 0 & 0 & 1 \\ 0 & 0 & 1 & 0 \end{bmatrix} \times \begin{bmatrix} 0 \\ 0 \\ 1 \\ 0 \end{bmatrix} = \begin{bmatrix} 0 \\ 0 \\ 0 \\ 1 \end{bmatrix}$$

$$\begin{bmatrix} 0 \\ 0 \\ 0 \\ 1 \end{bmatrix} = \begin{bmatrix} 0 \\ 1 \end{bmatrix} \otimes \begin{bmatrix} 0 \\ 1 \end{bmatrix} = |1\rangle \otimes |1\rangle = |11\rangle$$

Table 34.1 shows the resulting quantum states of CX gate operations, where the first qubit flips only if the second qubit is 1. Figure 34.13 illustrates how the CX gate is represented in a circuit diagram. Note that in quantum computing qubit strings are often enumerated from the right end of the string to the left: $\dots |q_2\rangle \otimes |q_1\rangle \otimes |q_0\rangle$; this is the standard adopted for the examples in this chapter from now on.

Another useful conditional gate, which appears on a number of quantum algorithms, is the CCX gate, also known as the *Toffoli gate*, involving three qubits (Fig. 33.14).

Table 34.2 shows resulting quantum states of the Toffoli gate: qubit q2 flips only if q1 and q0 are $|1\rangle$.

Table 34.1 CX gate table, where q1 changes only if q0 is $|1\rangle$	Input	Result
	$|00\rangle$	$|00\rangle$
	$|01\rangle$	$|11\rangle$
	$|10\rangle$	$|10\rangle$
	$|11\rangle$	$|01\rangle$

Table 34.2 Toffoli gate table

Input	Result
$|000\rangle$	$|000\rangle$
$|001\rangle$	$|001\rangle$
$|010\rangle$	$|010\rangle$
$|011\rangle$	$|111\rangle$
$|100\rangle$	$|100\rangle$
$|101\rangle$	$|101\rangle$
$|110\rangle$	$|110\rangle$
$|111\rangle$	$|011\rangle$

The equation for describing a 2-qubits system $|q_1\rangle \otimes |q_0\rangle$ combines two state vectors $|\Psi\rangle$ and $|\Phi\rangle$ as follows. Consider:

$$|\psi\rangle = \alpha_1|0\rangle + \alpha_2|1\rangle \text{ for } q_0$$

$$|\phi\rangle = \beta_1|0\rangle + \beta_2|1\rangle \text{ for } q_1$$

Then,

$$|\Psi\rangle \otimes |\Phi\rangle = \alpha_0\beta_0|00\rangle + \alpha_0\beta_1|01\rangle + \alpha_1\beta_0|10\rangle + \alpha_1\beta_1|11\rangle$$

The above represents a new quantum state with four amplitude coefficients, which can be written as:

$$|A\rangle = \alpha_0|00\rangle + \alpha_1|01\rangle + \alpha_2|10\rangle + \alpha_3|11\rangle$$

Consider this equation:

$$||\Psi\rangle = \frac{1}{4}|00\rangle + \frac{1}{4}|01\rangle + \frac{1}{4}|10\rangle + \frac{1}{4}|11\rangle$$

The above is saying that each of the four quantum states have equal probability of 25% each of being returned.

Now, it should be straightforward to work out how to describe quantum systems with more qubits. For instance, a system with four qubits looks like this:

$$
\begin{aligned}
|B\rangle = {} & \beta_0|0000\rangle + \beta_1|0001\rangle + \beta_2|0010\rangle + \beta_3|0011\rangle + \\
& \beta_4|0100\rangle + \beta_5|0101\rangle + \beta_6|0110\rangle + \beta_7|0111\rangle + \\
& \beta_8|1000\rangle + \beta_9|1001\rangle + \beta_{10}|1010\rangle + \beta_{11}|1011\rangle + \\
& \beta_{12}|1100\rangle + \beta_{13}|1101\rangle + \beta_{14}|0110\rangle + \beta_{15}|1111\rangle
\end{aligned}
$$

A linear increase of the number of qubits extends the capacity of representing information on a quantum computer exponentially. With qubits in superposition, a quantum computer can handle all possible values of some input data simultaneously. This endows the machine with massive parallelism. However, we do not have access to the information until the qubits are measured.

Quantum algorithms require a different way of thinking than the way one normally approaches programming; for instance, it is not possible to store quantum states on a working memory for accessing later in the algorithm. This is due to the so-called *non-cloning principle* of quantum physics: it is impossible to make a copy of a quantum system. It is possible, however, to move the state of a set of qubits to another set of qubits, but in effect this deletes the information from the original qubits. To program a quantum computer requires manipulations of qubits so that the states that correspond to the desired outcome have a much higher probability of being measured than all the other possibilities.

Decoherence is problematic because it poses limitations on the number of successive gates we can use in a circuit (a.k.a. the circuit depth). The more gates we use, the higher the chances that the qubits will decohere. And this inevitably causes errors. In particular, running a circuit which is deeper than the critical depth for which a quantum device can maintain coherence will result in measurement outcomes sampled from an effectively classical distribution, sadly defeating the whole purpose of using a quantum computer. At the time of writing, QPUs do not have more than a few dozen qubits and are unable to maintain a desired quantum state for longer than a few microseconds.

One way to mitigate errors is to run the algorithms, which are not too deep, many times and then select the result that appeared most. Additional post processing on the measurement outcomes that tries to undo the effect of the noise by solving an inverse problem can also be carried out. Increasingly sophisticated error correction methods are also being developed. And better hardware technology is also developing fast. But as stated above fault-tolerant quantum computation is still a long way from being realised.

34.5 Quantum Vocal Synthesizer

This section introduces an interactive vocal synthesizer with parameters determined by a *quantum hyper-die*. The system listens to a tune chanted on a microphone and counts the number of notes it can detect in the signal. Then, it synthesizes the same amount of sounds as the number of notes that it counted in the tune. The synthesized vocal sounds are not intended to imitate the listened tune. Rather, they are 'quantum' responses, whose make-up is defined by the quantum hyper-die.

The system comprises two components connected through the Internet using the SSH (Secure Shell) protocol: a client and server (Fig. 34.15). The client operates on a standard laptop computer and the server on a Rigetti's Forest quantum computer, located in Berkeley, California.

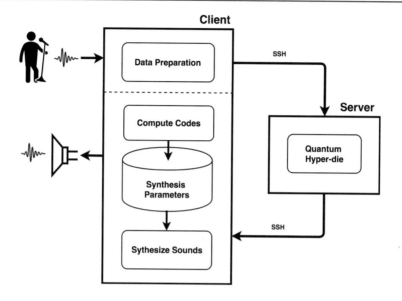

Fig. 34.15 The interactive quantum vocal system architecture

The server runs the hyper-die quantum circuit depicted in Fig. 34.19 and sends measurements to the client. The client takes care of analysing the chanted tune, preparing data to set up the server, and synthesizing sounds based on the results of the measurements.

The system is programmed in Python and uses pyQuil, a Python library developed by Rigetti to write quantum programs [4]. The core of the vocal synthesiser is implemented using the programming language Csound [10]. The Csound code is called from within Python.

The audio spectrum of singing human voice has the appearance of a pattern of 'hills and valleys'. The 'hills' are referred to as *formants* (Fig. 34.16). A vocal sound usually has between three to five distinct formants. Each of them comprises a set of sound partials.

Fig. 34.16 Generalized spectrum of the human voice with three formants

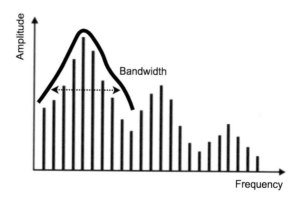

A formant is described by a frequency, which is the frequency of its most prominent partial, and an amplitude, which is the energy of this frequency. A third descriptor is the formant's bandwidth, which is the width of the 'hill'. It is calculated as the difference between the highest and the lowest frequencies in the formant set. Frequencies and bandwidths are quantified in Hz and amplitudes in dB.

Normally, the first three formants of a vocal sound characterise its phonetic timbre. For instance, they define whether a vowel is open (e.g., as in /a/ in the word 'back') or close (e.g., as in /o/ in the word 'too'); e.g., the frequency of the first formant of an open vowel is higher than that of a close vowel.

Traditionally, the vocal system has been modelled as a system consisting of two modules: a source module and a resonator module. The source module produces an excitation signal. Then, this signal is altered by the acoustic response of the resonator. The excitation signal is intended to simulate the waveform produced by the vibration of the glottis. The throat, nasal cavity and mouth function as resonating chambers whereby particular frequencies of the excitation signal are emphasised and others are attenuated (Fig. 34.17).

There are a number of methods to synthesise simulations of singing voice [20]. The synthesis method used here is known as FOF, which is an acronym for *Fonctions d'Onde Formantique*, or Formant Wave Functions, in English [21].

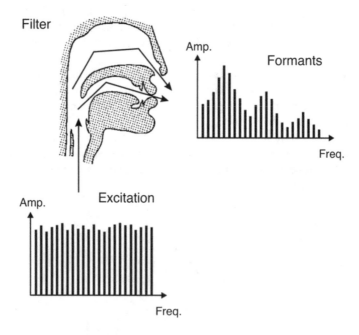

Fig. 34.17 Vocal system

The core of the synthesizer comprises five formant generators in parallel to produce five formants (Fig. 34.18). Each FOF generator requires 15 input parameters to produce a formant. A detailed explanation of FOF is beyond the scope of this chapter. For the sake of simplicity, we shall focus here on three parameters only: formant's frequency (fq), formant's amplitude (amp) and formant's bandwidth (bw).

Each formant generator is controlled by three linear functions. The functions vary the generator's input frequency, amplitude and bandwidth, from initial to end values. For instance, fq1s is the starting frequency value for generator Formant 1, whereas fq1e is the ending value. These variations are continuous and last through the entire duration of the sound.

The outputs from the oscillators are summed and a vibrato generator is applied, which is also controlled by linear functions. Vibrato renders the result more realistic to our ears. Then, an ADSR (short for attack, decay, sustain and release) function

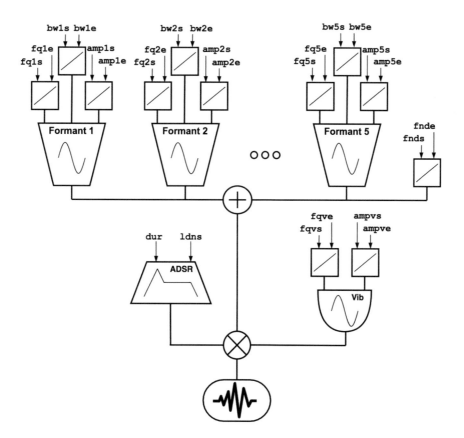

Fig. 34.18 Synthesizer's layout

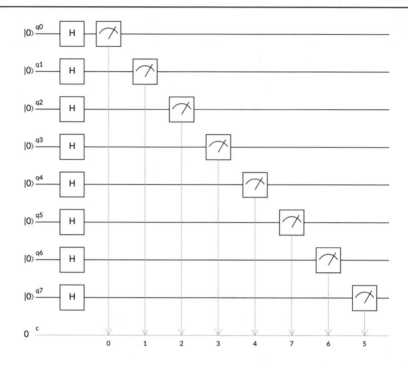

Fig. 34.19 The quantum hyper-die circuit. Hadamard gates put all 9 qubits in superposition

shapes the overall amplitude of the sound. Other parameters for the synthesizer are the resulting sound's fundamental frequency, or pitch (fnd), its loudness (ldns) and its duration (dur).

The quantum hyper-die is a simple quantum circuit that puts 9 qubits in superposition and measures them (Fig. 34.19). This results in a set of 9 measurements, which are processed by the client to produce codes of three bits each. These codes are used to retrieve synthesis parameter values from a database. The database contains valid values for all synthesis parameters shown in Fig. 34.18, plus other ones that are not shown.

For instance, consider the list of measurements $[c_8, c_7, c_6, c_5, c_4, c_3, c_2, c_1, c_0]$. Codes are produced by combining three elements from the measurements list according to a bespoke combinatorial formula. For example, $(c_8\ c_7\ c_6)$, $(c_6\ c_7\ c_8)$, $(c_5\ c_4\ c_3)$, $(c_3\ c_4\ c_5)$, $(c_2\ c_1\ c_0)$, $(c_0\ c_1\ c_2)$ and so forth. Given a list of synthesis parameter values $[p_0, p_1, p_2, p_3, p_4, p_5, p_6, p_7]$, the decimal value of a code gives an index to retrieve a value for the synthesizer. For instance, the code $(0\ 1\ 0)$, which yields the decimal number 2, would retrieve p_2.

Each synthesis parameter is coupled with a unique code formation for retrieval. For instance, $(c_8\ c_7\ c_6)$ is coupled with the starting frequency for the first formant (fq1s) and $(c_6\ c_7\ c_8)$ with the ending frequency for the first formant (fq1e). And $(c_5\ c_4\ c_3)$ is coupled with the starting frequency for the second formant (fq2s), and so on. The database holds different lists of synthesis parameters, which can be customised.

As an illustration, let us consider a simple database with the following lists of fundamental frequencies and durations, and frequencies, amplitudes and bandwidths for formants 1, 2 and 3:

fnd = [277.2, 185.0, 207.6, 415.3, 155.6, 311.2, 369.9, 233.1].
dur = [3.25, 2.0, 2.75, 4.0, 1.5, 3.75, 2.5, 4.5].
fq1 = [310.0, 270.0, 290.0, 350.0, 650.0, 400.0, 430.0, 470.0].
fq2 = [600.0, 1150.0, 800.0, 1870.0, 1080.0, 1620.0, 1700.0, 1040.0].
fq3 = [2250.0, 2100.0, 2800.0, 2650.0, 2500.0, 2900.0, 2600.0, 2750.0].
amp1 = [0.0, 0.0, 0.0, 0.0, 0.0, 0.0, 0.0, 0.0].
amp2 = [−5, −7, −11, −6, −14, −9, −20, −30].
amp3 = [−9, −21, −12, −32, −17, −16, −10, −18].
bw1 = [35, 60, 45, 70, 80, 75, 58, 85].
bw2 = [65, 70, 90, 75, 83, 95, 60, 87].
bw3 = [128, 115, 110, 112, 98, 104, 124, 120].

For this example, the server returned the following measurements: [0, 0, 0, 0, 0, 1, 0, 0, 1].

Then, the system produces the respective codes and retrieves the parameters for the synthesiser. For instance, the code $(x_0\ x_1\ x_2)$ is equal to 000. Therefore, it retrieves the first element of fq1 for the starting frequency of the first formant generator (fg1s), which is 310.0 Hz. Table 34.3 shows the retrieved values for the aforementioned parameters.

Figure 34.21 shows a spectrogram snapshot taken at two seconds in the sound, showing three prominent formants, whose frequencies match the input parameters yielded by the quantum hyper-die.

Note that the synthesizer reads amplitudes in terms of attenuations from a hard-coded reference dB value. As a convention, the first formant is always set to this reference, hence the values in the amp1 list are all 0.0 dB. The other amplitudes are calculated by subtracting the negative values from this reference.

Figure 34.20 shows a formant analysis graph of the synthesized sound. Each line corresponds to a formant detected in the signal. Note the first formant is practically constant at 310 Hz throughout the duration of the sound. The third formant, however, raised slightly; i.e., from 1080.0 Hz to 2100.0 Hz.

Table 34.3 Retrieved synthesis parameters with codes produced from quantum measurements

Code	Binary	Decimal	Parameter	Retrieved value
$(c_8\ c_7\ c_6)$	000	0	fq1s	310.0 Hz
$(c_6\ c_7\ c_8)$	000	0	fq1e	310.0 Hz
$(c_5\ c_4\ c_3)$	001	1	fq2s	1150.0 Hz
$(c_3\ c_4\ c_5)$	100	4	fq2e	1080.0 Hz
$(c_2\ c_1\ c_0)$	001	1	fq3s	2100.0 Hz
$(c_0\ c_1\ c_2)$	100	4	fq3e	2500.0 Hz
$(c_7\ c_6\ c_5)$	000	0	amp1s	0.0 dB
$(c_5\ c_6\ c_7)$	000	0	amp1e	0.0 dB
$(c_4\ c_3\ c_2)$	010	2	amp2s	−11 dB
$(c_2\ c_3\ c_4)$	010	2	amp2e	−11 dB
$(c_8\ c_5\ c_2)$	000	0	amp3s	−9 dB
$(c_2\ c_5\ c_8)$	000	0	amp3e	−9 dB
$(c_7\ c_4\ c_3)$	001	1	bw1s	60 Hz
$(c_3\ c_4\ c_7)$	100	4	bw1e	80 Hz
$(c_6\ c_3\ c_0)$	011	3	bw2s	75 Hz
$(c_0\ c_3\ c_6)$	110	6	bw2e	60 Hz
$(c_8\ c_7\ c_0)$	001	1	bw3s	115 Hz
$(c_0\ c_7\ c_8)$	100	4	bw3e	98 Hz
$(c_8\ c_1\ c_0)$	001	1	fnds	185.0 Hz
$(c_0\ c_1\ c_8)$	100	4	fnde	155.6 Hz
$(c_5\ c_3\ c_1)$	010	2	dur	2.75 s

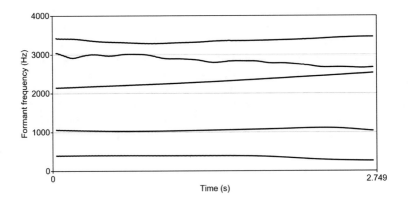

Fig. 34.20 Formant analysis revealing five salient spectral components in the sound

	Step	Pitch	Duration
Table 34.4 Pitch and duration codes generated for each step of the random walk example	1	110	100
	2	010	110
	3	010	110
	4	110	100
	5	100	101
	6	100	001
	7	000	001
	8	000	000
	9	001	100
	10	000	000
	11	100	100
	12	100	110
	13	000	010
	14	010	010
	15	011	011
	16	111	001
	17	011	001
	18	111	101
	19	111	101
	20	101	100
	21	001	000
	22	000	001
	23	000	101
	24	000	001

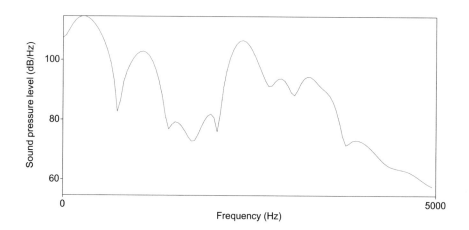

Fig. 34.21 Spectrogram analysis snapshot taken at two seconds

34.6 Quantum Walk Sequencer

This section presents a system that generates sequences of musical notes using a quantum walk algorithm. For a detailed discussion on quantum random walks, please refer to [22].

As with the quantum vocal synthesiser above, the system consists of two components: a client and a server (Fig. 34.22). The server runs the quantum random walk circuit and sends a list of measurements to the client. Then, the client translates those measurements into a sequence of musical notes, which are encoded as MIDI information [23]. MIDI is a protocol that allows computers, musical instruments and other hardware to communicate. The difference of encoding the results with MIDI rather than synthesizing sounds is that we can connect third party music software to visualize or play back the music.

As we have briefly seen earlier in this chapter, in a random walk algorithm, a "walker" starts on a certain node of a graph and has an equal probability of travelling through any connected edge to an adjacent node. This process is then repeated as many times as required. The nodes can represent tasks to be performed once the walker lands on them, or information to handle; e.g., a musical note to be played or appended to a list.

In classical random walk, the walker inhabits a definite node at any one moment in time. But in quantum walk, it will be in a superposition of all nodes it can possibly visit in a given moment. Metaphorically, we could say that the walker is on all viable nodes simultaneously, until we observe it.

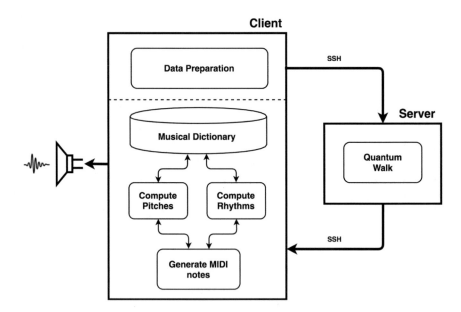

Fig. 34.22 The quantum walk music system architecture

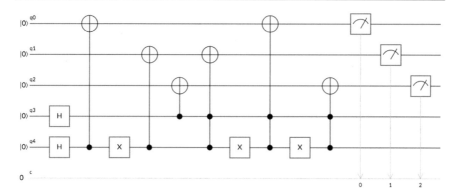

Fig. 34.23 Quantum walk circuit

The circuit (Fig. 34.23) was designed to walk through the edges of a cube to visit eight vertices, each of which is represented as a three bits long binary number (Fig. 34.24). The circuit uses five qubits: three (q0, q1, and q2) to encode the eight vertices of the cube {000, 001, ..., 111} and two (q3 and q4) to encode the possible routes that the walker can take from a given vertex, one of which is to stay put. The diagram shows a sequence of 10 operations before measurements, the first of which are the two H gates applied to q3 and q4, then a CX with q4 and q0, and so on.

We refer to the first three qubits as *input qubits* and the last two as *die qubits*. The die qubits act as controls for X gates to invert the state of input qubits.

Fig. 34.24 Cube representation of the quantum walk routes and nodes

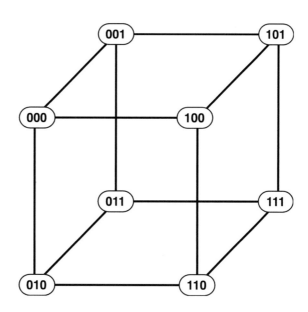

For every vertex on the cube, the edges connect three neighbouring vertices whose codes differ by changing only one bit of the origin's code. For instance, vertex 111 is connected to 110, 101 and 011. Therefore, upon measurement the system returns one of four possible outputs:

- the original input with inverted q0
- the original input with inverted q1
- the original input with inverted q2
- the original input unchanged.

The quantum walk algorithm runs as follows: the input qubits are armed with the state representing a node of departure and two die qubits are armed in superposition (H gate). Then, the input qubits are measured and the results are stored in a classical memory. This causes the whole system to decohere. Depending on the values yielded by the die qubits, the conditional gates will invert the input qubits accordingly. Note that we measure and store only input qubits; the value of the die can be lost. The result of the measurement is then used to arm the input qubits for the next step of the walk, and the cycle continues for a number of steps. The number of steps is established at the initial data preparation stage. (In fact, each step is run for thousands of times, or thousands of shots in quantum computing terminology.)

As a trace table example, let us assume the following input: 001, where q0 is armed to $|0\rangle$, q1 to $|0\rangle$ and q2 to $|1\rangle$. Upon measurement, let us suppose that the die yielded q3 = 0 and q4 = 1. The second operation on the circuit diagram is a CX gate where q4 acts a conditional to invert q0. Right at the second operation the state vector of q0 is inverted because q4 = 1. As the rest of the circuit does not incur any further action on the input qubits, the system returns 101. Should the dice have yielded q3 = 0 and q4 = 0 instead, then the fourth operation would have inverted q1. The X gate (third operation) would have inverted q4, which would subsequently act as a conditional to invert q1. The result in this case would have been 011.

The cube in Fig. 34.24 functions as an underlying common abstract representation of simple musical grammars, whose isomorphic digraphs are shown in Figs. 34.25 and 34.26. One of the grammars encodes rules for sequencing pitches (Fig. 34.25) and the other rules for sequencing durations of musical notes (Fig. 34.26), respectively. The system holds musical dictionaries associating vertices with pitches and note durations.

In order to generate a music sequence, the system starts with a given note; for instance, a half note C4, whose codes for pitch and duration are 000 and 100, respectively. This initial note is given to the system at the data preparation stage. Then, for every new note the server runs the quantum walk circuit twice, once with input qubits armed with the code for pitch and then armed with the code for duration. The results from the measurements are then used to establish the next note. For instance, if the first run goes to 001 and the second to 000, then the

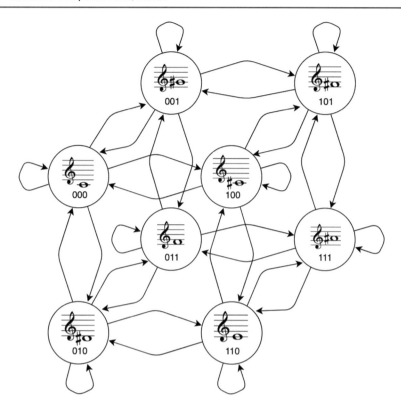

Fig. 34.25 Digraph representation of a grammar for pitches

resulting note is quarter note G4 sharp. The measurements are used to re-arm the circuit for the next note and so on.

An important component of music is silence. Note in Fig. 34.26 that the grammar for durations includes 4 pauses: 001, 010, 101 and 111. When the walker lands on a pause, the pitch of the note is discarded and a silence takes place for the duration of the respective pause. The dictionaries of notes and durations are modifiable and there are tools to change the dictionary during the generation of a sequence. The length of the sequence and the dictionaries are set up at the data preparation stage.

Due to the statistical nature of quantum computation, it is often necessary to execute a quantum algorithm multiple times in order to obtain results that are statistically sound. This enables one to inspect if the outcomes reflect the envisaged amplitude distribution of the quantum states. And running a circuit multiple times mitigates the effect of errors caused by undesired decoherence.

In quantum computing, the times an algorithm is run is referred to as *shots*. For each shot, the measurements are stored in standard digital memory, and in the case of our quantum walk algorithm, the result that occurred more frequently is selected. Figure 34.27 shows histograms from running three steps of the quantum walk algorithms for 50 shots for generating pitches. Starting on 000, then the walker moves to 010, goes back to 000 and then it goes to 100. In this case the generated pitched were: D#3, C3 and C#3.

An example of a music sequence generated by the system is shown in Fig. 34.28. In this case the system ran for 24 steps, 500 shots each. The initial pitch was 110 and the initial duration was 100. Table 34.4 shows the codes generated at each step of the walk.

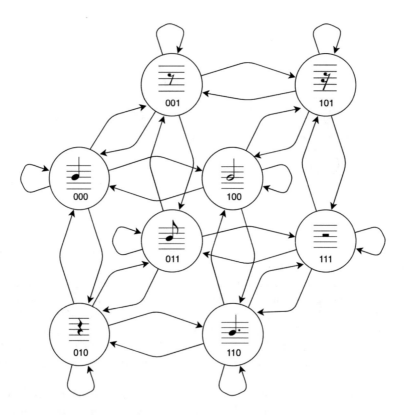

Fig. 34.26 Digraph representation of a grammar of durations

Fig. 34.27 Histograms from 3 steps of the quantum walk algorithms for 50 shots each. For each step, the system selects the result that occurred more frequently: 010, 000 and 100, respectively

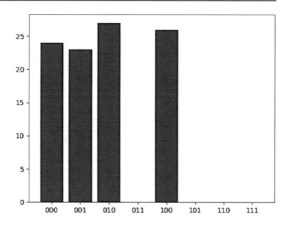

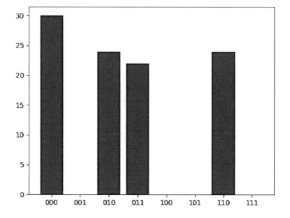

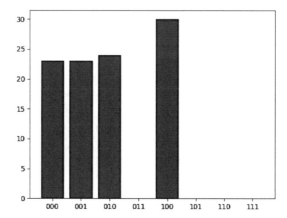

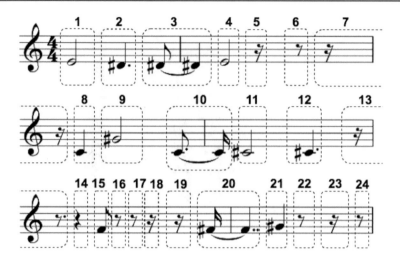

Fig. 34.28 A music sequence generated by the quantum walk system

34.7 Concluding Remarks

Admittedly, the two quantum systems introduced above could as well be implemented on standard digital computers. At this stage, we are not advocating any quantum advantage for musical applications. What we advocate, however, is that the music technology community should be quantum-ready for when quantum computing hardware becomes more sophisticated, widely available, and possibly advantageous for creativity and business. In the process of learning and experimenting with this new technology, novel approaches, creative ideas, and innovative applications are bound to emerge.

The method introduced above to control the vocal synthesiser certainly begs further development. The codes to retrieve synthesis parameter values were assembled with three bits taken from a string of nine measurements. The algorithm to assemble the codes is as arbitrary as the association of codes to specific parameters; e.g., what is the rationale of allocating $(c_8\ c_7\ c_6)$ to retrieve fq1s? Or why $(c_8\ c_7\ c_6)$ instead of $(c_0\ c_1\ c_2)$ or perhaps $(c_2\ c_2\ c_2)$?

Research is needed in order to forge stronger couplings between quantum computational processes and the synthesis parameters. Quantum computing should be used here to generate codes that are meaningful; it should be harnessed to yield values for producing targeted vocalizations; e.g., to sing syllables or words.

The complete vocal synthesiser shown above requires 52 parameter values to produce a sound. Moreover, the linear functions in fact need to be piecewise linear functions with various breakpoints in order to simulate transitions of vocal articulations. Therefore, the synthesis parameters' search space to produce a desired sung utterance is vast. It is here that quantum search algorithms may provide an advantageous solution [24] in the near future.

The quantum walk sequencer is an example of a first attempt at designing quantum versions of classic algorithmic music composition techniques. The shortcoming is that the sequencer has a limited number of musical parameters to work with; e.g., only eight notes. A larger number of parameters would require a much larger quantum circuit. But this increases the problem of decoherence, as mentioned earlier. Improved quantum hardware and better error correction methods will enable circuits with greater number qubits and gates in the future. In the meantime, simulators are available for research [1, 2].

It has been argued that quantum walk (on real quantum hardware) is faster than classical random walk to navigate vast mathematical spaces [25]. Quantum walk is an area of much interest for computer music. In addition to its generative uses, quantum walk is applicable as a search algorithm and in machine learning [26].

Musicians started experimenting with computers very early on in the history of computing, and paved the way for today's thriving music industry. CSIR's Mk1 was one of only a handful of electronic computers in existence at the time. And the mainframe used to compose the *Illiac Suite* string quartet was one of the first computers built in a university in the USA, comprising thousands of vacuum tubes.

It is often said that today's quantum computers are in a development stage comparable to those clunky mainframes built in the mid of the last century. Time is ripe for musicians to embrace this emerging technology.

Acknowledgements I am thankful to Dr. Konstantinos Meichanetzidis at the Department of Computer Science of the University of Oxford for inspiring discussions and advice.

References

1. Microsoft Quantum Development Kit. Retrieved September 17, 2019, from https://www.microsoft.com/en-gb/quantum/development-kit.
2. Quantum Programming Studio. Retrieved January 02, 2020, from https://quantum-circuit.com/.
3. IBM, Q. Retrieved September 17, 2019, from https://www.ibm.com/quantum-computing/.
4. Rigetti Quantum Cloud Services. Retrieved September 17, 2019, from https://www.rigetti.com/qcs.
5. Kais, S. (2014). *Quantum information and computation for chemistry*. Hoboken, NJ (USA): John Wiley & Sons Inc.
6. Bernstein, D., & Lange, T. (2017). Post-quantum cryptography. *Nature, 549,* 188–194.
7. Manabrea, L. F. (1843). *Sketch of the analytical engine invented by Charles Babbage*. (A. Lovelace, Trans.). London, UK: R. & J. E. Taylor. Retrieved April 30, 2020, from https://johnrhudson.me.uk/computing/Menabrea_Sketch.pdf.
8. Doornbusch, P. (2004). Computer sound synthesis in 1951: The music of CSIRAC. *Computer Music Journal, 28*(1), 10–25.
9. Hiller, L. A., & Isaacson, L. M. (1959). *Experimental music: Composition with an electronic computer*. New York, NY (USA): McGraw-Hill.
10. Boulanger, R. (Ed.). (2000). *The csound book: Perspectives in software synthesis, sound design, signal processing, and programming*. Cambridge, MA: The MIT Press.

11. Kirke, A., & Miranda, E. R. (2017). Experiments in sound and music quantum computing. In E. R. Miranda (Ed.), *Guide to unconventional computing for music*. Cham (Switzerland): Springer International Publishing.

12. Kirke, A. (2019). Applying quantum hardware to non-scientific problems: Grover's algorithm and rule-based algorithmic music composition. *International Journal of Unconventional Computing, 14*(3–4), 349–374.

13. Miranda, E. R. (2021). Creative quantum computing: Inverse FFT sound synthesis, adaptive sequencing and musical composition. In A. Adamatzky (Ed.), *Alternative computing*. Singapore: World Scientific. Available on arXiv: t.b.a.

14. Cherubini, L. (1884). *A treatise on counterpoint & fugue*. New York, NY (USA): Novello, Ewer and Co. Retrieved January 05, 2020, from https://archive.org/details/treatiseoncounte002279mbp.

15. Miranda, E. R. (2001). *Composing music with computers*. Oxford (UK): Elsevier Focal Press.

16. Grumbling, E., & Horowitz, M (Eds.) (2019). *Quantum computing: Progress and prospects*. Washington, DC: National Academies Press. https://doi.org/10.17226/25196

17. Rieffel, E., & Polak, W. (2011). *Quantum computing: A gentle introduction*. Cambridge, MA: The MIT Press.

18. Mermin, N. D. (2007). *Quantum computer science: An introduction*. Cambridge, UK: Cambridge University Press.

19. Bernhardt, C. (2019). *Quantum computing for everyone*. Cambridge, MA: The MIT Press.

20. Miranda, E. R. (1998). *Computer sound synthesis for the electronic musician*. Oxford, UK: Focal Press.

21. Rodet, X., Potard, Y., & Barriere, J.-B. (1984). The CHANT project: From synthesis of the singing voice to synthesis in general. *Computer Music Journal, 8*(3), 15–31.

22. Ambainis, A. (2008). Quantum random walks—New method for designing quantum algorithms. In V. Geffert, J. Karhumäki, A. Bertoni, B. Preneel, P. Návrat, & M. Bieliková (eds.) *SOFSEM 2008: theory and practice of computer science*. Lecture Notes in Computer Science, 4910. Berlin, Germany: Springer.

23. The official MIDI specification. MIDI Association. Retrieved April 08, 2020, from https://www.midi.org/.

24. Giri, P. R., & Korepin, V. E. (2017). A review on quantum search algorithms. *Quantum Information Processing, 16*(12), 1–36.

25. Kendon, V. M. (2006). A random walk approach to quantum algorithms. *Philosophical Transactions of the Royal Society, 364*, 3407–3422.

26. Dernbach, S., Mohseni-Kabir, A., Pal, S., Gepner, M., & Towsley, D. (2019). Quantum walk neural networks with feature dependent coins. *Applied Network Science, 4*. Article number: 76.

Eduardo Reck Miranda is Professor in Computer Music and head the Interdisciplinary Centre for Computer Music Research (ICCMR) at the University of Plymouth, UK. He studied music, philosophy and informatics in Brazil before he graduated with an M.Sc. in Music Technology from the University of York, UK. Subsequently he received a Ph.D. on the topic of sound design with Artificial Intelligence (AI) from the University of Edinburgh, UK. Before joining the University of Plymouth, he worked at Sony Computer Science Laboratory in Paris, France, as a research scientist in the fields of AI, speech and evolution of language. He also is a composer working at the crossroads of music and science. His distinctive music is informed by his unique background as a classically trained composer and AI scientist with an early involvement in electroacoustic and avant-garde pop music. E-mail: eduardo.miranda@plymouth.ac.uk.

Printed in the United States
by Baker & Taylor Publisher Services